Butterworths Guide Insolvency Rules

Look Chan Ho
MA, BCL (Oxon), LLM (Cantab), LLM (NYU),
Attorney-at-Law and Solicitor
Freshfields Bruckhaus Deringer LLP

Helen Smithson
ACCA, MIPA, MABRP
Technical Senior Manager, Ernst & Young LLP

With contributions from Emma Gateaud

Butterworths Guide to the Insolvency Rules

Members of the LexisNexis Group worldwide

United Kingdom	3 Baxter's Place, Leith Walk Edinburgh EH1 3AF
Australia	LexisNexis Butterworths, Chatswood, New South Wales
Austria	LexisNexis Verlag ARD Orac GmbH & Co KG, Vienna
Benelux	LexisNexis Benelux, Amsterdam
Canada	LexisNexis Canada, Markham, Ontario
China	LexisNexis China, Beijing and Shanghai
France	LexisNexis SA, Paris
Germany	LexisNexis Deutschland GmbH, Munster
Hong Kong	LexisNexis Hong Kong, Hong Kong
India	LexisNexis India, New Delhi
Italy	Editore, Milan
Japan	LexisNexis Japan, Tokyo
Malaysia	Malayan Law Journal Sdn Bhd, Kuala Lumpur
New Zealand	LexisNexis NZ Ltd, Wellington
Poland	Wydawnictwo Prawnicze LexisNexis Sp, Warsaw
Singapore	LexisNexis Singapore, Singapore
South Africa	LexisNexis Butterworths, Durban
USA	LexisNexis, Dayton, Ohio

© Reed Elsevier (UK) Ltd 2010
Published by LexisNexis Butterworths

All rights reserved. No part of this publication may be reproduced in any material form (including photocopying or storing it in any medium by electronic means and whether or not transiently or incidentally to some other use of this publication) without the written permission of the copyright owner except in accordance with the provisions of the Copyright, Designs and Patents Act 1988 or under the terms of a licence issued by the Copyright Licensing Agency Ltd, 90 Tottenham Court Road, London, England W1T 4LP. Applications for the copyright owner's written permission to reproduce any part of this publication should be addressed to the publisher.
Warning: The doing of an unauthorised act in relation to a copyright work may result in both a civil claim for damages and criminal prosecution.

Crown copyright material is reproduced with the permission of the Controller of HMSO and the Queen's Printer for Scotland. Parliamentary copyright material is reproduced with the permission of the Controller of Her Majesty's Stationery Office on behalf of Parliament.
A CIP Catalogue record for this book is available from the British Library.

ISBN 13: 9781405744928

Printed and bound in the UK by CPI Antony Rowe, Chippenham and Eastbourne

Visit LexisNexis Butterworths at www.lexisnexis.co.uk

Preface

This book is organised into thematic chapters, with a final chapter dealing with miscellaneous topics which did not readily fit elsewhere. Chapters 1–4 and 10 were written by Helen Smithson and Chapters 5–9 by Look Chan Ho. The title of the book is *Butterworths Guide to the Insolvency Rules*, but as some of the modernising provisions required amendments to primary legislation we have included discussion of the Legislative Reform (Insolvency) (Miscellaneous Provisions) Order 2010. Transitional provisions are considered at the end of each chapter.

In Scotland, company voluntary arrangements and administrations are reserved areas of insolvency law. As a consequence some of the 2010 changes apply to these two processes. The approach we have adopted in this book is to deal with legislative changes in England and Wales in the first part of each chapter and then, if appropriate, to describe their application to Scotland.

As this book goes to press, work is in progress to further modernise and streamline the Insolvency Rules: the Insolvency Service has published a consultation draft of Insolvency Rules for 2012. We understand that limited changes to substance are planned and therefore we hope that our work will survive a little longer!

Finally, we would like to express our gratitude to the partners, directors and staff of Freshfields Bruckhaus Deringer LLP and Ernst & Young LLP for their support for and assistance with this project. Helen Smithson would particularly like to thank Julian Shepherd. Look Chan Ho would particularly like to thank Emma Gateaud. We would also like to thank all those outside our respective firms with whom we have had the opportunity to discuss the new Rules and their implications.

We have endeavoured to state the law as at 31 August 2010.

Look Chan Ho
Freshfields Bruckhaus Deringer LLP
Helen Smithson
Ernst & Young LLP

Contents

Preface	v
Table of Statutes	xiii
Table of Statutory Instruments	xv
Table of Cases	xix
Chapter 1 Advertising and gazetting	**1**
Introduction	1
Standard contents – general	1
Standard contents for advertising in the Gazette	2
All cases	2
Additional requirements for companies	2
Additional requirements for bankrupts	3
General provisions relating to advertising in the Gazette	3
Standard contents for advertising other than in the Gazette	3
All cases	3
Non-Gazette notices – additional requirements for companies	4
Non-Gazette notices – additional requirements for bankrupts	4
Other amendments	4
No requirement to advertise annual meetings in voluntary liquidations	4
Application to Scotland	5
Standard contents	5
Transitional provisions	5
Chapter 2 Electronic communications and websites	**7**
Introduction	7
Scope of application of the new provisions (England and Wales)	7
Electronic communications	7
General	7
Recipient to have given consent to electronic communication	8
Right to request a hard copy	8
Authentication	8
Delivery	8
Electronic communications – the courts	8

Contents

Practical considerations	9
Use of websites	10
Practical considerations	12
Application to Scotland	12
Electronic communication	12
Use of websites	13
Transitional provisions	13
Chapter 3 Meetings and resolutions	**15**
Introduction	15
Remote attendance at meetings	15
What is meant by "remote means"?	16
Responsibilities of the person summoning the meeting	16
Giving notice of a meeting held by remote means	16
Request for a place to be specified for a meeting	17
Excluded persons and complaints	18
Meetings of creditors' and liquidation committees	19
Practical considerations	20
Annual meetings in voluntary liquidations	22
Notice required for meetings	22
Resolutions by correspondence	22
Notice of meetings by advertisement only	23
Requisitioned meetings	23
Proofs and proxies for use at meetings	23
Chairman's discretion to allow a vote	23
Appeals against a chairman's decision	24
Quorum	24
Suspension and adjournment of meetings	24
Suspension	24
Mandatory adjournment	24
Discretionary adjournment	24
Time limit for adjournment	25
Use of proofs and proxies	25
Majority to approve CVA proposals	25
Minutes or other record of proceedings	25
Application to Scotland	26
Summoning meetings under section 3 of the Insolvency Act 1986 to	

consider a CVA proposal	26
Chairman of meeting as proxy holder (CVA)	26
Entitlement to vote (CVA)	26
Requisite majorities (CVA)	26
Entitlement to vote (administration)	27
Notice of meetings by advertisement only (administration)	27
Suspension and adjournment (administration)	27
Meetings held by remote means	27
Transitional provisions	28
Chapter 4 Creditors' and liquidation committees	**29**
Introduction	29
Membership of the committee – eligibility	29
Certificate of (amended) constitution of the committee	29
Committee meetings	30
First meeting of the committee	30
Meeting held at the request of a committee member	30
Resolutions	30
Termination of membership of the committee	31
Composition of the liquidation committee when creditors have been paid in full	31
Creditors' committee in liquidation following administration	31
Scotland	32
Creditors' committees in administration	32
Transitional provisions	32
Chapter 5 Court procedure and practice	**33**
Applications	33
Enforcement procedures	33
Court file and records	34
General	34
Transitional provisions	34
Chapter 6 Voluntary arrangements	**37**
Statutory insolvency procedure	37
Improving visibility for creditors	39
Content of the proposal made by the directors	39
Contents of a proposal made by an insolvency practitioner	39
Statement of affairs	39

Contents

Notice of moratorium	40
Time recording information	40
CVAs: a more flexible tool	40
Summoning of meetings	40
Requisite majorities (creditors)	41
Procedural changes to increase speed and efficiency	41
Supervisor's accounts and reports	42
Specific issues in relation to IVAs	42
Contents of proposal	42
Annulment of bankruptcy order	43
Nominee's report	43
Transitional provisions	43
Chapter 7 Disclaimer	**45**
Liquidation	45
Notice of disclaimer	45
Records	46
Application by interested party	46
Bankruptcy	46
Notice of disclaimer	46
Records	47
Application by interested party	47
Transitional provisions	47
Chapter 8 Public and private examinations	**49**
Public examination	49
Public examination in a winding up	50
Public examination in a bankruptcy	51
Private examination	51
Transitional provisions	52
Chapter 9 Office holders' remuneration and expenses	**55**
The concept of and approach to insolvency expenses	55
Lundy Granite	57
Liquidation expenses	58
Basis of remuneration	58
Apportionment of set fee remuneration	60
Remuneration of new liquidator	60
Creditors' entitlement to information on liquidator's remuneration	

and expenses	60
Creditors' claim that remuneration is or other expenses are excessive	62
Administration expenses	62
Basis of remuneration	63
Apportionment of set fee remuneration	64
Remuneration of new administrator	64
Pre-administration costs	64
Creditors' entitlement to information on administrator's remuneration and expenses	69
Creditors' claim that remuneration is or other expenses are excessive	70
Rent as an administration expense	71
Trustee in bankruptcy's remuneration	77
Basis of remuneration	77
Apportionment of set fee remuneration	78
Remuneration of new trustee	78
Creditors' entitlement to information on liquidator's remuneration and expenses	78
Creditors' claim that remuneration is or other expenses are excessive	80
Transitional provisions	80
Chapter 10 Miscellaneous legislative amendments	**85**
Introduction	85
Notice of deemed approval of administrator's proposals	85
Claims and distributions – administration, liquidation and bankruptcy	85
Definition of a debt in a winding up	85
Proving claims	86
Appeal against a decision on a proof	86
Interest	86
Redemption of security by an office holder	87
Notice of intended dividend	87
Admission or rejection of proofs	87
Postponement or cancellation of dividend	87
Notice of declaration of dividend	87
Section 110 arrangements – disclosure	88
Other distributions to members in specie	88
Scotland: procedure for drawing a dividend in administration	88

Contents

Office holders' powers – liquidator and trustee in bankruptcy	89
Redemption of security by liquidator or trustee	90
Amendments specific to bankruptcy	90
Service of a bankruptcy petition	90
Amendment of a petition	90
Petitioner seeking dismissal or permission to withdraw	91
Bankrupt carrying on a business	91
Application for annulment under section 282(1)(b) of the Insolvency Act 1986 – trustee's remuneration	91
Annulment – post-commencement interest	92
Individual Insolvency Register	92
Voluntary arrangements	92
Bankruptcies	92
Information not to be included on the register where persons at risk of violence	93
Other provisions relating to persons at risk of violence	93
Application to Scotland	94
Block transfer orders	94
Use of prescribed forms	95
Application to Scotland	95
Changes in language	96
Procedures relating to the EC Regulation	96
Application to Scotland	96
Transitional provisions	96
Appendix I The Insolvency Rules 1986 (as amended)	99
Appendix II The Legislative Reform (Insolvency) (Miscellaneous Provisions) Order 2010	815
Appendix III Commentary for stakeholders on the draft Insolvency Modernisation Rules	827
Index	**841**

Table of Statutes

Paragraph references printed in **bold** type indicate where the Statute is set out in part or in full.

C

Companies Act 2006
- s 360a(1) 3.2
- Pt 26 (ss 895–901)
  .... 6.2, 6.20

D

Deeds of Arrangement Act 1914
  .... 6.2

I

Insolvency Act 1986
  .... 1.2, 3.2, 3.32, 5.3, 6.2, 8.1, 9.5
- Pt 1 (ss 1–7b) 1.15
- s 1a 6.7, 6.17
- 4(3) 6.5
- 4a(3) 6.6
- (6) 6.6
- Pt 2 (ss 8–27) 1.15
- s 92a 9.19
- 93 .... 1.15, 3.30
- s 95 .... 1.15
- 104a 9.19, 9.62
- 105 .... 3.30, 9.62
- 110 .... 10.15
  - (2) 10.14
  - (4) 10.14
- 112 .... 8.4
- 133 .... 8.3
- 134 .... 5.4
- 156 .... 9.7
- 176a(2)(a) 9.35
  - (5) 10.13
- 178 .... 7.4
  - (3) 7.3
  - (4) 7.1
  - (5) 7.6, 7.7
- 236 .... 5.5, 8.11
- 246a 3.1, 3.57
  - (2) 3.57
  - (3) 3.4
  - (5) 3.3
  - (6) 3.5, 3.19
  - (8) 3.4
  - (9) 3.7
- 246b 2.15

Insolvency Act 1986 – *cont.*
- s 246b(2) 2.27
- 247(3)(b) 9.62
- 251n 5.5, 8.13
- 253 .... 6.31
- 256(1)(aa) 6.32
- 256a 6.35
  - (3) 6.32
- 257 .... 6.32
- 261(2)(b) 6.32
- 282(1)(b) 10.33
- 290 .... 8.4
- 315 .... 7.10
  - (2) 7.3
  - (3) 7.2
- 316 .... 7.11
  - (1) 7.10
- 364 .... 5.4
- 366 .... 5.5, 8.14
- 379a 3.1, 3.57
  - (2) 3.4
  - (4) 3.3
  - (5) 3.5
  - (7) 3.4
  - (50) 3.22
- 379b 2.15
- Sch a1 .... 6.7
- Sch b1
- para 3(1) 9.34
  - (a) 10.49, 10.50
- 10 .... 5.8, 7.12, 8.16, 9.61
- 13(1)(f) 9.31
- 14 .... 5.8, 7.12, 8.16, 9.61
- 22 .... 5.8, 7.12, 8.16, 9.61
- 49 .... 9.34
  - (1) 9.31
- 52(1)(b) 9.35
- 53 .... 9.34
- 59(1) 9.41
- 65(3) 9.41
- 83 .... 3.30, 3.59, 5.8, 7.12, 8.16, 9.61, 9.62
- Sch 1
- para 13 .... 9.41
- Sch 4 .... 10.22
- Sch 5 .... 10.23

Insolvency Act 2000
  .... 6.6, 6.7

Table of Statutory Instruments

Paragraph references printed in **bold** type indicate where the Statutory Instruments is set out in part or in full

C

Civil Procedure Rules 1998, SI 1998/3132
.... 5.7

I

Insolvency Rules 1986, SI 1986/1925
.... 2.15, 3.2
Pt 1 (rr 1.1–1.56) 6.1
r 1.3 .... 6.36
    (2)(a)–(q) 6.9
        (r) 6.9
   1.5(1) 6.13
    (4) 6.13
   1.9 .... 3.49
    (1) 6.18
   1.10 .... 6.36
    (1) 6.12
   1.13(1) 3.10
   1.14(4) 3.50
   1.14za 3.57
   1.14aa 3.50, 3.52
   1.15aa 3.53
   1.16a, 1.16b 3.53
   1.19(1) 6.19
   1.19(2) 3.46, 6.19
   1.20 .... 6.22
   1.21(4a) 6.23
   1.22(1) 6.24
   1.26a 6.25
    (3) 6.26
    (4) 6.27, 6.29
    (6) 6.28
   1.31 .... 10.49
   1.37 .... 6.14
   1.40(2a) 6.16
   1.42(1a) 6.16
   1.46 .... 10.51
   1.50 .... 10.42
    (6) 3.37
   1.52 .... 6.21
   1.53(4a) 6.23
   1.55 .... 6.17
   1.56 .... 6.15, 10.39
   2.25(3a) 10.2
   2.26b 3.57
   2.26c 3.54, 10.16, 10.21
    (3)(c) 3.54, 10.21
   2.27c 3.56
   2.30 .... 10.39
   2.32a 3.55
   2.33 .... 9.34

Insolvency Rules 1986, SI 1986/1925 – *cont.*
  r 2.33(2a)(a), (b) 9.32
    (5), (5a) 10.2
   2.33a 10.39, 10.40, 10.43
   2.34 .... 3.40
    (1) 1.4
   2.35 .... 3.40
    (3) 3.10
   2.36a–2.36d 4.12
   2.36d 3.57
   2.36e 3.57, 4.12
   2.36f–2.36r 4.12
   2.37 .... 3.13
    (1) 10.2
   2.37a 3.33
    (5) 3.38
   2.41 .... 10.21
   2.44a 3.47
   2.47 .... 6.30, 9.36, 9.37, 10.51
   2.48a 9.36, 9.37
    (4) 9.39
   2.50(2) 4.2
   2.52(3) 3.20, 4.6
    (3a) 4.5
   2.52(4), (5) 3.20
   2.57(1) 4.8
   2.61(5) 4.7
   2.67 .... 9.24, 9.43, 9.48
    (1)(a) 9.41
    (c) 9.31
    (h) 9.33, 9.41
   2.67a 9.33, 9.34, 9.35
   2.72, 2.73 .... 10.5
  r 2.78(2) 10.7
    (4a) 10.7
   2.88 .... 10.8
   2.92(4) 10.9
   2.95(4) 1.10
   2.96 .... 10.11
   2.96a 10.12
   2.98(2) 10.13
   2.106 .... 9.31, 9.38
    (2) 9.25
    (c) 9.29, 9.36, 9.37
    (3a), (3b) 9.25
    (3c) 9.26, 9.28
    (5) 9.26, 9.28
    (6) 9.27, 9.28
   2.107, 2.108 .... 9.26, 9.28
   2.109 .... 9.38
   2.109a 9.28, 9.31
   2.109b 9.30, 9.31
   2.109c 9.29, 9.31

Table of Statutory Instruments

Insolvency Rules 1986, SI 1986/1925 – *cont.*
- r 2.130 .... 10.50
- 3.5 .... 10.39
- 3.9(1) 3.10
- 3.11a 3.36
  - (4a) 3.38
- 3.15 .... 3.47
- 3.16(2) 4.2
- 3.17(4) 4.3
- 3.18(3) 4.4
- 3.18(4) 3.20
  - (5) 3.20, 4.6
- 3.23(1) 4.8
- 3.27 .... 4.7
- 4.15(2) 4.4, 10.21
- 4.35 .... 10.39
- 4.49b 9.19
  - (1)(d) 9.62
  - (j) 9.62
- 4.49c 9.19
  - (1)–(7) 9.62
- 4.49d 9.19, 9.21, 9.62
- 4.49e 9.17, 9.18, 9.19, 9.62
  - (5) 9.21
- 4.54 .... 3.31
- r 4.54(6)(a) 1.14
- 4.57 .... 3.34
- 4.59 .... 3.33
- 4.60(1) 3.10
- 4.61 .... 3.13
- 4.63a 3.32
- 4.65 .... 3.40
- 4.68 .... 3.37
  - (4a) 3.38
- 4.71 .... 3.47
- 4.77 .... 10.5
- 4.83(4a) 10.7
- 4.93 .... 10.8
- 4.97 .... 10.24
  - (4) 10.9
- 4.108 .... 9.21
  - (3) 9.62
- 4.108a 9.62
- 4.125 .... 9.62
- 4.126(5), (6) 9.62
- 4.127 .... 9.13, 9.17, 9.20, 9.62
  - (2) 9.9
  - (c) 9.15, 9.19
  - (3a)–(3c) 9.10, 9.14
  - (5), (5a) 9.14
  - (7) 9.14
- 4.127a 9.14
- 4.129a 9.10, 9.14
- 4.130 .... 9.10, 9.14
- 4.131 .... 9.20, 9.62
  - (1b) 9.62
- 4.131a 9.14
- 4.131b 9.16, 9.17
- 4.131c 9.15, 9.17
- 4.148a 9.10, 9.14
- 4.153(6) 4.3
- 4.156(4) 3.20, 4.6
- 4.167 .... 4.7

Insolvency Rules 1986, SI 1986/1925 – *cont.*
- r 4.171 .... 4.9
- 4.171a(5) 4.9
- 4.173, 4.174 .... 4.10
- 4.174a 4.9, 4.10
- 4.175–4.178 .... 4.10
- 4.187(4) 7.4
- 4.190a 7.5, 7.12
- 4.191a 7.7
- 4.211(2) 8.5
- 4.212(2) 8.6
  - (3), (3a) 8.8
  - (4) 8.7
- 4.218 .... 9.43, 9.48
  - (1) 9.8
    - (a) 9.41
    - (c) 9.7
  - (3)(a)(ii) 9.41
- 4.220 .... 9.10, 9.14
- 4.223 .... 9.62
- 4.288(2) 1.6
- Pt 5 (rr 5.1–5.68) 6.1
- r 5.3(2)(s) 6.31
- r 5.3 .... 6.36
- 5.5(1) 6.13
- 5.14a, 5.14b 6.35
- 5.18(1) 3.10
- 5.22(6) 3.37
- 5.23 .... 6.19
- 5.31a 6.25
- 5.43 .... 6.19
- 5.55(2) 6.32
- 5.60(3a) 6.33
- 5.66 .... 6.17
- 5.67 .... 6.34
- 5.68 .... 10.39
- 6.14(6) 10.25
- 6.15a 10.25
- 6.22 .... 10.26
- 6.32(1) 10.28
- 6.61 .... 10.39
- 6.78a, 6.78b 9.57
- 6.78c 9.57
  - (5) 9.59
- 6.79 .... 3.31
- 6.81 .... 3.31
- 6.83 .... 3.34
- 6.84 .... 3.31
- 6.85 .... 3.33
- 6.86(1) 3.10
- 6.87 .... 3.13
- 6.88a 3.32
- 6.91 .... 3.40
- 6.93a 3.37
- 6.94(4a) 3.38
- 6.95 .... 3.47
- 6.99 .... 10.5
- 6.117 .... 10.24
  - (4) 10.9
- 6.126 .... 9.59
- 6.138 .... 9.57, 9.58
  - (2) 9.50
  - (c) 9.55, 9.57
  - (3a) 9.50, 9.52

Insolvency Rules 1986, SI 1986/1925 – *cont.*
r 6.138(3b) 9.51, 9.52
  (3c) 9.52, 9.54
  (5) 9.52, 9.54
  (6) 9.53, 9.54
 6.140a 9.52, 9.54
 6.141 .... 9.52, 9.54
 6.142 .... 9.58
 6.142a 9.54, 9.57
 6.142b 9.57
 6.142c 9.55, 9.57
 6.151(5) 4.3
 6.153(2) 4.4
  (4) 3.20, 4.6
 6.158(1) 4.7
 6.162 .... 4.7
 6.172(3) 8.9
  (4)–(5a) 8.10
 6.178(4) 7.8
 6.181a 7.9
 6.183 .... 7.11
 6.207 .... 10.30
 6.207a 10.31
 6.211(5) 10.33
 6a.2a 10.34
 6a.3 .... 10.34
 6a.4 .... 10.35
 6a.5 .... 10.36
 Pt 7 (rr 7.1–7.64) 5.1,
 r 7.6 .... 5.2
  7.6a 5.2, 5.8, 9.61, 9.62
 7.8 .... 3.56
 Pt 7, Ch 1a (ss 7.10a–7.10d)
   .... 10.44
 r 7.10b 10.45
 7.10d 10.45
 7.19(3) 5.3
 7.22(a) 5.4
 7.23(2) 5.5
 7.31a(3)–(7) 5.6, 5.7
 7.51a 5.7
 7.53, 7.54 .... 5.7
 7.58 .... 5.7
 11.2 .... 10.10
 11.3 .... 10.11
 11.4 .... 10.12
 11.6(2a) 10.13
 12.2(1) 9.8
 Pt 12a (rr 12a.1–12a.57)
   .... 3.1, 7.7, 8.5
 Pt 12a, Ch 2 (rr 12a.6–12a.15)
   .... 2.1
 r 12a.6(2) 2.2
  (3)(a), (b) 2.2
 12a.7 .... 2.3
 12a.9 .... 7.4
  (2) 2.6
 12a.10 .... 2.11
  (1) 2.4
  (2) 2.7
   (b) 2.13, 2.14
  (3) 2.7, 2.9
 12a.11 .... 2.5, 2.11

Insolvency Rules 1986, SI 1986/1925 – *cont.*
r 12a.12(2) 2.16, 2.17
  (3) 2.17
 12a.13 .. 2.16, 2.18, 2.19, 2.21, 2.23,
           2.24
 12a.14 .... 2.2
  (1) 2.8
  (3), (4) 2.8
  (5) 2.9
 12a.21 .... 3.39
 12a.22 .... 3.27
  (3) 3.8
  (4) 3.9, 3.11
  (7) 3.13
 12a.23 .... 3.23
  (1) 3.14
 12a.24 .... 3.17, 3.23, 3.29
 12a.25 .... 3.15, 3.23
 12a.26 .... 3.19
 12a.27 .... 3.19, 3.23, 3.27
 12a.27(4) 3.23
 12a.33 .... 1.4
  (2) 1.6
 12a.34 .... 1.4, 1.7
 12a.35 .... 1.4, 1.8
 12a.36 .... 1.4
 12a.37 .... 1.9
 12a.38 .... 1.4
 12a.39 .... 1.4, 1.12
 12a.40 .... 1.4, 1.13
 12a.41 .... 1.4, 1.10
 12a.41(2) 1.4
 12a.51 .... 10.41
 13.12 .... 10.4
 r 13.13(4B) 1.4
 13.13(5) 1.4
 Sch 4
 Form 2.2B 9.31
  4.7 .... 10.20
  4.52 .... 4.11
  7.1a 5.2
 Sch 6 .... 9.13
Insolvency (Amendment) Rules 2010, SI
 2010/686 .... 1.1, 1.3, 1.15, 3.31, 5.1,
  5.2, 6.8, 6.20, 6.21, 6.23, 6.24,
  7.3, 8.2, 8.8, 9.1, 9.8, 9.17,
  9.24, 9.31, 9.36, 9.49, 9.57
 r 6(2) 1.14
 r 502(5) 3.6
  503(6) 3.6
 Sch 4
 para 1 .... 6.36, 8.16, 9.61
  (6) 9.62
 2 .... 9.61, 9.62
  (1)(a) 7.12
  3(1), (2) 6.36
Insolvency (Amendment) (No. 2) Rules
 2010, SI 2010/734
 r 13 .... 3.30, 9.62
Insolvency (Scotland) Rules 1986, SI
 1986/1915 .... 1.15, 2.1
 r 1.1b 2.26

Table of Statutory Instruments

Insolvency (Scotland) Rules 1986, SI 1986/1915 – *cont.*
    r 1.1c, r 1.1d 2.27
       2.25c 2.26
       2.25d, 2.25e 2.27
          a–R 4.12, 4.13
       7.21a, 7.21b 1.15
       7.30 .... 10.2, 10.47
    Sch 5 .... 10.47
    Form 2.16BZ 10.2
       4.7 .... 10.21
Insolvency (Scotland) Amendment Rules 2010, SI 2010/688
    .... 1.1, 1.3

L

Legislative Reform (Insolvency) (Miscellaneous Provisions) Order 2010, SI 2010/18
    art 6(3), (4) 9.62
    art 8 .... 6.35
       12(1), (2) 9.62

Table of Cases

A

ABC Coupler and Engineering Co Ltd (No 3), Re [1970] 1 All ER 650, [1970] 1 WLR 702, 114 Sol Jo 242, 209 Estates Gazette 1197 .... 9.7
Ansett Australia Ground Staff Superannuation Plan v Ansett Australia [2002] VSC 576 .... 9.7
Atlantic Computer Systems plc, Re [1992] Ch 505, [1992] 1 All ER 476, [1992] 2 WLR 367, [1991] BCLC 606, [1990] BCC 859, CA 9.7, 9.42, 9.43, 9.45, 9.46, 9.47

B

Beloit Walmsley Ltd, Re [2008] EWHC 1888 (Ch), [2009] 1 BCLC 584, [2008] BPIR 1445 .... 5.7, 6.7
Bridgewater Engineering Co, Re (1879) 12 Ch D 181, 48 LJ Ch 389 .... 9.7

C

Casterbridge Properties Ltd (in liq), Re, Jeeves v Official Receiver [2003] EWCA Civ 1246, [2003] 4 All ER 1041, [2004] 1 WLR 602, [2004] 1 BCLC 96, [2003] BCC 912, [2004] BPIR 46, [2003] All ER (D) 504 (Jul) 8.3

D

Downer Enterprises Ltd, Re [1974] 2 All ER 1074, [1974] 1 WLR 1460, 118 Sol Jo 829 .... 9.7

F

Franbar Holdings Ltd v Patel [2008] EWHC 1534 (Ch), [2009] Bus LR D14, [2009] 1 BCLC 1, [2008] BCC 885, [2008] All ER (D) 14 (Jul) 5.6, 5.7

G

Goldacre (Offices) Ltd v Nortel Networks UK Ltd (in administration) [2010] 3 WLR 171, [2010] 09 EG 168, [2009] EWHC 3389 (Ch), [2010] All ER (D) 54 (Jan) .. 9.7, 9.40, 9.41, 9.48

J

Johnson Machine and Tool Ltd, Re [2010] EWHC 582 (Ch), [2010] NLJR 805, [2010] All ER (D) 271 (May) 9.24, 9.31, 9.32

K

Kayley Vending Ltd, Re [2009] EWHC 904 (Ch), [2009] BCC 578, [2009] All ER (D) 203 (Oct) 9.31
Kentish Homes Ltd, Re (1993) 91 LGR 592, [1993] BCLC 1375, [1993] BCC 212, [1993] 13 LS Gaz R 36, 137 Sol Jo LB 45 .... 9.6

L

Lancashire Cotton Spinning Co, Re, ex p Carnelley (1887) 35 Ch D 656, 56 LJ Ch 761, 36 WR 305, 57 LT 511, CA 9.7
Lomas v Rab Market Cycles (Master) Fund Ltd [2009] EWHC 2545 (Ch), [2009] All ER (D) 313 (Oct) 9.41, 9.43
London Metallurgical Co, Re [1895] 1 Ch 758, 64 LJ Ch 442, 2 Mans 276, 13 R 436, 43 WR 476, 39 Sol Jo 363, 72 LT 421, 11 TLR 308 ...... 9.4
Lundy Granite Co, Re, ex p Heavan (1871) 6 Ch App 462, 35 JP 692, 40 LJ Ch 588, 19 WR 609, 24 LT 922 ...... 9.7, 9.41, 9.42, 9.43, 9.44, 9.48

O

Oak Pitts Colliery Co, Re (1882) 21 Ch D 322, 51 LJ Ch 768, 30 WR 759, [1881–5] All ER Rep 1157, 47 LT 7, CA 9.7

P

Pantmaenog Timber Co Ltd (in liq), Re [2003] UKHL 49, [2004] 1 AC 158, [2003] 4 All ER 18, [2003] 3 WLR 767, [2003] 2 BCLC 257, [2003] BCC 659, [2003] NLJR 1346, (2003) Times, 7 August, 147 Sol Jo LB 936, [2004] BPIR 139, [2003] All ER (D) 553 (Jul) 8.1, 8.3
Paramount Airways Ltd (in administration), Re [1993] Ch 223, [1992] 3 All ER 1, [1992] 3 WLR 690, [1992] BCLC 710, [1992] BCC 416, 136 Sol Jo LB 97, CA 9.5
Perpetual Trustee Co Ltd v BNY Corporate Trustee Services Ltd [2009] EWCA Civ 1160, [2010] 3 WLR 87, [2010] 1 BCLC 747, (2009) Times, 16 November, [2010] BPIR 174, [2009] All ER (D) 87 (Nov) 9.45
Polly Peck International plc (in administration) (No 2), Re; Marangos Hotel Co Ltd v Stone [1998] 3 All ER 812, 1 ITELR 289, [1998] 2 BCLC 185, [1998] All ER (D) 194, CA 9.5
Progress Assurance Co, Re, ex p Liverpool Exchange Co (1870) LR 9 Eq 370, 39 LJ Ch 504, 22 LT 707 ...... 9.7

R

Raleigh v Illinois Dept of Revenue 530 US 15 (2000) 9.2

S

SE Services Ltd, Re (9 August 2006, unreported) 9.31
SSSL Realisations (2002) Ltd (in liq), Re EWCA Civ 7, [2006] Ch 610, [2006] 2 WLR 1369, [2007] 1 BCLC 29, (2006) Times, 20 January, [2006] BPIR 457, [2006] All ER (D) 98 (Jan), sub nom Squires (liquidators of SSSL Realisations (2002) Ltd) v AIG Europe (UK) Ltd [2006] BCC 233 ...... 7.1
Shackell & Co v Chorlton & Sons [1895] 1 Ch 378, 64 LJ Ch 353, 2 Mans 233, 13 R 301, 43 WR 394, 72 LT 188 ...... 9.7
South Kensington Co-operative Stores, Re (1881) 17 Ch D 161, 50 LJ Ch 446, 29 WR 662, 44 LT 471 ...... 9.7
Sporting Options plc, Re [2004] EWHC 3128 (Ch), [2005] BCC 88, [2005] BPIR 435, [2004] All ER (D) 30 (Dec) 2.22
Springfield Retail, Re [2010] CSOH 115 ...... 9.48
Squires (liquidators of SSSL Realisations (2002) Ltd) v AIG Europe (UK) Ltd. See SSSL Realisations (2002) Ltd (in liq), Re; Re Save Group plc (in liq)

T

Toshoku Finance UK plc, Re, Kahn v IRC [2002] UKHL 6, [2002] 3 All ER 961, [2002] 1 WLR 671, [2002] STC 368, [2002] 1 BCLC 598, [2002] BCC 110, (2002) Times, 25 February, [2002] All ER (D) 276 (Feb) 9.7, 9.41, 9.42, 9.44, 9.46, 9.48

Travelers Casualty & Surety Co of America v Pacific Gas & Electric Co 549 US 443 (2007) 9.2

Trident Fashions, Re, Exeter City Council v Bairstow [2007] EWHC 400 (Ch), [2007] 4 All ER 437, [2007] Bus LR 813, [2007] 2 P & CR 129, [2007] RA 109, [2007] 2 BCLC 455, [2007] BCC 236, (2007) Times, 6 April, [2007] All ER (D) 45 (Mar) 9.7, 9.42, 9.47

U

Unadkat & Co (Accountants) Ltd v Bhardwaj (former liquidator of Isher Fashions Ltd) [2006] EWHC 2785 (Ch), [2007] BCC 452 .... 9.8

Chapter 1

Advertising and gazetting

Introduction

[1.1] The changes in advertising and gazetting, introduced by the Insolvency (Amendment) Rules 2010 (IR 2010) and the Insolvency (Scotland) (Amendment) Rules 2010 (IR Scotland 2010), build on amendments made in April 2009.[1] Before discussing the 2010 changes, it may be helpful to summarise the amendments made in the previous year.

---

[1] Introduced by the Legislative Reform (Insolvency) (Advertising Requirements) Order 2009 (SI 2009/864), the Insolvency (Amendment) Rules 2009 (SI 2009/642) and the Insolvency (Scotland) Amendment Rules 2009 (SI 2009/662).

[1.2] Broadly speaking, the 2009 amendments provide that where there is a requirement to advertise a notice under the Act or Rules, the notice must be published in the Gazette and may be advertised in such other manner as the office holder thinks fit. Mandatory newspaper advertising was thus abolished and the use of the phrase "such other manner" made it clear that the discretionary advertising could be in any medium. The Insolvency Service issued guidance on the use of discretionary advertising and stated that the reason for the 2009 amendments was to "achieve better targeted publicity in insolvency proceedings".[1]

---

[1] *Dear IP*, Issue 39, Chapter 15, Article 37.

[1.3] IR 2010 have introduced further changes to advertising requirements, principally to standardise the content of notices which are advertised under the Act or the Rules. IR Scotland 2010 make corresponding changes to the content of notices for company voluntary arrangements and administrations.

Standard contents – general

[1.4] All notices which are advertised must include standard contents. Additional content may be prescribed by the specific rule to which the notice relates. For example, a notice of an initial meeting of creditors in administration must contain standard contents and the information prescribed in r 2.34(1).

The term "standard contents" is defined in r 13.13(4B) and makes a distinction between the content of notices to be gazetted and that of notices to be advertised in any other way. Standard contents for Gazette notices is set out in rr 12A.33–12A.35 and standard contents for a notice to be advertised in any other way is contained in rr 12A.38–12A.40. The Rules provide that information prescribed as standard contents for a notice may be omitted if it is not reasonably practicable to obtain it.[1]

[1.4] Advertising and gazetting

[1] Rule 12A.36 for Gazette notices and r 12A.41(2) for non-Gazette notices.

Standard contents for advertising in the Gazette

[1.5] There are requirements which apply in all cases and additional requirements which vary depending on whether the notice is in respect of a company or a bankrupt.

All cases

[1.6] All notices advertised in the Gazette, with the exception of notices advertised under r 4.228(2), must contain the following information as standard, in so far as it is applicable to the particular notice:

(a) the name and postal address of the office holder acting in the proceedings;
(b) the capacity in which the office holder is acting and the date of appointment;
(c) either an e-mail address, or a telephone number, through which the office holder may be contacted;
(d) the name of any person other than the office holder (if any) who may be contacted regarding the proceedings;
(e) the number assigned to the office holder by the Secretary of State; and
(f) the court name and any number assigned to the proceedings by the court.[1]

[1] Rule 12A.33(2).

Additional requirements for companies

[1.7] Company notices must contain the following additional information:

(a) the registered name of the company;
(b) its registered number;
(c) its registered office, or if an unregistered company, the postal address of its principal place of business;
(d) any principal trading address if this is different from its registered office;
(e) any name under which it was registered in the 12 months prior to the date of the commencement of the proceedings which are the subject of the Gazette notice; and
(f) any name or style (other than its registered name) under which—
  (i) the company carried on business; and
  (ii) any debt owed to a creditor was incurred.[1]

[1] Rule 12A.34.

Additional requirements for bankrupts

[1.8] Bankruptcy notices must include the following:

(a) the bankrupt's full name and residential address;
(b) any other address at which the bankrupt has resided in the period of 12 months preceding the making of the bankruptcy order;
(c) the bankrupt's date of birth;
(d) the bankrupt's occupation;
(e) any other name by which the bankrupt has been known;
(f) any name or style (other than the bankrupt's own name) under which—
  (i) the bankrupt carried on business; and
  (ii) any debt owed to a creditor was incurred.[1]

[1] Rule 12A.35.

General provisions relating to advertising in the Gazette

[1.9] Former r 12.20 is reproduced as r 12A.37. It provides for a Gazette notice to be evidence of facts stated in the notice and for notices to be corrected in the event of variation of an advertised court order or any matter having been erroneously or inaccurately gazetted.

Standard contents for advertising other than in the Gazette

All cases

[1.10] As stated at the beginning of this chapter, notices advertised other than in the Gazette can be advertised in any manner that the office holder thinks fit. This could include, for example, advertising on a website, television or radio. In view of the variety of media which could be used, the Rules provide that the information contained in non-Gazette notices must be included in such a way that it is reasonably likely that a person reading, hearing or seeing the advertisement will be able to read, hear or see the information contained in the notice.[1]

[1] Rule 12A.41(1).

[1.11] All notices which are to be advertised other than in the Gazette must contain the following information, in so far as it is applicable to the particular notice:

(a) the name and postal address of the office holder acting in the proceedings to which the notice relates;
(b) the capacity in which the office holder is acting; and
(c) either an e-mail address, or a telephone number, through which the office holder may be contacted.

[1.11] Advertising and gazetting

There are additional requirements depending on whether the notice relates to a company or a bankrupt. These requirements are set out below.

Non-Gazette notices – additional requirements for companies

[1.12] The notice must state:

(a) the registered name of the company;
(b) its registered number;
(c) any name under which it was registered in the 12 months prior to the date of the commencement of the proceedings which are the subject of the notice; and
(d) any name or style (other than its registered name) under which—
    (i) the company carried on business; and
    (ii) any debt owed to a creditor was incurred.[1]

---

[1] Rule 12A.39.

Non-Gazette notices – additional requirements for bankrupts

[1.13] The notice must state:

(a) the bankrupt's full name and address;
(b) any other address at which the bankrupt has resided in the period of 12 months preceding the making of the bankruptcy order;
(c) the bankrupt's date of birth;
(d) the bankrupt's occupation;
(e) any other name by which the bankrupt has been known;
    (i) the bankrupt carried on business; and
    (ii) any debt owed to a creditor was incurred.[1]

---

[1] Rule 12A.40.

Other amendments

No requirement to advertise annual meetings in voluntary liquidations

[1.14] Rule 6(2) of IR 2010 provides that the requirement to advertise a meeting in the Gazette under r 4.54(6)(a) does not apply to meetings convened under ss 93 or 95 of the Insolvency Act 1986 (annual meetings in voluntary liquidations).

Application to Scotland

Standard contents

[1.15] The Insolvency (Scotland) Rules 1986 are amended to provide for standard contents in notices published or advertised in company voluntary arrangements or administrations.[1] As is the case for England and Wales, the content of the notice varies depending on whether it is advertised in the Gazette or by other means.[2] The requirements mirror those for companies in England and Wales.

[1] Rule 7.21A, inserted by the IR Scotland 2010, prescribes the content for notices advertised in accordance with Pts I and II of the Act and Pts 1 and 2 of the Insolvency (Scotland) Rules 1986.
[2] Rules 7.21A and 7.21B respectively.

Transitional provisions

[1.16] The change described in paragraph 1.14 only applies to voluntary liquidations which started before 6 April 2010 (because annual meetings are not required for liquidations starting on or after 6 April 2010). The rest of the changes described in this chapter apply to cases where the insolvency commences or, in the case of a voluntary arrangement, the nominee agrees to act, on or after 6 April 2010, with the following exceptions:

- An administration by court order made on or after 6 April 2010 on an application made before 6 April 2010
- An administration commencing on or after 6 April 2010 which was preceded by a liquidation which started before 6 April 2010
- A liquidation commencing on or after 6 April 2010 which was preceded by an administration which started before 6 April 2010
- A liquidation commencing on or after 6 April 2010 which was preceded by an administration by court order where the application was made before 6 April 2010
- A compulsory liquidation commencing on or after 6 April 2010 which was immediately preceded by a voluntary liquidation starting before 6 April 2010.

Chapter 2

Electronic communications and websites

Introduction

[2.1] The Insolvency (Amendment) Rules 2010 (IR 2010) introduce important new provisions enabling office holders to communicate with stakeholders by electronic means and to publish documents on a website as an alternative to sending them by post. The provisions are contained in Ch 2 of Pt 12A of the Rules. Equivalent amendments have been made to the Insolvency (Scotland) Rules 1986 for company voluntary arrangements and administrations.

Scope of application of the new provisions (England and Wales)

[2.2] The new provisions can be used in respect of any notice or other document required to be given, delivered or sent under the Insolvency Act 1986 (IA 1986) or Insolvency Rules 1986, except for the following:

- The submission of documents to Companies House[1]
- The service of a statutory demand[2]
- The filing of any notice or other document with the court unless electronic delivery is permitted under a different rule or the court has provided an electronic working scheme for the proceedings to which the document relates.[3]

---

[1] Rule 12A.6(2).
[2] Rule 12A.6(3)(b).
[3] Rules 12A.6(3)(a) and 12A.14.

Electronic communications

General

[2.3] Any notice or other document required to be given, delivered or sent must be in writing, unless the court orders otherwise. Where electronic delivery is permitted, a document in electronic form is treated as being in writing if a copy of it can be produced in legible form.[1]

---

[1] Rule 12A.7.

[2.4] Electronic communications and websites

Recipient to have given consent to electronic communication

[2.4] A notice or other document may only be given, delivered or sent by electronic means if the intended recipient has consented to electronic delivery (and has not revoked that consent) and has provided an electronic address for delivery. Consent may be given in relation to a specific case or may be general.[1]

[1] Rule 12A.10(1).

Right to request a hard copy

[2.5] Any document which is sent electronically must include, or be accompanied by, a statement that the recipient may request a hard copy of the document. The statement must include a telephone number, e-mail address and postal address which may be used to request a hard copy. If the recipient requests a hard copy, it must be sent, free of charge, within five business days of receipt of the request.[1]

[1] Rule 12A.11.

Authentication

[2.6] A document or information sent in electronic form is sufficiently authenticated if the identity of the sender is confirmed in a manner specified by the recipient or, if no manner has been specified, it contains a statement of the identity of the sender and the recipient has no grounds to doubt the truth of it.[1]

[1] Rule 12A.9(2).

Delivery

[2.7] In the absence of evidence to the contrary, a document is presumed to have been delivered if the sender can produce a copy of the electronic message which contains the notice or document, or to which the notice or document was attached, shows the date and time of the message and contains the electronic address supplied by the intended recipient.[1] As regards timing of delivery, a document is deemed to have been delivered no later than 9 a m on the next business day after it was sent.[2]

[1] Rule 12A.10(2). "Evidence to the contrary" would presumably include a delivery failure notice.
[2] Rule 12A.10(3).

Electronic communications – the courts

[2.8] No petition, application, notice or other document may be delivered or made to a court by electronic means unless one of two exceptions applies.[1] The first exception is for cases where electronic delivery of documents to a court is permitted by another rule (for example, r 2.19 which allows the holder of a qualifying floating charge holder to file a notice of appointment of administrator with the court out of hours as an attachment to an e-mail).

The second exception is if the court provides an electronic working scheme for the proceedings to which the document relates, the requirements of the scheme are complied with and the communication is sent to the electronic address provided by the court and is accompanied by any payment due to the court.[2] If the court provides an electronic working scheme, it will be set out in a practice direction.[3] Practice Direction 5C of the Civil Procedure Rules provides for an electronic working scheme to operate from 1 April 2010 in the Chancery Division of the High Court at the Royal Courts of Justice, including the Bankruptcy and Companies Courts.

[1] Rule 12A.14(1).
[2] Rule 12A.14(3).
[3] Rule 12A.14(4).

[2.9] It should be noted that where an electronic working scheme applies, an electronic communication will only be treated as delivered to the court at the time that it is recorded by the court as having been received.[1] There is no deemed delivery.[2]

[1] Rule 12A.14(5).
[2] Contrast with r 12A.10(3) which provides for deemed delivery of documents to other parties.

Practical considerations

[2.10] Electronic communication has a number of advantages. It can save on printing and postage costs and time spent filling envelopes, particularly in cases with a large number of recipients and or where the documents are bulky. Documents can be delivered quickly, which is particularly useful if there are postal difficulties or recipients are based overseas. In some cases, the insolvent entity may have conducted its business largely or even entirely by electronic means and it is helpful to have a procedure in the Rules by which this can continue, without incurring the time and expense of applications to court.

[2.11] The provisions of rr 12A.10–11 are drafted widely enough to facilitate electronic communication with a variety of different stakeholders, for example, creditors, shareholders, other insolvency office holders, directors and the debtor in personal insolvency.

[2.12] Office holders may need to amend their systems to capture e-mail addresses. This could be done by including a form with the initial communication to the stakeholders concerned, including a 'tick box' for consent to electronic communications and space for the stakeholder to insert the electronic address. Office holders might also consider including a statement to the effect that it is important that the stakeholder keeps the office holder notified of changes of electronic address.

Particular care will need to be taken in recording electronic addresses. A typographical error in a postal address may not be fatal to delivery of the document, but a mistake in keying an e-mail address will almost certainly result in the document either being delivered to the wrong recipient or not being delivered at all.

[2.13] If the sender receives a 'delivery failure' notice, he or she will probably wish to check that the electronic address has been keyed correctly from the information supplied by the stakeholder. If the address which has been keyed is not the same as the address supplied by the recipient, the document cannot have been properly delivered under the provisions of r 12A.10(2)(b). If a 'delivery failure' notice is received for other reasons (for example, if the e-mail account has been closed), it would seem logical for it to be treated in the same way as a postal document returned as 'not known at this address' or 'addressee gone away'.

A further possibility is that an 'out of office' message will be received. It is suggested that in such cases, if the requirements of r 12A.10 have been complied with, the document is deemed to have been delivered and it is the responsibility of the recipient (having consented to electronic communication in the first place) to make arrangements for e-mails to be reviewed or forwarded in his or her absence, in the same way as documents received in the post.

[2.14] Other matters to consider might include:

- If there are attachments, should they be sent in a 'read only' format, to prevent alteration, or will the recipient need to be able to edit the document, for example, to fill in details of a claim?
- Is the file format one which is widely used?
- How bulky is the attachment? Can the document be opened and printed easily?
- What are the effects on system resources of e-mailing a large number of stakeholders simultaneously?
- Is the sender able to print out a copy of the document which contains all the e-mail addresses to which the document has been sent (in order to comply with r 12A.10(2)(b))? Some systems only show the first few addresses when an e-mail is printed out.

Use of websites

[2.15] Sections 246B and 379B of the IA 1986 provide that where any provision of the Act or Rules requires the office holder to give, deliver, furnish or send a notice or other document or information to any person, that requirement is satisfied by making the information available on a website.[1]

---

[1] Introduced by art 3 of the Legislative Reform (Insolvency) (Miscellaneous Provisions) Order 2010 (SI 2010/18).

[2.16] Rules 12A.12 and 12A.13 set out the detailed procedure for using websites. The office holder must send the person concerned a notice stating that the document is available for viewing on a website. The notice must specify the website address and provide any password required. It must also state that a hard copy of the document may be requested and must provide a telephone number, e-mail address and postal address which may be used to request a hard copy.[1]

[1] Rule 12A.12(2).

[2.17] If the office holder is asked for a hard copy of the document it must be sent within five business days of receipt of the request. The office holder is not allowed to charge the recipient a fee for providing the document.

The document must be available on the website for a period of not less than three months after the date on which the notice is sent and must be in a format which enables it to be downloaded from the website within a reasonable period of time.[1]

Where a document is published on a website as an alternative to being sent out electronically or by post, it is deemed delivered on the later of:
- the day on which it was first made available on the website; or
- the date on which the notice under r 12A.12(2) was delivered.

[1] Rule 12A.12(3).

[2.18] In some cases, the cost of sending individual notices each time a document is placed on a website may be prohibitive and so the Rules provide for the office holder to be able to apply to court for permission to send a notice only once.[1] If the court is satisfied that the expense of sending individual notices would, on account of the number of persons entitled to receive them, be disproportionate to the benefit, it may allow the office holder to send to each person one notice stating that all relevant documents will be made available for viewing and downloading on a website. The notice must include the website address and any password needed to access the document. The notice must also state that a hard copy can be requested and give a telephone number, e-mail address and postal address which can be used for this purpose.

[1] Rule 12A.13.

[2.19] A document published on a website in accordance with r 12A.13 must be available on the website for a period of not less than 12 months from the later of:
- the date on which the document was first published on the website; and
- the date on which the notice was sent.

It must be in a format that will enable it to be downloaded from the website within a reasonable time.

[2.20] Where a hard copy is requested, it must be sent within five business days of receipt of the request, if the request is received after publication of the document on the website, or within five business days of publication on the website if the request is received before the document is published. The office holder is not allowed to charge the recipient a fee for providing the document.

[2.21] Electronic communications and websites

[2.21] Where a document is published on a website in accordance with r 12A.13, it is deemed to be sent or delivered on the day that it is first published on the website or, if later, the date on which the notice was delivered to the recipient.

Practical considerations

[2.22] These are useful provisions which have the potential to reduce costs and enable quicker communication with stakeholders. The Rules reflect decisions in cases, reported and unreported, where the courts have permitted documents such as administrators' proposals to be published on a website, as an alternative to sending by post.[1]

---

[1] For example, *Sporting Options plc, Re* [2004] EWHC 3128 (Ch), [2005] BCC 88, [2005] BPIR 435.

[2.23] Office holders will need to consider whether to use their own firm's website, the insolvent entity's website, or a website set up specifically for publishing documents relating to insolvency proceedings. Whichever is chosen, it will be necessary to ensure that the website will be available for the 'life' of the document, which will be at least 3 or 12 months depending on whether a court order was obtained under r 12A.13, and may well extend beyond the closure of the case. It is probably also desirable to have all the documents relating to particular a case available on the same website.

[2.24] The legislation stipulates that a document placed on a website pursuant to rr 12A.12 or 12A.13 must be in a format which will enable it to be downloaded within a reasonable time. It will be advisable to consider the likely volume of traffic to the site, particularly in large and or high profile cases, the size of the document files to be published and whether the system resources available will be adequate.

[2.25] Office holders will also need to consider whether the area of the website or the document should be password-protected to restrict access. The approach adopted may depend on whether the document contains any personal data (for example, individuals' names and addresses) or confidential information and how wide a circulation is required under the Act or Rules or is otherwise desirable.

Application to Scotland

Electronic communication

[2.26] Rules 1.1B and 2.25C of the Insolvency (Scotland) Rules 1986 provide for electronic delivery of documents in company voluntary arrangements and administrations respectively. The provisions mirror those for England and Wales.

Use of websites

[2.27] The provisions of s 246B of the Act do not apply to liquidation or receivership in Scotland.[1] This means that websites can only be used in company voluntary arrangements and administrations. The supporting legislation is contained in rr 1.1C and 1.1D and 2.25D and 2.25E. Again, the provisions mirror those for England and Wales.

[1] Section 246B(2).

Transitional provisions

[2.28] The new rules relating to electronic communications and the use of websites apply on or after 6 April 2010 in all cases, regardless of the date of commencement of the insolvency process.

Chapter 3

Meetings and resolutions

Introduction

[3.1] The new legislation makes various changes to requirements and procedures relating to meetings. The principal changes, as they affect England and Wales, are summarised below and are described in more detail later in the chapter. Changes in Scotland are discussed at the end of the chapter.

- Meetings summoned under the Insolvency Act 1986 (IA 1986) or Rules, including meetings of creditors' or liquidation committees, can be held by remote attendance, if the person summoning the meeting considers it appropriate.[1]
- Annual meetings are not required in voluntary liquidations which started on or after 6 April 2010.
- The minimum notice requirement for meetings of creditors or contributories (other than final meetings) in liquidation or bankruptcy is reduced from 21 to 14 days.
- In liquidation and bankruptcy, resolutions can be passed by correspondence (as is the case in administration) unless the Insolvency Act requires a resolution to be passed at a meeting.
- In administration, notice of meetings can be given by advertisement only, with the permission of the court. This is now consistent with liquidation and bankruptcy.
- Inconsistencies have been removed from rules relating to requisitioned meetings, lodging of proofs and proxies for voting purposes, the chairman's discretion to allow a vote, appeals and suspension and adjournment of meetings.
- The rules relating to quorum for meetings have been moved to Pt 12A of the Rules.
- In a company voluntary arrangement (CVA), the requisite majority of creditors for approving a CVA is slightly amended.
- Amendments are made to the information to be contained in the minutes or record of proceedings.

---

[1] Sections 246A and 379A of the IA 1986, introduced by art 3 of the Legislative Reform (Insolvency) (Miscellaneous Provisions) Order 2010 ("the Legislative Reform Order 2010").

Remote attendance at meetings

[3.2] Any meeting of creditors, members (other than a company meeting in a members' voluntary liquidation) or contributories summoned under the Act or Rules may be held by remote means. Company meetings in a members' voluntary winding up are excluded because they are convened in accordance

[3.2] Meetings and resolutions

with the requirements of the company's Articles of Association and the Companies Act 2006 instead.[1]

---

[1] It is possible for a company meeting to be held by electronic means—see s 360A(1), Companies Act 2006.

What is meant by "remote means"?

[3.3] The IA 1986 provides that a meeting is held by remote means if it is attended by persons who are not present together at the same place, but are nonetheless able to exercise their rights to speak or vote. To be able to speak, a person must be able to communicate during the meeting any information or opinions he or she has on the business of the meeting with all those who are present. In this context, communication can be oral or written. A participant is able to exercise a right to vote if he or she is able to vote during the meeting on resolutions put to the vote and his or her vote can be taken into account in determining whether or not such resolutions are passed at the same time as the votes of all the other persons attending the meeting.[1]

---

[1] Sections 246A(5) and 379A(4).

Responsibilities of the person summoning the meeting

[3.4] The IA 1986 makes it clear that the person summoning the meeting (the convenor) must decide whether it is appropriate for the meeting to be summoned by remote means.[1] In making the decision, the convenor must have regard to the legitimate interests of those attending the meeting in the efficient despatch of the business of the meeting.[2]

---

[1] Sections 246A(3) and 379A(2).
[2] Sections 246A(8) and 379A(7).

[3.5] The convenor is also responsible for choosing the medium in which the meeting is to be held remotely. He or she may make whatever arrangements he or she thinks appropriate to enable those attending the meeting to exercise their rights to speak or vote, to ensure the identification of those attending the meeting and the security of any electronic means used to enable attendance.[1]

---

[1] Sections 246A(6) and 379A(5).

Giving notice of a meeting held by remote means

[3.6] The number of days notice required to be given of a meeting of creditors, contributories or members held by remote means is the same as it would have been if the meeting were held in the conventional way. Before sending out a notice of a meeting to be held by remote means, the person completing the form must insert details of the arrangements proposed.[1]

Similarly, if forms have to be completed after the meeting to record that it was held, the person completing the form must include a statement to the effect that the meeting was held without a place being specified.²

1   Rule 502(5), Insolvency (Amendment) Rules 2010 (IR 2010).
2   Rule 502(6), IR 2010.

Request for a place to be specified for a meeting

[3.7] Those summoned to a 'remote' meeting may be able to insist that the meeting is held in the conventional way instead, by making a request for the convenor to specify a place for the meeting. The convenor must specify a place for the meeting if requested to do so by at least 10% in value of the creditors or contributories, in the case of a creditors' or contributories' meeting, or members holding at least 10% of the voting rights in the case of a members' meeting.¹

1   Sections 246A(9) and 379A(8).

[3.8] A request for a meeting to be held at a place must be made within seven business days of the date on which the convenor sent the notice of the meeting.¹ The request must be accompanied by a list of the creditors, contributories or members (as the case may be) making or concurring with the request and must include the amounts of their debts, values (in the case of contributories) or voting rights. Those concurring with the request must provide written confirmation of their concurrence.

1   Rule 12A.22(3).

[3.9] If the convenor considers that the request has been properly made, he or she must take the following steps:¹

(a)   give notice to all those previously invited to the meeting that it is to be held at a specified place. The notice must state whether the time and date are to remain the same;
(b)   set a venue for the meeting;
(c)   give at least 14 days' notice of the venue to all those previously given notice of the meeting.

The meeting must be held not later than 28 days after the original date for the meeting and, as stated above, at least 14 days' notice must be given.

1   Rule 12A.22(4).

[3.10] The usual rules relating to venue will apply to a meeting requested under r 12A.22 and so in choosing where to hold the meeting, the convenor must have regard to the convenience of those invited to attend.¹

1   Rules 1.13(1), 2.35(3), 3.9(1), 4.60(1), 5.18(1), 6.86(1).

[3.11] The notice of the venue under (c) above may be given at the same time as the notice in (a) or at a different time.[1] This two-stage process for giving notice is presumably designed to cater for situations where the convenor is unable to confirm the venue at the time that he or she has to give notice that the arrangements have changed.

[1] Rule 12A.22(4).

[3.12] Where the convenor has specified a place for the meeting in response to a request, the chairman of the meeting must attend the meeting by being present in person.

[3.13] The convenor cannot charge the person(s) who have requested a place for the meeting the expenses of, or a deposit in respect of, such a meeting. This is prohibited by ss 246A(9) and 379A(8) of the Act, which provide that the rules relating to deposits and expenses of summoning meetings do not apply.[1]

[1] Rule 12A.22(7). The rules which are excluded are rr 2.37(3), (4), (5) and (6), 4.61 and 6.87.

Excluded persons and complaints

[3.14] An excluded person is someone who has taken all steps necessary to attend a meeting under the arrangements made by the convenor, but those arrangements do not permit the person to attend the whole or part of the meeting.[1]

[1] Rule 12A.23(1).

[3.15] Where, during the course of a meeting, the chairman becomes aware that there is an excluded person, the chairman has several options. He or she can:

(a) Continue the meeting
(b) Declare the meeting void and convene the meeting again
(c) Declare the meeting valid up to the point that the person was excluded and adjourn the meeting
(d) Suspend the meeting for a period up to one hour without an adjournment and without prejudice to (a) to (c) above.

If the chairman decides to continue the meeting, the meeting is valid unless either the chairman decides, as a result of a complaint under r 12A.25, to declare the proceedings void and hold the meeting again, or the court directs otherwise.

[3.16] An excluded person may ask to be provided with an indication of what occurred during the period of claimed exclusion. Such a request must be made either to the chairman of the meeting, during the meeting, or to the office holder, after the meeting. The request must be made as soon as reasonably practicable and no later than 4 p m on the business day following the day of the exclusion. If the person to whom the request is made is satisfied that the person was excluded, he or she must provide the indication as soon as reasonably practicable and no later than 4 p m on the business day after the day on which the request was made. The legislation does not stipulate that the request or indication has to be in writing and so presumably either or both could be dealt with by telephone.

[3.17] Any person who either claims to be an excluded person or who attends the meeting and claims to have been adversely affected by the actual or apparent exclusion of someone else may make a complaint. The complaint must be made to the chairman of the meeting, if it is made during the meeting, or to the office holder if it is made afterwards. A complaint must be made as soon as reasonably practicable and no later than 4 p m on the business day following the day on which the person was or appeared to be excluded or, where an indication was requested under r 12A.24, the day on which the indication was received.

[3.18] The chairman of the meeting or office holder (the relevant person) must consider the complaint and if satisfied that there has been prejudice, take such steps as he or she thinks appropriate to remedy the matter. If during the period of exclusion a resolution was voted on and the excluded person asserts how they would have voted, the relevant person must consider whether the vote would have changed the outcome of the resolution. If more than one person was excluded, the combined effect of the votes has to be considered. If the effect would have been to change the result, the relevant person must:

(a) count the intended vote as being cast in accordance with the excluded person's stated intention
(b) amend the record of the meeting, and
(c) where those attending the meeting have been notified of the result, notify them of the change.

The relevant person must also notify the complainant in writing of any decision.

Meetings of creditors' and liquidation committees

[3.19] Meetings of creditors' committees or liquidation committees can also be held by remote means if the office holder considers it appropriate.[1] He or she is responsible for choosing the medium in which the meeting is to be held remotely and must make appropriate arrangements to enable those attending the meeting to exercise their rights to speak or vote, to ensure the identification of those attending the meeting and the security of any electronic means used to enable attendance.

[1] Rules 12A.26 and 12A.27.

[3.20] It should be noted that where a creditors' or liquidation committee is to be held by remote means, the office holder must give seven business days' notice of the meeting rather than five business days if a place is specified.[1]

[1] Rules 2.52(4) and (5), 3.18(4) and (5), 4.156(3) and (4) and 6.153(3) and (4).

[3.21] Any one committee member can request that a place is specified for the meeting instead of it being held by remote means. A request has to be made within five business days of the date on which the office holder sent the notices of the meeting.

[3.22] If the office holder receives a valid request he or she must take the following steps:

(a) Give notice to all those previously invited to the meeting that it is to be held at a specified place. The notice must state whether the time and date are to remain the same.
(b) Set a venue for the meeting.
(c) Give at least five business days' notice of the venue to all those previously given notice of the meeting.

The meeting must be held no later than seven business days after the date of the original meeting.

[3.23] Where the convenor has specified a place for the meeting in response to a request, the chairman of the meeting must attend the meeting by being present in person.[1]

The Rules relating to remote attendance at committee meetings do not make any provision for excluded persons or complaints that a person has been excluded.[2]

---

[1] Rule 12A.27(4).
[2] The only provisions relating to excluded persons are in rr 12A.23 to 12A.25 which only apply to meetings convened under ss 246A(6) or 379A(5) of the Act—ie meetings of creditors, contributories or members.

Practical considerations

[3.24] It is useful to have the ability to be able to hold meetings by remote means, particularly if participants would otherwise have to incur time and expense in travelling long distances or if there is a risk of transport disruptions. It may encourage greater stakeholder participation and representation in insolvency processes. The legislation gives the convenor of the meeting flexibility to choose any suitable medium, which could include, for example, telephone conference call, video conferencing or a web meeting. It should be remembered that the convenor is responsible for ensuring that the chosen medium is appropriate: the aim is for the business of the meeting to be carried out efficiently and the arrangements should ensure security and confidentiality and must enable participants to exercise their rights to speak and vote. Convenors might wish to consider the following when deciding whether to hold a meeting by remote means:

(a) Will all those to be invited to the meeting have access to the technology which is proposed to be used?
(b) Are there any known obstacles to participants being able to use the technology?
(c) Is any of the business of the meeting confidential? If so, how can the convenor of the meeting ensure that only those who are entitled to attend the meeting are present and can take part in the proceedings?

(d) How easy is it to record and count votes using the chosen medium?
(e) Are sensitive or contentious issues are likely to be discussed? If so, would it be better to hold the meeting face to face?
(f) Does the meeting need to be arranged quickly? If so, and there are few participants, it may be easier to arrange a telephone or web meeting than to arrange a place to meet.
(g) What is the likelihood of someone requesting a place to be specified for the meeting?
(h) If there is a subsequent request for a place to be specified, could one be found in sufficient time to give the required notice of the place and to comply with any other requirements under the Act or Rules regarding the timing of the meeting (for example, the requirement to hold an initial meeting of creditors in administration within ten weeks of the company entering administration)?
(i) Will staff be available to assist in setting up the equipment and resolving any technological problems which may occur during the course of the meeting?
(j) Is there a back-up plan in case the equipment or connection fails?

[3.25] Remote meetings may be best suited to circumstances where there are relatively few participants and they are known to be satisfied to deal with the business of the meeting by remote means, rather than have to travel to a location, for example. It could be more difficult for a chairman to control a large meeting or to gauge its mood if the meeting is held by remote means. That is not to say that such challenges cannot be overcome and no doubt the use of the new provisions and technology will evolve over time.

[3.26] Security and confidentiality issues will need to be considered. Some telephone conferencing systems provide for the person dialling in to be announced when they join and leave the call, but these measures do not prevent someone else in the room from listening in. Convenors of meetings may also wish to consider using pin codes and changing the codes for different meetings. Bearing in mind security and confidentiality, when advertising a notice of a meeting to be held by remote means, it may be advisable not to divulge too much information in the notice about the arrangements for the meeting (for example, dial-in details or pin codes for telephone conference calls). The notice might instead ask those claiming to be eligible to participate in the meeting to contact the office holder for further information. This would enable credentials to be checked before disclosing access numbers and codes.

[3.27] If a valid request is made for a meeting to be held at a place, the convenor has only a short time in which to comply. It may be prudent to identify a potential venue in advance, in case a request is received. It is not clear whether it is necessary to re-advertise the meeting with details of the venue.[1]

---

[1] Rules 12A.22 and 12A.27 state that the convenor or office holder must give notice of the venue to all those who received the original notice, but do not stipulate that the venue has to be advertised.

[3.28] If someone claims to be excluded from a meeting, the person chairing the meeting or the office holder will need to consider carefully which course of action to take, bearing in mind the implications for the validity of the proceedings if a participant, or would-be participant, is not satisfied with the decision. The course of action chosen may depend on the length of exclusion, the effect it had on participants and what occurred during the period of exclusion.

[3.29] Important decisions regarding meeting arrangements and the conduct of the meeting should be documented carefully, as should any requests received or indications made under r 12A.24.

Annual meetings in voluntary liquidations

[3.30] Sections 93 and 105 of the IA 1986 have been amended to remove the requirement to hold annual meetings in voluntary liquidations in England and Wales.

It should be noted that annual meetings are only abolished for voluntary liquidations where the resolution to wind up was passed on or after 6 April 2010, and paragraph 83 creditors' voluntary liquidations which started on or after 6 April 2010.[1] Annual meetings are still required in voluntary liquidations which started before 6 April 2010.

---

[1] A paragraph 83 creditors' voluntary liquidation is a liquidation which follows on from administration under the provisions of para 83 of Sch B1 to the IA 1986. Initially, the requirements for a paragraph 83 creditors' voluntary liquidation starting on or after 6 April 2010 but preceded by an administration which started before 6 April 2010 were unclear. The position was clarified in r 13 of the Insolvency (Amendment) (No 2) Rules 2010.

Notice required for meetings

[3.31] Where minimum notice periods for meetings (other than final meetings) are prescribed in the Rules, IR 2010 remove inconsistencies by making the notice period 14 days rather than 21 days. It should be noted that the notice period for a final meeting of creditors in a liquidation or bankruptcy remains unchanged at 28 days.

Examples of notice periods which have changed from 21 to 14 days are:

- Meetings to ascertain the wishes of creditors or contributories (r 4.54).
- First meeting of creditors in a bankruptcy (r 6.79).
- General meetings of creditors in a bankruptcy (r 6.81).
- Notice to bankrupt of a meeting of creditors (r 6.84).

Resolutions by correspondence

[3.32] New rr 4.63A (liquidation) and 6.88A (bankruptcy) enable the office holder to seek the passing of resolutions of creditors or contributories by correspondence without holding a meeting. However, if the Insolvency Act requires a resolution to be passed at a meeting, it cannot be passed by correspondence.

The procedure for passing a resolution by correspondence corresponds with that for resolutions by correspondence in administration.

Notice of meetings by advertisement only

[3.33] New r 2.37A allows notice of any meeting in administration to be given by advertisement only, rather than individual notice, with the permission of the court. This provision already existed in liquidation and bankruptcy.[1]

In considering whether to give permission, the court must have regard to the cost of advertisement, the amount of assets available and the extent of the interest of creditors, members or any particular class of either.

---

[1] Rules 4.59 and 6.85 respectively.

Requisitioned meetings

[3.34] Rules 4.57 and 6.83 are amended in liquidation and bankruptcy to reduce the period within which an office holder must fix a venue for a requisitioned meeting from 35 days of receipt of the request to 28 days. The period of notice required for the meeting is reduced from 21 days to 14 days. These requirements are consistent with administration.

Proofs and proxies for use at meetings

[3.35] The liquidation and bankruptcy rules are amended, for consistency with administration and administrative receivership, to provide that notices of creditors' meetings must state that proofs and (if applicable) proxies must be lodged not later than 12 p m on the business day before the date fixed for the meeting. Previously, the time and date specified had to be not more than four days before the date fixed for the meeting.

[3.36] In administrative receivership, new r 3.11A prescribes the information which must be included in a creditor's claim for voting purposes. The required content is consistent with that for proving a debt in administration, liquidation or bankruptcy.

Chairman's discretion to allow a vote

[3.37] The Rules are amended to give the chairman of a meeting of creditors in a winding up by the court or bankruptcy discretion to allow a creditor to vote if satisfied that the requirements for entitlement to vote were not met as a result of circumstances beyond the creditor's control.[1] This now corresponds to the position in administration, administrative receivership and creditors' voluntary liquidation.

---

[1] Rules 4.68 and 6.93A.

Appeals against a chairman's decision

[3.38] The administration, administrative receivership, liquidation and bankruptcy rules are amended to provide that any application to court to appeal against a decision of the chairman with regard to a vote must be made no later than 21 days after the date of the meeting.[1] The time limit for appealing against a decision in a voluntary arrangement meeting remains unchanged.[2]

[1] Rules 2.39(5), 3.12(4A), 4.70(4A) and 6.94(4A).
[2] A longer period applies in voluntary arrangements—see rr 1.50(6) and 5.22(6).

Quorum

[3.39] Rule 12.4A is revoked and replaced by new r 12A.21.

In practice, there is little effect as r 12A.21 re-states the provisions of the old r 12.4A without any change in substance.

Suspension and adjournment of meetings

[3.40] Various amendments are made to the administration, liquidation and bankruptcy rules to provide a standardised approach to suspending and adjourning meetings of creditors or contributories.[1]

[1] Rules 2.34, 2.35, 4.65 and 6.91.

Suspension

[3.41] The chairman may declare a meeting suspended, without an adjournment, for a period of up to one hour. This may be done only once during the course of the meeting.

Mandatory adjournment

[3.42] The chairman must adjourn a meeting in either of the following circumstances:

- If within 30 minutes of the time fixed for the start of the meeting there is no person present to act as chairman. The meeting is adjourned to the same time and place in the following week, or if that is not a business day, to the business day following.
- If the meeting resolves that it should be adjourned. The meeting is adjourned to such time and place as seem to be appropriate to the chairman in the circumstances.

Discretionary adjournment

[3.43] The chairman may adjourn a meeting to such time and place as seem to be appropriate to the chairman in the circumstances if:

- within 30 minutes of the time fixed for the start of the meeting those attending do not constitute a quorum; or
- there is not the requisite majority for approval of the administrator's proposals; or
- the chairman considers it appropriate.

Time limit for adjournment

[3.44] An adjournment may not be for a period of more than 14 days, subject to the direction of the court. If there is more than one adjournment the final adjournment must not be to a day later than 14 days after the date on which the meeting was originally held.

Use of proofs and proxies

[3.45] Where a meeting is adjourned, proofs and proxies may be used if lodged at any time up to 12 p m hours on the business day immediately before the adjourned meeting.

Majority to approve CVA proposals

[3.46] The majority of creditors required to approve a proposal or a modification to a proposal is now three-quarters or more in value.[1] Previously it was a majority in excess of three-quarters in value.

---

[1] Rule 1.19(2).

Minutes or other record of proceedings

[3.47] The Rules relating to minutes or other records of proceedings in administration, administrative receivership, liquidation and bankruptcy are standardised to provide that the following information must be included:[1]

- A list of the creditors or contributories who attended, either personally or by proxy.
- The names and addresses of those elected to the committee (if one is established).
- A record of every resolution passed.

Minutes of a meeting in administration no longer have to entered in the company's minute book. They are kept as part of the record of proceedings instead.

---

[1] Rules 2.44A, 3.15, 4.71 and 6.95.

Application to Scotland

[3.48] Various changes are made to meeting procedures in CVAs or administrations in Scotland, in order to align the position with England and Wales. The principal changes are described below.

Summoning meetings under section 3 of the Insolvency Act 1986 to consider a CVA proposal

[3.49] Rule 1.9 is expanded to provide that notices calling the meeting must be sent by the nominee at least 14 days before the day of the meeting. They are to be sent to all the creditors specified in the statement of affairs and any other creditors of whose address the nominee is aware and to all persons who are to the best of the nominee's belief members of the company. Rule 1.14 is also expanded to provide that meetings must be summoned to begin between 10 am and 4 p m on a business day.[1]

[1] Rule 1.14(4).

Chairman of meeting as proxy holder (CVA)

[3.50] New r 1.14AA is inserted which provides that the chairman may not use a proxy in his or her favour to vote to increase or reduce the remuneration or expenses of the nominee or supervisor unless the proxy specifically directs him to vote in that way.

Entitlement to vote (CVA)

[3.51] The rule on creditors' entitlement to vote is expanded to provide that a creditor is entitled to vote at any meeting if the creditor, either at the meeting or before it, has submitted a claim to the responsible insolvency practitioner and the claim has been accepted in whole or in part.[1]

[1] Rule 1.15A(4).

[3.52] A new rule is inserted to clarify members' entitlement to vote.[1] Members vote according to the rights attaching to their shares in accordance with the company's Articles of Association. In this context, the term "shares" includes any other interests which that person has as a member of the company.

[1] Rule 1.15AA.

Requisite majorities (CVA)

[3.53] New rules are inserted setting out the requisite majorities to pass resolutions at creditors' and members' meetings.[1] They also deal with creditors' votes to be left out of account and how the votes of connected parties are to be dealt with. They align the position with England and Wales.

[1] Rules 1.16A and 1.16B.

Entitlement to vote (administration)

[3.54] New r 2.26C is inserted dealing with entitlement to vote. In order to vote at any meeting of creditors in administration a creditor must submit a claim to the administrator at or before the meeting. The claim must be made out by or under the direction of the creditor and, unless the administrator dispenses with the requirement, have attached to it an account or voucher which constitutes prima facie evidence of the debt. The claim must also contain the information specified in r 2.26C(3)(c).

Notice of meetings by advertisement only (administration)

[3.55] In administration, but not in any other procedures, the court may order that notice of any meeting may be given by advertisement and not by individual notice to the persons concerned. In considering whether to make the order, the court must have regard to the cost of advertisement, the amount of assets available and the extent of the interest of creditors, members or any particular class of either.[1]

[1] Rule 2.32A.

Suspension and adjournment (administration)

[3.56] New r 2.27C sets out the procedure for suspending or adjourning any meeting of creditors in administration. Rule 7.8 does not apply. The procedure corresponds to that for creditors' meetings in England and Wales, as described earlier in this chapter.

Meetings held by remote means

[3.57] In Scotland, the provisions of s 246A of the Act apply to meetings of creditors, contributories and members in CVAs and administrations.[1] Creditors' committee meetings in administrations can also be held by remote means.

The procedure follows that for England and Wales. The supporting legislation is contained in rr 1.14ZA, 2.26B, 2.36D and 2.36E.

Meetings in receivership, liquidation or personal insolvency cannot be held by remote means.

[1] See s 246A(2), which provides that this section does not apply to winding up or receivership in Scotland. Section 379A deals with personal insolvency and the personal insolvency provisions of the IA 1986 do not apply in Scotland.

Transitional provisions

[3.58] The provisions relating to remote attendance at meetings apply in all cases on or after 6 April 2010, regardless of the date on which the insolvency process commenced.

[3.59] The abolition of annual meetings in voluntary liquidations applies to liquidations commencing on or after 6 April 2010, including a creditors' voluntary liquidation under para 83 of Sch B1 following on from an administration which started before 6 April 2010.

[3.60] The other changes described in this chapter apply to cases where the insolvency commences or, in the case of a CVA, the nominee agrees to act, on or after 6 April 2010, with the following exceptions:

- An administration by court order made on or after 6 April 2010 on an application made before 6 April 2010.
- An administration commencing on or after 6 April 2010 which was immediately preceded by a liquidation which started before 6 April 2010.
- A liquidation commencing on or after 6 April 2010 which was preceded by an administration which started before 6 April 2010.
- A liquidation commencing on or after 6 April 2010 which was preceded by an administration by court order where the application for the administration order was made before 6 April 2010.
- A compulsory liquidation commencing on or after 6 April 2010 which was immediately preceded by a voluntary liquidation starting before 6 April 2010.

Chapter 4

Creditors' and liquidation committees

Introduction

[4.1] In addition to new provisions enabling committee meetings to be held by remote means, which are discussed in Chapter 3, there are various amendments to existing rules relating to the constitution, formalities, meetings and resolutions of creditors' and liquidation committees. The changes are designed to harmonise the requirements, as far as possible, across the administration, administrative receivership, liquidation and bankruptcy processes.

The Insolvency (Scotland) (Amendment) Rules 2010 (IR Scotland 2010) introduce new rules for creditors' committees in administration. None of the other changes described in this chapter affect Scotland.

Membership of the committee – eligibility

[4.2] The administration and administrative receivership rules have been amended to make it clear that a creditor can be a member of a committee provided that the creditor's claim has not been wholly disallowed for voting purposes, nor wholly rejected for the purpose of distribution or dividend, and the claim is not wholly secured.[1] Previously, it was not clear whether a creditor whose vote or claim had been admitted in part, or was part secured, was eligible to be a member of a creditors' committee in administration or administrative receivership. The position is now consistent with that in liquidation and bankruptcy.

---

[1] Rules 2.50(2) and 3.16(2).

Certificate of (amended) constitution of the committee

[4.3] As part of the initiative to remove unnecessary burdens on the court, it is no longer necessary to file in court, in an administration or liquidation, the certificate of constitution or amended constitution of the committee. This aligns the position with administrative receivership. There is still a requirement to file the certificate in court in a bankruptcy and the rules are amended to provide that it must be filed as soon as reasonably practicable.[1]

The requirement to file the certificate with the registrar of companies (in company procedures) has been retained. The administrative receivership and liquidation rules are amended, for consistency with administration, to provide that the certificate must be sent as soon as reasonably practicable.[2]

---

[1] Rule 6.151(5).

[2] Rules 3.17(4) and 4.153(6).

Committee meetings

First meeting of the committee

[4.4] The administrative receivership, liquidation and bankruptcy rules have been amended to provide that the first meeting of the committee must be held within six weeks, rather than three months as previously.[1] In administrative receivership and bankruptcy the meeting must be held within six weeks of the establishment of the committee and in liquidation it must be held within six weeks of the establishment of the committee or of the liquidator's appointment, whichever is the later.

[1] Rules 3.18(3), 4.15(2) and 6.153(2).

Meeting held at the request of a committee member

[4.5] The administration rules have been amended to provide that if a member of the committee requests a meeting it must be held within 21 days of receipt of the request.[1] Previously, the requirement was to hold the meeting within 14 days. The amendment means that the time limit is now consistent with the other insolvency processes.

[1] Rule 2.52(3A).

[4.6] The Rules have been changed for all processes to provide that the office holder must give five business days' notice of the venue for a committee meeting. Previously, the requirement was to give seven days' notice, which could include weekends and public holidays. If the meeting is to be held by remote means rather than at a physical location, seven business days' notice must be given.[1] The ability of committee members to waive notice is unchanged.

The change to business days means that notice periods will have to be computed carefully if the meeting is to be held soon after a public holiday.

[1] Rules 2.52(3), 3.18(5), 4.156(4) and 6.153(4).

Resolutions

[4.7] The Rules previously provided for committee resolutions to be passed by post, as an alternative to a meeting. The Insolvency (Amendment) Rules 2010 (IR 2010) now permit resolutions to be passed by other means (for example, e-mail).[1]

The previous requirement, in administration, to place a copy of committee resolutions in the company's minute book has been replaced by a requirement to keep a copy of the resolutions with the record of the proceedings.[2]

[1] Rules 2.61, 3.27, 4.167, 6.162.
[2] Rule 2.61(5).

Termination of membership of the committee

[4.8] The administration, administrative receivership and bankruptcy rules are amended to provide that membership of the committee comes to an end three months after the date on which the committee member concerned ceases to be a creditor.[1] Previously, membership came to an end immediately on ceasing to be a creditor, which could cause difficulties if, as a consequence, the number of committee members fell below the required minimum of three and there was still business to be conducted. The three months grace period should make it easier to finalise committee business. Alternatively, it will allow more time to find a replacement committee member.

[1] Rules 2.57(1), 3.23(1) and 6.158(1).

Composition of the liquidation committee when creditors have been paid in full

[4.9] Rule 4.171 has been replaced by a new r 4.174A. The changes of substance are that there is no longer a prescribed form for the liquidator's certificate[1] and the requirement to file the certificate in court in a winding up by the court has been abolished.

[1] Rule 4.171A(5) does however specify the information which must be included.

Creditors' committee in liquidation following administration

[4.10] Rules 4.173 to 4.178 deal with the continuation of a creditors' committee formed in an administration in a subsequent winding up by the court. There is no change in substance to the previous rules, except that r 4.174 is replaced by new r 4.174A which provides that in a solvent winding up[1] the liquidator must summon a meeting of contributories on 14 days' notice to elect (if the meeting so wishes) up to three contributory members.

[1] In this context a solvent winding up is a winding up by the court in which creditors have been paid in full, not a members' voluntary liquidation.

[4.11] A new form has been prescribed for giving notice to Companies House of the continuation of the committee. It is Form F9.4 and accompanies Form 4.52 which is the certificate of constitution of the committee. Form F9.4 is to be used in all cases where the event giving rise to the requirement to file the form arose on or after 6 April 2010.[1]

[1] Rule 4, Registrar's (Amendment) Rules 2010.

Scotland

Creditors' committees in administration

[4.12] The previous r 2.36, which applied Chapter 3 of Part 3 of the Insolvency (Scotland) Rules 1986, is replaced and new rr 2.36A–R are inserted. The new Rules set out in detail the procedure for establishing a committee, its functions, dealings, the conduct of meetings and the passing of resolutions. The Rules mirror those for administration creditors' committees in England and Wales.

Transitional provisions

[4.13] In England and Wales, the changes described in this chapter apply to all cases where the commencement date is on or after 6 April 2010, with the exception of the following:

- An administration by court order made on or after 6 April 2010 on an application made before 6 April 2010.
- An administration commencing on or after 6 April 2010 which was preceded by a liquidation which started before 6 April 2010.
- A liquidation commencing on or after 6 April 2010 which was preceded by an administration which started before 6 April 2010.
- A liquidation commencing on or after 6 April 2010 which was preceded by an administration by court order where the application was made before 6 April 2010.

In Scotland, new rr 2.36A–R apply to all administrations which started on or after 6 April 2010, except where a petition for an administration order had been presented before 6 April 2010 or the administration was preceded by a liquidation which started before 6 April 2010.

Chapter 5

Court procedure and practice

[5.1] The Insolvency (Amendment) Rules 2010 (IR 2010) made a number of amendments to Part 7 of the Insolvency Rules 1986 (IR 1986) relating to court procedures and practice. This chapter reviews the key amendments.

Applications

[5.2] In relation to applications to court, IR 2010 has removed the distinction in IR 1986 between an originating application[1] and an ordinary application.[2] Note that the distinction between these two types of applications remains relevant for court administrative purposes in the new Application Notice (Form 7.1A).

The new r 7.6A, replacing the former r 7.6, provides that unless the court otherwise directs, the hearing of an application must be in open court.

---

[1] Namely, an application to the court which is not an application in pending proceedings before the court.
[2] Namely, any other application to the court.

Enforcement procedures

[5.3] Some amendments have been made to deal with the delivery of arrested persons to prison and the discharge of arrest warrants.

The new r 7.19(3) provides that where a warrant for the arrest of a person is issued by the High Court, the warrant may be discharged by the county court where the person who is the subject of the warrant (a) has been brought before a county court exercising insolvency jurisdiction, and (b) has given a satisfactory undertaking to the county court to comply with his obligations under the Insolvency Act 1986 (IA 1986) or the IR 1986.

[5.4] The amended r 7.22(a) provides that when a person (the arrested person) is arrested under a warrant issued by the court under s 134 of the IA 1986 (officer of company failing to attend for public examination), or s 364 (arrest of debtor or bankrupt), the apprehending officer must deliver the arrested person into the custody of (i) the court, or (ii) where the court is not ready and able to deal with the arrested person, the governor of the prison named in the warrant (or another prison if that prison is not able to accommodate the arrested person). The prison governor who must keep the arrested person in custody until such time as the court otherwise orders must produce that person before the court at its next sitting.

[5.5] Similarly, the amended r 7.23(2) provides that when a person arrested under a warrant issued under s 236 (inquiry into insolvent company's dealings), s 251N (the equivalent in relation to debt relief orders) or s 366 (the equivalent in bankruptcy) of the IA 1986 cannot immediately be brought up for examination, the arresting officer shall deliver the arrested person into the custody of the governor of the prison named in the warrant (or another prison if that prison is not able to accommodate the arrested person). The prison governor shall keep the arrested person in custody and produce him before the court as it may from time to time direct.

Court file and records

[5.6] The new r 7.31A replaces the former rr 7.26–7.31 in relation to the maintenance and rights to inspect court file and records. Certain persons such as office holder and creditors are entitled to inspect the court file as a matter of right, subject to the court's contrary direction.[1] Any person who is not otherwise entitled to inspect the court file may do so if he has the permission of the court.[2]

Rule 7.31A also makes clear that anyone entitled to inspect the court file may also obtain a copy of any document or documents contained in the file.

[1] Rule 7.31A(3)–(5) and (7).
[2] Rule 7.31A(6). See *Franbar Holdings Ltd v Patel* [2008] EWHC 1534 (Ch), [2009] Bus LR D14, [2009] 1 BCLC 1 in relation to the court's exercise of discretion under the former r 7.31(4).

General

[5.7] The new r 7.51A, replacing the former r 7.51, sets out the application of the Civil Procedure Rules (CPR) to insolvency proceedings.[1]

The former rr 7.53 and 7.54 dealing with court attendance have been deleted because they are no longer necessary.

In relation to security in court, the former r 7.58 has been deleted because security in court is covered by the CPR.

[1] The application of the CPR to insolvency proceedings does not confer on the court a power to depart from a time limit imposed by primary legislation: *Beloit Walmsley Ltd, Re* [2008] EWHC 1888 (Ch), [2009] 1 BCLC 584, [2008] BPIR 1445.

Transitional provisions

[5.8] Other than the new r 7.6A, the amendments discussed above apply where:[1]

(a) a person agrees to act as nominee in respect of a proposal for a company voluntary arrangement on or after 6 April 2010;
(b) a company enters administration on or after 6 April 2010, except where—

(i) it enters administration by virtue of an administration order under para 10 of Sch B1 to the IA 1986 on an application made before 6 April 2010;
(ii) the administration is immediately preceded by a voluntary liquidation in respect of which the resolution to wind up was passed before 6 April 2010; or
(iii) the administration is immediately preceded by a liquidation on the making of a winding-up order on a petition which was presented before 6 April 2010;

(c) in a receivership, a receiver or manager is appointed in respect of a company on or after 6 April 2010;
(d) a company goes into liquidation upon the passing on or after 6 April 2010 of a resolution to wind up;
(e) a company goes into voluntary liquidation under para 83 of Sch B1 to the IA 1986, except where the preceding administration—
(i) commenced before 6 April 2010; or
(ii) is an administration which commenced by virtue of an administration order under para 10 of Sch B1 to the IA 1986 on an application which was made before 6 April 2010;
(f) a company goes into liquidation on the making of a winding-up order on a petition presented on or after 6 April 2010, except where the liquidation is immediately preceded by—
(i) an administration under para 10 of Sch B1 to the IA 1986 where the administration order was made on an application made before 6 April 2010;
(ii) an administration in respect of which the appointment of an administrator under para 14 or 22 of Sch B1 to the Act took effect before 6 April 2010; or
(iii) a voluntary liquidation in respect of which the resolution to wind up was passed before 6 April 2010;
(g) a person agrees to act as nominee in respect of a proposal for an individual voluntary arrangement on or after 6 April 2010;
(h) a debt relief order is made on or after 6 April 2010;
(i) a bankruptcy order is made on a petition presented on or after 6 April 2010.

---

[1] Paragraph 1 of Sch 4 to IR 2010. The new r 7.6A applies on and after 6 April 2010 in all cases (para 2 of Sch 4 to IR 2010).

Chapter 6

Voluntary arrangements

[6.1] The Insolvency (Amendment) Rules 2010 (IR 2010) have made a number of amendments to Part 1 and Part 5 of the Insolvency Rules 1986 (IR 1986) respectively relating to company voluntary arrangements (CVA) and individual voluntary arrangements (IVA). This chapter examines the key amendments in relation to company voluntary arrangements.

Many of the amendments to the provisions relating to IVAs mirror those made in relation to CVAs and this chapter focuses on company voluntary arrangements, highlighting only significant differences or key additional provisions in relation to IVAs.

Statutory insolvency procedure

[6.2] Introduced by the Insolvency Act 1986 (IA 1986), CVAs allow companies[1] to bind their creditors into arrangements, including for the composition of their debts and provide an alternative to the procedures available under corporate law.[2]

---

[1] Prior to 1986, individuals, unlike companies, could enter into voluntary arrangements with their creditors under the Deeds of Arrangement Act 1914. However, such arrangements did not bind dissenting creditors who could petition for bankruptcy. Therefore, a procedure for IVAs was also introduced to replace the disappearing deeds of arrangement.

[2] Such as schemes of arrangements now under Part 26 of the Companies Act 2006.

[6.3] Despite being a creature of insolvency statute and constituting "insolvency proceedings" for the purposes of Council Regulation (EC) No 1346/2000 of 29 May 2000 on insolvency proceedings (EC Insolvency Regulation),[1] CVAs can be used outside of an insolvency context, since the statute does not set out any requirement for the company to be insolvent or any tests relating to its ability to pay its debts.

---

[1] "Voluntary arrangements under insolvency legislation" are listed in Annex A of the EC Insolvency Regulation.

[6.4] As a result, CVAs can be proposed not only by an insolvency practitioner (if the company is in administration or liquidation) but also by the directors of a company where the company is not in any insolvency proceeding. CVAs, when proposed by the directors, can therefore be an effective tool to rescue companies by allowing directors to retain the management of the company[1] and to avoid the potential negative publicity arising from the appointment of an administrator or liquidator.

---

[1] The role of a supervisor appointed in a CVA differs from that of an administrator or liquidator.

[6.5] Voluntary arrangements

[6.5] One of the essential attractions of the CVA is that, once approved by the creditors' meetings, it binds all the creditors of the debtor entitled to vote at the creditors' meeting (even if they did not attend the meeting or voted against it). An important caveat to this, often identified as a cause for CVAs' lack of popularity, is that the rights of secured creditors cannot be affected by a CVA without their consent.[1]

---

[1] Section 4(3) of the IA 1986.

[6.6] Although the CVA procedure still requires a meeting of the company's shareholders, if the decision reached at that meeting conflicts with that of the creditors' meetings, this no longer[1] prevents the CVA from taking effect but simply gives the member a right to apply to court.[2] A member's application to court could ultimately result in the CVA being amended in line with the shareholders' decision[3] but the court is likely to be reluctant to undermine the agreement of the company and its creditors.

---

[1] Prior to the Insolvency Act 2000 amending the CVA procedure, the CVA proposal had to be approved by both the creditors' meeting and the shareholders' meeting.
[2] Section 4A(3) of the IA 1986.
[3] Under s 4A(6) of the IA 1986, the court may order the decision of the company meeting to have effect instead of the decision of the creditors' meeting or make such other order as it thinks fit.

[6.7] Furthermore, CVAs do not require the involvement of the court and can therefore be relatively inexpensive to put in place. However, to date, they have not become a popular tool.[1] Why? The finger of blame has been pointed to any or all or the following: insolvency practitioners' lack of familiarity with the procedure; the inability to bind secured creditors; the lack of availability of a moratorium (although this issue has largely been resolved by the Insolvency Act 2000 which introduced an optional moratorium procedure for "small companies");[2] and the lack of finality in respect of creditors not given notice of the creditors' meeting.[3]

---

[1] Based on figures on the Insolvency Service's website (http://www.insolvency.gov.uk/otherinformation/statistics/201005/pressnotables.pdf), there were approximately 726 CVAs in 2009, compared with 4,161 administrations in the same period. A recent use of a CVA is demonstrated in *HMRC v Portsmouth City Football Club* [2010] EWHC 2013 (Ch).
[2] Section 1A of and Sch A1 to the IA 1986.
[3] Under s 6(3) of the IA 1986, a person not given notice of the creditors' meeting may, by the end of the period of 28 days beginning with the day on which he became aware that the meeting had taken place, apply to the court to challenge the CVA on the grounds that the CVA unfairly prejudiced his interests or there was some material irregularity at or in relation to the creditors' meeting or shareholders' meeting. Note that this 28-day period cannot be tolled: *Beloit Walmsley Ltd, Re* [2008] EWHC 1888 (Ch), [2009] 1 BCLC 584, [2008] BPIR 1445.

[6.8] The changes introduced by IR 2010 fall within two trends which have emerged in the past few years in insolvency law: (i) to improve visibility for creditors in insolvency proceedings; and (ii) to provide alternative and flexible tools to administration and liquidation procedures.

Improving visibility for creditors

Content of the proposal made by the directors

[6.9] IR 2010 introduce a new r 1.3(2)(r), which broadens the required content of a CVA proposal made by directors.[1] It states that the proposal should include "such other matters (if any) as the directors consider appropriate for ensuring that members and creditors are enabled to reach an informed decision on the proposal".

---

[1] Rule 1.3(2)(a) to (q), left intact by IR 2010, sets out in detail certain matters which must be included in such a proposal.

[6.10] Whilst in the past, directors might have been able to satisfy their duties by relying on an exhaustive statutory list for the content of the proposal, directors are now required to consider additional matters that creditors and members would want to know. Directors may be further guided by the Appendix of SIP 3 which sets out issues which should be included in the proposal, but the new rule will mean that directors must complete an additional step and consider which issues creditors or members would need to know.

[6.11] This new rule is based on the former r 1.10(b) (now deleted by IR 2010) relating to the content of proposals made by insolvency practitioners. This broadly drafted requirement to consider any matters which the creditors would need to reach an informed decision was always part of an insolvency practitioner's duties when making a CVA proposal and is now brought into the scope of directors' duties.

This desire to give more visibility to the creditors echoes the recent SIP 16 relating to pre-pack administrations, under which administrators are required to make disclosures to creditors explaining the rationale for the pre-pack.

Contents of a proposal made by an insolvency practitioner

[6.12] Under the amended r 1.10(1), a proposal made by an insolvency practitioner must contain all such matters as would need to be set out in a proposal by the directors with the addition of "the nature and amount of its preferential creditors" (note that the old r 1.10(1)(a) referred to the names and addresses of the company's preferential creditors which are no longer necessary).

Statement of affairs

[6.13] Under the amended r 1.5(1) directors are required to deliver a statement of the company's affairs at the same time as the proposal is delivered to the nominee.[1] Previously, the statement of affairs had to be delivered within seven days of the delivery of the proposal.

Rule 1.5(4) is also altered slightly in that the statement must now be verified by a statement of truth made by at least one director. The old rule required two or more directors to certify the statement as correct, to the best of their knowledge and belief (or by the company secretary and at least one director).

[6.13] Voluntary arrangements

[1] The equivalent provision for IVA is r 5.5(1).

[6.14] These changes have also been mirrored in the amended r 1.37 relating to the delivery of a statement of affairs when a moratorium has been obtained in relation to small companies.

[6.15] IR 2010 also introduce a new r 1.56, which allows the court, on the application of the nominee, the directors or any person appearing to it to have an interest, to direct that specified information may be omitted from any statement of affairs required to be sent to the creditors where the disclosure of such information would be likely to prejudice the conduct of the CVA or might reasonably be expected to lead to violence against any person.

Notice of moratorium

[6.16] A new r 1.40(2A) is introduced in relation to the notices to be placed by nominees regarding the coming into force of a moratorium. In addition to the standard contents, the notice to be issued by the nominee must now also state "the nature of the business of the company, that a moratorium under section 1A of the Insolvency Act 1986 has come into force, and the date upon which the moratorium came into force".

This change is also mirrored for the notice to be placed by the nominee regarding the end of the moratorium (r 1.42(1A)).

Time recording information

[6.17] In line with a desire to improve visibility and accountability to creditors, a new r 1.55 is introduced,[1] under which a nominee (if the CVA has not yet been approved) and a supervisor (when the CVA has been approved) are required to provide a statement setting out, inter alia, the number of hours spent on the CVA (including staff assigned to the CVA) and the average hourly rate within 28 days of receipt of a request by (i) any director of the company or (ii) where the proposal has been approved, any creditor or member of the company in respect of the arrangement. No request may be made pursuant to this rule more than two years after the nominee/supervisor has ceased to act in relation to the proposal or voluntary arrangement.

[1] The equivalent provision for IVA is r 5.66.

CVAs: a more flexible tool

Summoning of meetings

[6.18] The amended r 1.9(1) no longer contains the minimum 14-day requirement which was previously imposed between the date of filing of the nominee's report at court and the date on which creditors' and members' meetings are to be held. This, it is hoped, will speed up the CVA process, thus making it a more attractive tool.

CVAs: a more flexible tool [6.24]

Requisite majorities (creditors)

[6.19] A key amendment introduced by IR 2010 is the change to the requisite majority at creditors' meetings to approve CVA proposals.

Prior to the new rules, resolutions at creditors' meetings to approve the proposal or modify it required a majority *in excess of three-quarters in value of the creditors* present (or by proxy) and voting on the resolution. Any other resolution could be passed with a majority in excess of one half of the creditors present and voting.

However, the new r 1.19(2) provides a slightly lower threshold to be met. A resolution to approve the CVA proposal is now passed "when a majority of three-quarters or more (in value) of those present and voting in person or by proxy" vote in favour of it. Similarly, in respect of other resolutions, they are passed "when a majority (in value) of those present and voting in person or by proxy" vote in favour (new r 1.19(1)).[1]

---

[1] The equivalent provisions for IVA are rr 5.23 and 5.43.

[6.20] With this change, IR 2010 bring the requisite majorities for acceptance of a CVA proposal closer to the wording used in relation to schemes of arrangements under Part 26 of the Companies Act 2006, which requires a majority in number representing 75% in value of the creditors. However, it remains that for CVAs there is no requirement for a majority in number.

[6.21] These changes are mirrored in the amended r 1.52, relating to majorities required in creditors' meetings where a moratorium has been obtained.

[6.22] It is noteworthy that IR 2010 did not make any changes to the requisite majorities for members' meetings, which still require the consent of "more than one-half in value of the members present in person or by proxy and voting on the resolution" for any resolution to be passed (r 1.20).

Procedural changes to increase speed and efficiency

[6.23] IR 2010 have introduced a number of amendments which seek to increase speed and efficiency in the CVA process.

A new r 1.21(4A) is introduced, which allows the chairman, once only during the course of a meeting (of the creditors or of the members), to declare the meeting suspended for any period up to one hour. Where a moratorium has been obtained, the new r 1.53(4A) mirrors the new r 1.21(4A).

[6.24] The amended r 1.22(1) now prescribes that if a CVA is approved, a resolution *must* be taken by the creditors, where two or more supervisors are appointed, on the question whether acts to be done in connection with the arrangement may be done by one or more of them or must be done by all. The amended rule thus places the emphasis on a clear delimitation of powers between joint supervisors and reflects a desire to encourage an efficient decision-making process.

Supervisor's accounts and reports

[6.25] The former r 1.26, which set out the supervisor's duties regarding accounts and reports, has been removed and replaced by a new r 1.26A.[1]

As under the old rule, where a CVA authorises or requires a supervisor to carry on the business of the company, to realise its assets or otherwise to administer or dispose of any of its funds, the new rule also requires the supervisor to keep accounts and records of the supervisor's acts and dealings in connection with the CVA, including records of receipts and payment of money.

[1] The equivalent provision for IVA is r 5.31A.

[6.26] However, a new rule is introduced (r 1.26A(3)) which requires the supervisor to preserve accounts and records which "were kept by any other person who has acted as supervisor of the arrangement and are in the supervisor's possession." This new rule, it is hoped, will help to ensure a seamless transition where one supervisor is replaced by another.

[6.27] The new r 1.26A(4) also amends the requirements relating to the contents of the annual report to be sent to the company's stakeholders. First, it is no longer a requirement to send this report to the court. The supervisor is now only required to send the report to the company's creditors of whose addresses the supervisor is aware, rather than all the creditors bound by the CVA.

[6.28] Secondly, the supervisor must now send "a report on the progress and prospects for the full implementation of the voluntary arrangement". This appears to broaden the supervisor's duties, which previously were to send "an abstract of such receipts and payments [as required to be kept under the former rule 1.26(2) and now under rule 1.26A(6)] accompanied by his comments on the progress and efficacy of the arrangement".

[6.29] The focus is now on the progress and prospects for the full implementation of the CVA, rather than simply on the payments and receipts and this r 1.26A(4) applies to all supervisors (whether or not they are authorised or required by the CVA to carry on the business of the company, to realise its assets or otherwise to administer or dispose of any of its funds).

[6.30] It is not entirely apparent whether this amendment will result in significant changes in terms of the contents of the report. However, it seems to demonstrate a move towards an administration style of "progress report" as required under r 2.47 (in relation to administrations) and aims to increase visibility for creditors.

Specific issues in relation to IVAs

Contents of proposal

[6.31] Under the new r 5.3(s), an IVA proposal must now contain a statement regarding whether a proposal for an IVA in respect of the debtor was submitted, either to a meeting of the debtor's creditors or to the court in connection with an application for an interim order under s 253 of the IA 1986, within the 24 months preceding the date on which the proposal is delivered to the nominee, and if so the outcome.

Annulment of bankruptcy order

[6.32] Under the amended r 5.55(2), an Official Receiver may not make an application to annul a bankruptcy order under s 261(2)(b) of the IA 1986 before the expiry of a period of 42 days beginning with the day on which the nominee filed the report of the creditors' meeting with the court (where the creditors' meeting was summoned under s 257 pursuant to a report to the court under s 256(1)(aa)) or the day on which the result of the creditors' meeting was notified to the creditors (where the creditors' meeting was summoned under s 257 pursuant to a report to the debtor's creditors under s 256A(3)).

[6.33] A new r 5.60(3A) is introduced, which prescribes that the notice to be made by the Secretary of State in relation to the annulment of a bankruptcy order must contain "the name of the former bankrupt, the date on which the bankruptcy order was made, that the bankruptcy order has been annulled, the date of the annulling order, and the grounds of the annulment."

[6.34] A new r 5.67 is introduced to protect individuals who have entered into voluntary arrangements from violence. The court may, on application of the debtor, supervisor or Official Receiver or the Secretary of State, order that the debtor's address be removed from court files, the insolvency register or any notice published by the Secretary of State. Such an application must be supported by a witness statement.

Nominee's report

[6.35] In order to remove certain burdensome requirements, art 8 of the Legislative Reform (Insolvency) (Miscellaneous Provisions) Order 2010 has amended s 256A of the IA 1986, substituting a requirement for the nominee to report to the creditors for the requirement to report to the court where there is no pending application for an interim order. New rr 5.14A and 5.14B give effect to this amendment.

Thus there is now a distinction between IVAs where there has been an interim order, in which case the nominee continues to report to the court, and IVAs without an interim order in which is there will be no report to the court.

Transitional provisions

[6.36] Generally, the amendments discussed above apply where:[1]

(a) a person agrees to act as nominee in respect of a proposal for a CVA on or after 6 April 2010;
(b) a person agrees to act as nominee in respect of a proposal for an IVA on or after 6 April 2010.

The amendments relating to the preparation of proposals for CVAs made to rr 1.3 and 1.10 apply where a copy of the proposal is delivered to the intended nominee on or after 6 April 2010.[2]

[6.36] Voluntary arrangements

The amendments made by r 5.3 (contents of IVA proposals) apply where a copy of the proposal is delivered to the intended nominee on or after 6 April 2010.[3]

---

[1] Paragraph 1 of Sch 4 to IR 2010.
[2] Paragraph 3(1) of Sch 4 to IR 2010.
[3] Paragraph 3(2) of Sch 4 to IR 2010.

Chapter 7

Disclaimer

[7.1] Pursuant to s 178 of the Insolvency Act 1986 (IA 1986), a liquidator may by the giving of the prescribed notice disclaim any onerous property of the company.[1] The effect of a disclaimer is to determine the rights, interests and liabilities of the company in or in respect of the property disclaimed (s 178(4)).

---

[1] Onerous property means any unprofitable contract and any other property of the company which is unsaleable or not readily saleable or is such that it may give rise to a liability to pay money or perform any other onerous act (s 178(3)). See also *SSSL Realisations (2002) Ltd (in liquidation), Re* [2006] EWCA Civ 7, [2006] Ch 610, [2006] 2 WLR 1369.

[7.2] Similarly, pursuant to s 315 of the IA 1986, the trustee in bankruptcy may, by the giving of the prescribed notice, disclaim any onerous property of the bankrupt.[1] The effect of a disclaimer is to determine the rights, interests and liabilities of the bankrupt and his estate in or in respect of the property disclaimed, and to discharge the trustee from all personal liability in respect of that property as from the commencement of his trusteeship (s 315(3)).

---

[1] Onerous property means any unprofitable contract and any other property comprised in the bankrupt's estate which is unsaleable or not readily saleable, or is such that it may give rise to a liability to pay money or perform any other onerous act (s 315(2)).

[7.3] The Insolvency (Amendment) Rules 2010 (IR 2010) have amended the procedural rules that liquidators and trustees in bankruptcy need to follow when disclaiming onerous property.

The chapter considers the key amendments made by IR 2010 relating to the disclaimer procedures.

Liquidation

Notice of disclaimer

[7.4] There is now no longer any requirement for the notice of disclaimer to be filed with the court or for the court to seal the notice and endorse it with the date of filing.

Instead, the amended r 4.187 provides that the notice of disclaimer must be authenticated[1] and dated by the liquidator. As soon as reasonably practicable after authenticating the notice of disclaimer, the liquidator must send a copy of the notice to the registrar of companies and to the Chief Land Registrar if the disclaimer is of registered land.

For the purposes of s 178, the date of the prescribed notice is that on which the liquidator authenticated it.[2]

---

[1] See r 12A.9 for different methods of authentication.

[7.4] Disclaimer

² Rule 4.187(4).

Records

[7.5] There is now no longer a duty on the liquidator to notify the court as to the persons he has sent the notice of disclaimer. Instead, the new r 4.190A, replacing the former r 4.190, provides that the liquidator must include in his records of the insolvency a record of:

(a) the persons to whom he has sent or given copies of the notice of disclaimer, showing their names and addresses, and the nature of their respective interests;
(b) the dates on which the copies of the notice of disclaimer were sent or given to those persons;
(c) the date on which a copy of the notice of disclaimer was sent to the registrar of companies; and
(d) (where applicable) the date on which a copy of the notice was sent to the Chief Land Registrar.

Application by interested party

[7.6] Section 178(5) of the IA 1986 provides that a notice of disclaimer shall not be given in respect of any property if:

(a) a person interested in the property has applied in writing to the liquidator requiring the liquidator to decide whether he will disclaim or not, and
(b) the period of 28 days beginning with the day on which that application was made, or such longer period as the court may allow, has expired without a notice of disclaimer having been given under s 178 in respect of that property.

[7.7] The new r 4.191A, replacing the former r 4.191, has slightly recast the procedural rules that an interested party has to follow when making an application to the liquidator under s 178(5). The application must be delivered to the liquidator personally, by electronic means in accordance with Part 12A, or by any other means of delivery which enables proof of receipt of the application by the liquidator to be provided, if requested.

Bankruptcy

Notice of disclaimer

[7.8] There remains a requirement for the notice of disclaimer to be filed with the court, although there is no longer any requirement for the court to seal the notice and endorse it with the date of filing.

Instead, the amended r 6.178 provides that the notice of disclaimer must be authenticated and dated by the trustee. As soon as reasonably practicable after authenticating the notice of disclaimer, the trustee must file a copy of the notice with the court and send a copy of the notice to the Chief Land Registrar if the disclaimer is of registered land.

Transitional provisions **[7.12]**

For the purposes of s 315, the date of the prescribed notice is that on which the trustee authenticates it.[1]

[1] Rule 6.178(4).

Records

[7.9] There is now no longer a duty on the trustee to notify the court as to the persons he has sent the notice of disclaimer. Instead, the new r 6.181A, replacing the former r 6.181, provides that the trustee must include in his records of the insolvency a record of:

(a) the persons to whom that trustee has sent or given copies of the notice of disclaimer, showing their names and addresses, and the nature of their respective interests;
(b) the dates on which the copies of the notice of disclaimer were sent or given to those persons;
(c) the date on which a copy of the notice of disclaimer was filed with the court; and
(d) (where applicable) the date on which a copy of the notice was sent to the Chief Land Registrar.

Application by interested party

[7.10] Section 316(1) of the IA 1986 provides that notice of disclaimer shall not be given under s 315 in respect of any property if:

(a) a person interested in the property has applied in writing to the trustee requiring him to decide whether he will disclaim or not, and
(b) the period of 28 days beginning with the day on which that application was made has expired without a notice of disclaimer having been given under s 315 in respect of that property.

[7.11] The amended r 6.183 has slightly recast the procedural rules that an interested party has to follow when making an application to the trustee under s 316. The application must be delivered to the trustee personally, by electronic means in accordance with Part 12A, or by any other means of delivery which enables proof of receipt of the application by the trustee to be provided, if requested.

Transitional provisions

[7.12] The amendments discussed above apply where:[1]

(a) a company goes into liquidation upon the passing on or after 6 April 2010 of a resolution to wind up;
(b) a company goes into voluntary liquidation under para 83 of Sch B1 to the IA 1986, except where the preceding administration—
 (i) commenced before 6 April 2010; or
 (ii) is an administration which commenced by virtue of an administration order under para 10 of Sch B1 to the IA 1986 on an application which was made before 6 April 2010;

47

[7.12] Disclaimer

(c) a company goes into liquidation on the making of a winding-up order on a petition presented on or after 6 April 2010, except where the liquidation is immediately preceded by—
  (i) an administration under para 10 of Sch B1 to the IA 1986 where the administration order was made on an application made before 6 April 2010;
  (ii) an administration in respect of which the appointment of an administrator under para 14 or 22 of Sch B1 to the IA 1986 took effect before 6 April 2010; or
  (iii) a voluntary liquidation in respect of which the resolution to wind up was passed before 6 April 2010;

(d) a bankruptcy order is made on a petition presented on or after 6 April 2010.

---

[1] Paragraph 1 of Sch 4 to IR 2010. Note that the former r 4.190 was revoked by r 5 of IR 2010 and this revocation applies on and after 6 April 2010 in all cases (para 2 (1)(a) of Sch 4 to IR 2010). This seems to be a mistake as the revocation does not match the transitional provisions applicable to r 4.190A which replaces the former r 4.190.

Chapter 8

Public and private examinations

[8.1] The ability and duty of office holders to investigate the conduct and affairs of the insolvency entity or bankrupt is an important element of insolvency law:

> 'Facilities for investigations and examinations form an important part of the scheme for policing and enforcing obedience to the requirements of the Insolvency Act 1986 . . . and other legislation such as corporate and finance regulation legislation. There rests upon an official liquidator a public responsibility to investigate past activities connected with the company and, in appropriate cases, to report findings to the Director of Public Prosecutions. For winding up provides, short of investigations by the Serious Frauds Office, what is generally the only opportunity for subjecting the affairs of a company to the sort of close and detailed scrutiny which is capable of revealing the existence and extent of any frauds which may have been committed by those involved in its promotion and management. Publicity, discovery, and deterrence are the principal objects of both investigations and examinations.'[1]

---

[1] Andrew R Keay, *McPherson's Law of Company Liquidation* (2nd edn, 2009), Sweet & Maxwell, p 910 (footnote omitted). See also *Pantmaenog Timber Co (in liquidation)* [2003] UKHL 49, [2003] 4 All ER 1041, [2004] 1 AC 158 at [56].

[8.2] This chapter considers the procedural rules for two means of interrogation, public and private examinations, in particular the key amendments made by the Insolvency (Amendment) Rules 2010 (IR 2010).

Public examination

[8.3] A public examination requires a court order that the relevant person be publicly examined. Only the Official Receiver may apply for a public examination.

Section 133 of the Insolvency Act 1986 (IA 1986) provides that in a compulsory liquidation, the Official Receiver may at any time before the dissolution of the company apply to the court for the public examination of any person who

(a) is or has been an officer of the company; or
(b) has acted as liquidator or administrator of the company or as receiver or manager of its property; or
(c) is or has been concerned, or has taken part, in the promotion, formation or management of the company.

The court is required to direct that the person to whom the application relates be publicly examined as to the promotion, formation or management of the company or as to the conduct of its business and affairs, or his conduct or dealings in relation to the company, unless it is satisfied that there is no useful purpose to be served by such an examination.[1]

[8.3] Public and private examinations

[1] *Casterbridge Properties Ltd (in liquidation), Re, Jeeves v Official Receiver* [2003] EWCA Civ 1246, [2003] 4 All ER 1041, [2004] 1 WLR 602. The court could also direct a public examination on the application of the liquidator in a voluntary winding up under s 112 of the IA 1986: *Pantmaenog Timber Co (in liquidation)* [2003] UKHL 49, [2003] 4 All ER 1041, [2004] 1 AC 158 at [56].

[8.4] Section 290 of the IA 1986 provides that where a bankruptcy order has been made, the Official Receiver may at any time before the discharge of the bankrupt apply to the court for the public examination of the bankrupt. The court shall then direct that the bankrupt be publicly examined as to his affairs, dealings and property.

"Parliament intended that public examination should be ordered in corporate insolvency – should the official receiver think it appropriate – as in individual insolvency."[1] Thus the procedural rules for examination are the same in both corporate insolvency and personal bankruptcy.

The key amendments made by IR 2010 will be discussed below.

[1] *Casterbridge Properties Ltd (in liquidation), Re, Jeeves v Official Receiver* [2003] EWCA Civ 1246, [2003] 4 All ER 1041, [2004] 1 WLR 602 at [52].

Public examination in a winding up

[8.5] The amended r 4.211(2) provides that where the application for examination relates to a person who is or has been concerned, or has taken part, in the promotion, formation or management of the company, the application shall be accompanied by a report by the Official Receiver indicating whether, in the Official Receiver's opinion, it is likely that service of the order on the person can be effected at a known address in accordance with any means permitted by the new Part 12A of the Insolvency Rules 1986.[1]

[1] Prior to IR 2010, service was restricted to postal service.

[8.6] The original r 4.212(2) contained a requirement for the Official Receiver to give notice of the examination to every creditor and contributory of the company identified in the company's statement of affairs. There is no longer such requirement in the amended r 4.212(2).

[8.7] Where the Official Receiver thinks fit, notice of the court's examination order shall be gazetted and may be advertised in such other manner as the Official Receiver thinks fit, not less than 14 days before the date fixed for the examination.[1] However, the amended r 4.212(4) provides that where the court's order relates to a person who is or has been concerned, or has taken part, in the promotion, formation or management of the company, unless the court otherwise directs, there shall be no publication of the court's order before at least five business days have elapsed since the examinee was served with the order.

[1] Rule 4.212(3).

[8.8] A new r 4.212(3A) provides that the notice of the court's order must include the purpose of the hearing and the venue for the hearing.

Public examination in a bankruptcy

[8.9] The original r 6.172(3) contained a requirement for the Official Receiver to give notice of the examination to every creditor of the bankrupt identified in the bankrupt's statement of affairs. There is no longer such requirement in the amended r 6.172(3).

[8.10] Where the Official Receiver thinks fit, notice of the court's examination order shall be gazetted and may be advertised in such other manner as the Official Receiver thinks fit, not less than 14 days before the date fixed for the examination.[1] A new r 6.172(5A) provides that the notice of the court's order must include the purpose of the hearing and the venue for the hearing.

---

[1] Rule 6.172(4) and (5).

Private examination

[8.11] Section 236 of the IA 1986 permits the court, on the application of the office holder,[1] to summon to appear before it (a) any officer of the company, (b) any person known or suspected to have in his possession any property of the company or supposed to be indebted to the company, or (c) any person whom the court thinks capable of giving information concerning the promotion, formation, business, dealings, affairs or property of the company.

---

[1] Namely, the Official Receiver, administrator, administrative receiver, liquidator or provisional liquidator, as the case may be.

[8.12] The court may require any such person to submit to the court an account of his dealings with the company or to produce any books, papers or other records in his possession or under his control relating to the company or the matters concerning the promotion, formation, business, dealings, affairs or property of the company.

[8.13] In the context of debt relief orders, s 251N of the IA 1986 permits the court, on the application of the Official Receiver, to summon to appear before it (a) the debtor, (b) the debtor's spouse or former spouse or the debtor's civil partner or former civil partner, and (c) any person appearing to the court to be able to give information or assistance concerning the debtor or his dealings, affairs and property.

[8.14] At any time after a bankruptcy order has been made, s 366 permits the court, on the application of the Official Receiver or the trustee of the bankrupt's estate, to summon to appear before it (a) the bankrupt or the bankrupt's spouse or former spouse or civil partner or former civil partner, (b) any person known or believed to have any property comprised in the bankrupt's estate in his possession or to be indebted to the bankrupt, and (c) any person appearing to the court to be able to give information concerning the bankrupt or the bankrupt's dealings, affairs or property.

[8.15] Public and private examinations

[8.15] The procedural rules for examination are the same in both corporate insolvency and personal bankruptcy. The key amendments made by IR 2010 are to be found in the amended r 9.5(2) which now provides expressly that copies of questions put to the respondent or proposed to be put to the respondent are not open to inspection without an order of the court by any person other than (a) the applicant for an order under the applicable section, or (b) any person who could have applied for such an order in respect of the affairs of the same insolvent.

Transitional provisions

[8.16] The amendments discussed above apply where:[1]

(a) a company enters administration on or after 6 April 2010, except where—
    (i) it enters administration by virtue of an administration order under para 10 of Sch B1 to the IA 1986 on an application made before 6 April 2010;
    (ii) the administration is immediately preceded by a voluntary liquidation in respect of which the resolution to wind up was passed before 6 April 2010; or
    (iii) the administration is immediately preceded by a liquidation on the making of a winding-up order on a petition which was presented before 6 April 2010;

(b) in a receivership, a receiver or manager is appointed in respect of a company on or after 6 April 2010;

(c) a company goes into liquidation upon the passing on or after 6 April 2010 of a resolution to wind up;

(d) a company goes into voluntary liquidation under para 83 of Sch B1 to the IA 1986, except where the preceding administration—
    (i) commenced before 6 April 2010; or
    (ii) is an administration which commenced by virtue of an administration order under para 10 of Sch B1 to the IA 1986 on an application which was made before 6 April 2010;

(e) a company goes into liquidation on the making of a winding-up order on a petition presented on or after 6 April 2010, except where the liquidation is immediately preceded by—
    (i) an administration under para 10 of Sch B1 to the IA 1986 where the administration order was made on an application made before 6 April 2010;
    (ii) an administration in respect of which the appointment of an administrator under para 14 or 22 of Sch B1 to the IA 1986 took effect before 6 April 2010; or
    (iii) a voluntary liquidation in respect of which the resolution to wind up was passed before 6 April 2010;

(f) a debt relief order is made on or after 6 April 2010;

(g) a bankruptcy order is made on a petition presented on or after 6 April 2010.

[1] Paragraph 1 of Sch 4 to IR 2010.

Chapter 9

Office holders' remuneration and expenses

[9.1] A key part of the Insolvency (Amendment) Rules 2010 (IR 2010) concerns office holders' remuneration and expenses. This chapter considers the key reforms in this respect effected by IR 2010, together with some recent judicial developments.

Before considering the statutory reforms, it may be helpful to identify the operation of insolvency expenses within the corpus of insolvency law.

The concept of and approach to insolvency expenses

[9.2] The corpus of insolvency law concerns in essence how an asset deficit is to be managed in a way fair to all participants. An essential limb of that corpus is the distribution of assets among the claimants, while respecting as much as possible the claimants' pre-insolvency entitlements. As the US Supreme Court has also repeatedly held, "[c]reditors' entitlements in bankruptcy arise in the first instance from the underlying substantive law creating the debtor's obligation, subject to any qualifying or contrary provisions of the Bankruptcy Code".[1] Once the pre-insolvency entitlements are established, the claimants' rights to payment from the insolvent estate and their priority status are solely a matter of insolvency law, primarily a matter of legislative policy informed by such normative standards as equality, fairness, liberty and efficiency.

---

[1] *Raleigh v Illinois Dept of Revenue* 530 US 15, 20 (2000); *Travelers Casualty & Surety Co of America v Pacific Gas & Electric Co* 549 US 443, 450 (2007).

[9.3] Insolvency expenses are post-insolvency entitlements which by statute generally have priority over creditors' pre-insolvency entitlements. In liquidation terminology, pre-insolvency debts are provable, while post-insolvency claims are payable in full (though not provable).

[9.4] Like the ranking of creditors' pre-insolvency entitlements, the priority of insolvency expenses is also primarily a matter of insolvency distribution policy.[1]

---

[1] It has been correctly said that "[q]uestions of priority may arise, but they will only be of importance where there is a deficiency in the assets, and not where everybody can be paid in full": *Re London Metallurgical Co* [1895] 1 Ch 758 at 763.

[9.5] The determination of insolvency distribution policy is a question for legislative chambers, not judicial chambers. For the court's business is to apply the insolvency distribution policy laid down by Parliament, not to conduct policy seminars. This explains why judicial discretion is inherently improper

[9.5] Office holders' remuneration and expenses

when dealing with the priority of claims in insolvency. Mummery LJ put the matter lucidly in these terms, when rejecting the possibility of a remedial constructive trust under English law:[1]

> 'Parliament has . . . sanctioned a scheme for . . . distribution of assets designed to achieve a fair distribution of the insolvent company's property among the unsecured creditors. This scheme, now contained in the Insolvency Act 1986 was described . . . in *Re Paramount Airways* [1993] Ch 223 at 230, as "a coherent, modernised and expanded code". The provisions of that code apply both to the case of an insolvent company which has gone into formal liquidation and to one in respect of which an administration order has been made. The essential characteristic of the statutory scheme is that the liquidator or administrator is bound to deal with the assets of the company as directed by statute for the benefit of all creditors who come in to prove a valid claim. There is a statutory obligation on the administrators . . . to treat the general creditors in a particular way. A question may arise as to whether a particular asset was or was not the beneficial property of the company at the date of the commencement of the winding up (or administration). If it is established in a dispute that it is not an asset of the company then it never becomes subject of the statutory insolvency scheme . . . If, on the other hand, the asset is the absolute beneficial property of the company there is no general power in the liquidator, the administrators or the court to amend or modify the statutory scheme so as to transfer that asset or to declare it to be held for the benefit of another person. To do that would be to give a preference to another person who enjoys no preference under the statutory scheme.
>
> In brief, the position is that there is no prospect of the court in this case granting a remedial constructive trust to the applicants . . . , since the effect of the statutory scheme applicable on an insolvency is to shut out a remedy which would, if available, have the effect of conferring a priority not accorded by the provisions of the statutory insolvency scheme. In her eloquent address, [counsel] submitted that "the law moves". That is true. But it cannot be legitimately moved by judicial decision down a road signed "No Entry" by Parliament. The insolvency road is blocked off to remedial constructive trusts, at least when judge driven in a vehicle of discretion . . .
>
> To a trust lawyer and, even more so to an insolvency lawyer, the prospect of a court imposing such a trust is inconceivable and . . . even the most enthusiastic student of the law of restitution would be forced to recognise that the scheme imposed by statute for a fair distribution of the assets of an insolvent company precludes the application of the equitable principles manifested in the remedial constructive trust developed by such courts as the Supreme Court of Canada.'

---

[1] *Polly Peck International plc (in administration) (No 2)* [1998] 3 All ER 812 at 826–827, 1 ITELR 289, CA.

[9.6] It follows that what constitutes an insolvency expense should be purely a matter of statutory construction and using judicial discretion to label as an insolvency expense what would otherwise be a general unsecured claim is inherently inapposite. For the effect of labelling such an unsecured claim an insolvency expense is to confer insolvency priority by judicial discretion. Similarly, using judicial discretion to disallow what would otherwise be an insolvency expense (as in *Kentish Homes Ltd, Re*)[1] is equally impermissible, for its effect is to downgrade insolvency priority by judicial discretion.

[1] (1993) 91 LGR 592, [1993] BCLC 1375.

Lundy Granite

[9.7] In a liquidation, pre-insolvency debts are provable, while post-insolvency expenses are payable in full (though not provable). However, certain pre-insolvency debts would become payable as expenses if they fall within the principle in *Lundy Granite Co, Re, ex p Heavan*.[1] The principle "permits, on equitable grounds, the concept of a liability incurred as an expense of the liquidation to be expanded to include liabilities incurred before the liquidation in respect of property afterwards retained by the liquidator for the benefit of the insolvent estate".[2]

The Supreme Court of Victoria, after a careful review of the English authorities,[3] accurately summarised the operation of the *Lundy Granite* principle in respect of rent as follows:

> 'First, prima facie claims under pre-liquidation leases are provable; they are not payable as expenses of the winding-up, the importance of preserving *pari passu* distribution being emphasised. Second, although rent is not incurred by the liquidator (the obligation existing in the pre-liquidation lease) the ambit of the administration expense is expanded where the liquidator actively retains (as opposed to passively holds) or uses the premises for the purposes of the winding-up. In those circumstances rent accruing during that period of retention or use will be an expense of the winding-up. Third, the rent will not be an expense of the winding up where the retention or use is agreed to or acquiesced in by the landlord so as to secure mutual benefits for both the purposes of the winding-up and the landlord.'[4]

It is important to note that the *Lundy Granite* principle does not mean that whether debts should count as insolvency expenses is a matter for the discretion of the court. The principle serves only to illuminate the process of statutory construction. Accordingly, in context of liquidation expenses, Lord Hoffmann said:

> '[The *Lundy Granite* principle] was not . . . a general test for deciding what counted as an expense of the liquidation. Expenses incurred after the liquidation date need no further equitable reason why they should be paid. Of course it will generally be true that such expenses will have been incurred by the liquidator for the purposes of the liquidation. It is not the business of the liquidator to incur expenses for any other purpose. But this is not at all the same thing as saying that the expenses will necessarily be for the benefit of estate. They may simply be liabilities which, as liquidator, he has to pay. For example, there will be the fees payable to fund the Insolvency Service, ranking as paragraph (c) in rule 4.218(1), where the benefit to the estate may seem somewhat remote . . .
>
> Rule 4.218 determines what counts as expenses, subject only to the limited discretion under section 156 of the 1986 Act to re-arrange the priorities of expenses inter se. The court will of course interpret rule 4.218 to include debts which, under the *Lundy Granite* principle, are deemed to be expenses of the liquidation. Ordinarily this means that debts such as rents under a lease will be treated as coming within paragraph (a), but the principle may possibly enlarge the scope of other paragraphs as well. But the application of that principle does not involve an exercise of discretion any more than the application of any other legal principle to the particular facts of the case.'[5]

The above approach also applies to administration expenses.[6]

[9.7] Office holders' remuneration and expenses

It is with the above conceptual background that we now consider the amendments made by IR 2010.

1   (1871) LR 6 Ch App 462 (CA).
2   *Toshoku Finance UK plc, Re, Kahn v IRC* [2002] UKHL 6, [2002] 3 All ER 961, [2002] 1 WLR 671 at [29].
3   Including, *Progress Assurance Co, Re, ex p Liverpool Exchange Co* (1870) LR 9 Eq 370; *In re Bridgewater Engineering Co* (1879) 12 Ch D 181; *In re Oak Pits Colliery Co* (1882) 21 Ch D 322 (CA); *In re South Kensington Co-operative Stores* (1881) 17 Ch D 161; *Lancashire Cotton Spinning Co, Re, ex p Carnelley* (1887) 35 Ch D 656, CA; *Shackell & Co v Chorlton & Sons* [1895] 1 Ch 378; *ABC Coupler and Engineering Co Ltd (No 3)* [1970] 1 All ER 650, [1970] 1 WLR 702; *Downer Enterprises Ltd, Re* [1974] 2 All ER 1074, [1974] 1 WLR 1460.
4   *Ansett Australia Ground Staff Superannuation Plan v Ansett Australia* [2002] VSC 576 at [321].
5   *Re Toshoku Finance UK* [2002] UKHL 6, [2002] 1 WLR 671 at [30] and [38].
6   *Trident Fashions, Re, Exeter City Council v Bairstow* [2007] EWHC 400 (Ch), [2007] 4 All ER 437, [2007] 2 BCLC 455; *Goldacre (Offices) Ltd v Nortel Networks UK Ltd (in administration)* [2009] EWHC 3389 (Ch), [2010] 3 WLR 171. The contrary approach in *Atlantic Computer Systems plc, Re* [1992] Ch 505, [1992] 1 All ER 476, CA that whether debts should count as insolvency expenses is a matter for the court's discretion must be discarded. See further discussion below and also Look Chan Ho, 'Sealing administration expenses, puncturing rescue culture?' (2007) 23 Insolvency Law & Practice 26.

Liquidation expenses[1]

1   The focus of this section is on insolvent liquidation, although occasional references to members' voluntary liquidation will also be made.

[9.8] Rules 4.218(1) and 12.2(1) of the Insolvency Rules 1986 both provide that all fees, costs, charges and other expenses incurred in the course of the liquidation are to be regarded as expenses of the liquidation. *Toshoku* confirmed that r 4.218 contains an exhaustive list of items of liquidation expenses.[2] None of this is changed by IR 2010.

The key IR 2010 changes are discussed below.

2   Subject to r 4.220. See *Unadkat & Co (Accountants) v Bhardwaj (former liquidator of Isher Fashions Ltd)* [2006] EWHC 2785 (Ch), [2007] BCC 452.

Basis of remuneration

[9.9] The amended r 4.127(2) sets out the three bases for fixing a liquidator's remuneration:

(a)   a percentage of the value of the assets which are realised or distributed, or of the one value and the other in combination;
(b)   by reference to the time properly given by the liquidator and his staff in attending to matters arising in the winding-up;
(c)   a set amount.[1]

The bases of remuneration above may be used in any combination and different bases may be used in respect of different things done by the liquidator.[2]

Where the percentage basis of remuneration is used, different percentages may be fixed in respect of different things done by the liquidator.[3]

---

[1] See r 4.148A in respect of members' voluntary liquidation.
[2] Rule 4.127(3A).
[3] Rule 4.127(3B).

[9.10] Where the liquidator is not the Official Receiver, it is for the liquidation committee (if there is one) to determine:

(a) which of the three bases set out above are to be fixed and (where appropriate) in what combination,
(b) the percentage or percentages (if any) to be fixed, and
(c) the applicable set amount.[1]

If there is no liquidation committee, or the committee does not make the requisite determination, the liquidator's remuneration may be fixed (in accordance with the bases mentioned above) by a resolution of a meeting of creditors.[2]

---

[1] Rule 4.127(3C). Note that if the basis of the liquidator's remuneration has been fixed by the liquidation committee and the liquidator considers the rate or amount to be insufficient or the basis to be inappropriate, the liquidator may request that the rate or amount be increased or the basis changed by resolution of the creditors (r 4.129A). Further, if the liquidator considers that the basis of remuneration fixed by the liquidation committee or by resolution of the creditors is insufficient or inappropriate, the liquidator may apply to the court for an order changing it or increasing its amount or rate (r 4.130).
[2] Rule 4.127(5).

[9.11] Where the liquidation is immediately preceded by an administration and the liquidator was the erstwhile administrator, the basis of remuneration fixed in the administration continues to apply in the liquidation.[1]

---

[1] Rule 4.127(5A).

[9.12] In the case of a creditors' voluntary liquidation (CVL), if the basis of the liquidator's remuneration is not fixed in any of the above ways, it shall, on application by the liquidator, be fixed by the court; but such an application may not be made by the liquidator unless the liquidator has first sought fixing of the basis in accordance with above methods, and in any event may not be made more than 18 months after the date of the liquidator's appointment.[1]

---

[1] Rule 4.127(7).

[9.13] In the case of a compulsory liquidation, if the basis of the liquidator's remuneration is not fixed or treated as fixed in accordance with r 4.127, the liquidator (not being the Official Receiver) shall be entitled by way of remuneration for his services in accordance with the scale set out in Sch 6 to the Insolvency Rules 1986.[1]

[9.13] Office holders' remuneration and expenses

[1] Rule 4.127A.

[9.14] Where, after the basis of the liquidator's remuneration has been fixed, there is a material and substantial change in the circumstances which were taken into account in fixing it, the liquidator may request that it be changed in accordance with the same rules applicable to the original basis of remuneration. The liquidator's request must be made to the same body that fixed the original basis of remuneration.[1]

[1] Rule 4.131A.

Apportionment of set fee remuneration

[9.15] In a case in which the basis of the liquidator's remuneration is a set amount under r 4.127(2)(c) and the liquidator (former liquidator) ceases (for whatever reason) to hold office before the time has elapsed or the work has been completed in respect of which the amount was set, application may be made for determination of what portion of the amount should be paid to the former liquidator or the former liquidator's personal representative in respect of the time which has actually elapsed or the work which has actually been done. Application must be made to the same body that fixed the original basis of remuneration.[1]

[1] New r 4.131C.

Remuneration of new liquidator

[9.16] If a new liquidator (not being the Official Receiver) is appointed in place of another, any determination, resolution or court order in effect immediately before the former liquidator ceased to hold office continues to apply in respect of the remuneration of the new liquidator until a further determination, resolution or court order is made.[1]

[1] New r 4.131B.

Creditors' entitlement to information on liquidator's remuneration and expenses

[9.17] IR 2010 has facilitated the creditors' right to challenge office holders' remuneration and expenses.

One begins with the newly created liquidator's obligations to send yearly progress reports to creditors and members.[1] The progress report must include the following information:

- details of the basis fixed for the remuneration of the liquidator under r 4.127 (or if not fixed at the date of the report, the steps taken during the period of the report to fix it);

- if the basis of remuneration has been fixed, a statement of (i) the remuneration charged by the liquidator during the period of the report, and (ii) where the report is the first to be made after the basis has been fixed, the remuneration charged by the liquidator during the periods covered by the previous reports, together with a description of the things done by the liquidator during those periods in respect of which the remuneration was charged, irrespective in either case of whether payment was made in respect of that remuneration during that period;[2]
- a statement of the expenses incurred by the liquidator during the period of the report, irrespective of whether payment was made in respect of them during that period;
- a statement of the creditors' right to request information under r 4.49E and their right to challenge the liquidator's remuneration and expenses.

[1] Section 92A of the Insolvency Act 1986 (IA 1986) and r 4.49C for MVL; s 104A of the IA 1986 and r 4.49C for CVL; r 4.49B for compulsory liquidation.
[2] Except where the basis for the remuneration is a set amount under r 4.127(2)(c), in which case it may be shown as that amount without any apportionment to the period of the report.

[9.18] Then, at least eight weeks before holding a final meeting, the liquidator must send to each creditor known to the liquidator a draft of the report which the liquidator intends to lay before the meeting.[1] The draft report must include the following information:

- details of remuneration charged and expenses incurred by the liquidator;
- details of the basis fixed for the liquidator's remuneration;
- a statement of the creditors' right to request information under r 4.49E and their right to challenge the liquidator's remuneration and expenses.

[1] New r 4.49D.

[9.19] Pursuant to the new r 4.49E, within 21 days of receipt of the progress report or draft report (or within seven business days of receipt of the progress report where the report is for the purpose of a creditors' meeting to receive the liquidator's resignation), a creditor may make a request in writing to the liquidator for further information about remuneration or expenses set out in the progress report or draft report, provided that the creditor is a secured creditor, has the concurrence of at least 5% in value of the unsecured creditors (including the creditor in question) or has the permission of the court. The liquidator must, within 14 days of receipt of the request, provide the requested information, unless he considers that:

(i) the time or cost of preparation of the information would be excessive, or
(ii) disclosure of the information would be prejudicial to the conduct of the liquidation or might reasonably be expected to lead to violence against any person, or
(iii) the liquidator is subject to an obligation of confidentiality in respect of the information, in which case he must give reasons for not providing all of the information.

[9.19] Office holders' remuneration and expenses

Any creditor may apply to the court within 21 days of (a) the giving by the liquidator of reasons for not providing all of the information asked for, or (b) the expiry of the 14-day deadline for the provision of the requested information, and the court may make such order as it thinks just.

Creditors' claim that remuneration is or other expenses are excessive

[9.20] The amended r 4.131 provides for the circumstances in which a creditor could challenge the liquidator's remuneration and expenses.

Any secured creditor, or any unsecured creditor with either the concurrence of at least 10% in value of the creditors (including that creditor) or the permission of the court, may apply for one or more orders on the grounds that:

(a) the remuneration charged by the liquidator,
(b) the basis fixed for the liquidator's remuneration under r 4.127, or
(c) expenses incurred by the liquidator,

is or are, in all the circumstances,[1] excessive, or in the case of the basis fixed for the liquidator's remuneration, inappropriate.

---

[1] The reference to "all the circumstances" presumably means that a successful challenge has to cross a fairly high threshold.

[9.21] Any such application must, subject to any order of the court under r 4.49E(5), be made no later than eight weeks (or, in a case falling within r 4.108, four weeks) after receipt by the applicant of the progress report, or the draft report under r 4.49D, which first reports the charging of the remuneration or the incurring of the expenses in question.

[9.22] If the court considers the application to be well-founded, it must make one or more of the following orders:

(a) reducing the amount of remuneration which the liquidator was entitled to charge;
(b) fixing the basis of remuneration at a reduced rate or amount;
(c) changing the basis of remuneration;
(d) that some or all of the remuneration or expenses in question be treated as not being expenses of the liquidation;
(e) that the liquidator or the liquidator's personal representative pay to the company the amount of the excess of remuneration or expenses or such part of the excess as the court may specify.

[9.23] The court may also make any other order that it thinks just. Presumably the court could in some circumstances order a third party to pay to the company the amount of the excess expenses it received from the liquidator.

Administration expenses

[9.24] As in the case of liquidation expenses, what constitutes an administration expense is purely a matter of statutory construction, a process informed by the *Lundy Granite* principle in respect of certain pre-insolvency claims such as rent. Rule 2.67 sets out a complete code as to the priorities in an administration.[1] IR 2010 does not change this approach.

The key IR 2010 changes are discussed below.

[1] *Johnson Machine and Tool Ltd, Re* [2010] EWHC 582 (Ch) at [8], [2010] NLJR 805.

Basis of remuneration

[9.25] The amended r 2.106(2) sets out the three bases for fixing an administrator's remuneration:

(a) a percentage of the value of the property with which he has to deal;
(b) by reference to the time properly given by the administrator and his staff in attending to matters arising in the administration; and
(c) a set amount.

The bases of remuneration above may be used in any combination and different bases may be used in respect of different things done by the administrator.[1]

Where the percentage basis of remuneration is used, different percentages may be fixed in respect of different things done by the administrator.[2]

[1] Rule 2.106(3A).
[2] Rule 2.106(3B).

[9.26] It is for the creditors' committee (if there is one) to determine:

(a) which of the three bases set out above are to be fixed and (where appropriate) in what combination,
(b) the percentage or percentages (if any) to be fixed, and
(c) the applicable set amount.[1]

If there is no creditors' committee, or the committee does not make the requisite determination, the administrator's remuneration may be fixed (in accordance with the bases mentioned above) by a resolution of a meeting of creditors.[2]

[1] Rule 2.106(3C). Note that if the basis of the administrator's remuneration has been fixed by the creditors' committee and the administrator considers the rate or amount to be insufficient or the basis to be inappropriate, the administrator may request that the rate or amount be increased or the basis changed by resolution of the creditors (amended r 2.107). Further, if the administrator considers that the basis of remuneration fixed by the creditors' committee or by resolution of the creditors is insufficient or inappropriate, the administrator may apply to the court for an order changing it or increasing its amount or rate (amended r 2.108).
[2] Rule 2.106(5).

[9.27] If the basis of the administrator's remuneration is not fixed in any of the above ways, it shall, on application by the administrator, be fixed by the court; but such an application may not be made by the administrator unless the administrator has first sought fixing of the basis in accordance with above

[9.27] Office holders' remuneration and expenses

methods, and in any event may not be made more than 18 months after the date of the administrator's appointment.[1]

---
[1] Rule 2.106(6).

[9.28] Where, after the basis of the administrator's remuneration has been fixed, there is a material and substantial change in the circumstances which was taken into account in fixing it, the administrator may request that it be changed in accordance with the same rules applicable to the original basis of remuneration. The administrator's request must be made to the same body that fixed the original basis of remuneration.[1]

---
[1] New r 2.109A.

Apportionment of set fee remuneration

[9.29] In a case in which the basis of the administrator's remuneration is a set amount under r 2.106(2)(c) and the administrator (former administrator) ceases (for whatever reason) to hold office before the time has elapsed or the work has been completed in respect of which the amount was set, application may be made for determination of what portion of the amount should be paid to the former administrator or the former administrator's personal representative in respect of the time which has actually elapsed or the work which has actually been done. Application must be made to the same body that fixed the original basis of remuneration.[1]

---
[1] New r 2.109C.

Remuneration of new administrator

[9.30] If a new administrator is appointed in place of another, any determination, resolution or court order in effect immediately before the former administrator ceased to hold office continues to apply in respect of the remuneration of the new administrator until a further determination, resolution or court order is made.[1]

---
[1] New r 2.109B.

Pre-administration costs

[9.31] Prior to IR 2010, the court could as a matter of discretion allow an administrator's pre-appointment costs to be recovered as an expense of the administration pursuant to para 13(1)(f) of Sch B1 to the IA 1986:

> '[I]t was appropriate to use the power contained in paragraph 13 of Schedule B1 to make an order on a discretionary basis, rather than to find that pre- appointment costs were in all cases part of the costs of the Applicant that must be allowed under Rule 2.67(1)(c) . . . [I]t was appropriate in the exercise of this discretion to make

the order sought where the court is satisfied that the balance of benefit arising from the incurring of pre-appointment costs is in favour of the creditors rather than (in a pre-pack case) the management as potential purchasers of the business.'[1]

However, such allowance was appropriate only in limited circumstances and the position is neatly summarised below which serves as a prelude to the IR 2010 reform:

'The legitimacy of pre-packs and the jurisdiction to make an order allowing pre-appointment costs are not in doubt: see *Re Kayley Vending Ltd* [2009] BCC 578. The jurisdiction, as that case demonstrates, is a discretionary one, founded not on any right of the applicant to treat the pre-appointment costs as his costs of the application, but on the discretionary power of the Court under para 13 of Schedule B1 of the Insolvency Act 1986 to make "any other order which the court thinks appropriate" . . .

In *Re SE Services Ltd* (9th August 2006) HHJ Norris QC (as he then was) drew a distinction between an administration that was plainly for the benefit of creditors and one where the balance of advantage appeared to lie heavily with the management. In the former but not the latter case, it would be appropriate to allow the pre-appointment costs. In that case, he was considering . . . the situation in which the particular administration purpose was obtaining for creditors a better result than would ensue in a liquidation. It is thus clear that crossing that threshold (which, as is well known, is a relatively modest one) does not without more justify the treatment of pre-appointment costs as an administration expense.

There are many cases in which it is not clear one way or the other where the balance of advantage as between creditors and purchasing directors lies. In the present cases, there was evidence before the Court demonstrating compliance with SIP 16 (the details and significance of which are lucidly explained by Judge Cooke in the *Kayley Vending* case) and I was satisfied that the proposed administration and pre-pack would be reasonably likely to result in a somewhat better result for creditors as a whole than would be the case in a winding-up, though the outlook was still bleak for unsecured creditors, who would receive a modest return on a best case scenario in each case. The return would nevertheless be better than in a liquidation, not least because of the elimination of employee claims, as employees would continue to be engaged in the ongoing business which was being sold. However, in applying the test advanced by Judge Norris, a different comparison is called for. What the court is called upon to compare is whether the advantage to the purchasing directors in retaining a business shorn of debt is clearly outweighed by the advantage derived by creditors from the pre-pack. Where the directors (or a company which they control or have a substantial connection with) are the purchasers, it is rarely possible to establish clearly that the balance of advantage is in the creditors' favour. As the onus is in my judgment on those seeking to treat pre-appointment costs as administration expenses to justify the appropriateness of that course, I did not consider it right to add what would appear to many creditors to be insult to the injury already suffered by them by subjecting them to the burden of such costs . . .

I have one other consideration in mind. Most administrations are out-of-court appointments. I enquired of [counsel] what happened to pre-appointment costs in the case of an out-of-court appointment and was told that their payment is often approved as part of the administrator's proposals under para 49(1) of Schedule B1. If that is correct, the approach seems misconceived, as the proposals to be considered under that paragraph are "for achieving the purpose of the administration". This has nothing to do with pre-appointment costs. Whilst the basis of the administrator's remuneration forms part of the proposals, remuneration may only be fixed as a percentage of the value of the property with which he has to deal (which may or may not be sufficient to cover the pre-appointment costs) or by reference to time properly spent in attending to "the matters arising in the administration":

rule 2.106 of the Insolvency Rules 1986. Pre-appointment costs do not reflect time spent on any matter arising in the administration, but on matters arising pre-administration. Nor do I see any basis for treating such costs as an administration expense under rule 2.67(1) of the Insolvency Rules 1986, which sets out a complete code as to the priorities in an administration. It does not seem to me, therefore, that it lies within the power of the creditors to approve any payment to the administrators in respect of pre-appointment costs which would not otherwise count as an administration expense.

Given, therefore, the difficulties that I perceive in ever treating pre-appointment costs as an administration expense in an out-of-court appointment, it would be wrong to allow such costs just because (as in the present cases) there happened to be administration applications to the court in the context of pending petitions for winding-up.

This observation highlights one other point. In the *SE Services case*, the order that Judge Norris was asked to make (as recorded in *Kayley Vending*) related to "considering and completing form 2.2B". In cases such as the present, there are also costs associated with the preparation by the insolvency practitioner of a witness statement complying with the guidance given by Judge Cooke in the *Kayley Vending* case. Even where it is appropriate to make a costs order in respect of this pre-appointment activity, a distinction may, and often will, need to be made between the costs associated with advising the directors as to the appropriate way of dealing with the insolvency and the subsequent costs of the proposed administrator in considering and preparing the form 2.2B and any necessary witness statement, following the advice that administration is the appropriate route. It may be in any given case that the appropriate course is not that administration is the appropriate route, but that the company should go into liquidation, or enter into a voluntary arrangement . . . , or even continue to trade out of its difficulties. In those cases, the same costs of obtaining advice as to the appropriate course of action would have been incurred, and the burden of costs would have followed whatever arrangement the insolvency practitioner made with his appointors. Where the decision is made to seek an administration order, the subsequent costs may in an appropriate case properly be treated as an administration expense, but the prior costs burden of seeking insolvency advice should in cases such as the present ordinarily lie where they fall.

It follows that the scope of a costs order in a case such as the present (when appropriately to be made) should in my judgment ordinarily be to deal, and deal only, with those additional costs that the bringing of the administration application occasions, and not advice given before any decision to seek administration has been made, or the pre-administration costs of considering and arranging the pre-pack. If the costs occasioned by insolvency advice would have been incurred in any event, even if no decision to go down the administration route had been made, it will rarely (if ever) be appropriate to order those costs to be paid as an administration expense. The justification for ordering such costs to be treated as an administration expense is that it is unfair that the applicants should bear those costs which are in truth costs occasioned for the benefit of creditors generally.

It follows also from this that there should ordinarily be evidence confirming that the applicant (rather than the company itself) is personally liable for the costs, and as to the amount of and justification for the relevant costs, bearing in mind the distinctions I have drawn in the previous paragraph. The court should be in a position to assess the costs summarily in most cases.

In addition, it will commonly be the case in cases such as the present that the largest element of costs incurred by potential administrators will be referable to the negotiation of the terms of the pre-pack sale, ascertaining what assets are to be sold, arranging any valuation advice and considering whether to market the business or go for a pre-pack. These are not really costs of preparing the Form 2.2B or witness statement; they produce the factual situation reported on by those documents. Ordinarily, therefore, they would not fall properly to be treated as an administration expense.'[2]

---

[1] *Re Kayley Vending* [2009] EWHC 904 (Ch), [2009] BCC 578 at [32]-[33]. For a critique of this approach, see Look Chan Ho, 'Interrogating and indulging prepacks: *Re Kayley Vending*' (2009) 2 Corporate Rescue and Insolvency 168.

[2] *Johnson Machine and Tool Ltd, Re* [2010] EWHC 582 (Ch) at [2], [4], [5], [8]-[13], [2010] NLJR 805.

[9.32] IR 2010 introduces the concept of pre-administration costs as an item of administration expense. Pre-administration costs are fees charged and expenses incurred by the administrator, or another person qualified to act as an insolvency practitioner, before the company entered administration but "with a view to" its doing so.[1]

As there is no definition of "with a view to", the court might find the following passage in *Johnson Machine and Tool Ltd, Re* instructive:

> 'Pre-appointment costs do not reflect time spent on any matter arising in the administration, but on matters arising pre-administration . . .
>
> A distinction may, and often will, need to be made between the costs associated with advising the directors as to the appropriate way of dealing with the insolvency and the subsequent costs of the proposed administrator . . . following the advice that administration is the appropriate route. It may be in any given case that the appropriate course is not that administration is the appropriate route, but that the company should go into liquidation, or enter into a voluntary arrangement . . . In those cases, the same costs of obtaining advice as to the appropriate course of action would have been incurred, and the burden of costs would have followed whatever arrangement the insolvency practitioner made with his appointors. Where the decision is made to seek an administration order, the subsequent costs may in an appropriate case properly be treated as an administration expense, but the prior costs burden of seeking insolvency advice should in cases such as the present ordinarily lie where they fall . . .
>
> In addition, it will commonly be the case in cases such as the present that the largest element of costs incurred by potential administrators will be referable to the negotiation of the terms of the pre-pack sale, ascertaining what assets are to be sold, arranging any valuation advice and considering whether to market the business or go for a pre-pack . . . Ordinarily . . . they would not fall properly to be treated as an administration expense.'[2]

Accordingly, insolvency practitioners should heed the following judicial advice:

> 'In the case of an insolvency practitioner giving advice to a company prior to the commencement of an insolvency process, the liability to pay his fees (unless he is acting "on spec") will, subject to anything else that may be agreed in any given case, be the company's. If there is no advance payment, that leaves the insolvency practitioner at risk of having nothing but a claim as unsecured creditor in the ensuing insolvency process. Insolvency practitioners are able to protect themselves either by insisting on payment in advance, or by contracting personally with or taking a guarantee from the directors or others. If they do neither of those things, they are at risk, but the rewards of the ensuing appointment that often occurs are in many cases more than adequate to justify that risk. Those rewards are however less

[9.32] Office holders' remuneration and expenses

certain in the case of a pre-pack, involving an immediate pre-arranged sale of the business and assets, as the real work is most often done pre-appointment. That highlights the need for insolvency practitioners to take steps to protect themselves, if they feel in need of protection.'[3]

---

[1] Rule 2.33(2A)(a). "Unpaid pre-administration costs" are pre-administration costs which had not been paid when the company entered administration (r 2.33(2A)(b)).
[2] *Re Johnson Machine and Tool Co* [2010] EWHC 582 (Ch), [2010] BCC 382 at [8], [10] and [13].
[3] *Re Johnson Machine and Tool Co* [2010] EWHC 582 (Ch), [2010] BCC 382 at [3].

[9.33] Pursuant to the amended r 2.67(h), unpaid pre-administration costs are payable as an administration expense provided they are approved under the new r 2.67A. Such pre-administration costs rank pari passu with the administrator's remuneration.

[9.34] Pursuant to the amended r 2.33, the administrator's statement of proposals under para 49 of Sch B1 to the IA 1986 must include the details of any pre-administration costs charged or incurred by the administrator or, to the administrator's knowledge, by any other person qualified to act as an insolvency practitioner. They must encompass:

(a) details of any agreement under which the fees were charged and expenses incurred, including the parties to the agreement and the date on which the agreement was made,
(b) details of the work done for which the fees were charged and expenses incurred,
(c) an explanation of why the work was done before the company entered administration and how it would further the achievement of the objective of administration set out in para 3(1) of Sch B1,
(d) the amount of the pre-administration costs,
(e) the amounts of pre-administration costs which have already been paid,
(f) the identity of the person who made the payment or, if more than one person made the payment, the identity of each such person and of the amounts paid by each such person,
(g) the amounts of unpaid pre-administration costs, and
(h) a statement that the payment of unpaid pre-administration costs as an expense of the administration is (i) subject to approval under r 2.67A, and (ii) not part of the proposals subject to approval under para 53 of Sch B1.

[9.35] The approval process under r 2.67A is as follows:

First, where there a creditors' committee, it is for the committee to determine whether and to what extent the unpaid pre-administration costs should be approved for payment.[1]

Secondly, if there is no creditors' committee or the committee does not make the necessary determination, or if it does do so but the administrator or other insolvency practitioner who has charged fees or incurred expenses as pre-administration costs considers the amount determined to be insufficient, determination of whether and to what extent the unpaid pre-administration costs are approved for payment will be by resolution of a meeting of creditors, unless the administrator has made a statement under para 52(1)(b) of Sch B1.[2]

If the administrator has made a statement under para 52(1)(b), determination of whether and to what extent the unpaid pre-administration costs are approved for payment will be (i) by the approval of each secured creditor of the company, or (ii) if the administrator has made, or intends to make, a distribution to preferential creditors, by the approval of each secured creditor of the company and preferential creditors whose debts amount to more than 50% of the preferential debts of the company, disregarding debts of any creditor who does not respond to an invitation to give or withhold approval.[3]

Thirdly, the administrator (where the fees were charged or expenses incurred by the administrator) or other insolvency practitioner (where the fees were charged or expenses incurred by that practitioner) may apply to the court for a determination of whether and to what extent the unpaid pre-administration costs are approved for payment if there is no determination in one of the ways above, or there is such a determination but the administrator or other insolvency practitioner who has charged fees or incurred expenses as pre-administration costs considers the amount determined to be insufficient.

---

[1] The administrator must call a meeting of the creditors' committee if so requested by another insolvency practitioner who has charged fees or incurred expenses as pre-administration costs, and the administrator must give notice of the meeting within 28 days of receipt of the request. If the administrator fails to call a meeting, the other insolvency practitioner may apply to the court for an order requiring the administrator to do so.

[2] Namely, a statement that the company has insufficient property to enable a distribution to be made to unsecured creditors other than by virtue of s 176A(2)(a) of the IA 1986.

[3] The administrator must call a meeting of the creditors if so requested by another insolvency practitioner who has charged fees or incurred expenses as pre-administration costs, and the administrator must give notice of the meeting within 28 days of receipt of the request. If the administrator fails to call a meeting, the other insolvency practitioner may apply to the court for an order requiring the administrator to do so.

Creditors' entitlement to information on administrator's remuneration and expenses

[9.36] IR 2010 has facilitated the creditors' right to challenge administrators' remuneration and expenses.

One begins with the expanded scope of progress reports to creditors. The progress report must include the following information:[1]

- details of the basis fixed for the remuneration of the administrator under r 2.106 (or if not fixed at the date of the report, the steps taken during the period of the report to fix it);
- if the basis of remuneration has been fixed, a statement of (i) the remuneration charged by the administrator during the period of the report, and (ii) where the report is the first to be made after the basis has been fixed, the remuneration charged by the administrator during the periods covered by the previous reports, together with a description of the things done by the administrator during those periods in respect of which the remuneration was charged, irrespective in either case of whether payment was made in respect of that remuneration during the period of the report;[2]

[9.36] Office holders' remuneration and expenses

- a statement of the expenses incurred by the administrator during the period of the report, irrespective of whether payment was made in respect of them during that period;
- where approval of pre-administration costs is needed, a statement in the first progress report after the approval setting out the date of the approval and the amounts approved;
- so long as any of the pre-administration costs remain unapproved, a statement either (i) of any steps taken to get approval, or (ii) that the administrator has decided, or (as the case may be) another insolvency practitioner entitled to seek approval has told the administrator of that practitioner's decision, not to seek approval;
- a statement of the creditors' right to request information under the new r 2.48A and their right to challenge the administrator's remuneration and expenses.

[1] Amended r 2.47.
[2] Except where the basis for the remuneration is a set amount under r 2.106(2)(c), in which case it may be shown as that amount without any apportionment to the period of the report.

[9.37] Pursuant to r 2.48A, within 21 days of receipt of the progress report, a creditor may make a request in writing to the administrator for further information about remuneration or expenses (other than pre-administration costs) set out in the progress report, provided that the creditor is a secured creditor, has the concurrence of at least 5% in value of the unsecured creditors (including the creditor in question), or has the permission of the court. The administrator must, within 14 days of receipt of the request, provide the requested information, unless he considers that:

(i) the time or cost of preparation of the information would be excessive, or
(ii) disclosure of the information would be prejudicial to the conduct of the administration or might reasonably be expected to lead to violence against any person, or
(iii) the administrator is subject to an obligation of confidentiality in respect of the information,

in which case he must give reasons for not providing all of the information.

Any creditor may apply to the court within 21 days of (a) the giving by the administrator of reasons for not providing all of the information asked for, or (b) the expiry of the 14-day deadline for the provision of the requested information, and the court may make such order as it thinks just.

Creditors' claim that remuneration is or other expenses are excessive

[9.38] The amended r 2.109 provides for the circumstances in which a creditor could challenge the administrator's remuneration and expenses.

Any secured creditor, or any unsecured creditor with either the concurrence of at least 10% in value of the unsecured creditors (including that creditor) or the permission of the court, may apply to the court for one or more orders on the grounds that:

(a) the remuneration charged by the administrator,
(b) the basis fixed for the administrator's remuneration under r 2.106, or
(c) expenses incurred by the administrator,

is or are, in all the circumstances,[1] excessive or, in the case of the basis fixed for the administrator's remuneration, inappropriate.

---

[1] The reference to "all the circumstances" presumably means that a successful challenge has to cross a fairly high threshold.

[9.39] Any such application must, subject to any order of the court under r 2.48A(4), be made no later than eight weeks after receipt by the applicant of the progress report which first reports the charging of the remuneration or the incurring of the expenses in question.

If the court considers the application to be well-founded, it must make one or more of the following orders:

(a) reducing the amount of remuneration which the administrator was entitled to charge;
(b) fixing the basis of remuneration at a reduced rate or amount;
(c) changing the basis of remuneration;
(d) that some or all of the remuneration or expenses in question be treated as not being expenses of the administration;
(e) that the administrator or the administrator's personal representative pay to the company the amount of the excess of remuneration or expenses or such part of the excess as the court may specify.

The court may also make any other order that it thinks just. Presumably the court could in some circumstances order a third party to pay to the company the amount of the excess expenses it received from the administrator.

Rent as an administration expense

[9.40] Some controversy has arisen following the recent decision in *Goldacre (Offices) Ltd v Nortel Networks UK Ltd (in administration)* concerning whether rent under two pre-administration leases falling due during the course of the administration was payable as an expense of the administration in circumstances where since the date of the administration, the administrators had been using only a relatively small part of the premises for the more efficient conduct of the administration.

[9.41] The court held that the administrators were liable to pay the rent as it fell due in full as an administration expense so long as the administrators retained or used any part of the premises demised under each such lease for the benefit of the administration. The rent would fall within either the original r 2.67(1)(a)[1] or the original 2.67(1)(h).[2] The court reasoned as follows:

> 'Given the closeness of the opening words of rule 4.218(1)(a) as it stood at the time of *Toshoku* (and indeed as the rule now stands, though the relevant part is now para.4.218(3)(a)(ii) and a number of other words have been added) to the opening words of rule 2.67(1)(a), my inclination would be to regard rent as falling within rule 2.67(1)(a). It seems to me that that subparagraph, were the matter free from

authority, would be apt to refer to all of the expenses incurred by the administrator in performing his functions in the administration of the company, making no distinction for this purpose between expenses incurred on his own account for which he was entitled to be reimbursed, and expenses incurred on behalf of the company . . .

It is however not necessary for me to reach a final view on the point because if the rent does not fall within (a), it falls in my judgment within (f) – the disbursement is a necessary one because the application of the *Lundy Granite* principle requires rent to be paid. It is clear from other provisions of the Insolvency Act 1986 that the administrator has power to make payments whether or not they are necessary in any ordinary sense of that word. They may, for example, be merely "incidental" to the performance of his functions within para.13 of Schedule 1, without being "necessary" (both words being used in that paragraph) and his powers under para.59(1) of Schedule B1 enable him to do (and therefore to incur liability in respect of) anything 'necessary or expedient' for the management of the affairs, business and property of the company. It would be surprising if necessary expenses had a measure of priority, but liabilities incurred merely incidentally or through expediency had no priority whatsoever. That suggests either that (a) should be construed more broadly, or "necessary" given an extended meaning, or both . . .

[W]hatever the precise extent of the meaning of the word "necessary", it is plainly apt, in my judgment, to extend to a case where the *Lundy Granite* principle applies. Briggs J [in *Lomas v RAB Market Cycles (Master) Fund* [2009] EWHC 2545 (Ch)] at para.98 [*sic*] considered the Lundy Granite principle to apply to administrations . . .

I do not accept the reasons that [counsel for the administrators] has advanced for not regarding rent as an administration expense in the present case. The *Lundy Granite* principle seems, in my judgment, clearly to apply, and the Court's jurisdiction to order payment derives from the relevant rules which, properly construed in accordance with the *Lundy Granite* principle, compel payment. Any failure on the part of the administrators to recognise this unfairly harms the applicant landlord, and there can be no doubting the appropriateness of the Court directing the administrators to act in accordance with the mandatory requirements of the rules, properly construed . . .

I am urged also to construe the rules in accordance with the underlying importance, which I do not dispute for one moment, of the rescue culture upon which the Insolvency Act 1986 is based. [Counsel for the landlord], however, pointed out that in a number of the older cases where the *Lundy Granite* principle was developed, liquidators were in fact carrying on business for the purpose of the winding up in an endeavour to sell the business as a going concern, which is what administrators now do, certainly in the early stages, very often. That did not prevent the *Lundy Granite* principle from emerging and is no reason, in my judgment, for excluding it in the present case. As, moreover, administrators now have power (with the permission of the Court) to make distributions to unsecured creditors under para.65(3) of Schedule B1, administrations may come to resemble liquidations, and it would be surprising were the *Lundy Granite* principle to apply to the one and not the other . . .

[A] liquidator electing to hold leasehold premises can do so only on the terms and conditions contained in the lease, and . . . any liability incurred while the lease is being enjoyed or retained for the benefit of the liquidation is payable in full as a liquidation expense. The same principle in my judgment applies in an administration. As Lord Hoffmann recognised in *Toshoku* at para.28, the liability to pay rent is not treated as an expense having priority until (and lasts only so long as) the office holder makes use of or decides to retain the property. Subject to that, any such liability accruing during that period is in my judgment to be treated as an expense having the requisite priority . . .

> [T]he court might have a discretion as to whether or not to allow forfeiture proceedings to be brought or to allow distress to issue, but there is no discretion to declare something to be or not to be a liquidation expense. The same principle applies, in my judgment, to administrations.'[3]

The above reasoning seems entirely orthodox. However, Gabriel Moss QC[4] and Lexa Hilliard QC[5] have sought to criticise the decision in no uncertain terms. This commentator does not find their criticisms persuasive, which are to be evaluated in turn below.

---

[1] Namely, expenses properly incurred by the administrator in performing his functions in the administration of the company.
[2] Namely, expenses properly incurred by the administrator in performing his functions in the administration of the company.
[3] [2009] EWHC 3389 (Ch), [2010] 3 WLR 171 at [9], [11], [13], [16], [17], [20] and [27].
[4] Gabriel Moss QC, 'Pearly gates for retail administrations? Rent payable as an expense: *Goldacre (Office) Ltd v Nortel Networks UK Ltd (In Administration)*' (2010) 23(5) Insolvency Intelligence 76.
[5] Lexa Hilliard QC, 'All that glistens isn't *Goldacre*' (R3 Presentation, 22 April 2010) (on file with Look Chan Ho).

[9.42] Mr Moss's criticisms take the following steps.

The first step begins with the expenses principle enunciated in *Re Atlantic Computer Systems* whose principal proposition for present purposes is neatly summarised in *Re Trident Fashions*:[1]

> '[I]n *Atlantic Computer*, the Court of Appeal laid down a flexible approach to the circumstances in which administrators should be required to pay liabilities, whether under pre-administration engagements or arising during the administration... In particular, the principles applicable in liquidations were to be applied flexibly, with no automatic presumption that, for example, the rent on premises let to the company before the administration but used by the company during, and for the benefit of, the administration should be paid as an expense.'

Mr Moss argues that:

> 'although *Toshoku* disapproves of the Court of Appeal's view that post-liquidation expenses are subject to any discretion, there is no disapproval in any shape or form of the Court of Appeal's rulings or statements in relation to administration and the more flexible approach to expenses . . . Thus, although the *Toshoku* case corrected the analysis of post-liquidation liabilities in *Atlantic Computers*, nothing was said to undermine the Court of Appeal's approach to administration expenses, including the status of pre-administration liabilities such as rent . . . The *Lundy Granite* principle does not apply with full force in administrations, as the Court of Appeal in *Atlantic* held and there is a discretion in the court in deciding whether or not a pre-administration liability is to be treated *as if* it were an expense.'[2]

---

[1] [2007] EWHC 400 (Ch), [2007] 2 BCLC 455 at [27].
[2] Moss at pp 77 and 79.

[9.43] With great respect, this extreme narrowing of *Toshoku* is hard to sustain. We ought to take it as settled that the *Atlantic Computer* approach is wrong in relation to post-administration liabilities in light of *Re Trident Fashions*.

As regards pre-administration liabilities, it is difficult to see how *Atlantic Computer* can remain good law.

In the case of liquidation expenses, the *Lundy Granite* principle serves merely to inform the interpretation of r 4.218 in order to encompass certain pre-liquidation liabilities.

There is now a "substantial alignment of the administration expenses regime with that applicable to liquidation".[1] Accordingly, in the same way that the *Lundy Granite* principle helps interpret the scope of r 4.218, the principle also helps interpret the scope of r 2.67. *Toshoku* maintains that the application of this principle does not involve an exercise of discretion any more than the application of any other legal principle to the particular facts of the case.

[1] *Lomas v Rab Market Cycles (Master) Fund Ltd* [2009] EWHC 2545 (Ch) at [101], [2009] All ER (D) 313 (Oct).

[9.44] What is more, Mr Moss's narrow reading of *Toshoku* suggests that in an administration, the court has a discretion whether or not to apply the *Lundy Granite* principle because the principle does not apply with full force in an administration. But such selective application of the *Lundy Granite* principle would appear inconsistent with it being an aid to statutory interpretation and would probably lead to opaque, conclusory judicial reasoning. On Mr Moss's argument, the application of the *Lundy Granite* principle would seem relevant only after the court has decided whether a particular pre-administration liability should be treated as an administration expense. Depending on the conclusion it has already reached, the court would then say it applies or ignores the *Lundy Granite* principle as a matter of discretion. Such *ex post* application of the *Lundy Granite* principle has no explanatory force; it does not explain why a particular pre-administration liability should be treated as an administration expense.

[9.45] Secondly, Mr Moss argues that the judge in *Goldacre* failed to understand the nature of administration:

> 'Administration does not necessarily involve a liquidation type distribution and the primary goal is in fact the rescue of the company. Moreover, even in most cases, where leave to distribute is given, prior to such leave an administration operates very much like a pre-Enterprise Act 2002 administration and is not at all like liquidation. Administrations are definitely not coming to "resemble liquidations".'[1]

This view of the current administration regime is questionable. An administration is no longer "an interim and temporary regime" in the *Atlantic Computer* era.[2] Administrations these days are often straight substitutes for liquidation, performing exactly the same role from the point of view of the company's creditors (though minus some of the statutory functions which only the liquidator is empowered to perform in the public interest).[3]

At any rate, the differences between administration and liquidation are for present purposes dwarfed by the statutory assimilation of administration expenses to liquidation expenses.

¹ Moss at p 79.
² *Atlantic Computer Systems plc, Re* [1992] Ch 505 at 528, [1992] 1 All ER 476, CA.
³ Cf. *Perpetual Trustee Co Ltd v BNY Corporate Trustee Services Ltd* [2009] EWCA Civ 1160, [2010] 1 BCLC 747, [2010] 3 WLR 87 at [43].

[9.46] Thirdly, in arguing that *Atlantic Computer* remains good law, Mr Moss seeks support from this sentence in Briggs J's judgment in *Lomas v RAB Market Cycles (Master) Fund*:

> 'under the *Lundy Granite* principle itself, the retention by administrators of property for the benefit of the administration *may* mean that liabilities incurred by reason of that retention, although unsecured, become administration expenses.'¹

Also Briggs J apparently did not quarrel with counsel's submission that:

> 'although for the purposes of liquidators' expenses, the decision of the House of Lords in *Re Toshoku Finance UK plc* . . . had removed what was previously thought by some to be a general discretion in the court to identify particular debts as expenses, the flexible approach to that question in the context of administration adopted . . . in *Re Atlantic Computer Systems plc* . . . remains good law'.²

However, Briggs J did not expressly approve the application of *Atlantic Computer* either and in fact went on to note the alignment between the administration expenses regime and the liquidation expenses regime.

¹ At [101] (emphasis added).
² At [98].

[9.47] Further, if Briggs J was indeed confirming that *Atlantic Computer* remains good law, one would have expected a clearer statement in light of *Trident Fashions*. Although Mr Moss is strictly correct that *Trident Fashions* "decides nothing . . . in relation to pre-administration liabilities under post-Enterprise Act administrations",¹ *Trident Fashions* is premised on assimilating administration expenses to liquidation expenses. In these circumstances, how likely is it that Briggs J confirmed without much discussion a bifurcation—that the *Atlantic Computer* approach applied to pre-administration liabilities and the *Toshoku* approach applied only to post-administration liabilities?

¹ Moss at p 78.

[9.48] Ms Hilliard levies a different criticism against *Goldacre*:

> '[The judge] made no distinction between expenses that arise out of obligations incurred post-administration and those arising out of contracts (such as leases) entered into pre-administration . . . [The judge] proceeded on the assumption that the *Lundy Granite* principle applied in administrations but then failed to pay any heed to Lord Hoffmann's injunction [in *Toshoku*] that there had to be equitable grounds for permitting payment to a creditor of amounts arising out of a pre-administration contract. Once it is accepted that there must be an equitable justification for allowing a landlord priority over unsecured creditors before allowing him to be paid as an expense, there is considerable scope to argue that any priority given should be limited to what is a fair sum arising under the pre-

administration contract in contrast to the entirety of the sums due under the lease to which [the judge] concluded the landlord was entitled.'

With respect, this seems to be a misreading of both *Goldacre* and *Toshoku*. The judge in *Goldacre* had to consider the *Lundy Granite* principle precisely because he was faced with a pre-administration liability. As regards the need for "equitable grounds for permitting payment to a creditor of amounts arising out of a pre-administration contract", the application of the *Lundy Granite* principle itself supplies the equitable reason. Lord Hoffmann in *Toshoku* said thus:[1]

> 'The principle evolved from . . . *Lundy Granite* is . . . one which permits, on equitable grounds, the concept of a liability incurred as an expense of the liquidation to be expanded to include liabilities incurred before the liquidation in respect of property afterwards retained by the liquidator for the benefit of the insolvent estate. Although it was originally based upon a statutory discretion to allow a distress or execution against the company's assets, the courts quickly recognised that its effect could be to promote a creditor from merely having a claim in the liquidation to having a prior right to payment in full. As in the case of other equitable doctrines, the discretion hardened into principle.'

As mentioned above, the *Lundy Granite* principle now functions to inform the interpretation of r 4.218 and r 2.67. Once the outcome of interpretation is settled, there is no warrant for any further equitable grounds to alter the outcome.

Indeed, *Goldacre* and the approach advocated here also find currency in Scotland. The Scottish Court of Session (Lord Menzies) in *Re Springfield Retail*[2] at [31] held as follows:

> '[I]n light of the decision of the House of Lords in *Toshoku* and the changes to the rules I do not consider that the court has any discretion in deciding what is or is not an expense of the administration. This falls to be decided by applying the *Lundy Granite* principle, as explained in *Toshoku*. Counsel for the respondents pointed out that the observations of Lord Hoffmann at paragraph 38 of his speech in *Toshoku* relate only to liquidations, and not to administrations. There might have been some force in this argument were it not for the changes which were made to the rules following *Toshoku*, and which have the effect of making the provisions for expenses in administrations substantially the same as the provisions for expenses in liquidations. In England, the terms of Rule 2.67 are substantially the same as those of Rule 4.218, and in Scotland Rule 2.39B adopts the terms of Rule 4.67 mutatis mutandis. I agree with the reasoning of David Richards J in *Exeter City Council v Bairstow* . . . In light of this reasoning, the observations of Lord Hoffmann at paragraph 38 of Toshoku must apply to administrations. It follows that I agree with the decision of Judge Purle Q.C. sitting as a High Court Judge in *Goldacre* . . . that the matter is now to be considered exclusively by reference to the rules and that if the rental liability falls within the rules, then that is payable as a matter of mandatory obligation, not as a matter of discretion, either on the part of the administrator or on the part of the court.'

---

[1] At [29].
[2] [2010] CSOH 115.

Trustee in bankruptcy's remuneration

[9.49] The changes effected by IR 2010 in respect of trustee in bankruptcy's remuneration tracks the liquidation regime. The key IR 2010 changes are discussed below.

Basis of remuneration

[9.50] The amended r 6.138(2) sets out the three bases for fixing a trustee's remuneration:

(a) a percentage of the value of the assets in the bankrupt's estate which are realised or distributed, or of the one value and the other in combination,
(b) by reference to the time properly given by the insolvency practitioner (as trustee), and his staff in attending to matters arising in the bankruptcy, and
(c) a set amount.

The bases of remuneration above may be used in any combination and different bases may be used in respect of different things done by the trustee.[1]

---

[1] Rule 6.138(3A).

[9.51] Where the percentage basis of remuneration is used, different percentages may be fixed in respect of different things done by the trustee.[1]

---

[1] Rule 6.138(3B).

[9.52] Where the trustee is not the Official Receiver, it is for the creditors' committee (if there is one) to determine:

(a) which of the three bases set out above are to be fixed and (where appropriate) in what combination,
(b) the percentage or percentages (if any) to be fixed; and
(c) the applicable set amount.[1]

If there is no creditors' committee, or the committee does not make the requisite determination, the trustee's remuneration may be fixed (in accordance with the bases mentioned above) by a resolution of a meeting of creditors.[2]

---

[1] Rule 6.138(3C). Note that if the basis of the trustee's remuneration has been fixed by the creditors' committee and the trustee considers the rate or amount to be insufficient or the basis to be inappropriate, the trustee may request that the rate or amount be increased or the basis changed by resolution of the creditors (new r 6.140A). Further, if the trustee considers that the basis of remuneration fixed by the creditors' committee or by resolution of the creditors is insufficient or inappropriate, the trustee may apply to the court for an order changing it or increasing its amount or rate (amended r 6.141).
[2] Rule 6.138(5).

[9.53] If the basis of the trustee's remuneration is not fixed in any of the above ways within 18 months after the date of the trustee's appointment, the trustee

[9.53] Office holders' remuneration and expenses

(not being the Official Receiver) shall be entitled by way of remuneration for his services in accordance with the scale set out in Sch 6 to the Insolvency Rules 1986.[1]

[1] Rule 6.138(6).

[9.54] Where, after the basis of the trustee's remuneration has been fixed, there is a material and substantial change in the circumstances which were taken into account in fixing it, the trustee may request that it be changed in accordance with the same rules applicable to the original basis of remuneration. The trustee's request must be made to the same body that fixed the original basis of remuneration.[1]

[1] New r 6.142A.

Apportionment of set fee remuneration

[9.55] In a case in which the basis of the trustee's remuneration is a set amount under r 6.138(2)(c) and the trustee (former liquidator) ceases (for whatever reason) to hold office before the time has elapsed or the work has been completed in respect of which the amount was set, application may be made for determination of what portion of the amount should be paid to the former trustee or the former trustee's personal representative in respect of the time which has actually elapsed or the work which has actually been done. Application must be made to the same body that fixed the original basis of remuneration.[1]

[1] New r 6.142C.

Remuneration of new trustee

[9.56] If a new liquidator (not being the Official Receiver) is appointed in place of another, any determination, resolution or court order in effect immediately before the former trustee ceased to hold office continues to apply in respect of the remuneration of the new trustee until a further determination, resolution or court order is made.[1]

[1] New r 6.142B.

Creditors' entitlement to information on liquidator's remuneration and expenses

[9.57] IR 2010 has facilitated the creditors' right to challenge a trustee's remuneration and expenses.

One begins with the newly created trustee's obligations to send yearly progress reports to creditors.[1] The progress report must include the following information:

- details of the basis fixed for the remuneration of the trustee under r 6.138 (or if not fixed at the date of the report, the steps taken during the period of the report to fix it);
- if the basis of remuneration has been fixed, a statement of (i) the remuneration charged by the trustee during the period of the report, and (ii) where the report is the first to be made after the basis has been fixed, the remuneration charged by the trustee during the periods covered by the previous reports, together with a description of the things done by the trustee during those periods in respect of which the remuneration was charged, irrespective in either case of whether payment was made in respect of that remuneration during that period;[2]
- a statement of the expenses incurred by the trustee during the period of the report, irrespective of whether payment was made in respect of them during that period;
- a statement of the creditors' right to request information under the new r 6.78C and their right to challenge the trustee's remuneration and expenses.

Moreover, at least eight weeks before holding a final meeting, the trustee must send to the bankrupt and each creditor known to the trustee a draft of the report which the trustee intends to lay before the meeting.[3] The draft report must include the following information:

- details of remuneration charged and expenses incurred by the trustee;
- details of the basis fixed for the trustee's remuneration;
- a statement of the creditors' right to request information under r 6.78C and their right to challenge the trustee's remuneration and expenses.

Pursuant to r 6.78C, within 21 days of receipt of the progress report or draft report (or seven business days of receipt of the progress report where the report is for the purpose of a creditors' meeting to receive the trustee's resignation), a creditor may make a request in writing to the trustee for further information about remuneration or expenses set out in the progress report or draft report, provided that the creditor is a secured creditor, has the concurrence of at least 5% in value of the unsecured creditors (including the creditor in question) or has the permission of the court. The trustee must, within 14 days of receipt of the request, provide the requested information, unless he considers that:

(i) the time or cost of preparation of the information would be excessive, or
(ii) disclosure of the information would be prejudicial to the conduct of the bankruptcy or might reasonably be expected to lead to violence against any person, or
(iii) the trustee is subject to an obligation of confidentiality in respect of the information,

in which case he must give reasons for not providing all of the information.

Any creditor may apply to the court within 21 days of (a) the giving by the trustee of reasons for not providing all of the information asked for, or (b) the expiry of the 14-day deadline for the provision of the requested information, and the court may make such order as it thinks just.

---

[1] New r 6.78A.
[2] Except where the basis for the remuneration is a set amount under r 6.138(2)(c), in which case it may be shown as that amount without any apportionment to the period of the report.

[3] New r 6.78B.

Creditors' claim that remuneration is or other expenses are excessive

[9.58] The amended r 6.142 provides for the circumstances in which a creditor could challenge the trustee's remuneration and expenses.

Any secured creditor, or any unsecured creditor with either the concurrence of at least 10% in value of the creditors (including that creditor) or the permission of the court, or the bankrupt, may apply for one or more orders on the grounds that:

(a)   the remuneration charged by the trustee,
(b)   the basis fixed for the trustee's remuneration under r 6.138, or
(c)   expenses incurred by the trustee,

is or are, in all the circumstances,[1] excessive or, in the case of the basis fixed for the trustee's remuneration, inappropriate.

[1] The reference to "all the circumstances" presumably means that a successful challenge has to cross a fairly high threshold.

[9.59] Any such application must, subject to any order of the court under r 6.78C(5), be made no later than eight weeks (or, in a case falling within r 6.126, four weeks) after receipt by the applicant of the progress report, or the draft report under r 6.78B, which first reports the charging of the remuneration or the incurring of the expenses in question.

[9.60] If the court considers the application to be well-founded, it must make one or more of the following orders:

(a)   reducing the amount of remuneration which the trustee was entitled to charge;
(b)   fixing the basis of remuneration at a reduced rate or amount;
(c)   changing the basis of remuneration;
(d)   that some or all of the remuneration or expenses in question be treated as not being bankruptcy expenses;
(e)   that the trustee or the trustee's personal representative pay to such person as the court may specify as property comprised in the bankrupt's estate the amount of the excess of remuneration or expenses or such part of the excess as the court may specify.

The court may also make any other order that it thinks just. Presumably the court could in some circumstances order a third party to disgorge the amount of the excess expenses it received from the trustee.

Transitional provisions

[9.61] The amendments discussed above apply where:[1]

(a)   a company enters administration on or after 6 April 2010, except where—

(i) it enters administration by virtue of an administration order under para 10 of Sch B1 to the IA 1986 on an application made before 6 April 2010;
(ii) the administration is immediately preceded by a voluntary liquidation in respect of which the resolution to wind up was passed before 6 April 2010; or
(iii) the administration is immediately preceded by a liquidation on the making of a winding-up order on a petition which was presented before 6 April 2010;
(b) a company goes into liquidation upon the passing on or after 6 April 2010 of a resolution to wind up;
(c) a company goes into voluntary liquidation under para 83 of Sch B1 to the IA 1986, except where the preceding administration—
(i) commenced before 6 April 2010; or
(ii) is an administration which commenced by virtue of an administration order under para 10 of Sch B1 to the IA 1986 on an application which was made before 6 April 2010;
(d) a company goes into liquidation on the making of a winding-up order on a petition presented on or after 6 April 2010, except where the liquidation is immediately preceded by—
(i) an administration under para 10 of Sch B1 to the IA 1986 where the administration order was made on an application made before 6 April 2010;
(ii) an administration in respect of which the appointment of an administrator under para 14 or 22 of Sch B1 to the Act took effect before 6 April 2010; or
(iii) a voluntary liquidation in respect of which the resolution to wind up was passed before 6 April 2010;
(e) a bankruptcy order is made on a petition presented on or after 6 April 2010.

---

1   Paragraph 1 of Sch 4 to IR 2010. The new r 7.6A applies on and after 6 April 2010 in all cases (para 2 of Sch 4 to IR 2010).

[9.62] Note, however, the transitional provisions applicable to cases in which, under para 83 of Sch B1 to the IA 1986, companies move, on or after 6 April 2010, to creditors' voluntary liquidation (CVL) from administration entered before 6 April 2010. The position is summarised in a paper prepared by the Insolvency Service, reproduced below.

'1. This paper considers how the amendments to the Insolvency Rules 1986 ("the 1986 Rules") made by the Insolvency (Amendment) Rules 2010 ("the Amendment Rules") apply in cases in which, under paragraph 83 of Schedule B1 ("paragraph 83") to the Insolvency Act 1986 ("the 1986 Act"), companies move, on or after 6 April 2010, to creditors' voluntary liquidation ("CVL") from administration entered before 6 April 2010. In this paper, those cases are referred to as "transitional paragraph 83 cases" (and except for references to "transitional Rule 13" – see paragraph 6 below – references to Rules are to Rules (new, amended or unamended as the case may be) of the 1986 Rules).

2. Article 6(3) and (4) of the Legislative Reform (Insolvency) (Miscellaneous Provisions) Order 2010 ("the LRO") inserts a new section 104A into, and amends section 105 of, the 1986 Act. The effect is to replace annual creditors' meetings in CVL with a requirement for the liquidator to send

3. periodic progress reports to the creditors.
3. Article 12(1) and (2) of the LRO provides that those amendments do not apply where the resolution to wind up is passed before 6 April 2010. By virtue of section 247(3) (b) of the 1986 Act and paragraph 83(6) (b), that also means that those amendments do not apply where the notice under paragraph 83 of moving from administration to CVL is registered before that date. Thus they do apply where the noticed is registered on or after that date, including in transitional paragraph 83 cases.
4. The Amendment Rules contain several amendments giving effect to article 6(3) and (4) of the LRO. Paragraph 1(6) of Schedule 4 to the Amendment Rules provides that those amendments do not apply in transitional paragraph 83 cases.
5. That, however, is inconsistent with article 12(1) and (2) of the LRO, because that article applies the LRO amendments where the paragraph 83 notice is registered on or after that date irrespective of the date of entry into administration or of application therefor.
6. Accordingly, Rule 13 of the Insolvency (Amendment) (No. 2) Rules 2010 ("transitional Rule 13") provides:

"Where a company goes into voluntary liquidation under paragraph 83 of Schedule B1 to the Act in a case in which article 12(1) and (2) of the Legislative Reform (Insolvency) (Miscellaneous Provisions) Order 2010 causes section 104A of the Act and the amendments to section 105 of the Act to apply, the amendments to the Insolvency Rules 1986 made by the Insolvency (Amendment) Rules 2010 apply to the extent necessary to give effect to section 104A and the amendments to section 105 notwithstanding that by virtue of paragraph 1(6)(a) or (b) of Schedule 4 to the Insolvency (Amendment) Rules 2010 those amendments to the Insolvency Rules 1986 would otherwise not apply."

This means that the amendments, revocations and new Rules in the Amendment Rules providing for progress reports and removing the requirement to hold annual meetings will apply in transitional paragraph 83 cases even though other amendments, revocations and new Rules in the Amendment Rules will not apply in those cases.
7. The problem with applying transitional Rule 13 is that there is no simple division of amendments, revocations and new Rules in the Amendment Rules into those which provide for progress reports and remove the requirement to hold annual meetings and those which do other things. The Amendment Rules are drafted so as to be applied as a whole or not at all. They are not drafted in so that in transitional paragraph 83 cases, some of the amendments, revocations and new Rules will apply and some not. That means that textual analysis is required to determine how provisions for progress reports in the Amendment Rules are to apply in transitional paragraph 83 cases when those provisions also refer to other things provided for in the Amendment Rules but not in the unamended 1986 Rules, and also how provisions in the unamended 1986 Rules are to apply in transitional paragraph 83 cases when they refer to annual meetings as well as other things.
8. The following paragraphs suggest how transitional Rule 13 is to be applied in respect of particular amendments, revocations and new Rules in the Amendment Rules.
9. New Rule 4.49B sets out the basic provision for progress reports in windings up by the court. Since new section 104A and section 105 of the 1986 Act do not apply to windings up by the court, that new Rule does not in itself apply in transitional paragraph 83 cases. It is, however, relevant because of references to it in new Rules 4.49C and 4.49E, which apply to CVLs.
10. In new Rule 4.49C, which is the basic provision for progress reports in CVLs:

a. paragraphs (1) to (3), (6) and (7) will apply without difficulty in transitional paragraph 83 cases;
b. paragraph (4) provides that a progress report in a CVL is not required for any period which ends after the liquidator has sent a draft final report to creditors under new Rule 4.49D: since new Rule 4.49D does not itself apply in transitional paragraph 83 cases, there will be no such period in transitional paragraph 83 cases and therefore, in effect, paragraph (4) does not apply in transitional paragraph 83 cases;
c. paragraph (5) provides for the content of progress reports in CVLs by reference to new Rule 4.49B, which in turn refers to new Rule 4.49E and amended Rules 4.127 and 4.131:
  i. although Rules 127 and 131 are amended by the Amendment Rules, the references to them in new Rule 4.49B(1)(d) and (j) are equally capable of being to the unamended Rules 127 and 131, and therefore pose no problem in transitional paragraph 83 cases;
  ii. since new Rule 4.49E does not itself apply in transitional paragraph 83 cases, the reference to it in new Rule 4.49B (1) (j) is meaningless and therefore it can be treated as not being there, with the practical consequence that new Rule 4.49B (1) (j) should be read as if the words "right to request information under Rule 4.49E and their" were not there.
11. New Rules 4.49E (as mentioned above), 4.108A, 4.126(5) and (6) and 4.131(1B) and substituted 4.108(3) do not apply in transitional paragraph 83 cases (nor, obviously, do the amendments to Rule 4.125, which has no CVL application), because they do not fall within transitional Rule 13. The references therein to progress reports are therefore irrelevant in transitional paragraph 83 cases.
12. Rule 4.223 must be complied with in transitional paragraph 83 cases even though it is being revoked as duplicating progress reports, because it does not fall within transitional Rule 13, and therefore paragraph 1(6) of Schedule 4 to the Amendment Rules applies."

Chapter 10

Miscellaneous legislative amendments

Introduction

[10.1] This chapter deals with various amendments not covered elsewhere in the book. They apply only in England and Wales, except where otherwise stated.

Notice of deemed approval of administrator's proposals

[10.2] In administrations where the administrator's proposals are deemed approved under r 2.33(5) there is now a requirement to give notice of the deemed approval to the court, the registrar of companies and the creditors. Notice must be given as soon as reasonably practicable after the expiry of the period set out in r 2.37(1) (that is, eight business days from the date on which the proposals were sent out). A copy of the proposals must be attached to the notice sent to the court and to creditors who have not previously received them.[1] There is a prescribed form for sending notice to the registrar of companies, Form F2.18.[2]

There is an equivalent amendment for Scotland.[3] The new prescribed form is Form 2.16BZ(Scot).[4]

---

[1] Rule 2.33(5A).
[2] Prescribed by the Registrar's (Amendment) Rules 2010.
[3] Rule 2.25(3A).
[4] Prescribed by r 7.30 and Sch 5 to the Insolvency (Scotland) Rules 1986.

Claims and distributions – administration, liquidation and bankruptcy

[10.3] Various amendments are made to the rules relating to the submission and agreement of claims, to provide greater consistency between administration, liquidation and bankruptcy procedures and also to clarify the relevant date for claims where a liquidation was immediately preceded by an administration, or vice versa. The main changes are described below.

Definition of a debt in a winding up

[10.4] Rule 13.12 is amended to provide that in the case of a winding up immediately preceded by an administration, a debt means a debt or liability to which the company is subject at the date on which the company entered administration.

[10.5] Miscellaneous legislative amendments

Proving claims

[10.5] Rule 2.72 is amended to provide that where a company was in liquidation when it entered administration, a creditor's claim is calculated as at the date of liquidation. Where an administration is immediately preceded by a winding up, a creditor who has proved in the winding up is deemed to have proved in the administration.

The rules which enabled an office holder to require claims to be verified by affidavit have been revoked.[1]

---
[1] Rules 2.73, 4.77 and 6.99.

Appeal against a decision on a proof

[10.6] A member of a company in administration who is dissatisfied with an administrator's decision to admit or reject a creditor's proof may apply to the court for the decision to be reversed or varied. An application must be made within 21 days of becoming aware of the administrator's decision.[1] The member must, however, be able to demonstrate an economic interest in the matter. The court must not disallow the proof (in whole or in part) unless the member shows that there is (or would be but for the amount claimed in the proof), or that it is likely that there will be (or would be but for the amount claimed in the proof) a surplus of assets to which the company would be entitled.[2]

---
[1] Rule 2.78(2).
[2] Rule 2.78(4A).

[10.7] An equivalent provision already existed in the liquidation rules, enabling a contributory to be able to appeal against a liquidator's decision. Rule 4.83 is amended to provide that the contributory must be able to show there is (or would be but for the amount claimed in the proof), or that it is likely that there will be (or would be but for the amount claimed in the proof) a surplus of assets to which the company would be entitled.[1]

---
[1] Rule 4.83(4A).

Interest

[10.8] Rule 2.88 is amended to clarify the relevant date for purposes of determining the periods for which interest can be claimed. The relevant date is the date on which the company entered administration unless the administration was immediately preceded by a winding up in which case it is the date on which the company went into liquidation. Rule 4.93 is similarly amended to provide that in a liquidation the relevant date is the date on which the company went into liquidation or, if the liquidation was immediately preceded by an administration, the date on which the company entered administration.

Redemption of security by an office holder

[10.9] In cases where a secured creditor has called on a liquidator or trustee in bankruptcy to elect whether or not to redeem the security, the Rules are amended to reduce the amount of time the office holder has in which to exercise the power to redeem security or determine not to exercise it. The time limit is now three months (previously it was six months), to correspond with administration.[1]

---

[1] Rules 4.97(4) and 6.117(4) and r 2.92(4).

Notice of intended dividend

[10.10] The period in which a liquidator or trustee in bankruptcy must declare a dividend is also reduced. Rule 11.2 is amended to provide that the notice of intended dividend must state the office holder's intention to declare a dividend within a period of two months, rather than four months as previously. This now corresponds with administration.[1]

---

[1] Rule 2.95(4).

Admission or rejection of proofs

[10.11] Rules 2.96 (administration) and 11.3 (liquidation and bankruptcy) are amended to provide that the last date for dealing with proofs is five business days (previously seven days) from the last date for proving.

Postponement or cancellation of dividend

[10.12] A new r 2.96A is inserted to provide for postponement or cancellation of a dividend where an application has been made to court for a decision on a proof to be reversed or varied or for a proof to be expunged or for a reduction of the amount claimed. This corresponds to existing r 11.4 in liquidation and bankruptcy.

Notice of declaration of dividend

[10.13] A notice of declaration of dividend in administration no longer has to state how the administrator proposes to distribute the dividend.[1] In liquidation, r 11.6 is amended by the insertion of sub-para 2A which provides that where in a winding up other than members' voluntary liquidation, the liquidator intends to make a distribution to unsecured creditors, the notice must state the value of the prescribed part except where the court has made an order under s 176A(5) of the IA 1986 (IA 1986).

---

[1] Rule 2.98(2). Sub-paragraph (f) revoked.

[10.14] Miscellaneous legislative amendments

Section 110 arrangements – disclosure

[10.14] Where there has been an arrangement under s 110 of the IA 1986 and a distribution has taken place pursuant to sub-s (2) or (4) of that section, the liquidator must state the estimated value of the following in any account or summary of receipts and payments required to be included in accounts or reports to members or creditors:

(i) the property transferred to the transferee;
(ii) the property received from the transferee; and
(iii) the property distributed to members pursuant to s 110(2) or (4).

The details of the basis of valuation must be included as a note to the account or summary of receipts and payments.

Other distributions to members in specie

[10.15] In a members' voluntary liquidation, where there has been a distribution of property to members in its existing form other than pursuant to an arrangement under s 110 of the Act, the liquidator must include the following in any account or summary of receipts and payments required to be included in accounts or reports to members:

(a) the estimated value of the property distributed among the members during the period to which the account relates, and as a note to the account or summary of receipts and payments;
(b) details of the basis of valuation.

Scotland: procedure for drawing a dividend in administration

[10.16] New r 2.26C is inserted, setting out the procedure for obtaining an adjudication as to entitlement to vote (which was dealt with in Chapter 3) and to a dividend. The creditor must submit a claim to the administrator not later than eight weeks before the end of the accounting period. It must be made out by, or under the direction of, the creditor, have attached to it an account or voucher (according to the nature of the debt claimed) which constitutes prima facie evidence of the debt and state the following matters:

(i) the creditor's name and address;
(ii) if the creditor is a company, its registered number;
(iii) the total amount of the creditor's claim (including value added tax) as at the date on which the company entered administration (or, if the company was in liquidation when it entered administration, the date on which it went into liquidation) less any payments that have been made to the creditor after that date in respect of that claim;
(iv) whether or not the claim includes outstanding uncapitalised interest;
(v) particulars of how and when the debt was incurred by the company;
(vi) particulars of any security held, the date on which it was given and the value which the creditor puts on it;
(vii) details of any reservation of title in respect of goods to which the debt refers; and
(viii) the name, address and authority of the person making out the proof, if other than the creditor.

[10.17] The administrator may dispense with the requirement to attach an account or voucher in respect of any debt or any class of debt.

[10.18] A claim which has been accepted in whole or in part for the purpose of drawing a dividend in respect of any accounting period, shall be deemed to have been resubmitted for the purpose of obtaining an adjudication as to the creditor's entitlement to a dividend in respect of any subsequent accounting period.

[10.19] A creditor who has submitted a claim may at any time submit a further claim specifying a different amount. However, a secured creditor is not entitled to submit a further claim specifying a different value for the security at any time after the administrator has required the creditor to discharge, convey or assign the security.

[10.20] Where an administration is immediately preceded by a winding up, a creditor who has proved a debt in the winding up is deemed to have proved it in the administration.

[10.21] It should be noted that there is an inconsistency between rr 2.26C and 2.41 regarding the form and content of claims. Rule 2.26C does not require a creditor's claim to be in a prescribed form, but it must contain the information set out in sub-para 3(c). Rule 2.41 (which applies r 4.15(2)(a)) requires a statement of claim to be submitted on Form 4.7(Scot), but, unlike r 2.26C(3)(c), the administrator may dispense with the requirement.[1] The information requirements of r 2.26C(3)(c) and Form 4.7(Scot) are also different.[2] It appears that the intention was that r 2.26C(3)(c) should be followed, in order to align the position with administration in England and Wales, where there is prescribed content for a creditors' claim (and the administrator cannot dispense with it) but no prescribed form.

---

[1] The author is grateful to David A. Bennett W.S. for pointing out the inconsistency.
[2] Rule 2.26C(3)(c) requires additional information—namely the registered number of the creditor, if it is a company, and the name, address and authority of the person making out the proof if other than the creditor.

Office holders' powers – liquidator and trustee in bankruptcy

[10.22] Schedule 4 to the IA 1986 is amended to provide that a liquidator in a voluntary winding up or winding up by the court does not need sanction in order to compromise all calls, debts and claims existing between a company and its contributories or debtors.[1]

---

[1] Paragraph 3 amended and para 6A inserted by the Legislative Reform (Insolvency) (Miscellaneous Provisions) Order 2010.

[10.23] In bankruptcy, Sch 5 is amended to provide that a trustee does not need sanction in order to order to compromise or refer to arbitration any debts, claims or liabilities existing between a bankrupt and any debtor of the bankrupt, or to make any compromise or arrangement in respect of claims in respect of the estate which are made or are capable of being made by the trustee.[1]

It should be noted that sanction is still required in order to compromise creditors' claims.

---

[1] Paragraph 6 deleted and paras 9A and 9B inserted by the Legislative Reform (Insolvency) (Miscellaneous Provisions) Order 2010.

Redemption of security by liquidator or trustee

[10.24] The time limit for a liquidator or trustee in bankruptcy to elect whether or not to redeem security, following written notice from the secured creditor, is reduced from six months to three months.[1]

---

[1] Rules 4.97 and 6.117, as amended.

Amendments specific to bankruptcy

Service of a bankruptcy petition

[10.25] The Rules now provide for a bankruptcy petition to be served outside England and Wales, with the permission of the court and in such manner as the court may direct.[1]

Service of a bankruptcy petition is now proved by a certificate of service rather than an affidavit. The certificate must include the following information:

(a)   the name of the debtor,
(b)   the name of the petitioner,
(c)   the court in which the petition was filed and the court reference number,
(d)   the date of the petition,
(e)   whether the copy served was a sealed copy,
(f)   the date on which service was effected, and
(g)   the manner in which service was effected.

The certificate of service must be filed in court as soon as reasonably practicable after service, and in any event not less than five business days before the hearing of the petition.[2]

---

[1] Rule 6.14(6).
[2] Rule 6.15A.

Amendment of a petition

[10.26] A petition may be amended at any time after presentation with the permission of the court, on such terms as the court thinks fit to impose.[1]

Amendments under this rule are no longer restricted amendments in respect of the omission of any creditor or any debt.

[1] Rule 6.22.

Petitioner seeking dismissal or permission to withdraw

[10.27] Before 6 April 2010, if a petitioner sought to have the petition dismissed or withdrawn, it had to file with the court an affidavit, specifying the grounds of the application and the circumstances in which it was made. This was required in all cases unless the court ordered otherwise.

[10.28] From 6 April 2010, rules are amended to provide that the petitioner must file a witness statement (containing equivalent information to the affidavit) with the court if a creditor has given notice of intention to appear on the petition. In other cases a witness statement is required if the court so orders.[1]

[1] Rule 6.32(1).

Bankrupt carrying on a business

[10.29] The requirement for a bankrupt carrying on a business to supply details of sales and purchases and profit or loss not less than once every six months is amended to provide that the information must be supplied when required by the trustee.[1]

[1] Rule 6.200(5).

Application for annulment under section 282(1)(b) of the Insolvency Act 1986 – trustee's remuneration

[10.30] Rule 6.207 is amended to provide that the trustee's report to court (where the trustee is not the Official Receiver) must include details of the trustee's remuneration, the basis fixed for the remuneration and the expenses incurred by the trustee.

[10.31] The IR 2010 insert a new r 6.207A, enabling the person applying for annulment to challenge the trustee's remuneration charged or expenses incurred on the grounds that it is, in all the circumstances, excessive. The challenge is made by way of an application to court, which must be made no later than five business days before the date of the hearing. The application must be accompanied by a copy of any evidence which the applicant intends to adduce in support. The applicant must send a copy of the application and any supporting evidence to the trustee at the same time that the application is made.

[10.32] If the court annuls the bankruptcy order and considers the application to be well-founded it must make one or more of the following orders:

(a) reducing the amount of remuneration which the trustee was entitled to charge;
(b) that some or all of the remuneration or expenses in question be treated as not being bankruptcy expenses;
(c) that the trustee or the trustee's personal representative pay to the applicant the amount of the excess of remuneration or expenses or such part of the excess as the court may specify.

The court may also make any other order that it thinks just.

Annulment – post-commencement interest

[10.33] In determining whether to annul a bankruptcy order under s 282(1)(b) of the Act, the court may take into account whether any sums have been paid or payment of any sums has been secured in respect of post-commencement interest on the debts which have been proved.[1]

---

[1] Rule 6.211(5).

Individual Insolvency Register

Voluntary arrangements

[10.34] Rule 6A.2A is amended to standardise the information which must be entered on the register in respect of all types of individual voluntary arrangement. Rule 6A.3 extends the period for which information must be kept on the register, by providing that three months must have elapsed from the date on which the Secretary of State receives notice of a court order revoking the arrangement or notice that the arrangement has been implemented in full or terminated.

Bankruptcies

[10.35] Rule 6A.4 is amended to provide that if a bankruptcy order is rescinded by the court, the bankruptcy register must record that an order has been made, the date on which it was made and (if different) the date on which it has effect.

[10.36] Rule 6A.5 extends the period of time for which information must be kept on the register when a bankruptcy has been annulled or a bankrupt has been discharged. In the case of annulment other than on the grounds that the bankruptcy order should not have been made, the time period is three months from the date on which notice of annulment was given to the Secretary of State. Where a bankrupt has been discharged, the time limit is three months from the date of discharge. If the bankruptcy has been annulled on the grounds that the bankruptcy order should not have been made or the bankruptcy order has been rescinded, the time period is 28 days from the date on which notice of annulment was given to the Secretary of State or the date on which the Secretary of State received a copy of the order of recission.

Information not to be included on the register where persons at risk of violence

[10.37] The court may, on the application of the debtor, the supervisor of an individual voluntary arrangement, the trustee in bankruptcy, the Official Receiver or the Secretary of State, order that the details entered onto the Individual Insolvency Register must not include details of the debtor's current address. "Current address" means not only the debtor's current residential address but also any address at which the debtor currently carries on business.

[10.38] The court may make such an order where disclosure of the address might reasonably be expected to lead to violence against the debtor or a person who normally resides with the debtor as a member of the debtor's family.

Further provisions relating to persons at risk of violence are discussed below.

Other provisions relating to persons at risk of violence

[10.39] Amendments are made to the Rules to allow the court to order that certain information is not to be made publicly available if disclosure might reasonably be expected to lead to violence against the person concerned or, in the case of a debtor in personal insolvency, a person who normally resides with the debtor as a member of the debtor's family.

- IVA and bankruptcy—in addition to not making the debtor's current address available in the Individual Insolvency Register, the court may order that, in bankruptcy, the debtor's address is not included in the court file open to inspection but is kept in a separate file not open to inspection, or is not included in certain notices or the bankruptcy order or the full title of the proceedings;
- Administrator's statement of proposals—the court may order that some or all of the information in the statement of affairs or, in a case where the statement of affairs has not been submitted, the names and addresses of the creditors and details of their debts must not be sent to the registrar of companies or to creditor or members;[1]
- Statements of affairs—the court may order that the statement of affairs, or a specified part of it, shall not be disclosed or filed with the registrar of companies or in court, or be sent to creditors (as the case may be). These provisions do not apply in voluntary liquidation to the extent that ss 95, 98 and 99 of the Act do not permit limited disclosure.[2]

[1] Rule 2.33A.
[2] Rules 1.56, 2.30, 3.5, 4.35, 5.68 and 6.61.

[10.40] In administration, there are provisions allowing a creditor to apply for disclosure. If there is a material change in circumstances rendering the limit on disclosure or any part of it unnecessary, the administrator must as soon as reasonably practicable apply to court for the order or any part of it to be rescinded.[1]

[1] Rule 2.33A.

[10.41] In other instances, the office holder may use his or her discretion not to disclose information, without the need to apply to court. For example, if an office holder considers that a document forming part of the records of the proceedings

(a) should be treated as confidential, or
(b) is of such a nature that its disclosure would be prejudicial to the conduct of the proceedings or might reasonably be expected to lead to violence against any person,

the office holder may decline to allow it to be inspected by any person who would otherwise be entitled to inspect it. The persons who may be refused inspection include members of a liquidation committee or creditors' committee. A person who has been refused inspection may apply to court for the decision to be overruled.[1]

[1] Rule 12A.51.

Application to Scotland

[10.42] In voluntary arrangements, r 1.50 provides that the court on the application of the nominee, the directors or any person appearing to the court to have an interest, may direct that specified information may be omitted from any statement of affairs required to be sent to creditors where the disclosure of such information would be likely to prejudice the conduct of the voluntary arrangement or might reasonably be expected to lead to violence against any person.

[10.43] In administrations, new r 2.33A enables the administrator to apply to court for limited disclosure of the administrator's proposals if the administrator thinks that disclosure of information contained in the statement of affairs or the list of creditors (in cases where a statement of affairs has not been submitted) would prejudice the conduct of the administration or might reasonably be expected to lead to violence against any person. There are provisions allowing a creditor to apply for disclosure. If there is a material change in circumstances rendering the limit on disclosure or any part of it unnecessary, the administrator must as soon as reasonably practicable apply to court for the order or any part of it to be rescinded.

Block transfer orders

[10.44] Part 7 of the Rules includes a new Ch 1A, dealing with the procedure for block transfer orders by the court. A block transfer may be made by the court where an insolvency office holder has died, retired from practice or is otherwise unable or unwilling to continue in office and it has become expedient to transfer some or all of his or her cases to one or more office holders in a single transaction.[1]

[1] Rule 7.10B.

[10.45] The Rules set out the procedure for making an application, the requirements for giving notice, the information which must accompany the application and how the costs of the application are to be dealt with. Where an application relates to the appointment of an administrator, the costs of making that application are to be paid as an expense of the administration, unless the court orders otherwise. In any other case, the court will decide to what extent, if any, the costs of making the application should be paid as an expense of the insolvency proceedings. The factors to which the court must have regard in making a decision include:

(a) the reasons for making the application;
(b) the number of cases to which the application relates;
(c) the value of the assets comprised in those cases; and
(d) the nature and extent of the costs involved.

Any appointment made under a block transfer order must be notified to the Secretary of State as soon as reasonably practicable. It must also be notified to the creditors and such other persons as the court may direct, in such manner as the court may direct.[1]

---

[1] Rule 7.10D.

Use of prescribed forms

[10.46] In anticipation of greater use of electronic communication and delivery of documents, there is a move away from prescribed forms. No new forms have been prescribed in the Insolvency Rules (some new forms have however been prescribed under Companies House rules) and some forms have been revoked where they are considered to be unnecessary. Where forms have to be delivered to Companies House, the information content is prescribed in the Insolvency Rules but the format of the document and manner of delivery is prescribed by the Registrar's (Amendment) Rules 2010. Forms prescribed under the Registrar's Rules are to be used in all cases (regardless of the date of commencement) except where the event which creates the obligation to send the document occurred before 6 April 2010.[1]

---

[1] Rule 4, Registrar's (Amendment) Rules 2010.

Application to Scotland

[10.47] In Scotland, forms are prescribed in the Insolvency (Scotland) Rules.[1] There are no changes to prescribed forms except that there is a new form for giving notice of deemed approval of the administrator's proposals, as discussed earlier in this chapter.

---

[1] Rule 7.30 and Sch 5.

[10.48] Miscellaneous legislative amendments

Changes in language

[10.48] Various amendments have been made to the Rules to modernise the language. The following terms have been replaced:

Old term	New term
Affidavit	Statement of truth
Deponent	Person making the statement/nominated person
Ex parte	Without notice to any other party
Leave of the court	Permission of the court

These changes apply in all cases on or after 6 April 2010.

Procedures relating to the EC Regulation

[10.49] Rule 1.31 is amended to make it clear that where a member state liquidator applies to court for a voluntary arrangement to be converted into winding up proceedings, winding up proceedings are:

(a) administration proceedings whose purposes are limited to the winding up of the company through administration and are to exclude the purpose contained in para 3(1)(a) of Sch B1 to the Act;
(b) a creditors' voluntary winding up; or
(c) a winding up by the court.

[10.50] Rule 2.130 is amended to provide that where a member state liquidator applies for the conversion of an administration into winding up, the winding up proceedings may be creditors' voluntary liquidation or a winding up by the court. Alternatively, the court may order that the purposes of administration are to be limited to the winding up of the company through administration and are to exclude the purpose contained in para 3(1)(a) of Sch B1 to the Act.

Application to Scotland

[10.51] Equivalent amendments have been made in Scotland.[1]

---

[1] Rules 1.46 and 2.47.

Transitional provisions

[10.52] Unless otherwise stated, the amendments apply to cases where the insolvency commences or, in the case of a voluntary arrangement, the nominee agrees to act, on or after 6 April 2010, with the following exceptions:

- An administration by court order made on or after 6 April 2010 on an application made before 6 April 2010

- An administration commencing on or after 6 April 2010 which was immediately preceded by a liquidation which started before 6 April 2010
- A liquidation commencing on or after 6 April 2010 which was preceded by an administration which started before 6 April 2010
- A liquidation commencing on or after 6 April 2010 which was preceded by an administration by court order where the application for the administration order was made before 6 April 2010
- A compulsory liquidation commencing on or after 6 April 2010 which was immediately preceded by a voluntary liquidation starting before 6 April 2010.

Appendix I

Insolvency Rules 1986

SI 1986/1925

INSOLVENCY RULES 1986
Made: 10th November 1986

Authority: Insolvency Act 1986, ss 411, 412

INTRODUCTORY PROVISIONS

0.1 Citation and commencement
These Rules may be cited as the Insolvency Rules 1986 and shall come into force on 29th December 1986.

NOTES

Initial Commencement

Specified date
  Specified date: 29 December 1986: see above.

[0.2 Construction and interpretation]
  [(1) In these Rules—
    "the Act" means the Insolvency Act 1986 (any reference to a numbered section being to a section of that Act);
    "the Companies Act" means [the Companies Act 2006];
    "CPR" means the Civil Procedure Rules 1998 and "CPR" followed by a Part or rule by number means the Part or rule with that number in those Rules;
    "RSC" followed by an Order by number means the Order with that number set out in Schedule 1 to the CPR; and
    "the Rules" means the Insolvency Rules 1986.
  (2) . . .
  (3) Subject to [paragraph (1)], Part 13 of the Rules has effect for their interpretation and application.]

NOTES

Amendment
  Substituted by SI 1999/1022, r 3, Schedule, para 1.
    Date in force: 26 April 1999: see SI 1999/1022, r 1.
  Para (1): words "the Companies Act 2006" in square brackets substituted by SI 2009/2472, rr 3, 4.
    Date in force: 1 October 2009: see SI 2009/2472, r 1; for transitional provisions see r 2 thereof.
  Para (2): revoked by SI 2010/686, r 2, Sch 1, para 2(1), (2).
    Date in force: 6 April 2010: see SI 2010/686, r 1; for transitional provisions and further effect see rr 6(1), 7, Sch 4, para 1, Sch 5 thereto.
  Para (3): words "paragraph (1)" in square brackets substituted by SI 2010/686, r 2, Sch 1, para 2(1), (3).

Date in force: 6 April 2010: see SI 2010/686, r 1; for transitional provisions and further effect see rr 6(1), 7, Sch 4, para 1, Sch 5 thereto.

0.3 Extent

(1) Parts 1, 2 and 4 of the Rules, and Parts 7 to 13 as they relate to company insolvency, apply in relation to companies which the courts in England and Wales have jurisdiction to wind up.

[(2) Rule 3.1 applies to all receivers to whom Part III of the Act applies, Rule 3.39 and 3.40 apply to all receivers who are not administrative receivers, and the remainder of Part 3 of the Rules applies to administrative receivers appointed otherwise than under section 51 (Scottish Receivership).]

(3) Parts 5 and 6 of the Rules, and Parts 7 to 13 as they relate to individual insolvency, extend to England and Wales only.

NOTES

Initial Commencement

Specified date
Specified date: 29 December 1986: see r 0.1.

Amendment
Para (2): substituted by SI 2003/1730, r 3.
Date in force: 15 September 2003: see SI 2003/1730, r 1(2).

THE FIRST GROUP OF PARTS

COMPANY INSOLVENCY; COMPANIES WINDING UP

PART 1

COMPANY VOLUNTARY ARRANGEMENTS

CHAPTER 1

PRELIMINARY

1.1 Scope of this Part; interpretation

(1) The Rules in this Part apply where, pursuant to Part I of the Act, it is intended to make, and there is made, a proposal to a company and its creditors for a voluntary arrangement, that is to say, a composition in satisfaction of its debts or a scheme of arrangement of its affairs.

(2) In this Part—
    [(a) Chapter 2 applies where the proposal for the voluntary arrangement is made by the directors of the company and
        (i) the company is neither in liquidation nor is [the company in administration]; and
        (ii) no steps have been taken to obtain a moratorium under Schedule A1 to the Act in connection with the proposal;]
    (b) Chapter 3 applies where the company is in liquidation or [the company is in administration], and the proposal is made by the liquidator or (as the case may be) the administrator, he in either case being the nominee for the purposes of the proposal;
    [(c) Chapter 4 applies in the same case as Chapter 3, but where the nominee is not the liquidator or administrator;
    (d) Chapter 5 applies in all the three cases mentioned in sub-paragraphs (a) to (c) above;

(e) Chapters 7 and 8 apply to all voluntary arrangements with or without a moratorium; and
(f) Chapter 9 applies where the proposal is made by the directors of an eligible company with a view to obtaining a moratorium].

(3) In Chapters 3, 4 and 5, the liquidator or the administrator is referred to as "the responsible insolvency practitioner".

[(4) In this Part, a reference to an "eligible company" is to a company that is eligible for a moratorium in accordance with paragraph 2 of Schedule A1 to the Act.]

NOTES

Initial Commencement

Specified date

Specified date: 29 December 1986: see r 0.1.

Amendment

Para (2): sub-para (a) substituted by SI 2002/2712, r 3(1), Schedule, Pt 1, para 1(a).
Date in force: 1 January 2003: see SI 2002/2712, r 1(1); for effect see rr 1(2), 3(2) thereof.
Para (2): in sub-para (a)(i) words "the company in administration" in square brackets substituted by SI 2003/1730, r 4, Sch 1, Pt 1, para 1(a).
Date in force: 15 September 2003: see SI 2003/1730, r 1(2).
Para (2): in sub-para (b) words "the company is in administration" in square brackets substituted by SI 2003/1730, r 4, Sch 1, Pt 1, para 1(b).
Date in force: 15 September 2003: see SI 2003/1730, r 1(2).
Para (2): sub-paras (c)–(f) substituted, for sub-paras (c), (d) as originally enacted, by SI 2002/2712, r 3(1), Schedule, Pt 1, para 1(b).
Date in force: 1 January 2003: see SI 2002/2712, r 1(1); for effect see rr 1(2), 3(2) thereof.
Para (4): inserted by SI 2002/2712, r 3(1), Schedule, Pt 1, para 1(c).
Date in force: 1 January 2003: see SI 2002/2712, r 1(1); for effect see rr 1(2), 3(2) thereof.

CHAPTER 2

PROPOSAL BY DIRECTORS

1.2 . . .

. . .

NOTES

Amendment

Revoked by SI 2010/686, r 5.
Date in force: 6 April 2010: see SI 2010/686, r 1; for transitional provisions see r 6(1), Sch 4, paras 1, 2(1)(a) thereto.

1.3 Contents of proposal

(1) The directors' proposal shall provide a short explanation why, in their opinion, a voluntary arrangement under Part I of the Act is desirable, and give reasons why the company's creditors may be expected to concur with such an arrangement.

(2) The following matters shall be stated, or otherwise dealt with, in the directors' proposal—
(a) the following matters, so far as within the directors' immediate knowledge—
(i) the company's assets, with an estimate of their respective values,

(ii) the extent (if any) to which the assets are charged in favour of creditors,
(iii) the extent (if any) to which particular assets are to be excluded from the voluntary arrangement;
(b) particulars of any property, other than assets of the company itself, which is proposed to be included in the arrangement, the source of such property and the terms on which it is to be made available for inclusion;
(c) the nature and amount of the company's liabilities (so far as within the directors' immediate knowledge), the manner in which they are proposed to be met, modified, postponed or otherwise dealt with by means of the arrangement, and (in particular)—
  (i) how it is proposed to deal with preferential creditors (defined in section 4(7)) and creditors who are, or claim to be, secured,
  (ii) how persons connected with the company (being creditors) are proposed to be treated under the arrangement, and
  (iii) whether there are, to the directors' knowledge, any circumstances giving rise to the possibility, in the event that the company should go into liquidation, of claims under—
    section 238 (transactions at an undervalue),
    section 239 (preferences),
    section 244 (extortionate credit transactions), or
    section 245 (floating charges invalid);
    and, where any such circumstances are present, whether, and if so how, it is proposed under the voluntary arrangement to make provision for wholly or partly indemnifying the company in respect of such claims;
[(ca) an estimate (to the best of the directors' knowledge and belief and subject to paragraph (4)) of—
  (i) the value of the prescribed part, should the company go into liquidation if the proposal for the voluntary arrangement is not accepted, whether or not section 176A is to be disapplied; and
  (ii) the value of the company's net property on the date that the estimate is made;]
(d) whether any, and if so what, guarantees have been given of the company's debts by other persons, specifying which (if any) of the guarantors are persons connected with the company;
(e) the proposed duration of the voluntary arrangement;
(f) the proposed dates of distributions to creditors, with estimates of their amounts;
[(fa) how it is proposed to deal with the claim of any person who is bound by the arrangement by virtue of section 5(2)(b)(ii);]
(g) the amount proposed to be paid to the nominee (as such) by way of remuneration and expenses;
(h) the manner in which it is proposed that the supervisor of the arrangement should be remunerated, and his expenses defrayed;
(j) whether, for the purposes of the arrangement, any guarantees are to be offered by directors, or other persons, and whether (if so) any security is to be given or sought;
(k) the manner in which funds held for the purposes of the arrangement are to be banked, invested or otherwise dealt with pending distribution to creditors;
(l) the manner in which funds held for the purpose of payment to creditors, and not so paid on the termination of the arrangement, are to be dealt with;

(m) the manner in which the business of the company is proposed to be conducted during the course of the arrangement;
(n) details of any further credit facilities which it is intended to arrange for the company, and how the debts so arising are to be paid;
(o) the functions which are to be undertaken by the supervisor of the arrangement; . . .
[(p) the name, address and qualification of the person proposed as supervisor of the voluntary arrangement, and confirmation that he is either qualified to act as an insolvency practitioner in relation to the company or is an authorised person in relation to the company][; . . .
(q) whether the EC Regulation will apply and, if so, whether the proceedings will be main proceedings, secondary proceedings or territorial proceedings][; and
(r) such other matters (if any) as the directors consider appropriate for ensuring that members and creditors are enabled to reach an informed decision on the proposal].

(3) With the agreement in writing of the nominee, the directors' proposal may be amended at any time up to delivery of the [nominee's] report to the court under section 2(2).

[(4) Nothing in paragraph (2)(ca) is to be taken as requiring the estimate referred to in that paragraph to include any information, the disclosure of which could seriously prejudice the commercial interests of the company. If such information is excluded from the calculation the estimate shall be accompanied by a statement to that effect.]

NOTES

Initial Commencement

Specified date

Specified date: 29 December 1986: see r 0.1.

Amendment

Para (2): sub-para (ca) inserted by SI 2003/1730, r 4, Sch 1, Pt 1, para 2(1).
Date in force: 15 September 2003: see SI 2003/1730, r 1(2).
Para (2): sub-para (fa) inserted by SI 2002/2712, r 3(1), Schedule, Pt 1, para 2(a).
Date in force: 1 January 2003: see SI 2002/2712, r 1(1); for effect see rr 1(2), 3(2) thereof.
Para (2): in sub-para (o) word omitted revoked by SI 2002/1307, rr 3(1), 4(2)(a).
Date in force: 31 May 2002: see SI 2002/1307, r 1.
Para (2): sub-para (p) substituted by SI 2002/2712, r 3(1), Schedule, Pt 1, para 2(b).
Date in force: 1 January 2003: see SI 2002/2712, r 1(1); for effect see rr 1(2), 3(2) thereof.
Para (2): sub-para (q) and word (omitted) immediately preceding it inserted by SI 2002/1307, rr 3(1), 4(2)(b).
Date in force: 31 May 2002: see SI 2002/1307, r 1.
Para (2): in sub-para (p) word omitted revoked by SI 2010/686, r 2, Sch 1, para 3(1), (2)(a).
Date in force: 6 April 2010: see SI 2010/686, r 1; for transitional provisions see r 6(1), Sch 4, paras 1, 3(1) thereto.
Para (2): sub-para (r) and word "; and" immediately preceding it inserted by SI 2010/686, r 2, Sch 1, para 3(1), (2)(b).
Date in force: 6 April 2010: see SI 2010/686, r 1; for transitional provisions see r 6(1), Sch 4, paras 1, 3 thereto.
Para (3): word "nominee's" in square brackets substituted by SI 2010/686, r 2, Sch 1, para 3(1), (3).
Date in force: 6 April 2010: see SI 2010/686, r 1; for transitional provisions see r 6(1), Sch 4, para 1 thereto.
Para (4): inserted by SI 2003/1730, r 4, Sch 1, Pt 1, para 2(2).

Date in force: 15 September 2003: see SI 2003/1730, r 1(2).

1.4 Notice to intended nominee

(1) The directors shall give to the intended nominee written notice of their proposal.

(2) The notice, accompanied by a copy of the proposal, shall be delivered either to the nominee himself, or to a person authorised to take delivery of documents on his behalf.

(3) If the intended nominee agrees to act, he shall cause a copy of the notice to be endorsed to the effect that it has been received by him on a specified date; and the period of 28 days referred to in section 2(2) then runs from that date.

(4) The copy of the notice so endorsed shall be returned by the nominee [as soon as reasonably practicable] to the directors at an address specified by them in the notice for that purpose.

NOTES

Initial Commencement

Specified date

Specified date: 29 December 1986: see r 0.1.

Amendment

Para (4): words "as soon as reasonably practicable" in square brackets substituted by SI 2009/642, rr 4, 5.

Date in force: 6 April 2009: see SI 2009/642, r 1; for transitional provisions see r 3 thereof.

1.5 Statement of affairs

(1) The directors shall, [at the same time as the] proposal is delivered to the nominee, . . . deliver to him a statement of the company's affairs.

(2) The statement shall comprise the following particulars (supplementing or amplifying, so far as is necessary for clarifying the state of the company's affairs, those already given in the directors' proposal)—

- (a) a list of the company's assets, divided into such categories as are appropriate for easy identification, with estimated values assigned to each category;
- (b) in the case of any property on which a claim against the company is wholly or partly secured, particulars of the claim and its amount, and of how and when the security was created;
- (c) the names and addresses of the company's preferential creditors (defined in section 4(7)), with the amounts of their respective claims;
- (d) the names and addresses of the company's unsecured creditors, with the amounts of their respective claims;
- (e) particulars of any debts owed by or to the company to or by persons connected with it;
- (f) the names and addresses of the company's members, with details of their respective shareholdings;
- (g) such other particulars (if any) as the nominee may in writing require to be furnished for the purposes of making his report to the court on the directors' proposal.

(3) The statement of affairs shall be made up to a date not earlier than 2 weeks before the date of the notice to the nominee under Rule 1.4.

However, the nominee may allow an extension of that period to the nearest practicable date (not earlier than 2 months before the date of the notice under Rule 1.4); and if he does so, he shall give his reasons in his report to the court on the directors' proposal.

[(4) The statement must be verified by a statement of truth made by at least one director.]

NOTES

Initial Commencement

Specified date

Specified date: 29 December 1986: see r 0.1.

Amendment

Para (1): words "at the same time as the" in square brackets substituted by SI 2010/686, r 2, Sch 1, para 4(1), (2)(a).
Date in force: 6 April 2010: see SI 2010/686, r 1; for transitional provisions see r 6(1), Sch 4, para 1 thereto.
Para (1): words omitted revoked by SI 2010/686, r 2, Sch 1, para 4(1), (2)(b).
Date in force: 6 April 2010: see SI 2010/686, r 1; for transitional provisions see r 6(1), Sch 4, para 1 thereto.
Para (4): substituted by SI 2010/686, r 2, Sch 1, para 4(1), (3).
Date in force: 6 April 2010: see SI 2010/686, r 1; for transitional provisions see r 6(1), Sch 4, para 1 thereto.

1.6 Additional disclosure for assistance of nominee

(1) If it appears to the nominee that he cannot properly prepare his report on the basis of information in the directors' proposal and statement of affairs, he may call on the directors to provide him with—

- (a) further and better particulars as to the circumstances in which, and the reasons why, the company is insolvent or (as the case may be) threatened with insolvency;
- (b) particulars of any previous proposals which have been made in respect of the company under Part I of the Act;
- (c) any further information with respect to the company's affairs which the nominee thinks necessary for the purposes of his report.

(2) The nominee may call on the directors to inform him, with respect to any person who is, or at any time in the 2 years preceding the notice under Rule 1.4 has been, a director or officer of the company, whether and in what circumstances (in those 2 years or previously) that person—

- (a) has been concerned in the affairs of any other company (whether or not incorporated in England and Wales) which has become insolvent, or
- (b) has himself been adjudged bankrupt or entered into an arrangement with his creditors.

(3) For the purpose of enabling the nominee to consider their proposal and prepare his report on it, the directors must give [the nominee such access to the company's accounts and records as the nominee may require].

NOTES

Initial Commencement

Specified date

Specified date: 29 December 1986: see r 0.1.

Amendment
Para (3): words from "the nominee such" to "nominee may require" in square brackets substituted by SI 2010/686, r 2, Sch 1, para 5.
Date in force: 6 April 2010: see SI 2010/686, r 1; for transitional provisions see r 6(1), Sch 4, para 1 thereto.

1.7 Nominee's report on the proposal

(1) With his report to the court under section 2 the nominee shall deliver—
  (a) a copy of the directors' proposal (with amendments, if any, authorised under Rule 1.3(3)); and
  (b) a copy or summary of the company's statement of affairs.

(2) If the nominee makes known his opinion [that the directors' proposal has a reasonable prospect of being approved and implemented and] that meetings of the company and its creditors should be summoned under section 3, his report shall have annexed to it his comments on the proposal.

If his opinion is otherwise, he shall give his reasons for that opinion.

(3) The court shall cause the nominee's report to be endorsed with the date on which it is filed in court. Any director, member or creditor of the company is entitled, at all reasonable times on any business day, to inspect the file.

(4) The nominee shall send a copy of his report, and of his comments (if any), to the company.

NOTES

Initial Commencement

Specified date
Specified date: 29 December 1986: see r 0.1.

Amendment
Para (2): words "that the directors' proposal has a reasonable prospect of being approved and implemented and" in square brackets inserted by SI 2002/2712, r 3(1), Schedule, Pt 1, para 3.
Date in force: 1 January 2003: see SI 2002/2712, r 1(1); for effect see rr 1(2), 3(2) thereof.

[1.8 Replacement of nominee]

[(1) Where a person other than the nominee intends to apply to the court under section 2(4) for the nominee to be replaced, (except in any case where the nominee has died) he shall give to the nominee at least [5 business] days' notice of his application.

(2) Where the nominee intends to apply to the court under section 2(4) of the Act to be replaced, he shall give at least [5 business] days' notice of his application to the person intending to make the proposal.

(3) No appointment of a replacement nominee shall be made by the court unless there is filed in court a statement by the replacement nominee—
  (a) indicating his consent to act, and
  (b) that he is qualified to act as an insolvency practitioner in relation to the company or is an authorised person in relation to the company.]

NOTES

Amendment
Substituted by SI 2002/2712, r 3(1), Schedule, Pt 1, para 4.
Date in force: 1 January 2003: see SI 2002/2712, r 1(1); for effect see rr 1(2), 3(2) thereof.

Para (1): words "5 business" in square brackets substituted by SI 2010/686, r 2, Sch 1, para 6.
Date in force: 6 April 2010: see SI 2010/686, r 1; for transitional provisions see r 6(1), Sch 4, para 1 thereto.
Para (2): words "5 business" in square brackets substituted by SI 2010/686, r 2, Sch 1, para 6.
Date in force: 6 April 2010: see SI 2010/686, r 1; for transitional provisions see r 6(1), Sch 4, para 1 thereto.

1.9 Summoning of meetings under s 3

(1) If in his report the nominee states that in his opinion meetings of the company and its creditors should be summoned to consider the directors' proposal, the date on which the meetings are to be held shall be not . . . more than 28, days from that on which the nominee's report is filed in court under Rule 1.7.

(2) Notices calling the meetings shall be sent by the nominee, at least 14 days before the day fixed for them to be held—

(a) in the case of the creditors' meeting, to all the creditors specified in the statement of affairs, and any other creditors of the company of [whose address the nominee] is otherwise aware; and

(b) in the case of the meeting of members of the company, to all persons who are, to the best of the nominee's belief, members of it.

(3) Each notice sent under this Rule shall specify the court to which the nominee's report under section 2 has been delivered and shall state the effect of [Rule 1.19(2)], (3) and (4) (requisite majorities (creditors)); and with each notice there shall be sent—

(a) a copy of the directors' proposal;

(b) a copy of the statement of affairs or, if the nominee thinks fit, a summary of it (the summary to include a list of creditors and the amount of their debts); and

(c) the nominee's comments on the proposal.

NOTES

Initial Commencement

Specified date

Specified date: 29 December 1986: see r 0.1.

Amendment

Para (1): words omitted revoked by SI 2010/686, r 2, Sch 1, para 7(1), (2).
Date in force: 6 April 2010: see SI 2010/686, r 1; for transitional provisions see r 6(1), Sch 4, para 1 thereto.
Para (2): in sub-para (a) words "whose address the nominee" in square brackets substituted by SI 2010/686, r 2, Sch 1, para 7(1), (3).
Date in force: 6 April 2010: see SI 2010/686, r 1; for transitional provisions see r 6(1), Sch 4, para 1 thereto.
Para (3): words "Rule 1.19(2)" in square brackets substituted by SI 2010/686, r 2, Sch 1, para 7(1), (4).
Date in force: 6 April 2010: see SI 2010/686, r 1; for transitional provisions see r 6(1), Sch 4, para 1 thereto.

CHAPTER 3

PROPOSAL BY ADMINISTRATOR OR LIQUIDATOR (HIMSELF THE NOMINEE)

1.10 Preparation of proposal

[(1) The responsible insolvency practitioner's proposal must specify all such matters as under Rule 1.3 (subject to paragraph (3) below) in Chapter 2 the directors of the company would be required to include in a proposal by them, with the addition, where the company is in administration or liquidation, of the nature and amount of its preferential creditors.]

(2) Where the company is being wound up by the court, the insolvency practitioner shall give notice of the proposal to the official receiver.

[(3) The administrator or liquidator shall include, in place of the estimate required by Rule 1.3(2)(ca), a statement which contains—

(a) to the best of the administrator or liquidator's knowledge and belief—
  (i) an estimate of the value of the prescribed part (whether or not he proposes to make an application to court under section 176A(5) or section 176A(3) applies), and
  (ii) an estimate of the value of the company's net property, and
(b) whether, and, if so, why, the administrator or liquidator proposes to make an application to court under section 176A(5).

(4) Nothing in this Rule is to be taken as requiring any such estimate to include any information, the disclosure of which could seriously prejudice the commercial interests of the company. If such information is excluded from the calculation the estimate shall be accompanied by a statement to that effect.]

NOTES

Initial Commencement

Specified date

Specified date: 29 December 1986: see r 0.1.

Amendment

Para (1): substituted by SI 2010/686, r 2, Sch 1, para 8.
  Date in force: 6 April 2010: see SI 2010/686, r 1; for transitional provisions see r 6(1), Sch 4, paras 1, 3 thereto.
Paras (3), (4): inserted by SI 2003/1730, r 4, Sch 1, Pt 1, para 3(b).
  Date in force: 15 September 2003: see SI 2003/1730, r 1(2).

1.11 Summoning of meetings under s 3

(1) The responsible insolvency practitioner shall fix a venue for the creditors' meeting and the company meeting, and give at least 14 days' notice of the meetings—

(a) in the case of the creditors' meeting, to all the creditors specified in the company's statement of affairs, and to any other creditors of [whose address the insolvency practitioner is otherwise] aware; and
(b) in the case of the company meeting, to all persons who are, to the best of his belief, members of the company.

(2) Each notice sent out under this Rule shall state the effect of Rule 1.19(1), (3) and (4) (requisite majorities (creditors)); and with it there shall be sent—

(a) a copy of the responsible insolvency practitioner's proposal, and
(b) a copy of the statement of affairs or, if he thinks fit, a summary of it (the summary to include a list of creditors and the amounts of their debts).

NOTES

Initial Commencement

Specified date
Specified date: 29 December 1986: see r 0.1.

Amendment
Para (1): in sub-para (a) words "whose address the insolvency practitioner is otherwise" in square brackets substituted by SI 2010/686, r 2, Sch 1, para 9.
Date in force: 6 April 2010: see SI 2010/686, r 1; for transitional provisions see r 6(1), Sch 4, para 1 thereto.

CHAPTER 4

PROPOSAL BY ADMINISTRATOR OR LIQUIDATOR (ANOTHER INSOLVENCY PRACTITIONER THE NOMINEE)

1.12 Preparation of proposal and notice to nominee

(1) The responsible insolvency practitioner shall give notice to the intended nominee, and prepare his proposal for a voluntary arrangement, in the same manner as is required of the directors, in the case of a proposal by them, under Chapter 2.

(2) Rule 1.2 applies to the responsible insolvency practitioner as it applies to the directors; and Rule 1.4 applies as regards the action to be taken by the nominee.

(3) The content of the proposal shall be as required by Rule 1.3 [(and, where relevant, Rule 1.10)], reading references to the directors as referring to the responsible insolvency practitioner.

(4) Rule 1.6 applies in respect of the information to be furnished to the nominee, reading references to the directors as referring to the responsible insolvency practitioner.

(5) With the proposal the responsible insolvency practitioner shall provide a copy of the company's statement of affairs.

(6) Where the company is being wound up by the court, the responsible insolvency practitioner shall send a copy of the proposal to the official receiver, accompanied by the name and address of the insolvency practitioner [or authorised person] who has agreed to act as nominee.

(7) Rules 1.7 to 1.9 apply as regards a proposal under this Chapter as they apply to a proposal under Chapter 2.

NOTES

Initial Commencement

Specified date
Specified date: 29 December 1986: see r 0.1.

Amendment
Para (3): words in square brackets inserted by SI 1987/1919, r 3(1), Schedule, Part 1, para 4.
Para (6): words "or authorised person" in square brackets inserted by SI 2002/2712, r 3(1), Schedule, Pt 1, para 5.
Date in force: 1 January 2003: see SI 2002/2712, r 1(1); for effect see rr 1(2), 3(2) thereof.

CHAPTER 5

PROCEEDINGS ON A PROPOSAL MADE BY THE DIRECTORS, OR BY THE ADMINISTRATOR, OR BY THE LIQUIDATOR

SECTION A: MEETINGS OF COMPANY'S CREDITORS AND MEMBERS

[1.13 Summoning of meetings]

[(1) Subject as follows, in fixing the venue for the creditors' meeting and the company meeting, [the nominee must] have regard primarily to the convenience of the creditors.

(2) Meetings shall in each case be summoned for commencement between 10.00 and 16.00 hours on a business day.

(3) The meetings may be held on the same day or on different days. If held on the same day, the meetings shall be held in the same place, but in either case the creditors' meeting shall be fixed for a time in advance of the company meeting.

(4) Where the meetings are not held on the same day, they shall be held within [5 business] days of each other.

(5) With every notice summoning either meeting there shall be sent out forms of proxy.]

NOTES

Amendment

Substituted by SI 2003/1730, r 4, Sch 1, Pt 1, para 4.
    Date in force: 15 September 2003: see SI 2003/1730, r 1(2).
Para (1): words "the nominee must" in square brackets substituted by SI 2010/686, r 2, Sch 1, para 10(1), (2).
    Date in force: 6 April 2010: see SI 2010/686, r 1; for transitional provisions see r 6(1), Sch 4, para 1 thereto.
Para (4): words "5 business" in square brackets substituted by SI 2010/686, r 2, Sch 1, para 10(1), (3).
    Date in force: 6 April 2010: see SI 2010/686, r 1; for transitional provisions see r 6(1), Sch 4, para 1 thereto.

1.14 The chairman at meetings

(1) Subject as follows, at both the creditors' meeting and the company meeting, and at any combined meeting, the [nominee must] be chairman.

(2) If for any reason he is unable to attend, he may nominate another person to act as chairman in his place; but a person so nominated must be . . .—

[(a)   a person qualified to act as an insolvency practitioner in relation to the company;
(b)   an authorised person in relation to the company; or
(c)   an employee of the [nominee] or his firm who is experienced in insolvency matters].

NOTES

Initial Commencement

Specified date

    Specified date: 29 December 1986: see r 0.1.

Amendment

Para (1): words "nominee must" in square brackets substituted by SI 2010/686, r 2, Sch 1, para 11(1), (2).
    Date in force: 6 April 2010: see SI 2010/686, r 1; for transitional provisions see r 6(1), Sch 4, para 1 thereto.

Para (2): word omitted revoked by SI 2002/2712, r 3(1), Schedule, Pt 1, para 7(a).
Date in force: 1 January 2003: see SI 2002/2712, r 1(1); for effect see rr 1(2), 3(2) thereof.
Para (2): sub-paras (a)–(c) substituted, for sub-paras (a), (b) as originally enacted, by SI 2002/2712, r 3(1), Schedule, Pt 1, para 7(b).
Date in force: 1 January 2003: see SI 2002/2712, r 1(1); for effect see rr 1(2), 3(2) thereof.
Para (2): in sub-para (c) word "nominee" in square brackets substituted by SI 2010/686, r 2, Sch 1, para 11(1), (3).
Date in force: 6 April 2010: see SI 2010/686, r 1; for transitional provisions see r 6(1), Sch 4, para 1 thereto.

1.15 The chairman as proxy-holder

The chairman shall not by virtue of any proxy held by him vote to increase or reduce the amount of the remuneration or expenses of the nominee or the supervisor of the proposed arrangement, unless the proxy specifically directs him to vote in that way.

NOTES

Initial Commencement

Specified date

Specified date: 29 December 1986: see r 0.1.

1.16 Attendance by company officers

(1) At least 14 days' notice to attend the meetings shall be given by the [nominee]—
(a) to all directors of the company, and
(b) to any persons in whose case the [nominee] thinks that their presence is required as being officers of the company, or as having been directors or officers of it at any time in the 2 years immediately preceding the date of the notice.

(2) The chairman may, if he thinks fit, exclude any present or former director or officer from attendance at a meeting, either completely or for any part of it; and this applies whether or not a notice under this Rule has been sent to the person excluded.

NOTES

Initial Commencement

Specified date

Specified date: 29 December 1986: see r 0.1.

Amendment

Para (1): word "nominee" in square brackets in both places it occurs substituted by SI 2010/686, r 2, Sch 1, para 12.
Date in force: 6 April 2010: see SI 2010/686, r 1; for transitional provisions see r 6(1), Sch 4, para 1 thereto.

SECTION B: VOTING RIGHTS AND MAJORITIES

[1.17 Entitlement to vote (creditors)]

[(1) Subject as follows, every creditor who has notice of the creditors' meeting is entitled to vote at the meeting or any adjournment of it.

(2) Votes are calculated according to the amount of the creditor's debt as at the date of the meeting or, where the company is being wound up or is [in administration],

the date of its going into liquidation or (as the case may be) [when the company entered administration].

(3) A creditor may vote in respect of a debt for an unliquidated amount or any debt whose value is not ascertained and for the purposes of voting (but not otherwise) his debt shall be valued at £1 unless the chairman agrees to put a higher value on it.]

NOTES

Amendment

Substituted, together with r 1.17A, for r 1.17 as originally enacted, by SI 2002/2712, r 3(1), Schedule, Pt 1, para 8.
Date in force: 1 January 2003: see SI 2002/2712, r 1(1); for effect see rr 1(2), 3(2) thereof.
Para (2): words "in administration" and "when the company entered administration" in square brackets substituted by SI 2003/1730, r 4, Sch 1, Pt 1, para 5.
Date in force: 15 September 2003: see SI 2003/1730, r 1(2).

[1.17A Procedure for admission of creditors' claims for voting purposes]

[(1) Subject as follows, at any creditors' meeting the chairman shall ascertain the entitlement of persons wishing to vote and shall admit or reject their claims accordingly.

(2) The chairman may admit or reject a claim in whole or in part.

(3) The chairman's decision on any matter under this Rule or under paragraph (3) of Rule 1.17 is subject to appeal to the court by any creditor or member of the company.

(4) If the chairman is in doubt whether a claim should be admitted or rejected, he shall mark it as objected to and allow votes to be cast in respect of it, subject to such votes being subsequently declared invalid if the objection to the claim is sustained.

(5) If on an appeal the chairman's decision is reversed or varied, or votes are declared invalid, the court may order another meeting to be summoned, or make such order as it thinks just.
The court's power to make an order under this paragraph is exercisable only if it considers that the circumstances giving rise to the appeal give rise to unfair prejudice or material irregularity.

(6) An application to the court by way of appeal against the chairman's decision shall not be made after the end of the period of 28 days beginning with the first day on which the report required by section 4(6) has been made to the court.

(7) The chairman is not personally liable for any costs incurred by any person in respect of an appeal under this Rule.]

NOTES

Amendment

Substituted, together with r 1.17, for r 1.17 as originally enacted, by SI 2002/2712, r 3(1), Schedule, Pt 1, para 8.
Date in force: 1 January 2003: see SI 2002/2712, r 1(1); for effect see rr 1(2), 3(2) thereof.]

1.18 Voting rights (members)

(1) Subject as follows, members of the company at their meeting vote according to the rights attaching to their shares respectively in accordance with the articles.

(2) . . .

(3) References in this Rule to a person's shares include any other interest which he may have as a member of the company.

NOTES

Initial Commencement

Specified date
Specified date: 29 December 1986: see r 0.1.

Amendment
Para (2): revoked by SI 2002/2712, r 3(1), Schedule, Pt 1, para 9.
Date in force: 1 January 2003: see SI 2002/2712, r 1(1); for effect see rr 1(2), 3(2) thereof.

1.19 Requisite majorities (creditors)

[(1) Subject to paragraph (2), at the creditors' meeting, a resolution is passed when a majority (in value) of those present and voting in person or by proxy have voted in favour of it.

(2) A resolution to approve the proposal or a modification is passed when a majority of three-quarters or more (in value) of those present and voting in person or by proxy have voted in favour of it.]

(3) In the following cases there is to be left out of account a creditor's vote in respect of any claim or part of a claim—

- (a) where written notice of the claim was not given, either at the meeting or before it, to the chairman or [nominee];
- (b) where the claim or part is secured;
- (c) where the claim is in respect of a debt wholly or partly on, or secured by, a current bill of exchange or promissory note, unless the creditor is willing—
  - (i) to treat the liability to him on the bill or note of every person who is liable on it antecedently to the company, and against whom a bankruptcy order has not been made (or in the case of a company, which has not gone into liquidation), as a security in his hands, and
  - (ii) to estimate the value of the security and (for the purpose of entitlement to vote, but not of any distribution under the arrangement) to deduct it from his claim.

(4) Any resolution is invalid if those voting against it include more than half in value of the creditors, counting in these latter only those—

- (a) to whom notice of the meeting was sent;
- (b) whose votes are not to be left out of account under paragraph (3); and
- (c) who are not, to the best of the chairman's belief, persons connected with the company.

(5) It is for the chairman of the meeting to decide whether under this Rule—

- (a) a vote is to be left out of account in accordance with paragraph (3), or
- (b) a person is a connected person for the purposes of paragraph (4)(c);

and in relation to the second of these two cases the chairman is entitled to rely on the information provided by the company's statement of affairs or otherwise in accordance with this Part of the Rules.

(6) If the chairman uses a proxy contrary to Rule 1.15, his vote with that proxy does not count towards any majority under this Rule.

[(7) The chairman's decision on any matter under this Rule is subject to appeal to the court by any creditor or member and paragraphs (5) to (7) of Rule 1.17A apply as regards such an appeal.]

NOTES

Initial Commencement

Specified date

Specified date: 29 December 1986: see r 0.1.

Amendment

Paras (1), (2): substituted by SI 2010/686, r 2, Sch 1, para 13(1), (2).
Date in force: 6 April 2010: see SI 2010/686, r 1; for transitional provisions see r 6(1), Sch 4, para 1 thereto.
Para (3): in sub-para (a) word "nominee" in square brackets substituted by SI 2010/686, r 2, Sch 1, para 13(1), (3).
Date in force: 6 April 2010: see SI 2010/686, r 1; for transitional provisions see r 6(1), Sch 4, para 1 thereto.
Para (7): substituted by SI 2002/2712, r 3(1), Schedule, Pt 1, para 10.
Date in force: 1 January 2003: see SI 2002/2712, r 1(1); for effect see rr 1(2), 3(2) thereof.

1.20 Requisite majorities (members)

(1) Subject as follows, and to any express provision made in the articles, at a company meeting any resolution is to be regarded as passed if voted for by more than one-half [in value] of the members present in person or by proxy and voting on the resolution.

[The value of members is determined by reference to the number of votes conferred on each member by the company's articles.]

(2) ...

(3) If the chairman uses a proxy contrary to Rule 1.15, his vote with that proxy does not count towards any majority under this Rule.

NOTES

Initial Commencement

Specified date

Specified date: 29 December 1986: see r 0.1.

Amendment

Para (1): words in square brackets inserted by SI 1987/1919, r 3(1), Schedule, Part 1, para 5.
Para (2): revoked by SI 2002/2712, r 3(1), Schedule, Pt 1, para 11.
Date in force: 1 January 2003: see SI 2002/2712, r 1(1); for effect see rr 1(2), 3(2) thereof.

[1.21 Proceedings to obtain agreement on the proposal]

[(1) If the chairman thinks fit, the creditors' meeting and the company meeting may be held together.

(2) The chairman may, and shall if it is so resolved at the meeting in question, adjourn that meeting for not more than 14 days.

(3) If there are subsequently further adjournments, the final adjournment shall not be to a day later than 14 days after the date on which the meeting in question was originally held.

(4) In the case of a proposal by the directors, if the meetings are adjourned under paragraph (2), notice of the fact shall be given by the nominee [as soon as reasonably practicable] to the court.

[(4A) Once only in the course of a meeting the chairman may, without an adjournment, declare it suspended for any period up to 1 hour.]

(5) If following the final adjournment of the creditors' meeting the proposal (with or without modifications) has not been approved by the creditors, it is deemed rejected.]

NOTES

Amendment

Substituted by SI 2002/2712, r 3(1), Schedule, Pt 1, para 12.
Date in force: 1 January 2003: see SI 2002/2712, r 1(1); for effect see rr 1(2), 3(2) thereof.
Para (4): words "as soon as reasonably practicable" in square brackets substituted by SI 2009/642, rr 4, 5.
Date in force: 6 April 2009: see SI 2009/642, r 1; for transitional provisions see r 3 thereof.
Para (4A): inserted by SI 2010/686, r 2, Sch 1, para 14.
Date in force: 6 April 2010: see SI 2010/686, r 1; for transitional provisions see r 6(1), Sch 4, para 1 thereto.

SECTION C: IMPLEMENTATION OF THE ARRANGEMENT

1.22 Resolutions to follow approval

[(1) If the voluntary arrangement is approved (with or without modifications) by the creditors' meeting, a resolution [must] be taken by the creditors, where two or more supervisors are appointed, on the question whether acts to be done in connection with the arrangement may be done by any one or more of them, or must be done by all of them.]

(2) . . .

(3) If at either meeting a resolution is moved for the appointment of some person other than the nominee to be supervisor of the arrangement, there must be produced to the chairman, at or before the meeting—

(a) that person's written consent to act (unless he is present and then and there signifies his consent), and

(b) his written confirmation that he is qualified to act as an insolvency practitioner in relation to the company [or is an authorised person in relation to the company].

NOTES

Initial Commencement

Specified date

Specified date: 29 December 1986: see r 0.1.

Amendment

Para (1): substituted by SI 2002/2712, r 3(1), Schedule, Pt 1, para 13(a).
Date in force: 1 January 2003: see SI 2002/2712, r 1(1); for effect see rr 1(2), 3(2) thereof.
Para (1): word "must" in square brackets substituted by SI 2010/686, r 2, Sch 1, para 15.
Date in force: 6 April 2010: see SI 2010/686, r 1; for transitional provisions see r 6(1), Sch 4, para 1 thereto.
Para (2): revoked by SI 2002/2712, r 3(1), Schedule, Pt 1, para 13(b).
Date in force: 1 January 2003: see SI 2002/2712, r 1(1); for effect see rr 1(2), 3(2) thereof.
Para (3): in sub-para (b) words "or is an authorised person in relation to the company" in square brackets inserted by SI 2002/2712, r 3(1), Schedule, Pt 1, para 13(c).
Date in force: 1 January 2003: see SI 2002/2712, r 1(1); for effect see rr 1(2), 3(2) thereof.

[1.22A Notice of order made under section 4A(6)]

[(1) This Rule applies where the court makes an order under section 4A(6).

(2) The member of the company who applied for the order shall serve sealed copies of it on—

(a) the supervisor of the voluntary arrangement; and
(b) the directors of the company.

(3) Service on the directors may be effected by service of a single copy on the company at its registered office.

(4) The directors or (as the case may be) the supervisor shall [as soon as reasonably practicable] after receiving a copy of the court's order, give notice of it to all persons who were sent notice of the creditors' or company meetings or who, not having been sent such notice, are affected by the order.

(5) The person on whose application the order of the court was made shall, within [5 business] days of the order, deliver [a copy] to the registrar of companies.]

NOTES

Amendment

Inserted by SI 2002/2712, r 3(1), Schedule, Pt 1, para 14.
    Date in force: 1 January 2003: see SI 2002/2712, r 1(1); for effect see rr 1(2), 3(2) thereof.
Para (4): words "as soon as reasonably practicable" in square brackets substituted by SI 2009/642, rr 4, 5.
    Date in force: 6 April 2009: see SI 2009/642, r 1; for transitional provisions see r 3 thereof.
Para (5): words "5 business" in square brackets substituted by SI 2010/686, r 2, Sch 1, para 16.
    Date in force: 6 April 2010: see SI 2010/686, r 1; for transitional provisions see r 6(1), Sch 4, para 1 thereto.
Para (5): words "a copy" in square brackets substituted by SI 2009/2472, rr 3, 5.
    Date in force: 1 October 2009: see SI 2009/2472, r 1; for transitional provisions see r 2 thereof.

1.23 Hand-over of property etc to supervisor

(1) [Where the decision approving the voluntary arrangement has effect under section 4A—]

(a) the directors, or
(b) where the company is in liquidation or is [in administration], and a person other than the responsible insolvency practitioner is appointed as supervisor of the voluntary arrangement, the insolvency practitioner,

shall [as soon as reasonably practicable] do all that is required for putting the supervisor into possession of the assets included in the arrangement.

(2) Where the company is in liquidation or is [in administration], the supervisor shall on taking possession of the assets discharge any balance due to the insolvency practitioner by way of remuneration or on account of—

(a) fees, costs, charges and expenses properly incurred and payable under the Act or the Rules, and
(b) any advances made in respect of the company, together with interest on such advances at the rate specified in section 17 of the Judgments Act 1838 at the date on which the company went into liquidation or (as the case may be) [entered administration].

(3) Alternatively, the supervisor must, before taking possession, give the responsible insolvency practitioner a written undertaking to discharge any such balance out of the first realisation of assets.

(4) The insolvency practitioner has a charge on the assets included in the voluntary arrangement in respect of any sums due as above until they have been discharged, subject only to the deduction from realisations by the supervisor of the proper costs and expenses of such realisations.

(5) The supervisor shall from time to time out of the realisation of assets discharge all guarantees properly given by the responsible insolvency practitioner for the benefit of the company, and shall pay all the insolvency practitioner's expenses.

(6) References in this Rule to the responsible insolvency practitioner include, where a company is being wound up by the court, the official receiver, whether or not in his capacity as liquidator; and any sums due to the official receiver take priority over those due to a liquidator.

NOTES

Initial Commencement

Specified date

Specified date: 29 December 1986: see r 0.1.

Amendment

Para (1): words "Where the decision approving the voluntary arrangement has effect under section 4A—" in square brackets substituted by SI 2002/2712, r 3(1), Schedule, Pt 1, para 15.
Date in force: 1 January 2003: see SI 2002/2712, r 1(1); for effect see rr 1(2), 3(2) thereof.
Para (1): in sub-para (b) words "in administration" in square brackets substituted by SI 2003/1730, r 4, Sch 1, Pt 1, para 6(a).
Date in force: 15 September 2003: see SI 2003/1730, r 1(2).
Para (1): words "as soon as reasonably practicable" in square brackets substituted by SI 2009/642, rr 4, 5.
Date in force: 6 April 2009: see SI 2009/642, r 1; for transitional provisions see r 3 thereof.
Para (2): words "in administration" in square brackets substituted by SI 2003/1730, r 4, Sch 1, Pt 1, para 6(b)(i).
Date in force: 15 September 2003: see SI 2003/1730, r 1(2).
Para (2): in sub-para (b) words "entered administration" in square brackets substituted by SI 2003/1730, r 4, Sch 1, Pt 1, para 6(b)(ii).
Date in force: 15 September 2003: see SI 2003/1730, r 1(2).

1.24 Report of meetings

(1) A report of the meetings shall be prepared by the person who was chairman of them.

(2) The report shall—

[(a) state whether the proposal for a voluntary arrangement was approved by the creditors of the company alone or by both the creditors and members of the company and in either case whether such approval was with any modifications;]

(b) set out the resolutions which were taken at each meeting, and the decision on each one;

(c) list the creditors and members of the company (with their respective values) who were present or represented at the meetings, and how they voted on each resolution; . . .

[(ca) state whether, in the opinion of the supervisor, (i) the EC Regulation applies to the voluntary arrangement and (ii) if so, whether the proceedings are main proceedings, secondary proceedings or territorial proceedings; and]

(d) include such further information (if any) as the chairman thinks it appropriate to make known to the court.

(3) A copy of the chairman's report shall, within 4 [business] days of the meetings being held, be filed in court; and the court shall cause that copy to be endorsed with the date of filing.

(4) In respect of each of the meetings, the persons to whom notice of its result is to be sent by the chairman under section 4(6) are all of those who were sent notice of the meeting under this Part of the Rules.

The notice shall be sent [as soon as reasonably practicable] after a copy of the chairman's report is filed in court under paragraph (3).

(5) [If the decision approving the voluntary arrangement has effect under section 4A] (whether or not in the form proposed), the supervisor shall [as soon as reasonably practicable] send a copy of the chairman's report to the registrar of companies.

NOTES

Initial Commencement

Specified date

Specified date: 29 December 1986: see r 0.1.

Amendment

Para (2): sub-para (a) substituted by SI 2002/2712, r 3(1), Schedule, Pt 1, para 16(a).
Date in force: 1 January 2003: see SI 2002/2712, r 1(1); for effect see rr 1(2), 3(2) thereof.
Para (2): in sub-para (c) word omitted revoked by SI 2002/1307, rr 3(1), 4(3)(a).
Date in force: 31 May 2002: see SI 2002/1307, r 1.
Para (2): sub-para (ca) inserted by SI 2002/1307, rr 3(1), 4(3)(b).
Date in force: 31 May 2002: see SI 2002/1307, r 1.
Para (3): word "business" in square brackets inserted by SI 2010/686, r 2, Sch 1, para 17(1), (2).
Date in force: 6 April 2010: see SI 2010/686, r 1; for transitional provisions see r 6(1), Sch 4, para 1 thereto.
Para (4): words "as soon as reasonably practicable" in square brackets substituted by SI 2010/686, r 2, Sch 1, para 17(1), (3).
Date in force: 6 April 2010: see SI 2010/686, r 1; for transitional provisions see r 6(1), Sch 4, para 1 thereto.
Para (5): words "If the decision approving the voluntary arrangement has effect under section 4A" in square brackets substituted by SI 2002/2712, r 3(1), Schedule, Pt 1, para 16(b).
Date in force: 1 January 2003: see SI 2002/2712, r 1(1); for effect see rr 1(2), 3(2) thereof.
Para (5): words "as soon as reasonably practicable" in square brackets substituted by SI 2009/642, rr 4, 5.
Date in force: 6 April 2009: see SI 2009/642, r 1; for transitional provisions see r 3 thereof.

1.25 Revocation or suspension of the arrangement

(1) This Rule applies where the court makes an order of revocation or suspension under section 6.

(2) The person who applied for the order shall serve sealed copies of it—
- (a) on the supervisor of the voluntary arrangement, and
- (b) on the directors of the company or the administrator or liquidator (according to who made the proposal for the arrangement).

Service on the directors may be effected by service of a single copy of the order on the company at its registered office.

(3) If the order includes a direction by the court under section 6(4)(b) for any further meetings to be summoned, notice shall also be given (by the person who

applied for the order) to whoever is, in accordance with the direction, required to summon the meetings.

(4) The directors or (as the case may be) the administrator or liquidator shall—
- (a) [as soon as reasonably practicable] after receiving a copy of the court's order, give notice of it to all persons who were sent notice of the creditors' and company meetings or who, not having been sent that notice, appear to be affected by the order;
- (b) within [5 business] days of their receiving a copy of the order (or within such longer period as the court may allow), give notice to the court whether it is intended to make a revised proposal to the company and its creditors, or to invite re-consideration of the original proposal.

(5) The person on whose application the order of revocation or suspension was made shall, within [5 business] days after the making of the order, deliver a copy of the order to the registrar of companies.

NOTES

Initial Commencement

Specified date

Specified date: 29 December 1986: see r 0.1.

Amendment

Para (4): in sub-para (a) words "as soon as reasonably practicable" in square brackets substituted by SI 2009/642, rr 4, 5.
Date in force: 6 April 2009: see SI 2009/642, r 1; for transitional provisions see r 3 thereof.
Para (4): in sub-para (b) words "5 business" in square brackets substituted by SI 2010/686, r 2, Sch 1, para 18.
Date in force: 6 April 2010: see SI 2010/686, r 1; for transitional provisions see r 6(1), Sch 4, para 1 thereto.
Para (5): words "5 business" in square brackets substituted by SI 2010/686, r 2, Sch 1, para 18.
Date in force: 6 April 2010: see SI 2010/686, r 1; for transitional provisions see r 6(1), Sch 4, para 1 thereto.

[1.26A Supervisor's accounts and reports]

[(1) Paragraph (2) applies where the voluntary arrangement authorises or requires the supervisor—
- (a) to carry on the business of the company or trade on its behalf or in its name; or
- (b) to realise assets of the company; or
- (c) otherwise to administer or dispose of any of its funds.

(2) The supervisor must keep accounts and records of the supervisor's acts and dealings in, and in connection with, the arrangement, including in particular records of all receipts and payments of money.

(3) The supervisor must preserve any accounts and records in paragraph (2) which—
- (a) were kept by any other person who has acted as supervisor of the arrangement; and
- (b) are in the supervisor's possession.

(4) Subject to paragraph (5), the supervisor must in respect of each period of 12 months ending with the anniversary of the commencement of the arrangement send within 2 months of the end of that period a report on the progress and prospects for the full implementation of the voluntary arrangement to—
- (a) the registrar of companies;
- (b) the company;

(c) all those of the company's creditors who are bound by the voluntary arrangement of whose address the supervisor is aware;
(d) subject to paragraph (7) below, the members of the company; and
(e) if the company is not in liquidation, the company's auditors (if any) for the time being.

(5) The supervisor is released from an obligation to send a report under paragraph (4), if an obligation to send a final report under Rule 1.29 arises in the period of 2 months mentioned in paragraph (4).

(6) Where the supervisor is authorised or required to do any of the things mentioned in paragraph (1)(a) to (c), the report required to be sent pursuant to paragraph (4) must include or be accompanied by—
(a) an abstract of receipts and payments required to be recorded by virtue of paragraph (2); or
(b) where there have been no such receipts and payments, a statement to that effect.

(7) The court may, on application by the supervisor dispense with the sending under this Rule of abstracts or reports to members of the company, either altogether or on the basis that the availability of the abstract or report to members is to be advertised by the supervisor in a specified manner.]

NOTES

Amendment

Substituted, for r 1.26 as originally enacted, by SI 2010/686, r 2, Sch 1, para 19.
Date in force: 6 April 2010: see SI 2010/686, r 1; for transitional provisions see r 6(1), Sch 4, para 1 thereto.

1.27 Production of accounts and records to Secretary of State

(1) The Secretary of State may at any time during the course of the voluntary arrangement or after its completion [or termination] require the supervisor to produce for inspection—
(a) his records and accounts in respect of the arrangement, and
(b) copies of abstracts and reports prepared in compliance with Rule [1.26A].

(2) The Secretary of State may require production either at the premises of the supervisor or elsewhere; and it is the duty of the supervisor to comply with any requirement imposed on him under this Rule.

(3) The Secretary of State may cause any accounts and records produced to him under this Rule to be audited; and the supervisor shall give to the Secretary of State such further information and assistance as he needs for the purposes of his audit.

NOTES

Initial Commencement

Specified date

Specified date: 29 December 1986: see r 0.1.

Amendment

Para (1): words "or termination" in square brackets inserted by SI 2002/2712, r 3(1), Schedule, Pt 1, para 17.
Date in force: 1 January 2003: see SI 2002/2712, r 1(1); for effect see rr 1(2), 3(2) thereof.
Para (1): in sub-para (b) reference to "1.26A" in square brackets substituted by SI 2010/686, r 2, Sch 1, para 20.

Date in force: 6 April 2010: see SI 2010/686, r 1; for transitional provisions see r 6(1), Sch 4, para 1 thereto.

1.28 Fees, costs, charges and expenses

(1) The fees, costs, charges and expenses that may be incurred for any of the purposes of the voluntary arrangement are—
- (a) any disbursements made by the nominee prior to the [decision approving the arrangement taking effect under section 4A], and any remuneration for his services as such agreed between himself and the company (or, as the case may be, the administrator or liquidator);
- (b) any fees, costs, charges or expenses which—
  - (i) are sanctioned by the terms of the arrangement, or
  - (ii) would be payable, or correspond to those which would be payable, in an administration or winding up.

NOTES

Initial Commencement

Specified date
Specified date: 29 December 1986: see r 0.1.

Amendment
Para (1): in sub-para (a) words "decision approving the arrangement taking effect under section 4A" in square brackets substituted by SI 2002/2712, r 3(1), Schedule, Pt 1, para 18.
Date in force: 1 January 2003: see SI 2002/2712, r 1(1); for effect see rr 1(2), 3(2) thereof.

[1.29 Completion or termination of the arrangement]

[(1) Not more than 28 days after the final completion or termination of the voluntary arrangement, the supervisor shall send to creditors and members of the company who are bound by it a notice that the voluntary arrangement has been fully implemented or (as the case may be) has terminated.

(2) With the notice there shall be sent to each creditor and member a copy of a report by the supervisor summarising all receipts and payments made by him in pursuance of the arrangement, and explaining in relation to implementation of the arrangement any departure from the proposals as they originally took effect, or (in the case of termination of the arrangement) explaining the reasons why the arrangement has terminated.

(3) The supervisor shall, within the 28 days mentioned above, send to the registrar of companies and to the court a copy of the notice to creditors and members under paragraph (1), together with a copy of the report under paragraph (2), and the supervisor shall not vacate office until after such copies have been sent.

[(4) In the report under paragraph (2), the supervisor shall include a statement as to the amount paid, if any, to unsecured creditors by virtue of the application of section 176A (prescribed part).]]

NOTES

Amendment
Substituted by SI 2002/2712, r 3(1), Schedule, Pt 1, para 19.
Date in force: 1 January 2003: see SI 2002/2712, r 1(1); for effect see rr 1(2), 3(2) thereof.
Para (4): inserted by SI 2003/1730, r 4, Sch 1, Pt 1, para 7.
Date in force: 15 September 2003: see SI 2003/1730, r 1(2).

CHAPTER 6

. . .

NOTES

Amendment

Revoked by SI 2002/2712, r 3(1), Schedule, Pt 1, para 20.
Date in force: 1 January 2003: see SI 2002/2712, r 1(1); for effect see rr 1(2), 3(2) thereof.

1.30 . . .

. . .

NOTES

Amendment

Revoked by SI 2002/2712, r 3(1), Schedule, Pt 1, para 20.
Date in force: 1 January 2003: see SI 2002/2712, r 1(1); for effect see rr 1(2), 3(2) thereof.

[CHAPTER 7

EC REGULATION—CONVERSION OF VOLUNTARY ARRANGEMENT INTO WINDING UP]

NOTES

Amendment

Inserted by SI 2002/1307, rr 3(1), 4(4).
Date in force: 31 May 2002: see SI 2002/1307, r 1.

[1.31 Application for conversion into winding up]

[[(1) Where a member State liquidator proposes to apply to the court for conversion of a voluntary arrangement into winding-up proceedings, a witness statement complying with Rule 1.32 must be prepared and filed in court in support of the application.

(1A) In this Rule, and in Rules 1.32 and 1.33, "conversion into winding-up proceedings" means an order under Article 37 of the EC Regulation (conversion of earlier proceedings) that the voluntary arrangement is converted into—

    (a)   administration proceedings whose purposes are limited to the winding up of the company through administration and are to exclude the purpose contained in paragraph 3(1)(a) of Schedule B1 to the Act;
    (b)   a creditors' voluntary winding up; or
    (c)   a winding up by the court.]

(2) An application under this Rule shall be by originating application.

(3) The application and the [witness statement] required under this Rule shall be served upon—

    (a)   the company; and
    (b)   the supervisor.]

NOTES

Amendment

Inserted by SI 2002/1307, rr 3(1), 4(4).
Date in force: 31 May 2002: see SI 2002/1307, r 1.
Paras (1), (1A): substituted, for para (1) as previously enacted, by SI 2010/686, r 2, Sch 1, para 21(1), (2).
Date in force: 6 April 2010: see SI 2010/686, r 1; for transitional provisions see r 6(1), Sch 4, para 1 thereto.
Para (3): words "witness statement" in square brackets substituted by SI 2010/686, r 2, Sch 1, para 21(1), (3).
Date in force: 6 April 2010: see SI 2010/686, r 1; for transitional provisions see r 6(1), Sch 4, paras 1, 2(1)(b), (2)–(4) thereto.

[1.32 Contents of [witness statement]]

[(1) The [witness statement] shall state—
  (a) that main proceedings have been opened in relation to the company in a member State other than the United Kingdom;
  (b) the [belief of the person making the statement] that the conversion of the voluntary arrangement into [winding-up proceedings] would prove to be in the interests of the creditors in the main proceedings;
  [(c) the opinion of the person making the statement as to whether the company ought to go into voluntary liquidation or be wound up by the court; and]
  (d) all other matters that, in the opinion of the member State liquidator, would assist the court—
    (i) in deciding whether to make such an order, and
    (ii) if the court were to do so, in considering the need for any consequential provision that would be necessary or desirable.
(2) [A witness statement] under this Rule shall be [made] by, or on behalf of, the member State liquidator.]

NOTES

Amendment

Inserted by SI 2002/1307, rr 3(1), 4(4).
Date in force: 31 May 2002: see SI 2002/1307, r 1.
Provision heading: words "witness statement" in square brackets substituted by SI 2010/686, r 2, Sch 1, para 22(1), (2).
Date in force: 6 April 2010: see SI 2010/686, r 1; for transitional provisions see r 6(1), Sch 4, paras 1, 2(1)(b), (2)–(4) thereto.
Para (1): words "witness statement" in square brackets substituted by SI 2010/686, r 2, Sch 1, para 22(1), (3)(a).
Date in force: 6 April 2010: see SI 2010/686, r 1; for transitional provisions see r 6(1), Sch 4, paras 1, 2(1)(b), (2)–(4) thereto.
Para (1): in sub-para (b) words "belief of the person making the statement" in square brackets substituted by SI 2010/686, r 2, Sch 1, para 22(1), (3)(b)(i).
Date in force: 6 April 2010: see SI 2010/686, r 1; for transitional provisions see r 6(1), Sch 4, paras 1, 2(1)(b), (2)–(4) thereto.
Para (1): in sub-para (b) words "winding-up proceedings" in square brackets substituted by SI 2010/686, r 2, Sch 1, para 22(1), (3)(b)(ii).
Date in force: 6 April 2010: see SI 2010/686, r 1; for transitional provisions see r 6(1), Sch 4, paras 1, 2(1)(b), (2)–(4) thereto.
Para (1): sub-para (c) substituted by SI 2010/686, r 2, Sch 1, para 22(1), (3)(c).
Date in force: 6 April 2010: see SI 2010/686, r 1; for transitional provisions see r 6(1), Sch 4, paras 1, 2(1)(b), (2)–(4) thereto.

Para (2): words "A witness statement" in square brackets substituted by SI 2010/686, r 2, Sch 1, para 22(1), (4)(a).
 Date in force: 6 April 2010: see SI 2010/686, r 1; for transitional provisions see r 6(1), Sch 4, paras 1, 2(1)(b), (2)–(4) thereto.
Para (2): word "made" in square brackets substituted by SI 2010/686, r 2, Sch 1, para 22(1), (4)(b).
 Date in force: 6 April 2010: see SI 2010/686, r 1; for transitional provisions see r 6(1), Sch 4, paras 1, 2(1)(b), (2)–(4) thereto.

[1.33 Power of court]

[(1) On hearing the application for conversion into [winding-up proceedings] the court may make such order as it thinks [just].

(2) If the court makes an order for conversion into [winding-up proceedings] the order may contain all such consequential provisions as the court deems necessary or desirable.

(3) Without prejudice to the generality of paragraph (1), an order under that paragraph may provide that the company be wound up as if a resolution for voluntary winding up under section 84 were passed on the day on which the order is made.

(4) Where the court makes an order for conversion into [winding-up proceedings] under paragraph (1), any expenses properly incurred as expenses of the administration of the voluntary arrangement in question shall be a first charge on the company's assets.]

NOTES

Amendment
 Inserted by SI 2002/1307, rr 3(1), 4(4).
  Date in force: 31 May 2002: see SI 2002/1307, r 1.
Para (1): words "winding-up proceedings" in square brackets substituted by SI 2010/686, r 2, Sch 1, para 23.
 Date in force: 6 April 2010: see SI 2010/686, r 1; for transitional provisions see r 6(1), Sch 4, para 1 thereto.
Para (1): word "just" in square brackets substituted by SI 2010/686, r 2, Sch 1, para 1.
 Date in force: 6 April 2010: see SI 2010/686, r 1; for transitional provisions see r 6(1), Sch 4, paras 1, 2(1)(b) thereto.
Para (2): words "winding-up proceedings" in square brackets substituted by SI 2010/686, r 2, Sch 1, para 23.
 Date in force: 6 April 2010: see SI 2010/686, r 1; for transitional provisions see r 6(1), Sch 4, para 1 thereto.
Para (4): words "winding-up proceedings" in square brackets substituted by SI 2010/686, r 2, Sch 1, para 23.
 Date in force: 6 April 2010: see SI 2010/686, r 1; for transitional provisions see r 6(1), Sch 4, para 1 thereto.

[CHAPTER 8

EC REGULATION—MEMBER STATE LIQUIDATOR]

NOTES

Amendment
 Inserted by SI 2002/1307, rr 3(1), 4(4).
  Date in force: 31 May 2002: see SI 2002/1307, r 1.

[1.34 Interpretation of creditor and notice to member State liquidator]

[(1) This Rule applies where a member State liquidator has been appointed in relation to the company.

(2) Where the supervisor is obliged to give notice to, or provide a copy of a document (including an order of court) to, the court, the registrar of companies or the official receiver, the supervisor shall give notice or provide copies, as appropriate, to the member State liquidator.

(3) Paragraph (2) is without prejudice to the generality of the obligations imposed by Article 31 of the EC Regulation (duty to cooperate and communicate information).]

NOTES

Amendment

Inserted by SI 2002/1307, rr 3(1), 4(4).
Date in force: 31 May 2002: see SI 2002/1307, r 1.

[CHAPTER 9

OBTAINING A MORATORIUM

NOTES

Amendment

Inserted by SI 2002/2712, r 3(1), Schedule, Pt 1, para 21.
Date in force: 1 January 2003: see SI 2002/2712, r 1(1); for effect see rr 1(2), 3(2) thereof.

[SECTION A: OBTAINING A MORATORIUM]

NOTES

Amendment

Inserted by SI 2002/2712, r 3(1), Schedule, Pt 1, para 21.
Date in force: 1 January 2003: see SI 2002/2712, r 1(1); for effect see rr 1(2), 3(2) thereof.

[1.35 Preparation of proposal by directors and submission to nominee]

[(1) The document containing the proposal referred to in paragraph 6(1)(a) of Schedule A1 to the Act shall—

(a) be prepared by the directors;
(b) comply with the requirements of paragraphs (1) and (2) of Rule 1.3 (save that the reference to preferential creditors shall be to preferential creditors within the meaning of paragraph 31(8) of Schedule A1 to the Act); and
(c) state the address to which notice of the consent of the nominee to act and the documents referred to in Rule 1.38 shall be sent.

(2) With the agreement in writing of the nominee, the directors may amend the proposal at any time before submission to them by the nominee of the statement required by paragraph 6(2) of Schedule A1 to the Act.]

NOTES

Amendment

Inserted by SI 2002/2712, r 3(1), Schedule, Pt 1, para 21.
Date in force: 1 January 2003: see SI 2002/2712, r 1(1); for effect see rr 1(2), 3(2) thereof.

[1.36 Delivery of documents to the intended nominee etc]

[(1) The documents required to be delivered to the nominee pursuant to paragraph 6(1) of Schedule A1 to the Act shall be delivered to the nominee himself or to a person authorised to take delivery of documents on his behalf.

(2) On receipt of the documents, the nominee shall [as soon as reasonably practicable] issue an acknowledgement of receipt of the documents to the directors which shall indicate the date on which the documents were received.]

NOTES

Amendment

Inserted by SI 2002/2712, r 3(1), Schedule, Pt 1, para 21.
    Date in force: 1 January 2003: see SI 2002/2712, r 1(1); for effect see rr 1(2), 3(2) thereof.
Para (2): words "as soon as reasonably practicable" in square brackets substituted by SI 2009/642, rr 4, 5.
    Date in force: 6 April 2009: see SI 2009/642, r 1; for transitional provisions see r 3 thereof.

[1.37 Statement of affairs]

[(1) The statement of the company's affairs required to be delivered to the nominee pursuant to paragraph 6(1)(b) of Schedule A1 to the Act shall be delivered to the nominee [at the same time as] the delivery to him of the document setting out the terms of the proposed voluntary arrangement . . ..

(2) The statement of affairs shall comprise the same particulars as required by Rule 1.5(2) (supplementing or amplifying, so far as is necessary for clarifying the state of the company's affairs, those already given in the directors' proposal).

(3) The statement of affairs shall be made up to a date not earlier than 2 weeks before the date of the delivery of the document containing the proposal for the voluntary arrangement to the nominee under Rule 1.36(1).
However, the nominee may allow an extension of that period to the nearest practicable date (not earlier than 2 months before the date of delivery of the documents referred to in Rule 1.36(1)) and if he does so, he shall give a statement of his reasons in writing to the directors.

[(4) The statement of affairs must be verified by a statement of truth made by at least one director.]]

NOTES

Amendment

Inserted by SI 2002/2712, r 3(1), Schedule, Pt 1, para 21.
    Date in force: 1 January 2003: see SI 2002/2712, r 1(1); for effect see rr 1(2), 3(2) thereof.
Para (1): words "at the same time as" in square brackets substituted by SI 2010/686, r 2, Sch 1, para 24(1), (2)(a).
    Date in force: 6 April 2010: see SI 2010/686, r 1; for transitional provisions see r 6(1), Sch 4, para 1 thereto.
Para (1): words omitted revoked by SI 2010/686, r 2, Sch 1, para 24(1), (2)(b).
    Date in force: 6 April 2010: see SI 2010/686, r 1; for transitional provisions see r 6(1), Sch 4, para 1 thereto.
Para (4): substituted by SI 2010/686, r 2, Sch 1, para 24(1), (3).
    Date in force: 6 April 2010: see SI 2010/686, r 1; for transitional provisions see r 6(1), Sch 4, para 1 thereto.

[1.38 The nominee's statement]

[(1) The nominee shall submit to the directors the statement required by paragraph 6(2) of Schedule A1 to the Act within 28 days of the submission to him of the document setting out the terms of the proposed voluntary arrangement.

(2) The statement shall have annexed to it—

(a) the nominee's comments on the proposal, unless the statement contains an opinion in the negative on any of the matters referred to in paragraph 6(2)(a) and (b) of Schedule A1 to the Act, in which case he shall instead give his reasons for that opinion, and

(b) where he is willing to act in relation to the proposed arrangement, a statement of his consent to act.]

NOTES

Amendment

Inserted by SI 2002/2712, r 3(1), Schedule, Pt 1, para 21.
Date in force: 1 January 2003: see SI 2002/2712, r 1(1); for effect see rr 1(2), 3(2) thereof.

[1.39 Documents submitted to the court to obtain moratorium]

[(1) Where pursuant to paragraph 7 of Schedule A1 to the Act the directors file the document and statements referred to in that paragraph in court, those documents shall be delivered together with 4 copies of a schedule listing them within 3 [business] days of the date of the submission to them of the nominee's statement under paragraph 6(2) of Schedule A1 to the Act.

(2) When the directors file the document and statements referred to in paragraph (1), they shall also file—

(a) a copy of any statement of reasons made by the nominee pursuant to Rule 1.37(3); and

(b) a copy of the nominee's comments on the proposal submitted to them pursuant to Rule 1.38(2).

(3) The copies of the schedule shall be endorsed by the court with the date on which the documents were filed in court and 3 copies of the schedule sealed by the court shall be returned by the court to the person who filed the documents in court.

(4) The statement of affairs required to be filed under paragraph 7(1)(b) of Schedule A1 to the Act shall comprise the same particulars as required by Rule 1.5(2).]

NOTES

Amendment

Inserted by SI 2002/2712, r 3(1), Schedule, Pt 1, para 21.
Date in force: 1 January 2003: see SI 2002/2712, r 1(1); for effect see rr 1(2), 3(2) thereof.
Para (1): word "business" in square brackets substituted by SI 2010/686, r 2, Sch 1, para 25.
Date in force: 6 April 2010: see SI 2010/686, r 1; for transitional provisions see r 6(1), Sch 4, para 1 thereto.

[1.40 Notice and advertisement of beginning of a moratorium]

[(1) After receiving the copies of the schedule endorsed by the court under Rule 1.39(3), the directors shall [as soon as reasonably practicable] serve 2 of them on the nominee and one on the company.

[(2) On receipt of the copies of the schedule pursuant to paragraph (1), the nominee—

(a) as soon as reasonably practicable shall cause a notice of the coming into force of the moratorium to be gazetted; and
(b) may advertise the notice in such other manner as the nominee thinks fit.]
[(2A) In addition to the standard contents, the notice under paragraph (2) must state—
(a) the nature of the business of the company;
(b) that a moratorium under section 1A has come into force; and
(c) the date upon which the moratorium came into force.]

(3) The nominee shall [as soon as reasonably practicable] notify the registrar of companies, the company and any petitioning creditor of the company of whose [address the nominee] is aware of the coming into force of the moratorium and such notification shall specify the date on which the moratorium came into force [and the court at which the documents to obtain the moratorium were filed].

(4) The nominee shall give notice of the coming into force of the moratorium specifying the date on which it came into force to—
(a) any [enforcement officer] or other officer who, to his knowledge, is charged with an execution or other legal process against the company or its property; and
(b) any person who, to his knowledge, has distrained against the company or its property.]

NOTES

Amendment

Inserted by SI 2002/2712, r 3(1), Schedule, Pt 1, para 21.
    Date in force: 1 January 2003: see SI 2002/2712, r 1(1); for effect see rr 1(2), 3(2) thereof.
Para (1): words "as soon as reasonably practicable" in square brackets substituted by SI 2009/642, rr 4, 5.
    Date in force: 6 April 2009: see SI 2009/642, r 1; for transitional provisions see r 3 thereof.
Para (2): substituted by SI 2009/642, rr 4, 6.
    Date in force: 6 April 2009: see SI 2009/642, r 1; for transitional provisions see r 3 thereof.
Para (2A): inserted by SI 2010/686, r 2, Sch 1, para 26(1), (2).
    Date in force: 6 April 2010: see SI 2010/686, r 1; for transitional provisions see r 6(1), Sch 4, para 1 thereto.
Para (3): words "as soon as reasonably practicable" in square brackets substituted by SI 2009/642, rr 4, 5.
    Date in force: 6 April 2009: see SI 2009/642, r 1; for transitional provisions see r 3 thereof.
Para (3): words "address the nominee" in square brackets substituted by SI 2010/686, r 2, Sch 1, para 26(1), (3)(a).
    Date in force: 6 April 2010: see SI 2010/686, r 1; for transitional provisions see r 6(1), Sch 4, para 1 thereto.
Para (3): words "and the court at which the documents to obtain the moratorium were filed" in square brackets inserted by SI 2010/686, r 2, Sch 1, para 26(1), (3)(b).
    Date in force: 6 April 2010: see SI 2010/686, r 1; for transitional provisions see r 6(1), Sch 4, para 1 thereto.
Para (4): in sub-para (a) words "enforcement officer" in square brackets substituted by SI 2005/527, r 4.
    Date in force: 1 April 2005: see SI 2005/527, r 1(2).

[1.41 Notice of extension of moratorium]

[(1) The nominee shall [as soon as reasonably practicable] notify the registrar of companies and the court of a decision taking effect pursuant to paragraph 36 of Schedule A1 to the Act to extend or further extend the moratorium and such notice shall specify the new expiry date of the moratorium.

(2) Where an order is made by the court extending or further extending or renewing or continuing a moratorium, the nominee shall [as soon as reasonably practicable] after receiving a copy of the same give notice to the registrar of companies and with the notice shall send [a copy] of the order.]

NOTES

Amendment

Inserted by SI 2002/2712, r 3(1), Schedule, Pt 1, para 21.
Date in force: 1 January 2003: see SI 2002/2712, r 1(1); for effect see rr 1(2), 3(2) thereof.
Para (1): words "as soon as reasonably practicable" in square brackets substituted by SI 2009/642, rr 4, 5.
Date in force: 6 April 2009: see SI 2009/642, r 1; for transitional provisions see r 3 thereof.
Para (2): words "as soon as reasonably practicable" in square brackets substituted by SI 2009/642, rr 4, 5.
Date in force: 6 April 2009: see SI 2009/642, r 1; for transitional provisions see r 3 thereof.
Para (2): words "a copy" in square brackets substituted by SI 2009/2472, rr 3, 6.
Date in force: 1 October 2009: see SI 2009/2472, r 1; for transitional provisions see r 2 thereof.

[1.42 Notice and advertisement of end of moratorium]
[[(1) After the moratorium comes to an end, the nominee—
  (a) as soon as reasonably practicable shall cause a notice of its coming to an end and the date on which it came to an end to be gazetted; and
  (b) may advertise the notice in such other manner as the nominee thinks fit.]
[(1A) In addition to the standard contents, the notice under paragraph (1) must state—
  (a) the nature of the business of the company;
  (b) that a moratorium under section 1A has come to an end; and
  (c) the date upon which the moratorium came to an end.]
(2) The nominee shall [as soon as reasonably practicable] give notice of the ending of the moratorium to the registrar of companies, the court, the company and any creditor of the company of whose [address the nominee] is aware and such notice shall specify the date on which the moratorium came to an end.]

NOTES

Amendment

Inserted by SI 2002/2712, r 3(1), Schedule, Pt 1, para 21.
Date in force: 1 January 2003: see SI 2002/2712, r 1(1); for effect see rr 1(2), 3(2) thereof.
Para (1): substituted by SI 2009/642, rr 4, 7.
Date in force: 6 April 2009: see SI 2009/642, r 1; for transitional provisions see r 3 thereof.
Para (1A): inserted by SI 2010/686, r 2, Sch 1, para 27(1), (2).
Date in force: 6 April 2010: see SI 2010/686, r 1; for transitional provisions see r 6(1), Sch 4, para 1 thereto.
Para (2): words "as soon as reasonably practicable" in square brackets substituted by SI 2009/642, rr 4, 5.
Date in force: 6 April 2009: see SI 2009/642, r 1; for transitional provisions see r 3 thereof.
Para (2): words "address the nominee" in square brackets substituted by SI 2010/686, r 2, Sch 1, para 27(1), (3).

Date in force: 6 April 2010: see SI 2010/686, r 1; for transitional provisions see r 6(1), Sch 4, para 1 thereto.

[SECTION B: PROCEEDINGS DURING A MORATORIUM]

NOTES

Amendment

Inserted by SI 2002/2712, r 3(1), Schedule, Pt 1, para 21.
Date in force: 1 January 2003: see SI 2002/2712, r 1(1); for effect see rr 1(2), 3(2) thereof.

[1.43 Disposal of charged property etc during a moratorium]

[(1) This Rule applies in any case where the company makes an application to the court under paragraph 20 of Schedule A1 to the Act for [permission] to dispose of property of the company which is subject to a security, or goods in possession of the company under an agreement to which that paragraph relates.

(2) The court shall fix a venue for the hearing of the application and the company shall [as soon as reasonably practicable] give notice of the venue to the person who is the holder of the security or, as the case may be, the owner under the agreement.

(3) If an order is made, the company shall [as soon as reasonably practicable] give notice of it to that person or owner.

(4) The court shall send 2 sealed copies of the order to the company, who shall send one of them to that person or owner.]

NOTES

Amendment

Inserted by SI 2002/2712, r 3(1), Schedule, Pt 1, para 21.
Date in force: 1 January 2003: see SI 2002/2712, r 1(1); for effect see rr 1(2), 3(2) thereof.
Para (1): word "permission" in square brackets substituted by SI 2010/686, r 2, Sch 1, para 1.
Date in force: 6 April 2010: see SI 2010/686, r 1; for transitional provisions see r 6(1), Sch 4, paras 1, 2(1)(b) thereto.
Para (2): words "as soon as reasonably practicable" in square brackets substituted by SI 2009/642, rr 4, 5.
Date in force: 6 April 2009: see SI 2009/642, r 1; for transitional provisions see r 3 thereof.
Para (3): word "as soon as reasonably practicable" in square brackets substituted by SI 2009/642, rr 4, 5.
Date in force: 6 April 2009: see SI 2009/642, r 1; for transitional provisions see r 3 thereof.

[SECTION C: NOMINEES]

NOTES

Amendment

Inserted by SI 2002/2712, r 3(1), Schedule, Pt 1, para 21.
Date in force: 1 January 2003: see SI 2002/2712, r 1(1); for effect see rr 1(2), 3(2) thereof.

[1.44 Withdrawal of nominee's consent to act]

[Where the nominee withdraws his consent to act he shall, pursuant to paragraph 25(5) of Schedule A1 to the Act, [as soon as reasonably practicable] give notice of his withdrawal and the reason for withdrawing his consent to act to—

(a)   the registrar of companies;
(b)   the court;
(c)   the company; and
(d)   any creditor of the company of whose claim [and address the nominee] is aware.]

NOTES

Amendment

Inserted by SI 2002/2712, r 3(1), Schedule, Pt 1, para 21.
   Date in force: 1 January 2003: see SI 2002/2712, r 1(1); for effect see rr 1(2), 3(2) thereof.
Words "as soon as reasonably practicable" in square brackets substituted by SI 2009/642, rr 4, 5.
   Date in force: 6 April 2009: see SI 2009/642, r 1; for transitional provisions see r 3 thereof.
In para (d) word "and address the nominee" in square brackets substituted by SI 2010/686, r 2, Sch 1, para 28.
   Date in force: 6 April 2010: see SI 2010/686, r 1; for transitional provisions see r 6(1), Sch 4, para 1 thereto.

[1.45 Replacement of nominee by the court]

[(1) Where the directors intend to make an application to the court under paragraph 28 of Schedule A1 to the Act for the nominee to be replaced, they shall give to the nominee at least [5 business] days' notice of their application.

(2) Where the nominee intends to make an application to the court under that paragraph to be replaced, he shall give to the directors at least [5 business] days' notice of his application.

(3) No appointment of a replacement nominee shall be made by the court unless there is filed in court a statement by the replacement nominee indicating [that the replacement nominee—

(a)   consents to act; and
(b)   is qualified to act as an insolvency practitioner in relation to the company or is an authorised person in relation to the company].]

NOTES

Amendment

Inserted by SI 2002/2712, r 3(1), Schedule, Pt 1, para 21.
   Date in force: 1 January 2003: see SI 2002/2712, r 1(1); for effect see rr 1(2), 3(2) thereof.
Para (1): words "5 business" in square brackets substituted by SI 2010/686, r 2, Sch 1, para 29(1), (2).
   Date in force: 6 April 2010: see SI 2010/686, r 1; for transitional provisions see r 6(1), Sch 4, para 1 thereto.
Para (2): words "5 business" in square brackets substituted by SI 2010/686, r 2, Sch 1, para 29(1), (2).
   Date in force: 6 April 2010: see SI 2010/686, r 1; for transitional provisions see r 6(1), Sch 4, para 1 thereto.
Para (3): words from "that the replacement nominee—" to "to the company" in square brackets substituted by SI 2010/686, r 2, Sch 1, para 29(1), (3).

Date in force: 6 April 2010: see SI 2010/686, r 1; for transitional provisions see r 6(1), Sch 4, para 1 thereto.

[1.46 Notification of appointment of a replacement nominee]
[Where a person is appointed as a replacement nominee, he shall [as soon as reasonably practicable] give notice of his appointment to—
(a) the registrar of companies;
(b) the court (in any case where he was not appointed by the court); and
(c) the person whom he has replaced as nominee.]

NOTES

Amendment
Inserted by SI 2002/2712, r 3(1), Schedule, Pt 1, para 21.
Date in force: 1 January 2003: see SI 2002/2712, r 1(1); for effect see rr 1(2), 3(2) thereof.
Words "as soon as reasonably practicable" in square brackets substituted by SI 2009/642, rr 4, 5.
Date in force: 6 April 2009: see SI 2009/642, r 1; for transitional provisions see r 3 thereof.

[1.47 Applications to court under paragraphs 26 or 27 of Schedule A1 to the Act]
[Where any person intends to make an application to the court pursuant to paragraph 26 or 27 of Schedule A1 to the Act, he shall give to the nominee at least [5 business] days' notice of his application.]

NOTES

Amendment
Inserted by SI 2002/2712, r 3(1), Schedule, Pt 1, para 21.
Date in force: 1 January 2003: see SI 2002/2712, r 1(1); for effect see rr 1(2), 3(2) thereof.
Words "5 business" in square brackets substituted by SI 2010/686, r 2, Sch 1, para 30.
Date in force: 6 April 2010: see SI 2010/686, r 1; for transitional provisions see r 6(1), Sch 4, para 1 thereto.

[SECTION D: CONSIDERATION OF PROPOSALS WHERE MORATORIUM OBTAINED]

NOTES

Amendment
Inserted by SI 2002/2712, r 3(1), Schedule, Pt 1, para 21.
Date in force: 1 January 2003: see SI 2002/2712, r 1(1); for effect see rr 1(2), 3(2) thereof.

[1.48 Summoning of meetings; procedure at meetings etc]
[(1) Where the nominee summons meetings of creditors and the company pursuant to paragraph 29(1) of Schedule A1 to the Act, each of those meetings shall be summoned for a date that is not more than 28 days from the date on which the moratorium came into force.

(2) Notices calling the creditors' meetings shall be sent by the nominee to all creditors specified in the statement of affairs and any other creditors of the company of whose address he is aware at least 14 days before the day fixed for the meeting.

(3) Notices calling the company meeting shall be sent by the nominee to all persons who are, to the best of the nominee's belief, members of the company at least 14 days before the day fixed for the meeting.

[(4) Each notice sent under this Rule must—
- (a) specify—
  - (i) the court in which the documents relating to the obtaining of the moratorium were filed and
  - (ii) the court reference; and
- (b) state the effect of paragraphs (2) to (4) of Rule 1.52 (requisite majorities (creditors)).

(4A) With each notice there must be sent—
- (a) a copy of the directors' proposal;
- (b) a copy of the statement of affairs or, if the nominee thinks fit, a summary of it (the summary to include a list of creditors and the amount of their debts); and
- (c) the nominee's comments on the proposal.]

(5) The provisions of Rules 1.13 to 1.16 shall apply.]

NOTES

Amendment

Inserted by SI 2002/2712, r 3(1), Schedule, Pt 1, para 21.
Date in force: 1 January 2003: see SI 2002/2712, r 1(1); for effect see rr 1(2), 3(2) thereof.
Paras (4), (4A): substituted, for para (4) as originally enacted, by SI 2010/686, r 2, Sch 1, para 31.
Date in force: 6 April 2010: see SI 2010/686, r 1; for transitional provisions see r 6(1), Sch 4, para 1 thereto.

[1.49 Entitlement to vote (creditors)]

[(1) Subject as follows, every creditor who has notice of the creditors' meeting is entitled to vote at the meeting or any adjournment of it.

(2) Votes are calculated according to the amount of the creditor's debt as at the beginning of the moratorium, after deducting any amounts paid in respect of that debt after that date.

(3) A creditor may vote in respect of a debt for an unliquidated amount or any debt whose value is not ascertained and for the purposes of voting (but not otherwise) his debt shall be valued at £1 unless the chairman agrees to put a higher value on it.]

NOTES

Amendment

Inserted by SI 2002/2712, r 3(1), Schedule, Pt 1, para 21.
Date in force: 1 January 2003: see SI 2002/2712, r 1(1); for effect see rr 1(2), 3(2) thereof.

[1.50 Procedure for admission of creditors' claims for voting purposes]

[(1) Subject as follows, at any creditors' meeting the chairman shall ascertain the entitlement of persons wishing to vote and shall admit or reject their claims accordingly.

(2) The chairman may admit or reject a claim in whole or in part.

(3) The chairman's decision on any matter under this Rule or under paragraph (3) of Rule 1.49 is subject to appeal to the court by any creditor or member of the company.

(4) If the chairman is in doubt whether a claim should be admitted or rejected, he shall mark it as objected to and allow votes to be cast in respect of it, subject to such votes being subsequently declared invalid if the objection to the claim is sustained.

(5) If on an appeal the chairman's decision is reversed or varied, or votes are declared invalid, the court may order another meeting to be summoned, or make such order as it thinks just.

The court's power to make an order under this paragraph is exercisable only if it considers that the circumstances giving rise to the appeal are such as give rise to unfair prejudice or material irregularity.

(6) An application to the court by way of appeal against the chairman's decision shall not be made after the end of the period of 28 days beginning with the first day on which the report required by paragraph 30(3) of Schedule A1 to the Act has been made to the court.

(7) The chairman is not personally liable for any costs incurred by any person in respect of an appeal under this Rule.]

NOTES

Amendment

Inserted by SI 2002/2712, r 3(1), Schedule, Pt 1, para 21.
Date in force: 1 January 2003: see SI 2002/2712, r 1(1); for effect see rr 1(2), 3(2) thereof.

[1.51 Voting rights (members)]
[Rule 1.18 shall apply.]

NOTES

Amendment

Inserted by SI 2002/2712, r 3(1), Schedule, Pt 1, para 21.
Date in force: 1 January 2003: see SI 2002/2712, r 1(1); for effect see rr 1(2), 3(2) thereof.

[1.52 Requisite majorities (creditors)]

[[(1) Subject to paragraph (2), at the creditors' meeting, a resolution is passed when a majority (in value) of those present and voting in person or by proxy have voted in favour of it.

(2) A resolution to approve the proposal or a modification is passed when a majority of three-quarters or more (in value) of those present and voting in person or by proxy have voted in favour of it.]

(3) At a meeting of the creditors for any resolution to pass extending (or further extending) a moratorium, or to bring a moratorium to an end before the end of the period of any extension, there must be a majority in excess of three quarters in value of the creditors present in person or by proxy and voting on the resolution. For this purpose paragraph (4)(b) below shall not apply and a secured creditor is entitled to vote in respect of the amount of his claim without deducting the value of his security.

(4) In the following cases there is to be left out of account a creditor's vote in respect of any claim or part of a claim—

(a) where written notice of the claim was not given, either at the meeting or before it, to the chairman or [nominee];

(b) where the claim or part is secured;

(c) where the claim is in respect of a debt wholly or partly on, or secured by, a current bill of exchange or promissory note, unless the creditor is willing—

(i) to treat the liability to him on the bill or note of every person who is liable on it antecedently to the company, and against whom a bankruptcy order has not been made (or, in the case of a company, which has not gone into liquidation), as a security in his hands, and

(ii) to estimate the value of the security and (for the purpose of entitlement to vote, but not of any distribution under the arrangement) to deduct it from his claim.

(5) Any resolution is invalid if those voting against it include more than half in value of the creditors, counting in these latter only those—

(a) who have notice of the meeting;
(b) whose votes are not to be left out of account under paragraph (4); and
(c) who are not, to the best of the chairman's belief, persons connected with the company.

(6) It is for the chairman of the meeting to decide whether under this Rule—

(a) a vote is to be left out of account in accordance with paragraph [(4)], or
(b) a person is a connected person for the purposes of paragraph (5)(c);

and in relation to the second of these two cases the chairman is entitled to rely on the information provided by the statement of the company's affairs or otherwise in accordance with this Part of the Rules.

(7) If the chairman uses a proxy contrary to Rule 1.15 as it applies by virtue of Rule [1.48(5)], his vote with that proxy does not count towards any majority under this Rule.

(8) The chairman's decision on any matter under this Rule is subject to appeal to the court by any creditor or member and paragraphs (5) to (7) of Rule 1.50 apply as regards such an appeal.]

NOTES

Amendment

Inserted by SI 2002/2712, r 3(1), Schedule, Pt 1, para 21.
Date in force: 1 January 2003: see SI 2002/2712, r 1(1); for effect see rr 1(2), 3(2) thereof.
Paras (1), (2): substituted by SI 2010/686, r 2, Sch 1, para 32(1), (2).
Date in force: 6 April 2010: see SI 2010/686, r 1; for transitional provisions see r 6(1), Sch 4, para 1 thereto.
Para (4): in sub-para (a) word "nominee" in square brackets substituted by SI 2010/686, r 2, Sch 1, para 32(1), (3).
Date in force: 6 April 2010: see SI 2010/686, r 1; for transitional provisions see r 6(1), Sch 4, para 1 thereto.
Para (6): in sub-para (a) reference to "(4)" in square brackets substituted by SI 2003/1730, r 4, Sch 1, Pt 1, para 8(a).
Date in force: 15 September 2003: see SI 2003/1730, r 1(2).
Para (7): reference to "1.48(5)" in square brackets substituted by SI 2003/1730, r 4, Sch 1, Pt 1, para 8(b).
Date in force: 15 September 2003: see SI 2003/1730, r 1(2).

[1.53 Requisite majorities (members) and proceedings to obtain agreement on the proposal]

[(1) Rule 1.20 shall apply.

(2) If the chairman thinks fit, the creditors' meeting and the company meeting may be held together.

(3) The chairman may, and shall if it is so resolved at the meeting in question, adjourn that meeting, but any adjournment shall not be to a day which is more than 14 days after the date on which the moratorium (including any extension) ends.

(4) If the meetings are adjourned under paragraph (3), notice of the fact shall be given by the nominee [as soon as reasonably practicable] to the court.

[(4A) Once only in the course of a meeting the chairman may, without an adjournment, declare it suspended for any period up to 1 hour.]

(5) If following the final adjournment of the creditors' meeting the proposal (with or without modifications) has not been approved by the creditors, it is deemed rejected.]

NOTES

Amendment

Inserted by SI 2002/2712, r 3(1), Schedule, Pt 1, para 21.
Date in force: 1 January 2003: see SI 2002/2712, r 1(1); for effect see rr 1(2), 3(2) thereof.
Para (4): words "as soon as reasonably practicable" in square brackets substituted by SI 2009/642, rr 4, 5.
Date in force: 6 April 2009: see SI 2009/642, r 1; for transitional provisions see r 3 thereof.
Para (4A): inserted by SI 2010/686, r 2, Sch 1, para 33.
Date in force: 6 April 2010: see SI 2010/686, r 1; for transitional provisions see r 6(1), Sch 4, para 1 thereto.

[1.54 Implementation of the arrangement]

[(1) Where a decision approving the arrangement has effect under paragraph 36 of Schedule A1 to the Act, the directors shall [as soon as reasonably practicable] do all that is required for putting the supervisor into possession of the assets included in the arrangement.

(2) Subject to paragraph (3), Rules 1.22, 1.22A and 1.24 to 1.29 apply.

(3) The provisions referred to in paragraph (2) are modified as follows—

(a) in paragraph (1) of Rule 1.22A the reference to section 4A(6) is to be read as a reference to paragraph 36(5) of Schedule A1 to the Act;

(b) in paragraph (4) of Rule 1.24 the reference to section 4(6) is to be read as a reference to paragraph 30(3) of Schedule A1 to the Act;

(c) in paragraph (5) of Rule 1.24 the reference to section 4A is to be read as a reference to paragraph 36 of Schedule A1 to the Act;

(d) in paragraph (1) of Rule 1.25 the reference to section 6 is to be read as a reference to paragraph 38 of Schedule A1 to the Act and the references in paragraphs (2) and (4) to the administrator or liquidator shall be ignored;

(e) in paragraph (3) of Rule 1.25 the reference to section 6(4)(b) is to be read as a reference to paragraph 38 (4)(b) of Schedule A1 to the Act; and

(f) in sub-paragraph (a) of paragraph (1) of Rule 1.28 the reference to section 4A is to be read as a reference to paragraph 36 of Schedule A1 to the Act.]

NOTES

Amendment

Inserted by SI 2002/2712, r 3(1), Schedule, Pt 1, para 21.
Date in force: 1 January 2003: see SI 2002/2712, r 1(1); for effect see rr 1(2), 3(2) thereof.
Para (1): words "as soon as reasonably practicable" in square brackets substituted by SI 2009/642, rr 4, 5.
Date in force: 6 April 2009: see SI 2009/642, r 1; for transitional provisions see r 3 thereof.

[CHAPTER 10

TIME RECORDING INFORMATION]

NOTES

Amendment

Inserted by SI 2010/686, r 2, Sch 1, para 34.
Date in force: 6 April 2010: see SI 2010/686, r 1; for transitional provisions see r 6(1), Sch 4, para 1 thereto.

[1.55 Provision by nominee or supervisor of information about time spent on a proposal or voluntary arrangement]

[(1) Subject as set out in this Rule, a person ("the relevant person") who has acted or is acting as—

(a) a nominee in respect of a proposed voluntary arrangement; or

(b) a supervisor in respect of a voluntary arrangement

must, on request in writing by any person mentioned in paragraph (2), supply free of charge to that person a statement of the kind described in paragraph (3).

(2) The persons referred to in paragraph (1) are—

(a) any director of the company;

(b) where the proposal has been approved, any creditor or member of the company in respect of the arrangement.

(3) The statement referred to in paragraph (1)—

(a) must cover the period beginning with the date of the appointment of the relevant person as nominee or supervisor, as the case may be, and ending—

(i) with the date next before the date of making the request on which the relevant person has completed any period as nominee or supervisor, or both, which is a multiple of 6 months or,

(ii) where the relevant person has ceased to act as nominee or supervisor, the date upon which the person so ceased; and

(b) must comprise the following details—

(i) the total number of hours spent on the voluntary arrangement by the relevant person whether as nominee or supervisor, or both, and any staff assigned to the voluntary arrangement during that period;

(ii) for each grade of individual so engaged, the average hourly rate at which any work carried out by individuals in that grade is charged; and

(iii) the number of hours spent by each grade of staff during that period.

(4) No request pursuant to this Rule may be made where more than 2 years has elapsed since the relevant person ceased to act in any capacity in relation to the proposal or any voluntary arrangement arising out of the approval of the proposal.

(5) Any statement required to be provided to any person under this Rule must be supplied within 28 days of the date of the receipt of the request by the person required to supply it.]

NOTES

Amendment

Inserted by SI 2010/686, r 2, Sch 1, para 34.

Date in force: 6 April 2010: see SI 2010/686, r 1; for transitional provisions see r 6(1), Sch 4, para 1 thereto.

[CHAPTER 11
OMISSION OF INFORMATION FROM STATEMENT OF AFFAIRS]

NOTES

Amendment

Inserted by SI 2010/686, r 2, Sch 1, para 34.
Date in force: 6 April 2010: see SI 2010/686, r 1; for transitional provisions see r 6(1), Sch 4, para 1 thereto.

[1.56 Omission of Information from Statement of Affairs]
[The court, on the application of the nominee, the directors or any person appearing to it to have an interest, may direct that specified information may be omitted from any statement of affairs required to be sent to the creditors where the disclosure of such information would be likely to prejudice the conduct of the voluntary arrangement or might reasonably be expected to lead to violence against any person.]

NOTES

Amendment

Inserted by SI 2010/686, r 2, Sch 1, para 34.
Date in force: 6 April 2010: see SI 2010/686, r 1; for transitional provisions see r 6(1), Sch 4, para 1 thereto.

[PART 2
ADMINISTRATION PROCEDURE]

NOTES

Amendment

Substituted by SI 2003/1730, r 5(1), Sch 1, Pt 2, para 9.
Date in force: 15 September 2003: see SI 2003/1730, r 1(2); for effect and the continuing operation of this Part where a provision made by or under any enactment preserves the Insolvency Act 1986, old Pt II after that date see r 5(2)–(4) thereof.

[CHAPTER 1
PRELIMINARY]

NOTES

Amendment

Substituted by SI 2003/1730, r 5(1), Sch 1, Pt 2, para 9.
Date in force: 15 September 2003: see SI 2003/1730, r 1(2); for effect and the continuing operation of this Part where a provision made by or under any enactment preserves the Insolvency Act 1986, old Pt II after that date see r 5(2)–(4) thereof.

[2.1 Introductory and interpretation]
[(1) In this Part—

(a) Chapter 2 applies in relation to the appointment of an administrator by the court;
(b) Chapter 3 applies in relation to the appointment of an administrator by the holder of a qualifying floating charge under paragraph 14;
(c) Chapter 4 applies in relation to the appointment of an administrator by the company or the directors under paragraph 22;
(d) The following Chapters apply in all the cases mentioned in sub-paragraphs (a)-(c) above:
—Chapter 5: Process of administration;
—Chapter 6: Meetings and reports;
—Chapter 7: The creditors' committee;
—Chapter 8: Disposal of charged property;
—Chapter 9: Expenses of the administration;
—Chapter 10: Distributions to creditors;
—Chapter 11: The administrator;
—Chapter 12: Ending administration;
—Chapter 13: Replacing administrator;
—Chapter 14: EC Regulation—conversion of administration into winding up;
—Chapter 15: EC Regulation—member State liquidator.

(2) In this Part of these Rules a reference to a numbered paragraph shall, unless otherwise stated, be to the paragraph so numbered in Schedule B1 to the Act.]

NOTES

Amendment

Substituted, together with rr 2.2–2.133, for rr 2.1–2.6, 2.6A (inserted by SI 1987/1919, reg 3(1), Schedule, Pt 1, para 7), 2.7–2.46, 2.46A (inserted by SI 1987/1919, reg 3(1), Schedule, Pt 1, para 19), 2.47–2.58, 2.59–2.62 (inserted by SI 2002/1307, rr 3(1), 5(8)), by SI 2003/1730, r 5(1), Sch 1, Pt 2, para 9.
Date in force: 15 September 2003: see SI 2003/1730, r 1(2); for effect and the continuing operation of this Part where a provision made by or under any enactment preserves the Insolvency Act 1986, old Pt II after that date see r 5(2)–(4) thereof.

[CHAPTER 2

APPOINTMENT OF ADMINISTRATOR BY COURT]

NOTES

Amendment

Substituted by SI 2003/1730, r 5(1), Sch 1, Pt 2, para 9.
Date in force: 15 September 2003: see SI 2003/1730, r 1(2); for effect and the continuing operation of this Part where a provision made by or under any enactment preserves the Insolvency Act 1986, old Pt II after that date see r 5(2)–(4) thereof.

[2.2 [Witness statement] in support of administration application]

[(1) Where it is proposed to apply to the court for an administration order to be made in relation to a company, the administration application shall be in Form 2.1B and [a witness statement] complying with Rule 2.4 must be prepared . . . with a view to its being filed with the court in support of the application.

(2) If the administration application is to be made by the company or by the directors, the [witness statement] shall be made by one of the directors, or the secretary

of the company, stating himself to make it on behalf of the company or, as the case may be, on behalf of the directors.

(3) If the application is to be made by creditors, the [witness statement] shall be made by a person acting under the authority of them all, whether or not himself one of their number. In any case there must be stated in the [witness statement] the nature of his authority and the means of his knowledge of the matters to which the [witness statement] relates.

(4) If the application is to be made by the supervisor of a voluntary arrangement under Part I of the Act, it is to be treated as if it were an application by the company.]

NOTES

Amendment

Substituted, together with rr 2.1, 2.3–2.133, for rr 2.1–2.6, 2.6A (inserted by SI 1987/1919, reg 3(1), Schedule, Pt 1, para 7), 2.7–2.46, 2.46A (inserted by SI 1987/1919, reg 3(1), Schedule, Pt 1, para 19), 2.47–2.58, 2.59–2.62 (inserted by SI 2002/1307, rr 3(1), 5(8)), by SI 2003/1730, r 5(1), Sch 1, Pt 2, para 9.
Date in force: 15 September 2003: see SI 2003/1730, r 1(2); for effect and the continuing operation of this Part where a provision made by or under any enactment preserves the Insolvency Act 1986, old Pt II after that date see r 5(2)–(4) thereof.
Provision heading: words "Witness statement" in square brackets substituted by SI 2010/686, r 2, Sch 1, para 35(1), (2).
Date in force: 6 April 2010: see SI 2010/686, r 1; for transitional provisions see r 6(1), Sch 4, paras 1, 2(1)(b), (2)–(4) thereto.
Para (1): words "a witness statement" in square brackets substituted by SI 2010/686, r 2, Sch 1, para 35(1), (3)(a).
Date in force: 6 April 2010: see SI 2010/686, r 1; for transitional provisions see r 6(1), Sch 4, paras 1, 2(1)(b), (2)–(4) thereto.
Para (1): words omitted revoked by SI 2010/686, r 2, Sch 1, para 35(1), (3)(b).
Date in force: 6 April 2010: see SI 2010/686, r 1; for transitional provisions see r 6(1), Sch 4, paras 1, 2(1)(b), (2)–(4) thereto.
Para (2): words "witness statement" in square brackets substituted by SI 2010/686, r 2, Sch 1, para 35(1), (4).
Date in force: 6 April 2010: see SI 2010/686, r 1; for transitional provisions see r 6(1), Sch 4, paras 1, 2(1)(b), (2)–(4) thereto.
Para (3): words "witness statement" in square brackets in each place they occur substituted by SI 2010/686, r 2, Sch 1, para 35(1), (4).
Date in force: 6 April 2010: see SI 2010/686, r 1; for transitional provisions see r 6(1), Sch 4, paras 1, 2(1)(b), (2)–(4) thereto.

[2.3 Form of application]

[(1) If made by the company or by the directors, the application shall state the name of the company and its address for service, which (in the absence of special reasons to the contrary) is that of the company's registered office.

(2) If the application is made by the directors, it shall state that it is so made under paragraph 12(1)(b); but from and after making it is to be treated for all purposes as the application of the company.

(3) If made by a single creditor, the application shall state his name and address for service.

(4) If the application is made by two or more creditors, it shall state that it is so made (naming them); but from and after making it is to be treated for all purposes as the application of only one of them, named in the application as applying on behalf of himself and other creditors. An address for service for that one shall be specified.

(5) There shall be attached to the application a written statement which shall be in Form 2.2B by each of the persons proposed to be administrator stating—
    (a)   that he consents to accept appointment;
    (b)   details of any prior professional relationship(s) that he has had with the company to which he is to be appointed as administrator; and

(c) his opinion that it is reasonably likely that the purpose of administration will be achieved.]

NOTES

Amendment

Substituted, together with rr 2.1, 2.2, 2.4–2.133, for rr 2.1–2.6, 2.6A (inserted by SI 1987/1919, reg 3(1), Schedule, Pt 1, para 7), 2.7–2.46, 2.46A (inserted by SI 1987/1919, reg 3(1), Schedule, Pt 1, para 19), 2.47–2.58, 2.59–2.62 (inserted by SI 2002/1307, rr 3(1), 5(8)), by SI 2003/1730, r 5(1), Sch 1, Pt 2, para 9.

Date in force: 15 September 2003: see SI 2003/1730, r 1(2); for effect and the continuing operation of this Part where a provision made by or under any enactment preserves the Insolvency Act 1986, old Pt II after that date see r 5(2)–(4) thereof.

[2.4 Contents of application and [witness statement] in support]

[(1) The administration application shall contain a statement of the applicant's belief that the company is, or is likely to become, unable to pay its debts, except where the applicant is the holder of a qualifying floating charge and is making the application in reliance on paragraph 35.

(2) There shall be attached to the application [a witness statement] in support which shall contain—

- (a) a statement of the company's financial position, specifying (to the best of the applicant's knowledge and belief) the company's assets and liabilities, including contingent and prospective liabilities;
- (b) details of any security known or believed to be held by creditors of the company, and whether in any case the security is such as to confer power on the holder to appoint an administrative receiver or to appoint an administrator under paragraph 14. If an administrative receiver has been appointed, that fact shall be stated;
- (c) details of any insolvency proceedings in relation to the company including any petition that has been presented for the winding up of the company so far as within the immediate knowledge of the applicant;
- (d) where it is intended to appoint a number of persons as administrators, details of the matters set out in paragraph 100(2) regarding the exercise of the function of the administrators; and
- (e) any other matters which, in the opinion of those intending to make the application for an administration order, will assist the court in deciding whether to make such an order, so far as lying within the knowledge or belief of the applicant.

(3) Where the application is made by the holder of a qualifying floating charge in reliance on paragraph 35, he shall give sufficient details in the [witness statement] in support to satisfy the court that he is entitled to appoint an administrator under paragraph 14.

(4) The [witness statement] shall state whether, in the opinion of the person making the application, (i) the EC Regulation will apply and (ii) if so, whether the proceedings will be main proceedings[, secondary proceedings] or territorial proceedings.]

NOTES

Amendment

Substituted, together with rr 2.1–2.3, 2.5–2.133, for rr 2.1–2.6, 2.6A (inserted by SI 1987/1919, reg 3(1), Schedule, Pt 1, para 7), 2.7–2.46, 2.46A (inserted by SI 1987/1919, reg 3(1), Schedule, Pt 1, para 19), 2.47–2.58, 2.59–2.62 (inserted by SI 2002/1307, rr 3(1), 5(8)), by SI 2003/1730, r 5(1), Sch 1, Pt 2, para 9.

Date in force: 15 September 2003: see SI 2003/1730, r 1(2); for effect and the continuing operation of this Part where a provision made by or under any enactment preserves the Insolvency Act 1986, old Pt II after that date see r 5(2)–(4) thereof.
Provision heading: words "witness statement" in square brackets substituted by SI 2010/686, r 2, Sch 1, para 36(1), (2).
Date in force: 6 April 2010: see SI 2010/686, r 1; for transitional provisions see r 6(1), Sch 4, paras 1, 2(1)(b), (2)–(4) thereto.
Para (2): words "a witness statement" in square brackets substituted by SI 2010/686, r 2, Sch 1, para 36(1), (3).
Date in force: 6 April 2010: see SI 2010/686, r 1; for transitional provisions see r 6(1), Sch 4, paras 1, 2(1)(b), (2)–(4) thereto.
Para (3): words "witness statement" in square brackets substituted by SI 2010/686, r 2, Sch 1, para 36(1), (4).
Date in force: 6 April 2010: see SI 2010/686, r 1; for transitional provisions see r 6(1), Sch 4, paras 1, 2(1)(b), (2)–(4) thereto.
Para (4): words "witness statement" in square brackets substituted by SI 2010/686, r 2, Sch 1, para 36(1), (4).
Date in force: 6 April 2010: see SI 2010/686, r 1; for transitional provisions see r 6(1), Sch 4, paras 1, 2(1)(b), (2)–(4) thereto.
Para (4): words ", secondary proceedings" in square brackets inserted by SI 2010/686, r 2, Sch 1, para 36(1), (5).
Date in force: 6 April 2010: see SI 2010/686, r 1; for transitional provisions see r 6(1), Sch 4, para 1 thereto.

[2.5 Filing of application]

[(1) The application (and all supporting documents) shall be filed with the court, with a sufficient number of copies for service and use as provided by Rule 2.6.

(2) Each of the copies filed shall have applied to it the seal of the court and be issued to the applicant; and on each copy there shall be endorsed the date and time of filing.

(3) The court shall fix a venue for the hearing of the application and this also shall be endorsed on each copy of the application issued under paragraph (2).

(4) After the application is filed, it is the duty of the applicant to notify the court in writing of the existence of any insolvency proceedings, and any insolvency proceedings under the EC Regulation, in relation to the company, as soon as he becomes aware of them.]

NOTES

Amendment

Substituted, together with rr 2.1–2.4, 2.6–2.133, for rr 2.1–2.6, 2.6A (inserted by SI 1987/1919, reg 3(1), Schedule, Pt 1, para 7), 2.7–2.46, 2.46A (inserted by SI 1987/1919, reg 3(1), Schedule, Pt 1, para 19), 2.47–2.58, 2.59–2.62 (inserted by SI 2002/1307, rr 3(1), 5(8)), by SI 2003/1730, r 5(1), Sch 1, Pt 2, para 9.
Date in force: 15 September 2003: see SI 2003/1730, r 1(2); for effect and the continuing operation of this Part where a provision made by or under any enactment preserves the Insolvency Act 1986, old Pt II after that date see r 5(2)–(4) thereof.

[2.6 Service of application]

[(1) In the following paragraphs of this Rule, references to the application are to a copy of the application issued by the court under Rule 2.5(2) together with the [witness statement required by Rule 2.4] and the documents attached to the application.

(2) Notification for the purposes of paragraph 12(2) shall be by way of service in accordance with Rule 2.8, verified in accordance with Rule 2.9.

(3) The application shall be served in addition to those persons referred to in paragraph 12(2)—

 (a)   if an administrative receiver has been appointed, on him;

(b) if there is pending a petition for the winding-up of the company, on the petitioner (and also on the provisional liquidator, if any);

(c) if a member State liquidator has been appointed in main proceedings in relation to the company, on him;

(d) on the person proposed as administrator;

(e) on the company, if the application is made by anyone other than the company;

(f) if a supervisor of a voluntary arrangement under Part I of the Act has been appointed, on him.]

NOTES

Amendment

Substituted, together with rr 2.1–2.5, 2.7–2.133, for rr 2.1–2.6, 2.6A (inserted by SI 1987/1919, reg 3(1), Schedule, Pt 1, para 7), 2.7–2.46, 2.46A (inserted by SI 1987/1919, reg 3(1), Schedule, Pt 1, para 19), 2.47–2.58, 2.59–2.62 (inserted by SI 2002/1307, rr 3(1), 5(8)), by SI 2003/1730, r 5(1), Sch 1, Pt 2, para 9.

Date in force: 15 September 2003: see SI 2003/1730, r 1(2); for effect and the continuing operation of this Part where a provision made by or under any enactment preserves the Insolvency Act 1986, old Pt II after that date see r 5(2)–(4) thereof.

Para (1): words "witness statement required by Rule 2.4" in square brackets substituted by SI 2010/686, r 2, Sch 1, para 37.

Date in force: 6 April 2010: see SI 2010/686, r 1; for transitional provisions see r 6(1), Sch 4, paras 1, 2(1)(b), (2)–(4) thereto.

[2.6A . . .]
[. . .]

NOTES

Amendment

Substituted, together with rr 2.1–2.133, for rr 2.1–2.6, 2.6A, 2.7–2.46, 2.46A (inserted by SI 1987/1919, reg 3(1), Schedule, Pt 1, para 19), 2.47–2.58, 2.59–2.62 (inserted by SI 2002/1307, rr 3(1), 5(8)), by SI 2003/1730, r 5(1), Sch 1, Pt 2, para 9.

Date in force: 15 September 2003: see SI 2003/1730, r 1(2); for effect and the continuing operation of this Part where a provision made by or under any enactment preserves the Insolvency Act 1986, old Pt II after that date see r 5(2)–(4) thereof.

[2.7 Notice to [officers charged with execution of writs or other process], etc]
[The applicant shall as soon as reasonably practicable after filing the application give notice of its being made to—

(a) any [enforcement officer] or other officer who to his knowledge is charged with an execution or other legal process against the company or its property; and

(b) any person who to his knowledge has distrained against the company or its property.]

NOTES

Amendment

Substituted, together with rr 2.1–2.6, 2.8–2.133, for rr 2.1–2.6, 2.6A (inserted by SI 1987/1919, reg 3(1), Schedule, Pt 1, para 7), 2.7–2.46, 2.46A (inserted by SI 1987/1919, reg 3(1), Schedule, Pt 1, para 19), 2.47–2.58, 2.59–2.62 (inserted by SI 2002/1307, rr 3(1), 5(8)), by SI 2003/1730, r 5(1), Sch 1, Pt 2, para 9.

Date in force: 15 September 2003: see SI 2003/1730, r 1(2); for effect and the continuing operation of this Part where a provision made by or under any enactment preserves the Insolvency Act 1986, old Pt II after that date see r 5(2)–(4) thereof.

Provision heading: words "officers charged with execution of writs or other process" in square brackets substituted by SI 2005/527, r 5(a).

Date in force: 1 April 2005: see SI 2005/527, r 1(2).

In para (a) words "enforcement officer" in square brackets substituted by SI 2005/527, r 5(b).

Date in force: 1 April 2005: see SI 2005/527, r 1(2).

[2.8 Manner in which service to be effected]

[(1) Service of the application in accordance with Rule 2.6 shall be effected by the applicant, or his solicitor, or by a person instructed by him or his solicitor, not less than 5 [business] days before the date fixed for the hearing.

(2) Service shall be effected as follows—
- (a) on the company (subject to paragraph (3) below), by delivering the documents to its registered office;
- (b) on any other person (subject to paragraph (4) below), by delivering the documents to his proper address;
- (c) in either case, in such other manner as the court may direct.

(3) If delivery to a company's registered office is not practicable, service may be effected by delivery to its last known principal place of business in England and Wales.

(4) Subject to paragraph (5), for the purposes of paragraph (2)(b) above, a person's proper address is any which he has previously notified as his address for service; but if he has not notified any such address, service may be effected by delivery to his usual or last known address.

(5) In the case of a person who—
- (a) is an authorised deposit-taker or former authorised deposit-taker;
- (b)
    - (i) has appointed, or is or may be entitled to appoint, an administrative receiver of the company, or
    - (ii) is, or may be, entitled to appoint an administrator of the company under paragraph 14; and
- (c) has not notified an address for service,

the proper address is the address of an office of that person where, to the knowledge of the applicant, the company maintains a bank account or, where no such office is known to the applicant, the registered office of that person, or, if there is no such office, his usual or last known address.

(6) . . .]

NOTES

Amendment

Substituted, together with rr 2.1–2.7, 2.9–2.133, for rr 2.1–2.6, 2.6A (inserted by SI 1987/1919, reg 3(1), Schedule, Pt 1, para 7), 2.7–2.46, 2.46A (inserted by SI 1987/1919, reg 3(1), Schedule, Pt 1, para 19), 2.47–2.58, 2.59–2.62 (inserted by SI 2002/1307, rr 3(1), 5(8)), by SI 2003/1730, r 5(1), Sch 1, Pt 2, para 9.

Date in force: 15 September 2003: see SI 2003/1730, r 1(2); for effect and the continuing operation of this Part where a provision made by or under any enactment preserves the Insolvency Act 1986, old Pt II after that date see r 5(2)–(4) thereof.

Para (1): word "business" in square brackets inserted by SI 2010/686, r 2, Sch 1, para 38(1), (2).

Date in force: 6 April 2010: see SI 2010/686, r 1; for transitional provisions see r 6(1), Sch 4, para 1 thereto.

Para (6): revoked by SI 2010/686, r 2, Sch 1, para 38(1), (3).

Date in force: 6 April 2010: see SI 2010/686, r 1; for transitional provisions see r 6(1), Sch 4, para 1 thereto.

[2.9 Proof of service]

[(1) Service of the application must be verified by a certificate of service.

(1A) The certificate of service must be sufficient to identify the application served and must specify—
- (a) the name and registered number of the company,
- (b) the address of the registered office of the company,
- (c) the name of the applicant,
- (d) the court to which the application was made and the court reference number,
- (e) the date of the application,
- (f) whether the copy served was a sealed copy,
- (g) the date on which service was effected, and
- (h) the manner in which service was effected.]

(2) The [certificate of service] shall be filed with the court as soon as reasonably practicable after service, and in any event not less than 1 [business] day before the hearing of the application.]

NOTES

Amendment

Substituted, together with rr 2.1–2.8, 2.10–2.133, for rr 2.1–2.6, 2.6A (inserted by SI 1987/1919, reg 3(1), Schedule, Pt 1, para 7), 2.7–2.46, 2.46A (inserted by SI 1987/1919, reg 3(1), Schedule, Pt 1, para 19), 2.47–2.58, 2.59–2.62 (inserted by SI 2002/1307, rr 3(1), 5(8)), by SI 2003/1730, r 5(1), Sch 1, Pt 2, para 9.

Date in force: 15 September 2003: see SI 2003/1730, r 1(2); for effect and the continuing operation of this Part where a provision made by or under any enactment preserves the Insolvency Act 1986, old Pt II after that date see r 5(2)–(4) thereof.

Paras (1), (1A): substituted, for para (1) as previously enacted, by SI 2010/686, r 2, Sch 1, para 39(1), (2).

Date in force: 6 April 2010: see SI 2010/686, r 1; for transitional provisions see r 6(1), Sch 4, para 1 thereto.

Para (2): words "certificate of service" in square brackets substituted by SI 2010/686, r 2, Sch 1, para 39(1), (3)(a).

Date in force: 6 April 2010: see SI 2010/686, r 1; for transitional provisions see r 6(1), Sch 4, para 1 thereto.

Para (2): word "business" in square brackets inserted by SI 2010/686, r 2, Sch 1, para 39(1), (3)(b).

Date in force: 6 April 2010: see SI 2010/686, r 1; for transitional provisions see r 6(1), Sch 4, para 1 thereto.

[2.10 Application to appoint specified person as administrator by holder of qualifying floating charge]

[(1) Where the holder of a qualifying floating charge applies to the court under paragraph 36(1)(b), he shall produce to the court—
- (a) the written consent of all holders of any prior qualifying floating charge;
- (b) a written statement in the Form 2.2B made by the specified person proposed by him as administrator; and
- (c) sufficient evidence to satisfy the court that he is entitled to appoint an administrator under paragraph 14.

(2) If an administration order is made appointing the specified person, the costs of the person who made the administration application and the applicant under paragraph 36(1)(b) shall, unless the court otherwise orders, be paid as an expense of the administration.]

NOTES

Amendment

Substituted, together with rr 2.1–2.9, 2.11–2.133, for rr 2.1–2.6, 2.6A (inserted by SI 1987/1919, reg 3(1), Schedule, Pt 1, para 7), 2.7–2.46, 2.46A (inserted by SI 1987/1919, reg 3(1), Schedule, Pt 1, para 19), 2.47–2.58, 2.59–2.62 (inserted by SI 2002/1307, rr 3(1), 5(8)), by SI 2003/1730, r 5(1), Sch 1, Pt 2, para 9.

Date in force: 15 September 2003: see SI 2003/1730, r 1(2); for effect and the continuing operation of this Part where a provision made by or under any enactment preserves the Insolvency Act 1986, old Pt II after that date see r 5(2)–(4) thereof.

CHAPTER 2

. . .

NOTES

Amendment

Substituted by SI 2003/1730, r 5(1), Sch 1, Pt 2, para 9.

Date in force: 15 September 2003: see SI 2003/1730, r 1(2); for effect and the continuing operation of this Part where a provision made by or under any enactment preserves the Insolvency Act 1986, old Pt II after that date see r 5(2)–(4) thereof.

[2.11 Application where company in liquidation]

[(1) Where an administration application is made under paragraph 37 or paragraph 38, the [witness statement required by Rule 2.4] shall contain—

(a) full details of the existing insolvency proceedings, the name and address of the liquidator, the date he was appointed and by whom;

(b) the reasons why it has subsequently been considered appropriate that an administration application should be made;

(c) all other matters that would, in the opinion of the applicant, assist the court in considering the need to make provisions in respect of matters arising in connection with the liquidation; and

(d) the details required in Rules 2.4(2) and (4).

(2) Where the application is made by the holder of a qualifying floating charge he shall set out sufficient evidence in the [witness statement required by Rule 2.4] to satisfy the court that he is entitled to appoint an administrator under paragraph 14.]

NOTES

Amendment

Substituted, together with rr 2.1–2.10, 2.12–2.133, for rr 2.1–2.6, 2.6A (inserted by SI 1987/1919, reg 3(1), Schedule, Pt 1, para 7), 2.7–2.46, 2.46A (inserted by SI 1987/1919, reg 3(1), Schedule, Pt 1, para 19), 2.47–2.58, 2.59–2.62 (inserted by SI 2002/1307, rr 3(1), 5(8)), by SI 2003/1730, r 5(1), Sch 1, Pt 2, para 9.

Date in force: 15 September 2003: see SI 2003/1730, r 1(2); for effect and the continuing operation of this Part where a provision made by or under any enactment preserves the Insolvency Act 1986, old Pt II after that date see r 5(2)–(4) thereof.

Para (1): words "witness statement required by Rule 2.4" in square brackets substituted by SI 2010/686, r 2, Sch 1, para 40(1), (2).

Date in force: 6 April 2010: see SI 2010/686, r 1; for transitional provisions see r 6(1), Sch 4, para 1 thereto.

Para (2): word "witness statement required by Rule 2.4" in square brackets substituted by SI 2010/686, r 2, Sch 1, para 40(1), (3).

Date in force: 6 April 2010: see SI 2010/686, r 1; for transitional provisions see r 6(1), Sch 4, paras 1, 2(1)(b), (2)–(4) thereto.

[2.12 The hearing]
[(1) At the hearing of the administration application, any of the following may appear or be represented—
- (a) the applicant;
- (b) the company;
- (c) one or more of the directors;
- (d) if an administrative receiver has been appointed, that person;
- (e) any person who has presented a petition for the winding-up of the company;
- (f) the person proposed for appointment as administrator;
- (g) if a member State liquidator has been appointed in main proceedings in relation to the company, that person;
- (h) any person that is the holder of a qualifying floating charge;
- (j) any supervisor of a voluntary arrangement under Part I of the Act;
- (k) with the permission of the court, any other person who appears to have an interest justifying his appearance.

(2) If the court makes an administration order, it shall be in Form 2.4B.

(3) If the court makes an administration order, the costs of the applicant, and of any person whose costs are allowed by the court, are payable as an expense of the administration.]

NOTES

Amendment
Substituted, together with rr 2.1–2.11, 2.13–2.133, for rr 2.1–2.6, 2.6A (inserted by SI 1987/1919, reg 3(1), Schedule, Pt 1, para 7), 2.7–2.46, 2.46A (inserted by SI 1987/1919, reg 3(1), Schedule, Pt 1, para 19), 2.47–2.58, 2.59–2.62 (inserted by SI 2002/1307, rr 3(1), 5(8)), by SI 2003/1730, r 5(1), Sch 1, Pt 2, para 9.

Date in force: 15 September 2003: see SI 2003/1730, r 1(2); for effect and the continuing operation of this Part where a provision made by or under any enactment preserves the Insolvency Act 1986, old Pt II after that date see r 5(2)–(4) thereof.

[2.13]
[Where the court makes an administration order in relation to a company upon an application under paragraph 37 or 38, the court shall include in the order—
- (a) in the case of a liquidator appointed in a voluntary winding-up, his removal from office;
- (b) details concerning the release of the liquidator;
- (c) provision for payment of the expenses of the liquidation;
- (d) provisions regarding any indemnity given to the liquidator;
- (e) provisions regarding the handling or realisation of any of the company's assets in the hands of or under the control of the liquidator;
- (f) such provision as the court thinks [just] with respect to matters arising in connection with the liquidation; and
- (g) such other provisions as the court shall think [just].]

NOTES

Amendment
Substituted, together with rr 2.1–2.12, 2.14–2.133, for rr 2.1–2.6, 2.6A (inserted by SI 1987/1919, reg 3(1), Schedule, Pt 1, para 7), 2.7–2.46, 2.46A (inserted by SI 1987/1919,

reg 3(1), Schedule, Pt 1, para 19), 2.47–2.58, 2.59–2.62 (inserted by SI 2002/1307, rr 3(1), 5(8)), by SI 2003/1730, r 5(1), Sch 1, Pt 2, para 9.
    Date in force: 15 September 2003: see SI 2003/1730, r 1(2); for effect and the continuing operation of this Part where a provision made by or under any enactment preserves the Insolvency Act 1986, old Pt II after that date see r 5(2)–(4) thereof.
In paras (f), (g) word "just" in square brackets substituted by SI 2010/686, r 2, Sch 1, para 1.
    Date in force: 6 April 2010: see SI 2010/686, r 1; for transitional provisions see r 6(1), Sch 4, paras 1, 2(1)(b) thereto.

[2.14 Notice of administration order]

[(1) If the court makes an administration order, it shall as soon as reasonably practicable send two sealed copies of the order to the person who made the application.

(2) The applicant shall send a sealed copy of the order as soon as reasonably practicable to the person appointed as administrator.

(3) If the court makes an order under paragraph 13(1)(d) or any other order under paragraph 13(1)(f), it shall give directions as to the persons to whom, and how, notice of that order is to be given.]

NOTES

Initial Commencement

Specified date

Specified date: 29 December 1986: see r 0.1.

Amendment

Substituted, together with rr 2.1–2.13, 2.15–2.133, for rr 2.1–2.6, 2.6A (inserted by SI 1987/1919, reg 3(1), Schedule, Pt 1, para 7), 2.7–2.46, 2.46A (inserted by SI 1987/1919, reg 3(1), Schedule, Pt 1, para 19), 2.47–2.58, 2.59–2.62 (inserted by SI 2002/1307, rr 3(1), 5(8)), by SI 2003/1730, r 5(1), Sch 1, Pt 2, para 9.
    Date in force: 15 September 2003: see SI 2003/1730, r 1(2); for effect and the continuing operation of this Part where a provision made by or under any enactment preserves the Insolvency Act 1986, old Pt II after that date see r 5(2)–(4) thereof.

[CHAPTER 3

APPOINTMENT OF ADMINISTRATOR BY HOLDER OF FLOATING CHARGE]

NOTES

Amendment

Substituted by SI 2003/1730, r 5(1), Sch 1, Pt 2, para 9.
    Date in force: 15 September 2003: see SI 2003/1730, r 1(2); for effect and the continuing operation of this Part where a provision made by or under any enactment preserves the Insolvency Act 1986, old Pt II after that date see r 5(2)–(4) thereof.

[2.15 Notice of intention to appoint]

[(1) The prescribed form for the notice of intention to appoint for the purposes of paragraph 44(2) is Form 2.5B.

(2) For the purposes of paragraph 44(2), a copy of Form 2.5B shall be filed with the court at the same time as it is sent in accordance with paragraph 15(1) to the holder of any prior qualifying floating charge.

(3) The provisions of Rule 2.8(2) to 2.8(6) shall apply to the sending of a notice under this Rule as they apply to the manner in which service of an administration application is effected under that Rule.]

NOTES

Initial Commencement

Specified date

Specified date: 29 December 1986: see r 0.1.

Amendment

Substituted, together with rr 2.1–2.14, 2.16–2.133, for rr 2.1–2.6, 2.6A (inserted by SI 1987/1919, reg 3(1), Schedule, Pt 1, para 7), 2.7–2.46, 2.46A (inserted by SI 1987/1919, reg 3(1), Schedule, Pt 1, para 19), 2.47–2.58, 2.59–2.62 (inserted by SI 2002/1307, rr 3(1), 5(8)), by SI 2003/1730, r 5(1), Sch 1, Pt 2, para 9.

Date in force: 15 September 2003: see SI 2003/1730, r 1(2); for effect and the continuing operation of this Part where a provision made by or under any enactment preserves the Insolvency Act 1986, old Pt II after that date see r 5(2)–(4) thereof.

[2.16 Notice of appointment]

[(1) The notice of appointment for the purposes of an appointment under paragraph 14 shall be in Form 2.6B.

(2) The copies of the notice filed with the court, shall be accompanied by—

    (a)   the administrator's written statement in Form 2.2B; and

    (b)   either—

        (i)   evidence that the person making the appointment has given such notice as may be required by paragraph 15(1)(a); or

        (ii)   copies of the written consent of all those required to give consent in accordance with paragraph 15(1)(b); and

    (c)   a statement of those matters provided for in paragraph 100(2), if applicable.

(3) The statutory declaration on Form 2.6B shall be made not more than 5 business days before the form is filed with the court.

(4) Written consent may be given by the holder of a prior qualifying floating charge where a notice of intention to appoint an administrator has been given and filed with the court in accordance with Rule 2.15 above, by completing the section provided on Form 2.5B and returning to the appointor a copy of the form.

(5) Where the holder of a prior qualifying floating charge does not choose to complete the section provided on Form 2.5B to indicate his consent, or no such form has been sent to him, his written consent shall include—

    (a)   details of the name, address of registered office and registered number of the company in respect of which the appointment is proposed to be made;

    (b)   details of the charge held by him including the date it was registered and, where applicable, any financial limit and any deeds of priority;

    (c)   his name and address;

    (d)   the name and address of the holder of the qualifying floating charge who is proposing to make the appointment;

    (e)   the date that notice of intention to appoint was given;

    (f)   the name of the proposed administrator;

    (g)   a statement of consent to the proposed appointment,

and it shall be [authenticated] and dated.

(6) This Rule and the following Rule are subject to Rule 2.19, the provisions of which apply when an appointment is to be made out of court business hours.]

NOTES

Amendment

Substituted, together with rr 2.1–2.15, 2.17–2.133, for rr 2.1–2.6, 2.6A (inserted by SI 1987/1919, reg 3(1), Schedule, Pt 1, para 7), 2.7–2.46, 2.46A (inserted by SI 1987/1919, reg 3(1), Schedule, Pt 1, para 19), 2.47–2.58, 2.59–2.62 (inserted by SI 2002/1307, rr 3(1), 5(8)), by SI 2003/1730, r 5(1), Sch 1, Pt 2, para 9.
: Date in force: 15 September 2003: see SI 2003/1730, r 1(2); for effect and the continuing operation of this Part where a provision made by or under any enactment preserves the Insolvency Act 1986, old Pt II after that date see r 5(2)–(4) thereof.

Para (5): word "authenticated" in square brackets substituted by SI 2010/686, r 2, Sch 1, para 1.
: Date in force: 6 April 2010: see SI 2010/686, r 1; for transitional provisions see r 6(1), Sch 4, paras 1, 2(1)(b) thereto.

[2.17]

[(1) Three copies of the notice of appointment shall be filed with the court and shall have applied to them the seal of the court and be endorsed with the date and time of filing.

(2) The court shall issue two of the sealed copies of the notice of appointment to the person making the appointment, who shall as soon as reasonably practicable send one of the sealed copies to the administrator.]

NOTES

Amendment

Substituted, together with rr 2.1–2.16, 2.18–2.133, for rr 2.1–2.6, 2.6A (inserted by SI 1987/1919, reg 3(1), Schedule, Pt 1, para 7), 2.7–2.46, 2.46A (inserted by SI 1987/1919, reg 3(1), Schedule, Pt 1, para 19), 2.47–2.58, 2.59–2.62 (inserted by SI 2002/1307, rr 3(1), 5(8)), by SI 2003/1730, r 5(1), Sch 1, Pt 2, para 9.
: Date in force: 15 September 2003: see SI 2003/1730, r 1(2); for effect and the continuing operation of this Part where a provision made by or under any enactment preserves the Insolvency Act 1986, old Pt II after that date see r 5(2)–(4) thereof.

CHAPTER 3

. . .

NOTES

Amendment

Substituted by SI 2003/1730, r 5(1), Sch 1, Pt 2, para 9.
: Date in force: 15 September 2003: see SI 2003/1730, r 1(2); for effect and the continuing operation of this Part where a provision made by or under any enactment preserves the Insolvency Act 1986, old Pt II after that date see r 5(2)–(4) thereof.

. . .

NOTES

Amendment

Substituted by SI 2003/1730, r 5(1), Sch 1, Pt 2, para 9.

Date in force: 15 September 2003: see SI 2003/1730, r 1(2); for effect and the continuing operation of this Part where a provision made by or under any enactment preserves the Insolvency Act 1986, old Pt II after that date see r 5(2)–(4) thereof.

[2.18]

[Where, after receiving notice that an administration application has been made, the holder of a qualifying floating charge appoints an administrator in reliance on paragraph 14, he shall as soon as reasonably practicable send a copy of the notice of appointment to the person making the administration application and to the court in which the application has been made.]

NOTES

Amendment

Substituted, together with rr 2.1–2.17, 2.19–2.133, for rr 2.1–2.6, 2.6A (inserted by SI 1987/1919, reg 3(1), Schedule, Pt 1, para 7), 2.7–2.46, 2.46A (inserted by SI 1987/1919, reg 3(1), Schedule, Pt 1, para 19), 2.47–2.58, 2.59–2.62 (inserted by SI 2002/1307, rr 3(1), 5(8)), by SI 2003/1730, r 5(1), Sch 1, Pt 2, para 9.

Date in force: 15 September 2003: see SI 2003/1730, r 1(2); for effect and the continuing operation of this Part where a provision made by or under any enactment preserves the Insolvency Act 1986, old Pt II after that date see r 5(2)–(4) thereof.

[2.19 Appointment taking place out of court business hours]

[(1) The holder of a qualifying floating charge may file a notice of appointment with the court, notwithstanding that the court is not open for public business. When the court is closed (and only when it is closed) a notice of appointment may be filed with the court by faxing that form [or sending it as an attachment to an e-mail in accordance with paragraphs (3) and (3A)]. The notice of appointment shall be in Form 2.7B.

(2) The filing of a notice in accordance with this Rule shall have the same effect for all purposes as a notice of appointment filed in accordance with Rule 2.16 with the court specified in the notice as having jurisdiction in the case.

[(3) The notice must be—
   (a) faxed to a designated telephone number, or
   (b) sent as an attachment by e-mail to a designated e-mail address,
which must be provided by the Court Service for that purpose.

(3A) The Secretary of State must publish the designated telephone number and e-mail address on The Insolvency Service website and, on request to The Insolvency Service, make them available in writing.]

(4) The appointor shall ensure that[—]
   [(a)] a fax transmission report detailing the time and date of the fax transmission [and the telephone number to which the notice was faxed] and containing a copy of the first page (in part or in full) of the document faxed is created by the fax machine that is used to fax the form[, or
   (b) a hard copy of the e-mail is created detailing the time and date of the e-mail and the address to which it was sent and containing a copy of the document sent as an attachment,
as the case may be; and the appointor must retain the report or hard copy].

(5) The appointment shall take effect from the date and time of [the fax transmission or sending of the e-mail]. The appointor shall notify the administrator, as soon as reasonably practicable, that the notice has been filed.

(6) The copy of the faxed notice of appointment [, or the e-mail (or a hard copy of the e-mail) containing the notice of appointment, as (in either case) received by

the Court Service,] shall be forwarded as soon as reasonably practicable to the court specified in the notice as the court having jurisdiction in the case, to be placed on the relevant court file.

(7) The appointor shall take three copies of the notice of appointment that was faxed to the designated telephone number, together with the transmission report [or hard copy required by paragraph (4)] and all the necessary supporting documents listed on Form 2.7B, to the court on the next day that the court is open for business.

(8) The appointor shall attach to the notice a statement providing full reasons for the out of hours filing of the notice of appointment, including why it would have been damaging to the company and its creditors not to have so acted.

(9) The copies of the notice shall be sealed by the court and shall be endorsed with the date and time when, according to the appointor's fax transmission report [or hard copy of the e-mail], the notice was faxed [or sent] and the date when the notice and accompanying documents were delivered to the court.

(10) The administrator's appointment shall cease to have effect if the requirements of paragraph (7) are not completed within the time period indicated in that paragraph.

(11) Where any question arises in respect of the date and time that the notice of appointment was filed with the court it shall be a presumption capable of rebuttal that the date and time shown on the appointor's fax transmission report [or hard copy of the e-mail] is the date and time at which the notice was so filed.

(12) The court shall issue two of the sealed copies of the notice of appointment to the person making the appointment, who shall, as soon as reasonably practicable, send one of the copies to the administrator.]

NOTES

Amendment

Substituted, together with rr 2.1–2.18, 2.20–2.133, for rr 2.1–2.6, 2.6A (inserted by SI 1987/1919, reg 3(1), Schedule, Pt 1, para 7), 2.7–2.46, 2.46A (inserted by SI 1987/1919, reg 3(1), Schedule, Pt 1, para 19), 2.47–2.58, 2.59–2.62 (inserted by SI 2002/1307, rr 3(1), 5(8)), by SI 2003/1730, r 5(1), Sch 1, Pt 2, para 9.
Date in force: 15 September 2003: see SI 2003/1730, r 1(2); for effect and the continuing operation of this Part where a provision made by or under any enactment preserves the Insolvency Act 1986, old Pt II after that date see r 5(2)–(4) thereof.
Para (1): words from "or sending it" to "(3) and (3A)" in square brackets substituted by SI 2010/686, r 2, Sch 1, para 41(1), (2).
Date in force: 6 April 2010: see SI 2010/686, r 1; for transitional provisions see r 6(1), Sch 4, para 1 thereto.
Paras (3), (3A): substituted, for para (3) as previously enacted , by SI 2010/686, r 2, Sch 1, para 41(1), (3).
Date in force: 6 April 2010: see SI 2010/686, r 1; for transitional provisions see r 6(1), Sch 4, para 1 thereto.
Para (4): sub-para (a) designated as such by SI 2010/686, r 2, Sch 1, para 41(1), (4)(a).
Date in force: 6 April 2010: see SI 2010/686, r 1; for transitional provisions see r 6(1), Sch 4, para 1 thereto.
Para (4): in sub-para (a) words "and the telephone number to which the notice was faxed" in square brackets inserted by SI 2010/686, r 2, Sch 1, para 41(1), (4)(b).
Date in force: 6 April 2010: see SI 2010/686, r 1; for transitional provisions see r 6(1), Sch 4, para 1 thereto.
Para (4): words from ", or (b)" to "or hard copy" in square brackets inserted by SI 2010/686, r 2, Sch 1, para 41(1), (4)(c).
Date in force: 6 April 2010: see SI 2010/686, r 1; for transitional provisions see r 6(1), Sch 4, para 1 thereto.
Para (5): words "the fax transmission or sending of the e-mail" in square brackets substituted by SI 2010/686, r 2, Sch 1, para 41(1), (5).
Date in force: 6 April 2010: see SI 2010/686, r 1; for transitional provisions see r 6(1), Sch 4, para 1 thereto.
Para (6): words from ", or the e-mail" to "the Court Service," in square brackets substituted by SI 2010/686, r 2, Sch 1, para 41(1), (6).

Date in force: 6 April 2010: see SI 2010/686, r 1; for transitional provisions see r 6(1), Sch 4, para 1 thereto.
Para (7): words "or hard copy required by paragraph (4)" in square brackets substituted by SI 2010/686, r 2, Sch 1, para 41(1), (7).
Date in force: 6 April 2010: see SI 2010/686, r 1; for transitional provisions see r 6(1), Sch 4, para 1 thereto.
Para (9): words "or hard copy of the e-mail" in square brackets inserted by SI 2010/686, r 2, Sch 1, para 41(1), (8)(a).
Date in force: 6 April 2010: see SI 2010/686, r 1; for transitional provisions see r 6(1), Sch 4, para 1 thereto.
Para (9): word "or sent" in square brackets inserted by SI 2010/686, r 2, Sch 1, para 41(1), (8)(b).
Date in force: 6 April 2010: see SI 2010/686, r 1; for transitional provisions see r 6(1), Sch 4, para 1 thereto.
Para (11): words "or hard copy of the e-mail" in square brackets inserted by SI 2010/686, r 2, Sch 1, para 41(1), (9).
Date in force: 6 April 2010: see SI 2010/686, r 1; for transitional provisions see r 6(1), Sch 4, para 1 thereto.

[CHAPTER 4

APPOINTMENT OF ADMINISTRATOR BY COMPANY OR DIRECTORS]

NOTES

Amendment

Substituted by SI 2003/1730, r 5(1), Sch 1, Pt 2, para 9.
Date in force: 15 September 2003: see SI 2003/1730, r 1(2); for effect and the continuing operation of this Part where a provision made by or under any enactment preserves the Insolvency Act 1986, old Pt II after that date see r 5(2)–(4) thereof.

[2.20 Notice of intention to appoint]

[(1) The notice of intention to appoint an administrator for the purposes of paragraph 26 shall be in Form 2.8B.

(2) A copy of the notice of intention to appoint must, in addition to the persons specified in paragraph 26, be given to—

- (a) any [enforcement officer] who, to the knowledge of the person giving the notice, is charged with execution or other legal process against the company;
- (b) any person who, to the knowledge of the person giving the notice, has distrained against the company or its property;
- (c) any supervisor of a voluntary arrangement under Part I of the Act; and
- (d) the company, if the company is not intending to make the appointment.

(3) The provisions of Rule 2.8(2) to [2.8(5)] shall apply to the sending or giving of a notice under this Rule as they apply to the manner in which service of an administration application is effected under that Rule.]

NOTES

Amendment

Substituted, together with rr 2.1–2.19, 2.21–2.133, for rr 2.1–2.6, 2.6A (inserted by SI 1987/1919, reg 3(1), Schedule, Pt 1, para 7), 2.7–2.46, 2.46A (inserted by SI 1987/1919, reg 3(1), Schedule, Pt 1, para 19), 2.47–2.58, 2.59–2.62 (inserted by SI 2002/1307, rr 3(1), 5(8)), by SI 2003/1730, r 5(1), Sch 1, Pt 2, para 9.
Date in force: 15 September 2003: see SI 2003/1730, r 1(2); for effect and the continuing operation of this Part where a provision made by or under any enactment preserves the Insolvency Act 1986, old Pt II after that date see r 5(2)–(4) thereof.

Para (2): in sub-para (a) words "enforcement officer" in square brackets substituted by SI 2005/527, r 6.
Date in force: 1 April 2005: see SI 2005/527, r 1(2).
Para (3): reference to "2.8(5)" in square brackets substituted by SI 2010/686, r 2, Sch 1, para 42.
Date in force: 6 April 2010: see SI 2010/686, r 1; for transitional provisions see r 6(1), Sch 4, paras 1, 2(1)(b) thereto.

[2.21]

[The statutory declaration on Form 2.8B shall be made not more than 5 business days before the notice is filed with the court.]

NOTES

Amendment

Substituted, together with rr 2.1–2.20, 2.22–2.133, for rr 2.1–2.6, 2.6A (inserted by SI 1987/1919, reg 3(1), Schedule, Pt 1, para 7), 2.7–2.46, 2.46A (inserted by SI 1987/1919, reg 3(1), Schedule, Pt 1, para 19), 2.47–2.58, 2.59–2.62 (inserted by SI 2002/1307, rr 3(1), 5(8)), by SI 2003/1730, r 5(1), Sch 1, Pt 2, para 9.
Date in force: 15 September 2003: see SI 2003/1730, r 1(2); for effect and the continuing operation of this Part where a provision made by or under any enactment preserves the Insolvency Act 1986, old Pt II after that date see r 5(2)–(4) thereof.

[2.22]

[The notice of intention to appoint shall be accompanied by either a copy of the resolution of the company to appoint an administrator (where the company intends to make the appointment) or a record of the decision of the directors (where the directors intend to make the appointment).]

NOTES

Amendment

Substituted, together with rr 2.1–2.21, 2.23–2.133, for rr 2.1–2.6, 2.6A (inserted by SI 1987/1919, reg 3(1), Schedule, Pt 1, para 7), 2.7–2.46, 2.46A (inserted by SI 1987/1919, reg 3(1), Schedule, Pt 1, para 19), 2.47–2.58, 2.59–2.62 (inserted by SI 2002/1307, rr 3(1), 5(8)), by SI 2003/1730, r 5(1), Sch 1, Pt 2, para 9.
Date in force: 15 September 2003: see SI 2003/1730, r 1(2); for effect and the continuing operation of this Part where a provision made by or under any enactment preserves the Insolvency Act 1986, old Pt II after that date see r 5(2)–(4) thereof.

[2.23 Notice of appointment]

[(1) The notice of appointment for the purposes of an appointment under paragraph 22 shall be in Form 2.9B or Form 2.10B, as appropriate.
(2) The copies of the notice filed with the court shall be accompanied by—
- (a) the administrator's written statement in Form 2.2B;
- (b) the written consent of all those persons to whom notice was given in accordance with paragraph 26(1) unless the period of notice set out in paragraph 26(1) has expired; and
- (c) a statement of the matters provided for in paragraph 100(2), where applicable.]

NOTES

Amendment

Substituted, together with rr 2.1–2.22, 2.24–2.133, for rr 2.1–2.6, 2.6A (inserted by SI 1987/1919, reg 3(1), Schedule, Pt 1, para 7), 2.7–2.46, 2.46A (inserted by SI 1987/1919, reg 3(1), Schedule, Pt 1, para 19), 2.47–2.58, 2.59–2.62 (inserted by SI 2002/1307, rr 3(1), 5(8)), by SI 2003/1730, r 5(1), Sch 1, Pt 2, para 9.

Date in force: 15 September 2003: see SI 2003/1730, r 1(2); for effect and the continuing operation of this Part where a provision made by or under any enactment preserves the Insolvency Act 1986, old Pt II after that date see r 5(2)–(4) thereof.

[2.24]

[The statutory declaration on Form 2.9B or Form 2.10B shall be made not more than 5 business days before the notice is filed with the court.]

NOTES

Amendment

Substituted, together with rr 2.1–2.23, 2.25–2.133, for rr 2.1–2.6, 2.6A (inserted by SI 1987/1919, reg 3(1), Schedule, Pt 1, para 7), 2.7–2.46, 2.46A (inserted by SI 1987/1919, reg 3(1), Schedule, Pt 1, para 19), 2.47–2.58, 2.59–2.62 (inserted by SI 2002/1307, rr 3(1), 5(8)), by SI 2003/1730, r 5(1), Sch 1, Pt 2, para 9.

Date in force: 15 September 2003: see SI 2003/1730, r 1(2); for effect and the continuing operation of this Part where a provision made by or under any enactment preserves the Insolvency Act 1986, old Pt II after that date see r 5(2)–(4) thereof.

[2.25]

[Where a notice of intention to appoint an administrator has not been given, the notice of appointment shall be accompanied by the documents specified in Rule 2.22 above.]

NOTES

Amendment

Substituted, together with rr 2.1–2.24, 2.26–2.133, for rr 2.1–2.6, 2.6A (inserted by SI 1987/1919, reg 3(1), Schedule, Pt 1, para 7), 2.7–2.46, 2.46A (inserted by SI 1987/1919, reg 3(1), Schedule, Pt 1, para 19), 2.47–2.58, 2.59–2.62 (inserted by SI 2002/1307, rr 3(1), 5(8)), by SI 2003/1730, r 5(1), Sch 1, Pt 2, para 9.

Date in force: 15 September 2003: see SI 2003/1730, r 1(2); for effect and the continuing operation of this Part where a provision made by or under any enactment preserves the Insolvency Act 1986, old Pt II after that date see r 5(2)–(4) thereof.

[2.26]

[(1) Three copies of the notice of appointment shall be filed with the court and shall have applied to them the seal of the court and be endorsed with the date and time of filing.

(2) The court shall issue two of the sealed copies of the notice of appointment to the person making the appointment who shall as soon as reasonably practicable send one of the sealed copies to the administrator.]

NOTES

Amendment

Substituted, together with rr 2.1–2.25, 2.27–2.133, for rr 2.1–2.6, 2.6A (inserted by SI 1987/1919, reg 3(1), Schedule, Pt 1, para 7), 2.7–2.46, 2.46A (inserted by SI 1987/1919,

reg 3(1), Schedule, Pt 1, para 19), 2.47–2.58, 2.59–2.62 (inserted by SI 2002/1307, rr 3(1), 5(8)), by SI 2003/1730, r 5(1), Sch 1, Pt 2, para 9.

Date in force: 15 September 2003: see SI 2003/1730, r 1(2); for effect and the continuing operation of this Part where a provision made by or under any enactment preserves the Insolvency Act 1986, old Pt II after that date see r 5(2)–(4) thereof.

[CHAPTER 5
PROCESS OF ADMINISTRATION]

NOTES

Amendment

Substituted by SI 2003/1730, r 5(1), Sch 1, Pt 2, para 9.

Date in force: 15 September 2003: see SI 2003/1730, r 1(2); for effect and the continuing operation of this Part where a provision made by or under any enactment preserves the Insolvency Act 1986, old Pt II after that date see r 5(2)–(4) thereof.

[2.27 Notification and advertisement of administrator's appointment]

[[(1) The notice of appointment to be given by the administrator as soon as reasonably practicable after appointment under paragraph 46(2)(b) shall be gazetted . . . and may be advertised in such other manner as the administrator thinks fit.]

[(1A) In addition to the standard contents, the notice under paragraph (1) must state—

(a) that an administrator has been appointed,

(b) the date of the appointment, and

(c) the nature of the business of the company.]

(2) The administrator shall, as soon as reasonably practicable after the date specified in paragraph 46(6), give notice of his appointment—

(a) if a receiver or an administrative receiver has been appointed, to him;

(b) if there is pending a petition for the winding up of the company, to the petitioner (and also to the provisional liquidator, if any);

(c) to any [enforcement officer] who, to the administrator's knowledge, is charged with execution or other legal process against the company;

(d) to any person who, to the administrator's knowledge, has distrained against the company or its property; and

(e) any supervisor of a voluntary arrangement under Part I of the Act.

(3) Where, under a provision of Schedule B1 to the Act or these Rules, the administrator is required to send a notice of his appointment to any person [other than the registrar of companies] he shall do so in Form 2.12B.]

NOTES

Amendment

Substituted, together with rr 2.1–2.26, 2.28–2.133, for rr 2.1–2.6, 2.6A (inserted by SI 1987/1919, reg 3(1), Schedule, Pt 1, para 7), 2.7–2.46, 2.46A (inserted by SI 1987/1919, reg 3(1), Schedule, Pt 1, para 19), 2.47–2.58, 2.59–2.62 (inserted by SI 2002/1307, rr 3(1), 5(8)), by SI 2003/1730, r 5(1), Sch 1, Pt 2, para 9.

Date in force: 15 September 2003: see SI 2003/1730, r 1(2); for effect and the continuing operation of this Part where a provision made by or under any enactment preserves the Insolvency Act 1986, old Pt II after that date see r 5(2)–(4) thereof.

Para (1): substituted by SI 2009/642, rr 4, 8.

Date in force: 6 April 2009: see SI 2009/642, r 1; for transitional provisions see r 3 thereof.

Para (1): words omitted revoked by SI 2010/686, r 2, Sch 1, para 43(1), (2).

Date in force: 6 April 2010: see SI 2010/686, r 1; for transitional provisions see r 6(1), Sch 4, para 1 thereto.

Para (1A): inserted by SI 2010/686, r 2, Sch 1, para 43(1), (3).

Date in force: 6 April 2010: see SI 2010/686, r 1; for transitional provisions see r 6(1), Sch 4, para 1 thereto.

Para (2): in sub-para (c) words "enforcement officer" in square brackets substituted by SI 2005/527, r 7.

Date in force: 1 April 2005: see SI 2005/527, r 1(2).

Para (3): words "other than the registrar of companies" in square brackets inserted by SI 2010/686, r 2, Sch 1, para 43(1), (4).

Date in force: 6 April 2010: see SI 2010/686, r 1; for transitional provisions see r 6(1), Sch 4, paras 1, 2(1)(b) thereto.

See Further

See further, in relation to the application of this rule, with modifications, in respect of bank administration and applications for bank administration: the Bank Administration (England and Wales) Rules 2009, SI 2009/357, rr 58–61.

[2.28 Notice requiring statement of affairs]

[(1) In this Chapter "relevant person" shall have the meaning given to it in paragraph 47(3).

(2) The administrator shall send notice in Form 2.13B to each relevant person whom he determines appropriate requiring him to prepare and submit a statement of the company's affairs.

(3) The notice shall inform each of the relevant persons—

(a) of the names and addresses of all others (if any) to whom the same notice has been sent;

(b) of the time within which the statement must be delivered;

(c) of the effect of paragraph 48(4) (penalty for non-compliance); and

(d) of the application to him, and to each other relevant person, of section 235 (duty to provide information, and to attend on the administrator, if required).

(4) The administrator shall furnish each relevant person to whom he has sent notice in Form 2.13B with the forms required for the preparation of the statement of affairs.]

NOTES

Initial Commencement

Specified date

Specified date: 29 December 1986: see r 0.1.

Amendment

Substituted, together with rr 2.1–2.27, 2.29–2.133, for rr 2.1–2.6, 2.6A (inserted by SI 1987/1919, reg 3(1), Schedule, Pt 1, para 7), 2.7–2.46, 2.46A (inserted by SI 1987/1919, reg 3(1), Schedule, Pt 1, para 19), 2.47–2.58, 2.59–2.62 (inserted by SI 2002/1307, rr 3(1), 5(8)), by SI 2003/1730, r 5(1), Sch 1, Pt 2, para 9.

Date in force: 15 September 2003: see SI 2003/1730, r 1(2); for effect and the continuing operation of this Part where a provision made by or under any enactment preserves the Insolvency Act 1986, old Pt II after that date see r 5(2)–(4) thereof.

See Further

See further, in relation to the application of this rule, with modifications, in respect of bank administration and applications for bank administration: the Bank Administration (England and Wales) Rules 2009, SI 2009/357, rr 58–61.

[2.29 Verification and filing]

[(1) The statement of the company's affairs shall be in Form 2.14B, contain all the particulars required by that form and be verified by a statement of truth by the relevant person.

(2) The administrator may require any relevant person to submit a statement of concurrence in Form 2.15B stating that he concurs in the statement of affairs. Where the administrator does so, he shall inform the person making the statement of affairs of that fact.

(3) The statement of affairs shall be delivered by the relevant person making the statement of truth, together with a copy, to the administrator. The relevant person shall also deliver a copy of the statement of affairs to all those persons whom the administrator has required to make a statement of concurrence.

(4) A person required to submit a statement of concurrence shall do so before the end of the period of 5 business days (or such other period as the administrator may agree) beginning with the day on which the statement of affairs being concurred with is received by him.

(5) A statement of concurrence may be qualified in respect of matters dealt with in the statement of affairs, where the maker of the statement of concurrence is not in agreement with the relevant person, or he considers the statement of affairs to be erroneous or misleading, or he is without the direct knowledge necessary for concurring with it.

(6) Every statement of concurrence shall be verified by a statement of truth and be delivered to the administrator by the person who makes it, together with a copy of it.

(7) Subject to Rule 2.30 below, the administrator shall as soon as reasonably practicable send to the registrar of companies . . . a copy of the statement of affairs and any statement of concurrence.]

NOTES

Amendment

Substituted, together with rr 2.1–2.28, 2.30–2.133, for rr 2.1–2.6, 2.6A (inserted by SI 1987/1919, reg 3(1), Schedule, Pt 1, para 7), 2.7–2.46, 2.46A (inserted by SI 1987/1919, reg 3(1), Schedule, Pt 1, para 19), 2.47–2.58, 2.59–2.62 (inserted by SI 2002/1307, rr 3(1), 5(8)), by SI 2003/1730, r 5(1), Sch 1, Pt 2, para 9.
Date in force: 15 September 2003: see SI 2003/1730, r 1(2); for effect and the continuing operation of this Part where a provision made by or under any enactment preserves the Insolvency Act 1986, old Pt II after that date see r 5(2)–(4) thereof.
Para (7): words omitted revoked by SI 2010/686, r 2, Sch 1, para 44.
Date in force: 6 April 2010: see SI 2010/686, r 1; for transitional provisions see r 6(1), Sch 4, para 1 thereto.

See Further

See further, in relation to the application of this rule, with modifications, in respect of bank administration and applications for bank administration: the Bank Administration (England and Wales) Rules 2009, SI 2009/357, rr 58–61.

[2.30 Limited disclosure]

[(1) Where the administrator thinks that it would prejudice the conduct of the administration [or might reasonably be expected to lead to violence against any person] for the whole or part of the statement of the company's affairs to be disclosed, he may apply to the court for an order of limited disclosure in respect of the statement, or any specified part of it.

(2) The court may, on such application, order that the statement or, as the case may be, the specified part of it, shall not be filed with the registrar of companies.

(3) The administrator shall as soon as reasonably practicable send to the registrar of companies . . . a copy of the order and the statement of affairs (to the extent provided by the order) and any statement of concurrence.

(4) If a creditor seeks disclosure of a statement of affairs or a specified part of it in relation to which an order has been made under this Rule, he may apply to the court for an order that the administrator disclose it or a specified part of it. The application shall be supported by written evidence in the form of [a witness statement].

(5) The applicant shall give the administrator notice of his application at least 3 [business] days before the hearing.

(6) The court may make any order for disclosure subject to any conditions as to confidentiality, duration, the scope of the order in the event of any change of circumstances, or other matters as it sees [just].

(7) If there is a material change in circumstances rendering the limit on disclosure or any part of it unnecessary, the administrator shall, as soon as reasonably practicable after the change, apply to the court for the order or any part of it to be rescinded.

(8) The administrator shall, as soon as reasonably practicable after the making of an order under paragraph (7) above, file with the registrar of companies . . . a copy of the statement of affairs to the extent provided by the order.

(9) When the statement of affairs is filed in accordance with paragraph (8), the administrator shall, where he has sent a statement of proposals under paragraph 49, provide the creditors with a copy of the statement of affairs as filed, or a summary thereof.

(10) The provisions of Part 31 of the CPR shall not apply to an application under this Rule.]

NOTES

Amendment

Substituted, together with rr 2.1–2.29, 2.31–2.133, for rr 2.1–2.6, 2.6A (inserted by SI 1987/1919, reg 3(1), Schedule, Pt 1, para 7), 2.7–2.46, 2.46A (inserted by SI 1987/1919, reg 3(1), Schedule, Pt 1, para 19), 2.47–2.58, 2.59–2.62 (inserted by SI 2002/1307, rr 3(1), 5(8)), by SI 2003/1730, r 5(1), Sch 1, Pt 2, para 9.
  Date in force: 15 September 2003: see SI 2003/1730, r 1(2); for effect and the continuing operation of this Part where a provision made by or under any enactment preserves the Insolvency Act 1986, old Pt II after that date see r 5(2)–(4) thereof.
Para (1): words "or might reasonably be expected to lead to violence against any person" in square brackets inserted by SI 2010/686, r 2, Sch 1, para 45(1), (2).
  Date in force: 6 April 2010: see SI 2010/686, r 1; for transitional provisions see r 6(1), Sch 4, para 1 thereto.
Para (3): words omitted revoked by SI 2010/686, r 2, Sch 1, para 45(1), (3).
  Date in force: 6 April 2010: see SI 2010/686, r 1; for transitional provisions see r 6(1), Sch 4, para 1 thereto.
Para (4): words "a witness statement" in square brackets substituted by SI 2010/686, r 2, Sch 1, para 45(1), (4).
  Date in force: 6 April 2010: see SI 2010/686, r 1; for transitional provisions see r 6(1), Sch 4, paras 1, 2(1)(b), (2)–(4) thereto.
Para (5): word "business" in square brackets inserted by SI 2010/686, r 2, Sch 1, para 45(1), (5).
  Date in force: 6 April 2010: see SI 2010/686, r 1; for transitional provisions see r 6(1), Sch 4, para 1 thereto.
Para (6): word "just" in square brackets substituted by SI 2010/686, r 2, Sch 1, para 1.
  Date in force: 6 April 2010: see SI 2010/686, r 1; for transitional provisions see r 6(1), Sch 4, paras 1, 2(1)(b) thereto.
Para (8): words omitted revoked by SI 2010/686, r 2, Sch 1, para 45(1), (6).
  Date in force: 6 April 2010: see SI 2010/686, r 1; for transitional provisions see r 6(1), Sch 4, para 1 thereto.

See Further

See further, in relation to the application of this rule, with modifications, in respect of bank administration and applications for bank administration: the Bank Administration (England and Wales) Rules 2009, SI 2009/357, rr 58–61.

...

NOTES

Amendment

Substituted by SI 2003/1730, r 5(1), Sch 1, Pt 2, para 9.
Date in force: 15 September 2003: see SI 2003/1730, r 1(2); for effect and the continuing operation of this Part where a provision made by or under any enactment preserves the Insolvency Act 1986, old Pt II after that date see r 5(2)–(4) thereof.

[2.31 Release from duty to submit statement of affairs; extension of time]

[(1) The power of the administrator under paragraph 48(2) to give a release from the obligation imposed by paragraph 47(1), or to grant an extension of time, may be exercised at the administrator's own discretion, or at the request of any relevant person.

(2) A relevant person may, if he requests a release or extension of time and it is refused by the administrator, apply to the court for it.

(3) The court may, if it thinks that no sufficient cause is shown for the application, dismiss it without a hearing but it shall not do so without giving the relevant person at least [5 business] days' notice, upon receipt of which the relevant person may request the court to list the application for a without notice hearing. If the application is not dismissed the court shall fix a venue for it to be heard, and give notice to the relevant person accordingly.

(4) The relevant person shall, at least 14 days before the hearing, send to the administrator a notice stating the venue and accompanied by a copy of the application and of any evidence which he (the relevant person) intends to adduce in support of it.

(5) The administrator may appear and be heard on the application and, whether or not he appears, he may file a written report of any matters which he considers ought to be drawn to the court's attention.
If such a report is filed, a copy of it shall be sent by the administrator to the relevant person, not later than 5 [business] days before the hearing.

(6) Sealed copies of any order made on the application shall be sent by the court to the relevant person and the administrator.

(7) On any application under this Rule the relevant person's costs shall be paid in any event by him and, unless the court otherwise orders, no allowance towards them shall be made [as an expense of the administration].]

NOTES

Amendment

Substituted, together with rr 2.1–2.30, 2.32–2.133, for rr 2.1–2.6, 2.6A (inserted by SI 1987/1919, reg 3(1), Schedule, Pt 1, para 7), 2.7–2.46, 2.46A (inserted by SI 1987/1919, reg 3(1), Schedule, Pt 1, para 19), 2.47–2.58, 2.59–2.62 (inserted by SI 2002/1307, rr 3(1), 5(8)), by SI 2003/1730, r 5(1), Sch 1, Pt 2, para 9.
Date in force: 15 September 2003: see SI 2003/1730, r 1(2); for effect and the continuing operation of this Part where a provision made by or under any enactment preserves the Insolvency Act 1986, old Pt II after that date see r 5(2)–(4) thereof.
Para (3): words "5 business" in square brackets substituted by SI 2010/686, r 2, Sch 1, para 46(1), (2).
Date in force: 6 April 2010: see SI 2010/686, r 1; for transitional provisions see r 6(1), Sch 4, para 1 thereto.
Para (5): word "business" in square brackets inserted by SI 2010/686, r 2, Sch 1, para 46(1), (3).
Date in force: 6 April 2010: see SI 2010/686, r 1; for transitional provisions see r 6(1), Sch 4, para 1 thereto.
Para (7): words "as an expense of the administration" in square brackets substituted by SI 2010/686, r 2, Sch 1, para 46(1), (4).

Date in force: 6 April 2010: see SI 2010/686, r 1; for transitional provisions see r 6(1), Sch 4, para 1 thereto.

See Further

See further, in relation to the application of this rule, with modifications, in respect of bank administration and applications for bank administration: the Bank Administration (England and Wales) Rules 2009, SI 2009/357, rr 58–61.

CHAPTER 4

. . .

NOTES

Amendment

Substituted by SI 2003/1730, r 5(1), Sch 1, Pt 2, para 9.
Date in force: 15 September 2003: see SI 2003/1730, r 1(2); for effect and the continuing operation of this Part where a provision made by or under any enactment preserves the Insolvency Act 1986, old Pt II after that date see r 5(2)–(4) thereof.

[2.32 Expenses of statement of affairs]

[(1) A relevant person making the statement of [affairs of the company] or statement of concurrence shall be allowed, and paid by the administrator [as an expense of the administration], any expenses incurred by the relevant person in so doing which the administrator considers reasonable.

(2) Any decision by the administrator under this Rule is subject to appeal to the court.

(3) Nothing in this Rule relieves a relevant person from any obligation with respect to the preparation, verification and submission of the statement of affairs, or to the provision of information to the administrator.]

NOTES

Amendment

Substituted, together with rr 2.1–2.31, 2.33–2.133, for rr 2.1–2.6, 2.6A (inserted by SI 1987/1919, reg 3(1), Schedule, Pt 1, para 7), 2.7–2.46, 2.46A (inserted by SI 1987/1919, reg 3(1), Schedule, Pt 1, para 19), 2.47–2.58, 2.59–2.62 (inserted by SI 2002/1307, rr 3(1), 5(8)), by SI 2003/1730, r 5(1), Sch 1, Pt 2, para 9.
Date in force: 15 September 2003: see SI 2003/1730, r 1(2); for effect and the continuing operation of this Part where a provision made by or under any enactment preserves the Insolvency Act 1986, old Pt II after that date see r 5(2)–(4) thereof.
Para (1): words "affairs of the company" in square brackets substituted by SI 2010/686, r 2, Sch 1, para 47(1), (2).
Date in force: 6 April 2010: see SI 2010/686, r 1; for transitional provisions see r 6(1), Sch 4, para 1 thereto.
Para (1): words "as an expense of the administration" in square brackets substituted by SI 2010/686, r 2, Sch 1, para 47(1), (3).
Date in force: 6 April 2010: see SI 2010/686, r 1; for transitional provisions see r 6(1), Sch 4, para 1 thereto.

See Further

See further, in relation to the application of this rule, with modifications, in respect of bank administration and applications for bank administration: the Bank Administration (England and Wales) Rules 2009, SI 2009/357, rr 58–61.

[2.33 Administrator's proposals]

[(1) The administrator shall, under paragraph 49, make a statement which he shall send to the registrar of companies . . ..

(2) The statement shall include, in addition to those matters set out in paragraph 49—

- (a) details of the court where the proceedings are and the relevant court reference number;
- (b) the full name, registered address, registered number and any other trading names of the company;
- (c) details relating to his appointment as administrator, including the date of appointment and the person making the application or appointment and, where there are joint administrators, details of the matters set out in paragraph 100(2);
- (d) the names of the directors and secretary of the company and details of any shareholdings in the company they may have;
- (e) an account of the circumstances giving rise to the appointment of the administrator;
- (f) if a statement of the company's affairs has been submitted, a copy or summary of it, with the administrator's comments, if any;
- (g) if an order limiting the disclosure of the statement of affairs (under Rule 2.30) has been made, a statement of that fact, as well as—
    - (i) details of who provided the statement of affairs;
    - (ii) the date of the order of limited disclosure; and
    - (iii) the details or a summary of the details that are not subject to that order;
- (h) if a full statement of affairs is not provided, the names, addresses and debts of the creditors including details of any security held;
- (j) if no statement of affairs has been submitted, details of the financial position of the company at the latest practicable date (which must, unless the court otherwise orders, be a date not earlier than that on which the company entered administration), a list of the company's creditors including their names, addresses and details of their debts, including any security held, and an explanation as to why there is no statement of affairs;
- (k) the basis upon which it is proposed that the administrator's remuneration should be fixed under Rule 2.106;
- [(ka) a statement complying with paragraph (2B) of any pre-administration costs charged or incurred by the administrator or, to the administrator's knowledge, by any other person qualified to act as an insolvency practitioner;]
- (l) (except where the administrator proposes a voluntary arrangement in relation to the company and subject to paragraph (3))—
    - (i) to the best of the administrator's knowledge and belief—
        - (aa) an estimate of the value of the prescribed part (whether or not he proposes to make an application to court under section 176A(5) or section 176A(3) applies); and
        - (bb) an estimate of the value of the company's net property; and
    - (ii) whether, and, if so, why, the administrator proposes to make an application to court under section 176A(5);
- (m) [a statement (which must comply with paragraph (2C) where that paragraph applies) of] how it is envisaged the purpose of the administration will be achieved and how it is proposed that the administration shall end. . . .;
- (n) where the administrator has decided not to call a meeting of creditors, his reasons;

(o) the manner in which the affairs and business of the company—
    (i) have, since the date of the administrator's appointment, been managed and financed, including, where any assets have been disposed of, the reasons for such disposals and the terms upon which such disposals were made; and
    (ii) will, if the administrator's proposals are approved, continue to be managed and financed;
(p) whether—
    (i) the EC Regulation applies; and
    (ii) if so, whether the proceedings are main proceedings[, secondary proceedings] or territorial proceedings; and
(q) such other information (if any) as the administrator thinks necessary to enable creditors to decide whether or not to vote for the adoption of the proposals.

[(2A) In this Part—
(a) "pre-administration costs" are—
    (i) fees charged, and
    (ii) expenses incurred,

by the administrator, or another person qualified to act as an insolvency practitioner, before the company entered administration but with a view to its doing so; and

(b) "unpaid pre-administration costs" are pre-administration costs which had not been paid when the company entered administration.

(2B) A statement of pre-administration costs complies with this paragraph if it includes—
(a) details of any agreement under which the fees were charged and expenses incurred, including the parties to the agreement and the date on which the agreement was made,
(b) details of the work done for which the fees were charged and expenses incurred,
(c) an explanation of why the work was done before the company entered administration and how it would further the achievement of an objective in sub-paragraph (1) of paragraph 3 in accordance with sub-paragraphs (2) to (4) of that paragraph,
(d) a statement of the amount of the pre-administration costs, setting out separately—
    (i) the fees charged by the administrator,
    (ii) the expenses incurred by the administrator,
    (iii) the fees charged (to the administrator's knowledge) by any other person qualified to act as an insolvency practitioner (and, if more than one, by each separately), and
    (iv) the expenses incurred (to the administrator's knowledge) by any other person qualified to act as an insolvency practitioner (and, if more than one, by each separately),
(e) a statement of the amounts of pre-administration costs which have already been paid (set out separately as under sub-paragraph (d)),
(f) the identity of the person who made the payment or, if more than one person made the payment, the identity of each such person and of the amounts paid by each such person set out separately as under sub-paragraph (d),
(g) a statement of the amounts of unpaid pre-administration costs (set out separately as under sub-paragraph (d)), and
(h) a statement that the payment of unpaid pre-administration costs as an expense of the administration is—

(i) subject to approval under Rule 2.67A, and

(ii) not part of the proposals subject to approval under paragraph 53.

(2C) This paragraph applies where it is proposed that the administration will end by the company moving to a creditors' voluntary liquidation; and in that case, the statement required by paragraph (2)(m) must include—

(a) details of the proposed liquidator;

(b) where applicable, the declaration required by section 231; and

(c) a statement that the creditors may, before the proposals are approved, nominate a different person as liquidator in accordance with paragraph 83(7)(a) and Rule 2.117A(2)(b).]

(3) Nothing in paragraph (2)(l) is to be taken as requiring any such estimate to include any information, the disclosure of which could seriously prejudice the commercial interests of the company. If such information is excluded from the calculation the estimate shall be accompanied by a statement to that effect.

(4) Where the court orders, upon an application by the administrator under paragraph 107, an extension of the period of time in paragraph 49(5), the administrator [must as soon as reasonably practicable after the making of the order—

(a) notify in Form 2.18B every creditor of the company and every member of the company of whose address (in either case) the administrator is aware, and

(b) send a copy of the notification to the registrar of companies].

(5) Where the administrator has made a statement under paragraph 52(1) and has not called an initial meeting of creditors, the proposals sent out under this Rule and paragraph 49 will (if no meeting has been requisitioned under paragraph 52(2) within the period set out in Rule 2.37(1)) be deemed to have been approved by the creditors.

[(5A) Where proposals are deemed under paragraph (5) to have been approved, the administrator must, as soon as reasonably practicable after expiry of the period set out in Rule 2.37(1), give notice of the date on which they were deemed to have been approved to the registrar of companies, the court and the creditors; and a copy of the proposals must be attached to the notice given to the court and to creditors who have not previously received them.]

(6) Where the administrator intends to apply to the court (or file a notice under paragraph 80(2)) for the administration to cease at a time before he has sent a statement of his proposals to creditors in accordance with paragraph 49, he shall, at least [7 business] days before he makes such an application (or files such a notice), send to all creditors of the company (so far as he is aware of their addresses) a report containing the information required by paragraphs (2)(a)-(p) of this Rule.

[(7) Where the administrator wishes to publish a notice under paragraph 49(6), the notice shall be advertised in such manner as the administrator thinks fit.

[(7A) In addition to the standard contents, the notice under paragraph (7) must state—

(a) that members can write for a copy of the statement of proposals for achieving the purpose of administration; and

(b) the address to which to write.]]

(8) This notice must be published as soon as reasonably practicable after the administrator sends his statement of proposals to the company's creditors but no later than 8 weeks (or such other period as may be agreed by the creditors or as the court may order) from the date that the company entered administration.]

NOTES

Amendment

Substituted, together with rr 2.1–2.32, 2.34–2.133, for rr 2.1–2.6, 2.6A (inserted by SI 1987/1919, reg 3(1), Schedule, Pt 1, para 7), 2.7–2.46, 2.46A (inserted by SI 1987/1919,

reg 3(1), Schedule, Pt 1, para 19), 2.47–2.58, 2.59–2.62 (inserted by SI 2002/1307, rr 3(1), 5(8)), by SI 2003/1730, r 5(1), Sch 1, Pt 2, para 9.
  Date in force: 15 September 2003: see SI 2003/1730, r 1(2); for effect and the continuing operation of this Part where a provision made by or under any enactment preserves the Insolvency Act 1986, old Pt II after that date see r 5(2)–(4) thereof.
Para (1): words omitted revoked by SI 2010/686, r 2, Sch 1, para 48(1), (2).
  Date in force: 6 April 2010: see SI 2010/686, r 1; for transitional provisions see r 6(1), Sch 4, para 1 thereto.
Para (2): sub-para (ka) inserted by SI 2010/686, r 2, Sch 1, para 48(1), (3)(a).
  Date in force: 6 April 2010: see SI 2010/686, r 1; for transitional provisions see r 6(1), Sch 4, para 1 thereto.
Para (2): in sub-para (m) words from "a statement (which" to "paragraph applies) of" in square brackets inserted by SI 2010/686, r 2, Sch 1, para 48(1), (3)(b)(i).
  Date in force: 6 April 2010: see SI 2010/686, r 1; for transitional provisions see r 6(1), Sch 4, para 1 thereto.
Para (2): in sub-para (m) words omitted revoked by SI 2010/686, r 2, Sch 1, para 48(1), (3)(b)(ii).
  Date in force: 6 April 2010: see SI 2010/686, r 1; for transitional provisions see r 6(1), Sch 4, para 1 thereto.
Para (2): in sub-para (p)(ii) words ", secondary proceedings" in square brackets inserted by SI 2010/686, r 2, Sch 1, para 48(1), (3)(c).
  Date in force: 6 April 2010: see SI 2010/686, r 1; for transitional provisions see r 6(1), Sch 4, para 1 thereto.
Paras (2A)–(2C): inserted by SI 2010/686, r 2, Sch 1, para 48(1), (4).
  Date in force: 6 April 2010: see SI 2010/686, r 1; for transitional provisions see r 6(1), Sch 4, para 1 thereto.
Para (4): words from "must as soon" to "registrar of companies" in square brackets substituted by SI 2010/686, r 2, Sch 1, para 48(1), (5).
  Date in force: 6 April 2010: see SI 2010/686, r 1; for transitional provisions see r 6(1), Sch 4, para 1 thereto.
Para (5A): inserted by SI 2010/686, r 2, Sch 1, para 48(1), (6).
  Date in force: 6 April 2010: see SI 2010/686, r 1; for transitional provisions see r 6(1), Sch 4, para 1 thereto.
Para (6): words "7 business" in square brackets substituted by SI 2010/686, r 2, Sch 1, para 48(1), (7).
  Date in force: 6 April 2010: see SI 2010/686, r 1; for transitional provisions see r 6(1), Sch 4, para 1 thereto.
Paras (7), (7A): substituted, for para (7) as originally enacted, by SI 2009/642, rr 4, 9.
  Date in force: 6 April 2009: see SI 2009/642, r 1; for transitional provisions see r 3 thereof.
Para (7A): further substituted by SI 2010/686, r 2, Sch 1, para 48(1), (8).
  Date in force: 6 April 2010: see SI 2010/686, r 1; for transitional provisions see r 6(1), Sch 4, para 1 thereto.

See Further

See further, in relation to the application of this rule, with modifications, in respect of bank administration and applications for bank administration: the Bank Administration (England and Wales) Rules 2009, SI 2009/357, rr 58–61.

[2.33A Limited disclosure of para 49 statement]

[(1) Where the administrator thinks that it would prejudice the conduct of the administration or might reasonably be expected to lead to violence against any person for any of the matters specified in Rule 2.33(2)(h) and (j) to be disclosed, the administrator may apply to the court for an order of limited disclosure in respect of any specified part of the statement under paragraph 49.

(2) The court may, on such application, order that some or all of the specified part of the statement must not be sent to the registrar of companies or to creditors or members of the company as otherwise required by paragraph 49(4).

(3) The administrator must as soon as reasonably practicable send to the persons specified in paragraph 49(4) the statement under paragraph 49 (to the extent provided

by the order) and an indication of the nature of the matter in relation to which the order was made.

(4) The administrator must also send a copy of the order to the registrar of companies.

(5) A creditor who seeks disclosure of a part of a statement under paragraph 49 in relation to which an order has been made under this Rule may apply to the court for an order that the administrator disclose it. The application must be supported by written evidence in the form of a witness statement.

(6) The applicant must give the administrator notice of the application at least 3 business days before the hearing.

(7) The court may make any order for disclosure subject to any conditions as to confidentiality, duration, the scope of the order in the event of any change of circumstances, or other matters as it sees just.

(8) If there is a material change in circumstances rendering the limit on disclosure or any part of it unnecessary, the administrator must, as soon as reasonably practicable after the change, apply to the court for the order or any part of it to be rescinded.

(9) The administrator must, as soon as reasonably practicable after the making of an order under paragraph (8), send to the persons specified in paragraph 49(4) a copy of the statement under paragraph 49 to the extent provided by the order.

(10) The provisions of CPR Part 31 do not apply to an application under this Rule.]

NOTES

Amendment

Inserted by SI 2010/686, r 2, Sch 1, para 49.
Date in force: 6 April 2010: see SI 2010/686, r 1; for transitional provisions see r 6(1), Sch 4, para 1 thereto.

[CHAPTER 6

MEETINGS AND REPORTS]

NOTES

Amendment

Substituted by SI 2003/1730, r 5(1), Sch 1, Pt 2, para 9.
Date in force: 15 September 2003: see SI 2003/1730, r 1(2); for effect and the continuing operation of this Part where a provision made by or under any enactment preserves the Insolvency Act 1986, old Pt II after that date see r 5(2)–(4) thereof.

[SECTION A: CREDITORS' MEETINGS]

NOTES

Amendment

Substituted by SI 2003/1730, r 5(1), Sch 1, Pt 2, para 9.
Date in force: 15 September 2003: see SI 2003/1730, r 1(2); for effect and the continuing operation of this Part where a provision made by or under any enactment preserves the Insolvency Act 1986, old Pt II after that date see r 5(2)–(4) thereof.

[2.34 Meetings to consider administrator's proposals]

[[(1) As soon as reasonably practicable after an invitation to the initial creditors' meeting has been sent to the creditors in compliance with the requirements of paragraph 51(1), the administrator [must have gazetted a notice which, in addition to the standard contents, must state—

(a) that an initial creditors' meeting is to take place; and
(b) the venue fixed for the meeting].]

[(1A) The information required to be gazetted under paragraph (1) may also be advertised in such other manner as the administrator thinks fit.]

(2) Notice in Form 2.19B to attend the meeting shall be sent out at the same time to any directors or officers of the company (including persons who have been directors or officers in the past) whose presence at the meeting is, in the administrator's opinion, required.

(3) Where the court orders an extension to the period set out in paragraph 51(2)(b) the administrator shall send a notice in Form 2.18B to each person to whom he is required to send notice by paragraph 49(4).

(4) If at the meeting there is not the requisite majority for approval of the administrator's proposals (with modifications, if any), the chairman may, and shall if a resolution is passed to that effect, adjourn the meeting for not more than 14 days . . . (subject to any direction by the court).

[(5) If there are subsequently further adjournments, the final adjournment must not be to a day later than 14 days after the date on which the meeting was originally held, subject to any direction of the court.

(6) Where a meeting is adjourned under this Rule, proofs and proxies may be used if lodged at any time up to 12.00 hours on the business day immediately before the adjourned meeting.]]

NOTES

Amendment

Substituted, together with rr 2.1–2.33, 2.35–2.133, for rr 2.1–2.6, 2.6A (inserted by SI 1987/1919, reg 3(1), Schedule, Pt 1, para 7), 2.7–2.46, 2.46A (inserted by SI 1987/1919, reg 3(1), Schedule, Pt 1, para 19), 2.47–2.58, 2.59–2.62 (inserted by SI 2002/1307, rr 3(1), 5(8)), by SI 2003/1730, r 5(1), Sch 1, Pt 2, para 9.
Date in force: 15 September 2003: see SI 2003/1730, r 1(2); for effect and the continuing operation of this Part where a provision made by or under any enactment preserves the Insolvency Act 1986, old Pt II after that date see r 5(2)–(4) thereof.
Para (1): substituted by SI 2009/642, rr 4, 10(a).
Date in force: 6 April 2009: see SI 2009/642, r 1; for transitional provisions see r 3 thereof.
Para (1): words from "must have gazetted" to "for the meeting" in square brackets substituted by SI 2010/686, r 2, Sch 1, para 50(1), (2).
Date in force: 6 April 2010: see SI 2010/686, r 1; for transitional provisions see r 6(1), Sch 4, para 1 thereto.
Para (1A): inserted by SI 2009/642, rr 4, 10(b).
Date in force: 6 April 2009: see SI 2009/642, r 1; for transitional provisions see r 3 thereof.
Para (4): words omitted revoked by SI 2010/686, r 2, Sch 1, para 50(1), (3).
Date in force: 6 April 2010: see SI 2010/686, r 1; for transitional provisions see r 6(1), Sch 4, para 1 thereto.
Paras (5), (6): inserted by SI 2010/686, r 2, Sch 1, para 50(1), (4).
Date in force: 6 April 2010: see SI 2010/686, r 1; for transitional provisions see r 6(1), Sch 4, para 1 thereto.

See Further

See further, in relation to the application of this rule, with modifications, in respect of bank administration and applications for bank administration: the Bank Administration (England and Wales) Rules 2009, SI 2009/357, rr 58–61.

[2.35 Creditors' meetings generally]

[(1) This Rule applies to creditors' meetings summoned by the administrator under—

(a) paragraph 51 (initial creditors' meeting);
(b) paragraph 52(2) (at the request of the creditors);
(c) paragraph 54(2) (to consider revision to the administrator's proposals);
(d) paragraph 56(1) (further creditors' meetings); and
(e) paragraph 62 (general power to summon meetings of creditors).

(2) Notice of any of the meetings set out in paragraph (1) above shall be in Form 2.20B.

(3) In fixing the venue for the meeting, the administrator shall have regard to the convenience of creditors and the meeting shall be summoned for commencement between 10.00 and 16.00 hours on a business day, unless the court otherwise directs.

(4) Subject to paragraphs (6) and (7) below, at least 14 days' notice of the meeting shall be given to all creditors who are known to the administrator and had claims against the company at the date when the company entered administration unless that creditor has subsequently been paid in full; and the notice shall—

(a) specify the purpose of the meeting;
(b) contain a statement of the effect of Rule 2.38 (entitlement to vote); and
(c) contain the forms of proxy.

[(4A) As soon as reasonably practicable after notice of the meeting has been given, the administrator must have gazetted a notice which, in addition to the standard contents, must state—

(a) that a creditors' meeting is to take place;
(b) the venue fixed for the meeting;
(c) the purpose of the meeting; and
(d) a statement of the effect of Rule 2.38 (entitlement to vote).]

(5) If within 30 minutes from the time fixed for commencement of the meeting there is no person present to act as chairman, the meeting stands adjourned to the same time and place in the following week or, if that is not a business day, to the business day immediately following.

[(6A) If within 30 minutes from the time fixed for the commencement of the meeting those persons attending the meeting do not constitute a quorum, the chairman may adjourn the meeting to such time and place as the chairman may appoint.

(6B) Once only in the course of the meeting the chairman may, without an adjournment, declare the meeting suspended for any period up to 1 hour.

(6C) The chairman may, and must if the meeting so resolves, adjourn the meeting to such time and place as seems to the chairman to be appropriate in the circumstances.

An adjournment under this paragraph must not be for a period of more than 14 days, subject to the direction of the court.

(6D) If there are subsequently further adjournments, the final adjournment must not be to a day later than 14 days after the date on which the meeting was originally held.

(6E) Where a meeting is adjourned under this Rule, proofs and proxies may be used if lodged at any time up to 12.00 hours on the business day immediately before the adjourned meeting.

(6F) Paragraph (3) applies with regard to the venue fixed for a meeting adjourned under this Rule.]

(7) . . .]

NOTES

Amendment

Substituted, together with rr 2.1–2.34, 2.36–2.133, for rr 2.1–2.6, 2.6A (inserted by SI 1987/1919, reg 3(1), Schedule, Pt 1, para 7), 2.7–2.46, 2.46A (inserted by SI 1987/1919, reg 3(1), Schedule, Pt 1, para 19), 2.47–2.58, 2.59–2.62 (inserted by SI 2002/1307, rr 3(1), 5(8)), by SI 2003/1730, r 5(1), Sch 1, Pt 2, para 9.

Date in force: 15 September 2003: see SI 2003/1730, r 1(2); for effect and the continuing operation of this Part where a provision made by or under any enactment preserves the Insolvency Act 1986, old Pt II after that date see r 5(2)–(4) thereof.

Para (4A): inserted by SI 2010/686, r 2, Sch 1, para 51(1), (2).

Date in force: 6 April 2010: see SI 2010/686, r 1; for transitional provisions see r 6(1), Sch 4, para 1 thereto.

Paras (6A)–(6F): substituted, for para (6) as previously enacted, by SI 2010/686, r 2, Sch 1, para 51(1), (3).

Date in force: 6 April 2010: see SI 2010/686, r 1; for transitional provisions see r 6(1), Sch 4, para 1 thereto.

Para (7): revoked by SI 2010/686, r 2, Sch 1, para 51(1), (4).

Date in force: 6 April 2010: see SI 2010/686, r 1; for transitional provisions see r 6(1), Sch 4, para 1 thereto.

See Further

See further, in relation to the application of this rule, with modifications, in respect of bank administration and applications for bank administration: the Bank Administration (England and Wales) Rules 2009, SI 2009/357, rr 58–61.

[2.36 The chairman at meetings]

[(1) At any meeting of creditors summoned by the administrator, either he shall be chairman, or a person nominated by him in writing to act in his place.

(2) A person so nominated must be either—

(a) one who is qualified to act as an insolvency practitioner in relation to the company; or

(b) an employee of the administrator or his firm who is experienced in insolvency matters.

[(3) Where the chairman holds a proxy which includes a requirement to vote for a particular resolution and no other person proposes that resolution—

(a) the chairman must propose it unless the chairman considers that there is good reason for not doing so, and

(b) if the chairman does not propose it, the chairman must as soon as reasonably practicable after the meeting notify the principal of the reason why not.]]

NOTES

Amendment

Substituted, together with rr 2.1–2.35, 2.37–2.133, for rr 2.1–2.6, 2.6A (inserted by SI 1987/1919, reg 3(1), Schedule, Pt 1, para 7), 2.7–2.46, 2.46A (inserted by SI 1987/1919, reg 3(1), Schedule, Pt 1, para 19), 2.47–2.58, 2.59–2.62 (inserted by SI 2002/1307, rr 3(1), 5(8)), by SI 2003/1730, r 5(1), Sch 1, Pt 2, para 9.

Date in force: 15 September 2003: see SI 2003/1730, r 1(2); for effect and the continuing operation of this Part where a provision made by or under any enactment preserves the Insolvency Act 1986, old Pt II after that date see r 5(2)–(4) thereof.

Para (3): inserted by SI 2010/686, r 2, Sch 1, para 52.

Date in force: 6 April 2010: see SI 2010/686, r 1; for transitional provisions see r 6(1), Sch 4, para 1 thereto.

See Further
> See further, in relation to the application of this rule, with modifications, in respect of bank administration and applications for bank administration: the Bank Administration (England and Wales) Rules 2009, SI 2009/357, rr 58–61.

[2.37 Meeting requisitioned by creditors]

[(1) The request for a creditors' meeting under paragraph 52(2) or 56(1) shall be in Form 2.21B. A request for an initial creditors' meeting shall be made within [8 business] days of the date on which the administrator's statement of proposals is sent out. A request under paragraph 52(2) or 56(1) shall include—

(a) a list of the creditors concurring with the request, showing the amounts of their respective debts in the administration;

(b) from each creditor concurring, written confirmation of his concurrence; and

(c) a statement of the purpose of the proposed meeting,

but [sub-paragraphs (a) and (b) do] not apply if the requisitioning creditor's debt is alone sufficient without the concurrence of other creditors.

(2) A meeting requested under paragraph 52(2) or 56(1) shall be held within 28 days of the administrator's receipt of the notice requesting the meeting.

(3) The expenses of summoning and holding a meeting at the request of a creditor shall be paid by that person, who shall deposit with the administrator security for their payment.

(4) The sum to be deposited shall be such as the administrator may determine, and he shall not act without the deposit having been made.

(5) The meeting may resolve that the expenses of summoning and holding it are to be payable out of the assets of the company as an expense of the administration.

(6) To the extent that any deposit made under this Rule is not required for the payment of expenses of summoning and holding the meeting, it shall be repaid to the person who made it.]

NOTES

Amendment
> Substituted, together with rr 2.1–2.36, 2.38–2.133, for rr 2.1–2.6, 2.6A (inserted by SI 1987/1919, reg 3(1), Schedule, Pt 1, para 7), 2.7–2.46, 2.46A (inserted by SI 1987/1919, reg 3(1), Schedule, Pt 1, para 19), 2.47–2.58, 2.59–2.62 (inserted by SI 2002/1307, rr 3(1), 5(8)), by SI 2003/1730, r 5(1), Sch 1, Pt 2, para 9.
>> Date in force: 15 September 2003: see SI 2003/1730, r 1(2); for effect and the continuing operation of this Part where a provision made by or under any enactment preserves the Insolvency Act 1986, old Pt II after that date see r 5(2)–(4) thereof.
>
> Para (1): words "8 business" in square brackets substituted by SI 2010/686, r 2, Sch 1, para 53(1), (2)(a).
>> Date in force: 6 April 2010: see SI 2010/686, r 1; for transitional provisions see r 6(1), Sch 4, para 1 thereto.
>
> Para (1): words "sub-paragraphs (a) and (b) do" in square brackets substituted by SI 2010/686, r 2, Sch 1, para 53(1), (2)(b).
>> Date in force: 6 April 2010: see SI 2010/686, r 1; for transitional provisions see r 6(1), Sch 4, para 1 thereto.

See Further
> See further, in relation to the application of this rule, with modifications, in respect of bank administration and applications for bank administration: the Bank Administration (England and Wales) Rules 2009, SI 2009/357, rr 58–61.

[2.37A Notice of meetings by advertisement only]

[(1) The court may order that notice of any meeting be given by advertisement and not by individual notice to the persons concerned.

(2) In considering whether to act under this Rule, the court must have regard to the cost of advertisement, the amount of assets available and the extent of the interest of creditors, members or any particular class of either.]

NOTES

Amendment

Inserted by SI 2010/686, r 2, Sch 1, para 54.
Date in force: 6 April 2010: see SI 2010/686, r 1; for transitional provisions see r 6(1), Sch 4, para 1 thereto.

[2.38 Entitlement to vote]

[(1) Subject as follows, at a meeting of creditors in administration proceedings a person is entitled to vote only if—

(a) he has given to the administrator, not later than 12.00 hours on the business day before the day fixed for the meeting, details in writing of the debt which—
 (i) he claims to be due to him from the company; or
 (ii) in relation to a member State liquidator, is claimed to be due to creditors in proceedings in relation to which he holds office;
(b) the claim has been duly admitted under [Rule 2.39 or] this Rule; and
(c) there has been lodged with the administrator any proxy which he intends to be used on his behalf,

and details of the debt must include any calculation for the purposes of Rules 2.40 to 2.42.

(2) The chairman of the meeting may allow a creditor to vote, notwithstanding that he has failed to comply with paragraph (1)(a), if satisfied that the failure was due to circumstances beyond the creditor's control.

(3) The chairman of the meeting may call for any document or other evidence to be produced to him, where he thinks it necessary for the purpose of substantiating the whole or any part of the claim.

(4) Votes are calculated according to the amount of a creditor's claim as at the date on which the company entered administration, less any payments that have been made to him after that date in respect of his claim and any adjustment by way of set-off in accordance with Rule 2.85 as if that Rule were applied on the date that the votes are counted.

(5) A creditor shall not vote in respect of a debt for an unliquidated amount, or any debt whose value is not ascertained, except where the chairman agrees to put upon the debt an estimated minimum value for the purpose of entitlement to vote and admits the claim for that purpose.

(6) No vote shall be cast by virtue of a claim more than once on any resolution put to the meeting.

(7) Where—
(a) a creditor is entitled to vote under this Rule [and Rule 2.39];
(b) has lodged his claim in one or more sets of other proceedings; and
(c) votes (either in person or by proxy) on a resolution put to the meeting; and
(d) the member State liquidator casts a vote in respect of the same claim,

only the creditor's vote shall be counted.

(8) Where—

(a) a creditor has lodged his claim in more than one set of other proceedings; and
(b) more than one member State liquidator seeks to vote by virtue of that claim,

the entitlement to vote by virtue of that claim is exercisable by the member State liquidator in main proceedings, whether or not the creditor has lodged his claim in the main proceedings.

(9) For the purposes of paragraph (6), the claim of a creditor and of any member State liquidator in relation to the same debt are a single claim.

(10) For the purposes of paragraphs (7) and (8), "other proceedings" means main proceedings, secondary proceedings or territorial proceedings in another member State.]

NOTES

Amendment

Substituted, together with rr 2.1–2.37, 2.39–2.133, for rr 2.1–2.6, 2.6A (inserted by SI 1987/1919, reg 3(1), Schedule, Pt 1, para 7), 2.7–2.46, 2.46A (inserted by SI 1987/1919, reg 3(1), Schedule, Pt 1, para 19), 2.47–2.58, 2.59–2.62 (inserted by SI 2002/1307, rr 3(1), 5(8)), by SI 2003/1730, r 5(1), Sch 1, Pt 2, para 9.
Date in force: 15 September 2003: see SI 2003/1730, r 1(2); for effect and the continuing operation of this Part where a provision made by or under any enactment preserves the Insolvency Act 1986, old Pt II after that date see r 5(2)–(4) thereof.
Para (1): in sub-para (b) words "Rule 2.39 or" in square brackets substituted by SI 2010/686, r 2, Sch 1, para 55(1), (2).
Date in force: 6 April 2010: see SI 2010/686, r 1; for transitional provisions see r 6(1), Sch 4, para 1 thereto.
Para (7): in sub-para (a) words "and Rule 2.39" in square brackets inserted by SI 2010/686, r 2, Sch 1, para 55(1), (3).
Date in force: 6 April 2010: see SI 2010/686, r 1; for transitional provisions see r 6(1), Sch 4, para 1 thereto.

See Further

See further, in relation to the application of this rule, with modifications, in respect of bank administration and applications for bank administration: the Bank Administration (England and Wales) Rules 2009, SI 2009/357, rr 58–61.

[2.39 Admission and rejection of claims]

[(1) At any creditors' meeting the chairman has power to admit or reject a creditor's claim for the purpose of his entitlement to vote; and the power is exercisable with respect to the whole or any part of the claim.

(2) The chairman's decision under this Rule, or in respect of any matter arising under Rule 2.38, is subject to appeal to the court by any creditor.

(3) If the chairman is in doubt whether a claim should be admitted or rejected, he shall mark it as objected to and allow the creditor to vote, subject to his vote being subsequently declared invalid if the objection to the claim is sustained.

(4) If on an appeal the chairman's decision is reversed or varied, or a creditor's vote is declared invalid, the court may order that another meeting be summoned, or make such other order as it thinks [just].

[(5) An application to the court by way of appeal under this Rule against a decision of the chairman must be made not later than 21 days after the date of the meeting.]

(6) Neither the administrator nor any person nominated by him to be chairman is personally liable for costs incurred by any person in respect of an appeal to the court under this Rule, unless the court makes an order to that effect.]

NOTES

Amendment

Substituted, together with rr 2.1–2.38, 2.40–2.133, for rr 2.1–2.6, 2.6A (inserted by SI 1987/1919, reg 3(1), Schedule, Pt 1, para 7), 2.7–2.46, 2.46A (inserted by SI 1987/1919, reg 3(1), Schedule, Pt 1, para 19), 2.47–2.58, 2.59–2.62 (inserted by SI 2002/1307, rr 3(1), 5(8)), by SI 2003/1730, r 5(1), Sch 1, Pt 2, para 9.

Date in force: 15 September 2003: see SI 2003/1730, r 1(2); for effect and the continuing operation of this Part where a provision made by or under any enactment preserves the Insolvency Act 1986, old Pt II after that date see r 5(2)–(4) thereof.

Para (4): word "just" in square brackets substituted by SI 2010/686, r 2, Sch 1, para 1.

Date in force: 6 April 2010: see SI 2010/686, r 1; for transitional provisions see r 6(1), Sch 4, paras 1, 2(1)(b) thereto.

Para (5): substituted by SI 2010/686, r 2, Sch 1, para 56.

Date in force: 6 April 2010: see SI 2010/686, r 1; for transitional provisions see r 6(1), Sch 4, para 1 thereto.

See Further

See further, in relation to the application of this rule, with modifications, in respect of bank administration and applications for bank administration: the Bank Administration (England and Wales) Rules 2009, SI 2009/357, rr 58–61.

[2.40 Secured creditors]

[(1) At a meeting of creditors a secured creditor is entitled to vote only in respect of the balance (if any) of his debt after deducting the value of his security as estimated by him.

(2) However, in a case where the administrator has made a statement under paragraph 52(1)(b) and an initial creditors' meeting has been requisitioned under paragraph 52(2) then a secured creditor is entitled to vote in respect of the full value of his debt without any deduction of the value of his security.]

NOTES

Amendment

Substituted, together with rr 2.1–2.39, 2.41–2.133, for rr 2.1–2.6, 2.6A (inserted by SI 1987/1919, reg 3(1), Schedule, Pt 1, para 7), 2.7–2.46, 2.46A (inserted by SI 1987/1919, reg 3(1), Schedule, Pt 1, para 19), 2.47–2.58, 2.59–2.62 (inserted by SI 2002/1307, rr 3(1), 5(8)), by SI 2003/1730, r 5(1), Sch 1, Pt 2, para 9.

Date in force: 15 September 2003: see SI 2003/1730, r 1(2); for effect and the continuing operation of this Part where a provision made by or under any enactment preserves the Insolvency Act 1986, old Pt II after that date see r 5(2)–(4) thereof.

See Further

See further, in relation to the application of this rule, with modifications, in respect of bank administration and applications for bank administration: the Bank Administration (England and Wales) Rules 2009, SI 2009/357, rr 58–61.

[2.41 Holders of negotiable instruments]

[A creditor shall not vote in respect of a debt on, or secured by, a current bill of exchange or promissory note, unless he is willing—

- (a) to treat the liability to him on the bill or note of every person who is liable on it antecedently to the company, and against whom a bankruptcy order has not been made (or, in the case of a company, which has not gone into liquidation), as a security in his hands; and
- (b) to estimate the value of the security and, for the purpose of his entitlement to vote [(but not for dividend)], to deduct it from his claim.]

NOTES

Amendment

Substituted, together with rr 2.1–2.40, 2.42–2.133, for rr 2.1–2.6, 2.6A (inserted by SI 1987/1919, reg 3(1), Schedule, Pt 1, para 7), 2.7–2.46, 2.46A (inserted by SI 1987/1919, reg 3(1), Schedule, Pt 1, para 19), 2.47–2.58, 2.59–2.62 (inserted by SI 2002/1307, rr 3(1), 5(8)), by SI 2003/1730, r 5(1), Sch 1, Pt 2, para 9.

Date in force: 15 September 2003: see SI 2003/1730, r 1(2); for effect and the continuing operation of this Part where a provision made by or under any enactment preserves the Insolvency Act 1986, old Pt II after that date see r 5(2)–(4) thereof.

In para (b) words "(but not for dividend)" in square brackets inserted by SI 2010/686, r 2, Sch 1, para 57.

Date in force: 6 April 2010: see SI 2010/686, r 1; for transitional provisions see r 6(1), Sch 4, para 1 thereto.

See Further

See further, in relation to the application of this rule, with modifications, in respect of bank administration and applications for bank administration: the Bank Administration (England and Wales) Rules 2009, SI 2009/357, rr 58–61.

[2.42 Hire-purchase, conditional sale and chattel leasing agreements]

[(1) Subject as follows, an owner of goods under a hire-purchase or chattel leasing agreement, or a seller of goods under a conditional sale agreement, is entitled to vote in respect of the amount of the debt due and payable to him by the company on the date that the company entered administration.

(2) In calculating the amount of any debt for this purpose, no account shall be taken of any amount attributable to the exercise of any right under the relevant agreement, so far as the right has become exercisable solely by virtue of the making of an administration application, a notice of intention to appoint an administrator or any matter arising as a consequence, or of the company entering administration.]

NOTES

Amendment

Substituted, together with rr 2.1–2.41, 2.43–2.133, for rr 2.1–2.6, 2.6A (inserted by SI 1987/1919, reg 3(1), Schedule, Pt 1, para 7), 2.7–2.46, 2.46A (inserted by SI 1987/1919, reg 3(1), Schedule, Pt 1, para 19), 2.47–2.58, 2.59–2.62 (inserted by SI 2002/1307, rr 3(1), 5(8)), by SI 2003/1730, r 5(1), Sch 1, Pt 2, para 9.

Date in force: 15 September 2003: see SI 2003/1730, r 1(2); for effect and the continuing operation of this Part where a provision made by or under any enactment preserves the Insolvency Act 1986, old Pt II after that date see r 5(2)–(4) thereof.

See Further

See further, in relation to the application of this rule, with modifications, in respect of bank administration and applications for bank administration: the Bank Administration (England and Wales) Rules 2009, SI 2009/357, rr 58–61.

[2.43 Resolutions]

[(1) Subject to paragraph (2), at a creditors' meeting in administration proceedings, a resolution is passed when a majority (in value) of those present and voting, in person or by proxy, have voted in favour of it.

(2) Any resolution is invalid if those voting against it include more than half in value of the creditors to whom notice of the meeting was sent and who are not, to the best of the chairman's belief, persons connected with the company.]

NOTES

Amendment

Substituted, together with rr 2.1–2.42, 2.44–2.133, for rr 2.1–2.6, 2.6A (inserted by SI 1987/1919, reg 3(1), Schedule, Pt 1, para 7), 2.7–2.46, 2.46A (inserted by SI 1987/1919, reg 3(1), Schedule, Pt 1, para 19), 2.47–2.58, 2.59–2.62 (inserted by SI 2002/1307, rr 3(1), 5(8)), by SI 2003/1730, r 5(1), Sch 1, Pt 2, para 9.

Date in force: 15 September 2003: see SI 2003/1730, r 1(2); for effect and the continuing operation of this Part where a provision made by or under any enactment preserves the Insolvency Act 1986, old Pt II after that date see r 5(2)–(4) thereof.

See Further

See further, in relation to the application of this rule, with modifications, in respect of bank administration and applications for bank administration: the Bank Administration (England and Wales) Rules 2009, SI 2009/357, rr 58–61.

[2.44A Minutes]

[(1) The chairman of the meeting must cause minutes of its proceedings to be kept.

(2) The minutes must be authenticated by the chairman, and be retained by the chairman as part of the records of the administration.

(3) The chairman must also cause to be made up and kept a list of all the creditors who attended the meeting.

(4) The minutes must include—
- (a) a list of the names of creditors who attended (personally or by proxy) and their claims,
- (b) if a creditors' committee has been established, the names and addresses of those elected to be members of the committee, and
- (c) a record of every resolution passed.]

NOTES

Amendment

Substituted, for r 2.44 as previously enacted, by SI 2010/686, r 2, Sch 1, para 58.

Date in force: 6 April 2010: see SI 2010/686, r 1; for transitional provisions see r 6(1), Sch 4, para 1 thereto.

[2.45 Revision of the administrator's proposals]

[(1) The administrator shall, under paragraph 54, make a statement setting out the proposed revisions to his proposals which he shall attach to Form 2.22B and send to all those to whom he is required to send a copy of his revised proposals.

(2) The statement of revised proposals shall include—
- (a) details of the court where the proceedings are and the relevant court reference number;
- (b) the full name, registered address, registered number and any other trading names of the company;
- (c) details relating to his appointment as administrator, including the date of appointment and the person making the administration application or appointment;
- (d) the names of the directors and secretary of the company and details of any shareholdings in the company they may have;
- (e) a summary of the initial proposals and the reason(s) for proposing a revision;

(f) details of the proposed revision including details of the administrator's assessment of the likely impact of the proposed revision upon creditors generally or upon each class of creditors (as the case may be);

(g) where a proposed revision relates to the ending of the administration by a creditors' voluntary liquidation and the nomination of a person to be the proposed liquidator of the company,

[(i) details of the proposed liquidator,

(ii) where applicable, the declaration required by section 231, and

(iii) a statement that the creditors may, before the proposals are approved, nominate a different person as liquidator in accordance with paragraph 83(7)(a) and Rule 2.117A(2)(b)]; and

(h) any other information that the administrator thinks necessary to enable creditors to decide whether or not to vote for the proposed revisions.

(3) Subject to paragraph 54(3), within 5 [business] days of sending out the statement in paragraph (1) above, the administrator shall send a copy of the statement to every member of the company.

(4) [Any notice to be published by the administrator acting under paragraph 54(3) shall be advertised in such manner as the administrator thinks fit.]

[(5) The notice must be published as soon as reasonably practicable after the administrator sends the statement to the creditors and in addition to the standard contents must state—

(a) that members can write for a copy of the statement of revised proposals for the administration; and

(b) the address to which to write.]]

NOTES

Amendment

Substituted, together with rr 2.1–2.44, 2.46–2.133, for rr 2.1–2.6, 2.6A (inserted by SI 1987/1919, reg 3(1), Schedule, Pt 1, para 7), 2.7–2.46, 2.46A (inserted by SI 1987/1919, reg 3(1), Schedule, Pt 1, para 19), 2.47–2.58, 2.59–2.62 (inserted by SI 2002/1307, rr 3(1), 5(8)), by SI 2003/1730, r 5(1), Sch 1, Pt 2, para 9.

Date in force: 15 September 2003: see SI 2003/1730, r 1(2); for effect and the continuing operation of this Part where a provision made by or under any enactment preserves the Insolvency Act 1986, old Pt II after that date see r 5(2)–(4) thereof.

Para (2): sub-para (g)(i)–(iii) substituted, for words as previously enacted, by SI 2010/686, r 2, Sch 1, para 59(1), (2).

Date in force: 6 April 2010: see SI 2010/686, r 1; for transitional provisions see r 6(1), Sch 4, para 1 thereto.

Para (3): word "business" in square brackets inserted by SI 2010/686, r 2, Sch 1, para 59(1), (3).

Date in force: 6 April 2010: see SI 2010/686, r 1; for transitional provisions see r 6(1), Sch 4, para 1 thereto.

Para (4): words from "Any notice to" to "administrator thinks fit." in square brackets substituted by SI 2009/642, rr 4, 11.

Date in force: 6 April 2009: see SI 2009/642, r 1; for transitional provisions see r 3 thereof.

Para (5): substituted, for second sentence of para (4) as previously enacted, by SI 2010/686, r 2, Sch 1, para 59(1), (4).

Date in force: 6 April 2010: see SI 2010/686, r 1; for transitional provisions see r 6(1), Sch 4, para 1 thereto.

See Further

See further, in relation to the application of this rule, with modifications, in respect of bank administration and applications for bank administration: the Bank Administration (England and Wales) Rules 2009, SI 2009/357, rr 58–61.

[2.46 Notice to creditors]
[As soon as reasonably practicable after the conclusion of a meeting of creditors to consider the administrator's proposals or revised proposals, the administrator shall—

[(a)   send notice in Form 2.23B of the result of the meeting to every creditor and to every other person who received a copy of the original proposals,

(b)   attach a copy of the proposals considered at the meeting to the notice sent to each creditor who did not receive notice of the meeting but of whose claim the administrator has subsequently become aware, and

(c)   file with the court a copy of the proposals considered at the meeting and notice of the result of the meeting].]

NOTES

Amendment

Substituted, together with rr 2.1–2.45, 2.47–2.133, for rr 2.1–2.6, 2.6A (inserted by SI 1987/1919, reg 3(1), Schedule, Pt 1, para 7), 2.7–2.46, 2.46A (inserted by SI 1987/1919, reg 3(1), Schedule, Pt 1, para 19), 2.47–2.58, 2.59–2.62 (inserted by SI 2002/1307, rr 3(1), 5(8)), by SI 2003/1730, r 5(1), Sch 1, Pt 2, para 9.
Date in force: 15 September 2003: see SI 2003/1730, r 1(2); for effect and the continuing operation of this Part where a provision made by or under any enactment preserves the Insolvency Act 1986, old Pt II after that date see r 5(2)–(4) thereof.
Paras (a)–(c) substituted, for paras (a), (b) as previously enacted, by SI 2010/686, r 2, Sch 1, para 60.
Date in force: 6 April 2010: see SI 2010/686, r 1; for transitional provisions see r 6(1), Sch 4, para 1 thereto.

See Further

See further, in relation to the application of this rule, with modifications, in respect of bank administration and applications for bank administration: the Bank Administration (England and Wales) Rules 2009, SI 2009/357, rr 58–61.

CHAPTER 5

. . .

NOTES

Amendment

Substituted by SI 2003/1730, r 5(1), Sch 1, Pt 2, para 9.
Date in force: 15 September 2003: see SI 2003/1730, r 1(2); for effect and the continuing operation of this Part where a provision made by or under any enactment preserves the Insolvency Act 1986, old Pt II after that date see r 5(2)–(4) thereof.

[2.46A . . .]
[. . .]

NOTES

Amendment

Substituted, together with rr 2.1–2.133, for rr 2.1–2.6, 2.6A (inserted by SI 1987/1919, reg 3(1), Schedule, Pt 1, para 7), 2.7–2.46, 2.46A, 2.47–2.58, 2.59–2.62 (inserted by SI 2002/1307, rr 3(1), 5(8)), by SI 2003/1730, r 5(1), Sch 1, Pt 2, para 9.
Date in force: 15 September 2003: see SI 2003/1730, r 1(2); for effect and the continuing operation of this Part where a provision made by or under any enactment preserves the Insolvency Act 1986, old Pt II after that date see r 5(2)–(4) thereof.

[2.47 Reports to creditors]

[(1) "Progress report" means a report which includes—
- (a) details of the court where the proceedings are and the relevant court reference number;
- (b) full details of the company's name, address of registered office and registered number;
- (c) full details of the administrator's name and address, date of appointment and name and address of appointor, including any changes in office-holder, and, in the case of joint administrators, their functions as set out in the statement made for the purposes of paragraph 100(2);
- (d) details of any extensions to the initial period of appointment;
- [(da) details of the basis fixed for the remuneration of the administrator under Rule 2.106 (or if not fixed at the date of the report, the steps taken during the period of the report to fix it);
- (db) if the basis of remuneration has been fixed, a statement of—
  - (i) the remuneration charged by the administrator during the period of the report (subject to paragraph (2A)), and
  - (ii) where the report is the first to be made after the basis has been fixed, the remuneration charged by the administrator during the periods covered by the previous reports (subject to paragraph (2A)), together with a description of the things done by the administrator during those periods in respect of which the remuneration was charged,

  irrespective in either case of whether payment was made in respect of that remuneration during the period of the report;
- (dc) a statement of the expenses incurred by the administrator during the period of the report, irrespective of whether payment was made in respect of them during that period;]
- (e) details of progress during the period of the report, including a receipts and payments account (as detailed in paragraph (2) below);
- (f) details of any assets that remain to be realised; . . .
- [(fa) a statement of the creditors' right to request information under Rule 2.48A and their right to challenge the administrator's remuneration and expenses under Rule 2.109; and]
- (g) any other relevant information for the creditors.

[(2) A receipts and payments account must be in the form of an abstract showing receipts and payments during the period of the report and, where the administrator has ceased to act, must also include a statement as to the amount paid to unsecured creditors by virtue of the application of section 176A.

(2A) Where the basis for the remuneration is a set amount under Rule 2.106(2)(c), it may be shown as that amount without any apportionment to the period of the report.

(2B) Where the administrator has made a statement of pre-administration costs under Rule 2.33(2)(ka)—
- (a) if they are approved under Rule 2.67A, the first progress report after the approval must include a statement setting out the date of the approval and the amounts approved;
- (b) each successive report, so long as any of the costs remain unapproved, must include a statement either—
  - (i) of any steps taken to get approval, or
  - (ii) that the administrator has decided, or (as the case may be) another insolvency practitioner entitled to seek approval has told the administrator of that practitioner's decision, not to seek approval.]

[(3) The progress report must, except where paragraph (3A) or (3B) applies, cover the period of 6 months commencing on the date on which the company entered administration and every subsequent period of 6 months.

(3A) The period to be covered by a progress report ends on the date when an administrator ceases to act, and the period to be covered by each subsequent progress report is each successive period of 6 months beginning immediately after that date (subject to the further application of this paragraph when another administrator ceases to act).

(3B) The sending of a progress report to creditors under Rule 2.112 (application for extension of administration) also satisfies paragraph (3) or (3A) of this Rule in respect of the period covered by that report; and the period to be covered by each subsequent progress report under this Rule is each successive period of 6 months beginning with the end of the period covered by the report under Rule 2.112.]

[(4) The administrator must, within 1 month of the end of the period covered by the report, send—
 (a) a copy to the creditors attached to Form 2.24B, and
 (b) a copy to the registrar of companies;
but this paragraph does not apply when the period covered by the report is that of a final progress report under Rule 2.110.]

(5) The court may, on the administrator's application, extend the period of 1 month mentioned in paragraph (4) above, or make such other order in respect of the content of the report as it thinks [just].

(6) If the administrator makes default in complying with this Rule, he is liable to a fine and, for continued contravention, to a daily default fine.]

NOTES

Amendment

Substituted, together with rr 2.1–2.46, 2.48–2.133, for rr 2.1–2.6, 2.6A (inserted by SI 1987/1919, reg 3(1), Schedule, Pt 1, para 7), 2.7–2.46, 2.46A (inserted by SI 1987/1919, reg 3(1), Schedule, Pt 1, para 19), 2.47–2.58, 2.59–2.62 (inserted by SI 2002/1307, rr 3(1), 5(8)), by SI 2003/1730, r 5(1), Sch 1, Pt 2, para 9.
 Date in force: 15 September 2003: see SI 2003/1730, r 1(2); for effect and the continuing operation of this Part where a provision made by or under any enactment preserves the Insolvency Act 1986, old Pt II after that date see r 5(2)–(4) thereof.
Para (1): sub-paras (da)–(dc) inserted by SI 2010/686, r 2, Sch 1, para 61(1), (2)(a).
 Date in force: 6 April 2010: see SI 2010/686, r 1; for transitional provisions see r 6(1), Sch 4, para 1 thereto.
Para (1): in sub-para (f) word omitted revoked by SI 2010/686, r 2, Sch 1, para 61(1), (2)(b).
 Date in force: 6 April 2010: see SI 2010/686, r 1; for transitional provisions see r 6(1), Sch 4, para 1 thereto.
Para (1): sub-para (fa) inserted by SI 2010/686, r 2, Sch 1, para 61(1), (2)(c).
 Date in force: 6 April 2010: see SI 2010/686, r 1; for transitional provisions see r 6(1), Sch 4, para 1 thereto.
Paras (2), (2A), (2B): substituted, for para (2) as previously enacted, by SI 2010/686, r 2, Sch 1, para 61(1), (3).
 Date in force: 6 April 2010: see SI 2010/686, r 1; for transitional provisions see r 6(1), Sch 4, para 1 thereto.
Paras (3), (3A), (3B): substituted, for para (3) as previously enacted, by SI 2010/686, r 2, Sch 1, para 61(1), (4).
 Date in force: 6 April 2010: see SI 2010/686, r 1; for transitional provisions see r 6(1), Sch 4, para 1 thereto.
Para (4): substituted by SI 2010/686, r 2, Sch 1, para 61(1), (5).
 Date in force: 6 April 2010: see SI 2010/686, r 1; for transitional provisions see r 6(1), Sch 4, para 1 thereto.
Para (5): word "just" in square brackets substituted by SI 2010/686, r 2, Sch 1, para 1.
 Date in force: 6 April 2010: see SI 2010/686, r 1; for transitional provisions see r 6(1), Sch 4, paras 1, 2(1)(b) thereto.

See Further

See further, in relation to the application of this rule, with modifications, in respect of bank administration and applications for bank administration: the Bank Administration (England and Wales) Rules 2009, SI 2009/357, rr 58–61.

[2.48 Correspondence instead of creditors' meetings]

[(1) The administrator may seek to obtain the passing of a resolution by the creditors by sending a notice in Form 2.25B to every creditor who is entitled to be notified of a creditors' meeting under Rule 2.35(4).

(2) In order to be counted, votes must be received by the administrator by 12.00 hours on the closing date specified on Form 2.25B and must be accompanied by the statement in writing on entitlement to vote required by Rule 2.38 [unless it has already been given to the administrator under that Rule].

(3) If any votes are received without the statement as to entitlement, or the administrator decides that the creditor is not entitled to vote according to Rules 2.38 and 2.39, then that creditor's votes shall be disregarded.

(4) The closing date shall be set at the discretion of the administrator. In any event it must not be set less than 14 days from the date of issue of the Form 2.25B.

(5) For any business to be transacted the administrator must receive at least 1 valid Form 2.25B by the closing date specified by him.

(6) If no valid Form 2.25B is received by the closing date specified then the administrator shall call a meeting of the creditors in accordance with Rule 2.35.

(7) Any single creditor, or a group of creditors, of the company whose debt(s) amount to at least 10% of the total debts of the company may, within 5 business days from the date of the administrator sending out a resolution or proposals, require him to summon a meeting of creditors to consider the matters raised therein in accordance with Rule 2.37. Any meeting called under this Rule shall be conducted in accordance with Rule 2.35.

(8) ...

(9) A reference in these Rules to anything done, or required to be done, at, or in connection with, or in consequence of, a creditors' meeting includes a reference to anything done in the course of correspondence in accordance with this Rule.]

NOTES

Amendment

Substituted, together with rr 2.1–2.47, 2.49–2.133, for rr 2.1–2.6, 2.6A (inserted by SI 1987/1919, reg 3(1), Schedule, Pt 1, para 7), 2.7–2.46, 2.46A (inserted by SI 1987/1919, reg 3(1), Schedule, Pt 1, para 19), 2.47–2.58, 2.59–2.62 (inserted by SI 2002/1307, rr 3(1), 5(8)), by SI 2003/1730, r 5(1), Sch 1, Pt 2, para 9.

Date in force: 15 September 2003: see SI 2003/1730, r 1(2); for effect and the continuing operation of this Part where a provision made by or under any enactment preserves the Insolvency Act 1986, old Pt II after that date see r 5(2)–(4) thereof.

Para (2): words "unless it has already been given to the administrator under that Rule" in square brackets inserted by SI 2010/686, r 2, Sch 1, para 62(1), (2).

Date in force: 6 April 2010: see SI 2010/686, r 1; for transitional provisions see r 6(1), Sch 4, para 1 thereto.

Para (8): revoked by SI 2010/686, r 2, Sch 1, para 62(1), (3).

Date in force: 6 April 2010: see SI 2010/686, r 1; for transitional provisions see r 6(1), Sch 4, para 1 thereto.

See Further

See further, in relation to the application of this rule, with modifications, in respect of bank administration and applications for bank administration: the Bank Administration (England and Wales) Rules 2009, SI 2009/357, rr 58–61.

[2.48A Creditors' request for further information]
[(1) If—
- (a) within 21 days of receipt of a progress report under Rule 2.47—
  - (i) a secured creditor, or
  - (ii) an unsecured creditor with the concurrence of at least 5% in value of the unsecured creditors (including the creditor in question), or
- (b) with the permission of the court upon an application made within that period of 21 days, any unsecured creditor,

makes a request in writing to the administrator for further information about remuneration or expenses (other than pre-administration costs) set out in a statement required by Rule 2.47(1)(db) or (dc), the administrator must, within 14 days of receipt of the request, comply with paragraph (2).

(2) The administrator complies with this paragraph by either—
- (a) providing all of the information asked for, or
- (b) so far as the administrator considers that—
  - (i) the time or cost of preparation of the information would be excessive, or
  - (ii) disclosure of the information would be prejudicial to the conduct of the administration or might reasonably be expected to lead to violence against any person, or
  - (iii) the administrator is subject to an obligation of confidentiality in respect of the information,

giving reasons for not providing all of the information.

(3) Any creditor, who need not be the same as the creditor who requested further information under paragraph (1), may apply to the court within 21 days of—
- (a) the giving by the administrator of reasons for not providing all of the information asked for, or
- (b) the expiry of the 14 days provided for in paragraph (1),

and the court may make such order as it thinks just.

(4) Without prejudice to the generality of paragraph (3), the order of the court under that paragraph may extend the period of 8 weeks provided for in Rule 2.109(1B) by such further period as the court thinks just.]

NOTES

Amendment

Inserted by SI 2010/686, r 2, Sch 1, para 63.
Date in force: 6 April 2010: see SI 2010/686, r 1; for transitional provisions see r 6(1), Sch 4, para 1 thereto.

[SECTION B: COMPANY MEETINGS]

NOTES

Amendment

Substituted by SI 2003/1730, r 5(1), Sch 1, Pt 2, para 9.
Date in force: 15 September 2003: see SI 2003/1730, r 1(2); for effect and the continuing operation of this Part where a provision made by or under any enactment preserves the Insolvency Act 1986, old Pt II after that date see r 5(2)–(4) thereof.

[2.49 Venue and conduct of company meeting]
[(1) Where the administrator summons a meeting of members of the company, he shall fix a venue for it having regard to their convenience.

(2) The chairman of the meeting shall be the administrator or a person nominated by him in writing to act in his place.

(3) A person so nominated must be either—
- (a) one who is qualified to act as an insolvency practitioner in relation to the company; or
- (b) an employee of the administrator or his firm who is experienced in insolvency matters.

(4) If within 30 minutes from the time fixed for commencement of the meeting there is no person present to act as chairman, the meeting stands adjourned to the same time and place in the following week or, if that is not a business day, to the business day immediately following.

[(5A) Subject to anything to the contrary in the Act and these Rules, the meeting must be summoned and conducted—
- (a) in the case of a company incorporated—
  - (i) in England and Wales, or in Wales, or
  - (ii) outside the United Kingdom other than in an EEA state,

  in accordance with the law of England and Wales, including any applicable provision in or made under the Companies Act;
- (b) in the case of a company incorporated in an EEA state other than the United Kingdom, in accordance with the law of that state applicable to meetings of the company.]

(7) The chairman of the meeting shall cause minutes of its proceedings to be entered in the company's minute book.]

NOTES

Amendment

Substituted, together with rr 2.1–2.48, 2.50–2.133, for rr 2.1–2.6, 2.6A (inserted by SI 1987/1919, reg 3(1), Schedule, Pt 1, para 7), 2.7–2.46, 2.46A (inserted by SI 1987/1919, reg 3(1), Schedule, Pt 1, para 19), 2.47–2.58, 2.59–2.62 (inserted by SI 2002/1307, rr 3(1), 5(8)), by SI 2003/1730, r 5(1), Sch 1, Pt 2, para 9.

Date in force: 15 September 2003: see SI 2003/1730, rule 1(2).

Para (5A): substituted, for paras (5), (6) as previously enacted, by SI 2010/686, r 2, Sch 1, para 64(1), (2).

Date in force: 6 April 2010: see SI 2010/686, r 1; for transitional provisions see r 6(1), Sch 4, para 1 thereto.

See Further

See further, in relation to the application of this rule, with modifications, in respect of bank administration and applications for bank administration: the Bank Administration (England and Wales) Rules 2009, SI 2009/357, rr 58–61.

[CHAPTER 7

THE CREDITORS' COMMITTEE]

NOTES

Amendment

Substituted by SI 2003/1730, r 5(1), Sch 1, Pt 2, para 9.

Date in force: 15 September 2003: see SI 2003/1730, r 1(2); for effect and the continuing operation of this Part where a provision made by or under any enactment preserves the Insolvency Act 1986, old Pt II after that date see r 5(2)–(4) thereof.

[2.50 Constitution of committee]
[(1) Where it is resolved by a creditors' meeting to establish a creditors' committee for the purposes of the administration, the committee shall consist of at least 3 and not more than 5 creditors of the company elected at the meeting.

[(2) A person claiming to be a creditor is entitled to be a member of the committee provided that—
   (a) that person's claim has neither been wholly disallowed for voting purposes, nor wholly rejected for the purpose of distribution or dividend; and
   (b) the claim mentioned in sub-paragraph (a) is not fully secured.]

(3) A body corporate may be a member of the committee, but it cannot act as such otherwise than by a representative appointed under Rule 2.55 below.]

NOTES

Amendment

Substituted, together with rr 2.1–2.49, 2.51–2.133, for rr 2.1–2.6, 2.6A (inserted by SI 1987/1919, reg 3(1), Schedule, Pt 1, para 7), 2.7–2.46, 2.46A (inserted by SI 1987/1919, reg 3(1), Schedule, Pt 1, para 19), 2.47–2.58, 2.59–2.62 (inserted by SI 2002/1307, rr 3(1), 5(8)), by SI 2003/1730, r 5(1), Sch 1, Pt 2, para 9.
   Date in force: 15 September 2003: see SI 2003/1730, r 1(2); for effect and the continuing operation of this Part where a provision made by or under any enactment preserves the Insolvency Act 1986, old Pt II after that date see r 5(2)–(4) thereof.
Para (2): substituted by SI 2010/686, r 2, Sch 1, para 65(1), (2).
   Date in force: 6 April 2010: see SI 2010/686, r 1; for transitional provisions see r 6(1), Sch 4, para 1 thereto.

See Further

See further, in relation to the application of this rule, with modifications, in respect of bank administration and applications for bank administration: the Bank Administration (England and Wales) Rules 2009, SI 2009/357, rr 58–61.

[2.51 Formalities of establishment]
[(1) The creditors' committee does not come into being, and accordingly cannot act, until the administrator has issued a certificate in Form 2.26B of its due constitution.

[(1A) If the chairman of the creditors' meeting which resolves to establish the committee is not the administrator, the chairman must as soon as reasonably practicable give notice of the resolution to the administrator and inform the administrator of the names and addresses of the persons elected to be members of the committee.]

(2) No person may act as a member of the committee unless and until he has agreed to do so and, unless the relevant proxy or authorisation contains a statement to the contrary, such agreement may be given by his proxy-holder . . . present at the meeting establishing the committee [or, in the case of a corporation, by its duly appointed representative].

(3) The administrator's certificate of the committee's due constitution shall not be issued [before the minimum number of members set out in Rule 2.50 elected] to be members of the committee have agreed to act and shall be issued as soon as reasonably practicable thereafter.

(4) As and when the others (if any) agree to act, the administrator shall issue an amended certificate in Form 2.26B.

(5) The certificate, and any amended certificate, shall be . . . sent to the registrar of companies by the administrator, as soon as reasonably practicable.

(6) If after the first establishment of the committee there is any change in its membership, the administrator shall as soon as reasonably practicable report the change to the [registrar of companies by filing an amended certificate].]

NOTES

Amendment

Substituted, together with rr 2.1–2.50, 2.52–2.133, for rr 2.1–2.6, 2.6A (inserted by SI 1987/1919, reg 3(1), Schedule, Pt 1, para 7), 2.7–2.46, 2.46A (inserted by SI 1987/1919, reg 3(1), Schedule, Pt 1, para 19), 2.47–2.58, 2.59–2.62 (inserted by SI 2002/1307, rr 3(1), 5(8)), by SI 2003/1730, r 5(1), Sch 1, Pt 2, para 9.
 Date in force: 15 September 2003: see SI 2003/1730, r 1(2); for effect and the continuing operation of this Part where a provision made by or under any enactment preserves the Insolvency Act 1986, old Pt II after that date see r 5(2)–(4) thereof.
Para (1A): inserted by SI 2010/686, r 2, Sch 1, para 66(1), (2).
 Date in force: 6 April 2010: see SI 2010/686, r 1; for transitional provisions see r 6(1), Sch 4, para 1 thereto.
Para (2): words omitted revoked by SI 2010/686, r 2, Sch 1, para 66(1), (3)(a).
 Date in force: 6 April 2010: see SI 2010/686, r 1; for transitional provisions see r 6(1), Sch 4, para 1 thereto.
Para (2): words "or, in the case of a corporation, by its duly appointed representative" in square brackets inserted by SI 2010/686, r 2, Sch 1, para 66(1), (3)(b).
 Date in force: 6 April 2010: see SI 2010/686, r 1; for transitional provisions see r 6(1), Sch 4, para 1 thereto.
Para (3): words "before the minimum number of members set out in Rule 2.50 elected" in square brackets substituted by SI 2010/686, r 2, Sch 1, para 66(1), (4).
 Date in force: 6 April 2010: see SI 2010/686, r 1; for transitional provisions see r 6(1), Sch 4, para 1 thereto.
Para (5): words omitted revoked by SI 2010/686, r 2, Sch 1, para 66(1), (5).
 Date in force: 6 April 2010: see SI 2010/686, r 1; for transitional provisions see r 6(1), Sch 4, paras 1, 2(1)(b) thereto.
Para (6): words "registrar of companies by filing an amended certificate" in square brackets substituted by SI 2010/686, r 2, Sch 1, para 66(1), (6).
 Date in force: 6 April 2010: see SI 2010/686, r 1; for transitional provisions see r 6(1), Sch 4, paras 1, 2(1)(b) thereto.

See Further

See further, in relation to the application of this rule, with modifications, in respect of bank administration and applications for bank administration: the Bank Administration (England and Wales) Rules 2009, SI 2009/357, rr 58–61.

[2.52 Functions and meetings of the committee]

[(1) [In addition to any functions conferred on the creditors' committee by any provision of the Act,] the creditors' committee shall assist the administrator in discharging his functions, and act in relation to him in such manner as may be agreed from time to time.

(2) Subject as follows, meetings of the committee shall be held when and where determined by the administrator.

[(3) The administrator must call a first meeting of the committee to take place within 6 weeks of the committee's establishment.

 (3A) After the calling of the first meeting, the administrator must call a meeting—
  (a) if so requested by a member of the committee or the member's representative (the meeting then to be held within 21 days of the request being received by the administrator); and
  (b) for a specified date, if the committee has previously resolved that a meeting be held on that date.]

(4) [Subject to paragraph (5),] the administrator shall give [5 business] days' written notice of the venue of any meeting to every member of the committee (or his

representative designated for that purpose), unless in any case the requirement of notice has been waived by or on behalf of any member. Waiver may be signified either at or before the meeting.

[(5) Where the administrator has determined that a meeting should be conducted and held in the manner referred to in Rule 12A.26(2), the notice period mentioned in paragraph (4) is 7 business days.]]

NOTES

Amendment

Substituted, together with rr 2.1–2.51, 2.53–2.133, for rr 2.1–2.6, 2.6A (inserted by SI 1987/1919, reg 3(1), Schedule, Pt 1, para 7), 2.7–2.46, 2.46A (inserted by SI 1987/1919, reg 3(1), Schedule, Pt 1, para 19), 2.47–2.58, 2.59–2.62 (inserted by SI 2002/1307, rr 3(1), 5(8)), by SI 2003/1730, r 5(1), Sch 1, Pt 2, para 9.

Date in force: 15 September 2003: see SI 2003/1730, r 1(2); for effect and the continuing operation of this Part where a provision made by or under any enactment preserves the Insolvency Act 1986, old Pt II after that date see r 5(2)–(4) thereof.

Para (1): words from "In addition to" to "of the Act" in square brackets inserted by SI 2010/686, r 2, Sch 1, para 67(1), (2).

Date in force: 6 April 2010: see SI 2010/686, r 1; for transitional provisions see r 6(1), Sch 4, para 1 thereto.

Paras (3), (3A): substituted, for para (3) as previously enacted, by SI 2010/686, r 2, Sch 1, para 67(1), (3).

Date in force: 6 April 2010: see SI 2010/686, r 1; for transitional provisions see r 6(1), Sch 4, para 1 thereto.

Para (4): words "Subject to paragraph (5)," in square brackets inserted by SI 2010/686, r 2, Sch 1, para 67(1), (4)(a).

Date in force: 6 April 2010: see SI 2010/686, r 1; for transitional provisions see r 6(1), Sch 4, para 1 thereto.

Para (4): words "5 business" in square brackets substituted by SI 2010/686, r 2, Sch 1, para 67(1), (4)(b).

Date in force: 6 April 2010: see SI 2010/686, r 1; for transitional provisions see r 6(1), Sch 4, para 1 thereto.

Para (5): inserted by SI 2010/686, r 2, Sch 1, para 67(1), (5).

Date in force: 6 April 2010: see SI 2010/686, r 1; for transitional provisions see r 6(1), Sch 4, para 1 thereto.

See Further

See further, in relation to the application of this rule, with modifications, in respect of bank administration and applications for bank administration: the Bank Administration (England and Wales) Rules 2009, SI 2009/357, rr 58–61.

[2.53 The chairman at meetings]

[[(1) The chairman at any meeting of the creditors' committee must be the administrator, or a person appointed by the administrator in writing to act.]

(2) A person so [appointed] must be either—
- (a) one who is qualified to act as an insolvency practitioner in relation to the company; or
- (b) an employee of the administrator or his firm who is experienced in insolvency matters.]

NOTES

Amendment

Substituted, together with rr 2.1–2.52, 2.54–2.133, for rr 2.1–2.6, 2.6A (inserted by SI 1987/1919, reg 3(1), Schedule, Pt 1, para 7), 2.7–2.46, 2.46A (inserted by SI 1987/1919, reg 3(1), Schedule, Pt 1, para 19), 2.47–2.58, 2.59–2.62 (inserted by SI 2002/1307, rr 3(1), 5(8)), by SI 2003/1730, r 5(1), Sch 1, Pt 2, para 9.

Date in force: 15 September 2003: see SI 2003/1730, r 1(2); for effect and the continuing operation of this Part where a provision made by or under any enactment preserves the Insolvency Act 1986, old Pt II after that date see r 5(2)–(4) thereof.

Para (1): substituted by SI 2010/686, r 2, Sch 1, para 68(1), (2).

Date in force: 6 April 2010: see SI 2010/686, r 1; for transitional provisions see r 6(1), Sch 4, para 1 thereto.

Para (2): word "appointed" in square brackets substituted by SI 2010/686, r 2, Sch 1, para 68(1), (3).

Date in force: 6 April 2010: see SI 2010/686, r 1; for transitional provisions see r 6(1), Sch 4, para 1 thereto.

See Further

See further, in relation to the application of this rule, with modifications, in respect of bank administration and applications for bank administration: the Bank Administration (England and Wales) Rules 2009, SI 2009/357, rr 58–61.

[**2.54 Quorum**]
[A meeting of the committee is duly constituted if due notice of it has been given to all the members, and at least 2 members are present or represented.]

NOTES

Amendment

Substituted, together with rr 2.1–2.53, 2.55–2.133, for rr 2.1–2.6, 2.6A (inserted by SI 1987/1919, reg 3(1), Schedule, Pt 1, para 7), 2.7–2.46, 2.46A (inserted by SI 1987/1919, reg 3(1), Schedule, Pt 1, para 19), 2.47–2.58, 2.59–2.62 (inserted by SI 2002/1307, rr 3(1), 5(8)), by SI 2003/1730, r 5(1), Sch 1, Pt 2, para 9.

Date in force: 15 September 2003: see SI 2003/1730, r 1(2); for effect and the continuing operation of this Part where a provision made by or under any enactment preserves the Insolvency Act 1986, old Pt II after that date see r 5(2)–(4) thereof.

See Further

See further, in relation to the application of this rule, with modifications, in respect of bank administration and applications for bank administration: the Bank Administration (England and Wales) Rules 2009, SI 2009/357, rr 58–61.

[**2.55 Committee-members' representatives**]
[(1) A member of the committee may, in relation to the business of the committee, be represented by another person duly authorised by him for that purpose.

(2) A person acting as a committee-member's representative must hold a letter of authority entitling him so to act (either generally or specially) and [authenticated] by or on behalf of the committee-member, and for this purpose any proxy . . . in relation to any meeting of creditors of the company shall, unless it contains a statement to the contrary, be treated as a letter of authority to act generally [authenticated] by or on behalf of the committee-member.

(3) The chairman at any meeting of the committee may call on a person claiming to act as a committee-member's representative to produce his letter of authority, and may exclude him if it appears that his authority is deficient.

[(4) No member may be represented by—
- (a) another member of the committee;
- (b) a person who is at the same time representing another committee member;
- (c) a body corporate;
- (d) an undischarged bankrupt;
- (e) a disqualified director; or

(f) a person who is subject to a bankruptcy restrictions order (including an interim order), a bankruptcy restrictions undertaking, a debt relief restrictions order (including an interim order) or a debt relief restrictions undertaking.]

(5) ...

(6) Where a member's representative [authenticates] any document on the member's behalf, the fact that he so [authenticates] must be stated below his [authentication].]

NOTES

Amendment

Substituted, together with rr 2.1–2.54, 2.56–2.133, for rr 2.1–2.6, 2.6A (inserted by SI 1987/1919, reg 3(1), Schedule, Pt 1, para 7), 2.7–2.46, 2.46A (inserted by SI 1987/1919, reg 3(1), Schedule, Pt 1, para 19), 2.47–2.58, 2.59–2.62 (inserted by SI 2002/1307, rr 3(1), 5(8)), by SI 2003/1730, r 5(1), Sch 1, Pt 2, para 9.

Date in force: 15 September 2003: see SI 2003/1730, r 1(2); for effect and the continuing operation of this Part where a provision made by or under any enactment preserves the Insolvency Act 1986, old Pt II after that date see r 5(2)–(4) thereof.

Para (2): word "authenticated" in square brackets in both places it occurs substituted by SI 2010/686, r 2, Sch 1, para 1.

Date in force: 6 April 2010: see SI 2010/686, r 1; for transitional provisions see r 6(1), Sch 4, paras 1, 2(1)(b) thereto.

Para (2): words omitted revoked by SI 2010/686, r 2, Sch 1, para 69(1), (2).

Date in force: 6 April 2010: see SI 2010/686, r 1; for transitional provisions see r 6(1), Sch 4, para 1 thereto.

Para (4): substituted by SI 2010/686, r 2, Sch 1, para 69(1), (3).

Date in force: 6 April 2010: see SI 2010/686, r 1; for transitional provisions see r 6(1), Sch 4, para 1 thereto.

Para (5): revoked by SI 2010/686, r 2, Sch 1, para 69(1), (4).

Date in force: 6 April 2010: see SI 2010/686, r 1; for transitional provisions see r 6(1), Sch 4, para 1 thereto.

Para (6): word "authenticates" in square brackets in both places it occurs substituted by SI 2010/686, r 2, Sch 1, para 1.

Date in force: 6 April 2010: see SI 2010/686, r 1; for transitional provisions see r 6(1), Sch 4, paras 1, 2(1)(b) thereto.

Para (6): word "authentication" in square brackets substituted by SI 2010/686, r 2, Sch 1, para 1.

Date in force: 6 April 2010: see SI 2010/686, r 1; for transitional provisions see r 6(1), Sch 4, paras 1, 2(1)(b) thereto.

See Further

See further, in relation to the application of this rule, with modifications, in respect of bank administration and applications for bank administration: the Bank Administration (England and Wales) Rules 2009, SI 2009/357, rr 58–61.

CHAPTER 6

...

NOTES

Amendment

Substituted by SI 2003/1730, r 5(1), Sch 1, Pt 2, para 9.

Date in force: 15 September 2003: see SI 2003/1730, r 1(2); for effect and the continuing operation of this Part where a provision made by or under any enactment preserves the Insolvency Act 1986, old Pt II after that date see r 5(2)–(4) thereof.

[2.56 Resignation]

[A member of the committee may resign by notice in writing delivered to the administrator.]

NOTES

Amendment

Substituted, together with rr 2.1–2.55, 2.57–2.133, for rr 2.1–2.6, 2.6A (inserted by SI 1987/1919, reg 3(1), Schedule, Pt 1, para 7), 2.7–2.46, 2.46A (inserted by SI 1987/1919, reg 3(1), Schedule, Pt 1, para 19), 2.47–2.58, 2.59–2.62 (inserted by SI 2002/1307, rr 3(1), 5(8)), by SI 2003/1730, r 5(1), Sch 1, Pt 2, para 9.

Date in force: 15 September 2003: see SI 2003/1730, r 1(2); for effect and the continuing operation of this Part where a provision made by or under any enactment preserves the Insolvency Act 1986, old Pt II after that date see r 5(2)–(4) thereof.

See Further

See further, in relation to the application of this rule, with modifications, in respect of bank administration and applications for bank administration: the Bank Administration (England and Wales) Rules 2009, SI 2009/357, rr 58–61.

[2.57 Termination of membership]

[(1) Membership of the creditors' committee is automatically terminated if the member—

(a) becomes bankrupt. . .; or

(b) at 3 consecutive meetings of the committee is neither present nor represented (unless at the third of those meetings it is resolved that this Rule is not to apply in his case); or

[(c) ceases to be a creditor and a period of 3 months has elapsed from the date that that member ceased to be a creditor or is found never to have been a creditor].

(2) However, if the cause of termination is the member's bankruptcy, his trustee in bankruptcy replaces him as a member of the committee.]

NOTES

Amendment

Substituted, together with rr 2.1–2.56, 2.58–2.133, for rr 2.1–2.6, 2.6A (inserted by SI 1987/1919, reg 3(1), Schedule, Pt 1, para 7), 2.7–2.46, 2.46A (inserted by SI 1987/1919, reg 3(1), Schedule, Pt 1, para 19), 2.47–2.58, 2.59–2.62 (inserted by SI 2002/1307, rr 3(1), 5(8)), by SI 2003/1730, r 5(1), Sch 1, Pt 2, para 9.

Date in force: 15 September 2003: see SI 2003/1730, r 1(2); for effect and the continuing operation of this Part where a provision made by or under any enactment preserves the Insolvency Act 1986, old Pt II after that date see r 5(2)–(4) thereof.

Para (1): in sub-para (a) words omitted revoked by SI 2004/584, r 5.

Date in force: 1 April 2004: see SI 2004/584, r 1(2).

Para (1): sub-para (c) substituted by SI 2010/686, r 2, Sch 1, para 70.

Date in force: 6 April 2010: see SI 2010/686, r 1; for transitional provisions see r 6(1), Sch 4, para 1 thereto.

See Further

See further, in relation to the application of this rule, with modifications, in respect of bank administration and applications for bank administration: the Bank Administration (England and Wales) Rules 2009, SI 2009/357, rr 58–61.

[2.58 Removal]

[A member of the committee may be removed by resolution at a meeting of creditors' at least 14 days' notice having been given of the intention to move that resolution.]

NOTES

Amendment

Substituted, together with rr 2.1–2.57, 2.59–2.133, for rr 2.1–2.6, 2.6A (inserted by SI 1987/1919, reg 3(1), Schedule, Pt 1, para 7), 2.7–2.46, 2.46A (inserted by SI 1987/1919, reg 3(1), Schedule, Pt 1, para 19), 2.47–2.58, 2.59–2.62 (inserted by SI 2002/1307, rr 3(1), 5(8)), by SI 2003/1730, r 5(1), Sch 1, Pt 2, para 9.

Date in force: 15 September 2003: see SI 2003/1730, r 1(2); for effect and the continuing operation of this Part where a provision made by or under any enactment preserves the Insolvency Act 1986, old Pt II after that date see r 5(2)–(4) thereof.

See Further

See further, in relation to the application of this rule, with modifications, in respect of bank administration and applications for bank administration: the Bank Administration (England and Wales) Rules 2009, SI 2009/357, rr 58–61.

[CHAPTER 7

. . .]

NOTES

Amendment

Inserted by SI 2002/1307, rr 3(1), 5(8).
  Date in force: 31 May 2002: see SI 2002/1307, r 1.
Substituted by SI 2003/1730, r 5(1), Sch 1, Pt 2, para 9.
  Date in force: 15 September 2003: see SI 2003/1730, r 1(2); for effect and the continuing operation of this Part where a provision made by or under any enactment preserves the Insolvency Act 1986, old Pt II after that date see r 5(2)–(4) thereof.

[2.59 Vacancies]

[(1) The following applies if there is a vacancy in the membership of the creditors' committee.

(2) The vacancy need not be filled if the administrator and a majority of the remaining members of the committee so agree, provided that the total number of members does not fall below [3].

(3) The administrator may appoint any creditor (being qualified under the Rules to be a member of the committee) to fill the vacancy, if a majority of the other members of the committee agree to the appointment, and the creditor concerned consents to act.

[(4) Alternatively, a meeting of creditors may resolve that a creditor be appointed (with that creditor's consent) to fill the vacancy.

(5) Where the vacancy is filled by an appointment made by a creditors' meeting at which the administrator is not present, the chairman of the meeting must report to the administrator the appointment which has been made.]]

NOTES

Amendment

Substituted (for this rule as inserted by SI 2002/1307, rr 3(1), 5(8)), together with rr 2.1–2.58, 2.60–2.133, for rr 2.1–2.6, 2.6A (inserted by SI 1987/1919, reg 3(1), Schedule, Pt 1, para 7), 2.7–2.46, 2.46A (inserted by SI 1987/1919, reg 3(1), Schedule, Pt 1, para 19), 2.47–2.58, 2.59, 2.60–2.62 (inserted by SI 2002/1307, rr 3(1), 5(8)), by SI 2003/1730, r 5(1), Sch 1, Pt 2, para 9.

Date in force: 15 September 2003: see SI 2003/1730, r 1(2); for effect and the continuing operation of this Part where a provision made by or under any enactment preserves the Insolvency Act 1986, old Pt II after that date see r 5(2)–(4) thereof.

Para (2): reference to "3" in square brackets substituted by SI 2010/686, r 2, Sch 1, para 71(1), (2).
  Date in force: 6 April 2010: see SI 2010/686, r 1; for transitional provisions see r 6(1), Sch 4, para 1 thereto.
Paras (4), (5): inserted by SI 2010/686, r 2, Sch 1, para 71(1), (3).
  Date in force: 6 April 2010: see SI 2010/686, r 1; for transitional provisions see r 6(1), Sch 4, para 1 thereto.

See Further
  See further, in relation to the application of this rule, with modifications, in respect of bank administration and applications for bank administration: the Bank Administration (England and Wales) Rules 2009, SI 2009/357, rr 58–61.

[2.60 Procedure at meetings]

[(1) At any meeting of the creditors' committee, each member of it (whether present himself, or by his representative) has one vote; and a resolution is passed when a majority of the members present or represented have voted in favour of it.

[(2) Every resolution passed must be recorded in writing and authenticated by the chairman, either separately or as part of the minutes of the meeting, and the record must be kept with the records of the proceedings.]]

NOTES

Amendment

  Substituted (for this rule as inserted by SI 2002/1307, rr 3(1), 5(8)), together with rr 2.1–2.59, 2.61–2.133, for rr 2.1–2.6, 2.6A (inserted by SI 1987/1919, reg 3(1), Schedule, Pt 1, para 7), 2.7–2.46, 2.46A (inserted by SI 1987/1919, reg 3(1), Schedule, Pt 1, para 19), 2.47–2.58, 2.59 (inserted by SI 2002/1307, rr 3(1), 5(8)), 2.60, 2.61 (inserted by SI 2002/1307, rr 3(1), 5(8)), 2.62 (inserted by SI 2002/1307, rr 3(1), 5(8)), by SI 2003/1730, r 5(1), Sch 1, Pt 2, para 9.
    Date in force: 15 September 2003: see SI 2003/1730, r 1(2); for effect and the continuing operation of this Part where a provision made by or under any enactment preserves the Insolvency Act 1986, old Pt II after that date see r 5(2)–(4) thereof.
  Para (2): substituted, for paras (2), (3) as previously enacted, by SI 2010/686, r 2, Sch 1, para 72.
    Date in force: 6 April 2010: see SI 2010/686, r 1; for transitional provisions see r 6(1), Sch 4, para 1 thereto.

See Further
  See further, in relation to the application of this rule, with modifications, in respect of bank administration and applications for bank administration: the Bank Administration (England and Wales) Rules 2009, SI 2009/357, rr 58–61.

[2.61 Resolutions of creditors' committee [otherwise than at a meeting]]

[(1) In accordance with this Rule, the administrator may seek to obtain the agreement of members of the creditors' committee to a resolution by sending to every member (or his representative designated for the purpose) a copy of the proposed resolution.

(2) Where the administrator makes use of the procedure allowed by this Rule, he shall send out to members of the committee or their representatives (as the case may be) a copy of any proposed resolution on which a decision is sought, which shall be set out in such a way that agreement with or dissent from each separate resolution may be indicated by the recipient on the copy so sent.

(3) Any member of the committee may, within 7 business days from the date of the administrator sending out a resolution, require him to summon a meeting of the committee to consider matters raised by the resolution.

(4) In the absence of such a request, the resolution is deemed to have been passed by the committee if and when the administrator is notified in writing by a majority of the members that they concur with it.

(5) A copy of every resolution passed under this Rule, and a note that the committee's concurrence was obtained, shall be [kept with the records of the proceedings].]

NOTES

Amendment

Substituted (for this rule as inserted by SI 2002/1307, rr 3(1), 5(8)), together with rr 2.1–2.60, 2.62–2.133, for rr 2.1–2.6, 2.6A (inserted by SI 1987/1919, reg 3(1), Schedule, Pt 1, para 7), 2.7–2.46, 2.46A (inserted by SI 1987/1919, reg 3(1), Schedule, Pt 1, para 19), 2.47–2.58, 2.59 (inserted by SI 2002/1307, rr 3(1), 5(8)), 2.60 (inserted by SI 2002/1307, rr 3(1), 5(8)), 2.61, 2.62 (inserted by SI 2002/1307, rr 3(1), 5(8)), by SI 2003/1730, r 5(1), Sch 1, Pt 2, para 9.

Date in force: 15 September 2003: see SI 2003/1730, r 1(2); for effect and the continuing operation of this Part where a provision made by or under any enactment preserves the Insolvency Act 1986, old Pt II after that date see r 5(2)–(4) thereof.

Provision heading: words "otherwise than at a meeting" in square brackets substituted by SI 2010/686, r 2, Sch 1, para 73(1), (2).

Date in force: 6 April 2010: see SI 2010/686, r 1; for transitional provisions see r 6(1), Sch 4, para 1 thereto.

Para (5): words "kept with the records of the proceedings" in square brackets substituted by SI 2010/686, r 2, Sch 1, para 73(1), (3).

Date in force: 6 April 2010: see SI 2010/686, r 1; for transitional provisions see r 6(1), Sch 4, para 1 thereto.

See Further

See further, in relation to the application of this rule, with modifications, in respect of bank administration and applications for bank administration: the Bank Administration (England and Wales) Rules 2009, SI 2009/357, rr 58–61.

[CHAPTER 8

...]

NOTES

Amendment

Inserted by SI 2002/1307, rr 3(1), 5(8).
Date in force: 31 May 2002: see SI 2002/1307, r 1.
Substituted by SI 2003/1730, r 5(1), Sch 1, Pt 2, para 9.
Date in force: 15 September 2003: see SI 2003/1730, r 1(2); for effect and the continuing operation of this Part where a provision made by or under any enactment preserves the Insolvency Act 1986, old Pt II after that date see r 5(2)–(4) thereof.

[2.62 Information from administrator]

[(1) Where the committee resolves to require the attendance of the administrator under paragraph 57(3)(a), the notice to him shall be in writing [authenticated] by the majority of the members of the committee for the time being. A member's representative may [authenticate] for him.

(2) The meeting at which the administrator's attendance is required shall be fixed by the committee for a business day, and shall be held at such time and place as he determines.

(3) Where the administrator so attends, the members of the committee may elect any one of their number to be chairman of the meeting, in place of the administrator or a nominee of his.]

NOTES

Amendment

Substituted (for this rule as inserted by SI 2002/1307, rr 3(1), 5(8)), together with rr 2.1–2.61, 2.63–2.133, for rr 2.1–2.6, 2.6A (inserted by SI 1987/1919, reg 3(1), Schedule, Pt 1, para 7), 2.7–2.46, 2.46A (inserted by SI 1987/1919, reg 3(1), Schedule, Pt 1, para 19), 2.47–2.58, 2.59–2.61 (inserted by SI 2002/1307, rr 3(1), 5(8)), 2.62, by SI 2003/1730, r 5(1), Sch 1, Pt 2, para 9.

Date in force: 15 September 2003: see SI 2003/1730, r 1(2); for effect and the continuing operation of this Part where a provision made by or under any enactment preserves the Insolvency Act 1986, old Pt II after that date see r 5(2)–(4) thereof.

Para (1): words "authenticated" and "authenticate" in square brackets substituted by SI 2010/686, r 2, Sch 1, para 1.

Date in force: 6 April 2010: see SI 2010/686, r 1; for transitional provisions see r 6(1), Sch 4, paras 1, 2(1)(b) thereto.

See Further

See further, in relation to the application of this rule, with modifications, in respect of bank administration and applications for bank administration: the Bank Administration (England and Wales) Rules 2009, SI 2009/357, rr 58–61.

[2.63 Expenses of members]

[(1) Subject as follows, the administrator shall, out of the assets of the company, defray[, in the prescribed order of priority,] any reasonable travelling expenses directly incurred by members of the creditors' committee or their representatives in relation to their attendance at the committee's meetings, or otherwise on the committee's business, as an expense of the administration.

(2) Paragraph (1) does not apply to any meeting of the committee held within 6 weeks of a previous meeting, unless the meeting in question is summoned at the instance of the administrator.]

NOTES

Amendment

Substituted, together with rr 2.1–2.62, 2.64–2.133, for rr 2.1–2.6, 2.6A (inserted by SI 1987/1919, reg 3(1), Schedule, Pt 1, para 7), 2.7–2.46, 2.46A (inserted by SI 1987/1919, reg 3(1), Schedule, Pt 1, para 19), 2.47–2.58, 2.59–2.62 (inserted by SI 2002/1307, rr 3(1), 5(8)), by SI 2003/1730, r 5(1), Sch 1, Pt 2, para 9.

Date in force: 15 September 2003: see SI 2003/1730, r 1(2); for effect and the continuing operation of this Part where a provision made by or under any enactment preserves the Insolvency Act 1986, old Pt II after that date see r 5(2)–(4) thereof.

Para (1): words ", in the prescribed order of priority," in square brackets inserted by SI 2010/686, r 2, Sch 1, para 74.

Date in force: 6 April 2010: see SI 2010/686, r 1; for transitional provisions see r 6(1), Sch 4, para 1 thereto.

See Further

See further, in relation to the application of this rule, with modifications, in respect of bank administration and applications for bank administration: the Bank Administration (England and Wales) Rules 2009, SI 2009/357, rr 58–61.

[2.64 Members' dealing with the company]

[(1) Membership of the committee does not prevent a person from dealing with the company while the company is in administration, provided that any transactions in the course of such dealings are in good faith and for value.

(2) The court may, on the application of any person interested, set aside any transaction which appears to it to be contrary to the requirements of this Rule, and may give such consequential directions as it thinks [just] for compensating the company for any loss which it may have incurred in consequence of the transaction.]

NOTES

Amendment

Substituted, together with rr 2.1–2.63, 2.65–2.133, for rr 2.1–2.6, 2.6A (inserted by SI 1987/1919, reg 3(1), Schedule, Pt 1, para 7), 2.7–2.46, 2.46A (inserted by SI 1987/1919, reg 3(1), Schedule, Pt 1, para 19), 2.47–2.58, 2.59–2.62 (inserted by SI 2002/1307, rr 3(1), 5(8)), by SI 2003/1730, r 5(1), Sch 1, Pt 2, para 9.

Date in force: 15 September 2003: see SI 2003/1730, r 1(2); for effect and the continuing operation of this Part where a provision made by or under any enactment preserves the Insolvency Act 1986, old Pt II after that date see r 5(2)–(4) thereof.

Para (2): word "just" in square brackets substituted by SI 2010/686, r 2, Sch 1, para 1.

Date in force: 6 April 2010: see SI 2010/686, r 1; for transitional provisions see r 6(1), Sch 4, paras 1, 2(1)(b) thereto.

See Further

See further, in relation to the application of this rule, with modifications, in respect of bank administration and applications for bank administration: the Bank Administration (England and Wales) Rules 2009, SI 2009/357, rr 58–61.

[2.65 Formal defects]

[The acts of the creditors' committee established for any administration are valid notwithstanding any defect in the appointment, election or qualifications of any member of the committee or any committee-member's representative or in the formalities of its establishment.]

NOTES

Amendment

Substituted, together with rr 2.1–2.64, 2.66–2.133, for rr 2.1–2.6, 2.6A (inserted by SI 1987/1919, reg 3(1), Schedule, Pt 1, para 7), 2.7–2.46, 2.46A (inserted by SI 1987/1919, reg 3(1), Schedule, Pt 1, para 19), 2.47–2.58, 2.59–2.62 (inserted by SI 2002/1307, rr 3(1), 5(8)), by SI 2003/1730, r 5(1), Sch 1, Pt 2, para 9.

Date in force: 15 September 2003: see SI 2003/1730, r 1(2); for effect and the continuing operation of this Part where a provision made by or under any enactment preserves the Insolvency Act 1986, old Pt II after that date see r 5(2)–(4) thereof.

See Further

See further, in relation to the application of this rule, with modifications, in respect of bank administration and applications for bank administration: the Bank Administration (England and Wales) Rules 2009, SI 2009/357, rr 58–61.

[CHAPTER 8

DISPOSAL OF CHARGED PROPERTY]

NOTES

Amendment

Substituted by SI 2003/1730, r 5(1), Sch 1, Pt 2, para 9.
Date in force: 15 September 2003: see SI 2003/1730, r 1(2); for effect and the continuing operation of this Part where a provision made by or under any enactment preserves the Insolvency Act 1986, old Pt II after that date see r 5(2)–(4) thereof.

[2.66]

[(1) The following applies where the administrator applies to the court under paragraphs 71 or 72 for authority to dispose of property of the company which is subject to a security (other than a floating charge), or goods in the possession of the company under a hire purchase agreement.

(2) The court shall fix a venue for the hearing of the application, and the administrator shall as soon as reasonably practicable give notice of the venue to the person who is the holder of the security or, as the case may be, the owner under the agreement.

(3) If an order is made under paragraphs 71 or 72 the court shall send two sealed copies to the administrator.

(4) The administrator shall send one of them to that person who is the holder of the security or owner under the agreement.

[(5) The administrator must send a copy of the sealed order to the registrar of companies.]]

NOTES

Amendment

Substituted, together with rr 2.1–2.65, 2.67–2.133, for rr 2.1–2.6, 2.6A (inserted by SI 1987/1919, reg 3(1), Schedule, Pt 1, para 7), 2.7–2.46, 2.46A (inserted by SI 1987/1919, reg 3(1), Schedule, Pt 1, para 19), 2.47–2.58, 2.59–2.62 (inserted by SI 2002/1307, rr 3(1), 5(8)), by SI 2003/1730, r 5(1), Sch 1, Pt 2, para 9.
Date in force: 15 September 2003: see SI 2003/1730, r 1(2); for effect and the continuing operation of this Part where a provision made by or under any enactment preserves the Insolvency Act 1986, old Pt II after that date see r 5(2)–(4) thereof.
Para (5): substituted by SI 2010/686, r 2, Sch 1, para 75.
Date in force: 6 April 2010: see SI 2010/686, r 1; for transitional provisions see r 6(1), Sch 4, para 1 thereto.

See Further

See further, in relation to the application of this rule, with modifications, in respect of bank administration and applications for bank administration: the Bank Administration (England and Wales) Rules 2009, SI 2009/357, rr 58–61.

[CHAPTER 9

EXPENSES OF THE ADMINISTRATION]

NOTES

Amendment

Substituted by SI 2003/1730, r 5(1), Sch 1, Pt 2, para 9.

Date in force: 15 September 2003: see SI 2003/1730, r 1(2); for effect and the continuing operation of this Part where a provision made by or under any enactment preserves the Insolvency Act 1986, old Pt II after that date see r 5(2)–(4) thereof.

[2.67]
[(1) The expenses of the administration are payable in the following order of priority—

- (a) expenses properly incurred by the administrator in performing his functions in the administration of the company;
- (b) the cost of any security provided by the administrator in accordance with the Act or the Rules;
- (c) where an administration order was made, the costs of the applicant and any person appearing on the hearing of the application and where the administrator was appointed otherwise than by order of the court, any costs and expenses of the appointor in connection with the making of the appointment and the costs and expenses incurred by any other person in giving notice of intention to appoint an administrator;
- (d) any amount payable to a person employed or authorised, under Chapter 5 of this Part of the Rules, to assist in the preparation of a statement of affairs or statement of concurrence;
- (e) any allowance made, by order of the court, towards costs on an application for release from the obligation to submit a statement of affairs or statement of concurrence;
- (f) any necessary disbursements by the administrator in the course of the administration (including any expenses incurred by members of the creditors' committee or their representatives and allowed for by the administrator under Rule 2.63, but not including any payment of corporation tax in circumstances referred to in sub-paragraph (j) below);
- (g) the remuneration or emoluments of any person who has been employed by the administrator to perform any services for the company, as required or authorised under the Act or the Rules;
- [(h) the administrator's remuneration the basis of which has been fixed under Chapter 11 of this Part of the Rules and unpaid pre-administration costs approved under Rule 2.67A;]
- (j) the amount of any corporation tax on chargeable gains accruing on the realisation of any asset of the company (without regard to whether the realisation is effected by the administrator, a secured creditor, or a receiver or manager appointed to deal with a security).

(2) The priorities laid down by paragraph (1) of this Rule are subject to the power of the court to make orders under paragraph (3) of this Rule where the assets are insufficient to satisfy the liabilities.

(3) The court may, in the event of the assets being insufficient to satisfy the liabilities, make an order as to the payment out of the assets of the expenses incurred in the administration in such order of priority as the court thinks just.

[(4) For the purposes of paragraph 99(3), the former administrator's remuneration and expenses shall comprise all those items set out in paragraph (1) of this Rule.]]

NOTES

Amendment

Substituted, together with rr 2.1–2.66, 2.68–2.133, for rr 2.1–2.6, 2.6A (inserted by SI 1987/1919, reg 3(1), Schedule, Pt 1, para 7), 2.7–2.46, 2.46A (inserted by SI 1987/1919, reg 3(1), Schedule, Pt 1, para 19), 2.47–2.58, 2.59–2.62 (inserted by SI 2002/1307, rr 3(1), 5(8)), by SI 2003/1730, r 5(1), Sch 1, Pt 2, para 9.

Insolvency Rules 1986, reg 2.65

>   Date in force: 15 September 2003: see SI 2003/1730, r 1(2); for effect and the continuing operation of this Part where a provision made by or under any enactment preserves the Insolvency Act 1986, old Pt II after that date see r 5(2)–(4) thereof.
> Para (1): sub-para (h) substituted by SI 2010/686, r 2, Sch 1, para 76.
>   Date in force: 6 April 2010: see SI 2010/686, r 1; for transitional provisions see r 6(1), Sch 4, para 1 thereto.
> Para (4): inserted by SI 2005/527, r 8.
>   Date in force: 1 April 2005: see SI 2005/527, r 1(2); for transitional provisions in relation to any case where a company has entered administration or gone into liquidation, or a bankruptcy order has been made before that date see r 3(1) thereof.

See Further

> See further, in relation to the application of this rule, with modifications, in respect of bank administration and applications for bank administration: the Bank Administration (England and Wales) Rules 2009, SI 2009/357, rr 58–61.

[2.67A Pre-administration costs]

[(1) Where the administrator has made a statement of pre-administration costs under Rule 2.33(2)(ka), the creditors' committee may determine whether and to what extent the unpaid pre-administration costs set out in the statement are approved for payment.

(2) But if—
- (a) there is no creditors' committee, or
- (b) there is but it does not make the necessary determination, or
- (c) it does do so but the administrator or other insolvency practitioner who has charged fees or incurred expenses as pre-administration costs considers the amount determined to be insufficient,

paragraph (3) applies.

(3) When this paragraph applies, determination of whether and to what extent the unpaid pre-administration costs are approved for payment shall be—
- (a) by resolution of a meeting of creditors other than in a case falling in sub-paragraph (b), or
- (b) in a case where the administrator has made a statement under paragraph 52(1)(b)—
    - (i) by the approval of each secured creditor of the company, or
    - (ii) if the administrator has made, or intends to make, a distribution to preferential creditors, by the approval of—
        - (aa) each secured creditor of the company, and
        - (bb) preferential creditors whose debts amount to more than 50% of the preferential debts of the company, disregarding debts of any creditor who does not respond to an invitation to give or withhold approval.

(4) The administrator must call a meeting of the creditors' committee or of creditors if so requested for the purposes of paragraphs (1) to (3) by another insolvency practitioner who has charged fees or incurred expenses as pre-administration costs; and the administrator must give notice of the meeting within 28 days of receipt of the request.

(5) If—
- (a) there is no determination under paragraph (1) or (3), or
- (b) there is such a determination but the administrator or other insolvency practitioner who has charged fees or incurred expenses as pre-administration costs considers the amount determined to be insufficient,

the administrator (where the fees were charged or expenses incurred by the administrator) or other insolvency practitioner (where the fees were charged or expenses incurred by that practitioner) may apply to the court for a determination of whether and to what extent the unpaid pre-administration costs are approved for payment.

(6) Paragraphs (2) to (4) of Rule 2.108 apply to an application under paragraph (5) of this Rule as they do to an application under paragraph (1) of that Rule (references to the administrator being read as references to the insolvency practitioner who has charged fees or incurred expenses as pre-administration costs).

(7) Where the administrator fails to call a meeting of the creditors' committee or of creditors in accordance with paragraph (4), the other insolvency practitioner may apply to the court for an order requiring the administrator to do so.]

NOTES

Amendment

Inserted by SI 2010/686, r 2, Sch 1, para 77.
Date in force: 6 April 2010: see SI 2010/686, r 1; for transitional provisions see r 6(1), Sch 4, para 1 thereto.

[CHAPTER 10

DISTRIBUTIONS TO CREDITORS]

NOTES

Amendment

Substituted by SI 2003/1730, r 5(1), Sch 1, Pt 2, para 9.
Date in force: 15 September 2003: see SI 2003/1730, r 1(2); for effect and the continuing operation of this Part where a provision made by or under any enactment preserves the Insolvency Act 1986, old Pt II after that date see r 5(2)–(4) thereof.

[SECTION A: APPLICATION OF CHAPTER AND GENERAL]

NOTES

Amendment

Substituted by SI 2003/1730, r 5(1), Sch 1, Pt 2, para 9.
Date in force: 15 September 2003: see SI 2003/1730, r 1(2); for effect and the continuing operation of this Part where a provision made by or under any enactment preserves the Insolvency Act 1986, old Pt II after that date see r 5(2)–(4) thereof.

[2.68]

[(1) This Chapter applies where the administrator makes, or proposes to make, a distribution to any class of creditors [other than secured creditors]. Where the distribution is to a particular class of creditors, references in this Chapter to creditors shall, in so far as the context requires, be a reference to that class of creditors only.

(2) The administrator shall give notice to the creditors of his intention to declare and distribute a dividend in accordance with Rule 2.95.

(3) Where it is intended that the distribution is to be a sole or final dividend, the administrator shall, after the date specified in the notice referred to in paragraph (2)—
    (a)   defray any outstanding expenses of a liquidation (including any of the items mentioned in Rule 4.218) or provisional liquidation that immediately preceded the administration;
    (b)   defray any items payable in accordance with the provisions of paragraph 99;

(c) defray any amounts (including any debts or liabilities and his own remuneration and expenses) which would, if the administrator were to cease to be the administrator of the company, be payable out of the property of which he had custody or control in accordance with the provisions of paragraph 99; and

(d) declare and distribute that dividend without regard to the claim of any person in respect of a debt not already proved.

(4) The court may, on the application of any person, postpone the date specified in the notice.]

NOTES

Amendment

Substituted, together with rr 2.1–2.67, 2.69–2.133, for rr 2.1–2.6, 2.6A (inserted by SI 1987/1919, reg 3(1), Schedule, Pt 1, para 7), 2.7–2.46, 2.46A (inserted by SI 1987/1919, reg 3(1), Schedule, Pt 1, para 19), 2.47–2.58, 2.59–2.62 (inserted by SI 2002/1307, rr 3(1), 5(8)), by SI 2003/1730, r 5(1), Sch 1, Pt 2, para 9.

Date in force: 15 September 2003: see SI 2003/1730, r 1(2); for effect and the continuing operation of this Part where a provision made by or under any enactment preserves the Insolvency Act 1986, old Pt II after that date see r 5(2)–(4) thereof.

Para (1): words "other than secured creditors" in square brackets inserted by SI 2010/686, r 2, Sch 1, para 78.

Date in force: 6 April 2010: see SI 2010/686, r 1; for transitional provisions see r 6(1), Sch 4, para 1 thereto.

See Further

See further, in relation to the application of this rule, with modifications, in respect of bank administration and applications for bank administration: the Bank Administration (England and Wales) Rules 2009, SI 2009/357, rr 58–61.

[2.69 Debts of insolvent company to rank equally]

[Debts other than preferential debts rank equally between themselves in the administration and, after the preferential debts, shall be paid in full unless the assets are insufficient for meeting them, in which case they abate in equal proportions between themselves.]

NOTES

Amendment

Substituted, together with rr 2.1–2.68, 2.70–2.133, for rr 2.1–2.6, 2.6A (inserted by SI 1987/1919, reg 3(1), Schedule, Pt 1, para 7), 2.7–2.46, 2.46A (inserted by SI 1987/1919, reg 3(1), Schedule, Pt 1, para 19), 2.47–2.58, 2.59–2.62 (inserted by SI 2002/1307, rr 3(1), 5(8)), by SI 2003/1730, r 5(1), Sch 1, Pt 2, para 9.

Date in force: 15 September 2003: see SI 2003/1730, r 1(2); for effect and the continuing operation of this Part where a provision made by or under any enactment preserves the Insolvency Act 1986, old Pt II after that date see r 5(2)–(4) thereof.

See Further

See further, in relation to the application of this rule, with modifications, in respect of bank administration and applications for bank administration: the Bank Administration (England and Wales) Rules 2009, SI 2009/357, rr 58–61.

[2.70 Supplementary provisions as to dividend]

[(1) In the calculation and distribution of a dividend the administrator shall make provision for—

(a) any debts which appear to him to be due to persons who, by reason of the distance of their place of residence, may not have had sufficient time to tender and establish their proofs;
(b) any debts which are the subject of claims which have not yet been determined; and
(c) disputed proofs and claims.

(2) A creditor who has not proved his debt before the declaration of any dividend is not entitled to disturb, by reason that he has not participated in it, the distribution of that dividend or any other dividend declared before his debt was proved, but—
(a) when he has proved that debt he is entitled to be paid, out of any money for the time being available for the payment of any further dividend, any dividend or dividends which he has failed to receive; and
(b) any dividends payable under sub-paragraph (a) shall be paid before the money is applied to the payment of any such further dividend.

(3) No action lies against the administrator for a dividend; but if he refuses to pay a dividend the court may, if it thinks [just], order him to pay it and also to pay, out of his own money—
(a) interest on the dividend, at the rate for the time being specified in section 17 of the Judgments Act 1838, from the time when it was withheld; and
(b) the costs of the proceedings in which the order to pay is made.]

NOTES

Amendment

Substituted, together with rr 2.1–2.69, 2.71–2.133, for rr 2.1–2.6, 2.6A (inserted by SI 1987/1919, reg 3(1), Schedule, Pt 1, para 7), 2.7–2.46, 2.46A (inserted by SI 1987/1919, reg 3(1), Schedule, Pt 1, para 19), 2.47–2.58, 2.59–2.62 (inserted by SI 2002/1307, rr 3(1), 5(8)), by SI 2003/1730, r 5(1), Sch 1, Pt 2, para 9.

Date in force: 15 September 2003: see SI 2003/1730, r 1(2); for effect and the continuing operation of this Part where a provision made by or under any enactment preserves the Insolvency Act 1986, old Pt II after that date see r 5(2)–(4) thereof.

Para (3): word "just" in square brackets substituted by SI 2010/686, r 2, Sch 1, para 1.

Date in force: 6 April 2010: see SI 2010/686, r 1; for transitional provisions see r 6(1), Sch 4, paras 1, 2(1)(b) thereto.

See Further

See further, in relation to the application of this rule, with modifications, in respect of bank administration and applications for bank administration: the Bank Administration (England and Wales) Rules 2009, SI 2009/357, rr 58–61.

[2.71 Division of unsold assets]

[[(1)] The administrator may, with the permission of the creditors' committee, or if there is no creditors' committee, the creditors, divide in its existing form amongst the company's creditors, according to its estimated value, any property which from its peculiar nature or other special circumstances cannot be readily or advantageously sold.

[(2) The administrator must—
(a) in the receipts and payments account included in the final progress report under Chapter 12 of this Part, state the estimated value of the property divided amongst the creditors of the company during the period to which the report relates, and
(b) as a note to the account, provide details of the basis of the valuation.]]

NOTES

Amendment

Substituted, together with rr 2.1–2.70, 2.72–2.133, for rr 2.1–2.6, 2.6A (inserted by SI 1987/1919, reg 3(1), Schedule, Pt 1, para 7), 2.7–2.46, 2.46A (inserted by SI 1987/1919, reg 3(1), Schedule, Pt 1, para 19), 2.47–2.58, 2.59–2.62 (inserted by SI 2002/1307, rr 3(1), 5(8)), by SI 2003/1730, r 5(1), Sch 1, Pt 2, para 9.
Date in force: 15 September 2003: see SI 2003/1730, r 1(2); for effect and the continuing operation of this Part where a provision made by or under any enactment preserves the Insolvency Act 1986, old Pt II after that date see r 5(2)–(4) thereof.
Para (1): numbered as such by SI 2010/686, r 2, Sch 1, para 79(1), (2).
Date in force: 6 April 2010: see SI 2010/686, r 1; for transitional provisions see r 6(1), Sch 4, para 1 thereto.
Para (2): inserted by SI 2010/686, r 2, Sch 1, para 79(1), (3).
Date in force: 6 April 2010: see SI 2010/686, r 1; for transitional provisions see r 6(1), Sch 4, para 1 thereto.

See Further

See further, in relation to the application of this rule, with modifications, in respect of bank administration and applications for bank administration: the Bank Administration (England and Wales) Rules 2009, SI 2009/357, rr 58–61.

[SECTION B: MACHINERY OF PROVING A DEBT]

NOTES

Amendment

Substituted by SI 2003/1730, r 5(1), Sch 1, Pt 2, para 9.
Date in force: 15 September 2003: see SI 2003/1730, r 1(2); for effect and the continuing operation of this Part where a provision made by or under any enactment preserves the Insolvency Act 1986, old Pt II after that date see r 5(2)–(4) thereof.

[2.72 Proving a debt]

[(1) A person claiming to be a creditor of the company and wishing to recover his debt in whole or in part must (subject to any order of the court to the contrary) submit his claim in writing to the administrator.

(2) A creditor who claims is referred to as "proving" for his debt and a document by which he seeks to establish his claim is his "proof".

(3) Subject to the next paragraph, a proof must—
    (a)   be made out by, or under the direction of, the creditor and [authenticated] by him or a person authorised in that behalf; and
    (b)   state the following matters—
        (i)   the creditor's name and address;
        [(ia)   if the creditor is a company, its registered number;]
        [(ii)   the total amount of the creditor's claim (including value added tax) as at the date on which the company entered administration (or, if the company was in liquidation when it entered administration, the date on which it went into liquidation), less any payments made after that date in respect of the claim, any deduction under Rule 2.84 and any adjustment by way of set-off in accordance with Rule 2.85;]
        (iii)   whether or not the claim includes outstanding uncapitalised interest;
        (iv)   . . .
        (v)   . . .

(vi) particulars of how and when the debt was incurred by the company;

(vii) particulars of any security held, the date on which it was given and the value which the creditor puts on it;

(viii) details of any reservation of title in respect of goods to which the debt refers; and

(ix) the name, address and authority of the person [authenticating] the proof (if other than the creditor himself).

(4) There shall be specified in the proof details of any documents by reference to which the debt can be substantiated; but (subject as follows) it is not essential that such document be attached to the proof or submitted with it.

(5) The administrator may call for any document or other evidence to be produced to him, where he thinks it necessary for the purpose of substantiating the whole or any part of the claim made in the proof.

[(6) Where an administration is immediately preceded by a winding up, a creditor proving in the winding up is deemed to have proved in the administration.]]

NOTES

Amendment

Substituted, together with rr 2.1–2.71, 2.73–2.133, for rr 2.1–2.6, 2.6A (inserted by SI 1987/1919, reg 3(1), Schedule, Pt 1, para 7), 2.7–2.46, 2.46A (inserted by SI 1987/1919, reg 3(1), Schedule, Pt 1, para 19), 2.47–2.58, 2.59–2.62 (inserted by SI 2002/1307, rr 3(1), 5(8)), by SI 2003/1730, r 5(1), Sch 1, Pt 2, para 9.

Date in force: 15 September 2003: see SI 2003/1730, r 1(2); for effect and the continuing operation of this Part where a provision made by or under any enactment preserves the Insolvency Act 1986, old Pt II after that date see r 5(2)–(4) thereof.

Para (3): in sub-para (a) word "authenticated" in square brackets substituted by SI 2010/686, r 2, Sch 1, para 1.

Date in force: 6 April 2010: see SI 2010/686, r 1; for transitional provisions see r 6(1), Sch 4, paras 1, 2(1)(b) thereto.

Para (3): sub-para (b)(ia) inserted by SI 2010/686, r 2, Sch 1, para 80(1), (2)(a).

Date in force: 6 April 2010: see SI 2010/686, r 1; for transitional provisions see r 6(1), Sch 4, para 1 thereto.

Para (3): sub-para (b)(ii) substituted by SI 2010/686, r 2, Sch 1, para 80(1), (2)(b).

Date in force: 6 April 2010: see SI 2010/686, r 1; for transitional provisions see r 6(1), Sch 4, para 1 thereto.

Para (3): sub-paras (b)(iv), (v) revoked by SI 2010/686, r 2, Sch 1, para 80(1), (2)(c).

Date in force: 6 April 2010: see SI 2010/686, r 1; for transitional provisions see r 6(1), Sch 4, para 1 thereto.

Para (3): in sub-para (b)(ix) word "authenticating" in square brackets substituted by SI 2010/686, r 2, Sch 1, para 1.

Date in force: 6 April 2010: see SI 2010/686, r 1; for transitional provisions see r 6(1), Sch 4, paras 1, 2(1)(b) thereto.

Para (6): inserted by SI 2010/686, r 2, Sch 1, para 80(1), (5).

Date in force: 6 April 2010: see SI 2010/686, r 1; for transitional provisions see r 6(1), Sch 4, para 1 thereto.

See Further

See further, in relation to the application of this rule, with modifications, in respect of bank administration and applications for bank administration: the Bank Administration (England and Wales) Rules 2009, SI 2009/357, rr 58–61.

[2.73 . . .]
[. . .]

NOTES

Amendment

Substituted, together with rr 2.1–2.72, 2.74–2.133, for rr 2.1–2.6, 2.6A (inserted by SI 1987/1919, reg 3(1), Schedule, Pt 1, para 7), 2.7–2.46, 2.46A (inserted by SI 1987/1919, reg 3(1), Schedule, Pt 1, para 19), 2.47–2.58, 2.59–2.62 (inserted by SI 2002/1307, rr 3(1), 5(8)), by SI 2003/1730, r 5(1), Sch 1, Pt 2, para 9.

Date in force: 15 September 2003: see SI 2003/1730, r 1(2); for effect and the continuing operation of this Part where a provision made by or under any enactment preserves the Insolvency Act 1986, old Pt II after that date see r 5(2)–(4) thereof.

Revoked by SI 2010/686, r 5.

Date in force: 6 April 2010: see SI 2010/686, r 1; for transitional provisions see r 6(1), Sch 4, paras 1, 2(1)(a) thereto.

[2.74 Costs of proving]

[Unless the court otherwise orders—

(a) every creditor bears the cost of proving his own debt, including costs incurred in providing documents or evidence under Rule 2.72(5); and

(b) costs incurred by the administrator in estimating the quantum of a debt under Rule 2.81 are payable out of the assets as an expense of the administration.]

NOTES

Amendment

Substituted, together with rr 2.1–2.73, 2.75–2.133, for rr 2.1–2.6, 2.6A (inserted by SI 1987/1919, reg 3(1), Schedule, Pt 1, para 7), 2.7–2.46, 2.46A (inserted by SI 1987/1919, reg 3(1), Schedule, Pt 1, para 19), 2.47–2.58, 2.59–2.62 (inserted by SI 2002/1307, rr 3(1), 5(8)), by SI 2003/1730, r 5(1), Sch 1, Pt 2, para 9.

Date in force: 15 September 2003: see SI 2003/1730, r 1(2); for effect and the continuing operation of this Part where a provision made by or under any enactment preserves the Insolvency Act 1986, old Pt II after that date see r 5(2)–(4) thereof.

See Further

See further, in relation to the application of this rule, with modifications, in respect of bank administration and applications for bank administration: the Bank Administration (England and Wales) Rules 2009, SI 2009/357, rr 58–61.

[2.75 Administrator to allow inspection of proofs]

[The administrator shall, so long as proofs lodged with him are in his hands, allow them to be inspected, at all reasonable times on any business day, by any of the following persons—

(a) any creditor who has submitted a proof of debt (unless his proof has been wholly rejected for purposes of dividend or otherwise);

(b) any contributory of the company; and

(c) any person acting on behalf of either of the above.]

NOTES

Amendment

Substituted, together with rr 2.1–2.74, 2.76–2.133, for rr 2.1–2.6, 2.6A (inserted by SI 1987/1919, reg 3(1), Schedule, Pt 1, para 7), 2.7–2.46, 2.46A (inserted by SI 1987/1919, reg 3(1), Schedule, Pt 1, para 19), 2.47–2.58, 2.59–2.62 (inserted by SI 2002/1307, rr 3(1), 5(8)), by SI 2003/1730, r 5(1), Sch 1, Pt 2, para 9.

Date in force: 15 September 2003: see SI 2003/1730, r 1(2); for effect and the continuing operation of this Part where a provision made by or under any enactment preserves the Insolvency Act 1986, old Pt II after that date see r 5(2)–(4) thereof.

See Further

See further, in relation to the application of this rule, with modifications, in respect of bank administration and applications for bank administration: the Bank Administration (England and Wales) Rules 2009, SI 2009/357, rr 58–61.

[2.76 New administrator appointed]

[(1) If a new administrator is appointed in place of another, the former administrator [must as soon as reasonably practicable] transmit to him all proofs which he has received, together with an itemised list of them.

(2) The new administrator shall [authenticate] the list by way of receipt for the proofs, and return it to his predecessor.

[(3) From then on, all proofs of debt must be sent to and retained by the new administrator.]]

NOTES

Amendment

Substituted, together with rr 2.1–2.75, 2.77–2.133, for rr 2.1–2.6, 2.6A (inserted by SI 1987/1919, reg 3(1), Schedule, Pt 1, para 7), 2.7–2.46, 2.46A (inserted by SI 1987/1919, reg 3(1), Schedule, Pt 1, para 19), 2.47–2.58, 2.59–2.62 (inserted by SI 2002/1307, rr 3(1), 5(8)), by SI 2003/1730, r 5(1), Sch 1, Pt 2, para 9.

Date in force: 15 September 2003: see SI 2003/1730, r 1(2); for effect and the continuing operation of this Part where a provision made by or under any enactment preserves the Insolvency Act 1986, old Pt II after that date see r 5(2)–(4) thereof.

Para (1): word "must as soon as reasonably practicable" in square brackets substituted by SI 2010/686, r 2, Sch 1, para 81(1), (2).

Date in force: 6 April 2010: see SI 2010/686, r 1; for transitional provisions see r 6(1), Sch 4, para 1 thereto.

Para (2): word "authenticate" in square brackets substituted by SI 2010/686, r 2, Sch 1, para 1.

Date in force: 6 April 2010: see SI 2010/686, r 1; for transitional provisions see r 6(1), Sch 4, paras 1, 2(1)(b) thereto.

Para (3): inserted by SI 2010/686, r 2, Sch 1, para 81(1), (3).

Date in force: 6 April 2010: see SI 2010/686, r 1; for transitional provisions see r 6(1), Sch 4, para 1 thereto.

See Further

See further, in relation to the application of this rule, with modifications, in respect of bank administration and applications for bank administration: the Bank Administration (England and Wales) Rules 2009, SI 2009/357, rr 58–61.

[2.77 Admission and rejection of proofs for dividend]

[(1) A proof may be admitted for dividend either for the whole amount claimed by the creditor, or for part of that amount.

(2) If the administrator rejects a proof in whole or in part, he shall prepare a written statement of his reasons for doing so, and send it as soon as reasonably practicable to the creditor.]

NOTES

Amendment

Substituted, together with rr 2.1–2.76, 2.78–2.133, for rr 2.1–2.6, 2.6A (inserted by SI 1987/1919, reg 3(1), Schedule, Pt 1, para 7), 2.7–2.46, 2.46A (inserted by SI 1987/1919,

reg 3(1), Schedule, Pt 1, para 19), 2.47–2.58, 2.59–2.62 (inserted by SI 2002/1307, rr 3(1), 5(8)), by SI 2003/1730, r 5(1), Sch 1, Pt 2, para 9.
>Date in force: 15 September 2003: see SI 2003/1730, r 1(2); for effect and the continuing operation of this Part where a provision made by or under any enactment preserves the Insolvency Act 1986, old Pt II after that date see r 5(2)–(4) thereof.

See Further
>See further, in relation to the application of this rule, with modifications, in respect of bank administration and applications for bank administration: the Bank Administration (England and Wales) Rules 2009, SI 2009/357, rr 58–61.

[2.78 Appeal against decision on proof]

[(1) If a creditor is dissatisfied with the administrator's decision with respect to his proof (including any decision on the question of preference), he may apply to the court for the decision to be reversed or varied. The application must be made within 21 days of his receiving the statement sent under Rule 2.77(2).

(2) [A member or] any other creditor may, if dissatisfied with the administrator's decision admitting or rejecting the whole or any part of a proof, make such an application within 21 days of becoming aware of the administrator's decision.

(3) Where application is made to the court under this Rule, the court shall fix a venue for the application to be heard, notice of which shall be sent by the applicant to the creditor who lodged the proof in question (if it is not himself) and the administrator.

(4) The administrator shall, on receipt of the notice, file with the court the relevant proof, together (if appropriate) with a copy of the statement sent under Rule 2.77(2).

[(4A) Where the application is made by a member, the court must not disallow the proof (in whole or in part) unless the member shows that there is (or would be but for the amount claimed in the proof), or that it is likely that there will be (or would be but for the amount claimed in the proof), a surplus of assets to which the company would be entitled.]

(5) After the application has been heard and determined, the proof shall, unless it has been wholly disallowed, be returned by the court to the administrator.

(6) The administrator is not personally liable for costs incurred by any person in respect of an application under this Rule unless the court otherwise orders.]

NOTES

Amendment
>Substituted, together with rr 2.1–2.77, 2.79–2.133, for rr 2.1–2.6, 2.6A (inserted by SI 1987/1919, reg 3(1), Schedule, Pt 1, para 7), 2.7–2.46, 2.46A (inserted by SI 1987/1919, reg 3(1), Schedule, Pt 1, para 19), 2.47–2.58, 2.59–2.62 (inserted by SI 2002/1307, rr 3(1), 5(8)), by SI 2003/1730, r 5(1), Sch 1, Pt 2, para 9.
>>Date in force: 15 September 2003: see SI 2003/1730, r 1(2); for effect and the continuing operation of this Part where a provision made by or under any enactment preserves the Insolvency Act 1986, old Pt II after that date see r 5(2)–(4) thereof.
>Para (2): words "A member or" in square brackets inserted by SI 2010/686, r 2, Sch 1, para 82(1), (2).
>>Date in force: 6 April 2010: see SI 2010/686, r 1; for transitional provisions see r 6(1), Sch 4, para 1 thereto.
>Para (4A): inserted by SI 2010/686, r 2, Sch 1, para 82(1), (3).
>>Date in force: 6 April 2010: see SI 2010/686, r 1; for transitional provisions see r 6(1), Sch 4, para 1 thereto.

See Further
>See further, in relation to the application of this rule, with modifications, in respect of bank administration and applications for bank administration: the Bank Administration (England and Wales) Rules 2009, SI 2009/357, rr 58–61.

[2.79 **Withdrawal or variation of proof**]
[A creditor's proof may at any time, by agreement between himself and the administrator, be withdrawn or varied as to the amount claimed.]

NOTES

Amendment

Substituted, together with rr 2.1–2.78, 2.80–2.133, for rr 2.1–2.6, 2.6A (inserted by SI 1987/1919, reg 3(1), Schedule, Pt 1, para 7), 2.7–2.46, 2.46A (inserted by SI 1987/1919, reg 3(1), Schedule, Pt 1, para 19), 2.47–2.58, 2.59–2.62 (inserted by SI 2002/1307, rr 3(1), 5(8)), by SI 2003/1730, r 5(1), Sch 1, Pt 2, para 9.

Date in force: 15 September 2003: see SI 2003/1730, r 1(2); for effect and the continuing operation of this Part where a provision made by or under any enactment preserves the Insolvency Act 1986, old Pt II after that date see r 5(2)–(4) thereof.

See Further

See further, in relation to the application of this rule, with modifications, in respect of bank administration and applications for bank administration: the Bank Administration (England and Wales) Rules 2009, SI 2009/357, rr 58–61.

[2.80 **Expunging of proof by the court**]
[(1) The court may expunge a proof or reduce the amount claimed—
  (a) on the administrator's application, where he thinks that the proof has been improperly admitted, or ought to be reduced; or
  (b) on the application of a creditor, if the administrator declines to interfere in the matter.

(2) Where application is made to the court under this Rule, the court shall fix a venue for the application to be heard, notice of which shall be sent by the applicant—
  (a) in the case of an application by the administrator, to the creditor who made the proof; and
  (b) in the case of an application by a creditor, to the administrator and to the creditor who made the proof (if not himself).]

NOTES

Amendment

Substituted, together with rr 2.1–2.79, 2.81–2.133, for rr 2.1–2.6, 2.6A (inserted by SI 1987/1919, reg 3(1), Schedule, Pt 1, para 7), 2.7–2.46, 2.46A (inserted by SI 1987/1919, reg 3(1), Schedule, Pt 1, para 19), 2.47–2.58, 2.59–2.62 (inserted by SI 2002/1307, rr 3(1), 5(8)), by SI 2003/1730, r 5(1), Sch 1, Pt 2, para 9.

Date in force: 15 September 2003: see SI 2003/1730, r 1(2); for effect and the continuing operation of this Part where a provision made by or under any enactment preserves the Insolvency Act 1986, old Pt II after that date see r 5(2)–(4) thereof.

See Further

See further, in relation to the application of this rule, with modifications, in respect of bank administration and applications for bank administration: the Bank Administration (England and Wales) Rules 2009, SI 2009/357, rr 58–61.

[SECTION C: QUANTIFICATION OF CLAIMS]

NOTES

Amendment

Substituted by SI 2003/1730, r 5(1), Sch 1, Pt 2, para 9.

Date in force: 15 September 2003: see SI 2003/1730, r 1(2); for effect and the continuing operation of this Part where a provision made by or under any enactment preserves the Insolvency Act 1986, old Pt II after that date see r 5(2)–(4) thereof.

[**2.81 Estimate of quantum**]
[(1) The administrator shall estimate the value of any debt which, by reason of its being subject to any contingency or for any other reason, does not bear a certain value; and he may revise any estimate previously made, if he thinks fit by reference to any change of circumstances or to information becoming available to him. He shall inform the creditor as to his estimate and any revision of it.

(2) Where the value of a debt is estimated under this Rule, the amount provable in the administration in the case of that debt is that of the estimate for the time being.]

NOTES

Amendment
Substituted, together with rr 2.1–2.80, 2.82–2.133, for rr 2.1–2.6, 2.6A (inserted by SI 1987/1919, reg 3(1), Schedule, Pt 1, para 7), 2.7–2.46, 2.46A (inserted by SI 1987/1919, reg 3(1), Schedule, Pt 1, para 19), 2.47–2.58, 2.59–2.62 (inserted by SI 2002/1307, rr 3(1), 5(8)), by SI 2003/1730, r 5(1), Sch 1, Pt 2, para 9.
Date in force: 15 September 2003: see SI 2003/1730, r 1(2); for effect and the continuing operation of this Part where a provision made by or under any enactment preserves the Insolvency Act 1986, old Pt II after that date see r 5(2)–(4) thereof.

See Further
See further, in relation to the application of this rule, with modifications, in respect of bank administration and applications for bank administration: the Bank Administration (England and Wales) Rules 2009, SI 2009/357, rr 58–61.

[**2.82 Negotiable instruments, etc**]
[Unless the administrator allows, a proof in respect of money owed on a bill of exchange, promissory note, cheque or other negotiable instrument or security cannot be admitted unless there is produced the instrument or security itself or a copy of it, certified by the creditor or his authorised representative to be a true copy.]

NOTES

Amendment
Substituted, together with rr 2.1–2.81, 2.83–2.133, for rr 2.1–2.6, 2.6A (inserted by SI 1987/1919, reg 3(1), Schedule, Pt 1, para 7), 2.7–2.46, 2.46A (inserted by SI 1987/1919, reg 3(1), Schedule, Pt 1, para 19), 2.47–2.58, 2.59–2.62 (inserted by SI 2002/1307, rr 3(1), 5(8)), by SI 2003/1730, r 5(1), Sch 1, Pt 2, para 9.
Date in force: 15 September 2003: see SI 2003/1730, r 1(2); for effect and the continuing operation of this Part where a provision made by or under any enactment preserves the Insolvency Act 1986, old Pt II after that date see r 5(2)–(4) thereof.

See Further
See further, in relation to the application of this rule, with modifications, in respect of bank administration and applications for bank administration: the Bank Administration (England and Wales) Rules 2009, SI 2009/357, rr 58–61.

[**2.83 Secured creditors**]
[(1) If a secured creditor realises his security, he may prove for the balance of his debt, after deducting the amount realised.

(2) If a secured creditor voluntarily surrenders his security for the general benefit of creditors, he may prove for his whole debt, as if it were unsecured.]

NOTES

Amendment

Substituted, together with rr 2.1–2.82, 2.84–2.133, for rr 2.1–2.6, 2.6A (inserted by SI 1987/1919, reg 3(1), Schedule, Pt 1, para 7), 2.7–2.46, 2.46A (inserted by SI 1987/1919, reg 3(1), Schedule, Pt 1, para 19), 2.47–2.58, 2.59–2.62 (inserted by SI 2002/1307, rr 3(1), 5(8)), by SI 2003/1730, r 5(1), Sch 1, Pt 2, para 9.

Date in force: 15 September 2003: see SI 2003/1730, r 1(2); for effect and the continuing operation of this Part where a provision made by or under any enactment preserves the Insolvency Act 1986, old Pt II after that date see r 5(2)–(4) thereof.

See Further

See further, in relation to the application of this rule, with modifications, in respect of bank administration and applications for bank administration: the Bank Administration (England and Wales) Rules 2009, SI 2009/357, rr 58–61.

[2.84 Discounts]

[There shall in every case be deducted from the claim all trade and other discounts which would have been available to the company but for its administration except any discount for immediate, early or cash settlement.]

NOTES

Amendment

Substituted, together with rr 2.1–2.83, 2.85–2.133, for rr 2.1–2.6, 2.6A (inserted by SI 1987/1919, reg 3(1), Schedule, Pt 1, para 7), 2.7–2.46, 2.46A (inserted by SI 1987/1919, reg 3(1), Schedule, Pt 1, para 19), 2.47–2.58, 2.59–2.62 (inserted by SI 2002/1307, rr 3(1), 5(8)), by SI 2003/1730, r 5(1), Sch 1, Pt 2, para 9.

Date in force: 15 September 2003: see SI 2003/1730, r 1(2); for effect and the continuing operation of this Part where a provision made by or under any enactment preserves the Insolvency Act 1986, old Pt II after that date see r 5(2)–(4) thereof.

See Further

See further, in relation to the application of this rule, with modifications, in respect of bank administration and applications for bank administration: the Bank Administration (England and Wales) Rules 2009, SI 2009/357, rr 58–61.

[2.85 Mutual credits and set-off]

[(1) This Rule applies where the administrator, being authorised to make the distribution in question, has, pursuant to Rule 2.95 given notice that he proposes to make it.

(2) In this Rule "mutual dealings" means mutual credits, mutual debts or other mutual dealings between the company and any creditor of the company proving or claiming to prove for a debt in the administration but does not include any of the following—

(a) any debt arising out of an obligation incurred after the company entered administration;

(b) any debt arising out of an obligation incurred at a time when the creditor had notice that—
  (i) an application for an administration order was pending; or
  (ii) any person had given notice of intention to appoint an administrator;

(c) any debt arising out of an obligation where—
  (i) the administration was immediately preceded by a winding up; and

(ii) at the time the obligation was incurred the creditor had notice that a meeting of creditors had been summoned under section 98 or a petition for the winding up of the company was pending;
(d) any debt arising out of an obligation incurred during a winding up which immediately preceded the administration; or
(e) any debt which has been acquired by a creditor by assignment or otherwise, pursuant to an agreement between the creditor and any other party where that agreement was entered into—
  (i) after the company entered administration;
  (ii) at a time when the creditor had notice that an application for an administration order was pending;
  (iii) at a time when the creditor had notice that any person had given notice of intention to appoint an administrator;
  (iv) where the administration was immediately preceded by a winding up, at a time when the creditor had notice that a meeting of creditors had been summoned under section 98 or that a winding up petition was pending; or
  (v) during a winding up which immediately preceded the administration.

(3) An account shall be taken as at the date of the notice referred to in paragraph (1) of what is due from each party to the other in respect of the mutual dealings and the sums due from one party shall be set off against the sums due from the other.

(4) A sum shall be regarded as being due to or from the company for the purposes of paragraph (3) whether—
(a) it is payable at present or in the future;
(b) the obligation by virtue of which it is payable is certain or contingent; or
(c) its amount is fixed or liquidated, or is capable of being ascertained by fixed rules or as a matter of opinion.

(5) Rule 2.81 shall apply for the purposes of this Rule to any obligation to or from the company which, by reason of its being subject to any contingency or for any other reason, does not bear a certain value;

(6) Rules 2.86 to 2.88 shall apply for the purposes of this Rule in relation to any sums due to the company which—
(a) are payable in a currency other than sterling;
(b) are of a periodical nature; or
(c) bear interest.

(7) Rule 2.105 shall apply for the purposes of this Rule to any sum due to or from the company which is payable in the future.

(8) Only the balance (if any) of the account owed to the creditor is provable in the administration. Alternatively the balance (if any) owed to the company shall be paid to the administrator as part of the assets except where all or part of the balance results from a contingent or prospective debt owed by the creditor and in such a case the balance (or that part of it which results from the contingent or prospective debt) shall be paid if and when that debt becomes due and payable.

(9) In this Rule "obligation" means an obligation however arising, whether by virtue of an agreement, rule of law or otherwise.]

NOTES

Amendment

Substituted by SI 2005/527, r 9.
Date in force: 1 April 2005: see SI 2005/527, r 1(2); for transitional provisions in relation to any case where a company has entered administration or gone into liquidation, or a bankruptcy order has been made before that date see r 3(1) thereof.

Insolvency Rules 1986, reg 2.87

See Further

See further, in relation to the application of this rule, with modifications, in respect of bank administration and applications for bank administration: the Bank Administration (England and Wales) Rules 2009, SI 2009/357, rr 58–61.

[**2.86 Debt in foreign currency**]

[(1) For the purpose of proving a debt incurred or payable in a currency other than sterling, the amount of the debt shall be converted into sterling at the official exchange rate prevailing on the date when the company entered administration [or, if the administration was immediately preceded by a winding up, on the date that the company went into liquidation].

(2) "The official exchange rate" is the middle exchange rate on the London Foreign Exchange Market at the close of business, as published for the date in question. In the absence of any such published rate, it is such rate as the court determines.]

NOTES

Amendment

Substituted, together with rr 2.1–2.85, 2.87–2.133, for rr 2.1–2.6, 2.6A (inserted by SI 1987/1919, reg 3(1), Schedule, Pt 1, para 7), 2.7–2.46, 2.46A (inserted by SI 1987/1919, reg 3(1), Schedule, Pt 1, para 19), 2.47–2.58, 2.59–2.62 (inserted by SI 2002/1307, rr 3(1), 5(8)), by SI 2003/1730, r 5(1), Sch 1, Pt 2, para 9.
   Date in force: 15 September 2003: see SI 2003/1730, r 1(2); for effect and the continuing operation of this Part where a provision made by or under any enactment preserves the Insolvency Act 1986, old Pt II after that date see r 5(2)–(4) thereof.
Para (1): words from "or, if the" to "went into liquidation" in square brackets inserted by SI 2005/527, r 10.
   Date in force: 1 April 2005: see SI 2005/527, r 1(2); for transitional provisions in relation to any case where a company has entered administration or gone into liquidation, or a bankruptcy order has been made before that date see r 3(1) thereof.

See Further

See further, in relation to the application of this rule, with modifications, in respect of bank administration and applications for bank administration: the Bank Administration (England and Wales) Rules 2009, SI 2009/357, rr 58–61.

[**2.87 Payments of a periodical nature**]

[(1) In the case of rent and other payments of a periodical nature, the creditor may prove for any amounts due and unpaid up to the date when the company entered administration [or, if the administration was immediately preceded by a winding up, up to the date that the company went into liquidation].

(2) Where at that date any payment was accruing due, the creditor may prove for so much as would have fallen due at that date, if accruing from day to day.]

NOTES

Amendment

Substituted, together with rr 2.1–2.86, 2.88–2.133, for rr 2.1–2.6, 2.6A (inserted by SI 1987/1919, reg 3(1), Schedule, Pt 1, para 7), 2.7–2.46, 2.46A (inserted by SI 1987/1919, reg 3(1), Schedule, Pt 1, para 19), 2.47–2.58, 2.59–2.62 (inserted by SI 2002/1307, rr 3(1), 5(8)), by SI 2003/1730, r 5(1), Sch 1, Pt 2, para 9.
   Date in force: 15 September 2003: see SI 2003/1730, r 1(2); for effect and the continuing operation of this Part where a provision made by or under any enactment preserves the Insolvency Act 1986, old Pt II after that date see r 5(2)–(4) thereof.
Para (1): words from "or, if the" to "went into liquidation" in square brackets inserted by SI 2005/527, r 11.

Date in force: 1 April 2005: see SI 2005/527, r 1(2); for transitional provisions in relation to any case where a company has entered administration or gone into liquidation, or a bankruptcy order has been made before that date see r 3(1) thereof.

See Further

See further, in relation to the application of this rule, with modifications, in respect of bank administration and applications for bank administration: the Bank Administration (England and Wales) Rules 2009, SI 2009/357, rr 58–61.

[2.88 Interest]

[[(A1) In this Rule, "the relevant date" means the date on which the company entered administration or, if the administration was immediately preceded by a winding up, the date on which the company went into liquidation.]

(1) Where a debt proved in the administration bears interest, that interest is provable as part of the debt except in so far as it is payable in respect of any period after [the relevant date].

(2) In the following circumstances the creditor's claim may include interest on the debt for periods before [the relevant date], although not previously reserved or agreed.

(3) If the debt is due by virtue of a written instrument, and payable at a certain time, interest may be claimed for the period from that time to [the relevant date].

(4) If the debt is due otherwise, interest may only be claimed if, before [the relevant date], a demand for payment of the debt was made in writing by or on behalf of the creditor, and notice given that interest would be payable from the date of the demand to the date of payment.

(5) Interest under paragraph (4) may only be claimed for the period from the date of the demand to [the relevant date] and for all the purposes of the Act and the Rules shall be chargeable at a rate not exceeding that mentioned in paragraph (6).

(6) The rate of interest to be claimed under paragraphs (3) and (4) is the rate specified in section 17 of the Judgments Act 1838 on [the relevant date].

(7) ... any surplus remaining after payment of the debts proved shall, before being applied for any purpose, be applied in paying interest on those debts in respect of the periods during which they have been outstanding since [the relevant date].

(8) All interest payable under paragraph (7) ranks equally whether or not the debts on which it is payable rank equally.

(9) The rate of interest payable under paragraph (7) is whichever is the greater of the rate specified under paragraph (6) [and] the rate applicable to the debt apart from the administration.]

NOTES

Amendment

Substituted, together with rr 2.1–2.87, 2.89–2.133, for rr 2.1–2.6, 2.6A (inserted by SI 1987/1919, reg 3(1), Schedule, Pt 1, para 7), 2.7–2.46, 2.46A (inserted by SI 1987/1919, reg 3(1), Schedule, Pt 1, para 19), 2.47–2.58, 2.59–2.62 (inserted by SI 2002/1307, rr 3(1), 5(8)), by SI 2003/1730, r 5(1), Sch 1, Pt 2, para 9.
Date in force: 15 September 2003: see SI 2003/1730, r 1(2); for effect and the continuing operation of this Part where a provision made by or under any enactment preserves the Insolvency Act 1986, old Pt II after that date see r 5(2)–(4) thereof.
Para (A1): inserted by SI 2010/686, r 2, Sch 1, para 83(1), (2).
Date in force: 6 April 2010: see SI 2010/686, r 1; for transitional provisions see r 6(1), Sch 4, para 1 thereto.
Para (1): words "the relevant date" in square brackets substituted by SI 2010/686, r 2, Sch 1, para 83(1), (3).
Date in force: 6 April 2010: see SI 2010/686, r 1; for transitional provisions see r 6(1), Sch 4, para 1 thereto.
Para (2): words "the relevant date" in square brackets substituted by SI 2010/686, r 2, Sch 1, para 83(1), (4).

Date in force: 6 April 2010: see SI 2010/686, r 1; for transitional provisions see r 6(1), Sch 4, para 1 thereto.
Para (3): words "the relevant date" in square brackets substituted by SI 2010/686, r 2, Sch 1, para 83(1), (5).
Date in force: 6 April 2010: see SI 2010/686, r 1; for transitional provisions see r 6(1), Sch 4, para 1 thereto.
Para (4): words "the relevant date" in square brackets substituted by SI 2010/686, r 2, Sch 1, para 83(1), (6).
Date in force: 6 April 2010: see SI 2010/686, r 1; for transitional provisions see r 6(1), Sch 4, para 1 thereto.
Para (5): words "the relevant date" in square brackets substituted by SI 2010/686, r 2, Sch 1, para 83(1), (7).
Date in force: 6 April 2010: see SI 2010/686, r 1; for transitional provisions see r 6(1), Sch 4, para 1 thereto.
Para (6): words "the relevant date" in square brackets substituted by SI 2010/686, r 2, Sch 1, para 83(1), (8).
Date in force: 6 April 2010: see SI 2010/686, r 1.
Para (7): words omitted revoked by SI 2005/527, r 12(b).
Date in force: 1 April 2005: see SI 2005/527, r 1(2); for transitional provisions in relation to any case where a company has entered administration or gone into liquidation, or a bankruptcy order has been made before that date see r 3(1) thereof.
Para (7): words "the relevant date" in square brackets substituted by SI 2010/686, r 2, Sch 1, para 83(1), (9).
Date in force: 6 April 2010: see SI 2010/686, r 1; for transitional provisions see r 6(1), Sch 4, para 1 thereto.
Para (9): word "and" in square brackets substituted by SI 2010/686, r 2, Sch 1, para 83(1), (10).
Date in force: 6 April 2010: see SI 2010/686, r 1; for transitional provisions see r 6(1), Sch 4, para 1 thereto.

See Further

See further, in relation to the application of this rule, with modifications, in respect of bank administration and applications for bank administration: the Bank Administration (England and Wales) Rules 2009, SI 2009/357, rr 58–61.

[2.89 Debt payable at future time]

[A creditor may prove for a debt of which payment was not yet due on the date when the company entered administration, [or, if the administration was immediately preceded by a winding up, up to the date that the company went into liquidation] subject to Rule 2.105 (adjustment of dividend where payment made before time).]

NOTES

Amendment

Substituted, together with rr 2.1–2.88, 2.90–2.133, for rr 2.1–2.6, 2.6A (inserted by SI 1987/1919, reg 3(1), Schedule, Pt 1, para 7), 2.7–2.46, 2.46A (inserted by SI 1987/1919, reg 3(1), Schedule, Pt 1, para 19), 2.47–2.58, 2.59–2.62 (inserted by SI 2002/1307, rr 3(1), 5(8)), by SI 2003/1730, r 5(1), Sch 1, Pt 2, para 9.
Date in force: 15 September 2003: see SI 2003/1730, r 1(2); for effect and the continuing operation of this Part where a provision made by or under any enactment preserves the Insolvency Act 1986, old Pt II after that date see r 5(2)–(4) thereof.
Words from "or, if the" to "went into liquidation" in square brackets inserted by SI 2005/527, r 13.
Date in force: 1 April 2005: see SI 2005/527, r 1(2); for transitional provisions in relation to any case where a company has entered administration or gone into liquidation, or a bankruptcy order has been made before that date see r 3(1) thereof.

See Further

See further, in relation to the application of this rule, with modifications, in respect of bank administration and applications for bank administration: the Bank Administration (England

and Wales) Rules 2009, SI 2009/357, rr 58–61.

[2.90 Value of security]

[(1) A secured creditor may, with the agreement of the administrator or the [permission] of the court, at any time alter the value which he has, in his proof of debt, put upon his security.

(2) However, if a secured creditor—

(a) being the applicant for an administration order or the appointor of the administrator, has in the application or the notice of appointment put a value on his security; or

(b) has voted in respect of the unsecured balance of his debt,

he may re-value his security only with permission of the court.]

NOTES

Amendment

Substituted, together with rr 2.1–2.89, 2.91–2.133, for rr 2.1–2.6, 2.6A (inserted by SI 1987/1919, reg 3(1), Schedule, Pt 1, para 7), 2.7–2.46, 2.46A (inserted by SI 1987/1919, reg 3(1), Schedule, Pt 1, para 19), 2.47–2.58, 2.59–2.62 (inserted by SI 2002/1307, rr 3(1), 5(8)), by SI 2003/1730, r 5(1), Sch 1, Pt 2, para 9.

Date in force: 15 September 2003: see SI 2003/1730, r 1(2); for effect and the continuing operation of this Part where a provision made by or under any enactment preserves the Insolvency Act 1986, old Pt II after that date see r 5(2)–(4) thereof.

Para (1): word "permission" in square brackets substituted by SI 2010/686, r 2, Sch 1, para 1.

Date in force: 6 April 2010: see SI 2010/686, r 1; for transitional provisions see r 6(1), Sch 4, paras 1, 2(1)(b) thereto.

See Further

See further, in relation to the application of this rule, with modifications, in respect of bank administration and applications for bank administration: the Bank Administration (England and Wales) Rules 2009, SI 2009/357, rr 58–61.

[2.91 Surrender for non-disclosure]

[(1) If a secured creditor omits to disclose his security in his proof of debt, he shall surrender his security for the general benefit of creditors, unless the court, on application by him, relieves him from the effect of this Rule on the ground that the omission was inadvertent or the result of honest mistake.

(2) If the court grants that relief, it may require or allow the creditor's proof of debt to be amended, on such terms as may be just.

(3) Nothing in this Rule or the following two Rules may affect the rights in rem of creditors or third parties protected under Article 5 of the EC Regulation (third parties' rights in rem).]

NOTES

Amendment

Substituted, together with rr 2.1–2.90, 2.92–2.133, for rr 2.1–2.6, 2.6A (inserted by SI 1987/1919, reg 3(1), Schedule, Pt 1, para 7), 2.7–2.46, 2.46A (inserted by SI 1987/1919, reg 3(1), Schedule, Pt 1, para 19), 2.47–2.58, 2.59–2.62 (inserted by SI 2002/1307, rr 3(1), 5(8)), by SI 2003/1730, r 5(1), Sch 1, Pt 2, para 9.

Date in force: 15 September 2003: see SI 2003/1730, r 1(2); for effect and the continuing operation of this Part where a provision made by or under any enactment preserves the Insolvency Act 1986, old Pt II after that date see r 5(2)–(4) thereof.

See Further

See further, in relation to the application of this rule, with modifications, in respect of bank administration and applications for bank administration: the Bank Administration (England and Wales) Rules 2009, SI 2009/357, rr 58–61.

[2.92 Redemption by administrator]

[(1) The administrator may at any time give notice to a creditor whose debt is secured that he proposes, at the expiration of 28 days from the date of the notice, to redeem the security at the value put upon it in the creditor's proof.

(2) The creditor then has 21 days (or such longer period as the administrator may allow) in which, if he so wishes, to exercise his right to revalue his security (with the permission of the court, where Rule 2.90(2) applies).
If the creditor re-values his security, the administrator may only redeem at the new value.

(3) If the administrator redeems the security, the cost of transferring it is payable out of the assets.

(4) A secured creditor may at any time, by a notice in writing, call on the administrator to elect whether he will or will not exercise his power to redeem the security at the value then placed on it; and the administrator then has 3 months in which to exercise the power or determine not to exercise it.]

NOTES

Amendment

Substituted, together with rr 2.1–2.91, 2.93–2.133, for rr 2.1–2.6, 2.6A (inserted by SI 1987/1919, reg 3(1), Schedule, Pt 1, para 7), 2.7–2.46, 2.46A (inserted by SI 1987/1919, reg 3(1), Schedule, Pt 1, para 19), 2.47–2.58, 2.59–2.62 (inserted by SI 2002/1307, rr 3(1), 5(8)), by SI 2003/1730, r 5(1), Sch 1, Pt 2, para 9.

Date in force: 15 September 2003: see SI 2003/1730, r 1(2); for effect and the continuing operation of this Part where a provision made by or under any enactment preserves the Insolvency Act 1986, old Pt II after that date see r 5(2)–(4) thereof.

See Further

See further, in relation to the application of this rule, with modifications, in respect of bank administration and applications for bank administration: the Bank Administration (England and Wales) Rules 2009, SI 2009/357, rr 58–61.

[2.93 Test of security's value]

[(1) Subject as follows, the administrator, if he is dissatisfied with the value which a secured creditor puts on his security (whether in his proof or by way of re-valuation under [Rule 2.92]), may require any property comprised in the security to be offered for sale.

(2) The terms of sale shall be such as may be agreed, or as the court may direct; and if the sale is by auction, the administrator on behalf of the company, and the creditor on his own behalf, may appear and bid.

[(3) This Rule does not apply if the security has been revalued and the revaluation has been approved by the court.]]

NOTES

Amendment

Substituted, together with rr 2.1–2.92, 2.94–2.133, for rr 2.1–2.6, 2.6A (inserted by SI 1987/1919, reg 3(1), Schedule, Pt 1, para 7), 2.7–2.46, 2.46A (inserted by SI 1987/1919, reg 3(1), Schedule, Pt 1, para 19), 2.47–2.58, 2.59–2.62 (inserted by SI 2002/1307, rr 3(1), 5(8)), by SI 2003/1730, r 5(1), Sch 1, Pt 2, para 9.

Date in force: 15 September 2003: see SI 2003/1730, r 1(2); for effect and the continuing operation of this Part where a provision made by or under any enactment preserves the Insolvency Act 1986, old Pt II after that date see r 5(2)–(4) thereof.
Para (1): words "Rule 2.92" in square brackets substituted by SI 2010/686, r 2, Sch 1, para 84(1), (2).
Date in force: 6 April 2010: see SI 2010/686, r 1; for transitional provisions see r 6(1), Sch 4, para 1 thereto.
Para (3): inserted by SI 2010/686, r 2, Sch 1, para 84(1), (3).
Date in force: 6 April 2010: see SI 2010/686, r 1; for transitional provisions see r 6(1), Sch 4, para 1 thereto.

See Further

See further, in relation to the application of this rule, with modifications, in respect of bank administration and applications for bank administration: the Bank Administration (England and Wales) Rules 2009, SI 2009/357, rr 58–61.

[2.94 Realisation of security by creditor]

[If a creditor who has valued his security subsequently realises it (whether or not at the instance of the administrator)—

(a) the net amount realised shall be substituted for the value previously put by the creditor on the security; and

(b) that amount shall be treated in all respects as an amended valuation made by him.]

NOTES

Amendment

Substituted, together with rr 2.1–2.93, 2.95–2.133, for rr 2.1–2.6, 2.6A (inserted by SI 1987/1919, reg 3(1), Schedule, Pt 1, para 7), 2.7–2.46, 2.46A (inserted by SI 1987/1919, reg 3(1), Schedule, Pt 1, para 19), 2.47–2.58, 2.59–2.62 (inserted by SI 2002/1307, rr 3(1), 5(8)), by SI 2003/1730, r 5(1), Sch 1, Pt 2, para 9.
Date in force: 15 September 2003: see SI 2003/1730, r 1(2); for effect and the continuing operation of this Part where a provision made by or under any enactment preserves the Insolvency Act 1986, old Pt II after that date see r 5(2)–(4) thereof.

See Further

See further, in relation to the application of this rule, with modifications, in respect of bank administration and applications for bank administration: the Bank Administration (England and Wales) Rules 2009, SI 2009/357, rr 58–61.

[2.95 Notice of proposed distribution]

[(1) Where an administrator is proposing to make a distribution to creditors he shall give . . . notice of that fact.

(2) The notice given pursuant to paragraph (1) shall—

(a) be sent to—
  (i) all creditors whose addresses are known to the administrator; and
  (ii) where a member State liquidator has been appointed in relation to the company, to the member State liquidator;

(b) state whether the distribution is to preferential creditors or preferential creditors and unsecured creditors; and

(c) where the administrator proposes to make a distribution to unsecured creditors, state the value of the prescribed part, except where the court has made an order under section 176A(5).

[(3) Subject to paragraph (5)(b), before declaring a dividend the administrator shall by notice invite the creditors to prove their debts. Such notice—

(a) shall be gazetted; and

(b) may be advertised in such other manner as the administrator thinks fit.]

(4) A notice pursuant to [paragraph (1) or (3) must, in addition to the standard contents]—
- (a) state that it is the intention of the administrator to make a distribution to creditors within the period of 2 months from the last date for proving;
- (b) specify whether the proposed dividend is interim or final;
- (c) specify a date up to which proofs may be lodged being a date which—
  - (i) is the same date for all creditors; and
  - (ii) is not less than 21 days from that of the notice.

[(5) Where a dividend is to be declared for preferential creditors—
- (a) the notice pursuant to paragraph (1) need only to be given to those creditors in whose case the administrator has reason to believe that their debts are preferential; and
- (b) the notice pursuant to paragraph (3) need only be given if the administrator thinks fit.]]

NOTES

Amendment

Substituted, together with rr 2.1–2.94, 2.96–2.133, for rr 2.1–2.6, 2.6A (inserted by SI 1987/1919, reg 3(1), Schedule, Pt 1, para 7), 2.7–2.46, 2.46A (inserted by SI 1987/1919, reg 3(1), Schedule, Pt 1, para 19), 2.47–2.58, 2.59–2.62 (inserted by SI 2002/1307, rr 3(1), 5(8)), by SI 2003/1730, r 5(1), Sch 1, Pt 2, para 9.

Date in force: 15 September 2003: see SI 2003/1730, r 1(2); for effect and the continuing operation of this Part where a provision made by or under any enactment preserves the Insolvency Act 1986, old Pt II after that date see r 5(2)–(4) thereof.

Para (1): words omitted revoked by SI 2010/686, r 2, Sch 1, para 85(1), (2).

Date in force: 6 April 2010: see SI 2010/686, r 1; for transitional provisions see r 6(1), Sch 4, para 1 thereto.

Para (3): substituted by SI 2009/642, rr 4, 12(a).

Date in force: 6 April 2009: see SI 2009/642, r 1; for transitional provisions see r 3 thereof.

Para (4): words "paragraph (1) or (3) must, in addition to the standard contents" in square brackets substituted by SI 2010/686, r 2, Sch 1, para 85(1), (3).

Date in force: 6 April 2010: see SI 2010/686, r 1; for transitional provisions see r 6(1), Sch 4, para 1 thereto.

Para (5): substituted by SI 2009/642, rr 4, 12(b).

Date in force: 6 April 2009: see SI 2009/642, r 1; for transitional provisions see r 3 thereof.

See Further

See further, in relation to the application of this rule, with modifications, in respect of bank administration and applications for bank administration: the Bank Administration (England and Wales) Rules 2009, SI 2009/357, rr 58–61.

[2.96 Admission or rejection of proofs]

[(1) Unless he has already dealt with them, within [5 business] days of the last date for proving, the administrator shall—
- (a) admit or reject [(in whole or in part)] proofs submitted to him; or
- (b) make such provision in respect of them as he thinks fit.

(2) The administrator is not obliged to deal with proofs lodged after the last date for proving, but he may do so, if he thinks fit.

(3) In the declaration of a dividend no payment shall be made more than once by virtue of the same debt.

(4) Subject to Rule 2.104, where—
- (a) a creditor has proved; and
- (b) a member State liquidator has proved in relation to the same debt,

payment shall only be made to the creditor.]

NOTES

Amendment

Substituted, together with rr 2.1–2.95, 2.97–2.133, for rr 2.1–2.6, 2.6A (inserted by SI 1987/1919, reg 3(1), Schedule, Pt 1, para 7), 2.7–2.46, 2.46A (inserted by SI 1987/1919, reg 3(1), Schedule, Pt 1, para 19), 2.47–2.58, 2.59–2.62 (inserted by SI 2002/1307, rr 3(1), 5(8)), by SI 2003/1730, r 5(1), Sch 1, Pt 2, para 9.

Date in force: 15 September 2003: see SI 2003/1730, r 1(2); for effect and the continuing operation of this Part where a provision made by or under any enactment preserves the Insolvency Act 1986, old Pt II after that date see r 5(2)–(4) thereof.

Para (1): words "5 business" in square brackets substituted by SI 2010/686, r 2, Sch 1, para 86(1), (2)(a).

Date in force: 6 April 2010: see SI 2010/686, r 1; for transitional provisions see r 6(1), Sch 4, para 1 thereto.

Para (1): in sub-para (a) words "(in whole or in part)" in square brackets inserted by SI 2010/686, r 2, Sch 1, para 86(1), (2)(b).

Date in force: 6 April 2010: see SI 2010/686, r 1; for transitional provisions see r 6(1), Sch 4, para 1 thereto.

See Further

See further, in relation to the application of this rule, with modifications, in respect of bank administration and applications for bank administration: the Bank Administration (England and Wales) Rules 2009, SI 2009/357, rr 58–61.

[2.96A Postponement or cancellation of dividend]

[If in the period of 2 months referred to in Rule 2.95(4)(a)—

(a) the administrator has rejected a proof in whole or in part and application is made to the court for that decision to be reversed or varied, or

(b) application is made to the court for the administrator's decision on a proof to be reversed or varied, or for a proof to be expunged, or for a reduction of the amount claimed,

the administrator may postpone or cancel the dividend.]

NOTES

Amendment

Inserted by SI 2010/686, r 2, Sch 1, para 87.

Date in force: 6 April 2010: see SI 2010/686, r 1; for transitional provisions see r 6(1), Sch 4, para 1 thereto.

[2.97 Declaration of dividend]

[(1) Subject to paragraph (2), within the 2 month period referred to in Rule 2.95(4)(a) the administrator shall proceed to declare the dividend to one or more classes of creditor of which he gave notice.

(2) Except with the permission of the court, the administrator shall not declare a dividend so long as there is pending any application to the court to reverse or vary a decision of his on a proof, or to expunge a proof or to reduce the amount claimed.

[(3) If the court gives permission under paragraph (2), the administrator must make such provision in respect of the proof in question as the court directs.]]

NOTES

Amendment

Substituted, together with rr 2.1–2.96, 2.98–2.133, for rr 2.1–2.6, 2.6A (inserted by SI 1987/1919, reg 3(1), Schedule, Pt 1, para 7), 2.7–2.46, 2.46A (inserted by SI 1987/1919, reg 3(1), Schedule, Pt 1, para 19), 2.47–2.58, 2.59–2.62 (inserted by SI 2002/1307, rr 3(1), 5(8)), by SI 2003/1730, r 5(1), Sch 1, Pt 2, para 9.

Date in force: 15 September 2003: see SI 2003/1730, r 1(2); for effect and the continuing operation of this Part where a provision made by or under any enactment preserves the Insolvency Act 1986, old Pt II after that date see r 5(2)–(4) thereof.

Para (3): inserted by SI 2010/686, r 2, Sch 1, para 88.

Date in force: 6 April 2010: see SI 2010/686, r 1; for transitional provisions see r 6(1), Sch 4, para 1 thereto.

See Further

See further, in relation to the application of this rule, with modifications, in respect of bank administration and applications for bank administration: the Bank Administration (England and Wales) Rules 2009, SI 2009/357, rr 58–61.

[2.98 Notice of declaration of a dividend]

[(1) Where the administrator declares a dividend he shall give notice of that fact to all creditors who have proved their debts and, where a member State liquidator has been appointed in relation to the company, to the member State liquidator.

(2) The notice shall include the following particulars relating to the administration—

(a) amounts raised from the sale of assets, indicating (so far as practicable) amounts raised by the sale of particular assets;

(b) payments made by the administrator when acting as such;

(c) where the administrator proposed to make a distribution to unsecured creditors, the value of the prescribed part, except where the court has made an order under section 176A(5);

(d) provision (if any) made for unsettled claims, and funds (if any) retained for particular purposes;

(e) the total amount of dividend and the rate of dividend;

(f) ...

(g) whether, and if so when, any further dividend is expected to be declared.]

NOTES

Amendment

Substituted, together with rr 2.1–2.97, 2.99–2.133, for rr 2.1–2.6, 2.6A (inserted by SI 1987/1919, reg 3(1), Schedule, Pt 1, para 7), 2.7–2.46, 2.46A (inserted by SI 1987/1919, reg 3(1), Schedule, Pt 1, para 19), 2.47–2.58, 2.59–2.62 (inserted by SI 2002/1307, rr 3(1), 5(8)), by SI 2003/1730, r 5(1), Sch 1, Pt 2, para 9.

Date in force: 15 September 2003: see SI 2003/1730, r 1(2); for effect and the continuing operation of this Part where a provision made by or under any enactment preserves the Insolvency Act 1986, old Pt II after that date see r 5(2)–(4) thereof.

Para (2): sub-para (f) revoked by SI 2010/686, r 2, Sch 1, para 89.

Date in force: 6 April 2010: see SI 2010/686, r 1; for transitional provisions see r 6(1), Sch 4, para 1 thereto.

See Further

See further, in relation to the application of this rule, with modifications, in respect of bank administration and applications for bank administration: the Bank Administration (England and Wales) Rules 2009, SI 2009/357, rr 58–61.

[2.99 Payments of dividends and related matters]

[(1) The dividend may be distributed simultaneously with the notice declaring it.

(2) Payment of dividend may be made by post, or arrangements may be made with any creditor for it to be paid to him in another way, or held for his collection.

(3) Where a dividend is paid on a bill of exchange or other negotiable instrument, the amount of the dividend shall be endorsed on the instrument, or on a certified copy of it, if required to be produced by the holder for that purpose.]

NOTES

Amendment

Substituted, together with rr 2.1–2.98, 2.100–2.133, for rr 2.1–2.6, 2.6A (inserted by SI 1987/1919, reg 3(1), Schedule, Pt 1, para 7), 2.7–2.46, 2.46A (inserted by SI 1987/1919, reg 3(1), Schedule, Pt 1, para 19), 2.47–2.58, 2.59–2.62 (inserted by SI 2002/1307, rr 3(1), 5(8)), by SI 2003/1730, r 5(1), Sch 1, Pt 2, para 9.

Date in force: 15 September 2003: see SI 2003/1730, r 1(2); for effect and the continuing operation of this Part where a provision made by or under any enactment preserves the Insolvency Act 1986, old Pt II after that date see r 5(2)–(4) thereof.

See Further

See further, in relation to the application of this rule, with modifications, in respect of bank administration and applications for bank administration: the Bank Administration (England and Wales) Rules 2009, SI 2009/357, rr 58–61.

[2.100 Notice of no dividend, or no further dividend]

[If the administrator gives notice to creditors that he is unable to declare any dividend or (as the case may be) any further dividend, the notice shall contain a statement to the effect either—

(a)   that no funds have been realised; or

(b)   that the funds realised have already been distributed or used or allocated for defraying the expenses of administration.]

NOTES

Amendment

Substituted, together with rr 2.1–2.99, 2.101–2.133, for rr 2.1–2.6, 2.6A (inserted by SI 1987/1919, reg 3(1), Schedule, Pt 1, para 7), 2.7–2.46, 2.46A (inserted by SI 1987/1919, reg 3(1), Schedule, Pt 1, para 19), 2.47–2.58, 2.59–2.62 (inserted by SI 2002/1307, rr 3(1), 5(8)), by SI 2003/1730, r 5(1), Sch 1, Pt 2, para 9.

Date in force: 15 September 2003: see SI 2003/1730, r 1(2); for effect and the continuing operation of this Part where a provision made by or under any enactment preserves the Insolvency Act 1986, old Pt II after that date see r 5(2)–(4) thereof.

See Further

See further, in relation to the application of this rule, with modifications, in respect of bank administration and applications for bank administration: the Bank Administration (England and Wales) Rules 2009, SI 2009/357, rr 58–61.

[2.101 Proof altered after payment of dividend]

[(1) If after payment of dividend the amount claimed by a creditor in his proof is increased, the creditor is not entitled to disturb the distribution of the dividend; but he is entitled to be paid, out of any money for the time being available for the payment of any further dividend, any dividend or dividends which he has failed to receive.

(2) Any dividend or dividends payable under paragraph (1) shall be paid before the money there referred to is applied to the payment of any such further dividend.

(3) If, after a creditor's proof has been admitted, the proof is withdrawn or expunged, or the amount is reduced, the creditor is liable to repay to the administrator any amount overpaid by way of dividend.]

NOTES

Amendment

Substituted, together with rr 2.1–2.100, 2.102–2.133, for rr 2.1–2.6, 2.6A (inserted by SI 1987/1919, reg 3(1), Schedule, Pt 1, para 7), 2.7–2.46, 2.46A (inserted by SI 1987/1919, reg 3(1), Schedule, Pt 1, para 19), 2.47–2.58, 2.59–2.62 (inserted by SI 2002/1307, rr 3(1), 5(8)), by SI 2003/1730, r 5(1), Sch 1, Pt 2, para 9.

Date in force: 15 September 2003: see SI 2003/1730, r 1(2); for effect and the continuing operation of this Part where a provision made by or under any enactment preserves the Insolvency Act 1986, old Pt II after that date see r 5(2)–(4) thereof.

See Further

See further, in relation to the application of this rule, with modifications, in respect of bank administration and applications for bank administration: the Bank Administration (England and Wales) Rules 2009, SI 2009/357, rr 58–61.

[2.102 Secured creditors]

[(1) The following applies where a creditor re-values his security at a time when a dividend has been declared.

(2) If the revaluation results in a reduction of his unsecured claim ranking for dividend, the creditor shall [as soon as reasonably practicable] repay to the administrator, for the credit of the administration, any amount received by him as dividend in excess of that to which he would be entitled having regard to the revaluation of the security.

(3) If the revaluation results in an increase of his unsecured claim, the creditor is entitled to receive from the administrator, out of any money for the time being available for the payment of a further dividend, before any such further dividend is paid, any dividend or dividends which he has failed to receive, having regard to the revaluation of the security.

However, the creditor is not entitled to disturb any dividend declared (whether or not distributed) before the date of the revaluation.]

NOTES

Amendment

Substituted, together with rr 2.1–2.101, 2.103–2.133, for rr 2.1–2.6, 2.6A (inserted by SI 1987/1919, reg 3(1), Schedule, Pt 1, para 7), 2.7–2.46, 2.46A (inserted by SI 1987/1919, reg 3(1), Schedule, Pt 1, para 19), 2.47–2.58, 2.59–2.62 (inserted by SI 2002/1307, rr 3(1), 5(8)), by SI 2003/1730, r 5(1), Sch 1, Pt 2, para 9.

Date in force: 15 September 2003: see SI 2003/1730, r 1(2); for effect and the continuing operation of this Part where a provision made by or under any enactment preserves the Insolvency Act 1986, old Pt II after that date see r 5(2)–(4) thereof.

Para (2): words "as soon as reasonably practicable" in square brackets substituted by SI 2009/642, rr 4, 5.

Date in force: 6 April 2009: see SI 2009/642, r 1; for transitional provisions see r 3 thereof.

See Further

See further, in relation to the application of this rule, with modifications, in respect of bank administration and applications for bank administration: the Bank Administration (England and Wales) Rules 2009, SI 2009/357, rr 58–61.

Insolvency Rules 1986, reg 2.103

[2.103 Disqualification from dividend]
[If a creditor contravenes any provision of the Act or the Rules relating to the valuation of securities, the court may, on the application of the administrator, order that the creditor be wholly or partly disqualified from participation in any dividend.]

NOTES

Amendment
    Substituted, together with rr 2.1–2.102, 2.104–2.133, for rr 2.1–2.6, 2.6A (inserted by SI 1987/1919, reg 3(1), Schedule, Pt 1, para 7), 2.7–2.46, 2.46A (inserted by SI 1987/1919, reg 3(1), Schedule, Pt 1, para 19), 2.47–2.58, 2.59–2.62 (inserted by SI 2002/1307, rr 3(1), 5(8)), by SI 2003/1730, r 5(1), Sch 1, Pt 2, para 9.
    Date in force: 15 September 2003: see SI 2003/1730, r 1(2); for effect and the continuing operation of this Part where a provision made by or under any enactment preserves the Insolvency Act 1986, old Pt II after that date see r 5(2)–(4) thereof.

See Further
    See further, in relation to the application of this rule, with modifications, in respect of bank administration and applications for bank administration: the Bank Administration (England and Wales) Rules 2009, SI 2009/357, rr 58–61.

[2.104 Assignment of right to dividend]
[(1) If a person entitled to a dividend gives notice to the administrator that he wishes the dividend to be paid to another person, or that he has assigned his entitlement to another person, the administrator shall pay the dividend to that other accordingly.
    (2) A notice given under this Rule must specify the name and address of the person to whom payment is to be made.]

NOTES

Amendment
    Substituted, together with rr 2.1–2.103, 2.105–2.133, for rr 2.1–2.6, 2.6A (inserted by SI 1987/1919, reg 3(1), Schedule, Pt 1, para 7), 2.7–2.46, 2.46A (inserted by SI 1987/1919, reg 3(1), Schedule, Pt 1, para 19), 2.47–2.58, 2.59–2.62 (inserted by SI 2002/1307, rr 3(1), 5(8)), by SI 2003/1730, r 5(1), Sch 1, Pt 2, para 9.
    Date in force: 15 September 2003: see SI 2003/1730, r 1(2); for effect and the continuing operation of this Part where a provision made by or under any enactment preserves the Insolvency Act 1986, old Pt II after that date see r 5(2)–(4) thereof.

See Further
    See further, in relation to the application of this rule, with modifications, in respect of bank administration and applications for bank administration: the Bank Administration (England and Wales) Rules 2009, SI 2009/357, rr 58–61.

[2.105 Debt payable at future time]
[(1) Where a creditor has proved for a debt of which payment is not due at the date of the declaration of dividend, he is entitled to dividend equally with other creditors, but subject as follows.
    [(2) For the purpose of dividend (and no other purpose) the amount of the creditor's admitted proof (or, if a distribution has previously been made to him, the amount remaining outstanding in respect of his admitted proof) shall be reduced by applying the following formula—
$$X / 1.05^n$$
where—

(a) "X" is the value of the admitted proof; and
(b) "n" is the period beginning with the relevant date and ending with the date on which the payment of the creditor's debt would otherwise be due expressed in years and months in a decimalised form.

(3) In paragraph (2) "relevant date" means—
(a) in the case of an administration which was not immediately preceded by a winding up, the date that the company entered administration;
(b) in the case of an administration which was immediately preceded by a winding up, the date that the company went into liquidation.]

(3) . . .]

NOTES

Amendment

Substituted, together with rr 2.1–2.104, 2.106–2.133, for rr 2.1–2.6, 2.6A (inserted by SI 1987/1919, reg 3(1), Schedule, Pt 1, para 7), 2.7–2.46, 2.46A (inserted by SI 1987/1919, reg 3(1), Schedule, Pt 1, para 19), 2.47–2.58, 2.59–2.62 (inserted by SI 2002/1307, rr 3(1), 5(8)), by SI 2003/1730, r 5(1), Sch 1, Pt 2, para 9.
Date in force: 15 September 2003: see SI 2003/1730, r 1(2); for effect and the continuing operation of this Part where a provision made by or under any enactment preserves the Insolvency Act 1986, old Pt II after that date see r 5(2)–(4) thereof.
Para (2) and first para (3): substituted, for para (2) as originally enacted, by SI 2005/527, r 14(1).
Date in force: 1 April 2005: see SI 2005/527, r 1(2); for transitional provisions in relation to any case where a company has entered administration or gone into liquidation, or a bankruptcy order has been made before that date see r 3(1) thereof.
Second para (3): revoked by SI 2005/527, r 14(2).
Date in force: 1 April 2005: see SI 2005/527, r 1(2); for transitional provisions in relation to any case where a company has entered administration or gone into liquidation, or a bankruptcy order has been made before that date see r 3(1) thereof.

See Further

See further, in relation to the application of this rule, with modifications, in respect of bank administration and applications for bank administration: the Bank Administration (England and Wales) Rules 2009, SI 2009/357, rr 58–61.

[CHAPTER 11

THE ADMINISTRATOR]

NOTES

Amendment

Substituted by SI 2003/1730, r 5(1), Sch 1, Pt 2, para 9.
Date in force: 15 September 2003: see SI 2003/1730, r 1(2); for effect and the continuing operation of this Part where a provision made by or under any enactment preserves the Insolvency Act 1986, old Pt II after that date see r 5(2)–(4) thereof.

[2.106 Fixing of remuneration]

[(1) The administrator is entitled to receive remuneration for his services as such.
(2) [The basis of remuneration] shall be fixed . . .—
(a) as a percentage of the value of the property with which he has to deal; or
(b) by reference to the time properly given by the insolvency practitioner (as administrator) and his staff in attending to matters arising in the administration[; or
(c) as a set amount].

[(3A) The basis of remuneration may be fixed as any one or more of the bases set out in paragraph (2), and different bases may be fixed in respect of different things done by the administrator.

(3B) Where the basis of remuneration is fixed as set out in paragraph (2)(a), different percentages may be fixed in respect of different things done by the administrator.

(3C) It is for the creditors' committee (if there is one) to determine—
- (a) which of the bases set out in paragraph (2) are to be fixed and (where appropriate) in what combination under paragraph (3A), and
- (b) the percentage or percentages (if any) to be fixed under paragraphs (2)(a) and (3B) and the amount (if any) to be set under paragraph (2)(c).]

(4) In arriving at that determination, the committee shall have regard to the following matters—
- (a) the complexity (or otherwise) of the case;
- (b) any respects in which, in connection with the company's affairs, there falls on the administrator any responsibility of an exceptional kind or degree;
- (c) the effectiveness with which the administrator appears to be carrying out, or to have carried out, his duties as such; and
- (d) the value and nature of the property with which he has to deal.

(5) If there is no creditors' committee, or the committee does not make the requisite determination, [and the case does not fall within paragraph (5A), the basis of] the administrator's remuneration may be fixed (in accordance with [paragraphs (2), (3A) and (3B)]) by a resolution of a meeting of creditors; and paragraph (4) applies to them as it does to the creditors' committee.

[(5A) In a case where the administrator has made a statement under paragraph 52(1)(b), if there is no creditors' committee, or the committee does not make the requisite determination, [the basis of] the administrator's remuneration may be fixed (in accordance with [paragraphs (2), (3A) and (3B)]) by the approval of—
- (a) each secured creditor of the company: or
- (b) if the administrator has made or intends to make a distribution to preferential creditors—
  - (i) each secured creditor of the company; and
  - (ii) preferential creditors whose debts amount to more than 50% of the preferential debts of the company, disregarding debts of any creditor who does not respond to an invitation to give or withhold approval;

and paragraph (4) applies to them as it does to the creditors' committee.]

(6) If not fixed as above, [the basis of] the administrator's remuneration shall, on his application, be fixed by the court [and the provisions of paragraphs (2) to (4) apply as they do to the fixing of the basis of remuneration by the creditors' committee; but such an application may not be made by the administrator unless the administrator has first sought fixing of the basis in accordance with paragraph (3), (5) or (5A), and in any event may not be made more than 18 months after the date of the administrator's appointment].

(7) Where there are joint administrators, it is for them to agree between themselves as to how the remuneration payable should be apportioned. Any dispute arising between them may be referred—
- (a) to the court, for settlement by order; or
- (b) to the creditors' committee or a meeting of creditors, for settlement by resolution.

(8) If the administrator is a solicitor and employs his own firm, or any partner in it, to act on behalf of the company, profit costs shall not be paid unless this is authorised by the creditors' committee, the creditors or the court.

(9) . . .]

NOTES

Amendment

Substituted, together with rr 2.1–2.105, 2.107–2.133, for rr 2.1–2.6, 2.6A (inserted by SI 1987/1919, reg 3(1), Schedule, Pt 1, para 7), 2.7–2.46, 2.46A (inserted by SI 1987/1919, reg 3(1), Schedule, Pt 1, para 19), 2.47–2.58, 2.59–2.62 (inserted by SI 2002/1307, rr 3(1), 5(8)), by SI 2003/1730, r 5(1), Sch 1, Pt 2, para 9.

Date in force: 15 September 2003: see SI 2003/1730, r 1(2); for effect and the continuing operation of this Part where a provision made by or under any enactment preserves the Insolvency Act 1986, old Pt II after that date see r 5(2)–(4) thereof.

Para (2): words "The basis of remuneration" in square brackets substituted by SI 2010/686, r 2, Sch 1, para 90(1), (2)(a).

Date in force: 6 April 2010: see SI 2010/686, r 1; for transitional provisions see r 6(1), Sch 4, para 1 thereto.

Para (2): word omitted revoked by SI 2010/686, r 2, Sch 1, para 90(1), (2)(b).

Date in force: 6 April 2010: see SI 2010/686, r 1; for transitional provisions see r 6(1), Sch 4, para 1 thereto.

Para (2): sub-para (c) and word "; or" immediately preceding it inserted by SI 2010/686, r 2, Sch 1, para 90(1), (2)(c).

Date in force: 6 April 2010: see SI 2010/686, r 1; for transitional provisions see r 6(1), Sch 4, para 1 thereto.

Paras (3A)–(3C): substituted, for para (3) as previously enacted, by SI 2010/686, r 2, Sch 1, para 90(1), (3).

Date in force: 6 April 2010: see SI 2010/686, r 1; for transitional provisions see r 6(1), Sch 4, para 1 thereto.

Para (5): words "and the case does not fall within paragraph (5A), the basis of" in square brackets inserted by SI 2010/686, r 2, Sch 1, para 90(1), (4).

Date in force: 6 April 2010: see SI 2010/686, r 1; for transitional provisions see r 6(1), Sch 4, para 1 thereto.

Para (5): words "paragraphs (2), (3A) and (3B)" in square brackets substituted by SI 2010/686, r 2, Sch 1, para 90(1), (5).

Date in force: 6 April 2010: see SI 2010/686, r 1; for transitional provisions see r 6(1), Sch 4, para 1 thereto.

Para (5A): inserted by SI 2005/527, r 15(1).

Date in force: 1 April 2005: see SI 2005/527, r 1(2); for transitional provisions in relation to any case where a company has entered administration or gone into liquidation, or a bankruptcy order has been made before that date see r 3(1) thereof.

Para (5A): words "the basis of" in square brackets inserted by SI 2010/686, r 2, Sch 1, para 90(1), (6).

Date in force: 6 April 2010: see SI 2010/686, r 1; for transitional provisions see r 6(1), Sch 4, para 1 thereto.

Para (5A): words "paragraphs (2), (3A) and (3B)" in square brackets substituted by SI 2010/686, r 2, Sch 1, para 90(1), (5).

Date in force: 6 April 2010: see SI 2010/686, r 1; for transitional provisions see r 6(1), Sch 4, para 1 thereto.

Para (6): words "the basis of" in square brackets inserted by SI 2010/686, r 2, Sch 1, para 90(1), (7).

Date in force: 6 April 2010: see SI 2010/686, r 1; for transitional provisions see r 6(1), Sch 4, para 1 thereto.

Para (6): words from "and the provisions" to "the administrator's appointment" in square brackets inserted by SI 2010/686, r 2, Sch 1, para 90(1), (8).

Date in force: 6 April 2010: see SI 2010/686, r 1; for transitional provisions see r 6(1), Sch 4, para 1 thereto.

Para (9): revoked by SI 2005/527, r 15(2).

Date in force: 1 April 2005: see SI 2005/527, r 1(2); for transitional provisions in relation to any case where a company has entered administration or gone into liquidation, or a bankruptcy order has been made before that date see r 3(1) thereof.

See Further

See further, in relation to the application of this rule, with modifications, in respect of bank administration and applications for bank administration: the Bank Administration (England and Wales) Rules 2009, SI 2009/357, rr 58–61.

[2.107 Recourse to meeting of creditors]

[[(1)] If [the basis of] the administrator's remuneration has been fixed by the creditors' committee, and he considers the rate or amount to be insufficient, [or the basis to be inappropriate, the administrator may request that the rate or amount be increased or the basis changed] by resolution of the creditors.

[(2) In a case where the administrator has made a statement under paragraph 52(1)(b), if [the basis of] the administrator's remuneration has been fixed by the creditors' committee, and he considers the rate or amount to be insufficient, [or the basis to be inappropriate, the administrator may request that the rate or amount be increased or the basis changed] by the approval of—

(a) each secured creditor of the company: or
(b) if the administrator has made or intends to make a distribution to preferential creditors—
 (i) each secured creditor of the company; and
 (ii) preferential creditors whose debts amount to more than 50% of the preferential debts of the company, disregarding debts of any creditor who does not respond to an invitation to give or withhold approval.]]

NOTES

Amendment

Substituted, together with rr 2.1–2.106, 2.108–2.133, for rr 2.1–2.6, 2.6A (inserted by SI 1987/1919, reg 3(1), Schedule, Pt 1, para 7), 2.7–2.46, 2.46A (inserted by SI 1987/1919, reg 3(1), Schedule, Pt 1, para 19), 2.47–2.58, 2.59–2.62 (inserted by SI 2002/1307, rr 3(1), 5(8)), by SI 2003/1730, r 5(1), Sch 1, Pt 2, para 9.
 Date in force: 15 September 2003: see SI 2003/1730, r 1(2); for effect and the continuing operation of this Part where a provision made by or under any enactment preserves the Insolvency Act 1986, old Pt II after that date see r 5(2)–(4) thereof.
Para (1): numbered as such by SI 2005/527, r 16.
 Date in force: 1 April 2005: see SI 2005/527, r 1(2); for transitional provisions in relation to any case where a company has entered administration or gone into liquidation, or a bankruptcy order has been made before that date see r 3(1) thereof.
Para (1): words "the basis of" in square brackets inserted by SI 2010/686, r 2, Sch 1, para 91(1), (2)(a).
 Date in force: 6 April 2010: see SI 2010/686, r 1; for transitional provisions see r 6(1), Sch 4, para 1 thereto.
Para (1): words from "or the basis" to "the basis changed" in square brackets substituted by SI 2010/686, r 2, Sch 1, para 91(1), (2)(b).
 Date in force: 6 April 2010: see SI 2010/686, r 1; for transitional provisions see r 6(1), Sch 4, para 1 thereto.
Para (2): inserted by SI 2005/527, r 16.
 Date in force: 1 April 2005: see SI 2005/527, r 1(2); for transitional provisions in relation to any case where a company has entered administration or gone into liquidation, or a bankruptcy order has been made before that date see r 3(1) thereof.
Para (2): words "the basis of" in square brackets inserted by SI 2010/686, r 2, Sch 1, para 91(1), (2)(a).
 Date in force: 6 April 2010: see SI 2010/686, r 1; for transitional provisions see r 6(1), Sch 4, para 1 thereto.
Para (2): words from "or the basis" to "the basis changed" in square brackets substituted by SI 2010/686, r 2, Sch 1, para 91(1), (2)(b).
 Date in force: 6 April 2010: see SI 2010/686, r 1; for transitional provisions see r 6(1), Sch 4, para 1 thereto.

See Further

See further, in relation to the application of this rule, with modifications, in respect of bank administration and applications for bank administration: the Bank Administration (England and Wales) Rules 2009, SI 2009/357, rr 58–61.

[2.108 Recourse to the court]

[(1) If the administrator considers that the [basis of] remuneration fixed for him by the creditors' committee, or by resolution of the creditors, is insufficient [or inappropriate], he may apply to the court for an order [changing it or] increasing its amount or rate.

[(1A) In a case where the administrator has made a statement under paragraph 52(1)(b), if the administrator considers that the [basis of] remuneration fixed by the approval of the creditors in accordance with Rule 2.107(2) is insufficient [or inappropriate], he may apply to the court for an order [changing it or] increasing its amount or rate.]

[(1B) Where an application is made under paragraph (1A), the administrator must give notice to each of the creditors whose approval was sought under Rule 2.106(5A).]

(2) The administrator shall give at least 14 days' notice of his application to the members of the creditors' committee; and the committee may nominate one or more members to appear, or be represented, and to be heard on the application.

(3) If there is no creditors' committee, the administrator's notice of his application shall be sent to such one or more of the company's creditors as the court may direct, which creditors may nominate one or more of their number to appear or be represented.

(4) The court may, if it appears to be a proper case, order the costs of the administrator's application, including the costs of any member of the creditors' committee appearing or being represented on it, or any creditor so appearing or being represented, to be paid as an expense of the administration.]

NOTES

Amendment

Substituted, together with rr 2.1–2.107, 2.109–2.133, for rr 2.1–2.6, 2.6A (inserted by SI 1987/1919, reg 3(1), Schedule, Pt 1, para 7), 2.7–2.46, 2.46A (inserted by SI 1987/1919, reg 3(1), Schedule, Pt 1, para 19), 2.47–2.58, 2.59–2.62 (inserted by SI 2002/1307, rr 3(1), 5(8)), by SI 2003/1730, r 5(1), Sch 1, Pt 2, para 9.
  Date in force: 15 September 2003: see SI 2003/1730, r 1(2); for effect and the continuing operation of this Part where a provision made by or under any enactment preserves the Insolvency Act 1986, old Pt II after that date see r 5(2)–(4) thereof.
Para (1): words "basis of" in square brackets inserted by SI 2010/686, r 2, Sch 1, para 92(1), (2)(a).
  Date in force: 6 April 2010: see SI 2010/686, r 1; for transitional provisions see r 6(1), Sch 4, para 1 thereto.
Para (1): words "or inappropriate" in square brackets inserted by SI 2010/686, r 2, Sch 1, para 92(1), (2)(b).
  Date in force: 6 April 2010: see SI 2010/686, r 1; for transitional provisions see r 6(1), Sch 4, para 1 thereto.
Para (1): words "changing it or" in square brackets inserted by SI 2010/686, r 2, Sch 1, para 92(1), (2)(c).
  Date in force: 6 April 2010: see SI 2010/686, r 1; for transitional provisions see r 6(1), Sch 4, para 1 thereto.
Para (1A): inserted by SI 2005/527, r 17.
  Date in force: 1 April 2005: see SI 2005/527, r 1(2); for transitional provisions in relation to any case where a company has entered administration or gone into liquidation, or a bankruptcy order has been made before that date see r 3(1) thereof.
Para (1A): words "basis of" in square brackets inserted by SI 2010/686, r 2, Sch 1, para 92(1), (2)(a).

Date in force: 6 April 2010: see SI 2010/686, r 1; for transitional provisions see r 6(1), Sch 4, para 1 thereto.
Para (1A): words "or inappropriate" in square brackets inserted by SI 2010/686, r 2, Sch 1, para 92(1), (2)(b).
Date in force: 6 April 2010: see SI 2010/686, rule 1.
Para (1A): words "changing it or" in square brackets inserted by SI 2010/686, r 2, Sch 1, para 92(1), (2)(c).
Date in force: 6 April 2010: see SI 2010/686, r 1; for transitional provisions see r 6(1), Sch 4, para 1 thereto.
Para (1B): inserted by SI 2010/686, r 2, Sch 1, para 92(1), (3).
Date in force: 6 April 2010: see SI 2010/686, r 1; for transitional provisions see r 6(1), Sch 4, para 1 thereto.

See Further

See further, in relation to the application of this rule, with modifications, in respect of bank administration and applications for bank administration: the Bank Administration (England and Wales) Rules 2009, SI 2009/357, rr 58–61.

[2.109 Creditors' claim that remuneration is [or other expenses are] excessive]

[[(1) Any secured creditor, or any unsecured creditor with either the concurrence of at least 10% in value of the unsecured creditors (including that creditor) or the permission of the court, may apply to the court for one or more of the orders in paragraph (4).

(1A) Application may be made on the grounds that—
- (a) the remuneration charged by the administrator,
- (b) the basis fixed for the administrator's remuneration under Rule 2.106, or
- (c) expenses incurred by the administrator,

is or are, in all the circumstances, excessive or, in the case of an application under sub-paragraph (b), inappropriate.

(1B) The application must, subject to any order of the court under Rule 2.48A(4), be made no later than 8 weeks after receipt by the applicant of the progress report which first reports the charging of the remuneration or the incurring of the expenses in question ("the relevant report").]

(2) The court may, if it thinks that no sufficient cause is shown for a reduction, dismiss it without a hearing but it shall not do so without giving the applicant at least [5 business] days' notice, upon receipt of which the applicant may require the court to list the application for a without notice hearing. If the application is not dismissed, the court shall fix a venue for it to be heard, and give notice to the applicant accordingly.

(3) The applicant shall, at least 14 days before the hearing, send to the administrator a notice stating the venue and accompanied by a copy of the application, and of any evidence which the applicant intends to adduce in support of it.

[(4) If the court considers the application to be well-founded, it must make one or more of the following orders—
- (a) an order reducing the amount of remuneration which the administrator was entitled to charge;
- (b) an order fixing the basis of remuneration at a reduced rate or amount;
- (c) an order changing the basis of remuneration;
- (d) an order that some or all of the remuneration or expenses in question be treated as not being expenses of the administration;
- (e) an order that the administrator or the administrator's personal representative pay to the company the amount of the excess of remuneration or expenses or such part of the excess as the court may specify;

and may make any other order that it thinks just; but an order under sub-paragraph (b) or (c) may be made only in respect of periods after the period covered by the relevant report.]

(5) Unless the court orders otherwise, the costs of the application shall be paid by the applicant, and are not payable as an expense of the administration.]

NOTES

Amendment

Substituted, together with rr 2.1–2.108, 2.110–2.133, for rr 2.1–2.6, 2.6A (inserted by SI 1987/1919, reg 3(1), Schedule, Pt 1, para 7), 2.7–2.46, 2.46A (inserted by SI 1987/1919, reg 3(1), Schedule, Pt 1, para 19), 2.47–2.58, 2.59–2.62 (inserted by SI 2002/1307, rr 3(1), 5(8)), by SI 2003/1730, r 5(1), Sch 1, Pt 2, para 9.

Date in force: 15 September 2003: see SI 2003/1730, r 1(2); for effect and the continuing operation of this Part where a provision made by or under any enactment preserves the Insolvency Act 1986, old Pt II after that date see r 5(2)–(4) thereof.

Provision heading: words "or other expenses are" in square brackets inserted by SI 2010/686, r 2, Sch 1, para 93(1), (2).

Date in force: 6 April 2010: see SI 2010/686, r 1; for transitional provisions see r 6(1), Sch 4, para 1 thereto.

Paras (1), (1A), (1B): substituted, for para (1) as previously enacted, by SI 2010/686, r 2, Sch 1, para 93(1), (3).

Date in force: 6 April 2010: see SI 2010/686, r 1; for transitional provisions see r 6(1), Sch 4, para 1 thereto.

Para (2): words "5 business" in square brackets substituted by SI 2010/686, r 2, Sch 1, para 93(1), (4).

Date in force: 6 April 2010: see SI 2010/686, r 1; for transitional provisions see r 6(1), Sch 4, para 1 thereto.

Para (4): substituted by SI 2010/686, r 2, Sch 1, para 93(1), (5).

Date in force: 6 April 2010: see SI 2010/686, r 1; for transitional provisions see r 6(1), Sch 4, para 1 thereto.

See Further

See further, in relation to the application of this rule, with modifications, in respect of bank administration and applications for bank administration: the Bank Administration (England and Wales) Rules 2009, SI 2009/357, rr 58–61.

[2.109A Review of remuneration]

[(1) Where, after the basis of the administrator's remuneration has been fixed, there is a material and substantial change in the circumstances which were taken into account in fixing it, the administrator may request that it be changed.

(2) The request must be made—
   (a)   where the creditors' committee fixed the basis, to the committee;
   (b)   where the creditors fixed the basis, to the creditors;
   (c)   where the court fixed the basis, by application to the court;
and Rules 2.106 to 2.109 apply as appropriate.

(3) Any change in the basis for remuneration applies from the date of the request under paragraph (2) and not for any earlier period.]

NOTES

Amendment

Inserted by SI 2010/686, r 2, Sch 1, para 94.

Date in force: 6 April 2010: see SI 2010/686, r 1; for transitional provisions see r 6(1), Sch 4, para 1 thereto.

[2.109B Remuneration of new administrator]

[If a new administrator is appointed in place of another, any determination, resolution or court order in effect under the preceding provisions of this Chapter immediately before the former administrator ceased to hold office continues to apply in respect of the remuneration of the new administrator until a further determination, resolution or court order is made in accordance with those provisions.]

NOTES

Amendment

Inserted by SI 2010/686, r 2, Sch 1, para 94.
Date in force: 6 April 2010: see SI 2010/686, r 1; for transitional provisions see r 6(1), Sch 4, para 1 thereto.

[**2.109C Apportionment of set fee remuneration**]

[(1) In a case in which the basis of the administrator's remuneration is a set amount under Rule 2.106(2)(c) and the administrator ("the former administrator") ceases (for whatever reason) to hold office before the time has elapsed or the work has been completed in respect of which the amount was set, application may be made for determination of what portion of the amount should be paid to the former administrator or the former administrator's personal representative in respect of the time which has actually elapsed or the work which has actually been done.

(2) Application may be made—
- (a) by the former administrator or the former administrator's personal representative within the period of 28 days beginning with the date upon which the former administrator ceased to hold office, or
- (b) by the administrator for the time being in office if the former administrator or the former administrator's personal representative has not applied by the end of that period.

(3) Application must be made—
- (a) where the creditors' committee fixed the basis, to the committee;
- (b) where the creditors fixed the basis, to the creditors for a resolution determining the portion;
- (c) where the court fixed the basis, to the court for an order determining the portion.

(4) The applicant must give a copy of the application to the administrator for the time being in office or to the former administrator or the former administrator's personal representative, as the case may be ("the recipient").

(5) The recipient may within 21 days of receipt of the copy of the application give notice of intent to make representations to the creditors' committee or the creditors or to appear or be represented before the court, as the case may be.

(6) No determination may be made upon the application until expiry of the 21 days referred to in paragraph (5) or, if the recipient does give notice of intent in accordance with that paragraph, until the recipient has been afforded the opportunity to make representations or to appear or be represented, as the case may be.

(7) If the former administrator or the former administrator's personal representative (whether or not the original applicant) considers that the portion determined upon application to the creditors' committee or the creditors is insufficient, that person may apply—
- (a) in the case of a determination by the creditors' committee, to the creditors for a resolution increasing the portion;
- (b) in the case of a resolution of the creditors (whether under paragraph (1) or under sub-paragraph (a)), to the court for an order increasing the portion;

and paragraphs (4) to (6) apply as appropriate.]

NOTES

Amendment

Inserted by SI 2010/686, r 2, Sch 1, para 94.
Date in force: 6 April 2010: see SI 2010/686, r 1; for transitional provisions see r 6(1), Sch 4, para 1 thereto.

[CHAPTER 12

ENDING ADMINISTRATION]

NOTES

Amendment

Substituted by SI 2003/1730, r 5(1), Sch 1, Pt 2, para 9.
Date in force: 15 September 2003: see SI 2003/1730, r 1(2); for effect and the continuing operation of this Part where a provision made by or under any enactment preserves the Insolvency Act 1986, old Pt II after that date see r 5(2)–(4) thereof.

[2.110 Final progress reports]

[(1) In this Chapter reference to a progress report is to a report in the form specified in Rule 2.47.

(2) The final progress report means a progress report which includes a summary of—

(a) the administrator's proposals;
(b) any major amendments to, or deviations from, those proposals;
(c) the steps taken during the administration; and
(d) the outcome.]

NOTES

Amendment

Substituted, together with rr 2.1–2.109, 2.111–2.133, for rr 2.1–2.6, 2.6A (inserted by SI 1987/1919, reg 3(1), Schedule, Pt 1, para 7), 2.7–2.46, 2.46A (inserted by SI 1987/1919, reg 3(1), Schedule, Pt 1, para 19), 2.47–2.58, 2.59–2.62 (inserted by SI 2002/1307, rr 3(1), 5(8)), by SI 2003/1730, r 5(1), Sch 1, Pt 2, para 9.
Date in force: 15 September 2003: see SI 2003/1730, r 1(2); for effect and the continuing operation of this Part where a provision made by or under any enactment preserves the Insolvency Act 1986, old Pt II after that date see r 5(2)–(4) thereof.

See Further

See further, in relation to the application of this rule, with modifications, in respect of bank administration and applications for bank administration: the Bank Administration (England and Wales) Rules 2009, SI 2009/357, rr 58–61.

[2.111 Notice of automatic end of administration]

[(1) Where the appointment of an administrator has ceased to have effect, and the administrator is not required by any other Rule to give notice of that fact, he shall, as soon as reasonably practicable, and in any event within 5 business days of the date when the appointment has ceased, file a notice of automatic end of administration in Form 2.30B with the court. The notice shall be accompanied by a final progress report.

(2) A copy of the notice and accompanying document shall be sent as soon as reasonably practicable to the registrar of companies, and to all [other] persons who received a copy of the administrator's proposals.

(3) If the administrator makes default in complying with this Rule, he is liable to a fine and, for continued contravention, to a daily default fine.]

NOTES

Amendment

Substituted, together with rr 2.1–2.110, 2.112–2.133, for rr 2.1–2.6, 2.6A (inserted by SI 1987/1919, reg 3(1), Schedule, Pt 1, para 7), 2.7–2.46, 2.46A (inserted by SI 1987/1919, reg 3(1), Schedule, Pt 1, para 19), 2.47–2.58, 2.59–2.62 (inserted by SI 2002/1307, rr 3(1), 5(8)), by SI 2003/1730, r 5(1), Sch 1, Pt 2, para 9.
Date in force: 15 September 2003: see SI 2003/1730, r 1(2); for effect and the continuing operation of this Part where a provision made by or under any enactment preserves the Insolvency Act 1986, old Pt II after that date see r 5(2)–(4) thereof.
Para (2): word "other" in square brackets inserted by SI 2010/686, r 2, Sch 1, para 95.
Date in force: 6 April 2010: see SI 2010/686, r 1; for transitional provisions see r 6(1), Sch 4, paras 1, 2(1)(b) thereto.

[2.112 Applications for extension of administration]

[(1) An application to court for an extension of administration shall be accompanied by a progress report for the period since the last progress report (if any) or the date the company entered administration.

(2) When the administrator requests an extension of the period of the administration by consent of creditors, his request shall be accompanied by a progress report for the period since the last progress report (if any) or the date the company entered administration.

[(4) Where the court makes an order extending the administration, the administrator must give notice of the order to the creditors as soon as reasonably practicable, together with a copy of the progress report which accompanied the application to the court.

(5) Where the period of the administration has been extended by consent of creditors, the administrator must give notice to the creditors as soon as reasonably practicable.]]

NOTES

Amendment

Substituted, together with rr 2.1–2.111, 2.113–2.133, for rr 2.1–2.6, 2.6A (inserted by SI 1987/1919, reg 3(1), Schedule, Pt 1, para 7), 2.7–2.46, 2.46A (inserted by SI 1987/1919, reg 3(1), Schedule, Pt 1, para 19), 2.47–2.58, 2.59–2.62 (inserted by SI 2002/1307, rr 3(1), 5(8)), by SI 2003/1730, r 5(1), Sch 1, Pt 2, para 9.
Date in force: 15 September 2003: see SI 2003/1730, r 1(2); for effect and the continuing operation of this Part where a provision made by or under any enactment preserves the Insolvency Act 1986, old Pt II after that date see r 5(2)–(4) thereof.
Paras (4), (5): substituted, for para (3) as previously enacted, by SI 2010/686, r 2, Sch 1, para 96.
Date in force: 6 April 2010: see SI 2010/686, r 1; for transitional provisions see r 6(1), Sch 4, para 1 thereto.

[2.113 Notice of end of administration]

[(1) Where an administrator who was appointed under paragraph 14 or 22 gives notice that the purpose of administration has been sufficiently achieved he shall use Form 2.32B. The notice shall be accompanied by a final progress report.

(2) The administrator shall send a copy of the notice to the registrar of companies.

(3) Two copies of the notice shall be filed with the court and shall contain a statement that a copy of the notice has been sent to the registrar of companies. The

court shall endorse each copy with the date and time of filing. The appointment shall cease to have effect from that date and time.

(4) The court shall give a sealed copy of the notice to the administrator.

(5) The administrator shall, as soon as reasonably practicable, and within 5 business days, send a copy of the notice of end of administration (and the accompanying report) to every creditor of the company of whose claim and address he is aware, to all those persons [(except the registrar of companies—see paragraph (2))] who were notified of his appointment and to the company.

[(6) The requirements of paragraph 80(4) shall be taken to be complied with if, within 5 business days of filing the notice of end of administration with the court, the administrator has gazetted a notice undertaking to provide a copy of the notice of the end of administration to any creditor of the company.

(6A) The notice under Rule 2.113(6) may be advertised in such other manner as the administrator thinks fit.]

[(7) In addition to the standard contents, the notice under paragraph (6) must state—
 (a) the date that the administration ended; and
 (b) that creditors can write for a copy of the notice of end of administration and the address to which to write.]]

NOTES

Amendment

 Substituted, together with rr 2.1–2.112, 2.114–2.133, for rr 2.1–2.6, 2.6A (inserted by SI 1987/1919, reg 3(1), Schedule, Pt 1, para 7), 2.7–2.46, 2.46A (inserted by SI 1987/1919, reg 3(1), Schedule, Pt 1, para 19), 2.47–2.58, 2.59–2.62 (inserted by SI 2002/1307, rr 3(1), 5(8)), by SI 2003/1730, r 5(1), Sch 1, Pt 2, para 9.
  Date in force: 15 September 2003: see SI 2003/1730, r 1(2); for effect and the continuing operation of this Part where a provision made by or under any enactment preserves the Insolvency Act 1986, old Pt II after that date see r 5(2)–(4) thereof.
 Para (5): words "(except the registrar of companies—see paragraph (2))" insquare brackets inserted by SI 2010/686, r 2, Sch 1, para 97(1), (2).
  Date in force: 6 April 2010: see SI 2010/686, r 1; for transitional provisions see r 6(1), Sch 4, paras 1, 2(1)(b) thereto.
 Paras (6), (6A): substituted, for para (6) as originally enacted, by SI 2009/642, rr 4, 13.
  Date in force: 6 April 2009: see SI 2009/642, r 1; for transitional provisions see r 3 thereof.
 Para (7): substituted by SI 2010/686, r 2, Sch 1, para 97(1), (3).
  Date in force: 6 April 2010: see SI 2010/686, r 1; for transitional provisions see r 6(1), Sch 4, para 1 thereto.

See Further

 See further, in relation to the application of this rule, with modifications, in respect of bank administration and applications for bank administration: the Bank Administration (England and Wales) Rules 2009, SI 2009/357, rr 58–61.

[2.114 Application to court by administrator]

[(1) An application to court under paragraph 79 for an order ending an administration shall have attached to it a progress report for the period since the last progress report (if any) or the date the company entered administration and a statement indicating what the administrator thinks should be the next steps for the company (if applicable).

(2) Where the administrator applies to the court because the creditors' meeting has required him to, he shall also attach a statement to the application in which he shall indicate (giving reasons) whether or not he agrees with the creditors' requirement to him to make the application.

(3) When the administrator applies other than at the request of a creditors' meeting, he shall—
  (a) give notice in writing to the applicant for the administration order under which he was appointed, or the person by whom he was appointed and the creditors of his intention to apply to court at least [5 business] days before the date that he intends to makes his application; and
  (b) attach to his application to court a statement that he has notified the creditors, and copies of any response from creditors to that notification.

(4) Where the administrator applies to court under paragraph 79 in conjunction with a petition under section 124 for an order to wind up the company, he shall, in addition to the requirements of paragraph (3), notify the creditors whether he intends to seek appointment as liquidator.]

NOTES

Amendment

Substituted, together with rr 2.1–2.113, 2.115–2.133, for rr 2.1–2.6, 2.6A (inserted by SI 1987/1919, reg 3(1), Schedule, Pt 1, para 7), 2.7–2.46, 2.46A (inserted by SI 1987/1919, reg 3(1), Schedule, Pt 1, para 19), 2.47–2.58, 2.59–2.62 (inserted by SI 2002/1307, rr 3(1), 5(8)), by SI 2003/1730, r 5(1), Sch 1, Pt 2, para 9.
  Date in force: 15 September 2003: see SI 2003/1730, r 1(2); for effect and the continuing operation of this Part where a provision made by or under any enactment preserves the Insolvency Act 1986, old Pt II after that date see r 5(2)–(4) thereof.
  Para (3): in sub-para (a) words "5 business" in square brackets substituted by SI 2010/686, r 2, Sch 1, para 98.
  Date in force: 6 April 2010: see SI 2010/686, r 1; for transitional provisions see r 6(1), Sch 4, para 1 thereto.

See Further

See further, in relation to the application of this rule, with modifications, in respect of bank administration and applications for bank administration: the Bank Administration (England and Wales) Rules 2009, SI 2009/357, rr 58–61.

[2.115 Application to court by creditor]

[(1) Where a creditor applies to the court to end the administration a copy of the application shall be served on the administrator and the person who either made the application for the administration order or made the appointment. Where the appointment was made under paragraph 14, a copy of the application shall be served on the holder of the floating charge by virtue of which the appointment was made.

(2) Service shall be effected not less than 5 business days before the date fixed for the hearing. The administrator, applicant or appointor, or holder of the floating charge by virtue of which the appointment was made may appear at the hearing of the application.

(3) Where the court makes an order to end the administration, the court shall send a copy of the order to the administrator.]

NOTES

Amendment

Substituted, together with rr 2.1–2.114, 2.116–2.133, for rr 2.1–2.6, 2.6A (inserted by SI 1987/1919, reg 3(1), Schedule, Pt 1, para 7), 2.7–2.46, 2.46A (inserted by SI 1987/1919, reg 3(1), Schedule, Pt 1, para 19), 2.47–2.58, 2.59–2.62 (inserted by SI 2002/1307, rr 3(1), 5(8)), by SI 2003/1730, r 5(1), Sch 1, Pt 2, para 9.
  Date in force: 15 September 2003: see SI 2003/1730, r 1(2); for effect and the continuing operation of this Part where a provision made by or under any enactment preserves the Insolvency Act 1986, old Pt II after that date see r 5(2)–(4) thereof.

[2.116 Notification by administrator of court order]

[[(1)] Where the court makes an order to end the administration, the administrator [must send to the registrar of companies] a copy of the court order and a copy of his final progress report.

[(2) As soon as reasonably practicable, the adminstrator must send a copy of the notice and the final progress report to all other persons who received notice of the administrator's appointment.]]

NOTES

Amendment

Substituted, together with rr 2.1–2.115, 2.117–2.133, for rr 2.1–2.6, 2.6A (inserted by SI 1987/1919, reg 3(1), Schedule, Pt 1, para 7), 2.7–2.46, 2.46A (inserted by SI 1987/1919, reg 3(1), Schedule, Pt 1, para 19), 2.47–2.58, 2.59–2.62 (inserted by SI 2002/1307, rr 3(1), 5(8)), by SI 2003/1730, r 5(1), Sch 1, Pt 2, para 9.
    Date in force: 15 September 2003: see SI 2003/1730, r 1(2); for effect and the continuing operation of this Part where a provision made by or under any enactment preserves the Insolvency Act 1986, old Pt II after that date see r 5(2)–(4) thereof.

Para (1): numbered as such by SI 2010/686, r 2, Sch 1, para 99(1), (2).
    Date in force: 6 April 2010: see SI 2010/686, r 1; for transitional provisions see r 6(1), Sch 4, para 1 thereto.

Para (1): words "must send to the registrar of companies" in square brackets substituted by SI 2010/686, r 2, Sch 1, para 99(1), (3).
    Date in force: 6 April 2010: see SI 2010/686, r 1; for transitional provisions see r 6(1), Sch 4, paras 1, 2(1)(b) thereto.

Para (2): inserted by SI 2010/686, r 2, Sch 1, para 99(1), (4).
    Date in force: 6 April 2010: see SI 2010/686, r 1; for transitional provisions see r 6(1), Sch 4, para 1 thereto.

[2.117A Moving from administration to creditors' voluntary liquidation]

[(1) As soon as reasonably practicable after the day on which the registrar of companies registers the notice of moving from administration to creditors' voluntary liquidation sent by the administrator for the purposes of paragraph 83(3), the person who at that point ceases to be the administrator must (whether the administrator becomes the liquidator or not) send a final progress report (which must include details of the assets to be dealt with in the liquidation) to the registrar of companies and to all those who received notice of the administrator's appointment.

(2) For the purposes of paragraph 83(7)(a), a person is nominated by the creditors as liquidator by—

  (a) their approval of the statement of the proposed liquidator in the administrator's proposals or revised proposals, or

  (b) their nomination of a different person before their approval of the proposals or revised proposals.

(3) Where the creditors nominate a different person, the nomination must, where applicable, include the declaration required by section 231.]

NOTES

Amendment

Substituted, for r 2.117 as previously enacted, by SI 2010/686, r 2, Sch 1, para 100.
    Date in force: 6 April 2010: see SI 2010/686, r 1; for transitional provisions see r 6(1), Sch 4, para 1 thereto.

[2.118 Moving from administration to dissolution]

[(1) Where, for the purposes of paragraph 84(1), the administrator sends a notice of moving from administration to dissolution to the registrar of companies, [the administrator must] attach to that notice a final progress report.

(2) As soon as reasonably practicable a copy of the notice and the attached document shall be sent to all [other persons] who received notice of the administrator's appointment.

(3) Where a court makes an order under paragraph 84(7) it shall, where the applicant is not the administrator, give a copy of the order to the administrator.

(4) . . .]

NOTES

Amendment

Substituted, together with rr 2.1–2.117, 2.119–2.133, for rr 2.1–2.6, 2.6A (inserted by SI 1987/1919, reg 3(1), Schedule, Pt 1, para 7), 2.7–2.46, 2.46A (inserted by SI 1987/1919, reg 3(1), Schedule, Pt 1, para 19), 2.47–2.58, 2.59–2.62 (inserted by SI 2002/1307, rr 3(1), 5(8)), by SI 2003/1730, r 5(1), Sch 1, Pt 2, para 9.

Date in force: 15 September 2003: see SI 2003/1730, r 1(2); for effect and the continuing operation of this Part where a provision made by or under any enactment preserves the Insolvency Act 1986, old Pt II after that date see r 5(2)–(4) thereof.

Para (1): words "the administrator must" in square brackets substituted by SI 2010/686, r 2, Sch 1, para 101(1), (2).

Date in force: 6 April 2010: see SI 2010/686, r 1; for transitional provisions see r 6(1), Sch 4, para 1 thereto.

Para (2): words "other persons" in square brackets substituted by SI 2010/686, r 2, Sch 1, para 101(1), (3).

Date in force: 6 April 2010: see SI 2010/686, r 1; for transitional provisions see r 6(1), Sch 4, para 1 thereto.

Para (4): revoked by SI 2010/686, r 2, Sch 1, para 101(1), (4).

Date in force: 6 April 2010: see SI 2010/686, r 1; for transitional provisions see r 6(1), Sch 4, para 1 thereto.

See Further

See further, in relation to the application of this rule, with modifications, in respect of bank administration and applications for bank administration: the Bank Administration (England and Wales) Rules 2009, SI 2009/357, rr 58–61.

[CHAPTER 13

REPLACING ADMINISTRATOR]

NOTES

Amendment

Substituted by SI 2003/1730, r 5(1), Sch 1, Pt 2, para 9.

Date in force: 15 September 2003: see SI 2003/1730, r 1(2); for effect and the continuing operation of this Part where a provision made by or under any enactment preserves the Insolvency Act 1986, old Pt II after that date see r 5(2)–(4) thereof.

[2.119 Grounds for resignation]

[(1) The administrator may give notice of his resignation on grounds of ill health or because—

- (a) he intends ceasing to be in practice as an insolvency practitioner; or
- (b) there is some conflict of interest, or change of personal circumstances, which precludes or makes impracticable the further discharge by him of the duties of administrator.

(2) The administrator may, with the permission of the court, give notice of his resignation on grounds other than those specified in paragraph (1).]

NOTES

Amendment

Substituted, together with rr 2.1–2.118, 2.120–2.133, for rr 2.1–2.6, 2.6A (inserted by SI 1987/1919, reg 3(1), Schedule, Pt 1, para 7), 2.7–2.46, 2.46A (inserted by SI 1987/1919, reg 3(1), Schedule, Pt 1, para 19), 2.47–2.58, 2.59–2.62 (inserted by SI 2002/1307, rr 3(1), 5(8)), by SI 2003/1730, r 5(1), Sch 1, Pt 2, para 9.
Date in force: 15 September 2003: see SI 2003/1730, r 1(2); for effect and the continuing operation of this Part where a provision made by or under any enactment preserves the Insolvency Act 1986, old Pt II after that date see r 5(2)–(4) thereof.

See Further

See further, in relation to the application of this rule, with modifications, in respect of bank administration and applications for bank administration: the Bank Administration (England and Wales) Rules 2009, SI 2009/357, rr 58–61.

[2.120 Notice of intention to resign]

[(1) The administrator shall in all cases give at least [5 business] days' notice in Form 2.37B of his intention to resign, or to apply for the court's permission to do so, to the following persons—

(a) if there is a continuing administrator of the company, to him; and
(b) if there is a creditors' committee to it; but
(c) if there is no such administrator and no creditors' committee, to the company and its creditors.

(2) Where the administrator gives notice under paragraph (1), he shall also give notice to a member State liquidator, if such a person has been appointed in relation to the company.

(3) Where the administrator was appointed by the holder of a qualifying floating charge under paragraph 14, the notice of intention to resign shall also be sent to all holders of prior qualifying floating charges, and to the person who appointed the administrator. A copy of the notice shall also be sent to the holder of the floating charge by virtue of which the appointment was made.

(4) Where the administrator was appointed by the company or the directors of the company under paragraph 22, a copy of the notice of intention to resign shall also be sent to the appointor and all holders of a qualifying floating charge.]

NOTES

Amendment

Substituted, together with rr 2.1–2.119, 2.121–2.133, for rr 2.1–2.6, 2.6A (inserted by SI 1987/1919, reg 3(1), Schedule, Pt 1, para 7), 2.7–2.46, 2.46A (inserted by SI 1987/1919, reg 3(1), Schedule, Pt 1, para 19), 2.47–2.58, 2.59–2.62 (inserted by SI 2002/1307, rr 3(1), 5(8)), by SI 2003/1730, r 5(1), Sch 1, Pt 2, para 9.
Date in force: 15 September 2003: see SI 2003/1730, r 1(2); for effect and the continuing operation of this Part where a provision made by or under any enactment preserves the Insolvency Act 1986, old Pt II after that date see r 5(2)–(4) thereof.
Para (1): words "5 business" in square brackets substituted by SI 2010/686, r 2, Sch 1, para 102.
Date in force: 6 April 2010: see SI 2010/686, r 1; for transitional provisions see r 6(1), Sch 4, para 1 thereto.

See Further

See further, in relation to the application of this rule, with modifications, in respect of bank administration and applications for bank administration: the Bank Administration (England

and Wales) Rules 2009, SI 2009/357, rr 58–61.

[2.121 Notice of resignation]

[(1) The notice of resignation shall be in Form 2.38B.

(2) Where the administrator was appointed under an administration order, the notice shall be filed with the court, and a copy sent to the registrar of companies. A copy of the notice of resignation shall be sent not more than 5 business days after it has been filed with the court to all those to whom notice of intention to resign was sent.

(3) Where the administrator was appointed by the holder of a qualifying floating charge under paragraph 14, a copy of the notice of resignation shall be filed with the court and sent to the registrar of companies, and anyone else who received a copy of the notice of intention to resign, within 5 business days of the notice of resignation being sent to the holder of the floating charge by virtue of which the appointment was made.

(4) Where the administrator was appointed by the company or the directors under paragraph 22, a copy of the notice of resignation shall be filed with the court and sent to the registrar of companies and to anyone else who received notice of intention to resign within 5 business days of the notice of resignation being sent to either the company or the directors that made the appointment.]

NOTES

Amendment

Substituted, together with rr 2.1–2.120, 2.122–2.133, for rr 2.1–2.6, 2.6A (inserted by SI 1987/1919, reg 3(1), Schedule, Pt 1, para 7), 2.7–2.46, 2.46A (inserted by SI 1987/1919, reg 3(1), Schedule, Pt 1, para 19), 2.47–2.58, 2.59–2.62 (inserted by SI 2002/1307, rr 3(1), 5(8)), by SI 2003/1730, r 5(1), Sch 1, Pt 2, para 9.

Date in force: 15 September 2003: see SI 2003/1730, r 1(2); for effect and the continuing operation of this Part where a provision made by or under any enactment preserves the Insolvency Act 1986, old Pt II after that date see r 5(2)–(4) thereof.

See Further

See further, in relation to the application of this rule, with modifications, in respect of bank administration and applications for bank administration: the Bank Administration (England and Wales) Rules 2009, SI 2009/357, rr 58–61.

[2.122 Application to court to remove administrator from office]

[(1) Any application under paragraph 88 shall state the grounds on which it is requested that the administrator should be removed from office.

(2) Service of the notice of the application shall be effected on the administrator, the person who made the application for the administration order or the person who appointed the administrator, the creditors' committee (if any), the joint administrator (if any), and where there is neither a creditors' committee or joint administrator, to the company and all the creditors, including any floating charge holders not less than 5 business days before the date fixed for the application to be heard. Where the appointment was made under paragraph 14, the notice shall be served on the holder of the floating charge by virtue of which the appointment was made.

(3) Where a court makes an order removing the administrator it shall give a copy of the order to the applicant who as soon as reasonably practicable shall send a copy to the administrator.

(4) The applicant shall also within 5 business days of the order being made send a copy of the order to all those to whom notice of the application was sent.

(5) A copy of the order shall also be sent to the registrar of companies . . . within the same time period.]

NOTES

Amendment

Substituted, together with rr 2.1–2.121, 2.123–2.133, for rr 2.1–2.6, 2.6A (inserted by SI 1987/1919, reg 3(1), Schedule, Pt 1, para 7), 2.7–2.46, 2.46A (inserted by SI 1987/1919, reg 3(1), Schedule, Pt 1, para 19), 2.47–2.58, 2.59–2.62 (inserted by SI 2002/1307, rr 3(1), 5(8)), by SI 2003/1730, r 5(1), Sch 1, Pt 2, para 9.
Date in force: 15 September 2003: see SI 2003/1730, r 1(2); for effect and the continuing operation of this Part where a provision made by or under any enactment preserves the Insolvency Act 1986, old Pt II after that date see r 5(2)–(4) thereof.
Para (5): words omitted revoked by SI 2010/686, r 2, Sch 1, para 103.
Date in force: 6 April 2010: see SI 2010/686, r 1; for transitional provisions see r 6(1), Sch 4, para 1 thereto.

See Further

See further, in relation to the application of this rule, with modifications, in respect of bank administration and applications for bank administration: the Bank Administration (England and Wales) Rules 2009, SI 2009/357, rr 58–61.

[2.123 Notice of vacation of office when administrator ceases to be qualified to act]
[Where the administrator who has ceased to be qualified to act as an insolvency practitioner in relation to the company gives notice in accordance with paragraph 89, he shall also give notice to the registrar of companies . . ..]

NOTES

Amendment

Substituted, together with rr 2.1–2.122, 2.124–2.133, for rr 2.1–2.6, 2.6A (inserted by SI 1987/1919, reg 3(1), Schedule, Pt 1, para 7), 2.7–2.46, 2.46A (inserted by SI 1987/1919, reg 3(1), Schedule, Pt 1, para 19), 2.47–2.58, 2.59–2.62 (inserted by SI 2002/1307, rr 3(1), 5(8)), by SI 2003/1730, r 5(1), Sch 1, Pt 2, para 9.
Date in force: 15 September 2003: see SI 2003/1730, r 1(2); for effect and the continuing operation of this Part where a provision made by or under any enactment preserves the Insolvency Act 1986, old Pt II after that date see r 5(2)–(4) thereof.
Words omitted revoked by SI 2010/686, r 2, Sch 1, para 104.
Date in force: 6 April 2010: see SI 2010/686, r 1; for transitional provisions see r 6(1), Sch 4, para 1 thereto.

See Further

See further, in relation to the application of this rule, with modifications, in respect of bank administration and applications for bank administration: the Bank Administration (England and Wales) Rules 2009, SI 2009/357, rr 58–61.

[2.124 Administrator deceased]
[(1) Subject as follows, where the administrator has died, it is the duty of his personal representatives to give notice of the fact to the court, specifying the date of the death. This does not apply if notice has been given under either paragraph (2) or (3) of this Rule.

(2) If the deceased administrator was a partner in [or an employee of] a firm, notice may be given by a partner in the firm who is qualified to act as an insolvency practitioner, or is a member of any body recognised by the Secretary of State for the authorisation of insolvency practitioners.

(3) Notice of the death may be given by any person producing to the court the relevant death certificate or a copy of it.

(4) Where a person gives notice to the court under this Rule, he shall also give notice to the registrar of companies . . ..]

NOTES

Amendment

Substituted, together with rr 2.1–2.123, 2.125–2.133, for rr 2.1–2.6, 2.6A (inserted by SI 1987/1919, reg 3(1), Schedule, Pt 1, para 7), 2.7–2.46, 2.46A (inserted by SI 1987/1919, reg 3(1), Schedule, Pt 1, para 19), 2.47–2.58, 2.59–2.62 (inserted by SI 2002/1307, rr 3(1), 5(8)), by SI 2003/1730, r 5(1), Sch 1, Pt 2, para 9.

Date in force: 15 September 2003: see SI 2003/1730, r 1(2); for effect and the continuing operation of this Part where a provision made by or under any enactment preserves the Insolvency Act 1986, old Pt II after that date see r 5(2)–(4) thereof.

Para (2): words "or an employee of" in square brackets inserted by SI 2010/686, r 2, Sch 1, para 105(1), (2).

Date in force: 6 April 2010: see SI 2010/686, r 1; for transitional provisions see r 6(1), Sch 4, para 1 thereto.

Para (4): words omitted revoked by SI 2010/686, r 2, Sch 1, para 105(1), (3).

Date in force: 6 April 2010: see SI 2010/686, r 1; for transitional provisions see r 6(1), Sch 4, para 1 thereto.

See Further

See further, in relation to the application of this rule, with modifications, in respect of bank administration and applications for bank administration: the Bank Administration (England and Wales) Rules 2009, SI 2009/357, rr 58–61.

[2.125 Application to replace]

[(1) Where an application is made to court under paragraphs 91(1) or 95 to appoint a replacement administrator, the application shall be accompanied by a written statement in Form 2.2B by the person proposed to be the replacement administrator.

(2) Where the original administrator was appointed under an administration order, a copy of the application shall be served, in addition to those persons listed in paragraph 12(2) and Rule 2.6(3), on the person who made the application for the administration order.

(3) Where the application to court is made under paragraph 95, the application shall be accompanied by [a witness statement] setting out the applicant's belief as to the matters set out in that paragraph.

(4) Rule 2.8 shall apply to the service of an application under paragraphs 91(1) and 95 as it applies to service in accordance with Rule 2.6.

(5) Rules 2.9, 2.10, 2.12 and 2.14(1) and (2) apply to an application under paragraphs 91(1) and 95.]

NOTES

Amendment

Substituted, together with rr 2.1–2.124, 2.126–2.133, for rr 2.1–2.6, 2.6A (inserted by SI 1987/1919, reg 3(1), Schedule, Pt 1, para 7), 2.7–2.46, 2.46A (inserted by SI 1987/1919, reg 3(1), Schedule, Pt 1, para 19), 2.47–2.58, 2.59–2.62 (inserted by SI 2002/1307, rr 3(1), 5(8)), by SI 2003/1730, r 5(1), Sch 1, Pt 2, para 9.

Date in force: 15 September 2003: see SI 2003/1730, r 1(2); for effect and the continuing operation of this Part where a provision made by or under any enactment preserves the Insolvency Act 1986, old Pt II after that date see r 5(2)–(4) thereof.

Para (3): words "a witness statement" in square brackets substituted by SI 2010/686, r 2, Sch 1, para 106.

Date in force: 6 April 2010: see SI 2010/686, r 1; for transitional provisions see r 6(1), Sch 4, paras 1, 2(1)(b), (2)–(4) thereto.

See Further

See further, in relation to the application of this rule, with modifications, in respect of bank administration and applications for bank administration: the Bank Administration (England and Wales) Rules 2009, SI 2009/357, rr 58–61.

[2.126 Notification and advertisement of appointment of replacement administrator]
[Where a replacement administrator is appointed, the same provisions apply in respect of giving notice of, and advertising, the replacement appointment as in the case of the appointment (subject to Rule 2.128), and all statements, consents etc as are required shall also be required in the case of the appointment of a replacement. All forms and notices shall clearly identify that the appointment is of a replacement administrator.]

NOTES

Amendment

Substituted, together with rr 2.1–2.125, 2.127–2.133, for rr 2.1–2.6, 2.6A (inserted by SI 1987/1919, reg 3(1), Schedule, Pt 1, para 7), 2.7–2.46, 2.46A (inserted by SI 1987/1919, reg 3(1), Schedule, Pt 1, para 19), 2.47–2.58, 2.59–2.62 (inserted by SI 2002/1307, rr 3(1), 5(8)), by SI 2003/1730, r 5(1), Sch 1, Pt 2, para 9.

Date in force: 15 September 2003: see SI 2003/1730, r 1(2); for effect and the continuing operation of this Part where a provision made by or under any enactment preserves the Insolvency Act 1986, old Pt II after that date see r 5(2)–(4) thereof.

See Further

See further, in relation to the application of this rule, with modifications, in respect of bank administration and applications for bank administration: the Bank Administration (England and Wales) Rules 2009, SI 2009/357, rr 58–61.

[2.127 Notification and advertisement of appointment of joint administrator]
[Where, after an initial appointment has been made, an additional person or persons are to be appointed as joint administrator the same Rules shall apply in respect of giving notice of and advertising the appointment as in the case of the initial appointment, subject to Rule 2.128.]

NOTES

Amendment

Substituted, together with rr 2.1–2.126, 2.128–2.133, for rr 2.1–2.6, 2.6A (inserted by SI 1987/1919, reg 3(1), Schedule, Pt 1, para 7), 2.7–2.46, 2.46A (inserted by SI 1987/1919, reg 3(1), Schedule, Pt 1, para 19), 2.47–2.58, 2.59–2.62 (inserted by SI 2002/1307, rr 3(1), 5(8)), by SI 2003/1730, r 5(1), Sch 1, Pt 2, para 9.

Date in force: 15 September 2003: see SI 2003/1730, r 1(2); for effect and the continuing operation of this Part where a provision made by or under any enactment preserves the Insolvency Act 1986, old Pt II after that date see r 5(2)–(4) thereof.

See Further

See further, in relation to the application of this rule, with modifications, in respect of bank administration and applications for bank administration: the Bank Administration (England and Wales) Rules 2009, SI 2009/357, rr 58–61.

[2.128]
[The replacement or additional administrator shall send notice of the appointment . . . to the registrar of companies.]

Insolvency Rules 1986, reg 2.127

NOTES

Amendment

Substituted, together with rr 2.1–2.127, 2.129–2.133, for rr 2.1–2.6, 2.6A (inserted by SI 1987/1919, reg 3(1), Schedule, Pt 1, para 7), 2.7–2.46, 2.46A (inserted by SI 1987/1919, reg 3(1), Schedule, Pt 1, para 19), 2.47–2.58, 2.59–2.62 (inserted by SI 2002/1307, rr 3(1), 5(8)), by SI 2003/1730, r 5(1), Sch 1, Pt 2, para 9.

Date in force: 15 September 2003: see SI 2003/1730, r 1(2); for effect and the continuing operation of this Part where a provision made by or under any enactment preserves the Insolvency Act 1986, old Pt II after that date see r 5(2)–(4) thereof.

Words omitted revoked by SI 2010/686, r 2, Sch 1, para 107.

Date in force: 6 April 2010: see SI 2010/686, r 1; for transitional provisions see r 6(1), Sch 4, para 1 thereto.

See Further

See further, in relation to the application of this rule, with modifications, in respect of bank administration and applications for bank administration: the Bank Administration (England and Wales) Rules 2009, SI 2009/357, rr 58–61.

[2.129 Administrator's duties on vacating office]

[(1) Where the administrator ceases to be in office as such, in consequence of removal, resignation or cesser of qualification as an insolvency practitioner, he is under obligation as soon as reasonably practicable to deliver up to the person succeeding him as administrator the assets (after deduction of any expenses properly incurred and distributions made by him) and further to deliver up to that person—

(a) the records of the administration, including correspondence, proofs and other related papers appertaining to the administration while it was within his responsibility; and

(b) the company's books, papers and other records.

(2) If the administrator makes default in complying with this Rule, he is liable to a fine and, for continued contravention, to a daily default fine.]

NOTES

Amendment

Substituted, together with rr 2.1–2.128, 2.130–2.133, for rr 2.1–2.6, 2.6A (inserted by SI 1987/1919, reg 3(1), Schedule, Pt 1, para 7), 2.7–2.46, 2.46A (inserted by SI 1987/1919, reg 3(1), Schedule, Pt 1, para 19), 2.47–2.58, 2.59–2.62 (inserted by SI 2002/1307, rr 3(1), 5(8)), by SI 2003/1730, r 5(1), Sch 1, Pt 2, para 9.

Date in force: 15 September 2003: see SI 2003/1730, r 1(2); for effect and the continuing operation of this Part where a provision made by or under any enactment preserves the Insolvency Act 1986, old Pt II after that date see r 5(2)–(4) thereof.

See Further

See further, in relation to the application of this rule, with modifications, in respect of bank administration and applications for bank administration: the Bank Administration (England and Wales) Rules 2009, SI 2009/357, rr 58–61.

[CHAPTER 14

EC REGULATION: CONVERSION OF ADMINISTRATION INTO WINDING UP]

NOTES

Amendment

Substituted by SI 2003/1730, r 5(1), Sch 1, Pt 2, para 9.
Date in force: 15 September 2003: see SI 2003/1730, r 1(2); for effect and the continuing operation of this Part where a provision made by or under any enactment preserves the Insolvency Act 1986, old Pt II after that date see r 5(2)–(4) thereof.

[2.130 Application for conversion into winding up]

[[(1) Where a member State liquidator proposes to apply to the court for the conversion into winding-up proceedings of an administration, a witness statement complying with Rule 2.131 must be prepared and filed with the court in support of the application.

(1A) In this Rule, and in Rules 2.131 and 2.132, "conversion into winding-up proceedings" means an order under Article 37 of the EC Regulation (conversion of earlier proceedings) that—

(a) the purposes of the administration are to be limited to the winding up of the company through administration and are to exclude the purpose contained in sub- paragraph (a) of paragraph 3(1);

(b) the administration is converted into a creditors' voluntary winding up; or

(c) the administration is converted into a winding up by the court.]

(2) An application under this Rule shall be by originating application.

(3) The application and the [witness statement] required under this Rule shall be served upon—

(a) the company; and

(b) the administrator.]

NOTES

Amendment

Substituted, together with rr 2.1–2.129, 2.131–2.133, for rr 2.1–2.6, 2.6A (inserted by SI 1987/1919, reg 3(1), Schedule, Pt 1, para 7), 2.7–2.46, 2.46A (inserted by SI 1987/1919, reg 3(1), Schedule, Pt 1, para 19), 2.47–2.58, 2.59–2.62 (inserted by SI 2002/1307, rr 3(1), 5(8)), by SI 2003/1730, r 5(1), Sch 1, Pt 2, para 9.
Date in force: 15 September 2003: see SI 2003/1730, r 1(2); for effect and the continuing operation of this Part where a provision made by or under any enactment preserves the Insolvency Act 1986, old Pt II after that date see r 5(2)–(4) thereof.
Paras (1), (1A): substituted, for para (1) as previously enacted, by SI 2010/686, r 2, Sch 1, para 108(1), (2).
Date in force: 6 April 2010: see SI 2010/686, r 1; for transitional provisions see r 6(1), Sch 4, paras 1, 2(2)–(4) thereto.
Para (3): word "witness statement" in square brackets substituted by SI 2010/686, r 2, Sch 1, para 108(1), (3).
Date in force: 6 April 2010: see SI 2010/686, r 1; for transitional provisions see r 6(1), Sch 4, paras 1, 2(1)(b), (2)–(4) thereto.

[2.131 Contents of [witness statement]]

[(1) The [witness statement] shall state—

(a) that main proceedings have been opened in relation to the company in a member State other than the United Kingdom;

(b) the [belief of the person making the statement] that the conversion of the administration into [winding-up proceedings] would prove to be in the interests of the creditors in the main proceedings;

[(c) the opinion of the person making the statement as to whether the company ought to go into voluntary liquidation or be wound up by the court; and]

(d) all other matters that, in the opinion of the member State liquidator, would assist the court—
   (i) in deciding whether to make such an order; and
   (ii) if the court were to do so, in considering the need for any consequential provision that would be necessary or desirable.

(2) [A witness statement] under this rule shall be [made] by, or on behalf of, the member State liquidator.]

NOTES

Amendment

Substituted, together with rr 2.1–2.130, 2.132, 2.133, for rr 2.1–2.6, 2.6A (inserted by SI 1987/1919, reg 3(1), Schedule, Pt 1, para 7), 2.7–2.46, 2.46A (inserted by SI 1987/1919, reg 3(1), Schedule, Pt 1, para 19), 2.47–2.58, 2.59–2.62 (inserted by SI 2002/1307, rr 3(1), 5(8)), by SI 2003/1730, r 5(1), Sch 1, Pt 2, para 9.
  Date in force: 15 September 2003: see SI 2003/1730, r 1(2); for effect and the continuing operation of this Part where a provision made by or under any enactment preserves the Insolvency Act 1986, old Pt II after that date see r 5(2)–(4) thereof.
Provision heading: words "witness statement" in square brackets substituted by SI 2010/686, r 2, Sch 1, para 109(1), (2).
  Date in force: 6 April 2010: see SI 2010/686, r 1; for transitional provisions see r 6(1), Sch 4, paras 1, 2(1)(b), (2)–(4) thereto.
Para (1): word "witness statement" in square brackets substituted by SI 2010/686, r 2, Sch 1, para 109(1), (3)(a).
  Date in force: 6 April 2010: see SI 2010/686, r 1; for transitional provisions see r 6(1), Sch 4, paras 1, 2(1)(b), (2)–(4) thereto.
Para (1): in sub-para (b) words "belief of the person making the statement" in square brackets substituted by SI 2010/686, r 2, Sch 1, para 109(1), (3)(b)(i).
  Date in force: 6 April 2010: see SI 2010/686, r 1; for transitional provisions see r 6(1), Sch 4, paras 1, 2(1)(b), (2)–(4) thereto.
Para (1): in sub-para (b) words "winding-up proceedings" in square brackets substituted by SI 2010/686, r 2, Sch 1, para 109(1), (3)(b)(ii).
  Date in force: 6 April 2010: see SI 2010/686, r 1; for transitional provisions see r 6(1), Sch 4, paras 1, 2(1)(b), (2)–(4) thereto.
Para (1): sub-para (c) substituted by SI 2010/686, r 2, Sch 1, para 109(1), (3)(c).
  Date in force: 6 April 2010: see SI 2010/686, r 1; for transitional provisions see r 6(1), Sch 4, paras 1, 2(1)(b), (2)–(4) thereto.
Para (2): words "A witness statement" in square brackets substituted by SI 2010/686, r 2, Sch 1, para 109(1), (4)(a).
  Date in force: 6 April 2010: see SI 2010/686, r 1; for transitional provisions see r 6(1), Sch 4, paras 1, 2(1)(b), (2)–(4) thereto.
Para (2): word "made" in square brackets substituted by SI 2010/686, r 2, Sch 1, para 109(1), (4)(b).
  Date in force: 6 April 2010: see SI 2010/686, r 1; for transitional provisions see r 6(1), Sch 4, paras 1, 2(1)(b), (2)–(4) thereto.

[2.132 Power of court]

[(1) On hearing the application for conversion into [winding-up proceedings] the court may make such order as it thinks [just].

(2) If the court makes an order for conversion into [winding-up proceedings] the order may contain all such consequential provisions as the court deems necessary or desirable.

(3) Without prejudice to the generality of paragraph (1), an order under that paragraph may provide that the company be wound up as if a resolution for voluntary winding up under section 84 were passed on the day on which the order is made.]

NOTES

Amendment

Substituted, together with rr 2.1–2.131, 2.133, for rr 2.1–2.6, 2.6A (inserted by SI 1987/1919, reg 3(1), Schedule, Pt 1, para 7), 2.7–2.46, 2.46A (inserted by SI 1987/1919, reg 3(1), Schedule, Pt 1, para 19), 2.47–2.58, 2.59–2.62 (inserted by SI 2002/1307, rr 3(1), 5(8)), by SI 2003/1730, r 5(1), Sch 1, Pt 2, para 9.
Date in force: 15 September 2003: see SI 2003/1730, r 1(2); for effect and the continuing operation of this Part where a provision made by or under any enactment preserves the Insolvency Act 1986, old Pt II after that date see r 5(2)–(4) thereof.
Para (1): words "winding-up proceedings" in square brackets substituted by SI 2010/686, r 2, Sch 1, para 110.
Date in force: 6 April 2010: see SI 2010/686, r 1; for transitional provisions see r 6(1), Sch 4, para 1 thereto.
Para (1): word "just" in square brackets substituted by SI 2010/686, r 2, Sch 1, para 1.
Date in force: 6 April 2010: see SI 2010/686, r 1; for transitional provisions see r 6(1), Sch 4, paras 1, 2(1)(b) thereto.
Para (2): words "winding-up proceedings" in square brackets substituted by SI 2010/686, r 2, Sch 1, para 110.
Date in force: 6 April 2010: see SI 2010/686, r 1; for transitional provisions see r 6(1), Sch 4, para 1 thereto.

[CHAPTER 15

EC REGULATION: MEMBER STATE LIQUIDATOR]

NOTES

Amendment

Substituted by SI 2003/1730, r 5(1), Sch 1, Pt 2, para 9.
Date in force: 15 September 2003: see SI 2003/1730, r 1(2); for effect and the continuing operation of this Part where a provision made by or under any enactment preserves the Insolvency Act 1986, old Pt II after that date see r 5(2)–(4) thereof.

[2.133 Interpretation of creditor and notice to member State liquidator]

[(1) This Rule applies where a member State liquidator has been appointed in relation to the company.

(2) For the purposes of the Rules referred to in paragraph (3) the member State liquidator is deemed to be a creditor.

(3) The Rules referred to in paragraph (2) are Rules 2.34 (notice of creditors' meeting), 2.35(4) (creditors' meeting), 2.37 (requisitioning of creditors' meeting), 2.38 (entitlement to vote), 2.39 (admission and rejection of claims), 2.40 (secured creditors), 2.41 (holders of negotiable instruments), 2.42 (hire-purchase, conditional sale and chattel leasing agreements), 2.46 (notice to creditors), 2.47 (reports to creditors), 2.48 (correspondence instead of creditors' meeting), 2.50(2) (creditors' committee), 2.57(1)(b) and (c) (termination of membership of creditors' committee), 2.59(3) (vacancies in creditors' committee), 2.108(3) (administrator's remuneration—recourse to court) and 2.109 (challenge to administrator's remuneration).

(4) Paragraphs (2) and (3) are without prejudice to the generality of the right to participate referred to in paragraph 3 of Article 32 of the EC Regulation (exercise of creditor's rights).

(5) Where the administrator is obliged to give notice to, or provide a copy of a document (including an order of court) to, the court, the registrar of companies or the official receiver, the administrator shall give notice or provide copies, as the case may be, to the member State liquidator.

(6) Paragraph (5) is without prejudice to the generality of the obligations imposed by Article 31 of the EC Regulation (duty to co-operate and communicate information).]

NOTES

Amendment

Substituted, together with rr 2.1–2.132, for rr 2.1–2.6, 2.6A (inserted by SI 1987/1919, reg 3(1), Schedule, Pt 1, para 7), 2.7–2.46, 2.46A (inserted by SI 1987/1919, reg 3(1), Schedule, Pt 1, para 19), 2.47–2.58, 2.59–2.62 (inserted by SI 2002/1307, rr 3(1), 5(8)), by SI 2003/1730, r 5(1), Sch 1, Pt 2, para 9.

Date in force: 15 September 2003: see SI 2003/1730, r 1(2); for effect and the continuing operation of this Part where a provision made by or under any enactment preserves the Insolvency Act 1986, old Pt II after that date see r 5(2)–(4) thereof.

PART 3

ADMINISTRATIVE RECEIVERSHIP

CHAPTER 1

APPOINTMENT OF ADMINISTRATIVE RECEIVER

[3.1 Acceptance and confirmation of acceptance of appointment]

[(1) Where two or more persons are appointed as joint receivers or managers of a company's property under powers contained in an instrument, the acceptance of such an appointment shall be made by each of them in accordance with section 33 as if that person were a sole appointee, but the joint appointment takes effect only when all such persons have so accepted and is then deemed to have been made at the time at which the instrument of appointment was received by or on behalf of all such persons.

(2) Subject to the next paragraph, where a person is appointed as the sole or joint receiver of a company's property under powers contained in an instrument, the appointee shall, if he accepts the appointment, within [5 business] days confirm his acceptance in writing to the person appointing him.

(3) Paragraph (2) does not apply where an appointment is accepted in writing.

(4) Any acceptance or confirmation of acceptance of appointment as a receiver or manager of a company's property, whether under the Act or the Rules, may be given by any person (including, in the case of a joint appointment, any joint appointee) duly authorised for that purpose on behalf of the receiver or manager.

(5) In confirming acceptance the appointee or person authorised for that purpose shall state—

(a) the time and date of receipt of the instrument of appointment, and
(b) the time and date of acceptance.]

NOTES

Amendment

Substituted by SI 1987/1919, r 3(1), Schedule, Part 1, para 23.

Para (2): words "5 business" in square brackets substituted by SI 2010/686, r 2, Sch 1, para 111.

Date in force: 6 April 2010: see SI 2010/686, r 1; for transitional provisions see r 6(1), Sch 4, para 1 thereto.

3.2 Notice and advertisement of appointment

(1) This Rule relates to the notice which a person is required by section 46(1) to send and publish, when appointed as administrative receiver.

(2) The following matters shall be stated in the [notices sent to the company and the creditors]—

- (a) the registered name of the company, as at the date of the appointment, and its registered number;
- (b) any other name with which the company has been registered in the 12 months preceding that date;
- (c) any name under which the company has traded at any time in those 12 months, if substantially different from its then registered name;
- (d) the name and address of the administrative receiver, and the date of his appointment;
- (e) the name of the person by whom the appointment was made;
- (f) the date of the instrument conferring the power under which the appointment was made, and a brief description of the instrument;
- (g) a brief description of the assets of the company (if any) in respect of which the person appointed is not made the receiver.

[(3) Subject to paragraph (4), the notice of appointment to be given by the administrative receiver under section 46(1)(a) shall be gazetted and may be advertised in such other manner as the administrative receiver thinks fit.]

[(4) In addition to the standard contents, the notice under paragraph (3) must state—

- (a) that an administrative receiver has been appointed;
- (b) the date of the appointment;
- (c) the name of the person who made the appointment, and that the appointment was made by that person; and
- (d) the nature of the business of the company.]

NOTES

Initial Commencement

Specified date

Specified date: 29 December 1986: see r 0.1.

Amendment

Para (2): words "notices sent to the company and the creditors" in square brackets substituted by SI 1987/1919, r 3(1), Schedule, Pt 1, para 24.

Para (3): substituted by SI 2009/642, rr 4, 14.
Date in force: 6 April 2009: see SI 2009/642, r 1; for transitional provisions see r 3 thereof.

Para (4): substituted by SI 2010/686, r 2, Sch 1, para 112.
Date in force: 6 April 2010: see SI 2010/686, r 1; for transitional provisions see r 6(1), Sch 4, para 1 thereto.

CHAPTER 2

STATEMENT OF AFFAIRS AND REPORT TO CREDITORS

3.3 Notice requiring statement of affairs

(1) [Where] the administrative receiver determines to require a statement of the company's affairs to be made out and submitted to him in accordance with section 47, he shall send notice to each of the persons whom he considers should be made responsible under that section, requiring them to prepare and submit the statement.

(2) The persons to whom the notice is sent are referred to in this Chapter as "the [nominated persons]".
(3) The notice shall inform each of the [nominated persons]—
- (a) of the names and addresses of all others (if any) to whom the same notice has been sent;
- (b) of the time within which the statement must be delivered;
- (c) of the effect of section 47(6) (penalty for non-compliance); and
- (d) of the application to him, and to each of the other [nominated persons], of section 235 (duty to provide information, and to attend on the administrative receiver if required).

(4) The administrative receiver shall, on request, furnish each [nominated person] with [the forms required for the preparation of the statement of affairs].

NOTES

Initial Commencement

Specified date

Specified date: 29 December 1986: see r 0.1.

Amendment

Para (1): word "Where" in square brackets substituted by SI 1987/1919, r 3(1), Schedule, Pt 1, para 25(1).

Para (2): words "nominated persons" words in square brackets substituted by SI 2010/686, r 2, Sch 1, para 113(1), (2).
    Date in force: 6 April 2010: see SI 2010/686, r 1; for transitional provisions see r 6(1), Sch 4, paras 1, 2(1)(b) thereto.

Para (3): words "nominated persons" in square brackets in both places they occur substituted by SI 2010/686, r 2, Sch 1, para 113(1), (2).
    Date in force: 6 April 2010: see SI 2010/686, r 1; for transitional provisions see r 6(1), Sch 4, paras 1, 2(1)(b) thereto.

Para (4): words "nominated person" in square brackets substituted by SI 2010/686, r 2, Sch 1, para 113(1), (3).
    Date in force: 6 April 2010: see SI 2010/686, r 1; for transitional provisions see r 6(1), Sch 4, paras 1, 2(1)(b) thereto.

Para (4): words "the forms required for the preparation of the statement of affairs" in square brackets substituted by SI 1987/1919, r 3(1), Schedule, Pt 1, para 25(2).

3.4 Verification and filing

(1) The statement of affairs shall be in Form 3.2, shall contain all the particulars required by that form and shall be verified by [a statement of truth] by the [nominated persons] (using the same form).

(2) The administrative receiver may require any of the persons mentioned in section 47(3) to submit [a statement of concurrence], stating that he concurs [with the statement of affairs].

(3) [A statement] of concurrence may be qualified in respect of matters dealt with in the statement of affairs, where the maker of [the statement of concurrence] is not in agreement with the [nominated persons], or he considers the statement to be erroneous or misleading, or he is without the direct knowledge necessary for concurring with it.

(4) The statement of affairs shall be delivered to the receiver by the [nominated person] making the [statement of truth] (or by one of them, if more than one), together with a copy of the verified statement.

(5) Every [statement] of concurrence shall be delivered by the person who makes it, together with a copy.

(6) The administrative receiver shall retain the verified copy of the statement [of affairs] and the [statements] of concurrence (if any) as part of the records of the receivership.

NOTES

Initial Commencement

Specified date

Specified date: 29 December 1986: see r 0.1.

Amendment

Para (1): words "a statement of truth" in square brackets substituted by SI 2010/686, r 2, Sch 1, para 114(1), (2)(a).
　　Date in force: 6 April 2010: see SI 2010/686, r 1; for transitional provisions see r 6(1), Sch 4, paras 1, 2(1)(b) thereto.
Para (1): words "nominated persons" in square brackets substituted by SI 2010/686, r 2, Sch 1, para 114(1), (2)(b).
　　Date in force: 6 April 2010: see SI 2010/686, r 1; for transitional provisions see r 6(1), Sch 4, paras 1, 2(1)(b) thereto.
Para (2): words "a statement of concurrence" in square brackets substituted by SI 2010/686, r 2, Sch 1, para 114(1), (3)(a).
　　Date in force: 6 April 2010: see SI 2010/686, r 1; for transitional provisions see r 6(1), Sch 4, paras 1, 2(1)(b) thereto.
Para (2): words "with the statement of affairs" in square brackets substituted by SI 2010/686, r 2, Sch 1, para 114(1), (3)(b).
　　Date in force: 6 April 2010: see SI 2010/686, r 1; for transitional provisions see r 6(1), Sch 4, paras 1, 2(1)(b) thereto.
Para (3): words "A statement" in square brackets substituted by SI 2010/686, r 2, Sch 1, para 114(1), (4)(a).
　　Date in force: 6 April 2010: see SI 2010/686, r 1; for transitional provisions see r 6(1), Sch 4, paras 1, 2(1)(b) thereto.
Para (3): words "the statement of concurrence" in square brackets substituted by SI 2010/686, r 2, Sch 1, para 114(1), (4)(b).
　　Date in force: 6 April 2010: see SI 2010/686, r 1; for transitional provisions see r 6(1), Sch 4, paras 1, 2(1)(b) thereto.
Para (3): words "nominated persons" in square brackets substituted by SI 2010/686, r 2, Sch 1, para 114(1), (4)(c).
　　Date in force: 6 April 2010: see SI 2010/686, r 1; for transitional provisions see r 6(1), Sch 4, paras 1, 2(1)(b) thereto.
Para (4): words "nominated person" in square brackets substituted by SI 2010/686, r 2, Sch 1, para 114(1), (5)(a).
　　Date in force: 6 April 2010: see SI 2010/686, r 1; for transitional provisions see r 6(1), Sch 4, paras 1, 2(1)(b) thereto.
Para (4): words "statement of truth" in square brackets substituted by SI 2010/686, r 2, Sch 1, para 114(1), (5)(b).
　　Date in force: 6 April 2010: see SI 2010/686, r 1; for transitional provisions see r 6(1), Sch 4, paras 1, 2(1)(b) thereto.
Para (5): word "statement" in square brackets substituted by SI 2010/686, r 2, Sch 1, para 114(1), (6).
　　Date in force: 6 April 2010: see SI 2010/686, r 1; for transitional provisions see r 6(1), Sch 4, paras 1, 2(1)(b) thereto.
Para (6): words "of affairs" in square brackets inserted by SI 2010/686, r 2, Sch 1, para 114(1), (7)(a).
　　Date in force: 6 April 2010: see SI 2010/686, r 1; for transitional provisions see r 6(1), Sch 4, paras 1, 2(1)(b) thereto.
Para (6): word "statements" in square brackets substituted by SI 2010/686, r 2, Sch 1, para 114(1), (7)(b).
　　Date in force: 6 April 2010: see SI 2010/686, r 1; for transitional provisions see r 6(1), Sch 4, paras 1, 2(1)(b) thereto.

3.5 Limited disclosure

(1) Where the administrative receiver thinks that it would prejudice the conduct of the receivership [or might reasonably be expected to lead to violence against any

person] for the whole or part of the statement of affairs to be disclosed, he may apply to the court for an order of limited disclosure in respect of the statement or a specified part of it.

(2) The court may on the application order that the statement, or, as the case may be, the specified part of it, be not open to inspection otherwise than with [permission] of the court.

(3) The court's order may include directions as to the delivery of documents to the registrar of companies and the disclosure of relevant information to other persons.

NOTES

Initial Commencement

Specified date

Specified date: 29 December 1986: see r 0.1.

Amendment

Para (1): words "or might reasonably be expected to lead to violence against any person" in square brackets inserted by SI 2010/686, r 2, Sch 1, para 115.
Date in force: 6 April 2010: see SI 2010/686, r 1; for transitional provisions see r 6(1), Sch 4, para 1 thereto.
Para (2): word "permission" in square brackets substituted by SI 2010/686, r 2, Sch 1, para 1.
Date in force: 6 April 2010: see SI 2010/686, r 1; for transitional provisions see r 6(1), Sch 4, paras 1, 2(1)(b) thereto.

3.6 Release from duty to submit statement of affairs; extension of time

(1) The power of the administrative receiver under section 47(5) to give a release from the obligation imposed by that section, or to grant an extension of time, may be exercised at the receiver's own discretion, or at the request of any [nominated person].

(2) A [nominated person] may, if he requests a release or extension of time and it is refused by the receiver, apply to the court for it.

(3) The court may, if it thinks that no sufficient cause is shown for the application, dismiss it; but it shall not do so unless the applicant has had an opportunity to attend the court for [a hearing without notice to any other party], of which he has been given at least [5 business] days' notice.

If the application is not dismissed under this paragraph, the court shall fix a venue for it to be heard, and give notice to the [nominated person] accordingly.

(4) The [nominated person] shall, at least 14 days before the hearing, send to the receiver a notice stating the venue and accompanied by a copy of the application, and of any evidence which he (the [nominated person]) intends to adduce in support of it.

(5) The receiver may appear and be heard on the application; and, whether or not he appears, he may file a written report of any matters which he considers ought to be drawn to the court's attention.

If such a report is filed, a copy of it shall be sent by the receiver to the [nominated person], not later than 5 [business] days before the hearing.

(6) Sealed copies of any order made on the application shall be sent by the court to the [nominated person] and the receiver.

(7) On any application under this Rule the applicant's costs shall be paid in any event by him and, unless the court otherwise orders, no allowance towards them shall be made out of the assets under the administrative receiver's control.

NOTES

Initial Commencement

Specified date

Specified date: 29 December 1986: see r 0.1.

Amendment

Para (1): words "nominated person" in square brackets substituted by SI 2010/686, r 2, Sch 1, para 116(1), (2).
Date in force: 6 April 2010: see SI 2010/686, r 1; for transitional provisions see r 6(1), Sch 4, paras 1, 2(1)(b) thereto.

Para (2): words "nominated person" in square brackets substituted by SI 2010/686, r 2, Sch 1, para 116(1), (2).
Date in force: 6 April 2010: see SI 2010/686, r 1; for transitional provisions see r 6(1), Sch 4, paras 1, 2(1)(b) thereto.

Para (3): words "a hearing without notice to any other party" in square brackets substituted by SI 2010/686, r 2, Sch 1, para 116(1), (3)(a).
Date in force: 6 April 2010: see SI 2010/686, r 1; for transitional provisions see r 6(1), Sch 4, paras 1, 2(1)(b) thereto.

Para (3): words "5 business" in square brackets substituted by SI 2010/686, r 2, Sch 1, para 116(1), (3)(b).
Date in force: 6 April 2010: see SI 2010/686, r 1; for transitional provisions see r 6(1), Sch 4, para 1 thereto.

Para (3): words "nominated person" in square brackets substituted by SI 2010/686, r 2, Sch 1, para 116(1), (2).
Date in force: 6 April 2010: see SI 2010/686, r 1; for transitional provisions see r 6(1), Sch 4, paras 1, 2(1)(b) thereto.

Para (4): words "nominated person" in square brackets in both places they occur substituted by SI 2010/686, r 2, Sch 1, para 116(1), (2).
Date in force: 6 April 2010: see SI 2010/686, r 1; for transitional provisions see r 6(1), Sch 4, paras 1, 2(1)(b) thereto.

Para (5): words "nominated person" in square brackets substituted by SI 2010/686, r 2, Sch 1, para 116(1), (2).
Date in force: 6 April 2010: see SI 2010/686, r 1; for transitional provisions see r 6(1), Sch 4, paras 1, 2(1)(b) thereto.

Para (5): word "business" in square brackets inserted by SI 2010/686, r 2, Sch 1, para 116(1), (4).
Date in force: 6 April 2010: see SI 2010/686, r 1; for transitional provisions see r 6(1), Sch 4, para 1 thereto.

Para (6): words "nominated person" in square brackets substituted by SI 2010/686, r 2, Sch 1, para 116(1), (2).
Date in force: 6 April 2010: see SI 2010/686, r 1; for transitional provisions see r 6(1), Sch 4, paras 1, 2(1)(b) thereto.

3.7 Expenses of statement of affairs

(1) A [nominated person] making the statement of affairs and [statement of truth] shall be allowed, and paid by the administrative receiver out of his receipts, any expenses incurred by the [nominated person] in so doing which the receiver thinks reasonable.

(2) Any decision by the receiver under this Rule is subject to appeal to the court.

(3) Nothing in this Rule relieves a [nominated person] from any obligation with respect to the preparation, verification and submission of the statement of affairs, or to the provision of information to the receiver.

NOTES

Initial Commencement

Specified date

Specified date: 29 December 1986: see r 0.1.

Amendment

Para (1): words "nominated person" in square brackets in both places they occur substituted by SI 2010/686, r 2, Sch 1, para 117(1), (2)(a).
Date in force: 6 April 2010: see SI 2010/686, r 1; for transitional provisions see r 6(1), Sch 4, paras 1, 2(1)(b) thereto.
Para (1): words "statement of truth" in square brackets substituted by SI 2010/686, r 2, Sch 1, para 117(1), (2)(b).
Date in force: 6 April 2010: see SI 2010/686, r 1; for transitional provisions see r 6(1), Sch 4, paras 1, 2(1)(b) thereto.
Para (3): words "nominated person" in square brackets substituted by SI 2010/686, r 2, Sch 1, para 117(1), (3).
Date in force: 6 April 2010: see SI 2010/686, r 1; for transitional provisions see r 6(1), Sch 4, paras 1, 2(1)(b) thereto.

3.8 Report to creditors

[(1) If an administrative receiver gives notice under section 48(2)(b), the notice—
  (a) shall be gazetted; and
  (b) may be advertised in such other manner as the administrative receiver thinks fit.]

[(1A) In addition to the standard contents, the notice under paragraph (1) must state that creditors can write for a copy of the report and the address to which to write.]

(2) If he proposes to apply to the court to dispense with the holding of the meeting of unsecured creditors (otherwise required by section 48(2)), he shall in his report to creditors or (as the case may be) in the notice published as above, state the venue fixed by the court for the hearing of the application.

(3) Subject to any order of the court under Rule 3.5, the copy of the receiver's report which under section 48(1) is to be sent to the registrar of companies shall have attached to it a copy of any statement of affairs under section 47, and copies of any [statements] of concurrence.

(4) If the statement of affairs or [statements] of concurrence, if any, have not been submitted to the receiver by the time he sends a copy of his report to the registrar of companies, he shall send a copy of the statement [of affairs] and any [statements] of concurrence as soon thereafter as he receives them.

[(5) The receiver's report under section 48(1) shall state, to the best of his knowledge and belief—
  (a) an estimate of the value of the prescribed part (whether or not he proposes to make an application under section 176A(5) or whether section 176A(3) applies); and
  (b) an estimate of the value of the company's net property.

(6) Nothing in this Rule is to be taken as requiring any such estimate to include any information, the disclosure of which could seriously prejudice the commercial interests of the company.

If such information is excluded from the calculation the estimate shall be accompanied by a statement to that effect.

(7) The report shall also state whether, and if so why, the receiver proposes to make an application to court under section 176A(5).]

NOTES

Initial Commencement

Specified date

Specified date: 29 December 1986: see r 0.1.

Amendment

Para (1): substituted by SI 2009/642, rr 4, 15.
Date in force: 6 April 2009: see SI 2009/642, r 1; for transitional provisions see r 3 thereof.
Para (1A): inserted by SI 2010/686, r 2, Sch 1, para 118(1), (3).
Date in force: 6 April 2010: see SI 2010/686, r 1; for transitional provisions see r 6(1), Sch 4, para 1 thereto.
Para (3): word "statements" in square brackets substituted by SI 2010/686, r 2, Sch 1, para 118(1), (2).
Date in force: 6 April 2010: see SI 2010/686, r 1; for transitional provisions see r 6(1), Sch 4, para 1 thereto.
Para (4): word "statements" in square brackets in both places it occurs substituted by SI 2010/686, r 2, Sch 1, para 118(1), (2).
Date in force: 6 April 2010: see SI 2010/686, r 1; for transitional provisions see r 6(1), Sch 4, para 1 thereto.
Para (4): words "of affairs" in square brackets inserted by SI 2010/686, r 2, Sch 1, para 118(1), (4).
Date in force: 6 April 2010: see SI 2010/686, r 1; for transitional provisions see r 6(1), Sch 4, para 1 thereto.
Paras (5)–(7): inserted by SI 2003/1730, r 6, Sch 1, Pt 3, para 10.
Date in force: 15 September 2003: see SI 2003/1730, r 1(2).

CHAPTER 3

CREDITORS' MEETING

3.9 Procedure for summoning meeting under s 48(2)

(1) In fixing the venue for a meeting of creditors summoned under section 48(2), the administrative receiver shall have regard to the convenience of the persons who are invited to attend.

(2) The meeting shall be summoned for commencement between 10.00 and 16.00 hours on a business day, unless the court otherwise directs.

(3) At least 14 days' notice of the venue shall be given to all creditors of the company who . . . are known to the receiver and had claims against the company at the date of his appointment.

(4) With the notice summoning the meeting there shall be sent out forms of proxy.

(5) The notice shall include a statement to the effect that creditors whose claims are wholly secured are not entitled to attend or be represented at the meeting.

[(6) The administrative receiver—

- (a) as soon as reasonably practicable must also have gazetted a notice of the meeting; and
- (b) may advertise the notice of the meeting in such other manner as the administrative receiver thinks fit.

(6A) In addition to the standard contents, the notice under paragraph (6) must—

- (a) state that a meeting under section 48(2) is to take place;
- (b) include the statement required by paragraph (5); and
- (c) state the venue for the meeting.]

(7) The notice to creditors and the [notice given under paragraph (6)] shall contain a statement of the effect of Rule 3.11(1) below (voting rights).

NOTES

Initial Commencement

Specified date
  Specified date: 29 December 1986: see r 0.1.

Amendment
  Para (3): words omitted revoked by SI 2010/686, r 2, Sch 1, para 119(1), (2).
    Date in force: 6 April 2010: see SI 2010/686, r 1; for transitional provisions see r 6(1), Sch 4, para 1 thereto.
  Paras (6), (6A): substituted, for para (6) as previously enacted, by SI 2010/686, r 2, Sch 1, para 119(1), (3).
    Date in force: 6 April 2010: see SI 2010/686, r 1; for transitional provisions see r 6(1), Sch 4, para 1 thereto.
  Para (7): words "notice given under paragraph (6)" in square brackets substituted by SI 2009/642, rr 4, 16(b).
    Date in force: 6 April 2009: see SI 2009/642, r 1; for transitional provisions see r 3 thereof.

3.10 The chairman at the meeting

(1) The chairman at the creditors' meeting shall be the receiver, or a person nominated by him in writing to act in his place.

(2) A person so nominated must be either—
  (a) one who is qualified to act as an insolvency practitioner in relation to the company, or
  (b) an employee of the receiver or his firm who is experienced in insolvency matters.

NOTES

Initial Commencement

Specified date
  Specified date: 29 December 1986: see r 0.1.

3.11 Voting rights

(1) Subject as follows, at the creditors' meeting a person is entitled to vote only if—
  (a) he has given to the receiver, not later than 12.00 hours on the business day before the day fixed for the meeting, details in writing of the debt that he claims to be due to him from the company, and the claim has been duly admitted under [Rule 3.12 or] this Rule, and
  (b) there has been lodged with the administrative receiver any proxy which the creditor intends to be used on his behalf,
[and details of the debt must include any calculation for the purposes of paragraphs (6) and (7)].

(2) The chairman of the meeting may allow a creditor to vote, notwithstanding that he has failed to comply with paragraph (1)(a), if satisfied that the failure was due to circumstances beyond the creditor's control.

(3) The receiver or (if other) the chairman of the meeting may call for any document or other evidence to be produced to him where he thinks it necessary for the purpose of substantiating the whole or any part of the claim.

(4) Votes are calculated according to the amount of a creditor's debt as at the date of the appointment of the receiver, after deducting any amounts paid in respect of that debt after that date.

(5) A creditor shall not vote in respect of a debt for an unliquidated amount, or any debt whose value is not ascertained, except where the chairman agrees to put upon the debt an estimated minimum value for the purpose of entitlement to vote and admits the claim for that purpose.

[(5A) No vote may be cast by virtue of a claim more than once on any resolution put to the meeting.]

(6) A secured creditor is entitled to vote only in respect of the balance (if any) of his debt after deducting the value of his security as estimated by him.

(7) A creditor shall not vote in respect of a debt on, or secured by, a current bill of exchange or promissory note, unless he is willing—

(a) to treat the liability to him on the bill or note of every person who is liable on it antecedently to the company, and against whom a bankruptcy order has not been made (or, in the case of a company, which has not gone into liquidation), as a security in his hands, and

(b) to estimate the value of the security and, for the purpose of his entitlement to vote [(but not for dividend)], to deduct it from his claim.

NOTES

Initial Commencement

Specified date

Specified date: 29 December 1986: see r 0.1.

Amendment

Para (1): in sub-para (a) words "Rule 3.12 or" in square brackets substituted by SI 2010/686, r 2, Sch 1, para 120(1), (2).
Date in force: 6 April 2010: see SI 2010/686, r 1; for transitional provisions see r 6(1), Sch 4, para 1 thereto.

Para (1): words from "and details of" to "paragraphs (6) and (7)" in square brackets inserted by SI 2010/686, r 2, Sch 1, para 120(1), (3).
Date in force: 6 April 2010: see SI 2010/686, r 1; for transitional provisions see r 6(1), Sch 4, para 1 thereto.

Para (5A): inserted by SI 2010/686, r 2, Sch 1, para 120(1), (4).
Date in force: 6 April 2010: see SI 2010/686, r 1; for transitional provisions see r 6(1), Sch 4, para 1 thereto.

Para (7): in sub-para (b) words "(but not for dividend)" in square brackets inserted by SI 2010/686, r 2, Sch 1, para 120(1), (5).
Date in force: 6 April 2010: see SI 2010/686, r 1; for transitional provisions see r 6(1), Sch 4, para 1 thereto.

[3.11A Contents of claim]

[(1) The following matters must be stated in a creditor's claim under Rule 3.11—

(a) the creditor's name and address, and, if a company, its company registration number;

(b) the total amount of the claim (including any value added tax) as at the date of the appointment of the receiver, less all trade and other discounts available to the company, or which would have been available to the company but for the appointment, except for any discount for immediate, early or cash settlement;

(c) whether or not that amount includes outstanding uncapitalised interest;

(d) particulars of how and when the debt was incurred by the company;

(e) particulars of any security held, the date when it was given and the value which the creditor puts upon it;

(f) details of any reservation of title in respect of goods to which the debt refers; and

(g) the name, and address and authority of the person making out the claim (if other than the creditor himself).

(2) The claim must specify any documents by reference to which the debt can be substantiated; but it is not essential that such documents be attached to the claim or submitted with it.]

NOTES
Amendment
> Inserted by SI 2010/686, r 2, Sch 1, para 121.
> Date in force: 6 April 2010: see SI 2010/686, r 1; for transitional provisions see r 6(1), Sch 4, para 1 thereto.

3.12 Admission and rejection of claim

(1) At the creditors' meeting the chairman has power to admit or reject a creditor's claim for the purpose of his entitlement to vote; and the power is exercisable with respect to the whole or any part of the claim.

(2) The chairman's decision under this Rule, or in respect of any matter arising under Rule 3.11, is subject to appeal to the court by any creditor.

(3) If the chairman is in doubt whether a claim should be admitted or rejected, he shall mark it as objected to and allow the creditor to vote, subject to his vote being subsequently declared invalid if the objection to the claim is sustained.

(4) If on an appeal the chairman's decision is reversed or varied, or a creditor's vote is declared invalid, the court may order that another meeting be summoned, or make such other order as it thinks just.

[(4A) An application to the court by way of appeal under this Rule against a decision of the chairman must be made not later than 21 days after the date of the meeting.]

(5) Neither the receiver nor any person nominated by him to be chairman is personally liable for costs incurred by any person in respect of an appeal to the court under this Rule, unless the court makes an order to that effect.

NOTES
Initial Commencement
Specified date
> Specified date: 29 December 1986: see r 0.1.

Amendment
> Para (4A): inserted by SI 2010/686, r 2, Sch 1, para 122.
> Date in force: 6 April 2010: see SI 2010/686, r 1; for transitional provisions see r 6(1), Sch 4, para 1 thereto.

3.14 Adjournment

(1) The creditors' meeting shall not be adjourned, even if no quorum is present, unless the chairman decides that it is desirable; and in that case he shall adjourn it to such date, time and place as he thinks fit.

(2) Rule 3.9(1) and (2) applies, with necessary modifications, to any adjourned meeting.

[(2A) Once only in the course of a meeting the chairman may, without an adjournment, declare it suspended for any period up to 1 hour.]

(3) If there is no quorum, and the meeting is not adjourned, it is deemed to have been duly summoned and held.

NOTES

Initial Commencement

Specified date

Specified date: 29 December 1986: see r 0.1.

Amendment

Para (2A): inserted by SI 2010/686, r 2, Sch 1, para 123.
Date in force: 6 April 2010: see SI 2010/686, r 1; for transitional provisions see r 6(1), Sch 4, para 1 thereto.

3.15 Resolutions and minutes

(1) At the creditors' meeting, a resolution is passed when a majority (in value) of those present and voting in person or by proxy have voted in favour of it.

(2) The chairman of the meeting shall cause a record to be made of the proceedings [(including of every resolution passed)], and kept as part of the records of the receivership.

(3) The record shall include a list of the creditors who attended (personally or by proxy) and, if a creditors' committee has been established, the names and addresses of those elected to be members of the committee.

NOTES

Initial Commencement

Specified date

Specified date: 29 December 1986: see r 0.1.

Amendment

Para (2): words "(including of every resolution passed)" in square brackets inserted by SI 2010/686, r 2, Sch 1, para 124.
Date in force: 6 April 2010: see SI 2010/686, r 1; for transitional provisions see r 6(1), Sch 4, para 1 thereto.

CHAPTER 4

THE CREDITORS' COMMITTEE

3.16 Constitution of committee

(1) Where it is resolved by the creditors' meeting to establish a creditors' committee, the committee shall consist of at least 3 and not more than 5 creditors of the company elected at the meeting.

[(2) A person claiming to be a creditor is entitled to be a member of the committee provided that—
  (a) that person's claim has not been wholly disallowed for voting purposes; and
  (b) the claim mentioned in sub-paragraph (a) is not fully secured.]

(3) A body corporate may be a member of the committee, but it cannot act as such otherwise than by a representative appointed under Rule 3.21 below.

NOTES

Initial Commencement

Specified date

Specified date: 29 December 1986: see r 0.1.

Amendment

Para (2): substituted by SI 2010/686, r 2, Sch 1, para 125.
Date in force: 6 April 2010: see SI 2010/686, r 1; for transitional provisions see r 6(1), Sch 4, para 1 thereto.

3.17 Formalities of establishment

(1) The creditors' committee does not come into being, and accordingly cannot act, until the administrative receiver has issued a certificate of its due constitution.

[(1A) If the chairman of the creditors' meeting which resolves to establish the committee is not the administrative receiver, the chairman must as soon as reasonably practicable give notice of the resolution to the receiver and inform the receiver of the names and addresses of the persons elected to be members of the committee.]

[(2) No person may act as a member of the committee unless and until he has agreed to do so and, unless the relevant proxy or authorisation contains a statement to the contrary, such agreement may be given by his proxy-holder . . . present at the meeting establishing the committee [or, in the case of a corporation, by its duly appointed representative].

(2A) The receiver's certificate of the committee's due constitution shall not [be issued before the minimum number of members set out in Rule 3.16 elected] to be members of the committee have agreed to act [and must be issued as soon as reasonably practicable thereafter].]

(3) As and when the others (if any) agree to act, the receiver shall issue an amended certificate.

(4) The certificate, and any amended certificate, shall be sent by the receiver to the registrar of companies [as soon as reasonably practicable].

(5) If, after the first establishment of the committee, there is any change in its membership, [as soon as reasonably practicable] the receiver shall report the change to the registrar of companies.

NOTES

Initial Commencement

Specified date

Specified date: 29 December 1986: see r 0.1.

Amendment

Para (1A): inserted by SI 2010/686, r 2, Sch 1, para 126(1), (2).
Date in force: 6 April 2010: see SI 2010/686, r 1; for transitional provisions see r 6(1), Sch 4, para 1 thereto.

Paras (2), (2A): substituted, for para (2) as originally enacted, by SI 1987/1919, r 3(1), Schedule, Part 1, para 27.

Para (2): words omitted revoked by SI 2010/686, r 2, Sch 1, para 126(1), (3)(a).
Date in force: 6 April 2010: see SI 2010/686, r 1; for transitional provisions see r 6(1), Sch 4, para 1 thereto.

Para (2): words "or, in the case of a corporation, by its duly appointed representative" in square brackets inserted by SI 2010/686, r 2, Sch 1, para 126(1), (3)(b).
Date in force: 6 April 2010: see SI 2010/686, r 1; for transitional provisions see r 6(1), Sch 4, para 1 thereto.

Para (2A): words "be issued before the minimum number of members set out in Rule 3.16 elected" in square brackets substituted by SI 2010/686, r 2, Sch 1, para 126(1), (4)(a).
Date in force: 6 April 2010: see SI 2010/686, r 1; for transitional provisions see r 6(1), Sch 4, para 1 thereto.
Para (2A): words "and must be issued as soon as reasonably practicable thereafter" in square brackets inserted by SI 2010/686, r 2, Sch 1, para 126(1), (4)(b).
Date in force: 6 April 2010: see SI 2010/686, r 1; for transitional provisions see r 6(1), Sch 4, para 1 thereto.
Para (4): words "as soon as reasonably practicable" in square brackets inserted by SI 2010/686, r 2, Sch 1, para 126(1), (5).
Date in force: 6 April 2010: see SI 2010/686, r 1; for transitional provisions see r 6(1), Sch 4, para 1 thereto.
Para (5): words "as soon as reasonably practicable" in square brackets inserted by SI 2010/686, r 2, Sch 1, para 126(1), (6).
Date in force: 6 April 2010: see SI 2010/686, r 1; for transitional provisions see r 6(1), Sch 4, para 1 thereto.

3.18 Functions and meetings of the committee

(1) [In addition to any functions conferred on the creditors' committee by any provision of the Act,] the creditors' committee shall assist the administrative receiver in discharging his functions, and act in relation to him in such manner as may be agreed from time to time.

(2) Subject as follows, meetings of the committee shall be held when and where determined by the receiver.

[(3) The receiver must call a first meeting of the committee to take place within 6 weeks of the committee's establishment.

(3A) After the calling of the first meeting, the receiver must call a meeting—

(a) if so requested by a member of the committee or the member's representative (the meeting then to be held within 21 days of the request being received by the receiver); and

(b) for a specified date, if the committee has previously resolved that a meeting be held on that date.]

(4) [Subject to paragraph (5),] the receiver shall give [5 business] days' written notice of the venue of any meeting to every member (or his representative designated for that purpose), unless in any case the requirement of notice has been waived by or on behalf of any member.

Waiver may be signified either at or before the meeting.

[(5) Where the receiver has determined that a meeting should be conducted and held in the manner referred to in Rule 12A.26(2), the notice period mentioned in paragraph (4) is 7 business days.]

NOTES

Initial Commencement

Specified date

Specified date: 29 December 1986: see r 0.1.

Amendment

Para (1): words from "In addition to" to "of the Act," in square brackets inserted by SI 2010/686, r 2, Sch 1, para 127(1), (2).
Date in force: 6 April 2010: see SI 2010/686, r 1; for transitional provisions see r 6(1), Sch 4, para 1 thereto.
Paras (3), (3A): substituted, for para (3) as originally enacted, by SI 2010/686, r 2, Sch 1, para 127(1), (3).
Date in force: 6 April 2010: see SI 2010/686, r 1; for transitional provisions see r 6(1), Sch 4, para 1 thereto.
Para (4): words "Subject to paragraph (5)," in square brackets inserted by SI 2010/686, r 2, Sch 1, para 127(1), (4)(a).

Date in force: 6 April 2010: see SI 2010/686, r 1; for transitional provisions see r 6(1), Sch 4, para 1 thereto.
Para (4): words "5 business" in square brackets substituted by SI 2010/686, r 2, Sch 1, para 127(1), (4)(b).
Date in force: 6 April 2010: see SI 2010/686, r 1; for transitional provisions see r 6(1), Sch 4, para 1 thereto.
Para (5): inserted by SI 2010/686, r 2, Sch 1, para 127(1), (5).
Date in force: 6 April 2010: see SI 2010/686, r 1; for transitional provisions see r 6(1), Sch 4, para 1 thereto.

3.19 The chairman at meetings

[(1) The chairman at any meeting of the creditors' committee must be the administrative receiver, or a person appointed by the receiver in writing to act.]

(2) A person so [appointed] must be either—

(a) one who is qualified to act as an insolvency practitioner in relation to the company, or

(b) an employee of the receiver or his firm who is experienced in insolvency matters.

NOTES

Initial Commencement

Specified date

Specified date: 29 December 1986: see r 0.1.

Amendment

Para (1): substituted by SI 2010/686, r 2, Sch 1, para 128(1), (2).
Date in force: 6 April 2010: see SI 2010/686, r 1; for transitional provisions see r 6(1), Sch 4, para 1 thereto.
Para (2): word "appointed" in square brackets substituted by SI 2010/686, r 2, Sch 1, para 128(1), (3).
Date in force: 6 April 2010: see SI 2010/686, r 1; for transitional provisions see r 6(1), Sch 4, para 1 thereto.

3.20 Quorum

A meeting of the committee is duly constituted if due notice has been given to all the members, and at least 2 members are present or represented.

NOTES

Initial Commencement

Specified date

Specified date: 29 December 1986: see r 0.1.

3.21 Committee-members' representatives

(1) A member of the committee may, in relation to the business of the committee, be represented by another person duly authorised by him for that purpose.

(2) A person acting as a committee-member's representative must hold a letter of authority entitling him so to act (either generally or specially) and [authenticated] by or on behalf of the committee-member [, and for this purpose any proxy . . . in relation to any meeting of creditors of the company shall, unless it contains a statement to the contrary, be treated as a letter of authority to act generally [authenticated] by or on behalf of the committee-member].

(3) The chairman at any meeting of the committee may call on a person claiming to act as a committee-member's representative to produce his letter of authority, and may exclude him if it appears that his authority is deficient.

[(4) No member may be represented by—
- (a) another member of the committee;
- (b) a person who is at the same time representing another committee member;
- (c) a body corporate;
- (d) an undischarged bankrupt;
- (e) a disqualified director; or
- (f) a person who is subject to a bankruptcy restrictions order (including an interim order), a bankruptcy restrictions undertaking, a debt relief restrictions order (including an interim order) or a debt relief restrictions undertaking.]

(5) . . .

(6) Where a member's representative [authenticates] any document on the member's behalf, the fact that he so [authenticates] must be stated below his [authentication].

NOTES

Initial Commencement

Specified date

Specified date: 29 December 1986: see r 0.1.

Amendment

Para (2): word "authenticated" in square brackets in both places it occurs substituted by SI 2010/686, r 2, Sch 1, para 1.
Date in force: 6 April 2010: see SI 2010/686, r 1; for transitional provisions see r 6(1), Sch 4, paras 1, 2(1)(b) thereto.

Para (2): words from ", and for this purpose" to "the committee-member" in square brackets inserted by SI 1987/1919, r 3(1), Schedule, Pt 1, para 28.

Para (2): words omitted revoked by SI 2010/686, r 2, Sch 1, para 129(1), (2).
Date in force: 6 April 2010: see SI 2010/686, r 1; for transitional provisions see r 6(1), Sch 4, para 1 thereto.

Para (4): substituted by SI 2010/686, r 2, Sch 1, para 129(1), (3).
Date in force: 6 April 2010: see SI 2010/686, r 1; for transitional provisions see r 6(1), Sch 4, para 1 thereto.

Para (5): revoked by SI 2010/686, r 2, Sch 1, para 129(1), (4).
Date in force: 6 April 2010: see SI 2010/686, r 1; for transitional provisions see r 6(1), Sch 4, para 1 thereto.

Para (6): word "authenticates" in square brackets in both places it occurs substituted by SI 2010/686, r 2, Sch 1, para 1.
Date in force: 6 April 2010: see SI 2010/686, r 1; for transitional provisions see r 6(1), Sch 4, paras 1, 2(1)(b) thereto.

Para (6): word "authentication" in square brackets substituted by SI 2010/686, r 2, Sch 1, para 1.
Date in force: 6 April 2010: see SI 2010/686, r 1; for transitional provisions see r 6(1), Sch 4, paras 1, 2(1)(b) thereto.

3.22 Resignation

A member of the committee may resign by notice in writing delivered to the administrative receiver.

NOTES

Initial Commencement

Specified date

Specified date: 29 December 1986: see r 0.1.

3.23 Termination of membership

(1) Membership of the creditors' committee is automatically terminated if the member—

(a) becomes bankrupt. . ., or
(b) at 3 consecutive meetings of the committee is neither present nor represented (unless at the third of those meetings it is resolved that this Rule is not to apply in his case), or
[(c) ceases to be a creditor and a period of 3 months has elapsed from the date that that member ceased to be a creditor or is found never to have been a creditor].

(2) However, if the cause of termination is the member's bankruptcy, his trustee in bankruptcy replaces him as a member of the committee.

NOTES

Initial Commencement

Specified date

Specified date: 29 December 1986: see r 0.1.

Amendment

Para (1): in sub-para (a) words omitted revoked by SI 2004/584, r 7.
Date in force: 1 April 2004: see SI 2004/584, r 1(2).
Para (1): sub-para (c) substituted by SI 2010/686, r 2, Sch 1, para 130.
Date in force: 6 April 2010: see SI 2010/686, r 1; for transitional provisions see r 6(1), Sch 4, para 1 thereto.

3.24 Removal

A member of the committee may be removed by resolution at a meeting of creditors, at least 14 days' notice having been given of the intention to move that resolution.

NOTES

Initial Commencement

Specified date

Specified date: 29 December 1986: see r 0.1.

3.25 Vacancies

(1) The following applies if there is a vacancy in the membership of the creditors' committee.

(2) The vacancy need not be filled if the administrative receiver and a majority of the remaining members of the committee so agree, provided that the total number of members does not fall below [3].

(3) The receiver may appoint any creditor (being qualified under the Rules to be a member of the committee) to fill the vacancy, if a majority of the other members of the committee agree to the appointment and the creditor concerned consents to act.

[(4) Alternatively, a meeting of creditors may resolve that a creditor be appointed (with that creditor's consent) to fill the vacancy. In this case at least 14 days' notice must have been given of a resolution to make such an appointment (whether or not of a person named in the notice).

(5) Where the vacancy is filled by an appointment made by a creditors' meeting at which the receiver is not present, the chairman of the meeting must report to the receiver the appointment which has been made.]

NOTES

Initial Commencement

Specified date

Specified date: 29 December 1986: see r 0.1.

Amendment

Para (2): reference to "3" in square brackets substituted by SI 2010/686, r 2, Sch 1, para 131(1), (2).
Date in force: 6 April 2010: see SI 2010/686, r 1; for transitional provisions see r 6(1), Sch 4, para 1 thereto.
Paras (4), (5): inserted by SI 2010/686, r 2, Sch 1, para 131(1), (3).
Date in force: 6 April 2010: see SI 2010/686, r 1; for transitional provisions see r 6(1), Sch 4, para 1 thereto.

3.26 Procedure at meetings

(1) At any meeting of the committee, each member of it (whether present himself or by his representative) has one vote; and a resolution is passed when a majority of the members present or represented have voted in favour of it.

[(2) Every resolution passed must be recorded in writing and authenticated by the chairman, either separately or as part of the minutes of the meeting and the record must be kept with the records of the proceedings.]

NOTES

Initial Commencement

Specified date

Specified date: 29 December 1986: see r 0.1.

Amendment

Para (2): substituted, for paras (2), (3) as originally enacted, by SI 2010/686, r 2, Sch 1, para 132.
Date in force: 6 April 2010: see SI 2010/686, r 1; for transitional provisions see r 6(1), Sch 4, para 1 thereto.

3.27 Resolutions [otherwise than at a meeting]

(1) In accordance with this Rule, the administrative receiver may seek to obtain the agreement of members of the creditors' committee to a resolution by sending to every member (or his representative designated for the purpose) a copy of the proposed resolution.

(2) Where the receiver makes use of the procedure allowed by this Rule, he shall send out to members of the committee or their representatives (as the case may be) [a copy of any proposed resolution on which a decision is sought, which shall be set out in such a way that agreement with or dissent from each separate resolution may be indicated by the recipient on the copy so sent].

(3) Any member of the committee may, within 7 business days from the date of the receiver sending out a resolution, require him to summon a meeting of the committee to consider the matters raised by the resolution.

(4) In the absence of such a request, the resolution is deemed to have been passed by the committee if and when the receiver is notified in writing by a majority of the members that they concur with it.

(5) A copy of every resolution passed under this Rule, and a note that the committee's concurrence was obtained, shall be kept with the records of the receivership.

NOTES

Initial Commencement

Specified date

Specified date: 29 December 1986: see r 0.1.

Amendment

Provision heading: words "otherwise than at a meeting" in square brackets substituted by SI 2010/686, r 2, Sch 1, para 133.
Date in force: 6 April 2010: see SI 2010/686, r 1; for transitional provisions see r 6(1), Sch 4, para 1 thereto.

Para (2): words in square brackets substituted by SI 1987/1919, r 3(1), Schedule, Part 1, para 29.

3.28 Information from receiver

(1) Where the committee resolves to require the attendance of the administrative receiver under section 49(2), the notice to him shall be in writing [authenticated] by the majority of the members of the committee for the time being. A member's representative may [authenticate] for him.

(2) The meeting at which the receiver's attendance is required shall be fixed by the committee for a business day, and shall be held at such time and place as he determines.

(3) Where the receiver so attends, the members of the committee may elect any one of their number to be chairman of the meeting, in place of the receiver or any nominee of his.

NOTES

Initial Commencement

Specified date

Specified date: 29 December 1986: see r 0.1.

Amendment

Para (1): word "authenticated" in square brackets substituted by SI 2010/686, r 2, Sch 1, para 1.
Date in force: 6 April 2010: see SI 2010/686, r 1; for transitional provisions see r 6(1), Sch 4, paras 1, 2(1)(b) thereto.

Para (1): word "authenticate" in square brackets substituted by SI 2010/686, r 2, Sch 1, para 1.
Date in force: 6 April 2010: see SI 2010/686, r 1; for transitional provisions see r 6(1), Sch 4, paras 1, 2(1)(b) thereto.

3.29 Expenses of members

(1) Subject as follows, the administrative receiver shall out of the assets of the company defray[, in the prescribed order of priority,] any reasonable travelling

expenses directly incurred by members of the creditors' committee or their representatives in relation to their attendance at the committee's meetings, or otherwise on the committee's business, as an expense of the receivership.

(2) Paragraph (1) does not apply to any meeting of the committee held within 3 months of a previous meeting, unless the meeting in question is summoned at the instance of the administrative receiver.

NOTES

Initial Commencement

Specified date

Specified date: 29 December 1986: see r 0.1.

Amendment

Para (1): words ", in the prescribed order of priority," in square brackets inserted by SI 2010/686, r 2, Sch 1, para 134.
Date in force: 6 April 2010: see SI 2010/686, r 1; for transitional provisions see r 6(1), Sch 4, para 1 thereto.

3.30 Members' dealings with the company

(1) Membership of the committee does not prevent a person from dealing with the company while the receiver is acting, provided that any transactions in the course of such dealings are entered into in good faith and for value.

(2) The court may, on the application of any person interested, set aside a transaction which appears to it to be contrary to the requirements of this Rule, and may give such consequential directions as it thinks [just] for compensating the company for any loss which it may have incurred in consequence of the transaction.

NOTES

Initial Commencement

Specified date

Specified date: 29 December 1986: see r 0.1.

Amendment

Para (2): word "just" in square brackets substituted by SI 2010/686, r 2, Sch 1, para 1.
Date in force: 6 April 2010: see SI 2010/686, r 1; for transitional provisions see r 6(1), Sch 4, paras 1, 2(1)(b) thereto.

[3.30A Formal defects]

[The acts of the creditors' committee established for any administrative receivership are valid notwithstanding any defect in the appointment, election or qualifications of any member of the committee or any committee-member's representative or in the formalities of its establishment.]

NOTES

Amendment

Inserted by SI 1987/1919, r 3(1), Schedule, Part 1, para 30.

CHAPTER 5

THE ADMINISTRATIVE RECEIVER (MISCELLANEOUS)

3.31 Disposal of charged property

(1) The following applies where the administrative receiver applies to the court under section 43(1) for authority to dispose of property of the company which is subject to a security.

(2) The court shall fix a venue for the hearing of the application, and the receiver shall [as soon as reasonably practicable] give notice of the venue to the person who is the holder of the security.

[(3) If an order is made under section 43(1), the court must send two sealed copies to the administrative receiver.

(4) The administrative receiver must send one of them to that person who is the holder of the security.]

NOTES

Initial Commencement

Specified date

Specified date: 29 December 1986: see r 0.1.

Amendment

Para (2): word "as soon as reasonably practicable" in square brackets substituted by SI 2009/642, rr 4, 5.
Date in force: 6 April 2009: see SI 2009/642, r 1; for transitional provisions see r 3 thereof.
Paras (3), (4): substituted by SI 2010/686, r 2, Sch 1, para 135.
Date in force: 6 April 2010: see SI 2010/686, r 1; for transitional provisions see r 6(1), Sch 4, para 1 thereto.

3.32 Abstract of receipts and payments

(1) The administrative receiver shall—
   (a) within 2 months after the end of 12 months from the date of his appointment, and of every subsequent period of 12 months, and
   (b) within 2 months after he ceases to act as administrative receiver,
send to the registrar of companies, to the company and to the person by whom he was appointed, and to each member of the creditors' committee (if there is one), the requisite accounts of his receipts and payments as receiver.

(2) The court may, on the receiver's application, extend the period of 2 months referred to in paragraph (1).

(3) The accounts are to be in the form of an abstract showing—
   (a) receipts and payments during the relevant period of 12 months, or
   (b) where the receiver has ceased to act, receipts and payments during the period from the end of the last 12 month period to the time when he so ceased (alternatively, if there has been no previous abstract, receipts and payments in the period since his appointment as administrative receiver).

(4) This Rule is without prejudice to the receiver's duty to render proper accounts required otherwise than as above.

(5) If the administrative receiver makes default in complying with this Rule, he is liable to a fine and, for continued contravention, to a daily default fine.

NOTES

Initial Commencement

Specified date

Specified date: 29 December 1986: see r 0.1.

3.33 Resignation

(1) Subject as follows, before resigning his office the administrative receiver shall give at least [5 business] days' notice of his intention to do so to—

(a)   the person by whom he was appointed, . . .

(b)   the company or, if it is then in liquidation, its liquidator [, and

(c)   in any case, to the members of the creditors' committee (if any)].

(2) A notice given under this Rule shall specify the date on which the receiver intends his resignation to take effect.

(3) . . .

NOTES

Initial Commencement

Specified date

Specified date: 29 December 1986: see r 0.1.

Amendment

Para (1): words "5 business" in square brackets substituted by SI 2010/686, r 2, Sch 1, para 136(1), (2).
   Date in force: 6 April 2010: see SI 2010/686, r 1; for transitional provisions see r 6(1), Sch 4, para 1 thereto.

Para (1): word omitted revoked and sub-para (c) inserted, by SI 1987/1919, r 3(1), Schedule, Part 1, para 31.

Para (3): revoked by SI 2010/686, r 2, Sch 1, para 136(1), (3).
   Date in force: 6 April 2010: see SI 2010/686, r 1; for transitional provisions see r 6(1), Sch 4, para 1 thereto.

3.34 Receiver deceased

If the administrative receiver dies, the person by whom he was appointed shall, [as soon as reasonably practicable] on his becoming aware of the death, give notice of it to—

(a)   the registrar of companies, . . .

(b)   the company or, if it is in liquidation, the liquidator [, and

(c)   in any case, to the members of the creditors' committee (if any)].

NOTES

Initial Commencement

Specified date

Specified date: 29 December 1986: see r 0.1.

Amendment

Words "as soon as reasonably practicable" in square brackets substituted by SI 2009/642, rr 4, 5.
   Date in force: 6 April 2009: see SI 2009/642, r 1; for transitional provisions see r 3 thereof.

Word omitted revoked and para (c) inserted, by SI 1987/1919, r 3(1), Schedule, Part 1, para 32.

3.35 Vacation of office

(1) The administrative receiver, on vacating office on completion of the receivership, or in consequence of his ceasing to be qualified as an insolvency practitioner, shall [as soon as reasonably practicable] give notice of his doing so—

[(a) to the company or, if it is in liquidation, the liquidator, and]
(b) . . . , to the members of the creditors' committee (if any).

(2) Where the receiver's office is vacated, the notice to the registrar of companies which is required by section 45(4) may be given by means of an indorsement on the notice required by [section 871(2)] of the Companies Act (notice for the purposes of the register of charges).

NOTES

Initial Commencement

Specified date
Specified date: 29 December 1986: see r 0.1.

Amendment
Para (1): words "as soon as reasonably practicable" in square brackets substituted by SI 2009/642, rr 4, 5.
Date in force: 6 April 2009: see SI 2009/642, r 1; for transitional provisions see r 3 thereof.

Para (1): sub-para (a) substituted and words omitted from sub-para (b) revoked, by SI 1987/1919, r 3(1), Schedule, Part I, para 33.

Para (2): words "section 871(2)" in square brackets substituted by SI 2009/2472, rr 3, 9.
Date in force: 1 October 2009: see SI 2009/2472, r 1; for transitional provisions see r 2 thereof.

CHAPTER 6

. . .

NOTES

Amendment
Revoked by SI 2010/686, r 5.
Date in force: 6 April 2010: see SI 2010/686, r 1; for transitional provisions see r 6(1), Sch 4, para 1 thereto.

3.36 . . .
. . .

NOTES

Amendment
Revoked by SI 2010/686, r 5.
Date in force: 6 April 2010: see SI 2010/686, r 1; for transitional provisions see r 6(1), Sch 4, para 1 thereto.

3.37 . . .
. . .

NOTES

Amendment

Revoked by SI 2010/686, r 5.
Date in force: 6 April 2010: see SI 2010/686, r 1; for transitional provisions see r 6(1), Sch 4, para 1 thereto.

3.38 . . .
. . .

NOTES

Amendment

Revoked by SI 2010/686, r 5.
Date in force: 6 April 2010: see SI 2010/686, r 1; for transitional provisions see r 6(1), Sch 4, para 1 thereto.

[CHAPTER 7

SECTION 176A: THE PRESCRIBED PART]

NOTES

Amendment

Inserted by SI 2003/1730, r 6, Sch 1, Pt 3, para 11.
Date in force: 15 September 2003: see SI 2003/1730, r 1(2).

[3.39 Report to creditors]

[(1) This Rule applies where—
- (a) a receiver (other than an administrative receiver) is appointed by the court or otherwise under a charge which as created was a floating charge; and
- (b) section 176A applies.

(2) Within 3 months (or such longer period as the court may allow) of the date of his appointment the receiver shall send to creditors, details of whose names and addresses are available to him, notice of his appointment and a report which will include the following matters—
- (a) to the best of the receiver's knowledge and belief—
  - (i) an estimate of the value of the prescribed part (whether or not he proposes to make an application to the court under section 176A(5) or section 176A(3) applies); and
  - (ii) an estimate of the value of company's net property;
- (b) whether, and if so, why, he proposes to make an application to court under section 176A(5); and
- (c) whether he proposes to present a petition for the winding up of the company.

(3) Nothing in this Rule is to be taken as requiring any such estimate to include any information, the disclosure of which could seriously prejudice the commercial interests of the company. If such information is excluded from the calculation the estimate shall be accompanied by a statement to that effect.

Insolvency Rules 1986, reg 3.39

[(4) Where the requirements of paragraph (5) are satisfied, the receiver may, instead of sending the report required under paragraph (2)—
  (a)   cause a notice . . . to be gazetted; and
  (b)   may advertise the notice in such other manner as the receiver thinks fit.
[(4A) In addition to the standard contents, the notice under paragraph (4) must include a statement of the matters required to be included in the receiver's report under paragraph (2).]
(5) The requirements of this paragraph are that—
  (a)   full details of the unsecured creditors of the company are not available to the receiver; or
  (b)   the receiver thinks it is otherwise impracticable to send the report.]]

NOTES

Amendment

Inserted by SI 2003/1730, r 6, Sch 1, Pt 3, para 11.
  Date in force: 15 September 2003: see SI 2003/1730, r 1(2).
Paras (4), (5): substituted, for para (4) as originally enacted, by SI 2009/642, rr 4, 17.
  Date in force: 6 April 2009: see SI 2009/642, r 1; for transitional provisions see r 3 thereof.
Para (4): in sub-para (a) words omitted revoked by SI 2010/686, r 2, Sch 1, para 137(1), (2).
  Date in force: 6 April 2010: see SI 2010/686, r 1; for transitional provisions see r 6(1), Sch 4, para 1 thereto.
Para (4A): inserted by SI 2010/686, r 2, Sch 1, para 137(1), (3).
  Date in force: 6 April 2010: see SI 2010/686, r 1; for transitional provisions see r 6(1), Sch 4, para 1 thereto.

[3.40 Receiver to deal with prescribed part]

[Where Rule 3.39 applies—
  (a)   the receiver may present a petition for the winding up of the company if the ground of the petition is that in section 122(1)(f);
  (b)   where a liquidator or administrator has been appointed to the company, the receiver shall deliver up the sums representing the prescribed part to him;
  (c)   in any other case, the receiver shall apply to the court for directions as to the manner in which he is to discharge his duty under section 176A(2)(a) and shall act in accordance with such directions as are given by the court.]

NOTES

Amendment

Inserted by SI 2003/1730, r 6, Sch 1, Pt 3, para 11.
  Date in force: 15 September 2003: see SI 2003/1730, r 1(2).

PART 4

COMPANIES WINDING UP

CHAPTER 1

THE SCHEME OF THIS PART OF THE RULES

4.1 Voluntary winding up; winding up by the court

[(1) In a members' voluntary winding up, the Rules in this Part do not apply, except as follows—

(a) [Rules 4.3 and 4.35 apply] in the same way as [they apply] in a creditors' voluntary winding up;

[(aa) Rules 4.49C, 4.49E and 4.49F apply except so far as it is provided (expressly or by necessary implication) that they do not apply;

(ab) Rule 4.49G applies only in a members' voluntary winding up, and not otherwise;]

(b) Rule 4.72 (additional provisions concerning meetings in relation to [the Financial Services Authority] and [the scheme manager]) applies in the winding up of [authorised deposit-takers or former authorised deposit-takers], whether members' or creditors' voluntary or by the court;

(c) Chapters 9 (proof of debts in a liquidation), 10 (secured creditors), 15 (disclaimer) and 18 (special manager) apply wherever, and in the same way as, they apply in a creditors' voluntary winding up;

(d) Section F of Chapter 11 (the liquidator) applies only in a members' voluntary winding up, and not otherwise;

(e) Section G of that Chapter (court's power to set aside certain transactions; rule against solicitation) applies in any winding up, whether members' or creditors' voluntary or by the court;

(f) [Rules 4.126A and 4.182A apply] only in a members' voluntary winding up, and not otherwise; and

(g) Rule 4.223-CVL (liquidator's statements) applies in the same way as it applies in a creditors' voluntary winding up.]

(2) Subject as follows, the Rules in this Part apply both in a creditors' voluntary winding up and in a winding up by the court; and for this purpose a winding up is treated as a creditors' voluntary [winding up] if, and from the time when, the liquidator forms the opinion that the company will be unable to pay its debts in full, and determines accordingly to summon a creditors' meeting under section 95.

(3) The following Chapters, or Sections of Chapters, of this Part do not apply in a creditors' voluntary winding up—

Chapter 2—The statutory demand;
Chapter 3—Petition to winding-up order;
Chapter 4—Petition by contributories;
Chapter 5—Provisional liquidator;
[Chapter 11 (Section F)—The Liquidator in a members' voluntary winding up;]
Chapter 13—The liquidation committee where winding up follows immediately on administration;
Chapter 16—Settlement of list of contributories;
Chapter 17—Calls;
Chapter 19—Public examination of company officers and others; and
Chapter 21 (Section A)—Return of capital.
[Chapter 21 (Section C)—Dissolution after winding up].

(4) Where at the head of any Rule, or at the end of any paragraph of a Rule, there appear the words "(NO CVL APPLICATION)", this signifies that the Rule or, as the case may be, the paragraph does not apply in a creditors' voluntary winding up.

However, this does not affect the court's power to make orders under section 112 (exercise in relation to voluntary winding up of powers available in winding up by the court).

(5) Where to any Rule or paragraph there is given a number incorporating the letters "CVL", that signifies that the Rule or (as the case may be) the paragraph applies in a creditors' voluntary winding up, and not in a winding up by the court.

[(6) In a voluntary winding up which is commenced by the registration of a notice under paragraph 83(3) of Schedule B1 to the Act, the following provisions of this Part shall not apply—

Rules 4.34, 4.38, 4.49, 4.51, 4.53, 4.62, 4.101, 4.103, 4.106, 4.152, 4.153, 4.206–4.210.]

NOTES

Initial Commencement

Specified date

Specified date: 29 December 1986: see r 0.1.

Amendment

Para (1): substituted by SI 1987/1919, r 3(1), Schedule, Part 1, para 34.

Para (1): in sub-para (a) words "Rules 4.3 and 4.35 apply" in square brackets substituted by SI 2010/686, r 2, Sch 1, para 138(1), (2)(a)(i).
Date in force: 6 April 2010: see SI 2010/686, r 1; for transitional provisions see r 6(1), Sch 4, para 1 thereto.

Para (1): in sub-para (a) words "they apply" in square brackets substituted by SI 2010/686, r 2, Sch 1, para 138(1), (2)(a)(ii).
Date in force: 6 April 2010: see SI 2010/686, r 1; for transitional provisions see r 6(1), Sch 4, para 1 thereto.

Para (1): sub-paras (aa), (ab) inserted by SI 2010/686, r 2, Sch 1, para 138(1), (2)(b).
Date in force: 6 April 2010: see SI 2010/686, r 1; for transitional provisions see r 6(1), Sch 4, para 1 thereto.

Para (1): in sub-para (b) words "the Financial Services Authority" in square brackets substituted by SI 1998/1129, art 2, Sch 1, para 4(2).
Date in force: 1 June 1998: see SI 1998/1129, art 1.

Para (1): in sub-para (b) words "the scheme manager" in square brackets substituted by SI 2001/3649, art 378(1).
Date in force: 1 December 2001: see SI 2001/3649, art 1.

Para (1): in sub-para (b) words "authorised deposit-takers or former authorised deposit-takers" in square brackets substituted by SI 2001/3649, art 377(1), (3).
Date in force: 1 December 2001: see SI 2001/3649, art 1.

Para (1): in sub-para (f) words "Rules 4.126A and 4.182A apply" in square brackets substituted by SI 2010/686, r 2, Sch 1, para 138(1), (2)(c).
Date in force: 6 April 2010: see SI 2010/686, r 1; for transitional provisions see r 6(1), Sch 4, para 1 thereto.

Para (2): words "winding up" in square brackets inserted by SI 1997/1919, r 3(1), Schedule, Pt 1, para 34.

Para (3): entries "Chapter 11" and "Chapter 21 (Section C)" inserted by SI 1987/1919, r 3(1), Schedule, Part 1, para 34.

Para (6): inserted by SI 2003/1730, r 7, Sch 1, Pt 4, para 12.
Date in force: 15 September 2003: see SI 2003/1730, r 1(2).

4.2 Winding up by the court: the various forms of petition [(No CVL Application)]

(1) Insofar as the Rules in this Part apply to winding up by the court, they apply (subject as follows) whether the petition for winding up is presented under any of the several paragraphs of section 122(1), namely—

paragraph (a)—company special resolution for winding up by the court;
paragraph (b)—public company without certificate under [section 761] of the Companies Act;
paragraph (c)—old public company;
paragraph (d)—company not commencing business after formation, or suspending business;
paragraph (e)—number of company's members reduced below 2;
paragraph (f)—company unable to pay its debts;
[paragraph (fa)—end of moratorium without approval of voluntary arrangement;]
paragraph (g)—court's power under the "just and equitable" rule,

or under any enactment enabling the presentation of a winding-up petition.

(2) Except as provided by the following two paragraphs or by any particular Rule, the Rules apply whether the petition for winding up is presented by the company, the directors, one or more creditors, one or more contributories, the Secretary of State, the official receiver, or any person entitled under any enactment to present such a petition.

(3) Chapter 2 (statutory demand) has no application except in relation to an unpaid creditor of the company satisfying section 123(1)(a) (the first of the two cases specified, in relation to England and Wales, of the company being deemed unable to pay its debts within section 122(1)(f) or section 222(1) (the equivalent provision in relation to unregistered companies).

(4) Chapter 3 (petition to winding-up order) has no application to a petition for winding up presented by one or more contributories; and in relation to a petition so presented Chapter 4 has effect.

NOTES

Initial Commencement

Specified date

Specified date: 29 December 1986: see r 0.1.

Amendment

Provision-heading: words in square brackets inserted by SI 1987/1919, r 3(1), Schedule, Pt 1, para 35.

Para (1): words "section 761" in square brackets substituted by SI 2009/2472, rr 3, 11.
Date in force: 1 October 2009: see SI 2009/2472, r 1; for transitional provisions see r 2 thereof.

Para (1): words "paragraph (fa)—end of moratorium without approval of voluntary arrangement;" in square brackets inserted by SI 2002/2712, r 4(1), Schedule, Pt 2, para 22.
Date in force: 1 January 2003: see SI 2002/2712, r 1(1); for effect see rr 1(2), 4(2) thereof.

4.3 Time-limits

Where by any provision of the Act or the Rules about winding up, the time for doing anything is limited, the court may extend the time, either before or after it has expired, on such terms, if any, as it thinks [just].

NOTES

Initial Commencement

Specified date

Specified date: 29 December 1986: see r 0.1.

Amendment

Word "just" in square brackets substituted by SI 2010/686, r 2, Sch 1, para 1.
Date in force: 6 April 2010: see SI 2010/686, r 1; for transitional provisions see r 6(1), Sch 4, paras 1, 2(1)(b) thereto.

CHAPTER 2

THE STATUTORY DEMAND (NO CVL APPLICATION)

4.4 Preliminary

(1) This Chapter does not apply where a petition for the winding up of a company is presented under section 124 on or after the date on which the Rules come into force and the petition is based on failure to comply with a written demand served on the company before that date.

(2) A written demand served by a creditor on a company under section 123(1)(a) (registered companies) or 222(1)(a) (unregistered companies) is known . . . as "the statutory demand".

(3) The statutory demand must be dated, and be [authenticated] either by the creditor himself or by a person stating himself to be authorised to make the demand on the creditor's behalf.

NOTES

Initial Commencement

Specified date

Specified date: 29 December 1986: see r 0.1.

Amendment

Para (2): words omitted revoked by SI 2010/686, r 2, Sch 1, para 139.
   Date in force: 6 April 2010: see SI 2010/686, r 1; for transitional provisions see r 6(1), Sch 4, para 1 thereto.
Para (3): word "authenticated" in square brackets substituted by SI 2010/686, r 2, Sch 1, para 1.
   Date in force: 6 April 2010: see SI 2010/686, r 1; for transitional provisions see r 6(1), Sch 4, paras 1, 2(1)(b) thereto.

4.5 Form and content of statutory demand

(1) The statutory demand must state the amount of the debt and the consideration for it (or, if there is no consideration, the way in which it arises).

(2) If the amount claimed in the demand includes—
- (a) any charge by way of interest not previously notified to the company as included in its liability, or
- (b) any other charge accruing from time to time,

the amount or rate of the charge must be separately identified, and the grounds on which payment of it is claimed must be stated.

In either case the amount claimed must be limited to that which has accrued due at the date of the demand.

NOTES

Initial Commencement

Specified date

Specified date: 29 December 1986: see r 0.1.

4.6 Information to be given in statutory demand

(1) The statutory demand must include an explanation to the company of the following matters—
- (a) the purpose of the demand, and the fact that, if the demand is not complied with, proceedings may be instituted for the winding up of the company;
- (b) the time within which it must be complied with, if that consequence is to be avoided; . . .
- (c) the methods of compliance which are open to the company[; and
- (d) that the company has the right to make an application to the court for an injunction restraining the creditor from presenting or advertising a petition for the winding up of the company].

(2) Information must be provided for the company as to how an officer or representative of it may enter into communication with one or more named individuals, with a view to securing or compounding for the debt to the creditor's satisfaction.

In the case of any individual so named in the demand, his address and telephone number (if any) must be given.

NOTES

Initial Commencement

Specified date
>Specified date: 29 December 1986: see r 0.1.

Amendment
>Para (1): in sub-para (b) word omitted revoked by SI 2010/686, r 2, Sch 1, para 140(1), (2)(a).
>>Date in force: 6 April 2010: see SI 2010/686, r 1; for transitional provisions see r 6(1), Sch 4, para 1 thereto.
>
>Para (1): sub-para (d) and word "; and" immediately preceding it inserted by SI 2010/686, r 2, Sch 1, para 140(1), (2)(b).
>>Date in force: 6 April 2010: see SI 2010/686, r 1; for transitional provisions see r 6(1), Sch 4, para 1 thereto.

CHAPTER 3

PETITION TO WINDING-UP ORDER (NO CVL APPLICATION) (NO APPLICATION TO PETITION BY CONTRIBUTORIES)

[4.6A Injunction to restrain presentation or advertisement of petition]
[An application by a company for an injunction restraining a creditor from—
- (a) presenting a petition for the winding up of the company must be made to a court having jurisdiction to wind up the company;
- (b) advertising a petition for the winding up of a company must be made to the court in which the petition is pending.]

NOTES

Amendment
>Inserted by SI 2010/686, r 2, Sch 1, para 141.
>>Date in force: 6 April 2010: see SI 2010/686, r 1; for transitional provisions see r 6(1), Sch 4, para 1 thereto.

4.7 Presentation and filing of petition

(1) The petition, verified by [a statement of truth] in accordance with Rule 4.12 below, shall be filed in court.

[(2) No petition shall be filed unless there is produced on presentation of the petition a receipt for the deposit payable or paragraph (2A) applies.

(2A) This paragraph applies in any case where the Secretary of State has given written notice to the court that the petitioner has made suitable alternative arrangements for the payment of the deposit to the official receiver and such notice has not been revoked in relation to the petitioner in accordance with paragraph (2B).

(2B) A notice of the kind referred to in paragraph (2A) may be revoked in relation to the petitioner in whose favour it is given by a further notice in writing to the court stating that the earlier notice is revoked in relation to the petitioner.]

[(3) A petitioner who is a person other than the company must also deliver to the court one copy for service on the company.]

(4) There shall in any case be delivered with the petition—

- (a) if the company is in course of being wound up voluntarily, and a liquidator has been appointed, one copy of the petition to be sent to him;
- (b) [if the company is in administration], one copy [. . .] to be sent to the administrator;
- (c) if an administrative receiver has been appointed in relation to the company, one copy to be sent to him;
- (d) if there is in force for the company a voluntary arrangement under Part I of the Act, one copy for the supervisor of the arrangement; . . .
- [(da) if a member State liquidator has been appointed in main proceedings in relation to the company, one copy to be sent to him; and]
- (e) if the company is [an authorised deposit-taker or a former authorised deposit-taker] and the petitioner is not the [Financial Services Authority], one copy to be sent to the [Authority].

(5) Each of the copies delivered shall have applied to it the seal of the court, and shall be issued to the petitioner.

(6) The court shall fix a venue for the hearing of the petition; and this shall be endorsed on any copy issued to the petitioner under paragraph (5).

[(7) Where a petition is filed at the instance of a company's administrator the petition shall—

- (a) be expressed to be the petition of the company by its administrator,
- (b) state the name of the administrator, [the court case number and the date that the company entered administration], and
- [(c) where applicable, contain an application under paragraph 79 of Schedule B1, requesting that the appointment of the administrator shall cease to have effect].

[(8) Any petition filed in relation to a company in respect of which there is in force a voluntary arrangement under Part I of the Act or which is in administration shall be presented to the court to which the nominee's report under section 2 was submitted or the court having jurisdiction for the administration.]

(9) Any petition such as is mentioned in paragraph (7) above or presented by the supervisor of a voluntary arrangement under Part I of the Act in force for the company shall be treated as if it were a petition filed by contributories, and Chapter 4 in this Part of the Rules shall apply accordingly.

(10) Where a petition contains a request for the appointment of a person as liquidator in accordance with section 140 (appointment of former administrator or supervisor as liquidator) the person whose appointment is sought shall, not less than 2 [business] days before the return day for the petition, file in court a report including particulars of—

- (a) a date on which he notified creditors of the company, either in writing or at a meeting of creditors, of the intention to seek his appointment as liquidator, such date to be at least [7 business] days before the day on which the report under this paragraph is filed, and
- (b) details of any response from creditors to that notification, including any objections to his appointment.]

NOTES

Initial Commencement

Specified date

Specified date: 29 December 1986: see r 0.1.

Amendment

Para (1): words "a statement of truth" in square brackets substituted by SI 2010/686, r 2, Sch 1, para 141(1), (2).
　　Date in force: 6 April 2010: see SI 2010/686, r 1; for transitional provisions see r 6(1), Sch 4, paras 1, 2(1)(b) thereto.
Paras (2), (2A), (2B): substituted, for para (2) as originally enacted, by SI 2004/584, r 8(a).
　　Date in force: 1 April 2004: see SI 2004/584, r 1(2).
Para (3): substituted by SI 2010/686, r 2, Sch 1, para 142(1), (3).
　　Date in force: 6 April 2010: see SI 2010/686, r 1; for transitional provisions see r 6(1), Sch 4, para 1 thereto.
Para (4): in sub-para (b) words "if the company is in administration" in square brackets substituted by SI 2003/1730, r 7, Sch 1, Pt 4, para 13(a).
　　Date in force: 15 September 2003: see SI 2003/1730, r 1(2).
Para (4): in sub-para (b) words omitted inserted by SI 2003/1730, r 7, Sch 1, Pt 4, para 13(a).
　　Date in force: 15 September 2003: see SI 2003/1730, r 1(2).
Para (4): in sub-para (b) words omitted revoked by SI 2004/584, r 8(b).
　　Date in force: 1 April 2004: see SI 2004/584, r 1(2).
Para (4): in sub-para (d) word omitted revoked by SI 2002/1307, rr 3(1), 6(1)(a).
　　Date in force: 31 May 2002: see SI 2002/1307, r 1.
Para (4): sub-para (da) inserted by SI 2002/1307, rr 3(1), 6(1)(b).
　　Date in force: 31 May 2002: see SI 2002/1307, r 1.
Para (4): in sub-para (e) words "an authorised deposit-taker or a former authorised deposit-taker" in square brackets substituted by SI 2001/3649, art 377(1), (4).
　　Date in force: 1 December 2001: see SI 2001/3649, art 1.
Para (4): in sub-para (e) words "Financial Services Authority" in square brackets substituted by SI 1998/1129, art 2, Sch 1, para 4(3)(a).
　　Date in force: 1 June 1998: see SI 1998/1129, art 1.
Para (4): in sub-para (e) word "Authority" in square brackets substituted by SI 1998/1129, art 2, Sch 1, para 4(3)(b).
　　Date in force: 1 June 1998: see SI 1998/1129, art 1.
Paras (7)–(10): inserted by SI 1987/1919, r 3(1), Schedule, Pt 1, para 36.
Para (7): in sub-para (b) words "the court case number and the date that the company entered administration" in square brackets substituted by SI 2003/1730, r 7, Sch 1, Pt 4, para 13(b).
　　Date in force: 15 September 2003: see SI 2003/1730, r 1(2).
Para (7): sub-para (c) substituted by SI 2005/527, r 18.
　　Date in force: 1 April 2005: see SI 2005/527, r 1(2).
Para (8): substituted by SI 2003/1730, r 7, Sch 1, Pt 4, para 13(d).
　　Date in force: 15 September 2003: see SI 2003/1730, r 1(2).
Para (10): word "business" in square brackets inserted by SI 2010/686, r 2, Sch 1, para 142(1), (4)(a).
　　Date in force: 6 April 2010: see SI 2010/686, r 1; for transitional provisions see r 6(1), Sch 4, para 1 thereto.
Para (10): in sub-para (a) words "7 business" in square brackets substituted by SI 2010/686, r 2, Sch 1, para 142(1), (4)(b).
　　Date in force: 6 April 2010: see SI 2010/686, r 1; for transitional provisions see r 6(1), Sch 4, para 1 thereto.

4.8 Service of petition

(1) The following paragraphs apply as regards service of the petition on the company (where the petitioner is other than the company itself); and references to the petition are to a copy of the petition bearing the seal of the court in which it is presented.

(2) Subject as follows, the petition shall be served at the company's registered office, that is to say—
　　(a)　the place which is specified, in the company's statement delivered under [section 9] of the Companies Act as the intended situation of its registered office on incorporation, or

(b) if notice has been given by the company to the registrar of companies under [section 87] of that Act (change of registered office), the place specified in that notice or, as the case may be, in the last such notice.

(3) Service of the petition at the registered office may be effected in any of the following ways—

(a) it may be handed to a person who there and then acknowledges himself to be, or to the best of the server's knowledge, information and belief is, a director or other officer, or employee, of the company; or

(b) it may be handed to a person who there and then acknowledges himself to be authorised to accept service of documents on the company's behalf; or

(c) in the absence of any such person as is mentioned in sub-paragraph (a) or (b), it may be deposited at or about the registered office in such a way that it is likely to come to the notice of a person attending at the office.

[(4) If for any reason service at the registered office is not practicable, or the company has no registered office or is an unregistered company, the petition may be served on the company by leaving it at the company's last known principal place of business in such a way that it is likely to come to the attention of a person attending there, or by delivering it to the secretary or some director, manager or principal officer of the company, wherever that person may be found.]

(5) In the case of an [overseas] company, service may be effected in any manner provided for by [section 1139(2)] of the Companies Act.

(6) If for any reason it is impracticable to effect service as provided by paragraphs (2) to (5), the petition may be served in such other manner as the court may [approve or] direct.

(7) Application for [permission] of the court under paragraph (6) may be made [by an application without notice to any other party], [supported by a witness statement] stating what steps have been taken to comply with paragraphs (2) to (5), and the reasons why it is impracticable to effect service as there provided.

NOTES

Initial Commencement

Specified date

Specified date: 29 December 1986: see r 0.1.

Amendment

Para (2): in sub-para (a) words "section 9" in square brackets substituted by SI 2009/2472, rr 3, 12(1), (2)(a).
Date in force: 1 October 2009: see SI 2009/2472, r 1; for transitional provisions see r 2 thereof.

Para (2): in sub-para (b) words "section 87" in square brackets substituted by SI 2009/2472, rr 3, 12(1), (2)(b).
Date in force: 1 October 2009: see SI 2009/2472, r 1; for transitional provisions see r 2 thereof.

Para (4): substituted by SI 1987/1919, r 3(1), Schedule, Part 1, para 37(1).

Para (5): word "overseas" in square brackets substituted by SI 2009/2472, rr 3, 12(1), (3).
Date in force: 1 October 2009: see SI 2009/2472, r 1; for transitional provisions see r 2 thereof.

Para (5): words "section 1139(2)" in square brackets substituted by SI 2009/2472, rr 3, 12(1), (3).
Date in force: 1 October 2009: see SI 2009/2472, r 1; for transitional provisions see r 2 thereof.

Para (6): words "approve or" in square brackets inserted by SI 1987/1919, r 3(1), Schedule, Part 1, para 37(2).

Para (7): word "permission" in square brackets substituted by SI 2010/686, r 2, Sch 1, para 1.
    Date in force: 6 April 2010: see SI 2010/686, r 1; for transitional provisions see r 6(1), Sch 4, paras 1, 2(1)(b) thereto.
Para (7): words "by an application without notice to any other party" in square brackets substituted by SI 2010/686, r 2, Sch 1, para 143(1), (2)(a).
    Date in force: 6 April 2010: see SI 2010/686, r 1; for transitional provisions see r 6(1), Sch 4, paras 1, 2(1)(b) thereto.
Para (7): words "supported by a witness statement" in square brackets substituted by SI 2010/686, r 2, Sch 1, para 143(1), (2)(b).
    Date in force: 6 April 2010: see SI 2010/686, r 1; for transitional provisions and further effect see rr 6(1), 7, Sch 4, paras 1, 2(1)(b), (2)–(4), Sch 5 thereto.

[4.9A Proof of Service]

[(1) Service of the petition must be proved by a certificate of service.

(2) The certificate of service must be sufficient to identify the petition served and must specify—

(a) the name and registered number of the company,
(b) the address of the registered office of the company,
(c) the name of the petitioner,
(d) the court in which the petition was filed and the court reference number,
(e) the date of the petition,
(f) whether the copy served was a sealed copy,
(g) the date on which service was effected, and
(h) the manner in which service was effected.

(3) Where substituted service has been ordered, the certificate of service must have attached to it a sealed copy of the order.

(4) The certificate of service must be filed in court as soon as reasonably practicable after service, and in any event not less than 5 business days before the hearing of the petition.]

NOTES

Amendment

Substituted, for r 4.9 as originally enacted, by SI 2010/686, r 2, Sch 1, para 144.
    Date in force: 6 April 2010: see SI 2010/686, r 1; for transitional provisions see r 6(1), Sch 4, para 1 thereto.

4.10 Other persons to receive copies of petition

(1) If to the petitioner's knowledge the company is in course of being wound up voluntarily, a copy of the petition shall be sent by him to the liquidator.

(2) If to the petitioner's knowledge an administrative receiver has been appointed in relation to the company, or [the company is in administration], a copy of the petition shall be sent by him to the receiver or, as the case may be, the administrator.

(3) If to the petitioner's knowledge there is in force for the company a voluntary arrangement under Part I of the Act, a copy of the petition shall be sent by him to the supervisor of the voluntary arrangement.

[(3A) If to the petitioner's knowledge, there is a member State liquidator appointed in main proceedings in relation to the company, a copy of the petition shall be sent by him to that person.
This does not apply if the petitioner referred to in this paragraph is a member State liquidator.]

(4) If the company is [an authorised institution or former authorised institution within the meaning of the Banking Act 1987] a copy of the petition shall be sent by the petitioner to the [Financial Services Authority].

This does not apply if the petitioner is the [Financial Services Authority] itself.

(5) A copy of the petition which is required by this Rule to be sent shall be despatched on the next business day after the day on which the petition is served on the company.

NOTES

Initial Commencement

Specified date

Specified date: 29 December 1986: see r 0.1.

Amendment

Para (2): words "the company is in administration" in square brackets substituted by SI 2003/1730, r 7, Sch 1, Pt 4, para 14.
Date in force: 15 September 2003: see SI 2003/1730, r 1(2).
Para (3A): inserted by SI 2002/1307, rr 3(1), 6(2).
Date in force: 31 May 2002: see SI 2002/1307, r 1.

Para (4): words from "an authorised" to "Banking Act 1987" in square brackets substituted by SI 1987/1919, r 3(1), Schedule, Pt 1, para 38.

Para (4): words "Financial Services Authority" in square brackets in both places they occur substituted by SI 1998/1129, art 2, Sch 1, para 4(4).
Date in force: 1 June 1998: see SI 1998/1129, art 1.

[4.11 Advertisement of petition]

[(1) Unless the court otherwise directs, the petitioner shall give notice of the petition.

(2) The notice shall be gazetted.

(3) Where compliance with paragraph (2) is not reasonably practicable, the court may direct that instead of the notice being gazetted, it shall be given in such other manner as the court thinks [just].

(4) The notice must be made to appear—
- (a) if the petitioner is the company itself, not less than 7 business days before the day appointed for the hearing; and
- (b) otherwise, not less than 7 business days after service of the petition on the company, nor less than 7 business days before the day so appointed.

[(5) In addition to the standard contents, the notice under paragraph (4) must state—
- (a) that a petition has been presented for the winding up of the company;
- (b) in the case of an overseas company, the address at which service of the petition was effected;
- (c) the name and address of the petitioner;
- (d) the date on which the petition was presented;
- (e) the venue fixed for the hearing of the petition;
- (f) the name and address of the petitioner's solicitor (if any); and
- (g) that any person intending to appear at the hearing (whether to support or oppose the petition) must give notice of that intention in accordance with Rule 4.16.]

(6) If notice of the petition is not given in accordance with this Rule, the court may dismiss it.]

NOTES

Amendment

Substituted by SI 2009/642, rr 4, 18.

Date in force: 6 April 2009: see SI 2009/642, r 1; for transitional provisions see r 3 thereof.
Para (3): word "just" in square brackets substituted by SI 2010/686, r 2, Sch 1, para 1.
Date in force: 6 April 2010: see SI 2010/686, r 1; for transitional provisions see r 6(1), Sch 4, paras 1, 2(1)(b) thereto.
Para (5): substituted by SI 2010/686, r 2, Sch 1, para 145.
Date in force: 6 April 2010: see SI 2010/686, r 1; for transitional provisions see r 6(1), Sch 4, para 1 thereto.

Modification
References to solicitors etc modified to include references to bodies recognised under the Administration of Justice Act 1985, s 9, by the Solicitors' Incorporated Practices Order 1991, SI 1991/2684, arts 4, 5, Sch 1.

4.12 Verification of petition

(1) The petition shall be verified by [a statement of truth].

(2) If the petition is in respect of debts due to different creditors, the debts to each creditor must be separately verified.

[(3A) A statement of truth which is not contained in or endorsed upon the petition which it verifies must be sufficient to identify the petition and must specify—

    (a)   the name and registered number of the company,

    (b)   the name of the petitioner, and

    (c)   the court in which the petition is to be presented.]

(4) The [statement of truth must be authenticated]—

    (a)   by the petitioner (or if there are two or more petitioners, any one of them), or

    (b)   by some person such as a director, company secretary or similar company officer, or a solicitor, who has been concerned in the matters giving rise to the presentation of the petition, or

    (c)   by some responsible person who is duly authorised to [authenticate the statement of truth] and has the requisite knowledge of those matters.

(5) Where the [person authenticating the statement of truth] is not the petitioner himself, or one of the petitioners, he must in the [statement of truth] identify himself and state—

    (a)   the capacity in which, and the authority by which, he [authenticates] it, and

    (b)   the means of his knowledge of the matters [verified in the statement of truth].

(6) . . .

(7) [A statement of truth] verifying more than one petition shall include in its title the names of the companies to which it relates and shall set out, in respect of each company, the statements relied on by the petitioner; and a clear and legible photocopy of the [statement of truth must be filed] with each petition which it verifies.

[(8) The [statement of truth] shall state whether, in the opinion of the person making the application, (i) the EC Regulation will apply and (ii) if so, whether the proceedings will be main proceedings[, secondary proceedings] or territorial proceedings.]

NOTES

Initial Commencement

Specified date
    Specified date: 29 December 1986: see r 0.1.

Amendment

Para (1): words "a statement of truth" in square brackets substituted by SI 2010/686, r 2, Sch 1, para 146(1), (2).
　　Date in force: 6 April 2010: see SI 2010/686, r 1; for transitional provisions see r 6(1), Sch 4, paras 1, 2(1)(b) thereto.
Para (3A): substituted, for para (3) as originally enacted, by SI 2010/686, r 2, Sch 1, para 146(1), (3).
　　Date in force: 6 April 2010: see SI 2010/686, r 1; for transitional provisions see r 6(1), Sch 4, paras 1, 2(1)(b) thereto.
Para (4): words "statement of truth must be authenticated" in square brackets substituted by SI 2010/686, r 2, Sch 1, para 146(1), (4)(a).
　　Date in force: 6 April 2010: see SI 2010/686, r 1; for transitional provisions see r 6(1), Sch 4, paras 1, 2(1)(b) thereto.
Para (4): in sub-para (c) words "authenticate the statement of truth" in square brackets substituted by SI 2010/686, r 2, Sch 1, para 146(1), (4)(b).
　　Date in force: 6 April 2010: see SI 2010/686, r 1; for transitional provisions see r 6(1), Sch 4, paras 1, 2(1)(b) thereto.
Para (5): words "person authenticating the statement of truth" in square brackets substituted by SI 2010/686, r 2, Sch 1, para 146(1), (5)(a).
　　Date in force: 6 April 2010: see SI 2010/686, r 1; for transitional provisions see r 6(1), Sch 4, paras 1, 2(1)(b) thereto.
Para (5): words "statement of truth" in square brackets substituted by SI 2010/686, r 2, Sch 1, para 146(1), (5)(b).
　　Date in force: 6 April 2010: see SI 2010/686, r 1; for transitional provisions see r 6(1), Sch 4, paras 1, 2(1)(b) thereto.
Para (5): in sub-para (a) word "authenticates" in square brackets substituted by SI 2010/686, r 2, Sch 1, para 146(1), (5)(c).
　　Date in force: 6 April 2010: see SI 2010/686, r 1; for transitional provisions see r 6(1), Sch 4, paras 1, 2(1)(b) thereto.
Para (5): in sub-para (b) words "verified in the statement of truth" in square brackets substituted by SI 2010/686, r 2, Sch 1, para 146(1), (5)(d).
　　Date in force: 6 April 2010: see SI 2010/686, r 1; for transitional provisions see r 6(1), Sch 4, paras 1, 2(1)(b) thereto.
Para (6): revoked by SI 2010/686, r 2, Sch 1, para 146(1), (6).
　　Date in force: 6 April 2010: see SI 2010/686, r 1; for transitional provisions see r 6(1), Sch 4, para 1 thereto.
Para (7): words "A statement of truth" in square brackets substituted by SI 2010/686, r 2, Sch 1, para 146(1), (7)(a).
　　Date in force: 6 April 2010: see SI 2010/686, r 1; for transitional provisions see r 6(1), Sch 4, paras 1, 2(1)(b) thereto.
Para (7): words "statement of truth must be filed" in square brackets substituted by SI 2010/686, r 2, Sch 1, para 146(1), (7)(b).
　　Date in force: 6 April 2010: see SI 2010/686, r 1; for transitional provisions see r 6(1), Sch 4, paras 1, 2(1)(b) thereto.
Para (8): inserted by SI 2005/527, r 20.
　　Date in force: 1 April 2005: see SI 2005/527, r 1(2).
Para (8): words "statement of truth" in square brackets substituted by SI 2010/686, r 2, Sch 1, para 146(1), (8)(a).
　　Date in force: 6 April 2010: see SI 2010/686, r 1; for transitional provisions see r 6(1), Sch 4, paras 1, 2(1)(b) thereto.
Para (8): words ", secondary proceedings" in square brackets inserted by SI 2010/686, r 2, Sch 1, para 146(1), (8)(b).
　　Date in force: 6 April 2010: see SI 2010/686, r 1; for transitional provisions see r 6(1), Sch 4, para 1 thereto.

4.13 Persons entitled to copy of petition

Every director, contributory or creditor of the company is entitled to be furnished by the solicitor for the petitioner (or by the petitioner himself, if acting in person) with a copy of the petition within 2 [business] days after requiring it, on payment of the appropriate fee.

NOTES

Initial Commencement

Specified date

Specified date: 29 December 1986: see r 0.1.

Amendment

Word "business" in square brackets inserted by SI 2010/686, r 2, Sch 1, para 147.
Date in force: 6 April 2010: see SI 2010/686, r 1; for transitional provisions see r 6(1), Sch 4, para 1 thereto.

Modification

References to solicitors etc modified to include references to bodies recognised under the Administration of Justice Act 1985, s 9, by the Solicitors' Incorporated Practices Order 1991, SI 1991/2684, arts 4, 5, Sch 1.

4.14 Certificate of compliance

(1) The petitioner or his solicitor shall, at least 5 [business] days before the hearing of the petition, file in court a certificate of compliance with the Rules relating to service and advertisement.

(2) The certificate shall show—

(a) the date of presentation of the petition,

(b) the date fixed for the hearing, and

[(c) the date or dates on which the petition was served and notice of it was given in compliance with the Rules].

[A copy or, where this is not reasonably practicable, a description of the form and content of any notice given shall be filed in court with the certificate.]

(3) Non-compliance with this Rule is a ground on which the court may, if it thinks [just], dismiss the petition.

NOTES

Initial Commencement

Specified date

Specified date: 29 December 1986: see r 0.1.

Amendment

Para (1): word "business" in square brackets inserted by SI 2010/686, r 2, Sch 1, para 148.
Date in force: 6 April 2010: see SI 2010/686, r 1; for transitional provisions see r 6(1), Sch 4, para 1 thereto.
Para (2): sub-para (c) substituted by SI 2009/642, rr 4, 19(a).
Date in force: 6 April 2009: see SI 2009/642, r 1; for transitional provisions see r 3 thereof.
Para (2): words from "A copy or," to "with the certificate." in square brackets substituted by SI 2009/642, rr 4, 19(b).
Date in force: 6 April 2009: see SI 2009/642, r 1; for transitional provisions see r 3 thereof.
Para (3): word "just" in square brackets substituted by SI 2010/686, r 2, Sch 1, para 1.
Date in force: 6 April 2010: see SI 2010/686, r 1; for transitional provisions see r 6(1), Sch 4, paras 1, 2(1)(b) thereto.

Modification

References to solicitors etc modified to include references to bodies recognised under the Administration of Justice Act 1985, s 9, by the Solicitors' Incorporated Practices Order 1991, SI 1991/2684, arts 4, 5, Sch 1.

See Further

See further, in relation the application of this rule, with modifications, in respect of the procedure for the appointment of a bank liquidator and the operation of bank insolvency under the Banking Act 2009, Pt 2: the Bank Insolvency (England and Wales) Rules 2009, SI 2009/356, rr 3(3)–(8), 13.

4.15 [Permission] for petitioner to withdraw

If at least 5 [business] days before the hearing the petitioner, on an [application without notice to any other party], satisfies the court that—

(a) the petition has not been advertised, and

(b) no notices (whether in support or in opposition) have been received by him with reference to the petition, and

(c) the company consents to an order being made under this Rule,

the court may order that the petitioner has [permission] to withdraw the petition on such terms as to costs as the parties may agree.

NOTES

Initial Commencement

Specified date

Specified date: 29 December 1986: see r 0.1.

Amendment

Provision heading: word "Permission" in square brackets substituted by SI 2010/686, r 2, Sch 1, para 1.
 Date in force: 6 April 2010: see SI 2010/686, r 1; for transitional provisions see r 6(1), Sch 4, paras 1, 2(1)(b) thereto.
Word "business" in square brackets inserted by SI 2010/686, r 2, Sch 1, para 149(1), (2).
 Date in force: 6 April 2010: see SI 2010/686, r 1; for transitional provisions see r 6(1), Sch 4, para 1 thereto.
Words "application without notice to any other party" in square brackets substituted by SI 2010/686, r 2, Sch 1, para 149(1), (3).
 Date in force: 6 April 2010: see SI 2010/686, r 1; for transitional provisions see r 6(1), Sch 4, paras 1, 2(1)(b) thereto.
Word "permission" in square brackets substituted by SI 2010/686, r 2, Sch 1, para 1.
 Date in force: 6 April 2010: see SI 2010/686, r 1; for transitional provisions see r 6(1), Sch 4, paras 1, 2(1)(b) thereto.

See Further

See further, in relation the application of this rule, with modifications, in respect of the procedure for the appointment of a bank liquidator and the operation of bank insolvency under the Banking Act 2009, Pt 2: the Bank Insolvency (England and Wales) Rules 2009, SI 2009/356, rr 3(3)–(8), 14.

4.16 Notice of appearance

(1) Every person who intends to appear on the hearing of the petition shall give to the petitioner notice of his intention in accordance with this Rule.

(2) The notice shall specify—

(a) the name and address of the person giving it, and any telephone number and reference which may be required for communication with him or with any other person (to be also specified in the notice) authorised to speak or act on his behalf;

(b) whether his intention is to support or oppose the petition; and

(c) the amount and nature of his debt.

(3) The notice shall be sent to the petitioner at the address shown for him in the court records, or in the advertisement of the petition required by Rule 4.11; or it may be sent to his solicitor.

(4) The notice shall be sent so as to reach the addressee not later than 16.00 hours on the business day before that which is appointed for the hearing (or, where the hearing has been adjourned, for the adjourned hearing).

(5) A person failing to comply with this Rule may appear on the hearing of the petition only with the [permission] of the court.

NOTES

Initial Commencement

Specified date

Specified date: 29 December 1986: see r 0.1.

Amendment

Para (5): word "permission" in square brackets substituted by SI 2010/686, r 2, Sch 1, para 1.
Date in force: 6 April 2010: see SI 2010/686, r 1; for transitional provisions see r 6(1), Sch 4, paras 1, 2(1)(b) thereto.

Modification

References to solicitors etc modified to include references to bodies recognised under the Administration of Justice Act 1985, s 9, by the Solicitors' Incorporated Practices Order 1991, SI 1991/2684, arts 4, 5, Sch 1.

4.17 List of appearances

(1) The petitioner shall prepare for the court a list of the persons (if any) who have given notice under Rule 4.16, specifying their names and addresses and (if known to him) their respective solicitors.

(2) Against the name of each creditor in the list it shall be stated whether his intention is to support the petition, or to oppose it.

(3) On the day appointed for the hearing of the petition, a copy of the list shall be handed to the court before the commencement of the hearing.

(4) If any [permission] is given under Rule 4.16(5), the petitioner shall add to the list the same particulars in respect of the person to whom [permission] has been given.

NOTES

Initial Commencement

Specified date

Specified date: 29 December 1986: see r 0.1.

Amendment

Para (4): word "permission" in square brackets in both places it occurs substituted by SI 2010/686, r 2, Sch 1, para 1.
Date in force: 6 April 2010: see SI 2010/686, r 1; for transitional provisions see r 6(1), Sch 4, paras 1, 2(1)(b) thereto.

Modification

References to solicitors etc modified to include references to bodies recognised under the Administration of Justice Act 1985, s 9, by the Solicitors' Incorporated Practices Order 1991, SI 1991/2684, arts 4, 5, Sch 1.

4.18 [Witness statement] in opposition

(1) If the company intends to oppose the petition, its [witness statement] in opposition shall be filed in court not less than [5 business] days before the date fixed for the hearing.

(2) A copy of the [witness statement] shall be sent by the company to the petitioner, [as soon as reasonably practicable] after filing.

NOTES

Initial Commencement

Specified date

Specified date: 29 December 1986: see r 0.1.

Amendment

Provision heading: words "Witness statement" in square brackets substituted by SI 2010/686, r 2, Sch 1, para 150(1), (2).
Date in force: 6 April 2010: see SI 2010/686, r 1; for transitional provisions and further effect see rr 6(1), 7, Sch 4, paras 1, 2(1)(b), (2)–(4), Sch 5 thereto.

Para (1): words "witness statement" in square brackets substituted by SI 2010/686, r 2, Sch 1, para 150(1), (3)(a).
Date in force: 6 April 2010: see SI 2010/686, r 1; for transitional provisions and further effect see rr 6(1), 7, Sch 4, paras 1, 2(1)(b), (2)–(4), Sch 5 thereto.

Para (1): words "5 business" in square brackets substituted by SI 2010/686, r 2, Sch 1, para 150(1), (3)(b).
Date in force: 6 April 2010: see SI 2010/686, r 1; for transitional provisions see r 6(1), Sch 4, para 1 thereto.

Para (2): words "witness statement" in square brackets substituted by SI 2010/686, r 2, Sch 1, para 150(1), (4).
Date in force: 6 April 2010: see SI 2010/686, r 1; for transitional provisions and further effect see rr 6(1), 7, Sch 4, paras 1, 2(1)(b), (2)–(4), Sch 5 thereto.

Para (2): words "as soon as reasonably practicable" in square brackets substituted by SI 2009/642, rr 4, 5.
Date in force: 6 April 2009: see SI 2009/642, r 1; for transitional provisions see r 3 thereof.

[4.18A Adjournment]

[(1) If the court adjourns the hearing of the petition, the following applies.

(2) Unless the court otherwise directs, the petitioning creditor must forthwith send—
   (a)   to the company, and
   (b)   where any creditor has given notice under Rule 4.16 but was not present at the hearing, to that creditor,
notice of the making of the order of adjournment. The notice must state the venue for the adjourned hearing.]

NOTES

Amendment

Inserted by SI 2010/686, r 2, Sch 1, para 151.
Date in force: 6 April 2010: see SI 2010/686, r 1; for transitional provisions see r 6(1), Sch 4, para 1 thereto.

4.19 Substitution of creditor or contributory for petitioner

(1) This Rule applies where a person petitions and is subsequently found not entitled to do so, or where the petitioner—

(a) fails to advertise his petition within the time prescribed by the Rules or such extended time as the court may allow, or

(b) consents to withdraw his petition, or to allow it to be dismissed, consents to an adjournment, or fails to appear in support of his petition when it is called on in court on the day originally fixed for the hearing, or on a day to which it is adjourned, or

(c) appears, but does not apply for an order in the terms of the prayer of his petition.

(2) The court may, on such terms as it thinks just, substitute as petitioner any creditor or contributory who in its opinion would have a right to present a petition, and who is desirous of prosecuting it.

[(2A) Where a member State liquidator has been appointed in main proceedings in relation to the company, without prejudice to paragraph (2), the court may, on such terms as it thinks just, substitute the member State liquidator as petitioner, where he is desirous of prosecuting the petition.]

(3) An order of the court under this Rule may, where a petitioner fails to advertise his petition within the time prescribed by these Rules, or consents to withdraw his petition, be made at any time.

NOTES

Initial Commencement

Specified date

Specified date: 29 December 1986: see r 0.1.

Amendment

Para (2A): inserted by SI 2002/1307, rr 3(1), 6(3).
Date in force: 31 May 2002: see SI 2002/1307, r 1.

4.20 Notice and settling of winding-up order

(1) When a winding-up order has been made, the court shall [s soon as reasonably practicable] give notice of the fact to the official receiver.

(2) The petitioner and every other person who has appeared on the hearing of the petition shall, not later than the business day following that on which the order is made, leave at the court all the documents required for enabling the order to be completed [as soon as reasonably practicable].

(3) It is not necessary for the court to appoint a venue for any person to attend to settle the order, unless in any particular case the special circumstances make an appointment necessary.

NOTES

Initial Commencement

Specified date

Specified date: 29 December 1986: see r 0.1.

Amendment

Para (1): words "as soon as reasonably practicable" in square brackets substituted by SI 2009/642, rr 4, 5.
Date in force: 6 April 2009: see SI 2009/642, r 1; for transitional provisions see r 3 thereof.
Para (2): words "as soon as reasonably practicable" in square brackets substituted by SI 2009/642, rr 4, 5.

Date in force: 6 April 2009: see SI 2009/642, r 1; for transitional provisions see r 3 thereof.

4.21 Transmission and advertisement of order

(1) When the winding-up order has been made, 3 copies of it, sealed with the seal of the court, shall be sent [as soon as reasonably practicable] by the court to the official receiver.

(2) The official receiver shall cause a sealed copy of the order to be served on the company by prepaid letter addressed to it at its registered office (if any) or, if there is no registered office, at its principal or last known principal place of business.

Alternatively, the order may be served on such other person or persons, or in such other manner, as the court directs.

(3) The official receiver shall forward to the registrar of companies the copy of the order which by section 130(1) is directed to be so forwarded by the company.

[(4) The official receiver—

(a) as soon as reasonably practicable shall cause notice of the order to be gazetted; and

(b) may advertise notice of the order in such other manner as the official receiver thinks fit.]

[(5) In addition to the standard contents a notice under paragraph (4) must state—

(a) that a winding-up order has been made in respect of the company; and

(b) the date of the order.]

NOTES

Initial Commencement

Specified date

Specified date: 29 December 1986: see r 0.1.

Amendment

Para (1): words "as soon as reasonably practicable" in square brackets substituted by SI 2009/642, rr 4, 5.
Date in force: 6 April 2009: see SI 2009/642, r 1; for transitional provisions see r 3 thereof.
Para (4): substituted by SI 2009/642, rr 4, 20.
Date in force: 6 April 2009: see SI 2009/642, r 1; for transitional provisions see r 3 thereof.
Para (5): inserted by SI 2010/686, r 2, Sch 1, para 152.
Date in force: 6 April 2010: see SI 2010/686, r 1; for transitional provisions see r 6(1), Sch 4, para 1 thereto.

See Further

See further, in relation to the application of this rule, for the purposes of the European Grouping of Territorial Cooperation Regulations 2007, SI 2007/1949: the European Grouping of Territorial Cooperation Regulations 2007, SI 2007/1949, regs 2, 7, 10, Schedule, Pt 3.
See further, in relation the application of this rule, with modifications, in respect of the procedure for the appointment of a bank liquidator and the operation of bank insolvency under the Banking Act 2009, Pt 2: the Bank Insolvency (England and Wales) Rules 2009, SI 2009/356, rr 3(3)–(8), 19.

[4.21A Expenses of voluntary arrangement]

[Where a winding-up order is made and there is at the time of the presentation of the petition in force for the company a voluntary arrangement under Part I of the Act, any expenses properly incurred as expenses of the administration of the arrangement in question shall be [payable in priority to any expenses of the liquidation].]

NOTES

Amendment

Inserted by SI 1987/1919, r 3(1), Schedule, Part 1, para 39.

Words "payable in priority to any expenses of the liquidation" in square brackets substituted by SI 2008/737, rr 3, 7(2).
Date in force: 6 April 2008: see SI 2008/737, r 1(1); for transitional provisions see r 2 thereof.

[4.21B Petition dismissed]

[(1) Unless the court otherwise directs, when a petition is dismissed, as soon as reasonably practicable the petitioner shall give notice of the dismissal. Such notice shall be—
- (a) gazetted; or
- (b) advertised in accordance with any directions of the court.

[(2) In addition to the standard contents, the notice published under paragraph (1) must state—
- (a) that a petition for the winding up of the company has been dismissed;
- (b) in the case of an overseas company, the address at which service of the petition was effected;
- (c) the name and address of the petitioner;
- (d) the date on which the petition was presented;
- (e) the date on which the petition was gazetted or otherwise advertised; and
- (f) the date of the hearing at which the petition was dismissed.]

(3) Where—
- (a) the petitioner is not the company itself; and
- (b) the petitioner has not complied with paragraphs (1) and (2) within 21 days of the date of the hearing at which the petition was dismissed,

the company may give notice of the dismissal itself. Such notice shall be gazetted.]

NOTES

Amendment

Inserted by SI 2009/642, rr 4, 21.
Date in force: 6 April 2009: see SI 2009/642, r 1; for transitional provisions see r 3 thereof.

Para (2): substituted by SI 2010/686, r 2, Sch 1, para 153.
Date in force: 6 April 2010: see SI 2010/686, r 1; for transitional provisions see r 6(1), Sch 4, para 1 thereto.

CHAPTER 4

PETITION BY CONTRIBUTORIES (NO CVL APPLICATION)

4.22 Presentation and service of petition

(1) The petition shall specify the grounds on which it is presented . . . and shall be filed in court with one copy for service under this Rule.

[(1A) No petition shall be filed unless there is produced with it the receipt for the deposit payable on presentation.]

(2) The court shall fix a hearing for a day ("the return day") on which, unless the court otherwise directs, the petitioner and the company shall attend before the registrar [or district judge for—
- (a) directions to be given in relation to the procedure on the petition; or

(b) where—
   (i) the petition is presented under Rule 4.7(9), and
   (ii) the court considers it just in all the circumstances,

the hearing of the petition].

(3) On fixing the return day, the court shall return to the petitioner a sealed copy of the petition for service, endorsed with the return day and time of hearing.

(4) The petitioner shall, at least 14 days before the return day, serve a sealed copy of the petition on the company.

[(5) Where a member State liquidator has been appointed in main proceedings in relation to the company, the petitioner shall send a copy of the petition to him.]

NOTES

Initial Commencement

Specified date
   Specified date: 29 December 1986: see r 0.1.

Amendment
   Para (1): words omitted revoked by SI 1987/1919, r 3(1), Schedule, Part 1, para 40(1).
   Para (1A): inserted by SI 1987/1919, r 3(1), Schedule, Part 1, para 40(2).
   Para (2): words from "or district judge" to "of the petition" in square brackets substituted by SI 2010/686, r 2, Sch 1, para 154.
      Date in force: 6 April 2010: see SI 2010/686, r 1; for transitional provisions see r 6(1), Sch 4, paras 1, 2(1)(b) thereto.
   Para (5): inserted by SI 2002/1307, rr 3(1), 6(4).
      Date in force: 31 May 2002: see SI 2002/1307, r 1.

4.23 Return of petition

(1) On the return day, or at any time after it, the court [must or, where the petition is presented under Rule 4.7(9), may] give such directions as it thinks appropriate with respect to the following matters—
   (a) service of the petition, whether in connection with the venue for a further hearing, or for any other purpose;
   (b) whether particulars of claim and defence are to be delivered, and generally as to the procedure on the petition;
   (c) whether and if so by what means, the petition is to be advertised;
   (d) the manner in which any evidence is to be adduced at any hearing before the judge and in particular (but without prejudice to the generality of the above) as to—
      (i) the taking of evidence wholly or in part by [witness statement] or orally;
      (ii) the cross-examination of any [persons authenticating witness statements];
      (iii) the matters to be dealt with in evidence;
   (e) any other matter affecting the procedure on the petition or in connection with the hearing and disposal of the petition.

(2) In giving directions under paragraph (1)(a), the court shall have regard to whether any of the persons specified in Rule 4.10 should be served with a copy of the petition.

NOTES

Initial Commencement

Specified date

Specified date: 29 December 1986: see r 0.1.

Amendment

Para (1): words "must or, where the petition is presented under Rule 4.7(9), may" in square brackets substituted by SI 2010/686, r 2, Sch 1, para 155(1), (2)(a).
Date in force: 6 April 2010: see SI 2010/686, r 1; for transitional provisions see r 6(1), Sch 4, paras 1, 2(1)(b) thereto.
Para (1): in sub-para (d)(i) words "witness statement" in square brackets substituted by SI 2010/686, r 2, Sch 1, para 155(1), (2)(b).
Date in force: 6 April 2010: see SI 2010/686, r 1; for transitional provisions and further effect see rr 6(1), 7, Sch 4, paras 1, 2(1)(b), (2)–(4), Sch 5 thereto.
Para (1): in sub-para (d)(ii) words "persons authenticating witness statements" in square brackets substituted by SI 2010/686, r 2, Sch 1, para 155(1), (2)(c).
Date in force: 6 April 2010: see SI 2010/686, r 1; for transitional provisions and further effect see rr 6(1), 7, Sch 4, paras 1, 2(1)(b), (2)–(4), Sch 5 thereto.

4.24 Application of Rules in Chapter 3

The following Rules in Chapter 3 apply, with the necessary modifications—
Rule 4.16 (notice of appearance);
Rule 4.17 (list of appearances);
Rule 4.20 (notice and settling of winding-up order); . . .
Rule 4.21 (transmission and advertisement of order)[; and
Rule 4.21A (expenses of voluntary arrangement)].

NOTES

Initial Commencement

Specified date

Specified date: 29 December 1986: see r 0.1.

Amendment

Word omitted revoked and words in square brackets inserted, by SI 1987/1919, r 3(1), Schedule, Part 1, para 41.

CHAPTER 5

PROVISIONAL LIQUIDATOR (NO CVL APPLICATION)

4.25 Appointment of provisional liquidator

[(1) An application to the court for the appointment of a provisional liquidator under section 135 may be made by—
- (a) the petitioner;
- (b) a creditor of the company;
- (c) a contributory;
- (d) the company;
- (e) the Secretary of State;
- (f) a temporary administrator;
- (g) a member State liquidator appointed in main proceedings; or
- (h) any person who under any enactment would be entitled to present a petition for the winding up of the company.]

(2) The application must be supported by [a witness statement] stating—
- (a) the grounds on which it is proposed that a provisional liquidator should be appointed;
- (b) if some person other than the official receiver is proposed to be appointed, that the person has consented to act and, to the best of the applicant's belief, is qualified to act as an insolvency practitioner in relation to the company;
- (c) whether or not the official receiver has been informed of the application and, if so, has been furnished with a copy of it;
- (d) whether to the applicant's knowledge—
  - (i) there has been proposed or is in force for the company a voluntary arrangement under Part I of the Act, or
  - (ii) an administrator or administrative receiver is acting in relation to the company, or
  - (iii) a liquidator has been appointed for its voluntary winding up; and
- (e) the applicant's estimate of the value of the assets in respect of which the provisional liquidator is to be appointed.

(3) The applicant shall send copies of the application and of the [witness statement] in support to the official receiver, who may attend the hearing and make any representations which he thinks appropriate.

If for any reason it is not practicable to comply with this paragraph, the official receiver must be informed of the application in sufficient time for him to be able to attend.

(4) The court may on the application, if satisfied that sufficient grounds are shown for the appointment, make it on such terms as it thinks [just].

NOTES

Initial Commencement

Specified date

Specified date: 29 December 1986: see r 0.1.

Amendment

Para (1): substituted by SI 2002/1307, rr 3(1), 6(5).
Date in force: 31 May 2002: see SI 2002/1307, r 1.
Para (2): words "a witness statement" in square brackets substituted by SI 2010/686, r 2, Sch 1, para 156(1), (2).
Date in force: 6 April 2010: see SI 2010/686, r 1; for transitional provisions and further effect see rr 6(1), 7, Sch 4, paras 1, 2(1)(b), (2)–(4), Sch 5 thereto.
Para (3): words "witness statement" in square brackets substituted by SI 2010/686, r 2, Sch 1, para 156(1), (3).
Date in force: 6 April 2010: see SI 2010/686, r 1; for transitional provisions and further effect see rr 6(1), 7, Sch 4, paras 1, 2(1)(b), (2)–(4), Sch 5 thereto.
Para (4): word "just" in square brackets substituted by SI 2010/686, r 2, Sch 1, para 1.
Date in force: 6 April 2010: see SI 2010/686, r 1; for transitional provisions see r 6(1), Sch 4, paras 1, 2(1)(b) thereto.

See Further

See further, in relation to the application of this rule, with modifications, in respect of bank administration and applications for bank administration: the Bank Administration (England and Wales) Rules 2009, SI 2009/357, rr 58–61.

[4.25A Notice of Appointment]

[(1) Where a provisional liquidator has been appointed the court shall [as soon as reasonably practicable] give notice of the fact to the official receiver.

(2) A copy of that notice shall at the same time be sent by the court to the provisional liquidator where he is not the official receiver.

[(3) Unless the court otherwise directs, on receipt of the notice of appointment, as soon as reasonably practicable the provisional liquidator shall give notice of that appointment. Such notice—
- (a) shall be gazetted; and
- (b) may be advertised in such other manner as the provisional liquidator thinks fit.]

[(4) In addition to the standard contents, the notice under paragraph (3) must state—
- (a) that a provisional liquidator has been appointed; and
- (b) the date of the appointment.]]

NOTES

Amendment

Inserted by SI 1987/1919, r 3(1), Schedule, Part 1, para 42.

Para (1): words "as soon as reasonably practicable" in square brackets substituted by SI 2009/642, rr 4, 5.
Date in force: 6 April 2009: see SI 2009/642, r 1; for transitional provisions see r 3 thereof.

Para (3): inserted by SI 2009/642, rr 4, 22.
Date in force: 6 April 2009: see SI 2009/642, r 1; for transitional provisions see r 3 thereof.

Para (4): inserted by SI 2010/686, r 2, Sch 1, para 157.
Date in force: 6 April 2010: see SI 2010/686, r 1; for transitional provisions see r 6(1), Sch 4, para 1 thereto.

See Further

See further, in relation to the application of this rule, with modifications, in respect of bank administration and applications for bank administration: the Bank Administration (England and Wales) Rules 2009, SI 2009/357, rr 58–61.

4.26 Order of appointment

(1) The order appointing the provisional liquidator shall specify the functions to be carried out by him in relation to the company's affairs.

(2) The court shall, [as soon as reasonably practicable] after the order is made, send sealed copies of the order as follows—
- (a) if the official receiver is appointed, [three] copies to him;
- (b) if a person other than the official receiver is appointed—
  - (i) [three] copies to that person, and
  - (ii) one copy to the official receiver;
- (c) if there is an administrative receiver acting in relation to the company, one copy to him.

[(3) Of the three copies of the order sent to the official receiver under paragraph (2)(a), or to another person under paragraph (2)(b)(i)—
  - (i) one shall in each case be sent by the recipient to the company, or if a liquidator has been appointed for the company's voluntary winding-up, to him; and
  - (ii) one shall be sent . . . to the registrar of companies.]

NOTES

Initial Commencement

Specified date

Specified date: 29 December 1986: see r 0.1.

Amendment

Para (2): words "as soon as reasonably practicable" in square brackets substituted by SI 2009/642, rr 4, 5.
  Date in force: 6 April 2009: see SI 2009/642, r 1; for transitional provisions see r 3 thereof.
Para (2): in sub-para (a) word "three" in square brackets substituted by SI 2005/527, r 21(a)(i).
  Date in force: 1 April 2005: see SI 2005/527, r 1(2).
Para (2): in sub-para (b)(i) word "three" in square brackets substituted by SI 2005/527, r 21(a)(ii).
  Date in force: 1 April 2005: see SI 2005/527, r 1(2).
Para (3): substituted by SI 2005/527, r 21(b).
  Date in force: 1 April 2005: see SI 2005/527, r 1(2).
Para (3): in sub-para (ii) words omitted revoked by SI 2010/686, r 2, Sch 1, para 158.
  Date in force: 6 April 2010: see SI 2010/686, r 1; for transitional provisions see r 6(1), Sch 4, para 1 thereto.

See Further

See further, in relation to the application of this rule, with modifications, in respect of bank administration and applications for bank administration: the Bank Administration (England and Wales) Rules 2009, SI 2009/357, rr 58–61.

4.27 Deposit

(1) Before an order appointing the official receiver as provisional liquidator is issued, the applicant for it shall deposit with him, or otherwise secure to his satisfaction, such sum as the court directs to cover the official receiver's remuneration and expenses.

(2) If the sum deposited or secured subsequently proves to be insufficient, the court may, on application by the official receiver, order that an additional sum be deposited or secured. If the order is not complied with within 2 [business] days after service of it on the person to whom it is directed, the court may discharge the order appointing the provisional liquidator.

(3) If a winding-up order is made after a provisional liquidator has been appointed, any money deposited under this Rule shall (unless it is required by reason of insufficiency of assets for payment of remuneration and expenses of the provisional liquidator) be repaid to the person depositing it (or as that person may direct) [as an expense of the liquidation], in the prescribed order of priority.

NOTES

Initial Commencement

Specified date

Specified date: 29 December 1986: see r 0.1.

Amendment

Para (2): word "business" in square brackets inserted by SI 2010/686, r 2, Sch 1, para 159.
  Date in force: 6 April 2010: see SI 2010/686, r 1; for transitional provisions see r 6(1), Sch 4, para 1 thereto.
Para (3): words "as an expense of the liquidation" in square brackets substituted by SI 2008/737, rr 3, 7(1).

Date in force: 6 April 2008: see SI 2008/737, r 1(1); for transitional provisions see r 2 thereof.

4.28 Security

(1) The following applies where an insolvency practitioner is appointed to be provisional liquidator under section 135.

(2) The cost of providing the security required under the Act shall be paid in the first instance by the provisional liquidator; but—

(a) if a winding-up order is not made, the person so appointed is entitled to be reimbursed out of the property of the company, and the court may make an order on the company accordingly, and

(b) if a winding-up order is made, he is entitled to be reimbursed [as an expense of the liquidation] in the prescribed order of priority.

NOTES

Initial Commencement

Specified date

Specified date: 29 December 1986: see r 0.1.

Amendment

Para (2): in sub-para (b) words "as an expense of the liquidation" in square brackets substituted by SI 2008/737, rr 3, 7(1).
Date in force: 6 April 2008: see SI 2008/737, r 1(1); for transitional provisions see r 2 thereof.

See Further

See further, in relation the application of this rule, with modifications, in respect of the procedure for the appointment of a bank liquidator and the operation of bank insolvency under the Banking Act 2009, Pt 2: the Bank Insolvency (England and Wales) Rules 2009, SI 2009/356, rr 3(3)–(8), 23.
See further, in relation to the application of this rule, with modifications, in respect of bank administration and applications for bank administration: the Bank Administration (England and Wales) Rules 2009, SI 2009/357, rr 58–61.

4.29 Failure to give or keep up security

(1) If the provisional liquidator fails to give or keep up his security, the court may remove him, and make such order as it thinks [just] as to costs.

(2) If an order is made under this Rule removing the provisional liquidator, or discharging the order appointing him, the court shall give directions as to whether any, and if so what, steps should be taken for the appointment of another person in his place.

NOTES

Initial Commencement

Specified date

Specified date: 29 December 1986: see r 0.1.

Amendment

Para (1): word "just" in square brackets substituted by SI 2010/686, r 2, Sch 1, para 1.
Date in force: 6 April 2010: see SI 2010/686, r 1; for transitional provisions see r 6(1), Sch 4, paras 1, 2(1)(b) thereto.

See Further

See further, in relation the application of this rule, with modifications, in respect of the procedure for the appointment of a bank liquidator and the operation of bank insolvency under the Banking Act 2009, Pt 2: the Bank Insolvency (England and Wales) Rules 2009, SI 2009/356, rr 3(3)–(8), 24.

See further, in relation to the application of this rule, with modifications, in respect of bank administration and applications for bank administration: the Bank Administration (England and Wales) Rules 2009, SI 2009/357, rr 58–61.

4.30 Remuneration

(1) The remuneration of the provisional liquidator (other than the official receiver) shall be fixed by the court from time to time on his application.

(2) In fixing his remuneration, the court shall take into account—

- (a) the time properly given by him (as provisional liquidator) and his staff in attending to the company's affairs;
- (b) the complexity (or otherwise) of the case;
- (c) any respects in which, in connection with the company's affairs, there falls on the provisional liquidator any responsibility of an exceptional kind or degree;
- (d) the effectiveness with which the provisional liquidator appears to be carrying out, or to have carried out, his duties; and
- (e) the value and nature of the property with which he has to deal.

(3) [Without prejudice to any order the court may make as to costs, the provisional liquidator's remuneration (whether the official receiver or another) shall be paid to him, and the amount of any expenses incurred by him (including the remuneration and expenses of any special manager appointed under section 177) reimbursed—

- (a) if a winding-up order is not made, out of the property of the company], and
- (b) if a winding-up order is made, [as an expense of the liquidation], in the prescribed order of priority,

or, in either case (the relevant funds being insufficient), out of the deposit under Rule 4.27.

[(3A) Unless the court otherwise directs, in a case falling within paragraph (3)(a) above the provisional liquidator may retain out of the company's property such sums or property as are or may be required for meeting his remuneration and expenses.]

(4) Where a person other than the official receiver has been appointed provisional liquidator, and the official receiver has taken any steps for the purpose of obtaining a statement of affairs or has performed any other duty under the Rules, he shall pay the official receiver such sum (if any) as the court may direct.

NOTES

Initial Commencement

Specified date

Specified date: 29 December 1986: see r 0.1.

Amendment

Para (3): words from "Without prejudice" to "of the company" in square brackets substituted by SI 1987/1919, r 3(1), Schedule, Pt 1, para 43(1).

Para (3): in sub-para (b) words "as an expense of the liquidation" in square brackets substituted by SI 2008/737, rr 3, 7(1).

Date in force: 6 April 2008: see SI 2008/737, r 1(1); for transitional provisions see r 2 thereof.

Para (3A): inserted by SI 1987/1919, r 3(1), Schedule, Pt 1, para 43(2).

See Further

See further, in relation the application of this rule, with modifications, in respect of the procedure for the appointment of a bank liquidator and the operation of bank insolvency under the Banking Act 2009, Pt 2: the Bank Insolvency (England and Wales) Rules 2009, SI 2009/356, rr 3(3)–(8), 25.

See further, in relation to the application of this rule, with modifications, in respect of bank administration and applications for bank administration: the Bank Administration (England and Wales) Rules 2009, SI 2009/357, rr 58–61.

4.31 Termination of appointment

(1) The appointment of the provisional liquidator may be terminated by the court on his application, or on that of any of the persons specified in Rule 4.25(1).

(2) If the provisional liquidator's appointment terminates, in consequence of the dismissal of the winding-up petition or otherwise, the court may give such directions as it thinks [just] with respect to the accounts of his administration or any other matters which it thinks appropriate.

(3) . . .

[(4) Notice of termination of the appointment of a provisional liquidator must be given by the provisional liquidator, unless the termination is on the making of a winding-up order or the court otherwise directs. Such notice—

(a) as soon as reasonably practicable must be sent to the registrar of companies;
(b) as soon as reasonably practicable must be gazetted; and
(c) may be advertised in such other manner as the provisional liquidator thinks fit.

(5) In addition to the standard contents, a notice under paragraph (4)(b) or (c) must state—

(a) that the appointment as provisional liquidator has been terminated;
(b) the date of that termination; and
(c) that the appointment terminated otherwise than on the making of a winding-up order.]

NOTES

Initial Commencement

Specified date

Specified date: 29 December 1986: see r 0.1.

Amendment

Para (1): word "just" in square brackets substituted by SI 2010/686, r 2, Sch 1, para 1.
Date in force: 6 April 2010: see SI 2010/686, r 1; for transitional provisions see r 6(1), Sch 4, paras 1, 2(1)(b) thereto.

Para (3): revoked by SI 1987/1919, r 3(1), Schedule, Pt 1, para 44.

Paras (4), (5): substituted, for para (3) (as inserted by SI 2009/642, rr 4, 23), by SI 2010/686, r 2, Sch 1, para 160.
Date in force: 6 April 2010: see SI 2010/686, r 1; for transitional provisions see r 6(1), Sch 4, para 1 thereto.

See Further

See further, in relation the application of this rule, with modifications, in respect of the procedure for the appointment of a bank liquidator and the operation of bank insolvency under the Banking Act 2009, Pt 2: the Bank Insolvency (England and Wales) Rules 2009, SI 2009/356, rr 3(3)–(8), 26.

See further, in relation to the application of this rule, with modifications, in respect of bank administration and applications for bank administration: the Bank Administration (England and Wales) Rules 2009, SI 2009/357, rr 58–61.

CHAPTER 6

STATEMENT OF AFFAIRS AND OTHER INFORMATION

4.32 Notice requiring statement of affairs (No CVL Application)

(1) The following applies where the official receiver determines to require a statement of the company's affairs to be made out and submitted to him in accordance with section 131.

(2) He shall send notice to each of the persons whom he considers should be made responsible under that section, requiring them to prepare and submit the statement.

(3) The persons to whom that notice is sent are referred to in this Chapter as "the [nominated persons]".

(4) The notice shall inform each of the [nominated persons]—

- (a) of the names and addresses of all others (if any) to whom the same notice has been sent;
- (b) of the time within which the statement must be delivered;
- (c) of the effect of section 131(7) (penalty for non-compliance); and
- (d) of the application to him, and to each of the other [nominated persons], of section 235 (duty to provide information, and to attend on the official receiver if required).

(5) The official receiver shall, on request, furnish a [nominated person] with instructions for the preparation of the statement and with the forms required for that purpose.

NOTES

Initial Commencement

Specified date

Specified date: 29 December 1986: see r 0.1.

Amendment

Para (3): words "nominated persons" in square brackets substituted by SI 2010/686, r 2, Sch 1, para 161(1), (2).
Date in force: 6 April 2010: see SI 2010/686, r 1; for transitional provisions see r 6(1), Sch 4, paras 1, 2(1)(b) thereto.
Para (4): words "nominated persons" in square brackets in both places they occur substituted by SI 2010/686, r 2, Sch 1, para 161(1), (2).
Date in force: 6 April 2010: see SI 2010/686, r 1; for transitional provisions see r 6(1), Sch 4, paras 1, 2(1)(b) thereto.
Para (5): words "nominated person" in square brackets substituted by SI 2010/686, r 2, Sch 1, para 161(1), (3).
Date in force: 6 April 2010: see SI 2010/686, r 1; for transitional provisions see r 6(1), Sch 4, paras 1, 2(1)(b) thereto.

See Further

See further, in relation the application of this rule, with modifications, in respect of the procedure for the appointment of a bank liquidator and the operation of bank insolvency under the Banking Act 2009, Pt 2: the Bank Insolvency (England and Wales) Rules 2009, SI 2009/356, rr 3(3)–(8), 27.

4.33 Verification and filing (No CVL Application)

(1) The statement of affairs shall be in Form 4.17, shall contain all the particulars required by that form and shall be verified by [a statement of truth] by the [persons making the statement of affairs] (using the same form).

(2) The official receiver may require any of the persons mentioned in section 131(3) to submit [a statement of concurrence verified by a statement of truth], stating that he concurs in the statement of affairs.

(3) [A statement] of concurrence made under paragraph (2) may be qualified in respect of matters dealt with in the statement of affairs, where the [maker of the statement of concurrence] is not in agreement with the [persons making the statement of affairs], or he considers the statement to be erroneous or misleading, or he is without the direct knowledge necessary for concurring in the statement.

(4) The statement of affairs shall be delivered to the official receiver by the [nominated person] (or by one of them, if more than one), together with a copy of the verified statement.

(5) Every [statement] of concurrence shall be delivered to the official receiver by the person who makes it, together with a copy.

[(6) The official receiver must send the verified copy of the statement of affairs and any statements of concurrence to the registrar of companies.]

(7) ...

NOTES

Initial Commencement

Specified date

Specified date: 29 December 1986: see r 0.1.

Amendment

Para (1): words "a statement of truth" in square brackets substituted by SI 2010/686, r 2, Sch 1, para 162(1), (2)(a).
Date in force: 6 April 2010: see SI 2010/686, r 1; for transitional provisions see r 6(1), Sch 4, paras 1, 2(1)(b) thereto.

Para (1): words "persons making the statement of affairs" in square brackets substituted by SI 2010/686, r 2, Sch 1, para 162(1), (2)(b).
Date in force: 6 April 2010: see SI 2010/686, r 1; for transitional provisions see r 6(1), Sch 4, paras 1, 2(1)(b) thereto.

Para (2): words "a statement of concurrence verified by a statement of truth" in square brackets substituted by SI 2010/686, r 2, Sch 1, para 162(1), (3).
Date in force: 6 April 2010: see SI 2010/686, r 1; for transitional provisions see r 6(1), Sch 4, paras 1, 2(1)(b) thereto.

Para (3): words "A statement" in square brackets substituted by SI 2010/686, r 2, Sch 1, para 162(1), (4)(a).
Date in force: 6 April 2010: see SI 2010/686, r 1; for transitional provisions see r 6(1), Sch 4, paras 1, 2(1)(b) thereto.

Para (3): words "maker of the statement of concurrence" in square brackets substituted by SI 2010/686, r 2, Sch 1, para 162(1), (4)(b).
Date in force: 6 April 2010: see SI 2010/686, r 1; for transitional provisions see r 6(1), Sch 4, paras 1, 2(1)(b) thereto.

Para (3): words "persons making the statement of affairs" in square brackets substituted by SI 2010/686, r 2, Sch 1, para 162(1), (4)(c).
Date in force: 6 April 2010: see SI 2010/686, r 1; for transitional provisions see r 6(1), Sch 4, paras 1, 2(1)(b) thereto.

Para (4): words "nominated person" in square brackets substituted by SI 2010/686, r 2, Sch 1, para 162(1), (5).
Date in force: 6 April 2010: see SI 2010/686, r 1; for transitional provisions see r 6(1), Sch 4, paras 1, 2(1)(b) thereto.

Para (5): word "statement" in square brackets substituted by SI 2010/686, r 2, Sch 1, para 162(1), (6).
Date in force: 6 April 2010: see SI 2010/686, r 1; for transitional provisions see r 6(1), Sch 4, paras 1, 2(1)(b) thereto.

Para (6): substituted by SI 2010/686, r 2, Sch 1, para 162(1), (7).
Date in force: 6 April 2010: see SI 2010/686, r 1; for transitional provisions see r 6(1), Sch 4, para 1 thereto.

Para (7): revoked by SI 2010/686, r 2, Sch 1, para 162(1), (8).
Date in force: 6 April 2010: see SI 2010/686, r 1; for transitional provisions see r 6(1), Sch 4, paras 1, 2(1)(b) thereto.

Insolvency Rules 1986, reg 4.33

See Further
See further, in relation the application of this rule, with modifications, in respect of the procedure for the appointment of a bank liquidator and the operation of bank insolvency under the Banking Act 2009, Pt 2: the Bank Insolvency (England and Wales) Rules 2009, SI 2009/356, rr 3(3)–(8), 28.

4.34 Statement of affairs—CVL

(1) This Rule applies with respect to the statement of affairs made out by the liquidator under section 95(3) or (as the case may be) by the directors under section 99(1).

(2) Where it is made out by the liquidator, the statement of affairs shall be delivered by him to the registrar of companies within [5 business] days after the creditors' meeting summoned under section 95(2).

[(3) Where it is made out by the directors under section 99(1) the statement of affairs shall be delivered by them to the liquidator in office following the creditors' meeting summoned under section 98 [as soon as reasonably practicable] after that meeting has been held; and he shall, within [5 business] days, deliver it to the registrar of companies.

(4) A statement of affairs under section 99(1) may be made up to a date not more than 14 days before that on which the resolution for voluntary winding up is passed by the company.]

[(5) The liquidator may require any of the directors who has not submitted the statement of affairs to submit a statement of concurrence verified by a statement of truth, stating that that director concurs in the statement of affairs.

(6) A statement of concurrence made under paragraph (5) may be qualified in respect of matters dealt with in the statement of affairs, where the maker of the statement of concurrence—

- (a) is not in agreement with the persons making the statement of affairs, or
- (b) considers the statement to be erroneous or misleading, or
- (c) is without the direct knowledge necessary for concurring in the statement.

(7) Every statement of concurrence must be delivered to the liquidator by the person who makes it, together with a copy.]

NOTES

Initial Commencement

Specified date
Specified date: 29 December 1986: see r 0.1.

Amendment
Para (2): words "5 business" in square brackets substituted by SI 2010/686, r 2, Sch 1, para 163(1), (2).
Date in force: 6 April 2010: see SI 2010/686, r 1; for transitional provisions see r 6(1), Sch 4, para 1 thereto.

Paras (3), (4): substituted, for para (3) as originally enacted, by SI 1987/1919, r 3(1), Schedule, Part 1, para 45.

Para (3): words "as soon as reasonably practicable" in square brackets substituted by SI 2009/642, rr 4, 5.
Date in force: 6 April 2009: see SI 2009/642, r 1; for transitional provisions see r 3 thereof.

Para (3): words "5 business" in square brackets substituted by SI 2010/686, r 2, Sch 1, para 163(1), (2).
Date in force: 6 April 2010: see SI 2010/686, r 1; for transitional provisions see r 6(1), Sch 4, para 1 thereto.

Paras (5)–(7): inserted by SI 2010/686, r 2, Sch 1, para 163(1), (3).

Date in force: 6 April 2010: see SI 2010/686, r 1; for transitional provisions see r 6(1), Sch 4, para 1 thereto.

[4.34A Copy Statement of affairs—CVL]

[Where a liquidator is nominated by the company at a general meeting held on a day prior to that on which the creditors' meeting summoned under section 98 is held, the directors shall [as soon as reasonably practicable] after his nomination or the making of the statement of affairs, whichever is the later, deliver to him a copy of the statement of affairs.]

NOTES

Amendment

Inserted by SI 1987/1919, r 3(1), Schedule, Part 1, para 46.

Words "as soon as reasonably practicable" in square brackets substituted by SI 2009/642, rr 4, 5.

Date in force: 6 April 2009: see SI 2009/642, r 1; for transitional provisions see r 3 thereof.

4.35 Limited disclosure . . .

(1) Where the official receiver [or liquidator] thinks that it would prejudice the conduct of the liquidation [or might reasonably be expected to lead to violence against any person] for the whole or part of the statement of affairs to be disclosed, he may apply to the court for an order of limited disclosure in respect of the statement, or any specified part of it.

(2) The court may on the application order that the statement or, as the case may be, the specified part of it be not filed [with the registrar of companies].

[(3) The official receiver or liquidator must as soon as reasonably practicable send to the registrar of companies a copy of the order and the statement of affairs (to the extent provided by the order) and any statement of concurrence.

(4) In a voluntary winding up, this Rule does not apply so far as section 95, 98 or 99 does not permit limited disclosure.]

NOTES

Initial Commencement

Specified date

Specified date: 29 December 1986: see r 0.1.

Amendment

Provision heading: words omitted revoked by SI 2010/686, r 2, Sch 1, para 164(1), (2).

Date in force: 6 April 2010: see SI 2010/686, r 1; for transitional provisions see r 6(1), Sch 4, para 1 thereto.

Para (1): words "or liquidator" in square brackets inserted by SI 2010/686, r 2, Sch 1, para 164(1), (3)(a).

Date in force: 6 April 2010: see SI 2010/686, r 1; for transitional provisions see r 6(1), Sch 4, para 1 thereto.

Para (1): words "or might reasonably be expected to lead to violence against any person" in square brackets inserted by SI 2010/686, r 2, Sch 1, para 164(1), (3)(b).

Date in force: 6 April 2010: see SI 2010/686, r 1; for transitional provisions see r 6(1), Sch 4, para 1 thereto.

Para (2): words "with the registrar of companies" in square brackets substituted by SI 2010/686, r 2, Sch 1, para 164(1), (4).

Date in force: 6 April 2010: see SI 2010/686, r 1; for transitional provisions see r 6(1), Sch 4, para 1 thereto.

Paras (3), (4): inserted by SI 2010/686, r 2, Sch 1, para 164(1), (5).

Date in force: 6 April 2010: see SI 2010/686, r 1; for transitional provisions see r 6(1), Sch 4, para 1 thereto.

See Further

See further, in relation the application of this rule, with modifications, in respect of the procedure for the appointment of a bank liquidator and the operation of bank insolvency under the Banking Act 2009, Pt 2: the Bank Insolvency (England and Wales) Rules 2009, SI 2009/356, rr 3(3)–(8), 29.

4.36 Release from duty to submit statement of affairs; extension of time (No CVL Application)

(1) The power of the official receiver under section 131(5) to give a release from the obligation imposed by that section, or to grant an extension of time, may be exercised at the official receiver's own discretion, or at the request of any [nominated person].

(2) A [nominated person] may, if he requests a release or extension of time and it is refused by the official receiver, apply to the court for it.

(3) The court may, if it thinks that no sufficient cause is shown for the application, dismiss it; but it shall not do so unless the applicant has had an opportunity to attend the court for [a] hearing, of which he has been given at least [5 business] days' notice [but which is without notice to any other party].

If the application is not dismissed under this paragraph, the court shall fix a venue for it to be heard, and give notice to the [nominated person] accordingly.

(4) The [nominated person] shall, at least 14 days before the hearing, send to the official receiver a notice stating the venue and accompanied by a copy of the application, and of any evidence which he (the [nominated person]) intends to adduce in support of it.

(5) The official receiver may appear and be heard on the application; and, whether or not he appears, he may file a written report of any matters which he considers ought to be drawn to the court's attention.

If such a report is filed, a copy of it shall be sent by the official receiver to the [nominated person], not later than 5 [business] days before the hearing.

(6) Sealed copies of any order made on the application shall be sent by the court to the [nominated person] and the official receiver.

(7) On any application under this Rule the applicant's costs shall be paid in any event by him and, [unless and to the extent that the court otherwise orders, shall not be an expense of the liquidation].

NOTES

Initial Commencement

Specified date

Specified date: 29 December 1986: see r 0.1.

Amendment

Words "nominated person" in square brackets in each place they occur substituted by SI 2010/686, r 2, Sch 1, para 165(1), (2).
Date in force: 6 April 2010: see SI 2010/686, r 1; for transitional provisions see r 6(1), Sch 4, paras 1, 2(1)(b) thereto.

Para (3): word "a" in square brackets substituted by SI 2010/686, r 2, Sch 1, para 165(1), (3)(a).
Date in force: 6 April 2010: see SI 2010/686, r 1; for transitional provisions see r 6(1), Sch 4, paras 1, 2(1)(b) thereto.

Para (3): words "5 business" in square brackets substituted by SI 2010/686, r 2, Sch 1, para 165(1), (3)(b).
Date in force: 6 April 2010: see SI 2010/686, r 1; for transitional provisions see r 6(1), Sch 4, para 1 thereto.

Para (3): words "but which is without notice to any other party" in square brackets inserted by SI 2010/686, r 2, Sch 1, para 165(1), (3)(c).
> Date in force: 6 April 2010: see SI 2010/686, r 1; for transitional provisions see r 6(1), Sch 4, paras 1, 2(1)(b) thereto.

Para (5): word "business" in square brackets inserted by SI 2010/686, r 2, Sch 1, para 165(1), (4).
> Date in force: 6 April 2010: see SI 2010/686, r 1; for transitional provisions see r 6(1), Sch 4, para 1 thereto.

Para (7): words "unless and to the extent that the court otherwise orders, shall not be an expense of the liquidation" in square brackets substituted by SI 2008/737, rr 3, 7(3).
> Date in force: 6 April 2008: see SI 2008/737, r 1(1); for transitional provisions see r 2 thereof.

See Further
> See further, in relation the application of this rule, with modifications, in respect of the procedure for the appointment of a bank liquidator and the operation of bank insolvency under the Banking Act 2009, Pt 2: the Bank Insolvency (England and Wales) Rules 2009, SI 2009/356, rr 3(3)–(8), 30.

4.37 Expenses of statement of affairs (No CVL Application)

(1) If any [nominated person] cannot himself prepare a proper statement of affairs, the official receiver may, [as an expense of the liquidation], employ some person or persons to assist in the preparation of the statement.

(2) At the request of any [nominated person], made on the grounds that he cannot himself prepare a proper statement, the official receiver may authorise an allowance, payable [as an expense of the liquidation], towards expenses to be incurred by the [nominated person] in employing some person or persons to assist him in preparing it.

(3) Any such request by the [nominated person] shall be accompanied by an estimate of the expenses involved; and the official receiver shall only authorise the employment of a named person or a named firm, being in either case approved by him.

(4) An authorisation given by the official receiver under this Rule shall be subject to such conditions (if any) as he thinks fit to impose with respect to the manner in which any person may obtain access to relevant books and papers.

(5) Nothing in this Rule relieves a [nominated person] from any obligation with respect to the preparation, verification and submission of the statement of affairs, or to the provision of information to the official receiver or the liquidator.

(6) Any payment [made as an expense of the liquidation] under this Rule shall be made in the prescribed order of priority.

(7) Paragraphs (2) to (6) of this Rule may be applied, on application to the official receiver by any [nominated person], in relation to the making of [a statement of concurrence verified by a statement of truth].

NOTES

Initial Commencement

Specified date
> Specified date: 29 December 1986: see r 0.1.

Amendment
> Words "nominated person" in square brackets in each place they occur substituted by SI 2010/686, r 2, Sch 1, para 166(1), (2).
> > Date in force: 6 April 2010: see SI 2010/686, r 1; for transitional provisions see r 6(1), Sch 4, paras 1, 2(1)(b) thereto.
>
> Para (1): words "as an expense of the liquidation" in square brackets substituted by SI 2008/737, rr 3, 7(4)(a).
> > Date in force: 6 April 2008: see SI 2008/737, r 1(1); for transitional provisions see r 2 thereof.

Para (2): words "as an expense of the liquidation" in square brackets substituted by SI 2008/737, rr 3, 7(1).
> Date in force: 6 April 2008: see SI 2008/737, r 1(1); for transitional provisions see r 2 thereof.

Para (6): words "made as an expense of the liquidation" in square brackets substituted by SI 2008/737, rr 3, 7(4)(b).
> Date in force: 6 April 2008: see SI 2008/737, r 1(1); for transitional provisions see r 2 thereof.

Para (7): words "a statement of concurrence verified by a statement of truth" in square brackets substituted by SI 2010/686, r 2, Sch 1, para 166(1), (3).
> Date in force: 6 April 2010: see SI 2010/686, r 1; for transitional provisions see r 6(1), Sch 4, paras 1, 2(1)(b) thereto.

See Further

> See further, in relation the application of this rule, with modifications, in respect of the procedure for the appointment of a bank liquidator and the operation of bank insolvency under the Banking Act 2009, Pt 2: the Bank Insolvency (England and Wales) Rules 2009, SI 2009/356, rr 3(3)–(8), 31.

4.38 Expenses of statement of affairs—CVL

(1) Payment may be made out of the company's assets, either before or after the commencement of the winding up, of any reasonable and necessary expenses of preparing the statement of affairs under section 99.

Any such payment is an expense of the liquidation.

(2) Where such a payment is made before the commencement of the winding up, the director presiding at the creditors' meeting held under section 98 shall inform the meeting of the amount of the payment and the identity of the person to whom it was made.

(3) The liquidator appointed under section 100 may make such a payment (subject to the next paragraph); but if there is a liquidation committee, he must give the committee at least [5 business] days' notice of his intention to make it.

(4) Such a payment shall not be made by the liquidator to himself, or to any associate of his, otherwise than with the approval of the liquidation committee, the creditors, or the court.

(5) This Rule is without prejudice to the powers of the court under Rule 4.219 (voluntary winding up superseded by winding up by the court).

NOTES

Initial Commencement

Specified date

> Specified date: 29 December 1986: see r 0.1.

Amendment

> Para (3): words "5 business" in square brackets substituted by SI 2010/686, r 2, Sch 1, para 167.
> > Date in force: 6 April 2010: see SI 2010/686, r 1; for transitional provisions see r 6(1), Sch 4, para 1 thereto.

4.39 Submission of accounts (No CVL Application)

(1) Any of the persons specified in section 235(3) shall, at the request of the official receiver, furnish him with accounts of the company of such nature, as at such date, and for such period, as he may specify.

(2) The period specified may begin from a date up to 3 years preceding the date of the presentation of the winding-up petition, or from an earlier date to which audited accounts of the company were last prepared.

(3) The court may, on the official receiver's application, require accounts for any earlier period.

(4) Rule 4.37 applies (with the necessary modifications) in relation to accounts to be furnished under this Rule as it applies in relation to the statement of affairs.

(5) The accounts shall, if the official receiver so requires, be verified by [a statement of truth] and (whether or not so verified) delivered to him within 21 days of the request under paragraph (1), or such longer period as he may allow.

(6) . . .

NOTES

Initial Commencement

Specified date

Specified date: 29 December 1986: see r 0.1.

Amendment

Para (5): words "a statement of truth" in square brackets substituted by SI 2010/686, r 2, Sch 1, para 168(1), (2).
   Date in force: 6 April 2010: see SI 2010/686, r 1; for transitional provisions see r 6(1), Sch 4, paras 1, 2(1)(b) thereto.
Para (6): revoked by SI 2010/686, r 2, Sch 1, para 168(1), (3).
   Date in force: 6 April 2010: see SI 2010/686, r 1; for transitional provisions see r 6(1), Sch 4, para 1 thereto.

See Further

See further, in relation the application of this rule, with modifications, in respect of the procedure for the appointment of a bank liquidator and the operation of bank insolvency under the Banking Act 2009, Pt 2: the Bank Insolvency (England and Wales) Rules 2009, SI 2009/356, rr 3(3)–(8), 32.

4.40 Submission of accounts—CVL

(1) Any of the persons specified in section 235(3) shall, at the request of the liquidator, furnish him with accounts of the company of such nature, as at such date, and for such period, as he may specify.

(2) The specified period for the accounts may begin from a date up to 3 years preceding the date of the resolution for winding up, or from an earlier date to which audited accounts of the company were last prepared.

(3) The accounts shall, if the liquidator so requires, be verified [by a statement of truth] and (whether or not so verified) delivered to him, with [the statement of truth] if required, within 21 days from the request under paragraph (1), or such longer period as he may allow.

NOTES

Initial Commencement

Specified date

Specified date: 29 December 1986: see r 0.1.

Amendment

Para (3): words "by a statement of truth" in square brackets substituted by SI 2010/686, r 2, Sch 1, para 169(1), (2)(a).
   Date in force: 6 April 2010: see SI 2010/686, r 1; for transitional provisions see r 6(1), Sch 4, paras 1, 2(1)(b) thereto.
Para (3): words "the statement of truth" in square brackets substituted by SI 2010/686, r 2, Sch 1, para 169(1), (2)(b).

Date in force: 6 April 2010: see SI 2010/686, r 1; for transitional provisions see r 6(1), Sch 4, paras 1, 2(1)(b) thereto.

4.41 Expenses of preparing accounts—CVL

(1) Where a person is required under Rule 4.40—CVL to furnish accounts, the liquidator may, with the sanction of the liquidation committee (if there is one) and [as an expense of the liquidation], employ some person or persons to assist in the preparation of the accounts.

(2) At the request of the person subject to the requirement, the liquidator may, with that sanction, authorise an allowance, payable [as an expense of the liquidation], towards expenses to be incurred by that person in employing others to assist him in preparing the accounts.

(3) Any such request shall be accompanied by an estimate of the expenses involved; and the liquidator shall only authorise the employment of a named person or a named firm, being in either case approved by him.

NOTES

Initial Commencement

Specified date

Specified date: 29 December 1986: see r 0.1.

Amendment

Para (1): words "as an expense of the liquidation" in square brackets substituted by SI 2008/737, rr 3, 7(5).
Date in force: 6 April 2008: see SI 2008/737, r 1(1); for transitional provisions see r 2 thereof.
Para (2): words "as an expense of the liquidation" in square brackets substituted by SI 2008/737, rr 3, 7(1).
Date in force: 6 April 2008: see SI 2008/737, r 1(1); for transitional provisions see r 2 thereof.

4.42 Further disclosure (No CVL Application)

(1) The official receiver may at any time require the [nominated persons], or any one or more of them, to submit (in writing) further information amplifying, modifying or explaining any matter contained in the statement of affairs, or in accounts submitted in pursuance of the Act or the Rules.

(2) The information shall, if the official receiver so directs, be verified by [a statement of truth], and (whether or not so verified) delivered to him within 21 days of the requirement under paragraph (1), or such longer period as he may allow.

(3) . . .

NOTES

Initial Commencement

Specified date

Specified date: 29 December 1986: see r 0.1.

Amendment

Para (1): words "nominated persons" in square brackets substituted by SI 2010/686, r 2, Sch 1, para 170(1), (2).
Date in force: 6 April 2010: see SI 2010/686, r 1; for transitional provisions see r 6(1), Sch 4, paras 1, 2(1)(b) thereto.
Para (2): words "a statement of truth" in square brackets substituted by SI 2010/686, r 2, Sch 1, para 170(1), (3).

Date in force: 6 April 2010: see SI 2010/686, r 1; for transitional provisions see r 6(1), Sch 4, paras 1, 2(1)(b) thereto.

Para (3): revoked by SI 2010/686, r 2, Sch 1, para 170(1), (4).
Date in force: 6 April 2010: see SI 2010/686, r 1; for transitional provisions see r 6(1), Sch 4, para 1 thereto.

See Further

See further, in relation the application of this rule, with modifications, in respect of the procedure for the appointment of a bank liquidator and the operation of bank insolvency under the Banking Act 2009, Pt 2: the Bank Insolvency (England and Wales) Rules 2009, SI 2009/356, rr 3(3)–(8), 33.

CHAPTER 7

INFORMATION TO CREDITORS AND CONTRIBUTORIES

4.43 Reports by official receiver (No CVL Application)

[(1)] The official receiver shall, at least once after the making of the winding-up order, send a report to creditors and contributories with respect to the proceedings in the winding up, and the state of the company's affairs.

[(1A) The official receiver shall also include in the report under paragraph (1)—
  (a) to the best of his knowledge and belief—
    (i) an estimate of the value of the prescribed part (whether or not he proposes to make an application to the court under section 176A(5) or section 176A(3) applies);
    (ii) an estimate of the value of the company's net property; and
  (b) whether, and if so, why, he proposes to make an application to court under section 176A(5).

(1B) Nothing in this Rule is to be taken as requiring any such estimate to include any information, the disclosure of which could seriously prejudice the commercial interests of the company. If such information is excluded from the calculation the estimate shall be accompanied by a statement to that effect.]

[(2) . . .]

NOTES

Initial Commencement

Specified date

Specified date: 29 December 1986: see r 0.1.

Amendment

Para (1): numbered as such by SI 1987/1919, r 3(1), Schedule, Pt 1, para 47.

Paras (1A), (1B): inserted by SI 2003/1730, r 7, Sch 1, Pt 4, para 15.
Date in force: 15 September 2003: see SI 2003/1730, r 1(2).

Para (2): revoked by SI 2010/686, r 2, Sch 1, para 171.
Date in force: 6 April 2010: see SI 2010/686, r 1; for transitional provisions see r 6(1), Sch 4, paras 1, 2(1)(b) thereto.

4.44 Meaning of "creditors"

Any reference in this Chapter to creditors is to creditors of the company who are known to the official receiver or (as the case may be) the liquidator . . ..

NOTES

Initial Commencement

Specified date

Specified date: 29 December 1986: see r 0.1.

Amendment

Words omitted revoked by SI 2010/686, r 2, Sch 1, para 172.
Date in force: 6 April 2010: see SI 2010/686, r 1; for transitional provisions see r 6(1), Sch 4, para 1 thereto.

See Further

See further, in relation the application of this rule, with modifications, in respect of the procedure for the appointment of a bank liquidator and the operation of bank insolvency under the Banking Act 2009, Pt 2: the Bank Insolvency (England and Wales) Rules 2009, SI 2009/356, rr 3(3)–(8), 35.

4.45 Report where statement of affairs lodged (No CVL Application)

(1) Where a statement of affairs has been submitted . . ., the official receiver shall send out to creditors and contributories a report containing a summary of the statement [(if he thinks fit, as amplified, modified or explained by virtue of Rule 4.42)] and such observations (if any) as he thinks fit to make with respect to it, or to the affairs of the company in general.

(2) The official receiver need not comply with paragraph (1) if he has previously reported to creditors and contributories with respect to the company's affairs (so far as known to him) and he is of opinion that there are no additional matters which ought to be brought to their attention.

NOTES

Initial Commencement

Specified date

Specified date: 29 December 1986: see r 0.1.

Amendment

Para (1): words omitted revoked by SI 2010/686, r 2, Sch 1, para 173.
Date in force: 6 April 2010: see SI 2010/686, r 1; for transitional provisions see r 6(1), Sch 4, paras 1, 2(1)(b) thereto.

See Further

See further, in relation the application of this rule, with modifications, in respect of the procedure for the appointment of a bank liquidator and the operation of bank insolvency under the Banking Act 2009, Pt 2: the Bank Insolvency (England and Wales) Rules 2009, SI 2009/356, rr 3(3)–(8), 36.

4.46 Statement of affairs dispensed with (No CVL Application)

(1) This Rule applies where, in the company's case, release from the obligation to submit a statement of affairs has been granted by the official receiver or the court.

(2) As soon as may be after the release has been granted, the official receiver shall send to creditors and contributories a report containing a summary of the company's affairs (so far as within his knowledge), and his observations (if any) with respect to it, or to the affairs of the company in general.

(3) The official receiver need not comply with paragraph (2) if he has previously reported to creditors and contributories with respect to the company's affairs (so far as

known to him) and he is of opinion that there are no additional matters which ought to be brought to their attention.

NOTES

Initial Commencement

Specified date

Specified date: 29 December 1986: see r 0.1.

See Further

See further, in relation the application of this rule, with modifications, in respect of the procedure for the appointment of a bank liquidator and the operation of bank insolvency under the Banking Act 2009, Pt 2: the Bank Insolvency (England and Wales) Rules 2009, SI 2009/356, rr 3(3)–(8), 37.

4.47 General rule as to reporting (No CVL Application)

(1) The court may, on the official receiver's application, relieve him of any duty imposed on him by this Chapter, or authorise him to carry out the duty in a way other than there required.

(2) In considering whether to act under this Rule, the court shall have regard to the cost of carrying out the duty, to the amount of the assets available, and to the extent of the interest of creditors or contributories, or any particular class of them.

NOTES

Initial Commencement

Specified date

Specified date: 29 December 1986: see r 0.1.

See Further

See further, in relation the application of this rule, with modifications, in respect of the procedure for the appointment of a bank liquidator and the operation of bank insolvency under the Banking Act 2009, Pt 2: the Bank Insolvency (England and Wales) Rules 2009, SI 2009/356, rr 3(3)–(8), 38.

4.48 Winding up stayed (No CVL Application)

(1) If proceedings in the winding up are stayed by order of the court, any duty of the official receiver to send reports under the preceding Rules in this Chapter ceases.

(2) Where the court grants a stay, it may include in its order such requirements on the company as it thinks [just] with a view to bringing the stay to the notice of creditors and contributories.

NOTES

Initial Commencement

Specified date

Specified date: 29 December 1986: see r 0.1.

Amendment

Para (2): word "just" in square brackets substituted by SI 2010/686, r 2, Sch 1, para 1.
Date in force: 6 April 2010: see SI 2010/686, r 1; for transitional provisions see r 6(1), Sch 4, paras 1, 2(1)(b) thereto.

Insolvency Rules 1986, reg 4.48

See Further

See further, in relation the application of this rule, with modifications, in respect of the procedure for the appointment of a bank liquidator and the operation of bank insolvency under the Banking Act 2009, Pt 2: the Bank Insolvency (England and Wales) Rules 2009, SI 2009/356, rr 3(3)–(8), 39.

4.49 Information to creditors and contributories—CVL

[(1)] The liquidator shall, within 28 days of a meeting held under section 95 or 98, send to creditors and contributories of the company—
- (a) a copy or summary of the statement of affairs, and
- (b) a report of the proceedings at the meeting.

[(2) The report under paragraph (1) shall also include—
- (a) to the best of the liquidator's knowledge and belief—
  - (i) an estimate of the value of the prescribed part (whether or not he proposes to make an application to court under section 176A(5) or section 176A(3) applies); and
  - (ii) an estimate of the value of the company's net property; and
- (b) whether, and if so, why, the liquidator proposes to make an application to court under section 176A(5).

(3) Nothing in this Rule is to be taken as requiring any such estimate to include any information, the disclosure of which could seriously prejudice the commercial interests of the company. If such information is excluded from the calculation the estimate shall be accompanied by a statement to that effect.]

NOTES

Initial Commencement

Specified date

Specified date: 29 December 1986: see r 0.1.

Amendment

Para (1): numbered as such by SI 2003/1730, r 7, Sch 1, Pt 4, para 16.
Date in force: 15 September 2003: see SI 2003/1730, r 1(2).
Paras (2), (3): inserted by SI 2003/1730, r 7, Sch 1, Pt 4, para 16.
Date in force: 15 September 2003: see SI 2003/1730, r 1(2).

[4.49A Further information where liquidation follows administration]

[Where under section 140 the court appoints as the company's liquidator a person who was formerly its administrator [or a person is appointed as liquidator upon the registration of a notice under paragraph 83(3) of Schedule B1 to the Act] and that person becomes aware of creditors not formerly known to him in his capacity as administrator, he shall send to those creditors a copy of any statement or report sent by him to creditors under [Rule 2.33], so noted as to indicate that it is being sent under this Rule.]

NOTES

Amendment

Inserted by SI 1987/1919, r 3(1), Schedule, Pt 1, para 49.
Words from "or a person" to "to the Act" in square brackets inserted by SI 2003/1730, r 7, Sch 1, Pt 4, para 17.
Date in force: 15 September 2003: see SI 2003/1730, r 1(2).
Words "Rule 2.33" in square brackets substituted by SI 2003/1730, r 7, Sch 1, Pt 4, para 17.

Date in force: 15 September 2003: see SI 2003/1730, r 1(2).

[4.49B Reports to creditors and members—winding up by the court (No CVL Application)]
[(1) "Progress report" means a report which includes—
- (a) details of the court where the proceedings are and the relevant court reference number;
- (b) full details of the company's name, address of registered office and registered number;
- (c) full details of the liquidator's name and address and date of appointment, including any changes in office-holder;
- (d) details of the basis fixed for the remuneration of the liquidator under Rule 4.127 (or if not fixed at the date of the report, the steps taken during the period of the report to fix it);
- (e) if the basis of remuneration has been fixed, a statement of—
  - (i) the remuneration charged by the liquidator during the period of the report (subject to paragraph (3)), and
  - (ii) where the report is the first to be made after the basis has been fixed, the remuneration charged by the liquidator during the periods covered by the previous reports (subject to paragraph (3)), together with a description of the things done by the liquidator during those periods in respect of which the remuneration was charged,

  irrespective in either case of whether payment was made in respect of that remuneration during that period;
- (f) a statement of the expenses incurred by the liquidator during the period of the report, irrespective of whether payment was made in respect of them during that period;
- (g) details of progress during the period of the report, including a receipts and payments account (as detailed in paragraph (2));
- (h) details of any assets that remain to be realised;
- (j) a statement of the creditors' right to request information under Rule 4.49E and their right to challenge the liquidator's remuneration and expenses under Rule 4.131; and
- (k) any other relevant information for the creditors.

(2) A receipts and payments account must be in the form of an abstract showing receipts and payments during the period of the report and, where the liquidator has ceased to act, must also include a statement as to the amount paid to unsecured creditors by virtue of the application of section 176A.

(3) Where the basis for the remuneration is a set amount under Rule 4.127(2)(c), it may be shown as that amount without any apportionment to the period of the report.

(4) The progress report must, except where paragraph (5) or (6) applies, cover the period of 1 year commencing on the date on which the liquidator is appointed and every subsequent period of 1 year.

(5) The period to be covered by a progress report ends on the date when a liquidator ceases to act, and the period to be covered by each subsequent progress report is each successive period of 1 year beginning immediately after that date (subject to the further application of this paragraph when another liquidator ceases to act).

(6) A progress report is not required for any period which ends after the liquidator has sent a draft report to creditors under Rule 4.49D.

(7) The liquidator must send a copy of the progress report within 2 months of the end of the period covered by the report, to the registrar of companies, to the members of the company and to the creditors.

(8) The court may, on the liquidator's application, extend the period of 2 months mentioned in paragraph (7), or make such other order in respect of the content of the report as it thinks just.

(9) This Rule does not apply where the liquidator is the official receiver.]

NOTES

Amendment

> Inserted by SI 2010/686, r 2, Sch 1, para 174.
> > Date in force: 6 April 2010: see SI 2010/686, r 1; for transitional provisions see r 6(1), Sch 4, para 1 thereto.

[4.49C CVL Progress reports—voluntary winding up]

[(1) This Rule applies for the purposes of sections 92A and 104A.

(2) The prescribed period for which the liquidator must produce a progress report, except when the liquidator ceases to act (in which case paragraph (3) applies) and subject to paragraph (4), is the period of 1 year commencing on the date on which the liquidator is appointed and every subsequent period of 1 year.

(3) When a liquidator ceases to act, and subject to paragraph (4)—
- (a) the prescribed period for which the liquidator must produce a progress report ends on the date of that liquidator's ceasing to act, and
- (b) the prescribed period for which the new liquidator (if any) must produce a progress report is the period of 1 year commencing immediately after that date and every subsequent period of 1 year (subject to the further application of this paragraph when that new liquidator ceases to act).

(4) A progress report is not required for any period which ends after the liquidator has sent a draft report to creditors under Rule 4.49D (final report to creditors).

(5) The prescribed matters to which a progress report must relate are those set out in Rule 4.49B(1)(b) to (j), (2) and (3); and for that purpose in a members' voluntary winding up—
- (a) the reference in Rule 4.49B(1)(d) to Rule 4.127 is to be read as a reference to Rule 4.148A,
- (b) the reference in Rule 4.49B(1)(j) to—
  - (i) the creditors' right to request information is to be read as a reference to the members' right to request information,
  - (ii) Rule 4.131 is to be read as a reference to Rule 4.148C, and
- (c) the reference in Rule 4.49B(3) to Rule 4.127(2)(c) is to be read as a reference to Rule 4.148A(2)(c).

(6) The prescribed person (in addition to members and creditors) to whom the liquidator must send a copy of a progress report is the registrar of companies.

(7) The prescribed period commencing with the end of the period prescribed in sub-paragraph (a) or (b) of paragraph (3) within which the liquidator must send a copy of a progress report to members, creditors and the registrar of companies is 2 months.]

NOTES

Amendment

> Inserted by SI 2010/686, r 2, Sch 1, para 174.
> > Date in force: 6 April 2010: see SI 2010/686, r 1; for transitional provisions see r 6(1), Sch 4, para 1 thereto.

[4.49D Final report to creditors]

[(1) The liquidator must, at least 8 weeks before holding a final meeting in accordance with section 106 or 146, send to each creditor known to the liquidator a draft of the report which the liquidator intends to lay before the meeting under Rule 4.125 or 4.126.

(2) The draft report must—
- (a) contain such matters and be in such terms as would comply with Rule 4.125 or 4.126, as the case may be, if the report were to be laid before a meeting as soon as reasonably practicable after the draft had been sent to creditors, and
- (b) be accompanied by a statement of the creditors' right to request information under Rule 4.49E and their right to challenge the liquidator's remuneration and expenses under Rule 4.131.

(3) The liquidator may not send a draft report to creditors under this Rule before giving notice under Rule 4.186 of intention to declare a final dividend or that no dividend or further dividend will be declared.

(4) If any creditor has applied to the court under Rule 4.131 and given a copy of the application to the liquidator, the final meeting may not be held until the application (including any appeal) has been disposed of and the liquidator has complied with any order of the court.

(5) This Rule does not apply where the liquidator is the official receiver.]

NOTES

Amendment

Inserted by SI 2010/686, r 2, Sch 1, para 174.
Date in force: 6 April 2010: see SI 2010/686, r 1; for transitional provisions see r 6(1), Sch 4, para 1 thereto.

[4.49E Creditors' and members' request for further information]

[(1) If—
- (a) within the period mentioned in paragraph (2)—
  - (i) a secured creditor, or
  - (ii) an unsecured creditor with the concurrence of at least 5% in value of the unsecured creditors (including the creditor in question), or
  - (iii) members of the company in a members' voluntary winding up with at least 5% of the total voting rights of all the members having the right to vote at general meetings of the company, or
- (b) with the permission of the court upon an application made within the period mentioned in paragraph (2)—
  - (i) any unsecured creditor, or
  - (ii) any member of the company in a members' voluntary winding up,

makes a request in writing to the liquidator for further information about remuneration or expenses set out in a progress report in accordance with Rule 4.49B(1)(e) or (f) (including by virtue of Rule 4.49C(5)) or in a draft report under Rule 4.49D, the liquidator must, within 14 days of receipt of the request, comply with paragraph (3) except to the extent that the request is in respect of matter in a draft report under Rule 4.49D or a progress report required by Rule 4.108 which (in either case) was previously included in a progress report not required by Rule 4.108.

(2) The period referred to in paragraph (1)(a) and (b) is—
- (a) 7 business days of receipt (by the last of them in the case of an application by more than one member) of the progress report where it is required by Rule 4.108, and

(b) 21 days of receipt (by the last of them in the case of an application by more than one member) of the report or draft report in any other case.
(3) The liquidator complies with this paragraph by either—
(a) providing all of the information asked for, or
(b) so far as the liquidator considers that—
(i) the time or cost of preparation of the information would be excessive, or
(ii) disclosure of the information would be prejudicial to the conduct of the liquidation or might reasonably be expected to lead to violence against any person, or
(iii) the liquidator is subject to an obligation of confidentiality in respect of the information,

giving reasons for not providing all of the information.
(4) Any creditor, and any member of the company in a members' voluntary winding up, who need not be the same as the creditors or members who asked for the information, may apply to the court within 21 days of—
(a) the giving by the liquidator of reasons for not providing all of the information asked for, or
(b) the expiry of the 14 days provided for in paragraph (1),
and the court may make such order as it thinks just.
(5) Without prejudice to the generality of paragraph (4), the order of the court under that paragraph may extend the period of 8 weeks or, as the case may be, 4 weeks provided for in Rule 4.131(1B) or 4.148C(2) by such further period as the court thinks just.
(6) This Rule does not apply where the liquidator is the official receiver.]

NOTES

Amendment

Inserted by SI 2010/686, r 2, Sch 1, para 174.
Date in force: 6 April 2010: see SI 2010/686, r 1; for transitional provisions see r 6(1), Sch 4, para 1 thereto.

[4.49F Arrangements under s 110 (acceptance of shares, etc, as consideration for sale of company property)]

[(1) Where there has been an arrangement under section 110 and a distribution to members has taken place pursuant to subsection (2) or (4) of that section, the liquidator must comply with paragraph (2) in respect of any account or report which the liquidator is required to prepare pursuant to any of the following—
(a) section 92A (progress report to company at year's end);
(b) section 94 (final meeting prior to dissolution—members' voluntary winding up);
(c) section 104A (progress report to company and creditors at year's end);
(d) section 106 (final meeting prior to dissolution—creditors' voluntary winding up);
(e) Rule 4.49B (reports to creditors and members—winding up by the court);
(f) Rule 4.49D (final report to creditors);
(g) Rule 4.108 (creditors' meeting to receive liquidator's resignation);
(h) Rule 4.126 (final meeting—creditors' voluntary liquidation);
(j) Rule 4.142 (company meeting to receive liquidator's resignation).
(2) The liquidator must—

(a) in any account or summary of receipts and payments which is required to be included in the account or report, state the estimated value of—
(i) the property transferred to the transferee;
(ii) the property received from the transferee; and
(iii) the property distributed to members pursuant to section 110(2) or (4),

during the period to which the account or report relates, and
(b) as a note to the account or summary of receipts and payments, provide details of the basis of the valuation.]

NOTES

Amendment

Inserted by SI 2010/686, r 2, Sch 1, para 174.
Date in force: 6 April 2010: see SI 2010/686, r 1; for transitional provisions see r 6(1), Sch 4, para 1 thereto.

[4.49G Other distributions to members in specie]

[(1) In a members' voluntary winding up, where there has been a distribution of property to members in its existing form other than pursuant to an arrangement under section 110, the liquidator must comply with paragraph (2) in respect of any account or report which the liquidator is required to prepare pursuant to any of the following—
(a) section 92A (progress report to company at year's end);
(b) section 94 (final meeting prior to dissolution);
(c) Rule 4.142 (company meeting to receive liquidator's resignation)
(2) The liquidator must—
(a) in any account or summary of receipts and payments which is required to be included in the account or report, state the estimated value of the property distributed amongst the members of the company during the period to which the account or report relates, and
(b) as a note to the account or summary of receipts and payments, provide details of the basis of the valuation.]

NOTES

Amendment

Inserted by SI 2010/686, r 2, Sch 1, para 174.
Date in force: 6 April 2010: see SI 2010/686, r 1; for transitional provisions see r 6(1), Sch 4, para 1 thereto.

CHAPTER 8

MEETINGS OF CREDITORS AND CONTRIBUTORIES

SECTION A: RULES OF GENERAL APPLICATION

4.50 First meetings (No CVL Application)

(1) If under section 136(5) the official receiver decides to summon meetings of the company's creditors and contributories for the purpose of nominating a person to be liquidator in place of himself, he shall fix a venue for each meeting, in neither case more than 4 months from the date of the winding-up order.

(2) When for each meeting a venue has been fixed, notice of the meetings shall be given . . .—

(a) in the case of the creditors' meeting, to every creditor who is known to the official receiver . . .; and

(b) in the case of the contributories' meeting, to every person appearing (by the company's books or otherwise) to be a contributory of the company.

[(3) Notice for each meeting must be given at least 14 days before the date fixed for it.]

[(4) The notice to creditors must state that proofs and (if applicable) proxies must be lodged at a specified place not later than 12.00 hours on the business day before the date fixed for the meeting in order for creditors to be entitled to vote at the meeting; and the same applies in respect of contributories and their proxies.]

[(5) Notice of the meetings shall be gazetted and may be advertised in such other manner as the official receiver thinks fit.]

[(5A) In addition to the standard contents, a notice under paragraph (5) must state—

(a) that a meeting of the creditors or contributories is to take place;
(b) the venue fixed for the meeting; and
(c) the time and date by which, and place at which, creditors must lodge proxies and hitherto unlodged proofs in order to be entitled to vote at the meeting.]

(6) Where the official receiver receives a request by creditors under section 136(5)(c) for meetings of creditors and contributories to be summoned, and it appears to him that the request is properly made in accordance with the Act, he shall—

(a) withdraw any notices previously given by him under section 136(5)(b) (that he has decided not to summon such meetings),
(b) fix the venue of each meeting for not more than 3 months from his receipt of the creditors' request, and
(c) act in accordance with paragraphs (2) to (5) above, as if he had decided under section 136 to summon the meetings.

(7) Meetings summoned by the official receiver under this Rule are known respectively as "the first meeting of creditors" and "the first meeting of contributories", and jointly as "the first meetings in the liquidation".

(8) Where the company is [an authorised deposit-taker or a former authorised deposit-taker], additional notices are required by Rule 4.72.

NOTES

Initial Commencement

Specified date

Specified date: 29 December 1986: see r 0.1.

Amendment

Para (2): first words omitted revoked by SI 2010/686, r 2, Sch 1, para 175(1), (2)(a).
    Date in force: 6 April 2010: see SI 2010/686, r 1; for transitional provisions see r 6(1), Sch 4, para 1 thereto.

Para (2): in sub-para (a) words omitted revoked by SI 2010/686, r 2, Sch 1, para 175(1), (2)(b).
    Date in force: 6 April 2010: see SI 2010/686, r 1; for transitional provisions see r 6(1), Sch 4, para 1 thereto.

Para (3): substituted by SI 2010/686, r 2, Sch 1, para 175(1), (3).
    Date in force: 6 April 2010: see SI 2010/686, r 1; for transitional provisions see r 6(1), Sch 4, para 1 thereto.

Para (4): substituted by SI 2010/686, r 2, Sch 1, para 175(1), (4).
    Date in force: 6 April 2010: see SI 2010/686, r 1; for transitional provisions see r 6(1), Sch 4, para 1 thereto.

Para (5): substituted by SI 2009/642, rr 4, 24.
    Date in force: 6 April 2009: see SI 2009/642, r 1; for transitional provisions see r 3 thereof.

Para (5A): inserted by SI 2010/686, r 2, Sch 1, para 175(1), (5).
Date in force: 6 April 2010: see SI 2010/686, r 1; for transitional provisions see r 6(1), Sch 4, para 1 thereto.
Para (8): words "an authorised deposit-taker or a former authorised deposit-taker" in square brackets substituted by SI 2001/3649, art 377(1), (5).
Date in force: 1 December 2001: see SI 2001/3649, art 1.

4.51 First meeting of creditors—CVL

(1) This Rule applies in the case of a meeting of creditors summoned by the liquidator under section 95 (where, in what starts as a members' voluntary winding up, he forms the opinion that the company will be unable to pay its debts) or a meeting under section 98 (first meeting of creditors in a creditors' voluntary winding up).

(2) The notice summoning the meeting shall [state the name of the company and the registered number of the company, and] specify a venue for the meeting and the time (not earlier than 12.00 hours on the business day before the day fixed for the meeting) by which, and the place at which, creditors must lodge [any [proofs and] proxies necessary to entitle them to vote at the meeting].

(3) Where the company is [an authorised deposit-taker or a former authorised deposit-taker], additional notices are required by Rule 4.72.

NOTES

Initial Commencement

Specified date

Specified date: 29 December 1986: see r 0.1.

Amendment

Para (2): words "state the name of the company and the registered number of the company, and" in square brackets inserted by SI 2005/527, r 22.
Date in force: 1 April 2005: see SI 2005/527, r 1(2).
Para (2): words from "any" to "at the meeting" in square brackets substituted by SI 1987/1919, r 3(1), Schedule, Pt 1, para 51.
Para (2): words "proofs and" in square brackets inserted by SI 2010/686, r 2, Sch 1, para 176.
Date in force: 6 April 2010: see SI 2010/686, r 1; for transitional provisions see r 6(1), Sch 4, para 1 thereto.
Para (3): words "an authorised deposit-taker or a former authorised deposit-taker" in square brackets substituted by SI 2001/3649, art 377(1), (6).
Date in force: 1 December 2001: see SI 2001/3649, art 1.

4.52 Business at first meetings in the liquidation (No CVL Application)

(1) At the first meeting of creditors, no resolutions shall be taken other than the following—

- (a) a resolution to appoint a named insolvency practitioner to be liquidator, or two or more insolvency practitioners as joint liquidators;
- (b) a resolution to establish a liquidation committee;
- (c) (unless it has been resolved to establish a liquidation committee) a resolution specifying the terms on which the liquidator is to be remunerated, or to defer consideration of that matter;
- (d) (if, and only if, two or more persons are appointed to act jointly as liquidator) a resolution specifying whether acts are to be done by both or all of them, or by only one;
- (e) (where the meeting has been requisitioned under section 136), a resolution authorising payment . . . as an expense of the liquidation, of the cost of summoning and holding the meeting and any meeting of contributories so requisitioned and held;

(f) a resolution to adjourn the meeting . . .;
(g) any other resolution which the chairman thinks it right to allow for special reasons.

(2) The same applies as regards the first meeting of contributories, but that meeting shall not pass any resolution to the effect of paragraph (1)(c) or (e).

[(3A) The meeting may be adjourned, either in accordance with a resolution under paragraph (1)(f) or if the chairman thinks fit, but for not more than 14 days from the date on which it was fixed to commence, subject to any direction of the court.

(3B) If there are subsequently further adjournments, the final adjournment must not be to a day later than 14 days after the date on which the meeting was originally held, subject to any direction of the court.

(3C) Where a meeting is adjourned under this Rule, proofs and proxies may be used if lodged at any time up to 12.00 hours on the business day immediately before the adjourned meeting.]

NOTES

Initial Commencement

Specified date

Specified date: 29 December 1986: see r 0.1.

Amendment

Para (1): in sub-para (e) words omitted revoked by SI 2008/737, rr 3, 7(6).
Date in force: 6 April 2008: see SI 2008/737, r 1(1); for transitional provisions see r 2 thereof.
Para (1): sub-para (f) revoked by SI 2010/686, r 2, Sch 1, para 177(1), (2).
Date in force: 6 April 2010: see SI 2010/686, r 1; for transitional provisions see r 6(1), Sch 4, para 1 thereto.
Paras (3A)–(3C): substituted, for para (3) as originally enacted, by SI 2010/686, r 2, Sch 1, para 177(1), (3).
Date in force: 6 April 2010: see SI 2010/686, r 1; for transitional provisions see r 6(1), Sch 4, para 1 thereto.

4.53 Business at meeting under s 95 or 98—CVL

Rule 4.52(1), except sub-paragraph (e), applies to a creditors' meeting under section 95 or 98.

NOTES

Initial Commencement

Specified date

Specified date: 29 December 1986: see r 0.1.

[4.53A Effect of adjournment of company meeting—CVL]

[Where a company meeting at which a resolution for voluntary winding up is to be proposed is adjourned, any resolution passed at a meeting under section 98 held before the holding of the adjourned company meeting only has effect on and from the passing by the company of a resolution for winding up.]

NOTES

Amendment

Inserted by SI 1987/1919, r 3(1), Schedule, Part 1, para 52.

[4.53B Report by director, etc—CVL]

[(1) At any meeting held under section 98 where the statement of affairs laid before the meeting does not state the company's affairs as at the date of the meeting, the directors of the company shall cause to be made to the meeting, either by the director presiding at the meeting or by another person with knowledge of the relevant matters, a report (written or oral) on any material transactions relating to the company occurring between the date of the making of the statement of affairs and that of the meeting.

(2) Any such report shall be recorded in the minutes of the meeting kept under Rule 4.71.]

NOTES

Amendment

Inserted by SI 1987/1919, r 3(1), Schedule, Part 1, para 52.

[4.53C CVL Additional contents of notices gazetted or advertised under s 95]

[In addition to the statement of duty required under subsection (2A) of section 95, and to the standard contents, notices under paragraphs (c) and (d) of that subsection must state—

    (a)   the purpose of the meeting; and
    (b)   the venue fixed for the meeting.]

NOTES

Amendment

Inserted by SI 2010/686, r 2, Sch 1, para 178.
Date in force: 6 April 2010: see SI 2010/686, r 1; for transitional provisions see r 6(1), Sch 4, para 1 thereto.

[4.53D CVL Additional contents of notices gazetted or advertised under s 98]

[In addition to the content required by section 98(2), and the standard contents, notices under section 98(1A) (c) or (d) must state—

    (a)   the purpose of the meeting; and
    (b)   the venue fixed for the meeting.]

NOTES

Amendment

Inserted by SI 2010/686, r 2, Sch 1, para 178.
Date in force: 6 April 2010: see SI 2010/686, r 1; for transitional provisions see r 6(1), Sch 4, para 1 thereto.

4.54 General power to call meetings

(1) The official receiver or the liquidator may at any time summon and conduct meetings of creditors or of contributories for the purpose of ascertaining their wishes in all matters relating to the liquidation; and in relation to any meeting summoned under the Act or the Rules, the person summoning it is referred to as "the convener".

(2) When (in either case) a venue for the meeting has been fixed, notice of it shall be given by the convener—

    (a)   in the case of a creditors' meeting, to every creditor who is known to him . . .; and

(b) in the case of a meeting of contributories, to every person appearing (by the company's books or otherwise) to be a contributory of the company.

(3) Notice of the meeting shall be given at least [14] days before the date fixed for it, and shall specify the purpose of the meeting.

[(4) The notice must state that proofs and (if applicable) proxies must be lodged at a specified place not later than 12.00 hours on the business day before the date fixed for the meeting in order for creditors to be entitled to vote at the meeting; and the same applies in respect of contributories and their proxies. (NO CVL APPLICATION)]

[(5–CVL) The notice must state that proofs and (if applicable) proxies must be lodged at a specified place not later than 12.00 hours on the business day before the date fixed for the meeting in order for creditors to be entitled to vote at the meeting.]

[(6) Notice of the meeting—
(a) shall be gazetted; and
(b) may be advertised in such other manner as the convenor thinks fit.]

[(7) In addition to the standard contents, the notice under paragraph (6) must state—
(a) who summoned the meeting;
(b) if the meeting was summoned by a creditor, the fact that it was so summoned and the section of the Act under which it was summoned;
(c) the purpose for which the meeting was summoned;
(d) the venue fixed for the meeting; and
(e) the time and date by which, and place at which, creditors must lodge proxies and hitherto unlodged proofs in order to be entitled to vote at the meeting.]

NOTES

Initial Commencement

Specified date

Specified date: 29 December 1986: see r 0.1.

Amendment

Para (2): in sub-para (a) words omitted revoked by SI 2010/686, r 2, Sch 1, para 179(1), (2).
  Date in force: 6 April 2010: see SI 2010/686, r 1; for transitional provisions see r 6(1), Sch 4, para 1 thereto.
Para (3): reference to "14" in square brackets substituted by SI 2010/686, r 2, Sch 1, para 179(1), (3).
  Date in force: 6 April 2010: see SI 2010/686, r 1; for transitional provisions see r 6(1), Sch 4, para 1 thereto.
Para (4): substituted by SI 2010/686, r 2, Sch 1, para 179(1), (4).
  Date in force: 6 April 2010: see SI 2010/686, r 1; for transitional provisions see r 6(1), Sch 4, para 1 thereto.
Para (5): substituted by SI 2010/686, r 2, Sch 1, para 179(1), (5).
  Date in force: 6 April 2010: see SI 2010/686, r 1; for transitional provisions see r 6(1), Sch 4, para 1 thereto.
Para (6): substituted by SI 2009/642, rr 4, 25.
  Date in force: 6 April 2009: see SI 2009/642, r 1; for transitional provisions see r 3 thereof.
Para (7): inserted by SI 2010/686, r 2, Sch 1, para 179(1), (6).
  Date in force: 6 April 2010: see SI 2010/686, r 1; for transitional provisions see r 6(1), Sch 4, para 1 thereto.

See Further

See further, in relation the application of this rule, with modifications, in respect of the procedure for the appointment of a bank liquidator and the operation of bank insolvency under the Banking Act 2009, Pt 2: the Bank Insolvency (England and Wales) Rules 2009, SI 2009/356, rr 3(3)–(8), 42.

See further, in relation to the disapplication of para (6)(a) above where the notice is of a meeting to be held under the Insolvency Act 1986, s 93 or s 105: the Insolvency (Amendment) Rules 2010, SI 2010/686, r 6(2).

4.55 The chairman at meetings (No CVL Application)

(1) This Rule applies both to a meeting of creditors and to a meeting of contributories.

(2) Where the convener of the meeting is the official receiver, he, or a person nominated by him, shall be chairman.

A nomination under this paragraph shall be in writing, unless the nominee is another official receiver or a deputy official receiver.

(3) Where the convener is other than the official receiver, the chairman shall be he, or a person nominated in writing by him.

A person nominated under this paragraph must be either—

- (a) one who is qualified to act as an insolvency practitioner in relation to the company, or
- (b) an employee of the liquidator or his firm who is experienced in insolvency matters.

NOTES

Initial Commencement

Specified date

Specified date: 29 December 1986: see r 0.1.

4.56 The chairman at meetings—CVL

(1) This rule applies both to a meeting of creditors (except a meeting under [section 95 or 98]) and to a meeting of contributories.

(2) The liquidator, or a person nominated by him in writing to act, shall be chairman of the meeting.

A person nominated under this paragraph must be either—

- (a) one who is qualified to act as an insolvency practitioner in relation to the company, or
- (b) an employee of the liquidator or his firm who is experienced in insolvency matters.

NOTES

Initial Commencement

Specified date

Specified date: 29 December 1986: see r 0.1.

Amendment

Para (1): words in square brackets substituted by SI 1987/1919, r 3(1), Schedule, Part 1, para 53.

4.57 Requisitioned meetings

(1) Any request by creditors to the liquidator (whether or not the official receiver) for a meeting of creditors or contributories, or meetings of both, to be summoned shall be accompanied by—

- (a) a list of the creditors concurring with the request and the amount of their respective claims in the winding up;

(b) from each creditor concurring, written confirmation of his concurrence; and

(c) a statement of the purpose of the proposed meeting.

Sub-paragraphs (a) and (b) do not apply if the requisitioning creditor's debt is alone sufficient, without the concurrence of other creditors.

(2) The liquidator shall, if he considers the request to be properly made in accordance with the Act, fix a venue for the meeting, not more than [28] days from his receipt of the request.

(3) The liquidator shall give [14] days' notice of the meeting, and the venue for it, to creditors.

(4) Paragraphs (1) to (3) above apply to the requisitioning by contributories of contributories' meetings, with the following modifications—

(a) for the reference in paragraph (1)(a) to the creditors' respective claims substitute the contributories' respective values (being the amounts for which they may vote at any meeting); and

(b) the persons to be given notice under paragraph (3) are those appearing (by the company's books or otherwise) to be contributories of the company.

(NO CVL APPLICATION)

NOTES

Initial Commencement

Specified date

Specified date: 29 December 1986: see r 0.1.

Amendment

Para (2): reference to "28" in square brackets substituted by SI 2010/686, r 2, Sch 1, para 180(1), (2).
  Date in force: 6 April 2010: see SI 2010/686, r 1; for transitional provisions see r 6(1), Sch 4, para 1 thereto.
Para (3): reference to "14" in square brackets substituted by SI 2010/686, r 2, Sch 1, para 180(1), (3).
  Date in force: 6 April 2010: see SI 2010/686, r 1; for transitional provisions see r 6(1), Sch 4, para 1 thereto.

See Further

See further, in relation the application of this rule, with modifications, in respect of the procedure for the appointment of a bank liquidator and the operation of bank insolvency under the Banking Act 2009, Pt 2: the Bank Insolvency (England and Wales) Rules 2009, SI 2009/356, rr 3(3)–(8), 44, 45.

4.58 Attendance at meetings of company's personnel

(1) This Rule applies to meetings of creditors and to meetings of contributories.

(2) Whenever a meeting is summoned, the convener shall give at least [14] days' notice to such of the company's personnel as he thinks should be told of, or be present at, the meeting.

"The company's personnel" means the persons referred to in paragraphs (a) to (d) of section 235(3) (present and past officers, employees, etc).

(3) If the meeting is adjourned, the chairman of the meeting shall, unless for any reason he thinks it unnecessary or impracticable, give notice of the adjournment to such (if any) of the company's personnel as he considers appropriate, being persons who were not themselves present at the meeting.

(4) The convener may, if he thinks fit, give notice to any one or more of the company's personnel that he is, or they are, required to be present at the meeting, or to be in attendance.

(5) In the case of any meeting, any one or more of the company's personnel, and any other persons, may be admitted, but—
- (a) they must have given reasonable notice of their wish to be present, and
- (b) it is a matter for the chairman's discretion whether they are to be admitted or not, and his decision is final as to what (if any) intervention may be made by any of them.

(6) If it is desired to put questions to any one of the company's personnel who is not present, the chairman may adjourn the meeting with a view to obtaining his attendance.

(7) Where one of the company's personnel is present at a meeting, only such questions may be put to him as the chairman may in his discretion allow.

NOTES

Initial Commencement

Specified date

Specified date: 29 December 1986: see r 0.1.

Amendment

Para (2): reference to "14" in square brackets substituted by SI 2010/686, r 2, Sch 1, para 181.

Date in force: 6 April 2010: see SI 2010/686, r 1; for transitional provisions see r 6(1), Sch 4, para 1 thereto.

See Further

See further, in relation the application of this rule, with modifications, in respect of the procedure for the appointment of a bank liquidator and the operation of bank insolvency under the Banking Act 2009, Pt 2: the Bank Insolvency (England and Wales) Rules 2009, SI 2009/356, rr 3(3)–(8), 46.

4.59 Notice of meetings by advertisement only

(1) In the case of any meeting of creditors or contributories to be held under the Act or the Rules, the court may order that notice of the meeting be given by . . . advertisement, and not by individual notice to the persons concerned.

(2) In considering whether to act under this Rule, the court shall have regard to the cost of . . . advertisement, to the amount of the assets available, and to the extent of the interest of creditors or of contributories, or any particular class of either of them.

[(3) In addition to the standard contents, the advertisement must state—
- (a) the venue fixed for the meeting;
- (b) that proofs and (if applicable) proxies must be lodged at a specified place not later than 12.00 hours on the business day before the date fixed for the meeting;
- (c) the date of the court order or the date of the resolution to wind up.]

NOTES

Initial Commencement

Specified date

Specified date: 29 December 1986: see r 0.1.

Amendment

Para (1): word omitted revoked by SI 2010/686, r 2, Sch 1, para 182(1), (2).

Date in force: 6 April 2010: see SI 2010/686, r 1; for transitional provisions see r 6(1), Sch 4, para 1 thereto.

Para (2): word omitted revoked by SI 2010/686, r 2, Sch 1, para 182(1), (2).
   Date in force: 6 April 2010: see SI 2010/686, r 1; for transitional provisions see r 6(1), Sch 4, para 1 thereto.
Para (3): inserted by SI 2010/686, r 2, Sch 1, para 182(1), (3).
   Date in force: 6 April 2010: see SI 2010/686, r 1; for transitional provisions see r 6(1), Sch 4, para 1 thereto.

See Further

See further, in relation the application of this rule, with modifications, in respect of the procedure for the appointment of a bank liquidator and the operation of bank insolvency under the Banking Act 2009, Pt 2: the Bank Insolvency (England and Wales) Rules 2009, SI 2009/356, rr 3(3)–(8), 47.

4.60 Venue

(1) In fixing the venue for a meeting of creditors or contributories, the convener shall have regard to the convenience of the persons (other than whoever is to be chairman) who are invited to attend.

(2) Meetings shall in all cases be summoned for commencement between the hours of 10.00 and 16.00 hours on a business day, unless the court otherwise directs.

(3) With every notice summoning a meeting of creditors or contributories there shall be sent out forms of proxy.

NOTES

Initial Commencement

Specified date

   Specified date: 29 December 1986: see r 0.1.

See Further

See further, in relation the application of this rule, with modifications, in respect of the procedure for the appointment of a bank liquidator and the operation of bank insolvency under the Banking Act 2009, Pt 2: the Bank Insolvency (England and Wales) Rules 2009, SI 2009/356, rr 3(3)–(8), 48.

4.61 Expenses of summoning meetings

(1) Subject as follows, the expenses of summoning and holding a meeting of creditors or contributories at the instance of any person other than the official receiver or the liquidator shall be paid by that person, who shall deposit with the liquidator security for their payment.

(2) The sum to be deposited shall be such as the official receiver or liquidator (as the case may be) determines to be appropriate; and neither shall act without the deposit having been made.

(3) Where a meeting of creditors is so summoned, it may vote that the expenses of summoning and holding it, and of summoning and holding any meeting of contributories requisitioned at the same time, shall be payable . . . as an expense of the liquidation.

(4) Where a meeting of contributories is summoned on the requisition of contributories, it may vote that the expenses of summoning and holding it shall be payable [as an expense of the liquidation], but subject to the right of creditors to be paid in full, with interest.

(5) To the extent that any deposit made under this Rule is not required for the payment of expenses of summoning and holding a meeting, it shall be repaid to the person who made it.

NOTES

Initial Commencement

Specified date

Specified date: 29 December 1986: see r 0.1.

Amendment

Para (3): words omitted revoked by SI 2008/737, rr 3, 7(7).
Date in force: 6 April 2008: see SI 2008/737, r 1(1); for transitional provisions see r 2 thereof.
Para (4): words "as an expense of the liquidation" in square brackets substituted by SI 2008/737, rr 3, 7(1).
Date in force: 6 April 2008: see SI 2008/737, r 1(1); for transitional provisions see r 2 thereof.

See Further

See further, in relation the application of this rule, with modifications, in respect of the procedure for the appointment of a bank liquidator and the operation of bank insolvency under the Banking Act 2009, Pt 2: the Bank Insolvency (England and Wales) Rules 2009, SI 2009/356, rr 3(3)–(8), 49.

4.62 Expenses of meeting under s 98—CVL

(1) Payment may be made . . ., either before or after the commencement of the winding up, of any reasonable and necessary expenses incurred in connection with the summoning, advertisement and holding of a creditors' meeting under section 98.

Any such payment is an expense of the liquidation.

(2) Where such payments are made before the commencement of the winding up, the director presiding at the creditors' meeting shall inform the meeting of their amount and the identity of the persons to whom they were made.

(3) The liquidator appointed under section 100 may make such a payment (subject to the next paragraph); but if there is a liquidation committee, he must give the committee at least [5 business] days' notice of his intention to make the payment.

(4) Such a payment shall not be made by the liquidator to himself, or to any associate of his, otherwise than with the approval of the liquidation committee, the creditors, or the court.

(5) This Rule is without prejudice to the powers of the court under Rule 4.219 (voluntary winding up superseded by winding up by the court).

NOTES

Initial Commencement

Specified date

Specified date: 29 December 1986: see r 0.1.

Amendment

Para (1): words omitted revoked by SI 2008/737, rr 3, 7(8).
Date in force: 6 April 2008: see SI 2008/737, r 1(1); for transitional provisions see r 2 thereof.
Para (3): words "5 business" in square brackets substituted by SI 2010/686, r 2, Sch 1, para 183.
Date in force: 6 April 2010: see SI 2010/686, r 1; for transitional provisions see r 6(1), Sch 4, para 1 thereto.

4.63 Resolutions

(1) [Subject as follows,] at a meeting of creditors or contributories, a resolution is passed when a majority (in value) of those present and voting, in person or by proxy, have voted in favour of the resolution.

The value of contributories is determined by reference to the number of votes conferred on each contributory by the company's articles.

(2) In the case of a resolution for the appointment of a liquidator—

(a) . . . if on any vote there are two nominees for appointment, the person who obtains the most support is appointed;

(b) if there are three or more nominees, and one of them has a clear majority over both or all the others together, that one is appointed; and

(c) in any other case, the chairman of the meeting shall continue to take votes (disregarding at each vote any nominee who has withdrawn and, if no nominee has withdrawn, the nominee who obtained the least support last time), until a clear majority is obtained for any one nominee.

[(2A) . . .]

(3) The chairman may at any time put to the meeting a resolution for the joint appointment of any two or more nominees.

(4) Where a resolution is proposed which affects a person in respect of his remuneration or conduct as liquidator, or as proposed or former liquidator, the vote of that person, and of any partner or employee of his, shall not be reckoned in the majority required for passing the resolution.

This paragraph applies with respect to a vote given by a person [(whether personally or on his behalf by a proxy-holder)] either as creditor or contributory or as [proxy-holder] for a creditor or a contributory (but subject to Rule 8.6 in Part 8 of the Rules).

NOTES

Initial Commencement

Specified date

Specified date: 29 December 1986: see r 0.1.

Amendment

Para (1): words "Subject as follows" in square brackets inserted by SI 1987/1919, r 3(1), Schedule, Pt 1, para 54(1).

Para (2): in sub-para (a) words omitted revoked by SI 2010/686, r 2, Sch 1, para 184(1), (2).
Date in force: 6 April 2010: see SI 2010/686, r 1; for transitional provisions see r 6(1), Sch 4, para 1 thereto.

Para (2A): revoked by SI 2010/686, r 2, Sch 1, para 184(1), (3).
Date in force: 6 April 2010: see SI 2010/686, r 1; for transitional provisions see r 6(1), Sch 4, para 1 thereto.

Para (4): words "(whether personally or on his behalf by a proxy-holder)" in square brackets inserted by SI 1987/1919, r 3(1), Schedule, Part 1, para 54(4)(a).

Para (4): words "proxy-holder" in square brackets substituted by SI 1987/1919, r 3(1), Schedule, Part 1, para 54(4)(b).

See Further

See further, in relation the application of this rule, with modifications, in respect of the procedure for the appointment of a bank liquidator and the operation of bank insolvency under the Banking Act 2009, Pt 2: the Bank Insolvency (England and Wales) Rules 2009, SI 2009/356, rr 3(3)–(8), 50.

[4.63A Resolutions by correspondence]

[(1) The liquidator may seek to obtain the passing of a resolution by creditors or contributories without holding a meeting by giving notice of the resolution to every creditor or contributory who is entitled to be notified of a meeting at which the resolution could be passed.

(2) In order to be counted, votes must be received by the liquidator in writing by 12.00 hours on the closing date specified in the notice, and in the case of votes cast by creditors must be accompanied by a proof of debt as required by Rule 4.67(1)(a) unless it has already been lodged under that Rule.

(3) If any vote cast by a creditor is received without a proof of debt, or the liquidator decides that the creditor or contributory is not entitled to vote according to Rules 4.67 to 4.70, then that creditor's or contributory's vote must be disregarded.

(4) The closing date shall be set at the discretion of the liquidator; but in any event it must not be set less than 14 days from the giving of notice provided for in paragraph (1).

(5) For the resolution to be passed, the liquidator must receive at least one valid vote by the closing date specified in the notice.

(6) If no valid vote is received by the closing date specified, the liquidator must call a meeting of creditors or contributories at which the resolution could be passed.

(7) Creditors whose debts amount to at least 10% of the total debts of the company may, within 5 business days from the giving of notice provided for in paragraph (1), require the liquidator to summon a meeting of creditors to consider the resolution.

(8) Contributories representing at least 10% of the total voting rights of all contributories having the right to vote at a meeting of contributories may, within 5 business days from the giving of notice provided for in paragraph (1), require the liquidator to summon a meeting of contributories to consider the resolution.

(9) A reference in these Rules to a resolution passed at a creditors' or contributories' meeting includes a reference to a resolution passed under this Rule.

(10) This Rule does not apply in respect of any resolution which the Act requires to be passed at a meeting.]

NOTES

Amendment

Inserted by SI 2010/686, r 2, Sch 1, para 185.
Date in force: 6 April 2010: see SI 2010/686, r 1; for transitional provisions see r 6(1), Sch 4, para 1 thereto.

4.64 Chairman of meeting as proxy-holder

Where the chairman at a meeting of creditors or contributories holds a proxy which requires him to vote for a particular resolution, and no other person proposes that resolution—

(a) he shall himself propose it, unless he considers that there is good reason for not doing so, and

(b) if he does not propose it, he shall [as soon as reasonably practicable] after the meeting notify his principal of the reason why not.

NOTES

Initial Commencement

Specified date

Specified date: 29 December 1986: see r 0.1.

Amendment

In para (b) words "as soon as reasonably practicable" in square brackets substituted by SI 2009/642, rr 4, 5.

Date in force: 6 April 2009: see SI 2009/642, r 1; for transitional provisions see r 3 thereof.

See Further

See further, in relation the application of this rule, with modifications, in respect of the procedure for the appointment of a bank liquidator and the operation of bank insolvency under the Banking Act 2009, Pt 2: the Bank Insolvency (England and Wales) Rules 2009, SI 2009/356, rr 3(3)–(8), 51.

4.65 Suspension and adjournment

(1) This Rule applies to meetings of creditors and to meetings of contributories.

(2) Once only in the course of any meeting, the chairman may, in his discretion and without an adjournment, declare the meeting suspended for any period up to one hour.

(3) The chairman at any meeting may in his discretion, and shall if the meeting so resolves, adjourn it to such time and place as seems to him to be appropriate in the circumstances.

This is subject to Rule 4.113(3) [or, as the case may be, 4.144—CVL (3),] in a case where the liquidator or his nominee is chairman, and a resolution has been proposed for the liquidator's removal.

(4) If within a period of 30 minutes from the time appointed for the commencement of a meeting a quorum is not present, then [the chairman may, at his discretion, adjourn the meeting to such time and place as he may appoint].

(5) An adjournment under this Rule shall not be for a period of more than [14] days; and Rule 4.60(1) and (2) applies.

[(6A) If within 30 minutes from the time appointed for commencement of a meeting there is no person present to act as chairman, the meeting stands adjourned to the same time and place in the following week or, if that is not a business day, to the business day immediately following.

(6B) Paragraph (6A) applies to further adjournments of a final meeting.

(6C) In the case of any other meeting, further adjournment must be to the same time and place in the following week or, if either—

(a) that is not a business day, or
(b) whether or not it is a business day, it is later than 14 days after the date on which the meeting in question was originally held,

to the same time and place on the business day immediately preceding which is not later than 14 days after the date on which the meeting in question was originally held.]

(7) Where a meeting is adjourned under this Rule, proofs and proxies may be used if lodged at any time up to midday on the business day immediately before the adjourned meeting.

NOTES

Initial Commencement

Specified date

Specified date: 29 December 1986: see r 0.1.

Amendment

Paras (3), (4): words in square brackets inserted or substituted by SI 1987/1919, r 3(1), Schedule, Part 1, para 55.

Para (5): reference to "14" in square brackets substituted by SI 2010/686, r 2, Sch 1, para 186(1), (2).

Date in force: 6 April 2010: see SI 2010/686, r 1; for transitional provisions see r 6(1), Sch 4, para 1 thereto.

Paras (6A)–(6C): substituted, for para (6) as originally enacted, by SI 2010/686, r 2, Sch 1, para 186(1), (3).

Date in force: 6 April 2010: see SI 2010/686, r 1; for transitional provisions see r 6(1), Sch 4, para 1 thereto.

See Further

See further, in relation the application of this rule, with modifications, in respect of the procedure for the appointment of a bank liquidator and the operation of bank insolvency under the Banking Act 2009, Pt 2: the Bank Insolvency (England and Wales) Rules 2009, SI 2009/356, rr 3(3)–(8), 52.

4.67 Entitlement to vote (creditors)

(1) Subject as follows in this Rule and the next, at a meeting of creditors a person is entitled to vote as a creditor only if—
- (a) there has been duly lodged (. . . by the time and date stated in the notice of the meeting) a proof of the debt
  - [(i) claimed to be due to him from the company, or
  - (ii) in relation to a member State liquidator, is claimed to be due to creditors in proceedings in relation to which he holds office], and the claim has been admitted under Rule 4.70 for the purpose of entitlement to vote, and
- (b) there has been lodged, by the time and date stated in the notice of the meeting, any proxy requisite for that entitlement.

(2) The court may, in exceptional circumstances, by order declare the creditors, or any class of them, entitled to vote at creditors' meetings, without being required to prove their debts.

Where a creditor is so entitled, the court may, on the application of the liquidator, make such consequential orders as it thinks [just] (as for example an order treating a creditor as having proved his debt for the purpose of permitting payment of dividend).

(3) A creditor shall not vote in respect of a debt for an unliquidated amount, or any debt whose value is not ascertained, except where the chairman agrees to put upon the debt an estimated minimum value for the purpose of entitlement to vote and admits his proof for that purpose.

(4) A secured creditor is entitled to vote only in respect of the balance (if any) of his debt after deducting the value of his security as estimated by him.

(5) A creditor shall not vote in respect of a debt on, or secured by, a current bill of exchange or promissory note, unless he is willing—
- (a) to treat the liability to him on the bill or note of every person who is liable on it antecedently to the company, and against whom a bankruptcy order has not been made (or, in the case of a company, which has not gone into liquidation), as a security in his hands, and
- (b) to estimate the value of the security and (for the purpose of entitlement to vote, but not for dividend) to deduct it from his proof.

[(6) No vote shall be cast by virtue of a debt more than once on any resolution put to the meeting.

(7) Where—
- (a) a creditor is entitled to vote under this Rule and Rule 4.70 (admission of proof),
- (b) has lodged his claim in one or more sets of other proceedings, and
- (c) votes (either in person or by proxy) on a resolution put to the meeting, only the creditor's vote shall be counted.

(8) Where—
- (a) a creditor has lodged his claim in more than one set of other proceedings, and
- (b) more than one member State liquidator seeks to vote by virtue of that claim,

the entitlement to vote by virtue of that claim is exercisable by the member State liquidator in main proceedings, whether or not the creditor has lodged his claim in the main proceedings.

(9) For the purposes of paragraphs (7) and (8), "other proceedings" means main proceedings, secondary proceedings or territorial proceedings in another member State.]

NOTES

Initial Commencement

Specified date

Specified date: 29 December 1986: see r 0.1.

Amendment

Para (1): in sub-para (a) words omitted revoked by SI 2010/686, r 2, Sch 1, para 187.
Date in force: 6 April 2010: see SI 2010/686, r 1; for transitional provisions see r 6(1), Sch 4, para 1 thereto.
Para (1): words from "(i) claimed to be" to "he holds office" in square brackets substituted by SI 2002/1307, rr 3(1), 6(6)(a).
Date in force: 31 May 2002: see SI 2002/1307, r 1.
Para (2): word "just" in square brackets substituted by SI 2010/686, r 2, Sch 1, para 1.
Date in force: 6 April 2010: see SI 2010/686, r 1; for transitional provisions see r 6(1), Sch 4, paras 1, 2(1)(b) thereto.
Paras (6)–(9): inserted by SI 2002/1307, rr 3(1), 6(6)(b).
Date in force: 31 May 2002: see SI 2002/1307, r 1.

See Further

See further, in relation the application of this rule, with modifications, in respect of the procedure for the appointment of a bank liquidator and the operation of bank insolvency under the Banking Act 2009, Pt 2: the Bank Insolvency (England and Wales) Rules 2009, SI 2009/356, rr 3(3)–(8), 53.

4.68 Chairman's discretion to allow vote—...

At a creditors' meeting [in a creditors' voluntary winding up or a winding up by the court], the chairman may allow a creditor to vote, notwithstanding that he has failed to comply with Rule 4.67(1)(a), if satisfied that the failure was due to circumstances beyond the creditor's control.

NOTES

Initial Commencement

Specified date

Specified date: 29 December 1986: see r 0.1.

Amendment

Provision heading: reference omitted revoked by SI 2010/686, r 2, Sch 1, para 188(1), (2).
Date in force: 6 April 2010: see SI 2010/686, r 1; for transitional provisions see r 6(1), Sch 4, para 1 thereto.
Words "in a creditors' voluntary winding up or a winding up by the court" in square brackets inserted by SI 2010/686, r 2, Sch 1, para 188(1), (3).
Date in force: 6 April 2010: see SI 2010/686, r 1; for transitional provisions see r 6(1), Sch 4, para 1 thereto.

4.69 Entitlement to vote (contributories)

At a meeting of contributories, voting rights are as at a general meeting of the company, subject to any provision in the articles affecting entitlement to vote, either generally or at a time when the company is in liquidation.

NOTES

Initial Commencement

Specified date

Specified date: 29 December 1986: see r 0.1.

See Further

See further, in relation the application of this rule, with modifications, in respect of the procedure for the appointment of a bank liquidator and the operation of bank insolvency under the Banking Act 2009, Pt 2: the Bank Insolvency (England and Wales) Rules 2009, SI 2009/356, rr 3(3)–(8), 54.

4.70 Admission and rejection of proof (creditors' meeting)

(1) At any creditors' meeting the chairman has power to admit or reject a creditors' proof for the purpose of his entitlement to vote; and the power is exercisable with respect to the whole or any part of the proof.

(2) The chairman's decision under this Rule, or in respect of any matter arising under Rule 4.67, is subject to appeal to the court by any creditor or contributory.

(3) If the chairman is in doubt whether a proof should be admitted or rejected, he shall mark it as objected to and allow the creditor to vote, subject to his vote being subsequently declared invalid if the objection to the proof is sustained.

(4) If on an appeal the chairman's decision is reversed or varied, or a creditor's vote is declared invalid, the court may order that another meeting be summoned, or make such other order as it thinks just.

[(4A) An application to the court by way of appeal under this Rule against a decision of the chairman must be made not later than 21 days after the date of the meeting.]

(5) Neither the official receiver, nor any person nominated by him to be chairman, is personally liable for costs incurred by any person in respect of an application under this Rule; and the chairman (if other than the official receiver or a person so nominated) is not so liable unless the court makes an order to that effect.
(NO CVL APPLICATION)

(6–CVL) The liquidator or his nominee as chairman is not personally liable for costs incurred by any person in respect of an application under this Rule, unless the court makes an order to that effect.

NOTES

Initial Commencement

Specified date

Specified date: 29 December 1986: see r 0.1.

Amendment

Para (4A): inserted by SI 2010/686, r 2, Sch 1, para 189.
Date in force: 6 April 2010: see SI 2010/686, r 1; for transitional provisions see r 6(1), Sch 4, para 1 thereto.

See Further

See further, in relation the application of this rule, with modifications, in respect of the procedure for the appointment of a bank liquidator and the operation of bank insolvency under the Banking Act 2009, Pt 2: the Bank Insolvency (England and Wales) Rules 2009, SI 2009/356, rr 3(3)–(8), 55.

Insolvency Rules 1986, reg 4.71

4.71 Record of proceedings

(1) At any meeting, the chairman shall cause minutes of the proceedings to be kept. The minutes shall be [authenticated] by him, and retained as part of the records of the liquidation.

(2) The chairman shall also cause to be made up and kept a list of all the creditors or, as the case may be, contributories who attended the meeting.

(3) The minutes of the meeting shall include a record of every resolution passed [and if a liquidation committee has been established, the names and addresses of those elected to be members of the committee].

(4) . . .

NOTES

Initial Commencement

Specified date
    Specified date: 29 December 1986: see r 0.1.

Amendment
    Para (1): word "authenticated" in square brackets substituted by SI 2010/686, r 2, Sch 1, para 1.
        Date in force: 6 April 2010: see SI 2010/686, r 1; for transitional provisions see r 6(1), Sch 4, paras 1, 2(1)(b) thereto.
    Para (3): words from "and if a" to "of the committee" in square brackets inserted by SI 2010/686, r 2, Sch 1, para 190(1), (2) (as amended by SI 2010/734, rr 2, 4).
        Date in force: 6 April 2010: see SI 2010/686, r 1; for transitional provisions see r 6(1), Sch 4, para 1 thereto.
    Para (4): revoked by SI 2010/686, r 2, Sch 1, para 190(1), (3).
        Date in force: 6 April 2010: see SI 2010/686, r 1; for transitional provisions see r 6(1), Sch 4, para 1 thereto.

See Further
    See further, in relation the application of this rule, with modifications, in respect of the procedure for the appointment of a bank liquidator and the operation of bank insolvency under the Banking Act 2009, Pt 2: the Bank Insolvency (England and Wales) Rules 2009, SI 2009/356, rr 3(3)–(8), 56.

SECTION B: WINDING UP OF RECOGNISED BANKS, ETC

4.72 Additional provisions as regards certain meetings

(1) This Rule applies where a company goes, or proposes to go, into liquidation and it is [an authorised deposit-taker or a former authorised deposit-taker].

(2) Notice of any meeting of the company at which it is intended to propose a resolution for its winding up shall be given by the directors to the [Financial Services Authority] and [to the scheme manager established under section 212(1) of the Financial Services and Markets Act 2000].

(3) Notice to the [Authority] and [the scheme manager] shall be the same as given to members of the company.

(4) Where a creditors' meeting is summoned by the liquidator under section 95 or, in a creditors' voluntary winding up, is summoned under section 98, the same notice of the meeting must be given to the [Authority] and [the scheme manager] as is given to creditors under Rule 4.51—CVL.

(5) Where the company is being wound up by the court, notice of the first meetings of creditors and contributories shall be given to the [Authority] and [the scheme manager] by the official receiver.

(6) Where in the winding up (whether voluntary or by the court) a meeting of creditors or contributories or of the company is summoned for the purpose of—

    (a)   receiving the liquidator's resignation, or

(b) removing the liquidator, or
(c) appointing a new liquidator,
the person summoning the meeting and giving notice of it shall also give notice to the [Authority] and [the scheme manager].

(7) [The scheme manager] is entitled to be represented at any meeting of which it is required by this Rule to be given notice; and Schedule 1 to the Rules has effect with respect to the voting rights of [the scheme manager] at such a meeting.

NOTES

Initial Commencement

Specified date

Specified date: 29 December 1986: see r 0.1.

Amendment

Para (1): words "an authorised deposit-taker or a former authorised deposit-taker" in square brackets substituted by SI 2001/3649, art 377(1), (7).
Date in force: 1 December 2001: see SI 2001/3649, art 1.
Para (2): words "Financial Services Authority" in square brackets substituted by SI 1998/1129, art 2, Sch 1, para 4(5)(a).
Date in force: 1 June 1998: see SI 1998/1129, art 1.
Para (2): words "to the scheme manager established under section 212(1) of the Financial Services and Markets Act 2000" in square brackets substituted by SI 2001/3649, art 378(2)(a).
Date in force: 1 December 2001: see SI 2001/3649, art 1.
Para (3): word "Authority" in square brackets substituted by SI 1998/1129, art 2, Sch 1, para 4(5)(b).
Date in force: 1 June 1998: see SI 1998/1129, art 1.
Paras (3)–(7): words "The scheme manager" and words "the Scheme Manager" in square brackets in each place they occur substituted by SI 2001/3649, art 378(2)(b).
Date in force: 1 December 2001: see SI 2001/3649, art 1.
Para (4): word "Authority" in square brackets substituted by SI 1998/1129, art 2, Sch 1, para 4(5)(b).
Date in force: 1 June 1998: see SI 1998/1129, art 1.
Para (5): word "Authority" in square brackets substituted by SI 1998/1129, art 2, Sch 1, para 4(5)(b).
Date in force: 1 June 1998: see SI 1998/1129, art 1.
Para (6): word "Authority" in square brackets substituted by SI 1998/1129, art 2, Sch 1, para 4(5)(b).
Date in force: 1 June 1998: see SI 1998/1129, art 1.

CHAPTER 9

PROOF OF DEBTS IN A LIQUIDATION

SECTION A: PROCEDURE FOR PROVING

4.73 Meaning of "prove"

(1) Where a company is being wound up by the court, a person claiming to be a creditor of the company and wishing to recover his debt in whole or in part must (subject to any order of the court under Rule 4.67(2)) submit his claim in writing to the liquidator. (NO CVL APPLICATION)

(2–CVL) In a voluntary winding up (whether members' or creditors') the liquidator may require a person claiming to be a creditor of the company and wishing to recover his debt in whole or in part, to submit the claim in writing to him.

(3) A creditor who claims (whether or not in writing) is referred to as "proving" for his debt; and a document by which he seeks to establish his claim is his "proof".

(4) Subject to the next paragraph, a proof must be in the form known as "proof of debt" (whether the form prescribed by the Rules, or a substantially similar form),

Insolvency Rules 1986, reg 4.73

which shall be made out by or under the directions of the creditor, and [authenticated] by him or a person authorised in that behalf. (NO CVL APPLICATION)

(5) Where a debt is due to a Minister of the Crown or a Government Department, the proof need not be in that form, provided that there are shown all such particulars of the debt as are required in the form used by other creditors, and as are relevant in the circumstances. (NO CVL APPLICATION)

(6–CVL) The creditor's proof may be in any form.

(7) . . .

[(8) Where a winding up is immediately preceded by an administration, a creditor proving in the administration shall be deemed to have proved in the winding up.]

NOTES

Initial Commencement

Specified date

Specified date: 29 December 1986: see r 0.1.

Amendment

Para (4): word "authenticated" in square brackets substituted by SI 2010/686, r 2, Sch 1, para 1.
Date in force: 6 April 2010: see SI 2010/686, r 1; for transitional provisions see r 6(1), Sch 4, paras 1, 2(1)(b) thereto.
Para (7): revoked by SI 2010/686, r 2, Sch 1, para 191.
Date in force: 6 April 2010: see SI 2010/686, r 1; for transitional provisions see r 6(1), Sch 4, para 1 thereto.
Para (8): inserted by SI 2003/1730, r 7, Sch 1, Pt 4, para 18.
Date in force: 15 September 2003: see SI 2003/1730, r 1(2).

See Further

See further, in relation the application of this rule, with modifications, in respect of the procedure for the appointment of a bank liquidator and the operation of bank insolvency under the Banking Act 2009, Pt 2: the Bank Insolvency (England and Wales) Rules 2009, SI 2009/356, rr 3(3)–(8), 57.

[**4.74 Supply of Forms (No CVL Application)**]
[A form of proof shall be sent to any creditor of the company by the liquidator where the creditor so requests.]

NOTES

Amendment

Substituted by SI 2004/584, r 9.
Date in force: 1 April 2004: see SI 2004/584, r 1(2).

See Further

See further, in relation the application of this rule, with modifications, in respect of the procedure for the appointment of a bank liquidator and the operation of bank insolvency under the Banking Act 2009, Pt 2: the Bank Insolvency (England and Wales) Rules 2009, SI 2009/356, rr 3(3)–(8), 58.

4.75 Contents of proof (No CVL Application)

[(1) Subject to Rule 4.73(5), the following matters shall be stated in a creditor's proof of debt—

(a) the creditor's name and address, and, if a company, its company registration number;

(b) the total amount of his claim (including any Value Added Tax) as at the date on which the company went into liquidation [(or, if the liquidation was immediately preceded by an administration, the date on which the company entered administration), less any payments made after that date in respect of the claim and any deduction under Rule 4.89];
(c) whether or not that amount includes outstanding uncapitalised interest;
(d) particulars of how and when the debt was incurred by the company;
(e) particulars of any security held, the date when it was given and the value which the creditor puts upon it;
(f) details of any reservation of title in respect of goods to which the debt refers; and
(g) the name, and address and authority of the person [authenticating] the proof (if other than the creditor himself).]

(2) There shall be specified in the proof any documents by reference to which the debt can be substantiated; but (subject as follows) it is not essential that such documents be attached to the proof or submitted with it.

(3) The liquidator, or the chairman or convener of any meeting, may call for any document or other evidence to be produced to him, where he thinks it necessary for the purpose of substantiating the whole or any part of the claim made in the proof.

NOTES

Initial Commencement

Specified date

Specified date: 29 December 1986: see r 0.1.

Amendment

Para (1): substituted by SI 2004/584, r 10.
Date in force: 1 April 2004: see SI 2004/584, r 1(2).
Para (1): in sub-para (b) words from "(or, if the liquidation" to "under Rule 4.89" in square brackets inserted by SI 2010/686, r 2, Sch 1, para 192.
Date in force: 6 April 2010: see SI 2010/686, r 1; for transitional provisions see r 6(1), Sch 4, para 1 thereto.
Para (1): in sub-para (g) word "authenticating" in square brackets substituted by SI 2010/686, r 2, Sch 1, para 1.
Date in force: 6 April 2010: see SI 2010/686, r 1; for transitional provisions see r 6(1), Sch 4, paras 1, 2(1)(b) thereto.

See Further

See further, in relation the application of this rule, with modifications, in respect of the procedure for the appointment of a bank liquidator and the operation of bank insolvency under the Banking Act 2009, Pt 2: the Bank Insolvency (England and Wales) Rules 2009, SI 2009/356, rr 3(3)–(8), 59.

4.76 Particulars of creditor's claim—CVL

The liquidator, or the convener or chairman of any meeting, may, if he thinks it necessary for the purpose of clarifying or substantiating the whole or any part of a creditor's claim made in his proof, call for details of any matter specified in paragraphs (a) to (h) of Rule 4.75(1), or for the production to him of such documentary or other evidence as he may require.

NOTES

Initial Commencement

Specified date
　　Specified date: 29 December 1986: see r 0.1.

4.77 . . .
. . .

NOTES

Amendment
　　Revoked by SI 2010/686, r 5.
　　　　Date in force: 6 April 2010: see SI 2010/686, r 1; for transitional provisions see r 6(1), Sch 4, paras 1, 2(1)(a), (2)–(4) thereto.

4.78 Cost of proving

(1) Subject as follows, every creditor bears the cost of proving his own debt, including such as may be incurred in providing documents or evidence under Rule 4.75(3) or 4.76—CVL.

(2) Costs incurred by the liquidator in estimating the quantum of a debt under Rule 4.86 (debts not bearing a certain value) are payable . . . as an expense of the liquidation.

(3) Paragraphs (1) and (2) apply unless the court otherwise orders.

NOTES

Initial Commencement

Specified date
　　Specified date: 29 December 1986: see r 0.1.

Amendment
　　Para (2): words omitted revoked by SI 2008/737, rr 3, 7(9).
　　　　Date in force: 6 April 2008: see SI 2008/737, r 1(1); for transitional provisions see r 2 thereof.

See Further
　　See further, in relation the application of this rule, with modifications, in respect of the procedure for the appointment of a bank liquidator and the operation of bank insolvency under the Banking Act 2009, Pt 2: the Bank Insolvency (England and Wales) Rules 2009, SI 2009/356, rr 3(3)–(8), 61.

4.79 Liquidator to allow inspection of proofs

The liquidator shall, so long as proofs lodged with him are in his hands, allow them to be inspected, at all reasonable times on any business day, by any of the following persons—
　　(a)　　any creditor who has submitted his proof of debt (unless his proof has been wholly rejected for purposes of dividend or otherwise);
　　(b)　　any contributory of the company;
　　(c)　　any person acting on behalf of either of the above.

NOTES

Initial Commencement

Specified date

Specified date: 29 December 1986: see r 0.1.

See Further

See further, in relation the application of this rule, with modifications, in respect of the procedure for the appointment of a bank liquidator and the operation of bank insolvency under the Banking Act 2009, Pt 2: the Bank Insolvency (England and Wales) Rules 2009, SI 2009/356, rr 3(3)–(8), 62.

4.80 Transmission of proofs to liquidator (No CVL Application)

(1) Where a liquidator is appointed, the official receiver shall [as soon as reasonably practicable] transmit to him all the proofs which he has so far received, together with an itemised list of them.

(2) The liquidator shall [authenticate] the list by way of receipt for the proofs, and return it to the official receiver.

(3) From then on, all proofs of debt shall be sent to the liquidator, and retained by him.

NOTES

Initial Commencement

Specified date

Specified date: 29 December 1986: see r 0.1.

Amendment

Para (1): words "as soon as reasonably practicable" in square brackets substituted by SI 2009/642, rr 4, 5.
  Date in force: 6 April 2009: see SI 2009/642, r 1; for transitional provisions see r 3 thereof.
Para (2): word "authenticate" in square brackets substituted by SI 2010/686, r 2, Sch 1, para 1.
  Date in force: 6 April 2010: see SI 2010/686, r 1; for transitional provisions see r 6(1), Sch 4, paras 1, 2(1)(b) thereto.

4.81 New liquidator appointed

(1) If a new liquidator is appointed in place of another, the former liquidator [must as soon as reasonably practicable] transmit to him all proofs which he has received, together with an itemised list of them.

(2) The new liquidator shall [authenticate] the list by way of receipt for the proofs, and return it to his predecessor.

[(3) From then on, all proofs of debt must be sent to and retained by the new liquidator.]

NOTES

Initial Commencement

Specified date

Specified date: 29 December 1986: see r 0.1.

Amendment
> Para (1): words "must as soon as reasonably practicable" in square brackets substituted by SI 2010/686, r 2, Sch 1, para 193(1), (2).
>> Date in force: 6 April 2010: see SI 2010/686, r 1; for transitional provisions see r 6(1), Sch 4, para 1 thereto.
>
> Para (2): word "authenticate" in square brackets substituted by SI 2010/686, r 2, Sch 1, para 1.
>> Date in force: 6 April 2010: see SI 2010/686, r 1; for transitional provisions see r 6(1), Sch 4, paras 1, 2(1)(b) thereto.
>
> Para (3): inserted by SI 2010/686, r 2, Sch 1, para 193(1), (3).
>> Date in force: 6 April 2010: see SI 2010/686, r 1; for transitional provisions see r 6(1), Sch 4, para 1 thereto.

See Further
> See further, in relation the application of this rule, with modifications, in respect of the procedure for the appointment of a bank liquidator and the operation of bank insolvency under the Banking Act 2009, Pt 2: the Bank Insolvency (England and Wales) Rules 2009, SI 2009/356, rr 3(3)–(8), 63.

4.82 Admission and rejection of proofs for dividend

(1) A proof may be admitted for dividend either for the whole amount claimed by the creditor, or for part of that amount.

(2) If the liquidator rejects a proof in whole or in part, he shall prepare a written statement of his reasons for doing so, and send it [as soon as reasonably practicable] to the creditor.

NOTES

Initial Commencement

Specified date
> Specified date: 29 December 1986: see r 0.1.

Amendment
> Para (2): word "as soon as reasonably practicable" in square brackets substituted by SI 2009/642, rr 4, 5.
>> Date in force: 6 April 2009: see SI 2009/642, r 1; for transitional provisions see r 3 thereof.

See Further
> See further, in relation the application of this rule, with modifications, in respect of the procedure for the appointment of a bank liquidator and the operation of bank insolvency under the Banking Act 2009, Pt 2: the Bank Insolvency (England and Wales) Rules 2009, SI 2009/356, rr 3(3)–(8), 64.

4.83 Appeal against decision on proof

(1) If a creditor is dissatisfied with the liquidator's decision with respect to his proof (including any decision on the question of preference), he may apply to the court for the decision to be reversed or varied.

The application must be made within 21 days of his receiving the statement sent under Rule 4.82(2).

(2) A contributory or any other creditor may, if dissatisfied with the liquidator's decision admitting or rejecting the whole or any part of a proof, make such an application within 21 days of becoming aware of the liquidator's decision.

(3) Where application is made to the court under this Rule, the court shall fix a venue for the application to be heard, notice of which shall be sent by the applicant to the creditor who lodged the proof in question (if it is not himself) and to the liquidator.

(4) The liquidator shall, on receipt of the notice, file in court the relevant proof, together (if appropriate) with a copy of the statement sent under Rule 4.82(2).

[(4A) Where the application is made by a contributory, the court must not disallow the proof (in whole or in part) unless the contributory shows that there is (or would be but for the amount claimed in the proof), or that it is likely that there will be (or would be but for the amount claimed in the proof), a surplus of assets to which the company would be entitled.]

(5) After the application has been heard and determined, the proof shall, unless it has been wholly disallowed, be returned by the court to the liquidator.

(6) The official receiver is not personally liable for costs incurred by any person in respect of an application under this Rule; and the liquidator (if other than the official receiver) is not so liable unless the court makes an order to that effect.

NOTES

Initial Commencement

Specified date

Specified date: 29 December 1986: see r 0.1.

Amendment

Para (4A): inserted by SI 2010/686, r 2, Sch 1, para 194.
Date in force: 6 April 2010: see SI 2010/686, r 1; for transitional provisions see r 6(1), Sch 4, para 1 thereto.

See Further

See further, in relation the application of this rule, with modifications, in respect of the procedure for the appointment of a bank liquidator and the operation of bank insolvency under the Banking Act 2009, Pt 2: the Bank Insolvency (England and Wales) Rules 2009, SI 2009/356, rr 3(3)–(8), 65.

4.84 Withdrawal or variation of proof

A creditor's proof may at any time, by agreement between himself and the liquidator, be withdrawn or varied as to the amount claimed.

NOTES

Initial Commencement

Specified date

Specified date: 29 December 1986: see r 0.1.

See Further

See further, in relation the application of this rule, with modifications, in respect of the procedure for the appointment of a bank liquidator and the operation of bank insolvency under the Banking Act 2009, Pt 2: the Bank Insolvency (England and Wales) Rules 2009, SI 2009/356, rr 3(3)–(8), 66.

4.85 Expunging of proof by the court

(1) The court may expunge a proof or reduce the amount claimed—
- (a) on the liquidator's application, where he thinks that the proof has been improperly admitted, or ought to be reduced; or
- (b) on the application of a creditor, if the liquidator declines to interfere in the matter.

(2) Where application is made to the court under this Rule, the court shall fix a venue for the application to be heard, notice of which shall be sent by the applicant—

(a) in the case of an application by the liquidator, to the creditor who made the proof, and

(b) in the case of an application by a creditor, to the liquidator and to the creditor who made the proof (if not himself).

NOTES

Initial Commencement

Specified date

Specified date: 29 December 1986: see r 0.1.

See Further

See further, in relation the application of this rule, with modifications, in respect of the procedure for the appointment of a bank liquidator and the operation of bank insolvency under the Banking Act 2009, Pt 2: the Bank Insolvency (England and Wales) Rules 2009, SI 2009/356, rr 3(3)–(8), 67.

SECTION B: QUANTIFICATION OF CLAIM

4.86 Estimate of quantum

(1) The liquidator shall estimate the value of any debt which, by reason of its being subject to any contingency or for any other reason, does not bear a certain value; and he may revise any estimate previously made, if he thinks fit by reference to any change of circumstances or to information becoming available to him.

He shall inform the creditor as to his estimate and any revision of it.

(2) Where the value of a debt is estimated under this Rule, or by the court under section 168(3) or (5), the amount provable in the winding up in the case of that debt is that of the estimate for the time being.

NOTES

Initial Commencement

Specified date

Specified date: 29 December 1986: see r 0.1.

See Further

See further, in relation the application of this rule, with modifications, in respect of the procedure for the appointment of a bank liquidator and the operation of bank insolvency under the Banking Act 2009, Pt 2: the Bank Insolvency (England and Wales) Rules 2009, SI 2009/356, rr 3(3)–(8), 68, 72.

4.87 Negotiable instruments, etc

Unless the liquidator allows, a proof in respect of money owed on a bill of exchange, promissory note, cheque or other negotiable instrument or security cannot be admitted unless there is produced the instrument or security itself or a copy of it, certified by the creditor or his authorised representative to be a true copy.

NOTES

Initial Commencement

Specified date

Specified date: 29 December 1986: see r 0.1.

Insolvency Rules 1986, reg 4.90

See Further

See further, in relation the application of this rule, with modifications, in respect of the procedure for the appointment of a bank liquidator and the operation of bank insolvency under the Banking Act 2009, Pt 2: the Bank Insolvency (England and Wales) Rules 2009, SI 2009/356, rr 3(3)–(8), 69.

4.88 Secured creditors

(1) If a secured creditor realises his security, he may prove for the balance of his debt, after deducting the amount realised.

(2) If a secured creditor voluntarily surrenders his security for the general benefit of creditors, he may prove for his whole debt, as if it were unsecured.

NOTES

Initial Commencement

Specified date

Specified date: 29 December 1986: see r 0.1.

See Further

See further, in relation the application of this rule, with modifications, in respect of the procedure for the appointment of a bank liquidator and the operation of bank insolvency under the Banking Act 2009, Pt 2: the Bank Insolvency (England and Wales) Rules 2009, SI 2009/356, rr 3(3)–(8), 70.

4.89 Discounts

There shall in every case be deducted from the claim all trade and other discounts which would have been available to the company but for its liquidation, except any discount for immediate, early or cash settlement.

NOTES

Initial Commencement

Specified date

Specified date: 29 December 1986: see r 0.1.

See Further

See further, in relation the application of this rule, with modifications, in respect of the procedure for the appointment of a bank liquidator and the operation of bank insolvency under the Banking Act 2009, Pt 2: the Bank Insolvency (England and Wales) Rules 2009, SI 2009/356, rr 3(3)–(8), 71.

[4.90 Mutual credits and set-off]

[(1) This Rule applies where, before the company goes into liquidation there have been mutual credits, mutual debts or other mutual dealings between the company and any creditor of the company proving or claiming to prove for a debt in the liquidation.

(2) The reference in paragraph (1) to mutual credits, mutual debts or other mutual dealings does not include—
    (a)   any debt arising out of an obligation incurred at a time when the creditor had notice that—
        (i)   a meeting of creditors had been summoned under section 98; or
        (ii)   a petition for the winding up of the company was pending;
    (b)   any debt arising out of an obligation where—
        (i)   the liquidation was immediately preceded by an administration; and

(ii) at the time the obligation was incurred the creditor had notice that an application for an administration order was pending or a person had given notice of intention to appoint an administrator;
(c) any debt arising out of an obligation incurred during an administration which immediately preceded the liquidation; or
(d) any debt which has been acquired by a creditor by assignment or otherwise, pursuant to an agreement between the creditor and any other party where that agreement was entered into—
(i) after the company went into liquidation;
(ii) at a time when the creditor had notice that a meeting of creditors had been summoned under section 98;
(iii) at a time when the creditor had notice that a winding up petition was pending;
(iv) where the liquidation was immediately preceded by an administration, at a time when the creditor had notice that an application for an administration order was pending or a person had given notice of intention to appoint an administrator; or
(v) during an administration which immediately preceded the liquidation.

(3) An account shall be taken of what is due from each party to the other in respect of the mutual dealings, and the sums due from one party shall be set off against the sums due from the other.

(4) A sum shall be regarded as being due to or from the company for the purposes of paragraph (3) whether—
(a) it is payable at present or in the future;
(b) the obligation by virtue of which it is payable is certain or contingent; or
(c) its amount is fixed or liquidated, or is capable of being ascertained by fixed rules or as a matter of opinion.

(5) Rule 4.86 shall also apply for the purposes of this Rule to any obligation to or from the company which, by reason of its being subject to any contingency or for any other reason, does not bear a certain value.

(6) Rules 4.91 to 4.93 shall apply for the purposes of this Rule in relation to any sums due to the company which—
(a) are payable in a currency other than sterling;
(b) are of a periodical nature; or
(c) bear interest.

(7) Rule 11.13 shall apply for the purposes of this Rule to any sum due to or from the company which is payable in the future.

(8) Only the balance (if any) of the account owed to the creditor is provable in the liquidation. Alternatively the balance (if any) owed to the company shall be paid to the liquidator as part of the assets except where all or part of the balance results from a contingent or prospective debt owed by the creditor and in such a case the balance (or that part of it which results from the contingent or prospective debt) shall be paid if and when that debt becomes due and payable.

(9) In this Rule "obligation" means an obligation however arising, whether by virtue of an agreement, rule of law or otherwise.]

NOTES

Amendment

Substituted by SI 2005/527, r 23.
Date in force: 1 April 2005: see SI 2005/527, r 1(2); for transitional provisions in relation to any case where a company has entered administration or gone into liquidation, or a bankruptcy order has been made before that date see r 3(1) thereof.

4.91 Debt in foreign currency

(1) For the purpose of proving a debt incurred or payable in a currency other than sterling, the amount of the debt shall be converted into sterling at the official exchange rate prevailing on the date when the company went into liquidation [or, if the liquidation was immediately preceded by an administration, on the date that the company entered administration].

(2) "The official exchange rate" is the [middle exchange rate on the London Foreign Exchange Market at the close of business], as published for the date in question. In the absence of any such published rate, it is such rate as the court determines.

NOTES

Initial Commencement

Specified date

Specified date: 29 December 1986: see r 0.1.

Amendment

Para (1): words from "or, if the" to "company entered administration" in square brackets inserted by SI 2005/527, r 24.
Date in force: 1 April 2005: see SI 2005/527, r 1(2); for transitional provisions in relation to any case where a company has entered administration or gone into liquidation, or a bankruptcy order has been made before that date see r 3(1) thereof.
Para (2): words "middle exchange rate on the London Foreign Exchange Market at the close of business" in square brackets substituted by SI 2003/1730, r 7, Sch 1, Pt 4, para 20.
Date in force: 15 September 2003: see SI 2003/1730, r 1(2).

See Further

See further, in relation the application of this rule, with modifications, in respect of the procedure for the appointment of a bank liquidator and the operation of bank insolvency under the Banking Act 2009, Pt 2: the Bank Insolvency (England and Wales) Rules 2009, SI 2009/356, rr 3(3)–(8), 74.

4.92 Payments of a periodical nature

(1) In the case of rent and other payments of a periodical nature, the creditor may prove for any amounts due and unpaid up to the date when the company went into liquidation [or, if the liquidation was immediately preceded by an administration, up to the date that the company entered administration].

(2) Where at that date any payment was accruing due, the creditor may prove for so much as would have fallen due at that date, if accruing from day to day.

NOTES

Initial Commencement

Specified date

Specified date: 29 December 1986: see r 0.1.

Amendment

Para (1): words from "or, if the" to "company entered administration" in square brackets inserted by SI 2005/527, r 25.
Date in force: 1 April 2005: see SI 2005/527, r 1(2); for transitional provisions in relation to any case where a company has entered administration or gone into liquidation, or a bankruptcy order has been made before that date see r 3(1) thereof.

See Further

See further, in relation the application of this rule, with modifications, in respect of the procedure for the appointment of a bank liquidator and the operation of bank insolvency

under the Banking Act 2009, Pt 2: the Bank Insolvency (England and Wales) Rules 2009, SI 2009/356, rr 3(3)–(8), 75.

4.93 Interest

[(A1) In this Rule, "the relevant date" means the date on which the company went into liquidation or, if the liquidation was immediately preceded by an administration, the date on which the company entered administration.]

(1) Where a debt proved in the liquidation bears interest, that interest is provable as part of the debt except in so far as it is payable in respect of any period after [the relevant date].

(2) In the following circumstances the creditor's claim may include interest on the debt for periods before [the relevant date], although not previously reserved or agreed.

(3) If the debt is due by virtue of a written instrument, and payable at a certain time, interest may be claimed for the period from that time to [the relevant date].

(4) If the debt is due otherwise, interest may only be claimed if, before [the relevant date], a demand for payment of the debt was made in writing by or on behalf of the creditor, and notice given that interest would be payable from the date of the demand to the date of payment.

(5) Interest under paragraph (4) may only be claimed for the period from the date of the demand to [the relevant date] [and for all the purposes of the Act and the Rules shall be chargeable at a rate not exceeding that mentioned in paragraph (6)].

[(6) The rate of interest to be claimed under paragraphs (3) and (4) is the rate specified in section 17 of the Judgments Act 1838 on [the relevant date].]

NOTES

Initial Commencement

Specified date

Specified date: 29 December 1986: see r 0.1.

Amendment

Para (A1): inserted by SI 2010/686, r 2, Sch 1, para 195(1), (2).
Date in force: 6 April 2010: see SI 2010/686, r 1; for transitional provisions see r 6(1), Sch 4, para 1 thereto.
Para (1): words "the relevant date" in square brackets substituted by SI 2010/686, r 2, Sch 1, para 195(1), (3).
Date in force: 6 April 2010: see SI 2010/686, r 1; for transitional provisions see r 6(1), Sch 4, para 1 thereto.
Para (2): words "the relevant date" in square brackets substituted by SI 2010/686, r 2, Sch 1, para 195(1), (4).
Date in force: 6 April 2010: see SI 2010/686, r 1; for transitional provisions see r 6(1), Sch 4, para 1 thereto.
Para (3): words "the relevant date" in square brackets substituted by SI 2010/686, r 2, Sch 1, para 195(1), (5).
Date in force: 6 April 2010: see SI 2010/686, r 1; for transitional provisions see r 6(1), Sch 4, para 1 thereto.
Para (4): words "the relevant date" in square brackets substituted by SI 2010/686, r 2, Sch 1, para 195(1), (6).
Date in force: 6 April 2010: see SI 2010/686, r 1; for transitional provisions see r 6(1), Sch 4, para 1 thereto.
Para (5): words "the relevant date" in square brackets substituted by SI 2010/686, r 2, Sch 1, para 195(1), (7).
Date in force: 6 April 2010: see SI 2010/686, r 1; for transitional provisions see r 6(1), Sch 4, para 1 thereto.

Para (5): words "and for all the purposes of the Act and the Rules shall be chargeable at a rate not exceeding that mentioned in paragraph (6)" in square brackets inserted by SI 1987/1919, r 3(1), Schedule, Part 1, para 59(1).

Para (6): substituted by SI 1987/1919, r 3(1), Schedule, Part 1, para 59(2).

Para (6): words "the relevant date" in square brackets substituted by SI 2010/686, r 2, Sch 1, para 195(1), (8).
>   Date in force: 6 April 2010: see SI 2010/686, r 1; for transitional provisions see r 6(1), Sch 4, para 1 thereto.

See Further

See further, in relation the application of this rule, with modifications, in respect of the procedure for the appointment of a bank liquidator and the operation of bank insolvency under the Banking Act 2009, Pt 2: the Bank Insolvency (England and Wales) Rules 2009, SI 2009/356, rr 3(3)–(8), 76.

4.94 Debt payable at future time

A creditor may prove for a debt of which payment was not yet due on the date when the company went into liquidation, [or, if the liquidation was immediately preceded by an administration, on the date that the company entered administration] but subject to Rule 11.13 in Part II of the Rules (adjustment of dividend where payment made before time).

NOTES

Initial Commencement

Specified date

Specified date: 29 December 1986: see r 0.1.

Amendment

Words from "or, if the" to "company entered administration" in square brackets inserted by SI 2005/527, r 27.
>   Date in force: 1 April 2005: see SI 2005/527, r 1(2); for transitional provisions in relation to any case where a company has entered administration or gone into liquidation, or a bankruptcy order has been made before that date see r 3(1) thereof.

See Further

See further, in relation the application of this rule, with modifications, in respect of the procedure for the appointment of a bank liquidator and the operation of bank insolvency under the Banking Act 2009, Pt 2: the Bank Insolvency (England and Wales) Rules 2009, SI 2009/356, rr 3(3)–(8), 77.

CHAPTER 10
SECURED CREDITORS

4.95 Value of security

(1) A secured creditor may, with the agreement of the liquidator or the [permission] of the court, at any time alter the value which he has, in his proof of debt, put upon his security.

(2) However, if a secured creditor—

    (a)   being the petitioner, has in the petition put a value on his security, or

    (b)   has voted in respect of the unsecured balance of his debt,

he may re-value his security only with [permission] of the court. (NO CVL APPLICATION)

NOTES

Initial Commencement

Specified date

Specified date: 29 December 1986: see r 0.1.

Amendment

Para (1): word "permission" in square brackets substituted by SI 2010/686, r 2, Sch 1, para 1.
Date in force: 6 April 2010: see SI 2010/686, r 1; for transitional provisions see r 6(1), Sch 4, paras 1, 2(1)(b) thereto.
Para (2): word "permission" in square brackets substituted by SI 2010/686, r 2, Sch 1, para 1.
Date in force: 6 April 2010: see SI 2010/686, r 1; for transitional provisions see r 6(1), Sch 4, paras 1, 2(1)(b) thereto.

See Further

See further, in relation the application of this rule, with modifications, in respect of the procedure for the appointment of a bank liquidator and the operation of bank insolvency under the Banking Act 2009, Pt 2: the Bank Insolvency (England and Wales) Rules 2009, SI 2009/356, rr 3(3)–(8), 78.

4.96 Surrender for non-disclosure

(1) If a secured creditor omits to disclose his security in his proof of debt, he shall surrender his security for the general benefit of creditors, unless the court, on application by him, relieves him [from] the effect of this Rule on the ground that the omission was inadvertent or the result of honest mistake.

(2) If the court grants that relief, it may require or allow the creditor's proof of debt to be amended, on such terms as may be just.

[(3) Nothing in this Rule or the following two Rules may affect the rights in rem of creditors or third parties protected under Article 5 of the EC Regulation (third parties' rights in rem).]

NOTES

Initial Commencement

Specified date

Specified date: 29 December 1986: see r 0.1.

Amendment

Para (1): word "from" in square brackets substituted by SI 2010/686, r 2, Sch 1, para 196.
Date in force: 6 April 2010: see SI 2010/686, r 1; for transitional provisions see r 6(1), Sch 4, para 1 thereto.
Para (3): inserted by SI 2002/1307, rr 3(1), 6(8).
Date in force: 31 May 2002: see SI 2002/1307, r 1.

See Further

See further, in relation the application of this rule, with modifications, in respect of the procedure for the appointment of a bank liquidator and the operation of bank insolvency under the Banking Act 2009, Pt 2: the Bank Insolvency (England and Wales) Rules 2009, SI 2009/356, rr 3(3)–(8), 79.

4.97 Redemption by liquidator

(1) The liquidator may at any time give notice to a creditor whose debt is secured that he proposes, at the expiration of 28 days from the date of the notice, to redeem the security at the value put upon it in the creditor's proof.

(2) The creditor then has 21 days (or such longer period as the liquidator may allow) in which, if he so wishes, to exercise his right to revalue his security (with the [permission] of the court, where Rule 4.95(2) applies).
If the creditor re-values his security, the liquidator may only redeem at the new value.

(3) If the liquidator redeems the security, the cost of transferring it is payable [as an expense of the liquidation].

(4) A secured creditor may at any time, by a notice in writing, call on the liquidator to elect whether he will or will not exercise his power to redeem the security at the value then placed on it; and the liquidator then has [3 months] in which to exercise the power or determine not to exercise it.

NOTES

Initial Commencement

Specified date

Specified date: 29 December 1986: see r 0.1.

Amendment

Para (2): word "permission" in square brackets substituted by SI 2010/686, r 2, Sch 1, para 1.
Date in force: 6 April 2010: see SI 2010/686, r 1; for transitional provisions see r 6(1), Sch 4, paras 1, 2(1)(b) thereto.
Para (3): words "as an expense of the liquidation" in square brackets substituted by SI 2008/737, rr 3, 7(1).
Date in force: 6 April 2008: see SI 2008/737, r 1(1); for transitional provisions see r 2 thereof.
Para (4): words "3 months" in square brackets substituted by SI 2010/686, r 2, Sch 1, para 197.
Date in force: 6 April 2010: see SI 2010/686, r 1; for transitional provisions see r 6(1), Sch 4, para 1 thereto.

See Further

See further, in relation the application of this rule, with modifications, in respect of the procedure for the appointment of a bank liquidator and the operation of bank insolvency under the Banking Act 2009, Pt 2: the Bank Insolvency (England and Wales) Rules 2009, SI 2009/356, rr 3(3)–(8), 80.

4.98 Test of security's value

(1) Subject as follows, the liquidator, if he is dissatisfied with the value which a secured creditor puts on his security (whether in his proof or by way of re-valuation under Rule 4.97), may require any property comprised in the security to be offered for sale.

(2) The terms of sale shall be such as may be agreed, or as the court may direct; and if the sale is by auction, the liquidator on behalf of the company, and the creditor on his own behalf, may appear and bid.

[(3) This Rule does not apply if the security has been revalued and the revaluation has been approved by the court.]

NOTES

Initial Commencement

Specified date

Specified date: 29 December 1986: see r 0.1.

Amendment

Para (3): inserted by SI 2010/686, r 2, Sch 1, para 198.

Date in force: 6 April 2010: see SI 2010/686, r 1; for transitional provisions see r 6(1), Sch 4, para 1 thereto.

See Further

See further, in relation the application of this rule, with modifications, in respect of the procedure for the appointment of a bank liquidator and the operation of bank insolvency under the Banking Act 2009, Pt 2: the Bank Insolvency (England and Wales) Rules 2009, SI 2009/356, rr 3(3)–(8), 81.

4.99 Realisation of security by creditor

If a creditor who has valued his security subsequently realises it (whether or not at the instance of the liquidator)—

(a) the net amount realised shall be substituted for the value previously put by the creditor on the security, and

(b) that amount shall be treated in all respects as an amended valuation made by him.

NOTES

Initial Commencement

Specified date

Specified date: 29 December 1986: see r 0.1.

See Further

See further, in relation the application of this rule, with modifications, in respect of the procedure for the appointment of a bank liquidator and the operation of bank insolvency under the Banking Act 2009, Pt 2: the Bank Insolvency (England and Wales) Rules 2009, SI 2009/356, rr 3(3)–(8), 82.

CHAPTER 11

THE LIQUIDATOR

SECTION A: APPOINTMENT AND ASSOCIATED FORMALITIES

4.100 Appointment by creditors or contributories (No CVL Application)

(1) This Rule applies where a person is appointed as liquidator either by a meeting of creditors or by a meeting of contributories.

(2) The chairman of the meeting shall certify the appointment, but not unless and until the person appointed has provided him with a written statement to the effect that he is an insolvency practitioner, duly qualified under the Act to be the liquidator, and that he consents so to act.

[(3) The liquidator's appointment is effective from the date on which the appointment is certified, that date to be endorsed on the certificate.

(4) The chairman of the meeting (if not himself the official receiver) shall send the certificate to the official receiver.

(5) The official receiver shall in any case send the certificate to the liquidator . . ..]

NOTES

Initial Commencement

Specified date

Specified date: 29 December 1986: see r 0.1.

Amendment

Paras (3)–(5): substituted by SI 1987/1919, r 3(1), Schedule, Part 1, para 60.

Para (5): words omitted revoked by SI 2010/686, r 2, Sch 1, para 199.
Date in force: 6 April 2010: see SI 2010/686, r 1; for transitional provisions see r 6(1), Sch 4, para 1 thereto.

See Further

See further, in relation the application of this rule, with modifications, in respect of the procedure for the appointment of a bank liquidator and the operation of bank insolvency under the Banking Act 2009, Pt 2: the Bank Insolvency (England and Wales) Rules 2009, SI 2009/356, rr 3(3)–(8), 84.

4.101 Appointment by creditors or by the company—CVL

(1) This Rule applies where a person is appointed as liquidator either by a meeting of creditors or by a meeting of the company.

(2) Subject as follows, the chairman of the meeting shall certify the appointment, but not unless and until the person appointed has provided him with a written statement to the effect that he is an insolvency practitioner, duly qualified under the Act to be the liquidator, and that he consents so to act; the liquidator's appointment [takes effect upon the passing of the resolution for that appointment].

(3) The chairman shall send the certificate [as soon as reasonably practicable] to the liquidator, who shall keep it as part of the records of the liquidation.

(4) Paragraphs (2) and (3) need not be complied with in the case of a liquidator appointed by a company meeting and replaced by another liquidator appointed on the same day by a creditors' meeting.

NOTES

Initial Commencement

Specified date

Specified date: 29 December 1986: see r 0.1.

Amendment

Para (2): words in square brackets substituted by SI 1987/1919, r 3(1), Schedule, Part 1, para 61.

Para (3): words "as soon as reasonably practicable" in square brackets substituted by SI 2009/642, rr 4, 5.
Date in force: 6 April 2009: see SI 2009/642, r 1; for transitional provisions see r 3 thereof.

[4.101A Power to fill vacancy in office of liquidator—CVL]

[Where a vacancy in the office of liquidator occurs in the manner mentioned in section 104 a meeting of creditors to fill the vacancy may be convened by any creditor or, if there were more liquidators than one, by the continuing liquidators.]

NOTES

Amendment

Inserted by SI 1987/1919, r 3(1), Schedule, Part 1, para 62.

[4.101B Official receiver not to be appointed liquidator]

[The official receiver may not be appointed as liquidator by any meeting of creditors, contributories or the company.]

NOTES

Amendment

Inserted by SI 2010/686, r 2, Sch 1, para 200.
Date in force: 6 April 2010: see SI 2010/686, r 1; for transitional provisions see r 6(1), Sch 4, para 1 thereto.

4.102 Appointment by the court (No CVL Application)

(1) This Rule applies where the liquidator is appointed by the court under section 139(4) (different persons nominated by creditors and contributories) or section 140 (liquidation following administration or voluntary arrangement).

(2) The court's order shall not issue unless and until the person appointed has filed in court a statement to the effect that he is an insolvency practitioner, duly qualified under the Act to be the liquidator, and that he consents so to act.

(3) Thereafter, the court shall send 2 copies of the order to the official receiver. One of the copies shall be sealed, and this shall be sent to the person appointed as liquidator.

(4) The liquidator's appointment takes effect from the date of the order.

[(4A) . . .]

[(5) Within 28 days from appointment, the liquidator shall . . .—
  (a) give notice of it to all creditors and contributories of the company of whom the liquidator is aware; or
  (b) advertise it in accordance with any directions given by the court.]

(6) In his notice . . . under this Rule the liquidator shall—
  (a) state whether he proposes to summon meetings of creditors and contributories for the purpose of establishing a liquidation committee, or proposes to summon only a meeting of creditors for that purpose, and
  (b) if he does not propose to summon any such meeting, set out the powers of the creditors under the Act to require him to summon one.

NOTES

Initial Commencement

Specified date

Specified date: 29 December 1986: see r 0.1.

Amendment

Para (4A): inserted by SI 2009/642, rr 4, 26(a).
Date in force: 6 April 2009: see SI 2009/642, r 1; for transitional provisions see r 3 thereof.
Para (4A): revoked by SI 2010/686, r 2, Sch 1, para 201(1), (2).
Date in force: 6 April 2010: see SI 2010/686, r 1; for transitional provisions see r 6(1), Sch 4, para 1 thereto.
Para (5): substituted by SI 2009/642, rr 4, 26(b).
Date in force: 6 April 2009: see SI 2009/642, r 1; for transitional provisions see r 3 thereof.
Para (5): word omitted revoked by SI 2010/686, r 2, Sch 1, para 201(1), (3).
Date in force: 6 April 2010: see SI 2010/686, r 1; for transitional provisions see r 6(1), Sch 4, para 1 thereto.
Para (6): words omitted revoked by SI 2009/642, rr 4, 26(c).
Date in force: 6 April 2009: see SI 2009/642, r 1; for transitional provisions see r 3 thereof.

4.103 Appointment by the court—CVL

(1) This Rule applies where the liquidator is appointed by the court under section 100(3) or 108.

(2) The court's order shall not issue unless and until the person appointed has filed in court a statement to the effect that he is an insolvency practitioner, duly qualified under the Act to be the liquidator, and that he consents so to act.

(3) Thereafter, the court shall send a sealed copy of the order to the liquidator, whose appointment takes effect from the date of the order.

[(4) Within 28 days from appointment, the liquidator shall—
- (a) give notice of it to all creditors of the company of whom the liquidator is aware; or
- (b) advertise it in accordance with any directions given by the court.]

NOTES

Initial Commencement

Specified date

Specified date: 29 December 1986: see r 0.1.

Amendment

Para (4): substituted by SI 2009/642, rr 4, 27.
Date in force: 6 April 2009: see SI 2009/642, r 1; for transitional provisions see r 3 thereof.

4.104 Appointment by Secretary of State (No CVL Application)

(1) This Rule applies where the official receiver applies to the Secretary of State to appoint a liquidator in place of himself, or refers to the Secretary of State the need for an appointment.

(2) If the Secretary of State makes an appointment, he shall send [a copy] of the certificate of appointment to the official receiver, who shall transmit [it] to the person appointed. . ..

(3) The certificate shall specify the date from which the liquidator's appointment is to be effective.

NOTES

Initial Commencement

Specified date

Specified date: 29 December 1986: see r 0.1.

Amendment

Para (2): words "a copy" in square brackets substituted by SI 2010/686, r 2, Sch 1, para 202(1), (2)(a).
Date in force: 6 April 2010: see SI 2010/686, r 1; for transitional provisions see r 6(1), Sch 4, para 1 thereto.
Para (2): word "it" in square brackets substituted by SI 2010/686, r 2, Sch 1, para 202(1), (2)(b).
Date in force: 6 April 2010: see SI 2010/686, r 1; for transitional provisions see r 6(1), Sch 4, para 1 thereto.
Para (2): words omitted revoked by SI 2010/686, r 2, Sch 1, para 202(1), (2)(c).
Date in force: 6 April 2010: see SI 2010/686, r 1; for transitional provisions see r 6(1), Sch 4, para 1 thereto.

4.105 Authentication of liquidator's appointment

A copy of the certificate of the liquidator's appointment or (as the case may be) a sealed copy of the court's order [or a copy of the notice registered in accordance with paragraph 83(3) of Schedule B1 to the Act], may in any proceedings be adduced as proof that the person appointed is duly authorised to exercise the powers and perform the duties of liquidator in the company's winding up.

NOTES

Initial Commencement

Specified date

Specified date: 29 December 1986: see r 0.1.

Amendment

Words from "or a copy" to "to the Act" in square brackets inserted by SI 2003/1730, r 7, Sch 1, Pt 4, para 21.
Date in force: 15 September 2003: see SI 2003/1730, r 1(2).

See Further

See further, in relation the application of this rule, with modifications, in respect of the procedure for the appointment of a bank liquidator and the operation of bank insolvency under the Banking Act 2009, Pt 2: the Bank Insolvency (England and Wales) Rules 2009, SI 2009/356, rr 3(3)–(8), 85.

[4.106A Appointment to be gazetted and registered]

[(1) A liquidator appointed in a voluntary winding up in addition to giving notice of the appointment in accordance with section 109(1) may advertise the notice in such other manner as the liquidator thinks fit.

(2) A liquidator appointed in a winding up by the court -
   (a) as soon as reasonably practicable must have gazetted a notice of the appointment; and
   (b) may advertise the notice in such other manner as the liquidator thinks fit.

(3) In addition to the standard contents, the notice must state—
   (a) that a liquidator has been appointed; and
   (b) the date of the appointment.

(4) As soon as reasonably practicable a liquidator appointed in a winding up by the court must notify the appointment to the registrar of companies.

(5) At first instance the liquidator must bear the expense of giving notice under this Rule.

(6) The liquidator is entitled to be reimbursed for such expenditure as an expense of the liquidation.]

NOTES

Amendment

Substituted, for r 4.106 as originally enacted, SI 2010/686, r 2, Sch 1, para 203.
Date in force: 6 April 2010: see SI 2010/686, r 1; for transitional provisions see r 6(1), Sch 4, para 1 thereto.

4.107 Hand-over of assets to liquidator (No CVL Application)

(1) This Rule applies only where the liquidator is appointed in succession to the official receiver acting as liquidator.

(2) When the liquidator's appointment takes effect, the official receiver shall [as soon as reasonably practicable] do all that is required for putting him into possession of the assets.

(3) On taking possession of the assets, the liquidator shall discharge any balance due to the official receiver on account of—

(a) expenses properly incurred by him and payable under the Act or the Rules, and

(b) any advances made by him in respect of the assets, together with interest on such advances at the rate specified in section 17 of the Judgments Act 1838 at the date of the winding-up order.

(4) Alternatively, the liquidator may (before taking office) give to the official receiver a written undertaking to discharge any such balance out of the first realisation of assets.

(5) The official receiver has a charge on the assets in respect of any sums due to him under paragraph (3). But, where the liquidator has realised assets with a view to making those payments, the official receiver's charge does not extend in respect of sums deductible by the liquidator from the proceeds of realisation, as being expenses properly incurred therein.

(6) The liquidator shall from time to time out of the realisation of assets discharge all guarantees properly given by the official receiver for the benefit of the estate, and shall pay all the official receiver's expenses.

(7) The official receiver shall give to the liquidator all such information relating to the affairs of the company and the course of the winding up as he (the official receiver) considers to be reasonably required for the effective discharge by the liquidator of his duties as such.

(8) The liquidator shall also be furnished with a copy of any report made by the official receiver under Chapter 7 of this Part of the Rules.

NOTES

Initial Commencement

Specified date

Specified date: 29 December 1986: see r 0.1.

Amendment

Para (2): words "as soon as reasonably practicable" in square brackets substituted by SI 2009/642, rr 4, 5.
Date in force: 6 April 2009: see SI 2009/642, r 1; for transitional provisions see r 3 thereof.

SECTION B: RESIGNATION AND REMOVAL; VACATION OF OFFICE

4.108 Creditors' meeting to receive liquidator's resignation

(1) Before resigning his office, the liquidator must call a meeting of creditors for the purpose of receiving his resignation.

[(1A) The liquidator must give at least 28 days' notice of the meeting.

(1B) The notice summoning the meeting must—

(a) indicate that the purpose or one of the purposes of the meeting is to receive the liquidator's resignation; and

(b) draw the attention of the creditors with respect to the liquidator's release to Rule 4.121 or, as the case may be, Rule 4.122.]

(2) A copy of the notice shall at the same time also be sent to the official receiver. (NO CVL APPLICATION)

[(3) The notice to creditors under paragraph (1A) must be accompanied by an account of the liquidator's administration of the winding up including—

(a) where appropriate, a statement that the liquidator has reconciled the account with that held by the Secretary of State in respect of the winding up; and
(b) a progress report for the period—
  (i) commencing with the later of the date of—
   (aa) the appointment of the liquidator; and
   (bb) the day immediately following the end of the period of the last progress report; and
  (ii) ending with the date of the meeting.]

(4) Subject as follows, the liquidator may only proceed under this Rule on grounds of ill health or because—
(a) he intends ceasing to be in practice as an insolvency practitioner, or
(b) there is some conflict of interest or change of personal circumstances which precludes or makes impracticable the further discharge by him of the duties of liquidator.

(5) Where two or more persons are acting as liquidator jointly, any one of them may proceed under this Rule (without prejudice to the continuation in office of the other or others) on the ground that, in his opinion and that of the other or others, it is no longer expedient that there should continue to be the present number of joint liquidators.

[(6) [Except where Rule 4.108A applies,] if there is no quorum present at the meeting summoned to receive the liquidator's resignation, the meeting is deemed to have been held, a resolution is deemed to have been passed that the liquidator's resignation be accepted and the creditors are deemed not to have resolved against the liquidator having his release.

(7) Where paragraph (6) applies any reference in the Rules to a resolution that the liquidator's resignation be accepted is replaced by a reference to the making of a written statement, [authenticated] by the person who, had there been a quorum present, would have been chairman of the meeting, that no quorum was present and that the liquidator may resign.]

NOTES

Initial Commencement

Specified date

Specified date: 29 December 1986: see r 0.1.

Amendment

Paras (1A), (1B): substituted, for second sentence of para (1) as originally enacted, by SI 2010/686, r 2, Sch 1, para 204(1), (2).
  Date in force: 6 April 2010: see SI 2010/686, r 1; for transitional provisions see r 6(1), Sch 4, para 1 thereto.
Para (3): substituted by SI 2010/686, r 2, Sch 1, para 204(1), (3) (as amended by SI 2010/734, rr 2, 5).
  Date in force: 6 April 2010: see SI 2010/686, r 1; for transitional provisions see r 6(1), Sch 4, para 1 thereto.

Paras (6), (7): inserted by SI 1987/1919, r 3(1), Schedule, Part 1, para 64.

Para (6): words "Except where Rule 4.108A applies," in square brackets inserted by SI 2010/686, r 2, Sch 1, para 204(1), (4).
  Date in force: 6 April 2010: see SI 2010/686, r 1; for transitional provisions see r 6(1), Sch 4, para 1 thereto.
Para (7): word "authenticated" in square brackets substituted by SI 2010/686, r 2, Sch 1, para 1.
  Date in force: 6 April 2010: see SI 2010/686, r 1; for transitional provisions see r 6(1), Sch 4, paras 1, 2(1)(b) thereto.

See Further

See further, in relation the application of this rule, with modifications, in respect of the procedure for the appointment of a bank liquidator and the operation of bank insolvency under the Banking Act 2009, Pt 2: the Bank Insolvency (England and Wales) Rules 2009, SI 2009/356, rr 3(3)–(8), 87.

[4.108A Resignation (application under Rule 4.131)]

[(1) This Rule applies where at the date of a meeting summoned for the purpose of receiving the liquidator's resignation, an application made to the court under Rule 4.131 (including any appeal) has not been disposed of.

(2) At the meeting no resolution may be put regarding the liquidator's release.

(3) If at the meeting the liquidator's resignation is accepted, the meeting must be adjourned (notwithstanding anything in Rule 4.65 (suspension and adjournment)) to a day not less than 14 days after the day on which the application under Rule 4.131 (including any appeal) has been disposed of.

(4) The liquidator must give at least 14 days' notice of the meeting adjourned in accordance with paragraph (3) to the creditors.

(5) At the meeting adjourned in accordance with paragraph (3)—
- (a) a revised version of the account which accompanied the notice of the meeting must be laid showing any changes required as a result, or arising out of the application under Rule 4.131; and
- (b) a resolution must be put for the release of the liquidator whose resignation has been accepted.

(6) If there is no quorum present at the adjourned meeting, the meeting is deemed to have been held and the creditors are deemed to have resolved that the liquidator be released.

(7) Where the creditors have resolved at the adjourned meeting that the liquidator be released (or are deemed to have so resolved by virtue of paragraph (5)), the chairman of the meeting (or the person who, had there been a quorum present would have been chairman of the meeting) must send as soon as reasonably practicable a certificate to that effect with a copy of the revised account to—
- (a) the official receiver; and (NO CVL APPLICATION)
- (b) the registrar of companies.

(8) The official receiver must file a copy of the certificate in court.

(9) If at the meeting the liquidator's resignation is not accepted, the liquidator must not summon any further meeting under Rule 4.108 until the application under Rule 4.131 (including any appeal) has been disposed of.

(10) Paragraph (7) is subject to the powers of the court on an application being made to it by the liquidator under Rule 4.111 (permission to resign granted by the court).

(11) Rule 4.108 applies to any such further meeting with the modification that the progress report required to accompany the notice of the meeting must show any changes from the report which accompanied the notice of the earlier meeting called to receive the liquidator's resignation, and in particular any changes required as a result of the application under Rule 4.131 and any further remuneration charged or expenses incurred.

(12) The creditors' rights under Rules 4.49E and 4.131 do not apply in respect of any matter included in that report which—
- (a) was included in the report which accompanied the notice of the earlier meeting called to receive the liquidator's resignation; or
- (b) was the subject of the order of the court on the application made to it by the liquidator under Rule 4.131.]

NOTES

Amendment

Inserted by SI 2010/686, r 2, Sch 1, para 205.
Date in force: 6 April 2010: see SI 2010/686, r 1; for transitional provisions see r 6(1), Sch 4, para 1 thereto.

4.109 Action following acceptance of resignation (No CVL Application)

(1) This Rule applies where a meeting is summoned to receive the liquidator's resignation.

(2) If the chairman of the meeting is other than the official receiver, and there is passed at the meeting any of the following resolutions—

(a) that the liquidator's resignation be accepted,
(b) that a new liquidator be appointed,
(c) that the resigning liquidator be not given his release,

the chairman shall, within 3 [business days of the date of the resolution], send to the official receiver a copy of the resolution.

If it has been resolved to accept the liquidator's resignation, the chairman shall send to the official receiver a certificate to that effect.

(3) If the creditors have resolved to appoint a new liquidator, the certificate of his appointment shall also be sent to the official receiver within that time; and Rule 4.100 shall be complied with in respect of it.

(4) If the liquidator's resignation is accepted, the notice of it required by section 172(6) shall be given by him [as soon as reasonably practicable] after the [resolution has been passed]; and he shall send a copy of the notice to the official receiver.

The notice shall be accompanied by a copy of the account sent to creditors under Rule 4.108(3).

(5) The official receiver shall file a copy of the notice in court.

(6) The liquidator's resignation is effective as from the date on which the official receiver files the copy notice in court, that date to be endorsed on the copy notice.

NOTES

Initial Commencement

Specified date

Specified date: 29 December 1986: see r 0.1.

Amendment

Para (2): words "business days of the date of the resolution" in square brackets substituted by SI 2010/686, r 2, Sch 1, para 206(1), (2).
Date in force: 6 April 2010: see SI 2010/686, r 1; for transitional provisions see r 6(1), Sch 4, para 1 thereto.

Para (4): words "as soon as reasonably practicable" in square brackets substituted by SI 2009/642, rr 4, 5.
Date in force: 6 April 2009: see SI 2009/642, r 1; for transitional provisions see r 3 thereof.

Para (4): words "resolution has been passed" in square brackets substituted by SI 2010/686, r 2, Sch 1, para 206(1), (3).
Date in force: 6 April 2010: see SI 2010/686, r 1; for transitional provisions see r 6(1), Sch 4, para 1 thereto.

4.110 Action following acceptance of resignation—CVL

(1) This Rule applies where a meeting is summoned to receive the liquidator's resignation.

(2) If his resignation is accepted, the notice of it required by section 171(5) shall be given by him [as soon as reasonably practicable] after the [resolution has been passed].

(3) Where a new liquidator is appointed in place of the one who has resigned, the certificate of his appointment shall be delivered [as soon as reasonably practicable] by the chairman of the meeting to the new liquidator.

NOTES

Initial Commencement

Specified date
>Specified date: 29 December 1986: see r 0.1.

Amendment
>Para (2): words "as soon as reasonably practicable" in square brackets substituted by SI 2009/642, rr 4, 5.
>>Date in force: 6 April 2009: see SI 2009/642, r 1; for transitional provisions see r 3 thereof.
>
>Para (2): words "resolution has been passed" in square brackets substituted by SI 2010/686, r 2, Sch 1, para 207.
>>Date in force: 6 April 2010: see SI 2010/686, r 1; for transitional provisions see r 6(1), Sch 4, para 1 thereto.
>
>Para (3): words "as soon as reasonably practicable" in square brackets substituted by SI 2009/642, rr 4, 5.
>>Date in force: 6 April 2009: see SI 2009/642, r 1; for transitional provisions see r 3 thereof.

4.111 [Permission] to resign granted by the court

(1) If at a creditors' meeting summoned to accept the liquidator's resignation it is resolved that it be not accepted, the court may, on the liquidator's application, make an order giving him [permission] to resign.

(2) The court's order may include such provision as it thinks [just] with respect to matters arising in connection with the resignation, and shall determine the date from which the liquidator's release is effective.

(3) The court shall send two sealed copies of the order to the liquidator, who shall send one of the copies [as soon as reasonably practicable] to the official receiver. (NO CVL APPLICATION)

(4–CVL) The court shall send two sealed copies of the order to the liquidator, who shall [as soon as reasonably practicable] send one of them to the registrar of companies.

(5) On sending notice of his resignation to the court, the liquidator shall send a copy of it to the official receiver. (NO CVL APPLICATION)

NOTES

Initial Commencement

Specified date
>Specified date: 29 December 1986: see r 0.1.

Amendment
>Provision heading: word "Permission" in square brackets substituted by SI 2010/686, r 2, Sch 1, para 1.
>>Date in force: 6 April 2010: see SI 2010/686, r 1; for transitional provisions see r 6(1), Sch 4, paras 1, 2(1)(b) thereto.

Para (1): word "permission" in square brackets substituted by SI 2010/686, r 2, Sch 1, para 1.
: Date in force: 6 April 2010: see SI 2010/686, r 1; for transitional provisions see r 6(1), Sch 4, paras 1, 2(1)(b) thereto.
Para (2): word "just" in square brackets substituted by SI 2010/686, r 2, Sch 1, para 1.
: Date in force: 6 April 2010: see SI 2010/686, r 1; for transitional provisions see r 6(1), Sch 4, paras 1, 2(1)(b) thereto.
Para (3): words "as soon as reasonably practicable" in square brackets substituted by SI 2009/642, rr 4, 5.
: Date in force: 6 April 2009: see SI 2009/642, r 1; for transitional provisions see r 3 thereof.
Para (4): words "as soon as reasonably practicable" in square brackets substituted by SI 2009/642, rr 4, 5.
: Date in force: 6 April 2009: see SI 2009/642, r 1; for transitional provisions see r 3 thereof.

4.112 Advertisement of resignation

Where a new liquidator is appointed in place of one who has resigned, the former shall, in giving notice of his appointment, state that his predecessor has resigned and (if it be the case) that he has been given his release.

NOTES

Initial Commencement

Specified date

: Specified date: 29 December 1986: see r 0.1.

See Further

: See further, in relation the application of this rule, with modifications, in respect of the procedure for the appointment of a bank liquidator and the operation of bank insolvency under the Banking Act 2009, Pt 2: the Bank Insolvency (England and Wales) Rules 2009, SI 2009/356, rr 3(3)–(8), 89.

4.113 Meeting of creditors to remove liquidator (No CVL Application)

(1) Where a meeting of creditors is summoned for the purpose of removing the liquidator, the notice summoning it shall indicate that this is the purpose, or one of the purposes, of the meeting; and the notice shall draw the attention of creditors to section 174(4) with respect to the liquidator's release.

(2) A copy of the notice shall at the same time also be sent to the official receiver.

(3) At the meeting, a person other than the liquidator or his nominee may be elected to act as chairman; but if the liquidator or his nominee is chairman and a resolution has been proposed for the liquidator's removal, the chairman shall not adjourn the meeting without the consent of at least one-half (in value) of the creditors present (in person or by proxy) and entitled to vote.

(4) Where the chairman of the meeting is other than the official receiver, and there is passed at the meeting any of the following resolutions—

(a) that the liquidator be removed,
(b) that a new liquidator be appointed,
(c) that the removed liquidator be not given his release,

the chairman shall, within 3 [business] days, send to the official receiver a copy of the resolution.

If it has been resolved to remove the liquidator, the chairman shall send to the official receiver a certificate to that effect.

(5) If the creditors have resolved to appoint a new liquidator, the certificate of his appointment shall also be sent to the official receiver within that time; and Rule 4.100 above shall be complied with in respect of it.

NOTES

Initial Commencement

Specified date

Specified date: 29 December 1986: see r 0.1.

Amendment

Para (4): word "business" in square brackets inserted by SI 2010/686, r 2, Sch 1, para 208. Date in force: 6 April 2010: see SI 2010/686, r 1; for transitional provisions see r 6(1), Sch 4, para 1 thereto.

See Further

See further, in relation the application of this rule, with modifications, in respect of the procedure for the appointment of a bank liquidator and the operation of bank insolvency under the Banking Act 2009, Pt 2: the Bank Insolvency (England and Wales) Rules 2009, SI 2009/356, rr 3(3)–(8), 90.

4.114 Meeting of creditors to remove liquidator—CVL

(1) A meeting held under section 171(2)(b) for the removal of the liquidator shall be summoned by him if requested by 25 per cent in value of the company's creditors, excluding those who are connected with it.

(2) The notice summoning the meeting shall indicate that the removal of the liquidator is the purpose, or one of the purposes, of the meeting; and the notice shall draw the attention of creditors to section 173(2) with respect to the liquidator's release.

(3) At the meeting, a person other than the liquidator or his nominee may be elected to act as chairman; but if the liquidator or his nominee is chairman and a resolution has been proposed for the liquidator's removal, the chairman shall not adjourn the meeting without the consent of at least one-half (in value) of the creditors present (in person or by proxy) and entitled to vote.

NOTES

Initial Commencement

Specified date

Specified date: 29 December 1986: see r 0.1.

4.115 Court's power to regulate meetings under Rules 4.113, 4.114—CVL

Where a meeting under Rule 4.113 or 4.114—CVL is to be held, or is proposed to be summoned, the court may, on the application of any creditor, give directions as to the mode of summoning it, the sending out and return of forms of proxy, the conduct of the meeting, and any other matter which appears to the court to require regulation or control under this Rule.

NOTES

Initial Commencement

Specified date

Specified date: 29 December 1986: see r 0.1.

See Further

See further, in relation the application of this rule, with modifications, in respect of the procedure for the appointment of a bank liquidator and the operation of bank insolvency

under the Banking Act 2009, Pt 2: the Bank Insolvency (England and Wales) Rules 2009, SI 2009/356, rr 3(3)–(8), 91.

4.116 Procedure on removal (No CVL Application)

(1) Where the creditors have resolved that the liquidator be removed, the official receiver shall file in court the certificate of removal.

(2) The resolution is effective as from the date on which the official receiver files the certificate of removal in court, and that date shall be endorsed on the certificate.

[(3) The official receiver must send a copy of the certificate, so endorsed, as soon as reasonably practicable to—
  (a) the removed liquidator;
  (b) the new liquidator (if appointed); and
  (c) the registrar of companies.]

(4) The official receiver shall not file the certificate in court unless and until the Secretary of State has certified to him that the removed liquidator has reconciled his account with that held by the Secretary of State in respect of the winding up.

NOTES

Initial Commencement

Specified date

Specified date: 29 December 1986: see r 0.1.

Amendment

Para (3): substituted by SI 2010/686, r 2, Sch 1, para 209.
  Date in force: 6 April 2010: see SI 2010/686, r 1; for transitional provisions see r 6(1), Sch 4, para 1 thereto.

See Further

See further, in relation the application of this rule, with modifications, in respect of the procedure for the appointment of a bank liquidator and the operation of bank insolvency under the Banking Act 2009, Pt 2: the Bank Insolvency (England and Wales) Rules 2009, SI 2009/356, rr 3(3)–(8), 92.

4.117 Procedure on removal—CVL

Where the creditors have resolved that the liquidator be removed, the chairman of the creditors' meeting shall [as soon as reasonably practicable]—
  (a) if at the meeting another liquidator was not appointed, send the certificate of the liquidator's removal to the registrar of companies, and
  (b) otherwise, deliver the certificate to the new liquidator, who shall send it to the registrar.

NOTES

Initial Commencement

Specified date

Specified date: 29 December 1986: see r 0.1.

Amendment

Words "as soon as reasonably practicable" in square brackets substituted by SI 2009/642, rr 4, 5.
  Date in force: 6 April 2009: see SI 2009/642, r 1; for transitional provisions see r 3 thereof.

4.118 Advertisement of removal

Where a new liquidator is appointed in place of one removed, the former shall, in giving notice of his appointment, state that his predecessor has been removed and (if it be the case) that he has been given his release.

NOTES

Initial Commencement

Specified date

Specified date: 29 December 1986: see r 0.1.

See Further

See further, in relation the application of this rule, with modifications, in respect of the procedure for the appointment of a bank liquidator and the operation of bank insolvency under the Banking Act 2009, Pt 2: the Bank Insolvency (England and Wales) Rules 2009, SI 2009/356, rr 3(3)–(8), 93.

4.119 Removal of liquidator by the court (No CVL Application)

(1) This Rule applies where application is made to the court for the removal of the liquidator, or for an order directing the liquidator to summon a meeting of creditors for the purpose of removing him.

(2) The court may, if it thinks that no sufficient cause is shown for the application, dismiss it; but it shall not do so unless the applicant has had an opportunity to attend the court for [a] hearing, of which he has been given at least [5 business] days' notice [but which is without notice to any other party].

If the application is not dismissed under this paragraph, the court shall fix a venue for it to be heard.

(3) The court may require the applicant to make a deposit or give security for the costs to be incurred by the liquidator on the application.

(4) The applicant shall, at least 14 days before the hearing, send to the liquidator and the official receiver a notice stating the venue and accompanied by a copy of the application, and of any evidence which he intends to adduce in support of it.

(5) Subject to any contrary order of the court, the costs of the application are not payable [as an expense of the liquidation].

(6) Where the court removes the liquidator—

    (a) it shall send copies of the order of removal to him and to the official receiver;

    (b) the order may include such provision as the court thinks [just] with respect to matters arising in connection with the removal; and

    (c) if the court appoints a new liquidator, Rule 4.102 applies.

NOTES

Initial Commencement

Specified date

Specified date: 29 December 1986: see r 0.1.

Amendment

Para (2): word "a" in square brackets substituted by SI 2010/686, r 2, Sch 1, para 210(1), (2)(a).

Date in force: 6 April 2010: see SI 2010/686, r 1; for transitional provisions see r 6(1), Sch 4, paras 1, 2(1)(b) thereto.

Para (2): words "5 business" in square brackets substituted by SI 2010/686, r 2, Sch 1, para 210(1), (2)(b).

Date in force: 6 April 2010: see SI 2010/686, r 1; for transitional provisions see r 6(1), Sch 4, para 1 thereto.
Para (2): words "but which is without notice to any other party" in square brackets inserted by SI 2010/686, r 2, Sch 1, para 210(1), (2)(c).
Date in force: 6 April 2010: see SI 2010/686, r 1; for transitional provisions see r 6(1), Sch 4, paras 1, 2(1)(b) thereto.
Para (5): words "as an expense of the liquidation" in square brackets substituted by SI 2008/737, rr 3, 7(1).
Date in force: 6 April 2008: see SI 2008/737, r 1(1); for transitional provisions see r 2 thereof.
Para (6): in sub-para (b) word "just" in square brackets substituted by SI 2010/686, r 2, Sch 1, para 1.
Date in force: 6 April 2010: see SI 2010/686, r 1; for transitional provisions see r 6(1), Sch 4, paras 1, 2(1)(b) thereto.

See Further

See further, in relation the application of this rule, with modifications, in respect of the procedure for the appointment of a bank liquidator and the operation of bank insolvency under the Banking Act 2009, Pt 2: the Bank Insolvency (England and Wales) Rules 2009, SI 2009/356, rr 3(3)–(8), 94.

4.120 Removal of liquidator by the court—CVL

(1) This Rule applies where application is made to the court for the removal of the liquidator, or for an order directing the liquidator to summon a creditors' meeting for the purpose of removing him.

(2) The court may, if it thinks that no sufficient cause is shown for the application, dismiss it; but it shall not do so unless the applicant has had an opportunity to attend the court for [a] hearing, of which he has been given at least [5 business] days' notice [but which is without notice to any other party].

If the application is not dismissed under this paragraph, the court shall fix a venue for it to be heard.

(3) The court may require the applicant to make a deposit or give security for the costs to be incurred by the liquidator on the application.

(4) The applicant shall, at least 14 days before the hearing, send to the liquidator a notice stating the venue and accompanied by a copy of the application, and of any evidence which he intends to adduce in support of it.

(5) Subject to any contrary order of the court, the costs of the application are not payable [as an expense of the liquidation].

(6) Where the court removes the liquidator—
- (a) it shall send 2 copies of the order of removal to him, one to be sent by him [as soon as reasonably practicable] to the registrar of companies, with notice of his ceasing to act;
- (b) the order may include such provision as the court thinks [just] with respect to matters arising in connection with the removal; and
- (c) if the court appoints a new liquidator, Rule 4.103–CVL applies.

NOTES

Initial Commencement

Specified date

Specified date: 29 December 1986: see r 0.1.

Amendment

Para (2): word "a" in square brackets substituted by SI 2010/686, r 2, Sch 1, para 211(1), (2)(a).
Date in force: 6 April 2010: see SI 2010/686, r 1; for transitional provisions see r 6(1), Sch 4, paras 1, 2(1)(b) thereto.

Para (2): words "5 business" in square brackets substituted by SI 2010/686, r 2, Sch 1, para 211(1), (2)(b).
    Date in force: 6 April 2010: see SI 2010/686, r 1; for transitional provisions see r 6(1), Sch 4, para 1 thereto.

Para (2): words "but which is without notice to any other party" in square brackets inserted by SI 2010/686, r 2, Sch 1, para 211(1), (2)(c).
    Date in force: 6 April 2010: see SI 2010/686, r 1; for transitional provisions see r 6(1), Sch 4, paras 1, 2(1)(b) thereto.

Para (5): words "as an expense of the liquidation" in square brackets substituted by SI 2008/737, rr 3, 7(1).
    Date in force: 6 April 2008: see SI 2008/737, r 1(1); for transitional provisions see r 2 thereof.

Para (6): in sub-para (a) words "as soon as reasonably practicable" in square brackets substituted by SI 2009/642, rr 4, 5.
    Date in force: 6 April 2009: see SI 2009/642, r 1; for transitional provisions see r 3 thereof.

Para (6): in sub-para (b) word "just" in square brackets substituted by SI 2010/686, r 2, Sch 1, para 1.
    Date in force: 6 April 2010: see SI 2010/686, r 1; for transitional provisions see r 6(1), Sch 4, paras 1, 2(1)(b) thereto.

4.121 Release of resigning or removed liquidator (No CVL Application)

(1) [Subject to paragraph (1A),] where the liquidator's resignation is accepted by a meeting of creditors which has not resolved against his release, he has his release from when his resignation is effective under Rule 4.109.

[(1A) Where the liquidator's resignation is accepted under Rule 4.108A, the liquidator's release is effective as from the date on which the official receiver files the copy of the certificate under paragraph (8) of that Rule in court, that date to be endorsed on the copy certificate.]

(2) Where the liquidator is removed by a meeting of creditors which has not resolved against his release, the fact of his release shall be stated in the certificate of removal.

(3) Where—

(a) the liquidator resigns, and the creditors' meeting called to receive his resignation has resolved against his release, or

(b) he is removed by a creditors' meeting which has so resolved, or is removed by the court,

he must apply to the Secretary of State for his release.

(4) When the Secretary of State gives the release, he shall certify it accordingly, and send the certificate to the official receiver, to be filed in court.

(5) A copy of the certificate shall be sent by the Secretary of State to the former liquidator, whose release is effective from the date of the certificate.

NOTES

Initial Commencement

Specified date

    Specified date: 29 December 1986: see r 0.1.

Amendment

Para (1): words "Subject to paragraph (1A)," in square brackets inserted by SI 2010/686, r 2, Sch 1, para 212(1), (2).
    Date in force: 6 April 2010: see SI 2010/686, r 1; for transitional provisions see r 6(1), Sch 4, para 1 thereto.

Para (1A): inserted by SI 2010/686, r 2, Sch 1, para 212(1), (3).
    Date in force: 6 April 2010: see SI 2010/686, r 1; for transitional provisions see r 6(1), Sch 4, para 1 thereto.

See Further

See further, in relation the application of this rule, with modifications, in respect of the procedure for the appointment of a bank liquidator and the operation of bank insolvency under the Banking Act 2009, Pt 2: the Bank Insolvency (England and Wales) Rules 2009, SI 2009/356, rr 3(3)–(8), 95.

4.122 Release of resigning or removed liquidator—CVL

(1) [Subject to paragraph (1A),] where the liquidator's resignation is accepted by a meeting of creditors which has not resolved against his release, he has his release from when he gives notice of his resignation to the registrar of companies.

[(1A) Where the liquidator's resignation is accepted under Rule 4.108A, the liquidator's release is effective as from the date of the certificate.]

(2) Where the liquidator is removed by a creditors' meeting which has not resolved against his release, the fact of his release shall be stated in the certificate of removal.

(3) Where—
- (a) the liquidator resigns, and the creditors' meeting called to receive his resignation has resolved against his release, or
- (b) he is removed by a creditors' meeting which has so resolved, or is removed by the court,

he must apply to the Secretary of State for his release.

(4) When the Secretary of State gives the release, he shall certify it accordingly, and send the certificate to the registrar of companies.

(5) A copy of the certificate shall be sent by the Secretary of State to the former liquidator, whose release is effective from the date of the certificate.

NOTES

Initial Commencement

Specified date

Specified date: 29 December 1986: see r 0.1.

Amendment

Para (1): words "Subject to paragraph (1A)," in square brackets inserted by SI 2010/686, r 2, Sch 1, para 213(1), (2).
Date in force: 6 April 2010: see SI 2010/686, r 1; for transitional provisions see r 6(1), Sch 4, para 1 thereto.
Para (1A): inserted by SI 2010/686, r 2, Sch 1, para 213(1), (3).
Date in force: 6 April 2010: see SI 2010/686, r 1; for transitional provisions see r 6(1), Sch 4, para 1 thereto.

4.123 Removal of liquidator by Secretary of State (No CVL Application)

(1) If the Secretary of State decides to remove the liquidator, he shall before doing so notify the liquidator and the official receiver of his decision and the grounds of it, and specify a period within which the liquidator may make representations against implementation of the decision.

(2) If the Secretary of State directs the removal of the liquidator, he shall [as soon as reasonably practicable]—
- (a) file notice of his decision in court, and
- (b) send notice to the liquidator and the official receiver.

(3) If the liquidator is removed by direction of the Secretary of State—
- (a) Rule 4.121 applies as regards the liquidator obtaining his release, as if he had been removed by the court, and
- (b) the court may make any such order in his case as it would have power to make if he had been so removed.

NOTES

Initial Commencement

Specified date

Specified date: 29 December 1986: see r 0.1.

Amendment

Para (2): words "as soon as reasonably practicable" in square brackets substituted by SI 2009/642, rr 4, 5.
Date in force: 6 April 2009: see SI 2009/642, r 1; for transitional provisions see r 3 thereof.

SECTION C: RELEASE ON COMPLETION OF ADMINISTRATION

4.124 Release of official receiver (No CVL Application)

(1) The official receiver shall, before giving notice to the Secretary of State under section 174(3) (that the winding up is for practical purposes complete), send out notice of his intention to do so to all creditors [of which he is aware].

(2) The notice shall in each case be accompanied by a summary of the official receiver's receipts and payments as liquidator.

[(2A) The summary of receipts and payments referred to in paragraph (2) shall also include a statement as to the amount paid to unsecured creditors by virtue of the application of section 176A (prescribed part).]

(3) The Secretary of State, when he has determined the date from which the official receiver is to have his release, shall give notice to the court that he has done so. The notice shall be accompanied by the summary referred to in paragraph (2).

NOTES

Initial Commencement

Specified date

Specified date: 29 December 1986: see r 0.1.

Amendment

Para (1): words "of which he is aware" in square brackets substituted by SI 2004/584, r 11.
Date in force: 1 April 2004: see SI 2004/584, r 1(2).
Para (2A): inserted by SI 2003/1730, r 7, Sch 1, Pt 4, para 22.
Date in force: 15 September 2003: see SI 2003/1730, r 1(2).

4.125 Final meeting (No CVL Application)

(1) Where the liquidator is other than the official receiver, he shall give at least 28 days' notice of the final meeting of creditors to be held under section 146. The notice shall be sent to all creditors [of which he is aware]. . ..

[(1A) The final meeting must not be held unless Rule 4.49D has been complied with; and if for that reason the meeting is not held—

    (a)   the liquidator must give notice of that fact as soon as reasonably practicable to all to whom notice of the meeting was given, and

    (b)   fresh notice of the meeting complying with this Rule must be given when Rule 4.49D has been complied with.

(1B) The liquidator—

    (a)   at least 1 month before the meeting is held must have gazetted a notice of the meeting; and

    (b)   may advertise the notice in such other manner as the liquidator thinks fit.

(1C) In addition to the standard contents, the notice under paragraph (1B) must state—
- (a) who summoned the meeting;
- (b) if the meeting was summoned at the request of a creditor, the fact that it was so summoned and the section of the Act under which it was requested;
- (c) the purpose for which the meeting is summoned;
- (d) the venue fixed for the meeting; and
- (e) the time and date by which, and place at which, creditors must lodge proxies and hitherto unlodged proofs in order to be entitled to vote at the meeting.]

(2) The liquidator's report laid before the meeting under that section shall contain an account of the liquidator's administration of the winding up, including—
- (a) a summary of his receipts and payments, [including details of remuneration charged and expenses incurred by the liquidator,]
- [(ab) details of the basis fixed for the liquidator's remuneration, and]
- (b) a statement by him that he has reconciled his account with that which is held by the Secretary of State in respect of the winding up.

[(2A) The liquidator's report shall also contain a statement as to the amount paid to unsecured creditors by virtue of the application of section 176A (prescribed part).]

[(2B) Where the liquidator has sent a progress report to creditors in accordance with Rule 4.49B, the report to be laid at the final meeting of creditors must also—
- (a) contain a receipts and payments account in the form of an abstract showing the receipts and payments during the period since the last progress report, and
- (b) include—
  - (i) details of the remuneration charged and expenses incurred by the liquidator during that period, and
  - (ii) a description of the things done by the liquidator during that period in respect of which that remuneration was charged and those expenses incurred.

(2C) In any case where the basis of the liquidator's remuneration had not been fixed by the date to which the last progress report was made up, the receipts and payments account required by paragraph (2B)(a) must also include details of the remuneration charged in the period of any preceding progress report in which details of remuneration were not included.

(2D) Where the basis of remuneration has been fixed as a set amount only, it is sufficient compliance with paragraph (2B)(b) for the liquidator to state the amount which has been set and to supply details of the expenses charged within the period in question.]

(3) At the final meeting, the creditors may question the liquidator with respect to any matter contained in his report, and may resolve against him having his release.

(4) The liquidator shall give notice to the court that the final meeting has been held; and the notice shall state whether or not he has been given his release, and be accompanied by a copy of the report laid before the final meeting. A copy of the notice shall be sent by the liquidator to the [Secretary of State].

(5) If there is no quorum present at the final meeting, the liquidator shall report to the court that a final meeting was summoned in accordance with the Rules, but there was no quorum present; and the final meeting is then deemed to have been held, and the creditors not to have resolved against the liquidator having his release.

(6) If the creditors at the final meeting have not so resolved, the liquidator is released when the notice under paragraph (4) is filed in court. If they have so resolved, the liquidator must obtain his release from the Secretary of State and Rule 4.121 applies accordingly.

NOTES

Initial Commencement

Specified date

Specified date: 29 December 1986: see r 0.1.

Amendment

Para (1): words "of which he is aware" in square brackets substituted by SI 2004/584, r 12.
Date in force: 1 April 2004: see SI 2004/584, r 1(2).
Para (1): words omitted revoked by SI 2010/686, r 2, Sch 1, para 214(1), (2).
Date in force: 6 April 2010: see SI 2010/686, r 1; for transitional provisions see r 6(1), Sch 4, para 1 thereto.
Paras (1A)–(1C): inserted by SI 2010/686, r 2, Sch 1, para 214(1), (3).
Date in force: 6 April 2010: see SI 2010/686, r 1; for transitional provisions see r 6(1), Sch 4, para 1 thereto.
Para (2): in sub-para (a) words "including details of remuneration charged and expenses incurred by the liquidator," in square brackets substituted by SI 2010/686, r 2, Sch 1, para 214(1), (4).
Date in force: 6 April 2010: see SI 2010/686, r 1; for transitional provisions see r 6(1), Sch 4, para 1 thereto.
Para (2): sub-para (ab) inserted by SI 2010/686, r 2, Sch 1, para 214(1), (4).
Date in force: 6 April 2010: see SI 2010/686, r 1; for transitional provisions see r 6(1), Sch 4, para 1 thereto.
Para (2A): inserted by SI 2003/1730, r 7, Sch 1, Pt 4, para 23.
Date in force: 15 September 2003: see SI 2003/1730, r 1(2).
Paras (2B)–(2D): inserted by SI 2010/686, r 2, Sch 1, para 214(1), (5).
Date in force: 6 April 2010: see SI 2010/686, r 1; for transitional provisions see r 6(1), Sch 4, para 1 thereto.
Para (4): words "Secretary of State" in square brackets substituted by SI 2005/527, r 28.
Date in force: 1 April 2005: see SI 2005/527, r 1(2).

[4.125A Rule as to reporting]

[(1) The court may, on the liquidator or official receiver's application, relieve him of any duty imposed on him by Rule 4.124 or 4.125, or authorise him to carry out the duty in a way other than there required.

(2) In considering whether to act under this Rule, the court shall have regard to the cost of carrying out the duty, to the amount of the assets available, and to the extent of the interest of creditors or contributories, or any particular class of them.]

NOTES

Amendment

Inserted by SI 2004/584, r 13.
Date in force: 1 April 2004: see SI 2004/584, r 1(2).

See Further

See further, in relation the application of this rule, with modifications, in respect of the procedure for the appointment of a bank liquidator and the operation of bank insolvency under the Banking Act 2009, Pt 2: the Bank Insolvency (England and Wales) Rules 2009, SI 2009/356, rr 3(3)–(8), 97.

4.126 Final meeting—CVL

(1) The liquidator shall give at least 28 days' notice of the final meeting of creditors to be held under section 106. The notice shall be sent to all creditors who [are known to the liquidator].

[(1A) In addition to information required by subsection (2) of section 106 and the standard contents, the advertisement required by that subsection must state the time and date by which, and place at which, creditors must lodge proxies and hitherto unlodged proofs in order to be entitled to vote at the meeting.

(1B) In addition to the notice required by paragraph (1) and the advertisement required by section 106(2), the liquidator may advertise notice of the meeting in such other manner as the liquidator thinks fit.

(1C) In addition to the standard contents, notice under paragraph (1B) must state—
- (a) the purpose of the meeting;
- (b) the venue fixed for the meeting; and
- (c) the time and date by which, and place at which, creditors must lodge proxies and hitherto unlodged proofs in order to be entitled to vote at the meeting.

(1D) The final meeting must not be held unless Rule 4.49D has been complied with; and if for that reason the meeting is not held—
- (a) the liquidator must give notice of that fact as soon as reasonably practicable to all to whom notice of the meeting was given, and
- (b) fresh notice of the meeting complying with this Rule must be given when Rule 4.49D has been complied with.

(1E) The liquidator's report laid before the meeting of creditors under section 106 must contain an account of the liquidator's administration of the winding up, including—
- (a) a summary of the liquidator's receipts and payments, including at least the following items separately specified (except where the amount for an item is zero)—
    - (i) the total of all receipts, with separate specification thereunder of—
        - (aa) receipts from trading carried on by the liquidator;
        - (bb) payments made in the course of trading carried on by the liquidator;
        - (cc) the source of all other receipts;
        - (dd) payments to redeem securities;
        - (ee) costs of execution; and
        - (ff) net realisations;
    - (ii) the cost of employing a solicitor;
    - (iii) other legal costs;
    - (iv) the liquidator's remuneration;
    - (v) the cost of employing an auctioneer;
    - (vi) the cost of employing a valuer;
    - (vii) the costs of taking possession of and maintaining the company's property;
    - (viii) the cost of advertising in the Gazette and other newspapers;
    - (ix) incidental outlays;
    - (x) a statement of the total of costs and charges incurred;
    - (xi) the amount paid to holders of debentures of each class of debenture, setting out the amount paid per debenture, the nominal value of each debenture in each class and the total amount paid in respect of each class;
    - (xii) the aggregate numbers of preferential and unsecured creditors and the aggregate amounts paid out to them, the aggregates for preferential and unsecured creditors set out separately unless all creditors have been paid in full;
    - (xiii) statements of the aggregate dividend paid on each pound of preferential and of unsecured debt and of the estimate of the value of the company's net property which had been made under Rule 4.49(2)(a)(ii);

(xiv) the amount of interest paid under section 189;
(xv) the amount paid to contributories in respect of each class of share, setting out the amount per share and the nominal value of each share in each class;
(xvi) a statement of the total amount paid to holders of debentures, preferential and unsecured creditors and contributories;
(xvii) a statement of assets which have proved to be unrealisable, including the value of those assets which had been made for the purpose of Rule 4.49(2)(a)(ii);
(xviii) the amounts paid into the Insolvency Services Account, set out separately, in respect of—
  (aa) unclaimed dividends payable to creditors in the winding up;
  (bb) other unclaimed dividends in the winding up;
  (cc) moneys held by the company in trust in respect of dividends or other sums due before the commencement of the winding up to any person as a member of the company;
(b) details of the basis fixed for the liquidator's remuneration and by whom it was fixed;
(c) a statement by the liquidator that the account included in the report has been reconciled with that which is held by the Secretary of State in respect of the winding up;
(d) any other statement which the liquidator thinks it desirable to make.]

(2) At the final meeting, the creditors may question the liquidator with respect to any matter contained in the account required under [section 106] [or paragraph (4) of this Rule], and may resolve against the liquidator having his release.

(3) Where the creditors have so resolved, he must obtain his release from the Secretary of State; and Rule 4.122—CVL applies accordingly.

[(4) The account of the winding up required under section 106 shall also include a statement as to the amount paid to unsecured creditors by virtue of the application of section 176A (prescribed part).]

[(5) Where the liquidator has sent a progress report to creditors in accordance with section 104A, the report to be laid at the final meeting of creditors must also—
(a) contain a receipts and payments account in the form of an abstract showing the receipts and payments during the period since the last progress report, and
(b) include—
  (i) details of the remuneration charged and expenses incurred by the liquidator during that period, and
  (ii) a description of the things done by the liquidator during that period in respect of which that remuneration was charged and those expenses incurred.

(6) In any case where the basis of the liquidator's remuneration had not been fixed by the date to which the last progress report was made up, the receipts and payments account required by paragraph (5)(a) must also include details of the remuneration charged in the period of any preceding progress report in which details of remuneration were not included.

(7) Where the basis of remuneration has been fixed as a set amount only, it is sufficient compliance with paragraph (5)(b) for the liquidator to state the amount which has been set and to supply details of the expenses charged within the period in question.]

NOTES

Initial Commencement

Specified date

Specified date: 29 December 1986: see r 0.1.

Amendment

Para (1): words "are known to the liquidator" words in square brackets substituted by SI 2010/686, r 2, Sch 1, para 215(1), (2).
Date in force: 6 April 2010: see SI 2010/686, r 1; for transitional provisions see r 6(1), Sch 4, para 1 thereto.
Paras (1A)–(1E): inserted by SI 2010/686, r 2, Sch 1, para 215(1), (3).
Date in force: 6 April 2010: see SI 2010/686, r 1; for transitional provisions see r 6(1), Sch 4, para 1 thereto.
Para (2): words "section 106" in square brackets substituted by SI 2010/686, r 2, Sch 1, para 215(1), (4).
Date in force: 6 April 2010: see SI 2010/686, r 1; for transitional provisions see r 6(1), Sch 4, para 1 thereto.
Para (2): words "or paragraph (4) of this Rule" in square brackets inserted by SI 2003/1730, r 7, Sch 1, Pt 4, para 24(a).
Date in force: 15 September 2003: see SI 2003/1730, r 1(2).
Para (4): inserted by SI 2003/1730, r 7, Sch 1, Pt 4, para 24(b).
Date in force: 15 September 2003: see SI 2003/1730, r 1(2).
Paras (5)–(7): inserted by SI 2010/686, r 2, Sch 1, para 215(1), (5).
Date in force: 6 April 2010: see SI 2010/686, r 1; for transitional provisions see r 6(1), Sch 4, para 1 thereto.

[4.126A Final meeting in members' voluntary liquidation (No CVL Application)]

[(1) In addition to the information required by section 94(2) and the standard contents, the advertisement required by that subsection must state the time and date by which, and place at which, members must lodge proxies in order to be entitled to vote.

(2) In addition to the advertisement required by section 94(2), the liquidator may advertise notice of the meeting in such other manner as the liquidator thinks fit.

(3) In addition to the standard contents, notice given under paragraph (2) must state—

    (a)   the purpose of the meeting,
    (b)   the venue fixed for the meeting, and
    (c)   the time and date by which, and place at which, members must lodge proxies in order to be entitled to vote at the meeting.

(4) The liquidator's report laid before the meeting of the company under section 94 must contain an account of the liquidator's administration of the winding up, including (except where the amount for an item is zero)—

    (a)   a summary of the liquidator's receipts and payments, including at least the following items separately specified—
        (i)   the total of all receipts, with separate specification thereunder of—
            (aa) receipts from trading carried on by the liquidator;
            (bb) payments made in the course of trading carried on by the liquidator;
            (cc) the source of all other receipts;
            (dd) payments to redeem securities;
            (ee) costs of execution; and
            (ff) net realisations;
        (ii)   the cost of employing a solicitor;
        (iii) other legal costs;
        (iv) the liquidator's remuneration;

(v) the cost of employing an auctioneer;
(vi) the cost of employing a valuer;
(vii) the costs of taking possession of and maintaining the company's property;
(viii) the cost of advertising in the Gazette and other newspapers;
(ix) incidental outlays;
(x) a statement of the total of costs and charges incurred;
(xi) the amount paid to holders of debentures of each class of debenture, setting out the amount paid per debenture, the nominal value of each debenture in each class and the total amount paid in respect of each class;
(xii) the aggregate amount paid out to creditors;
(xiii) the amount of interest paid under section 189;
(xiv) the amount paid to contributories in respect of each class of share, setting out the amount per share and the nominal value of each share in each class;
(xv) a statement of the total amount paid to holders of debentures, preferential and unsecured creditors and contributories;
(xvi) a statement of assets which have proved to be unrealisable, including the value of those assets which had been made for the purpose of Rule 4.49(2)(a)(ii);
(xvii) the amounts paid into the Insolvency Services Account, set out separately, in respect of—
(aa) unclaimed dividends payable to creditors in the winding up;
(bb) other unclaimed dividends in the winding up;
(cc) moneys held by the company in trust in respect of dividends or other sums due before the commencement of the winding up to any person as a member of the company;
(b) details of the basis fixed for the liquidator's remuneration and by whom it was fixed;
(c) any other statement which the liquidator thinks it desirable to make.]

NOTES

Amendment
Inserted by SI 2010/686, r 2, Sch 1, para 216.
Date in force: 6 April 2010: see SI 2010/686, r 1; for transitional provisions see r 6(1), Sch 4, para 1 thereto.

SECTION D: REMUNERATION

4.127 Fixing of remuneration

(1) The liquidator is entitled to receive remuneration for his services as such.
(2) [The basis of remuneration] shall be fixed . . .—
(a) as a percentage of the value of the assets which are realised or distributed, or of the one value and the other in combination, or
(b) by reference to the time properly given by the insolvency practitioner (as liquidator) and his staff in attending to matters arising in the winding up[, or
(c) as a set amount].
[(3A) The basis of remuneration may be fixed as any one or more of the bases set out in paragraph (2), and different bases may be fixed in respect of different things done by the liquidator.

(3B) Where the basis of remuneration is fixed as set out in paragraph (2)(a), different percentages may be fixed in respect of different things done by the liquidator.

(3C) Where the liquidator is other than the official receiver, and subject to paragraph (5A), it is for the liquidation committee (if there is one) to determine—

(a) which of the bases set out in paragraph (2) are to be fixed and (where appropriate) in what combination under paragraph (3A), and

(b) the percentage or percentages (if any) to be fixed under paragraphs (2)(a) and (3B) and the amount (if any) to be set under paragraph (2)(c).]

(4) In arriving at that determination, the committee shall have regard to the following matters—

(a) the complexity (or otherwise) of the case,

(b) any respects in which, in connection with the winding up, there falls on the insolvency practitioner (as liquidator) any responsibility of an exceptional kind or degree,

(c) the effectiveness with which the insolvency practitioner appears to be carrying out, or to have carried out, his duties as liquidator, and

(d) the value and nature of the assets with which the liquidator has to deal.

(5) If there is no liquidation committee, or the committee does not make the requisite determination, [and subject to paragraph (5A), the basis of] the liquidator's remuneration may be fixed (in accordance with [paragraphs (2), (3A) and (3B)]) by a resolution of a meeting of creditors; and paragraph (4) applies to them as it does to the liquidation committee.

[(5A) Where—

(a) a company which is in administration moves into winding up under paragraph 83 of Schedule B1 to the Act and the administrator becomes the liquidator, or

(b) a winding-up order is made immediately upon the appointment of an administrator ceasing to have effect and the court under section 140(1) appoints as liquidator the person whose appointment as administrator has ceased to have effect,

the basis of remuneration fixed under Rule 2.106 is treated as having been fixed under this Rule and paragraphs (4) and (5) do not apply.]

[(6) Where the liquidator is not the official receiver and [the basis of] his remuneration is not fixed as above [within 18 months after the date of the liquidator's appointment], the liquidator shall be entitled to remuneration fixed in accordance with the provisions of Rule 4.127A [(NO CVL APPLICATION)].]

[(7–CVL) If not fixed as above, the basis of the liquidator's remuneration shall, on application by the liquidator, be fixed by the court, and the provisions of paragraphs (2) to (4) apply as they do to the fixing of the basis of remuneration by the liquidation committee; but such an application may not be made by the liquidator unless the liquidator has first sought fixing of the basis in accordance with paragraph (3C) or (5), and in any event may not be made more than 18 months after the date of the liquidator's appointment.]

NOTES

Initial Commencement

Specified date

Specified date: 29 December 1986: see r 0.1.

Amendment

Para (2): words "The basis of remuneration" in square brackets substituted by SI 2010/686, r 2, Sch 1, para 217(1), (2)(a).

Date in force: 6 April 2010: see SI 2010/686, r 1; for transitional provisions see r 6(1), Sch 4, para 1 thereto.
Para (2): word omitted revoked by SI 2010/686, r 2, Sch 1, para 217(1), (2)(b).
Date in force: 6 April 2010: see SI 2010/686, r 1; for transitional provisions see r 6(1), Sch 4, para 1 thereto.
Para (2): sub-para (c) and word ", or" immediately preceding it inserted by SI 2010/686, r 2, Sch 1, para 217(1), (2)(c).
Date in force: 6 April 2010: see SI 2010/686, r 1; for transitional provisions see r 6(1), Sch 4, para 1 thereto.
Paras (3A)–(3C): substituted, for para (3) as originally enacted, by SI 2010/686, r 2, Sch 1, para 217(1), (3).
Date in force: 6 April 2010: see SI 2010/686, r 1; for transitional provisions see r 6(1), Sch 4, para 1 thereto.
Para (5): words "and subject to paragraph (5A), the basis of" in square brackets inserted by SI 2010/686, r 2, Sch 1, para 217(1), (4)(a).
Date in force: 6 April 2010: see SI 2010/686, r 1; for transitional provisions see r 6(1), Sch 4, para 1 thereto.
Para (5): words "paragraphs (2), (3A) and (3B)" in square brackets substituted by SI 2010/686, r 2, Sch 1, para 217(1), (4)(b).
Date in force: 6 April 2010: see SI 2010/686, r 1; for transitional provisions see r 6(1), Sch 4, para 1 thereto.
Para (5A): inserted by SI 2010/686, r 2, Sch 1, para 217(1), (5).
Date in force: 6 April 2010: see SI 2010/686, r 1; for transitional provisions see r 6(1), Sch 4, para 1 thereto.
Para (6): substituted by SI 2004/584, r 14.
Date in force: 1 April 2004: see SI 2004/584, r 1(2); for transitional provisions see r 3 thereof.
Para (6): words "the basis of" in square brackets inserted by SI 2010/686, r 2, Sch 1, para 217(1), (6)(a).
Date in force: 6 April 2010: see SI 2010/686, r 1; for transitional provisions see r 6(1), Sch 4, para 1 thereto.
Para (6): words "within 18 months after the date of the liquidator's appointment" in square brackets inserted by SI 2010/686, r 2, Sch 1, para 217(1), (6)(b).
Date in force: 6 April 2010: see SI 2010/686, r 1; for transitional provisions see r 6(1), Sch 4, para 1 thereto.
Para (6): words "(NO CVL APPLICATION)" in square brackets inserted by SI 2010/686, r 2, Sch 1, para 217(1), (6)(c).
Date in force: 6 April 2010: see SI 2010/686, r 1; for transitional provisions see r 6(1), Sch 4, para 1 thereto.
Para (7): inserted by SI 2010/686, r 2, Sch 1, para 217(1), (7).
Date in force: 6 April 2010: see SI 2010/686, r 1; for transitional provisions see r 6(1), Sch 4, para 1 thereto.

See Further

See further, in relation the application of this rule, with modifications, in respect of the procedure for the appointment of a bank liquidator and the operation of bank insolvency under the Banking Act 2009, Pt 2: the Bank Insolvency (England and Wales) Rules 2009, SI 2009/356, rr 3(3)–(8), 98.

[4.127A Liquidator's entitlement to remuneration where it is not fixed under Rule 4.127 [(No CVL Application)]]

[(1) This Rule applies where the liquidator is not the official receiver and [the basis of] his remuneration is not fixed [or treated as fixed] in accordance with Rule 4.127.

(2) The liquidator shall be entitled by way of remuneration for his services as such, to such sum as is arrived at by—

    (a)   first applying the realisation scale set out in Schedule 6 to the monies received by him from the realisation of the assets of the company (including any Value Added Tax thereon but after deducting any sums paid to secured creditors in respect of their securities and any sums spent out of money received in carrying on the business of the company); and

(b) then by adding to the sum arrived at under sub-paragraph (a) such sum as is arrived at by applying the distribution scale set out in Schedule 6 to the value of assets distributed to creditors of the company (including payments made in respect of preferential debts) and to contributories.]

NOTES

Amendment

Inserted by SI 2004/584, r 15.
Date in force: 1 April 2004: see SI 2004/584, r 1(2); for transitional provisions see r 3 thereof.
Provision heading: words "(No CVL Application)" in square brackets inserted by SI 2010/686, r 2, Sch 1, para 218(1), (2).
Date in force: 6 April 2010: see SI 2010/686, r 1; for transitional provisions see r 6(1), Sch 4, para 1 thereto.
Para (1): words "the basis of" in square brackets inserted by SI 2010/686, r 2, Sch 1, para 218(1), (3)(a).
Date in force: 6 April 2010: see SI 2010/686, r 1; for transitional provisions see r 6(1), Sch 4, para 1 thereto.
Para (1): words "or treated as fixed" in square brackets inserted by SI 2010/686, r 2, Sch 1, para 218(1), (3)(b).
Date in force: 6 April 2010: see SI 2010/686, r 1; for transitional provisions see r 6(1), Sch 4, para 1 thereto.

See Further

See further, in relation the application of this rule, with modifications, in respect of the procedure for the appointment of a bank liquidator and the operation of bank insolvency under the Banking Act 2009, Pt 2: the Bank Insolvency (England and Wales) Rules 2009, SI 2009/356, rr 3(3)–(8), 99.

[4.127B Liquidator's remuneration where he realises assets on behalf of chargeholder]

[(1) This Rule applies where the liquidator is not the official receiver and realises assets on behalf of a secured creditor.

(2) Where the assets realised for a secured creditor are subject to a charge which when created was a mortgage or a fixed charge, the liquidator shall be entitled to such sum by way of remuneration as is arrived at by applying the realisation scale set out in Schedule 6 to the monies received by him in respect of the assets realised (including any sums received in respect of Value Added Tax thereon but after deducting any sums spent out of money received in carrying on the business of the company).

(3) Where the assets realised for a secured creditor are subject to a charge which when created was a floating charge, the liquidator shall be entitled to such sum by way of remuneration as is arrived at by—

(a) first applying the realisation scale set out in Schedule 6 to monies received by him from the realisation of those assets (including any Value Added Tax thereon but ignoring any sums received which are spent in carrying on the business of the company); and

(b) then by adding to the sum arrived at under sub-paragraph (a) such sum as is arrived at by applying the distribution scale set out in Schedule 6 to the value of the assets distributed to the holder of the charge] [and payments made in respect of preferential debts].

[(4) The sum to which the liquidator is entitled under paragraph (2) or (3) shall be taken out of the proceeds of the realisation effected under that paragraph.]

NOTES

Amendment

Inserted by SI 2004/584, r 15.

Date in force: 1 April 2004: see SI 2004/584, r 1(2); for transitional provisions see r 3 thereof.

Para (3): in sub-para (b) words "and payments made in respect of preferential debts" in square brackets inserted by SI 2005/527, r 29.

Date in force: this amendment shall apply in any case where, on or after 1 April 2004, a winding-up order has been made or a resolution for the winding up of a company has been passed or a bankruptcy order has been made, before 1 April 2005: see SI 2005/527, rr 1(2), 3(2).

Para (4): inserted by SI 2010/686, r 2, Sch 1, para 219.

Date in force: 6 April 2010: see SI 2010/686, r 1; for transitional provisions see r 6(1), Sch 4, para 1 thereto.

See Further

See further, in relation the application of this rule, with modifications, in respect of the procedure for the appointment of a bank liquidator and the operation of bank insolvency under the Banking Act 2009, Pt 2: the Bank Insolvency (England and Wales) Rules 2009, SI 2009/356, rr 3(3)–(8), 100.

See further, in relation to the application of this rule, with modifications, in respect of bank administration and applications for bank administration: the Bank Administration (England and Wales) Rules 2009, SI 2009/357, rr 58–61.

4.128 Other matters affecting remuneration

(1) ...

(2) Where there are joint liquidators, it is for them to agree between themselves as to how the remuneration payable should be apportioned. Any dispute arising between them may be referred—

(a) to the court, for settlement by order, or

(b) to the liquidation committee or a meeting of creditors, for settlement by resolution.

(3) If the liquidator is a solicitor and employs his own firm, or any partner in it, to act on behalf of the company, profit costs shall not be paid unless this is authorised by the liquidation committee, the creditors or the court.

NOTES

Initial Commencement

Specified date

Specified date: 29 December 1986: see r 0.1.

Amendment

Para (1): revoked by SI 2004/584, r 16.

Date in force: 1 April 2004: see SI 2004/584, r 1(2); for transitional provisions see r 3 thereof.

Modification

References to solicitors etc modified to include references to bodies recognised under the Administration of Justice Act 1985, s 9, by the Solicitors' Incorporated Practices Order 1991, SI 1991/2684, arts 4, 5, Sch 1.

See Further

See further, in relation the application of this rule, with modifications, in respect of the procedure for the appointment of a bank liquidator and the operation of bank insolvency under the Banking Act 2009, Pt 2: the Bank Insolvency (England and Wales) Rules 2009, SI 2009/356, rr 3(3)–(8), 101.

[4.129A Recourse of liquidator to meeting of creditors]

[If the basis of the liquidator's remuneration has been fixed by the liquidation committee, or by the creditors' committee under Rule 2.106(3C) in a case falling within Rule 4.127(5A) in which the administrator had not requested an increase under Rule 2.107, and the liquidator considers the rate or amount to be insufficient or the basis to be inappropriate, the liquidator may request that the rate or amount be increased or the basis changed by resolution of the creditors.]

NOTES

Amendment

Substituted, for r 4.129 as originally enacted, by SI 2010/686, r 2, Sch 1, para 220.
Date in force: 6 April 2010: see SI 2010/686, r 1; for transitional provisions see r 6(1), Sch 4, para 1 thereto.

4.130 Recourse to the court

[(1) If the liquidator considers that the basis of remuneration fixed by the liquidation committee, or by resolution of the creditors, or as under Rule 4.127(5A) or (6), is insufficient or inappropriate, the liquidator may apply to the court for an order changing it or increasing its amount or rate.]

(2) The liquidator shall give at least 14 days' notice of his application to the members of the liquidation committee; and the committee may nominate one or more members to appear or be represented, and to be heard, on the application.

(3) If there is no liquidation committee, the liquidator's notice of his application shall be sent to such one or more of the company's creditors as the court may direct, which creditors may nominate one or more of their number to appear or be represented.

(4) The court may, if it appears to be a proper case, order the costs of the liquidator's application, including the costs of any member of the liquidation committee appearing [or being represented] on it, or any creditor so appearing [or being represented], to be paid [as an expense of the liquidation].

NOTES

Initial Commencement

Specified date

Specified date: 29 December 1986: see r 0.1.

Amendment

Para (1): substituted by SI 2010/686, r 2, Sch 1, para 221.
Date in force: 6 April 2010: see SI 2010/686, r 1; for transitional provisions see r 6(1), Sch 4, para 1 thereto.

Para (4): words "or being represented" in square brackets in both places they occur inserted by SI 1987/1919, r 3(1), Schedule, Pt 1, para 65.

Para (4): words "as an expense of the liquidation" in square brackets substituted by SI 2008/737, rr 3, 7(1).
Date in force: 6 April 2008: see SI 2008/737, r 1(1); for transitional provisions see r 2 thereof.

See Further

See further, in relation the application of this rule, with modifications, in respect of the procedure for the appointment of a bank liquidator and the operation of bank insolvency under the Banking Act 2009, Pt 2: the Bank Insolvency (England and Wales) Rules 2009, SI 2009/356, rr 3(3)–(8), 130.

4.131 Creditors' claim that remuneration is [or other expenses are] excessive

[(1) Any secured creditor, or any unsecured creditor with either the concurrence of at least 10% in value of the creditors (including that creditor) or the permission of the court, may apply to the court for one or more of the orders in paragraph (4).

(1A) Application may be made on the grounds that—
- (a) the remuneration charged by the liquidator,
- (b) the basis fixed for the liquidator's remuneration under Rule 4.127, or
- (c) expenses incurred by the liquidator,

is or are, in all the circumstances, excessive or, in the case of an application under sub-paragraph (b), inappropriate.

(1B) The application must, subject to any order of the court under Rule 4.49E(5), be made no later than 8 weeks (or, in a case falling within Rule 4.108, 4 weeks) after receipt by the applicant of the progress report, or the draft report under Rule 4.49D, which first reports the charging of the remuneration or the incurring of the expenses in question ("the relevant report").]

(2) The court may, if it thinks that no sufficient cause is shown for a reduction, dismiss the application; but it shall not do so unless the applicant has had an opportunity to attend the court for [a] hearing, of which he has been given at least [5 business] days' notice [but which is without notice to any other party].

If the application is not dismissed under this paragraph, the court shall fix a venue for it to be heard, and give notice to the applicant accordingly.

(3) The applicant shall, at least 14 days before the hearing, send to the liquidator a notice stating the venue and accompanied by a copy of the application, and of any evidence which the applicant intends to adduce in support of it.

[(4) If the court considers the application to be well-founded, it must make one or more of the following orders—
- (a) an order reducing the amount of remuneration which the liquidator was entitled to charge;
- (b) an order fixing the basis of remuneration at a reduced rate or amount;
- (c) an order changing the basis of remuneration;
- (d) an order that some or all of the remuneration or expenses in question be treated as not being expenses of the liquidation;
- (e) an order that the liquidator or the liquidator's personal representative pay to the company the amount of the excess of remuneration or expenses or such part of the excess as the court may specify;

and may make any other order that it thinks just; but an order under sub-paragraph (b) or (c) may be made only in respect of periods after the period covered by the relevant report.]

(5) Unless the court orders otherwise, the costs of the application shall be paid by the applicant, and are not payable [as an expense of the liquidation].

NOTES

Initial Commencement

Specified date

Specified date: 29 December 1986: see r 0.1.

Amendment

Provision heading: words "or other expenses are" in square brackets inserted by SI 2010/686, r 2, Sch 1, para 222(1), (2).
Date in force: 6 April 2010: see SI 2010/686, r 1; for transitional provisions see r 6(1), Sch 4, para 1 thereto.
Paras (1), (1A), (1B): substituted, for para (1) as originally enacted, by SI 2010/686, r 2, Sch 1, para 222(1), (3).

Date in force: 6 April 2010: see SI 2010/686, r 1; for transitional provisions see r 6(1), Sch 4, para 1 thereto.

Para (2): word "a" in square brackets substituted by SI 2010/686, r 2, Sch 1, para 222(1), (4)(a).

Date in force: 6 April 2010: see SI 2010/686, r 1; for transitional provisions see r 6(1), Sch 4, paras 1, 2(1)(b) thereto.

Para (2): words "5 business" in square brackets substituted by SI 2010/686, r 2, Sch 1, para 222(1), (4)(b).

Date in force: 6 April 2010: see SI 2010/686, r 1; for transitional provisions see r 6(1), Sch 4, para 1 thereto.

Para (2): words "but which is without notice to any other party" in square brackets inserted by SI 2010/686, r 2, Sch 1, para 222(1), (4)(c).

Date in force: 6 April 2010: see SI 2010/686, r 1; for transitional provisions see r 6(1), Sch 4, paras 1, 2(1)(b) thereto.

Para (4): substituted by SI 2010/686, r 2, Sch 1, para 222(1), (5).

Date in force: 6 April 2010: see SI 2010/686, r 1; for transitional provisions see r 6(1), Sch 4, para 1 thereto.

Para (5): words "as an expense of the liquidation" in square brackets substituted by SI 2008/737, rr 3, 7(1).

Date in force: 6 April 2008: see SI 2008/737, r 1(1); for transitional provisions see r 2 thereof.

See Further

See further, in relation the application of this rule, with modifications, in respect of the procedure for the appointment of a bank liquidator and the operation of bank insolvency under the Banking Act 2009, Pt 2: the Bank Insolvency (England and Wales) Rules 2009, SI 2009/356, rr 3(3)–(8), 104.

[4.131A Review of remuneration]

[(1) Where, after the basis of the liquidator's remuneration has been fixed, there is a material and substantial change in the circumstances which were taken into account in fixing it, the liquidator may request that it be changed.

(2) The request must be made—

(a) where the liquidation committee fixed the basis, to the committee;
(b) where the creditors fixed the basis, to the creditors;
(c) where the court fixed the basis, by application to the court;
(d) where the remuneration was determined by application of the realisation scale under Rule 4.127A, to the liquidation committee if there is one or otherwise to the creditors;

and subject to paragraph (3), Rules 4.127 to 4.131 apply as appropriate.

(3) Where Rule 4.129A is applied in accordance with paragraph (2) of this Rule, ignore the words "in which the administrator had not requested an increase under Rule 2.107".

(4) Any change in the basis for remuneration applies from the date of the request under paragraph (2) and not for any earlier period.

(5) This Rule does not apply where the liquidator is the official receiver.]

NOTES

Amendment

Inserted by SI 2010/686, r 2, Sch 1, para 223.
Date in force: 6 April 2010: see SI 2010/686, r 1; for transitional provisions see r 6(1), Sch 4, para 1 thereto.

[4.131B Remuneration of new liquidator]

[(1) If a new liquidator is appointed in place of another, any determination, resolution or court order in effect under the preceding provisions of this Section of this

Chapter immediately before the former liquidator ceased to hold office continues to apply in respect of the remuneration of the new liquidator until a further determination, resolution or court order is made in accordance with those provisions.

(2) This Rule does not apply where the new liquidator is the official receiver.]

NOTES

Amendment

 Inserted by SI 2010/686, r 2, Sch 1, para 223.
  Date in force: 6 April 2010: see SI 2010/686, r 1; for transitional provisions see r 6(1), Sch 4, para 1 thereto.

[**4.131C Apportionment of set fee remuneration**]

[(1) In a case in which the basis of the liquidator's remuneration is a set amount under Rule 4.127(2)(c) and the liquidator ("the former liquidator") ceases (for whatever reason) to hold office before the time has elapsed or the work has been completed in respect of which the amount was set, application may be made for determination of what portion of the amount should be paid to the former liquidator or the former liquidator's personal representative in respect of the time which has actually elapsed or the work which has actually been done.

(2) Application may be made—
- (a) by the former liquidator or the former liquidator's personal representative within the period of 28 days beginning with the date upon which the former liquidator ceased to hold office, or
- (b) by the liquidator for the time being in office if the former liquidator or the former liquidator's personal representative has not applied by the end of that period.

(3) Application must be made—
- (a) where the liquidation committee fixed the basis, to the committee;
- (b) where the creditors fixed the basis, to the creditors for a resolution determining the portion;
- (c) where the court fixed the basis, to the court for an order determining the portion.

(4) The applicant must give a copy of the application to the liquidator for the time being in office or to the former liquidator or the former liquidator's personal representative, as the case may be ("the recipient").

(5) The recipient may within 21 days of receipt of the copy of the application give notice of intent to make representations to the liquidation committee or the creditors or to appear or be represented before the court, as the case may be.

(6) No determination may be made upon the application until expiry of the 21 days referred to in paragraph (5) or, if the recipient does give notice of intent in accordance with that paragraph, until the recipient has been afforded the opportunity to make representations or to appear or be represented, as the case may be.

(7) If the former liquidator or the former liquidator's personal representative (whether or not the original applicant) considers that the portion determined upon application to the liquidation committee or the creditors is insufficient, that person may apply—
- (a) in the case of a determination by the liquidation committee, to the creditors for a resolution increasing the portion;
- (b) in the case of a resolution of the creditors (whether under paragraph (1) or under sub-paragraph (a)), to the court for an order increasing the portion;

and paragraphs (4) to (6) apply as appropriate.]

NOTES

Amendment

Inserted by SI 2010/686, r 2, Sch 1, para 223.
Date in force: 6 April 2010: see SI 2010/686, r 1; for transitional provisions see r 6(1), Sch 4, para 1 thereto.

SECTION E: SUPPLEMENTARY PROVISIONS

4.132 Liquidator deceased (No CVL Application)

(1) Subject as follows, where the liquidator (other than the official receiver) has died, it is the duty of his personal representatives to give notice of the fact to the official receiver, specifying the date of the death.

This does not apply if notice has been given under any of the following paragraphs of this Rule.

(2) If the deceased liquidator was a partner in [or an employee of] a firm, notice may be given to the official receiver by a partner in the firm who is qualified to act as an insolvency practitioner, or is a member of any body recognised by the Secretary of State for the authorisation of insolvency practitioners.

(3) Notice of the death may be given by any person producing to the official receiver the relevant death certificate or a copy of it.

(4) The official receiver shall give notice to the court, for the purpose of fixing the date of the deceased liquidator's release.

NOTES

Initial Commencement

Specified date

Specified date: 29 December 1986: see r 0.1.

Amendment

Para (2): words "or an employee of" in square brackets inserted by SI 2010/686, r 2, Sch 1, para 224.
Date in force: 6 April 2010: see SI 2010/686, r 1; for transitional provisions see r 6(1), Sch 4, para 1 thereto.

4.133 Liquidator deceased—CVL

(1) Subject as follows, where the liquidator has died, it is the duty of his personal representatives to give notice of the fact, and of the date of death, to the registrar of companies and to the liquidation committee (if any) or a member of that committee.

(2) In the alternative, notice of the death may be given—

(a) if the deceased liquidator was a partner in [or an employee of] a firm, by a partner [in the firm] qualified to act as an insolvency practitioner or who is a member of any body approved by the Secretary of State for the authorisation of insolvency practitioners, or

(b) by any person, if he delivers with the notice a copy of the relevant death certificate.

NOTES

Initial Commencement

Specified date

Specified date: 29 December 1986: see r 0.1.

Amendment

Para (2): in sub-para (a) words "or an employee of" in square brackets inserted by SI 2010/686, r 2, Sch 1, para 225(1), (2)(a).
Date in force: 6 April 2010: see SI 2010/686, r 1; for transitional provisions see r 6(1), Sch 4, para 1 thereto.

Para (2): in sub-para (a) words "in the firm" in square brackets inserted by SI 2010/686, r 2, Sch 1, para 225(1), (2)(b).
Date in force: 6 April 2010: see SI 2010/686, r 1; for transitional provisions see r 6(1), Sch 4, para 1 thereto.

4.134 Loss of qualification as insolvency practitioner (No CVL Application)

(1) This Rule applies where the liquidator vacates office on ceasing to be qualified to act as an insolvency practitioner in relation to the company.

(2) He shall [as soon as reasonably practicable] give notice of his doing so to the official receiver, who shall give notice to the Secretary of State.

The official receiver shall file in court a copy of his notice under this paragraph.

(3) Rule 4.121 applies as regards the liquidator obtaining his release, as if he had been removed by the court.

NOTES

Initial Commencement

Specified date

Specified date: 29 December 1986: see r 0.1.

Amendment

Para (2): words "as soon as reasonably practicable" in square brackets substituted by SI 2009/642, rr 4, 5.
Date in force: 6 April 2009: see SI 2009/642, r 1; for transitional provisions see r 3 thereof.

See Further

See further, in relation the application of this rule, with modifications, in respect of the procedure for the appointment of a bank liquidator and the operation of bank insolvency under the Banking Act 2009, Pt 2: the Bank Insolvency (England and Wales) Rules 2009, SI 2009/356, rr 3(3)–(8), 108.

4.135 Loss of qualification as insolvency practitioner—CVL

(1) This Rule applies where the liquidator vacates office on ceasing to be qualified to act as an insolvency practitioner in relation to the company.

(2) He shall [as soon as reasonably practicable] give notice of his doing so to the registrar of companies and the Secretary of State.

(3) Rule 4.122—CVL applies as regards the liquidator obtaining his release, as if he had been removed by the court.

NOTES

Initial Commencement

Specified date

Specified date: 29 December 1986: see r 0.1.

Amendment

Para (2): words "as soon as reasonably practicable" in square brackets substituted by SI 2009/642, rr 4, 5.

Date in force: 6 April 2009: see SI 2009/642, r 1; for transitional provisions see r 3 thereof.

4.136 Vacation of office on making of winding-up order—CVL

Where the liquidator vacates office in consequence of the court making a winding-up order against the company, Rule 4.122—CVL applies as regards his obtaining his release, as if he had been removed by the court.

NOTES

Initial Commencement

Specified date

Specified date: 29 December 1986: see r 0.1.

[4.137 Notice to official receiver of intention to vacate office (No CVL Application)]

[(1) Where the liquidator intends to vacate office, whether by resignation or otherwise, he shall give notice of his intention to the official receiver together with notice of any creditors' meeting to be held in respect of his vacation of office, including any meeting to receive his resignation.

(2) The notice to the official receiver must be given at least 21 days before any such creditors' meeting.

(3) Where there remains any property of the company which has not been realised, applied, distributed or otherwise fully dealt with in the winding up, the liquidator shall include in his notice to the official receiver details of the nature of that property, its value (or the fact that it has no value), its location, any action taken by the liquidator to deal with that property or any reason for his not dealing with it, and the current position in relation to it.]

NOTES

Amendment

Substituted by SI 1987/1919, r 3(1), Schedule, Part 1, para 66.

See Further

See further, in relation the application of this rule, with modifications, in respect of the procedure for the appointment of a bank liquidator and the operation of bank insolvency under the Banking Act 2009, Pt 2: the Bank Insolvency (England and Wales) Rules 2009, SI 2009/356, rr 3(3)–(8), 110.

4.138 Liquidator's duties on vacating office

(1) Where the liquidator ceases to be in office as such, in consequence of removal, resignation or cesser of qualification as an insolvency practitioner, he is under obligation [as soon as reasonably practicable] to deliver up to the person succeeding him as liquidator the assets (after deduction of any expenses properly incurred, and distributions made, by him) and further to deliver up to that person—

 (a) the records of the liquidation, including correspondence, proofs and other related papers appertaining to the administration while it was within his responsibility, and
 (b) the company's books, papers and other records.

(2) . . .

[(3) Where the liquidator vacates office under section 172(8) (final meeting of creditors), he shall deliver up to the official receiver the company's books, papers and other records which have not already been disposed of in accordance with general regulations in the course of the liquidation. (NO CVL APPLICATION)]

NOTES

Initial Commencement

Specified date

Specified date: 29 December 1986: see r 0.1.

Amendment

Para (1): words "as soon as reasonably practicable" in square brackets substituted by SI 2009/642, rr 4, 5.
Date in force: 6 April 2009: see SI 2009/642, r 1; for transitional provisions see r 3 thereof.
Para (2): revoked by SI 2004/584, r 17.
Date in force: 1 April 2004: see SI 2004/584, r 1(2).

Para (3): inserted by SI 1987/1919, r 3(1), Schedule, Part 1, para 67.

See Further

See further, in relation the application of this rule, with modifications, in respect of the procedure for the appointment of a bank liquidator and the operation of bank insolvency under the Banking Act 2009, Pt 2: the Bank Insolvency (England and Wales) Rules 2009, SI 2009/356, rr 3(3)–(8), 111.

SECTION F: THE LIQUIDATOR IN A MEMBERS' VOLUNTARY WINDING UP

4.139 Appointment by the company

(1) This Rule applies where the liquidator is appointed by a meeting of the company.

(2) Subject as follows, the chairman of the meeting shall certify the appointment, but not unless and until the person appointed has provided him with a written statement to the effect that he is an insolvency practitioner, duly qualified under the Act to be the liquidator, and that he consents so to act.

(3) The chairman shall send the certificate [as soon as reasonably practicable] to the liquidator, who shall keep it as part of the records of the liquidation.

(4) Not later than 28 days from his appointment, the liquidator shall give notice of it to all creditors of the company of whom he is aware in that period.

NOTES

Initial Commencement

Specified date

Specified date: 29 December 1986: see r 0.1.

Amendment

Para (3): words "as soon as reasonably practicable" in square brackets substituted by SI 2009/642, rr 4, 5.
Date in force: 6 April 2009: see SI 2009/642, r 1; for transitional provisions see r 3 thereof.

4.140 Appointment by the court

(1) This Rule applies where the liquidator is appointed by the court under section 108.

(2) The court's order shall not issue unless and until the person appointed has filed in court a statement to the effect that he is an insolvency practitioner, duly qualified under the Act to be the liquidator, and that he consents so to act.

(3) Thereafter, the court shall send a sealed copy of the order to the liquidator, whose appointment takes effect from the date of the order.

(4) Not later than 28 days from his appointment, the liquidator shall give notice of it to all creditors of the company of whom he is aware in that period.

NOTES

Initial Commencement

Specified date

Specified date: 29 December 1986: see r 0.1.

4.141 Authentication of liquidator's appointment

A copy of the certificate of the liquidator's appointment or (as the case may be) a sealed copy of the court's order appointing him may in any proceedings be adduced as proof that the person appointed is duly authorised to exercise the powers and perform the duties of liquidator in the company's winding up.

NOTES

Initial Commencement

Specified date

Specified date: 29 December 1986: see r 0.1.

4.142 Company meeting to receive liquidator's resignation

(1) Before resigning his office, the liquidator must call a meeting of the company for the purpose of receiving his resignation. The notice summoning the meeting shall indicate that this is the purpose, or one of the purposes, of it.

(2) The notice under paragraph (1) must be accompanied by an account of the liquidator's administration of the winding up, including—

(a) a summary of his receipts and payments, and

(b) a statement by him that he has reconciled his account with that which is held by the Secretary of State in respect of the winding up.

(3) Subject as follows, the liquidator may only proceed under this Rule on grounds of ill health or because—

(a) he intends ceasing to be in practice as an insolvency practitioner, or

(b) there is some conflict of interest or change of personal circumstances which precludes or makes impracticable the further discharge by him of the duties of liquidator.

(4) Where two or more persons are acting as liquidator jointly, any one of them may proceed under this Rule (without prejudice to the continuation in office of the other or others) on the ground that, in his opinion or that of the other or others, it is no longer expedient that there should continue to be the present number of joint liquidators.

[(4A) If there is no quorum present at the meeting summoned to receive the liquidator's resignation, the meeting is deemed to have been held.]

(5) The notice of the liquidator's resignation required by section 171(5) shall be given by him [as soon as reasonably practicable] after the meeting.

(6) Where a new liquidator is appointed in place of one who has resigned, the former shall, in giving notice of his appointment, state that his predecessor has resigned.

NOTES

Initial Commencement

Specified date

Specified date: 29 December 1986: see r 0.1.

Amendment

Para (4A): inserted by SI 1987/1919, r 3(1), Schedule, Part 1, para 68.

Para (5): words "as soon as reasonably practicable" in square brackets substituted by SI 2009/642, rr 4, 5.

Date in force: 6 April 2009: see SI 2009/642, r 1; for transitional provisions see r 3 thereof.

4.143 Removal of liquidator by the court

(1) This Rule applies where application is made to the court for the removal of the liquidator, or for an order directing the liquidator to summon a company meeting for the purpose of removing him.

(2) The court may, if it thinks that no sufficient cause is shown for the application, dismiss it; but it shall not do so unless the applicant has had an opportunity to attend the court for [a] hearing, of which he has been given at least [5 business] days' notice [but which is without notice to any other party].

If the application is not dismissed under this paragraph, the court shall fix a venue for it to be heard.

(3) The court may require the applicant to make a deposit or give security for the costs to be incurred by the liquidator on the application.

(4) The applicant shall, at least 14 days before the hearing, send to the liquidator a notice stating the venue and accompanied by a copy of the application, and of any evidence which he intends to adduce in support of it.

Subject to any contrary order of the court, the costs of the application are not payable [as an expense of the liquidation].

(5) Where the court removes the liquidator—

   (a)   it shall send 2 copies of the order of removal to him, one to be sent by him [as soon as reasonably practicable] to the registrar of companies, with notice of his ceasing to act;

   (b)   the order may include such provision as the court thinks [just] with respect to matters arising in connection with the removal; and

   (c)   if the court appoints a new liquidator, Rule 4.140 applies.

NOTES

Initial Commencement

Specified date

Specified date: 29 December 1986: see r 0.1.

Amendment

Para (2): word "a" in square brackets substituted by SI 2010/686, r 2, Sch 1, para 226(1), (2)(a).

Date in force: 6 April 2010: see SI 2010/686, r 1; for transitional provisions see r 6(1), Sch 4, paras 1, 2(1)(b) thereto.

Para (2): words "5 business" in square brackets substituted by SI 2010/686, r 2, Sch 1, para 226(1), (2)(b).

Date in force: 6 April 2010: see SI 2010/686, r 1; for transitional provisions see r 6(1), Sch 4, para 1 thereto.

Para (2): words "but which is without notice to any other party" in square brackets inserted by SI 2010/686, r 2, Sch 1, para 226(1), (2)(c).
  Date in force: 6 April 2010: see SI 2010/686, r 1; for transitional provisions see r 6(1), Sch 4, paras 1, 2(1)(b) thereto.
Para (4): words "as an expense of the liquidation" in square brackets substituted by SI 2008/737, rr 3, 7(1).
  Date in force: 6 April 2008: see SI 2008/737, r 1(1); for transitional provisions see r 2 thereof.
Para (5): in sub-para (a) words "as soon as reasonably practicable" in square brackets substituted by SI 2009/642, rr 4, 5.
  Date in force: 6 April 2009: see SI 2009/642, r 1; for transitional provisions see r 3 thereof.
Para (5): in sub-para (b) word "just" in square brackets substituted by SI 2010/686, r 2, Sch 1, para 1.
  Date in force: 6 April 2010: see SI 2010/686, r 1; for transitional provisions see r 6(1), Sch 4, paras 1, 2(1)(b) thereto.

4.144 Release of resigning or removed liquidator

(1) Where the liquidator resigns, he has his release from the date on which he gives notice of his resignation to the registrar of companies.

(2) Where the liquidator is removed by a meeting of the company, he shall [as soon as reasonably practicable] give notice to the registrar of companies of his ceasing to act.

(3) Where the liquidator is removed by the court, he must apply to the Secretary of State for his release.

(4) When the Secretary of State gives the release, he shall certify it accordingly, and send the certificate to the registrar of companies.

(5) A copy of the certificate shall be sent by the Secretary of State to the former liquidator, whose release is effective from the date of the certificate.

NOTES

Initial Commencement

Specified date

  Specified date: 29 December 1986: see r 0.1.

Amendment

Para (2): words "as soon as reasonably practicable" in square brackets substituted by SI 2009/642, rr 4, 5.
  Date in force: 6 April 2009: see SI 2009/642, r 1; for transitional provisions see r 3 thereof.

4.145 Liquidator deceased

(1) Subject as follows, where the liquidator has died, it is the duty of his personal representatives to give notice of the fact, and of the date of death, to the company's directors, or any one of them, and to the registrar of companies.

(2) In the alternative, notice of the death may be given—
 (a) if the deceased liquidator was a partner in [or an employee of] a firm, by a partner [in the firm] qualified to act as an insolvency practitioner or who is a member of any body approved by the Secretary of State for the authorisation of insolvency practitioners, or
 (b) by any person, if he delivers with the notice a copy of the relevant death certificate.

NOTES

Initial Commencement

Specified date

Specified date: 29 December 1986: see r 0.1.

Amendment

Para (2): in sub-para (a) words "or an employee of" in square brackets inserted by SI 2010/686, r 2, Sch 1, para 227(1), (2)(a).
Date in force: 6 April 2010: see SI 2010/686, r 1; for transitional provisions see r 6(1), Sch 4, para 1 thereto.
Para (2): in sub-para (a) words "in the firm" in square brackets inserted by SI 2010/686, r 2, Sch 1, para 227(1), (2)(b).
Date in force: 6 April 2010: see SI 2010/686, r 1; for transitional provisions see r 6(1), Sch 4, para 1 thereto.

4.146 Loss of qualification as insolvency practitioner

(1) This Rule applies where the liquidator vacates office on ceasing to be qualified to act as an insolvency practitioner in relation to the company.

(2) He shall [as soon as reasonably practicable] give notice of his doing so to the registrar of companies and the Secretary of State.

(3) Rule 4.144 applies as regards the liquidator obtaining his release, as if he had been removed by the court.

NOTES

Initial Commencement

Specified date

Specified date: 29 December 1986: see r 0.1.

Amendment

Para (2): words "as soon as reasonably practicable" in square brackets substituted by SI 2009/642, rr 4, 5.
Date in force: 6 April 2009: see SI 2009/642, r 1; for transitional provisions see r 3 thereof.

4.147 Vacation of office on making of winding-up order

Where the liquidator vacates office in consequence of the court making a winding-up order against the company, Rule 4.144 applies as regards his obtaining his release, as if he had been removed by the court.

NOTES

Initial Commencement

Specified date

Specified date: 29 December 1986: see r 0.1.

4.148 Liquidator's duties on vacating office

Where the liquidator ceases to be in office as such, in consequence of removal, resignation or cesser of qualification as an insolvency practitioner, he is under obligation [as soon as reasonably practicable] to deliver up to the person succeeding him as liquidator the assets (after deduction of any expenses properly incurred, and distributions made, by him) and further to deliver up to that person—

(a) the records of the liquidation, including correspondence, proofs and other related papers appertaining to the administration while it was within his responsibility, and

(b) the company's books, papers and other records.

NOTES

Initial Commencement

Specified date

Specified date: 29 December 1986: see r 0.1.

Amendment

Words "as soon as reasonably practicable" in square brackets substituted by SI 2009/642, rr 4, 5.
Date in force: 6 April 2009: see SI 2009/642, r 1; for transitional provisions see r 3 thereof.

[4.148A Remuneration of liquidator in members' voluntary winding up]

[(1) The liquidator is entitled to receive remuneration for his services as such.

(2) [The basis of remuneration shall be fixed]—

(a) as a percentage of the value of the assets which are realised or distributed, or of the one value and the other in combination, or

(b) by reference to the time properly given by the insolvency practitioner (as liquidator) and his staff in attending to matters arising in the winding up[, or

(c) as a set amount.

(2A) The basis of remuneration may be fixed as any one or more of the bases set out in paragraph (2), and different bases may be fixed in respect of different things done by the liquidator.

(2B) Where the basis of remuneration is fixed as set out in paragraph (2)(a), different percentages may be fixed in respect of different things done by the liquidator.

(2C) It is for the company in general meeting to determine—

(a) which of the bases set out in paragraph (2) are to be fixed and (where appropriate) in what combination under paragraph (2A), and

(b) the percentage or percentages (if any) to be fixed under paragraphs (2)(a) and (2B) and the amount (if any) to be set under paragraph (2)(c)].

(3) In arriving at that determination the company in general meeting shall have regard to the matters set out in paragraph (4) of Rule 4.127.

[(4) If not fixed as above, the basis of the liquidator's remuneration shall, on application by the liquidator, be fixed by the court, and the provisions of paragraphs (2) to (3) apply as they do to the fixing of the basis of remuneration by the company in general meeting; but such an application may not be made by the liquidator unless the liquidator has first sought fixing of the basis in accordance with paragraph (2C), and in any event may not be made more than 18 months after the date of the liquidator's appointment.]

(5) Rule 4.128 [and Rule 4.127B] shall apply in relation to the remuneration of the liquidator in respect of the matters there mentioned and for this purpose references in that Rule to "the liquidation committee" and "a meeting of creditors" shall be read as references to the company in general meeting.

[(6) If the liquidator considers that the basis of the remuneration fixed by the company in general meeting is insufficient or inappropriate, the liquidator may apply to the court for an order changing it or increasing its amount or rate.]

(7) The liquidator shall give at least 14 days' notice of an application under paragraph [(4) or] (6) to the company's contributories, or such one or more of them as the court may direct, and the contributories may nominate any one or more of their number to appear or be represented.

(8) The court may, if it appears to be a proper case, order the costs of the liquidator's application, including the costs of any contributory appearing or being represented on it, to be paid [as an expense of the liquidation].]

NOTES

Amendment

Inserted by SI 1987/1919, r 3(1), Schedule, Part 1, para 69.

Para (2): words "The basis of remuneration shall be fixed" in square brackets substituted by SI 2010/686, r 2, Sch 1, para 228(1), (2).
Date in force: 6 April 2010: see SI 2010/686, r 1; for transitional provisions see r 6(1), Sch 4, para 1 thereto.

Para (2): sub-para (c), word ", or" immediately preceding it and paras (2A)–(2C) substituted, for words in para (2) as originally enacted, by SI 2010/686, r 2, Sch 1, para 228(1), (3).
Date in force: 6 April 2010: see SI 2010/686, r 1; for transitional provisions see r 6(1), Sch 4, para 1 thereto.

Para (4): substituted by SI 2010/686, r 2, Sch 1, para 228(1), (4).
Date in force: 6 April 2010: see SI 2010/686, r 1; for transitional provisions see r 6(1), Sch 4, para 1 thereto.

Para (5): words "and Rule 4.127B" in square brackets inserted by SI 2005/527, r 30.
Date in force: this amendment shall apply in any case where, on or after 1 April 2004, a winding-up order has been made or a resolution for the winding up of a company has been passed or a bankruptcy order has been made, before 1 April 2005: see SI 2005/527, rr 1(2), 3(2).

Para (6): substituted by SI 2010/686, r 2, Sch 1, para 228(1), (5).
Date in force: 6 April 2010: see SI 2010/686, r 1; for transitional provisions see r 6(1), Sch 4, para 1 thereto.

Para (7): words "(4) or" in square brackets inserted by SI 2010/686, r 2, Sch 1, para 228(1), (6).
Date in force: 6 April 2010: see SI 2010/686, r 1; for transitional provisions see r 6(1), Sch 4, para 1 thereto.

Para (8): words "as an expense of the liquidation" in square brackets substituted by SI 2008/737, rr 3, 7(1).
Date in force: 6 April 2008: see SI 2008/737, r 1(1); for transitional provisions see r 2 thereof.

[4.148B . . .]
[. . .]

NOTES

Amendment

Inserted by SI 2004/584, r 19.
Date in force: 1 April 2004: see SI 2004/584, r 1(2); for transitional provisions see r 3 thereof.
Revoked by SI 2010/686, r 5.
Date in force: 6 April 2010: see SI 2010/686, r 1; for transitional provisions see r 6(1), Sch 4, para 1 thereto.

[4.148C Members' claim that remuneration is excessive]

[(1) Members of the company with at least 10% of the total voting rights of all the members having the right to vote at general meetings of the company, or any member with the permission of the court, may apply to the court for one or more of the orders in paragraph (6) on the grounds that—

    (a)   the remuneration charged by the liquidator,
    (b)   the basis fixed for the liquidator's remuneration under Rule 4.148A, or
    (c)   expenses incurred by the liquidator,

is or are, in all the circumstances, excessive or, in the case of an application under sub-paragraph (b), inappropriate.

(2) Application must, subject to any order of the court under Rule 4.49E(5), be made no later than 8 weeks (or 4 weeks when the liquidator has resigned in accordance with Rule 4.142) after receipt by the applicant of the report or account which first reports the charging of the remuneration or the incurring of the expenses in question ("the relevant report").

(3) The court may, if it thinks that no sufficient cause is shown for a reduction, dismiss the application; but it must not do so unless the applicant has had the opportunity to attend the court for a hearing of which the applicant has been given at least 5 business days' notice but which is without notice to any other party.

(4) If the application is not dismissed under paragraph (3), the court must fix a venue for it to be heard and give notice to the applicant accordingly.

(5) The applicant must at least 14 days before the hearing send to the liquidator a notice stating the venue and accompanied by a copy of the application and of any evidence which the applicant intends to adduce in support of it.

(6) If the court considers the application to be well-founded, it must make one or more of the following orders—

    (a)   an order reducing the amount of remuneration which the liquidator was entitled to charge;
    (b)   an order fixing the basis of remuneration at a reduced rate or amount;
    (c)   an order changing the basis of remuneration;
    (d)   an order that some or all of the remuneration or expenses in question be treated as not being expenses of the liquidation;
    (e)   an order that the liquidator or the liquidator's personal representative pay to the company the amount of the excess of remuneration or expenses or such part of the excess as the court may specify;

and may make any other order that it thinks just; but an order under sub-paragraph (b) or (c) may be made only in respect of periods after the period covered by the relevant report.

(7) Unless the court orders otherwise, the costs of the application must be paid by the applicant and are not payable as an expense of the liquidation.]

NOTES

Amendment

    Inserted by SI 2010/686, r 2, Sch 1, para 229.
        Date in force: 6 April 2010: see SI 2010/686, r 1; for transitional provisions see r 6(1), Sch 4, para 1 thereto.

[4.148D Remuneration of new liquidator]

[If a new liquidator is appointed in place of another, any determination or court order in effect under Rule 4.148A immediately before the former liquidator ceased to hold office continues to apply in respect of the remuneration of the new liquidator until a further determination or court order is made in accordance with that Rule.]

NOTES

Amendment

Inserted by SI 2010/686, r 2, Sch 1, para 229.
Date in force: 6 April 2010: see SI 2010/686, r 1; for transitional provisions see r 6(1), Sch 4, para 1 thereto.

[4.148E Apportionment of fixed fee remuneration]

[(1) In a case in which the basis of the liquidator's remuneration is a set amount under Rule 4.148A(2)(c) and the liquidator ("the former liquidator") ceases (for whatever reason) to hold office before the time has elapsed or the work has been completed in respect of which the amount was set, application may be made for determination of what portion of the amount should be paid to the former liquidator or the former liquidator's personal representative in respect of the time which has actually elapsed or the work which has actually been done.

(2) Application may be made—

(a) by the former liquidator or the former liquidator's personal representative within the period of 28 days beginning with the date upon which the former liquidator ceased to hold office, or

(b) by the liquidator for the time being in office if the former liquidator or the former liquidator's personal representative has not applied by the end of that period.

(3) Application must be made—

(a) where the company in general meeting fixed the basis, to the company for a resolution determining the portion;

(b) where the court fixed the basis, to the court for an order determining the portion.

(4) The applicant must give a copy of the application to the liquidator for the time being in office or to the former liquidator or the former liquidator's personal representative, as the case may be ("the recipient").

(5) The recipient may within 21 days of receipt of the copy of the application give notice of intent to make representations to the company in general meeting or to appear or be represented before the court, as the case may be.

(6) No determination may be made upon the application until expiry of the 21 days referred to in paragraph (5) or, if the recipient does give notice of intent in accordance with that paragraph, until the recipient has been afforded the opportunity to make representations or to appear or be represented, as the case may be.

(7) If the former liquidator or the former liquidator's personal representative (whether or not the original applicant) considers that the portion determined upon application to the company in general meeting is insufficient, that person may apply to the court for an order increasing the portion; and paragraphs (4) to (6) apply as appropriate.]

NOTES

Amendment

Inserted by SI 2010/686, r 2, Sch 1, para 229.
Date in force: 6 April 2010: see SI 2010/686, r 1; for transitional provisions see r 6(1), Sch 4, para 1 thereto.

SECTION G: RULES APPLYING IN EVERY WINDING UP, WHETHER VOLUNTARY OR BY THE COURT

4.149 Power of court to set aside certain transactions

(1) If in the administration of the estate the liquidator enters into any transaction with a person who is an associate of his, the court may, on the application of any person interested, set the transaction aside and order the liquidator to compensate the company for any loss suffered in consequence of it.

(2) This does not apply if either—

(a) the transaction was entered into with the prior consent of the court, or

(b) it is shown to the court's satisfaction that the transaction was for value, and that it was entered into by the liquidator without knowing, or having any reason to suppose, that the person concerned was an associate.

(3) Nothing in this Rule is to be taken as prejudicing the operation of any rule of law or equity with respect to a liquidator's dealings with trust property, or the fiduciary obligations of any person.

NOTES

Initial Commencement

Specified date

Specified date: 29 December 1986: see r 0.1.

See Further

See further, in relation the application of this rule, with modifications, in respect of the procedure for the appointment of a bank liquidator and the operation of bank insolvency under the Banking Act 2009, Pt 2: the Bank Insolvency (England and Wales) Rules 2009, SI 2009/356, rr 3(3)–(8), 112.

4.150 Rule against solicitation

(1) Where the court is satisfied that any improper solicitation has been used by or on behalf of the liquidator in obtaining proxies or procuring his appointment, it may order that no remuneration [be allowed as an expense of the liquidation] to any person by whom, or on whose behalf, the solicitation was exercised.

(2) An order of the court under this Rule overrides any resolution of the liquidation committee or the creditors, or any other provision of the Rules relating to the liquidator's remuneration.

NOTES

Initial Commencement

Specified date

Specified date: 29 December 1986: see r 0.1.

Amendment

Para (1): words "be allowed as an expense of the liquidation" in square brackets substituted by SI 2008/737, rr 3, 7(10).

Date in force: 6 April 2008: see SI 2008/737, r 1(1); for transitional provisions see r 2 thereof.

See Further

See further, in relation the application of this rule, with modifications, in respect of the procedure for the appointment of a bank liquidator and the operation of bank insolvency

under the Banking Act 2009, Pt 2: the Bank Insolvency (England and Wales) Rules 2009, SI 2009/356, rr 3(3)–(8), 113.

CHAPTER 12

THE LIQUIDATION COMMITTEE

4.151 Preliminary (No CVL Application)
For the purposes of this Chapter—
(a) an "insolvent winding up" is where the company is being wound up on grounds which include inability to pay its debts, and
(b) a "solvent winding up" is where the company is being wound up on grounds which do not include that one.

NOTES

Initial Commencement

Specified date
Specified date: 29 December 1986: see r 0.1.

4.152 Membership of committee
(1) Subject to Rule 4.154 below, the liquidation committee shall consist as follows—
(a) in any case of at least 3, and not more than 5, creditors of the company, elected by the meeting of creditors held under section 141 of the Act, and
(b) also, in the case of a solvent winding up, where the contributories' meeting held under that section so decides, of up to 3 contributories, elected by that meeting.
(NO CVL APPLICATION)
(2–CVL) The committee must have at least 3 members before it can be established.
(3) Any creditor of the company (other than one whose debt is fully secured) is eligible to be a member of the committee, so long as—
(a) he has lodged a proof of his debt, and
(b) his proof has neither been wholly disallowed for voting purposes, nor wholly rejected for purposes of distribution or dividend.
(4) No person can be a member as both a creditor and a contributory.
(5) A body corporate may be a member of the committee, but it cannot act as such otherwise than by a representative appointed under Rule 4.159.
(6) Members of the committee elected or appointed to represent the creditors are called "creditor members"; and those elected or appointed to represent the contributories are called "contributory members".
[(7) The following categories of person are to be regarded as additional creditor members—
(a) a representative of the Financial Services Authority who exercises the right under section 371 (4)(b) of the Financial Services and Markets Act 2000 to be a member of the committee;
(b) a representative of the scheme manager who exercises the right under section 215(4) of that Act to be a member of the committee.]

Insolvency Rules 1986, reg 4.152

NOTES

Initial Commencement

Specified date

Specified date: 29 December 1986: see r 0.1.

Amendment

Para (7): substituted by SI 2001/3649, art 379.
Date in force: 1 December 2001: see SI 2001/3649, art 1.

See Further

See further, in relation the application of this rule, with modifications, in respect of the procedure for the appointment of a bank liquidator and the operation of bank insolvency under the Banking Act 2009, Pt 2: the Bank Insolvency (England and Wales) Rules 2009, SI 2009/356, rr 3(3)–(8), 115.

4.153 Formalities of establishment

(1) The liquidation committee does not come into being, and accordingly cannot act, until the liquidator has issued a certificate of its due constitution.

(2) If the chairman of the meeting which resolves to establish the committee is not the liquidator, he shall [as soon as reasonably practicable] give notice of the resolution to the liquidator (or, as the case may be, the person appointed as liquidator by that same meeting), and inform him of the names and addresses of the persons elected to be members of the committee.

[(3) No person may act as a member of the committee unless and until he has agreed to do so and, unless the relevant proxy or authorisation contains a statement to the contrary, such agreement may be given by his proxy-holder . . . present at the meeting establishing the committee [or, in the case of a corporation, by its duly appointed representative].

(3A) The liquidator's certificate of the committee's due constitution shall not [be issued] before the minimum number of persons (in accordance with Rule 4.152) who are to be members of the committee have agreed to act [and must be issued as soon as reasonably practicable thereafter].]

(4) As and when the others (if any) agree to act, the liquidator shall issue an amended certificate.

(5) . . .

(6–CVL) The certificate, and any amended certificate, shall be sent by the liquidator to the registrar of companies [as soon as reasonably practicable].

(7) . . .

(8–CVL) If after the first establishment of the committee there is any change in its membership, [as soon as reasonably practicable] the liquidator shall report the change to the registrar of companies.

NOTES

Initial Commencement

Specified date

Specified date: 29 December 1986: see r 0.1.

Amendment

Para (2): words "as soon as reasonably practicable" in square brackets substituted by SI 2009/642, rr 4, 5.
Date in force: 6 April 2009: see SI 2009/642, r 1; for transitional provisions see r 3 thereof.

Paras (3), (3A): substituted, for para (3) as originally enacted, by SI 1987/1919, r 3(1), Schedule, Part 1, para 71.

Para (3): words omitted revoked by SI 2010/686, r 2, Sch 1, para 230(1), (2)(a).
Date in force: 6 April 2010: see SI 2010/686, r 1; for transitional provisions see r 6(1), Sch 4, para 1 thereto.

Para (3): words "or, in the case of a corporation, by its duly appointed representative" in square brackets inserted by SI 2010/686, r 2, Sch 1, para 230(1), (2)(b).
Date in force: 6 April 2010: see SI 2010/686, r 1; for transitional provisions see r 6(1), Sch 4, para 1 thereto.

Para (3A): words "be issued" in square brackets substituted by SI 2010/686, r 2, Sch 1, para 230(1), (3)(a).
Date in force: 6 April 2010: see SI 2010/686, r 1; for transitional provisions see r 6(1), Sch 4, para 1 thereto.

Para (3A): words "and must be issued as soon as reasonably practicable thereafter" in square brackets inserted by SI 2010/686, r 2, Sch 1, para 230(1), (3)(b).
Date in force: 6 April 2010: see SI 2010/686, r 1; for transitional provisions see r 6(1), Sch 4, para 1 thereto.

Para (5): revoked by SI 2010/686, r 2, Sch 1, para 230(1), (4).
Date in force: 6 April 2010: see SI 2010/686, r 1; for transitional provisions see r 6(1), Sch 4, para 1 thereto.

Para (6): words "as soon as reasonably practicable" in square brackets inserted by SI 2010/686, r 2, Sch 1, para 230(1), (5).
Date in force: 6 April 2010: see SI 2010/686, r 1; for transitional provisions see r 6(1), Sch 4, para 1 thereto.

Para (7): revoked by SI 2010/686, r 2, Sch 1, para 230(1), (6).
Date in force: 6 April 2010: see SI 2010/686, r 1; for transitional provisions see r 6(1), Sch 4, para 1 thereto.

Para (8): words "as soon as reasonably practicable" in square brackets inserted by SI 2010/686, r 2, Sch 1, para 230(1), (7).
Date in force: 6 April 2010: see SI 2010/686, r 1; for transitional provisions see r 6(1), Sch 4, para 1 thereto.

See Further

See further, in relation the application of this rule, with modifications, in respect of the procedure for the appointment of a bank liquidator and the operation of bank insolvency under the Banking Act 2009, Pt 2: the Bank Insolvency (England and Wales) Rules 2009, SI 2009/356, rr 3(3)–(8), 116.

4.154 Committee established by contributories (No CVL Application)

(1) The following applies where the creditors' meeting under section 141 does not decide that a liquidation committee should be established, or decides that a committee should not be established.

(2) The meeting of contributories under that section may appoint one of their number to make application to the court for an order to the liquidator that a further creditors' meeting be summoned for the purpose of establishing a liquidation committee; and—

    (a) the court may, if it thinks that there are special circumstances to justify it, make that order, and

    (b) the creditors' meeting summoned by the liquidator in compliance with the order is deemed to have been summoned under section 141.

(3) If the creditors' meeting so summoned does not establish a liquidation committee, a meeting of contributories may do so.

(4) The committee shall then consist of at least 3, and not more than 5, contributories elected by that meeting; and Rule 4.153 applies, [substituting for the reference in paragraph (3A) of that Rule to Rule 4.152 a reference to this paragraph].

NOTES

Initial Commencement

Specified date

Specified date: 29 December 1986: see r 0.1.

Amendment

Para (4): words in square brackets substituted by SI 1987/1919, r 3(1), Schedule, Part 1, para 72.

See Further

See further, in relation the application of this rule, with modifications, in respect of the procedure for the appointment of a bank liquidator and the operation of bank insolvency under the Banking Act 2009, Pt 2: the Bank Insolvency (England and Wales) Rules 2009, SI 2009/356, rr 3(3)–(8), 117.

4.155 Obligations of liquidator to committee

(1) Subject as follows, it is the duty of the liquidator to report to the members of the liquidation committee all such matters as appear to him to be, or as they have indicated to him as being, of concern to them with respect to the winding up.

(2) In the case of matters so indicated to him by the committee, the liquidator need not comply with any request for information where it appears to him that—

(a) the request is frivolous or unreasonable, or

(b) the cost of complying would be excessive, having regard to the relative importance of the information, or

(c) there are not sufficient assets to enable him to comply.

(3) Where the committee has come into being more than 28 days after the appointment of the liquidator, he shall report to them, in summary form, what actions he has taken since his appointment, and shall answer all such questions as they may put to him regarding his conduct of the winding up hitherto.

(4) A person who becomes a member of the committee at any time after its first establishment is not entitled to require a report to him by the liquidator, otherwise than in summary form, of any matters previously arising.

(5) Nothing in this Rule disentitles the committee, or any member of it, from having access to the liquidator's records of the liquidation, or from seeking an explanation of any matter within the committee's responsibility.

NOTES

Initial Commencement

Specified date

Specified date: 29 December 1986: see r 0.1.

See Further

See further, in relation the application of this rule, with modifications, in respect of the procedure for the appointment of a bank liquidator and the operation of bank insolvency under the Banking Act 2009, Pt 2: the Bank Insolvency (England and Wales) Rules 2009, SI 2009/356, rr 3(3)–(8), 118.

4.156 Meetings of the committee

(1) Subject as follows, meetings of the liquidation committee shall be held when and where determined by the liquidator.

(2) The liquidator shall call a first meeting of the committee to take place within [6 weeks] of his appointment or of the committee's establishment (whichever is the later); and thereafter he shall call a meeting—
- (a) if so requested by a creditor member of the committee or his representative (the meeting then to be held within 21 days of the request being received by the liquidator), and
- (b) for a specified date, if the committee has previously resolved that a meeting be held on that date.

(3) [Subject to paragraph (4),] the liquidator shall give [5 business] days' written notice of the venue of a meeting to every member of the committee (or his representative, if designated for that purpose), unless in any case the requirement of the notice has been waived by or on behalf of any member.

Waiver may be signified either at or before the meeting.

[(4) Where the liquidator has determined that a meeting should be conducted and held in the manner referred to in Rule 12A.26(2), the notice period mentioned in paragraph (3) is 7 business days.

(5) In addition to any functions conferred on a committee by any provision of the Act, a committee must assist the liquidator in discharging the liquidator's functions and act in relation to that liquidator in such manner as may from time to time be agreed.]

NOTES

Initial Commencement

Specified date

Specified date: 29 December 1986: see r 0.1.

Amendment

Para (2): words "6 weeks" in square brackets substituted by SI 2010/686, r 2, Sch 1, para 231(1), (2).
Date in force: 6 April 2010: see SI 2010/686, r 1; for transitional provisions see r 6(1), Sch 4, para 1 thereto.
Para (3): words "Subject to paragraph (4)," in square brackets inserted by SI 2010/686, r 2, Sch 1, para 231(1), (3)(a).
Date in force: 6 April 2010: see SI 2010/686, r 1; for transitional provisions see r 6(1), Sch 4, para 1 thereto.
Para (3): words "5 business" in square brackets substituted by SI 2010/686, r 2, Sch 1, para 231(1), (3)(b).
Date in force: 6 April 2010: see SI 2010/686, r 1; for transitional provisions see r 6(1), Sch 4, para 1 thereto.
Paras (4), (5): inserted by SI 2010/686, r 2, Sch 1, para 231(1), (4).
Date in force: 6 April 2010: see SI 2010/686, r 1; for transitional provisions see r 6(1), Sch 4, para 1 thereto.

See Further

See further, in relation the application of this rule, with modifications, in respect of the procedure for the appointment of a bank liquidator and the operation of bank insolvency under the Banking Act 2009, Pt 2: the Bank Insolvency (England and Wales) Rules 2009, SI 2009/356, rr 3(3)–(8), 119.

4.157 The chairman at meetings

(1) The chairman at any meeting of the liquidation committee shall be the liquidator, or a person [appointed by the liquidator in writing] to act.

(2) A person so [appointed] must be either—
- (a) one who is qualified to act as an insolvency practitioner in relation to the company, or

(b) an employee of the liquidator or his firm who is experienced in insolvency matters.

NOTES

Initial Commencement

Specified date

Specified date: 29 December 1986: see r 0.1.

Amendment

Para (1): words "appointed by the liquidator in writing" in square brackets substituted by SI 2010/686, r 2, Sch 1, para 232(1), (2).
Date in force: 6 April 2010: see SI 2010/686, r 1; for transitional provisions see r 6(1), Sch 4, para 1 thereto.
Para (2): word "appointed" in square brackets substituted by SI 2010/686, r 2, Sch 1, para 232(1), (3).
Date in force: 6 April 2010: see SI 2010/686, r 1; for transitional provisions see r 6(1), Sch 4, para 1 thereto.

See Further

See further, in relation the application of this rule, with modifications, in respect of the procedure for the appointment of a bank liquidator and the operation of bank insolvency under the Banking Act 2009, Pt 2: the Bank Insolvency (England and Wales) Rules 2009, SI 2009/356, rr 3(3)–(8), 120.

4.158 Quorum

(1) A meeting of the committee is duly constituted if due notice of it has been given to all the members, and at least 2 creditor members are present or represented.
(NO CVL APPLICATION)

(2-CVL) A meeting of the committee is duly constituted if due notice of it has been given to all the members, and at least 2 members are present or represented.

NOTES

Initial Commencement

Specified date

Specified date: 29 December 1986: see r 0.1.

4.159 Committee-members' representatives

(1) A member of the liquidation committee may, in relation to the business of the committee, be represented by another person duly authorised by him for that purpose.

(2) A person acting as a committee-member's representative must hold a letter of authority entitling him so to act (either generally or specially) and [authenticated] by or on behalf of the committee-member [, and for this purpose any proxy . . . in relation to any meeting of creditors (or, as the case may be, members or contributories) of the company shall, unless it contains a statement to the contrary, be treated as such a letter of authority to act generally [authenticated] by or on behalf of the committee-member].

(3) The chairman at any meeting of the committee may call on a person claiming to act as a committee-member's representative to produce his letter of authority, and may exclude him if it appears that his authority is deficient.

[(4) No member may be represented by—
(a) another member of the committee;
(b) a person who is at the same time representing another committee member;

(c) a body corporate;
(d) an undischarged bankrupt;
(e) a disqualified director; or
(f) a person who is subject to a bankruptcy restrictions order (including an interim order), a bankruptcy restrictions undertaking, a debt relief restrictions order (including an interim order) or a debt relief restrictions undertaking.]

(5) . . .

(6) Where a member's representative [authenticates] any document on the member's behalf, the fact that he so [authenticates] must be stated below his [authentication].

NOTES

Initial Commencement

Specified date

Specified date: 29 December 1986: see r 0.1.

Amendment

Para (2): word "authenticated" in square brackets in both places it occurs substituted by SI 2010/686, r 2, Sch 1, para 1.
 Date in force: 6 April 2010: see SI 2010/686, r 1; for transitional provisions see r 6(1), Sch 4, paras 1, 2(1)(b) thereto.

Para (2): words from "and for this purpose" to "the committee-member" in square brackets inserted by SI 1987/1919, r 3(1), Schedule, Pt 1, para 73.

Para (2): words omitted revoked by SI 2010/686, r 2, Sch 1, para 233(1), (2).
 Date in force: 6 April 2010: see SI 2010/686, r 1; for transitional provisions see r 6(1), Sch 4, para 1 thereto.

Para (4): substituted by SI 2010/686, r 2, Sch 1, para 233(1), (3).
 Date in force: 6 April 2010: see SI 2010/686, r 1; for transitional provisions see r 6(1), Sch 4, para 1 thereto.

Para (5): revoked by SI 2010/686, r 2, Sch 1, para 233(1), (4).
 Date in force: 6 April 2010: see SI 2010/686, r 1; for transitional provisions see r 6(1), Sch 4, para 1 thereto.

Para (6): word "authenticates" in square brackets in both places it occurs substituted by SI 2010/686, r 2, Sch 1, para 1.
 Date in force: 6 April 2010: see SI 2010/686, r 1; for transitional provisions see r 6(1), Sch 4, paras 1, 2(1)(b) thereto.

Para (6): word "authentication" in square brackets substituted by SI 2010/686, r 2, Sch 1, para 1.
 Date in force: 6 April 2010: see SI 2010/686, r 1; for transitional provisions see r 6(1), Sch 4, paras 1, 2(1)(b) thereto.

4.160 Resignation

A member of the liquidation committee may resign by notice in writing delivered to the liquidator.

NOTES

Initial Commencement

Specified date

Specified date: 29 December 1986: see r 0.1.

See Further

See further, in relation the application of this rule, with modifications, in respect of the procedure for the appointment of a bank liquidator and the operation of bank insolvency

under the Banking Act 2009, Pt 2: the Bank Insolvency (England and Wales) Rules 2009, SI 2009/356, rr 3(3)–(8), 123.

4.161 Termination of membership

(1) A person's membership of the liquidation committee is automatically terminated if—
- (a) he becomes bankrupt . . ., or
- (b) at 3 consecutive meetings of the committee he is neither present nor represented (unless at the third of those meetings it is resolved that this Rule is not to apply in his case).

(2) However, if the cause of termination is the member's bankruptcy, his trustee in bankruptcy replaces him as a member of the committee.

(3) The membership of a creditor member is also automatically terminated if he ceases to be, or is found never to have been, a creditor.

NOTES

Initial Commencement

Specified date

Specified date: 29 December 1986: see r 0.1.

Amendment

Para (1): in sub-para (a) words omitted revoked by SI 2004/584, r 21.
Date in force: 1 April 2004: see SI 2004/584, r 1(2).

See Further

See further, in relation the application of this rule, with modifications, in respect of the procedure for the appointment of a bank liquidator and the operation of bank insolvency under the Banking Act 2009, Pt 2: the Bank Insolvency (England and Wales) Rules 2009, SI 2009/356, rr 3(3)–(8), 124.

4.162 Removal

(1) A creditor member of the committee may be removed by resolution at a meeting of creditors; and a contributory member may be removed by a resolution of a meeting of contributories.

(2) In either case, 14 days' notice must be given of the intention to move the resolution.

NOTES

Initial Commencement

Specified date

Specified date: 29 December 1986: see r 0.1.

See Further

See further, in relation the application of this rule, with modifications, in respect of the procedure for the appointment of a bank liquidator and the operation of bank insolvency under the Banking Act 2009, Pt 2: the Bank Insolvency (England and Wales) Rules 2009, SI 2009/356, rr 3(3)–(8), 125.

4.163 Vacancy (creditor members)

(1) The following applies if there is a vacancy among the creditor members of the committee.

(2) The vacancy need not be filled if the liquidator and a majority of the remaining creditor members so agree, provided that the total number of members does not fall below [3].

(3) The liquidator may appoint any creditor (being qualified under the Rules to be a member of the committee) to fill the vacancy, if a majority of the other creditor members agree to the appointment, and the creditor concerned consents to act.

(4) Alternatively, a meeting of creditors may resolve that a creditor be appointed (with his consent) to fill the vacancy. In this case, at least 14 days' notice must have been given of the resolution to make such an appointment (whether or not of a person named in the notice).

(5) Where the vacancy is filled by an appointment made by a creditors' meeting at which the liquidator is not present, the chairman of the meeting shall report to the liquidator the appointment which has been made.

NOTES

Initial Commencement

Specified date

Specified date: 29 December 1986: see r 0.1.

Amendment

Para (2): reference to "3" in square brackets substituted by SI 2010/686, r 2, Sch 1, para 234. Date in force: 6 April 2010: see SI 2010/686, r 1; for transitional provisions see r 6(1), Sch 4, para 1 thereto.

See Further

See further, in relation the application of this rule, with modifications, in respect of the procedure for the appointment of a bank liquidator and the operation of bank insolvency under the Banking Act 2009, Pt 2: the Bank Insolvency (England and Wales) Rules 2009, SI 2009/356, rr 3(3)–(8), 126.

4.164 Vacancy (contributory members)

(1) The following applies if there is a vacancy among the contributory members of the committee.

(2) The vacancy need not be filled if the liquidator and a majority of the remaining contributory members so agree, provided that, in the case of a committee of contributory members only, the total number of members does not fall below [3].

(3) The liquidator may appoint any contributory member (being qualified under the Rules to be a member of the committee) to fill the vacancy, if a majority of the other contributory members agree to the appointment, and the contributory concerned consents to act.

(4) Alternatively, a meeting of contributories may resolve that a contributory be appointed (with his consent) to fill the vacancy. In this case, at least 14 days' notice must have been given of the resolution to make such an appointment (whether or not of a person named in the notice).

(5–CVL) Where the contributories make an appointment under paragraph (4), the creditor members of the committee may, if they think fit, resolve that the person appointed ought not to be a member of the committee; and—

(a) that person is not then, unless the court otherwise directs, qualified to act as a member of the committee, and

(b) on any application to the court for a direction under this paragraph the court may, if it thinks [just], appoint another person (being a contributory) to fill the vacancy on the committee.

(6) Where the vacancy is filled by an appointment made by a contributories' meeting at which the liquidator is not present, the chairman of the meeting shall report to the liquidator the appointment which has been made.

NOTES

Initial Commencement

Specified date

Specified date: 29 December 1986: see r 0.1.

Amendment

Para (2): reference to "3" in square brackets substituted by SI 2010/686, r 2, Sch 1, para 235.
Date in force: 6 April 2010: see SI 2010/686, r 1; for transitional provisions see r 6(1), Sch 4, para 1 thereto.

Para (5): in sub-para (b) word "just" in square brackets substituted by SI 2010/686, r 2, Sch 1, para 1.
Date in force: 6 April 2010: see SI 2010/686, r 1; for transitional provisions see r 6(1), Sch 4, paras 1, 2(1)(b) thereto.

See Further

See further, in relation the application of this rule, with modifications, in respect of the procedure for the appointment of a bank liquidator and the operation of bank insolvency under the Banking Act 2009, Pt 2: the Bank Insolvency (England and Wales) Rules 2009, SI 2009/356, rr 3(3)–(8), 127.

4.165 Voting rights and resolutions (No CVL Application)

(1) At any meeting of the committee, each member of it (whether present himself, or by his representative) has one vote; and a resolution is passed when a majority of the creditor members present or represented have voted in favour of it.

(2) Subject to the next paragraph, the votes of contributory members do not count towards the number required for passing a resolution, but the way in which they vote on any resolution shall be recorded.

(3) Paragraph (2) does not apply where, by virtue of Rule 4.154 or 4.171, the only members of the committee are contributories. In that case the committee is to be treated for voting purposes as if all its members were creditors.

(4) Every resolution passed shall be recorded in writing, either separately or as part of the minutes of the meeting. The record shall be [authenticated] by the chairman and kept with the records of the liquidation.

NOTES

Initial Commencement

Specified date

Specified date: 29 December 1986: see r 0.1.

Amendment

Para (4): word "authenticated" in square brackets substituted by SI 2010/686, r 2, Sch 1, para 1.
Date in force: 6 April 2010: see SI 2010/686, r 1; for transitional provisions see r 6(1), Sch 4, paras 1, 2(1)(b) thereto.

See Further

See further, in relation the application of this rule, with modifications, in respect of the procedure for the appointment of a bank liquidator and the operation of bank insolvency under the Banking Act 2009, Pt 2: the Bank Insolvency (England and Wales) Rules 2009, SI 2009/356, rr 3(3)–(8), 128.

4.166 Voting rights and resolutions—CVL

(1) At any meeting of the committee, each member of it (whether present himself, or by his representative) has one vote; and a resolution is passed when a majority of the members present or represented have voted in favour of it.

(2) Every resolution passed shall be recorded in writing, either separately or as part of the minutes of the meeting. The record shall be [authenticated] by the chairman and kept with the records of the liquidation.

NOTES

Initial Commencement

Specified date

Specified date: 29 December 1986: see r 0.1.

Amendment

Para (2): word "authenticated" in square brackets substituted by SI 2010/686, r 2, Sch 1, para 1.

Date in force: 6 April 2010: see SI 2010/686, r 1; for transitional provisions see r 6(1), Sch 4, paras 1, 2(1)(b) thereto.

4.167 Resolutions [otherwise than at a meeting]

(1) In accordance with this Rule, the liquidator may seek to obtain the agreement of members of the liquidation committee to a resolution by sending to every member (or his representative designated for the purpose) a copy of the proposed resolution.

(2) Where the liquidator makes use of the procedure allowed by this Rule, he shall send out to members of the committee or their representatives (as the case may be) [a copy of any proposed resolution on which a decision is sought, which shall be set out in such a way that agreement with or dissent from each separate resolution may be indicated by the recipient on the copy so sent].

(3) Any creditor member of the committee may, within 7 business days from the date of the liquidator sending out a resolution, require him to summon a meeting of the committee to consider the matters raised by the resolution. (NO CVL APPLICATION)

(4–CVL) Any member of the committee may, within 7 business days from the date of the liquidator sending out a resolution, require him to summon a meeting of the committee to consider the matters raised by the resolution.

(5) In the absence of such a request, the resolution is deemed to have been passed by the committee if and when the liquidator is notified in writing by a majority of the creditor members that they concur with it. (NO CVL APPLICATION)

(6–CVL) In the absence of such a request, the resolution is deemed to have been passed by the committee if and when the liquidator is notified in writing by a majority of the members that they concur with it.

(7) A copy of every resolution passed under this Rule, and a note that the committee's concurrence was obtained, shall be kept with the records of the liquidation.

NOTES

Initial Commencement

Specified date

Specified date: 29 December 1986: see r 0.1.

Amendment

Provision heading: words "otherwise than at a meeting" in square brackets substituted by SI 2010/686, r 2, Sch 1, para 236.

Date in force: 6 April 2010: see SI 2010/686, r 1; for transitional provisions see r 6(1), Sch 4, para 1 thereto.

Para (2): words in square brackets substituted by SI 1987/1919, r 3(1), Schedule, Part 1, para 74.

See Further

See further, in relation the application of this rule, with modifications, in respect of the procedure for the appointment of a bank liquidator and the operation of bank insolvency under the Banking Act 2009, Pt 2: the Bank Insolvency (England and Wales) Rules 2009, SI 2009/356, rr 3(3)–(8), 129.

4.168 Liquidator's reports

(1) The liquidator shall, as and when directed by the liquidation committee (but not more often than once in any period of 2 months), send a written report to every member of the committee setting out the position generally as regards the progress of the winding up and matters arising in connection with it, to which he (the liquidator) considers the committee's attention should be drawn.

(2) In the absence of such directions by the committee, the liquidator shall send such a report not less often than once in every period of 6 months.

(3) The obligations of the liquidator under this Rule are without prejudice to those imposed by Rule 4.155.

NOTES

Initial Commencement

Specified date

Specified date: 29 December 1986: see r 0.1.

See Further

See further, in relation the application of this rule, with modifications, in respect of the procedure for the appointment of a bank liquidator and the operation of bank insolvency under the Banking Act 2009, Pt 2: the Bank Insolvency (England and Wales) Rules 2009, SI 2009/356, rr 3(3)–(8), 130.

4.169 Expenses of members, etc

The liquidator shall defray [as an expense of the liquidation], in the prescribed order of priority, any reasonable travelling expenses directly incurred by members of the liquidation committee or their representatives in respect of their attendance at the committee's meetings, or otherwise on the committee's business.

NOTES

Initial Commencement

Specified date

Specified date: 29 December 1986: see r 0.1.

Amendment

Words "as an expense of the liquidation" in square brackets substituted by SI 2008/737, rr 3, 7(1).

Date in force: 6 April 2008: see SI 2008/737, r 1(1); for transitional provisions see r 2 thereof.

See Further

See further, in relation the application of this rule, with modifications, in respect of the procedure for the appointment of a bank liquidator and the operation of bank insolvency

under the Banking Act 2009, Pt 2: the Bank Insolvency (England and Wales) Rules 2009, SI 2009/356, rr 3(3)–(8), 131.

4.170 Dealings by committee-members and others

(1) This Rule applies to—

(a) any member of the liquidation committee,

(b) any committee-member's representative,

(c) any person who is an associate of a member of the committee or a committee-member's representative, and

(d) any person who has been a member of the committee at any time in the last 12 months.

(2) Subject as follows, a person to whom this Rule applies shall not enter into any transaction whereby he—

(a) receives [as an expense of the liquidation] any payment for services given or goods supplied in connection with the administration, or

(b) obtains any profit from the administration, or

(c) acquires any asset forming part of the estate.

(3) Such a transaction may be entered into by a person to whom this Rule applies—

(a) with the prior [permission] of the court, or

(b) if he does so as a matter of urgency, or by way of performance of a contract in force before the date on which the company went into liquidation, and obtains the court's [permission] for the transaction, having applied for it without undue delay, or

(c) with the prior sanction of the liquidation committee, where it is satisfied (after full disclosure of the circumstances) that the person will be giving full value in the transaction.

(4) Where in the committee a resolution is proposed that sanction be accorded for a transaction to be entered into which, without that sanction or the [permission] of the court, would be in contravention of this Rule, no member of the committee, and no representative of a member, shall vote if he is to participate directly or indirectly in the transaction.

(5) The court may, on the application of any person interested—

(a) set aside a transaction on the ground that it has been entered into in contravention of this Rule, and

(b) make with respect to it such other order as it thinks [just], including (subject to the following paragraph) an order requiring a person to whom this Rule applies to account for any profit obtained from the transaction and compensate the estate for any resultant loss.

(6) In the case of a person to whom this Rule applies as an associate of a member of the committee or of a committee-member's representative, the court shall not make any order under paragraph (5), if satisfied that he entered into the relevant transaction without having any reason to suppose that in doing so he would contravene this Rule.

(7) The costs of an application to the court for [permission] under this Rule are not payable [as an expense of the liquidation], unless the court so orders.

NOTES

Initial Commencement

Specified date

Specified date: 29 December 1986: see r 0.1.

Amendment
>Para (2): in sub-para (a) words "as an expense of the liquidation" in square brackets substituted by SI 2008/737, rr 3, 7(11).
>>Date in force: 6 April 2008: see SI 2008/737, r 1(1); for transitional provisions see r 2 thereof.
>
>Para (3): in sub-paras (a), (b) word "permission" in square brackets substituted by SI 2010/686, r 2, Sch 1, para 1.
>>Date in force: 6 April 2010: see SI 2010/686, r 1; for transitional provisions see r 6(1), Sch 4, paras 1, 2(1)(b) thereto.
>
>Para (4): word "permission" in square brackets substituted by SI 2010/686, r 2, Sch 1, para 1.
>>Date in force: 6 April 2010: see SI 2010/686, r 1; for transitional provisions see r 6(1), Sch 4, paras 1, 2(1)(b) thereto.
>
>Para (5): in sub-para (b) word "just" in square brackets substituted by SI 2010/686, r 2, Sch 1, para 1.
>>Date in force: 6 April 2010: see SI 2010/686, r 1; for transitional provisions see r 6(1), Sch 4, paras 1, 2(1)(b) thereto.
>
>Para (7): word "permission" in square brackets substituted by SI 2010/686, r 2, Sch 1, para 1.
>>Date in force: 6 April 2010: see SI 2010/686, r 1; for transitional provisions see r 6(1), Sch 4, paras 1, 2(1)(b) thereto.
>
>Para (7): words "as an expense of the liquidation" in square brackets substituted by SI 2008/737, rr 3, 7(1).
>>Date in force: 6 April 2008: see SI 2008/737, r 1(1); for transitional provisions see r 2 thereof.

See Further
>See further, in relation the application of this rule, with modifications, in respect of the procedure for the appointment of a bank liquidator and the operation of bank insolvency under the Banking Act 2009, Pt 2: the Bank Insolvency (England and Wales) Rules 2009, SI 2009/356, rr 3(3)–(8), 132.

[4.171A Composition of committee when creditors paid in full]

[(1) Where the creditors have been paid in full together with interest in accordance with section 189, the liquidator must—

(a) issue a certificate to that effect; and

(b) send to the registrar of companies a notification to that effect together with a copy of the certificate referred to in sub-paragraph (a).

(2) On the issue of a certificate pursuant to paragraph (1), the creditor members of the liquidation committee cease to be members of the committee.

(3) The committee continues in existence unless—

(a) it is abolished by a decision of a meeting of contributories; or

(b) the number of members is less than 3 and 28 days have elapsed since the issue of the liquidator's certificate.

(4) At any time in the period referred to in paragraph (3)(b) where the committee consists of less than 3 contributory members it is suspended and cannot act.

(5) The certificate referred to in paragraph (1)(a) must include the following information—

(a) the name of the liquidator; and

(b) a statement by the liquidator certifying that the creditors of the company have been paid in full together with interest in accordance with section 189;

and must be authenticated and dated by the liquidator.]

NOTES

Amendment
>Substituted, for r 4.171 as originally enacted, by SI 2010/686, r 2, Sch 1, para 237.

Date in force: 6 April 2010: see SI 2010/686, r 1; for transitional provisions see r 6(1), Sch 4, para 1 thereto.

4.172 Committee's functions vested in Secretary of State (No CVL Application)
(1) At any time when the functions of the liquidation committee are vested in the Secretary of State under section 141(4) or (5), requirements of the Act or the Rules about notices to be given, or reports to be made, to the committee by the liquidator do not apply, otherwise than as enabling the committee to require a report as to any matter.

(2) Where the committee's functions are so vested under section 141(5), they may be exercised by the official receiver.

NOTES

Initial Commencement

Specified date
Specified date: 29 December 1986: see r 0.1.

See Further
See further, in relation the application of this rule, with modifications, in respect of the procedure for the appointment of a bank liquidator and the operation of bank insolvency under the Banking Act 2009, Pt 2: the Bank Insolvency (England and Wales) Rules 2009, SI 2009/356, rr 3(3)–(8), 134.

[4.172A Formal defects]
[The acts of the liquidation committee established for any winding up are valid notwithstanding any defect in the appointment, election or qualifications of any member of the committee or any committee-member's representative or in the formalities of its establishment.]

NOTES

Amendment
Inserted by SI 1987/1919, r 3(1), Schedule, Part 1, para 75.

See Further
See further, in relation the application of this rule, with modifications, in respect of the procedure for the appointment of a bank liquidator and the operation of bank insolvency under the Banking Act 2009, Pt 2: the Bank Insolvency (England and Wales) Rules 2009, SI 2009/356, rr 3(3)–(8), 135.

CHAPTER 13

THE LIQUIDATION COMMITTEE WHERE WINDING UP FOLLOWS IMMEDIATELY ON ADMINISTRATION (NO CVL APPLICATION)

4.173 Preliminary
(1) The Rules in this Chapter apply where—
- (a) the winding-up order has been made [by the court upon an application under paragraph 79 of Schedule B1 to the Act], . . .
- (b) the court makes an order under section 140(1) of the Act appointing as liquidator the person who was previously the administrator;
- [(c) a creditors' committee was established under paragraph 57 of Schedule B1 to the Act, and

(d) as at the date of the making of the order under section 140(1) the committee has at least three, but not more than five, members (leaving out of account any member whose debt is fully secured)].

(2) In this Chapter, "insolvent winding up", "solvent winding up", "creditor member" and "contributory member" mean the same as in Chapter 12.

NOTES

Initial Commencement

Specified date

Specified date: 29 December 1986: see r 0.1.

Amendment

Para (1): in sub-para (a) words from "by the court" to "to the Act" in square brackets substituted by SI 2003/1730, r 7, Sch 1, Pt 4, para 25.
Date in force: 15 September 2003: see SI 2003/1730, r 1(2).
Para (1): in sub-para (a) word omitted revoked by SI 2010/686, r 2, Sch 1, para 238(1), (2)(a).
Date in force: 6 April 2010: see SI 2010/686, r 1; for transitional provisions see r 6(1), Sch 4, para 1 thereto.
Para (1): sub-paras (c), (d) inserted by SI 2010/686, r 2, Sch 1, para 238(1), (2)(b).
Date in force: 6 April 2010: see SI 2010/686, r 1; for transitional provisions see r 6(1), Sch 4, para 1 thereto.

[4.174A Continuation of creditors' committee]

[Where a committee of the kind mentioned in Rule 4.173 is in existence in the circumstances mentioned in that Rule—

(a) that committee is deemed to have been established under section 141;
(b) no action may be taken under section 141(1) to (3) to establish any other committee;
(c) in the case of a solvent winding up, the liquidator must, on not less than 14 days' notice summon a meeting of contributories, in order to elect (if it so wishes) contributory members of the liquidation committee, up to 3 in number; and
(d) pending the issue of the liquidator's certificate referred to in Rule 4.176 the committee is suspended and cannot act.]

NOTES

Amendment

Substituted, for r 4.174 as originally enacted, by SI 2010/686, r 2, Sch 1, para 239.
Date in force: 6 April 2010: see SI 2010/686, r 1; for transitional provisions see r 6(1), Sch 4, para 1 thereto.

4.175 . . .

. . .

NOTES

Amendment

Revoked by SI 2010/686, r 5.
Date in force: 6 April 2010: see SI 2010/686, r 1; for transitional provisions see r 6(1), Sch 4, para 1 thereto.

4.176 Liquidator's certificate

(1) The liquidator [must ascertain whether the members of the committee agree to continue to act as members of the committee; and if the minimum number of 3 members required by Rule 4.152 to form a committee have signified their agreement so to act, the liquidator must] issue a certificate of the liquidation committee's continuance, specifying the persons who are, or are to be, members of it.

(2) It shall be stated in the certificate whether or not the liquidator has summoned a meeting of contributories under [Rule 4.174A(c)], and whether (if so) the meeting has elected contributories to be members of the committee.

(3) ...

(4) No person may act, or continue to act, as a member of the committee unless and until he has agreed to do so. . ..

(5) As and when the others signify their agreement, the liquidator shall issue an amended certificate.

[(6) The liquidator must send the certificate in paragraph (1) or as the case may be the amended certificate in paragraph (5) to the registrar of companies.]

(7) If subsequently there is any change in the committee's membership, the liquidator [must send an amended certificate to the registrar of companies].

NOTES

Initial Commencement

Specified date
 Specified date: 29 December 1986: see r 0.1.

Amendment
 Para (1): words from "must ascertain whether" to "the liquidator must" in square brackets substituted by SI 2010/686, r 2, Sch 1, para 240(1), (2).
  Date in force: 6 April 2010: see SI 2010/686, r 1; for transitional provisions see r 6(1), Sch 4, para 1 thereto.
 Para (2): words "Rule 4.174A(c)" in square brackets substituted by SI 2010/686, r 2, Sch 1, para 240(1), (3).
  Date in force: 6 April 2010: see SI 2010/686, r 1; for transitional provisions see r 6(1), Sch 4, para 1 thereto.
 Para (3): revoked by SI 2010/686, r 2, Sch 1, para 240(1), (4).
  Date in force: 6 April 2010: see SI 2010/686, r 1; for transitional provisions see r 6(1), Sch 4, para 1 thereto.
 Para (4): words omitted revoked by SI 2010/686, r 2, Sch 1, para 240(1), (5).
  Date in force: 6 April 2010: see SI 2010/686, r 1; for transitional provisions see r 6(1), Sch 4, para 1 thereto.
 Para (6): substituted by SI 2010/686, r 2, Sch 1, para 240(1), (6).
  Date in force: 6 April 2010: see SI 2010/686, r 1; for transitional provisions see r 6(1), Sch 4, para 1 thereto.
 Para (7): words "must send an amended certificate to the registrar of companies" in square brackets substituted by SI 2010/686, r 2, Sch 1, para 240(1), (7).
  Date in force: 6 April 2010: see SI 2010/686, r 1; for transitional provisions see r 6(1), Sch 4, para 1 thereto.

4.177 Obligations of liquidator to committee

(1) As soon as [reasonably practicable] after the issue of the liquidator's certificate under Rule 4.176, the liquidator shall report to the liquidation committee what actions he has taken since the date on which the company went into liquidation.

(2) A person who becomes a member of the committee after [the date of issue of the liquidator's certificate] is not entitled to require a report to him by the liquidator, otherwise than in a summary form, of any matters previously arising.

(3) Nothing in this Rule disentitles the committee, or any member of it, from having access to the records of the liquidation (whether relating to the period when he

was administrator, or to any subsequent period), or from seeking an explanation of any matter within the committee's responsibility.

NOTES

Initial Commencement

Specified date

Specified date: 29 December 1986: see r 0.1.

Amendment

Para (1): words "reasonably practicable" in square brackets substituted by SI 2010/686, r 2, Sch 1, para 241(1), (2).
Date in force: 6 April 2010: see SI 2010/686, r 1; for transitional provisions see r 6(1), Sch 4, para 1 thereto.
Para (2): words "the date of issue of the liquidator's certificate" in square brackets substituted by SI 2010/686, r 2, Sch 1, para 241(1), (3).
Date in force: 6 April 2010: see SI 2010/686, r 1; for transitional provisions see r 6(1), Sch 4, para 1 thereto.

4.178 Application of Chapter 12

Except as provided above in this Chapter, Rules 4.155 to [4.172A] in Chapter 12 apply to the liquidation committee following the issue of the liquidator's certificate under Rule 4.176, as if it had been established under section 141.

NOTES

Initial Commencement

Specified date

Specified date: 29 December 1986: see r 0.1.

Amendment

Figure in square brackets substituted by SI 1987/1919, r 3(1), Schedule, Part 1, para 76.

CHAPTER 14

COLLECTION AND DISTRIBUTION OF COMPANY'S ASSETS BY LIQUIDATOR

4.179 General duties of liquidator (No CVL Application)

(1) The duties imposed on the court by the Act with regard to the collection of the company's assets and their application in discharge of its liabilities are discharged by the liquidator as an officer of the court subject to its control.

(2) In the discharge of his duties the liquidator, for the purposes of acquiring and retaining possession of the company's property, has the same powers as a receiver appointed by the High Court, and the court may on his application enforce such acquisition or retention accordingly.

NOTES

Initial Commencement

Specified date

Specified date: 29 December 1986: see r 0.1.

See Further

See further, in relation the application of this rule, with modifications, in respect of the procedure for the appointment of a bank liquidator and the operation of bank insolvency under the Banking Act 2009, Pt 2: the Bank Insolvency (England and Wales) Rules 2009, SI 2009/356, rr 3(3)–(8), 136.

4.180 Manner of distributing assets

(1) Whenever the liquidator has sufficient funds in hand for the purpose he shall, subject to the retention of such sums as may be necessary for the expenses of the winding up, declare and distribute dividends among the creditors in respect of the debts which they have respectively proved.

(2) The liquidator shall give notice of his intention to declare and distribute a dividend.

(3) Where the liquidator has declared a dividend, he shall give notice of it to the creditors, stating how the dividend is proposed to be distributed. The notice shall contain such particulars with respect to the company, and to its assets and affairs, as will enable the creditors to comprehend the calculation of the amount of the dividend and the manner of its distribution.

NOTES

Initial Commencement

Specified date

Specified date: 29 December 1986: see r 0.1.

See Further

See further, in relation the application of this rule, with modifications, in respect of the procedure for the appointment of a bank liquidator and the operation of bank insolvency under the Banking Act 2009, Pt 2: the Bank Insolvency (England and Wales) Rules 2009, SI 2009/356, rr 3(3)–(8), 138.

4.181 Debts of insolvent company to rank equally (No CVL Application)

[(1)] Debts other than preferential debts rank equally between themselves in the winding up and, after the preferential debts, shall be paid in full unless the assets are insufficient for meeting them, in which case they abate in equal proportions between themselves.

[(2) Paragraph (1) applies whether or not the company is unable to pay its debts.]

NOTES

Initial Commencement

Specified date

Specified date: 29 December 1986: see r 0.1.

Amendment

Para (1): numbered as such by SI 1987/1919, r 3(1), Schedule, Part 1, para 77.

Para (2): inserted by SI 1987/1919, r 3(1), Schedule, Part 1, para 77.

See Further

See further, in relation the application of this rule, with modifications, in respect of the procedure for the appointment of a bank liquidator and the operation of bank insolvency under the Banking Act 2009, Pt 2: the Bank Insolvency (England and Wales) Rules 2009, SI 2009/356, rr 3(3)–(8), 139.

4.182 Supplementary provisions as to dividend

(1) In the calculation and distribution of a dividend the liquidator shall make provision—

(a) for any debts which appear to him to be due to persons who, by reason of the distance of their place of residence, may not have had sufficient time to tender and establish their proofs,

(b) for any debts which are the subject of claims which have not yet been determined, and

(c) for disputed proofs and claims.

(2) A creditor who has not proved his debt before the declaration of any dividend is not entitled to disturb, by reason that he has not participated in it, the distribution of that dividend or any other dividend declared before his debt was proved, but—

(a) when he has proved that debt he is entitled to be paid, out of any money for the time being available for the payment of any further dividend, any dividend or dividends which he has failed to receive, and

(b) any dividend or dividends payable under sub-paragraph (a) shall be paid before that money is applied to the payment of any such further dividend.

(3) No action lies against the liquidator for a dividend; but if he refuses to pay a dividend the court may, if it thinks [just], order him to pay it and also to pay, out of his own money—

(a) interest on the dividend, at the rate for the time being specified in section 17 of the Judgments Act 1838, from the time when it was withheld, and

(b) the costs of the proceedings in which the order to pay is made.

NOTES

Initial Commencement

Specified date

Specified date: 29 December 1986: see r 0.1.

Amendment

Para (3): word "just" in square brackets substituted by SI 2010/686, r 2, Sch 1, para 1.
Date in force: 6 April 2010: see SI 2010/686, r 1; for transitional provisions see r 6(1), Sch 4, paras 1, 2(1)(b) thereto.

See Further

See further, in relation the application of this rule, with modifications, in respect of the procedure for the appointment of a bank liquidator and the operation of bank insolvency under the Banking Act 2009, Pt 2: the Bank Insolvency (England and Wales) Rules 2009, SI 2009/356, rr 3(3)–(8), 140.

[4.182A Distribution in members' voluntary winding up (No CVL Application)]

[[(1) In a members' voluntary winding up the liquidator may give notice of the intention to make a distribution to creditors. Such notice—

(a) shall be gazetted; and

(b) may be advertised in such other manner as the liquidator thinks fit.]

[(2) In addition to the standard contents, the notice under paragraph (1) must—

(a) state that the liquidator intends to make a distribution to creditors; and

(b) specify a date ("the last date for proving") up to which proofs may be lodged at a specified place, which must be the same date for all creditors and not less than 21 days from that of the notice.]

(3) The liquidator is not obliged to deal with proofs lodged after the last date for proving; but he may do so, if he thinks fit.

(4) A creditor who has not proved his debt before the last date for proving or after that date increases the claim in his proof is not entitled to disturb, by reason that he has not participated in it, either at all or, as the case may be, to the extent that his increased claim would allow, that distribution or any other distribution made before his debt was proved or his claim increased; but when he has proved his debt or, as the case may be, increased his claim, he is entitled to be paid, out of any money for the time being available for the payment of any further distribution, any distribution or distributions which he has failed to receive.

(5) Where the distribution proposed to be made is to be the only or the final distribution in that winding up, the liquidator may, subject to paragraph (6), make that distribution without regard to the claim of any person in respect of a debt not already proved.

(6) Where the distribution proposed to be made is one specified in paragraph (5), the notice given under paragraph (1) shall state the effect of paragraph (5).]

NOTES

Amendment

Inserted by SI 1987/1919, r 3(1), Schedule, Part 1, para 78.
Para (1): substituted by SI 2009/642, rr 4, 29.
Date in force: 6 April 2009: see SI 2009/642, r 1; for transitional provisions see r 3 thereof.
Para (2): substituted by SI 2010/686, r 2, Sch 1, para 242.
Date in force: 6 April 2010: see SI 2010/686, r 1; for transitional provisions see r 6(1), Sch 4, para 1 thereto.

4.183 Division of unsold assets

[(1)] Without prejudice to provisions of the Act about disclaimer, the liquidator may, with the permission of the liquidation committee [(or if there is no such committee, a meeting of the company's creditors)], divide in its existing form amongst the company's creditors, according to its estimated value, any property which from its peculiar nature or other special circumstances cannot be readily or advantageously sold.

[(2) The liquidator must comply with paragraph (3) in respect of any account or report which the liquidator is required to prepare pursuant to any of the following—

- (a) section 104A (progress report to company and creditors at year's end);
- (b) section 106 (final meeting prior to dissolution—creditors' voluntary winding up);
- (c) section 146 (duty to summon final meeting—winding up by the court);
- (d) Rule 4.49B (reports to creditors and members —winding up by the court);
- (e) Rule 4.49D (final report to creditors);
- (f) Rule 4.108 (creditors' meeting to receive liquidator's resignation);
- (g) Rule 4.125 (final meeting—winding up by the court);
- (h) Rule 4.126 (final meeting—creditors' voluntary liquidation).

(3) The liquidator must—

- (a) in any account or summary of receipts and payments which is required to be included in the account or report, state the estimated value of the property distributed amongst the creditors of the company during the period to which the account or report relates, and
- (b) as a note to the account or summary of receipts and payments, provide details of the basis of the valuation.]

NOTES

Initial Commencement

Specified date

Specified date: 29 December 1986: see r 0.1.

Amendment

Para (1): numbered as such by SI 2010/686, r 2, Sch 1, para 243(1), (2).
Date in force: 6 April 2010: see SI 2010/686, r 1; for transitional provisions see r 6(1), Sch 4, para 1 thereto.
Para (1): words "(or if there is no such committee, a meeting of the company's creditors)" in square brackets inserted by SI 2010/686, r 2, Sch 1, para 243(1), (3).
Date in force: 6 April 2010: see SI 2010/686, r 1; for transitional provisions see r 6(1), Sch 4, para 1 thereto.
Paras (2), (3): inserted by SI 2010/686, r 2, Sch 1, para 243(1), (4).
Date in force: 6 April 2010: see SI 2010/686, r 1; for transitional provisions see r 6(1), Sch 4, para 1 thereto.

See Further

See further, in relation the application of this rule, with modifications, in respect of the procedure for the appointment of a bank liquidator and the operation of bank insolvency under the Banking Act 2009, Pt 2: the Bank Insolvency (England and Wales) Rules 2009, SI 2009/356, rr 3(3)–(8), 141.

4.184 General powers of liquidator

(1) Any permission given by the liquidation committee [(or if there is no such committee, a meeting of the company's creditors)] or the court under [section 165(2) or] section 167(1)(a), or under the Rules, shall not be a general permission but shall relate to a particular proposed exercise of the liquidator's power in question; and a person dealing with the liquidator in good faith and for value is not concerned to enquire whether any such permission has been given.

(2) Where the liquidator has done anything without that permission, the court or the liquidation committee may, for the purpose of enabling him to meet his expenses out of the assets, ratify what he has done; but neither shall do so unless it is satisfied that the liquidator has acted in a case of urgency and has sought ratification without undue delay.

NOTES

Initial Commencement

Specified date

Specified date: 29 December 1986: see r 0.1.

Amendment

Para (1): words "(or if there is no such committee, a meeting of the company's creditors)" and "section 165(2) or" in square brackets inserted by SI 2005/527, r 31.
Date in force: 1 April 2005: see SI 2005/527, r 1(2).

See Further

See further, in relation the application of this rule, with modifications, in respect of the procedure for the appointment of a bank liquidator and the operation of bank insolvency under the Banking Act 2009, Pt 2: the Bank Insolvency (England and Wales) Rules 2009, SI 2009/356, rr 3(3)–(8), 142.

4.185 **Enforced delivery up of company's property (No CVL Application)**

(1) The powers conferred on the court by section 234 (enforced delivery of company property) are exercisable by the liquidator or, where a provisional liquidator has been appointed, by him.

(2) Any person on whom a requirement under section 234(2) is imposed by the liquidator or provisional liquidator shall, without avoidable delay, comply with it.

NOTES

Initial Commencement

Specified date

Specified date: 29 December 1986: see r 0.1.

See Further

See further, in relation the application of this rule, with modifications, in respect of the procedure for the appointment of a bank liquidator and the operation of bank insolvency under the Banking Act 2009, Pt 2: the Bank Insolvency (England and Wales) Rules 2009, SI 2009/356, rr 3(3)–(8), 143.

4.186 **Final distribution**

(1) When the liquidator has realised all the company's assets or so much of them as can, in his opinion, be realised without needlessly protracting the liquidation, he shall give notice, under Part 11 of the Rules, either—
 (a) of his intention to declare a final dividend, or
 (b) that no dividend, or further dividend, will be declared.

(2) The notice shall contain all such particulars as are required by Part 11 of the Rules and shall require claims against the assets to be established by a date specified in the notice.

(3) After that date, the liquidator shall—
 (a) defray any outstanding expenses of the winding up [as an expense of the liquidation], and
 (b) if he intends to declare a final dividend, declare and distribute that dividend without regard to the claim of any person in respect of a debt not already proved.

(4) The court may, on the application of any person, postpone the date specified in the notice.

NOTES

Initial Commencement

Specified date

Specified date: 29 December 1986: see r 0.1.

Amendment

Para (3): in sub-para (a) words "as an expense of the liquidation" in square brackets substituted by SI 2008/737, rr 3, 7(1).
 Date in force: 6 April 2008: see SI 2008/737, r 1(1); for transitional provisions see r 2 thereof.

See Further

See further, in relation the application of this rule, with modifications, in respect of the procedure for the appointment of a bank liquidator and the operation of bank insolvency under the Banking Act 2009, Pt 2: the Bank Insolvency (England and Wales) Rules 2009, SI 2009/356, rr 3(3)–(8), 144.

CHAPTER 15
DISCLAIMER

4.187 Liquidator's notice of disclaimer

(1) Where the liquidator disclaims property under section 178, the notice of disclaimer shall contain such particulars of the property disclaimed as enable it to be easily identified.

[(2) The notice of disclaimer must be authenticated and dated by the liquidator.]

[(3A) As soon as reasonably practicable after authenticating the notice of disclaimer, the liquidator must—

(a) send a copy of the notice to the registrar of companies; and

(b) in any case where the disclaimer is of registered land as defined in section 132(1) of the Land Registration Act 2002, send a copy of the notice to the Chief Land Registrar.]

(4) For the purposes of section 178, the date of the prescribed notice is that [on which the liquidator authenticated it].

NOTES

Initial Commencement

Specified date

Specified date: 29 December 1986: see r 0.1.

Amendment

Para (2): substituted by SI 2010/686, r 2, Sch 1, para 244(1), (2).
Date in force: 6 April 2010: see SI 2010/686, r 1; for transitional provisions see r 6(1), Sch 4, para 1 thereto.
Para (3A): substituted, for para (3) as originally enacted, by SI 2010/686, r 2, Sch 1, para 244(1), (3).
Date in force: 6 April 2010: see SI 2010/686, r 1; for transitional provisions see r 6(1), Sch 4, para 1 thereto.
Para (4): words "on which the liquidator authenticated it" in square brackets substituted by SI 2010/686, r 2, Sch 1, para 244(1), (4).
Date in force: 6 April 2010: see SI 2010/686, r 1; for transitional provisions see r 6(1), Sch 4, para 1 thereto.

See Further

See further, in relation the application of this rule, with modifications, in respect of the procedure for the appointment of a bank liquidator and the operation of bank insolvency under the Banking Act 2009, Pt 2: the Bank Insolvency (England and Wales) Rules 2009, SI 2009/356, rr 3(3)–(8), 145.
See further, in relation to the application of this rule, with modifications, in respect of bank administration and applications for bank administration: the Bank Administration (England and Wales) Rules 2009, SI 2009/357, rr 58–61.

4.188 Communication of disclaimer to persons interested

[(1) Within 7 business days after the date of the notice of disclaimer, the liquidator shall send or give copies of the notice to the persons mentioned in paragraphs (2) to (4).]

(2) Where the property disclaimed is of a leasehold nature, he shall send or give a copy to every person who (to his knowledge) claims under the company as underlessee or mortgagee.

(3) He shall in any case send or give a copy of the notice to every person who (to his knowledge)—

(a) claims an interest in the disclaimed property, or

(b) is under any liability in respect of the property, not being a liability discharged by the disclaimer.

(4) If the disclaimer is of an unprofitable contract, he shall send or give copies of the notice to all such persons as, to his knowledge, are parties to the contract or have interests under it.

(5) If subsequently it comes to the liquidator's knowledge, in the case of any person, that he has such an interest in the disclaimed property as would have entitled him to receive a copy of the notice of disclaimer in pursuance of paragraphs (2) to (4), the liquidator shall then [as soon as reasonably practicable] send or give to that person a copy of the notice.

But compliance with this paragraph is not required if—

(a) the liquidator is satisfied that the person has already been made aware of the disclaimer and its date, or

(b) the court, on the liquidator's application, orders that compliance is not required in that particular case.

NOTES

Initial Commencement

Specified date

Specified date: 29 December 1986: see r 0.1.

Amendment

Para (1): substituted by SI 2010/686, r 2, Sch 1, para 245.
Date in force: 6 April 2010: see SI 2010/686, r 1; for transitional provisions see r 6(1), Sch 4, para 1 thereto.
Para (5): words "as soon as reasonably practicable" in square brackets substituted by SI 2009/642, rr 4, 5.
Date in force: 6 April 2009: see SI 2009/642, r 1; for transitional provisions see r 3 thereof.

See Further

See further, in relation the application of this rule, with modifications, in respect of the procedure for the appointment of a bank liquidator and the operation of bank insolvency under the Banking Act 2009, Pt 2: the Bank Insolvency (England and Wales) Rules 2009, SI 2009/356, rr 3(3)–(8), 146.
See further, in relation to the application of this rule, with modifications, in respect of bank administration and applications for bank administration: the Bank Administration (England and Wales) Rules 2009, SI 2009/357, rr 58–61.

4.189 Additional notices

The liquidator disclaiming property may, without prejudice to his obligations under sections 178 to 180 and Rules 4.187 and 4.188, at any time [send or give copies of the] notice of the disclaimer to any persons who in his opinion ought, in the public interest or otherwise, to be informed of [the disclaimer].

NOTES

Initial Commencement

Specified date

Specified date: 29 December 1986: see r 0.1.

Amendment

Words "send or give copies of the" in square brackets substituted by SI 2010/686, r 2, Sch 1, para 246(1), (2).
Date in force: 6 April 2010: see SI 2010/686, r 1; for transitional provisions see r 6(1), Sch 4, para 1 thereto.
Words "the disclaimer" in square brackets substituted by SI 2010/686, r 2, Sch 1, para 246(1), (3).

Date in force: 6 April 2010: see SI 2010/686, r 1; for transitional provisions see r 6(1), Sch 4, para 1 thereto.

See Further

See further, in relation the application of this rule, with modifications, in respect of the procedure for the appointment of a bank liquidator and the operation of bank insolvency under the Banking Act 2009, Pt 2: the Bank Insolvency (England and Wales) Rules 2009, SI 2009/356, rr 3(3)–(8), 147.

See further, in relation to the application of this rule, with modifications, in respect of bank administration and applications for bank administration: the Bank Administration (England and Wales) Rules 2009, SI 2009/357, rr 58–61.

4.190 . . .

. . .

NOTES

Amendment

Revoked by SI 2010/686, r 5.
Date in force: 6 April 2010: see SI 2010/686, r 1; for transitional provisions see r 6(1), Sch 4, paras 1, 2(1)(a), (2)–(4) thereto.

[4.190A Records]

[The liquidator must include in the liquidator's records of the insolvency a record of—

(a) the persons to whom that liquidator has sent or given copies of the notice of disclaimer under the two preceding Rules, showing their names and addresses, and the nature of their respective interests;

(b) the dates on which the copies of the notice of disclaimer were sent or given to those persons;

(c) the date on which, as required by Rule 4.187(3)(a), a copy of the notice of disclaimer was sent to the registrar of companies; and

(d) (where applicable) the date on which, as required by Rule 4.187(3)(b), a copy of the notice was sent to the Chief Land Registrar.]

NOTES

Amendment

Substituted, for r 4.190 as originally enacted, by SI 2010/686, r 2, Sch 1, para 247.
Date in force: 6 April 2010: see SI 2010/686, r 1; for transitional provisions see r 6(1), Sch 4, para 1 thereto.

[4.191A Application to interested party under s 178(5)]

[(1) The following applies where, in the case of any property, application is made to the liquidator by an interested party under section 178(5).

(2) The application must be delivered to the liquidator—

(a) personally;

(b) by electronic means in accordance with Part 12A; or

(c) by any other means of delivery which enables proof of receipt of the application by the liquidator to be provided, if requested.]

NOTES

Amendment

Substituted, for r 4.191 as originally enacted, by SI 2010/686, r 2, Sch 1, para 247.

Date in force: 6 April 2010: see SI 2010/686, r 1; for transitional provisions see r 6(1), Sch 4, para 1 thereto.

4.192 Interest in property to be declared on request

(1) If, in the case of property which the liquidator has the right to disclaim, it appears to him that there is some person who claims, or may claim, to have an interest in the property, he may give notice to that person calling on him to declare within 14 days whether he claims any such interest and, if so, the nature and extent of it.

(2) Failing compliance with the notice, the liquidator is entitled to assume that the person concerned has no such interest in the property as will prevent or impede its disclaimer.

NOTES

Initial Commencement

Specified date

Specified date: 29 December 1986: see r 0.1.

See Further

See further, in relation the application of this rule, with modifications, in respect of the procedure for the appointment of a bank liquidator and the operation of bank insolvency under the Banking Act 2009, Pt 2: the Bank Insolvency (England and Wales) Rules 2009, SI 2009/356, rr 3(3)–(8), 150.

See further, in relation to the application of this rule, with modifications, in respect of bank administration and applications for bank administration: the Bank Administration (England and Wales) Rules 2009, SI 2009/357, rr 58–61.

4.193 Disclaimer presumed valid and effective

Any disclaimer of property by the liquidator is presumed valid and effective, unless it is proved that he has been in breach of his duty with respect to the giving of notice of disclaimer, or otherwise under sections 178 to 180, or under this Chapter of the Rules.

NOTES

Initial Commencement

Specified date

Specified date: 29 December 1986: see r 0.1.

See Further

See further, in relation the application of this rule, with modifications, in respect of the procedure for the appointment of a bank liquidator and the operation of bank insolvency under the Banking Act 2009, Pt 2: the Bank Insolvency (England and Wales) Rules 2009, SI 2009/356, rr 3(3)–(8), 151.

See further, in relation to the application of this rule, with modifications, in respect of bank administration and applications for bank administration: the Bank Administration (England and Wales) Rules 2009, SI 2009/357, rr 58–61.

4.194 Application for exercise of court's powers under s 181

(1) This Rule applies with respect to an application by any person under section 181 for an order of the court to vest or deliver disclaimed property.

(2) The application must be made within 3 months of the applicant becoming aware of the disclaimer, or of his receiving a copy of the liquidator's notice of disclaimer sent under Rule 4.188, whichever is the earlier.

(3) The applicant shall with his application file [a witness statement]—

(a) stating whether he applies under paragraph (a) of section 181(2) (claim of interest in the property) or under paragraph (b) (liability not discharged);

(b) specifying the date on which he received a copy of the liquidator's notice of disclaimer, or otherwise became aware of the disclaimer; and

(c) specifying the grounds of his application and the order which he desires the court to make under section 181.

(4) The court shall fix a venue for the hearing of the application; and the applicant shall, not later than [5 business] days before the date fixed, give to the liquidator notice of the venue, accompanied by copies of the application and the [witness statement required by] paragraph (3).

(5) On the hearing of the application, the court may give directions as to other persons (if any) who should be sent or given notice of the application and the grounds on which it is made.

(6) Sealed copies of any order made on the application shall be sent by the court to the applicant and the liquidator.

(7) In a case where the property disclaimed is of a leasehold nature, and section 179 applies to suspend the effect of the disclaimer, there shall be included in the court's order a direction giving effect to the disclaimer.

This paragraph does not apply if, at the time when the order is issued, other applications under section 181 are pending in respect of the same property.

NOTES

Initial Commencement

Specified date

Specified date: 29 December 1986: see r 0.1.

Amendment

Para (3): words "a witness statement" in square brackets substituted by SI 2010/686, r 2, Sch 1, para 248(1), (2).
Date in force: 6 April 2010: see SI 2010/686, r 1; for transitional provisions and further effect see rr 6(1), 7, Sch 4, paras 1, 2(1)(b), (2)–(4), Sch 5 thereto.
Para (4): words "5 business" in square brackets substituted by SI 2010/686, r 2, Sch 1, para 248(1), (3)(a).
Date in force: 6 April 2010: see SI 2010/686, r 1; for transitional provisions see r 6(1), Sch 4, para 1 thereto.
Para (4): words "witness statement required by" in square brackets substituted by SI 2010/686, r 2, Sch 1, para 248(1), (3)(b).
Date in force: 6 April 2010: see SI 2010/686, r 1; for transitional provisions and further effect see rr 6(1), 7, Sch 4, paras 1, 2(1)(b), (2)–(4), Sch 5 thereto.

See Further

See further, in relation the application of this rule, with modifications, in respect of the procedure for the appointment of a bank liquidator and the operation of bank insolvency under the Banking Act 2009, Pt 2: the Bank Insolvency (England and Wales) Rules 2009, SI 2009/356, rr 3(3)–(8), 152.
See further, in relation to the application of this rule, with modifications, in respect of bank administration and applications for bank administration: the Bank Administration (England and Wales) Rules 2009, SI 2009/357, rr 58–61.

CHAPTER 16

SETTLEMENT OF LIST OF CONTRIBUTORIES (NO CVL APPLICATION)

4.195 Preliminary

The duties of the court with regard to the settling of the list of contributories are, by virtue of the Rules, delegated to the liquidator.

NOTES

Initial Commencement

Specified date

Specified date: 29 December 1986: see r 0.1.

See Further

See further, in relation the application of this rule, with modifications, in respect of the procedure for the appointment of a bank liquidator and the operation of bank insolvency under the Banking Act 2009, Pt 2: the Bank Insolvency (England and Wales) Rules 2009, SI 2009/356, rr 3(3)–(8), 153.

4.196 Duty of liquidator to settle list

(1) Subject as follows, the liquidator shall, as soon as may be after his appointment, exercise the court's power to settle a list of the company's contributories for the purposes of section 148 and, with the court's approval, rectify the register of members.

(2) The liquidator's duties under this Rule are performed by him as an officer of the court subject to the court's control.

NOTES

Initial Commencement

Specified date

Specified date: 29 December 1986: see r 0.1.

See Further

See further, in relation the application of this rule, with modifications, in respect of the procedure for the appointment of a bank liquidator and the operation of bank insolvency under the Banking Act 2009, Pt 2: the Bank Insolvency (England and Wales) Rules 2009, SI 2009/356, rr 3(3)–(8), 155.

4.197 Form of list

(1) The list shall identify—
- (a) the several classes of the company's shares (if more than one), and
- (b) the several classes of contributories, distinguishing between those who are contributories in their own right and those who are so as representatives of, or liable for the debts of, others.

(2) In the case of each contributory there shall in the list be stated—
- (a) his address,
- (b) the number and class of shares, or the extent of any other interest to be attributed to him, and
- (c) if the shares are not fully paid up, the amounts which have been called up and paid in respect of them (and the equivalent, if any, where his interest is other than shares).

NOTES

Initial Commencement

Specified date

Specified date: 29 December 1986: see r 0.1.

See Further

See further, in relation the application of this rule, with modifications, in respect of the procedure for the appointment of a bank liquidator and the operation of bank insolvency under the Banking Act 2009, Pt 2: the Bank Insolvency (England and Wales) Rules 2009, SI 2009/356, rr 3(3)–(8), 156.

4.198 Procedure for settling list

(1) Having settled the list, the liquidator shall [as soon as reasonably practicable] give notice, to every person included in the list, that he has done so.

(2) The notice given to each person shall state—

- (a) in what character, and for what number of shares or what interest, he is included in the list,
- (b) what amounts have been called up and paid up in respect of the shares or interest, and
- (c) that in relation to any shares or interest not fully paid up, his inclusion in the list may result in the unpaid capital being called.

(3) The notice shall inform any person to whom it is given that, if he objects to any entry in, or omission from, the list, he should so inform the liquidator in writing within 21 days from the date of the notice.

(4) On receipt of any such objection, the liquidator shall within 14 days give notice to the objector either—

- (a) that he has amended the list (specifying the amendment), or
- (b) that he considers the objection to be not well-founded and declines to amend the list.

The notice shall in either case inform the objector of the effect of Rule 4.199.

NOTES

Initial Commencement

Specified date

Specified date: 29 December 1986: see r 0.1.

Amendment

Para (1): words "as soon as reasonably practicable" in square brackets substituted by SI 2009/642, rr 4, 5.

Date in force: 6 April 2009: see SI 2009/642, r 1; for transitional provisions see r 3 thereof.

See Further

See further, in relation the application of this rule, with modifications, in respect of the procedure for the appointment of a bank liquidator and the operation of bank insolvency under the Banking Act 2009, Pt 2: the Bank Insolvency (England and Wales) Rules 2009, SI 2009/356, rr 3(3)–(8), 157.

4.199 Application to court for variation of the list

(1) If a person objects to any entry in, or exclusion from, the list of contributories as settled by the liquidator and, notwithstanding notice by the liquidator declining to amend the list, maintains his objection, he may apply to the court for an order removing the entry to which he objects or (as the case may be) otherwise amending the list.

(2) The application must be made within 21 days of the service on the applicant of the liquidator's notice under Rule 4.198(4).

NOTES

Initial Commencement

Specified date

Specified date: 29 December 1986: see r 0.1.

See Further

See further, in relation the application of this rule, with modifications, in respect of the procedure for the appointment of a bank liquidator and the operation of bank insolvency under the Banking Act 2009, Pt 2: the Bank Insolvency (England and Wales) Rules 2009, SI 2009/356, rr 3(3)–(8), 158.

4.200 Variation of, or addition to, the list

The liquidator may from time to time vary or add to the list of contributories as previously settled by him, but subject in all respects to the preceding Rules in this Chapter.

NOTES

Initial Commencement

Specified date

Specified date: 29 December 1986: see r 0.1.

See Further

See further, in relation the application of this rule, with modifications, in respect of the procedure for the appointment of a bank liquidator and the operation of bank insolvency under the Banking Act 2009, Pt 2: the Bank Insolvency (England and Wales) Rules 2009, SI 2009/356, rr 3(3)–(8), 159.

4.201 Costs not to fall on official receiver

The official receiver is not personally liable for any costs incurred by a person in respect of an application to set aside or vary his act or decision in settling the list of contributories, or varying or adding to the list; and the liquidator (if other than the official receiver) is not so liable unless the court makes an order to that effect.

NOTES

Initial Commencement

Specified date

Specified date: 29 December 1986: see r 0.1.

CHAPTER 17

CALLS (NO CVL APPLICATION)

4.202 Calls by liquidator

Subject as follows, the powers conferred by the Act with respect to the making of calls on contributories are exercisable by the liquidator as an officer of the court subject to the court's control.

NOTES

Initial Commencement

Specified date

Specified date: 29 December 1986: see r 0.1.

See Further

See further, in relation the application of this rule, with modifications, in respect of the procedure for the appointment of a bank liquidator and the operation of bank insolvency under the Banking Act 2009, Pt 2: the Bank Insolvency (England and Wales) Rules 2009, SI 2009/356, rr 3(3)–(8), 161.

4.203 Control by liquidation committee

(1) Where the liquidator proposes to make a call, and there is a liquidation committee, he may summon a meeting of the committee for the purpose of obtaining its sanction.

(2) At least [5 business] days' notice of the meeting shall be given by the liquidator to each member of the committee.

(3) The notice shall contain a statement of the proposed amount of the call, and the purpose for which it is intended to be made.

NOTES

Initial Commencement

Specified date

Specified date: 29 December 1986: see r 0.1.

Amendment

Para (2): words "5 business" in square brackets substituted by SI 2010/686, r 2, Sch 1, para 249.
Date in force: 6 April 2010: see SI 2010/686, r 1; for transitional provisions see r 6(1), Sch 4, para 1 thereto.

See Further

See further, in relation the application of this rule, with modifications, in respect of the procedure for the appointment of a bank liquidator and the operation of bank insolvency under the Banking Act 2009, Pt 2: the Bank Insolvency (England and Wales) Rules 2009, SI 2009/356, rr 3(3)–(8), 162.

4.204 Application to court for [permission] to make a call

(1) For the purpose of obtaining the [permission] of the court for the making of a call on any contributories of the company, the liquidator shall apply [without notice to any other party], supporting his application by [witness statement].

(2) There shall in the application be stated the amount of the proposed call, and the contributories on whom it is to be made.

(3) The court may direct that notice of the order be given to the contributories concerned, or to other contributories, or may direct that the notice be publicly advertised.

NOTES

Initial Commencement

Specified date

Specified date: 29 December 1986: see r 0.1.

Amendment

Provision heading: word "permission" in square brackets substituted by SI 2010/686, r 2, Sch 1, para 1.
Date in force: 6 April 2010: see SI 2010/686, r 1; for transitional provisions see r 6(1), Sch 4, paras 1, 2(1)(b) thereto.
Para (1): word "permission" in square brackets substituted by SI 2010/686, r 2, Sch 1, para 1.
Date in force: 6 April 2010: see SI 2010/686, r 1; for transitional provisions see r 6(1), Sch 4, paras 1, 2(1)(b) thereto.
Para (1): words "without notice to any other party" in square brackets substituted by SI 2010/686, r 2, Sch 1, para 250(1), (2)(a).
Date in force: 6 April 2010: see SI 2010/686, r 1; for transitional provisions see r 6(1), Sch 4, paras 1, 2(1)(b) thereto.
Para (1): words "witness statement" in square brackets substituted by SI 2010/686, r 2, Sch 1, para 250(1), (2)(b).
Date in force: 6 April 2010: see SI 2010/686, r 1; for transitional provisions and further effect see rr 6(1), 7, Sch 4, paras 1, 2(1)(b), (2)–(4), Sch 5 thereto.

See Further

See further, in relation the application of this rule, with modifications, in respect of the procedure for the appointment of a bank liquidator and the operation of bank insolvency under the Banking Act 2009, Pt 2: the Bank Insolvency (England and Wales) Rules 2009, SI 2009/356, rr 3(3)–(8), 163.

4.205 Making and enforcement of the call

(1) Notice of the call shall be given to each of the contributories concerned, and shall specify—

(a) the amount or balance due from him in respect of it, and

(b) whether the call is made with the sanction of the court or the liquidation committee.

(2) Payment of the amount due from any contributory may be enforced by order of the court.

NOTES

Initial Commencement

Specified date

Specified date: 29 December 1986: see r 0.1.

See Further

See further, in relation the application of this rule, with modifications, in respect of the procedure for the appointment of a bank liquidator and the operation of bank insolvency under the Banking Act 2009, Pt 2: the Bank Insolvency (England and Wales) Rules 2009, SI 2009/356, rr 3(3)–(8), 164.

CHAPTER 18

SPECIAL MANAGER

4.206 Appointment and remuneration

(1) An application made by the liquidator under section 177 for the appointment of a person to be special manager shall be supported by a report setting out the reasons for the application.

The report shall include the applicant's estimate of the value of the [business or property] in respect of which the special manager is to be appointed.

(2) This Chapter applies also with respect to an application by the provisional liquidator, where one has been appointed, and references to the liquidator are to be read accordingly as including the provisional liquidator. (NO CVL APPLICATION)

(3) The court's order appointing the special manager shall specify the duration of his appointment, which may be for a period of time, or until the occurrence of a specified event. Alternatively, the order may specify that the duration of the appointment is to be subject to a further order of the court.

(4) The appointment of a special manager may be renewed by order of the court.

(5) The special manager's remuneration shall be fixed from time to time by the court.

(6) The acts of the special manager are valid notwithstanding any defect in his appointment or qualifications.

NOTES

Initial Commencement

Specified date

Specified date: 29 December 1986: see r 0.1.

Amendment

Para (1): words "business or property" in square brackets substituted by SI 2010/686, r 2, Sch 1, para 251(1), (2)(a).

Date in force: 6 April 2010: see SI 2010/686, r 1; for transitional provisions see r 6(1), Sch 4, para 1 thereto.

See Further

See further, in relation the application of this rule, with modifications, in respect of the procedure for the appointment of a bank liquidator and the operation of bank insolvency under the Banking Act 2009, Pt 2: the Bank Insolvency (England and Wales) Rules 2009, SI 2009/356, rr 3(3)–(8), 165.

4.207 Security

(1) The appointment of the special manager does not take effect until the person appointed has given (or, being allowed by the court to do so, undertaken to give) security to the person who applies for him to be appointed.

(2) It is not necessary that security shall be given for each separate company liquidation; but it may be given either specially for a particular liquidation, or generally for any liquidation in relation to which the special manager may be employed as such.

(3) The amount of the security shall be not less than the value of the [business or property] in respect of which he is appointed, as estimated by the applicant in his report under Rule 4.206.

(4) When the special manager has given security to the person applying for his appointment, that person shall file in court a certificate as to the adequacy of the security.

(5) The cost of providing the security shall be paid in the first instance by the special manager; but—

(a) where a winding-up order is not made, he is entitled to be reimbursed out of the property of the company, and the court may make an order on the company accordingly, and

(b) where a winding-up order is made, he is entitled to be reimbursed [as an expense of the liquidation] in the prescribed order of priority.

(NO CVL APPLICATION)

(6-CVL) The cost of providing the security shall be paid in the first instance by the special manager; but he is entitled to be reimbursed [as an expense of the liquidation], in the prescribed order of priority.

NOTES

Initial Commencement

Specified date

Specified date: 29 December 1986: see r 0.1.

Amendment

Para (3): words "business or property" in square brackets substituted by SI 2010/686, r 2, Sch 1, para 251(1), (2)(b).
Date in force: 6 April 2010: see SI 2010/686, r 1; for transitional provisions see r 6(1), Sch 4, para 1 thereto.
Para (5): in sub-para (b) words "as an expense of the liquidation" in square brackets substituted by SI 2008/737, rr 3, 7(1).
Date in force: 6 April 2008: see SI 2008/737, r 1(1); for transitional provisions see r 2 thereof.
Para (6): words "as an expense of the liquidation" in square brackets substituted by SI 2008/737, rr 3, 7(1).
Date in force: 6 April 2008: see SI 2008/737, r 1(1); for transitional provisions see r 2 thereof.

See Further

See further, in relation the application of this rule, with modifications, in respect of the procedure for the appointment of a bank liquidator and the operation of bank insolvency under the Banking Act 2009, Pt 2: the Bank Insolvency (England and Wales) Rules 2009, SI 2009/356, rr 3(3)–(8), 166.

4.208 Failure to give or keep up security

(1) If the special manager fails to give the required security within the time stated for that purpose by the order appointing him, or any extension of that time that may be allowed, the liquidator shall report the failure to the court, which may thereupon discharge the order appointing the special manager.

(2) If the special manager fails to keep up his security, the liquidator shall report his failure to the court, which may thereupon remove the special manager, and make such order as it thinks [just] as to costs.

(3) If an order is made under this Rule removing the special manager, or discharging the order appointing him, the court shall give directions as to whether any, and if so what, steps should be taken for the appointment of another special manager in his place.

NOTES

Initial Commencement

Specified date

Specified date: 29 December 1986: see r 0.1.

Amendment

Para (2): word "just" in square brackets substituted by SI 2010/686, r 2, Sch 1, para 1.
Date in force: 6 April 2010: see SI 2010/686, r 1; for transitional provisions see r 6(1), Sch 4, paras 1, 2(1)(b) thereto.

See Further

See further, in relation the application of this rule, with modifications, in respect of the procedure for the appointment of a bank liquidator and the operation of bank insolvency under the Banking Act 2009, Pt 2: the Bank Insolvency (England and Wales) Rules 2009, SI 2009/356, rr 3(3)–(8), 167.

4.209 Accounting

(1) The special manager shall produce accounts, containing details of his receipts and payments, for the approval of the liquidator.

(2) The accounts shall be in respect of 3-month periods for the duration of the special manager's appointment (or for a lesser period, if his appointment terminates less than 3 months from its date, or from the date to which the last accounts were made up).

(3) When the accounts have been approved, the special manager's receipts and payments shall be added to those of the liquidator.

NOTES

Initial Commencement

Specified date

Specified date: 29 December 1986: see r 0.1.

See Further

See further, in relation the application of this rule, with modifications, in respect of the procedure for the appointment of a bank liquidator and the operation of bank insolvency under the Banking Act 2009, Pt 2: the Bank Insolvency (England and Wales) Rules 2009, SI 2009/356, rr 3(3)–(8), 168.

4.210 Termination of appointment

(1) The special manager's appointment terminates if the winding-up petition is dismissed or if, a provisional liquidator having been appointed, the latter is discharged without a winding-up order having been made. (NO CVL APPLICATION)

(2) If the liquidator is of opinion that the employment of the special manager is no longer necessary or profitable for the company, he shall apply to the court for directions, and the court may order the special manager's appointment to be terminated.

(3) The liquidator shall make the same application if a resolution of the creditors is passed, requesting that the appointment be terminated.

NOTES

Initial Commencement

Specified date

Specified date: 29 December 1986: see r 0.1.

See Further

See further, in relation the application of this rule, with modifications, in respect of the procedure for the appointment of a bank liquidator and the operation of bank insolvency under the Banking Act 2009, Pt 2: the Bank Insolvency (England and Wales) Rules 2009, SI 2009/356, rr 3(3)–(8), 169.

CHAPTER 19

PUBLIC EXAMINATION OF COMPANY OFFICERS AND OTHERS

4.211 Order for public examination

(1) If the official receiver applies to the court under section 133 for the public examination of any person, a copy of the court's order shall, [as soon as reasonably practicable] after its making, be served on that person.

(2) Where the application relates to a person falling within section 133(1)(c) (promoters, past managers, etc), it shall be accompanied by a report by the official receiver indicating—
- (a) the grounds on which the person is supposed to fall within that paragraph, and
- (b) whether, in the official receiver's opinion, it is likely that service of the order on the person can be effected . . . at a known address [in accordance with Chapter 3 of Part 12A, (service of court documents), and, if so, by what means].

(3) If in his report the official receiver gives it as his opinion that, in a case to which paragraph (2) applies, there is no reasonable certainty that service [at a known address in accordance with Chapter 3 of Part 12A] will be effective, the court may direct that the order be served by some means other than, or in [addition to, service in such manner].

(4) In a case to which paragraphs (2) and (3) apply, the court shall rescind the order if satisfied by the person to whom it is directed that he does not fall within section 133(1)(c).

NOTES

Initial Commencement

Specified date

Specified date: 29 December 1986: see r 0.1.

Amendment

Para (1): words "as soon as reasonably practicable" in square brackets substituted by SI 2009/642, rr 4, 5.
Date in force: 6 April 2009: see SI 2009/642, r 1; for transitional provisions see r 3 thereof.
Para (2): in sub-para (b) words omitted revoked by r 2, SI 2010/686, Sch 1, para 252(1), (2)(a).
Date in force: 6 April 2010: see SI 2010/686, r 1; for transitional provisions see r 6(1), Sch 4, para 1 thereto.
Para (2): in sub-para (b) words from "in accordance with" to "by what means" in square brackets inserted by SI 2010/686, r 2, Sch 1, para 252(1), (2)(b).
Date in force: 6 April 2010: see SI 2010/686, r 1; for transitional provisions see r 6(1), Sch 4, para 1 thereto.
Para (3): words "at a known address in accordance with Chapter 3 of Part 12A" in square brackets substituted by SI 2010/686, r 2, Sch 1, para 252(1), (3)(a).
Date in force: 6 April 2010: see SI 2010/686, r 1; for transitional provisions see r 6(1), Sch 4, para 1 thereto.
Para (3): words "addition to, service in such manner" in square brackets substituted by SI 2010/686, r 2, Sch 1, para 252(1), (3)(b).
Date in force: 6 April 2010: see SI 2010/686, r 1; for transitional provisions see r 6(1), Sch 4, para 1 thereto.

4.212 Notice of hearing

(1) The court's order shall appoint a venue for the examination of the person to whom it is directed ("the examinee"), and direct his attendance thereat.

(2) The official receiver shall give at least 14 days' notice of the hearing—
- (a) if a liquidator has been nominated or appointed, to him;
- (b) if a special manager has been appointed, to him; and
- (c) subject to any contrary direction of the court, to every creditor and contributory of the company who is known to the official receiver . . ..

[(3) Subject to paragraph (4), where the official receiver thinks fit, notice of the order—
- (a) shall be gazetted; and

(b) may be advertised in such other manner as the official receiver thinks fit, not less than 14 days before the date fixed for the hearing.]

[(3A) In addition to the standard contents, the notice under paragraph (3) must state—
(a) the purpose of the hearing; and
(b) the venue for the hearing.]

[(4) [Where the court's order relates to a person falling within section 133(1)(c),] unless the court otherwise directs, there shall be no publication under paragraph (3) before at least [5 business] days have elapsed since the examinee was served with the order.]

NOTES

Initial Commencement

Specified date

Specified date: 29 December 1986: see r 0.1.

Amendment

Para (2): in sub-para (c) words omitted revoked by SI 2010/686, r 2, Sch 1, para 253(1), (2).
Date in force: 6 April 2010: see SI 2010/686, r 1; for transitional provisions see r 6(1), Sch 4, para 1 thereto.

Para (3): substituted by SI 2009/642, rr 4, 30(a).
Date in force: 6 April 2009: see SI 2009/642, r 1; for transitional provisions see r 3 thereof.

Para (3A): inserted by SI 2010/686, r 2, Sch 1, para 253(1), (3).
Date in force: 6 April 2010: see SI 2010/686, r 1; for transitional provisions see r 6(1), Sch 4, para 1 thereto.

Para (4): inserted by SI 2009/642, rr 4, 30(b).
Date in force: 6 April 2009: see SI 2009/642, r 1; for transitional provisions see r 3 thereof.

Para (4): words "Where the court's order relates to a person falling within section 133(1)(c)," n square brackets inserted by SI 2010/686, r 2, Sch 1, para 253(1), (4)(a).
Date in force: 6 April 2010: see SI 2010/686, r 1; for transitional provisions see r 6(1), Sch 4, para 1 thereto.

Para (4): words "5 business" in square brackets substituted by SI 2010/686, r 2, Sch 1, para 253(1), (4)(b).
Date in force: 6 April 2010: see SI 2010/686, r 1; for transitional provisions see r 6(1), Sch 4, para 1 thereto.

4.213 Order on request by creditors or contributories

(1) A request to the official receiver by creditors or contributories under section 133(2) shall be made in writing and be accompanied by—
(a) a list of the creditors concurring with the request and the amounts of their respective claims in the liquidation or (as the case may be) of the contributories so concurring, with their respective values, and
(b) from each creditor or contributory concurring, written confirmation of his concurrence.

This paragraph does not apply if the requisitioning creditor's debt or, as the case may be, requisitioning contributory's shareholding is alone sufficient, without the concurrence of others.

(2) The request must specify the name of the proposed examinee, the relationship which he has, or has had, to the company [a statement of] and the reasons why his examination is requested.

(3) Before an application to the court is made on the request, the requisitionists shall deposit with the official receiver such sum as the latter may determine to be appropriate by way of security for the expenses of the hearing of a public examination, if ordered.

(4) Subject as follows, the official receiver shall, within 28 days of receiving the request, make the application to the court required by section 133(2).

(5) If the official receiver is of opinion that the request is an unreasonable one in the circumstances, he may apply to the court for an order relieving him from the obligation to make the application otherwise required by that subsection.

(6) If the court so orders, and the application for the order was made [without notice to any other party], notice of the order shall be given [as soon as reasonably practicable] by the official receiver to the requisitionists. If the application for an order is dismissed, the official receiver's application under section 133(2) shall be made [as soon as reasonably practicable] on conclusion of the hearing of the application first mentioned.

NOTES

Initial Commencement

Specified date

Specified date: 29 December 1986: see r 0.1.

Amendment

Para (2): words "a statement of" in square brackets inserted by SI 2010/686, r 2, Sch 1, para 254(1), (2).
Date in force: 6 April 2010: see SI 2010/686, r 1; for transitional provisions see r 6(1), Sch 4, para 1 thereto.
Para (6): words "without notice to any other party" in square brackets substituted by SI 2010/686, r 2, Sch 1, para 254(1), (3).
Date in force: 6 April 2010: see SI 2010/686, r 1; for transitional provisions see r 6(1), Sch 4, paras 1, 2(1)(b) thereto.
Para (6): words "as soon as reasonably practicable" in square brackets in both places they occur substituted by SI 2009/642, rr 4, 5.
Date in force: 6 April 2009: see SI 2009/642, r 1; for transitional provisions see r 3 thereof.

4.214 [Examinee] unfit for examination

(1) Where the examinee [is a person who lacks capacity within the meaning of the Mental Capacity Act 2005 (c 9) or] is suffering from any . . . physical affliction or disability rendering him unfit to undergo or attend for public examination, the court may, on [an application being made to it under this Rule], either stay the order for his public examination or direct that it shall be conducted in such manner and at such place as it thinks [just].

(2) Application under this Rule shall be made—
- (a) by a person who has been appointed by a court in the United Kingdom or elsewhere to manage the affairs of, or to represent, the examinee, or
- (b) by a relative or friend of the examinee whom the court considers to be a proper person to make the application, or
- (c) by the official receiver.

(3) Where the application is made by a person other than the official receiver, then—
- (a) it shall, unless the examinee is a [person who lacks capacity within the meaning of the Mental Capacity Act 2005], be supported by the [witness statement] of a registered medical practitioner as to the examinee's mental and physical condition;
- (b) at least 7 days' notice of the application shall be given to the official receiver and the liquidator (if other than the official receiver); and
- (c) before any order is made on the application, the applicant shall deposit with the official receiver such sum as the latter certifies to be necessary

for the additional expenses of any examination that may be ordered on the application.

An order made on the application may provide that the expenses of the examination are to be payable, as to a specified proportion, out of the deposit under sub-paragraph (c), instead of [as an expense of the liquidation].

(4) Where the application is made by the official receiver it may be made [without notice to any other party], and may be supported by evidence in the form of a report by the official receiver to the court.

NOTES

Initial Commencement

Specified date

Specified date: 29 December 1986: see r 0.1.

Amendment

Provision heading: word "Examinee" in square brackets substituted by SI 2010/686, r 2, Sch 1, para 255(1), (2).
Date in force: 6 April 2010: see SI 2010/686, r 1; for transitional provisions see r 6(1), Sch 4, para 1 thereto.

Para (1): words "is a person who lacks capacity within the meaning of the Mental Capacity Act 2005 (c 9) or" in square brackets inserted by SI 2007/1898, art 6, Sch 1, para 12(1), (2)(a)(ii).
Date in force: 1 October 2007: see SI 2007/1898, art 1.

Para (1): words omitted revoked by SI 2007/1898, art 6, Sch 1, para 12(1), (2)(a)(i).
Date in force: 1 October 2007: see SI 2007/1898, art 1.

Para (1): words "an application being made to it under this Rule" in square brackets substituted by SI 2010/686, r 2, Sch 1, para 255(1), (3).
Date in force: 6 April 2010: see SI 2010/686, r 1; for transitional provisions see r 6(1), Sch 4, para 1 thereto.

Para (1): word "just" in square brackets substituted by SI 2010/686, r 2, Sch 1, para 1.
Date in force: 6 April 2010: see SI 2010/686, r 1; for transitional provisions see r 6(1), Sch 4, paras 1, 2(1)(b) thereto.

Para (3): in sub-para (a) words "person who lacks capacity within the meaning of the Mental Capacity Act 2005" in square brackets substituted by SI 2007/1898, art 6, Sch 1, para 12(1), (2)(b).
Date in force: 1 October 2007: see SI 2007/1898, art 1.

Para (3): in sub-para (a) words "witness statement" in square brackets substituted by SI 2010/686, r 2, Sch 1, para 255(1), (4).
Date in force: 6 April 2010: see SI 2010/686, r 1; for transitional provisions and further effect see rr 6(1), 7, Sch 4, paras 1, 2(1)(b), (2)–(4), Sch 5 thereto.

Para (3): words "as an expense of the liquidation" in square brackets substituted by SI 2008/737, rr 3, 7(1).
Date in force: 6 April 2008: see SI 2008/737, r 1(1); for transitional provisions see r 2 thereof.

Para (4): words "without notice to any other party" in square brackets substituted by SI 2010/686, r 2, Sch 1, para 255(1), (5).
Date in force: 6 April 2010: see SI 2010/686, r 1; for transitional provisions see r 6(1), Sch 4, paras 1, 2(1)(b) thereto.

4.215 Procedure at hearing

(1) The examinee shall at the hearing be examined on oath; and he shall answer all such questions as the court may put, or allow to be put, to him.

(2) Any of the persons allowed by section 133(4) to question the examinee may, with the approval of the court (made known either at the hearing or in advance of it), appear by solicitor or counsel; or he may in writing authorise another person to question the examinee on his behalf.

(3) The examinee may at his own expense employ a solicitor with or without counsel, who may put to him such questions as the court may allow for the purpose of enabling him to explain or qualify any answers given by him, and may make representations on his behalf.

(4) There shall be made in writing such record of the examination as the court thinks proper. The record shall be read over either to or by the examinee, [authenticated] by him, and verified by [a statement of truth] at a venue fixed by the court.

(5) The written record may, in any proceedings (whether under the Act or otherwise) be used as evidence against the examinee of any statement made by him in the course of his public examination.

(6) If criminal proceedings have been instituted against the examinee, and the court is of opinion that the continuance of the hearing would be calculated to prejudice a fair trial of those proceedings, the hearing may be adjourned.

NOTES

Initial Commencement

Specified date

Specified date: 29 December 1986: see r 0.1.

Amendment

Para (4): word "authenticated" in square brackets substituted by SI 2010/686, r 2, Sch 1, para 1.
Date in force: 6 April 2010: see SI 2010/686, r 1; for transitional provisions see r 6(1), Sch 4, paras 1, 2(1)(b) thereto.
Para (4): words "a statement of truth" in square brackets substituted by SI 2010/686, r 2, Sch 1, para 256.
Date in force: 6 April 2010: see SI 2010/686, r 1; for transitional provisions see r 6(1), Sch 4, paras 1, 2(1)(b) thereto.

4.216 Adjournment

(1) The public examination may be adjourned by the court from time to time, either to a fixed date or generally.

(2) Where the examination has been adjourned generally, the court may at any time on the application of the official receiver or of the examinee—

(a) fix a venue for the resumption of the examination, and
(b) give directions as to the manner in which, and the time within which, notice of the resumed public examination is to be given to persons entitled to take part in it.

(3) Where application under paragraph (2) is made by the examinee, the court may grant it on terms that the expenses of giving the notices required by that paragraph shall be paid by him and that, before a venue for the resumed public examination is fixed, he shall deposit with the official receiver such sum as the latter considers necessary to cover those expenses.

NOTES

Initial Commencement

Specified date

Specified date: 29 December 1986: see r 0.1.

4.217 Expenses of examination

(1) Where a public examination of the examinee has been ordered by the court on a creditors' or contributories' requisition under Rule 4.213, the court may order that the expenses of the examination are to be paid, as to a specified proportion, out of the deposit under Rule 4.213(3), instead of [as an expense of the liquidation].

(2) In no case do the costs and expenses of a public examination fall on the official receiver personally.

NOTES

Initial Commencement

Specified date
   Specified date: 29 December 1986: see r 0.1.

Amendment
   Para (1): words "as an expense of the liquidation" in square brackets substituted by SI 2008/737, rr 3, 7(1).
      Date in force: 6 April 2008: see SI 2008/737, r 1(1); for transitional provisions see r 2 thereof.

CHAPTER 20

ORDER OF PAYMENT OF COSTS, ETC, OUT OF ASSETS

4.218 General rule as to priority

(1) [All fees, costs, charges and other expenses incurred in the course of the liquidation are to be regarded as expenses of the liquidation.

(2) The expenses of the liquidation are payable out of—
   (a) assets of the company available for the payment of general creditors, which shall be taken to include proceeds—
      (i) of any legal action which the liquidator has power to bring in his own name or in the name of the company, or
      (ii) arising from any award made under any arbitration or other dispute resolution procedure which the liquidator has power to bring in his own name or in the name of the company,
   which shall, for the purposes of this subparagraph, also include—
      (iii) any payments made under any compromise or other agreement intended to avoid legal action or recourse to arbitration or to any other dispute resolution procedure, and
      (iv) payments made as a result of a settlement of any such action, arrangement or procedure in lieu of or prior to any judgment being given or award being made;
   (b) subject as provided in Rules 4.218A to 4.218E, property comprised in or subject to a floating charge created by the company.

(3) Subject as provided in Rules 4.218A to 4.218E, the expenses are payable in the following order of priority—
   (a) expenses which—
      (i) are properly chargeable or incurred by the provisional liquidator in carrying out the functions conferred on him by the court;
      (ii) are properly chargeable or incurred by the official receiver or the liquidator in preserving, realising or getting in any of the assets of the company or otherwise in the preparation or conduct of any legal proceedings, arbitration or other dispute resolution procedures, which he has power to bring in his own name or bring or defend in the name of the company or in the preparation or

conduct of any negotiations intended to lead or leading to a settlement or compromise of any legal action or dispute to which the proceedings or procedures relate;

(iii) relate to the employment of a shorthand writer, if appointed by an order of the court made at the instance of the official receiver in connection with an examination; or

(iv) are incurred in holding an examination under Rule 4.214 (examinee unfit) where the application for it was made by the official receiver;]

(b) any other expenses incurred or disbursements made by the official receiver or under his authority, including those incurred or made in carrying on the business of the company;

[(c) the fees payable under any order made under section 414 [or section 415A], including those payable to the official receiver (other than the fee referred to in sub-paragraph (d)(i) below), and any remuneration payable to him under general regulations;

(d)

(i) the fee payable under any order made under section 414 for the performance by the official receiver of his general duties as official receiver;

(ii) any repayable deposit lodged under any such order as security for the fee mentioned in sub-paragraph (i);]

(e) the cost of any security provided by a provisional liquidator, liquidator or special manager in accordance with the Act or the Rules;

(f) the remuneration of the provisional liquidator (if any);

(g) any deposit lodged on an application for the appointment of a provisional liquidator;

(h) the costs of the petitioner, and of any person appearing on the petition whose costs are allowed by the court;

(j) the remuneration of the special manager (if any);

(k) any amount payable to a person employed or authorised, under Chapter 6 of this Part of the Rules, to assist in the preparation of a statement of affairs or of accounts;

(l) any allowance made, by order of the court, towards costs on an application for release from the obligation to submit a statement of affairs, or for an extension of time for submitting such a statement;

[(la) the costs of employing a shorthand writer in any case other than one appointed by an order of the court at the instance of the official receiver in connection with an examination;]

(m) any necessary disbursements by the liquidator in the course of his administration (including any expenses incurred by members of the liquidation committee or their representatives and allowed by the liquidator under Rule 4.169, but not including any payment of [corporation] tax in circumstances referred to in sub-paragraph (p) below);

(n) the remuneration or emoluments of any person who has been employed by the liquidator to perform any services for the company, as required or authorised by or under the Act or the Rules;

(o) the remuneration of the liquidator, up to any amount not exceeding that which is payable [under Schedule 6];

(p) the amount of any [corporation] tax on chargeable gains accruing on the realisation of any asset of the company (without regard to whether the realisation is effected by the liquidator, a secured creditor, or a receiver or manager appointed to deal with a security);

(q)   the balance, after payment of any sums due under sub-paragraph (o) above, of any remuneration due to the liquidator[;
(r)   any other expenses properly chargeable by the liquidator in carrying out his functions in the liquidation].

(2) ...
(3) ...

NOTES

Initial Commencement

Specified date

Specified date: 29 December 1986: see r 0.1.

Amendment

Paras (1)–(3): words from "All fees, costs," to "the official receiver;" in square brackets substituted, for para (1) as originally enacted, by SI 2008/737, rr 3, 4.
   Date in force: 6 April 2008: see SI 2008/737, r 1(1); for transitional provisions see r 2 thereof.

Para (3): sub-paras (c), (d) substituted by SI 1995/586, r 3, Schedule.

Para (3): in sub-para (c) words "or section 415A" in square brackets inserted by SI 2004/584, r 22.
   Date in force: 1 April 2004: see SI 2004/584, r 1(2).

Para (3): sub-para (la) inserted by SI 2002/2712, r 4(1), Schedule, Pt 2, para 23(b).
   Date in force: 1 January 2003: see SI 2002/2712, r 1(1); for effect see rr 1(2), 4(2) thereof.

Para (3): in sub-para (m) word "corporation" in square brackets substituted by SI 1987/1919, r 3(1), Schedule, Pt 1, para 79.

Para (3): in sub-para (o) words "under Schedule 6" in square brackets substituted by SI 2005/527, r 32.
   Date in force: this amendment shall apply in any case where, on or after 1 April 2004, a winding-up order has been made or a resolution for the winding up of a company has been passed or a bankruptcy order has been made, before 1 April 2005: see SI 2005/527, rr 1(2), 3(2).

Para (3): in sub-para (p) word "corporation" in square brackets substituted by SI 1987/1919, r 3(1), Schedule, Pt 1, para 79.

Para (3): sub-para (r) inserted by SI 2002/2712, r 4(1), Schedule, Pt 2, para 23(c).
   Date in force: 1 January 2003: see SI 2002/2712, r 1(1); for effect see rr 1(2), 4(2) thereof.

Paras (2), (3) (as originally enacted): revoked by SI 2002/2712, r 4(1), Schedule, Pt 2, para 23(d).
   Date in force: 1 January 2003: see SI 2002/2712, r 1(1); for effect see rr 1(2), 4(2) thereof.

See Further

See further, in relation the application of this rule, with modifications, in respect of the procedure for the appointment of a bank liquidator and the operation of bank insolvency under the Banking Act 2009, Pt 2: the Bank Insolvency (England and Wales) Rules 2009, SI 2009/356, rr 3(3)–(8), 170.

[4.218A Litigation expenses and property subject to a floating charge—general provisions]

[(1)   In this Rule and Rules 4.218B to 4.218E—
   (a)   "approval" and "authorisation" respectively mean:
      (i)   where yet to be incurred, the approval, and
      (ii) where already incurred, the authorisation,
   of expenses specified in section 176ZA(3);

(b) "the creditor" means—
  (i) a preferential creditor of the company, or
  (ii) a holder of a debenture secured by, or a holder of, a floating charge created by the company;
(c) "legal proceedings" means—
  (i) proceedings under sections 212, 213, 214, 238, 239, 244 and 423 and any arbitration or other dispute resolution proceedings invoked for purposes corresponding to those to which the sections relate and any other proceedings, including arbitration or other dispute resolution procedures, which a liquidator has power to bring in his own name for the purpose of preserving, realising, or getting in any of the assets of the company;
  (ii) legal actions and proceedings, arbitration or any other dispute resolution procedures which a liquidator has power to bring or defend in the name of the company, and
  (iii) negotiations intended to lead or leading to a settlement or compromise of any action, proceeding or procedure to which subparagraphs (i) or (ii) relate;
(d) "litigation expenses" means expenses of a liquidation which—
  (i) are properly chargeable or incurred in the preparation or conduct of any legal proceedings, and
  (ii) as expenses in the liquidation, exceed, or in the opinion of the liquidator are likely to exceed (and only in so far as they exceed or are likely to exceed), in the aggregate £5000.

(2) Litigation expenses shall not have the priority provided by section 176ZA over any claims to property comprised in or subject to a floating charge created by the company and shall not be paid out of any such property unless and until approved or authorised in accordance with Rules 4.218B to 4.218E.]

NOTES

Amendment

Inserted by SI 2008/737, rr 3, 5.
Date in force: 6 April 2008: see SI 2008/737, r 1(1); for transitional provisions see r 2 thereof.

See Further

See further, in relation the application of this rule, with modifications, in respect of the procedure for the appointment of a bank liquidator and the operation of bank insolvency under the Banking Act 2009, Pt 2: the Bank Insolvency (England and Wales) Rules 2009, SI 2009/356, rr 3(3)–(8), 171.

[4.218B Litigation expenses and property subject to a floating charge—requirement for approval or authorisation]

[(1) Subject to Rules 4.218C to 4.218E, paragraphs (2) and (3) or (4) apply where, in the course of winding up a company, the liquidator—
  (a) ascertains that property is comprised in or subject to a floating charge;
  (b) has himself instituted or proposes to institute or continue legal proceedings or is in the process of defending or proposes to defend any legal proceeding brought or likely to be brought against the company; and
  (c) prior to or at any stage in those proceedings, is of the opinion that—
    (i) the assets of the company available for payment of general creditors are or will be insufficient to pay litigation expenses; and

(ii) in order to pay litigation expenses he will have to have recourse to property comprised in or subject to a floating charge created by the company.

(2) As soon as reasonably practicable after the date on which he forms the opinion referred to in paragraph (1), the liquidator shall identify the creditor who, in his opinion at that time—

(a) has a claim to property comprised in or subject to a floating charge created by the company, and,

(b) taking into account the value of that claim and any subsisting property then comprised in or secured by such a charge, appears to the liquidator to be the creditor most immediately likely of any persons having such claims to receive some payment in respect of his claim but whose claim would not be paid in full ("the specified creditor").

(3) The liquidator shall request from the specified creditor the approval or authorisation of such amount for litigation expenses as the liquidator thinks fit.

(4) Where, in the liquidator's opinion, two or more creditors who are holders of debentures secured by, or holders of, floating charges created by the company, meet the condition in paragraph (2), the liquidator is to seek from each of them ("the specified creditors") approval or authorisation of such amount of litigation expenses as the liquidator thinks fit, apportioned between them ("the apportioned amount") according to the value of the property to the extent covered by their charges.

(5) For so long as the conditions specified in paragraph (1) subsist, the liquidator may, in the course of a winding up, make such further requests to the specified creditor or creditors for approval or authorisation of such further amount for litigation expenses as he thinks fit to be paid out of property comprised in or subject to a floating charge created by the company, taking into account any amount for litigation expenses previously approved or authorised and the value of the property comprised in or subject to the floating charge.]

NOTES

Amendment

Inserted by SI 2008/737, rr 3, 5.
Date in force: 6 April 2008: see SI 2008/737, r 1(1); for transitional provisions see r 2 thereof.

See Further

See further, in relation the application of this rule, with modifications, in respect of the procedure for the appointment of a bank liquidator and the operation of bank insolvency under the Banking Act 2009, Pt 2: the Bank Insolvency (England and Wales) Rules 2009, SI 2009/356, rr 3(3)–(8), 172.

[4.218C Litigation expenses and property subject to a floating charge—request for approval or authorisation]

[(1) All requests made by the liquidator for approval or authorisation shall be in writing whether in Form 4.74 or otherwise, and shall include the following—

(a) a statement describing the nature of the legal proceedings, including, where relevant, the statutory provision under which proceedings are or are to be brought and the grounds upon which the liquidator relies;

(b) where the power to bring those proceedings is subject to sanction, a statement that the liquidator has sought and been given the relevant permissions or an undertaking that the liquidator will seek the relevant permissions upon authorisation or approval being granted;

(c) a statement specifying the amount or apportioned amount of litigation expenses for which approval or authorisation is sought ("the specified amount");

(d) notice that approval or authorisation or other reply to the request must be made in writing (whether by way of Form 4.74 or otherwise) within 28 days from the date of its being received ("the specified time limit"); and

(e) a statement explaining the consequences of a failure to reply within the specified time limit.

(2) Where anything in paragraph (1) requires the inclusion of any information, the disclosure of which could be seriously prejudicial to the winding up of the company, the liquidator may—

(a) exclude such information from any of the above, provided that it is accompanied by a statement to that effect; or

(b) include it on terms—
  (i) that bind the creditor to keep the information confidential, and
  (ii) that include an undertaking on the part of the liquidator to apply to the court for an order that so much of the information as may be kept in the files of the court, not be open to public inspection.

(3) The creditor may within the specified time limit apply to the liquidator in writing for such further particulars as is reasonable and in such a case, the time limit specified in paragraph (1)(d) shall apply from the date of the creditor's receipt of the liquidator's response to any such request.

(4) Where the liquidator requires the approval or authorisation of two or more creditors, he shall send a request to each creditor in writing (whether by way of Form 4.74 or otherwise), containing the matters listed in paragraph (1) and also giving—

(a) the number of creditors concerned,

(b) the total value of their claims, or if not known, as it is estimated to be by the liquidator immediately prior to sending any such request, and

(c) to each preferential creditor, notice that approval or authorisation of the specified amount shall be taken to be given where a majority in value of those preferential creditors who respond within the specified time limit are in favour of it, or

(d) where Rule 4.218B(4) applies, notice to the specified creditors that the amount of litigation expenses will be apportioned between them in accordance with that rule and notice of the value of the portion allocated to, and the identity of, the specified creditors affected by that apportionment.]

NOTES

Amendment
    Inserted by SI 2008/737, rr 3, 5.
        Date in force: 6 April 2008: see SI 2008/737, r 1(1); for transitional provisions see r 2 thereof.

See Further
    See further, in relation the application of this rule, with modifications, in respect of the procedure for the appointment of a bank liquidator and the operation of bank insolvency under the Banking Act 2009, Pt 2: the Bank Insolvency (England and Wales) Rules 2009, SI 2009/356, rr 3(3)–(8), 173.

[4.218D Litigation expenses and property subject to a floating charge—grant of approval or authorisation]

[(1) Where the liquidator fails to include in his request any one of the matters, statements or notices required to be specified by paragraph (1) or paragraphs (1) and (4), of Rule 4.218C, as the case may be, the request for approval or authorisation shall be treated as not having been made.

Insolvency Rules 1986, reg 4.218D

(2) Subject to paragraphs (3), (4) and (5), approval or authorisation shall be taken to have been given where the specified amount has been requested by the liquidator, and—
- (a) that amount is approved or authorised within the specified time limit; or
- (b) a different amount is approved or authorised within the specified time limit and the liquidator considers it sufficient.

(3) Where the liquidator requires the approval or authorisation of two or more preferential creditors, approval or authorisation shall be taken to be given where a majority in value of those who respond within the specified time limit approve or authorise—
- (a) the specified amount, or
- (b) a different amount which the liquidator considers sufficient.

(4) Where a majority in value of two or more preferential creditors propose an amount other than that specified by the liquidator, they shall be taken to have approved or authorised an amount equal to the lowest of the amounts so proposed.

(5) In any case in which there is no response in writing within the specified time limit to the liquidator's request—
- (a) at all, or
- (b) at any time following the liquidator's provision of further particulars under Rule 4.218C(3),

the liquidator's request shall be taken to have been approved or authorised from the date of the expiry of that time limit.]

NOTES

Amendment

Inserted by SI 2008/737, rr 3, 5.
Date in force: 6 April 2008: see SI 2008/737, r 1(1); for transitional provisions see r 2 thereof.

See Further

See further, in relation the application of this rule, with modifications, in respect of the procedure for the appointment of a bank liquidator and the operation of bank insolvency under the Banking Act 2009, Pt 2: the Bank Insolvency (England and Wales) Rules 2009, SI 2009/356, rr 3(3)–(8), 174.

[4.218E Litigation expenses and property subject to a floating charge—application to court by the liquidator]

[(1) In the circumstances specified below the court may, upon the application of the liquidator, approve or authorise such amount of litigation expenses as it thinks [just].

(2) Save as provided by paragraph (3), application to the court by a liquidator for an order approving or authorising an amount for litigation expenses may only be made where—
- (a) the specified creditor (or, if more than one, any one of them) is or is intended to be a defendant in the legal proceedings in respect of which the litigation expenses have been or are to be incurred; or
- (b) the specified creditor has been requested to approve or authorise the amount specified under Rule 4.218C(1)(c) and has, in any case—
  - (i) declined to approve or authorise, as the case may be, the specified amount; or
  - (ii) has approved or authorised an amount which is less than the specified amount and which lesser amount the liquidator considers insufficient, or

(iii) made such application for further particulars or other response to the liquidator's request as is, in the liquidator's opinion, unreasonable.

(3) Where the liquidator is of the view that circumstances are such that he requires urgent approval or authorisation of litigation expenses, he may apply to the court for approval or authorisation either—

(a) without seeking approval or authorisation from the specified creditor; or

(b) if sought, prior to the expiry of the specified time limit.

(4) The court may grant such application for approval or authorisation—

(a) provided that the liquidator satisfies it of the urgency of the case, and

(b) subject to such terms and conditions as it thinks [just].

(5) The liquidator shall, at the same time as making any application to the court under this rule, send copies of it to the specified creditor or creditors, unless the court orders otherwise.

(6) The specified creditor (including any one or all of them where there are two or more such creditors) is entitled to be heard on any such application unless the court orders otherwise.

(7) The court may grant approval or authorisation subject to such terms and conditions as it may think [just], including terms and conditions relating to the amount or nature of the litigation expenses and as to any obligation to make further applications to the court under this Rule.

(8) The costs of the liquidator's application under this Rule, including the costs of any specified creditor appearing or represented on it, shall be an expense of the liquidation unless the court orders otherwise.]

NOTES

Amendment

Inserted by SI 2008/737, rr 3, 5.
Date in force: 6 April 2008: see SI 2008/737, r 1(1); for transitional provisions see r 2 thereof.
Para (1): word "just" in square brackets substituted by SI 2010/686, r 2, Sch 1, para 1.
Date in force: 6 April 2010: see SI 2010/686, r 1; for transitional provisions see r 6(1), Sch 4, paras 1, 2(1)(b) thereto.
Para (4): in sub-para (b) word "just" in square brackets substituted by SI 2010/686, r 2, Sch 1, para 1.
Date in force: 6 April 2010: see SI 2010/686, r 1; for transitional provisions see r 6(1), Sch 4, paras 1, 2(1)(b) thereto.
Para (7): word "just" in square brackets substituted by SI 2010/686, r 2, Sch 1, para 1.
Date in force: 6 April 2010: see SI 2010/686, r 1; for transitional provisions see r 6(1), Sch 4, paras 1, 2(1)(b) thereto.

See Further

See further, in relation the application of this rule, with modifications, in respect of the procedure for the appointment of a bank liquidator and the operation of bank insolvency under the Banking Act 2009, Pt 2: the Bank Insolvency (England and Wales) Rules 2009, SI 2009/356, rr 3(3)–(8), 175.

4.219 Winding up commencing as voluntary

In a winding up by the court which follows immediately on a voluntary winding up (whether members' voluntary or creditors' voluntary), such remuneration of the voluntary liquidator and costs and expenses of the voluntary liquidation as the court may allow are to rank in priority with the expenses specified in Rule [4.218(3)(a)].

Insolvency Rules 1986, reg 4.219

NOTES

Initial Commencement

Specified date

Specified date: 29 December 1986: see r 0.1.

Amendment

Reference to "4.218(3)(a)" in square brackets substituted by SI 2008/737, rr 3, 7(14).
Date in force: 6 April 2008: see SI 2008/737, r 1(1); for transitional provisions see r 2 thereof.

4.220 Saving for powers of the court

(1) In a winding up by the court, the priorities laid down by Rules 4.218 and 4.219 are subject to the power of the court to make orders under section 156, where the assets are insufficient to satisfy the liabilities.

(2) Nothing in those Rules applies to or affects the power of any court, in proceedings by or against the company, to order costs to be paid by the company, or the liquidator; nor do they affect the rights of any person to whom such costs are ordered to be paid.

NOTES

Initial Commencement

Specified date

Specified date: 29 December 1986: see r 0.1.

See Further

See further, in relation the application of this rule, with modifications, in respect of the procedure for the appointment of a bank liquidator and the operation of bank insolvency under the Banking Act 2009, Pt 2: the Bank Insolvency (England and Wales) Rules 2009, SI 2009/356, rr 3(3)–(8), 176.

CHAPTER 21

MISCELLANEOUS RULES

SECTION A: RETURN OF CAPITAL (NO CVL APPLICATION)

4.221 Application to court for order authorising return

(1) This Rule applies where the liquidator intends to apply to the court for an order authorising a return of capital.

(2) The application shall be accompanied by a list of the persons to whom the return is to be made.

(3) The list shall include the same details of those persons as appears in the settled list of contributories, with any necessary alterations to take account of matters after settlement of the list, and the amount to be paid to each person.

(4) Where the court makes an order authorising the return, it shall send a sealed copy of the order to the liquidator.

NOTES

Initial Commencement

Specified date

Specified date: 29 December 1986: see r 0.1.

See Further

See further, in relation the application of this rule, with modifications, in respect of the procedure for the appointment of a bank liquidator and the operation of bank insolvency under the Banking Act 2009, Pt 2: the Bank Insolvency (England and Wales) Rules 2009, SI 2009/356, rr 3(3)–(8), 177.

4.222 Procedure for return

(1) The liquidator shall inform each person to whom a return is made of the rate of return per share, and whether it is expected that any further return will be made.

(2) Any payments made by the liquidator by way of the return may be sent by post, unless for any reason another method of making the payment has been agreed with the payee.

NOTES

Initial Commencement

Specified date

Specified date: 29 December 1986: see r 0.1.

See Further

See further, in relation the application of this rule, with modifications, in respect of the procedure for the appointment of a bank liquidator and the operation of bank insolvency under the Banking Act 2009, Pt 2: the Bank Insolvency (England and Wales) Rules 2009, SI 2009/356, rr 3(3)–(8), 178.

. . .

NOTES

Amendment

Revoked by SI 2010/686, r 5.
 Date in force: 6 April 2010: see SI 2010/686, r 1; for transitional provisions see r 6(1), Sch 4, para 1 thereto.

4.223 . . .

. . .

NOTES

Amendment

Revoked by SI 2010/686, r 5.
 Date in force: 6 April 2010: see SI 2010/686, r 1; for transitional provisions see r 6(1), Sch 4, para 1 thereto.

SECTION C: DISSOLUTION AFTER WINDING UP

4.224 Secretary of State's directions under ss 203, 205

(1) Where the Secretary of State gives a direction under—
 (a) section 203 (where official receiver applies to registrar of companies for a company's early dissolution), or
 (b) section 205 (application by interested person for postponement of dissolution),
he shall send two copies of the direction to the applicant for it.

(2) Of those copies one shall be sent by the applicant to the registrar of companies, to comply with section 203(5) or, as the case may be, 205(6).

NOTES

Initial Commencement

Specified date

Specified date: 29 December 1986: see r 0.1.

4.225 Procedure following appeal under s 203(4) or 205(4)

Following an appeal under section 203(4) or 205(4) (against a decision of the Secretary of State under the applicable section) the court shall send two sealed copies of its order to the person in whose favour the appeal was determined; and that party shall send one of the copies to the registrar of companies to comply with section 203(5) or, as the case may be, 205(6).

NOTES

Initial Commencement

Specified date

Specified date: 29 December 1986: see r 0.1.

CHAPTER 22

[PERMISSION] TO ACT AS DIRECTOR, ETC, OF COMPANY WITH PROHIBITED NAME (SECTION 216 OF THE ACT)

NOTES

Amendment

Chapter heading: word "Permission" in square brackets substituted by SI 2010/686, r 2, Sch 1, para 1.
Date in force: 6 April 2010: see SI 2010/686, r 1; for transitional provisions see r 6(1), Sch 4, paras 1, 2(1)(b) thereto.

4.226 Preliminary

The Rules in this Chapter—

(a) relate to the [permission] required under section 216 (restriction on re-use of name of company in insolvent liquidation) for a person to act as mentioned in section 216(3) in relation to a company with a prohibited name, . . .

(b) prescribe the cases excepted from that provision, that is to say, those in which a person to whom the section applies may so act without that [permission] [, and

(c) apply to all windings up to which section 216 applies, whether or not the winding up commenced before the coming into force of the Rules].

NOTES

Initial Commencement

Specified date

Specified date: 29 December 1986: see r 0.1.

Amendment

In paras (a), (b) word "permission" in square brackets substituted by SI 2010/686, r 2, Sch 1, para 1.
Date in force: 6 April 2010: see SI 2010/686, r 1; for transitional provisions see r 6(1), Sch 4, paras 1, 2(1)(b) thereto.
In para (a) word omitted revoked by SI 1987/1919, r 3(1), Schedule, Pt 1, para 81.
Para (c) and word ", and" immediately preceding it inserted by SI 1987/1919, r 3(1), Schedule, Pt 1, para 81.

See Further

See further, in relation the application of this rule, with modifications, in respect of the procedure for the appointment of a bank liquidator and the operation of bank insolvency under the Banking Act 2009, Pt 2: the Bank Insolvency (England and Wales) Rules 2009, SI 2009/356, rr 3(3)–(8), 181.

[4.227A Application for permission under s 216(3)]

[(1) At least 14 days notice of any application for permission to act in any of the circumstances which would otherwise be prohibited by section 216(3) must be given by the applicant to the Secretary of State, who may—

(a) appear at the hearing of the application; and

(b) whether or not appearing at the hearing, make representations.

(2) When considering an application for permission under section 216, the court may call on the liquidator, or any former liquidator, of the liquidating company for a report of the circumstances in which that company became insolvent and the extent (if any) of the applicant's apparent responsibility for its doing so.]

NOTES

Amendment

Substituted, for r 4.227 as originally enacted, by SI 2010/686, r 2, Sch 1, para 257.
Date in force: 6 April 2010: see SI 2010/686, r 1; for transitional provisions see r 6(1), Sch 4, para 1 thereto.

[4.228 First excepted case]

[(1) This Rule applies where—

(a) a person ("the person") was within the period mentioned in section 216(1) a director, or shadow director, of an insolvent company that has gone into insolvent liquidation

(b) the person acts in all or any of the ways specified in section 216(3) in connection with, or for the purposes of, the carrying on (or proposed carrying on) of the whole or substantially the whole of the business of the insolvent company where that business (or substantially the whole of it) is (or is to be) acquired from the insolvent company under arrangements—

   (i) made by its liquidator; or

   (ii) made before the insolvent company entered into insolvent liquidation by an office-holder acting in relation to it as administrator, administrative receiver or supervisor of a voluntary arrangement under Part 1 of the Act.

(2) The person, will not be taken to have contravened section 216 if prior to his acting in the circumstances set out in paragraph (1) a notice is, in accordance with the requirements of paragraph (3),—

(a) given by the person, to every creditor of the insolvent company whose name and address—

   (i) is known by him; or

- (ii) is ascertainable by him on the making of such enquiries as are reasonable in the circumstances; and
- (b) published in the Gazette.

(3) The notice referred to in paragraph (2)—
- (a) may. . . be given and published before the completion of the arrangements referred to in paragraph (1)(b) but must be given and published no later than 28 days after that completion;
- (b) must state—
  - (i) the name and registered number of the insolvent company;
  - (ii) the name of the person;
  - (iii) that it is his intention to act (or, where the insolvent company has not entered insolvent liquidation, to act or continue to act) in all or any of the ways specified in section 216(3) in connection with, or for the purposes of, the carrying on of the whole or substantially the whole of the business of the insolvent company; and
  - (iv) the prohibited name or, where the company has not entered insolvent liquidation, the name under which the business is being, or is to be, carried on which would be a prohibited name in respect of the person in the event of the insolvent company entering insolvent liquidation; and
- (c) must in the case of notice given to each creditor of the company be given using Form 4.73.

(4) Notice may in particular be given under this Rule—
- (a) prior to the insolvent company entering insolvent liquidation where the business (or substantially the whole of the business) is, or is to be, acquired by another company under arrangements made by an office-holder acting in relation to the insolvent company as administrator, administrative receiver or supervisor of a voluntary arrangement (whether or not at the time of the giving of the notice the director is a director of that other company); or
- (b) at a time where the person is a director of another company where—
  - (i) the other company has acquired, or is to acquire, the whole, or substantially the whole, of the business of the insolvent company under arrangements made by its liquidator; and
  - (ii) it is proposed that after the giving of the notice a prohibited name should be adopted by the other company.]

NOTES

Amendment

Substituted by SI 2007/1974, r 3(1), (2).
   Date in force: 6 August 2007: see SI 2007/1974, r 1; for transitional provision see r 2 thereof.
Para (3): in sub-para (a) words omitted revoked by SI 2010/686, r 2, Sch 1, para 258.
   Date in force: 6 April 2010: see SI 2010/686, r 1; for transitional provisions see r 6(1), Sch 4, para 1 thereto.

See Further

See further, in relation the application of this rule, with modifications, in respect of the procedure for the appointment of a bank liquidator and the operation of bank insolvency under the Banking Act 2009, Pt 2: the Bank Insolvency (England and Wales) Rules 2009, SI 2009/356, rr 3(3)–(8), 184.

[4.229 Second excepted case]

[(1) Where a person to whom section 216 applies as having been a director or shadow director of the liquidating company applies for [permission] of the court under that section not later than 7 [business] days from the date on which the company went into liquidation, he may, during the period specified in paragraph (2) below, act in any of the ways mentioned in section 216(3), notwithstanding that he has not the [permission] of the court under that section.

(2) The period referred to in paragraph (1) begins with the day on which the company goes into liquidation and ends either on the day falling six weeks after that date or on the day on which the court disposes of the application for [permission] under section 216, whichever of those days occurs first.]

NOTES

Amendment

Substituted by SI 1987/1919, r 3(1), Schedule, Part 1, para 82.

Para (1): word "permission" in square brackets in both places it occurs substituted by SI 2010/686, r 2, Sch 1, para 1.

Date in force: 6 April 2010: see SI 2010/686, r 1; for transitional provisions see r 6(1), Sch 4, paras 1, 2(1)(b) thereto.

Para (1): word "business" in square brackets inserted by SI 2010/686, r 2, Sch 1, para 259.

Date in force: 6 April 2010: see SI 2010/686, r 1; for transitional provisions see r 6(1), Sch 4, para 1 thereto.

Para (2): word "permission" in square brackets substituted by SI 2010/686, r 2, Sch 1, para 1.

Date in force: 6 April 2010: see SI 2010/686, r 1; for transitional provisions see r 6(1), Sch 4, paras 1, 2(1)(b) thereto.

See Further

See further, in relation the application of this rule, with modifications, in respect of the procedure for the appointment of a bank liquidator and the operation of bank insolvency under the Banking Act 2009, Pt 2: the Bank Insolvency (England and Wales) Rules 2009, SI 2009/356, rr 3(3)–(8), 185.

4.230 Third excepted case

The court's [permission] under section 216(3) is not required where the company there referred to, though known by a prohibited name within the meaning of the section—

(a) has been known by that name for the whole of the period of 12 months ending with the day before the liquidating company went into liquidation, and

(b) has not at any time in those 12 months been dormant within the meaning of [section 1169(1), (2) and (3)(a)] of the Companies Act.

NOTES

Initial Commencement

Specified date

Specified date: 29 December 1986: see r 0.1.

Amendment

Word "permission" in square brackets substituted by SI 2010/686, r 2, Sch 1, para 1.

Date in force: 6 April 2010: see SI 2010/686, r 1; for transitional provisions see r 6(1), Sch 4, paras 1, 2(1)(b) thereto.

In para (b) words "section 1169(1), (2) and (3)(a)" in square brackets substituted by SI 2009/2472, rr 3, 14.

Date in force: 1 October 2009: see SI 2009/2472, r 1; for transitional provisions see r 2 thereof.

Insolvency Rules 1986, reg 4.230

See Further
See further, in relation the application of this rule, with modifications, in respect of the procedure for the appointment of a bank liquidator and the operation of bank insolvency under the Banking Act 2009, Pt 2: the Bank Insolvency (England and Wales) Rules 2009, SI 2009/356, rr 3(3)–(8), 186.

[CHAPTER 23

EC REGULATION—MEMBER STATE LIQUIDATOR]

NOTES

Amendment
Inserted by SI 2002/1307, rr 3(1), 6(9).
Date in force: 31 May 2002: see SI 2002/1307, r 1.

[4.231 Interpretation of creditor and notice to member State liquidator]
[(1) This Rule applies where a member State liquidator has been appointed in relation to the company.
(2) For the purposes of the Rules referred to in paragraph (3) the member State liquidator is deemed to be a creditor.
(3) The Rules referred to in paragraph (2) are Rules 4.43(1) (official receiver's report), 4.45(1) (report on statement of affairs), 4.46(2) (report where no statement of affairs), 4.47(2) (general rule on reporting), 4.48(2) (winding up stayed), 4.49 (information to creditors), 4.50(2) (notice of meetings), 4.51(2) (notice of creditors' meeting—CVL), 4.54 (power to call meetings), 4.57(1) (requisitioned meetings), 4.57(3), 4.67 (entitlement to vote (creditors)), 4.68 (chairman's discretion to allow vote—CVL), 4.70 (admission and rejection of proof (creditors' meeting)), 4.73 (meaning of "prove"), 4.74 (supply of forms), 4.75 (contents of proof), 4.76 (particulars of creditor's claim)..., 4.78 (cost of proving), 4.79 (inspection of proofs), 4.82 (admission and rejection of proofs for dividend), 4.83(1) (appeal against decision in relation to proof), 4.83(2), 4.84 (withdrawal or variation of proof), 4.85(1) (expunging of proof), 4.86 (estimate of quantum), 4.87 (negotiable instruments, etc), 4.88 (secured creditors), 4.89 (discounts), 4.90 (mutual credit and set-off), 4.91 (debt in foreign currency), 4.92 (payment of a periodical nature), 4.93 (interest), 4.94 (debt payable at future time), 4.101A (power to fill vacancy in office of liquidator), 4.102(5) (appointment by court), 4.103(4) (appointment by court), 4.113(1) (meeting of creditors to remove liquidator), 4.114(1) (meeting of creditors to remove liquidator), 4.115 (regulation of meetings), 4.124(1) (release of official receiver), 4.125(1) (final meeting), [4.125A(2) (rule on reporting),] 4.126(1) (final meeting), 4.131(1) (challenge to liquidator's remuneration), 4.152(1) (liquidation committee), 4.152(3) (eligibility for liquidation committee), 4.163(3) (vacancy on liquidation committee), 4.175(1) (liquidation committee), 4.180 (notice of dividend) and 4.212(2) (notice of public examination hearing).
(4) Paragraphs (2) and (3) are without prejudice to the generality of the right to participate referred to in paragraph 3 of Article 32 of the EC Regulation (exercise of creditor's rights).
(5) Where the liquidator is obliged to give notice to, or provide a copy of a document (including an order of court) to, the court, the registrar of companies or the official receiver, the liquidator shall give notice or provide copies, as the case may be, to the member State liquidator.
(6) Paragraph (5) is without prejudice to the generality of the obligations imposed by Article 31 of the EC Regulation (duty to cooperate and communicate information).]

NOTES

Amendment

Inserted by SI 2002/1307, rr 3(1), 6(9).
  Date in force: 31 May 2002: see SI 2002/1307, r 1.
Para (3): words omitted revoked by SI 2010/686, r 2, Sch 1, para 260.
  Date in force: 6 April 2010: see SI 2010/686, r 1; for transitional provisions see r 6(1), Sch 4, paras 1, 2(1)(b) thereto.
Para (3): words "4.125A(2) (rule on reporting)," in square brackets inserted by SI 2004/584, r 23.
  Date in force: 1 April 2004: see SI 2004/584, r 1(2).

THE SECOND GROUP OF PARTS

INDIVIDUAL INSOLVENCY; BANKRUPTCY

[PART 5

INDIVIDUAL VOLUNTARY ARRANGEMENTS]

NOTES

Amendment

Substituted, together with rr 5.1–5.38, for rr 5.1–5.5, 5.5A (as inserted by SI 1987/1919, r 3(1), Schedule, Pt I, para 85), 5.6–5.30, 5.31–5.34 (as inserted by SI 2002/1307, rr 3(1), 7(3)), by SI 2002/2712, r 5(1), Schedule, Pt 3, para 24.
  Date in force: 1 January 2003: see SI 2002/2712, r 1(1); for effect see rr 1(2), 5(2) thereof.

[CHAPTER 1

PRELIMINARY]

NOTES

Amendment

Substituted, together with rr 5.1–5.38, for rr 5.1–5.5, 5.5A (as inserted by SI 1987/1919, r 3(1), Schedule, Pt I, para 85), 5.6–5.30, 5.31–5.34 (as inserted by SI 2002/1307, rr 3(1), 7(3)), by SI 2002/2712, r 5(1), Schedule, Pt 3, para 24.
  Date in force: 1 January 2003: see SI 2002/2712, r 1(1); for effect see rr 1(2), 5(2) thereof.

[5.1 Introductory]

[(1) The Rules in this Part apply in relation to a voluntary arrangement under Part VIII of the Act[, except in relation to voluntary arrangements under section 263A, in relation to which only Chapters [7 and 10 to 14] of this Part shall apply].]

[(2) In this Part, in respect of voluntary arrangements other than voluntary arrangements under section 263A—

    (a)   Chapter 2 applies in all cases;
    (b)   Chapter 3 applies in cases where an application for an interim order is made;
    (c)   Chapter 4 applies in cases where no application for an interim order is or is to be made;
    (d)   except where otherwise stated, Chapters 5 and 6 apply in all cases;

(e) Chapter 8 applies where a bankrupt makes an application under section 261(2)(a); and
(f) Chapter 9 applies where the official receiver makes an application under section 261(2)(b).
(3) In this Part, in respect of voluntary arrangements under section 263A—
(a) Chapter 7 applies in all cases; and
(b) Chapter 10 applies where the official receiver makes an application under section 263D(3).
(4) In this Part, Chapters 11 [to 14] apply in all cases.]

NOTES

Amendment

Substituted, together with rr 5.2–5.38, for rr 5.2–5.5, 5.5A (as inserted by SI 1987/1919, r 3(1), Schedule, Pt I, para 85), 5.6–5.30, 5.31–5.34 (as inserted by SI 2002/1307, rr 3(1), 7(3)), by SI 2002/2712, r 5(1), Schedule, Pt 3, para 24.
Date in force: 1 January 2003: see SI 2002/2712, r 1(1); for effect see rr 1(2), 5(2) thereof.
Para (1): words from ", except in relation" to "Part shall apply" in square brackets inserted by SI 2003/1730, r 8, Sch 1, Pt 5, para 28(a).
Date in force: 1 April 2004: see SI 2003/1730, r 1(3).
Para (1): words "7 and 10 to 14" in square brackets substituted by SI 2010/686, r 2, Sch 1, para 261(1), (2).
Date in force: 6 April 2010: see SI 2010/686, r 1; for transitional provisions see r 6(1), Sch 4, para 1 thereto.
Paras (2)–(4): substituted, for para (2), by SI 2003/1730, r 8, Sch 1, Pt 5, para 28(b).
Date in force: 1 April 2004: see SI 2003/1730, r 1(3).
Para (4): words "to 14" in square brackets substituted by SI 2010/686, r 2, Sch 1, para 261(1), (3).
Date in force: 6 April 2010: see SI 2010/686, r 1; for transitional provisions see r 6(1), Sch 4, para 1 thereto.

[CHAPTER 2

PREPARATION OF THE DEBTOR'S PROPOSAL]

NOTES

Amendment

Substituted, together with rr 5.1–5.38, for rr 5.1–5.5, 5.5A (as inserted by SI 1987/1919, r 3(1), Schedule, Pt I, para 85), 5.6–5.30, 5.31–5.34 (as inserted by SI 2002/1307, rr 3(1), 7(3)), by SI 2002/2712, r 5(1), Schedule, Pt 3, para 24.
Date in force: 1 January 2003: see SI 2002/2712, r 1(1); for effect see rr 1(2), 5(2) thereof.

[5.2 Preparation of proposal]

[The debtor shall prepare for the intended nominee a proposal on which (with or without amendments to be made under Rule 5.3(3) below) to make his report to the court under section 256 or [the debtor's creditors under] section 256A.]

NOTES

Amendment

Substituted, together with rr 5.1, 5.3–5.38, for rr 5.1–5.5, 5.5A (as inserted by SI 1987/1919, r 3(1), Schedule, Pt I, para 85), 5.6–5.30, 5.31–5.34 (as inserted by SI 2002/1307, rr 3(1), 7(3)), by SI 2002/2712, r 5(1), Schedule, Pt 3, para 24.

Date in force: 1 January 2003: see SI 2002/2712, r 1(1); for effect see rr 1(2), 5(2) thereof.

Words "the debtor's creditors under" in square brackets inserted by SI 2010/686, r 2, Sch 1, para 262.

Date in force: 6 April 2010: see SI 2010/686, r 1; for transitional provisions see r 6(1), Sch 4, para 1 thereto.

[5.3 Contents of proposal]

[(1) The debtor's proposal shall provide a short explanation why, in his opinion, a voluntary arrangement under Part VIII is desirable, and give reasons why his creditors may be expected to concur with such an arrangement.

(2) The following matters shall be stated, or otherwise dealt with, in the proposal—

- (a) the following matters, so far as within the debtor's immediate knowledge—
  - (i) his assets, with an estimate of their respective values,
  - (ii) the extent (if any) to which the assets are charged in favour of creditors,
  - (iii) the extent (if any) to which particular assets are to be excluded from the voluntary arrangement;
- (b) particulars of any property, other than assets of the debtor himself, which is proposed to be included in the arrangement, the source of such property and the terms on which it is to be made available for inclusion;
- (c) the nature and amount of the debtor's liabilities (so far as within his immediate knowledge), the manner in which they are proposed to be met, modified, postponed or otherwise dealt with by means of the arrangement and (in particular)—
  - (i) how it is proposed to deal with preferential creditors (defined in section 258(7)) and creditors who are, or claim to be, secured,
  - (ii) how associates of the debtor (being creditors of his) are proposed to be treated under the arrangement, and
  - (iii) in any case where the debtor is an undischarged bankrupt, whether, to the debtor's knowledge, claims have been made under section 339 (transactions at an undervalue), section 340 (preferences) or section 343 (extortionate credit transactions), or where the debtor is not an undischarged bankrupt, whether there are circumstances which would give rise to the possibility of such claims in the event that he should be adjudged bankrupt,

and, where any such circumstances are present, whether, and if so how, it is proposed under the voluntary arrangement to make provision for wholly or partly indemnifying the insolvent estate in respect of such claims;

- (d) whether any, and if so what, guarantees have been given of the debtor's debts by other persons, specifying which (if any) of the guarantors are associates of his;
- (e) the proposed duration of the voluntary arrangement;
- (f) the proposed dates of distributions to creditors, with estimates of their amounts;
- (g) how it is proposed to deal with the claims of any person who is bound by the arrangement by virtue of section 260(2)(b)(ii);
- (h) the amount proposed to be paid to the nominee (as such) by way of remuneration and expenses;
- (j) the manner in which it is proposed that the supervisor of the arrangement should be remunerated, and his expenses defrayed;

(k)	whether, for the purposes of the arrangement, any guarantees are to be offered by any persons other than the debtor, and whether (if so) any security is to be given or sought;
(l)	the manner in which funds held for the purposes of the arrangement are to be banked, invested or otherwise dealt with pending distribution to creditors;
(m)	the manner in which funds held for the purpose of payment to creditors, and not so paid on the termination of the arrangement, are to be dealt with;
(n)	if the debtor has any business, the manner in which it is proposed to be conducted during the course of the arrangement;
(o)	details of any further credit facilities which it is intended to arrange for the debtor, and how the debts so arising are to be paid;
(p)	the functions which are to be undertaken by the supervisor of the arrangement;
(q)	the name, address and qualification of the person proposed as supervisor of the voluntary arrangement, and confirmation that he is, so far as the debtor is aware, qualified to act as an insolvency practitioner in relation to him or is an authorised person in relation to him; . . .
(r)	whether the EC Regulation will apply and, if so, whether the proceedings will be main proceedings or territorial proceedings;
[(s)	within the 24 months preceding the date on which the proposal is delivered to the nominee, whether a proposal for an individual voluntary arrangement in respect of the debtor was submitted—

    (i) to a meeting of the debtor's creditors for approval and if so,
        (aa) whether the proposal was approved and the arrangement completed, or
        (bb) whether the proposal was rejected or the arrangement was terminated and if so, in what respects it differs from the proposal in this Rule;
    (ii) to the court in connection with an application for an interim order under section 253 and if so, whether the interim order was made].

(3) With the agreement in writing of the nominee, the debtor's proposal may be amended at any time up to the delivery of the [nominee's] report to the court under section 256 or [to the debtor's creditors under] section 256A.]

NOTES

Amendment

Substituted, together with rr 5.1, 5.2, 5.4–5.38, for rr 5.1–5.5, 5.5A (as inserted by SI 1987/1919, r 3(1), Schedule, Pt I, para 85), 5.6–5.30, 5.31–5.34 (as inserted by SI 2002/1307, rr 3(1), 7(3)), by SI 2002/2712, r 5(1), Schedule, Pt 3, para 24.
    Date in force: 1 January 2003: see SI 2002/2712, r 1(1); for effect see rr 1(2), 5(2) thereof.
Para (2): in sub-para (q) word omitted revoked by SI 2010/686, r 2, Sch 1, para 263(1), (2)(a).
    Date in force: 6 April 2010: see SI 2010/686, r 1; for transitional provisions see r 6(1), Sch 4, paras 1, 3(2) thereto.
Para (2): sub-para (s) inserted by SI 2010/686, r 2, Sch 1, para 263(1), (2)(b).
    Date in force: 6 April 2010: see SI 2010/686, r 1; for transitional provisions see r 6(1), Sch 4, paras 1, 3(2) thereto.
Para (3): word "nominee's" in square brackets substituted by SI 2010/686, r 2, Sch 1, para 263(1), (3)(a).
    Date in force: 6 April 2010: see SI 2010/686, r 1; for transitional provisions see r 6(1), Sch 4, para 1 thereto.

Para (3): words "to the debtor's creditors under" in square brackets inserted by SI 2010/686, r 2, Sch 1, para 263(1), (3)(b).
> Date in force: 6 April 2010: see SI 2010/686, r 1; for transitional provisions see r 6(1), Sch 4, para 1 thereto.

[5.4 Notice to the intended nominee]

[(1) The debtor shall give to the intended nominee written notice of his proposal.

(2) The notice, accompanied by a copy of the proposal, shall be delivered either to the nominee himself, or to a person authorised to take delivery of documents on his behalf.

(3) If the intended nominee agrees to act, he shall cause a copy of the notice to be endorsed to the effect that it has been received by him on a specified date.

(4) The copy of the notice so endorsed shall be returned by the nominee [as soon as reasonably practicable] to the debtor at an address specified by him in the notice for that purpose.

(5) Where the debtor is an undischarged bankrupt and he gives notice of his proposal to the official receiver and (if any) the trustee, the notice must contain the name and address of the insolvency practitioner or (as the case may be) authorised person who has agreed to act as nominee.]

NOTES

Amendment

> Substituted, together with rr 5.1–5.3, 5.5–5.38, for rr 5.1–5.5, 5.5A (as inserted by SI 1987/1919, r 3(1), Schedule, Pt I, para 85), 5.6–5.30, 5.31–5.34 (as inserted by SI 2002/1307, rr 3(1), 7(3)), by SI 2002/2712, r 5(1), Schedule, Pt 3, para 24.
> Date in force: 1 January 2003: see SI 2002/2712, r 1(1); for effect see rr 1(2), 5(2) thereof.
> Para (4): words "as soon as reasonably practicable" in square brackets substituted by SI 2009/642, rr 4, 5.
> Date in force: 6 April 2009: see SI 2009/642, r 1; for transitional provisions see r 3 thereof.

[5.5 Statement of Affairs]

[(1) Subject to paragraph (2), the debtor shall, [at the same time as the] proposal is delivered to the nominee, . . .deliver to the nominee a statement of [the debtor's] affairs.

(2) Paragraph (1) shall not apply where the debtor is an undischarged bankrupt and he has already delivered a statement of affairs under section 272 (debtor's petition) or 288 (creditor's petition) but the nominee may require the debtor to submit a further statement supplementing or amplifying the statement of affairs already submitted.

(3) The statement of affairs shall comprise the following particulars (supplementing or amplifying, so far as is necessary for clarifying the state of the debtor's affairs, those already given in his proposal)—

(a) a list of his assets, divided into such categories as are appropriate for easy identification, with estimated values assigned to each category;

(b) in the case of any property on which a claim against the debtor is wholly or partly secured, particulars of the claim and its amount, and of how and when the security was created;

(c) the names and addresses of the debtor's preferential creditors (defined in section 258(7)), with the amounts of their respective claims;

(d) the names and addresses of the debtor's unsecured creditors, with the amounts of their respective claims;

(e) particulars of any debts owed by or to the debtor to or by persons who are associates of his;

(f) such other particulars (if any) as the nominee may in writing require to be furnished for the purposes of making his report [on the debtor's proposal] to the court [or to the debtor's creditors as the case may be].

(4) The statement of affairs shall be made up to a date not earlier than 2 weeks before the date of the notice to the nominee under Rule 5.4.

However, the nominee may allow an extension of that period to the nearest practicable date (not earlier than 2 months before the date of the notice under Rule 5.4); and if he does so, he shall give his reasons in his report . . . on the debtor's proposal.

[(5) The statement must be verified by a statement of truth made by the debtor.]]

NOTES

Amendment

Substituted, together with rr 5.1–5.4, 5.6–5.38, for rr 5.1–5.5, 5.5A (as inserted by SI 1987/1919, r 3(1), Schedule, Pt I, para 85), 5.6–5.30, 5.31–5.34 (as inserted by SI 2002/1307, rr 3(1), 7(3)), by SI 2002/2712, r 5(1), Schedule, Pt 3, para 24.
   Date in force: 1 January 2003: see SI 2002/2712, r 1(1); for effect see rr 1(2), 5(2) thereof.
Para (1): words "at the same time as the" in square brackets substituted by SI 2010/686, r 2, Sch 1, para 264(1), (2)(a).
   Date in force: 6 April 2010: see SI 2010/686, r 1; for transitional provisions see r 6(1), Sch 4, para 1 thereto.
Para (1): words omitted revoked by SI 2010/686, r 2, Sch 1, para 264(1), (2)(b).
   Date in force: 6 April 2010: see SI 2010/686, r 1; for transitional provisions see r 6(1), Sch 4, para 1 thereto.
Para (1): words "the debtor's" in square brackets substituted by SI 2010/686, r 2, Sch 1, para 264(1), (2)(c).
   Date in force: 6 April 2010: see SI 2010/686, r 1; for transitional provisions see r 6(1), Sch 4, para 1 thereto.
Para (3): in sub-para (f) words "on the debtor's proposal" in square brackets inserted by SI 2010/686, r 2, Sch 1, para 264(1), (3)(a).
   Date in force: 6 April 2010: see SI 2010/686, r 1; for transitional provisions see r 6(1), Sch 4, para 1 thereto.
Para (3): in sub-para (f) words "or to the debtor's creditors as the case may be" in square brackets substituted by SI 2010/686, r 2, Sch 1, para 264(1), (3)(b).
   Date in force: 6 April 2010: see SI 2010/686, r 1; for transitional provisions see r 6(1), Sch 4, para 1 thereto.
Para (4): words omitted revoked by SI 2010/686, r 2, Sch 1, para 264(1), (4).
   Date in force: 6 April 2010: see SI 2010/686, r 1; for transitional provisions see r 6(1), Sch 4, para 1 thereto.
Para (5): substituted by SI 2010/686, r 2, Sch 1, para 264(1), (5).
   Date in force: 6 April 2010: see SI 2010/686, r 1; for transitional provisions see r 6(1), Sch 4, para 1 thereto.

[5.5A . . .]
[. . .]

NOTES

Amendment

Substituted, together with rr 5.1–5.38, for rr 5.1–5.5, 5.6–5.30, 5.31–5.34 (as inserted by SI 2002/1307, rr 3(1), 7(3)), by SI 2002/2712, r 5(1), Schedule, Pt 3, para 24.

Date in force: 1 January 2003: see SI 2002/2712, r 1(1); for effect see rr 1(2), 5(2) thereof.

[5.6 Additional disclosure for assistance of nominee]
[(1) If it appears to the nominee that he cannot properly prepare his report on the basis of information in the debtor's proposal and statement of affairs, he may call on the debtor to provide him with—
- (a) further and better particulars as to the circumstances in which, and the reasons why, he is insolvent or (as the case may be) threatened with insolvency;
- [(aa) further and better particulars of any proposals of the kind, and within the period, referred to in Rule 5.3(2)(s) which have been submitted by the debtor;]
- (b) particulars of any previous proposals [other than those referred to in Rule 5.3(2)(s)] which have been made by [the debtor at any time] under Part VIII of the Act; [and]
- (c) any further information with respect to his affairs which the nominee thinks necessary for the purposes of his report.

(2) The nominee may call on the debtor to inform him whether and in what circumstances he has at any time—
- (a) been concerned in the affairs of any company (whether or not incorporated in England and Wales) which has become insolvent, or
- (b) been adjudged bankrupt, or entered into an arrangement with his creditors.

(3) For the purpose of enabling the nominee to consider the debtor's proposal and prepare his report on it, the latter must give [the nominee such access to the debtor's accounts and records as the nominee may require].]

NOTES

Amendment

Substituted, together with rr 5.1–5.5, 5.7–5.38, for rr 5.1–5.5, 5.5A (as inserted by SI 1987/1919, r 3(1), Schedule, Pt I, para 85), 5.6–5.30, 5.31–5.34 (as inserted by SI 2002/1307, rr 3(1), 7(3)), by SI 2002/2712, r 5(1), Schedule, Pt 3, para 24.
Date in force: 1 January 2003: see SI 2002/2712, r 1(1); for effect see rr 1(2), 5(2) thereof.
Para (1): sub-para (aa) inserted by SI 2010/686, r 2, Sch 1, para 265(1), (2)(a).
Date in force: 6 April 2010: see SI 2010/686, r 1; for transitional provisions see r 6(1), Sch 4, para 1 thereto.
Para (1): in sub-para (b) words "other than those referred to in Rule 5.3(2)(s)" in square brackets inserted by SI 2010/686, r 2, Sch 1, para 265(1), (2)(b)(i).
Date in force: 6 April 2010: see SI 2010/686, r 1; for transitional provisions see r 6(1), Sch 4, para 1 thereto.
Para (1): in sub-para (b) words "the debtor at any time" in square brackets substituted by SI 2010/686, r 2, Sch 1, para 265(1), (2)(b)(ii).
Date in force: 6 April 2010: see SI 2010/686, r 1; for transitional provisions see r 6(1), Sch 4, para 1 thereto.
Para (1): in sub-para (b) word "and" in square brackets inserted by SI 2010/686, r 2, Sch 1, para 265(1), (2)(b)(iii).
Date in force: 6 April 2010: see SI 2010/686, r 1; for transitional provisions see r 6(1), Sch 4, para 1 thereto.
Para (3): words "the nominee such access to the debtor's accounts and records as the nominee may require" in square brackets substituted by SI 2010/686, r 2, Sch 1, para 265(1), (3).
Date in force: 6 April 2010: see SI 2010/686, r 1; for transitional provisions see r 6(1), Sch 4, para 1 thereto.

Insolvency Rules 1986, reg 5.6

[CHAPTER 3

CASES IN WHICH AN APPLICATION FOR AN INTERIM ORDER IS MADE]

NOTES

Amendment

Substituted, together with rr 5.1–5.38, for rr 5.1–5.5, 5.5A (as inserted by SI 1987/1919, r 3(1), Schedule, Pt I, para 85), 5.6–5.30, 5.31–5.34 (as inserted by SI 2002/1307, rr 3(1), 7(3)), by SI 2002/2712, r 5(1), Schedule, Pt 3, para 24.

Date in force: 1 January 2003: see SI 2002/2712, r 1(1); for effect see rr 1(2), 5(2) thereof.

[5.7 Application for interim order]

[(1) An application to the court for an interim order under Part VIII of the Act shall be accompanied by [a witness statement] of the following matters—

(a) the reasons for making the application;

(b) particulars of any execution or other legal process or levying of any distress which, to the debtor's knowledge, has been commenced against him;

(c) that he is an undischarged bankrupt or (as the case may be) that he is able to petition for his own bankruptcy;

(d) that no previous application for an interim order has been made by or in respect of the debtor in the period of 12 months ending with the date of [the witness statement]; . . .

(e) that the nominee under the proposal (naming him) is willing to act in relation to the proposal and is a person who is either qualified to act as an insolvency practitioner in relation to the debtor or is authorised to act as nominee in relation to him[; and]

[(f) [whether] the debtor has . . . submitted to the official receiver either the document referred to at section 263B(1)(a) or the statement referred to at section 263B(1)(b) [and, if so, when and with what result]].

(2) A copy of the notice to the intended nominee under Rule 5.4, endorsed to the effect that he agrees so to act, and a copy of the debtor's proposal given to the nominee under that Rule, shall be [attached] to the [witness statement].

(3) On receiving the application and [the witness statement], the court shall fix a venue for the hearing of the application.

(4) The applicant shall give at least 2 [business] days' notice of the hearing—

(a) where the debtor is an undischarged bankrupt, to the bankrupt, the official receiver and the trustee (whichever of those three is not himself the applicant),

(b) where the debtor is not an undischarged bankrupt, to any creditor who (to the debtor's knowledge) has presented a bankruptcy petition against him, and

(c) in either case, to the nominee who has agreed to act in relation to the debtor's proposal.]

NOTES

Amendment

Substituted, together with rr 5.1–5.6, 5.8–5.38, for rr 5.1–5.5, 5.5A (as inserted by SI 1987/1919, r 3(1), Schedule, Pt I, para 85), 5.6–5.30, 5.31–5.34 (as inserted by SI 2002/1307, rr 3(1), 7(3)), by SI 2002/2712, r 5(1), Schedule, Pt 3, para 24.

Date in force: 1 January 2003: see SI 2002/2712, r 1(1); for effect see rr 1(2), 5(2) thereof.

Para (1): words "a witness statement" in square brackets substituted by SI 2010/686, r 2, Sch 1, para 266(1), (2)(a).
   Date in force: 6 April 2010: see SI 2010/686, r 1; for transitional provisions see r 6(1), Sch 4, paras 1, 2(1)(b), (2)–(4) thereto.
Para (1): in sub-para (d) words "the witness statement" in square brackets substituted by SI 2010/686, r 2, Sch 1, para 266(1), (2)(b).
   Date in force: 6 April 2010: see SI 2010/686, r 1; for transitional provisions see r 6(1), Sch 4, paras 1, 2(1)(b), (2)–(4) thereto.
Para (1): in sub-para (d) word omitted revoked by SI 2003/1730, r 8, Sch 1, Pt 5, para 29(a).
   Date in force: 1 April 2004: see SI 2003/1730, r 1(3).
Para (1): in sub-para (e) word "; and" in square brackets inserted by SI 2003/1730, r 8, Sch 1, Pt 5, para 29(b).
   Date in force: 1 April 2004: see SI 2003/1730, r 1(3).
Para (1): sub-para (f) inserted by SI 2003/1730, r 8, Sch 1, Pt 5, para 29(c).
   Date in force: 1 April 2004: see SI 2003/1730, r 1(3).
Para (1): in sub-para (f) word "whether" in square brackets substituted by SI 2010/686, r 2, Sch 1, para 266(1), (2)(c)(i).
   Date in force: 6 April 2010: see SI 2010/686, r 1; for transitional provisions see r 6(1), Sch 4, para 1 thereto.
Para (1): in sub-para (f) word omitted revoked by SI 2010/686, r 2, Sch 1, para 266(1), (2)(c)(ii).
   Date in force: 6 April 2010: see SI 2010/686, r 1; for transitional provisions see r 6(1), Sch 4, para 1 thereto.
Para (1): in sub-para (f) words "and, if so, when and with what result" in square brackets inserted by SI 2010/686, r 2, Sch 1, para 266(1), (2)(c)(iii).
   Date in force: 6 April 2010: see SI 2010/686, r 1; for transitional provisions see r 6(1), Sch 4, para 1 thereto.
Para (2): word "attached" in square brackets substituted by SI 2010/686, r 2, Sch 1, para 266(1), (3)(a).
   Date in force: 6 April 2010: see SI 2010/686, r 1; for transitional provisions see r 6(1), Sch 4, paras 1, 2(1)(b), (2)–(4) thereto.
Para (2): words "witness statement" in square brackets substituted by SI 2010/686, r 2, Sch 1, para 266(1), (3)(b).
   Date in force: 6 April 2010: see SI 2010/686, r 1; for transitional provisions see r 6(1), Sch 4, paras 1, 2(1)(b), (2)–(4) thereto.
Para (3): words "the witness statement" in square brackets substituted by SI 2010/686, r 2, Sch 1, para 266(1), (4).
   Date in force: 6 April 2010: see SI 2010/686, r 1; for transitional provisions see r 6(1), Sch 4, paras 1, 2(1)(b), (2)–(4) thereto.
Para (4): word "business" in square brackets inserted by SI 2010/686, r 2, Sch 1, para 266(1), (5).
   Date in force: 6 April 2010: see SI 2010/686, r 1; for transitional provisions see r 6(1), Sch 4, paras 1, 2(1)(b) thereto.

[5.8 Court in which application to be made]

[(1)   Except in the case of an undischarged bankrupt, an application to the court under Part VIII of the Act shall be made to a court in which the debtor would be entitled to present his own petition in bankruptcy under Rule [6.40A].

(2)   The application shall contain sufficient information to establish that it is brought in the appropriate court.

(3)   In the case of an undischarged bankrupt, such an application shall be made to the court having the conduct of his bankruptcy and shall be filed with the bankruptcy proceedings.]

NOTES

Amendment

Substituted, together with rr 5.1–5.7, 5.9–5.38, for rr 5.1–5.5, 5.5A (as inserted by SI 1987/1919, r 3(1), Schedule, Pt I, para 85), 5.6–5.30, 5.31–5.34 (as inserted by SI 2002/1307, rr 3(1), 7(3)), by SI 2002/2712, r 5(1), Schedule, Pt 3, para 24.

Date in force: 1 January 2003: see SI 2002/2712, r 1(1); for effect see rr 1(2), 5(2) thereof.

Para (1): reference to "6.40A" in square brackets substituted by SI 2010/686, r 2, Sch 1, para 267.

Date in force: 6 April 2010: see SI 2010/686, r 1; for transitional provisions see r 6(1), Sch 4, para 1 thereto.

[5.9 Hearing of the application]

[(1) Any of the persons who have been given notice under Rule 5.7(4) may appear or be represented at the hearing of the application.

(2) The court, in deciding whether to make an interim order on the application, shall take into account any representations made by or on behalf of any of those persons (in particular, whether an order should be made containing such provision as is referred to in section 255(3) and (4)).

(3) If the court makes an interim order, it shall fix a venue for consideration of the nominee's report. Subject to the following paragraph, the date for that consideration shall be not later than that on which the interim order ceases to have effect under section 255(6).

(4) If under section 256(4) an extension of time is granted for filing the nominee's report, the court shall, unless there appear to be good reasons against it, correspondingly extend the period for which the interim order has effect.]

NOTES

Amendment

Substituted, together with rr 5.1–5.8, 5.10–5.38, for rr 5.1–5.5, 5.5A (as inserted by SI 1987/1919, r 3(1), Schedule, Pt I, para 85), 5.6–5.30, 5.31–5.34 (as inserted by SI 2002/1307, rr 3(1), 7(3)), by SI 2002/2712, r 5(1), Schedule, Pt 3, para 24.

Date in force: 1 January 2003: see SI 2002/2712, r 1(1); for effect see rr 1(2), 5(2) thereof.

[5.10 Action to follow making of order]

[(1) Where an interim order is made, at least 2 sealed copies of the order shall be sent by the court to the person who applied for it; and that person shall serve one of the copies on the nominee under the debtor's proposal.

(2) The applicant shall also [as soon as reasonably practicable] give notice of the making of the order to any person who was given notice of the hearing pursuant to Rule 5.7(4) and was not present or represented at it.]

NOTES

Amendment

Substituted, together with rr 5.1–5.9, 5.11–5.38, for rr 5.1–5.5, 5.5A (as inserted by SI 1987/1919, r 3(1), Schedule, Pt I, para 85), 5.6–5.30, 5.31–5.34 (as inserted by SI 2002/1307, rr 3(1), 7(3)), by SI 2002/2712, r 5(1), Schedule, Pt 3, para 24.

Date in force: 1 January 2003: see SI 2002/2712, r 1(1); for effect see rr 1(2), 5(2) thereof.

Para (2): words "as soon as reasonably practicable" in square brackets substituted by SI 2009/642, rr 4, 5.

Date in force: 6 April 2009: see SI 2009/642, r 1; for transitional provisions see r 3 thereof.

[5.11 Nominee's report on the proposal]

[(1) Where the nominee makes his report to the court under section 256, he shall deliver 2 [business] copies of it to the court not less than 2 days before the interim order ceases to have effect.

(2) With his report the nominee shall deliver—
   (a) a copy of the debtor's proposal (with amendments, if any, authorised under Rule 5.3(3)); and
   (b) a copy or summary of any statement of affairs provided by the debtor.

(3) If the nominee makes known his opinion that the debtor's proposal has a reasonable prospect of being approved and implemented, and that a meeting of the debtor's creditors should be summoned under section 257, his report shall have annexed to it his comments on the debtor's proposal.

If his opinion is otherwise, he shall give his reasons for that opinion.

(4) The court shall upon receipt of the report cause one copy of the report to be endorsed with the date of its filing in court and returned to the nominee.

(5) . . .

(6) Where the debtor is an undischarged bankrupt, the nominee shall send to the official receiver and (if any) the trustee—
   (a) a copy of the debtor's proposal,
   (b) a copy of his (the nominee's) report and his comments accompanying it (if any), and
   (c) a copy or summary of the debtor's statement of affairs.

(7) Where the debtor is not an undischarged bankrupt, the nominee shall send a copy of each of the documents referred to in paragraph (6) to any person who has presented a bankruptcy petition against the debtor.]

NOTES

Amendment

Substituted, together with rr 5.1–5.10, 5.12–5.38, for rr 5.1–5.5, 5.5A (as inserted by SI 1987/1919, r 3(1), Schedule, Pt I, para 85), 5.6–5.30, 5.31–5.34 (as inserted by SI 2002/1307, rr 3(1), 7(3)), by SI 2002/2712, r 5(1), Schedule, Pt 3, para 24.

Date in force: 1 January 2003: see SI 2002/2712, r 1(1); for effect see rr 1(2), 5(2) thereof.

Para (1): word "business" in square brackets inserted by SI 2010/686, r 2, Sch 1, para 268(1), (2).

Date in force: 6 April 2010: see SI 2010/686, r 1; for transitional provisions see r 6(1), Sch 4, para 1 thereto.

Para (5): revoked by SI 2010/686, r 2, Sch 1, para 268(1), (3).

Date in force: 6 April 2010: see SI 2010/686, r 1; for transitional provisions see r 6(1), Sch 4, para 1 thereto.

. . .

NOTES

Amendment

Substituted, together with rr 5.1–5.38, for rr 5.1–5.5, 5.5A (as inserted by SI 1987/1919, r 3(1), Schedule, Pt I, para 85), 5.6–5.30, 5.31–5.34 (as inserted by SI 2002/1307, rr 3(1), 7(3)), by SI 2002/2712, r 5(1), Schedule, Pt 3, para 24.

Date in force: 1 January 2003: see SI 2002/2712, r 1(1); for effect see rr 1(2), 5(2) thereof.

[5.12 Replacement of nominee]

[(1) Where the debtor intends to apply to the court under section 256(3) for the nominee to be replaced, he shall give to the nominee at least [5 business] days' notice of his application.

(2) No appointment of a replacement nominee shall be made by the court unless there is filed in court a statement by the replacement nominee indicating [that the replacement nominee—

(a) consents to act; and
(b) is qualified to act as an insolvency practitioner in relation to the debtor or is an authorised person in relation to the debtor].]

NOTES

Amendment

Substituted, together with rr 5.1–5.11, 5.13–5.38, for rr 5.1–5.5, 5.5A (as inserted by SI 1987/1919, r 3(1), Schedule, Pt I, para 85), 5.6–5.30, 5.31–5.34 (as inserted by SI 2002/1307, rr 3(1), 7(3)), by SI 2002/2712, r 5(1), Schedule, Pt 3, para 24.

Date in force: 1 January 2003: see SI 2002/2712, r 1(1); for effect see rr 1(2), 5(2) thereof.

Para (1): words "5 business" in square brackets substituted by SI 2010/686, r 2, Sch 1, para 269(1), (2).

Date in force: 6 April 2010: see SI 2010/686, r 1; for transitional provisions see r 6(1), Sch 4, para 1 thereto.

Para (2): words from "that the replacement" to "to the debtor" in square brackets substituted by SI 2010/686, r 2, Sch 1, para 269(1), (3).

Date in force: 6 April 2010: see SI 2010/686, r 1; for transitional provisions see r 6(1), Sch 4, para 1 thereto.

[5.13 Consideration of nominee's report]

[(1) At the hearing by the court to consider the nominee's report, any of the persons who have been given notice under Rule 5.7(4) may appear or be represented.

(2) Rule 5.10 applies to any order made by the court at the hearing.]

NOTES

Amendment

Substituted, together with rr 5.1–5.12, 5.14–5.38, for rr 5.1–5.5, 5.5A (as inserted by SI 1987/1919, r 3(1), Schedule, Pt I, para 85), 5.6–5.30, 5.31–5.34 (as inserted by SI 2002/1307, rr 3(1), 7(3)), by SI 2002/2712, r 5(1), Schedule, Pt 3, para 24.

Date in force: 1 January 2003: see SI 2002/2712, r 1(1); for effect see rr 1(2), 5(2) thereof.

[CHAPTER 4

CASES WHERE NO INTERIM ORDER IS TO BE OBTAINED]

NOTES

Amendment

Substituted, together with rr 5.1–5.38, for rr 5.1–5.5, 5.5A (as inserted by SI 1987/1919, r 3(1), Schedule, Pt I, para 85), 5.6–5.30, 5.31–5.34 (as inserted by SI 2002/1307, rr 3(1), 7(3)), by SI 2002/2712, r 5(1), Schedule, Pt 3, para 24.

Date in force: 1 January 2003: see SI 2002/2712, r 1(1); for effect see rr 1(2), 5(2) thereof.

[5.14A Nominee's report]
[(1) This rule applies where the nominee has received the document and statement mentioned in section 256A(2).

(2) The nominee must within 14 days (or such longer period as the court may allow)—

- (a) if the nominee has the opinions in section 256A(3)(a) and (b), attach to the report the nominee's comments on the debtor's proposal and comply with paragraph (3); or
- (b) if the nominee does not have the opinions in section 256A(3)(a) and (b), comply with paragraph (5).

(3) Where paragraph (2)(a) applies, the nominee must deliver the documents in paragraph (4) to—

- (a) each of the debtor's creditors of whose address the nominee is aware;
- (b) where the debtor is an undischarged bankrupt, the official receiver and (if any) the trustee; and
- (c) any person who has presented a bankruptcy petition against the debtor.

(4) The documents are—

- (a) a copy of the report;
- (b) a copy of the nominee's comments attached to the report;
- (c) a copy of the debtor's proposal (with amendments, if any, authorised under Rule 5.3(3));
- (d) a copy or summary of any statement of affairs provided by the debtor; and
- (e) a copy of the notice referred to in Rule 5.4(3), and
- (f) a statement that no application for an interim order under section 253 is to be made.

(5) Where paragraph (2)(b) applies the nominee must—

- (a) deliver a copy of the report to each of the debtor's creditors of whose address the nominee is aware; and
- (b) give the reasons for that opinion to the debtor.]

NOTES

Amendment

Substituted, together with r 5.14B, for r 5.14 as previously enacted, by SI 2010/686, r 2, Sch 1, para 270.

Date in force: 6 April 2010: see SI 2010/686, r 1; for transitional provisions see r 6(1), Sch 4, para 1 thereto.

[5.14B Applications to the court]

[(1) Subject to paragraph (2), where a report has been made under section 256A any application relating to a voluntary arrangement or a proposal for a voluntary arrangement must be filed in the court in which the debtor would be entitled to present the debtor's petition in bankruptcy under Rule 6.40A.

(2) Where the debtor is an undischarged bankrupt, the appropriate court is the court having the conduct of the debtor's bankruptcy and any application must be filed with the bankruptcy proceedings.

(3) The report must contain sufficient information to identify the appropriate court in which to file an application relating to a voluntary arrangement or to a proposal for a voluntary arrangement.

(4) Where an application is made to the court in relation to any matter relating to a voluntary arrangement or a proposal for a voluntary arrangement, in addition to the

documents in support of the application, the applicant must file in court such other documents required by this Part as the applicant considers may assist the court in determining the application.

(5) Where the debtor intends to apply to the court under section 256A(4)(a) or (b) for the nominee to be replaced, the debtor must give to the nominee at least 5 business days' notice of the application.

(6) Where the nominee intends to apply to the court under section 256A(4)(b) to be replaced as nominee, the nominee must give to the debtor at least 5 business days' notice of the application.

(7) The court must not appoint a replacement nominee unless a statement by the replacement nominee indicating consent to act is filed in court.]

NOTES

Amendment

Substituted, together with r 5.14A, for r 5.14 as previously enacted, by SI 2010/686, r 2, Sch 1, para 270.
Date in force: 6 April 2010: see SI 2010/686, r 1; for transitional provisions see r 6(1), Sch 4, para 1 thereto.

5.15 ...

...

NOTES

Amendment

Revoked by SI 2010/686, r 5.
Date in force: 6 April 2010: see SI 2010/686, r 1; for transitional provisions see r 6(1), Sch 4, para 1 thereto.

5.16 ...

...

NOTES

Amendment

Revoked by SI 2010/686, r 5.
Date in force: 6 April 2010: see SI 2010/686, r 1; for transitional provisions see r 6(1), Sch 4, para 1 thereto.

[CHAPTER 5
CREDITORS' MEETINGS]

NOTES

Amendment

Substituted, together with rr 5.1–5.38, for rr 5.1–5.5, 5.5A (as inserted by SI 1987/1919, r 3(1), Schedule, Pt I, para 85), 5.6–5.30, 5.31–5.34 (as inserted by SI 2002/1307, rr 3(1), 7(3)), by SI 2002/2712, r 5(1), Schedule, Pt 3, para 24.
Date in force: 1 January 2003: see SI 2002/2712, r 1(1); for effect see rr 1(2), 5(2) thereof.

[5.17 Summoning of creditors' meeting]
[(1) If in his report the nominee states that in his opinion a meeting of creditors should be summoned to consider the debtor's proposal, the date on which the meeting is to be held shall be—
- (a) in a case where an interim order has not been obtained, . . . and not more than 28 days from that on which the [nominee received the document and statement in section 256A(2)]; and
- (b) in a case where an interim order is in force, not less than 14 days from the date on which the nominee's report is filed in court nor more than 28 days from that on which the report is considered by the court.

(2) Notices calling the meeting shall be sent by the nominee, at least 14 days before the day fixed for it to be held, to all the creditors [of the debtor of whose address the nominee is aware].

[(3) Each notice sent under this rule must specify—
- (a) in a case where an interim order has not been obtained, the court to which application must be made under Rule 5.14B(1) or (2) as the case may be; or
- (b) in a case where an interim order is in force, the court in which the nominee's report on the debtor's proposal has been filed under Rule 5.8; and must state the effect of Rule 5.23(2) to (4) (requisite majorities).

(3A) Unless they have been sent under Rule 5.14A, the following documents must be sent with every notice under paragraph (3)—
- (a) a copy of the proposal;
- (b) a copy of the statement of affairs or, if the nominee thinks fit, a summary of it (the summary to include a list of the creditors and the amounts of their debts); and
- (c) the nominee's report with the comments on the proposal annexed to it.]]

NOTES

Amendment

Substituted, together with rr 5.1–5.16, 5.18–5.38, for rr 5.1–5.5, 5.5A (as inserted by SI 1987/1919, r 3(1), Schedule, Pt I, para 85), 5.6–5.30, 5.31–5.34 (as inserted by SI 2002/1307, rr 3(1), 7(3)), by SI 2002/2712, r 5(1), Schedule, Pt 3, para 24.

Date in force: 1 January 2003: see SI 2002/2712, r 1(1); for effect see rr 1(2), 5(2) thereof.

Para (1): in sub-para (a) words omitted revoked by SI 2010/686, r 2, Sch 1, para 271(1), (2)(a).

Date in force: 6 April 2010: see SI 2010/686, r 1; for transitional provisions see r 6(1), Sch 4, para 1 thereto.

Para (1): in sub-para (a) words "nominee received the document and statement in section 256A(2)" in square brackets substituted by SI 2010/686, r 2, Sch 1, para 271(1), (2)(b).

Date in force: 6 April 2010: see SI 2010/686, r 1; for transitional provisions see r 6(1), Sch 4, para 1 thereto.

Para (2): words "of the debtor of whose address the nominee is aware" in square brackets substituted by SI 2010/686, r 2, Sch 1, para 271(1), (3).

Date in force: 6 April 2010: see SI 2010/686, r 1; for transitional provisions see r 6(1), Sch 4, para 1 thereto.

Paras (3), (3A): substituted, for para (3) as previously enacted, by SI 2010/686, r 2, Sch 1, para 271(1), (4).

Date in force: 6 April 2010: see SI 2010/686, r 1; for transitional provisions see r 6(1), Sch 4, para 1 thereto.

[5.18 Creditors' meeting: supplementary]
[(1) Subject as follows, in fixing the venue for the creditors' meeting, the nominee shall have regard to the convenience of creditors.

(2) The meeting shall be summoned for commencement between 10.00 and 16.00 hours on a business day.

(3) With every notice summoning the meeting there shall be sent out forms of proxy.]

NOTES

Amendment

Substituted, together with rr 5.1–5.17, 5.19–5.38, for rr 5.1–5.5, 5.5A (as inserted by SI 1987/1919, r 3(1), Schedule, Pt I, para 85), 5.6–5.30, 5.31–5.34 (as inserted by SI 2002/1307, rr 3(1), 7(3)), by SI 2002/2712, r 5(1), Schedule, Pt 3, para 24.

Date in force: 1 January 2003: see SI 2002/2712, r 1(1); for effect see rr 1(2), 5(2) thereof.

[5.19 The chairman at the meeting]

[(1) Subject as follows, the nominee shall be chairman of the creditors' meeting.

(2) If for any reason the nominee is unable to attend, he may nominate another person to act as chairman in his place; but a person so nominated must be—

- (a) a person qualified to act as an insolvency practitioner in relation to the debtor;
- (b) an authorised person in relation to the debtor; or
- (c) an employee of the nominee or his firm who is experienced in insolvency matters.]

NOTES

Amendment

Substituted, together with rr 5.1–5.18, 5.20–5.38, for rr 5.1–5.5, 5.5A (as inserted by SI 1987/1919, r 3(1), Schedule, Pt I, para 85), 5.6–5.30, 5.31–5.34 (as inserted by SI 2002/1307, rr 3(1), 7(3)), by SI 2002/2712, r 5(1), Schedule, Pt 3, para 24.

Date in force: 1 January 2003: see SI 2002/2712, r 1(1); for effect see rr 1(2), 5(2) thereof.

. . .

NOTES

Amendment

Substituted, together with rr 5.1–5.38, for rr 5.1–5.5, 5.5A (as inserted by SI 1987/1919, r 3(1), Schedule, Pt I, para 85), 5.6–5.30, 5.31–5.34 (as inserted by SI 2002/1307, rr 3(1), 7(3)), by SI 2002/2712, r 5(1), Schedule, Pt 3, para 24.

Date in force: 1 January 2003: see SI 2002/2712, r 1(1); for effect see rr 1(2), 5(2) thereof.

[5.20 The chairman as proxy-holder]

[The chairman shall not by virtue of any proxy held by him vote to increase or reduce the amount of the remuneration or expenses of the nominee or the supervisor of the proposed arrangement, unless the proxy specifically directs him to vote in that way.]

NOTES

Amendment

Substituted, together with rr 5.1–5.19, 5.21–5.38, for rr 5.1–5.5, 5.5A (as inserted by SI 1987/1919, r 3(1), Schedule, Pt I, para 85), 5.6–5.30, 5.31–5.34 (as inserted by SI 2002/1307, rr 3(1), 7(3)), by SI 2002/2712, r 5(1), Schedule, Pt 3, para 24.

Date in force: 1 January 2003: see SI 2002/2712, r 1(1); for effect see rr 1(2), 5(2) thereof.

[5.21 Entitlement to vote]

[(1) Subject as follows, every creditor who has notice of the creditors' meeting is entitled to vote at the meeting or any adjournment of it.

(2) A creditor's entitlement to vote is calculated as follows—

- (a) where the debtor is not an undischarged bankrupt and an interim order is in force, by reference to the amount of the debt owed to him as at the date of the interim order;
- (b) where the debtor is not an undischarged bankrupt and an interim order is not in force, by reference to the amount of the debt owed to him at the date of the meeting; and
- (c) where the debtor is an undischarged bankrupt, by reference to the amount of the debt owed to him as at the date of the bankruptcy order.

(3) A creditor may vote in respect of a debt for an unliquidated amount or any debt whose value is not ascertained, and for the purposes of voting (but not otherwise) his debt shall be valued at £1 unless the chairman agrees to put a higher value on it.]

NOTES

Amendment

Substituted, together with rr 5.1–5.20, 5.22–5.38, for rr 5.1–5.5, 5.5A (as inserted by SI 1987/1919, r 3(1), Schedule, Pt I, para 85), 5.6–5.30, 5.31–5.34 (as inserted by SI 2002/1307, rr 3(1), 7(3)), by SI 2002/2712, r 5(1), Schedule, Pt 3, para 24.

Date in force: 1 January 2003: see SI 2002/2712, r 1(1); for effect see rr 1(2), 5(2) thereof.

[5.22 Procedure for admission of creditors' claims for voting purposes]

[(1) Subject as follows, at the creditors' meeting the chairman shall ascertain the entitlement of persons wishing to vote and shall admit or reject their claims accordingly.

(2) The chairman may admit or reject a claim in whole or in part.

(3) The chairman's decision on any matter under this Rule or under paragraph (3) of Rule 5.21 is subject to appeal to the court by any creditor or by the debtor.

(4) If the chairman is in doubt whether a claim should be admitted or rejected, he shall mark it as objected to and allow votes to be cast in respect of it, subject to such votes being subsequently declared invalid if the objection to the claim is sustained.

(5) If on an appeal the chairman's decision is reversed or varied, or votes are declared invalid, the court may order another meeting to be summoned, or make such order as it thinks just.

The court's power to make an order under this paragraph is exercisable only if it considers that the circumstances giving rise to the appeal are such as give rise to unfair prejudice or material irregularity.

(6) An application to the court by way of appeal against the chairman's decision shall not be made after the end of the period of 28 days beginning with the first day on which—

[(a) where the creditors' meeting was summoned under section 257 pursuant to a report to the debtor's creditors under section 256A(3), the notice of the result of the meeting required by section 259(1)(a) has been given; or

(b) where the creditors' meeting was summoned under section 257 pursuant to a report to a court under section 256(1)(aa), the report required by section 259(1)(b) is made to the court].

(7) The chairman is not personally liable for any costs incurred by any person in respect of an appeal under this Rule.]

NOTES

Amendment

Substituted, together with rr 5.1–5.21, 5.23–5.38, for rr 5.1–5.5, 5.5A (as inserted by SI 1987/1919, r 3(1), Schedule, Pt I, para 85), 5.6–5.30, 5.31–5.34 (as inserted by SI 2002/1307, rr 3(1), 7(3)), by SI 2002/2712, r 5(1), Schedule, Pt 3, para 24.
Date in force: 1 January 2003: see SI 2002/2712, r 1(1); for effect see rr 1(2), 5(2) thereof.
Para (6): sub-paras (a), (b) substituted, for words as originally enacted, by SI 2010/686, r 2, Sch 1, para 272.
Date in force: 6 April 2010: see SI 2010/686, r 1; for transitional provisions see r 6(1), Sch 4, para 1 thereto.

[5.23 Requisite majorities]

[[(1) Subject to paragraph (2), at the creditors' meeting, a resolution is passed when a majority (in value) of those present and voting in person or by proxy have voted in favour of it.

(2) A resolution to approve the proposal or a modification is passed when a majority of three-quarters or more (in value) of those present and voting in person or by proxy have voted in favour of it.]

(3) In the following cases there is to be left out of account a creditor's vote in respect of any claim or part of a claim—

(a) where written notice of the claim was not given, either at the meeting or before it, to the chairman or the nominee;

(b) where the claim or part is secured;

(c) where the claim is in respect of a debt wholly or partly on, or secured by, a current bill of exchange or promissory note, unless the creditor is willing—

(i) to treat the liability to him on the bill or note of every person who is liable on it antecedently to the debtor, and against whom a bankruptcy order has not been made (or, in the case of a company, which has not gone into liquidation), as a security in his hands, and

(ii) to estimate the value of the security and (for the purpose of entitlement to vote, but not of any distribution under the arrangement) to deduct it from his claim.

(4) Any resolution is invalid if those voting against it include more than half in value of the creditors, counting in these latter only those—

(a) who have notice of the meeting;

(b) whose votes are not to be left out of account under paragraph (3); and

(c) who are not, to the best of the chairman's belief, associates of the debtor.

(5) It is for the chairman of the meeting to decide whether under this Rule—

(a) a vote is to be left out of account in accordance with the paragraph (3), or

(b) a person is an associate of the debtor for the purposes of paragraph (4)(c);

and in relation to the second of these cases the chairman is entitled to rely on the information provided by the debtor's statement of affairs or otherwise in accordance with this Part of the Rules.

(6) If the chairman uses a proxy contrary to Rule 5.20, his vote with that proxy does not count towards any majority under this Rule.

(7) The chairman's decision on any matter under this Rule is subject to appeal to the court by any creditor or by the debtor and paragraphs (5) to (7) of Rule 5.22 apply as regards such an appeal.]

NOTES

Amendment

Substituted, together with rr 5.1–5.22, 5.24–5.38, for rr 5.1–5.5, 5.5A (as inserted by SI 1987/1919, r 3(1), Schedule, Pt I, para 85), 5.6–5.30, 5.31–5.34 (as inserted by SI 2002/1307, rr 3(1), 7(3)), by SI 2002/2712, r 5(1), Schedule, Pt 3, para 24.
Date in force: 1 January 2003: see SI 2002/2712, r 1(1); for effect see rr 1(2), 5(2) thereof.
Paras (1), (2): substituted by SI 2010/686, r 2, Sch 1, para 273.
Date in force: 6 April 2010: see SI 2010/686, r 1; for transitional provisions see r 6(1), Sch 4, para 1 thereto.

[5.24 Proceedings to obtain agreement on the proposal]

[(1) On the day on which the creditors' meeting is held, it may from time to time be adjourned.

(2) If on that day the requisite majority for the approval of the voluntary arrangement (with or without modifications) has not been obtained, the chairman may, and shall if it is so resolved, adjourn the meeting for not more than 14 days.

(3) If there are subsequently further adjournments, the final adjournment shall not be to a day later than 14 days after that on which the meeting was originally held.

(4) If the meeting is adjourned under paragraph (2), notice of the fact shall be given by the chairman [as soon as reasonably practicable] to the court.

[(4A) Once only in the course of a meeting the chairman may, without an adjournment, declare it suspended for any period up to 1 hour.]

(5) If following any final adjournment of the meeting the proposal (with or without modifications) is not agreed to, it is deemed rejected.]

NOTES

Amendment

Substituted, together with rr 5.1–5.23, 5.25–5.38, for rr 5.1–5.5, 5.5A (as inserted by SI 1987/1919, r 3(1), Schedule, Pt I, para 85), 5.6–5.30, 5.31–5.34 (as inserted by SI 2002/1307, rr 3(1), 7(3)), by SI 2002/2712, r 5(1), Schedule, Pt 3, para 24.
Date in force: 1 January 2003: see SI 2002/2712, r 1(1); for effect see rr 1(2), 5(2) thereof.
Para (4): words "as soon as reasonably practicable" in square brackets substituted by SI 2009/642, rr 4, 5.
Date in force: 6 April 2009: see SI 2009/642, r 1; for transitional provisions see r 3 thereof.
Para (4A): inserted by SI 2010/686, r 2, Sch 1, para 274.
Date in force: 6 April 2010: see SI 2010/686, r 1; for transitional provisions see r 6(1), Sch 4, para 1 thereto.

[CHAPTER 6

IMPLEMENTATION OF THE ARRANGEMENT]

NOTES

Amendment

Substituted, together with rr 5.1–5.38, for rr 5.1–5.5, 5.5A (as inserted by SI 1987/1919, r 3(1), Schedule, Pt I, para 85), 5.6–5.30, 5.31–5.34 (as inserted by SI 2002/1307, rr 3(1), 7(3)), by SI 2002/2712, r 5(1), Schedule, Pt 3, para 24.
Date in force: 1 January 2003: see SI 2002/2712, r 1(1); for effect see rr 1(2), 5(2) thereof.

[5.25 Resolutions to follow approval]

[(1) If the voluntary arrangement is approved (with or without modifications), a resolution [must] be taken by the creditors, where two or more individuals are appointed to act as supervisor, on the question whether acts to be done in connection with the arrangement may be done by any one of them, or must be done by both or all.

(2) If at the creditors' meeting a resolution is moved for the appointment of some person other than the nominee to be supervisor of the arrangement, there must be produced to the chairman, at or before the meeting—

- (a) that person's written consent to act (unless he is present and then and there signifies his consent), and
- (b) his written confirmation that he is qualified to act as an insolvency practitioner in relation to the debtor or is an authorised person in relation to the debtor.]

NOTES

Amendment

Substituted, together with rr 5.1–5.24, 5.26–5.38, for rr 5.1–5.5, 5.5A (as inserted by SI 1987/1919, r 3(1), Schedule, Pt I, para 85), 5.6–5.30, 5.31–5.34 (as inserted by SI 2002/1307, rr 3(1), 7(3)), by SI 2002/2712, r 5(1), Schedule, Pt 3, para 24.
Date in force: 1 January 2003: see SI 2002/2712, r 1(1); for effect see rr 1(2), 5(2) thereof.
Para (1): word "must" in square brackets substituted by SI 2010/686, r 2, Sch 1, para 275.
Date in force: 6 April 2010: see SI 2010/686, r 1; for transitional provisions see r 6(1), Sch 4, para 1 thereto.

[5.26 Hand-over of property, etc to supervisor]

[(1) [As soon as reasonably practicable] after the approval of the voluntary arrangement, the debtor or, where the debtor is an undischarged bankrupt, the official receiver or the debtor's trustee, shall do all that is required for putting the supervisor into possession of the assets included in the arrangement.

(2) On taking possession of the assets in any case where the debtor is an undischarged bankrupt, the supervisor shall discharge any balance due to the official receiver and (if other) the trustee by way of remuneration or on account of—

- (a) fees, costs, charges and expenses properly incurred and payable under the Act or the Rules, and
- (b) any advances made in respect of the insolvent estate, together with interest on such advances at the rate specified in section 17 of the Judgments Act 1838 at the date of the bankruptcy order.

(3) Alternatively where the debtor is an undischarged bankrupt, the supervisor must, before taking possession, give the official receiver or the trustee a written undertaking to discharge any such balance out of the first realisation of assets.

(4) Where the debtor is an undischarged bankrupt, the official receiver and (if other) the trustee has a charge on the assets included in the voluntary arrangement in respect of any sums due as above until they have been discharged, subject only to the deduction from realisations by the supervisor of the proper costs and expenses of realisation.

Any sums due to the official receiver take priority over those due to a trustee.

(5) The supervisor shall from time to time out of the realisation of assets discharge all guarantees properly given by the official receiver or the trustee for the benefit of the estate, and shall pay all their expenses.]

NOTES

Amendment

Substituted, together with rr 5.1–5.25, 5.27–5.38, for rr 5.1–5.5, 5.5A (as inserted by SI 1987/1919, r 3(1), Schedule, Pt I, para 85), 5.6–5.30, 5.31–5.34 (as inserted by SI 2002/1307, rr 3(1), 7(3)), by SI 2002/2712, r 5(1), Schedule, Pt 3, para 24.

Date in force: 1 January 2003: see SI 2002/2712, r 1(1); for effect see rr 1(2), 5(2) thereof.

Para (1): words "As soon as reasonably practicable" in square brackets substituted by SI 2009/642, rr 4, 5.

Date in force: 6 April 2009: see SI 2009/642, r 1; for transitional provisions see r 3 thereof.

[5.27 Report of creditors' meeting]

[(1) A report of the creditors' meeting shall be prepared by the chairman of the meeting.

(2) The report shall—
- (a) state whether the proposal for a voluntary arrangement was approved or rejected and, if approved, with what (if any) modifications;
- (b) set out the resolutions which were taken at the meeting, and the decision on each one;
- (c) list the creditors (with their respective values) who were present or represented at the meeting, and how they voted on each resolution;
- (d) whether in the opinion of the supervisor,
  - (i) the EC Regulation applies to the voluntary arrangement, and
  - (ii) if so, whether the proceedings are main proceedings or territorial proceedings; and
- (e) include such further information (if any) as the chairman thinks it appropriate to make known to the court [or the debtor's creditors as the case may be].

(3) [Where the creditors' meeting was summoned under section 257 pursuant to a report to a court under section 256(1)(aa),] a copy of the chairman's report shall, within 4 [business] days of the meeting being held, be filed in court; and the court shall cause that copy to be endorsed with the date of filing.

(4) The persons to whom notice of the result is to be given, under section 259(1), are all those who were sent notice of the meeting under this Part of the Rules and any other creditor of [whose address] the chairman is aware, and where the debtor is an undischarged bankrupt, the official receiver and (if any) the trustee.

[(4A) The notice must be sent—
- (a) where the creditors' meeting was summoned under section 257 pursuant to a report to a court under section 256(1)(aa), as soon as reasonably practicable after a copy of the chairman's report is filed in court;
- (b) where the creditors' meeting was summoned under section 257 pursuant to a report to creditors under section 256A(3), within 4 business days of the meeting being held.]

(5) In a case where no interim order has been obtained the court shall not consider the chairman's report unless an application is made to the court under the Act or the Rules in relation to it.]

NOTES

Amendment

Substituted, together with rr 5.1–5.26, 5.28–5.38, for rr 5.1–5.5, 5.5A (as inserted by SI 1987/1919, r 3(1), Schedule, Pt I, para 85), 5.6–5.30, 5.31–5.34 (as inserted by SI 2002/1307, rr 3(1), 7(3)), by SI 2002/2712, r 5(1), Schedule, Pt 3, para 24.
Date in force: 1 January 2003: see SI 2002/2712, r 1(1); for effect see rr 1(2), 5(2) thereof.
Para (2): in sub-para (e) words "or the debtor's creditors as the case may be" in square brackets inserted by SI 2010/686, r 2, Sch 1, para 276(1), (2).
Date in force: 6 April 2010: see SI 2010/686, r 1; for transitional provisions see r 6(1), Sch 4, para 1 thereto.
Para (3): words from "Where the creditors'" to "under section 256(1)(aa)," in square brackets inserted by SI 2010/686, r 2, Sch 1, para 276(1), (3)(a).
Date in force: 6 April 2010: see SI 2010/686, r 1; for transitional provisions see r 6(1), Sch 4, para 1 thereto.
Para (3): word "business" in square brackets inserted by SI 2010/686, r 2, Sch 1, para 276(1), (3)(b).
Date in force: 6 April 2010: see SI 2010/686, r 1; for transitional provisions see r 6(1), Sch 4, para 1 thereto.
Para (4): words "whose address" in square brackets substituted by SI 2010/686, r 2, Sch 1, para 276(1), (4)(a).
Date in force: 6 April 2010: see SI 2010/686, r 1; for transitional provisions see r 6(1), Sch 4, para 1 thereto.
Para (4A): substituted, for second sentence of para (4) as previously enacted, by SI 2010/686, r 2, Sch 1, para 276(1), (4)(b).
Date in force: 6 April 2010: see SI 2010/686, r 1; for transitional provisions see r 6(1), Sch 4, para 1 thereto.

5.28 . . .
. . .

NOTES

Amendment

Revoked by SI 2003/1730, r 8, Sch 1, Pt 5, para 30.
Date in force: 1 April 2004: see SI 2003/1730, r 1(3).

[5.29 Reports to Secretary of State]

[[(1) As soon as reasonably practicable, and in any event, within the period of 14 days after a report that the creditors' meeting has approved the voluntary arrangement has been filed in court or sent to the creditors as the case may be, the chairman of the creditors' meeting must send to the Secretary of State the following information—
- (a) the name and address of the debtor;
- (b) the date on which the arrangement was approved by the creditors;
- (c) the name and address of the supervisor;
- (d) the debtor's gender;
- (e) the debtor's date of birth; and
- (f) any name by which the debtor was or is known, not being the name in which the debtor has entered into the voluntary arrangement.]

(2) A person who is appointed to act as supervisor of an individual voluntary arrangement (whether in the first instance or by way of replacement of another person previously appointed) shall [as soon as reasonably practicable] give written notice to the Secretary of State of his appointment.

If he vacates office as supervisor, he shall [as soon as reasonably practicable] give written notice of that fact also to the Secretary of State.]

NOTES

Amendment

Substituted, together with rr 5.1–5.28, 5.30–5.38, for rr 5.1–5.5, 5.5A (as inserted by SI 1987/1919, r 3(1), Schedule, Pt I, para 85), 5.6–5.30, 5.31–5.34 (as inserted by SI 2002/1307, rr 3(1), 7(3)), by SI 2002/2712, r 5(1), Schedule, Pt 3, para 24.
Date in force: 1 January 2003: see SI 2002/2712, r 1(1); for effect see rr 1(2), 5(2) thereof.
Para (1): substituted by SI 2010/686, r 2, Sch 1, para 277.
Date in force: 6 April 2010: see SI 2010/686, r 1; for transitional provisions see r 6(1), Sch 4, para 1 thereto.
Para (2): words "as soon as reasonably practicable" in square brackets in both places they occur substituted by SI 2009/642, rr 4, 5.
Date in force: 6 April 2009: see SI 2009/642, r 1; for transitional provisions see r 3 thereof.

. . .

NOTES

Amendment

Substituted, together with rr 5.1–5.38, for rr 5.1–5.5, 5.5A (as inserted by SI 1987/1919, r 3(1), Schedule, Pt I, para 85), 5.6–5.30, 5.31–5.34 (as inserted by SI 2002/1307, rr 3(1), 7(3)), by SI 2002/2712, r 5(1), Schedule, Pt 3, para 24.
Date in force: 1 January 2003: see SI 2002/2712, r 1(1); for effect see rr 1(2), 5(2) thereof.

[5.30 Revocation or suspension of the arrangement]

[(1) This Rule applies where the court makes an order of revocation or suspension under section 262.

(2) The person who applied for the order shall serve sealed copies of it—
   (a)   in a case where the debtor is an undischarged bankrupt, on the debtor, the official receiver and the trustee;
   (b)   in any other case, on the debtor; and
   (c)   in either case, on the supervisor of the voluntary arrangement.

(3) If the order includes a direction by the court under section 262(4)(b) for any further creditors' meeting to be summoned, notice shall also be given (by the person who applied for the order) to whoever is, in accordance with the direction, required to summon the meeting.

(4) The debtor or (where the debtor is an undischarged bankrupt) the trustee or (if there is no trustee) the official receiver shall—
   (a)   [as soon as reasonably practicable] after receiving a copy of the court's order, give notice of it to all persons who were sent notice of the creditors' meeting which approved the voluntary arrangement or who, not having been sent that notice, are affected by the order;
   (b)   within [5 business] days of their receiving a copy of the order (or within such longer period as the court may allow), give notice to the court whether it is intended to make a revised proposal to creditors, or to invite reconsideration of the original proposal.

(5) The person on whose application the order of revocation or suspension was made shall, within [5 business] days after the making of the order, give written notice of it to the Secretary of State and shall, in the case of an order of suspension, within [5 business] days of the expiry of any suspension order, given written notice of such expiry to the Secretary of State.]

NOTES
Amendment
Substituted, together with rr 5.1–5.29, 5.31–5.38, for rr 5.1–5.5, 5.5A (as inserted by SI 1987/1919, r 3(1), Schedule, Pt I, para 85), 5.6–5.30, 5.31–5.34 (as inserted by SI 2002/1307, rr 3(1), 7(3)), by SI 2002/2712, r 5(1), Schedule, Pt 3, para 24.
Date in force: 1 January 2003: see SI 2002/2712, r 1(1); for effect see rr 1(2), 5(2) thereof.
Para (4): in sub-para (a) words "as soon as reasonably practicable" in square brackets substituted by SI 2009/642, rr 4, 5.
Date in force: 6 April 2009: see SI 2009/642, r 1; for transitional provisions see r 3 thereof.
Para (4): in sub-para (b) words "5 business" in square brackets substituted by SI 2010/686, r 2, Sch 1, para 278.
Date in force: 6 April 2010: see SI 2010/686, r 1; for transitional provisions see r 6(1), Sch 4, para 1 thereto.
Para (5): words "5 business" in square brackets in both places they occur substituted by SI 2010/686, r 2, Sch 1, para 278.
Date in force: 6 April 2010: see SI 2010/686, r 1; for transitional provisions see r 6(1), Sch 4, para 1 thereto.

[. . .]

NOTES
Amendment
Inserted by SI 2002/1307, rr 3(1), 7(3).
Date in force: 31 May 2002: see SI 2002/1307, r 1.
Substituted, together with rr 5.1–5.38, for rr 5.1–5.5, 5.5A (as inserted by SI 1987/1919, r 3(1), Schedule, Pt I, para 85), 5.6–5.30, 5.31–5.34 (as inserted by SI 2002/1307, rr 3(1), 7(3)), by SI 2002/2712, r 5(1), Schedule, Pt 3, para 24.
Date in force: 1 January 2003: see SI 2002/2712, r 1(1); for effect see rr 1(2), 5(2) thereof.

[5.31A Supervisor's accounts and reports]
[(1) Paragraph (2) applies where the voluntary arrangement authorises or requires the supervisor—

(a) to carry on the business of the debtor or trade on behalf of or in the name of the debtor; or

(b) to realise assets of the debtor or (in a case where the debtor is an undischarged bankrupt) belonging to the estate; or

(c) otherwise to administer or dispose of any funds of the debtor or the estate.

(2) The supervisor must keep accounts and records of the supervisor's acts and dealings in, and in connection with, the arrangement, including in particular records of all receipts and payments of money.

(3) The supervisor must preserve any accounts and records in paragraph (2) which—

(a) were kept by any other person who has acted as supervisor of the arrangement; and

(b) are in the supervisor's possession.

(4) Subject to paragraph (5), the supervisor must in respect of each period of 12 months ending with the anniversary of the commencement of the arrangement send within 2 months of the end of that period a report on the progress and prospects for the full implementation of the voluntary arrangement to—
- (a) the debtor, and
- (b) all those of the debtor's creditors who are bound by the voluntary arrangement and of whose address the supervisor is aware.

(5) The supervisor is released from an obligation to send a report under paragraph (4), if an obligation to send a final report under Rule 5.34 arises in the period of 2 months mentioned in paragraph (4).

(6) Where the supervisor is authorised or required to do any of the things mentioned in paragraph (1)(a) to (c) the report required to be sent pursuant to paragraph (2) must include or be accompanied by—
- (a) an abstract of receipts and payments required to be recorded by virtue of paragraph (2); or
- (b) where there have been no such receipts and payments, a statement to that effect.]

NOTES

Amendment

Substituted, for r 5.31 as previously enacted, by SI 2010/686, r 2, Sch 1, para 279.
Date in force: 6 April 2010: see SI 2010/686, r 1; for transitional provisions see r 6(1), Sch 4, para 1 thereto.

[5.32 Production of accounts and records to Secretary of State]

[(1) The Secretary of State may at any time during the course of the voluntary arrangement or after its completion require the supervisor to produce for inspection—
- (a) his records and accounts in respect of the arrangement, and
- (b) copies of abstracts and reports prepared in compliance with Rule [5.31A].

(2) The Secretary of State may require production either at the premises of the supervisor or elsewhere; and it is the duty of the supervisor to comply with any requirement imposed on him under this Rule.

(3) The Secretary of State may cause any accounts and records produced to him under this Rule to be audited; and the supervisor shall give to the Secretary of State such further information and assistance as he needs for the purposes of his audit.]

NOTES

Amendment

Substituted (as inserted by SI 2002/1307, rr 3(1), 7(3)), together with rr 5.1–5.31, 5.33–5.38, for rr 5.1–5.5, 5.5A (as inserted by SI 1987/1919, r 3(1), Schedule, Pt I, para 85), 5.6–5.30; 5.31, 5.33, 5.34 (as inserted by SI 2002/1307, rr 3(1), 7(3)), by SI 2002/2712, r 5(1), Schedule, Pt 3, para 24.
Date in force: 1 January 2003: see SI 2002/2712, r 1(1); for effect see rr 1(2), 5(2) thereof.
Para (1): in sub-para (b) reference to "5.31A" in square brackets substituted by SI 2010/686, r 2, Sch 1, para 280.
Date in force: 6 April 2010: see SI 2010/686, r 1; for transitional provisions see r 6(1), Sch 4, para 1 thereto.

[5.33 Fees, costs, charges and expenses]

[The fees, costs, charges and expenses that may be incurred for any purposes of the voluntary arrangement are—

(a) any disbursements made by the nominee prior to the approval of the arrangement, and any remuneration for his services as such agreed between himself and the debtor, the official receiver or the trustee;

(b) any fees, costs, charges or expenses which—
   (i) are sanctioned by the terms of the arrangement, or
   (ii) would be payable, or correspond to those which would be payable, in the debtor's bankruptcy.]

NOTES

Amendment

Substituted (as inserted by SI 2002/1307, rr 3(1), 7(3)), together with rr 5.1–5.32, 5.34–5.38, for rr 5.1–5.5, 5.5A (as inserted by SI 1987/1919, r 3(1), Schedule, Pt I, para 85), 5.6–5.30; 5.31, 5.32, 5.34 (as inserted by SI 2002/1307, rr 3(1), 7(3)), by SI 2002/2712, r 5(1), Schedule, Pt 3, para 24.

Date in force: 1 January 2003: see SI 2002/2712, r 1(1); for effect see rr 1(2), 5(2) thereof.

[. . .]

NOTES

Amendment

Inserted by SI 2002/1307, rr 3(1), 7(3).

Date in force: 31 May 2002: see SI 2002/1307, r 1.

Substituted, together with rr 5.1–5.38, for rr 5.1–5.5, 5.5A (as inserted by SI 1987/1919, r 3(1), Schedule, Pt I, para 85), 5.6–5.30, 5.31–5.34 (as inserted by SI 2002/1307, rr 3(1), 7(3)), by SI 2002/2712, r 5(1), Schedule, Pt 3, para 24.

Date in force: 1 January 2003: see SI 2002/2712, r 1(1); for effect see rr 1(2), 5(2) thereof.

[5.34 Completion or termination of the arrangement]

[(1) Not more than 28 days after the final completion or termination of the voluntary arrangement, the supervisor shall send to all creditors of the debtor who are bound by the arrangement, and to the debtor, a notice that the arrangement has been fully implemented or (as the case may be) terminated.

(2) With the notice there shall be sent to each of those persons a copy of a report by the supervisor summarising all receipts and payments made by him in pursuance of the arrangement, and explaining any difference in the actual implementation of it as compared with the proposal as approved by the creditors' meeting or (in the case of termination of the arrangement) explaining the reasons why the arrangement has not been implemented in accordance with the proposal as approved by the creditors' meeting.

[(3) The Supervisor must not vacate office until paragraph (3A) has been complied with.

(3A) Within the period in paragraph (1), a copy of the notice under paragraph (1), together with a copy of the report under paragraph (2) must be—

(a) sent by the supervisor to the Secretary of State; and
(b) where the creditors' meeting was summoned under section 257 pursuant to a report to a court under section 256(1)(aa), filed with the court by the supervisor.]

(4) The court may, on application by the supervisor, extend the period of 28 days under paragraphs (1) . . ..]

NOTES

Amendment

Substituted (as inserted by SI 2002/1307, rr 3(1), 7(3)), together with rr 5.1–5.33, 5.35–5.38, for rr 5.1–5.5, 5.5A (as inserted by SI 1987/1919, r 3(1), Schedule, Pt I, para 85), 5.6–5.30, 5.31–5.33 (as inserted by SI 2002/1307, rr 3(1), 7(3)), by SI 2002/2712, r 5(1), Schedule, Pt 3, para 24.
Date in force: 1 January 2003: see SI 2002/2712, r 1(1); for effect see rr 1(2), 5(2) thereof.
Paras (3), (3A): substituted, for para (3) as originally enacted, by SI 2010/686, r 2, Sch 1, para 281(1), (2).
Date in force: 6 April 2010: see SI 2010/686, r 1; for transitional provisions see r 6(1), Sch 4, para 1 thereto.
Para (4): words omitted revoked by SI 2010/686, r 2, Sch 1, para 281(1), (3).
Date in force: 6 April 2010: see SI 2010/686, r 1; for transitional provisions see r 6(1), Sch 4, para 1 thereto.

[CHAPTER 7

FAST-TRACK VOLUNTARY ARRANGEMENT]

NOTES

Amendment

Substituted, together with Chapters 8–12, by SI 2003/1730, r 8, Sch 1, Pt 5, para 31.
Date in force: 1 April 2004: see SI 2003/1730, r 1(3).

[**5.35 Application of Chapter**]
[The Rules in this Chapter apply in relation to an individual debtor who intends to submit a proposal for a voluntary arrangement with his creditors to the official receiver in accordance with the provisions of section 263B.]

NOTES

Amendment

Substituted, together with rr 5.36–5.65, for rr 5.35–5.38 (substituted, together with rr 5.1–5.34, for rr 5.1–5.34, by SI 2002/2712, r 5(1), Schedule, Pt 3, para 24), by SI 2003/1730, r 8, Sch 1, Pt 5, para 31.
Date in force: 1 April 2004: see SI 2003/1730, r 1(3).

[**5.36 Interpretation**]
[In this Chapter—
"voluntary arrangement" means an individual voluntary arrangement under section 263A;
"proposal" means the document setting out the terms of the voluntary arrangement which the debtor is proposing.]

NOTES

Amendment

Substituted, together with rr 5.35, 5.37–5.65, for rr 5.35–5.38 (substituted, together with rr 5.1–5.34, for rr 5.1–5.34, by SI 2002/2712, r 5(1), Schedule, Pt 3, para 24), by SI 2003/1730, r 8, Sch 1, Pt 5, para 31.

Date in force: 1 April 2004: see SI 2003/1730, r 1(3).

[5.37 Contents of proposal]

[(1) The debtor's proposal submitted under section 263B(1) shall—
- (a) be accompanied by any fee payable to the official receiver for acting as nominee; and
- (b) contain—
  - (i) a statement that the debtor is eligible to propose a voluntary arrangement;
  - (ii) a short explanation why, in his opinion, a voluntary arrangement is desirable, and give reasons why his creditors may be expected to concur with such an arrangement; and
  - (iii) a statement that the debtor is aware that he commits an offence under section 262A if, for the purpose of obtaining the approval of his creditors to his proposal, he makes any false representation, or fraudulently does, or omits to do, anything.

(2) The following matters shall be stated, or otherwise dealt with, in the proposal—
- (a) the following matters, so far as within the debtor's immediate knowledge—
  - (i) his assets, with an estimate of their respective values;
  - (ii) the extent (if any) to which the assets are charged in favour of creditors; and
  - (iii) the extent (if any) to which particular assets are to be excluded from the voluntary arrangement;
- (b) particulars of any property, other than assets of the debtor himself, which is proposed to be included in the voluntary arrangement, the source of such property and the terms on which it is to be made available for inclusion;
- (c) the nature and amount of the debtor's liabilities (so far as within his immediate knowledge), the manner in which they are proposed to be met, modified, postponed or otherwise dealt with by means of the voluntary arrangement and (in particular)—
  - (i) how it is proposed to deal with preferential creditors (defined in section 258(7)) and creditors who are, or claim to be, secured;
  - (ii) how associates of the debtor (being creditors of his) are proposed to be treated under the voluntary arrangement; and
  - (iii) whether, to the debtor's knowledge, claims have been made under section 339 (transactions at an undervalue), section 340 (preferences), section 343 (extortionate credit transactions), or whether there are circumstances giving rise to the possibility of such claims,

and, where any such circumstances are present, whether, and if so how, it is proposed under the voluntary arrangement to make provision for wholly or partly indemnifying the insolvent estate in respect of such claims;

(d) whether any, and if so what, guarantees have been given of the debtor's debts by other persons, specifying which (if any) of the guarantors are associates of his;

(e) the proposed duration of the voluntary arrangement;

(f) the proposed dates of distributions to creditors, with estimates of their amounts;

(g) how it is proposed to deal with the claims of any person who is bound by the arrangement by virtue of section 263D(2)(c);

(h) an estimate of the fees and expenses that will be incurred in connection with the approval and implementation of the voluntary arrangement;

(j) whether, for the purposes of the voluntary arrangement, any guarantees are to be offered by any persons other than the debtor, and whether (if so) any security is to be given or sought;

(k) the manner in which funds held for the purpose of payment to creditors, and not so paid on the termination of the voluntary arrangement, are to be dealt with;

(l) the functions which are to be undertaken by the supervisor of the voluntary arrangement;

(m) an address of the official receiver to which correspondence with the official receiver is to be sent;

(n) the names and addresses of all the debtor's creditors so far as within his immediate knowledge; and

(o) whether the EC Regulation will apply and, if so, whether the proceedings will be main proceedings or territorial proceedings,

and the proposal shall be [authenticated] . . . by the debtor.

(3) The official receiver shall on request supply to the debtor the address referred to in paragraph (2)(m).]

NOTES

Amendment

Substituted, together with rr 5.35, 5.36, 5.38–5.65, for rr 5.35–5.38 (substituted, together with rr 5.1–5.34, for rr 5.1–5.34, by SI 2002/2712, r 5(1), Schedule, Pt 3, para 24), by SI 2003/1730, r 8, Sch 1, Pt 5, para 31.

Date in force: 1 April 2004: see SI 2003/1730, r 1(3).

Para (2): word "authenticated" in square brackets substituted by SI 2010/686, r 2, Sch 1, para 1.

Date in force: 6 April 2010: see SI 2010/686, r 1; for transitional provisions see r 6(1), Sch 4, paras 1, 2(1)(b) thereto.

Para (2): words omitted revoked by SI 2010/686, r 2, Sch 1, para 282.

Date in force: 6 April 2010: see SI 2010/686, r 1; for transitional provisions see r 6(1), Sch 4, paras 1, 2(1)(b) thereto.

[5.38 Requirement for the official receiver's decision]

[(1) Where the official receiver receives a proposal for a voluntary arrangement in accordance with Rule 5.37 he shall, within 28 days of its receipt, serve a notice on the debtor stating that—

(a) he agrees to act as nominee in relation to the proposal;

(b) he declines to act as nominee in relation to the proposal and specifying reasons for his decision; or

(c) on the basis of the information supplied to him he is unable to reach a decision as to whether to act and specifying what further information he requires.

(2) Where the debtor, pursuant to a request under paragraph (1)(c), supplies the information requested, the official receiver shall, within 28 days of the receipt of the information, serve a notice on the debtor in accordance with paragraph (1).]

NOTES

Amendment

Substituted, together with rr 5.35–5.37, 5.39–5.65, for rr 5.35–5.38 (substituted, together with rr 5.1–5.34, for rr 5.1–5.34, by SI 2002/2712, r 5(1), Schedule, Pt 3, para 24), by SI 2003/1730, r 8, Sch 1, Pt 5, para 31.

Date in force: 1 April 2004: see SI 2003/1730, r 1(3).

[5.39 Arrangements for approval of fast-track voluntary arrangement]

[(1) As soon as reasonably practicable after the official receiver agrees to act as nominee, he shall send to the creditors and any trustee who is not the official receiver—

    (a)   a copy of the proposal; and

    (b)   a notice inviting creditors to vote to approve or reject the debtor's proposal and stating that—

        (i)   if a majority . . . of three-quarters [or more] in value of creditors who vote approve the proposal, the official receiver will, as soon as reasonably practicable, [notify the Secretary of State] that the proposal has been approved;

        (ii)   under section 263F—

            (aa)   the debtor, a person who was entitled to participate in the arrangements made under section 263B(2), any trustee who is not the official receiver, or the official receiver, has 28 days from the date the official receiver [notifies the Secretary of State] under section 263C that the proposal has been approved to apply to the court to have the proposal set aside on the grounds set out in section 263F(1);

            (bb)   a creditor, who was not made aware of the arrangements under section 263B(2) at the time when they were made, has 28 days from the date on which he becomes aware of the voluntary arrangement, to apply to have the proposal set aside on the grounds set out in section 263F(1); and

        (iii)   creditors cannot propose modifications to the debtor's proposal; and

    (c)   for the creditors, a copy of Form 5.6 for their use.

(2) The notice shall include a date specified by the official receiver as the final date on which he will accept votes from creditors, being a date not less than 14 days and not more than 28 days from the date of the notice.]

NOTES

Amendment

Substituted, together with rr 5.35–5.38, 5.40–5.65, for rr 5.35–5.38 (substituted, together with rr 5.1–5.34, for rr 5.1–5.34, by SI 2002/2712, r 5(1), Schedule, Pt 3, para 24), by SI 2003/1730, r 8, Sch 1, Pt 5, para 31.

Date in force: 1 April 2004: see SI 2003/1730, r 1(3).

Para (1): in sub-para (b)(i) words omitted revoked by SI 2010/686, r 2, Sch 1, para 283(1), (2)(a).

Date in force: 6 April 2010: see SI 2010/686, r 1; for transitional provisions see r 6(1), Sch 4, para 1 thereto.

Para (1): in sub-para (b)(i) words "or more" in square brackets inserted by SI 2010/686, r 2, Sch 1, para 283(1), (2)(b).

Date in force: 6 April 2010: see SI 2010/686, r 1; for transitional provisions see r 6(1), Sch 4, para 1 thereto.
Para (1): in sub-para (b)(i) words "notify the Secretary of State" in square brackets substituted by SI 2010/686, r 2, Sch 1, para 283(1), (2)(c).
Date in force: 6 April 2010: see SI 2010/686, r 1; for transitional provisions see r 6(1), Sch 4, para 1 thereto.
Para (1): in sub-para (b)(ii)(aa) words "notifies the Secretary of State" in square brackets substituted by SI 2010/686, r 2, Sch 1, para 283(1), (3).
Date in force: 6 April 2010: see SI 2010/686, r 1; for transitional provisions see r 6(1), Sch 4, para 1 thereto.

[5.40 Approval by creditors]

[(1) All creditors who wish to vote shall give notice in Form 5.6 to the official receiver of their decision whether to accept or reject the debtor's proposal. Such notification shall be sent to the official receiver at the address specified in the notice.

[(2) That notice may be sent by a representative of a creditor if it is accompanied by a written authority for that representation authenticated by the creditor.]

(3) ...]

NOTES

Amendment

Substituted, together with rr 5.35–5.39, 5.41–5.65, for rr 5.35–5.38 (substituted, together with rr 5.1–5.34, for rr 5.1–5.34, by SI 2002/2712, r 5(1), Schedule, Pt 3, para 24), by SI 2003/1730, r 8, Sch 1, Pt 5, para 31.
Date in force: 1 April 2004: see SI 2003/1730, r 1(3).
Para (2): substituted by SI 2010/686, r 2, Sch 1, para 284(1), (2).
Date in force: 6 April 2010: see SI 2010/686, r 1; for transitional provisions see r 6(1), Sch 4, para 1 thereto.
Para (3): revoked by SI 2010/686, r 2, Sch 1, para 284(1), (3).
Date in force: 6 April 2010: see SI 2010/686, r 1; for transitional provisions see r 6(1), Sch 4, para 1 thereto.

[5.41 Entitlement to vote]

[(1) Subject as follows, any creditor who is sent a notice by the official receiver is entitled to vote for the approval or rejection of the proposal.

(2) A creditor's entitlement to vote is calculated by reference to the amount of the creditor's debt at the date of the bankruptcy order.

(3) A creditor may vote in respect of a debt for an unliquidated amount or any debt whose value is not ascertained, and for the purposes of voting (but not otherwise) his debt shall be valued at £1 unless the official receiver agrees to put a higher value on it.]

NOTES

Amendment

Substituted, together with rr 5.35–5.40, 5.42–5.65, for rr 5.35–5.38 (substituted, together with rr 5.1–5.34, for rr 5.1–5.34, by SI 2002/2712, r 5(1), Schedule, Pt 3, para 24), by SI 2003/1730, r 8, Sch 1, Pt 5, para 31.
Date in force: 1 April 2004: see SI 2003/1730, r 1(3).

[5.42 Procedure for admission of creditors' claims for voting purposes]

[(1) The official receiver has the power to admit or reject a creditor's claim for the purpose of his entitlement to vote, and the power is exercisable with respect to the whole or part of the claim.

(2) The official receiver's decision on entitlement to vote is subject to appeal to the court by any creditor or the debtor.

(3) If on appeal the official receiver's decision is reversed or varied, or votes are declared invalid, the court may order another vote to be held, or make such order as it thinks just.
The court's power to make an order under this paragraph is exercisable only if it considers that the circumstances giving rise to the appeal are such as give rise to unfair prejudice or material irregularity.

(4) An application to the court by way of appeal against the official receiver's decision shall not be made after the end of the period of 28 days beginning with the day on which the [official receiver is] required by section 263C [to notify the Secretary of State].

(5) The official receiver is not personally liable for any costs incurred by any person in respect of an appeal under this Rule.]

NOTES

Amendment

Substituted, together with rr 5.35–5.41, 5.43–5.65, for rr 5.35–5.38 (substituted, together with rr 5.1–5.34, for rr 5.1–5.34, by SI 2002/2712, r 5(1), Schedule, Pt 3, para 24), by SI 2003/1730, r 8, Sch 1, Pt 5, para 31.
Date in force: 1 April 2004: see SI 2003/1730, r 1(3).
Para (4): words "official receiver is" in square brackets substituted by SI 2010/686, r 2, Sch 1, para 285(1), (2)(a).
Date in force: 6 April 2010: see SI 2010/686, r 1; for transitional provisions see r 6(1), Sch 4, para 1 thereto.
Para (4): words "to notify the Secretary of State" in square brackets substituted by SI 2010/686, r 2, Sch 1, para 285(1), (2)(b).
Date in force: 6 April 2010: see SI 2010/686, r 1; for transitional provisions see r 6(1), Sch 4, para 1 thereto.

[5.43 Requisite majorities]

[(1) A proposal is approved by the creditors if [three-quarters or more] in value of the creditors who vote approve the proposal.

(2) In the following cases there is to be left out of account a creditor's vote in respect of any claim or part of a claim—

- (a) where the claim or part is secured;
- (b) where the claim is in respect of a debt wholly or partly on, or secured by, a current bill of exchange or promissory note, unless the creditor is willing—
    - (i) to treat the liability to him on the bill or note of every person who is liable on it antecedently to the debtor, and against whom a bankruptcy order has not been made (or in the case of a company, which has not gone into liquidation), as a security in his hands; and
    - (ii) to estimate the value of the security and (for the purpose of entitlement to vote, but not of any distribution under the arrangement) to deduct it from his claim.

[(3) A proposal is not approved if those voting against it include more than half in value of the creditors, counting in the latter only those—

- (a) who gave notice to the official receiver in accordance with Rule 5.40;
- (b) whose votes are not to be left out of account under paragraph (2); and
- (c) who are not, to the best of the official receiver's belief, associates of the debtor.

(4) It is for the official receiver to decide whether, under this Rule a person is an associate of the debtor for the purposes of paragraph (3)(c) and in relation to this he is

entitled to rely on the information provided by the debtor's statement of affairs or otherwise in accordance with this Part of the Rules.]]

NOTES

Amendment

Substituted, together with rr 5.35–5.42, 5.44–5.65, for rr 5.35–5.38 (substituted, together with rr 5.1–5.34, for rr 5.1–5.34, by SI 2002/2712, r 5(1), Schedule, Pt 3, para 24), by SI 2003/1730, r 8, Sch 1, Pt 5, para 31.
Date in force: 1 April 2004: see SI 2003/1730, r 1(3).
Para (1): words "three-quarters or more" in square brackets substituted by SI 2010/686, r 2, Sch 1, para 286.
Date in force: 6 April 2010: see SI 2010/686, r 1; for transitional provisions see r 6(1), Sch 4, para 1 thereto.
Paras (3), (4): inserted by SI 2004/584, r 24.
Date in force: 1 April 2004: see SI 2004/584, r 1(2).

[5.44 . . .]
[. . .]

NOTES

Amendment

Substituted, together with rr 5.35–5.43, 5.45–5.65, for rr 5.35–5.38 (substituted, together with rr 5.1–5.34, for rr 5.1–5.34, by SI 2002/2712, r 5(1), Schedule, Pt 3, para 24), by SI 2003/1730, r 8, Sch 1, Pt 5, para 31.
Date in force: 1 April 2004: see SI 2003/1730, r 1(3).
Revoked by SI 2010/686, r 5.
Date in force: 6 April 2010: see SI 2010/686, r 1; for transitional provisions see r 6(1), Sch 4, para 1 thereto.

[5.45 Notice of appointment as supervisor etc]
[(1) Where the official receiver is appointed to act as supervisor of a voluntary arrangement, he shall, as soon as reasonably practicable, give written notice of his appointment to the Secretary of State, and all creditors of [whose address the official receiver] is aware, and the trustee (if any) who is not the official receiver.
(2) If the official receiver vacates office as supervisor he [must, as soon as reasonably practicable after doing so,] give written notice of that fact to the Secretary of State.]

NOTES

Amendment

Substituted, together with rr 5.35–5.44, 5.46–5.65, for rr 5.35–5.38 (substituted, together with rr 5.1–5.34, for rr 5.1–5.34, by SI 2002/2712, r 5(1), Schedule, Pt 3, para 24), by SI 2003/1730, r 8, Sch 1, Pt 5, para 31.
Date in force: 1 April 2004: see SI 2003/1730, r 1(3).
Para (1): words "whose address the official receiver" in square brackets substituted by SI 2010/686, r 2, Sch 1, para 287(1), (2).
Date in force: 6 April 2010: see SI 2010/686, r 1; for transitional provisions see r 6(1), Sch 4, para 1 thereto.
Para (2): words "must, as soon as reasonably practicable after doing so," in square brackets substituted by SI 2010/686, r 2, Sch 1, para 287(1), (3).
Date in force: 6 April 2010: see SI 2010/686, r 1; for transitional provisions see r 6(1), Sch 4, para 1 thereto.

[5.46 Revocation of the fast-track voluntary arrangement]

[(1) This Rule applies where the court makes an order of revocation under section 263F.

(2) Where the person who applied for the order is—

- (a) the debtor, he shall serve a sealed copy of the order on the supervisor and any trustee of his estate who is not the official receiver;
- (b) the supervisor, he shall serve a sealed copy of the order on the debtor, and any trustee who is not the official receiver;
- (c) a trustee who is not the official receiver, he shall serve a sealed copy of the order on the debtor and the supervisor; and
- (d) a creditor, he shall serve a sealed copy of the order on the debtor, the supervisor and any trustee who is not the official receiver.

(3) The supervisor shall, as soon as reasonably practicable after receiving a copy of the order, give notice of it, to all persons who were sent a copy of the debtor's proposal under Rule 5.39 and all other persons who are affected by the order.

(4) The person on whose application the order was made shall, within [5 business] days after the making of the order, give written notice of it to the Secretary of State.]

NOTES

Amendment

Substituted, together with rr 5.35–5.45, 5.47–5.65, for rr 5.35–5.38 (substituted, together with rr 5.1–5.34, for rr 5.1–5.34, by SI 2002/2712, r 5(1), Schedule, Pt 3, para 24), by SI 2003/1730, r 8, Sch 1, Pt 5, para 31.
Date in force: 1 April 2004: see SI 2003/1730, r 1(3).
Para (4): words "5 business" in square brackets substituted by SI 2010/686, r 2, Sch 1, para 288.
Date in force: 6 April 2010: see SI 2010/686, r 1; for transitional provisions see r 6(1), Sch 4, para 1 thereto.

[5.47A Supervisor's accounts and reports]

[(1) The supervisor must keep accounts and records of the supervisor's acts and dealings in, and in connection with, the arrangement including in particular records of all receipts and payments of money.

(2) Subject to paragraph (3), the supervisor must in respect of each period of 12 months ending with the anniversary of the commencement of the arrangement send within 2 months of the end of that period a report on the progress and prospects for the full implementation of the voluntary arrangement to—

- (a) the debtor;
- (b) all those of the debtor's creditors who are bound by the voluntary arrangement of whose address the supervisor is aware;

(3) The supervisor is released from an obligation to send a report under paragraph (2), if an obligation to send a final report under Rule 5.50 arises in the period of 2 months mentioned in paragraph (2).]

NOTES

Amendment

Substituted, for r 5.47 as previously enacted, by SI 2010/686, r 2, Sch 1, para 289.
Date in force: 6 April 2010: see SI 2010/686, r 1; for transitional provisions see r 6(1), Sch 4, para 1 thereto.

[5.48 Fees, costs and expenses in respect of the performance of the functions of the official receiver]
[The fees, costs and expenses in respect of the performance by the official receiver of his functions in relation to the bankruptcy and those of the trustee who is not the official receiver (including those in connection with the employment of agents) shall be a first charge on any sums realised under the terms of the voluntary arrangement, and those of the official receiver in relation to the voluntary arrangement, shall be a second charge.]

NOTES

Amendment

> Substituted, together with rr 5.35–5.47, 5.49–5.65, for rr 5.35–5.38 (substituted, together with rr 5.1–5.34, for rr 5.1–5.34, by SI 2002/2712, r 5(1), Schedule, Pt 3, para 24), by SI 2003/1730, r 8, Sch 1, Pt 5, para 31.
> Date in force: 1 April 2004: see SI 2003/1730, r 1(3).

[5.49 Employment of agents by the supervisor]
[The supervisor may employ agents in connection with the realisation of any assets subject to the terms of the voluntary arrangement.]

NOTES

Amendment

> Substituted, together with rr 5.35–5.48, 5.50–5.65, for rr 5.35–5.38 (substituted, together with rr 5.1–5.34, for rr 5.1–5.34, by SI 2002/2712, r 5(1), Schedule, Pt 3, para 24), by SI 2003/1730, r 8, Sch 1, Pt 5, para 31.
> Date in force: 1 April 2004: see SI 2003/1730, r 1(3).

[5.50 Completion or termination of the fast-track voluntary arrangement]
[(1) Not more than 28 days after the final completion or termination of the voluntary arrangement, the supervisor shall send to all creditors of the debtor who are bound by the arrangement, and to the debtor, a notice that the voluntary arrangement has been fully implemented, [or (as] the case may be) terminated.

(2) With the notice there shall be sent to each of those persons a copy of a report by the supervisor summarising all receipts and payments made by him in pursuance of the voluntary arrangement, and explaining any difference in the actual implementation of it compared with the proposal as approved by the creditors.

(3) The supervisor shall, within the 28 days mentioned above, send to the Secretary of State a copy of the notice under paragraph (1), together with a copy of the report under paragraph (2), and he shall not vacate office until after such copies have been sent.

(4) The court may, on application by the supervisor, extend the period of 28 days under paragraphs (1) and (3).]

NOTES

Amendment

> Substituted, together with rr 5.35–5.49, 5.51–5.65, for rr 5.35–5.38 (substituted, together with rr 5.1–5.34, for rr 5.1–5.34, by SI 2002/2712, r 5(1), Schedule, Pt 3, para 24), by SI 2003/1730, r 8, Sch 1, Pt 5, para 31.
> Date in force: 1 April 2004: see SI 2003/1730, r 1(3).
> Para (1): words "or (as" in square brackets substituted by SI 2010/686, r 2, Sch 1, para 290.

Date in force: 6 April 2010: see SI 2010/686, r 1; for transitional provisions see r 6(1), Sch 4, para 1 thereto.

[CHAPTER 8

APPLICATION BY A BANKRUPT TO ANNUL A BANKRUPTCY ORDER UNDER SECTION 261(2)(A)]

NOTES

Amendment

Substituted, together with Chapters 7, 9–12, for Chapter 7, by SI 2003/1730, r 8, Sch 1, Pt 5, para 31.
Date in force: 1 April 2004: see SI 2003/1730, r 1(3).

[5.51 Application of this Chapter]
[The following Rules apply where a bankrupt applies for an annulment of a bankruptcy order under section 261(2)(a).]

NOTES

Amendment

Substituted, together with rr 5.35–5.50, 5.52–5.65, for rr 5.35–5.38 (substituted, together with rr 5.1–5.34, for rr 5.1–5.34, by SI 2002/2712, r 5(1), Schedule, Pt 3, para 24), by SI 2003/1730, r 8, Sch 1, Pt 5, para 31.
Date in force: 1 April 2004: see SI 2003/1730, r 1(3).

[5.52 Application to court]
[(1) An application to the court to annul a bankruptcy order under section 261(2)(a) shall specify the section under which it is made.
(2) The application shall be supported by [a witness statement] stating—
- (a) that the voluntary arrangement has been approved at a meeting of creditors;
- (b) the date of the approval by the creditors; and
- (c) that the 28 day period in section 262(3)(a) for applications to be made under section 262(1) has expired and no applications or appeal remain to be disposed of.

(3) The application and supporting [witness statement] shall be filed in court; and the court shall give to the bankrupt notice of the venue fixed for the hearing.
(4) The bankrupt shall give notice of the venue, accompanied by copies of the application and [witness statement] to the official receiver, any trustee who is not the official receiver, and the supervisor of the voluntary arrangement not less than [5 business] days before the date of the hearing.
(5) The official receiver, the supervisor of the voluntary arrangement and any trustee who is not the official receiver may attend the hearing or be represented and call to the attention of the court any matters which seem to him to be relevant.
(6) Where the court annuls a bankruptcy order, it shall send sealed copies of the order of annulment in Form 5.7 to the bankrupt, the official receiver, the supervisor of the voluntary arrangement and any trustee who is not the official receiver.]

NOTES

Amendment

Substituted, together with rr 5.35–5.51, 5.53–5.65, for rr 5.35–5.38 (substituted, together with rr 5.1–5.34, for rr 5.1–5.34, by SI 2002/2712, r 5(1), Schedule, Pt 3, para 24), by SI 2003/1730, r 8, Sch 1, Pt 5, para 31.
Date in force: 1 April 2004: see SI 2003/1730, r 1(3).
Para (2): words "a witness statement" in square brackets substituted by SI 2010/686, r 2, Sch 1, para 291(1), (2).
Date in force: 6 April 2010: see SI 2010/686, r 1; for transitional provisions see r 6(1), Sch 4, paras 1, 2(1)(b), (2)–(4) thereto.
Para (3): words "witness statement" in square brackets substituted by SI 2010/686, r 2, Sch 1, para 291(1), (3).
Date in force: 6 April 2010: see SI 2010/686, r 1; for transitional provisions see r 6(1), Sch 4, paras 1, 2(1)(b), (2)–(4) thereto.
Para (4): words "witness statement" in square brackets substituted by SI 2010/686, r 2, Sch 1, para 291(1), (4)(a).
Date in force: 6 April 2010: see SI 2010/686, r 1; for transitional provisions see r 6(1), Sch 4, paras 1, 2(1)(b), (2)–(4) thereto.
Para (4): words "5 business" in square brackets substituted by SI 2010/686, r 2, Sch 1, para 291(1), (4)(b).
Date in force: 6 April 2010: see SI 2010/686, r 1; for transitional provisions see r 6(1), Sch 4, para 1 thereto.

[5.53 Notice to creditors]

[(1) Where the official receiver has notified creditors of the debtor's bankruptcy, and the bankruptcy order is annulled, he shall, as soon as reasonably practicable, notify them of the annulment.

(2) Expenses incurred by the official receiver in giving notice under this Rule are a charge in his favour on the property of the former bankrupt, whether or not actually in his hands.

(3) Where any property is in the hands of a trustee or any person other than the former bankrupt himself, the official receiver's charge is valid subject only to any costs that may be incurred by the trustee or that other person in effecting realisation of the property for the purpose of satisfying the charge.]

NOTES

Amendment

Substituted, together with rr 5.35–5.52, 5.54–5.65, for rr 5.35–5.38 (substituted, together with rr 5.1–5.34, for rr 5.1–5.34, by SI 2002/2712, r 5(1), Schedule, Pt 3, para 24), by SI 2003/1730, r 8, Sch 1, Pt 5, para 31.
Date in force: 1 April 2004: see SI 2003/1730, r 1(3).

[CHAPTER 9

APPLICATION BY OFFICIAL RECEIVER TO ANNUL A BANKRUPTCY ORDER UNDER SECTION 261(2)(B)]

NOTES

Amendment

Substituted, together with Chapters 7, 8, 10–12, for Chapter 7, by SI 2003/1730, r 8, Sch 1, Pt 5, para 31.
Date in force: 1 April 2004: see SI 2003/1730, r 1(3).

[5.54 Application of this Chapter]
[The following Rules apply where the official receiver applies for an annulment of a bankruptcy order under section 261(2)(b).]

NOTES

Amendment

Substituted, together with rr 5.35–5.53, 5.55–5.65, for rr 5.35–5.38 (substituted, together with rr 5.1–5.34, for rr 5.1–5.34, by SI 2002/2712, r 5(1), Schedule, Pt 3, para 24), by SI 2003/1730, r 8, Sch 1, Pt 5, para 31.
Date in force: 1 April 2004: see SI 2003/1730, r 1(3).

[5.55 Application to court]
[(1) An application to the court to annul a bankruptcy order under section 261(2)(b) shall specify the section under which it is made.
[(2) The official receiver may not make an application under section 261(2)(b) before the expiry of the period of 42 days beginning with the day on which—
   (a)   where the creditors' meeting was summoned under section 257 pursuant to a report to a court under section 256(1)(aa), the nominee filed the report of the creditors' meeting with the court; or
   (b)   where the creditors' meeting was summoned under section 257 pursuant to a report to the debtor's creditors under section 256A(3), the result of the creditors' meeting was notified to the creditors.]
(3) The application shall be supported by a report stating the grounds on which it is made. It shall also state that—
   (a)   the time period for application in paragraph (2) above has expired; and
   (b)   the official receiver is not aware that any application or appeal remains to be disposed of.
(4) The application and the report shall be filed in court and the court shall give to the official receiver notice of the venue fixed for the hearing.
(5) The official receiver shall give notice of the venue, accompanied by copies of the application and the report to the bankrupt not less than [5 business] days before the date of the hearing.
(6) Where the court annuls a bankruptcy order, it shall send sealed copies of the order of annulment in Form 5.7 to the official receiver, any trustee who is not the official receiver, the supervisor of the voluntary arrangement and the bankrupt.]

NOTES

Amendment

Substituted, together with rr 5.35–5.54, 5.56–5.65, for rr 5.35–5.38 (substituted, together with rr 5.1–5.34, for rr 5.1–5.34, by SI 2002/2712, r 5(1), Schedule, Pt 3, para 24), by SI 2003/1730, r 8, Sch 1, Pt 5, para 31.
Date in force: 1 April 2004: see SI 2003/1730, r 1(3).
Para (2): substituted by SI 2010/686, r 2, Sch 1, para 292(1), (2).
Date in force: 6 April 2010: see SI 2010/686, r 1; for transitional provisions see r 6(1), Sch 4, para 1 thereto.
Para (5): words "5 business" in square brackets substituted by SI 2010/686, r 2, Sch 1, para 292(1), (3).
Date in force: 6 April 2010: see SI 2010/686, r 1; for transitional provisions see r 6(1), Sch 4, para 1 thereto.

[5.56 Notice to creditors]
[(1) Where the bankruptcy order is annulled, the official receiver shall notify all creditors of [whose address the official receiver] is aware of the annulment.

(2) Expenses incurred by the official receiver in giving notice under this Rule are a charge in his favour on the property of the former bankrupt, whether or not actually in his hands.

(3) Where any property is in the hands of a trustee or any person other than the former bankrupt himself, the official receiver's charge is valid subject only to any costs that may be incurred by the trustee or that other person in effecting realisation of the property for the purpose of satisfying the charge.]

NOTES

Amendment

Substituted, together with rr 5.35–5.55, 5.57–5.65, for rr 5.35–5.38 (substituted, together with rr 5.1–5.34, for rr 5.1–5.34, by SI 2002/2712, r 5(1), Schedule, Pt 3, para 24), by SI 2003/1730, r 8, Sch 1, Pt 5, para 31.

Date in force: 1 April 2004: see SI 2003/1730, r 1(3).

Para (1): words "whose address the official receiver" in square brackets substituted by SI 2010/686, r 2, Sch 1, para 293.

Date in force: 6 April 2010: see SI 2010/686, r 1; for transitional provisions see r 6(1), Sch 4, para 1 thereto.

[CHAPTER 10

APPLICATION BY OFFICIAL RECEIVER TO ANNUL A BANKRUPTCY ORDER UNDER SECTION 263D(3)]

NOTES

Amendment

Substituted, together with Chapters 7–9, 11, 12, for Chapter 7, by SI 2003/1730, r 8, Sch 1, Pt 5, para 31.

Date in force: 1 April 2004: see SI 2003/1730, r 1(3).

[5.57 Application of this Chapter]

[The following Rules apply where the official receiver applies for an annulment of a bankruptcy order under section 263D(3).]

NOTES

Amendment

Substituted, together with rr 5.35–5.56, 5.58–5.65, for rr 5.35–5.38 (substituted, together with rr 5.1–5.34, for rr 5.1–5.34, by SI 2002/2712, r 5(1), Schedule, Pt 3, para 24), by SI 2003/1730, r 8, Sch 1, Pt 5, para 31.

Date in force: 1 April 2004: see SI 2003/1730, r 1(3).

[5.58 Application to court]

[(1) An application to the court to annul a bankruptcy order under section 263D(3) shall specify the section under which it is made.

(2) An application under section 263D(3) shall be made within 21 days of the expiry of the relevant period set out in section 263D(4).

(3) The application shall be supported by a report stating the grounds on which it is made and a statement by the official receiver that he is not aware that any application or appeal under section 263F remains to be disposed of.

(4) The report shall be accompanied by a copy of the proposal for the voluntary arrangement and a copy of the report under section 263C.

(5) The application, together with the report and the documents in support, shall be filed in court and the court shall give to the official receiver notice of the venue fixed for the hearing.

(6) The official receiver shall give notice of the venue, accompanied by copies of the application and the report, to the bankrupt not less than [5 business] days before the date of the hearing.

(7) Where the court annuls a bankruptcy order, it shall send sealed copies of the order of annulment in Form 5.8 to the official receiver and the bankrupt.]

NOTES

Amendment

Substituted, together with rr 5.35–5.57, 5.59–5.65, for rr 5.35–5.38 (substituted, together with rr 5.1–5.34, for rr 5.1–5.34, by SI 2002/2712, r 5(1), Schedule, Pt 3, para 24), by SI 2003/1730, r 8, Sch 1, Pt 5, para 31.
Date in force: 1 April 2004: see SI 2003/1730, r 1(3).
Para (6): words "5 business" in square brackets substituted by SI 2010/686, r 2, Sch 1, para 294.
Date in force: 6 April 2010: see SI 2010/686, r 1; for transitional provisions see r 6(1), Sch 4, para 1 thereto.

[**5.59 Notice to creditors**]

[(1) Where the official receiver has notified creditors of the debtor's bankruptcy, and the bankruptcy order is annulled, he shall, as soon as reasonably practicable, notify them of the annulment.

(2) Expenses incurred by the official receiver in giving notice under this Rule are a charge in his favour on the property of the former bankrupt, whether or not actually in his hands.

(3) Where any property is in the hands of a trustee or any person other than the former bankrupt himself, the official receiver's charge is valid subject only to any costs that may be incurred by the trustee or that other person in effecting realisation of the property for the purpose of satisfying the charge.]

NOTES

Amendment

Substituted, together with rr 5.35–5.58, 5.60–5.65, for rr 5.35–5.38 (substituted, together with rr 5.1–5.34, for rr 5.1–5.34, by SI 2002/2712, r 5(1), Schedule, Pt 3, para 24), by SI 2003/1730, r 8, Sch 1, Pt 5, para 31.
Date in force: 1 April 2004: see SI 2003/1730, r 1(3).

[CHAPTER 11

OTHER MATTERS ARISING ON ANNULMENTS UNDER SECTIONS 261(2)(A), 261(2)(B) OR 263D(3)]

NOTES

Amendment

Substituted, together with Chapters 7–10, 12, for Chapter 7, by SI 2003/1730, r 8, Sch 1, Pt 5, para 31.
Date in force: 1 April 2004: see SI 2003/1730, r 1(3).

[5.60]

[(1) In an order under section 261(2)(a), 261(2)(b) or 263D(3) the court shall include provision permitting vacation of the registration of the bankruptcy petition as a pending action, and of the bankruptcy order, in the register of writs and orders affecting land.

(2) The court shall as soon as reasonably practicable give notice of the making of the order to the Secretary of State.

[(3) The former bankrupt may in writing within 28 days of the date of the order require the Secretary of State to give notice of the making of the order. As soon as reasonably practicable the notice shall be—
(a) gazetted; and
(b) advertised in the same manner as the bankruptcy order to which it relates was advertised.]

[(3A) In addition to the standard contents, the notice under paragraph (3) must state—
(a) the name of the former bankrupt;
(b) the date on which the bankruptcy order was made;
(c) that the bankruptcy order has been annulled;
(d) the date of the annulling order; and
(e) the grounds of the annulment.]

(4) . . .

(5) Where the former bankrupt has died, or is a person incapable of managing his affairs (within the meaning of Chapter 7 in Part 7 of the Rules), the references to him in [paragraph (3) is] to be read as referring to his personal representative or, as the case may be, a person appointed by the court to represent or act for him.]

NOTES

Amendment

Substituted, together with rr 5.35–5.59, 5.61–5.65, for rr 5.35–5.38 (substituted, together with rr 5.1–5.34, for rr 5.1–5.34, by SI 2002/2712, r 5(1), Schedule, Pt 3, para 24), by SI 2003/1730, r 8, Sch 1, Pt 5, para 31.
Date in force: 1 April 2004: see SI 2003/1730, r 1(3).
Para (3): substituted by SI 2009/642, rr 4, 31.
Date in force: 6 April 2009: see SI 2009/642, r 1; for transitional provisions see r 3 thereof.
Para (3A): inserted by SI 2010/686, r 2, Sch 1, para 295.
Date in force: 6 April 2010: see SI 2010/686, r 1; for transitional provisions see r 6(1), Sch 4, para 1 thereto.
Para (4): revoked by SI 2004/584, r 25(b).
Date in force: 1 April 2004: see SI 2004/584, r 1(2).
Para (5): words "paragraph (3) is" in square brackets substituted by SI 2005/527, r 34.
Date in force: 1 April 2005: see SI 2005/527, r 1(2).

[5.61 Trustee's final account]

[(1) Where a bankruptcy order is annulled under section 261(2)(a), 261(2)(b) or 263D(3), this does not of itself release the trustee from any duty or obligation, imposed on him by or under the Act or the Rules, to account for all his transactions in connection with the former bankrupt's estate.

(2) The trustee shall submit a copy of his final account to the Secretary of State as soon as reasonably practicable after the court's order annulling the bankruptcy order; and he shall file a copy of the final account in court.

(3) The final account must include a summary of the trustee's receipts and payments in the administration, and contain a statement to the effect that he has reconciled his account with that held by the Secretary of State in respect of the bankruptcy.

(4) The trustee is released from such time as the court may determine, having regard to whether paragraph (2) of this Rule has been complied with.]

NOTES

Amendment

Substituted, together with rr 5.35–5.60, 5.62–5.65, for rr 5.35–5.38 (substituted, together with rr 5.1–5.34, for rr 5.1–5.34, by SI 2002/2712, r 5(1), Schedule, Pt 3, para 24), by SI 2003/1730, r 8, Sch 1, Pt 5, para 31.
Date in force: 1 April 2004: see SI 2003/1730, r 1(3).

[CHAPTER 12

EC REGULATION: CONVERSION OF VOLUNTARY ARRANGEMENT INTO BANKRUPTCY]

NOTES

Amendment

Substituted, together with Chapters 7–11, for Chapter 7, by SI 2003/1730, r 8, Sch 1, Pt 5, para 31.
Date in force: 1 April 2004: see SI 2003/1730, r 1(3).

[5.62 Application for conversion of voluntary arrangement into bankruptcy]

[(1) Where a member State liquidator proposes to apply to the court for conversion under Article 37 of the EC Regulation (conversion of earlier proceedings) of a voluntary arrangement into a bankruptcy, [a witness statement] complying with Rule 5.63 must be prepared . . . and filed in court in support of the application.

(2) The application and the [witness statement] required under this Rule shall be served upon—
    (a)   the debtor; and
    (b)   the supervisor.]

NOTES

Amendment

Substituted, together with rr 5.35–5.61, 5.63–5.65, for rr 5.35–5.38 (substituted, together with rr 5.1–5.34, for rr 5.1–5.34, by SI 2002/2712, r 5(1), Schedule, Pt 3, para 24), by SI 2003/1730, r 8, Sch 1, Pt 5, para 31.
Date in force: 1 April 2004: see SI 2003/1730, r 1(3).
Para (1): words "a witness statement" in square brackets substituted by SI 2010/686, r 2, Sch 1, para 296(1), (2)(a).
Date in force: 6 April 2010: see SI 2010/686, r 1; for transitional provisions see r 6(1), Sch 4, paras 1, 2(1)(b), (2)–(4) thereto.
Para (1): words omitted revoked by SI 2010/686, r 2, Sch 1, para 296(1), (2)(b).
Date in force: 6 April 2010: see SI 2010/686, r 1; for transitional provisions see r 6(1), Sch 4, paras 1, 2(1)(b), (2)–(4) thereto.
Para (2): words "witness statement" in square brackets substituted by SI 2010/686, r 2, Sch 1, para 296(1), (3).
Date in force: 6 April 2010: see SI 2010/686, r 1; for transitional provisions see r 6(1), Sch 4, paras 1, 2(1)(b), (2)–(4) thereto.

[5.63 Contents of [witness statement]]

[(1) The [witness statement] shall state—

(a) that the main proceedings have been opened in relation to the debtor in a member State other than the United Kingdom;
(b) the [belief of the person making the witness statement] that the conversion of the voluntary arrangement into a bankruptcy would prove to be in the interests of the creditors in the main proceedings; and
(c) all other matters that, in the opinion of the member State liquidator, would assist the court—
  (i) in deciding whether to make an order under Rule 5.64; and
  (ii) if the court were to do so, in considering the need for any consequential provision that would be necessary or desirable.

(2) [A witness statement] under this Rule shall be [made] by, or on behalf of, the member State liquidator.]

NOTES

Amendment

Substituted, together with rr 5.35–5.62, 5.64, 5.65, for rr 5.35–5.38 (substituted, together with rr 5.1–5.34, for rr 5.1–5.34, by SI 2002/2712, r 5(1), Schedule, Pt 3, para 24), by SI 2003/1730, r 8, Sch 1, Pt 5, para 31.
Date in force: 1 April 2004: see SI 2003/1730, r 1(3).
Provision heading: words "witness statement" in square brackets substituted by SI 2010/686, r 2, Sch 1, para 297(1), (2).
Date in force: 6 April 2010: see SI 2010/686, r 1; for transitional provisions see r 6(1), Sch 4, paras 1, 2(1)(b), (2)–(4) thereto.
Para (1): words "witness statement" in square brackets substituted by SI 2010/686, r 2, Sch 1, para 297(1), (3)(a).
Date in force: 6 April 2010: see SI 2010/686, r 1; for transitional provisions see r 6(1), Sch 4, paras 1, 2(1)(b), (2)–(4) thereto.
Para (1): in sub-para (b) words "belief of the person making the witness statement" in square brackets substituted by SI 2010/686, r 2, Sch 1, para 297(1), (3)(b).
Date in force: 6 April 2010: see SI 2010/686, r 1; for transitional provisions see r 6(1), Sch 4, paras 1, 2(1)(b), (2)–(4) thereto.
Para (2): words "A witness statement" in square brackets substituted by SI 2010/686, r 2, Sch 1, para 297(1), (4)(a).
Date in force: 6 April 2010: see SI 2010/686, r 1; for transitional provisions see r 6(1), Sch 4, paras 1, 2(1)(b), (2)–(4) thereto.
Para (2): word "made" in square brackets substituted by SI 2010/686, r 2, Sch 1, para 297(1), (4)(b).
Date in force: 6 April 2010: see SI 2010/686, r 1; for transitional provisions see r 6(1), Sch 4, paras 1, 2(1)(b), (2)–(4) thereto.

[5.64 Power of court]

[(1) On hearing an application for conversion of a voluntary arrangement into a bankruptcy, the court may make such order as it thinks [just].

(2) If the court makes an order for conversion of a voluntary arrangement into a bankruptcy under paragraph (1), the order may contain all such consequential provisions as the court deems necessary or desirable.

(3) Where the court makes an order for conversion of a voluntary arrangement into a bankruptcy under paragraph (1), any expenses properly incurred as expenses of the administration of the voluntary arrangement in question shall be a first charge on the bankrupt's estate.]

NOTES

Amendment

Substituted, together with rr 5.35–5.63, 5.65, for rr 5.35–5.38 (substituted, together with rr 5.1–5.34, for rr 5.1–5.34, by SI 2002/2712, r 5(1), Schedule, Pt 3, para 24), by SI 2003/1730, r 8, Sch 1, Pt 5, para 31.

Date in force: 1 April 2004: see SI 2003/1730, r 1(3).

Para (1): word "just" in square brackets substituted by SI 2010/686, r 2, Sch 1, para 1.

Date in force: 6 April 2010: see SI 2010/686, r 1; for transitional provisions see r 6(1), Sch 4, paras 1, 2(1)(b) thereto.

[5.65 Notices to be given to member State liquidator]

[(1) This Rule applies where a member State liquidator has been appointed in relation to the debtor.

(2) Where the supervisor is obliged to give notice to, or provide a copy of a document (including an order of the court) to, the court or the official receiver, the supervisor shall give notice or provide copies, as appropriate, to the member State liquidator.]

NOTES

Amendment

Substituted, together with rr 5.35–5.64, for rr 5.35–5.38 (substituted, together with rr 5.1–5.34, for rr 5.1–5.34, by SI 2002/2712, r 5(1), Schedule, Pt 3, para 24), by SI 2003/1730, r 8, Sch 1, Pt 5, para 31.

Date in force: 1 April 2004: see SI 2003/1730, r 1(3).

[CHAPTER 13

INFORMATION ABOUT TIME SPENT ON A CASE TO BE PROVIDED BY PERSON ACTING AS NOMINEE OR SUPERVISOR]

NOTES

Amendment

Inserted by SI 2010/686, r 2, Sch 1, para 298.

Date in force: 6 April 2010: see SI 2010/686, r 1; for transitional provisions see r 6(1), Sch 4, para 1 thereto.

[5.66 Provision of information]

[(1) A person ("the relevant person") who has acted or is acting as—

(a) a nominee in respect of a proposed voluntary arrangement, or

(b) a supervisor in respect of a voluntary arrangement

must, on request in writing by any person mentioned in paragraph (2), supply free of charge to that person a statement complying with paragraph (3).

(2) The persons mentioned in this paragraph are—

(a) the debtor; and

(b) where the proposal has been approved, any creditor of the debtor in respect of the arrangement.

(3) The statement referred to in paragraph (1)—

(a) must cover the period beginning with the date of the appointment of the relevant person as nominee or supervisor, as the case may be, and ending—

(i) with the date next before the date of making the request on which the relevant person has completed any period as nominee or supervisor, or both, which is a multiple of 6 months, or
(ii) where the relevant person has ceased to act as nominee or supervisor, the date upon which the person so ceased; and
(b) must comprise the following details—
(i) the total number of hours spent on the voluntary arrangement by the relevant person whether as nominee or supervisor, or both, and any staff assigned to the voluntary arrangement during that period;
(ii) for each grade of individual so engaged, the average hourly rate at which any work carried out by individuals in that grade is charged; and
(iii) the number of hours spent by each grade of staff during that period.

(4) No request pursuant to this Rule may be made where more than 2 years has elapsed since the relevant person ceased to act in any capacity in relation to the proposal or any voluntary arrangement arising out of the approval of the proposal.

(5) Any statement required to be provided to any person under this Rule must be supplied within 28 days of the date of the receipt of the request by the person required to supply it.]

NOTES

Amendment

Inserted by SI 2010/686, r 2, Sch 1, para 298.
Date in force: 6 April 2010: see SI 2010/686, r 1; for transitional provisions see r 6(1), Sch 4, para 1 thereto.

[CHAPTER 14

PERSONS AT RISK OF VIOLENCE]

NOTES

Amendment

Inserted by SI 2010/686, r 2, Sch 1, para 298.
Date in force: 6 April 2010: see SI 2010/686, r 1; for transitional provisions see r 6(1), Sch 4, para 1 thereto.

[5.67 Persons at risk of violence]

[(1) The provisions of this Rule apply in any case where disclosure or continuing disclosure to other persons (whether to the public generally or to specific persons) of the current address or whereabouts of a debtor might reasonably be expected to lead to violence against the debtor or against a person who normally resides with the debtor as a member of the debtor's family.

(2) For the purposes of this Rule—
"current address" means, in relation to any debtor, the address of the debtor's current place of residence and any address at which the debtor currently carries on business;
"debtor" means a debtor who has entered into an individual voluntary arrangement.

(3) The court may, on the application of the debtor, the supervisor, the official receiver (whether acting as a supervisor or otherwise) or the Secretary of State, order that—
- (a) details of the debtor's current address be removed from any part of the court file of the proceedings in relation to the debtor which is open to inspection and be kept on a separate file not open to inspection;
- (b) the details in respect of the debtor to be entered onto the individual insolvency register under Rule 6A.2A in respect of an individual voluntary arrangement must not include details of the debtor's current address; and
- (c) that any notice published by the Secretary of State of the making of any order permitting vacation of the registration of a bankruptcy petition referred to in Rule 5.60, must not include details of the bankrupt's address.

(4) Where the court makes an order under paragraph (3), it may further order that the details in respect of the debtor to be entered onto the register referred to in paragraph (3) must instead include such other details of the debtor's addresses or whereabouts as the court thinks just, including details of any address at which the debtor has previously resided or carried on business.

(5) In any case where an application is made in respect of a debtor under or by virtue of this Rule, the application must be accompanied by a witness statement referring to this Rule and containing sufficient evidence to satisfy the court that paragraph (1) of this Rule applies to or in respect of that debtor.]

NOTES

Amendment

Inserted by SI 2010/686, r 2, Sch 1, para 298.
Date in force: 6 April 2010: see SI 2010/686, r 1; for transitional provisions see r 6(1), Sch 4, para 1 thereto.

[CHAPTER 15

OMISSION OF INFORMATION FROM STATEMENT OF AFFAIRS]

NOTES

Amendment

Inserted by SI 2010/686, r 2, Sch 1, para 298.
Date in force: 6 April 2010: see SI 2010/686, r 1; for transitional provisions see r 6(1), Sch 4, para 1 thereto.

[5.68 Omission of information from statement of affairs]

[The court, on the application of the nominee, the debtor or any person appearing to it to have an interest, may direct that specified information may be omitted from any statement of affairs required to be sent to the creditors where the disclosure of such information would be likely to prejudice the conduct of the voluntary arrangement or might reasonably be expected to lead to violence against any person.]

NOTES

Amendment

Inserted by SI 2010/686, r 2, Sch 1, para 298.

Date in force: 6 April 2010: see SI 2010/686, r 1; for transitional provisions see r 6(1), Sch 4, para 1 thereto.

[PART 5A

DEBT RELIEF ORDERS]

NOTES

Amendment

Inserted by SI 2009/642, rr 4, 32, Sch 1.
Date in force: 6 April 2009: see SI 2009/642, r 1.

[CHAPTER 1

PRELIMINARY]

NOTES

Amendment

Inserted by SI 2009/642, rr 4, 32, Sch 1.
Date in force: 6 April 2009: see SI 2009/642, r 1.

[5A.1 Scope of this part: introductory and interpretation]
[The Rules in this Part apply in relation to debt relief orders and applications for debt relief orders under Part 7A of the Act.]

NOTES

Amendment

Inserted by SI 2009/642, rr 4, 32, Sch 1.
Date in force: 6 April 2009: see SI 2009/642, r 1.

[5A.2 Excluded debts]
[For the purposes of that Part of the Act and this Part of the Rules—
"excluded debt" means—
- (a) any fine imposed for an offence and any obligation (including an obligation to pay a lump sum or to pay costs) arising under an order made in family proceedings or any obligation arising under a maintenance assessment made under the Child Support Act 1991
- (b) any obligation arising under a confiscation order made under section 1 of the Drug Trafficking Offences Act 1986 or section 1 of the Criminal Justice (Scotland) Act 1987 or section 71 of the Criminal Justice Act 1988 or under Parts 2, 3 or 4 of the Proceeds of Crime Act 2002; . . .
- (c) any debt or liability to which a debtor is or may become subject in respect of any sum paid or payable to the debtor as a student by way of a loan and which he receives before or after a debt relief order is made in respect of him[; and
- (d) any debt which consists in a liability to pay damages for negligence, nuisance or breach of a statutory, contractual or other duty, or to pay damages by virtue of Part 1 of the Consumer Protection Act 1987, being in either case damages in respect of the

death of or personal injury (including any disease or other impairment of physical or mental condition) to any person].

"Fine" and "family proceedings" have the meanings given by section 281(8) of the Act (which applies the Magistrates' Courts Act 1980 and the Matrimonial and Family Proceedings Act 1984).

"Loan" means a loan made pursuant to—

(a) regulations made under section 22(1) of the Teaching and Higher Education Act 1998, or

(b) the Education (Student Loans) Act 1990, or that Act as it continues in force by virtue of any savings made, in connection with its repeal by the Teaching and Higher Education Act 1998, by an order made under section 46(4) of that Act,

including any interest on the loan and any penalties or charges incurred in connection with it.]

NOTES

Amendment

Inserted by SI 2009/642, rr 4, 32, Sch 1.
Date in force: 6 April 2009: see SI 2009/642, r 1.
In definition "excluded debt" in para (b) word omitted revoked by SI 2010/686, r 2, Sch 1, para 299(1), (2)(a).
Date in force: 6 April 2010: see SI 2010/686, r 1; for transitional provisions see r 6(1), Sch 4, paras 1, 4 thereto.
In definition "excluded debt" para (d) and word "; and" immediately preceding it inserted by SI 2010/686, r 2, Sch 1, para 299(1), (2)(b).
Date in force: 6 April 2010: see SI 2010/686, r 1; for transitional provisions see r 6(1), Sch 4, paras 1, 4 thereto.

[5A.3 Application for a debt relief order—information to be in the application]

[(1) In addition to the matters referred to in section 251B(2)(a) and (b) of the Act and subject to paragraphs (5) to (11), an application for a debt relief order under section 251A must also state the matters set out in paragraphs (2) to (4) as they subsist at the date of the application.

(2) The application must state—

(a) the debtor's surname, forenames and occupation (if any);
(b) the debtor's gender and date of birth;
(c) the debtor's places of residence during the three years preceding the date of the application;
(d) any name or names used by the debtor for any purpose, if different from the above;
(e) the name, address and nature of any business carried on by the debtor, including any business carried on by—
   (i) a firm or partnership of which the debtor is a member;
   (ii) an agent or manager for the debtor or for such firm or partnership;
(f) any other liabilities (including those imposed by an order of the court) to which the debtor is subject;
(g) the address of the creditor to whom each debt is owed;
(h) the total amount of the debtor's monthly income from any source (see Rule 5A.8(1));
(i) the sources of that income and the amount from each source;
(j) particulars of the expenditure which the debtor claims is necessary to meet the monthly reasonable domestic needs of the debtor and the debtor's family, including the object and the amount of that expenditure (see Rule 5A.8(2));

(k) the total amount available from any source to meet the claimed monthly reasonable domestic needs of the debtor and his or her family (see Rule 5A.8(2)); and

(l) particulars of the debtor's property and its total estimated value (see Rule 5A.9 and 5A.10).

(3) The debtor shall also state in the application—
- (a) whether or not the debtor at the date of the application—
  - (i) has given a preference to any person during the period of two years prior to and ending with the application date;
  - (ii) has entered into a transaction with any person at an undervalue during the period of two years prior to and ending with the application date;
  - (iii) is domiciled in England and Wales;
  - (iv) at any time during the period of three years ending with the application date,
      - (aa) was ordinarily resident,
      - (bb) had a place of residence, or
      - (cc) carried on business,
      in England and Wales;
  - (v) is an undischarged bankrupt;
  - (vi) is subject to a debt relief order;
  - (vii) has been subject to a debt relief order in the six years preceding the date of the application;
  - (viii) is subject to an interim order or a voluntary arrangement under Part 8 of the Act; or
  - (ix) is subject to a bankruptcy restrictions order or undertaking or debt relief restrictions order or undertaking; and
- (b) whether at the date of the application—
  - (i) a bankruptcy petition has been presented by the debtor or by a creditor against the debtor;
  - (ii) a bankruptcy petition has been presented by the debtor, but the court has referred the debtor for the purpose of making an application for a debt relief order;
  - (iii) any debt management arrangements (see section 251F) are in force in respect of the debtor; and
  - (iv) any other legal action has been taken against the debtor in respect of any of the debtor's existing debts.

(4) In the application, the debtor must also—
- (a) consent to checks being made by the official receiver for the purpose of verifying that the debtor complies with the conditions to which the making of a debt relief order is subject;
- (b) state that the debtor is unable to pay his or her debts;
- (c) request a debt relief order, and
- (d) indicate the date on which the application is completed.

(5) The debtor shall submit to the approved intermediary such information and such documents by reference to which the information in the application, including information about each debt, the amount of the debt and the name and address of the creditor, may be substantiated.

(6) In making the application, the debtor must in every case deduct from the amount of the debt all trade and other discounts which are available to the debtor, except any discount for immediate, early or cash settlement.

(7) Subject to paragraph (8), where a debt was incurred or is payable in a currency other than sterling, the amount of the debt shall be converted into sterling at the official exchange rate prevailing on the application date.

(8) The official exchange rate is the middle exchange rate on the London foreign exchange market at the close of business, as published for the date in question or, in the absence of any such published rate for the date in question such rate as the official receiver determines.

(9) Where a debt consists of unpaid payments of a periodical nature, the amount of the debt shall consist of any amounts due and unpaid up to the date of the application.

(10) Where at the application date any payment was accruing due, the debt shall consist of so much as would have fallen due at that date, if accruing from day to day.

(11) A debtor may include a debt of which payment is not yet due at the date of the application, provided that it is for a liquidated sum payable at some certain future time.]

NOTES

Amendment

Inserted by SI 2009/642, rr 4, 32, Sch 1.
Date in force: 6 April 2009: see SI 2009/642, r 1.

[5A.4 Application for a debt relief order]

[(1) Subject to paragraphs (2) and (3), an application for a debt relief order must be completed and sent to the official receiver in electronic form and by electronic means.

(2) In this Rule, an application—

- (a) is sent by electronic means, if it is sent initially and received at its destination by means of electronic equipment for the processing (which expression includes digital compression) or storage of data and entirely created, transmitted, conveyed and received by wire, by radio, by optical means or by other electromagnetic means but does not include electronic facsimile transmission or mobile telephonic text messaging;
- (b) is completed in electronic form, if it is an application which is created, and sent, by electronic means;
- (c) in hard copy form, means an application completed and sent on paper and capable of being read (but is not the product of an electronic facsimile transmission).

(3) An application in electronic form sent by electronic means shall be treated as not having been submitted unless and until its receipt has been acknowledged by the official receiver in the same form and by the same means.

(4) In the event of any malfunction or error in the operation of the electronic form or means referred to, the official receiver shall notify the competent authorities and approved intermediaries—

- (a) that approved intermediaries may, for a specified period, complete and send applications in hard copy form; and
- (b) of the postal address to which such applications are to be sent and any terms or conditions to which their use is subject.]

NOTES

Amendment

Inserted by SI 2009/642, rr 4, 32, Sch 1.
Date in force: 6 April 2009: see SI 2009/642, r 1.

[5A.5 Approved intermediary]

[(1) The approved intermediary, as and when requested by a debtor who proposes to make an application for a debt relief order through him or her, shall create an application for a debt relief order in the name of the debtor.

(2) The approved intermediary through whom the application for a debt relief order is to be made may assist the debtor—
- (a) to identify what information is required to complete the application;
- (b) based upon the documentation and information supplied by the debtor, to ascertain whether—
  - (i) the debtor appears to have debts not exceeding the prescribed amount;
  - (ii) the debtor's surplus income does not exceed the prescribed amount; and
  - (iii) the value of the debtor's property does not exceed the prescribed amount; and
- (c) to ensure that the application (if any) is completed in full.

(3) The approved intermediary must draw the debtor's attention to—
- (a) all the conditions to which an application for, and the making of, a debt relief order is subject;
- (b) the possible consequences of the making by the debtor of any false representation or omission in the debtor's application; and
- (c) the fact that verification checks will be made for the purpose of verifying that the debtor complies with the conditions to which the making of a debt relief order is subject and the requirement for the debtor to consent to such checks being made.

(4) If and when instructed to do so by the debtor, the approved intermediary must send the application to the official receiver on behalf of the debtor.]

NOTES

Amendment

Inserted by SI 2009/642, rr 4, 32, Sch 1.
Date in force: 6 April 2009: see SI 2009/642, r 1.

[5A.6 Form, manner and reasons for refusal of application for debt relief order]

[(1) The official receiver must notify the debtor of his or her decision to refuse an application for a debt relief order in accordance with this Rule.

(2) The official receiver must send a notice in writing to the debtor stating—
- (a) that the official receiver has decided to refuse the debtor's application, and
- (b) the reason for which it has been refused.]

NOTES

Amendment

Inserted by SI 2009/642, rr 4, 32, Sch 1.
Date in force: 6 April 2009: see SI 2009/642, r 1.

[5A.7 Prescribed verification checks—conditions in paragraphs 1 to 8 of Schedule 4ZA]

[(1) In this Rule, "credit reference agency" means a person licensed to carry on a business comprising the furnishing of information relevant to the financial standing of individuals.

(2) For the purposes of subsections (4) and (5) of section 251D and the conditions specified in paragraphs 1 to 8 of Schedule 4ZA, the prescribed verification checks are those searches or enquiries specified in relation to the condition in paragraphs (3) to (8) below.

(3) For the purpose of verifying a debtor's connection with England and Wales on the application date, verification checks made in, or with, one or more of the following—
- (a) the electoral registers for the areas in England and Wales in which the debtor in, and at the date of, the debtor's application, claims to reside or to carry on business or to have resided or carried on business;
- (b) the individual insolvency register;
- (c) the bankruptcy restrictions register;
- (d) the debt relief restrictions register;
- (e) a credit reference agency.

(4) For the purpose of verifying that a debtor—
- (a) is not, on the determination date—
  - (i) an undischarged bankrupt;
  - (ii) subject to a bankruptcy restrictions order or undertaking;
  - (iii) subject to a debt relief restrictions order or undertaking;
  - (iv) subject to an individual voluntary arrangement; or
- (b) has not been the subject of a debt relief order in the period of 6 years ending with the determination date,

verification checks made in one or more of the registers specified in paragraph (5).

(5) The registers referred to in paragraph (4) are—
- (a) the individual insolvency register;
- (b) the bankruptcy restrictions register;
- (c) the debt relief restrictions register.

(6) For the purpose of verifying—
- (a) that the debtor is not, on the determination date, subject to an interim order;
- (b) whether a debtor's or creditor's bankruptcy petition has been presented against the debtor prior to the determination date;
- (c) where a bankruptcy petition has been presented against the debtor prior to the determination date, whether proceedings in relation to the petition have finally been disposed of before the determination date;
- (d) where a bankruptcy petition has been presented against the debtor prior to the determination date, the status of the proceedings in relation to the petition and whether the court has referred the debtor under section 274A(2) for the purpose of making an application for a debt relief order;
- (e) where a creditor's bankruptcy petition has been presented against the debtor prior to the determination date, the status of the proceedings in relation to the petition and whether the person who presented the petition has consented to the making of the application for a debt relief order,

verification checks made in, or with one or more of the sources specified in paragraph (7).

(7) The sources are—
- (a) the individual insolvency register;
- (b) county or other court records;
- (c) a credit reference agency.

(8) For the purpose of verifying that—
- (a) the amount of the debtor's overall indebtedness;
- (b) the amount of the debtor's monthly surplus income; or

(c) the total value of the debtor's property,

does not exceed the prescribed amount, verification checks made with a credit reference agency.]

NOTES

Amendment

Inserted by SI 2009/642, rr 4, 32, Sch 1.
Date in force: 6 April 2009: see SI 2009/642, r 1.

[5A.8 Determination of debtor's monthly surplus income]

[(1) For the purposes of this Part, the income of a debtor comprises every payment in the nature of income which is from time to time made to him or to which he from time to time becomes entitled, including any payment in respect of the carrying on of any business or in respect of any office or employment and (despite anything in section 11 or 12 of the Welfare Reform and Pensions Act 1999any payment under a pension scheme.

(2) In determining the monthly surplus income of a debtor, the official receiver shall take into account any contribution made by any member of the debtor's family to the amount necessary for the reasonable domestic needs of the debtor and his or her family.]

NOTES

Amendment

Inserted by SI 2009/642, rr 4, 32, Sch 1.
Date in force: 6 April 2009: see SI 2009/642, r 1.

[5A.9 Determination of value of a debtor's property]

[(1) Subject to Rule 5A.10, the official receiver in determining whether the condition in paragraph 8 of Schedule 4ZA to the Act is met shall regard as a debtor's property for the purposes of this Part—

- (a) all property belonging to or vested in the debtor on the determination date, and
- (b) any property which by virtue of any of the following provisions of this Part is comprised in or is treated as falling within the preceding sub-paragraph.

(2) References in this Part to property, in relation to a debtor, include references to any power exercisable by him or her over or in respect of property except in so far as the power is exercisable over or in respect of property which is not or is deemed not for the time being to be the property of the debtor and cannot be exercised for the benefit of the debtor;

and a power exercisable over or in respect of property is deemed for the purposes of this Part to vest in the person entitled to exercise it at the time of the transaction or event by virtue of which it is exercisable by that person (whether or not it becomes so exercisable at that time).

(3) For the purposes of any such provision in this Part, property belonging to or vested in the debtor so belongs or vests in him or her subject to the rights of any person other than the debtor (whether as a secured creditor of the debtor or otherwise) in relation thereto.]

Insolvency Rules 1986, reg 5A.9

NOTES

Amendment

Inserted by SI 2009/642, rr 4, 32, Sch 1.
Date in force: 6 April 2009: see SI 2009/642, r 1.

[**5A.10 Particular descriptions of property to be excluded for the purpose of determining the value of a person's property**]

[(1) For the purposes of Rule 5A.9, the official receiver shall disregard—
- (a) subject to paragraph (2), a single domestic motor vehicle belonging to or vested in the debtor provided that—
  - (i) it has been especially adapted for use by him or her because he or she has a physical impairment that has a substantial and long-term adverse effect on his or her ability to carry out normal day-to-day activities; or
  - (ii) the maximum potential realisable value of the vehicle is less than the prescribed amount;
- (b) subject to paragraph (3), such tools, books and other items of equipment as are necessary to the debtor for use personally by him in his employment, business or vocation;
- (c) such clothing, bedding, furniture, household equipment and provisions as are necessary for satisfying the basic domestic needs of the debtor and his or her family;
- (d) property held by the debtor on trust for any other person;
- (e) the right of nomination to a vacant ecclesiastical benefice;
- (f) a tenancy which is an assured tenancy or an assured agricultural occupancy, within the meaning of Part I of the Housing Act 1988, and the terms of which inhibit an assignment as mentioned in section 127(5) of the Rent Act 1977;
- (g) a protected tenancy, within the meaning of the Rent Act 1977, in respect of which, by virtue of any provision of Part IX of that Act, no premium can lawfully be required as a condition of assignment;
- (h) a tenancy of a dwelling-house by virtue of which the debtor is, within the meaning of the Rent (Agriculture) Act 1976, a protected occupier of the dwelling-house, and the terms of which inhibit an assignment as mentioned in section 127(5) of the Rent Act 1977, or
- (i) a secure tenancy, within the meaning of Part IV of the Housing Act 1985, which is not capable of being assigned, except in the cases mentioned in section 91(3) of that Act.

(2) Where—
- (a) a vehicle is to be disregarded by the official receiver by virtue of paragraph (1)(a)(i) of this Rule (adapted vehicle), and
- (b) it appears to the official receiver that the realisable value of the vehicle exceeds the cost of a reasonable replacement for it,

the official receiver shall disregard only the value of a reasonable replacement.

(3) Where—
- (a) property is to be disregarded by the official receiver by virtue of paragraph (1)(b) or (c) of this Rule (tools of trade, household effects, etc), and
- (b) it appears to the official receiver that the realisable value of the whole or any part of that property exceeds the cost of a reasonable replacement for that property or that part of it,

the official receiver shall disregard only the value of a reasonable replacement.

(4) For the purposes of this Rule,
- (a) the prescribed amount is £1000
- (b) property is a reasonable replacement for other property if it is reasonably adequate for meeting the needs met by the other property.

(5) This Rule has effect subject to the provisions of any enactment not contained in these Rules or in the Act under which any property is to be excluded from belonging to or being vested in the debtor for the purposes of the determination of a debt relief order.]

NOTES

Amendment

Inserted by SI 2009/642, rr 4, 32, Sch 1.
Date in force: 6 April 2009: see SI 2009/642, r 1.

[5A.11 Making of debt relief order—form of debt relief order]

[A debt relief order must be in writing and include the following particulars—
- (a) the name and address of the debtor;
- (b) the date of, and the reference number allocated to, the debtor's application;
- (c) a list of the debtor's qualifying debts as at the application date, specifying the amount owed and the creditor's name, address and reference (if any); and
- (d) the date on which the order was made.]

NOTES

Amendment

Inserted by SI 2009/642, rr 4, 32, Sch 1.
Date in force: 6 April 2009: see SI 2009/642, r 1.

[5A.12 Other steps to be taken by official receiver or debtor upon making of the order]

[(1) In addition to giving a copy of the order to the debtor, the official receiver must—
- (a) notify the approved intermediary through whom the debtor's application was made, of the making and date of the order; and
- (b) cause an entry to be made in the individual insolvency register in accordance with Rule 6A.5A.

(2) In any case in which there are other debt management arrangements or attachment of earnings orders in force in respect of the debtor, the official receiver must notify the court, or the body, as the case may be, responsible for making the debt management arrangements or orders, of the making of the debt relief order.]

NOTES

Amendment

Inserted by SI 2009/642, rr 4, 32, Sch 1.
Date in force: 6 April 2009: see SI 2009/642, r 1.

[5A.13 Prescribed information to be notified to creditor on making of debt relief order]
[The official receiver must notify each creditor to whom a qualifying debt specified in the order is owed, of—
- (a) the making, the date and the reference number of the order and its effect;
- (b) the matters to which a creditor may object under section 251K; and
- (c) the name, address and telephone number of the official receiver sending the notice and the address to which any objection under that section may or must be sent.]

NOTES

Amendment

Inserted by SI 2009/642, rr 4, 32, Sch 1.
Date in force: 6 April 2009: see SI 2009/642, r 1.

[5A.14 Creditor's objection]
[(1) In this Rule, "creditor" means a person specified in a debt relief order as a creditor to whom a specified qualifying debt is owed.

(2) A creditor who wishes to object to—
- (a) the making of an order;
- (b) the inclusion of the debt in the list of the debtor's qualifying debts; or
- (c) the details of the debt specified in the order,

must object in writing to the official receiver in accordance with this Rule.

(3) For an objection to be considered by the official receiver, it must be made during the moratorium period relating to the order and within 28 days of the date on which the creditor was notified of the making of the order and must include—
- (a) the name and address of the creditor;
- (b) the name of the debtor and the reference number of the order;
- (c) which of the matters under section 251K the creditor objects to;
- (d) a statement indicating at least one or more of the grounds listed in paragraph (4), upon which the creditor relies;
- (e) a statement indicating the facts upon which the creditor relies, and
- (f) information and documents in support of the grounds and the facts upon which the creditor relies.

(4) The grounds are that—
- (a) there is an error in, or an omission from, something specified in the debt relief order;
- (b) a bankruptcy order has been made in respect of the debtor;
- (c) the debtor has made a proposal under Part 8 of the Act;
- (d) the official receiver should not have been satisfied that—
    - (i) the debts specified in the order were qualifying debts of the debtor as at the application date;
    - (ii) the conditions specified in Part 1 of Schedule 4ZA to the Act were met;
    - (iii) the conditions specified in Part 2 of that Schedule were met or that any failure to meet such condition did not prevent him or her from making the order;
    - (iv) the condition in paragraph 7 of that Schedule was not met at any time after the order was made;
    - (v) the condition in paragraph 8 of that Schedule was not met at any time after the order was made.

(5) For the purposes of paragraph (4)(d)(iv) and (v) above, paragraph 7 and 8 of Schedule 4ZA to the Act are to be read as if references to the determination date were references to the time in question.]

NOTES

Amendment

Inserted by SI 2009/642, rr 4, 32, Sch 1.
Date in force: 6 April 2009: see SI 2009/642, r 1.

[**5A.15 Official receiver's response to objection**]
[(1) For the purposes of this Rule—
"the creditor" means the creditor specified in a debt relief order as a creditor to whom a qualifying debt is owed and who has made an objection in relation to that order under the Act and the Rules;
"the debt relief order" means the debt relief order in which the creditor is specified;
"the debtor" means the person subject to the debt relief order.
(2) If, after considering an objection in accordance with section 251K, the official receiver is minded to revoke or amend the debt relief order, he or she shall send to the debtor particulars of—
    (a)   the objection;
    (b)   the grounds and facts upon which the creditor relies; and
    (c)   the address to which the debtor's comments must be sent,
and invite the debtor to comment on them.
(3) Before deciding whether to revoke or amend the debt relief order, the official receiver shall consider any comments made by the debtor, provided they are made within 21 days after the particulars were sent to the debtor.
(4) The official receiver must—
    (a)   within 14 days of coming to a decision specified in section 251K(5)—
        (i)   send notice to the creditor under and in accordance with Rule 5A.16 of either the revocation or amendment of the debt relief order under section 251L; or
        (ii)   under Rule 5A.19(b), if he or she would not otherwise be treated as such, treat the creditor as a person interested in any application made under section 251M by the official receiver to the court for directions or an order in relation to any matter arising in connection with the debt relief order, to whom notice of the official receiver's application must be sent; or
        (iii)   send notice to the creditor of the official receiver's decision to take other steps in relation to the debtor and of the steps he or she proposes to take; or
    (b)   notify the creditor of the official receiver's decision to do none of the above.]

NOTES

Amendment

Inserted by SI 2009/642, rr 4, 32, Sch 1.
Date in force: 6 April 2009: see SI 2009/642, r 1.

[5A.16 Procedure to be followed when revoking or amending a debt relief order]

[(1) Subject to Rule 5A.27, the official receiver must as soon as reasonably practicable after deciding to revoke a debt relief order—
- (a) send notice of the decision to revoke to—
    - (i) the debtor; and
    - (ii) any creditor specified in the debt relief order as a creditor to whom a qualifying debt is owed; and
- (b) upon the revocation taking effect, provided that information concerning a debt relief order has not been deleted under Rule 6A.5B, cause the entry in the individual insolvency register relating to the debt relief order to be amended accordingly.

(2) The notice of the decision to revoke must—
- (a) identify the debtor and the date and reference number of the debt relief order;
- (b) state the reasons for revocation; and
- (c) specify the date (whether under subsection (5) or (7) of section 251L) on or from which the revocation has effect.

(3) Where—
- (a) a revocation is to take effect from a specified date, and
- (b) the official receiver thinks it appropriate to revoke the order under subsection (7) of section 251L with immediate effect at any time before that date,

any debtor or creditor to whom notice of the specified date has already been sent pursuant to paragraph (1), must be notified by the official receiver of the earlier date on which the revocation has effect.

(4) Upon amendment of a debt relief order, the official receiver shall as soon as reasonably practicable after the amendment—
- (a) send notice of the amendment to—
    - (i) the debtor; and
    - (ii) any creditor specified in the debt relief order as a creditor to whom a qualifying debt is owed;
- (b) in the notice of amendment—
    - (i) identify the debtor and the date and reference number of the debt relief order;
    - (ii) specify the amendment;
    - (iii) specify the date on which the amendment was made; and
    - (iv) state the reasons for it; and
- (c) cause the entry in the individual insolvency register relating to the amended debt relief order to be amended accordingly.]

NOTES

Amendment

Inserted by SI 2009/642, rr 4, 32, Sch 1.
Date in force: 6 April 2009: see SI 2009/642, r 1.

[5A.17 Notification of official receiver by debtor of matters in section 251J(3) or (5)]

[(1) As soon as reasonably practicable after the debtor becomes aware of—
- (a) an error in, or omission from, the information supplied to the official receiver in, or in support of, the application, he or she must notify the official receiver of—
    - (i) the nature of the error or omission; and
    - (ii) the reason for it;

(b) a change in his or her circumstances between the application date and the determination date that would affect (or would have affected) the determination of the application, he or she must notify the official receiver of—
(i) the nature of the change; and
(ii) the date of the change.
(2) Where a debt relief order is made and—
(a) there is an increase in the debtor's income during the moratorium period applicable to the order, the debtor shall notify the official receiver, as soon as reasonably practicable after the date of the increase, of—
(i) the amount of the increase;
(ii) the reason for it;
(iii) the date of the increase; and
(iv) its expected duration;
(b) the debtor acquires any property or any property is devolved upon him during that period, the debtor shall notify the official receiver, as soon as reasonably practicable after the date of the acquisition or the devolution, of—
(i) the nature of the acquisition or devolution;
(ii) the date of the acquisition or devolution;
(iii) the reason for it; and
(iv) its value;
(c) the debtor becomes aware of any error in or omission from any information supplied by him or her to the official receiver after the determination date, the debtor shall notify the official receiver, as soon as reasonably practicable after the date on which the debtor becomes aware of it, of—
(i) the nature of the error or omission;
(ii) the reason for it; and
(iii) the date on which the debtor becomes aware of it.]

NOTES

Amendment
Inserted by SI 2009/642, rr 4, 32, Sch 1.
Date in force: 6 April 2009: see SI 2009/642, r 1.

[5A.18 Persons at risk of violence—debt relief orders, debt relief restrictions orders and debt relief restrictions undertakings]

[(1) For the purposes of this Rule—
"debtor" means a person subject to a debt relief order, or a debt relief restrictions order or a debt relief restrictions undertaking; and
"current address" means in relation to any debtor the address of his or her current place of residence and any address at which he or she currently carries on business.
(2) This Rule applies in any case where disclosure or continuing disclosure to other persons (whether to the public generally or to specific persons) of the current address or whereabouts of a debtor might reasonably be expected to lead to violence against him or her or against a person who normally resides with him or her as a member of his or her family.
(3) The court may, subject to paragraph (6)—
(a) on the application of a debtor subject to a debt relief order or the official receiver in respect of such a debtor, order that—

(i) the details in respect of the debtor to be entered onto the individual insolvency register under Rule 6A.5A shall not include details of the debtor's current address; or
(ii) the details of the debtor's current address kept on the individual insolvency register under Part 6A shall be removed from such register;
(b) on the application of a debtor subject to a debt relief restrictions order or the official receiver in respect of such a debtor, order that—
(i) details of the debtor's current address shall be removed from any part of the court file of the proceedings in relation to the debtor which is open to inspection and be kept on a separate file not open to inspection;
(ii) the full of title of the proceedings shall be amended by the removal of the details of the debtor's current address from the description of the debtor;
(iii) the details in respect of the debtor to be entered onto the debt relief restrictions register under Rule 6A.7A shall not include details of the debtor's current address; or
(iv) the details of the debtor's current address kept on the debt relief restrictions register under Rule 6A shall be removed from such register;
(c) on the application of a debtor subject to a debt relief restrictions undertaking or the official receiver in respect of such a debtor, order that—
(i) the details of the debtor's current address shall be excluded from the details in respect of the debtor to be entered onto the debt relief restrictions register under Rule 6A.7A; or
(ii) the details of the debtor's current address kept on the debt relief restrictions register under Rule 6A shall be removed from such register.

(4) Where the court makes an order under paragraph (3), it may further order that—
(a) the full title of any proceedings; or
(b) the details in respect of the debtor kept on or to be entered onto the registers referred to in that paragraph,

as the case may be, shall instead include such other details of the debtor's addresses or whereabouts as the court thinks [just], including details of any address at which the debtor has previously resided or carried on business.

(5) Proceedings under this Rule may be ordered by the court to be transferred under Rule 7.11 on the application of the person in respect of whom the application is being made.

(6) In any case where an application is made by a debtor under or by virtue of this Rule, the application shall be accompanied by [a witness statement] referring to this Rule and containing sufficient evidence to satisfy the court to which the application was made, that this Rule applies to or in respect of that debtor.]

NOTES

Amendment

Inserted by SI 2009/642, rr 4, 32, Sch 1.
Date in force: 6 April 2009: see SI 2009/642, r 1.
Para (4): word "just" in square brackets substituted by SI 2010/686, r 2, Sch 1, para 1.
Date in force: 6 April 2010: see SI 2010/686, r 1; for transitional provisions see r 6(1), Sch 4, paras 1, 2(1)(b) thereto.
Para (6): words "a witness statement" in square brackets substituted by SI 2010/686, r 2, Sch 1, para 300.

Date in force: 6 April 2010: see SI 2010/686, r 1; for transitional provisions see r 6(1), Sch 4, paras 1, 2(1)(b), (2)–(4) thereto.

[5A.19 Application to court under section 251M]
[Where an application is made to the court under section 251M—
- (a) by a person who is dissatisfied by any act, omission or decision of the official receiver in connection with a debt relief order or an application for a debt relief order, if the person making the application—
    - (i) is the debtor, notice of the application to the court must be sent to the official receiver and to any creditor specified in the debt relief order or in the application for a debt relief order; or
    - (ii) is a person other than the debtor, notice of the application to the court must be sent to the official receiver and to the debtor;
- (b) by the official receiver for directions or an order in relation to any matter arising in connection with a debt relief order or an application for such an order, notice of the application must be sent by the official receiver to the debtor and to any person appearing to the official receiver to have an interest in the application.]

NOTES

Amendment

Inserted by SI 2009/642, rr 4, 32, Sch 1.
Date in force: 6 April 2009: see SI 2009/642, r 1.

[5A.20 Extension of moratorium period]
[Where the moratorium period applicable to a debt relief order is extended—
- (a) notice of the extension, and the period for which it is extended must be sent,
    - (i) where extended by the court, to the official receiver, who shall send a copy to the debtor subject to the debt relief order and to the creditors specified in it;
    - (ii) where extended by the official receiver, to the debtor subject to the debt relief order and to the creditors specified in it; and
- (b) the official receiver shall cause to be entered in the individual insolvency register that—
    - (i) such an extension has been made in relation to the debtor;
    - (ii) the date on which the extension was made;
    - (iii) its duration; and
    - (iv) the date of the anticipated end of the moratorium period.]

NOTES

Amendment

Inserted by SI 2009/642, rr 4, 32, Sch 1.
Date in force: 6 April 2009: see SI 2009/642, r 1.

[5A.21 Court in which applications under sections 251M (powers of court in relation to debt relief orders) or 251N (inquiry into debtor's dealings and property) to be made]
[(1) An application to the court by a debtor under section 251M(1) or by the official receiver under section 251M(2) or 251N shall, if the debtor is resident in England and Wales—

(a) be made to the High Court if the debtor has resided or carried on business in the London insolvency district for the greater part of the 6 months immediately preceding the making of the application, or for a longer period in those 6 months than in any other insolvency district, and

(b) in any other case, (subject to paragraph (2)) be made to the debtor's own county court, which is—
  (i) the county court for the insolvency district in which he or she has resided or carried on business for the longest period during those 6 months, or
  (ii) if he or she has for the greater part of those 6 months carried on business in one insolvency district and resided in another, the county court for that in which he or she has carried on business, or
  (iii) if he or she has during those 6 months carried on business in more than one insolvency district, the county court for that in which is, or has been for the longest period in those 6 months, his or her principal place of business.

(2) If, in a case not falling within paragraph (1)(a), it is more expedient for the debtor with a view to expediting the application—
(a) it may in any case be made to whichever court is specified by Schedule 2 to the Rules as being, in relation to the debtor's own county court, the nearest full-time court, and
(b) it may alternatively, in a case falling within paragraph (1)(b)(ii), be made to the court for the insolvency district in which he or she has resided for the greater part of the 6 months there referred to.

(3) If the debtor is not resident in England and Wales but has resided or carried on business in England and Wales within the 6 months immediately preceding the making of the application, the application—
(a) shall be made to the High Court if the debtor has resided or carried on business in the London insolvency district for the greater part of those 6 months, or for a longer period in those 6 months than in any other insolvency district, and
(b) in any other case, may (subject to paragraph (4)) be made either to the debtor's own county court or to the High Court.

(4) The provisions of paragraph (2) shall apply with any appropriate modifications in any case where in accordance with paragraph (3)(b) the application may be made to the debtor's own county court.

(5) If the debtor is not resident in England and Wales and has not resided or carried on business in England and Wales within the 6 months immediately preceding the making of the application, the application shall be made to the High Court.

(6) The application shall contain sufficient information to establish that it is brought in the appropriate court.]

NOTES

Amendment
Inserted by SI 2009/642, rr 4, 32, Sch 1.
Date in force: 6 April 2009: see SI 2009/642, r 1.

[5A.22 Referral of debtor, by court, to intermediary under section 274A]
[If, on the hearing of a debtor's bankruptcy petition, the court refers the debtor to an approved intermediary under section 274A for the purposes of making an application for a debt relief order, as soon as reasonably practicable after the making of the order of referral—

(a) the court shall send to the debtor a sealed copy of the order of referral, and

(b) the debtor shall send to the approved intermediary a copy of the order and copies of the debtor's petition and statement of affairs.]

NOTES

Amendment

Inserted by SI 2009/642, rr 4, 32, Sch 1.
Date in force: 6 April 2009: see SI 2009/642, r 1.

[5A.23 Creditor's bankruptcy petition—where creditor consents to making of application for a debt relief order]

[(1) This Rule applies where prior to the determination of an application, a creditor's petition for bankruptcy has been presented against a debtor and the proceedings in relation to that petition remain before the court.

(2) In this Rule,

"the petition" means the creditor's bankruptcy petition; and

"the debt" means the debt to which the creditor's bankruptcy petition relates.

(3) If, on the hearing of the petition, the petitioner consents to the making by the debtor of an application for a debt relief order in respect of the debt—

(a) the court shall—
 (i) refer the debtor to an approved intermediary (within the meaning of Part 7A) for the purpose of making an application for a debt relief order in relation to the debtor and the debt noting the consent of the creditor on the order for referral;
 (ii) stay the proceedings on the petition in relation to the debt on such terms and conditions as it thinks [just]; and

(b) the debtor shall send to the approved intermediary as soon as reasonably practicable after the making of the order of referral,
 (i) a sealed copy of the order, and
 (ii) copies of the petition and (if any), of the creditor's statutory demand.

(4) The approved intermediary shall, on receipt of the order and the copies, as soon as reasonably practicable after the application for a debt relief order has been made, send them to the official receiver endorsed with the name of the debtor and the number of the application to which they relate.

(5) If, following the reference by the court, a debt relief order is made in relation to the debt, the petition shall be dismissed in relation to it unless the court otherwise directs.]

NOTES

Amendment

Inserted by SI 2009/642, rr 4, 32, Sch 1.
Date in force: 6 April 2009: see SI 2009/642, r 1.
Para (3): in sub-para (a)(ii) word "just" in square brackets substituted by SI 2010/686, r 2, Sch 1, para 1.
Date in force: 6 April 2010: see SI 2010/686, r 1; for transitional provisions see r 6(1), Sch 4, paras 1, 2(1)(b) thereto.

[5A.24 Application for [permission] under Company Directors Disqualification Act 1986]

[(1) An application by a person—

(a) in relation to whom a moratorium period under a debt relief order applies, or
(b) in respect of whom a debt relief restrictions order or undertaking is in force,

for [permission] ("the applicant for [permission]"), under section 11 of the Company Directors Disqualification Act 1986, to act as director of, or to take part or be concerned in the promotion, formation or management of a company, shall be supported by [a witness statement] complying with this Rule.

(2) The [witness statement] must identify the company and specify—
(a) the nature of its business or intended business, and the place or places where that business is, or is to be, carried on;
(b) whether it is, or is to be, a private or a public company;
(c) the persons who are, or are to be, principally responsible for the conduct of its affairs (whether as directors, shadow directors, managers or otherwise);
(d) the manner and capacity in which the applicant for [permission] proposes to take part or be concerned in the promotion or formation of the company or, as the case may be, its management; and
(e) the emoluments and other benefits to be obtained from the directorship.

(3) If the company is already in existence, the [witness statement] must specify the date of its incorporation and the amount of its nominal and issued share capital; and if not, it must specify the amount, or approximate amount, of its proposed commencing share capital, and the sources from which that capital is to be obtained.

(4) Where the applicant for [permission] intends to take part or be concerned in the promotion or formation of a company, the [witness statement] must contain an undertaking by the applicant for [permission] that he or she will, within not less than [5 business] days of the company being incorporated, file in court a copy of its memorandum of association and certificate of incorporation under [section 15] of the Companies Act.

(5) The court shall fix a venue for the hearing of the application, and shall give notice to the applicant for [permission] accordingly.]

NOTES

Amendment

Inserted by SI 2009/642, rr 4, 32, Sch 1.
Date in force: 6 April 2009: see SI 2009/642, r 1.
Provision heading: word "permission" in square brackets substituted by SI 2010/686, r 2, Sch 1, para 1.
Date in force: 6 April 2010: see SI 2010/686, r 1; for transitional provisions see r 6(1), Sch 4, paras 1, 2(1)(b) thereto.
Para (1): word "permission" in square brackets in both places it occurs substituted by SI 2010/686, r 2, Sch 1, para 1.
Date in force: 6 April 2010: see SI 2010/686, r 1; for transitional provisions see r 6(1), Sch 4, paras 1, 2(1)(b) thereto.
Para (1): words "a witness statement" in square brackets substituted by SI 2010/686, r 2, Sch 1, para 301(1), (2).
Date in force: 6 April 2010: see SI 2010/686, r 1; for transitional provisions see r 6(1), Sch 4, paras 1, 2(1)(b), (2)–(4) thereto.
Para (2): words "witness statement" in square brackets substituted by SI 2010/686, r 2, Sch 1, para 301(1), (3).
Date in force: 6 April 2010: see SI 2010/686, r 1; for transitional provisions see r 6(1), Sch 4, paras 1, 2(1)(b), (2)–(4) thereto.
Para (2): in sub-para (d) word "permission" in square brackets substituted by SI 2010/686, r 2, Sch 1, para 1.
Date in force: 6 April 2010: see SI 2010/686, r 1; for transitional provisions see r 6(1), Sch 4, paras 1, 2(1)(b) thereto.

Para (3): words "witness statement" in square brackets substituted by SI 2010/686, r 2, Sch 1, para 301(1), (3).
Date in force: 6 April 2010: see SI 2010/686, r 1; for transitional provisions see r 6(1), Sch 4, paras 1, 2(1)(b), (2)–(4) thereto.
Para (4): word "permission" in square brackets in both places it occurs substituted by SI 2010/686, r 2, Sch 1, para 1.
Date in force: 6 April 2010: see SI 2010/686, r 1; for transitional provisions see r 6(1), Sch 4, paras 1, 2(1)(b) thereto.
Para (4): words "witness statement" in square brackets substituted by SI 2010/686, r 2, Sch 1, para 301(1), (3).
Date in force: 6 April 2010: see SI 2010/686, r 1; for transitional provisions see r 6(1), Sch 4, paras 1, 2(1)(b), (2)–(4) thereto.
Para (4): words "5 business" in square brackets substituted by SI 2010/686, r 2, Sch 1, para 301(1), (4).
Date in force: 6 April 2010: see SI 2010/686, r 1; for transitional provisions see r 6(1), Sch 4, para 1 thereto.
Para (4): words "section 15" in square brackets substituted by SI 2009/2472, rr 3, 15.
Date in force: 1 October 2009: see SI 2009/2472, r 1; for transitional provisions see r 2 thereof.
Para (5): word "permission" in square brackets substituted by SI 2010/686, r 2, Sch 1, para 1.
Date in force: 6 April 2010: see SI 2010/686, r 1; for transitional provisions see r 6(1), Sch 4, paras 1, 2(1)(b) thereto.

[5A.25 Application for [permission] under Company Directors Disqualification Act 1986— report of official receiver]

[(1) The applicant for [permission] shall, not less than 28 days before the date fixed for the hearing, give to the official receiver, notice of the venue, accompanied by copies of the application and the [witness statement] under Rule 5A.24.

(2) The official receiver may, not less than 14 days before the date fixed for the hearing, file in court a report of any matters which he considers ought to be drawn to the court's attention. A copy of the report shall be sent by him, as soon as reasonably practicable after it is filed, to the applicant for [permission].

(3) The applicant for [permission] may, not later than [5 business] days before the date of the hearing, file in court a notice specifying any statements in the official receiver's report which he or she intends to deny or dispute.

(4) If he or she gives notice under this paragraph, he or she shall send copies of it, not less than 4 [business] days before the date of the hearing, to the official receiver.

(5) The official receiver may appear on the hearing of the application, and may make representations and put to the applicant for [permission] such questions as the court may allow.]

NOTES

Amendment

Inserted by SI 2009/642, rr 4, 32, Sch 1.
Date in force: 6 April 2009: see SI 2009/642, r 1.
Provision heading: word "permission" in square brackets substituted by SI 2010/686, r 2, Sch 1, para 1.
Date in force: 6 April 2010: see SI 2010/686, r 1; for transitional provisions see r 6(1), Sch 4, paras 1, 2(1)(b) thereto.
Para (1): word "permission" in square brackets substituted by SI 2010/686, r 2, Sch 1, para 1.
Date in force: 6 April 2010: see SI 2010/686, r 1; for transitional provisions see r 6(1), Sch 4, paras 1, 2(1)(b) thereto.
Para (1): words "witness statement" in square brackets substituted by SI 2010/686, r 2, Sch 1, para 302(1), (2).
Date in force: 6 April 2010: see SI 2010/686, r 1; for transitional provisions see r 6(1), Sch 4, paras 1, 2(1)(b), (2)–(4) thereto.

Para (2): word "permission" in square brackets substituted by SI 2010/686, r 2, Sch 1, para 1.
> Date in force: 6 April 2010: see SI 2010/686, r 1; for transitional provisions see r 6(1), Sch 4, paras 1, 2(1)(b) thereto.

Para (3): word "permission" in square brackets substituted by SI 2010/686, r 2, Sch 1, para 1.
> Date in force: 6 April 2010: see SI 2010/686, r 1; for transitional provisions see r 6(1), Sch 4, paras 1, 2(1)(b) thereto.

Para (3): words "5 business" in square brackets substituted by SI 2010/686, r 2, Sch 1, para 302(1), (3).
> Date in force: 6 April 2010: see SI 2010/686, r 1; for transitional provisions see r 6(1), Sch 4, para 1 thereto.

Para (4): word "business" in square brackets inserted by SI 2010/686, r 2, Sch 1, para 302(1), (4).
> Date in force: 6 April 2010: see SI 2010/686, r 1; for transitional provisions see r 6(1), Sch 4, para 1 thereto.

Para (5): word "permission" in square brackets substituted by SI 2010/686, r 2, Sch 1, para 1.
> Date in force: 6 April 2010: see SI 2010/686, r 1; for transitional provisions see r 6(1), Sch 4, paras 1, 2(1)(b) thereto.

[5A.26 Application for [permission] under Company Directors Disqualification Act 1986—court's order on application]

[(1) If the court grants the application for [permission] under section 11 of the Company Directors Disqualification Act 1986, its order shall specify that which by virtue of the order the applicant has [permission] to do.

(2) The court may at the same time, having regard to any representations made by the official receiver on the hearing of the application, exercise in relation to the moratorium period or the debt relief order to which the applicant for [permission] is subject, any power which it has under section 251M.

(3) Whether or not the application is granted, copies of the order shall be sent by the court to the applicant and the official receiver.]

NOTES

Amendment

> Inserted by SI 2009/642, rr 4, 32, Sch 1.
> > Date in force: 6 April 2009: see SI 2009/642, r 1.
>
> Provision heading: word "permission" in square brackets substituted by SI 2010/686, r 2, Sch 1, para 1.
> > Date in force: 6 April 2010: see SI 2010/686, r 1; for transitional provisions see r 6(1), Sch 4, paras 1, 2(1)(b) thereto.
>
> Para (1): word "permission" in square brackets in both places it occurs substituted by SI 2010/686, r 2, Sch 1, para 1.
> > Date in force: 6 April 2010: see SI 2010/686, r 1; for transitional provisions see r 6(1), Sch 4, paras 1, 2(1)(b) thereto.
>
> Para (2): word "permission" in square brackets substituted by SI 2010/686, r 2, Sch 1, para 1.
> > Date in force: 6 April 2010: see SI 2010/686, r 1; for transitional provisions see r 6(1), Sch 4, paras 1, 2(1)(b) thereto.

[5A.27 Death of debtor at a time when a moratorium period under a debt relief order applies in relation to him or her]

[(1) This Rule applies where a debtor dies at a time when a moratorium period under a debt relief order applies in relation to him or her.

(2) The official receiver shall, as soon as reasonably practicable after receiving notice of the death of the debtor—

    (a)   revoke the debt relief order;

(b) cause a note of the fact and the date of the death to be entered on the individual insolvency register under Rule 6A.8; and
(c) send notice of the revocation—
   (i) to any creditor specified in the debt relief order as a creditor to whom a qualifying debt is owed, and
   (ii) to the personal representatives of the deceased debtor.
(3) In the notice of revocation, the official receiver shall—
   (a) identify the debtor;
   (b) state the reason for the revocation, and
   (c) specify the date on which the revocation took effect.]

NOTES

Amendment

Inserted by SI 2009/642, rr 4, 32, Sch 1.
Date in force: 6 April 2009: see SI 2009/642, r 1.

PART 6

BANKRUPTCY

CHAPTER 1

THE STATUTORY DEMAND

6.1 Form and content of statutory demand

(1) A statutory demand under section 268 must be dated, and be [authenticated] either by the creditor himself or by a person stating himself to be authorised to make the demand on the creditor's behalf.

(2) The statutory demand must specify whether it is made under section 268(1) (debt payable immediately) or section 268(2) (debt not so payable).

(3) The demand must state the amount of the debt, and the consideration for it (or, if there is no consideration, the way in which it arises) and—
   (a) if made under section 268(1) and founded on a judgment or order of a court, it must give details of the judgment or order, and
   (b) if made under section 268(2), it must state the grounds on which it is alleged that the debtor appears to have no reasonable prospect of paying the debt.

(4) If the amount claimed in the demand includes—
   (a) any charge by way of interest not previously notified to the debtor as a liability of his, or
   (b) any other charge accruing from time to time,
the amount or rate of the charge must be separately identified, and the grounds on which payment of it is claimed must be stated.
   In either case the amount claimed must be limited to that which has accrued due at the date of the demand.

(5) If the creditor holds any security in respect of the debt, the full amount of the debt shall be specified, but—
   (a) there shall in the demand be specified the nature of the security, and the value which the creditor puts upon it as at the date of the demand, and
   (b) the amount of which payment is claimed by the demand shall be the full amount of the debt, less the amount specified as the value of the security.

NOTES

Initial Commencement

Specified date

Specified date: 29 December 1986: see r 0.1.

Amendment

Para (1): word "authenticated" in square brackets substituted by SI 2010/686, r 2, Sch 1, para 1.
Date in force: 6 April 2010: see SI 2010/686, r 1; for transitional provisions see r 6(1), Sch 4, paras 1, 2(1)(b) thereto.

See Further

This rule is disapplied as respects a demand made by the Financial Services Authority (under the Financial Services and Markets Act 2000, s 372(4)(a)): see the Bankruptcy (Financial Services and Markets Act 2000) Rules 2001, SI 2001/3634, rr 3, 4.

6.2 Information to be given in statutory demand

(1) The statutory demand must include an explanation to the debtor of the following matters—

(a) the purpose of the demand, and the fact that, if the debtor does not comply with the demand, bankruptcy proceedings may be commenced against him;

(b) the time within which the demand must be complied with, if that consequence is to be avoided;

(c) the methods of compliance which are open to the debtor; and

(d) his right to apply to the court for the statutory demand to be set aside.

(2) The demand must specify one or more named individuals with whom the debtor may, if he wishes, enter into communication with a view to securing or compounding for the debt to the satisfaction of the creditor or (as the case may be) establishing to the creditor's satisfaction that there is a reasonable prospect that the debt will be paid when it falls due.

In the case of any individual so named in the demand, his address and telephone number (if any) must be given.

NOTES

Initial Commencement

Specified date

Specified date: 29 December 1986: see r 0.1.

See Further

This rule is disapplied as respects a demand made by the Financial Services Authority (under the Financial Services and Markets Act 2000, s 372(4)(a)) to an individual that he establish to the Authority's satisfaction that he has reasonable prospect of being able to pay a regulated activity debt when it falls due: see the Bankruptcy (Financial Services and Markets Act 2000) Rules 2001, SI 2001/3634, rr 3, 5.

6.3 Requirements as to service

(1) Rule 6.11 in Chapter 2 below has effect as regards service of the statutory demand, and proof of that service by [a certificate of service] to be filed with a bankruptcy petition.

(2) The creditor is, by virtue of the Rules, under an obligation to do all that is reasonable for the purpose of bringing the statutory demand to the debtor's attention

and, if practicable in the particular circumstances, to cause personal service of the demand to be effected.

(3) Where the statutory demand is for payment of a sum due under a judgment or order of any court and the creditor knows, or believes with reasonable cause—

(a) that the debtor has absconded or is keeping out of the way with a view to avoiding service, and

(b) there is no real prospect of the sum due being recovered by execution or other process,

[the creditor may advertise the demand in such manner as the creditor thinks fit]; and the time limited for compliance with the demand runs from the date of the advertisement's appearance or (as the case may be) its first appearance.

NOTES

Initial Commencement

Specified date

Specified date: 29 December 1986: see r 0.1.

Amendment

Para (1): words "a certificate of service" in square brackets substituted by SI 2010/686, r 2, Sch 1, para 303.

Date in force: 6 April 2010: see SI 2010/686, r 1; for transitional provisions see r 6(1), Sch 4, paras 1, 2(1)(b) thereto.

Para (3): words from "the creditor may" to "creditor thinks fit" in square brackets substituted by SI 2009/642, rr 4, 33.

Date in force: 6 April 2009: see SI 2009/642, r 1; for transitional provisions see r 3 thereof.

Modification

When demand is being made by the Financial Services Authority (under the Financial Services and Markets Act 2001, s 372(4)(a)), references to "the debtor" and "the creditor" are to be construed as references to "an individual" and "the authority" by virtue of the Bankruptcy (Financial Services and Markets Act 2000) Rules 2001, SI 2001/3634, rr 3, 6(1)(a), (b).

6.4 Application to set aside statutory demand

(1) The debtor may, within the period allowed by this Rule, apply to the appropriate court for an order setting the statutory demand aside.

That period is 18 days from the date of the service on him of the statutory demand or, where the demand is advertised . . . pursuant to Rule 6.3, from the date of the advertisement's appearance or (as the case may be) its first appearance.

[(2) Subject to paragraph (2A), an application to the court under this Rule must be made to the court to which the debtor would in accordance with Rule 6.40A present the petition for the debtor's bankruptcy.

(2A) A debtor may make an application to the High Court where the High Court is not the court to which the debtor would in accordance with Rule 6.40A present the petition for the debtor's bankruptcy if—

(a) the creditor issuing the statutory demand is a Minister of the Crown or a Government Department;

(b) the debt in respect of which the statutory demand is made, or a part of it equal to or exceeding the bankruptcy level (within the meaning of section 267), is the subject of a judgment or order of any court; and

(c) the statutory demand—
   (i) specifies the date of the judgment or order and the court in which it was obtained; and
   (ii) indicates the creditor's intention to present a bankruptcy petition against the debtor in the High Court.]

(3) As from (inclusive) the date on which the application is filed in court, the time limited for compliance with the statutory demand ceases to run, subject to any order of the court under Rule 6.5(6).

(4) The debtor's application shall be supported by [a witness statement]—

(a) specifying the date on which the statutory demand came into his hands, and

(b) stating the grounds on which he claims that it should be set aside.

. . .

[(5) The witness statement must have attached to it a copy of the statutory demand.]

NOTES

Initial Commencement

Specified date

Specified date: 29 December 1986: see r 0.1.

Amendment

Para (1): words "in a newspaper" in italics revoked by SI 2009/642, rr 4, 34.
Date in force: 6 April 2009: see SI 2009/642, r 1; for transitional provisions see r 3 thereof.
Paras (2), (2A): substituted, for para (2) as originally enacted, by SI 2010/686, r 2, Sch 1, para 304(1), (2).
Date in force: 6 April 2010: see SI 2010/686, r 1; for transitional provisions see r 6(1), Sch 4, para 1 thereto.
Para (4): words "a witness statement" in square brackets substituted by SI 2010/686, r 2, Sch 1, para 304(1), (3)(a).
Date in force: 6 April 2010: see SI 2010/686, r 1; for transitional provisions see r 6(1), Sch 4, paras 1, 2(1)(b), (2)–(4) thereto.
Para (4): words omitted revoked by SI 2010/686, r 2, Sch 1, para 304(1), (3)(b).
Date in force: 6 April 2010: see SI 2010/686, r 1; for transitional provisions see r 6(1), Sch 4, paras 1, 2(1)(b), (2)–(4) thereto.
Para (5): inserted by SI 2010/686, r 2, Sch 1, para 304(1), (4).
Date in force: 6 April 2010: see SI 2010/686, r 1; for transitional provisions see r 6(1), Sch 4, paras 1, 2(1)(b), (2)–(4) thereto.

Modification

Modified, in relation to a demand being made by the Financial Services Authority (under the Financial Services and Markets Act 2000, s 372(4)(a)), by the Bankruptcy (Financial Services and Markets Act 2000) Rules 2001, SI 2001/3634, rr 3, 7.

6.5 Hearing of application to set aside

(1) On receipt of an application under Rule 6.4, the court may, if satisfied that no sufficient cause is shown for it, dismiss it without giving notice to the creditor. As from (inclusive) the date on which the application is dismissed, the time limited for compliance with the statutory demand runs again.

(2) If the application is not dismissed under paragraph (1), the court shall fix a venue for it to be heard, and shall give at least [5 business] days' notice of it to—

(a) the debtor or, if the debtor's application was made by a solicitor acting for him, to the solicitor,

(b) the creditor, and

(c) whoever is named in the statutory demand as the person with whom the debtor may enter into communication with reference to the demand (or, if more than one person is so named, the first of them).

(3) On the hearing of the application, the court shall consider the evidence then available to it, and may either summarily determine the application or adjourn it, giving such directions as it thinks appropriate.

(4) The court may grant the application if—
- (a) the debtor appears to have a counterclaim, set-off or cross demand which equals or exceeds the amount of the debt or debts specified in the statutory demand; or
- (b) the debt is disputed on grounds which appear to the court to be substantial; or
- (c) it appears that the creditor holds some security in respect of the debt claimed by the demand, and either Rule 6.1(5) is not complied with in respect of it, or the court is satisfied that the value of the security equals or exceeds the full amount of the debt; or
- (d) the court is satisfied, on other grounds, that the demand ought to be set aside.

(5) Where the creditor holds some security in respect of his debt, and Rule 6.1(5) is complied with in respect of it but the court is satisfied that the security is undervalued in the statutory demand, the creditor may be required to amend the demand accordingly (but without prejudice to his right to present a bankruptcy petition by reference to the original demand).

(6) If the court dismisses the application, it shall make an order authorising the creditor to present a bankruptcy petition either [as soon as reasonably practicable], or on or after a date specified in the order.

A copy of the order shall be sent by the court [as soon as reasonably practicable] to the creditor.

NOTES

Initial Commencement

Specified date

Specified date: 29 December 1986: see r 0.1.

Amendment

Para (2): words "5 business" in square brackets substituted by SI 2010/686, r 2, Sch 1, para 305.

Date in force: 6 April 2010: see SI 2010/686, r 1; for transitional provisions see r 6(1), Sch 4, para 1 thereto.

Para (6): words "as soon as reasonably practicable" in square brackets in both places they occur substituted by SI 2009/642, rr 4, 5.

Date in force: 6 April 2009: see SI 2009/642, r 1; for transitional provisions see r 3 thereof.

Modification

References to solicitors etc modified to include references to bodies recognised under the Administration of Justice Act 1985, s 9, by the Solicitors' Incorporated Practices Order 1991, SI 1991/2684, arts 4, 5, Sch 1.

Modified, in relation to a demand being made by the Financial Services Authority (under the Financial Services and Markets Act 2000, s 372(4)(a)), by the Bankruptcy (Financial Services and Markets Act 2000) Rules 2001, SI 2001/3634, rr 3, 6.

CHAPTER 2

BANKRUPTCY PETITION (CREDITOR'S)

6.6 Preliminary

The Rules in this Chapter relate to a creditor's petition, and the making of a bankruptcy order thereon; and in those Rules "the debt" means, except where the context otherwise requires, the debt (or debts) in respect of which the petition is presented.

Those Rules also apply to a petition under section 264(1)(c) (supervisor of, or person bound by, voluntary arrangement), with any necessary modifications.

NOTES

Initial Commencement

Specified date

Specified date: 29 December 1986: see r 0.1.

6.7 Identification of debtor

(1) The petition shall state the following matters with respect to the debtor, so far as they are within the petitioner's knowledge—
- (a) his name, place of residence and occupation (if any);
- (b) the name or names in which he carries on business, if other than his true name, and whether, in the case of any business of a specified nature, he carries it on alone or with others;
- (c) the nature of his business, and the address or addresses at which he carries it on;
- (d) any name or names, other than his true name, in which he has carried on business at or after the time when the debt was incurred, and whether he has done so alone or with others;
- (e) any address or addresses at which he has resided or carried on business at or after that time, and the nature of that business;
- [(f) whether the debtor has his centre of main interests or an establishment in another member State].

(2) The particulars of the debtor given under this Rule determine the full title of the proceedings.

(3) If to the petitioner's personal knowledge the debtor has used any name other than the one specified under paragraph (1)(a), that fact shall be stated in the petition.

NOTES

Initial Commencement

Specified date

Specified date: 29 December 1986: see r 0.1.

Amendment

Para (1): sub-para (f) inserted by SI 2002/1307, rr 3(1), 8(1).
Date in force: 31 May 2002: see SI 2002/1307, r 1.

6.8 Identification of debt

(1) There shall be stated in the petition, with reference to every debt in respect of which it is presented—
- (a) the amount of the debt, the consideration for it (or, if there is no consideration, the way in which it arises) and the fact that it is owed to the petitioner;
- (b) when the debt was incurred or became due;
- (c) if the amount of the debt includes—
  - (i) any charge by way of interest not previously notified to the debtor as a liability of his, or
  - (ii) any other charge accruing from time to time,

  the amount or rate of the charge (separately identified) and the grounds on

which it is claimed to form part of the debt[, provided that such amount or rate must, in the case of a petition based on a statutory demand, be limited to that claimed in that demand];
  (d)   either—
        (i)   that the debt is for a liquidated sum payable immediately, and the debtor appears to be unable to pay it, or
        (ii) that the debt is for a liquidated sum payable at some certain, future time (that time to be specified), and the debtor appears to have no reasonable prospect of being able to pay it,
and, in either case (subject to section 269) that the debt is unsecured.
  (2) Where the debt is one for which, under section 268, a statutory demand must have been served on the debtor—
  (a)   there shall be specified the date and manner of service of the statutory demand, and
  (b)   it shall be stated that, to the best of the creditor's knowledge and belief—
        (i)   the demand has been neither complied with nor set aside in accordance with the Rules, and
        (ii) no application to set it aside is outstanding.
  (3) If the case is within section 268(1)(b) (debt arising under judgment or order of court; execution returned unsatisfied), the court from which the execution or other process issued shall be specified, and particulars shall be given relating to the return.

NOTES

Initial Commencement

Specified date

  Specified date: 29 December 1986: see r 0.1.

Amendment

  Para (1): words in square brackets in sub-para (c) inserted by SI 1987/1919, r 3(1), Schedule, Part 1, para 91.

[6.9A Court in which petition to be presented]
  [(1) If the debtor is resident in England and Wales, the petition must, in the following cases, be presented to the High Court—
  (a)   if the petition is presented by a Minister of the Crown or a Government Department, and either—
        (i)   in any statutory demand on which the petition is based the creditor has indicated the intention to present a bankruptcy petition to that Court, or
        (ii) the petition is presented under section 268(1)(b);
  (b)   if, for the greater part of the 6 months immediately preceding the presentation of the petition, the debtor—
        (i)   has carried on a business in the London insolvency district; or
        (ii) has not carried on a business in England and Wales but has resided in the London insolvency district; or
  (c)   if the petitioner is unable to ascertain the debtor's residence or place of business within England and Wales.
  (2) Where the debtor is resident in England and Wales and paragraph (1) does not apply, the petition must be presented to the debtor's own county court if the debtor—
  (a)   has carried on a business in England and Wales other than in the London insolvency district, or

(b) has not carried on a business in England and Wales and has resided outside the London insolvency district.

(3) In this Rule the debtor's own county court is—
(a) where the debtor has carried on a business within the 6 months immediately preceding the presentation of the petition, the county court for the insolvency district where for the greater part of that period of 6 months—
(i) the debtor carried on the business, or
(ii) the principal place of business was located, if the business was carried on in more than one insolvency district; or
(b) where the debtor has not carried on a business in the 6 months immediately preceding the presentation of the petition, the county court for the insolvency district where the debtor resided for the greater part of that 6 month period.

(4) If the debtor is not resident in England and Wales but was resident or carried on business in England and Wales within the 6 months immediately preceding the presentation of the petition, the petition—
(a) must be presented to the High Court if the debtor—
(i) carried on a business in the London insolvency district for a longer period in those 6 months than in any other insolvency district, or
(ii) did not carry on a business in England and Wales but resided in the London insolvency district for a longer period in those 6 months than in any other insolvency district; and
(b) in any other case, may be presented either to the debtor's own county court or to the High Court.

(5) The petition must be presented to the High Court if the debtor is not resident in England and Wales and—
(a) has not resided or carried on business in England and Wales within the 6 months immediately preceding the presentation of the petition, or
(b) the petitioner is unable to ascertain the debtor's residence or place of business.

(6) Notwithstanding any other provision of this Rule, where there is in force for the debtor a voluntary arrangement under Part 8 of the Act, the petition must be presented to the court to which the nominee's report under section 256 was submitted.

(7) The petition must contain sufficient information to establish that it is presented in the appropriate court.]

NOTES

Amendment

Substituted, for r 6.9 as originally enacted, by SI 2010/686, r 2, Sch 1, para 306.
Date in force: 6 April 2010: see SI 2010/686, r 1; for transitional provisions see r 6(1), Sch 4, para 1 thereto.

6.10 Procedure for presentation and filing

(1) The petition, verified by [a statement of truth] in accordance with Rule 6.12(1) below, shall be filed in court.

[(2) No petition shall be filed unless there is produced on presentation of the petition a receipt for the deposit payable or paragraph (2A) applies.

(2A) This paragraph applies in any case where the Secretary of State has given written notice to the court that the petitioner has made suitable alternative arrangements for the payment of the deposit to the official receiver and such notice has not been revoked in relation to the petitioner in accordance with paragraph (2B).

(2B) A notice of the kind referred to in paragraph (2A) may be revoked in relation to the petitioner in whose favour it is given by a further notice in writing to the court stating that the earlier notice is revoked in relation to the petitioner.]

(3) The following copies of the petition shall also be delivered to the court with the petition—

(a) one for service on the debtor, . . . [and]
(b) . . . [. . .
(c) if there is in force for the debtor a voluntary arrangement under Part VIII of the Act, and the petitioner is not the supervisor of the arrangement, one copy for him].

Each of these copies shall have applied to it the seal of the court, and shall be issued to the petitioner.

(4) The date and time of filing the petition shall be endorsed on the petition and on any copy issued under paragraph (3).

(5) The court shall fix a venue for hearing the petition, and this also shall be endorsed on the petition and on any copy so issued.

[(6) Where a petition contains a request for the appointment of a person as trustee in accordance with section 297(5) (appointment of former supervisor as trustee) the person whose appointment is sought shall, not less than 2 [business] days before the day appointed for hearing the petition, file in court a report including particulars of—

(a) a date on which he gave written notification to creditors bound by the arrangement of the intention to seek his appointment as trustee, such date to be at least [7 business] days before the day on which the report under this paragraph is filed, and
(b) details of any response from creditors to that notice, including any objections to his appointment.]

NOTES

Initial Commencement

Specified date

Specified date: 29 December 1986: see r 0.1.

Amendment

Para (1): word "a statement of truth" in square brackets substituted by SI 2010/686, r 2, Sch 1, para 307(1), (2).
Date in force: 6 April 2010: see SI 2010/686, r 1; for transitional provisions see r 6(1), Sch 4, paras 1, 2(1)(b) thereto.
Paras (2), (2A), (2B): substituted, for para (2) as originally enacted, by SI 2004/584, r 26.
Date in force: 1 April 2004: see SI 2004/584, r 1(2).

Para (3): in sub-para (a) word omitted revoked by SI 1987/1919, r 3(1), Schedule, Pt 1, para 93(1).

Para (3): in sub-para (a) word "and" in square brackets inserted by SI 2010/686, r 2, Sch 1, para 307(1), (3)(a).
Date in force: 6 April 2010: see SI 2010/686, r 1; for transitional provisions see r 6(1), Sch 4, paras 1, 2(1)(b) thereto.
Para (3): sub-para (b) revoked by SI 2010/686, r 2, Sch 1, para 307(1), (3)(b).
Date in force: 6 April 2010: see SI 2010/686, r 1; for transitional provisions see r 6(1), Sch 4, paras 1, 2(1)(b) thereto.

Para (3): sub-para (c) and word omitted immediately preceding it inserted by SI 1987/1919, r 3(1), Schedule, Pt 1, para 93(1).

Para (6): inserted by SI 1987/1919, r 3(1), Schedule, Part 1, para 93(2).
Para (6): word "business" in square brackets inserted by SI 2010/686, r 2, Sch 1, para 307(1), (4)(a).
Date in force: 6 April 2010: see SI 2010/686, r 1; for transitional provisions see r 6(1), Sch 4, para 1 thereto.

Para (6): in sub-para (a) words "7 business" in square brackets substituted by SI 2010/686, r 2, Sch 1, para 307(1), (4)(b).
   Date in force: 6 April 2010: see SI 2010/686, r 1; for transitional provisions see r 6(1), Sch 4, para 1 thereto.

6.11 Proof of service of statutory demand

(1) Where under section 268 the petition must have been preceded by a statutory demand, there must be filed in court, with the petition, [a certificate or certificates] proving service of the demand.

(2) [Every] [certificate must be verified by a statement of truth and] have [attached] to it a copy of the demand as served.

(3) Subject to the next paragraph, if the demand has been served personally on the debtor, the [certificate must be authenticated] by the person who effected that service.

(4) If service of the demand (however effected) has been acknowledged in writing either by the debtor himself, or by some person stating himself in the acknowledgement to be authorised to accept service on the debtor's behalf, the [certificate must be authenticated] either by the creditor or by a person acting on his behalf, and the acknowledgement of service must be [exhibited to the certificate].

(5) If neither paragraph (3) nor paragraph (4) applies, the [certificate or certificates must be authenticated] by a person [or persons] having direct personal knowledge of the means adopted for serving the statutory demand, and must—

  (a) give particulars of the steps which have been taken with a view to serving the demand [personally], and
  (b) state the means whereby (those steps having been ineffective) it was sought to bring the demand to the debtor's attention, and
  (c) specify a date by which, to the best of the knowledge, information and belief of the person [authenticating the certificate], the demand will have come to the debtor's attention.

(6) The steps of which particulars are given for the purposes of paragraph (5)(a) must be such as would have sufficed to justify an order for substituted service of a petition.

(7) If the [certificate] specifies a date for the purposes of compliance with paragraph (5)(c), then unless the court otherwise orders, that date is deemed for the purposes of the Rules to have been the date on which the statutory demand was served on the debtor.

(8) Where the creditor has taken advantage of Rule 6.3(3) (. . . advertisement), the [certificate must be authenticated] either by the creditor himself or by a person having direct personal knowledge of the circumstances; and there must be [specified in the certificate]—

  (a) the means of the creditor's knowledge or (as the case may be) belief required for the purposes of that Rule, and
  [(b) the method by which, and the date or dates on which the statutory demand was advertised under that rule];

and there shall be [exhibited to the certificate] [either a copy of any advertisement of the statutory demand or, where this is not reasonably practicable, the [certificate must contain or attach] a description of the contents of any such advertisement] of the statutory demand.

(9) The court may decline to file the petition if not satisfied that the creditor has discharged the obligation imposed on him by Rule 6.3(2).

NOTES

Initial Commencement

Specified date

   Specified date: 29 December 1986: see r 0.1.

Amendment

Para (1): words "a certificate or certificates" in square brackets substituted by SI 2010/686, r 2, Sch 1, para 308(1), (2).
   Date in force: 6 April 2010: see SI 2010/686, r 1; for transitional provisions see r 6(1), Sch 4, para 1 thereto.
Para (2): word "Every" in square brackets substituted by virtue of SI 1987/1919, r 3(1), Schedule, Pt 1, para 94(2).
Para (2): words "certificate must be verified by a statement of truth and" in square brackets substituted by SI 2010/686, r 2, Sch 1, para 308(1), (3)(a).
   Date in force: 6 April 2010: see SI 2010/686, r 1; for transitional provisions see r 6(1), Sch 4, para 1 thereto.
Para (2): word "attached" in square brackets substituted by SI 2010/686, r 2, Sch 1, para 308(1), (3)(b).
   Date in force: 6 April 2010: see SI 2010/686, r 1; for transitional provisions see r 6(1), Sch 4, para 1 thereto.
Para (3): words "certificate must be authenticated" in square brackets substituted by SI 2010/686, r 2, Sch 1, para 308(1), (4).
   Date in force: 6 April 2010: see SI 2010/686, r 1; for transitional provisions see r 6(1), Sch 4, para 1 thereto.
Para (4): words "certificate must be authenticated" in square brackets substituted by SI 2010/686, r 2, Sch 1, para 308(1), (5)(a).
   Date in force: 6 April 2010: see SI 2010/686, r 1; for transitional provisions see r 6(1), Sch 4, para 1 thereto.
Para (4): words "exhibited to the certificate" in square brackets substituted by SI 2010/686, r 2, Sch 1, para 308(1), (5)(b).
   Date in force: 6 April 2010: see SI 2010/686, r 1; for transitional provisions see r 6(1), Sch 4, para 1 thereto.
Para (5): words "certificate or certificates must be authenticated" in square brackets substituted by SI 2010/686, r 2, Sch 1, para 308(1), (6)(a).
   Date in force: 6 April 2010: see SI 2010/686, r 1; for transitional provisions see r 6(1), Sch 4, para 1 thereto.
Para (5): words "persons" in square brackets inserted by SI 1987/1919, r 3(1), Schedule, Pt 1, para 94(3)(b).
Para (5): in sub-para (a) word "personally" in square brackets inserted by SI 1987/1919, r 3(1), Schedule, Pt 1, para 94(3)(c).
Para (5): in sub-para (c) words "authenticating the certificate" in square brackets substituted by SI 2010/686, r 2, Sch 1, para 308(1), (6)(b).
   Date in force: 6 April 2010: see SI 2010/686, r 1; for transitional provisions see r 6(1), Sch 4, para 1 thereto.
Para (7): word "certificate" in square brackets substituted by SI 2010/686, r 2, Sch 1, para 308(1), (7).
   Date in force: 6 April 2010: see SI 2010/686, r 1; for transitional provisions see r 6(1), Sch 4, para 1 thereto.
Para (8): word omitted revoked by SI 2009/642, rr 4, 35(a)(i).
   Date in force: 6 April 2009: see SI 2009/642, r 1; for transitional provisions see r 3 thereof.
Para (8): words "certificate must be authenticated" in square brackets substituted by SI 2010/686, r 2, Sch 1, para 308(1), (8)(a).
   Date in force: 6 April 2010: see SI 2010/686, r 1; for transitional provisions see r 6(1), Sch 4, para 1 thereto.
Para (8): words "specified in the certificate" in square brackets substituted by SI 2010/686, r 2, Sch 1, para 308(1), (8)(b).
   Date in force: 6 April 2010: see SI 2010/686, r 1; for transitional provisions see r 6(1), Sch 4, para 1 thereto.
Para (8): sub-para (b) substituted by SI 2009/642, rr 4, 35(a)(ii).
   Date in force: 6 April 2009: see SI 2009/642, r 1; for transitional provisions see r 3 thereof.
Para (8): words "exhibited to the certificate" in square brackets substituted by SI 2010/686, r 2, Sch 1, para 308(1), (8)(c).
   Date in force: 6 April 2010: see SI 2010/686, r 1; for transitional provisions see r 6(1), Sch 4, para 1 thereto.

Para (8): words from "either a copy" to "any such advertisement" in square brackets substituted by SI 2009/642, rr 4, 35(b).
> Date in force: 6 April 2009: see SI 2009/642, r 1; for transitional provisions see r 3 thereof.

Para (8): words "certificate must contain or attach" in square brackets substituted by SI 2010/686, r 2, Sch 1, para 309(1), (8)(d).
> Date in force: 6 April 2010: see SI 2010/686, r 1; for transitional provisions see r 6(1), Sch 4, para 1 thereto.

Modification

When demand is being made by the Financial Services Authority (under the Financial Services and Markets Act 2001, s 372(4)(a)), references to "the debtor" and "the creditor" are to be construed as references to "an individual" and "the authority" by virtue of the Bankruptcy (Financial Services and Markets Act 2000) Rules 2001, SI 2001/3634, rr 3, 6(1).

6.12 Verification of petition

(1) The petition shall be verified by [a statement of truth].

(2) If the petition is in respect of debts to different creditors, the debts to each creditor must be separately verified.

[(3A) A statement of truth which is not contained in or endorsed upon the petition which it verifies must be sufficient to identify the petition and must specify—

- (a) the name of the debtor,
- (b) the name of the petitioner, and
- (c) the court in which the petition is to be presented.]

(4) The [statement of truth must be authenticated]—

- (a) by the petitioner (or if there are two or more petitioners, any one of them), or
- (b) by some person such as a director, company secretary or similar company officer, or a solicitor, who has been concerned in the matters giving rise to the presentation of the petition, or
- (c) by some responsible person who is duly authorised to [authenticate the statement of truth] and has the requisite knowledge of those matters.

(5) Where the [person authenticating the statement of truth] is not the petitioner himself, or one of the petitioners, he must in the [statement of truth] identify himself and state—

- (a) the capacity in which, and the authority by which, he [authenticates] it, and
- (b) the means of his knowledge of the matters [verified in the statement of truth].

(6) . . .

(7) If the petition is based upon a statutory demand, and more than 4 months have elapsed between the service of the demand and the presentation of the petition, the [petition must include a statement explaining] the reasons for the delay.

NOTES

Initial Commencement

Specified date
> Specified date: 29 December 1986: see r 0.1.

Amendment

Para (1): words "a statement of truth" in square brackets substituted by SI 2010/686, r 2, Sch 1, para 309(1), (2).
> Date in force: 6 April 2010: see SI 2010/686, r 1; for transitional provisions see r 6(1), Sch 4, paras 1, 2(1)(b) thereto.

Para (3A): substituted, for para (3) as originally enacted, by SI 2010/686, r 2, Sch 1, para 309(1), (3).
>Date in force: 6 April 2010: see SI 2010/686, r 1; for transitional provisions see r 6(1), Sch 4, paras 1, 2(1)(b) thereto.

Para (4): words "statement of truth must be authenticated" in square brackets substituted by SI 2010/686, r 2, Sch 1, para 309(1), (4)(a).
>Date in force: 6 April 2010: see SI 2010/686, r 1; for transitional provisions see r 6(1), Sch 4, paras 1, 2(1)(b) thereto.

Para (4): in sub-para (c) words "authenticate the statement of truth" in square brackets substituted by SI 2010/686, r 2, Sch 1, para 309(1), (4)(b).
>Date in force: 6 April 2010: see SI 2010/686, r 1; for transitional provisions see r 6(1), Sch 4, paras 1, 2(1)(b) thereto.

Para (5): words "person authenticating the statement of truth" in square brackets substituted by SI 2010/686, r 2, Sch 1, para 309(1), (5)(a).
>Date in force: 6 April 2010: see SI 2010/686, r 1; for transitional provisions see r 6(1), Sch 4, paras 1, 2(1)(b) thereto.

Para (5): word "statement of truth" in square brackets substituted by SI 2010/686, r 2, Sch 1, para 309(1), (5)(b).
>Date in force: 6 April 2010: see SI 2010/686, r 1; for transitional provisions see r 6(1), Sch 4, paras 1, 2(1)(b) thereto.

Para (5): in sub-para (a) word "authenticates" in square brackets substituted by SI 2010/686, r 2, Sch 1, paras 309(1), (5)(c).
>Date in force: 6 April 2010: see SI 2010/686, r 1; for transitional provisions see r 6(1), Sch 4, paras 1, 2(1)(b) thereto.

Para (5): in sub-para (b) words "verified in the statement of truth" in square brackets substituted by SI 2010/686, r 2, Sch 1, para 309(1), (5)(d).
>Date in force: 6 April 2010: see SI 2010/686, r 1; for transitional provisions see r 6(1), Sch 4, paras 1, 2(1)(b) thereto.

Para (6): revoked by SI 2010/686, r 2, Sch 1, para 309(1), (6).
>Date in force: 6 April 2010: see SI 2010/686, r 1; for transitional provisions see r 6(1), Sch 4, paras 1, 2(1)(b) thereto.

Para (7): words "petition must include a statement explaining" in square brackets substituted by SI 2010/686, r 2, Sch 1, para 309(1), (7).
>Date in force: 6 April 2010: see SI 2010/686, r 1; for transitional provisions see r 6(1), Sch 4, paras 1, 2(1)(b) thereto.

6.13 Notice to Chief Land Registrar

When the petition is filed, the court shall [as soon as reasonably practicable] send to the Chief Land Registrar notice of the petition together with a request that it may be registered in the register of pending actions.

NOTES

Initial Commencement

Specified date
>Specified date: 29 December 1986: see r 0.1.

Amendment
>Words "as soon as reasonably practicable" in square brackets substituted by SI 2009/642, rr 4, 5.
>>Date in force: 6 April 2009: see SI 2009/642, r 1; for transitional provisions see r 3 thereof.

6.14 Service of petition

(1) Subject as follows, the petition shall be served personally on the debtor by an officer of the court, or by the petitioning creditor or his solicitor, or by a person instructed by the creditor or his solicitor for that purpose; and service shall be effected by delivering to him a sealed copy of the petition.

(2) If the court is satisfied by [a witness statement] or other evidence on oath that prompt personal service cannot be effected because the debtor is keeping out of the way to avoid service of the petition or other legal process, or for any other cause, it may order substituted service to be effected in such manner as it thinks [just].

(3) Where an order for substituted service has been carried out, the petition is deemed duly served on the debtor.

[(4) If to the petitioner's knowledge there is in force for the debtor a voluntary arrangement under Part VIII of the Act, and the petitioner is not himself the supervisor of the arrangement, a copy of the petition shall be sent by him to the supervisor.]

[(5) If to the petitioner's knowledge, there is a member State liquidator appointed in main proceedings in relation to the bankrupt, a copy of the petition shall be sent by him to the member State liquidator.]

[(6) A bankruptcy petition may, with the permission of the court, be served outside England and Wales in such manner as the court may direct.]

NOTES

Initial Commencement

Specified date

Specified date: 29 December 1986: see r 0.1.

Amendment

Para (2): words "a witness statement" in square brackets substituted by SI 2010/686, r 2, Sch 1, para 310(1), (2).
Date in force: 6 April 2010: see SI 2010/686, r 1; for transitional provisions see r 6(1), Sch 4, paras 1, 2(1)(b), (2)–(4) thereto.

Para (2): word "just" in square brackets substituted by SI 2010/686, r 2, Sch 1, para 1.
Date in force: 6 April 2010: see SI 2010/686, r 1; for transitional provisions see r 6(1), Sch 4, paras 1, 2(1)(b) thereto.

Para (4): inserted by SI 1987/1919, r 3(1), Schedule, Part 1, para 95.

Para (5): inserted by SI 2002/1307, rr 3(1), 8(2).
Date in force: 31 May 2002: see SI 2002/1307, r 1.

Para (6): inserted by SI 2010/686, r 2, Sch 1, para 310(1), (3).
Date in force: 6 April 2010: see SI 2010/686, r 1; for transitional provisions see r 6(1), Sch 4, para 1 thereto.

Modification

References to solicitors etc modified to include references to bodies recognised under the Administration of Justice Act 1985, s 9, by the Solicitors' Incorporated Practices Order 1991, SI 1991/2684, arts 4, 5, Sch 1.

[6.15A Proof of service]

[(1) Service of the petition must be proved by a certificate of service.

(2) The certificate of service must be sufficient to identify the petition served and must specify—
    (a)   the name of the debtor,
    (b)   the name of the petitioner,
    (c)   the court in which the petition was filed and the court reference number,
    (d)   the date of the petition,
    (e)   whether the copy served was a sealed copy,
    (f)   the date on which service was effected, and
    (g)   the manner in which service was effected.

(3) Where substituted service has been ordered, the certificate of service must have attached to it a sealed copy of the order.

(4) The certificate of service must be filed in court as soon as reasonably practicable after service, and in any event not less than 5 business days before the hearing of the petition.]

NOTES

Amendment

> Substituted, for r 6.15 as originally enacted, by SI 2010/686, r 2, Sch 1, para 311.
> Date in force: 6 April 2010: see SI 2010/686, r 1; for transitional provisions see r 6(1), Sch 4, para 1 thereto.

6.16 Death of debtor before service

If the debtor dies before service of the petition, the court may order service to be effected on his personal representatives, or on such other persons as it thinks [just].

NOTES

Initial Commencement

Specified date

> Specified date: 29 December 1986: see r 0.1.

Amendment

> Word "just" in square brackets substituted by SI 2010/686, r 2, Sch 1, para 1.
> Date in force: 6 April 2010: see SI 2010/686, r 1; for transitional provisions see r 6(1), Sch 4, paras 1, 2(1)(b) thereto.

6.17 Security for costs (s 268(2) only)

(1) This Rule applies where the debt in respect of which the petition is presented is for a liquidated sum payable at some future time, it being claimed in the petition that the debtor appears to have no reasonable prospect of being able to pay it.

(2) The petitioning creditor may, on the debtor's application, be ordered to give security for the debtor's costs.

(3) The nature and amount of the security to be ordered is in the court's discretion.

(4) If an order is made under this Rule, there shall be no hearing of the petition until the whole amount of the security has been given.

NOTES

Initial Commencement

Specified date

> Specified date: 29 December 1986: see r 0.1.

6.18 Hearing of petition

(1) Subject as follows, the petition shall not be heard until at least 14 days have elapsed since it was served on the debtor.

(2) The court may, on such terms as it thinks [just], hear the petition at an earlier date, if it appears that the debtor has absconded, or the court is satisfied that it is a proper case for an expedited hearing, or the debtor consents to a hearing within the 14 days.

(3) Any of the following may appear and be heard, that is to say, the petitioning creditor, the debtor [, the supervisor of any voluntary arrangement under Part VIII of the Act in force for the debtor] and any creditor who has given notice under Rule 6.23 below.

NOTES

Initial Commencement

Specified date

Specified date: 29 December 1986: see r 0.1.

Amendment

Para (2): word "just" in square brackets substituted by SI 2010/686, r 2, Sch 1, para 1.
Date in force: 6 April 2010: see SI 2010/686, r 1; for transitional provisions see r 6(1), Sch 4, paras 1, 2(1)(b) thereto.

Para (3): words in square brackets inserted by SI 1987/1919, r 3(1), Schedule, Part 1, para 96.

6.20 . . .

. . .

NOTES

Amendment

Revoked by SI 2010/686, r 5.
Date in force: 6 April 2010: see SI 2010/686, r 1; for transitional provisions see r 6(1), Sch 4, paras 1, 2(1)(a) thereto.

6.21 Petition opposed by debtor

Where the debtor intends to oppose the petition, he shall not later than [5 business] days before the day fixed for the hearing—

(a) file in court a notice specifying the grounds on which he will object to the making of a bankruptcy order, and

(b) send a copy of the notice to the petitioning creditor or his solicitor.

NOTES

Initial Commencement

Specified date

Specified date: 29 December 1986: see r 0.1.

Amendment

Words "5 business" in square brackets substituted by SI 2010/686, r 2, Sch 1, para 312.
Date in force: 6 April 2010: see SI 2010/686, r 1; for transitional provisions see r 6(1), Sch 4, para 1 thereto.

Modification

References to solicitors etc modified to include references to bodies recognised under the Administration of Justice Act 1985, s 9, by the Solicitors' Incorporated Practices Order 1991, SI 1991/2684, arts 4, 5, Sch 1.

6.22 Amendment of petition

With the [permission] of the court (given on such terms, if any, as the court thinks [just] to impose), the petition may be amended at any time after presentation . . ..

NOTES

Initial Commencement

Specified date

Specified date: 29 December 1986: see r 0.1.

Amendment

Word "permission" in square brackets substituted by SI 2010/686, r 2, Sch 1, para 1.
Date in force: 6 April 2010: see SI 2010/686, r 1; for transitional provisions see r 6(1), Sch 4, paras 1, 2(1)(b) thereto.
Word "just" in square brackets substituted by SI 2010/686, r 2, Sch 1, para 1.
Date in force: 6 April 2010: see SI 2010/686, r 1; for transitional provisions see r 6(1), Sch 4, paras 1, 2(1)(b) thereto.
Words omitted revoked by SI 2010/686, r 2, Sch 1, para 313.
Date in force: 6 April 2010: see SI 2010/686, r 1; for transitional provisions see r 6(1), Sch 4, para 1 thereto.

6.23 Notice by persons intending to appear

(1) Every creditor who intends to appear on the hearing of the petition shall give to the petitioning creditor notice of his intention in accordance with this Rule.

(2) The notice shall specify—

(a) the name and address of the person giving it, and any telephone number and reference which may be required for communication with him or with any other person (to be also specified in the notice) authorised to speak or act on his behalf;

(b) whether his intention is to support or oppose the petition; and

(c) the amount and nature of his debt.

(3) The notice shall be sent so as to reach the addressee not later than 16.00 hours on the business day before that which is appointed for the hearing (or, where the hearing has been adjourned, for the adjourned hearing).

(4) A person failing to comply with this Rule may appear on the hearing of the petition only with the [permission] of the court.

NOTES

Initial Commencement

Specified date

Specified date: 29 December 1986: see r 0.1.

Amendment

Para (4): word "permission" in square brackets substituted by SI 2010/686, r 2, Sch 1, para 1.
Date in force: 6 April 2010: see SI 2010/686, r 1; for transitional provisions see r 6(1), Sch 4, paras 1, 2(1)(b) thereto.

6.24 List of appearances

(1) The petitioning creditor shall prepare for the court a list of the creditors (if any) who have given notice under Rule 6.23, specifying their names and addresses and (if known to him) their respective solicitors.

(2) Against the name of each creditor in the list it shall be stated whether his intention is to support the petition, or to oppose it.

(3) On the day appointed for the hearing of the petition, a copy of the list shall be handed to the court before the commencement of the hearing.

(4) If any [permission] is given under Rule 6.23(4), the petitioner shall add to the list the same particulars in respect of the person to whom [permission] has been given.

NOTES

Initial Commencement

Specified date

Specified date: 29 December 1986: see r 0.1.

Amendment

Para (4): word "permission" in square brackets in both places it occurs substituted by SI 2010/686, r 2, Sch 1, para 1.
Date in force: 6 April 2010: see SI 2010/686, r 1; for transitional provisions see r 6(1), Sch 4, paras 1, 2(1)(b) thereto.

Modification

References to solicitors etc modified to include references to bodies recognised under the Administration of Justice Act 1985, s 9, by the Solicitors' Incorporated Practices Order 1991, SI 1991/2684, arts 4, 5, Sch 1.

6.25 Decision on the hearing

(1) On the hearing of the petition, the court may make a bankruptcy order if satisfied that the statements in the petition are true, and that the debt on which it is founded has not been paid, or secured or compounded for.

(2) If the petition is brought in respect of a judgment debt, or a sum ordered by any court to be paid, the court may stay or dismiss the petition on the ground that an appeal is pending from the judgment or order, or that execution of the judgment has been stayed.

(3) A petition preceded by a statutory demand shall not be dismissed on the ground only that the amount of the debt was over-stated in the demand, unless the debtor, within the time allowed for complying with the demand, gave notice to the creditor disputing the validity of the demand on that ground; but, in the absence of such notice, the debtor is deemed to have complied with the demand if he has, within the time allowed, paid the correct amount.

NOTES

Initial Commencement

Specified date

Specified date: 29 December 1986: see r 0.1.

Modification

When demand is being made by the Financial Services Authority (under the Financial Services and Markets Act 2001, s 372(4)(a)), references to "the debtor" and "the creditor" are to be construed as references to "an individual" and "the authority" by virtue of the Bankruptcy (Financial Services and Markets Act 2000) Rules 2001, SI 2001/3634, rr 3, 6(1).

6.26 Non-appearance of creditor

If the petitioning creditor fails to appear on the hearing of the petition, no subsequent petition against the same debtor, either alone or jointly with any other person, shall be presented by the same creditor in respect of the same debt, without the [permission] of the court to which the previous petition was presented.

NOTES

Initial Commencement

Specified date

Specified date: 29 December 1986: see r 0.1.

Amendment

Word "permission" in square brackets substituted by SI 2010/686, r 2, Sch 1, para 1.
Date in force: 6 April 2010: see SI 2010/686, r 1; for transitional provisions see r 6(1), Sch 4, paras 1, 2(1)(b) thereto.

6.27 Vacating registration on dismissal of petition

If the petition is dismissed or withdrawn by [permission] of the court, an order shall be made at the same time permitting vacation of the registration of the petition as a pending action; and the court shall send to the debtor two sealed copies of the order.

NOTES

Initial Commencement

Specified date

Specified date: 29 December 1986: see r 0.1.

Amendment

Word "permission" in square brackets substituted by SI 2010/686, r 2, Sch 1, para 1.
Date in force: 6 April 2010: see SI 2010/686, r 1; for transitional provisions see r 6(1), Sch 4, paras 1, 2(1)(b) thereto.

6.28 Extension of time for hearing

(1) The petitioning creditor may, if the petition has not been served, apply to the court to appoint another venue for the hearing.

(2) The application shall state the reasons why the petition has not been served.

(3) No costs occasioned by the application shall be allowed in the proceedings except by order of the court.

(4) If the court appoints another day for the hearing, the petitioning creditor shall [as soon as reasonably practicable] notify any creditor who has given notice under Rule 6.23.

NOTES

Initial Commencement

Specified date

Specified date: 29 December 1986: see r 0.1.

Amendment

Para (4): words "as soon as reasonably practicable" in square brackets substituted by SI 2009/642, rr 4, 5.
Date in force: 6 April 2009: see SI 2009/642, r 1; for transitional provisions see r 3 thereof.

6.29 Adjournment

(1) If the court adjourns the hearing of the petition, the following applies.

(2) Unless the court otherwise directs, the petitioning creditor shall [as soon as reasonably practicable] send—

(a) to the debtor, and
(b) where any creditor has given notice under Rule 6.23 but was not present at the hearing, to him,
notice of the making of the order of adjournment. The notice shall state the venue for the adjourned hearing.

NOTES

Initial Commencement

Specified date

Specified date: 29 December 1986: see r 0.1.

Amendment

Para (2): words "as soon as reasonably practicable" in square brackets substituted by SI 2009/642, rr 4, 5.
Date in force: 6 April 2009: see SI 2009/642, r 1; for transitional provisions see r 3 thereof.

6.30 Substitution of petitioner

(1) This Rule applies where a creditor petitions and is subsequently found not entitled to do so, or where the petitioner—
 (a) consents to withdraw his petition or to allow it to be dismissed, or consents to an adjournment, or fails to appear in support of his petition when it is called on in court on the day originally fixed for the hearing, or on a day to which it is adjourned, or
 (b) appears, but does not apply for an order in the terms of the prayer of his petition.

(2) The court may, on such terms as it thinks just, order that there be substituted as petitioner any creditor who—
 (a) has under Rule 6.23 given notice of his intention to appear at the hearing,
 (b) is desirous of prosecuting the petition, and
 (c) was, at the date on which the petition was presented, in such a position in relation to the debtor as would have enabled him (the creditor) on that date to present a bankruptcy petition in respect of a debt or debts owed to him by the debtor [(or in the case of the member State liquidator, owed to creditors in proceedings in relation to which he holds office)], paragraphs (a) to (d) of section 267(2) being satisfied in respect of that debt or those debts.

NOTES

Initial Commencement

Specified date

Specified date: 29 December 1986: see r 0.1.

Amendment

Para (2): in sub-para (c) words from "(or in the" to "he holds office)" in square brackets inserted by SI 2002/1307, rr 3(1), 8(3).
Date in force: 31 May 2002: see SI 2002/1307, r 1.

6.31 Change of carriage of petition

(1) On the hearing of the petition, any person who claims to be a creditor of the debtor, and who has given notice under Rule 6.23 of his intention to appear at the

hearing, may apply to the court for an order giving him carriage of the petition in place of the petitioning creditor, but without requiring any amendment of the petition.

(2) The court may, on such terms as it thinks just, make a change of carriage order if satisfied that—
- (a) the applicant is an unpaid and unsecured creditor of the debtor, and
- (b) the petitioning creditor either—
  - (i) intends by any means to secure the postponement, adjournment or withdrawal of the petition, or
  - (ii) does not intend to prosecute the petition, either diligently or at all.

(3) The court shall not make the order if satisfied that the petitioning creditor's debt has been paid, secured or compounded for by means of—
- (a) a disposition of property made by some person other than the debtor, or
- (b) a disposition of the debtor's own property made with the approval of, or ratified by, the court.

(4) A change of carriage order may be made whether or not the petitioning creditor appears at the hearing.

(5) If the order is made, the person given the carriage of the petition is entitled to rely on all evidence previously adduced in the proceedings . . ..

NOTES

Initial Commencement

Specified date

Specified date: 29 December 1986: see r 0.1.

Amendment

Para (5): words omitted revoked by SI 2010/686, r 2, Sch 1, para 314.
Date in force: 6 April 2010: see SI 2010/686, r 1; for transitional provisions see r 6(1), Sch 4, paras 1, 2(1)(b), (2)–(4) thereto.

6.32 Petitioner seeking dismissal or [permission] to withdraw

[(1) Where the petitioner applies to the court for the petition to be dismissed, or for permission to withdraw it, the petitioner must, in any case where—
- (a) a creditor of the debtor has given notice under Rule 6.23 of intention to appear at the hearing of the petition, or
- (b) the court so orders,

file with the court a witness statement specifying the grounds of the application and the circumstances in which it is made.]

(2) If, since the petition was filed, any payment has been made to the petitioner by way of settlement (in whole or in part) of the debt or debts in respect of which the petition was brought, or any arrangement has been entered into for securing or compounding it or them, the [witness statement must also] state—
- (a) what dispositions of property have been made for the purposes of the settlement or arrangement, and
- (b) whether, in the case of any disposition, it was property of the debtor himself, or of some other person, and
- (c) whether, if it was property of the debtor, the disposition was made with the approval of, or has been ratified by, the court (if so, specifying the relevant court order).

(3) No order giving [permission] to withdraw a petition shall be given before the petition is heard.

NOTES

Initial Commencement

Specified date

Specified date: 29 December 1986: see r 0.1.

Amendment

Provision heading: word "permission" in square brackets substituted by SI 2010/686, r 2, Sch 1, para 1.
: Date in force: 6 April 2010: see SI 2010/686, r 1; for transitional provisions see r 6(1), Sch 4, paras 1, 2(1)(b) thereto.

Para (1): substituted by SI 2010/686, r 2, Sch 1, para 315(1), (2).
: Date in force: 6 April 2010: see SI 2010/686, r 1; for transitional provisions see r 6(1), Sch 4, para 1 thereto.

Para (2): words "witness statement must also" in square brackets substituted by SI 2010/686, r 2, Sch 1, para 315(1), (3).
: Date in force: 6 April 2010: see SI 2010/686, r 1; for transitional provisions see r 6(1), Sch 4, paras 1, 2(1)(b), (2)–(4) thereto.

Para (3): word "permission" in square brackets substituted by SI 2010/686, r 2, Sch 1, para 1.
: Date in force: 6 April 2010: see SI 2010/686, r 1; for transitional provisions see r 6(1), Sch 4, paras 1, 2(1)(b) thereto.

6.33 Settlement and content of bankruptcy order

(1) The bankruptcy order shall be settled by the court.

(2) The order shall—

    (a) state the date of the presentation of the petition on which the order is made, and the date and time of the making of the order, and

    [(b) contain a notice referring to the bankrupt's duties in relation to the official receiver under section 291, and in particular to the bankrupt's duty to give the official receiver such inventory of the bankrupt's estate and such other information, and to attend on the official receiver at such times, as the official receiver may reasonably require].

(3) Subject to section 346 (effect of bankruptcy on enforcement procedures), the order may include provision staying any action or proceeding against the bankrupt.

(4) Where the petitioning creditor is represented by a solicitor, the order shall be endorsed with the latter's name, address, telephone number and reference (if any).

NOTES

Initial Commencement

Specified date

Specified date: 29 December 1986: see r 0.1.

Amendment

Para (2): sub-para (b) substituted by SI 2010/686, r 2, Sch 1, para 316.
: Date in force: 6 April 2010: see SI 2010/686, r 1; for transitional provisions see r 6(1), Sch 4, para 1 thereto.

Modification

References to solicitors etc modified to include references to bodies recognised under the Administration of Justice Act 1985, s 9, by the Solicitors' Incorporated Practices Order 1991, SI 1991/2684, arts 4, 5, Sch 1.

6.34 Action to follow making of order

(1) At least two sealed copies of the bankruptcy order shall be sent [as soon as reasonably practicable] by the court to the official receiver, who shall [as soon as reasonably practicable] send one of them to the bankrupt.

[(2) Subject to the next paragraph, on receipt of the sealed copies of the bankruptcy order, the official receiver—
- (a) as soon as reasonably practicable shall—
  - (i) send notice of the making of the order to the Chief Land Registrar, for registration in the register of writs and orders affecting land;
  - (ii) cause notice of the order to be gazetted; and
- (b) may cause notice of the order to be advertised in such other manner as the official receiver thinks fit.]

[(2A) In addition to the standard contents, the notice to be gazetted and any notice to be advertised under paragraph (2) must state—
- (a) that a bankruptcy order has been made against the bankrupt;
- (b) the date and time of making of the bankruptcy order;
- (c) the name and address of the petitioning creditor; and
- (d) the date of presentation of the petition.]

(3) The court may, on the application of the bankrupt or a creditor, order the official receiver to suspend action under paragraph (2) [and [Rule 6A.4(2)]], pending a further order of the court.

An application under this paragraph shall be supported by [a witness statement] stating the grounds on which it is made.

(4) Where an order is made under paragraph (3), the applicant for the order shall [as soon as reasonably practicable] deliver a copy of it to the official receiver.

NOTES

Initial Commencement

Specified date

Specified date: 29 December 1986: see r 0.1.

Amendment

Para (1): words "as soon as reasonably practicable" in square brackets in both places they occur substituted by SI 2009/642, rr 4, 5.
Date in force: 6 April 2009: see SI 2009/642, r 1; for transitional provisions see r 3 thereof.

Para (2): substituted by SI 2009/642, rr 4, 36.
Date in force: 6 April 2009: see SI 2009/642, r 1; for transitional provisions see r 3 thereof.

Para (2A): inserted by SI 2010/686, r 2, Sch 1, para 317(1), (2).
Date in force: 6 April 2010: see SI 2010/686, r 1; for transitional provisions see r 6(1), Sch 4, para 1 thereto.

Para (3): words in square brackets beginning with the word "and" inserted by SI 1999/359, r 3, Schedule, para 4.
Date in force: 22 March 1999: see SI 1999/359, r 1.

Para (3): words "Rule 6A.4(2)" in square brackets substituted by SI 2005/527, r 35.
Date in force: 1 April 2005: see SI 2005/527, r 1(2).

Para (3): words "a witness statement" in square brackets substituted by SI 2010/686, r 2, Sch 1, para 317(1), (3).
Date in force: 6 April 2010: see SI 2010/686, r 1; for transitional provisions see r 6(1), Sch 4, paras 1, 2(1)(b), (2)–(4) thereto.

Para (4): words "as soon as reasonably practicable" in square brackets substituted by SI 2009/642, rr 4, 5.
Date in force: 6 April 2009: see SI 2009/642, r 1; for transitional provisions see r 3 thereof.

6.35 Amendment of title of proceedings

(1) At any time after the making of a bankruptcy order, the official receiver or the trustee may apply to the court for an order amending the full title of the proceedings.

[(2) Where such an order is made, as soon as reasonably practicable the official receiver shall send notice of it to the Chief Land Registrar for corresponding amendment of the register.]

[(3) If the official receiver thinks fit, notice of the order—
   (a) as soon as reasonably practicable, shall be gazetted; and
   (b) may be advertised in such other manner as the official receiver thinks fit.]

[(4) In addition to the standard contents, the notice under paragraph (3) must—
   (a) state that an amendment to the full title of the proceedings has been made; and
   (b) specify the amendment.]

NOTES

Initial Commencement

Specified date

Specified date: 29 December 1986: see r 0.1.

Amendment

Para (2): substituted by SI 2009/642, rr 4, 37(a).
   Date in force: 6 April 2009: see SI 2009/642, r 1; for transitional provisions see r 3 thereof.
Para (3): inserted by SI 2009/642, rr 4, 37(b).
   Date in force: 6 April 2009: see SI 2009/642, r 1; for transitional provisions see r 3 thereof.
Para (4): inserted by SI 2010/686, r 2, Sch 1, para 318.
   Date in force: 6 April 2010: see SI 2010/686, r 1; for transitional provisions see r 6(1), Sch 4, para 1 thereto.

6.36 . . .

. . .

NOTES

Amendment

Revoked by SI 2010/686, r 5.
   Date in force: 6 April 2010: see SI 2010/686, r 1; for transitional provisions see r 6(1), Sch 4, paras 1, 2(1)(a) thereto.

CHAPTER 3

BANKRUPTCY PETITION (DEBTOR'S)

6.37 Preliminary

The Rules in this Chapter relate to a debtor's petition, and the making of a bankruptcy order thereon.

NOTES

Initial Commencement

Specified date
   Specified date: 29 December 1986: see r 0.1.

6.38 Identification of debtor

(1) The petition shall state the following matters with respect to the debtor—
- (a) his name, place of residence and occupation (if any);
- (b) the name or names in which he carries on business, if other than his true name, and whether, in the case of any business of a specified nature, he carries it on alone or with others;
- (c) the nature of his business, and the address or addresses at which he carries it on;
- (d) any name or names, other than his true name, in which he has carried on business in the period in which any of his bankruptcy debts were incurred and, in the case of any such business, whether he has carried it on alone or with others; and
- (e) any address or addresses at which he has resided or carried on business during that period, and the nature of that business.

(2) The particulars of the debtor given under this Rule determine the full title of the proceedings.

(3) If the debtor has at any time used a name other than the one given under paragraph (1)(a), that fact shall be stated in the petition.

NOTES

Initial Commencement

Specified date
   Specified date: 29 December 1986: see r 0.1.

6.39 Admission of insolvency

(1) The petition shall contain the statement that the petitioner is unable to pay his debts, and a request that a bankruptcy order be made against him.

(2) If within the period of 5 years ending with the date of the petition the petitioner has been adjudged bankrupt, or has made a composition with his creditors in satisfaction of his debts or a scheme of arrangement of his affairs, or he has entered into any voluntary arrangement or been subject to an administration order under Part VI of the County Courts Act 1984, particulars of these matters shall be given in the petition.

[(3) If there is at the date of the petition in force for the debtor a voluntary arrangement under Part VIII of the Act, the particulars required by paragraph (2) above shall contain a statement to that effect and the name and address of the supervisor of the arrangement.]

NOTES

Initial Commencement

Specified date
   Specified date: 29 December 1986: see r 0.1.

Insolvency Rules 1986, reg 6.39

Amendment
Para (3): inserted by SI 1987/1919, r 3(1), Schedule, Part 1, para 98.

[6.40A Court in which petition to be presented]
[(1) If the debtor is resident in England and Wales, the petition—
- (a) must be presented to the High Court if, for the greater part of the 6 months immediately preceding the presentation of the petition, the debtor—
  - (i) has carried on a business in the London insolvency district; or
  - (ii) has not carried on a business in England and Wales but has resided in the London insolvency district; or
- (b) must be presented to the debtor's own county court (unless paragraph (5) applies) if the debtor—
  - (i) has carried on a business in England and Wales other than in the London insolvency district, or
  - (ii) has not carried on a business in England and Wales and has resided outside the London insolvency district.

(2) If the debtor is not resident in England and Wales but was resident or carried on business in England and Wales within the 6 months immediately preceding the presentation of the petition, the petition—
- (a) must be presented to the High Court if the debtor—
  - (i) carried on a business in the London insolvency district for a longer period in those 6 months than in any other insolvency district, or
  - (ii) did not carry on a business in England and Wales but resided in the London insolvency district for a longer period in those 6 months than in any other insolvency district; and
- (b) in any other case, may be presented either to the debtor's own county court or to the High Court.

(3) In a case not falling within either paragraph (1) or (2), the petition must be presented to the High Court.

(4) For the purposes of this Rule, what constitutes the debtor's own county court is to be determined in accordance with Rule 6.9A(3).

(5) Where, for whatever reason, it is not possible for the petition to be presented to the debtor's own county court, the debtor may, with a view to expediting the presentation of the petition, present the petition—
- (a) where Rule 6.9A(3)(a) applies, to—
  - (i) the court for the insolvency district in which the debtor resides, or
  - (ii) whichever court is specified by Schedule 2 to these Rules as being the nearest full time court in relation to—
    - (aa) the court in Rule 6.9A(3)(a), or
    - (bb) where the court in paragraph (i) is a county court, that court; or
- (b) where Rule 6.9A(3)(b) applies, whichever court is specified by Schedule 2 to these Rules as being the nearest full time court in relation to the court in that paragraph.

(6) Notwithstanding any other provision of this Rule, where there is in force for the debtor a voluntary arrangement under Part 8 of the Act, the petition must be presented to the court to which the nominee's report under section 256 was submitted.

(7) The petition must contain sufficient information to establish that it is presented to the appropriate court.]

NOTES

Amendment

Substituted, for r 6.40 as originally enacted, by SI 2010/686, r 2, Sch 1, para 319.
Date in force: 6 April 2010: see SI 2010/686, r 1; for transitional provisions see r 6(1), Sch 4, para 1 thereto.

6.41 Statement of affairs

(1) The petition shall be accompanied by a statement of the debtor's affairs, verified by [a statement of truth].

(2) Section B of Chapter 5 below applies with respect to the statement of affairs.

NOTES

Initial Commencement

Specified date

Specified date: 29 December 1986: see r 0.1.

Amendment

Para (1): words "a statement of truth" in square brackets substituted by SI 2010/686, r 2, Sch 1, para 320.
Date in force: 6 April 2010: see SI 2010/686, r 1; for transitional provisions see r 6(1), Sch 4, paras 1, 2(1)(b) thereto.

6.42 Procedure for presentation and filing

(1) The petition and the statement of affairs shall be filed in court, together with three copies of the petition, and [one copy] of the statement. No petition shall be filed unless there is produced with it the receipt for the deposit payable on presentation.

(2) [Subject to paragraph (2A),] the court may hear the petition [as soon as reasonably practicable]. If it does not do so, it shall fix a venue for the hearing.

[(2A) If the petition contains particulars of a voluntary arrangement under Part VIII of the Act in force for the debtor, the court shall fix a venue for the hearing and give at least 14 days' notice of it to the supervisor of the arrangement; the supervisor may appear and be heard on the petition.]

(3) Of the three copies of the petition delivered—
  (a) one shall be returned to the petitioner, endorsed with any venue fixed;
  (b) another, so endorsed, shall be [sent by the court to the official receiver; and]
  (c) the remaining copy shall be retained by the court, to be sent to an insolvency practitioner (if appointed under section 273(2)).

[(4) The copy of the statement of affairs shall be sent by the court to the official receiver.]

(5) ...

[(6) Where the court hears a petition [as soon as reasonably practicable], or it will in the opinion of the court otherwise expedite the delivery of any document to the official receiver, the court may, instead of sending that document to the official receiver, direct the bankrupt [as soon as reasonably practicable] to deliver it to him.

(7) Where a petition contains a request for the appointment of a person as trustee in accordance with section 297(5) (appointment of former supervisor as trustee) the person whose appointment is sought shall, not less than 2 [business] days before the day appointed for hearing the petition, file in court a report including particulars of—

(a) a date on which he gave written notification to creditors bound by the arrangement of the intention to seek his appointment as trustee, such date to be at least [7 business] days before the day on which the report under this paragraph is filed, and

(b) details of any response from creditors to that notice, including any objections to his appointment.]

NOTES

Initial Commencement

Specified date

Specified date: 29 December 1986: see r 0.1.

Amendment

Para (1): words "one copy" in square brackets substituted by SI 2005/527, r 36(a).
Date in force: 1 April 2005: see SI 2005/527, r 1(2).

Para (2): words "Subject to paragraph (2A)" in square brackets inserted by SI 1987/1919, r 3(1), Schedule, Pt 1, para 100(1).

Para (2): words "as soon as reasonably practicable" in square brackets substituted by SI 2009/642, rr 4, 5.
Date in force: 6 April 2009: see SI 2009/642, r 1; for transitional provisions see r 3 thereof.

Para (2A): inserted by SI 1987/1919, r 3(1), Schedule, Pt 1, para 100(2).

Para (3): words "sent by the court to the official receiver; and" in square brackets substituted by SI 1987/1919, r 3(1), Schedule, Pt 1, para 100(3).

Para (4): substituted by SI 2005/527, r 36(b).
Date in force: 1 April 2005: see SI 2005/527, r 1(2).

Para (5): revoked by SI 2010/686, r 2, Sch 1, para 321(1), (2).
Date in force: 6 April 2010: see SI 2010/686, r 1; for transitional provisions see r 6(1), Sch 4, para 1 thereto.

Paras (6): inserted by SI 1987/1919, r 3(1), Schedule, Pt 1, para 100(5).

Para (6): words "as soon as reasonably practicable" in square brackets in both places they occur substituted by SI 2009/642, rr 4, 5.
Date in force: 6 April 2009: see SI 2009/642, r 1; for transitional provisions see r 3 thereof.

Para (7): inserted by SI 1987/1919, r 3(1), Schedule, Pt 1, para 100(5).

Para (7): word "business" in square brackets inserted by SI 2010/686, r 2, Sch 1, para 321(1), (3)(a).
Date in force: 6 April 2010: see SI 2010/686, r 1; for transitional provisions see r 6(1), Sch 4, para 1 thereto.

Para (7): in sub-para (a) words "7 business" in square brackets substituted by SI 2010/686, r 2, Sch 1, para 321(1), (3)(b).
Date in force: 6 April 2010: see SI 2010/686, r 1; for transitional provisions see r 6(1), Sch 4, para 1 thereto.

6.43 Notice to Chief Land Registrar

When the petition is filed, the court shall [as soon as reasonably practicable] send to the Chief Land Registrar notice of the petition, for registration in the register of pending actions.

NOTES

Initial Commencement

Specified date

Specified date: 29 December 1986: see r 0.1.

Amendment

Words "as soon as reasonably practicable" in square brackets substituted by SI 2009/642, rr 4, 5.

Date in force: 6 April 2009: see SI 2009/642, r 1; for transitional provisions see r 3 thereof.

6.44 Report of insolvency practitioner

(1) If the court under section 273(2) appoints an insolvency practitioner to act in the debtor's case, it shall [as soon as reasonably practicable]—
  (a)   send to the person appointed—
      (i)   a sealed copy of the order of appointment, and
      (ii) copies of the petition and statement of affairs,
  (b)   fix a venue for the insolvency practitioner's report to be considered, and
  (c)   send notice of the venue to the insolvency practitioner and the debtor.

(2) The insolvency practitioner shall file his report in court . . . and send one copy of it to the debtor, so as to be in his hands not less than 3 [business] days before the date fixed for consideration of the report [, and a further copy to the official receiver].

(3) The debtor is entitled to attend when the report is considered, and shall attend if so directed by the court. If he attends, the court shall hear any representations which he makes with respect to any of the matters dealt with in the report.

(4) . . .

NOTES

Initial Commencement

Specified date

Specified date: 29 December 1986: see r 0.1.

Amendment

Para (1): words "as soon as reasonably practicable" in square brackets substituted by SI 2009/642, rr 4, 5.

Date in force: 6 April 2009: see SI 2009/642, r 1; for transitional provisions see r 3 thereof.

Para (2): words omitted revoked by SI 1987/1919, r 3(1), Schedule, Pt 1, para 101(1).

Para (2): word "business" in square brackets inserted by SI 2010/686, r 2, Sch 1, para 322.

Date in force: 6 April 2010: see SI 2010/686, r 1; for transitional provisions see r 6(1), Sch 4, para 1 thereto.

Para (2): words ", and a further copy to the official receiver" in square brackets inserted by SI 1987/1919, r 3(1), Schedule, Pt 1, para 101(1).

Para (4): revoked by SI 1987/1919, r 3(1), Schedule, Pt 1, para 101(2).

6.45 Settlement and content of bankruptcy order

(1) The bankruptcy order shall be settled by the court.

(2) The order shall—
  (a)   state the date of the presentation of the petition on which the order is made, and the date and time of the making of the order, and
  [(b) contain a notice referring to the bankrupt's duties in relation to the official receiver under section 291, and in particular to the bankrupt's duty to give the official receiver such inventory of the bankrupt's estate and such other information, and attend on the official receiver at such times, as the official receiver may reasonably require].

(3) Subject to section 346 (effect of bankruptcy on enforcement procedures), the order may include provision staying any action or proceeding against the bankrupt.

(4) Where the bankrupt is represented by a solicitor, the order shall be endorsed with the latter's name, address, telephone number and reference.

NOTES

Initial Commencement

Specified date

Specified date: 29 December 1986: see r 0.1.

Amendment

Para (2): sub-para (b) substituted by SI 2010/686, r 2, Sch 1, para 323.
Date in force: 6 April 2010: see SI 2010/686, r 1; for transitional provisions see r 6(1), Sch 4, para 1 thereto.

Modification

References to solicitors etc modified to include references to bodies recognised under the Administration of Justice Act 1985, s 9, by the Solicitors' Incorporated Practices Order 1991, SI 1991/2684, arts 4, 5, Sch 1.

6.46 Action to follow making of order

(1) At least two sealed copies of the bankruptcy order shall be sent [as soon as reasonably practicable] by the court to the official receiver, who [must (unless the official receiver is satisfied that the bankrupt has already received a copy of the order)] [as soon as reasonably practicable] send one of them to the bankrupt.

[(2) Subject to the next paragraph, on receipt of the sealed copies of the bankruptcy order, the official receiver—
- (a) as soon as reasonably practicable shall—
    - (i) send notice of the making of the order to the Chief Land Registrar, for registration in the register of writs and orders affecting land; and
    - (ii) cause notice of the order to be gazetted; and
- (b) may cause notice of the order to be advertised in such other manner as the official receiver thinks fit.]

[(2A) In addition to the standard contents, the notice to be gazetted under paragraph (2)(b) and any notice to be advertised under paragraph (2)(c) must state—
- (a) that a bankruptcy order has been made against the bankrupt;
- (b) the date and time of making of the bankruptcy order;
- (c) that the bankruptcy order was made on the debtor's own petition; and
- (d) the date of presentation of the petition.]

(3) The court may, on the application of the bankrupt or a creditor, order the official receiver to suspend action under paragraph (2) [and [Rule 6A.4(2)]], pending a further order of the court.

. . ..

[(3A) An application under this paragraph must be supported by a witness statement stating the grounds on which it is made.]

(4) Where an order is made under paragraph (3), the applicant shall [as soon as reasonably practicable] deliver a copy of it to the official receiver.

NOTES

Initial Commencement

Specified date

Specified date: 29 December 1986: see r 0.1.

Amendment

Para (1): words "as soon as reasonably practicable" in square brackets in both places they occur substituted by SI 2009/642, rr 4, 5.
    Date in force: 6 April 2009: see SI 2009/642, r 1; for transitional provisions see r 3 thereof.
Para (1): words from "must (unless the" to "of the order)" in square brackets substituted by SI 2010/686, r 2, Sch 1, para 324(1), (2).
    Date in force: 6 April 2010: see SI 2010/686, r 1; for transitional provisions see r 6(1), Sch 4, para 1 thereto.
Para (2): substituted by SI 2009/642, rr 4, 38.
    Date in force: 6 April 2009: see SI 2009/642, r 1; for transitional provisions see r 3 thereof.
Para (2A): inserted by SI 2010/686, r 2, Sch 1, para 324(1), (3).
    Date in force: 6 April 2010: see SI 2010/686, r 1; for transitional provisions see r 6(1), Sch 4, para 1 thereto.
Para (3): words in square brackets beginning with the word "and" inserted by SI 1999/359, r 3, Schedule, para 5.
    Date in force: 22 March 1999: see SI 1999/359, r 1.
Para (3): words "Rule 6A.4(2)" in square brackets substituted by SI 2005/527, r 37.
    Date in force: 1 April 2005: see SI 2005/527, r 1(2).
Para (3): words omitted revoked by SI 2010/686, r 2, Sch 1, para 324(1), (4).
    Date in force: 6 April 2010: see SI 2010/686, r 1; for transitional provisions see r 6(1), Sch 4, para 1 thereto.
Para (3A): inserted by SI 2010/686, r 2, Sch 1, para 324(1), (5).
    Date in force: 6 April 2010: see SI 2010/686, r 1; for transitional provisions see r 6(1), Sch 4, para 1 thereto.
Para (4): words "as soon as reasonably practicable" in square brackets substituted by SI 2009/642, rr 4, 5.
    Date in force: 6 April 2009: see SI 2009/642, r 1; for transitional provisions see r 3 thereof.

[6.46A Expenses of Voluntary arrangement]

[Where a bankruptcy order is made on a debtor's petition and there is at the time of the petition in force for the debtor a voluntary arrangement under Part VIII of the Act, any expenses properly incurred as expenses of the administration of the arrangement in question shall be a first charge on the bankrupt's estate.]

NOTES

Amendment

Inserted by SI 1987/1919, r 3(1), Schedule, Part 1, para 102.

6.47 Amendment of title of proceedings

(1) At any time after the making of the bankruptcy order, the official receiver or the trustee may apply to the court for an order amending the full title of the proceedings.

[(2) Where such an order is made, as soon as reasonably practicable the official receiver shall send notice of it to the Chief Land Registrar for corresponding amendment of the register.]

[(3) Where the official receiver thinks fit, notice of the order—

    (a)   as soon as reasonably practicable shall be gazetted; and

    (b)   may be advertised in such other manner as the official receiver thinks fit.]

[(4) In addition to the standard contents, the notice under paragraph (3) must—

    (a)   state that an amendment to the full title of the proceedings has been made; and

    (b)   specify the amendment.]

NOTES

Initial Commencement

Specified date

Specified date: 29 December 1986: see r 0.1.

Amendment

Para (2): substituted by SI 2009/642, rr 4, 39(a).
　　Date in force: 6 April 2009: see SI 2009/642, r 1; for transitional provisions see r 3 thereof.
Para (3): inserted by SI 2009/642, rr 4, 39(b).
　　Date in force: 6 April 2009: see SI 2009/642, r 1; for transitional provisions see r 3 thereof.
Para (4): inserted by SI 2010/686, r 2, Sch 1, para 325.
　　Date in force: 6 April 2010: see SI 2010/686, r 1; for transitional provisions see r 6(1), Sch 4, para 1 thereto.

6.48 . . .
. . .

NOTES

Amendment

Revoked by SI 2003/1730, r 9(1), Sch 1, Pt 6, para 34.
　　Date in force: 1 April 2004: see SI 2003/1730, r 1(3).

6.49 . . .
. . .

NOTES

Amendment

Revoked by SI 2003/1730, r 9(1), Sch 1, Pt 6, para 34.
　　Date in force: 1 April 2004: see SI 2003/1730, r 1(3).

6.50 . . .
. . .

NOTES

Amendment

Revoked by SI 2003/1730, r 9(1), Sch 1, Pt 6, para 34.
　　Date in force: 1 April 2004: see SI 2003/1730, r 1(3); for effect and the continuing operation of this rule see rr 2(3), (4), 9(2) thereof.

CHAPTER 4

THE INTERIM RECEIVER

6.51 Application for appointment of interim receiver

[(1) An application to the court for the appointment of an interim receiver under section 286 may be made by—
　　(a)　　a creditor;

(b) the debtor;
(c) an insolvency practitioner appointed under section 273(2);
(d) a temporary administrator, or
(e) a member State liquidator appointed in main proceedings.]

(2) The application must be supported by [a witness statement] stating—
  (a) the grounds on which it is proposed that the interim receiver should be appointed,
  (b) whether or not the official receiver has been informed of the application and, if so, has been furnished with a copy of it,
  (c) whether to the applicant's knowledge there has been proposed or is in force a voluntary arrangement under Part VIII of the Act, and
  (d) the applicant's estimate of the value of the property or business in respect of which the interim receiver is to be appointed.

(3) If an insolvency practitioner has been appointed under section 273, and it is proposed that he (and not the official receiver) should be appointed interim receiver, and it is not the insolvency practitioner himself who is the applicant under this Rule, the [witness statement] under paragraph (2) must state that he has consented to act.

(4) The applicant shall send copies of the application and the [witness statement] to the person proposed to be appointed interim receiver. If that person is the official receiver and an insolvency practitioner has been appointed under section 273 (and he is not himself the applicant), copies of the application and [witness statement] shall be sent by the applicant to the insolvency practitioner.

If, in any case where a copy of the application is to be sent to a person under this paragraph, it is for any reason not practicable to send a copy, that person must be informed of the application in sufficient time to enable him to be present at the hearing.

(5) The official receiver and (if appointed) the insolvency practitioner may attend the hearing of the application and make representations.

(6) The court may on the application, if satisfied that sufficient grounds are shown for the appointment, make it on such terms as it thinks [just].

NOTES

Initial Commencement

Specified date
  Specified date: 29 December 1986: see r 0.1.

Amendment
  Para (1): substituted by SI 2002/1307, rr 3(1), 8(4).
    Date in force: 31 May 2002: see SI 2002/1307, r 1.
  Para (2): words "a witness statement" in square brackets substituted by SI 2010/686, r 2, Sch 1, para 326(1), (2).
    Date in force: 6 April 2010: see SI 2010/686, r 1; for transitional provisions see r 6(1), Sch 4, paras 1, 2(1)(b), (2)–(4) thereto.
  Para (3): words "witness statement" in square brackets substituted by SI 2010/686, r 2, Sch 1, para 326(1), (3).
    Date in force: 6 April 2010: see SI 2010/686, r 1; for transitional provisions see r 6(1), Sch 4, paras 1, 2(1)(b), (2)–(4) thereto.
  Para (4): words "witness statement" in square brackets in both places they occur substituted by SI 2010/686, r 2, Sch 1, para 326(1), (3).
    Date in force: 6 April 2010: see SI 2010/686, r 1; for transitional provisions see r 6(1), Sch 4, paras 1, 2(1)(b), (2)–(4) thereto.
  Para (6): word "just" in square brackets substituted by SI 2010/686, r 2, Sch 1, para 1.
    Date in force: 6 April 2010: see SI 2010/686, r 1; for transitional provisions see r 6(1), Sch 4, paras 1, 2(1)(b) thereto.

6.52 Order of appointment

(1) The order appointing the interim receiver shall state the nature and a short description of the property of which the person appointed is to take possession, and the duties to be performed by him in relation to the debtor's affairs.

(2) The court shall, [as soon as reasonably practicable] after the order is made, send 2 sealed copies of it to the person appointed interim receiver (one of which shall be sent by him [as soon as reasonably practicable] to the debtor).

NOTES

Initial Commencement

Specified date

Specified date: 29 December 1986: see r 0.1.

Amendment

Para (2): words "as soon as reasonably practicable" in square brackets in both places they occur substituted by SI 2009/642, rr 4, 5.
Date in force: 6 April 2009: see SI 2009/642, r 1; for transitional provisions see r 3 thereof.

6.53 Deposit

(1) Before an order appointing the official receiver as interim receiver is issued, the applicant for it shall deposit with him, or otherwise secure to his satisfaction, such sum as the court directs to cover his remuneration and expenses.

(2) If the sum deposited or secured subsequently proves to be insufficient, the court may, on application by the official receiver, order that an additional sum be deposited or secured. If the order is not complied with within 2 [business] days after service on the person to whom the order is directed, the court may discharge the order appointing the interim receiver.

(3) If a bankruptcy order is made after an interim receiver has been appointed, any money deposited under this Rule shall (unless it is required by reason of insufficiency of assets for payment of remuneration and expenses of the interim receiver, or the deposit was made by the debtor out of his own property) be repaid to the person depositing it (or as that person may direct) out of the bankrupt's estate, in the prescribed order of priority.

NOTES

Initial Commencement

Specified date

Specified date: 29 December 1986: see r 0.1.

Amendment

Para (2): word "business" in square brackets inserted by SI 2010/686, r 2, Sch 1, para 327.
Date in force: 6 April 2010: see SI 2010/686, r 1; for transitional provisions see r 6(1), Sch 4, para 1 thereto.

6.54 Security

(1) The following applies where an insolvency practitioner is appointed to be interim receiver under section 286(2).

(2) The cost of providing the security required under the Act shall be paid in the first instance by the interim receiver; but—

(a) if a bankruptcy order is not made, the person so appointed is entitled to be reimbursed out of the property of the debtor, and the court may make an order on the debtor accordingly, and

(b) if a bankruptcy order is made, he is entitled to be reimbursed out of the estate in the prescribed order of priority.

NOTES

Initial Commencement

Specified date

Specified date: 29 December 1986: see r 0.1.

6.55 Failure to give or keep up security

(1) If the interim receiver fails to give or keep up his security, the court may remove him, and make such order as it thinks [just] as to costs.

(2) If an order is made under this Rule removing the interim receiver, or discharging the order appointing him, the court shall give directions as to whether any, and if so what, steps should be taken for the appointment of another person in his place.

NOTES

Initial Commencement

Specified date

Specified date: 29 December 1986: see r 0.1.

Amendment

Para (1): word "just" in square brackets substituted by SI 2010/686, r 2, Sch 1, para 1.
Date in force: 6 April 2010: see SI 2010/686, r 1; for transitional provisions see r 6(1), Sch 4, paras 1, 2(1)(b) thereto.

6.56 Remuneration

(1) The remuneration of the interim receiver (other than the official receiver) shall be fixed by the court from time to time on his application.

(2) In fixing the interim receiver's remuneration, the court shall take into account—

(a) the time properly given by him (as interim receiver) and his staff in attending to the debtor's affairs,

(b) the complexity (or otherwise) of the case,

(c) any respects in which, in connection with the debtor's affairs, there falls on the interim receiver any responsibility of an exceptional kind or degree,

(d) the effectiveness with which the interim receiver appears to be carrying out, or to have carried out, his duties as such, and

(e) the value and nature of the property with which he has to deal.

[(3) Without prejudice to any order the court may make as to costs, the interim receiver's remuneration (whether the official receiver or another) shall be paid to him, and the amount of any expenses incurred by him (including the remuneration and expenses of any special manager appointed under section 370) reimbursed—

(a) if a bankruptcy order is not made, out of the property of the debtor], and

(b) if a bankruptcy order is made, out of the estate in the prescribed order of priority, or, in either case (the relevant funds being insufficient), out of the deposit under Rule 6.53.

[(4) Unless the court otherwise directs, in a case falling within paragraph (3)(a) above the interim receiver may retain out of the debtor's property such sums or property as are or may be required for meeting his remuneration and expenses.]

NOTES

Initial Commencement

Specified date

Specified date: 29 December 1986: see r 0.1.

Amendment

Para (3): words in square brackets substituted by SI 1987/1919, r 3(1), Schedule, Part 1, para 103.

Para (4): inserted by SI 1987/1919, r 3(1), Schedule, Part 1, para 103.

6.57 Termination of appointment

(1) The appointment of the interim receiver may be terminated by the court on his application, or on that of the official receiver, the debtor or any creditor.

(2) If the interim receiver's appointment terminates, in consequence of the dismissal of the bankruptcy petition or otherwise, the court may give such directions as it thinks [just] with respect to the accounts of his administration and any other matters which it thinks appropriate.

(3) ...

NOTES

Initial Commencement

Specified date

Specified date: 29 December 1986: see r 0.1.

Amendment

Para (2): word "just" in square brackets substituted by SI 2010/686, r 2, Sch 1, para 1.
Date in force: 6 April 2010: see SI 2010/686, r 1; for transitional provisions see r 6(1), Sch 4, paras 1, 2(1)(b) thereto.

Para (3): revoked by SI 1987/1919, r 3(1), Schedule, Part 1, para 104.

CHAPTER 5

DISCLOSURE BY BANKRUPT WITH RESPECT TO THE STATE OF HIS AFFAIRS

SECTION A: CREDITOR'S PETITION

6.58 Preliminary

The Rules in this Section apply with respect to the statement of affairs required by section 288(1) to be submitted by the bankrupt, following a bankruptcy order made on a creditor's petition, and the further and other disclosure which is required of him in that case.

NOTES

Initial Commencement

Specified date
Specified date: 29 December 1986: see r 0.1.

6.59 The statement of affairs
The bankrupt's statement of affairs shall be in Form 6.33, and contain all the particulars required by that form.

NOTES

Initial Commencement

Specified date
Specified date: 29 December 1986: see r 0.1.

6.60 Verification and filing
(1) The bankrupt shall be furnished by the official receiver with instructions for the preparation of his statement of affairs, and the forms required for that purpose.
(2) The statement of affairs shall be verified by [a statement of truth] and delivered to the official receiver, together with one copy.
(3) The official receiver shall file the verified statement in court.
(4) . . .

NOTES

Initial Commencement

Specified date
Specified date: 29 December 1986: see r 0.1.

Amendment
Para (2): words "a statement of truth" in square brackets substituted by SI 2010/686, r 2, Sch 1, para 328(1), (2).
    Date in force: 6 April 2010: see SI 2010/686, r 1; for transitional provisions see r 6(1), Sch 4, paras 1, 2(1)(b) thereto.
Para (4): revoked by SI 2010/686, r 2, Sch 1, para 328(1), (3).
    Date in force: 6 April 2010: see SI 2010/686, r 1; for transitional provisions see r 6(1), Sch 4, paras 1, 2(1)(b) thereto.

6.61 Limited disclosure
(1) Where the official receiver thinks that it would prejudice the conduct of the bankruptcy [or might reasonably be expected to lead to violence against any person] for the whole or part of the statement of affairs to be disclosed, he may apply to the court for an order of limited disclosure in respect of the statement, or any specified part of it.
(2) The court may on the application order that the statement or, as the case may be, the specified part of it be not filed in court, or that it is to be filed separately and not be open to inspection otherwise than with [permission] of the court.

NOTES

Initial Commencement

Specified date

Specified date: 29 December 1986: see r 0.1.

Amendment

Para (1): words "or might reasonably be expected to lead to violence against any person" in square brackets inserted by SI 2010/686, r 2, Sch 1, para 329.
  Date in force: 6 April 2010: see SI 2010/686, r 1; for transitional provisions see r 6(1), Sch 4, paras 1, 2(1)(b), (2)–(4) thereto.

Para (2): word "permission" in square brackets substituted by SI 2010/686, r 2, Sch 1, para 1.
  Date in force: 6 April 2010: see SI 2010/686, r 1; for transitional provisions see r 6(1), Sch 4, paras 1, 2(1)(b) thereto.

6.62 Release from duty to submit statement of affairs; extension of time

(1) The power of the official receiver under section 288(3) to release the bankrupt from his duty to submit a statement of affairs, or to grant an extension of time, may be exercised at the official receiver's own discretion, or at the bankrupt's request.

(2) The bankrupt may, if he requests a release or extension of time and it is refused by the official receiver, apply to the court for it.

(3) The court may, if it thinks that no sufficient cause is shown for the application, dismiss it; but it shall not do so unless the bankrupt has had an opportunity to attend the court for [a] hearing, of which he has been given at least [5 business] days' notice [but which is without notice to any other party].

If the application is not dismissed under this paragraph, the court shall fix a venue for it to be heard, and give notice to the bankrupt accordingly.

(4) The bankrupt shall, at least 14 days before the hearing, send to the official receiver a notice stating the venue and accompanied by a copy of the application, and of any evidence which he (the bankrupt) intends to adduce in support of it.

(5) The official receiver may appear and be heard on the application; and, whether or not he appears, he may file a written report of any matters which he considers ought to be drawn to the court's attention.

If such a report is filed, a copy of it shall be sent by the official receiver to the bankrupt, not later than 5 [business] days before the hearing.

(6) Sealed copies of any order on the application shall be sent by the court to the bankrupt and the official receiver.

(7) On any application under this Rule the bankrupt's costs shall be paid in any event by him and, unless the court otherwise orders, no allowance towards them shall be made out of the estate.

NOTES

Initial Commencement

Specified date

Specified date: 29 December 1986: see r 0.1.

Amendment

Para (3): word "a" in square brackets substituted by SI 2010/686, r 2, Sch 1, para 330(1), (2)(a).
  Date in force: 6 April 2010: see SI 2010/686, r 1; for transitional provisions see r 6(1), Sch 4, paras 1, 2(1)(b) thereto.

Para (3): words "5 business" in square brackets substituted by SI 2010/686, r 2, Sch 1, para 330(1), (2)(b).

Date in force: 6 April 2010: see SI 2010/686, r 1; for transitional provisions see r 6(1), Sch 4, para 1 thereto.

Para (3): words "but which is without notice to any other party" in square brackets inserted by SI 2010/686, r 2, Sch 1, para 330(1), (2)(c).

Date in force: 6 April 2010: see SI 2010/686, r 1; for transitional provisions see r 6(1), Sch 4, paras 1, 2(1)(b) thereto.

Para (5): word "business" in square brackets inserted by SI 2010/686, r 2, Sch 1, para 330(1), (3).

Date in force: 6 April 2010: see SI 2010/686, r 1; for transitional provisions see r 6(1), Sch 4, para 1 thereto.

6.63 Expenses of statement of affairs

(1) If the bankrupt cannot himself prepare a proper statement of affairs, the official receiver may, at the expense of the estate, employ some person or persons to assist in the preparation of the statement.

(2) At the request of the bankrupt, made on the grounds that he cannot himself prepare a proper statement, the official receiver may authorise an allowance payable out of the estate (in accordance with the prescribed order of priority) towards expenses to be incurred by the bankrupt in employing some person or persons to assist him in preparing it.

(3) Any such request by the bankrupt shall be accompanied by an estimate of the expenses involved; and the official receiver shall only authorise the employment of a named person or a named firm, being in either case approved by him.

(4) An authorisation given by the official receiver under this Rule shall be subject to such conditions (if any) as he thinks fit to impose with respect to the manner in which any person may obtain access to relevant books and papers.

(5) Nothing in this Rule relieves the bankrupt from any obligation with respect to the preparation, verification and submission of his statement of affairs, or to the provision of information to the official receiver or the trustee.

NOTES

Initial Commencement

Specified date

Specified date: 29 December 1986: see r 0.1.

6.64 Requirement to submit accounts

(1) The bankrupt shall, at the request of the official receiver, furnish him with accounts relating to his affairs of such nature, as at such date and for such period as he may specify.

(2) The period specified may begin from a date up to 3 years preceding the date of the presentation of the bankruptcy petition.

(3) The court may, on the official receiver's application, require accounts in respect of any earlier period.

(4) Rule 6.63 applies (with the necessary modifications) in relation to accounts to be furnished under this Rule as it applies in relation to the statement of affairs.

NOTES

Initial Commencement

Specified date

Specified date: 29 December 1986: see r 0.1.

6.65 Submission and filing of accounts

(1) The accounts to be furnished under Rule 6.64 shall, if the official receiver so requires, be verified by [a statement of truth], and (whether or not so verified) delivered to him within 21 days of the request under Rule 6.64(1), or such longer period as he may allow.

(2) . . .

NOTES

Initial Commencement

Specified date

Specified date: 29 December 1986: see r 0.1.

Amendment

Para (1): words "a statement of truth" in square brackets substituted by SI 2010/686, r 2, Sch 1, para 331(1), (2).
Date in force: 6 April 2010: see SI 2010/686, r 1; for transitional provisions see r 6(1), Sch 4, paras 1, 2(1)(b) thereto.
Para (2): revoked by SI 2010/686, r 2, Sch 1, para 331(1), (3).
Date in force: 6 April 2010: see SI 2010/686, r 1; for transitional provisions see r 6(1), Sch 4, paras 1, 2(1)(b) thereto.

6.66 Further disclosure

(1) The official receiver may at any time require the bankrupt to submit (in writing) further information amplifying, modifying or explaining any matter contained in his statement of affairs, or in accounts submitted in pursuance of the Act or the Rules.

(2) The information shall, if the official receiver so directs, be verified by [a statement of truth], and (whether or not so verified) delivered to him within 21 days of the requirement under this Rule, or such longer period as he may allow.

(3) . . ..

NOTES

Initial Commencement

Specified date

Specified date: 29 December 1986: see r 0.1.

Amendment

Para (2): words "a statement of truth" in square brackets substituted by SI 2010/686, r 2, Sch 1, para 332(1), (2).
Date in force: 6 April 2010: see SI 2010/686, r 1; for transitional provisions see r 6(1), Sch 4, paras 1, 2(1)(b) thereto.
Para (3): revoked by SI 2010/686, r 2, Sch 1, para 332(1), (3).
Date in force: 6 April 2010: see SI 2010/686, r 1; for transitional provisions see r 6(1), Sch 4, paras 1, 2(1)(b) thereto.

SECTION B: DEBTOR'S PETITION

6.67 Preliminary

The Rules in this Section apply with respect to the statement of affairs required in the case of a person petitioning for a bankruptcy order to be made against him, and the further disclosure which is required of him in that case.

NOTES

Initial Commencement

Specified date

Specified date: 29 December 1986: see r 0.1.

6.68 Contents of statement

The statement of affairs required by Rule 6.41 to accompany the debtor's petition shall be in Form 6.28, and contain all the particulars required by that form.

NOTES

Initial Commencement

Specified date

Specified date: 29 December 1986: see r 0.1.

6.69 Requirement to submit accounts

(1) The bankrupt shall, at the request of the official receiver, furnish him with accounts relating to his affairs of such nature, as at such date and for such period as he may specify.

(2) The period specified may begin from a date up to 3 years preceding the date of the presentation of the bankruptcy petition.

(3) The court may, on the official receiver's application, require accounts in respect of any earlier period.

NOTES

Initial Commencement

Specified date

Specified date: 29 December 1986: see r 0.1.

6.70 Submission and filing of accounts

(1) The accounts to be furnished under Rule 6.69 shall, if the official receiver so requires, be verified by [a statement of truth], and (whether or not so verified) delivered to him within 21 days of the request under Rule 6.69, or such longer period as he may allow.

(2) . . .

NOTES

Initial Commencement

Specified date

Specified date: 29 December 1986: see r 0.1.

Amendment

Para (1): words "a statement of truth" in square brackets substituted by SI 2010/686, r 2, Sch 1, para 333(1), (2).

Date in force: 6 April 2010: see SI 2010/686, r 1; for transitional provisions see r 6(1), Sch 4, paras 1, 2(1)(b) thereto.

Para (2): revoked by SI 2010/686, r 2, Sch 1, para 333(1), (3).

Date in force: 6 April 2010: see SI 2010/686, r 1; for transitional provisions see r 6(1), Sch 4, paras 1, 2(1)(b) thereto.

6.71 Expenses of preparing accounts

(1) If the bankrupt cannot himself prepare proper accounts under Rule 6.69, the official receiver may, at the expense of the estate, employ some person or persons to assist in their preparation.

(2) At the request of the bankrupt, made on the grounds that he cannot himself prepare the accounts, the official receiver may authorise an allowance payable out of the estate (in accordance with the prescribed order of priority) towards expenses to be incurred by the bankrupt in employing some person or persons to assist him in their preparation.

(3) Any such request by the bankrupt shall be accompanied by an estimate of the expenses involved; and the official receiver shall only authorise the employment of a named person or a named firm, being in either case approved by him.

(4) An authorisation given by the official receiver under this Rule shall be subject to such conditions (if any) as he thinks fit to impose with respect to the manner in which any person may obtain access to relevant books and papers.

(5) Nothing in this Rule relieves the bankrupt from any obligation with respect to the preparation and submission of accounts, or to the provision of information to the official receiver or the trustee.

NOTES

Initial Commencement

Specified date

Specified date: 29 December 1986: see r 0.1.

6.72 Further disclosure

(1) The official receiver may at any time require the bankrupt to submit (in writing) further information amplifying, modifying or explaining any matter contained in his statement of affairs, or in accounts submitted in pursuance of the Act or the Rules.

(2) The information shall, if the official receiver so directs, be verified by [a statement of truth], and (whether or not so verified) delivered to him within 21 days from the date of the requirement under paragraph (1), or such longer period as he may allow.

(3) . . .

NOTES

Initial Commencement

Specified date

Specified date: 29 December 1986: see r 0.1.

Amendment

Para (2): words "a statement of truth" in square brackets substituted by SI 2010/686, r 2, Sch 1, para 334(1), (2).
  Date in force: 6 April 2010: see SI 2010/686, r 1; for transitional provisions see r 6(1), Sch 4, paras 1, 2(1)(b) thereto.
Para (3): revoked by SI 2010/686, r 2, Sch 1, para 334(1), (3).
  Date in force: 6 April 2010: see SI 2010/686, r 1; for transitional provisions see r 6(1), Sch 4, paras 1, 2(1)(b) thereto.

CHAPTER 6

INFORMATION TO CREDITORS

6.73 General duty of official receiver

[(1)] In accordance with this Chapter, the official receiver shall, at least once after the making of the bankruptcy order, send a report to creditors with respect to the bankruptcy proceedings, and the state of the bankrupt's affairs.

[(2) . . .]

NOTES

Initial Commencement

Specified date
   Specified date: 29 December 1986: see r 0.1.

Amendment
   Para (2): revoked by SI 2010/686, r 2, Sch 1, para 335.
      Date in force: 6 April 2010: see SI 2010/686, r 1; for transitional provisions see r 6(1), Sch 4, paras 1, 2(1)(b) thereto.

6.74 Those entitled to be informed

Any reference in this Chapter to creditors is to creditors of the bankrupt who are known to the official receiver . . ..

NOTES

Initial Commencement

Specified date
   Specified date: 29 December 1986: see r 0.1.

Amendment
   Words omitted revoked by SI 2010/686, r 2, Sch 1, para 336.
      Date in force: 6 April 2010: see SI 2010/686, r 1; for transitional provisions see r 6(1), Sch 4, para 1 thereto.

6.75 Report where statement of affairs lodged

(1) Where the bankrupt has submitted a statement of affairs, . . . the official receiver shall send out to creditors a report containing a summary of the statement [(if he thinks fit, as amplified, modified or explained by virtue of Rule 6.66 or 6.72)] and such observations (if any) as he thinks fit to make with respect to it or to the bankrupt's affairs generally.

(2) The official receiver need not comply with paragraph (1) if he has previously reported to creditors with respect to the bankrupt's affairs (so far as known to him) and he is of opinion that there are no additional matters which ought to be brought to their attention.

NOTES

Initial Commencement

Specified date
   Specified date: 29 December 1986: see r 0.1.

Amendment
   Para (1): words omitted revoked by SI 2010/686, r 2, Sch 1, para 337.

Date in force: 6 April 2010: see SI 2010/686, r 1; for transitional provisions see r 6(1), Sch 4, paras 1, 2(1)(b) thereto.

Para (1): words in square brackets inserted by SI 1987/1919, Schedule, Part 1, para 106.

6.76 Statement of affairs dispensed with

(1) This Rule applies where the bankrupt has been released from the obligation to submit a statement of affairs.

(2) As soon as may be after the release has been granted, the official receiver shall send to creditors a report containing a summary of the bankrupt's affairs (so far as within his knowledge), and his observations (if any) with respect to it or the bankrupt's affairs generally.

(3) The official receiver need not comply with paragraph (2) if he has previously reported to creditors with respect to the bankrupt's affairs (so far as known to him) and he is of opinion that there are no additional matters which ought to be brought to their attention.

NOTES

Initial Commencement

Specified date

Specified date: 29 December 1986: see r 0.1.

6.77 General rule as to reporting

(1) The court may, on the official receiver's application, relieve him of any duty imposed on him by this Chapter of the Rules, or authorise him to carry out the duty in a way other than there required.

(2) In considering whether to act as above, the court shall have regard to the cost of carrying out the duty, to the amount of the funds available in the estate, and to the extent of the interest of creditors or any particular class of them.

NOTES

Initial Commencement

Specified date

Specified date: 29 December 1986: see r 0.1.

6.78 Bankruptcy order annulled

If the bankruptcy order is annulled, the duty of the official receiver to send reports under the preceding Rules in this Chapter ceases.

NOTES

Initial Commencement

Specified date

Specified date: 29 December 1986: see r 0.1.

[6.78A Reports to creditors]

[(1) "Progress report" means a report which includes—
    (a) details of the court where the proceedings are and the relevant court reference number;

(b) the bankrupt's name;
(c) the title of the proceedings;
(d) full details of the trustee's name and address and date of appointment, including any changes in office-holder;
(e) details of the basis fixed for the remuneration of the trustee under Rule 6.138 (or if not fixed at the date of the report, the steps taken during the period of the report to fix it);
(f) if the basis of remuneration has been fixed, a statement of—
  (i) the remuneration charged by the trustee during the period of the report (subject to paragraph (2)), and
  (ii) where the report is the first to be made after the basis has been fixed, the remuneration charged by the trustee during the periods covered by the previous reports (subject to paragraph (2)), together with a description of the things done by the trustee during those periods in respect of which the remuneration was charged,

irrespective in either case of whether payment was made in respect of that remuneration during that period;

(g) a statement of the expenses incurred by the trustee during the period of the report, irrespective of whether payment was made in respect of them during that period;
(h) details of progress during the period of the report, including a receipts and payments account in the form of an abstract showing receipts and payments during the period of the report;
(j) details of any assets that remain to be realised;
(k) a statement of the creditors' right to request information under Rule 6.78C and their right to challenge the trustee's remuneration and expenses under Rule 6.142; and
(l) any other relevant information for the creditors.

(2) Where the basis for the remuneration is a set amount under Rule 6.138(2)(c), it may be shown as that amount without any apportionment to the period of the report.

(3) The progress report must, except where paragraph (4) or (5) applies, cover the period of 1 year commencing on the date on which the trustee is appointed and every subsequent period of 1 year.

(4) The period to be covered by a progress report ends on the date when a trustee ceases to act, and the period to be covered by each subsequent progress report is each successive period of 1 year beginning immediately after that date (subject to the further application of this paragraph when another trustee ceases to act).

(5) A progress report is not required for any period which ends after the trustee has sent a draft report to creditors under Rule 6.78B (final report to creditors).

(6) The trustee must send a copy of the progress report to the creditors within 2 months of the end of the period covered by the report.

(7) The court may, on the trustee's application, extend the period of 2 months mentioned in paragraph (6), or make such other order in respect of the content of the report as it thinks just.

(8) This Rule does not apply where the trustee is the official receiver.]

NOTES

Amendment

Inserted by SI 2010/686, r 2, Sch 1, para 338.
Date in force: 6 April 2010: see SI 2010/686, r 1; for transitional provisions see r 6(1), Sch 4, para 1 thereto.

[6.78B Final report to creditors and bankrupt]

[(1) The trustee must, at least 8 weeks before holding a final meeting in accordance with section 331, send to each creditor known to the trustee and to the bankrupt a draft of the report which the trustee intends to lay before the meeting under Rule 6.137.

(2) The draft report must—
- (a) contain such matters and be in such terms as would comply with Rule 6.137 if the report were to be laid before a meeting as soon as reasonably practicable after the draft had been sent to creditors, and
- (b) be accompanied by a statement of the creditors' right to request information under Rule 6.78C and their right to challenge the trustee's remuneration and expenses under Rule 6.142.

(3) The trustee may not send a draft report to creditors under this Rule before giving notice—
- (a) under Rule 11.2 of intention to declare a final dividend, or
- (b) under Rule 11.7 that no dividend or further dividend will be declared.

(4) If any creditor has applied to the court under Rule 6.142 and given a copy of the application to the trustee, the final meeting may not be held until the application (including any appeal) has been disposed of and the trustee has complied with any order of the court.

(5) This Rule does not apply where the trustee is the official receiver.]

NOTES

Amendment

Inserted by SI 2010/686, r 2, Sch 1, para 338.
Date in force: 6 April 2010: see SI 2010/686, r 1; for transitional provisions see r 6(1), Sch 4, para 1 thereto.

[6.78C Creditors' request for further information]

[(1) If—
- (a) within the period mentioned in paragraph (2)—
  - (i) a secured creditor, or
  - (ii) an unsecured creditor with the concurrence of at least 5% in value of the unsecured creditors (including the creditor in question), or
- (b) with the permission of the court upon an application made within the period mentioned in paragraph (2), any unsecured creditor,

makes a request in writing to the trustee for further information about remuneration or expenses set out in a progress report under Rule 6.78A(1)(f) or (g) or in a draft report under Rule 6.78B, the trustee must, within 14 days of receipt of the request, comply with paragraph (3) except to the extent that the request is in respect of matter in a draft report under Rule 6.78B or a progress report required by Rule 6.126 which (in either case) was previously included in a progress report not required by Rule 6.126.

(2) The period referred to in paragraph (1)(a) is—
- (a) 7 business days of receipt of the progress report where it is required by Rule 6.126, and
- (b) 21 days of receipt of the report or draft report in any other case.

(3) The trustee complies with this paragraph by either—
- (a) providing all of the information asked for, or
- (b) so far as the trustee considers that—
  - (i) the time or cost of preparation of the information would be excessive, or

(ii) disclosure of the information would be prejudicial to the conduct of the bankruptcy or might reasonably be expected to lead to violence against any person, or

(iii) the trustee is subject to an obligation of confidentiality in respect of the information,

giving reasons for not providing all of the information.

(4) Any creditor, who need not be the same as the creditor who asked for the information, may apply to the court within 21 days of—

(a) the giving by the trustee of reasons for not providing all of the information asked for, or

(b) the expiry of the 14 days provided for in paragraph (1),

and the court may make such order as it thinks just.

(5) Without prejudice to the generality of paragraph (4), the order of the court under that paragraph may extend the period of 8 weeks or, as the case may be, 4 weeks provided for in Rule 6.142(1B) by such further period as the court thinks just.

(6) This Rule does not apply where the trustee is the official receiver.]

NOTES

Amendment

Inserted by SI 2010/686, r 2, Sch 1, para 338.
Date in force: 6 April 2010: see SI 2010/686, r 1; for transitional provisions see r 6(1), Sch 4, para 1 thereto.

[6.78D Distribution of property in specie]

[(1) Where there has been a distribution of property to creditors under section 326, the trustee must comply with paragraph (2) in respect of any account or report which the trustee is required to prepare pursuant to any of the following—

(a) section 331 (final meeting);
(b) Rule 6.78A (reports to creditors);
(c) Rule 6.78B (final report to creditors);
(d) Rule 6.126 (creditors' meeting to receive trustee's resignation);
(e) Rule 6.137 (final meeting of creditors).

(2) The trustee must—

(a) in any account or summary of receipts and payments which is required to be included in the account or report, state the estimated value of the property distributed amongst the creditors during the period to which the account or report relates, and

(b) as a note to the account or summary of receipts and payments, provide details of the basis of the valuation.]

NOTES

Amendment

Inserted by SI 2010/686, r 2, Sch 1, para 338.
Date in force: 6 April 2010: see SI 2010/686, r 1; for transitional provisions see r 6(1), Sch 4, para 1 thereto.

CHAPTER 7

CREDITORS' MEETINGS

6.79 First meeting of creditors

(1) If under section 293(1) the official receiver decides to summon a meeting of creditors, he shall fix a venue for the meeting, not more than 4 months from the date of the bankruptcy order.

(2) When a venue has been fixed, notice of the meeting shall be given [to every creditor of the bankrupt who is known to the official receiver].

[(3) Notice must be given at least 14 days before the date fixed for the meeting.]

[(4) The notice to creditors must state that proofs and (if applicable) proxies must be lodged at a specified place not later than 12.00 hours on the business day before the date fixed for the meeting in order for creditors to be entitled to vote at the meeting.]

[(5) As soon as reasonably practicable, notice of the meeting shall also be gazetted and may be advertised in such other manner as the official receiver thinks fit.]

[(5A) In addition to the standard contents, the notice under paragraph (5) must state—

(a) the purpose for which the meeting is summoned;

(b) the venue fixed for the meeting; and

(c) the time and date by which, and place at which, creditors must lodge proxies and hitherto unlodged proofs in order to be entitled to vote at the meeting.]

(6) Where the official receiver receives a request by a creditor under section 294 for a meeting of creditors to be summoned, and it appears to him that the request is properly made in accordance with the Act, he shall—

(a) withdraw any notice already given by him under section 293(2) (that he has decided not to summon such a meeting), and

(b) fix the venue of the meeting for not more than 3 months from his receipt of the creditor's request, and

(c) act in accordance with paragraphs (2) to (5) above, as if he had decided under section 293(1) to summon the meeting.

(7) A meeting summoned by the official receiver under section 293 or 294 is known as "the first meeting of creditors".

NOTES

Initial Commencement

Specified date

Specified date: 29 December 1986: see r 0.1.

Amendment

Para (2): words "to every creditor of the bankrupt who is known to the official receiver" in square brackets substituted by SI 2010/686, r 2, Sch 1, para 339(1), (2).
  Date in force: 6 April 2010: see SI 2010/686, r 1; for transitional provisions see r 6(1), Sch 4, para 1 thereto.
Para (3): substituted by SI 2010/686, r 2, Sch 1, para 339(1), (3).
  Date in force: 6 April 2010: see SI 2010/686, r 1; for transitional provisions see r 6(1), Sch 4, para 1 thereto.
Para (4): substituted by SI 2010/686, r 2, Sch 1, para 339(1), (4).
  Date in force: 6 April 2010: see SI 2010/686, r 1; for transitional provisions see r 6(1), Sch 4, para 1 thereto.
Para (5): substituted by SI 2009/642, r 4, 40.
  Date in force: 6 April 2009: see SI 2009/642, r 1; for transitional provisions see r 3 thereof.
Para (5A): inserted by SI 2010/686, r 2, Sch 1, para 399(1), (5).

Date in force: 6 April 2010: see SI 2010/686, r 1; for transitional provisions see r 6(1), Sch 4, para 1 thereto.

6.80 Business at first meeting

(1) At the first meeting of creditors, no resolutions shall be taken other than the following—

- (a) a resolution to appoint a named insolvency practitioner to be trustee in bankruptcy or two or more named insolvency practitioners as joint trustees;
- (b) a resolution to establish a creditors' committee;
- (c) (unless it has been resolved to establish a creditors' committee) a resolution specifying the terms on which the trustee is to be remunerated, or to defer consideration of that matter;
- (d) (if, and only if, two or more persons are appointed to act jointly as trustee) a resolution specifying whether acts are to be done by both or all of them, or by only one;
- (e) (where the meeting has been requisitioned under section 294) a resolution authorising payment out of the estate, as an expense of the bankruptcy, of the cost of summoning and holding the meeting;
- (f) a resolution to adjourn the meeting . . .;
- (g) any other resolution which the chairman thinks it right to allow for special reasons.

[(2A) The meeting may be adjourned, either in accordance with a resolution under paragraph (1)(f) or if the chairman thinks fit, but for not more than 14 days from the date on which it was fixed to commence, subject to any direction of the court.

(2B) If there are subsequently further adjournments, the final adjournment must not be to a day later than 14 days after the date on which the meeting was originally held, subject to any direction of the court.

(2C) Where a meeting is adjourned under this Rule, proofs and proxies may be used if lodged at any time up to 12.00 hours on the business day immediately before the adjourned meeting.]

NOTES

Initial Commencement

Specified date

Specified date: 29 December 1986: see r 0.1.

Amendment

Para (1): in sub-para (f) words omitted revoked by SI 2010/686, r 2, Sch 1, para 340(1), (2).
Date in force: 6 April 2010: see SI 2010/686, r 1; for transitional provisions see r 6(1), Sch 4, para 1 thereto.
Paras (2A)–(2C): substituted, for para (2) as originally enacted, by SI 2010/686, r 2, Sch 1, para 340(1), (3).
Date in force: 6 April 2010: see SI 2010/686, r 1; for transitional provisions see r 6(1), Sch 4, para 1 thereto.

6.81 General power to call meetings

(1) The official receiver or the trustee may at any time summon and conduct meetings of creditors for the purpose of ascertaining their wishes in all matters relating to the bankruptcy.

In relation to any meeting of creditors, the person summoning it is referred to as "the convener".

(2) When a venue for the meeting has been fixed, notice of the meeting shall be given by the convener to every creditor who is known to him . . . .

The notice shall be given at least [14] days before the date fixed for the meeting.

[(3) The notice must specify the purpose for which the meeting is summoned and state that proofs and (if applicable) proxies must be lodged at a specified place not later than 12.00 hours on the business day before the date fixed for the meeting in order for creditors to be entitled to vote at the meeting.]

[(4) [As soon as reasonably practicable after sending notice of the meeting to the creditors under paragraph (2), the convener must give additional notice of the meeting.] Such notice—
- (a) shall be gazetted; and
- (b) may be advertised in such other manner as the convenor thinks fit.]

[(5) In addition to the standard contents, the notice under paragraph (4) must specify—
- (a) who summoned the meeting;
- (b) if the meeting was summoned at the request of a creditor, the fact that it was so summoned and the section of the Act under which it was requested;
- (c) the purpose for which the meeting is summoned;
- (d) the venue fixed for the meeting; and
- (e) the time and date by which, and place at which, creditors must lodge proxies and hitherto unlodged proofs in order to be entitled to vote at the meeting.]

NOTES

Initial Commencement

Specified date

Specified date: 29 December 1986: see r 0.1.

Amendment

Para (2): words omitted revoked by SI 2010/686, r 2, Sch 1, para 341(1), (2)(a).
    Date in force: 6 April 2010: see SI 2010/686, r 1; for transitional provisions see r 6(1), Sch 4, para 1 thereto.
Para (2): reference to "14" in square brackets substituted by SI 2010/686, r 2, Sch 1, para 341(1), (2)(b).
    Date in force: 6 April 2010: see SI 2010/686, r 1; for transitional provisions see r 6(1), Sch 4, para 1 thereto.
Para (3): substituted by SI 2010/686, r 2, Sch 1, para 341(1), (3).
    Date in force: 6 April 2010: see SI 2010/686, r 1; for transitional provisions see r 6(1), Sch 4, para 1 thereto.
Para (4): substituted by SI 2009/642, rr 4, 41.
    Date in force: 6 April 2009: see SI 2009/642, r 1; for transitional provisions see r 3 thereof.
Para (4): words from "As soon as" to "of the meeting." in square brackets substituted by SI 2010/686, r 2, Sch 1, para 341(1), (4).
    Date in force: 6 April 2010: see SI 2010/686, r 1; for transitional provisions see r 6(1), Sch 4, para 1 thereto.
Para (5): inserted by SI 2010/686, r 2, Sch 1, para 341(1), (5).
    Date in force: 6 April 2010: see SI 2010/686, r 1; for transitional provisions see r 6(1), Sch 4, para 1 thereto.

6.82 The chairman at a meeting

(1) Where the convener of a meeting is the official receiver, he, or a person nominated by him, shall be chairman.

A nomination under this paragraph shall be in writing, unless the nominee is another official receiver or a deputy official receiver.

(2) Where the convener is other than the official receiver, the chairman shall be he, or a person nominated by him in writing to act.

A person nominated under this paragraph must be either—
- (a) one who is qualified to act as an insolvency practitioner in relation to the bankrupt, or
- (b) an employee of the trustee or his firm who is experienced in insolvency matters.

NOTES

Initial Commencement

Specified date

Specified date: 29 December 1986: see r 0.1.

6.83 Requisitioned meetings

(1) A request by creditors to the official receiver for a meeting of creditors to be summoned shall be accompanied by—
- (a) a list of the creditors concurring with the request and the amount of their respective claims in the bankruptcy,
- (b) from each creditor concurring, written confirmation of his concurrence, and
- (c) a statement of the purpose of the proposed meeting.

Sub-paragraphs (a) and (b) do not apply if the requisitioning creditor's debt is alone sufficient, without the concurrence of other creditors.

(2) The official receiver, if he considers the request to be properly made in accordance with the Act, shall—
- (a) fix a venue for the meeting, to take place not more than [28] days from the receipt of the request, and
- (b) give [14] days' notice of the meeting, and of the venue for it, to creditors.

(3) Where a request for a creditors' meeting is made to the trustee, this Rule applies to him as it does to the official receiver.

[(4) This Rule shall not apply to voluntary arrangements under section 263A.]

NOTES

Initial Commencement

Specified date

Specified date: 29 December 1986: see r 0.1.

Amendment

Para (2): in sub-para (a) reference to "28" in square brackets substituted by SI 2010/686, r 2, Sch 1, para 342(1), (2)(a).
Date in force: 6 April 2010: see SI 2010/686, r 1; for transitional provisions see r 6(1), Sch 4, para 1 thereto.
Para (2): in sub-para (b) reference to "14" in square brackets substituted by SI 2010/686, r 2, Sch 1, para 342(1), (2)(b).
Date in force: 6 April 2010: see SI 2010/686, r 1; for transitional provisions see r 6(1), Sch 4, para 1 thereto.
Para (4): inserted by SI 2003/1730, r 9(1), Sch 1, Pt 6, para 35.
Date in force: 1 April 2004: see SI 2003/1730, r 1(3).

6.84 Attendance at meetings of bankrupt, etc

(1) Whenever a meeting of creditors is summoned, the convener shall give at least [14] days' notice of the meeting to the bankrupt.

(2) If the meeting is adjourned, the chairman of the meeting shall (unless for any reason it appears to him to be unnecessary or impracticable) give notice of the fact to the bankrupt, if the latter was not himself present at the meeting.

(3) The convener may, if he thinks fit, give notice to the bankrupt that he is required to be present, or in attendance.

(4) In the case of any meeting, the bankrupt or any other person may, if he has given reasonable notice of his wish to be present, be admitted; but this is at the discretion of the chairman.

The chairman's decision is final as to what (if any) intervention may be made by the bankrupt, or by any other person admitted to the meeting under this paragraph.

(5) If the bankrupt is not present, and it is desired to put questions to him, the chairman may adjourn the meeting with a view to obtaining his attendance.

(6) Where the bankrupt is present at a creditors' meeting, only such questions may be put to him as the chairman may in his discretion allow.

NOTES

Initial Commencement

Specified date

Specified date: 29 December 1986: see r 0.1.

Amendment

Para (1): reference to "14" in square brackets substituted by SI 2010/686, r 2, Sch 1, para 343.
Date in force: 6 April 2010: see SI 2010/686, r 1; for transitional provisions see r 6(1), Sch 4, para 1 thereto.

6.85 Notice of meetings by advertisement only

(1) In the case of any meeting to be held under the Act or the Rules, the court may order that notice of it be given by . . . advertisement, and not by individual notice to the persons concerned.

(2) In considering whether to act under this Rule, the court shall have regard to the cost of . . . advertisement, to the amount of the funds available in the estate, and to the extent of the interest of creditors or any particular class of them.

[(3) In addition to the standard contents, the advertisement must state—
  (a)   the venue fixed for the meeting;
  (b)   that proofs and (if applicable) proxies must be lodged at a specified place not later than 12.00 hours on the business day before the date fixed for the meeting; and
  (c)   the date of the court order.]

NOTES

Initial Commencement

Specified date

Specified date: 29 December 1986: see r 0.1.

Amendment

Para (1): word omitted revoked by SI 2010/686, r 2, Sch 1, para 344(1), (2).
Date in force: 6 April 2010: see SI 2010/686, r 1; for transitional provisions see r 6(1), Sch 4, para 1 thereto.
Para (2): word omitted revoked by SI 2010/686, r 2, Sch 1, para 344(1), (2).
Date in force: 6 April 2010: see SI 2010/686, r 1; for transitional provisions see r 6(1), Sch 4, para 1 thereto.
Para (3): inserted by SI 2010/686, r 2, Sch 1, para 344(1), (3).

Date in force: 6 April 2010: see SI 2010/686, r 1; for transitional provisions see r 6(1), Sch 4, para 1 thereto.

6.86 Venue of meetings

(1) In fixing the venue for a meeting of creditors, the person summoning the meeting shall have regard to the convenience of the creditors.

(2) Meetings shall in all cases be summoned for commencement between the hours of 10.00 and 16.00 hours on a business day, unless the court otherwise directs.

(3) With every notice summoning a creditors' meeting there shall be sent out forms of proxy.

NOTES

Initial Commencement

Specified date

Specified date: 29 December 1986: see r 0.1.

6.87 Expenses of summoning meetings

(1) Subject to paragraph (3) below, the expenses of summoning and holding a meeting of creditors at the instance of any person other than the official receiver or the trustee shall be paid by that person, who shall deposit security for their payment with the trustee or, if no trustee has been appointed, with the official receiver.

(2) The sum to be deposited shall be such as the trustee or (as the case may be) the official receiver determines to be appropriate; and neither shall act without the deposit having been made.

(3) Where a meeting is so summoned, it may vote that the expenses of summoning and holding it shall be payable out of the estate, as an expense of the bankruptcy.

(4) To the extent that any deposit made under this Rule is not required for the payment of expenses of summoning and holding the meeting, it shall be repaid to the person who made it.

NOTES

Initial Commencement

Specified date

Specified date: 29 December 1986: see r 0.1.

6.88 Resolutions

(1) [Subject as follows,] at a meeting of creditors, a resolution is passed when a majority (in value) of those present and voting, in person or by proxy, have voted in favour of the resolution.

(2) In the case of a resolution for the appointment of a trustee—

(a) if on any vote there are two nominees for appointment, the person who obtains the most support is appointed . . .;

(b) if there are three or more nominees, and one of them has a clear majority over both or all the others together, that one is appointed; and

(c) in any other case the chairman shall continue to take votes (disregarding at each vote any nominee who has withdrawn and, if no nominee has withdrawn, the nominee who obtained the least support last time), until a clear majority is obtained for any one nominee.

(3) The chairman may at any time put to the meeting a resolution for the joint appointment of any two or more nominees.

(4) Where a resolution is proposed which affects a person in respect of his remuneration or conduct as trustee, or as proposed or former trustee, the vote of that person, and of any partner or employee of his, shall not be reckoned in the majority required for passing the resolution.

This paragraph applies with respect to a vote given by a person [(whether personally or on his behalf by a proxy-holder)] either as creditor or as [proxy-holder] for a creditor (but subject to Rule 8.6 in Part 8 of the Rules).

NOTES

Initial Commencement

Specified date

Specified date: 29 December 1986: see r 0.1.

Amendment

Para (1): words "Subject as follows" in square brackets inserted by SI 1987/1919, r 3(1), Schedule, Part 1, para 107.

Para (2): in sub-para (a) words omitted revoked by SI 2010/686, r 2, Sch 1, para 345.
Date in force: 6 April 2010: see SI 2010/686, r 1; for transitional provisions see r 6(1), Sch 4, para 1 thereto.

Para (4): words in square brackets inserted or substituted by SI 1987/1919, r 3(1), Schedule, Part 1, para 107.

[6.88A Resolutions by correspondence]

[(1) The trustee may seek to obtain the passing of a resolution by creditors without holding a meeting by giving notice of the resolution to every creditor who is entitled to be notified of a meeting at which the resolution could be passed.

(2) In order to be counted, votes must be received by the trustee in writing by 12.00 hours on the closing date specified in the notice, and must be accompanied by a proof of debt as required by Rule 6.93(1)(a) unless it has already been lodged under that Rule.

(3) If any vote cast by a creditor is received without a proof of debt, or the trustee decides that the creditor is not entitled to vote according to Rules 6.93 to 6.94, then that creditor's vote must be disregarded.

(4) The closing date shall be set at the discretion of the trustee, but in any event it must not be set less than 14 days from the giving of notice provided for in paragraph (1).

(5) For the resolution to be passed, the trustee must receive at least one valid vote by the closing date specified in the notice.

(6) If no valid vote is received by the closing date specified, the trustee must call a meeting of creditors at which the resolution could be passed.

(7) Creditors whose debts amount to at least 10% of the bankrupt's total debts may, within 5 business days from the giving of notice provided for in paragraph (1), require the trustee to summon a meeting of creditors to consider the resolution.

(8) A reference in these Rules to a resolution passed at a creditors' meeting includes a reference to a resolution passed under this Rule.

(9) This Rule does not apply in respect of any resolution which the Act requires to be passed at a meeting.]

NOTES

Amendment

Inserted by SI 2010/686, r 2, Sch 1, para 346.

Date in force: 6 April 2010: see SI 2010/686, r 1; for transitional provisions see r 6(1), Sch 4, para 1 thereto.

6.89 Chairman of meeting as proxy-holder
Where the chairman at a meeting holds a proxy for a creditor, which requires him to vote for a particular resolution, and no other person proposes that resolution—
- (a) he shall himself propose it, unless he considers that there is good reason for not doing so, and
- (b) if he does not propose it, he shall [as soon as reasonably practicable] after the meeting notify his principal of the reason why not.

NOTES

Initial Commencement

Specified date
Specified date: 29 December 1986: see r 0.1.

Amendment
In para (b) words "as soon as reasonably practicable" in square brackets substituted by SI 2009/642, rr 4, 5.
Date in force: 6 April 2009: see SI 2009/642, r 1; for transitional provisions see r 3 thereof.

6.90 Suspension of meeting
Once only in the course of any meeting, the chairman may, in his discretion and without an adjournment, declare the meeting suspended for any period up to one hour.

NOTES

Initial Commencement

Specified date
Specified date: 29 December 1986: see r 0.1.

6.91 Adjournment
(1) The chairman at any meeting may, in his discretion, and shall if the meeting so resolves, adjourn it to such time and place as seems to him to be appropriate in the circumstances.
This is subject to Rule 6.129(3) in a case where the trustee or his nominee is chairman and a resolution has been proposed for the trustee's removal.

(2) If within a period of 30 minutes from the time appointed for the commencement of a meeting a quorum is not present, then [the chairman may, at his discretion, adjourn the meeting to such time and place as he may appoint].

(3) An adjournment under this Rule shall not be for a period of more than [14] days; and Rule 6.86(1) and (2) applies with regard to the venue of the adjourned meeting.

[(4A) If within 30 minutes from the time appointed for commencement of a meeting there is no person present to act as chairman, the meeting stands adjourned to the same time and place in the following week or, if that is not a business day, to the business day immediately following.

(4B) Paragraph (4A) applies to further adjournments of a final meeting.

(4C) In the case of any other meeting, further adjournment must be to the same time and place in the following week or, if either—
- (a) that is not a business day, or

(b) whether or not it is a business day, it is later than 14 days after the date on which the meeting in question was originally held,

to the same time and place on the business day immediately preceding which is not later than 14 days after the date on which the meeting in question was originally held.]

(5) Where a meeting is adjourned under this Rule, proofs and proxies may be used if lodged at any time up to midday on the business day immediately before the adjourned meeting.

NOTES

Initial Commencement

Specified date

Specified date: 29 December 1986: see r 0.1.

Amendment

Para (2): words in square brackets substituted by SI 1987/1919, r 3(1), Schedule, Part 1, para 108.

Para (3): reference to "14" in square brackets substituted by SI 2010/686, r 2, Sch 1, para 347(1), (2).

Date in force: 6 April 2010: see SI 2010/686, r 1; for transitional provisions see r 6(1), Sch 4, para 1 thereto.

Paras (4A)–(4C): substituted, for para (4) as originally enacted, by SI 2010/686, r 2, Sch 1, para 347(1), (3).

Date in force: 6 April 2010: see SI 2010/686, r 1; for transitional provisions see r 6(1), Sch 4, para 1 thereto.

6.93 Entitlement to vote

(1) Subject as follows [in this Rule and the next], at a meeting of creditors a person is entitled to vote as a creditor only if—

  (a) there has been duly lodged, by the time and date stated in the notice of the meeting, a proof of the debt
    [(i) claimed to be due to him from the bankrupt, or
    (ii) in relation to a member State liquidator, is claimed to be due to creditors in proceedings in relation to which he holds office], and the claim has been admitted under Rule 6.94 for the purpose of entitlement to vote, and
  (b) there has been lodged, by that time and date, any proxy requisite for that entitlement.

(2) The court may, in exceptional circumstances, by order declare the creditors, or any class of them, entitled to vote at creditors' meetings, without being required to prove their debts.

Where a creditor is so entitled, the court may, on the application of the trustee, make such consequential orders as it thinks [just] (as for example an order treating a creditor as having proved his debt for the purpose of permitting payment of dividend).

(3) A creditor shall not vote in respect of a debt for an unliquidated amount, or any debt whose value is not ascertained, except where the chairman agrees to put upon the debt an estimated minimum value for the purpose of entitlement to vote and admits his proof for that purpose.

(4) A secured creditor is entitled to vote only in respect of the balance (if any) of his debt after deducting the value of his security as estimated by him.

(5) A creditor shall not vote in respect of a debt on, or secured by, a current bill of exchange or promissory note, unless he is willing—

  (a) to treat the liability to him on the bill or note of every person who is liable on it antecedently to the bankrupt, and against whom a

bankruptcy order has not been made (or, in the case of a company, which has not gone into liquidation), as a security in his hands, and
- (b) to estimate the value of the security and (for the purpose of entitlement to vote, but not for dividend) to deduct it from his proof.

[(6) No vote shall be cast by virtue of a debt more than once on any resolution put to the meeting.

(7) Where—
- (a) a creditor is entitled to vote under this Rule and Rule 6.94 (admission of proof),
- (b) has lodged his claim in one or more sets of other proceedings, and
- (c) votes (either in person or by proxy) on a resolution put to the meeting, only the creditor's vote shall be counted.

(8) Where—
- (a) a creditor has lodged his claim in more than one set of other proceedings, and
- (b) more than one member State liquidator seeks to vote by virtue of that claim,

the entitlement to vote by virtue of that claim is exercisable by the member State liquidator in main proceedings, whether or not the creditor has lodged his claim in the main proceedings.

(9) For the purposes of paragraphs (7) and (8), "other proceedings" means main proceedings, secondary proceedings or territorial proceedings in another member State.]

NOTES

Initial Commencement

Specified date

Specified date: 29 December 1986: see r 0.1.

Amendment

Para (1): words "in this Rule and the next" in square brackets inserted by SI 2010/686, r 2, Sch 1, para 348.
Date in force: 6 April 2010: see SI 2010/686, r 1; for transitional provisions see r 6(1), Sch 4, para 1 thereto.
Para (1): in sub-para (a) words from "(i) claimed to be" to "he holds office" in square brackets substituted by SI 2002/1307, rr 3(1), 8(5)(a).
Date in force: 31 May 2002: see SI 2002/1307, r 1.
Para (2): word "just" in square brackets substituted by SI 2010/686, r 2, Sch 1, para 1.
Date in force: 6 April 2010: see SI 2010/686, r 1; for transitional provisions see r 6(1), Sch 4, paras 1, 2(1)(b) thereto.
Paras (6)–(9): inserted by SI 2002/1307, rr 3(1), 8(5)(b).
Date in force: 31 May 2002: see SI 2002/1307, r 1.

[6.93A Chairman's discretion to allow vote]

[At a creditors' meeting, the chairman may allow a creditor to vote, notwithstanding that the creditor has failed to comply with Rule 6.93(1)(a), if satisfied that the failure was due to circumstances beyond the creditor's control.]

NOTES

Amendment

Inserted by SI 2010/686, r 2, Sch 1, para 349.
Date in force: 6 April 2010: see SI 2010/686, r 1; for transitional provisions see r 6(1), Sch 4, para 1 thereto.

6.94 Admission and rejection of proof

(1) At any creditors' meeting the chairman has power to admit or reject a creditor's proof for the purpose of his entitlement to vote; and the power is exercisable with respect to the whole or any part of the proof.

(2) The chairman's decision under this Rule, or in respect of any matter arising under Rule 6.93, is subject to appeal to the court by any creditor, or by the bankrupt.

(3) If the chairman is in doubt whether a proof should be admitted or rejected, he shall mark it as objected to and allow the creditor to vote, subject to his vote being subsequently declared invalid if the objection to the proof is sustained.

(4) If on an appeal the chairman's decision is reversed or varied, or a creditor's vote is declared invalid, the court may order that another meeting be summoned, or make such other order as it thinks just.

[(4A) An application to the court by way of appeal under this Rule against a decision of the chairman must be made not later than 21 days after the date of the meeting.]

(5) Neither the official receiver nor any person nominated by him to be chairman is personally liable for costs incurred by any person in respect of an application to the court under this Rule; and the chairman (if other than the official receiver or a person so nominated) is not so liable unless the court makes an order to that effect.

NOTES

Initial Commencement

Specified date

Specified date: 29 December 1986: see r 0.1.

Amendment

Para (4A): inserted by SI 2010/686, r 2, Sch 1, para 350.
Date in force: 6 April 2010: see SI 2010/686, r 1; for transitional provisions see r 6(1), Sch 4, para 1 thereto.

6.95 Record of proceedings

(1) The chairman at any creditors' meeting shall cause minutes of the proceedings at the meeting, [authenticated] by him, to be retained by him as part of the records of the bankruptcy.

(2) He shall also cause to be made up and kept a list of all the creditors who attended the meeting.

(3) The minutes of the meeting shall include a record of every resolution passed; [and if a creditors' committee has been established, the names and addresses of those elected to be members of the committee].

NOTES

Initial Commencement

Specified date

Specified date: 29 December 1986: see r 0.1.

Amendment

Para (1): word "authenticated" in square brackets substituted by SI 2010/686, r 2, Sch 1, para 1.
Date in force: 6 April 2010: see SI 2010/686, r 1; for transitional provisions see r 6(1), Sch 4, paras 1, 2(1)(b) thereto.
Para (3): words from "and if a" to "of the committee" in square brackets substituted by SI 2010/686, r 2, Sch 1, para 351.

Date in force: 6 April 2010: see SI 2010/686, r 1; for transitional provisions see r 6(1), Sch 4, para 1 thereto.

CHAPTER 8

PROOF OF BANKRUPTCY DEBTS

SECTION A: PROCEDURE FOR PROVING

6.96 Meaning of "prove"

(1) A person claiming to be a creditor of the bankrupt and wishing to recover his debt in whole or in part must (subject to any order of the court under Rule 6.93(2)) submit his claim in writing to the official receiver, where acting as receiver and manager, or to the trustee.

(2) The creditor is referred to as "proving" for his debt; and the document by which he seeks to establish his claim is his "proof".

(3) Subject to the next two paragraphs, the proof must be in the form known as "proof of debt" (whether the form prescribed by the Rules, or a substantially similar form), which shall be made out by or under the directions of the creditor, and [authenticated] by him or a person authorised in that behalf.

(4) Where a debt is due to a Minister of the Crown or a Government Department, the proof need not be in that form, provided that there are shown all such particulars of the debt as are required in the form used by other creditors, and as are relevant in the circumstances.

(5) Where an existing trustee proves in a later bankruptcy under section 335(5), the proof must be in Form 6.38.

(6) . . .

NOTES

Initial Commencement

Specified date

Specified date: 29 December 1986: see r 0.1.

Amendment

Para (3): word "authenticated" in square brackets substituted by SI 2010/686, r 2, Sch 1, para 1.
Date in force: 6 April 2010: see SI 2010/686, r 1; for transitional provisions see r 6(1), Sch 4, paras 1, 2(1)(b) thereto.
Para (6): revoked by SI 2010/686, r 2, Sch 1, para 352.
Date in force: 6 April 2010: see SI 2010/686, r 1; for transitional provisions see r 6(1), Sch 4, para 1 thereto.

[6.97 Supply of forms]
[A form of proof shall be sent to any creditor of the bankrupt by the official receiver or trustee where the creditor so requests.]

NOTES

Amendment

Substituted by SI 2004/584, r 27.
Date in force: 1 April 2004: see SI 2004/584, r 1(2).

6.98 Contents of proof

[(1) Subject to Rule 6.96(4), the following matters shall be stated in a creditor's proof of debt—

(a) the creditor's name and address, and, if a company, its company registration number;

(b) the total amount of his claim (including any Value Added Tax) as at the date of the bankruptcy order[, less any deduction under Rule 6.110];

(c) whether or not that amount includes outstanding uncapitalised interest;

(d) particulars of how and when the debt was incurred by the debtor;

(e) particulars of any security held, the date when it was given and the value which the creditor puts upon it

(f) details of any reservation of title in respect of goods to which the debt refers; and

(g) the name, and address and authority of the person [authenticating] the proof (if other than the creditor himself).]

(2) There shall be specified in the proof any documents by reference to which the debt can be substantiated; but (subject as follows) it is not essential that such documents be attached to the proof or submitted with it.

(3) The trustee, [the official receiver, acting as receiver and manager] or the convener or chairman of any meeting, may call for any document or other evidence to be produced to him, where he thinks it necessary for the purpose of substantiating the whole or any part of the claim made in the proof.

NOTES

Initial Commencement

Specified date

Specified date: 29 December 1986: see r 0.1.

Amendment

Para (1): substituted by SI 2004/1070, r 2.
Date in force: 3 May 2004: see SI 2004/1070, r 1.
Para (1): in sub-para (b) words ", less any deduction under Rule 6.110" in square brackets inserted by SI 2010/686, r 2, Sch 1, para 353.
Date in force: 6 April 2010: see SI 2010/686, r 1; for transitional provisions see r 6(1), Sch 4, para 1 thereto.
Para (1): in sub-para (g) word "authenticating" in square brackets substituted by SI 2010/686, r 2, Sch 1, para 1.
Date in force: 6 April 2010: see SI 2010/686, r 1; for transitional provisions see r 6(1), Sch 4, paras 1, 2(1)(b) thereto.
Para (3): words "the official receiver, acting as receiver and manager" in square brackets inserted by SI 2004/584, r 28(2).
Date in force: 1 April 2004: see SI 2004/584, r 1(2).

6.99 . . .

. . .

NOTES

Amendment

Revoked by SI 2010/686, r 5.
Date in force: 6 April 2010: see SI 2010/686, r 1; for transitional provisions see r 6(1), Sch 4, paras 1, 2(1)(a) thereto.

6.100 Cost of proving

(1) Subject as follows, every creditor bears the cost of proving his own debt, including such as may be incurred in providing documents or evidence under Rule 6.98(3).

(2) Costs incurred by the trustee in estimating the value of a bankruptcy debt under section 322(3) (debts not bearing a certain value) fall on the estate, as an expense of the bankruptcy.

(3) Paragraphs (1) and (2) apply unless the court otherwise orders.

NOTES

Initial Commencement

Specified date

Specified date: 29 December 1986: see r 0.1.

6.101 Trustee to allow inspection of proofs

The trustee shall, so long as proofs lodged with him are in his hands, allow them to be inspected, at all reasonable times on any business day, by any of the following persons—

(a) any creditor who has submitted his proof of debt (unless his proof has been wholly rejected for purposes of dividend or otherwise),

(b) the bankrupt, and

(c) any person acting on behalf of either of the above.

NOTES

Initial Commencement

Specified date

Specified date: 29 December 1986: see r 0.1.

6.102 . . .

. . .

NOTES

Amendment

Revoked by SI 2010/686, r 5.
Date in force: 6 April 2010: see SI 2010/686, r 1; for transitional provisions see r 6(1), Sch 4, paras 1, 2(1)(a) thereto.

6.103 Transmission of proofs to trustee

(1) Where a trustee is appointed, the official receiver shall [as soon as reasonably practicable] transmit to him all the proofs which he has so far received, together with an itemised list of them.

(2) The trustee shall [authenticate] the list by way of receipt for the proofs, and return it to the official receiver.

(3) From then on, all proofs of debt shall be sent to the trustee and retained by him.

NOTES

Initial Commencement

Specified date

Specified date: 29 December 1986: see r 0.1.

Amendment

Para (1): words "as soon as reasonably practicable" in square brackets substituted by SI 2009/642, rr 4, 5.

Date in force: 6 April 2009: see SI 2009/642, r 1; for transitional provisions see r 3 thereof.

Para (2): word "authenticate" in square brackets substituted by SI 2010/686, r 2, Sch 1, para 1.

Date in force: 6 April 2010: see SI 2010/686, r 1; for transitional provisions see r 6(1), Sch 4, paras 1, 2(1)(b) thereto.

[6.103A New trustee appointed]

[(1) If a new trustee is appointed in place of another, the former trustee must as soon as reasonably practicable transmit to the new one all proofs which the former trustee has received, together with an itemised list of them.

(2) The new trustee must authenticate the list by way of receipt for the proofs, and return it to the former trustee.

(3) From then on, all proofs of debt must be sent to and retained by the new trustee.]

NOTES

Amendment

Inserted by SI 2010/686, r 2, Sch 1, para 354.

Date in force: 6 April 2010: see SI 2010/686, r 1; for transitional provisions see r 6(1), Sch 4, para 1 thereto.

6.104 Admission and rejection of proofs for dividend

(1) A proof may be admitted for dividend either for the whole amount claimed by the creditor, or for part of that amount.

(2) If the trustee rejects a proof in whole or in part, he shall prepare a written statement of his reasons for doing so, and send it [as soon as reasonably practicable] to the creditor.

NOTES

Initial Commencement

Specified date

Specified date: 29 December 1986: see r 0.1.

Amendment

Para (2): words "as soon as reasonably practicable" in square brackets substituted by SI 2009/642, rr .4, 5.

Date in force: 6 April 2009: see SI 2009/642, r 1; for transitional provisions see r 3 thereof.

6.105 Appeal against decision on proof

(1) If a creditor is dissatisfied with the trustee's decision with respect to his proof (including any decision on the question of preference), he may apply to the court for the decision to be reversed or varied.

The application must be made within 21 days of his receiving the statement sent under Rule 6.104(2).

(2) The bankrupt or any other creditor may, if dissatisfied with the trustee's decision admitting or rejecting the whole or any part of a proof, make such an application within 21 days of becoming aware of the trustee's decision.

(3) Where application is made to the court under this Rule, the court shall fix a venue for the application to be heard, notice of which shall be sent by the applicant to the creditor who lodged the proof in question (if it is not himself) and to the trustee.

(4) The trustee shall, on receipt of the notice, file in court the relevant proof, together (if appropriate) with a copy of the statement sent under Rule 6.104(2).

(5) After the application has been heard and determined, the proof shall, unless it has been wholly disallowed, be returned by the court to the trustee.

(6) The official receiver is not personally liable for costs incurred by any person in respect of an application under this Rule; and the trustee (if other than the official receiver) is not so liable unless the court makes an order to that effect.

NOTES

Initial Commencement

Specified date

Specified date: 29 December 1986: see r 0.1.

6.106 Withdrawal or variation of proof

A creditor's proof may at any time, by agreement between himself and the trustee, be withdrawn or varied as to the amount claimed.

NOTES

Initial Commencement

Specified date

Specified date: 29 December 1986: see r 0.1.

6.107 Expunging of proof by the court

(1) The court may expunge a proof or reduce the amount claimed—
- (a) on the trustee's application, where he thinks that the proof has been improperly admitted, or ought to be reduced; or
- (b) on the application of a creditor, if the trustee declines to interfere in the matter.

(2) Where application is made to the court under this Rule, the court shall fix a venue for the application to be heard, notice of which shall be sent by the applicant—
- (a) in the case of an application by the trustee, to the creditor who made the proof, and
- (b) in the case of an application by a creditor, to the trustee and to the creditor who made the proof (if not himself).

NOTES

Initial Commencement

Specified date

Specified date: 29 December 1986: see r 0.1.

SECTION B: QUANTIFICATION OF CLAIM

6.108 Negotiable instruments, etc

Unless the trustee allows, a proof in respect of money owed on a bill of exchange, promissory note, cheque or other negotiable instrument or security cannot be admitted unless there is produced the instrument or security itself or a copy of it, certified by the creditor or his authorised representative to be a true copy.

NOTES

Initial Commencement

Specified date

Specified date: 29 December 1986: see r 0.1.

6.109 Secured creditors

(1) If a secured creditor realises his security, he may prove for the balance of his debt, after deducting the amount realised.

(2) If a secured creditor voluntarily surrenders his security for the general benefit of creditors, he may prove for his whole debt, as if it were unsecured.

NOTES

Initial Commencement

Specified date

Specified date: 29 December 1986: see r 0.1.

6.110 Discounts

There shall in every case be deducted from the claim all trade and other discounts which would have been available to the bankrupt but for his bankruptcy, except any discount for immediate, early or cash settlement.

NOTES

Initial Commencement

Specified date

Specified date: 29 December 1986: see r 0.1.

6.111 Debt in foreign currency

(1) For the purpose of proving a debt incurred or payable in a currency other than sterling, the amount of the debt shall be converted into sterling at the official exchange rate prevailing on the date of the bankruptcy order.

(2) "The official exchange rate" is the [middle exchange rate on the London Foreign Exchange Market at the close of business], as published for the date in question. In the absence of any such published rate, it is such rate as the court determines.

NOTES

Initial Commencement

Specified date

Specified date: 29 December 1986: see r 0.1.

Amendment

Para (2): words "middle exchange rate on the London Foreign Exchange Market at the close of business" in square brackets substituted by SI 2003/1730, r 9(1), Sch 1, Pt 6, para 37. Date in force: 1 April 2004: see SI 2003/1730, r 1(3).

6.112 Payments of a periodical nature

(1) In the case of rent and other payments of a periodical nature, the creditor may prove for any amounts due and unpaid up to the date of the bankruptcy order.

(2) Where at that date any payment was accruing due, the creditor may prove for so much as would have fallen due at that date, if accruing from day to day.

NOTES

Initial Commencement

Specified date

Specified date: 29 December 1986: see r 0.1.

6.113 Interest

(1) In the following circumstances the creditor's claim may include interest on the debt for periods before the bankruptcy order; although not previously reserved or agreed.

(2) If the debt is due by virtue of a written instrument and payable at a certain time, interest may be claimed for the period from that time to the date of the bankruptcy order.

(3) If the debt is due otherwise, interest may only be claimed if, before the presentation of the bankruptcy petition, a demand for payment was made in writing by or on behalf of the creditor, and notice given that interest would be payable from the date of the demand to the date of payment [and for all the purposes of the Act and the Rules shall be chargeable at a rate not exceeding that mentioned in paragraph (5)].

[(4) Interest under paragraph (3) may only be claimed for the period from the date of the demand to that of the bankruptcy order.

(5) The rate of interest to be claimed under paragraphs (2) and (3) is the rate specified in section 17 of the Judgments Act 1838 on the date of the bankruptcy order.]

NOTES

Initial Commencement

Specified date

Specified date: 29 December 1986: see r 0.1.

Amendment

Para (3): words in square brackets inserted by SI 1987/1919, r 3(1), Schedule, Part 1, para 112(1).

Paras (4), (5): substituted for paras (3) (in part), (4) as originally enacted, by SI 1987/1919, r 3(1), Schedule, Part 1, para 112(2).

6.114 Debt payable at future time

A creditor may prove for a debt of which payment was not yet due at the date of the bankruptcy order, but subject to Rule 11.13 in Part 11 of the Rules (adjustment of dividend where payment made before time).

NOTES

Initial Commencement

Specified date

Specified date: 29 December 1986: see r 0.1.

CHAPTER 9
SECURED CREDITORS

6.115 Value of security

(1) A secured creditor may, with the agreement of the trustee or the [permission] of the court, at any time alter the value which he has, in his proof of debt, put upon his security.

(2) However, if a secured creditor—

(a) being the petitioner, has in the petition put a value on his security, or

(b) has voted in respect of the unsecured balance of his debt,

he may re-value his security only with [permission] of the court.

NOTES

Initial Commencement

Specified date

Specified date: 29 December 1986: see r 0.1.

Amendment

Para (1): word "permission" in square brackets substituted by SI 2010/686, r 2, Sch 1, para 1.
   Date in force: 6 April 2010: see SI 2010/686, r 1; for transitional provisions see r 6(1), Sch 4, paras 1, 2(1)(b) thereto.

Para (2): word "permission" in square brackets substituted by SI 2010/686, r 2, Sch 1, para 1.
   Date in force: 6 April 2010: see SI 2010/686, r 1; for transitional provisions see r 6(1), Sch 4, paras 1, 2(1)(b) thereto.

6.116 Surrender for non-disclosure

(1) If a secured creditor omits to disclose his security in his proof of debt, he shall surrender his security for the general benefit of creditors, unless the court, on application by him, relieves him from the effect of this Rule on the ground that the omission was inadvertent or the result of honest mistake.

(2) If the court grants that relief, it may require or allow the creditor's proof of debt to be amended, on such terms as may be just.

[(3) Nothing in this Rule or the following two Rules may affect the rights in rem of creditors or third parties protected under Article 5 of the EC Regulation (third parties' rights in rem).]

NOTES

Initial Commencement

Specified date

Specified date: 29 December 1986: see r 0.1.

Amendment

Para (3): inserted by SI 2002/1307, rr 3(1), 8(7).
Date in force: 31 May 2002: see SI 2002/1307, r 1.

6.117 Redemption by trustee

(1) The trustee may at any time give notice to a creditor whose debt is secured that he proposes, at the expiration of 28 days from the date of the notice, to redeem the security at the value put upon it in the creditor's proof.

(2) The creditor then has 21 days (or such longer period as the trustee may allow) in which, if he so wishes, to exercise his right to re-value his security (with the [permission] of the court, where Rule 6.115(2) applies).

If the creditor re-values his security, the trustee may only redeem at the new value.

(3) If the trustee redeems the security, the cost of transferring it is borne by the estate.

(4) A secured creditor may at any time, by a notice in writing, call on the trustee to elect whether he will or will not exercise his power to redeem the security at the value then placed on it; and the trustee then has [3 months] in which to exercise the power or determine not to exercise it.

NOTES

Initial Commencement

Specified date

Specified date: 29 December 1986: see r 0.1.

Amendment

Para (2): word "permission" in square brackets substituted by SI 2010/686, r 2, Sch 1, para 1.
Date in force: 6 April 2010: see SI 2010/686, r 1; for transitional provisions see r 6(1), Sch 4, paras 1, 2(1)(b) thereto.

Para (4): words "3 months" in square brackets substituted by SI 2010/686, r 2, Sch 1, para 355.
Date in force: 6 April 2010: see SI 2010/686, r 1; for transitional provisions see r 6(1), Sch 4, para 1 thereto.

6.118 Test of security's value

(1) Subject as follows, the trustee, if he is dissatisfied with the value which a secured creditor puts on his security (whether in his proof or by way of re-valuation under Rule 6.117), may require any property comprised in the security to be offered for sale.

(2) The terms of sale shall be such as may be agreed, or as the court may direct; and if the sale is by auction, the trustee on behalf of the estate, and the creditor on his own behalf, may appear and bid.

(3) This Rule does not apply if the security has been re-valued and the re-valuation has been approved by the court.

NOTES

Initial Commencement

Specified date

Specified date: 29 December 1986: see r 0.1.

6.119 Realisation of security by creditor

If a creditor who has valued his security subsequently realises it (whether or not at the instance of the trustee)—

- (a) the net amount realised shall be substituted for the value previously put by the creditor on the security; and
- (b) that amount shall be treated in all respects as an amended valuation made by him.

NOTES

Initial Commencement

Specified date

Specified date: 29 December 1986: see r 0.1.

CHAPTER 10

THE TRUSTEE IN BANKRUPTCY

SECTION A: APPOINTMENT AND ASSOCIATED FORMALITIES

6.120 Appointment by creditors' meeting

(1) This Rule applies where a person has been appointed trustee by resolution of a creditors' meeting.

(2) The chairman of the meeting shall certify the appointment, but not unless and until the person to be appointed has provided him with a written statement to the effect that he is an insolvency practitioner, duly qualified under the Act to act as trustee in relation to the bankrupt, and that he consents so to act.

[(3) The trustee's appointment is effective from the date on which the appointment is certified, that date to be endorsed on the certificate.

(4) The chairman of the meeting (if not himself the official receiver) shall send the certificate to the official receiver.

(5) The official receiver shall in any case send the certificate to the trustee . . ..]

NOTES

Initial Commencement

Specified date

Specified date: 29 December 1986: see r 0.1.

Amendment

Paras (3)–(5): substituted for paras (3), (4) as originally enacted, by SI 1987/1919, r 3(1), Schedule, Part 1, para 113.

Para (5): words omitted revoked by SI 2010/686, r 2, Sch 1, para 356.
Date in force: 6 April 2010: see SI 2010/686, r 1; for transitional provisions see r 6(1), Sch 4, para 1 thereto.

[6.120A Official receiver not to be appointed trustee]
[The official receiver may not be appointed as trustee by resolution of a creditors' meeting.]

NOTES

Amendment

>Inserted by SI 2010/686, r 2, Sch 1, para 357.
>>Date in force: 6 April 2010: see SI 2010/686, r 1; for transitional provisions see r 6(1), Sch 4, para 1 thereto.

6.121 Appointment by the court

(1) This Rule applies where the court under section 297. . . (4) or (5) appoints the trustee.

(2) The court's order shall not issue unless and until the person appointed has filed in court a statement to the effect that he is an insolvency practitioner, duly qualified under the Act to be the trustee, and that he consents so to act.

(3) Thereafter, the court shall send 2 copies of the order to the official receiver. One of the copies shall be sealed, and this shall be sent by him to the person appointed as trustee.

(4) The trustee's appointment takes effect from the date of the order.

NOTES

Initial Commencement

Specified date

>Specified date: 29 December 1986: see r 0.1.

Amendment

>Para (1): reference omitted revoked by SI 2003/1730, r 9(1), Sch 1, Pt 6, para 38.
>>Date in force: 1 April 2004: see SI 2003/1730, r 1(3).

6.122 Appointment by Secretary of State

(1) This Rule applies where the official receiver—
  (a) under section 295 or 300, refers to the Secretary of State the need for an appointment of a trustee, or
  (b) under section 296, applies to the Secretary of State to make the appointment.

(2) If the Secretary of State makes an appointment he shall send [a copy] of the certificate of appointment to the official receiver, who shall transmit [it] to the person appointed. . ..

The certificate shall specify the date from which the trustee's appointment is to be effective.

NOTES

Initial Commencement

Specified date

>Specified date: 29 December 1986: see r 0.1.

Amendment

>Para (2): words "a copy" in square brackets substituted by SI 2010/686, r 2, Sch 1, para 358(1), (2)(a).

Date in force: 6 April 2010: see SI 2010/686, r 1; for transitional provisions see r 6(1), Sch 4, para 1 thereto.
Para (2): word "it" in square brackets substituted by SI 2010/686, r 2, Sch 1, para 358(1), (2)(b).
Date in force: 6 April 2010: see SI 2010/686, r 1; for transitional provisions see r 6(1), Sch 4, para 1 thereto.
Para (2): words omitted revoked by SI 2010/686, r 2, Sch 1, para 358(1), (2)(c).
Date in force: 6 April 2010: see SI 2010/686, r 1; for transitional provisions see r 6(1), Sch 4, para 1 thereto.

6.123 Authentication of trustee's appointment

Where a trustee is appointed under any of [Rules 6.120, 6.121 and 6.122], a sealed copy of the order of appointment or (as the case may be) a copy of the certificate of his appointment may in any proceedings be adduced as proof that he is duly authorised to exercise the powers and perform the duties of trustee of the bankrupt's estate.

NOTES

Initial Commencement

Specified date

Specified date: 29 December 1986: see r 0.1.

Amendment

Words "Rules 6.120, 6.121 and 6.122" in square brackets substituted by SI 2010/686, r 2, Sch 1, para 359.
Date in force: 6 April 2010: see SI 2010/686, r 1; for transitional provisions see r 6(1), Sch 4, para 1 thereto.

6.124 Advertisement of appointment

[(1) A trustee who is appointed by a creditors' meeting, as soon as reasonably practicable after receiving the certificate of appointment, shall give notice of that appointment. Such notice—

(a) shall be gazetted; and

(b) may be advertised in other such manner as the trustee thinks fit.]

[(1A) In addition to the standard contents, the notice under paragraph (1) must state—

(a) that a trustee has been appointed by a creditors' meeting; and

(b) the date of the appointment.]

(2) The expense of giving the notice shall be borne in the first instance by the trustee; but he is entitled to be reimbursed by the estate, as an expense of the bankruptcy.

The same applies also in the case of the notice or advertisement under section 296(4) (appointment of trustee by Secretary of State), and of the notice or advertisement under section 297(7) (appointment by the court).

NOTES

Initial Commencement

Specified date

Specified date: 29 December 1986: see r 0.1.

Amendment

Para (1): substituted by SI 2009/642, rr 4, 42.
Date in force: 6 April 2009: see SI 2009/642, r 1; for transitional provisions see r 3 thereof.

Para (1A): inserted by SI 2010/686, r 2, Sch 1, para 360.
   Date in force: 6 April 2010: see SI 2010/686, r 1; for transitional provisions see r 6(1), Sch 4, para 1 thereto.

6.125 Hand-over of estate to trustee

(1) This Rule applies only where—
   (a) the bankrupt's estate vests in the trustee under Chapter IV of Part IX of the Act, following a period in which the official receiver is the receiver and manager of the estate according to section 287, or
   (b) the trustee is appointed in succession to the official receiver acting as trustee.

(2) When the trustee's appointment takes effect, the official receiver shall [as soon as reasonably practicable] do all that is required for putting him into possession of the estate.

(3) On taking possession of the estate, the trustee shall discharge any balance due to the official receiver on account of—
   (a) expenses properly incurred by him and payable under the Act or the Rules, and
   (b) any advances made by him in respect of the estate, together with interest on such advances at the rate specified in section 17 of the Judgments Act 1838 on the date of the bankruptcy order.

(4) Alternatively, the trustee may (before taking office) give to the official receiver a written undertaking to discharge any such balance out of the first realisation of assets.

(5) The official receiver has a charge on the estate in respect of any sums due to him under paragraph (3). But, where the trustee has realised assets with a view to making those payments, the official receiver's charge does not extend in respect of sums deductible by the trustee from the proceeds of realisation, as being expenses properly incurred therein.

(6) The trustee shall from time to time out of the realisation of assets discharge all guarantees properly given by the official receiver for the benefit of the estate, and shall pay all the official receiver's expenses.

(7) The official receiver shall give to the trustee all such information, relating to the affairs of the bankrupt and the course of the bankruptcy, as he (the official receiver) considers to be reasonably required for the effective discharge by the trustee of his duties in relation to the estate.

(8) The trustee shall also be furnished with any report of the official receiver under Chapter 6 of this Part of the Rules.

NOTES

Initial Commencement

Specified date

   Specified date: 29 December 1986: see r 0.1.

Amendment

   Para (2): words "as soon as reasonably practicable" in square brackets substituted by SI 2009/642, rr 4, 5.
      Date in force: 6 April 2009: see SI 2009/642, r 1; for transitional provisions see r 3 thereof.

SECTION B: RESIGNATION AND REMOVAL; VACATION OF OFFICE

6.126 Creditors' meeting to receive trustee's resignation

(1) Before resigning his office, the trustee must call a meeting of creditors for the purpose of receiving his resignation. . . .

[(1A) The trustee must give at least 28 days' notice of the meeting.

(1B) The notice summoning the meeting must—

(a) indicate that the purpose or one of the purposes of the meeting is to receive the trustee's resignation; and

(b) draw the attention of the creditors to Rule 6.142.

(1C) Notice of the meeting must be sent to the official receiver and to the bankrupt at the same time as it is sent to creditors.]

[(2) The notice to creditors and the bankrupt must be accompanied by an account of the trustee's administration of the bankrupt's estate, including—

(a) a statement that the trustee has reconciled the account with that held by the Secretary of State in respect of the bankruptcy; and

(b) a progress report for the period—

(i) commencing with the later of the date of—

(aa) the appointment of the trustee; and

(bb) the day immediately following the end of the period of the last progress report; and

(ii) ending with the date of the meeting.]

(3) Subject as follows, the trustee may only proceed under this Rule on grounds of ill health or because—

(a) he intends ceasing to be in practice as an insolvency practitioner, or

(b) there is some conflict of interest or change of personal circumstances which precludes or makes impracticable the further discharge by him of the duties of trustee.

(4) Where two or more persons are acting as trustee jointly, any one of them may proceed under this Rule (without prejudice to the continuation in office of the other or others) on the ground that, in his opinion and that of the other or others, it is no longer expedient that there should continue to be the present number of joint trustees.

[(5) [Except where Rule 6.126A applies,] if there is no quorum present at the meeting summoned to receive the trustee's resignation, the meeting is deemed to have been held, a resolution is deemed to have been passed that the trustee's resignation be accepted and the creditors are deemed not to have resolved against the trustee having his release.

(6) Where paragraph (5) applies any reference in the Rules to a resolution that the trustee's resignation be accepted is replaced by a reference to the making of a written statement, [authenticated] by the person who, had there been a quorum present, would have been chairman of the meeting, that no quorum was present and that the trustee may resign.]

NOTES

Initial Commencement

Specified date

Specified date: 29 December 1986: see r 0.1.

Amendment

Para (1): words omitted revoked by SI 2010/686, r 2, Sch 1, para 361(1), (2)(a).
Date in force: 6 April 2010: see SI 2010/686, r 1; for transitional provisions see r 6(1), Sch 4, para 1 thereto.
Paras (1A)–(1C): inserted by SI 2010/686, r 2, Sch 1, para 361(1), (2)(b).

Date in force: 6 April 2010: see SI 2010/686, r 1; for transitional provisions see r 6(1), Sch 4, para 1 thereto.
Para (2): substituted by SI 2010/686, r 2, Sch 1, para 361(1), (3).
Date in force: 6 April 2010: see SI 2010/686, r 1; for transitional provisions see r 6(1), Sch 4, para 1 thereto.
Paras (5), (6): inserted by SI 1987/1919, r 3(1), Schedule, Part 1, para 114.
Para (5): words "Except where Rule 6.126A applies," in square brackets inserted by SI 2010/686, r 2, Sch 1, para 361(1), (4).
Date in force: 6 April 2010: see SI 2010/686, r 1; for transitional provisions see r 6(1), Sch 4, para 1 thereto.
Para (6): word "authenticated" in square brackets substituted by SI 2010/686, r 2, Sch 1, para 1.
Date in force: 6 April 2010: see SI 2010/686, r 1; for transitional provisions see r 6(1), Sch 4, paras 1, 2(1)(b) thereto.

[6.126A Resignation (application under Rule 6.142)]

[(1) This Rule applies where at the date of a meeting summoned for the purpose of receiving the trustee's resignation, an application made to the court under Rule 6.142 (including any appeal) has not been disposed of.

(2) At the meeting no resolution may be put regarding the trustee's release.

(3) If at the meeting the trustee's resignation is accepted the meeting must be adjourned (notwithstanding anything in Rule 6.90 (suspension of meeting)) to a day not less than 14 days after the day on which the application under Rule 6.142 (including any appeal) has been disposed of.

(4) The trustee must give at least 14 days' notice of the meeting adjourned in accordance with paragraph (3) to the creditors.

(5) At the meeting adjourned in accordance with paragraph (3)—

(a) a revised version of the account which accompanied the notice of the meeting must be laid showing any changes required as a result, or arising out of the application under Rule 6.142; and

(b) a resolution for the release of the trustee whose resignation has been accepted must be put.

(6) If there is no quorum present at the adjourned meeting, the meeting is deemed to have been held and the creditors are deemed to have resolved that the trustee be released.

(7) Where the creditors have resolved at the adjourned meeting that the trustee be released (or are deemed to have so resolved by virtue of paragraph (5))—

(a) the chairman of the meeting (or the person who, had there been a quorum present would have been chairman of the meeting) must send as soon as reasonably practicable a certificate to that effect to the official receiver with a copy of the revised account; and

(b) the official receiver must file a copy of the certificate in court.

(8) If at the meeting the trustee's resignation is not accepted, the trustee must not summon any further meeting under Rule 6.126 until the application under Rule 6.142 (including any appeal) has been disposed of.

(9) Paragraph (7) is subject to the powers of the court on an application being made to it by the trustee under Rule 6.128 (permission to resign granted by the court).

(10) Rule 6.126 applies to any such further meeting with the modification that the account required to accompany the notice of the meeting must show any changes from the account which accompanied the notice of the earlier meeting called to receive the trustee's resignation, and in particular any changes required as a result of the application under Rule 6.142 and any further remuneration charged or expenses incurred.

(11) The creditors' rights under Rules 6.78C and 6.142 do not apply in respect of any matter included in that account which—

(a) was included in the account which accompanied the notice of the earlier meeting called to receive the trustee's resignation; or
(b) was the subject of the order of the court on the application made to it by the trustee under Rule 6.142.]

NOTES

Amendment

Inserted by SI 2010/686, r 2, Sch 1, para 362.
Date in force: 6 April 2010: see SI 2010/686, r 1; for transitional provisions see r 6(1), Sch 4, para 1 thereto.

6.127 Action following acceptance of resignation

(1) . . .
(2) . . .
(3) Where the chairman of the [creditors' meeting summoned for the purpose of receiving the trustee's resignation] is other than the official receiver, and there is passed at the meeting any of the following resolutions—

(a) that the trustee's resignation be accepted,
(b) that a new trustee be appointed,
(c) that the resigning trustee be not given his release,

the chairman shall, within 3 [business days of the date of the resolution], send to the official receiver a copy of the resolution.

If it has been resolved to accept the trustee's resignation, the chairman shall send to the official receiver a certificate to that effect.

(4) If the creditors have resolved to appoint a new trustee, the certificate of his appointment shall also be sent to the official receiver within that time; and Rule 6.120 above shall be complied with in respect of it.

(5) If the trustee's resignation is accepted, the notice of it required by section 298(7) shall be given by him [as soon as reasonably practicable] after the [resolution has been passed]; and he shall send a copy of the notice to the official receiver.

The notice shall be accompanied by a copy of the account sent to creditors under Rule 6.126(2).

(6) The official receiver shall file a copy of the notice in court.

(7) The trustee's resignation is effective as from the date on which the official receiver files the copy notice in court, that date to be endorsed on the copy notice.

NOTES

Initial Commencement

Specified date

Specified date: 29 December 1986: see r 0.1.

Amendment

Paras (1), (2): revoked by SI 2010/686, r 2, Sch 1, para 363(1), (2).
Date in force: 6 April 2010: see SI 2010/686, r 1; for transitional provisions see r 6(1), Sch 4, para 1 thereto.
Para (3): words "creditors' meeting summoned for the purpose of receiving the trustee's resignation" in square brackets substituted by SI 2010/686, r 2, Sch 1, para 363(1), (3)(a).
Date in force: 6 April 2010: see SI 2010/686, r 1; for transitional provisions see r 6(1), Sch 4, para 1 thereto.
Para (3): words "business days of the date of the resolution" in square brackets substituted by SI 2010/686, r 2, Sch 1, para 363(1), (3)(b).

Date in force: 6 April 2010: see SI 2010/686, r 1; for transitional provisions see r 6(1), Sch 4, para 1 thereto.
Para (5): words "as soon as reasonably practicable" in square brackets substituted by SI 2009/642, rr 4, 5.
Date in force: 6 April 2009: see SI 2009/642, r 1; for transitional provisions see r 3 thereto.
Para (5): words "resolution has been passed" in square brackets substituted by SI 2010/686, r 2, Sch 1, para 363(1), (4).
Date in force: 6 April 2010: see SI 2010/686, r 1; for transitional provisions see r 6(1), Sch 4, para 1 thereto.

6.128 [Permission] to resign granted by the court

(1) If at a creditors' meeting summoned to accept the trustee's resignation it is resolved that it be not accepted, the court may, on the trustee's application, make an order giving him [permission] to resign.

(2) The court's order under this Rule may include such provision as it thinks [just] with respect to matters arising in connection with the resignation, and shall determine the date from which the trustee's release is effective.

(3) The court shall send two sealed copies of the order to the trustee, who shall send one of the copies [as soon as reasonably practicable] to the official receiver.

(4) On sending notice of his resignation to the court, as required by section 298(7), the trustee shall send a copy of it to the official receiver.

NOTES

Initial Commencement

Specified date

Specified date: 29 December 1986: see r 0.1.

Amendment

Provision heading: word "Permission" in square brackets substituted by SI 2010/686, r 2, Sch 1, para 1.
Date in force: 6 April 2010: see SI 2010/686, r 1; for transitional provisions see r 6(1), Sch 4, paras 1, 2(1)(b) thereto.
Para (1): word "permission" in square brackets substituted by SI 2010/686, r 2, Sch 1, para 1.
Date in force: 6 April 2010: see SI 2010/686, r 1; for transitional provisions see r 6(1), Sch 4, paras 1, 2(1)(b) thereto.
Para (2): word "just" in square brackets substituted by SI 2010/686, r 2, Sch 1, para 1.
Date in force: 6 April 2010: see SI 2010/686, r 1; for transitional provisions see r 6(1), Sch 4, paras 1, 2(1)(b) thereto.
Para (3): words "as soon as reasonably practicable" in square brackets substituted by SI 2009/642, rr 4, 5.
Date in force: 6 April 2009: see SI 2009/642, r 1; for transitional provisions see r 3 thereto.

6.129 Meeting of creditors to remove trustee

(1) Where a meeting of creditors is summoned for the purpose of removing the trustee, the notice summoning it shall indicate that this is the purpose, or one of the purposes, of the meeting; and the notice shall draw the attention of creditors to section 299(3) with respect to the trustee's release.

(2) A copy of the notice shall at the same time also be sent to the official receiver.

(3) At the meeting, a person other than the trustee or his nominee may be elected to act as chairman; but if the trustee or his nominee is chairman and a resolution has been proposed for the trustee's removal, the chairman shall not adjourn the meeting without the consent of at least one-half (in value) of the creditors present (in person or by proxy) and entitled to vote.

(4) Where the chairman of the meeting is other than the official receiver, and there is passed at the meeting any of the following resolutions—
- (a) that the trustee be removed,
- (b) that a new trustee be appointed,
- (c) that the removed trustee be not given his release,

the chairman shall, within 3 [business] days, send to the official receiver a copy of the resolution.

If it has been resolved to remove the trustee, the chairman shall send to the official receiver a certificate to that effect.

(5) If the creditors have resolved to appoint a new trustee, the certificate of his appointment shall also be sent to the official receiver within that time; and rule 6.120 shall be complied with in respect of it.

NOTES

Initial Commencement

Specified date

Specified date: 29 December 1986: see r 0.1.

Amendment

Para (4): word "business" in square brackets inserted by SI 2010/686, r 2, Sch 1, para 364. Date in force: 6 April 2010: see SI 2010/686, r 1; for transitional provisions see r 6(1), Sch 4, para 1 thereto.

6.130 Court's power to regulate meeting under Rule 6.129

Where a meeting under Rule 6.129 is to be held, or is proposed to be summoned, the court may on the application of any creditor give directions as to the mode of summoning it, the sending out and return of forms of proxy, the conduct of the meeting, and any other matter which appears to the court to require regulation or control.

NOTES

Initial Commencement

Specified date

Specified date: 29 December 1986: see r 0.1.

6.131 Procedure on removal

(1) Where the creditors have resolved that the trustee be removed, the official receiver shall file the certificate of removal in court.

(2) The resolution is effective as from the date on which the official receiver files the certificate of removal in court, and that date shall be endorsed on the certificate.

(3) A copy of the certificate, so endorsed, shall be sent by the official receiver to the trustee who has been removed and, if a new trustee has been appointed, to him.

(4) The official receiver shall not file the certificate in court until the Secretary of State has certified to him that the removed trustee has reconciled his account with that held by the Secretary of State in respect of the bankruptcy.

NOTES

Initial Commencement

Specified date

Specified date: 29 December 1986: see r 0.1.

6.132 Removal of trustee by the court

(1) This Rule applies where application is made to the court for the removal of the trustee, or for an order directing the trustee to summon a meeting of creditors for the purpose of removing him.

(2) The court may, if it thinks that no sufficient cause is shown for the application, dismiss it; but it shall not do so unless the applicant has had an opportunity to attend the court for [a] hearing, of which he has been given at least [5 business] days' notice [but which is without notice to any other party].
If the application is not dismissed under this paragraph, the court shall fix a venue for it to be heard.

(3) The applicant shall, at least 14 days before the hearing, send to the trustee and the official receiver notice stating the venue so fixed; and the notice shall be accompanied by a copy of the application, and of any evidence which the applicant intends to adduce in support of it.

(4) Subject to any contrary order of the court, the costs of the application do not fall on the estate.

(5) Where the court removes the trustee—
   (a) it shall send copies of the order of removal to him and to the official receiver;
   (b) the order may include such provision as the court thinks [just] with respect to matters arising in connection with the removal; and
   (c) if the court appoints a new trustee, Rule 6.121 applies.

NOTES

Initial Commencement

Specified date

Specified date: 29 December 1986: see r 0.1.

Amendment

Para (2): word "a" in square brackets substituted by SI 2010/686, r 2, Sch 1, para 365(1), (2)(a).
   Date in force: 6 April 2010: see SI 2010/686, r 1; for transitional provisions see r 6(1), Sch 4, paras 1, 2(1)(b) thereto.
Para (2): words "5 business" in square brackets substituted by SI 2010/686, r 2, Sch 1, para 365(1), (2)(b).
   Date in force: 6 April 2010: see SI 2010/686, r 1; for transitional provisions see r 6(1), Sch 4, para 1 thereto.
Para (2): words "but which is without notice to any other party" in square brackets inserted by SI 2010/686, r 2, Sch 1, para 365(1), (2)(c).
   Date in force: 6 April 2010: see SI 2010/686, r 1; for transitional provisions see r 6(1), Sch 4, paras 1, 2(1)(b) thereto.
Para (5): in sub-para (b) word "just" in square brackets substituted by SI 2010/686, r 2, Sch 1, para 1.
   Date in force: 6 April 2010: see SI 2010/686, r 1; for transitional provisions see r 6(1), Sch 4, paras 1, 2(1)(b) thereto.

6.133 Removal of trustee by Secretary of State

(1) If the Secretary of State decides to remove the trustee, he shall before doing so notify the trustee and the official receiver of his decision and the grounds of it, and specify a period within which the trustee may make representations against implementation of the decision.

(2) If the Secretary of State directs the removal of the trustee, he shall [as soon as reasonably practicable]—

    (a)   file notice of his decision in court, and

    (b)   send notice to the trustee and the official receiver.

(3) If the trustee is removed by direction of the Secretary of State, the court may make any such order in his case as it would have power to make if he had been removed by itself.

NOTES

Initial Commencement

Specified date
    Specified date: 29 December 1986: see r 0.1.

Amendment
    Para (2): words "as soon as reasonably practicable" in square brackets substituted by SI 2009/642, rr 4, 5.
        Date in force: 6 April 2009: see SI 2009/642, r 1; for transitional provisions see r 3 thereof.

6.134 [Notice] of resignation or removal

Where a new trustee is appointed in place of one who has resigned or been removed, the new trustee shall, in the [notice] of his appointment, state that his predecessor has resigned or, as the case may be, been removed and (if it be the case) that he has been given his release.

NOTES

Initial Commencement

Specified date
    Specified date: 29 December 1986: see r 0.1.

Amendment
    Provision heading: word "Notice" in square brackets substituted by SI 2009/642, rr 4, 43.
        Date in force: 6 April 2009: see SI 2009/642, r 1; for transitional provisions see r 3 thereof.
    Word "notice" in square brackets substituted by SI 2009/642, rr 4, 43.
        Date in force: 6 April 2009: see SI 2009/642, r 1; for transitional provisions see r 3 thereof.

6.135 Release of resigning or removed trustee

(1) [Subject to paragraph (1A),] where the trustee's resignation is accepted by a meeting of creditors which has not resolved against his release, he has his release from when his resignation is effective under Rule 6.127.

[(1A) Where the trustee's resignation is accepted under Rule 6.126A, the trustee's release is effective as from the date on which the official receiver files the copy of the certificate under paragraph (7) of that Rule in court, that date to be endorsed on the copy certificate.]

(2) Where the trustee is removed by a meeting of creditors which has not resolved against his release, the fact of his release shall be stated in the certificate of removal.

(3) Where—
(a) the trustee resigns, and the creditors' meeting called to receive his resignation has resolved against his release, or
(b) he is removed by a creditors' meeting which has so resolved, or is removed by the court,
he must apply to the Secretary of State for his release.

(4) When the Secretary of State gives the release, he shall certify it accordingly, and send the certificate to the official receiver, to be filed in court.

(5) A copy of the certificate shall be sent by the Secretary of State to the former trustee, whose release is effective from the date of the certificate.

NOTES

Initial Commencement

Specified date

Specified date: 29 December 1986: see r 0.1.

Amendment

Para (1): words "Subject to paragraph (1A)," in square brackets inserted by SI 2010/686, r 2, Sch 1, para 366(1), (2).
Date in force: 6 April 2010: see SI 2010/686, r 1; for transitional provisions see r 6(1), Sch 4, para 1 thereto.
Para (1A): inserted by SI 2010/686, r 2, Sch 1, para 366(1), (3).
Date in force: 6 April 2010: see SI 2010/686, r 1; for transitional provisions see r 6(1), Sch 4, para 1 thereto.

SECTION C: RELEASE ON COMPLETION OF ADMINISTRATION

6.136 Release of official receiver

(1) The official receiver shall, before giving notice to the Secretary of State under section 299(2) (that the administration of the estate is for practical purposes complete), send out notice of his intention to do so to all creditors [of which he is aware], and to the bankrupt.

(2) The notice shall in each case be accompanied by a summary of the official receiver's receipts and payments as trustee.

(3) The Secretary of State, when he has under section 299(2) determined the date from which the official receiver is to have his release, shall give notice to the court that he has done so. The notice shall be accompanied by the summary referred to in paragraph (2).

NOTES

Initial Commencement

Specified date

Specified date: 29 December 1986: see r 0.1.

Amendment

Para (1): words "of which he is aware" in square brackets substituted by SI 2004/584, r 30.
Date in force: 1 April 2004: see SI 2004/584, r 1(2).

6.137 Final meeting of creditors

(1) Where the trustee is other than the official receiver, he shall give at least 28 days' notice of the final meeting of creditors to be held under section 331. The notice shall be sent to all creditors [of which he is aware], and to the bankrupt.

[(1A) The trustee—

(a) as soon as reasonably practicable after giving notice under paragraph (1) must have gazetted a notice of the final meeting; and
(b) may advertise notice of the meeting in such other manner as the trustee thinks fit.

(1B) In addition to the standard contents, the notice under paragraph (1A) must state—
(a) that the trustee has summoned the meeting;
(b) if the meeting was summoned at the request of a creditor, the fact that it was so summoned and the section of the Act under which it was summoned;
(c) the purpose for which the meeting was summoned;
(d) the venue fixed for the meeting; and
(e) the time and date by which, and place at which, creditors must lodge proxies and hitherto unlodged proofs in order to be entitled to vote at the meeting.

(1C) The final meeting must not be held unless Rule 6.78B has been complied with; and if for that reason the meeting is not held—
(a) the trustee must give notice of that fact as soon as reasonably practicable to all to whom notice of the meeting was given, and
(b) fresh notice of the meeting complying with this Rule must be given when Rule 6.78B has been complied with.]

(2) The trustee's report laid before the meeting under that section shall include—
(a) a summary of his receipts and payments, [including details of remuneration charged and expenses incurred by the trustee,
(ab) details of the basis fixed for the trustee's remuneration, and]
(b) a statement by him that he has reconciled his account with that which is held by the Secretary of State in respect of the bankruptcy.

[(2A) Where the trustee has sent a progress report to creditors in accordance with Rule 6.78A, the report to be laid at the final meeting of creditors must also—
(a) contain a receipts and payments account in the form of an abstract showing the receipts and payments during the period since the last progress report, and
(b) include—
(i) details of the remuneration charged and expenses incurred by the trustee during that period, and
(ii) a description of the things done by the trustee during that period in respect of which that remuneration was charged and those expenses incurred.

(2B) In any case where the basis of the trustee's remuneration had not been fixed by the date to which the last progress report was made up, the receipts and payments account required by paragraph (2A)(a) must also include details of the remuneration charged in the period of any preceding progress report in which details of remuneration were not included.

(2C) Where the basis of remuneration has been fixed as a set amount only, it is sufficient compliance with paragraph (2A)(b) for the trustee to state the amount which has been set and to supply details of the expenses charged within the period in question.]

(3) At the final meeting, the creditors may question the trustee with respect to any matter contained in his report, and may resolve against him having his release.

(4) The trustee shall give notice to the court that the final meeting has been held; and the notice shall state whether or not he has been given his release, and be accompanied by a copy of the report laid before the final meeting. A copy of the notice shall be sent by the trustee to the [Secretary of State].

(5) If there is no quorum present at the final meeting, the trustee shall report to the court that a final meeting was summoned in accordance with the Rules, but there was

no quorum present; and the final meeting is then deemed to have been held, and the creditors not to have resolved against the trustee having his release.

(6) If the creditors at the final meeting have not so resolved, the trustee is released when the notice under paragraph (4) is filed in court. If they have so resolved, the trustee must obtain his release from the Secretary of State, as provided by Rule 6.135.

NOTES

Initial Commencement

Specified date

Specified date: 29 December 1986: see r 0.1.

Amendment

Para (1): words "of which he is aware" in square brackets substituted by SI 2004/584, r 31.
Date in force: 1 April 2004: see SI 2004/584, r 1(2).
Paras (1A)–(1C): inserted by SI 2010/686, r 2, Sch 1, para 367(1), (2).
Date in force: 6 April 2010: see SI 2010/686, r 1; for transitional provisions see r 6(1), Sch 4, para 1 thereto.
Para (2): in sub-para (a) words "including details of remuneration charged and expenses incurred by the trustee," in square brackets and sub-para (ab) substituted by SI 2010/686, r 2, Sch 1, para 367(1), (3).
Date in force: 6 April 2010: see SI 2010/686, r 1; for transitional provisions see r 6(1), Sch 4, para 1 thereto.
Paras (2A)–(2C): inserted by SI 2010/686, r 2, Sch 1, para 367(1), (4).
Date in force: 6 April 2010: see SI 2010/686, r 1; for transitional provisions see r 6(1), Sch 4, para 1 thereto.
Para (4): words "Secretary of State" in square brackets substituted by SI 2005/527, r 38.
Date in force: 1 April 2005: see SI 2005/527, r 1(2).

[6.137A Rule as to reporting]

[(1) The court may, on the trustee or official receiver's application, relieve him of any duty imposed on him by Rules 6.136 or 6.137, or authorise him to carry out the duty in a way other than there required.

(2) In considering whether to act as above, the court shall have regard to the cost of carrying out the duty, to the amount of the funds available in the estate, and to the extent of the interest of creditors or any particular class of them.]

NOTES

Amendment

Inserted by SI 2004/584, r 32.
Date in force: 1 April 2004: see SI 2004/584, r 1(2).

SECTION D: REMUNERATION

6.138 Fixing of remuneration

(1) The trustee is entitled to receive remuneration for his services as such.
(2) [The basis of remuneration] shall be fixed . . .—
- (a) as a percentage of the value of the assets in the bankrupt's estate which are realised or distributed, or of the one value and the other in combination, or
- (b) by reference to the time properly given by the insolvency practitioner (as trustee) and his staff in attending to matters arising in the bankruptcy[, or
- (c) as a set amount].

[(3A) The basis of remuneration may be fixed as any one or more of the bases set out in paragraph (2), and different bases may be fixed in respect of different things done by the trustee.

(3B) Where remuneration is fixed as set out in paragraph (2)(a), different percentages may be fixed in respect of different things done by the trustee.

(3C) Where the trustee is other than the official receiver, it is for the creditors' committee (if there is one) to determine—

- (a) which of the bases set out in paragraph (2) are to be fixed and (where appropriate) in what combination under paragraph (3A), and
- (b) the percentage or percentages (if any) to be fixed under paragraphs (2)(a) and (3B) and the amount (if any) to be set under paragraph (2)(c).]

(4) In arriving at that determination, the committee shall have regard to the following matters—

- (a) the complexity (or otherwise) of the case,
- (b) any respects in which, in connection with the administration of the estate, there falls on the insolvency practitioner (as trustee) any responsibility of an exceptional kind or degree,
- (c) the effectiveness with which the insolvency practitioner appears to be carrying out, or to have carried out, his duties as trustee, and
- (d) the value and nature of the assets in the estate with which the trustee has to deal.

(5) If there is no creditors' committee, or the committee does not make the requisite determination, [the basis of] the trustee's remuneration may be fixed (in accordance with [paragraphs (2), (3A) and (3B)]) by a resolution of a meeting of creditors; and paragraph (4) applies to them as it does to the creditors' committee.

[(6) Where the trustee is not the official receiver and [the basis of] his remuneration is not fixed as above [within 18 months after the date of the trustee's appointment], the trustee shall be entitled to remuneration calculated in accordance with Rule 6.138A.]

NOTES

Initial Commencement

Specified date

Specified date: 29 December 1986: see r 0.1.

Amendment

Para (2): words "The basis of remuneration" in square brackets substituted by SI 2010/686, r 2, Sch 1, para 368(1), (2)(a).
Date in force: 6 April 2010: see SI 2010/686, r 1; for transitional provisions see r 6(1), Sch 4, para 1 thereto.
Para (2): word omitted revoked by SI 2010/686, r 2, Sch 1, para 368(1), (2)(b).
Date in force: 6 April 2010: see SI 2010/686, r 1; for transitional provisions see r 6(1), Sch 4, para 1 thereto.
Para (2): sub-para (c) and word ", or" immediately preceding it inserted by SI 2010/686, r 2, Sch 1, para 368(1), (2)(c).
Date in force: 6 April 2010: see SI 2010/686, r 1; for transitional provisions see r 6(1), Sch 4, para 1 thereto.
Paras (3A)–(3C): substituted, for para (3) as originally enacted, by SI 2010/686, r 2, Sch 1, para 368(1), (3).
Date in force: 6 April 2010: see SI 2010/686, r 1; for transitional provisions see r 6(1), Sch 4, para 1 thereto.
Para (5): words "the basis of" in square brackets inserted by SI 2010/686, r 2, Sch 1, para 368(1), (4)(a).
Date in force: 6 April 2010: see SI 2010/686, r 1; for transitional provisions see r 6(1), Sch 4, para 1 thereto.

Para (5): words "paragraphs (2), (3A) and (3B)" in square brackets substituted by SI 2010/686, r 2, Sch 1, para 368(1), (4)(b).
    Date in force: 6 April 2010: see SI 2010/686, r 1; for transitional provisions see r 6(1), Sch 4, para 1 thereto.
Para (6): substituted by SI 2004/584, r 33.
    Date in force: 1 April 2004: see SI 2004/584, r 1(2); for transitional provisions see r 3 thereof.
Para (6): words "the basis of" in square brackets inserted by SI 2010/686, r 2, Sch 1, para 368(1), (5)(a).
    Date in force: 6 April 2010: see SI 2010/686, r 1; for transitional provisions see r 6(1), Sch 4, para 1 thereto.
Para (6): words "within 18 months after the date of the trustee's appointment" in square brackets inserted by SI 2010/686, r 2, Sch 1, para 368(1), (5)(b).
    Date in force: 6 April 2010: see SI 2010/686, r 1; for transitional provisions see r 6(1), Sch 4, para 1 thereto.

[6.138A Trustee's remuneration where it is not fixed in accordance with Rule 6.138]

[(1) This Rule applies where the trustee is not the official receiver and his remuneration is not fixed in accordance with Rule 6.138.

(2) Subject to paragraph (3), the trustee shall be entitled by way of remuneration for his services as such, to such sum as is arrived at by—

(a) first applying the realisation scale set out in Schedule 6 to the monies received by him from the realisation of the assets of the bankrupt (including any Value Added Tax thereon but after deducting any sums paid to secured creditors in respect of their securities and any sums spent out of money received in carrying on the business of the bankrupt); and

(b) then by adding to the sum arrived at under sub-paragraph (a) such sum as is arrived at by applying the distribution scale set out in Schedule 6 to the value of assets distributed to creditors of the bankrupt (including sums paid in respect of preferential debts).

(3) That part of the trustee's remuneration calculated by reference to the realisation scale shall not exceed such sum as is arrived at by applying the realisation scale to such part of the bankrupt's assets as are required to pay the items referred to in paragraph (4).

(4) The items referred to in paragraph (3) are—

(a) the bankruptcy debts (including any interest payable by virtue of section 328(4)) to the extent required to be paid by these Rules (ignoring those debts paid otherwise than out of the proceeds of the realisation of the bankrupt's assets or which have been secured to the satisfaction of the court);

(b) the expenses of the bankruptcy other than—
   (i) fees or the remuneration of the official receiver; and
   (ii) any sums spent out of money received in carrying on the business of the bankrupt;

(c) fees payable by virtue of any order made under section 415; and

(d) the remuneration of the official receiver.]

NOTES

Amendment

Inserted by SI 2004/584, r 34.
    Date in force: 1 April 2004: see SI 2004/584, r 1(2); for transitional provisions see r 3 thereof.

6.139 Other matters affecting remuneration

[(1) Where the trustee (not being the official receiver) realises assets on behalf of a secured creditor, the trustee is entitled to such sum by way of remuneration as is arrived at by applying the realisation scale set out in Schedule 6 to the monies received by him in respect of the assets realised (including any Value Added Tax thereon).]

(2) Where there are joint trustees, it is for them to agree between themselves as to how the remuneration payable should be apportioned. Any dispute arising between them may be referred—

(a) to the court, for settlement by order, or

(b) to the creditors' committee or a meeting of creditors, for settlement by resolution.

(3) If the trustee is a solicitor and employs his own firm, or any partner in it, to act on behalf of the estate, profit costs shall not be paid unless this is authorised by the creditors' committee, the creditors or the court.

NOTES

Initial Commencement

Specified date

Specified date: 29 December 1986: see r 0.1.

Amendment

Para (1): substituted by SI 2004/584, r 35.
Date in force: 1 April 2004: see SI 2004/584, r 1(2); for transitional provisions see r 3 thereof.

Modification

References to solicitors etc modified to include references to bodies recognised under the Administration of Justice Act 1985, s 9, by the Solicitors' Incorporated Practices Order 1991, SI 1991/2684, arts 4, 5, Sch 1.

[6.140A Recourse of trustee to meeting of creditors]

[If the basis of the trustee's remuneration has been fixed by the creditors' committee and the trustee considers the rate or amount to be insufficient or the basis to be inappropriate, the trustee may request that the rate or amount be increased or the basis changed by resolution of the creditors.]

NOTES

Amendment

Substituted, for r 6.140 as originally enacted, by SI 2010/686, r 2, Sch 1, para 369.
Date in force: 6 April 2010: see SI 2010/686, r 1; for transitional provisions see r 6(1), Sch 4, para 1 thereto.

6.141 Recourse to the court

[(1) If the trustee considers that the basis of remuneration fixed by the creditors' committee, or by resolution of the creditors, or as under Rule 6.138(6), is insufficient or inappropriate, the trustee may apply to the court for an order changing it or increasing its amount or rate.]

(2) The trustee shall give at least 14 days' notice of his application to the members of the creditors' committee; and the committee may nominate one or more members to appear or be represented, and to be heard, on the application.

(3) If there is no creditors' committee, the trustee's notice of his application shall be sent to such one or more of the bankrupt's creditors as the court may direct, which creditors may nominate one or more of their number to appear or be represented.

(4) The court may, if it appears to be a proper case, order the costs of the trustee's application, including the costs of any member of the creditors' committee appearing [or being represented] on it, or any creditor so appearing [or being represented], to be paid out of the estate.

NOTES

Initial Commencement

Specified date
    Specified date: 29 December 1986: see r 0.1.

Amendment
    Para (1): substituted by SI 2010/686, r 2, Sch 1, para 370.
        Date in force: 6 April 2010: see SI 2010/686, r 1; for transitional provisions see r 6(1), Sch 4, para 1 thereto.
    Para (4): words in square brackets inserted by SI 1987/1919, r 3(1), Schedule, Part 1, para 115.

6.142 Creditor's claim that remuneration is [or other expenses are] excessive

[(1) Any secured creditor, or any unsecured creditor with either the concurrence of at least 10% in value of the creditors (including that creditor) or the permission of the court, or the bankrupt may apply to the court for one or more of the orders in paragraph (4).

(1A) Application by a creditor may be made on the grounds that—
    (a)   the remuneration charged by the trustee,
    (b)   the basis fixed for the trustee's remuneration under Rule 6.138, or
    (c)   expenses incurred by the trustee,
is or are, in all the circumstances, excessive or, in the case of an application under sub-paragraph (b), inappropriate.

(1B) Application by a creditor must, subject to any order of the court under Rule 6.78C(5), be made no later than 8 weeks (or in a case falling within Rule 6.126, 4 weeks) after receipt by the applicant of the progress report, or the draft report under Rule 6.78B, which first reports the charging of the remuneration or the incurring of the expenses in question ("the relevant report").

(1C) Application by the bankrupt may be made only on one or both of the grounds in paragraph (1A)(a) and (c) and no later than—
    (a)   8 weeks after receipt by the bankrupt of the draft report under Rule 6.78B, or
    (b)   in a case falling within Rule 6.126, 4 weeks after receipt by the bankrupt of notice under Rule 6.126(1C).]

[(2) When the application is made by a creditor, the court may dismiss it if it thinks that no sufficient cause is shown; but it must not do so unless the applicant has had an opportunity to attend the court for a hearing of which the applicant has been given at least 5 business days' notice but which is without notice to any other party.

(2A) Application may be made by the bankrupt only with the permission of the court; and without prejudice to the generality of the matters which the court may take into account, permission must not be given unless the bankrupt shows that there is (or would be but for the remuneration or expenses in question), or that it is likely that there will be (or would be but for the remuneration or expenses in question), a surplus of assets to which the bankrupt would be entitled.

(2B) If, as the case may be, the application is not dismissed under paragraph (2) or the bankrupt is given permission under paragraph (2A), the court must fix a venue for the application to be heard.]

(3) The applicant shall, at least 14 days before the hearing, send to the trustee a notice stating the venue so fixed; and the notice shall be accompanied by a copy of the application, and of any evidence which the applicant intends to adduce in support of it.

[(4) If the court considers the application to be well-founded, it must make one or more of the following orders—

(a) an order reducing the amount of remuneration which the trustee was entitled to charge;
(b) an order fixing the basis of remuneration at a reduced rate or amount;
(c) an order changing the basis of remuneration;
(d) an order that some or all of the remuneration or expenses in question be treated as not being bankruptcy expenses;
(e) an order that the trustee or the trustee's personal representative pay to such person as the court may specify as property comprised in the bankrupt's estate the amount of the excess of remuneration or expenses or such part of the excess as the court may specify;

and may make any other order that it thinks just; but an order under sub-paragraph (b) or (c) may be made only in respect of periods after the period covered by the relevant report.]

(5) Unless the court orders otherwise, the costs of the application shall be paid by the applicant, and do not fall on the estate.

NOTES

Initial Commencement

Specified date

Specified date: 29 December 1986: see r 0.1.

Amendment

Provision heading: words "or other expenses are" in square brackets inserted by SI 2010/686, r 2, Sch 1, para 371(1), (2).
Date in force: 6 April 2010: see SI 2010/686, r 1; for transitional provisions see r 6(1), Sch 4, para 1 thereto.
Paras (1), (1A)–(1C): substituted, for para (1) as originally enacted, by SI 2010/686, r 2, Sch 1, para 371(1), (3).
Date in force: 6 April 2010: see SI 2010/686, r 1; for transitional provisions see r 6(1), Sch 4, para 1 thereto.
Paras (2), (2A), (2B): substituted, for para (2) as originally enacted, by SI 2010/686, r 2, Sch 1, para 371(1), (4).
Date in force: 6 April 2010: see SI 2010/686, r 1; for transitional provisions see r 6(1), Sch 4, para 1 thereto.
Para (4): substituted by SI 2010/686, r 2, Sch 1, para 371(1), (5).
Date in force: 6 April 2010: see SI 2010/686, r 1; for transitional provisions see r 6(1), Sch 4, para 1 thereto.

[6.142A Review of remuneration]

[(1) Where, after the basis of the trustee's remuneration has been fixed, there is a material and substantial change in the circumstances which were taken into account in fixing it, the trustee may request that it be changed.

(2) The request must be made—

(a) where the creditors' committee fixed the basis, to the committee;
(b) where the creditors fixed the basis, to the creditors;
(c) where the court fixed the basis, by application to the court;
(d) where the remuneration was fixed by application of the realisation scale under Rule 6.138A, to the creditors' committee if there is one or otherwise to the creditors;

and Rules 6.138 to 6.142 apply as appropriate.

(3) Any change in the basis for remuneration applies from the date of the request under paragraph (2) and not for any earlier period.

(4) This Rule does not apply where the trustee is the official receiver.]

NOTES

Amendment

Inserted by SI 2010/686, r 2, Sch 1, para 372.
Date in force: 6 April 2010: see SI 2010/686, r 1; for transitional provisions see r 6(1), Sch 4, para 1 thereto.

[6.142B Remuneration of new trustee]

[(1) If a new trustee is appointed in place of another, any determination, resolution or court order in effect under the preceding provisions of this Section of this Chapter immediately before the former trustee ceased to hold office continues to apply in respect of the remuneration of the new trustee until a further determination, resolution or court order is made in accordance with those provisions.

(2) This Rule does not apply where the new trustee is the official receiver.]

NOTES

Amendment

Inserted by SI 2010/686, r 2, Sch 1, para 372.
Date in force: 6 April 2010: see SI 2010/686, r 1; for transitional provisions see r 6(1), Sch 4, para 1 thereto.

[6.142C Apportionment of set fee remuneration]

[(1) In a case in which the basis of the trustee's remuneration is a set amount under Rule 6.138(2)(c) and the trustee ("the former trustee") ceases (for whatever reason) to hold office before the time has elapsed or the work has been completed in respect of which the amount was set, application may be made for determination of what portion of the amount should be paid to the former trustee or the former trustee's personal representative in respect of the time which has actually elapsed or the work which has actually been done.

(2) Application may be made—
- (a) by the former trustee or the former trustee's personal representative within the period of 28 days beginning with the date upon which the former trustee ceased to hold office, or
- (b) by the trustee for the time being in office if the former trustee or the former trustee's personal representative has not applied by the end of that period.

(3) Application must be made—
- (a) where the creditors' committee fixed the basis, to the committee;
- (b) where the creditors fixed the basis, to the creditors for a resolution determining the portion;
- (c) where the court fixed the basis, to the court for an order determining the portion.

(4) The applicant must give a copy of the application to the trustee for the time being in office or to the former trustee or the former trustee's personal representative, as the case may be ("the recipient").

(5) The recipient may within 21 days of receipt of the copy of the application give notice of intent to make representations to the creditors' committee or the creditors or to appear or be represented before the court, as the case may be.

(6) No determination may be made upon the application until expiry of the 21 days referred to in paragraph (5) or, if the recipient does give notice of intent in accordance with that paragraph, until the recipient has been afforded the opportunity to make representations or to appear or be represented, as the case may be.

(7) If the former trustee or the former trustee's personal representative (whether or not the original applicant) considers that the portion determined upon application to the creditors' committee or the creditors is insufficient, that person may apply—

- (a) in the case of a determination by the creditors' committee, to the creditors for a resolution increasing the portion;
- (b) in the case of a resolution of the creditors (whether under paragraph (1) or under sub-paragraph (a)), to the court for an order increasing the portion,

and paragraphs (4) to (6) apply as appropriate.]

NOTES

Amendment

Inserted by SI 2010/686, r 2, Sch 1, para 372.
Date in force: 6 April 2010: see SI 2010/686, r 1; for transitional provisions see r 6(1), Sch 4, para 1 thereto.

SECTION E: SUPPLEMENTARY PROVISIONS

6.143 Trustee deceased

(1) Subject as follows, where the trustee (other than the official receiver) has died, it is the duty of his personal representatives to give notice of the fact to the official receiver, specifying the date of the death.

This does not apply if notice has been given under any of the following paragraphs of this Rule.

(2) If the deceased trustee was a partner in [or an employee of] a firm, notice may be given to the official receiver by a partner in the firm who is qualified to act as an insolvency practitioner, or is a member of any body recognised by the Secretary of State for the authorisation of insolvency practitioners.

(3) Notice of the death may be given by any person producing to the official receiver the relevant death certificate or a copy of it.

(4) The official receiver shall give notice to the court, for the purpose of fixing the date of the deceased trustee's release in accordance with section 299(3)(a).

NOTES

Initial Commencement

Specified date

Specified date: 29 December 1986: see r 0.1.

Amendment

Para (2): words "or an employee of" in square brackets inserted by SI 2010/686, r 2, Sch 1, para 373.
Date in force: 6 April 2010: see SI 2010/686, r 1; for transitional provisions see r 6(1), Sch 4, para 1 thereto.

6.144 Loss of qualification as insolvency practitioner

(1) This Rule applies where the trustee vacates office, under section 298(6), on his ceasing to be qualified to act as an insolvency practitioner in relation to the bankrupt.

(2) The trustee vacating office shall [as soon as reasonably practicable] give notice of his doing so to the official receiver, who shall give notice to the Secretary of State.

The official receiver shall file in court a copy of his notice under this paragraph.

(3) Rule 6.135 applies as regards the trustee obtaining his release, as if he had been removed by the court.

NOTES

Initial Commencement
Specified date

Specified date: 29 December 1986: see r 0.1.

Amendment

Para (2): words "as soon as reasonably practicable" in square brackets substituted by SI 2009/642, rr 4, 5.

Date in force: 6 April 2009: see SI 2009/642, r 1; for transitional provisions see r 3 thereof.

[6.145 Notice to official receiver of intention to vacate office]

[(1) Where the trustee intends to vacate office, whether by resignation or otherwise, he shall give notice of his intention to the official receiver together with notice of any creditors' meeting to be held in respect of his vacation of office, including any meeting to receive his resignation.

(2) The notice to the official receiver must given at least 21 days before any such creditors' meeting.

(3) Where there remains in the bankrupt's estate any property which has not been realised, applied, distributed or otherwise fully dealt with in the bankruptcy, the trustee shall include in his notice to the official receiver details of the nature of that property, its value (or the fact that it has no value), its location, any action taken by the trustee to deal with that property or any reason for his not dealing with it, and the current position in relation to it.]

NOTES

Amendment

Substituted by SI 1987/1919, r 3(1), Schedule, Part 1, para 116.

6.146 Trustee's duties on vacating office

(1) Where the trustee ceases to be in office as such, in consequence of removal, resignation or cesser of qualification as an insolvency practitioner, he is under obligation [as soon as reasonably practicable] to deliver up to the person succeeding him as trustee the assets of the estate (after deduction of any expenses properly incurred, and distributions made, by him) and further to deliver up to that person—

(a) the records of the bankruptcy, including correspondence, proofs and other related papers appertaining to the bankruptcy while it was within his responsibility, and

(b) the bankrupt's books, papers and other records.

(2) . . .

NOTES

Initial Commencement
Specified date

Specified date: 29 December 1986: see r 0.1.

Amendment

Para (1): words "as soon as reasonably practicable" in square brackets substituted by SI 2009/642, rr 4, 5.
Date in force: 6 April 2009: see SI 2009/642, r 1; for transitional provisions see r 3 thereof.
Para (2): revoked by SI 2004/584, r 36.
Date in force: 1 April 2004: see SI 2004/584, r 1(2).

6.147 Power of court to set aside certain transactions

(1) If in the administration of the estate the trustee enters into any transaction with a person who is an associate of his, the court may, on the application of any person interested, set the transaction aside and order the trustee to compensate the estate for any loss suffered in consequence of it.

(2) This does not apply if either—
   (a) the transaction was entered into with the prior consent of the court, or
   (b) it is shown to the court's satisfaction that the transaction was for value, and that it was entered into by the trustee without knowing, or having any reason to suppose, that the person concerned was an associate.

(3) Nothing in this Rule is to be taken as prejudicing the operation of any rule of law or equity with respect to a trustee's dealings with trust property, or the fiduciary obligations of any person.

NOTES

Initial Commencement

Specified date

Specified date: 29 December 1986: see r 0.1.

6.148 Rule against solicitation

(1) Where the court is satisfied that any improper solicitation has been used by or on behalf of the trustee in obtaining proxies or procuring his appointment, it may order that no remuneration out of the estate be allowed to any person by whom, or on whose behalf, the solicitation was exercised.

(2) An order of the court under this Rule overrides any resolution of the creditors' committee or the creditors, or any other provision of the Rules relating to the trustee's remuneration.

NOTES

Initial Commencement

Specified date

Specified date: 29 December 1986: see r 0.1.

6.149 Enforcement of trustee's obligations to official receiver

(1) The court may, on the application of the official receiver, make such orders as it thinks necessary for enforcement of the duties of the trustee under section 305(3) (information and assistance to be given; production and inspection of books and records relating to the bankruptcy).

(2) An order of the court under this Rule may provide that all costs of and incidental to the official receiver's application shall be borne by the trustee.

NOTES

Initial Commencement

Specified date

Specified date: 29 December 1986: see r 0.1.

CHAPTER 11
THE CREDITORS' COMMITTEE

6.150 Membership of creditors' committee

(1) The creditors' committee shall consist of at least 3, and not more than 5, members.

[(2) A person claiming to be a creditor is entitled to be a member of the committee provided that—

(a) that person has lodged a proof of debt;
(b) the proof mentioned in sub-paragraph (a) has neither been wholly disallowed for voting purposes, nor wholly rejected for the purpose of distribution or dividend; and
(c) the debt mentioned in sub-paragraph (a) is not fully secured.]

(3) A body corporate may be a member of the committee, but it cannot act as such otherwise than by a representative appointed under Rule 6.156.

NOTES

Initial Commencement

Specified date

Specified date: 29 December 1986: see r 0.1.

Amendment

Para (2): substituted by SI 2010/686, r 2, Sch 1, para 374.
Date in force: 6 April 2010: see SI 2010/686, r 1; for transitional provisions see r 6(1), Sch 4, para 1 thereto.

6.151 Formalities of establishment

(1) The creditors' committee does not come into being, and accordingly cannot act, until the trustee has issued a certificate of its due constitution.

(2) If the chairman of the creditors' meeting which resolves to establish the committee is not the trustee, he shall [as soon as reasonably practicable] give notice of the resolution to the trustee (or, as the case may be, the person appointed as trustee by that same meeting), and inform him of the names and addresses of the persons elected to be members of the committee.

[(3) No person may act as a member of the committee unless and until he has agreed to do so and, unless the relevant proxy [or authorisation] contains a statement to the contrary, such agreement may be given by his proxy-holder present at the meeting establishing the committee.

(3A) The trustee's certificate of the committee's due constitution shall not [be issued before the minimum number of members set out in Rule 6.150] elected to be members of the committee have agreed to act [and must be issued as soon as reasonably practicable thereafter].]

(4) As and when the others (if any) agree to act, the trustee shall issue an amended certificate.

(5) The certificate, and any amended certificate, shall be filed in court by the trustee [as soon as reasonably practicable].

[(6) If after the first establishment of the committee there is any change in its membership, as soon as reasonably practicable the trustee must file with the court notice of the change.]

NOTES

Initial Commencement

Specified date

Specified date: 29 December 1986: see r 0.1.

Amendment

Para (2): words "as soon as reasonably practicable" in square brackets substituted by SI 2009/642, rr 4, 5.
Date in force: 6 April 2009: see SI 2009/642, r 1; for transitional provisions see r 3 thereof.

Paras (3), (3A): substituted, for para (3) as originally enacted, by SI 1987/1919, r 3(1), Schedule, Part 1, para 117.

Para (3): words "or authorisation" in square brackets inserted by SI 2010/686, r 2, Sch 1, para 375(1), (2).
Date in force: 6 April 2010: see SI 2010/686, r 1; for transitional provisions see r 6(1), Sch 4, para 1 thereto.

Para (3A): words "be issued before the minimum number of members set out in Rule 6.150" in square brackets substituted by SI 2010/686, r 2, Sch 1, para 375(1), (3)(a).
Date in force: 6 April 2010: see SI 2010/686, r 1; for transitional provisions see r 6(1), Sch 4, para 1 thereto.

Para (3A): words "and must be issued as soon as reasonably practicable thereafter" in square brackets inserted by SI 2010/686, r 2, Sch 1, para 375(1), (3)(b).
Date in force: 6 April 2010: see SI 2010/686, r 1; for transitional provisions see r 6(1), Sch 4, para 1 thereto.

Para (5): words "as soon as reasonably practicable" in square brackets inserted by SI 2010/686, r 2, Sch 1, para 375(1), (4).
Date in force: 6 April 2010: see SI 2010/686, r 1; for transitional provisions see r 6(1), Sch 4, para 1 thereto.

Para (6): substituted by SI 2010/686, r 2, Sch 1, para 375(1), (5).
Date in force: 6 April 2010: see SI 2010/686, r 1; for transitional provisions see r 6(1), Sch 4, para 1 thereto.

6.152 Obligations of trustee to committee

(1) Subject as follows, it is the duty of the trustee to report to the members of the creditors' committee all such matters as appear to him to be, or as they have indicated to him as being, of concern to them with respect to the bankruptcy.

(2) In the case of matters so indicated to him by the committee, the trustee need not comply with any request for information where it appears to him that—

(a) the request is frivolous or unreasonable, or

(b) the cost of complying would be excessive, having regard to the relative importance of the information, or

(c) the estate is without funds sufficient for enabling him to comply.

(3) Where the committee has come into being more than 28 days after the appointment of the trustee, the latter shall report to them, in summary form, what actions he has taken since his appointment, and shall answer such questions as they may put to him regarding his conduct of the bankruptcy hitherto.

(4) A person who becomes a member of the committee at any time after its first establishment is not entitled to require a report to him by the trustee, otherwise than in summary form, of any matters previously arising.

(5) Nothing in this Rule disentitles the committee, or any member of it, from having access to the trustee's records of the bankruptcy, or from seeking an explanation of any matter within the committee's responsibility.

NOTES

Initial Commencement

Specified date

Specified date: 29 December 1986: see r 0.1.

6.153 Meetings of the committee

(1) Subject as follows, meetings of the creditors' committee shall be held when and where determined by the trustee.

(2) The trustee shall call a first meeting of the committee to take place within [6 weeks] of the committee's establishment . . .; and thereafter he shall call a meeting—

- (a) if so requested by a member of the committee or his representative (the meeting then to be held within 21 days of the request being received by the trustee), and
- (b) for a specified date, if the committee has previously resolved that a meeting be held on that date.

(3) [Subject to paragraph (4),] the trustee shall give [5 business] days' notice in writing of the venue of any meeting to every member of the committee (or his representative, if designated for that purpose), unless in any case the requirement of the notice has been waived by or on behalf of any member.

Waiver may be signified either at or before the meeting.

[(4) Where the trustee has determined that a meeting should be conducted and held in the manner referred to in Rule 12A.26(2), the notice period mentioned in paragraph (3) is 7 business days.

(5) In addition to any functions conferred on a committee by any provision of the Act, a committee must assist the trustee in discharging the trustee's functions and act in relation to that trustee in such manner as may from time to time be agreed.]

NOTES

Initial Commencement

Specified date

Specified date: 29 December 1986: see r 0.1.

Amendment

Para (2): words "6 weeks" in square brackets substituted by SI 2010/686, r 2, Sch 1, para 376(1), (2)(a).
    Date in force: 6 April 2010: see SI 2010/686, r 1; for transitional provisions see r 6(1), Sch 4, para 1 thereto.

Para (2): words omitted revoked by SI 2010/686, r 2, Sch 1, para 376(1), (2)(b).
    Date in force: 6 April 2010: see SI 2010/686, r 1; for transitional provisions see r 6(1), Sch 4, para 1 thereto.

Para (3): words "Subject to paragraph (4)," in square brackets inserted by SI 2010/686, r 2, Sch 1, para 376(1), (3)(a).
    Date in force: 6 April 2010: see SI 2010/686, r 1; for transitional provisions see r 6(1), Sch 4, para 1 thereto.

Para (3): words "5 business" in square brackets substituted by SI 2010/686, r 2, Sch 1, para 376(1), (3)(b).
    Date in force: 6 April 2010: see SI 2010/686, r 1; for transitional provisions see r 6(1), Sch 4, para 1 thereto.

Paras (4), (5): inserted by SI 2010/686, r 2, Sch 1, para 376(1), (4).

Insolvency Rules 1986, reg 6.153

Date in force: 6 April 2010: see SI 2010/686, r 1; for transitional provisions see r 6(1), Sch 4, para 1 thereto.

6.154 The chairman at meetings

(1) The chairman at any meeting of the creditors' committee shall be the trustee, or a person appointed by him in writing to act.

(2) A person so [appointed] must be either—
- (a) one who is qualified to act as an insolvency practitioner in relation to the bankrupt, or
- (b) an employee of the trustee or his firm who is experienced in insolvency matters.

NOTES

Initial Commencement

Specified date

Specified date: 29 December 1986: see r 0.1.

Amendment

Para (2): word "appointed" in square brackets substituted by SI 2010/686, r 2, Sch 1, para 377.

Date in force: 6 April 2010: see SI 2010/686, r 1; for transitional provisions see r 6(1), Sch 4, para 1 thereto.

6.155 Quorum

A meeting of the committee is duly constituted if due notice of it has been given to all the members and at least 2 of the members are present or represented.

NOTES

Initial Commencement

Specified date

Specified date: 29 December 1986: see r 0.1.

6.156 Committee-members' representatives

(1) A member of the creditors' committee may, in relation to the business of the committee, be represented by another person duly authorised by him for that purpose.

(2) A person acting as a committee-member's representative must hold a letter of authority entitling him so to act (either generally or [specially) and [authenticated] by or on behalf of the committee-member, and for this purpose any proxy in relation to any meeting of creditors of the bankrupt shall, unless it contains a statement to the contrary, be treated as such a letter of authority to act generally [authenticated] by or on behalf of the committee-member].

(3) The chairman at any meeting of the committee may call on a person claiming to act as a committee-member's representative to produce his letter of authority, and may exclude him if it appears that his authority is deficient.

[(4) No member may be represented by—
- (a) another member of the committee;
- (b) a person who is at the same time representing another committee member;
- (c) a body corporate;
- (d) an undischarged bankrupt;
- (e) a disqualified director; or

(f) a person who is subject to a bankruptcy restrictions order (including an interim order), a bankruptcy restrictions undertaking, a debt relief restrictions order (including an interim order) or a debt relief restrictions undertaking.]

(5) . . .

(6) Where the representative of a committee-member [authenticates] any document on the latter's behalf, the fact that he so [authenticates] must be stated below his [authentication].

[(7) The acts of the committee are valid notwithstanding any defect in the appointment or qualifications of any committee-member's representative.]

NOTES

Initial Commencement

Specified date

Specified date: 29 December 1986: see r 0.1.

Amendment

Para (2): words from "specially) and" to "the committee-member"in square brackets substituted by SI 1987/1919, r 3(1), Schedule, Part 1, para 118.

 Para (2): word "authenticated" in square brackets in both places it occurs substituted by SI 2010/686, r 2, Sch 1, para 1.
  Date in force: 6 April 2010: see SI 2010/686, r 1; for transitional provisions see r 6(1), Sch 4, paras 1, 2(1)(b) thereto.
 Para (4): substituted by SI 2010/686, r 2, Sch 1, para 378(1), (2).
  Date in force: 6 April 2010: see SI 2010/686, r 1; for transitional provisions see r 6(1), Sch 4, para 1 thereto.
 Para (5): revoked by SI 2010/686, r 2, Sch 1, para 378(1), (3).
  Date in force: 6 April 2010: see SI 2010/686, r 1; for transitional provisions see r 6(1), Sch 4, para 1 thereto.
 Para (6): word "authenticates" in square brackets in both place it occurs substituted by SI 2010/686, r 2, Sch 1, para 1.
  Date in force: 6 April 2010: see SI 2010/686, r 1; for transitional provisions see r 6(1), Sch 4, paras 1, 2(1)(b) thereto.
 Para (6): word "authentication" in square brackets substituted by SI 2010/686, r 2, Sch 1, para 1.
  Date in force: 6 April 2010: see SI 2010/686, r 1; for transitional provisions see r 6(1), Sch 4, paras 1, 2(1)(b) thereto.
Para (7): inserted by SI 1987/1919, r 3(1), Schedule, Part 1, para 118.

6.157 Resignation

A member of the creditors' committee may resign by notice in writing delivered to the trustee.

NOTES

Initial Commencement

Specified date

Specified date: 29 December 1986: see r 0.1.

6.158 Termination of membership

(1) A person's membership of the creditors' committee is automatically terminated if—

(a) he becomes bankrupt . . ., or

(b) at 3 consecutive meetings of the committee he is neither present nor represented (unless at the third of those meetings it is resolved that this Rule is not to apply in his case), or

[(c) ceases to be a creditor and a period of 3 months has elapsed from the date that that member ceased to be a creditor or is found never to have been a creditor].

(2) However, if the cause of termination is the member's bankruptcy, his trustee in bankruptcy replaces him as a member of the committee.

NOTES

Initial Commencement

Specified date

Specified date: 29 December 1986: see r 0.1.

Amendment

Para (1): in sub-para (a) words omitted revoked by SI 2004/584, r 38.
Date in force: 1 April 2004: see SI 2004/584, r 1(2).
Para (1): sub-para (c) substituted by SI 2010/686, r 2, Sch 1, para 379.
Date in force: 6 April 2010: see SI 2010/686, r 1; for transitional provisions see r 6(1), Sch 4, para 1 thereto.

6.159 Removal

A member of the creditors' committee may be removed by resolution at a meeting of creditors, at least 14 days' notice having been given of the intention to move that resolution.

NOTES

Initial Commencement

Specified date

Specified date: 29 December 1986: see r 0.1.

6.160 Vacancies

(1) The following applies if there is a vacancy in the membership of the creditors' committee.

(2) The vacancy need not be filled if the trustee and a majority of the remaining committee-members so agree, provided that the number of members does not fall below [3].

(3) The trustee may appoint any creditor (being qualified under the Rules to be a member of the committee) to fill the vacancy, if a majority of the other members of the committee agree to the appointment and the creditor concerned consents to act.

(4) Alternatively, a meeting of creditors may resolve that a creditor be appointed (with his consent) to fill the vacancy. In this case at least 14 days' notice must have been given of a resolution to make such an appointment (whether or not of a person named in the notice).

(5) Where the vacancy is filled by an appointment made by a creditors' meeting at which the trustee is not present, the chairman of the meeting shall report to the trustee the appointment which has been made.

NOTES

Initial Commencement

Specified date

Specified date: 29 December 1986: see r 0.1.

Amendment

Para (2): reference to "3" in square brackets substituted by SI 2010/686, r 2, Sch 1, para 380.
Date in force: 6 April 2010: see SI 2010/686, r 1; for transitional provisions see r 6(1), Sch 4, para 1 thereto.

6.161 Voting rights and resolutions

(1) At any meeting of the committee, each member (whether present himself, or by his representative) has one vote; and a resolution is passed when a majority of the members present or represented have voted in favour of it.

(2) Every resolution passed shall be recorded in writing, either separately or as part of the minutes of the meeting. The record shall be [authenticated] by the chairman and kept with the records of the bankruptcy.

NOTES

Initial Commencement

Specified date

Specified date: 29 December 1986: see r 0.1.

Amendment

Para (2): word "authenticated" in square brackets substituted by SI 2010/686, r 2, Sch 1, para 1.
Date in force: 6 April 2010: see SI 2010/686, r 1; for transitional provisions see r 6(1), Sch 4, paras 1, 2(1)(b) thereto.

6.162 Resolutions [otherwise than at a meeting]

(1) In accordance with this Rule, the trustee may seek to obtain the agreement of members of the creditors' committee to a resolution by sending to every member (or his representative designated for the purpose) a copy of the proposed resolution.

(2) Where the trustee makes use of the procedure allowed by this Rule, he shall send out to members of the committee or their representatives (as the case may be) [a copy of any proposed resolution on which a decision is sought, which shall be set out in such a way that agreement with or dissent from each separate resolution may be indicated by the recipient on the copy so sent].

(3) Any member of the committee may, within 7 [business] days from the date of the trustee sending out a resolution, require the trustee to summon a meeting of the committee to consider the matters raised by the resolution.

(4) In the absence of such a request, the resolution is deemed to have been carried in the committee if and when the trustee is notified in writing by a majority of the members that they concur with it.

(5) A copy of every resolution passed under this Rule, and a note that the concurrence of the committee was obtained, shall be kept with the records of the bankruptcy.

NOTES

Initial Commencement

Specified date

Specified date: 29 December 1986: see r 0.1.

Amendment

Provision heading: words "otherwise than at a meeting" in square brackets substituted by SI 2010/686, r 2, Sch 1, para 381.
    Date in force: 6 April 2010: see SI 2010/686, r 1; for transitional provisions see r 6(1), Sch 4, para 1 thereto.

Para (2): words in square brackets substituted by SI 1987/1919, r 3(1), Schedule, Part 1, para 119(1).

Para (3): word in square brackets inserted by SI 1987/1919, r 3(1), Schedule, Part 1, para 119(2).

6.163 Trustee's reports

(1) The trustee shall, as and when directed by the creditors' committee (but not more often than once in any period of 2 months), send a written report to every member of the committee setting out the position generally as regards the progress of the bankruptcy and matters arising in connection with it, to which he (the trustee) considers the committee's attention should be drawn.

(2) In the absence of any such directions by the committee, the trustee shall send such a report not less often than once in every period of 6 months.

(3) The obligations of the trustee under this Rule are without prejudice to those imposed by Rule 6.152.

NOTES

Initial Commencement

Specified date

Specified date: 29 December 1986: see r 0.1.

6.164 Expenses of members etc

The trustee shall defray out of the estate, in the prescribed order of priority, any reasonable travelling expenses directly incurred by members of the creditors' committee or their representatives in respect of their attendance at the committee's meetings, or otherwise on the committee's business.

NOTES

Initial Commencement

Specified date

Specified date: 29 December 1986: see r 0.1.

6.165 Dealings by committee-members and others

(1) This Rule applies to—
    (a)   any member of the creditors' committee,
    (b)   any committee-member's representative,
    (c)   any person who is an associate of a member of the committee or a committee-member's representative, and

(d) any person who has been a member of the committee at any time in the last 12 months.

(2) Subject as follows, a person to whom this Rule applies shall not enter into any transaction whereby he—

(a) receives out of the estate any payment for services given or goods supplied in connection with the estate's administration, or
(b) obtains any profit from the administration, or
(c) acquires any asset forming part of the estate.

(3) Such a transaction may be entered into by a person to whom this Rule applies—

(a) with the prior [permission] of the court, or
(b) if he does so as a matter of urgency, or by way of performance of a contract in force before the commencement of the bankruptcy, and obtains the court's [permission] for the transaction, having applied for it without undue delay, or
(c) with the prior sanction of the creditors' committee, where it is satisfied (after full disclosure of the circumstances) that the person will be giving full value in the transaction.

(4) Where in the committee a resolution is proposed that sanction be accorded for a transaction to be entered into which, without that sanction or the [permission] of the court, would be in contravention of this Rule, no member of the committee, and no representative of a member, shall vote if he is to participate directly or indirectly in the transaction.

(5) The court may, on the application of any person interested—

(a) set aside a transaction on the ground that it has been entered into in contravention of this Rule, and
(b) make with respect to it such other order as it thinks [just], including (subject to the following paragraph) an order requiring a person to whom this Rule applies to account for any profit obtained from the transaction and compensate the estate for any resultant loss.

(6) In the case of a person to whom this Rule applies as an associate of a member of the committee or of a committee-member's representative, the court shall not make any order under paragraph (5), if satisfied that he entered into the relevant transaction without having any reason to suppose that in doing so he would contravene this Rule.

(7) The costs of an application to the court for [permission] under this Rule do not fall on the estate, unless the court so orders.

NOTES

Initial Commencement

Specified date

Specified date: 29 December 1986: see r 0.1.

Amendment

Para (3): in sub-paras (a), (b) word "permission" in square brackets substituted by SI 2010/686, s 2, Sch 1, para 1.
 Date in force: 6 April 2010: see SI 2010/686, r 1; for transitional provisions see r 6(1), Sch 4, paras 1, 2(1)(b) thereto.
Para (4): word "permission" in square brackets substituted by SI 2010/686, r 2, Sch 1, para 1.
 Date in force: 6 April 2010: see SI 2010/686, r 1; for transitional provisions see r 6(1), Sch 4, paras 1, 2(1)(b) thereto.
Para (5): in sub-para (b) word "just" in square brackets substituted by SI 2010/686, r 2, Sch 1, para 1.
 Date in force: 6 April 2010: see SI 2010/686, r 1; for transitional provisions see r 6(1), Sch 4, paras 1, 2(1)(b) thereto.

Para (7): word "permission" in square brackets substituted by SI 2010/686, r 2, Sch 1, para 1.
> Date in force: 6 April 2010: see SI 2010/686, r 1; for transitional provisions see r 6(1), Sch 4, paras 1, 2(1)(b) thereto.

6.166 Committee's functions vested in Secretary of State

(1) At any time when the functions of the creditors' committee are vested in the Secretary of State under section 302(1) or (2), requirements of the Act or the Rules about notices to be given, or reports to be made, to the committee by the trustee do not apply, otherwise than as enabling the committee to require a report as to any matter.

(2) Where the committee's functions are so vested under section 302(2), they may be exercised by the official receiver.

NOTES

Initial Commencement

Specified date
> Specified date: 29 December 1986: see r 0.1.

CHAPTER 12
SPECIAL MANAGER

6.167 Appointment and remuneration

(1) An application made by the official receiver or trustee under section 370 for the appointment of a person to be special manager shall be supported by a report setting out the reasons for the application.
The report shall include the applicant's estimate of the value of the estate, property or business in respect of which the special manager is to be appointed.

(2) The court's order appointing the special manager shall specify the duration of his appointment, which may be for a period of time, or until the occurrence of a specified event. Alternatively, the order may specify that the duration of the appointment is to be subject to a further order of the court.

(3) The appointment of a special manager may be renewed by order of the court.

(4) The special manager's remuneration shall be fixed from time to time by the court.

NOTES

Initial Commencement

Specified date
> Specified date: 29 December 1986: see r 0.1.

6.168 Security

(1) The appointment of the special manager does not take effect until the person appointed has given (or, being allowed by the court to do so, undertaken to give) security to the person who applies for him to be appointed.

(2) It is not necessary that security shall be given for each separate bankruptcy; but it may be given either specially for a particular bankruptcy, or generally for any bankruptcy in relation to which the special manager may be employed as such.

(3) The amount of the security shall be not less than the value of the estate, property or business in respect of which he is appointed, as estimated by the applicant in his report under Rule 6.167(1).

(4) When the special manager has given security to the person applying for his appointment, that person's certificate as to the adequacy of the security shall be filed in court.

(5) The cost of providing the security shall be paid in the first instance by the special manager; but—

    (a)   where a bankruptcy order is not made, he is entitled to be reimbursed out of the property of the debtor, and the court may make an order on the debtor accordingly, and

    (b)   where a bankruptcy order is made, he is entitled to be reimbursed out of the estate in the prescribed order of priority.

NOTES

Initial Commencement

Specified date

    Specified date: 29 December 1986: see r 0.1.

6.169 Failure to give or keep up security

(1) If the special manager fails to give the required security within the time stated for that purpose by the order appointing him, or any extension of that time that may be allowed, the official receiver or trustee (as the case may be) shall report the failure to the court, which may thereupon discharge the order appointing the special manager.

(2) If the special manager fails to keep up his security, the official receiver or trustee shall report his failure to the court, which may thereupon remove the special manager, and make such order as it thinks [just] as to costs.

(3) If an order is made under this Rule removing the special manager, or discharging the order appointing him, the court shall give directions as to whether any, and if so what, steps should be taken for the appointment of another special manager in his place.

NOTES

Initial Commencement

Specified date

    Specified date: 29 December 1986: see r 0.1.

Amendment

    Para (2): word "just" in square brackets substituted by SI 2010/686, r 2, Sch 1, para 1.
        Date in force: 6 April 2010: see SI 2010/686, r 1; for transitional provisions see r 6(1), Sch 4, paras 1, 2(1)(b) thereto.

6.170 Accounting

(1) The special manager shall produce accounts, containing details of his receipts and payments, for the approval of the trustee.

(2) The accounts shall be in respect of 3-month periods for the duration of the special manager's appointment (or for a lesser period, if his appointment terminates less than 3 months from its date, or from the date to which the last accounts were made up).

(3) When the accounts have been approved, the special manager's receipts and payments shall be added to those of the trustee.

6.171 Termination of appointment

(1) The special manager's appointment terminates if the bankruptcy petition is dismissed or if, an interim receiver having been appointed, the latter is discharged without a bankruptcy order having been made.

(2) If the official receiver or the trustee is of opinion that the employment of the special manager is no longer necessary or profitable for the estate, he shall apply to the court for directions, and the court may order the special manager's appointment to be terminated.

(3) The official receiver or the trustee shall make the same application if a resolution of the creditors is passed, requesting that the appointment be terminated.

NOTES

Initial Commencement

Specified date

Specified date: 29 December 1986: see r 0.1.

CHAPTER 13

PUBLIC EXAMINATION OF BANKRUPT

6.172 Order for public examination

(1) If the official receiver applies to the court, under section 290, for the public examination of the bankrupt, a copy of the court's order shall, [as soon as reasonably practicable] after its making, be sent by the official receiver to the bankrupt.

(2) The order shall appoint a venue for the hearing, and direct the bankrupt's attendance thereat.

(3) The official receiver shall give at least 14 days' notice of the hearing—

   (a)   if a trustee has been nominated or appointed, to him;

   (b)   if a special manager has been appointed, to him; and

   (c)   subject to any contrary direction of the court, to every creditor of the bankrupt who is known to the official receiver . . . ..

[(4) Where the official receiver thinks fit, a notice of the order shall be gazetted not less than 14 days before the day fixed for the hearing.]

[(5) The official receiver may advertise the notice under paragraph (4) of this Rule in such other manner as the official receiver thinks fit.]

[(5A) In addition to the standard contents, notices under paragraphs (4) and (5) must state—

   (a)   the purpose of the hearing; and

   (b)   the venue fixed for the hearing.]

NOTES

Initial Commencement

Specified date

Specified date: 29 December 1986: see r 0.1.

Amendment

Para (1): words "as soon as reasonably practicable" in square brackets substituted by SI 2009/642, rr 4, 5.
    Date in force: 6 April 2009: see SI 2009/642, r 1; for transitional provisions see r 3 thereof.

Para (3): in sub-para (c) words omitted revoked by SI 2010/686, r 2, Sch 1, para 382(1), (2).
    Date in force: 6 April 2010: see SI 2010/686, r 1; for transitional provisions see r 6(1), Sch 4, para 1 thereto.

Para (4): substituted by SI 2009/642, rr 4, 44(a).
    Date in force: 6 April 2009: see SI 2009/642, r 1; for transitional provisions see r 3 thereof.

Para (5): inserted by SI 2009/642, rr 4, 44(b).
    Date in force: 6 April 2009: see SI 2009/642, r 1; for transitional provisions see r 3 thereof.

Para (5A): inserted by SI 2010/686, r 2, Sch 1, para 382(1), (3).
    Date in force: 6 April 2010: see SI 2010/686, r 1; for transitional provisions see r 6(1), Sch 4, para 1 thereto.

6.173 Order on request by creditors

(1) A request by a creditor to the official receiver, under section 290(2), for the bankrupt to be publicly examined shall be made in writing and be accompanied by—

    (a)   a list of the creditors concurring with the request and the amount of their respective claims in the bankruptcy,

    (b)   from each creditor concurring, written confirmation of his concurrence, and

    (c)   a statement of the reasons why the examination is requested.

Sub-paragraphs (a) and (b) do not apply if the requisitioning creditor's debt is alone sufficient, without the concurrence of others.

(2) Before an application to the court is made on the request, the requisitionist shall deposit with the official receiver such sum as the latter may determine to be appropriate by way of security for the expenses of the hearing of a public examination, if ordered.

(3) Subject as follows, the official receiver shall, within 28 days of receiving the request, make the application to the court required by section 290(2).

(4) If the official receiver is of opinion that the request is an unreasonable one in the circumstances, he may apply to the court for an order relieving him from the obligation to make the application otherwise required by that subsection.

(5) If the court so orders, and the application for the order was made [without notice to any other party], notice of the order shall be given [as soon as reasonably practicable] by the official receiver to the requisitionist. If the application for an order is dismissed, the official receiver's application under section 290(2) shall be made [as soon as reasonably practicable] on conclusion of the hearing of the application first mentioned.

NOTES

Initial Commencement

Specified date

    Specified date: 29 December 1986: see r 0.1.

Amendment

Para (5): words "without notice to any other party" in square brackets substituted by SI 2010/686, r 2, Sch 1, para 383.
    Date in force: 6 April 2010: see SI 2010/686, r 1; for transitional provisions see r 6(1), Sch 4, paras 1, 2(1)(b) thereto.

Para (5): words "as soon as reasonably practicable" in square brackets in both places they occur substituted by SI 2009/642, rr 4, 5.

Date in force: 6 April 2009: see SI 2009/642, r 1; for transitional provisions see r 3 thereof.

6.174 Bankrupt unfit for examination

(1) Where the bankrupt [is a person who lacks capacity within the meaning of the Mental Capacity Act 2005 or] is suffering from any . . . physical affliction or disability rendering him unfit to undergo or attend for public examination, the court may, on [an application being made to it under this Rule], either stay the order for his public examination or direct that it shall be conducted in such manner and at such place as it thinks [just].

(2) Application under this Rule shall be made—
- (a) by a person who has been appointed by a court in the United Kingdom or elsewhere to manage the affairs of, or to represent, the bankrupt, or
- (b) by a relative or friend of the bankrupt whom the court considers to be a proper person to make the application, or
- (c) by the official receiver.

(3) Where the application is made by a person other than the official receiver, then—
- (a) it shall, unless the bankrupt is a [person who lacks capacity within the meaning of the Mental Capacity Act 2005], be supported by [a witness statement] of a registered medical practitioner as to the bankrupt's mental and physical condition;
- (b) at least [5 business] days' notice of the application shall be given to the official receiver and the trustee (if any); and
- (c) before any order is made on the application, the applicant shall deposit with the official receiver such sum as the latter certifies to be necessary for the additional expenses of any examination that may be ordered on the application.

An order made on the application may provide that the expenses of the examination are to be payable, as to a specified proportion, out of the deposit under sub-paragraph (c), instead of out of the estate.

(4) Where the application is made by the official receiver, it may be made [without notice to any other party], and may be supported by evidence in the form of a report by the official receiver to the court.

NOTES

Initial Commencement

Specified date

Specified date: 29 December 1986: see r 0.1.

Amendment

Para (1): words "is a person who lacks capacity within the meaning of the Mental Capacity Act 2005 or" in square brackets inserted by SI 2007/1898, art 6, Sch 1, para 12(1), (3)(a)(ii).
Date in force: 1 October 2007: see SI 2007/1898, art 1.
Para (1): words omitted revoked by SI 2007/1898, art 6, Sch 1, para 12(1), (3)(a)(i).
Date in force: 1 October 2007: see SI 2007/1898, art 1.
Para (1): words "an application being made to it under this Rule" in square brackets substituted by SI 2010/686, r 2, Sch 1, para 384(1), (2).
Date in force: 6 April 2010: see SI 2010/686, r 1; for transitional provisions see r 6(1), Sch 4, paras 1, 2(1)(b) thereto.
Para (1): word "just" in square brackets substituted by SI 2010/686, r 2, Sch 1, para 1.
Date in force: 6 April 2010: see SI 2010/686, r 1; for transitional provisions see r 6(1), Sch 4, paras 1, 2(1)(b) thereto.

Para (3): in sub-para (a) words "person who lacks capacity within the meaning of the Mental Capacity Act 2005" in square brackets substituted by SI 2007/1898, art 6, Sch 1, para 12(1), (3)(b).
> Date in force: 1 October 2007: see SI 2007/1898, art 1.

Para (3): in sub-para (a) words "a witness statement" in square brackets substituted by SI 2010/686, r 2, Sch 1, para 384(1), (3)(a).
> Date in force: 6 April 2010: see SI 2010/686, r 1; for transitional provisions see r 6(1), Sch 4, paras 1, 2(1)(b), (2)–(4) thereto.

Para (3): in sub-para (b) words "5 business" in square brackets substituted by SI 2010/686, r 2, Sch 1, para 384(1), (3)(b).
> Date in force: 6 April 2010: see SI 2010/686, r 1; for transitional provisions see r 6(1), Sch 4, para 1 thereto.

Para (4): words "without notice to any other party" in square brackets substituted by SI 2010/686, r 2, Sch 1, para 384(1), (4).
> Date in force: 6 April 2010: see SI 2010/686, r 1; for transitional provisions see r 6(1), Sch 4, paras 1, 2(1)(b) thereto.

6.175 Procedure at hearing

(1) The bankrupt shall at the hearing be examined on oath; and he shall answer all such questions as the court may put, or allow to be put, to him.

(2) Any of the persons allowed by section 290(4) to question the bankrupt may, with the approval of the court (made known either at the hearing or in advance of it), appear by solicitor or counsel; or he may in writing authorise another person to question the bankrupt on his behalf.

(3) The bankrupt may at his own expense employ a solicitor with or without counsel, who may put to him such questions as the court may allow for the purpose of enabling him to explain or qualify any answers given by him, and may make representations on his behalf.

(4) There shall be made in writing such record of the examination as the court thinks proper. The record shall be read over either to or by the bankrupt, [authenticated] by him, and verified by [a statement of truth] at a venue fixed by the court.

(5) The written record may, in any proceedings (whether under the Act or otherwise) be used as evidence against the bankrupt of any statement made by him in the course of his public examination.

(6) If criminal proceedings have been instituted against the bankrupt, and the court is of opinion that the continuance of the hearing would be calculated to prejudice a fair trial of those proceedings, the hearing may be adjourned.

NOTES

Initial Commencement

Specified date
> Specified date: 29 December 1986: see r 0.1.

Amendment

Para (4): word "authenticated" in square brackets substituted by SI 2010/686, r 2, Sch 1, para 1.
> Date in force: 6 April 2010: see SI 2010/686, r 1; for transitional provisions see r 6(1), Sch 4, paras 1, 2(1)(b) thereto.

Para (4): words "a statement of truth" in square brackets substituted by SI 2010/686, r 2, Sch 1, para 385.
> Date in force: 6 April 2010: see SI 2010/686, r 1; for transitional provisions see r 6(1), Sch 4, paras 1, 2(1)(b) thereto.

6.176 Adjournment

(1) The public examination may be adjourned by the court from time to time, either to a fixed date or generally.

(2) Where the examination has been adjourned generally, the court may at any time on the application of the official receiver or of the bankrupt—

(a)   fix a venue for the resumption of the examination, and
(b)   give directions as to the manner in which, and the time within which, notice of the resumed public examination is to be given to persons entitled to take part in it.

(3) Where application under paragraph (2) is made by the bankrupt, the court may grant it on terms that the expenses of giving the notices required by that paragraph shall be paid by him and that, before a venue for the resumed public examination is fixed, he shall deposit with the official receiver such sum as the latter considers necessary to cover those expenses.

(4) Where the examination is adjourned . . ., the official receiver may, there and then, make application under section 279(3) (suspension of automatic discharge).

[(5) If, on the hearing of an application pursuant to paragraph (4), the court makes an order suspending the bankrupt's discharge, copies of such order shall be sent by the court to the official receiver, the trustee and the bankrupt.]

NOTES

Initial Commencement

Specified date

Specified date: 29 December 1986: see r 0.1.

Amendment

Para (4): word omitted revoked by SI 2010/686, r 2, Sch 1, para 386.
Date in force: 6 April 2010: see SI 2010/686, r 1; for transitional provisions see r 6(1), Sch 4, para 1 thereto.
Para (5): inserted by SI 1999/359, r 3, Schedule, para 6.
Date in force: 22 March 1999: see SI 1999/359, r 1.

6.177 Expenses of examination

(1) Where a public examination of the bankrupt has been ordered by the court on a creditors' requisition under Rule 6.173, the court may order that the expenses of the examination are to be paid, as to a specified proportion, out of the deposit under Rule 6.173(2), instead of out of the estate.

(2) In no case do the costs and expenses of a public examination fall on the official receiver personally.

NOTES

Initial Commencement

Specified date

Specified date: 29 December 1986: see r 0.1.

CHAPTER 14

DISCLAIMER

6.178 Trustee's notice of disclaimer

(1) Where the trustee disclaims property under section 315, the notice of disclaimer shall contain such particulars of the property disclaimed as enable it to be easily identified.

[(2) The notice of disclaimer must be authenticated and dated by the trustee.]

[(3) As soon as reasonably practicable after authenticating the notice of disclaimer, the trustee must—
- (a) file a copy of the notice with the court; and
- (b) in any case where the disclaimer is of registered land as defined in section 132(1) of the Land Registration Act 2002, send a copy of the notice to the Chief Land Registrar.]

(4) For the purposes of section 315, the date of the prescribed notice is that [on which the trustee authenticates it].

NOTES

Initial Commencement

Specified date

Specified date: 29 December 1986: see r 0.1.

Amendment

Para (2): substituted by SI 2010/686, r 2, Sch 1, para 387(1), (2).
 Date in force: 6 April 2010: see SI 2010/686, r 1; for transitional provisions see r 6(1), Sch 4, para 1 thereto.
Para (3): substituted by SI 2010/686, r 2, Sch 1, para 387(1), (3).
 Date in force: 6 April 2010: see SI 2010/686, r 1; for transitional provisions see r 6(1), Sch 4, para 1 thereto.
Para (4): words "on which the trustee authenticates it" in square brackets substituted by SI 2010/686, r 2, Sch 1, para 387(1), (4).
 Date in force: 6 April 2010: see SI 2010/686, r 1; for transitional provisions see r 6(1), Sch 4, para 1 thereto.

6.179 Communication of disclaimer to persons interested

[(1) Within 7 business days after the date of the notice of disclaimer, the trustee shall send or give copies of the notice to the persons mentioned in paragraphs (2) to (5).]

(2) Where the property disclaimed is of a leasehold nature, he shall send or give a copy to every person who (to his knowledge) claims under the bankrupt as underlessee or mortgagee.

(3) Where the disclaimer is of property in a dwelling-house, he shall send or give a copy to every person who (to his knowledge) is in occupation of, or claims a right to occupy, the house.

(4) He shall in any case send or give a copy of the notice to every person who (to his knowledge)—
- (a) claims an interest in the disclaimed property, or
- (b) is under any liability in respect of the property, not being a liability discharged by the disclaimer.

(5) If the disclaimer is of an unprofitable contract, he shall send or give copies of the notice to all such persons, as, to his knowledge, are parties to the contract or have interests under it.

(6) If subsequently it comes to the trustee's knowledge, in the case of any person, that he has such an interest in the disclaimed property as would have entitled him to

receive a copy of the notice of disclaimer in pursuance of paragraphs (2) to (5), the trustee shall then [as soon as reasonably practicable] send or give to that person a copy of the notice.

But compliance with this paragraph is not required if—

(a) the trustee is satisfied that the person has already been made aware of the disclaimer and its date, or

(b) the court, on the trustee's application, orders that compliance is not required in that particular case.

[(7) A notice or copy notice to be served on any person under the age of 18 in relation to the disclaimer of property in a dwelling-house is sufficiently served if sent or given to the parent or guardian of that person.]

NOTES

Initial Commencement

Specified date

Specified date: 29 December 1986: see r 0.1.

Amendment

Para (1): substituted by SI 2010/686, r 2, Sch 1, para 388.
Date in force: 6 April 2010: see SI 2010/686, r 1; for transitional provisions see r 6(1), Sch 4, para 1 thereto.
Para (6): words "as soon as reasonably practicable" in square brackets substituted by SI 2009/642, rr 4, 5.
Date in force: 6 April 2009: see SI 2009/642, r 1; for transitional provisions see r 3 thereof.
Para (7): inserted by SI 1987/1919, r 3(1), Schedule, Part 1, para 120.

6.180 Additional notices

The trustee disclaiming property may, without prejudice to his obligations under sections 315 to 319 and Rules 6.178 and 6.179, at any time [send or give copies of the] notice of the disclaimer to any persons who in his opinion ought, in the public interest or otherwise, to be informed of [the disclaimer].

NOTES

Initial Commencement

Specified date

Specified date: 29 December 1986: see r 0.1.

Amendment

Words "send or give copies of the" in square brackets substituted by SI 2010/686, r 2, Sch 1, para 389(1),(2).
Date in force: 6 April 2010: see SI 2010/686, r 1; for transitional provisions see r 6(1), Sch 4, para 1 thereto.
Words "the disclaimer" in square brackets substituted by SI 2010/686, r 2, Sch 1, para 389(1), (3).
Date in force: 6 April 2010: see SI 2010/686, r 1; for transitional provisions see r 6(1), Sch 4, para 1 thereto.

[6.181A Records]

[The trustee must include in that trustee's records of the insolvency a record of—

(a) the persons to whom that trustee has sent or given copies of the notice of disclaimer under the two preceding Rules, showing their names and addresses, and the nature of their respective interests;

(b) the dates on which the copies of the notice of disclaimer were sent or given to those persons;
(c) the date on which, as required by Rule 6.178(3)(a), a copy of the notice of disclaimer was filed with the court; and
(d) (where applicable) the date on which, as required by Rule 6.178(3)(b), a copy of the notice was sent to the Chief Land Registrar.]

NOTES

Amendment

Substituted, for r 6.181 as originally enacted, by SI 2010/686, r 2, Sch 1, para 390.
Date in force: 6 April 2010: see SI 2010/686, r 1; for transitional provisions see r 6(1), Sch 4, para 1 thereto.

6.182 Application for [permission] to disclaim

(1) Where under section 315(4) the trustee requires the [permission] of the court to disclaim property claimed for the bankrupt's estate under section 307 or 308, he may apply for that [permission] [without notice to any other party].

(2) The application must be accompanied by a report—
(a) giving such particulars of the property proposed to be disclaimed as enable it to be easily identified,
(b) setting out the reasons why, the property having been claimed for the estate, the court's [permission] to disclaim is now applied for, and
(c) specifying the persons (if any) who have been informed of the trustee's intention to make the application.

(3) If it is stated in the report that any [person has consented] to the disclaimer ..., a copy of that consent must be annexed to the report.

(4) The court may, on consideration of the application, grant the [permission] applied for; and it may, before granting [permission]—
(a) order that notice of the application be given to all such persons who, if the property is disclaimed, will be entitled to apply for a vesting or other order under section 320, and
(b) fix a venue for the hearing of the application under section 315(4).

NOTES

Initial Commencement

Specified date

Specified date: 29 December 1986: see r 0.1.

Amendment

Provision heading: word "permission" in square brackets substituted by SI 2010/686, r 2, Sch 1, para 1.
Date in force: 6 April 2010: see SI 2010/686, r 1; for transitional provisions see r 6(1), Sch 4, paras 1, 2(1)(b) thereto.
Para (1): word "permission" in square brackets in both places it occurs substituted by SI 2010/686, r 2, Sch 1, para 1.
Date in force: 6 April 2010: see SI 2010/686, r 1; for transitional provisions see r 6(1), Sch 4, paras 1, 2(1)(b) thereto.
Para (1): words "without notice to any other party" in square brackets substituted by SI 2010/686, r 2, Sch 1, para 391(1), (2).
Date in force: 6 April 2010: see SI 2010/686, r 1; for transitional provisions see r 6(1), Sch 4, paras 1, 2(1)(b) thereto.
Para (2): in sub-para (b) word "permission" in square brackets substituted by SI 2010/686, r 2, Sch 1, para 1.

Date in force: 6 April 2010: see SI 2010/686, r 1; for transitional provisions see r 6(1), Sch 4, paras 1, 2(1)(b) thereto.

Para (3): words "person has consented" in square brackets substituted by SI 2010/686, r 2, Sch 1, para 391(1), (3)(a).

Date in force: 6 April 2010: see SI 2010/686, r 1; for transitional provisions see r 6(1), Sch 4, para 1 thereto.

Para (3): words omitted revoked by SI 2010/686, Sch 1, para 391(1), (3)(b).r 2,

Date in force: 6 April 2010: see SI 2010/686, r 1; for transitional provisions see r 6(1), Sch 4, para 1 thereto.

Para (4): word "permission" in square brackets in both places it occurs substituted by SI 2010/686, r 2, Sch 1, para 1.

Date in force: 6 April 2010: see SI 2010/686, r 1; for transitional provisions see r 6(1), Sch 4, paras 1, 2(1)(b) thereto.

6.183 Application by interested party under s 316

[(1) The following applies where, in the case of any property, application is made to the trustee by an interested party under section 316.]

[(2) The application must be delivered to the trustee—
 (a) personally;
 (b) by electronic means in accordance with Part 12A; or
 (c) by any other means of delivery which enables proof of receipt of the application by the trustee to be provided, if requested.]

(3) This paragraph applies in a case where the property concerned cannot be disclaimed by the trustee without the [permission] of the court.

If within the period of 28 days mentioned in section 316(1) the trustee applies to the court for [permission] to disclaim, the court shall extend the time allowed by that section for giving notice of disclaimer to a date not earlier than the date fixed for the hearing of the application.

NOTES

Initial Commencement

Specified date

Specified date: 29 December 1986: see r 0.1.

Amendment

Para (1): substituted by SI 2010/686, r 2, Sch 1, para 392(1), (2).

Date in force: 6 April 2010: see SI 2010/686, r 1; for transitional provisions see r 6(1), Sch 4, para 1 thereto.

Para (2): substituted by SI 2010/686, r 2, Sch 1, para 392(1), (3).

Date in force: 6 April 2010: see SI 2010/686, r 1; for transitional provisions see r 6(1), Sch 4, para 1 thereto.

Para (3): word "permission" in square brackets in both places it occurs substituted by SI 2010/686, r 2, Sch 1, para 1.

Date in force: 6 April 2010: see SI 2010/686, r 1; for transitional provisions see r 6(1), Sch 4, paras 1, 2(1)(b) thereto.

6.184 Interest in property to be declared on request

(1) If, in the case of property which the trustee has the right to disclaim, it appears to him that there is some person who claims, or may claim, to have an interest in the property, he may give notice to that person calling on him to declare within 14 days whether he claims any such interest and, if so, the nature and extent of it.

(2) Failing compliance with the notice, the trustee is entitled to assume that the person concerned has no such interest in the property as will prevent or impede its disclaimer.

NOTES

Initial Commencement

Specified date

Specified date: 29 December 1986: see r 0.1.

6.185 Disclaimer presumed valid and effective

Any disclaimer of property by the trustee is presumed valid and effective, unless it is proved that he has been in breach of his duty with respect to the giving of notice of disclaimer, or otherwise under sections 315 to 319, or under this Chapter of the Rules.

NOTES

Initial Commencement

Specified date

Specified date: 29 December 1986: see r 0.1.

6.186 Application for exercise of court's powers under s 320

(1) This Rule applies with respect to an application by any person under section 320 for an order of the court to vest or deliver disclaimed property.

(2) The application must be made within 3 months of the applicant becoming aware of the disclaimer, or of his receiving a copy of the trustee's notice of disclaimer sent under Rule 6.179, whichever is the earlier.

(3) The applicant shall with his application file [a witness statement]—
- (a) stating whether he applies under paragraph (a) of section 320(2) (claim of interest in the property), under paragraph (b) (liability not discharged) or under paragraph (c) (occupation of dwelling-house);
- (b) specifying the date on which he received a copy of the trustee's notice of disclaimer, or otherwise became aware of the disclaimer; and
- (c) specifying the grounds of his application and the order which he desires the court to make under section 320.

(4) The court shall fix a venue for the hearing of the application; and the applicant shall, not later than [5 business] days before the date fixed, give to the trustee notice of the venue, accompanied by copies of the application and the [witness statement required by] paragraph (3).

(5) On the hearing of the application, the court may give directions as to other persons (if any) who should be sent or given notice of the application and the grounds on which it is made.

(6) Sealed copies of any order made on the application shall be sent by the court to the applicant and the trustee.

(7) In a case where the property disclaimed is of a leasehold nature, or is property in a dwelling-house, and section 317 or (as the case may be) section 318 applies to suspend the effect of the disclaimer, there shall be included in the court's order a direction giving effect to the disclaimer.

This paragraph does not apply if, at the time when the order is issued, other applications under section 320 are pending in respect of the same property.

NOTES

Initial Commencement

Specified date

Specified date: 29 December 1986: see r 0.1.

Amendment

Para (3): words "a witness statement" in square brackets substituted by SI 2010/686, r 2, Sch 1, para 393(1), (2).
Date in force: 6 April 2010: see SI 2010/686, r 1; for transitional provisions see r 6(1), Sch 4, paras 1, 2(1)(b), (2)–(4) thereto.
Para (4): words "5 business" in square brackets substituted by SI 2010/686, r 2, Sch 1, para 393(1), (3)(a).
Date in force: 6 April 2010: see SI 2010/686, r 1; for transitional provisions see r 6(1), Sch 4, para 1 thereto.
Para (4): words "witness statement required by" in square brackets substituted by SI 2010/686, r 2, Sch 1, para 393(1), (3)(b).
Date in force: 6 April 2010: see SI 2010/686, r 1; for transitional provisions see r 6(1), Sch 4, paras 1, 2(1)(b), (2)–(4) thereto.

CHAPTER 15
REPLACEMENT OF EXEMPT PROPERTY

6.187 Purchase of replacement property

(1) A purchase of replacement property under section 308(3) may be made either before or after the realisation by the trustee of the value of the property vesting in him under the section.

(2) The trustee is under no obligation, by virtue of the section, to apply funds to the purchase of a replacement for property vested in him, unless and until he has sufficient funds in the estate for that purpose.

NOTES

Initial Commencement

Specified date

Specified date: 29 December 1986: see r 0.1.

6.188 Money provided in lieu of sale

(1) The following applies where a third party proposes to the trustee that he (the former) should provide the estate with a sum of money enabling the bankrupt to be left in possession of property which would otherwise be made to vest in the trustee under section 308.

(2) The trustee may accept that proposal, if satisfied that it is a reasonable one, and that the estate will benefit to the extent of the value of the property in question less the cost of a reasonable replacement.

NOTES

Initial Commencement

Specified date

Specified date: 29 December 1986: see r 0.1.

CHAPTER 16
INCOME PAYMENTS ORDERS

6.189 Application for order

(1) Where the trustee applies for an income payments order under section 310, the court shall fix a venue for the hearing of the application.

(2) Notice of the application, and of the venue, shall be sent by the trustee to the bankrupt at least 28 days before the day fixed for the hearing, together with a copy of the trustee's application and a short statement of the grounds on which it is made.

(3) The notice shall inform the bankrupt that—
- (a) unless at least [5 business] days before the date fixed for the hearing he sends to the court and to the trustee written consent to an order being made in the terms of the application, he is required to attend the hearing, and
- (b) if he attends, he will be given an opportunity to show cause why the order should not be made, or an order should be made otherwise than as applied for by the trustee.

NOTES

Initial Commencement

Specified date

Specified date: 29 December 1986: see r 0.1.

Amendment

Para (3): in sub-para (a) words "5 business" in square brackets substituted by SI 2010/686, r 2, Sch 1, para 394.
Date in force: 6 April 2010: see SI 2010/686, r 1; for transitional provisions see r 6(1), Sch 4, para 1 thereto.

6.190 Action to follow making of order

(1) Where the court makes an income payments order, a sealed copy of the order shall, [as soon as reasonably practicable] after it is made, be sent by the trustee to the bankrupt.

(2) If the order is made under section 310(3)(b), a sealed copy of the order shall also be sent by the trustee to the person to whom the order is directed.

NOTES

Initial Commencement

Specified date

Specified date: 29 December 1986: see r 0.1.

Amendment

Para (1): words "as soon as reasonably practicable" in square brackets substituted by SI 2009/642, rr 4, 5.
Date in force: 6 April 2009: see SI 2009/642, r 1; for transitional provisions see r 3 thereof.

6.191 Variation of order

(1) If an income payments order is made under section 310(3)(a), and the bankrupt does not comply with it, the trustee may apply to the court for the order to be varied, so as to take effect under section 310(3)(b) as an order to the payor of the relevant income.

(2) The trustee's application under this Rule may be made [without notice to any other party].

(3) Sealed copies of any order made on the application shall, [as soon as reasonably practicable] after it is made, be sent by the court to the trustee and the bankrupt.

(4) In the case of an order varying or discharging an income payments order made under section 310(3)(b), an additional sealed copy shall be sent to the trustee, for transmission [as soon as reasonably practicable] to the payor of the relevant income.

NOTES

Initial Commencement

Specified date

Specified date: 29 December 1986: see r 0.1.

Amendment

Para (2): words "without notice to any other party" in square brackets substituted by SI 2010/686, r 2, Sch 1, para 395.
Date in force: 6 April 2010: see SI 2010/686, r 1; for transitional provisions see r 6(1), Sch 4, paras 1, 2(1)(b) thereto.
Para (3): words "as soon as reasonably practicable" in square brackets substituted by SI 2009/642, rr 4, 5.
Date in force: 6 April 2009: see SI 2009/642, r 1; for transitional provisions see r 3 thereof.
Para (4): words "as soon as reasonably practicable" in square brackets substituted by SI 2009/642, rr 4, 5.
Date in force: 6 April 2009: see SI 2009/642, r 1; for transitional provisions see r 3 thereof.

6.192 Order to payor of income: administration

(1) Where a person receives notice of an income payments order under section 310(3)(b), with reference to income otherwise payable by him to the bankrupt, he shall make the arrangements requisite for [compliance with the order as soon as reasonably practicable].

(2) When making any payment to the trustee, he may deduct the appropriate fee towards the clerical and administrative costs of compliance with the income payments order.

He shall give to the bankrupt a written statement of any amount deducted by him under this paragraph.

(3) Where a person receives notice of an income payments order imposing on him a requirement under section 310(3)(b), and either—

(a) he is then no longer liable to make to the bankrupt any payment of income, or

(b) having made payments in compliance with the order, he ceases to be so liable,

he shall [as soon as reasonably practicable] give notice of that fact to the trustee.

NOTES

Initial Commencement

Specified date

Specified date: 29 December 1986: see r 0.1.

Amendment

Para (1): words "compliance with the order as soon as reasonably practicable" in square brackets substituted by SI 2010/686, r 2, Sch 1, para 396.

Date in force: 6 April 2010: see SI 2010/686, r 1; for transitional provisions see r 6(1), Sch 4, para 1 thereto.

Para (3): words "as soon as reasonably practicable" in square brackets substituted by SI 2009/642, rr 4, 5.

Date in force: 6 April 2009: see SI 2009/642, r 1; for transitional provisions see r 3 thereof.

6.193 Review of order

(1) Where an income payments order is in force, either the trustee or the bankrupt may apply to the court for the order to be varied or discharged.

(2) If the application is made by the trustee, Rule 6.189 applies (with any necessary modification) as in the case of an application for an income payments order.

(3) If the application is made by the bankrupt, it shall be accompanied by a short statement of the grounds on which it is made.

(4) The court may, if it thinks that no sufficient cause is shown for the application, dismiss it; but it shall not do so unless the applicant has had an opportunity to attend the court for [a] hearing, of which he has been given at least [5 business] days' notice [but which is without notice to any other party].

If the application is not dismissed under this paragraph, the court shall fix a venue for it to be heard.

(5) At least 28 days before the date fixed for the hearing, the applicant shall send to the trustee or the bankrupt (whichever of them is not himself the applicant) notice of the venue, accompanied by a copy of the application.

Where the applicant is the bankrupt, the notice shall be accompanied by a copy of the statement of grounds under paragraph (3).

(6) The trustee may, if he thinks fit, appear and be heard on the application; and, whether or not he intends to appear, he may, not less than [5 business] days before the date fixed for the hearing, file a written report of any matters which he considers ought to be drawn to the court's attention.

If such a report is filed, a copy of it shall be sent by the trustee to the bankrupt.

(7) Sealed copies of any order made on the application shall, [as soon as reasonably practicable] after the order is made, be sent by the court to the trustee, the bankrupt and the payor (if other than the bankrupt).

NOTES

Initial Commencement

Specified date

Specified date: 29 December 1986: see r 0.1.

Amendment

Para (4): word "a" in square brackets substituted by SI 2010/686, r 2, Sch 1, para 397(1), (2)(a).

Date in force: 6 April 2010: see SI 2010/686, r 1; for transitional provisions see r 6(1), Sch 4, paras 1, 2(1)(b) thereto.

Para (4): words "5 business" in square brackets substituted by SI 2010/686, r 2, Sch 1, para 397(1), (2)(b).

Date in force: 6 April 2010: see SI 2010/686, r 1; for transitional provisions see r 6(1), Sch 4, para 1 thereto.

Para (4): words "but which is without notice to any other party" in square brackets inserted by SI 2010/686, r 2, Sch 1, para 397(1), (2)(c).

Date in force: 6 April 2010: see SI 2010/686, r 1; for transitional provisions see r 6(1), Sch 4, paras 1, 2(1)(b) thereto.

Para (6): words "5 business" in square brackets substituted by SI 2010/686, r 2, Sch 1, para 397(1), (3).

Date in force: 6 April 2010: see SI 2010/686, r 1; for transitional provisions see r 6(1), Sch 4, para 1 thereto.

Para (7): words "as soon as reasonably practicable" in square brackets substituted by SI 2009/642, rr 4, 5.
>Date in force: 6 April 2009: see SI 2009/642, r 1; for transitional provisions see r 3 thereof.

[CHAPTER 16A
INCOME PAYMENTS AGREEMENTS]

NOTES

Amendment

>Inserted by SI 2003/1730, r 9(1), Sch 1, Pt 6, para 39.
>Date in force: 1 April 2004: see SI 2003/1730, r 1(3).

[6.193A Approval of income payments agreements]

[(1) An income payments agreement can only be entered into prior to the discharge of the bankrupt.

(2) Where an income payments agreement is to be entered into between the official receiver or trustee and the bankrupt under section 310A(1), the official receiver or trustee shall provide an income payments agreement to the bankrupt for his approval.

(3) Within 14 days or such longer period as may be specified by the official receiver or trustee (whichever is appropriate) from the date on which the income payments agreement was sent, the bankrupt shall—

(a) if he decides to approve the draft income payments agreement, [authenticate] the agreement and return it to the official receiver or trustee (whichever is appropriate); or

(b) if he decides not to approve the agreement, notify the official receiver or trustee (whichever is appropriate) in writing of his decision.]

NOTES

Amendment

>Inserted by SI 2003/1730, r 9(1), Sch 1, Pt 6, para 39.
>Date in force: 1 April 2004: see SI 2003/1730, r 1(3).
>Para (3): in sub-para (a) word "authenticate" in square brackets substituted by SI 2010/686, r 2, Sch 1, para 1.
>Date in force: 6 April 2010: see SI 2010/686, r 1; for transitional provisions see r 6(1), Sch 4, paras 1, 2(1)(b) thereto.

[6.193B Acceptance of income payments agreements]

[(1) On receipt by the official receiver or trustee of the [authenticated] income payments agreement, the official receiver or trustee shall [authenticate] and date it.

(2) When the official receiver or the trustee [authenticates] and dates the income payments agreement, it shall come into force. A copy shall be sent to the bankrupt.

(3) Where the agreement provides for payments by a third person to the official receiver or trustee who is not the official receiver in accordance with section 310A(1)(b), a notice of the agreement shall be sent by the official receiver or trustee to that person.

(4) The notice shall contain—

(a) the full name and address of the bankrupt;

(b) a statement that an income payments agreement has been made, the date of it, and that it provides for the payment by the third person of sums

(c) the full name and address of the third person;
(d) a statement of the amount of money to be paid to the official receiver or trustee from the bankrupt's income, the period over which the payments are to be made, and the intervals at which the sums are to be paid; and
(e) the full name and address of the official receiver or trustee and the address or details of where the sums are to be paid.

(5) When making any payment to the official receiver or the trustee a person who has received notice of an income payments agreement with reference to income otherwise payable by him to the bankrupt may deduct the appropriate fee towards the clerical and administrative costs of compliance with the income payments agreement. He shall give to the bankrupt a written statement of any amount deducted by him under this paragraph.]

NOTES

Amendment

Inserted by SI 2003/1730, r 9(1), Sch 1, Pt 6, para 39.
Date in force: 1 April 2004: see SI 2003/1730, r 1(3).
Para (1): word "authenticated" in square brackets substituted by SI 2010/686, r 2, Sch 1, para 1.
Date in force: 6 April 2010: see SI 2010/686, r 1; for transitional provisions see r 6(1), Sch 4, paras 1, 2(1)(b) thereto.
Para (1): word "authenticate" in square brackets substituted by SI 2010/686, r 2, Sch 1, para 1.
Date in force: 6 April 2010: see SI 2010/686, r 1; for transitional provisions see r 6(1), Sch 4, paras 1, 2(1)(b) thereto.
Para (2): word "authenticates" in square brackets substituted by SI 2010/686, r 2, Sch 1, para 1.
Date in force: 6 April 2010: see SI 2010/686, r 1; for transitional provisions see r 6(1), Sch 4, paras 1, 2(1)(b) thereto.

[6.193C Variation of income payments agreements]

[(1) Where an application is made to court for variation of an income payments agreement, the application shall be accompanied by a copy of the agreement.

(2) Where the bankrupt applies to the court for variation of an income payments agreement under section 310A(6)(b), he shall send a copy of the application and notice of the venue to the official receiver or trustee (whichever is appropriate) at least 28 days before the date fixed for the hearing.

(3) When the official receiver or trustee applies to the court for variation of an income payments agreement under section 310A(6)(b), he shall send a copy of the application and notice of the venue to the bankrupt at least 28 days before the date fixed for the hearing.

(4) The court may order in Form 6.81 the variation of an income payments agreement under section 310A.

(5) Where the court orders an income payments agreement under section 310A(1)(a) to be varied, so as to take the form of an agreement under section 310A(1)(b) as an agreement providing that a third person is to make payments to the trustee or the official receiver, the official receiver or trustee shall send a notice in accordance with Rule 6.193B(3).

(6) When making any payment to the official receiver or the trustee a person who has received notice of an income payments agreement with reference to income otherwise payable by him to the bankrupt may deduct the appropriate fee towards the

clerical and administrative costs of compliance with the income payments agreement. He shall give to the bankrupt a written statement of any amount deducted by him under this paragraph.]

NOTES

Amendment

Inserted by SI 2003/1730, r 9(1), Sch 1, Pt 6, para 39.
Date in force: 1 April 2004: see SI 2003/1730, r 1(3).

CHAPTER 17

ACTION BY COURT UNDER SECTION 369; ORDER TO INLAND REVENUE OFFICIAL

6.194 Application for order

(1) An application by the official receiver or the trustee for an order under section 369 (order to [HM Revenue and Customs] official to produce documents) shall specify (with such particularity as will enable the order, if made, to be most easily complied with) the documents whose production to the court is desired, naming the official to whom the order is to be addressed.

(2) The court shall fix a venue for the hearing of the application.

(3) Notice of the venue, accompanied by a copy of the application, shall be sent by the applicant to the Commissioners [for HM Revenue and Customs] ("the Commissioners") at least 28 days before the hearing.

(4) The notice shall require the Commissioners, not later than [5 business] days before the date fixed for the hearing of the application, to inform the court whether they consent or object to the making of an order under the section.

(5) If the Commissioners consent to the making of an order, they shall inform the court of the name of the official to whom it should be addressed, if other than the one named in the application.

(6) If the Commissioners object to the making of an order, they shall secure that an officer of theirs attends the hearing of the application and, not less than [5 business] days before it, deliver to the court a statement in writing of their grounds of objection.

A copy of the statement shall be sent [as soon as reasonably practicable] to the applicant.

NOTES

Initial Commencement

Specified date

Specified date: 29 December 1986: see r 0.1.

Amendment

Para (1): words "HM Revenue and Customs" in square brackets substituted by SI 2010/686, r 2, Sch 1, para 398(1), (2).
   Date in force: 6 April 2010: see SI 2010/686, r 1; for transitional provisions see r 6(1), Sch 4, paras 1, 2(1)(b) thereto.
Para (3): words "for HM Revenue and Customs" in square brackets substituted by SI 2010/686, r 2, Sch 1, para 398(1), (3).
   Date in force: 6 April 2010: see SI 2010/686, r 1; for transitional provisions see r 6(1), Sch 4, paras 1, 2(1)(b) thereto.
Para (4): words "5 business" in square brackets substituted by SI 2010/686, r 2, Sch 1, para 398(1), (4).
   Date in force: 6 April 2010: see SI 2010/686, r 1; for transitional provisions see r 6(1), Sch 4, para 1 thereto.

Para (6): words "5 business" in square brackets substituted by SI 2010/686, r 2, Sch 1, para 398(1), (4).
> Date in force: 6 April 2010: see SI 2010/686, r 1; for transitional provisions see r 6(1), Sch 4, para 1 thereto.

Para (6): words "as soon as reasonably practicable" in square brackets substituted by SI 2009/642, rr 4, 5.
> Date in force: 6 April 2009: see SI 2009/642, r 1; for transitional provisions see r 3 thereto.

6.195 Making and service of the order

(1) If on the hearing of the application it appears to the court to be a proper case, the court may make the order applied for, with such modifications (if any) as appear appropriate having regard to any representations made on behalf of the Commissioners.

(2) The order—

(a) may be addressed to an [HM Revenue and Customs] official other than the one named in the application,

(b) shall specify a time, not less than 28 days after service on the official to whom the order is addressed, within which compliance is required, and

(c) may include requirements as to the manner in which documents to which the order relates are to be produced.

(3) A sealed copy of the order shall be served by the applicant on the official to whom it is addressed.

(4) If the official is unable to comply with the order because he has not the relevant documents in his possession, and has been unable to obtain possession of them, he shall deliver to the court a statement in writing as to the reasons for his non-compliance.

A copy of the statement shall be sent [as soon as reasonably practicable] by the official to the applicant.

NOTES

Initial Commencement

Specified date
> Specified date: 29 December 1986: see r 0.1.

Amendment
> Para (2): in sub-para (a) words "HM Revenue and Customs" in square brackets substituted by SI 2010/686, r 2, Sch 1, para 399.
>> Date in force: 6 April 2010: see SI 2010/686, r 1; for transitional provisions see r 6(1), Sch 4, paras 1, 2(1)(b) thereto.
>
> Para (4): words "as soon as reasonably practicable" in square brackets substituted by SI 2009/642, rr 4, 5.
>> Date in force: 6 April 2009: see SI 2009/642, r 1; for transitional provisions see r 3 thereto.

6.196 Custody of documents

Where in compliance with an order under section 369 original documents are produced, and not copies, any person who, by order of the court under section 369(2) (authorised disclosure to persons with right of inspection), has them in his possession or custody is responsible to the court for their safe keeping and return as and when directed.

NOTES

Initial Commencement

Specified date

Specified date: 29 December 1986: see r 0.1.

CHAPTER 18
MORTGAGED PROPERTY

6.197 Claim by mortgagee of land

(1) Any person claiming to be the legal or equitable mortgagee of land belonging to the bankrupt may apply to the court for an order directing that the land be sold.

"Land" includes any interest in, or right over, land.

(2) The court, if satisfied as to the applicant's title, may direct accounts to be taken and enquiries made to ascertain—

    (a) the principal, interest and costs due under the mortgage, and

    (b) where the mortgagee has been in possession of the land or any part of it, the rents and profits, dividends, interest, or other proceeds received by him or on his behalf.

Directions may be given by the court under this paragraph with respect to any mortgage (whether prior or subsequent) on the same property, other than that of the applicant.

(3) For the purpose of those accounts and enquiries, and of making title to the purchaser, any of the parties may be examined by the court, and shall produce on oath before the court all such documents in their custody or under their control relating to the estate of the bankrupt as the court may direct.

[The court may under this paragraph order any of the parties to clarify any matter which is in dispute in the proceedings or give additional information in relation to any such matter and CPR Part 18 (further information) shall apply to any such order.]

(4) In any proceedings between a mortgagor and mortgagee, or the trustee of either of them, the court may order accounts to be taken and enquiries made in like manner as in the Chancery Division of the High Court.

NOTES

Initial Commencement

Specified date

Specified date: 29 December 1986: see r 0.1.

Amendment

Para (3): words from "The court" to "any such order." in square brackets substituted by SI 1999/1022, r 3, Schedule, para 2.

Date in force: 26 April 1999: see SI 1999/1022, r 1.

6.198 Power of court to order sale

(1) The court may order that the land, or any specified part of it, be sold; and any party bound by the order and in possession of the land or part, or in receipt of the rents and profits from it, may be ordered to deliver up possession or receipt to the purchaser or to such other person as the court may direct.

(2) The court may permit the person having the conduct of the sale to sell the land in such manner as he thinks fit. Alternatively, the court may direct that the land be sold as directed by the order.

(3) The court's order may contain directions—
- (a) appointing the persons to have the conduct of the sale;
- (b) fixing the manner of sale (whether by contract conditional on the court's approval, private treaty, public auction, or otherwise);
- (c) settling the particulars and conditions of sale;
- (d) obtaining evidence of the value of the property, and fixing a reserve or minimum price;
- (e) requiring particular persons to join in the sale and conveyance;
- (f) requiring the payment of the purchase money into court, or to trustees or others;
- (g) if the sale is to be by public auction, fixing the security (if any) to be given by the auctioneer, and his remuneration.

(4) The court may direct that, if the sale is to be by public auction, the mortgagee may appear and bid on his own behalf.

[(5) Nothing in this Rule or the following Rule may affect the rights in rem of creditors or third parties protected under Article 5 of the EC Regulation (third parties' rights in rem).]

NOTES

Initial Commencement

Specified date

Specified date: 29 December 1986: see r 0.1.

Amendment

Para (5): inserted by SI 2002/1307, rr 3(1), 8(8).
Date in force: 31 May 2002: see SI 2002/1307, r 1.

6.199 Proceeds of sale

(1) The proceeds of sale shall be applied—
- (a) first, in payment of the expenses of the trustee, of and occasioned by the application to the court, of the sale and attendance thereat, and of any costs arising from the taking of accounts, and making of enquiries, as directed by the court under Rule 6.197; and
- (b) secondly, in payment of the amount found due to any mortgagee, for principal, interest and costs;

and the balance (if any) shall be retained by or paid to the trustee.

(2) Where the proceeds of the sale are insufficient to pay in full the amount found due to any mortgagee, he is entitled to prove as a creditor for any deficiency, and to receive dividends rateably with other creditors, but not so as to disturb any dividend already declared.

NOTES

Initial Commencement

Specified date

Specified date: 29 December 1986: see r 0.1.

CHAPTER 19

AFTER-ACQUIRED PROPERTY

6.200 Duties of bankrupt in respect of after-acquired property

(1) The notice to be given by the bankrupt to the trustee, under section 333(2), of property acquired by, or devolving upon, him, or of any increase of his income, shall be given within 21 days of his becoming aware of the relevant facts.

(2) Having served notice in respect of property acquired by or devolving upon him, the bankrupt shall not, without the trustee's consent in writing, dispose of it within the period of 42 days beginning with the date of the notice.

(3) If the bankrupt disposes of property before giving the notice required by this Rule or in contravention of paragraph (2), it is the duty [as soon as reasonably practicable] to disclose to the trustee the name and address of the disponee, and to provide any other information which may be necessary to enable the trustee to trace the property and recover it for the estate.

(4) Subject as follows, paragraphs (1) to (3) do not apply to property acquired by the bankrupt in the ordinary course of a business carried on by him.

(5) If the bankrupt carries on a business, he shall, [when required by the trustee], furnish to the trustee information with respect to it, showing the total of goods bought and sold (or, as the case may be, services supplied) and the profit or loss arising from the business.

The trustee may require the bankrupt to furnish fuller details (including accounts) of the business carried on by him.

NOTES

Initial Commencement

Specified date

Specified date: 29 December 1986: see r 0.1.

Amendment

Para (3): words "as soon as reasonably practicable" in square brackets substituted by SI 2009/642, rr 4, 5.
Date in force: 6 April 2009: see SI 2009/642, r 1; for transitional provisions see r 3 thereof.

Para (5): words "when required by the trustee" in square brackets substituted by SI 2010/686, r 2, Sch 1, para 400.
Date in force: 6 April 2010: see SI 2010/686, r 1; for transitional provisions see r 6(1), Sch 4, para 1 thereto.

6.201 Trustee's recourse to disponee of property

(1) Where property has been disposed of by the bankrupt, before giving the notice required by Rule 6.200 or otherwise in contravention of that Rule, the trustee may serve notice on the disponee, claiming the property as part of the estate by virtue of section 307(3).

(2) The trustee's notice under this Rule must be served within 28 days of his becoming aware of the disponee's identity and an address at which he can be served.

NOTES

Initial Commencement

Specified date

Specified date: 29 December 1986: see r 0.1.

6.202 Expenses of getting in property for the estate
Any expenses incurred by the trustee in acquiring title to after-acquired property shall be paid out of the estate, in the prescribed order of priority.

NOTES
Initial Commencement
Specified date
    Specified date: 29 December 1986: see r 0.1.

CHAPTER 20
[PERMISSION] TO ACT AS DIRECTOR, ETC

NOTES
Amendment
    Chapter heading: word "Permission" in square brackets substituted by SI 2010/686, r 2, Sch 1, para 1.
        Date in force: 6 April 2010: see SI 2010/686, r 1; for transitional provisions see r 6(1), Sch 4, paras 1, 2(1)(b) thereto.

[6.202A]
[In this Chapter a reference to a bankrupt includes a reference to a person in respect of whom a bankruptcy restrictions order is in force.]

NOTES
Amendment
    Inserted by SI 2003/1730, r 9(1), Sch 1, Pt 6, para 40.
        Date in force: 1 April 2004: see SI 2003/1730, r 1(3).

6.203 Application for [permission]
(1) An application by the bankrupt for [permission], under section 11 of the Company Directors Disqualification Act 1986, to act as director of, or to take part or be concerned in the promotion, formation or management of a company, shall be supported by [a witness statement] complying with this Rule.

(2) The [witness statement] must identify the company and specify—
    (a)   the nature of its business or intended business, and the place or places where that business is, or is to be, carried on,
    (b)   [in the case of a company which has not yet been incorporated,] whether it is, or is to be, a private or a public company,
    (c)   the persons who are, or are to be, principally responsible for the conduct of its affairs (whether as directors, shadow directors, managers or otherwise),
    (d)   the manner and capacity in which the applicant proposes to take part or be concerned in the promotion or formation of the company or, as the case may be, its management, and
    (e)   the emoluments and other benefits to be obtained from the directorship.

(3) . . .
(4) . . .
(5) The court shall fix a venue for the hearing of the bankrupt's application, and give notice to him accordingly.

NOTES

Initial Commencement

Specified date

Specified date: 29 December 1986: see r 0.1.

Amendment

Provision heading: word "permission" in square brackets substituted by SI 2010/686, r 2, Sch 1, para 1.
Date in force: 6 April 2010: see SI 2010/686, r 1; for transitional provisions see r 6(1), Sch 4, paras 1, 2(1)(b) thereto.
Para (1): word "permission" in square brackets substituted by SI 2010/686, r 2, Sch 1, para 1.
Date in force: 6 April 2010: see SI 2010/686, r 1; for transitional provisions see r 6(1), Sch 4, paras 1, 2(1)(b) thereto.
Para (1): words "a witness statement" in square brackets substituted by SI 2010/686, r 2, Sch 1, para 401(1), (2).
Date in force: 6 April 2010: see SI 2010/686, r 1; for transitional provisions see r 6(1), Sch 4, paras 1, 2(1)(b), (2)–(4) thereto.
Para (2): words "witness statement" in square brackets substituted by SI 2010/686, r 2, Sch 1, para 401(1), (3)(a).
Date in force: 6 April 2010: see SI 2010/686, r 1; for transitional provisions see r 6(1), Sch 4, paras 1, 2(1)(b), (2)–(4) thereto.
Para (2): in sub-para (b) words "in the case of a company which has not yet been incorporated," in square brackets inserted by SI 2010/686, r 2, Sch 1, para 401(1), (3)(b).
Date in force: 6 April 2010: see SI 2010/686, r 1; for transitional provisions see r 6(1), Sch 4, para 1 thereto.
Paras (3), (4): revoked by SI 2010/686, r 2, Sch 1, para 401(1), (4).
Date in force: 6 April 2010: see SI 2010/686, r 1; for transitional provisions see r 6(1), Sch 4, para 1 thereto.

6.204 Report of official receiver

(1) The bankrupt shall, not less than 28 days before the date fixed for the hearing, give to the official receiver and the trustee notice of the venue, accompanied by copies of the application and the [witness statement] under Rule 6.203.

(2) The official receiver may, not less than 14 days before the date fixed for the hearing, file in court a report of any matters which he considers ought to be drawn to the court's attention. A copy of the report shall be sent by him, [as soon as reasonably practicable] after it is filed, to the bankrupt and to the trustee.

(3) The bankrupt may, not later than [5 business] days before the date of the hearing, file in court a notice specifying any statements in the official receiver's report which he intends to deny or dispute.

If he gives notice under this paragraph, he shall send copies of it, not less than 4 days before the date of the hearing, to the official receiver and the trustee.

(4) The official receiver and the trustee may appear on the hearing of the application, and may make representations and put to the bankrupt such questions as the court may allow.

NOTES

Initial Commencement

Specified date

Specified date: 29 December 1986: see r 0.1.

Amendment

Para (1): words "witness statement" in square brackets substituted by SI 2010/686, r 2, Sch 1, para 401(1), (2).
    Date in force: 6 April 2010: see SI 2010/686, r 1; for transitional provisions see r 6(1), Sch 4, paras 1, 2(1)(b), (2)–(4) thereto.
Para (2): words "as soon as reasonably practicable" in square brackets substituted by SI 2009/642, rr 4, 5.
    Date in force: 6 April 2009: see SI 2009/642, r 1; for transitional provisions see r 3 thereof.
Para (3): words "5 business" in square brackets substituted by SI 2010/686, r 2, Sch 1, para 402(1), (3).
    Date in force: 6 April 2010: see SI 2010/686, r 1; for transitional provisions see r 6(1), Sch 4, para 1 thereto.

6.205 Court's order on application

(1) If the court grants the bankrupt's application for [permission] under section 11 of the Company Directors Disqualification Act 1986, its order shall specify that which by virtue of the order the bankrupt has [permission] to do.

(2) The court may at the same time, having regard to any representations made by the trustee on the hearing of the application—

    (a)   include in the order provision varying an income payments order [or an income payments agreement] already in force in respect of the bankrupt, or

    (b)   if no income payments order is in force, make one.

(3) Whether or not the application is granted, copies of the order shall be sent by the court to the bankrupt, the trustee and the official receiver.

NOTES

Initial Commencement

Specified date

    Specified date: 29 December 1986: see r 0.1.

Amendment

Para (1): word "permission" in square brackets in both places it occurs substituted by SI 2010/686, r 2, Sch 1, para 1.
    Date in force: 6 April 2010: see SI 2010/686, r 1; for transitional provisions see r 6(1), Sch 4, paras 1, 2(1)(b) thereto.
Para (2): in sub-para (a) words "or an income payments agreement" in square brackets inserted by SI 2003/1730, r 9(1), Sch 1, Pt 6, para 41.
    Date in force: 1 April 2004: see SI 2003/1730, r 1(3).

CHAPTER 21

ANNULMENT OF BANKRUPTCY ORDER

6.206 Application for annulment

(1) An application to the court under section 282(1) for the annulment of a bankruptcy order shall specify whether it is made—

    (a)   under subsection (1)(a) of the section (claim that the order ought not to have been made), or

    (b)   under subsection (1)(b) (debts and expenses of the bankruptcy all paid or secured).

(2) The application shall, in either case, be supported by [a witness statement] stating the grounds on which it is made; and, where it is made under section 282(1)(b),

there shall be set out in [the witness statement] all the facts by reference to which the court is, under the Act and the Rules, required to be satisfied before annulling the bankruptcy order.

(3) A copy of the application and [the witness statement in support must be filed with the court]; and the court shall give to the applicant notice of the venue fixed for the hearing.

(4) The applicant shall . . . give to the official receiver and (if other) the trustee notice of the venue, accompanied by copies of the application and the [witness statement] under paragraph (2)[—
    (a)   where the application is made under section 282(1)(a), in sufficient time to enable them to be present at the hearing, and
    (b)   where the application is made under section 282(1)(b), not less than 28 days before the hearing].

[(5) Where the application is made under section 282(1)(a), paragraph (4) shall additionally be complied with in relation to the person on whose petition the bankruptcy order was made.]

[(6) In this Chapter, where the applicant is not the bankrupt all notices, documents and [evidence] required to be given, sent or delivered to another party by the applicant shall also be given, sent or delivered to the bankrupt.]

NOTES

Initial Commencement

Specified date
    Specified date: 29 December 1986: see r 0.1.

Amendment

    Para (2): words "a witness statement" in square brackets substituted by SI 2010/686, r 2, Sch 1, para 403(1), (2)(a).
        Date in force: 6 April 2010: see SI 2010/686, r 1; for transitional provisions see r 6(1), Sch 4, paras 1, 2(1)(b), (2)–(4) thereto.
    Para (2): words "the witness statement" in square brackets substituted by SI 2010/686, r 2, Sch 1, para 403(1), (2)(b).
        Date in force: 6 April 2010: see SI 2010/686, r 1; for transitional provisions see r 6(1), Sch 4, paras 1, 2(1)(b), (2)–(4) thereto.
    Para (3): words "the witness statement in support must be filed with the court" in square brackets substituted by SI 2010/686, r 2, Sch 1, para 403(1), (3).
        Date in force: 6 April 2010: see SI 2010/686, r 1; for transitional provisions see r 6(1), Sch 4, paras 1, 2(1)(b), (2)–(4) thereto.
    Para (4): words omitted revoked by SI 1987/1919, r 3(1), Schedule, Pt 1, para 121(1).
    Para (4): words "witness statement" in square brackets substituted by SI 2010/686, r 2, Sch 1, para 403(1), (4).
        Date in force: 6 April 2010: see SI 2010/686, r 1; for transitional provisions see r 6(1), Sch 4, paras 1, 2(1)(b), (2)–(4) thereto.
    Para (4): sub-paras (a), (b) inserted by SI 1987/1919, r 3(1), Schedule, Pt 1, para 121(1).
    Para (5): inserted by SI 1987/1919, r 3(1), Schedule, Pt 1, para 121(2).
    Para (6): inserted by SI 2003/1730, r 9(1), Sch 1, Pt 6, para 42.
        Date in force: 1 April 2004: see SI 2003/1730, r 1(3).
    Para (6): word "evidence" in square brackets substituted by SI 2010/686, r 2, Sch 1, para 403(1), (5).
        Date in force: 6 April 2010: see SI 2010/686, r 1; for transitional provisions see r 6(1), Sch 4, paras 1, 2(1)(b), (2)–(4) thereto.

6.207 Report by trustee

(1) The following applies where the application is made under section 282(1)(b) (debts and expenses of the bankruptcy all paid or secured).

(2) Not less than 21 days before the date fixed for the hearing, the trustee or, if no trustee has been appointed, the official receiver shall file in court a report with respect to the following matters—
- (a) the circumstances leading to the bankruptcy;
- (b) (in summarised form) the extent of the bankrupt's assets and liabilities at the date of the bankruptcy order and at the date of the present application;
- (c) details of creditors (if any) who are known to him to have claims, but have not proved; and
- (d) such other matters as the person making the report considers to be, in the circumstances, necessary for the information of the court.

[(2A) Where the trustee is other than the official receiver, the report under paragraph (2) must also include a statement of—
- (a) the trustee's remuneration;
- (b) the basis fixed for the trustee's remuneration under Rule 6.138;
- (c) the expenses incurred by the trustee.]

(3) The report shall include particulars of the extent (if any) to which, and the manner in which, the debts and expenses of the bankruptcy have been paid or secured.

In so far as debts and expenses are unpaid but secured, the person making the report shall state in it whether and to what extent he considers the security to be satisfactory.

(4) A copy of the report shall be sent to the applicant [at the same time that it is filed in court]; and he may, if he wishes, file further [witness statements] in answer to statements made in the report.

Copies of any such [witness statements] shall be sent by the applicant to the official receiver and (if other) the trustee.

(5) If the trustee is other than the official receiver, a copy of his report shall be sent to the official receiver at least 21 days before the hearing. The official receiver may then file an additional report, a copy of which shall be sent to the applicant at least [5 business] days before the hearing.

NOTES

Initial Commencement

Specified date

Specified date: 29 December 1986: see r 0.1.

Amendment

Para (2A): inserted by SI 2010/686, r 2, Sch 1, para 404(1), (2).
Date in force: 6 April 2010: see SI 2010/686, r 1; for transitional provisions see r 6(1), Sch 4, para 1 thereto.
Para (4): words "at the same time that it is filed in court" in square brackets substituted by SI 2010/686, r 2, Sch 1, para 404(1), (3)(a).
Date in force: 6 April 2010: see SI 2010/686, r 1; for transitional provisions see r 6(1), Sch 4, para 1 thereto.
Para (4): words "witness statements" in square brackets in both places they occur substituted by SI 2010/686, r 2, Sch 1, para 404(1), (3)(b).
Date in force: 6 April 2010: see SI 2010/686, r 1; for transitional provisions see r 6(1), Sch 4, paras 1, 2(1)(b), (2)–(4) thereto.
Para (5): words "5 business" in square brackets substituted by SI 2010/686, r 2, Sch 1, para 404(1), (4).
Date in force: 6 April 2010: see SI 2010/686, r 1; for transitional provisions see r 6(1), Sch 4, para 1 thereto.

[6.207A Applicant's claim that remuneration is or expenses are excessive]

[(1) Where the trustee is other than the official receiver and application for annulment is made under section 282(1)(b), the applicant may also apply to the court for one or more of the orders in paragraph (4) on the ground that the remuneration charged or expenses incurred by the trustee is or are, in all the circumstances, excessive.

(2) Application under paragraph (1) must be made no later than 5 business days before the date fixed for the hearing of the application for annulment and be accompanied by a copy of any evidence which the applicant intends to adduce in support.

(3) The applicant under paragraph (1) must send a copy of the application and of any evidence accompanying it to the trustee at the same time that the application is made.

(4) If the court annuls the bankruptcy order under section 282(1)(b) and considers the application under paragraph (1) to be well-founded, it must also make one or more of the following orders—

(a) an order reducing the amount of remuneration which the trustee was entitled to charge;

(b) an order that some or all of the remuneration or expenses in question be treated as not being bankruptcy expenses;

(c) an order that the trustee or the trustee's personal representative pay to the applicant the amount of the excess of remuneration or expenses or such part of the excess as the court may specify;

and may make any other order that it thinks just.]

NOTES

Amendment

Inserted by SI 2010/686, r 2, Sch 1, para 405.
Date in force: 6 April 2010: see SI 2010/686, r 1; for transitional provisions see r 6(1), Sch 4, para 1 thereto.

6.208 Power of court to stay proceedings

(1) The court may, in advance of the hearing, make an interim order staying any proceedings which it thinks ought, in the circumstances of the application, to be stayed.

[(2) Except in relation to an application for an order staying all or any part of the proceedings in the bankruptcy, application for an order under this Rule may be made [without notice to any other party].

(3) Where application is made under this Rule for an order staying all or any part of the proceedings in the bankruptcy, the applicant shall send copies of the application to the official receiver and (if other) the trustee in sufficient time to enable them to be present at the hearing and (if they wish to do so) make representations.

(4) Where the court makes an order under this Rule staying all or any part of the proceedings in the bankruptcy, the rules in this Chapter nevertheless continue to apply to any application for, or other matters in connection with, the annulment of the bankruptcy order.

(5) If the court makes an order under this Rule, it shall send copies of the order to the applicant, the official receiver and (if other) the trustee.]

NOTES

Initial Commencement

Specified date

Specified date: 29 December 1986: see r 0.1.

Amendment

Paras (2)–(5): substituted, for para (2) as originally enacted, by SI 1987/1919, r 3(1), Schedule, Part 1, para 122.

Para (2): words "without notice to any other party" in square brackets substituted by SI 2010/686, r 2, Sch 1, para 406.

Date in force: 6 April 2010: see SI 2010/686, r 1; for transitional provisions see r 6(1), Sch 4, paras 1, 2(1)(b) thereto.

6.209 Notice to creditors who have not proved

Where the application for annulment is made under section 282(1)(b) and it has been reported to the court under Rule 6.207 that there are known creditors of the bankrupt who have not proved, the court may—

(a) direct the trustee [or, if no trustee has been appointed, the official receiver] to send notice of the application to such of those creditors as the court thinks ought to be informed of it, with a view to their proving their debts (if they so wish) within 21 days, and

(b) direct the trustee [or, if no trustee has been appointed, the official receiver] to advertise the fact that the application has been made, so that creditors who have not proved may do so within a specified time, and

(c) adjourn the application meanwhile, for any period not less than 35 days.

NOTES

Initial Commencement

Specified date

Specified date: 29 December 1986: see r 0.1.

Amendment

Words in square brackets inserted by SI 1987/1919, r 3(1), Schedule, Part 1, para 123.

6.210 The hearing

(1) The trustee shall attend the hearing of the application.

(2) The official receiver, if he is not the trustee, may attend, but is not required to do so unless he has filed a report under Rule 6.207.

(3) If the court makes an order on the application [or on an application under Rule 6.207A], it shall send copies of the order to the applicant, the official receiver and (if other) the trustee.

NOTES

Initial Commencement

Specified date

Specified date: 29 December 1986: see r 0.1.

Amendment

Para (3): words "or on an application under Rule 6.207A" in square brackets inserted by SI 2010/686, r 2, Sch 1, para 407.

Date in force: 6 April 2010: see SI 2010/686, r 1; for transitional provisions see r 6(1), Sch 4, para 1 thereto.

6.211 Matters to be proved under s 282(1)(b)

(1) This rule applies with regard to the matters which[—

(a)] must, in an application under section 282(1)(b), be proved to the satisfaction of the court[; and
(b) may be taken into account by the court on hearing such an application].

(2) Subject to the following paragraph, all bankruptcy debts which have been proved must have been[—
(a)] paid in full[, or
(b) secured in full to the satisfaction of the court].

(3) If a debt is disputed, or a creditor who has proved can no longer be traced, the bankrupt must have given such security (in the form of money paid into court, or a bond entered into with approved sureties) as the court considers adequate to satisfy any sum that may subsequently be proved to be due to the creditor concerned and (if the court thinks [just]) costs.

(4) Where under paragraph (3) security has been given in the case of an untraced creditor, the court may direct that particulars of the alleged debt, and the security, be advertised in such manner as it thinks [just].

If advertisement is ordered under this paragraph, and no claim on the security is made within 12 months from the date of the advertisement (or the first advertisement, if more than one), the court shall, on application in that behalf, order the security to be released.

[(5) In determining whether to annul a bankruptcy order under section 282(1)(b), the court may, if it thinks just and without prejudice to the generality of its discretion under section 282(1), take into account whether any sums have been paid or payment of any sums has been secured in respect of post-commencement interest on the bankruptcy debts which have been proved.

(6) For the purposes of paragraphs (2) and (5), security includes an undertaking given by a solicitor and accepted by the court.

(7) For the purposes of paragraph (5), "post-commencement interest" means interest on the bankruptcy debts at the rate specified in section 328(5) in respect of periods during which those debts have been outstanding since the commencement of the bankruptcy.]

NOTES

Initial Commencement

Specified date

Specified date: 29 December 1986: see r 0.1.

Amendment

Para (1): sub-para (a) designated as such by SI 2010/686, r 2, Sch 1, para 408(1), (2).
Date in force: 6 April 2010: see SI 2010/686, r 1; for transitional provisions see r 6(1), Sch 4, para 1 thereto.
Para (1): sub-para (b) and word "; and" immediately preceding it inserted by SI 2010/686, r 2, Sch 1, para 408(1), (2).
Date in force: 6 April 2010: see SI 2010/686, r 1; for transitional provisions see r 6(1), Sch 4, para 1 thereto.
Para (2): sub-para (a) designated as such by SI 2010/686, r 2, Sch 1, para 408(1), (3).
Date in force: 6 April 2010: see SI 2010/686, r 1; for transitional provisions see r 6(1), Sch 4, para 1 thereto.
Para (2): sub-para (b) and word ", or" immediately preceding it inserted by SI 2010/686, r 2, Sch 1, para 408(1), (3).
Date in force: 6 April 2010: see SI 2010/686, r 1; for transitional provisions see r 6(1), Sch 4, para 1 thereto.
Para (3): word "just" in square brackets substituted by SI 2010/686, r 2, Sch 1, para 1.
Date in force: 6 April 2010: see SI 2010/686, r 1; for transitional provisions see r 6(1), Sch 4, paras 1, 2(1)(b) thereto.
Para (4): word "just" in square brackets substituted by SI 2010/686, r 2, Sch 1, para 1.

Date in force: 6 April 2010: see SI 2010/686, r 1; for transitional provisions see r 6(1), Sch 4, paras 1, 2(1)(b) thereto.
Paras (5)–(7): inserted by SI 2010/686, r 2, Sch 1, para 408(1), (4).
Date in force: 6 April 2010: see SI 2010/686, r 1; for transitional provisions see r 6(1), Sch 4, para 1 thereto.

6.212 Notice to creditors

(1) Where the official receiver has notified creditors of the debtor's bankruptcy, and the bankruptcy order is annulled, he shall [as soon as reasonably practicable] notify them of the annulment.

(2) Expenses incurred by the official receiver in giving notice under this Rule are a charge in his favour on the property of the former bankrupt, whether or not actually in his hands.

(3) Where any property is in the hands of a trustee or any person other than the former bankrupt himself, the official receiver's charge is valid subject only to any costs that may be incurred by the trustee or that other person in effecting realisation of the property for the purpose of satisfying the charge.

NOTES

Initial Commencement

Specified date
Specified date: 29 December 1986: see r 0.1.

Amendment
Para (1): words "as soon as reasonably practicable" in square brackets substituted by SI 2009/642, rr 4, 5.
Date in force: 6 April 2009: see SI 2009/642, r 1; for transitional provisions see r 3 thereof.

[6.212A ...]
[...]

NOTES

Amendment
Revoked by SI 2003/1730, r 9(1), Sch 1, Pt 6, para 43.
Date in force: 1 April 2004: see SI 2003/1730, r 1(3); for the continuing operation of this rule in relation to a pre-commencement bankruptcy see rr 2(3), (4), 9(3)(a) thereof.

6.213 Other matters arising on annulment

(1) In an order under section [...] 282 the court shall include provision permitting vacation of the registration of the bankruptcy petition as a pending action, and of the bankruptcy order, in the register of writs and orders affecting land.

(2) The court shall [as soon as reasonably practicable] give notice of the making of the order to the Secretary of State.

[(3) Within 28 days of the making of the order, the former bankrupt may require the Secretary of State to give notice of the making of the order. As soon as reasonably practicable such notice shall be—
  (a) gazetted; and
  (b) advertised in the same manner as the bankruptcy order to which it relates was advertised.]

[(3A) In addition to the standard contents, the notice under paragraph (3) must state—
    (a) the name of the former bankrupt;
    (b) the date on which the bankruptcy order was made;
    (c) that the bankruptcy order against the former bankrupt has been annulled under section 282(1); and
    (d) the date of the annulment.]

(4) Any requirement by the former bankrupt under paragraph (3) shall be addressed to the Secretary of State in writing. . . .

(5) Where the former bankrupt has died, or is a person incapable of managing his affairs (within the meaning of Chapter 7 in Part 7 of the Rules), the references to him in paragraphs (3) and (4) are to be read as referring to his personal representative or, as the case may be, a person appointed by the court to represent or act for him.

NOTES

Initial Commencement
Specified date
    Specified date: 29 December 1986: see r 0.1.

Amendment
    Para (1): words omitted revoked, except in relation to a pre-commencement bankruptcy, by SI 2003/1730, rr 2(3), (4), 9(1), (3)(b), Sch 1, Pt 6, para 44.
        Date in force: 1 April 2004: see SI 2003/1730, r 1(3).
    Para (2): words "as soon as reasonably practicable" in square brackets substituted by SI 2009/642, rr 4, 5.
        Date in force: 6 April 2009: see SI 2009/642, r 1; for transitional provisions see r 3 thereof.
    Para (3): inserted by SI 2009/642, rr 4, 45.
        Date in force: 6 April 2009: see SI 2009/642, r 1; for transitional provisions see r 3 thereof.
    Para (3A): inserted by SI 2010/686, r 2, Sch 1, para 409.
        Date in force: 6 April 2010: see SI 2010/686, r 1; for transitional provisions see r 6(1), Sch 4, para 1 thereto.
    Para (4): words omitted revoked by SI 2004/584, r 39(b).
        Date in force: 1 April 2004: see SI 2004/584, r 1(2).

6.214 Trustee's final account

(1) Where a bankruptcy order is annulled under section [. . .] 282, this does not of itself release the trustee from any duty or obligation, imposed on him by or under the Act or the Rules, to account for all his transactions in connection with the former bankrupt's estate.

(2) The trustee shall submit a copy of his final account to the Secretary of State, as soon as practicable after the court's order annulling the bankruptcy order; and he shall file a copy of the final account in court.

(3) The final account must include a summary of the trustee's receipts and payments in the administration, and contain a statement to the effect that he has reconciled his account with that which is held by the Secretary of State in respect of the bankruptcy.

(4) The trustee is released from such time as the court may determine, having regard to whether—
    (a) paragraph (2) of this Rule has been complied with, and
    (b) any security given under Rule 6.211(3) has been, or will be, released.

NOTES

Initial Commencement

Specified date

Specified date: 29 December 1986: see r 0.1.

Amendment

Para (1): words omitted revoked, except in relation to a pre-commencement bankruptcy, by SI 2003/1730, rr 2(3), (4), 9(1), (3)(b), Sch 1, Pt 6, para 45.
Date in force: 1 April 2004: see SI 2003/1730, r 1(3).

[CHAPTER 21A

NOTICE UNDER SECTION 279(2)]

NOTES

Amendment

Inserted by SI 2003/1730, r 9(1), Sch 1, Pt 6, para 46.
Date in force: 1 April 2004: see SI 2003/1730, r 1(3); for the disapplication of this Chapter in relation to a pre-commencement bankruptcy see rr 2(3), (4), 9(3)(c) thereof.

[6.214A Notice under section 279(2) that an investigation of the conduct and affairs of a bankrupt is unnecessary or concluded]

[(1) Where the official receiver intends to file a notice that an investigation of the conduct and affairs of a bankrupt is unnecessary or concluded under section 279(2), he shall give notice in writing to all creditors of which he is aware and any trustee of his intention to file such a notice.

(2) Where a creditor or a trustee receives written notice of the official receiver's intention to file a notice under section 279(2) and he has any objection to the official receiver filing such a notice, he may, within 28 days of the date of such written notice, inform the official receiver in writing of his objection and give reasons for that objection.

(3) The official receiver shall not file a notice under section 279(2) until the period allowed for creditors or a trustee to object under paragraph (2) has expired.

[(4) Where the official receiver receives no objection from either a creditor or a trustee he may file a notice under section 279(2) by sending to the court two copies of Form 6.82. The court shall endorse each copy with the date of filing and shall return one copy to the official receiver. The official receiver shall send a copy of the endorsed form to the bankrupt.]

(5) Where the official receiver receives an objection under this Rule and he rejects that objection, he shall not file the notice under section 279(2) until he has—

(a) given notice of the rejection (and his reasons) to the complainant; and
(b) the period of time for an appeal by the complainant under Rule 7.50(2) has expired,

or an appeal under that Rule has been determined by the court.]

NOTES

Amendment

Inserted by SI 2003/1730, r 9(1), Sch 1, Pt 6, para 46.
Date in force: 1 April 2004: see SI 2003/1730, r 1(3); for the disapplication of this rule in relation to a pre-commencement bankruptcy see rr 2(3), (4), 9(3)(c) thereof.

Para (4): substituted by SI 2004/584, r 40.
Date in force: 1 April 2004: see SI 2004/584, r 1(2).

CHAPTER 22

DISCHARGE

[6.215 Application for suspension of discharge]

[(1) The following applies where the official receiver or any trustee who is not the official receiver applies to the court for an order under section 279(3) (suspension of automatic discharge), but not where the official receiver makes that application, pursuant to Rule 6.176(4), on the adjournment of the bankrupt's public examination.

(2) The official receiver or any trustee who is not the official receiver shall, with his application, file evidence in support setting out the reasons why it appears to him that such an order should be made.

(3) The court shall fix a venue for the hearing of the application, and give notice of it to the official receiver, the trustee who is not the official receiver, and the bankrupt.

(4) Copies of the official receiver's report under this Rule shall be sent by him to the bankrupt and any trustee who is not the official receiver, so as to reach them at least 21 days before the date fixed for the hearing.

(5) Copies of the trustee's evidence in support under this Rule shall be sent by him to the official receiver and the bankrupt, so as to reach them at least 21 days before the date fixed for the hearing.

(6) The bankrupt may, not later than [5 business] days before the date of the hearing, file in court a notice specifying any statements in the official receiver's or trustee's evidence in support which he intends to deny or dispute.

(7) If the bankrupt files a notice under paragraph (6), he shall send copies of it, not less than 4 [business] days before the date of the hearing, to the official receiver and any trustee who is not the official receiver.

(8) If the court makes an order suspending the bankrupt's discharge, copies of the order shall be sent by the court to the official receiver, any trustee who is not the official receiver and the bankrupt.]

NOTES

Amendment

Substituted by SI 2003/1730, r 9(1), Sch 1, Pt 6, para 47.
Date in force: 1 April 2004: see SI 2003/1730, r 1(3); for effect in relation to pre-commencement bankruptcies in the same way as they apply to post-commencement bankruptcies see rr 2(3), (4), 9(4) thereof.

Para (6): words "5 business" in square brackets substituted by SI 2010/686, r 2, Sch 1, para 410(1), (2).
Date in force: 6 April 2010: see SI 2010/686, r 1; for transitional provisions see r 6(1), Sch 4, para 1 thereto.

Para (7): word "business" in square brackets inserted by SI 2010/686, r 2, Sch 1, para 410(1), (3).
Date in force: 6 April 2010: see SI 2010/686, r 1; for transitional provisions see r 6(1), Sch 4, para 1 thereto.

[6.216 Lifting of suspension of discharge]

[(1) Where the court has made an order under section 279(3) that the period specified in section 279(1) shall cease to run, the bankrupt may apply to it for the order to be discharged.

(2) The court shall fix a venue for the hearing of the application; and the bankrupt shall, not less than 28 days before the date fixed for the hearing, give notice of the

venue to the official receiver and any trustee who is not the official receiver, accompanied in each case by a copy of the application.

(3) The official receiver and the trustee may appear and be heard on the bankrupt's application; and, whether or not they appear, the official receiver and trustee may file in court evidence in support of any matters which either of them considers ought to be drawn to the court's attention.

(4) If the court made an order under section 279(3)(b), the court may request a report from the official receiver or the trustee as to whether the conditions specified in the order have or have not been fulfilled.

(5) If a report is filed under paragraph (3) or (4), copies of it shall be sent by the official receiver or trustee to the bankrupt and to either the official receiver or trustee (depending on which has filed the report), not later than 14 days before the hearing.

(6) The bankrupt may, not later than [5 business] days before the date of the hearing, file in court a notice specifying any statements in the official receiver's or trustee's report which he intends to deny or dispute.
If he files a notice under this paragraph, he shall send copies of it, not less than 4 [business] days before the date of the hearing, to the official receiver and the trustee.

(7) If on the bankrupt's application the court discharges the order under section 279(3) (being satisfied that the period specified in section 279(1) should begin to run again), it shall issue to the bankrupt a certificate that it has done so, with effect from a specified date and shall send copies of the certificate to the official receiver and the trustee.]

NOTES

Amendment

Substituted by SI 2003/1730, r 9(1), Sch 1, Pt 6, para 48.
Date in force: 1 April 2004: see SI 2003/1730, r 1(3); for effect in relation to pre-commencement bankruptcies in the same way as they apply to post-commencement bankruptcies see rr 2(3), (4), 9(4) thereof.
Para (6): words "5 business" in square brackets substituted by SI 2010/686, r 2, Sch 1, para 411(1), (2)(a).
Date in force: 6 April 2010: see SI 2010/686, r 1; for transitional provisions see r 6(1), Sch 4, para 1 thereto.
Para (6): word "business" in square brackets inserted by SI 2010/686, r 2, Sch 1, para 411(1), (2)(b).
Date in force: 6 April 2010: see SI 2010/686, r 1; for transitional provisions see r 6(1), Sch 4, para 1 thereto.

6.217 Application by bankrupt for discharge

(1) If the bankrupt applies under section 280 for an order discharging him from bankruptcy, he shall give to the official receiver notice of the application, and deposit with him such sum as the latter may require to cover his costs of the application.

(2) The court, if satisfied that paragraph (1) has been complied with, shall fix a venue for the hearing of the application, and give at least 42 days' notice of it to the official receiver and the bankrupt.

(3) The official receiver shall give notice accordingly—
    (a)   to the trustee, and
    (b)   to every creditor who, to the official receiver's knowledge, has a claim outstanding against the estate which has not been satisfied.

(4) Notices under paragraph (3) shall be given not later than 14 days before the date fixed for the hearing of the bankrupt's application.

Insolvency Rules 1986, reg 6.217

NOTES

Initial Commencement

Specified date

Specified date: 29 December 1986: see r 0.1.

6.218 Report of official receiver

(1) Where the bankrupt makes an application under section 280, the official receiver shall, at least 21 days before the date fixed for the hearing of the application, file in court a report containing the following information with respect to the bankrupt—

(a) any failure by him to comply with his obligations under Parts VIII to XI of the Act;
(b) the circumstances surrounding the present bankruptcy, and those surrounding any previous bankruptcy of his;
(c) the extent to which, in the present and in any previous bankruptcy, his liabilities have exceeded his assets; and
(d) particulars of any distribution which has been, or is expected to be, made to creditors in the present bankruptcy or, if such is the case, that there has been and is to be no distribution;

and the official receiver shall include in his report any other matters which in his opinion ought to be brought to the court's attention.

(2) The official receiver shall send a copy of the report to the bankrupt and the trustee, so as to reach them at least 14 days before the date of the hearing of the application under section 280.

(3) The bankrupt may, not later than [5 business] days before the date of the hearing, file in court a notice specifying any statements in the official receiver's report which he intends to deny or dispute.

If he gives notice under this paragraph, he shall send copies of it, not less than 4 days before the date of the hearing, to the official receiver and the trustee.

(4) The official receiver, the trustee and any creditor may appear on the hearing of the bankrupt's application, and may make representations and put to the bankrupt such questions as the court may allow.

NOTES

Initial Commencement

Specified date

Specified date: 29 December 1986: see r 0.1.

Amendment

Para (3): words "5 business" in square brackets substituted by SI 2010/686, r 2, Sch 1, para 412.

Date in force: 6 April 2010: see SI 2010/686, r 1; for transitional provisions see r 6(1), Sch 4, para 1 thereto.

6.219 Order of discharge on application

(1) An order of the court under section 280(2)(b) (discharge absolutely) or (c) (discharge subject to conditions with respect to income or property) shall bear the date on which it is made, but does not take effect until such time as it is drawn up by the court.

(2) The order then has effect retrospectively to the date on which it was made.

(3) Copies of any order made by the court on an application by the bankrupt for discharge under section 280 shall be sent by the court to the bankrupt, the trustee and the official receiver.

NOTES

Initial Commencement

Specified date

Specified date: 29 December 1986: see r 0.1.

6.220 Certificate of discharge

(1) Where it appears to the court that a bankrupt is discharged, whether by expiration of time or otherwise, the court shall, on his application, issue to him a certificate of his discharge, and the date from which it is effective.

[(2) The discharged bankrupt may require [within 28 days of the order] the Secretary of State to give notice of the discharge. As soon as reasonably practicable such notice shall be—
 (a) gazetted; and
 (b) advertised in such manner as the bankruptcy order to which it relates was advertised.]

[(2A) In addition to the standard contents, a notice under paragraph (2) must state—
 (a) the name of the former bankrupt;
 (b) the date of the bankruptcy order;
 (c) that a certificate of discharge has been issued;
 (d) the date of the certificate; and
 (e) the date from which the discharge is effective.]

(3) Any requirement by the former bankrupt under paragraph (2) shall be addressed to the Secretary of State in writing. . . .

(4) Where the former bankrupt has died, or is a person incapable of managing his affairs (within the meaning of Chapter 7 in Part 7 of the Rules), the references to him in paragraphs (2) and (3) are to be read as referring to his personal representative or, as the case may be, a person appointed by the court to represent or act for him.

NOTES

Initial Commencement

Specified date

Specified date: 29 December 1986: see r 0.1.

Amendment

 Para (2): substituted by SI 2009/642, rr 4, 46.
  Date in force: 6 April 2009: see SI 2009/642, r 1; for transitional provisions see r 3 thereof.
 Para (2): words "within 28 days of the order" in square brackets inserted by SI 2010/686, r 2, Sch 1, para 413(1), (2).
  Date in force: 6 April 2010: see SI 2010/686, r 1; for transitional provisions see r 6(1), Sch 4, para 1 thereto.
 Para (2A): inserted by SI 2010/686, r 3, Sch 1, para 413(1), (3).
  Date in force: 6 April 2010: see SI 2010/686, r 1; for transitional provisions see r 6(1), Sch 4, para 1 thereto.
 Para (3): words omitted revoked by SI 2010/686, r 2, Sch 1, para 413(1), (4).
  Date in force: 6 April 2010: see SI 2010/686, r 1; for transitional provisions see r 6(1), Sch 4, para 1 thereto.

6.221 Deferment of issue of order pending appeal

An order made by the court on an application by the bankrupt for discharge under section 280 shall not be issued or gazetted until the time allowed for appealing has expired or, if an appeal is entered, until the appeal has been determined.

NOTES

Initial Commencement

Specified date

Specified date: 29 December 1986: see r 0.1.

6.222 Costs under this Chapter

In no case do any costs or expenses arising under this Chapter fall on the official receiver personally.

NOTES

Initial Commencement

Specified date

Specified date: 29 December 1986: see r 0.1.

6.223 Bankrupt's debts surviving discharge

Discharge does not release the bankrupt from any obligation arising under a confiscation order made under section 1 of the Drug Trafficking Offences Act 1986 [or section 1 of the Criminal Justice (Scotland) Act 1987] [or section 71 of the Criminal Justice Act 1988] [or under Parts 2, 3 or 4 of the Proceeds of Crime Act 2002].

NOTES

Initial Commencement

Specified date

Specified date: 29 December 1986: see r 0.1.

Amendment

Words "or section 1 of the Criminal Justice (Scotland) Act 1987" in square brackets inserted by SI 1987/1919, r 3(1), Schedule, Pt 1, para 127.

Words "or section 71 of the Criminal Justice Act 1988" in square brackets inserted by SI 1989/397, r 3(1), Schedule, para 1.

Words "or under Parts 2, 3 or 4 of the Proceeds of Crime Act 2002" in square brackets inserted by SI 2003/1730, r 9(1), Sch 1, Pt 6, para 49.

Date in force: 1 April 2004: see SI 2003/1730, r 1(3).

[CHAPTER 22A

...]

NOTES

Amendment

Inserted by SI 1999/359, r 3, Schedule, para 8.

Date in force: 22 March 1999: see SI 1999/359, r 1.

Revoked by SI 2003/1730, r 9(1), Sch 1, Pt 6, para 50.
Date in force: 1 April 2004: see SI 2003/1730, r 1(3).

[6.223A . . .]
[. . .]

NOTES

Amendment

Inserted by SI 1999/359, r 3, Schedule, para 8.
Date in force: 22 March 1999: see SI 1999/359, r 1.
Revoked by SI 2003/1730, r 9(1), Sch 1, Pt 6, para 50.
Date in force: 1 April 2004: see SI 2003/1730, r 1(3).

[6.223B . . .]
[. . .]

NOTES

Amendment

Inserted by SI 1999/359, r 3, Schedule, para 8.
Date in force: 22 March 1999: see SI 1999/359, r 1.
Revoked by SI 2003/1730, r 9(1), Sch 1, Pt 6, para 50.
Date in force: 1 April 2004: see SI 2003/1730, r 1(3).

[6.223C . . .]
[. . .]

NOTES

Amendment

Inserted by SI 1999/359, r 3, Schedule, para 8.
Date in force: 22 March 1999: see SI 1999/359, r 1.
Revoked by SI 2003/1730, r 9(1), Sch 1, Pt 6, para 50.
Date in force: 1 April 2004: see SI 2003/1730, r 1(3).

CHAPTER 23

ORDER OF PAYMENT OF COSTS, ETC, OUT OF ESTATE

6.224 General rule as to priority

(1) The expenses of the bankruptcy are payable out of the estate in the following order of priority—

[(a) expenses or costs which—
　(i) are properly chargeable or incurred by the official receiver or the trustee in preserving, realising or getting in any of the assets of the bankrupt or otherwise relating to the conduct of any legal proceedings which he has power to bring (whether the claim on which the proceedings are based forms part of the estate or otherwise) or defend;
　(ii) relate to the employment of a shorthand writer, if appointed by an order of the court made at the instance of the official receiver in connection with an examination; or

(iii) are incurred in holding an examination under Rule 6.174 (examinee unfit) where the application was made by the official receiver;]

(b) any other expenses incurred or disbursements made by the official receiver or under his authority, including those incurred or made in carrying on the business of a debtor or bankrupt;

[(c) the fees payable under any order made under section 415 [or 415A], including those payable to the official receiver (other than the fee referred to in sub-paragraph (d)(i) below), and any remuneration payable to him under general regulations;

(d)
(i) the fee payable under any order made under section 415 for the performance by the official receiver of his general duties as official receiver;
(ii) any repayable deposit lodged under any such order as security for the fee mentioned in sub-paragraph (i) (except where the deposit is applied to the payment of the remuneration of an insolvency practitioner appointed under section 273 (debtor's petition));]

(e) the cost of any security provided by an interim receiver, trustee or special manager in accordance with the Act or the Rules;

(f) the remuneration of the interim receiver (if any);

(g) any deposit lodged on an application for the appointment of an interim receiver;

(h) the costs of the petitioner, and of any person appearing on the petition whose costs are allowed by the court;

(j) the remuneration of the special manager (if any);

(k) any amount payable to a person employed or authorised, under Chapter 5 of this Part of the Rules, to assist in the preparation of a statement of affairs or of accounts;

(l) any allowance made, by order of the court, towards costs on an application for release from the obligation to submit a statement of affairs, or for an extension of time for submitting such a statement;

[(la) the costs of employing a shorthand writer in any case other than one appointed by an order of the court at the instance of the official receiver in connection with an examination;]

(m) any necessary disbursements by the trustee in the course of his administration (including any expenses incurred by members of the creditors' committee or their representatives and allowed by the trustee under Rule 6.164, but not including any payment of capital gains tax in circumstances referred to in sub-paragraph (p) below);

(n) the remuneration or emoluments of any person (including the bankrupt) who has been employed by the trustee to perform any services for the estate, as required or authorised by or under the Act or the Rules;

(o) the remuneration of the trustee, up to any amount not exceeding that which is payable [under Schedule 6];

(p) the amount of any capital gains tax on chargeable gains accruing on the realisation of any asset of the bankrupt (without regard to whether the realisation is effected by the trustee, a secured creditor, or a receiver or manager appointed to deal with a security);

(q) the balance, after payment of any sums due under sub-paragraph (o) above, of any remuneration due to the trustee[;

(r) any other expenses properly chargeable by the trustee in carrying out his functions in the bankruptcy].

(2) . . .
(3) . . .

NOTES

Initial Commencement

Specified date
  Specified date: 29 December 1986: see r 0.1.

Amendment
  Para (1): sub-para (a) substituted by SI 2002/2712, r 6(1), Schedule, Pt 4, para 25(a).
    Date in force: 1 January 2003: see SI 2002/2712, r 1(1); for effect see rr 1(2), 6(2) thereof.
  Para (1): sub-paras (c), (d) substituted by SI 1995/586, r 3, Schedule.
  Para (1): in sub-para (c) words "or 415A" in square brackets inserted by SI 2004/584, r 41.
    Date in force: 1 April 2004: see SI 2004/584, r 1(2).
  Para (1): sub-para (la) inserted by SI 2002/2712, r 6(1), Schedule, Pt 4, para 25(b).
    Date in force: 1 January 2003: see SI 2002/2712, r 1(1); for effect see rr 1(2), 6(2) thereof.
  Para (1): in sub-para (o) words "under Schedule 6" in square brackets substituted by SI 2005/527, r 39.
    Date in force: this amendment shall apply in any case where, on or after 1 April 2004, a winding-up order has been made or a resolution for the winding up of a company has been passed or a bankruptcy order has been made, before 1 April 2005: see SI 2005/527, rr 1(2), 3(2).
  Para (1): sub-para (r) inserted by SI 2002/2712, r 6(1), Schedule, Pt 4, para 25(c).
    Date in force: 1 January 2003: see SI 2002/2712, r 1(1); for effect see rr 1(2), 6(2) thereof.
  Paras (2), (3): revoked by SI 2002/2712, r 6(1), Schedule, Pt 4, para 25(d).
    Date in force: 1 January 2003: see SI 2002/2712, r 1(1); for effect see rr 1(2), 6(2) thereof.

CHAPTER 24
SECOND BANKRUPTCY

6.225 Scope of this Chapter

(1) The Rules in this Chapter relate to the manner in which, in the case of a second bankruptcy, the trustee in the earlier bankruptcy is to deal with property and money to which section 334(3) applies, until there is a trustee of the estate in the later bankruptcy.

(2) "The earlier bankruptcy", "the later bankruptcy" and "the existing trustee" have the meanings given by section 334(1).

NOTES

Initial Commencement

Specified date
  Specified date: 29 December 1986: see r 0.1.

6.226 General duty of existing trustee

(1) Subject as follows, the existing trustee shall take into his custody or under his control all such property and money, in so far as he has not already done so as part of his duties as trustee in the earlier bankruptcy.

(2) Where any of that property consists of perishable goods, or goods the value of which is likely to diminish if they are not disposed of, the existing trustee has power to sell or otherwise dispose of those goods.

(3) The proceeds of any such sale or disposal shall be held, under the existing trustee's control, with the other property and money comprised in the bankrupt's estate.

NOTES

Initial Commencement

Specified date

Specified date: 29 December 1986: see r 0.1.

6.227 Delivery up to later trustee

The existing trustee shall, as and when requested by the trustee for the purposes of the later bankruptcy, deliver up to the latter all such property and money as is in his custody or under his control in pursuance of Rule 6.226.

NOTES

Initial Commencement

Specified date

Specified date: 29 December 1986: see r 0.1.

6.228 Existing trustee's expenses

Any expenses incurred by the existing trustee in compliance with section 335(1) and this Chapter of the Rules shall be defrayed out of, and are a charge on, all such property and money as is referred to in section 334(3), whether in the hands of the existing trustee or of the trustee for the purposes of the later bankruptcy.

NOTES

Initial Commencement

Specified date

Specified date: 29 December 1986: see r 0.1.

CHAPTER 25

CRIMINAL BANKRUPTCY

6.229 Presentation of petition

(1) In criminal bankruptcy, the petition under section 264(1)(d) shall be presented to the High Court, and accordingly [Rule 6.9A] in Chapter 2 (court in which other petitions to be presented) does not apply.

(2) This does not affect the High Court's power to order that the proceedings be transferred.

NOTES

Initial Commencement

Specified date

Specified date: 29 December 1986: see r 0.1.

Amendment

Para (1): words "Rule 6.9A" in square brackets substituted by SI 2010/686, r 2, Sch 1, para 414.

Date in force: 6 April 2010: see SI 2010/686, r 1; for transitional provisions see r 6(1), Sch 4, para 1 thereto.

6.230 Status and functions of Official Petitioner

(1) Subject as follows, the Official Petitioner is to be regarded for all purposes of the Act and the Rules as a creditor of the bankrupt.

(2) He may attend or be represented at any meeting of creditors, and is to be given any notice under the Act or the Rules which is required or authorised to be given to creditors; and the requirements of the Rules as to the lodging or use of proxies do not apply.

NOTES

Initial Commencement

Specified date

Specified date: 29 December 1986: see r 0.1.

6.231 Interim receivership

Chapter 4 of this Part of the Rules applies in criminal bankruptcy only in so far as it provides for the appointment of the official receiver as interim receiver.

NOTES

Initial Commencement

Specified date

Specified date: 29 December 1986: see r 0.1.

6.232 Proof of bankruptcy debts and notice of order

(1) The making of a bankruptcy order on a criminal bankruptcy petition does not affect the right of creditors to prove for their debts arising otherwise than in consequence of the criminal proceedings.

(2) A person specified in a criminal bankruptcy order as having suffered loss or damage shall be treated as a creditor of the bankrupt; and a copy of the order is sufficient evidence of his claim, subject to its being shown by any party to the bankruptcy proceedings that the loss or damage actually suffered was more or (as the case may be) less than the amount specified in the order.

(3) The requirements of the Rules with respect to the proof of debts do not apply to the Official Petitioner.

[(4) In criminal bankruptcy, forms of proof shall be sent out by the official receiver within 12 weeks from the making of the bankruptcy order, to every creditor who is known to him, ...]

(5) The official receiver shall, within those 12 weeks, send to every such creditor notice of the making of the bankruptcy order.

NOTES

Initial Commencement

Specified date

Specified date: 29 December 1986: see r 0.1.

Insolvency Rules 1986, reg 6.232

Amendment

Para (4): substituted by SI 1987/1919, r 3(1), Schedule, Part 1, para 128.

Para (4): words omitted revoked by SI 2010/686, r 2, Sch 1, para 415.
Date in force: 6 April 2010: see SI 2010/686, r 1; for transitional provisions see r 6(1), Sch 4, para 1 thereto.

6.233 Meetings under the Rules

(1) The following Rules in Chapter 6 of this Part do not apply in criminal bankruptcy—

Rules 6.79 and 6.80 (first meeting of creditors, and business thereat);

Rule 6.82(2) (the chairman, if other than the official receiver);

Rule 6.88(2) and (3) (resolution for appointment of trustee).

(2) Rule 6.97 (supply of forms for proof of debts) does not apply.

NOTES

Initial Commencement

Specified date

Specified date: 29 December 1986: see r 0.1.

6.234 Trustee in bankruptcy; creditors' committee; annulment of bankruptcy order

(1) [Chapter 10] of this Part of the Rules does not apply in criminal bankruptcy, except Rules 6.136 (release of official receiver) and 6.147 (power of court to set aside transactions).

(2) [Chapter 11] (creditors' committee) does not apply.

(3) Chapter 21 (annulment of bankruptcy order) applies to an application to the court under section 282(2) as it applies to an application under section 282(1), with any necessary modifications.

NOTES

Initial Commencement

Specified date

Specified date: 29 December 1986: see r 0.1.

Amendment

Paras (1), (2): words in square brackets substituted by SI 1987/1919, r 3(1), Schedule, Part 1, para 129.

CHAPTER 26

MISCELLANEOUS RULES IN BANKRUPTCY

6.235 ...

...

NOTES

Amendment

Revoked by SI 2010/686, r 5.
Date in force: 6 April 2010: see SI 2010/686, r 1; for transitional provisions see r 6(1), Sch 4, paras 1, 2(1)(a) thereto.

[6.235A Application for redirection order]

[(1) This Rule applies where the official receiver or trustee in bankruptcy applies to the court under section 371(1) (re-direction of bankrupt's letters etc).

(2) The application shall be made without notice to the bankrupt or any other person, unless the court directs otherwise.

(3) The applicant shall with his application, where he is the official receiver, file a report, and where he is the trustee in bankruptcy, [a witness statement], setting out the reasons why such an order is sought.

(4) The court shall fix a venue for the hearing of the application if the court thinks [just] and give notice to the applicant.

(5) The court may make an order on such conditions as it thinks [just].

(6) The order shall identify the person on whom it is to be served, and need not be served on the bankrupt unless the court directs otherwise.]

NOTES

Amendment

Inserted by SI 2005/527, r 40.
Date in force: 1 April 2005: see SI 2005/527, r 1(2).
Para (3): words "a witness statement" in square brackets substituted by SI 2010/686, r 2, Sch 1, para 416.
Date in force: 6 April 2010: see SI 2010/686, r 1; for transitional provisions see r 6(1), Sch 4, paras 1, 2(1)(b), (2)–(4) thereto.
Para (4): word "just" in square brackets substituted by SI 2010/686, r 2, Sch 1, para 1.
Date in force: 6 April 2010: see SI 2010/686, r 1; for transitional provisions see r 6(1), Sch 4, paras 1, 2(1)(b) thereto.
Para (5): word "just" in square brackets substituted by SI 2010/686, r 2, Sch 1, para 1.
Date in force: 6 April 2010: see SI 2010/686, r 1; for transitional provisions see r 6(1), Sch 4, paras 1, 2(1)(b) thereto.

[6.235B Persons at risk of violence]

[(1) The provisions of this Rule apply in any case where disclosure or continuing disclosure to other persons (whether to the public generally or to specific persons) of the current address or whereabouts of a debtor might reasonably be expected to lead to violence against the debtor or against a person who normally resides with the debtor as a member of the debtor's family.

(2) For the purposes of this Rule—

"current address" means, in relation to any debtor, the address of the debtor's current place of residence and any address at which the debtor currently carries on business; and

"debtor" means a person who is subject to a bankruptcy order, a bankruptcy restrictions order or a bankruptcy restrictions undertaking.

(3) The court may, on the application of the debtor, the official receiver, the trustee or the Secretary of State, order that—

(a) details of the debtor's current address be removed from any part of the court file of the proceedings in relation to the debtor which is open to inspection and be kept on a separate file not open to inspection;

(b) the details in respect of the debtor to be entered in the bankruptcy order must not include details of the debtor's current address;

(c) the full title of the proceedings must be amended by the removal of the details of the debtor's current address from the description of the debtor;

(d) the details of the debtor to be included in any notice gazetted or otherwise advertised must not include details of the debtor's current address;

(e) the details in respect of the debtor to be entered onto the individual insolvency register under Rule 6A.4 or the bankruptcy restrictions register under Rule 6A.6 must not include details of the debtor's current address; or

(f) the details of the debtor's current address kept on the individual insolvency register or the bankruptcy restrictions register must be removed from such register.

(4) Where the court makes an order under paragraph (3)(b) to (f), it may further order that—

(a) the description of the debtor to be inserted in the bankruptcy order,
(b) the full title of the proceedings,
(c) the details of the debtor required to be included in any notice to be gazetted or otherwise advertised, or
(d) the details in respect of the debtor kept or to be entered on to the registers referred to in paragraph (3)(d) and (e),

as the case may be, must instead include such other details of the debtor's addresses or whereabouts as the court thinks just, including details of any address at which the debtor has previously resided or carried on business.

(5) Where the court makes an order under paragraph (3)(c)—

(a) the official receiver must as soon as reasonably practicable send notice of it to the Chief Land Registrar, for corresponding amendment of the register; and
(b) if official receiver thinks fit, the official receiver may cause notice of the order to be—
    (i) gazetted, or
    (ii) both gazetted and given in such other manner as the official receiver thinks fit.

(6) Any notice of the amendment of the title of the proceedings to be published in accordance with paragraph (5) must contain—

(a) the standard contents with the exception of the current address of the debtor,
(b) the amended title of the proceedings, and
(c) the date of the bankruptcy order,

but must not include the description under which the proceedings were previously published.

(7) In any case where an application is made in respect of a debtor under or by virtue of this Rule, the application must be accompanied by a witness statement referring to this Rule and containing sufficient evidence to satisfy the court that paragraph (1) of this Rule applies to or in respect of that debtor.]

NOTES

Amendment

Inserted by SI 2010/686, r 2, Sch 1, para 417.
Date in force: 6 April 2010: see SI 2010/686, r 1; for transitional provisions see r 6(1), Sch 4, para 1 thereto.

6.236 Consolidation of petitions

Where two or more bankruptcy petitions are presented against the same debtor, the court may order the consolidation of the proceedings, on such terms as it thinks [just].

NOTES

Initial Commencement

Specified date

Specified date: 29 December 1986: see r 0.1.

Amendment

Word "just" in square brackets substituted by SI 2010/686, r 2, Sch 1, para 1.
Date in force: 6 April 2010: see SI 2010/686, r 1; for transitional provisions see r 6(1), Sch 4, paras 1, 2(1)(b) thereto.

[6.237 Bankrupt's Home—Notification of property falling within section 283A]

[(1) Where it appears to a trustee that section 283A(1) applies, the trustee shall give notice in Form 6.83 as soon as reasonably practicable to—
   (a) the bankrupt;
   (b) the bankrupt's spouse [or civil partner] (in a case falling within section 283A(1)(b)); and
   (c) a former spouse [or former civil partner] of the bankrupt (in a case falling within section 283A(1)(c)).

(2) A notice under paragraph (1) shall contain—
   (a) the name of the bankrupt;
   (b) the address of the dwelling-house; and
   (c) if the dwelling-house is registered land, the title number.

(3) A trustee shall not give notice under paragraph (1) any later than 14 days before the expiry of the three year period under section 283A(2) or 283A(5).]

NOTES

Amendment

Substituted, together with rr 6.237A–6.237E, for this rule as originally enacted, by SI 2003/1730, r 9(1), Sch 1, Pt 6, para 51.
Date in force: 1 April 2004: see SI 2003/1730, r 1(3).
Para (1): in sub-para (b) words "or civil partner" in square brackets inserted by SI 2005/2114, art 2(18), Sch 18, Pt 1, para 1(1), (2)(a).
Date in force: 5 December 2005: see SI 2005/2114, art 1.
Para (1): in sub-para (c) words "or former civil partner" in square brackets inserted by SI 2005/2114, art 2(18), Sch 18, Pt 1, para 1(1), (2)(b).
Date in force: 5 December 2005: see SI 2005/2114, art 1.

[6.237A Application in respect of the vesting of an interest in a dwelling-house (registered land)]

[(1) Paragraph (2) applies where—
   (a) property comprised in the bankrupt's estate consists of an interest in a dwelling-house which at the date of bankruptcy was the sole or principal residence of—
      (i) the bankrupt;
      (ii) the bankrupt's spouse [or civil partner]; or
      (iii) a former spouse [or former civil partner] of the bankrupt; and
   (b) the dwelling-house is registered land; and
   (c) an entry has been made, or entries have been made, in the individual register or registers of the dwelling-house relating to the bankrupt's bankruptcy or the individual register or registers has or have been altered to reflect the vesting of the bankrupt's interest in a trustee in bankruptcy.

(2) Where an interest of a kind mentioned in paragraph (1) ceases to be comprised in the bankrupt's estate and vests in the bankrupt under either section 283A(2) or 283A(4) of the Act, or under section 261(8) of the Enterprise Act 2002, the trustee shall, within [5 business] days of the vesting, make such application or applications to the Chief Land Registrar as shall be necessary to show in the individual register or registers of the dwelling-house that the interest has vested in the bankrupt.

(3) An application under paragraph (2) shall be made in accordance with the Land Registration Act 2002 and shall be accompanied by—

(a) evidence of the trustee's appointment (where not previously provided to the Chief Land Registrar); and

(b) a certificate from the trustee stating that the interest has vested in the bankrupt under section 283A(2) or 283A(4) of the Act or section 261(8) of the Enterprise Act 2002 (whichever is appropriate).

(4) As soon as reasonably practicable after making an application under paragraph (2), the trustee shall notify the bankrupt and if the dwelling-house was the sole or principal residence of his spouse or former spouse [or civil partner or former civil partner], such person, that the application has been made.

(5) The trustee shall notify every person who (to his knowledge) either claims an interest in the dwelling-house, or is under any liability in respect of the dwelling-house that an application has been made.]

NOTES

Amendment

Substituted, together with rr 6.237, 6.237B–6.237E, for r 6.237 as originally enacted, by SI 2003/1730, r 9(1), Sch 1, Pt 6, para 51.
Date in force: 1 April 2004: see SI 2003/1730, r 1(3).
Para (1): in sub-para (a)(ii) words "or civil partner" in square brackets inserted by SI 2005/2114, art 2(18), Sch 18, Pt 1, para 1(1), (3)(a).
Date in force: 5 December 2005: see SI 2005/2114, art 1.
Para (1): in sub-para (a)(iii) words "or former civil partner" in square brackets inserted by SI 2005/2114, art 2(18), Sch 18, Pt 1, para 1(1), (3)(b).
Date in force: 5 December 2005: see SI 2005/2114, art 1.
Para (2): words "5 business" in square brackets substituted by SI 2010/686, r 2, Sch 1, para 418.
Date in force: 6 April 2010: see SI 2010/686, r 1; for transitional provisions see r 6(1), Sch 4, para 1 thereto.
Para (4): words "or civil partner or former civil partner" in square brackets inserted by SI 2005/2114, art 2(18), Sch 18, Pt 1, para 1(1), (3)(c).
Date in force: 5 December 2005: see SI 2005/2114, art 1.

[6.237B Vesting of bankrupt's interest (unregistered land)]

[(1) Where an interest in a dwelling-house which at the date of the bankruptcy was the sole or principal residence of—

(a) the bankrupt;
(b) the bankrupt's spouse [or civil partner]; or
(c) a former spouse [or former civil partner] of the bankrupt,

ceases to be comprised in the bankrupt's estate and vests in the bankrupt under either section 283A(2) or 283A(4) of the Act or section 261(8) of the Enterprise Act 2002 and the dwelling-house is unregistered land, the trustee shall issue the bankrupt with a certificate as to the vesting in Form 6.84 as soon as reasonably practicable.

(2) A certificate issued under paragraph (1) shall be conclusive proof that the interest mentioned in paragraph (1) has vested in the bankrupt.

(3) As soon as reasonably practicable after issuing the certificate under paragraph (1) the trustee shall, if the dwelling-house was the sole or principal

residence of the bankrupt's spouse or former spouse [or civil partner or former civil partner], notify such person, that the application has been made.

(4) The trustee shall notify every person who (to his knowledge) either claims an interest in the dwelling-house, or is under any liability in respect of the dwelling-house that an application has been made.]

NOTES

Amendment

Substituted, together with rr 6.237, 6.237A, 6.237C–6.237E, for r 6.237 as originally enacted, by SI 2003/1730, r 9(1), Sch 1, Pt 6, para 51.
Date in force: 1 April 2004: see SI 2003/1730, r 1(3).
Para (1): in sub-para (b) words "or civil partner" in square brackets inserted by SI 2005/2114, art 2(18), Sch 18, Pt 1, para 1(1), (4)(a).
Date in force: 5 December 2005: see SI 2005/2114, art 1.
Para (1): in sub-para (c) words "or former civil partner" in square brackets inserted by SI 2005/2114, art 2(18), Sch 18, Pt 1, para 1(1), (4)(b).
Date in force: 5 December 2005: see SI 2005/2114, art 1.
Para (3): words "or civil partner or former civil partner" in square brackets inserted by SI 2005/2114, art 2(18), Sch 18, Pt 1, para 1(1), (4)(c).
Date in force: 5 December 2005: see SI 2005/2114, art 1.

[6.237C]

[The court may substitute for the period of three years mentioned in section 283A(2) such longer period as the court thinks just and reasonable in all the circumstances of the case.]

NOTES

Amendment

Substituted, together with rr 6.237, 6.237A, 6.237B, 6.237D, 6.237E, for r 6.237 as originally enacted, by SI 2003/1730, r 9(1), Sch 1, Pt 6, para 51.
Date in force: 1 April 2004: see SI 2003/1730, r 1(3).

[6.237CA Vesting of bankrupt's estate—substituted period]

[For the purposes of section 283A(2) for the period of three years set out therein there shall be substituted, where the trustee in bankruptcy has sent notice to the bankrupt that he considers—

(a) the continued vesting of the property in the bankrupt's estate to be of no benefit to creditors; or

(b) the re-vesting to the bankrupt will facilitate a more efficient administration of the bankrupt's estate,

the period of one month from the date of that notice.]

NOTES

Amendment

Inserted by SI 2004/584, r 42.
Date in force: 1 April 2004: see SI 2004/584, r 1(2).

[6.237D Charging Order]

[(1) This Rule applies where the trustee applies to the court under section 313 for an order imposing a charge on property consisting of an interest in a dwelling-house.

(2) The respondents to the application shall be—

(a) any spouse or former spouse [or civil partner or former civil partner] of the bankrupt having or claiming to have an interest in the property;
(b) any other person appearing to have an interest in the property; and
(c) such other persons as the court may direct.

(3) The trustee shall make a report to the court, containing the following particulars—
(a) the extent of the bankrupt's interest in the property which is the subject of the application;
(b) the amount which, at the date of the application, remains owing to unsecured creditors of the bankrupt; and
(c) an estimate of the cost of realising the interest.

(4) The terms of the charge to be imposed shall be agreed between the trustee and the bankrupt or, failing agreement, shall be settled by the court.

(5) The rate of interest applicable under section 313(2) is the rate specified in section 17 of the Judgments Act 1838 on the day on which the charge is imposed, and the rate so applicable shall be stated in the court's order imposing the charge.

(6) The court's order shall also—
(a) describe the property to be charged;
(b) state whether the title to the property is registered and, if it is, specify the title number;
(c) set out the extent of the bankrupt's interest in the property which has vested in the trustee;
(d) indicate, by reference to any, or the total, amount which is payable otherwise than to the bankrupt out of the estate and of interest on that amount, how the amount of the charge to be imposed is to be ascertained;
(e) set out the conditions (if any) imposed by the court under section 3(1) of the Charging Orders Act 1979; and
(f) identify the date any property charged under section 313 shall cease to be comprised in the bankrupt's estate and shall, subject to the charge (and any prior charge), vest in the bankrupt.

(7) Unless the court is of the opinion that a different date is appropriate, the date referred to in paragraph (6)(f) shall be that of the registration of the charge in accordance with section 3(2) of the Charging Orders Act 1979.

(8) Where the court order is capable of giving rise to an application or applications under the Land Charges Act 1972 or the Land Registration Act 2002, the trustee shall, as soon as reasonably practicable after the making of the court order or at the appropriate time, make the appropriate application or applications to the Chief Land Registrar.

(9) In paragraph (8) an "appropriate application" is—
(a) an application under section 6(1)(a) of the Land Charges Act 1972 (application for registration in the register of writs and orders affecting land); or
(b) an application under the Land Registration Act 2002 for an entry in the register in respect of the charge imposed by the order; and such application under that Act as shall be necessary to show in the individual register or registers of the dwelling-house that the interest has vested in the bankrupt.

[(10) In determining the value of the bankrupt's interest for the purposes of paragraph (6)(c), the court shall disregard that part of the value of the property in which the bankrupt's interest subsists which is equal to the value of—
(a) any loans secured by mortgage or other charge against the property;
(b) any other third party interest; and
(c) the reasonable costs of sale.]]

NOTES

Amendment

Substituted, together with rr 6.237, 6.237A–6.237C, 6.237E, for r 6.237 as originally enacted, by SI 2003/1730, r 9(1), Sch 1, Pt 6, para 51.
Date in force: 1 April 2004: see SI 2003/1730, r 1(3).
Para (2): in sub-para (a) words "or civil partner or former civil partner" in square brackets inserted by SI 2005/2114, art 2(18), Sch 18, Pt 1, para 1(1), (5).
Date in force: 5 December 2005: see SI 2005/2114, art 1.
Para (10): inserted by SI 2004/584, r 43.
Date in force: 1 April 2004: see SI 2004/584, r 1(2).

[6.237E Interpretation]

[(1) In Rules 6.237 and 6.237A, "registered land" has the same meaning as in section 132(1) of the Land Registration Act 2002.

(2) In Rules 6.237A and 6.237D, "individual register" has the same meaning as in the Land Registration Rules 2003.]

NOTES

Amendment

Substituted, together with rr 6.237, 6.237A–6.237D, for r 6.237 as originally enacted, by SI 2003/1730, r 9(1), Sch 1, Pt 6, para 51.
Date in force: 1 April 2004: see SI 2003/1730, r 1(3).

[CHAPTER 27

EC REGULATION—MEMBER STATE LIQUIDATOR]

NOTES

Amendment

Inserted by SI 2002/1307, rr 3(1), 8(9).
Date in force: 31 May 2002: see SI 2002/1307, r 1.

[6.238 Interpretation of creditor and notice to member State liquidator]

[(1) This Rule applies where a member State liquidator has been appointed in relation to the bankrupt.

(2) For the purposes of the Rules referred to in paragraph (3) a member State liquidator is deemed to be a creditor.

(3) The Rules referred to in paragraph (2) are Rules 6.73(1) (duty of official receiver), 6.75(1) (report of official receiver), 6.76(2) (report of official receiver), 6.79(2) (creditors' meeting), 6.81 (power to call creditors' meeting), 6.83 (requisitioned meetings), 6.93 (entitlement to vote), 6.94 (admission and rejection of proof), 6.96 (meaning of "prove"), 6.97 (supply of forms), 6.98 (contents of proof). . ., 6.100 (cost of proving), 6.101 (inspection of proofs), 6.104 (admission and rejection of proofs for dividend), 6.105(1) (appeal against decision on proof), 6.105(2), 6.106 (withdrawal or variation of proofs), 6.107(1) (expunging of proof), 6.108 (negotiable instruments, etc), 6.109 (secured creditors), 6.110 (discounts), 6.111 (debts in foreign currency), 6.112 (payments of a periodical nature), 6.113 (interest), 6.114 (debt payable at future time), 6.126(1) (resignation of trustee), 6.136(1) (release of official receiver), 6.137(1) (final meeting), 6.142(1) (challenge to remuneration), 6.150(2)

(creditors' committee), 6.160(3) (vacancy on creditors' committee), 6.172(3) (request for public examination), 6.212(1) (notice of annulment) and 6.217(3) (application by bankrupt for discharge).

(4) Paragraphs (2) and (3) are without prejudice to the generality of the right to participate referred to in paragraph 3 of Article 32 of the EC Regulation (exercise of creditor's rights).

(5) Where the trustee is obliged to give notice to, or provide a copy of a document (including an order of court) to, the court or the official receiver, the trustee shall give notice or provide copies, as the case may be, to the member State liquidator.

(6) Paragraph (5) is without prejudice to the generality of the obligations imposed by Article 31 of the EC Regulation (duty to cooperate and communicate information).]

NOTES

Amendment

Inserted by SI 2002/1307, rr 3(1), 8(9).
Date in force: 31 May 2002: see SI 2002/1307, r 1.
Para (3): words omitted revoked by SI 2010/686, r 2, Sch 1, para 419.
Date in force: 6 April 2010: see SI 2010/686, r 1; for transitional provisions see r 6(1), Sch 4, paras 1, 2(1)(b), (2)–(4) thereto.

[6.239 Interpretation of creditor and notice to member State liquidator appointed in main proceedings]

[(1) This Rule applies, in addition to Rule 6.238, where a member State liquidator has been appointed in main proceedings in relation to the bankrupt.

(2) For the purposes of the Rules referred to in paragraph (3) the member State liquidator is deemed to be a creditor.

(3) The Rules referred to in paragraph (2) are Rules 6.18(3) (hearing of petition), 6.23(1) (notice of intention to appear), 6.28(4) (extension of time), 6.30(2) (substitution of petitioner), 6.31(1) (change of carriage of petition) and 6.218(4) (report of official receiver).

(4) Paragraphs (2) and (3) are without prejudice to the generality of the right to participate referred to in paragraph 3 of Article 32 of the EC Regulation (exercise of creditor's rights).]

NOTES

Amendment

Inserted by SI 2002/1307, rr 3(1), 8(9).
Date in force: 31 May 2002: see SI 2002/1307, r 1.

[CHAPTER 28

BANKRUPTCY RESTRICTIONS ORDER]

NOTES

Amendment

Inserted by SI 2003/1730, r 9(1), Sch 1, Pt 6, para 52.
Date in force: 1 April 2004: see SI 2003/1730, r 1(3).

[6.240]
[In this and the following two Chapters, "Secretary of State" includes the official receiver acting in accordance with paragraph 1(2)(b) of Schedule 4A to the Act.]

NOTES

Amendment

Inserted by SI 2003/1730, r 9(1), Sch 1, Pt 6, para 52.
Date in force: 1 April 2004: see SI 2003/1730, r 1(3).

[6.241 Application for bankruptcy restrictions order]

[(1) Where the Secretary of State applies to the court for a bankruptcy restrictions order under paragraph 1 of Schedule 4A to the Act, the application shall be supported by a report by the Secretary of State.

(2) The report shall include—

(a) a statement of the conduct by reference to which it is alleged that it is appropriate for a bankruptcy restrictions order to be made; and

(b) the evidence on which the Secretary of State relies in support of the application.

(3) Any evidence in support of an application for a bankruptcy restrictions order provided by persons other than the Secretary of State shall be by way of [a witness statement].

(4) The date for the hearing shall be no earlier than 8 weeks from the date when the court fixes the venue for the hearing.

(5) . . .]

NOTES

Amendment

Inserted by SI 2003/1730, r 9(1), Sch 1, Pt 6, para 52.
Date in force: 1 April 2004: see SI 2003/1730, r 1(3).
Para (3): words "a witness statement" in square brackets substituted by SI 2010/686, r 2, Sch 1, para 420(1), (2).
Date in force: 6 April 2010: see SI 2010/686, r 1; for transitional provisions see r 6(1), Sch 4, paras 1, 2(1)(b), (2)–(4) thereto.
Para (5): revoked by SI 2010/686, r 2, Sch 1, para 420(1), (3).
Date in force: 6 April 2010: see SI 2010/686, r 1; for transitional provisions see r 6(1), Sch 4, paras 1, 2(1)(b), (2)–(4) thereto.

[6.242 Service on the defendant]

[(1) The Secretary of State shall serve notice of the application and the venue fixed by the court on the bankrupt not more than 14 days after the application is made at court.

(2) Service shall be accompanied by a copy of the application, together with copies of the report by the Secretary of State, any other evidence filed with the court in support of the application, and an acknowledgement of service.

(3) The defendant shall file in court an acknowledgement of service of the application indicating whether or not he contests the application not more than 14 days after service on him of the application.

(4) Where the defendant has failed to file an acknowledgement of service and the time period for doing so has expired, the defendant may attend the hearing of the application but may not take part in the hearing unless the court gives permission.]

NOTES

Amendment

Inserted by SI 2003/1730, r 9(1), Sch 1, Pt 6, para 52.

Date in force: 1 April 2004: see SI 2003/1730, r 1(3).

[6.243 The bankrupt's evidence]

[(1) If the bankrupt wishes to oppose the application, he shall within 28 days of the service of the application and evidence of the Secretary of State, file in court any evidence which he wishes the court to take into consideration, and shall serve a copy of such evidence upon the Secretary of State within 3 [business] days of filing it at court.

(2) The Secretary of State shall, within 14 days from receiving the copy of the bankrupt's evidence, file in court any further evidence in reply he wishes the court to take into consideration and shall as soon as reasonably practicable serve a copy of that evidence upon the bankrupt.]

NOTES

Amendment

Inserted by SI 2003/1730, r 9(1), Sch 1, Pt 6, para 52.
Date in force: 1 April 2004: see SI 2003/1730, r 1(3).
Para (1): word "business" in square brackets inserted by SI 2010/686, r 2, Sch 1, para 421.
Date in force: 6 April 2010: see SI 2010/686, r 1; for transitional provisions see r 6(1), Sch 4, para 1 thereto.

[6.244 Making a bankruptcy restrictions order]

[(1) The court may make a bankruptcy restrictions order against the bankrupt, whether or not the latter appears, and whether or not he has filed evidence in accordance with Rule 6.243.

(2) Where the court makes a bankruptcy restrictions order, it shall send two sealed copies to the Secretary of State.

(3) As soon as reasonably practicable after receipt of the sealed copy of the order, the Secretary of State shall send a sealed copy of the order to the bankrupt.]

NOTES

Amendment

Inserted by SI 2003/1730, r 9(1), Sch 1, Pt 6, para 52.
Date in force: 1 April 2004: see SI 2003/1730, r 1(3).

[CHAPTER 29
INTERIM BANKRUPTCY RESTRICTIONS ORDER]

NOTES

Amendment

Inserted by SI 2003/1730, r 9(1), Sch 1, Pt 6, para 52.
Date in force: 1 April 2004: see SI 2003/1730, r 1(3).

[6.245 Application for interim bankruptcy restrictions order]

[(1) Where the Secretary of State applies for an interim bankruptcy restrictions order under paragraph 5 of Schedule 4A to the Act, the court shall fix a venue for the hearing.

(2) Notice of an application for an interim bankruptcy restrictions order shall be given to the bankrupt at least 2 business days before the date set for the hearing unless the court directs otherwise.

(3) . . .]

NOTES

Amendment

Inserted by SI 2003/1730, r 9(1), Sch 1, Pt 6, para 52.
Date in force: 1 April 2004: see SI 2003/1730, r 1(3).
Para (3): revoked by SI 2010/686, r 2, Sch 1, para 422.
Date in force: 6 April 2010: see SI 2010/686, r 1; for transitional provisions see r 6(1), Sch 4, paras 1, 2(1)(b) thereto.

[6.246 The case against the defendant]

[(1) The Secretary of State shall file a report in court as evidence in support of any application for an interim bankruptcy restrictions order.

(2) The report shall include evidence of the bankrupt's conduct which is alleged to constitute the grounds for the making of an interim bankruptcy restrictions order and evidence of matters which relate to the public interest in making the order.

(3) Any evidence by persons other than the Secretary of State in support of an application for an interim bankruptcy restrictions order shall be by way of [a witness statement].]

NOTES

Amendment

Inserted by SI 2003/1730, r 9(1), Sch 1, Pt 6, para 52.
Date in force: 1 April 2004: see SI 2003/1730, r 1(3).
Para (3): words "a witness statement" in square brackets substituted by SI 2010/686, r 2, Sch 1, para 423.
Date in force: 6 April 2010: see SI 2010/686, r 1; for transitional provisions see r 6(1), Sch 4, paras 1, 2(1)(b), (2)–(4) thereto.

[6.247 Making an interim bankruptcy restrictions order]

[(1) The bankrupt may file in court any evidence which he wishes the court to take into consideration and may appear at the hearing for an interim bankruptcy restrictions order.

(2) The court may make an interim bankruptcy restrictions order against the bankrupt, whether or not the latter appears, and whether or not he has filed evidence.

(3) Where the court makes an interim bankruptcy restrictions order, it shall send two sealed copies of the order shall be sent, as soon as reasonably practicable, to the Secretary of State.

(4) As soon as reasonably practicable after receipt of the sealed copies of the order, the Secretary of State shall send a copy of the order to the bankrupt.]

NOTES

Amendment

Inserted by SI 2003/1730, r 9(1), Sch 1, Pt 6, para 52.
Date in force: 1 April 2004: see SI 2003/1730, r 1(3).

[6.248 Application to set aside an interim bankruptcy restrictions order]

[(1) A bankrupt may apply to the court to set aside an interim bankruptcy restrictions order.

(2) An application by the bankrupt to set aside an interim bankruptcy restrictions order shall be supported by [a witness statement] stating the grounds on which the application is made.

(3) Where a bankrupt applies to set aside an interim bankruptcy restrictions order under paragraph (1), he shall send to the Secretary of State, not less than [5 business] days before the hearing—

- (a) notice of his application;
- (b) notice of the venue;
- (c) a copy of his application; and
- (d) a copy of the supporting [witness statement].

(4) The Secretary of State may attend the hearing and call the attention of the court to any matters which seem to him to be relevant, and may himself give evidence or call witnesses.

(5) Where the court sets aside an interim bankruptcy restrictions order two sealed copies of the order shall be sent, as soon as reasonably practicable, to the Secretary of State by the court.

(6) As soon as reasonably practicable after receipt of the sealed copies of the order, the Secretary of State shall send a sealed copy of the order to the bankrupt.]

NOTES

Amendment

Inserted by SI 2003/1730, r 9(1), Sch 1, Pt 6, para 52.
Date in force: 1 April 2004: see SI 2003/1730, r 1(3).
Para (2): words "a witness statement" in square brackets substituted by SI 2010/686, r 2, Sch 1, para 424(1), (2).
Date in force: 6 April 2010: see SI 2010/686, r 1; for transitional provisions see r 6(1), Sch 4, paras 1, 2(1)(b), (2)–(4) thereto.
Para (3): words "5 business" in square brackets substituted by SI 2010/686, r 2, Sch 1, para 424(1), (3)(a).
Date in force: 6 April 2010: see SI 2010/686, r 1; for transitional provisions see r 6(1), Sch 4, para 1 thereto.
Para (3): in sub-para (d) words "witness statement" in square brackets substituted by SI 2010/686, r 2, Sch 1, para 424(1), (3)(b).
Date in force: 6 April 2010: see SI 2010/686, r 1; for transitional provisions see r 6(1), Sch 4, paras 1, 2(1)(b), (2)–(4) thereto.

[CHAPTER 30

BANKRUPTCY RESTRICTIONS UNDERTAKING]

NOTES

Amendment

Inserted by SI 2003/1730, r 9(1), Sch 1, Pt 6, para 52.
Date in force: 1 April 2004: see SI 2003/1730, r 1(3).

[6.249 Acceptance of the bankruptcy restrictions undertaking]

[A bankruptcy restrictions undertaking [authenticated] by the bankrupt shall be deemed to have been accepted by the Secretary of State for the purposes of paragraph 9 of Schedule 4A of the Act when the undertaking is [authenticated] by the Secretary of State.]

NOTES

Amendment

> Inserted by SI 2003/1730, r 9(1), Sch 1, Pt 6, para 52.
> Date in force: 1 April 2004: see SI 2003/1730, r 1(3).
> Word "authenticated" in square brackets in both places it occurs substituted by SI 2010/686, r 2, Sch 1, para 1.
> > Date in force: 6 April 2010: see SI 2010/686, r 1; for transitional provisions see r 6(1), Sch 4, paras 1, 2(1)(b) thereto.

[6.250 Notification to the court]

[As soon as reasonably practicable after a bankruptcy restrictions undertaking has been accepted by the Secretary of State, a copy shall be sent to the bankrupt and filed in court and sent to the official receiver if he is not the applicant.]

NOTES

Amendment

> Inserted by SI 2003/1730, r 9(1), Sch 1, Pt 6, para 52.
> Date in force: 1 April 2004: see SI 2003/1730, r 1(3).

[6.251 Application under paragraph 9(3) of Schedule 4A to the Act to annul a bankruptcy restrictions undertaking]

[(1) An application under paragraphs 9(3)(a) or (b) of Schedule 4A to the Act shall be supported by [a witness statement] stating the grounds on which it is made.

(2) The bankrupt shall give notice of the application and the venue, together with a copy of the [witness statement] supporting his application to the Secretary of State at least 28 days before the date fixed for the hearing.

(3) The Secretary of State may attend the hearing and call the attention of the court to any matters which seem to him to be relevant, and may himself give evidence or call witnesses.

(4) The court shall send a sealed copy of any order annulling or varying the bankruptcy restrictions undertaking to the Secretary of State and the bankrupt.]

NOTES

Amendment

> Inserted by SI 2003/1730, r 9(1), Sch 1, Pt 6, para 52.
> Date in force: 1 April 2004: see SI 2003/1730, r 1(3).
> Para (1): words "a witness statement" in square brackets substituted by SI 2010/686, r 2, Sch 1, para 425(1), (2).
> > Date in force: 6 April 2010: see SI 2010/686, r 1; for transitional provisions see r 6(1), Sch 4, paras 1, 2(1)(b), (2)–(4) thereto.
> Para (2): words "witness statement" in square brackets substituted by SI 2010/686, r 2, Sch 1, para 425(1), (3).
> > Date in force: 6 April 2010: see SI 2010/686, r 1; for transitional provisions see r 6(1), Sch 4, paras 1, 2(1)(b), (2)–(4) thereto.

[CHAPTER 31

DEBT RELIEF RESTRICTIONS ORDER]

NOTES

Amendment

Inserted by SI 2009/642, rr 4, 47.
Date in force: 6 April 2009: see SI 2009/642, r 1.

[6.252 Interpretation]
[In this Chapter and in Chapter 32, "Secretary of State" includes the official receiver acting in accordance with paragraph 1(2)(b) of Schedule 4ZB to the Act.]

NOTES

Amendment

Inserted by SI 2009/642, rr 4, 47.
Date in force: 6 April 2009: see SI 2009/642, r 1.

[6.253 Application for debt relief restrictions order]
[(1) Where the Secretary of State applies to the court for a debt relief restrictions order to be made in relation to a person in respect of whom a debt relief order has been made under paragraph 1 of Schedule 4ZB to the Act, the application shall be supported by a report by the Secretary of State.

(2) The report shall include—

(a) a statement of the conduct by reference to which it is alleged that it is appropriate for a debt relief restrictions order to be made; and

(b) the evidence on which the Secretary of State relies in support of the application.

(3) Any evidence in support of an application for a debt relief restrictions order provided by persons other than the Secretary of State shall be by way of [a witness statement].

(4) The date for the hearing shall be no earlier than 8 weeks from the date when the court fixes the venue for the hearing.

(5) . . .]

NOTES

Amendment

Inserted by SI 2009/642, rr 4, 47.
Date in force: 6 April 2009: see SI 2009/642, r 1.
Para (3): words "a witness statement" in square brackets substituted by SI 2010/686, r 2, Sch 1, para 426(1), (2).
Date in force: 6 April 2010: see SI 2010/686, r 1; for transitional provisions see r 6(1), Sch 4, paras 1, 2(1)(b), (2)–(4) thereto.
Para (5): revoked by SI 2010/686, r 2, Sch 1, para 426(1), (3).
Date in force: 6 April 2010: see SI 2010/686, r 1; for transitional provisions see r 6(1), Sch 4, paras 1, 2(1)(b) thereto.

[6.254 Service on the defendant]
[(1) The Secretary of State shall serve notice of the application and the venue fixed by the court on the debtor not more than 14 days after the application is made at court.

(2) Service shall be accompanied by a copy of the application, together with copies of the report by the Secretary of State, any other evidence filed with the court in support of the application, and an acknowledgement of service.

(3) The defendant shall file in court an acknowledgement of service of the application indicating whether or not he contests the application not more than 14 days after service on him of the application.

(4) Where the defendant has failed to file an acknowledgement of service and the time period for doing so has expired, the defendant may attend the hearing of the application but may not take part in the hearing unless the court gives permission.]

NOTES

Amendment

Inserted by SI 2009/642, rr 4, 47.
Date in force: 6 April 2009: see SI 2009/642, r 1.

[6.255 The debtor's evidence]

[(1) If the debtor wishes to oppose the application, he shall within 28 days of the service of the application and evidence of the Secretary of State, file in court any evidence which he wishes the court to take into consideration, and shall serve a copy of such evidence upon the Secretary of State within 3 [business] days of filing it at court.

(2) The Secretary of State shall, within 14 days from receiving the copy of the debtor's evidence, file in court any further evidence in reply he wishes the court to take into consideration and shall as soon as reasonably practicable serve a copy of that evidence upon the debtor.]

NOTES

Amendment

Inserted by SI 2009/642, rr 4, 47.
Date in force: 6 April 2009: see SI 2009/642, r 1.
Para (1): word "business" in square brackets inserted by SI 2010/686, r 2, Sch 1, para 427.
Date in force: 6 April 2010: see SI 2010/686, r 1; for transitional provisions see r 6(1), Sch 4, para 1 thereto.

[6.256 Making a debt relief restrictions order]

[(1) The court may make a debt relief restrictions order against the debtor, whether or not the latter appears and whether or not he has filed evidence in accordance with Rule 6.255.

(2) Where the court makes a debt relief restrictions order, it shall send two sealed copies to the Secretary of State.

(3) As soon as reasonably practicable after receipt of the sealed copy of the order, the Secretary of State shall send a sealed copy of the order to the debtor.]

NOTES

Amendment

Inserted by SI 2009/642, rr 4, 47.
Date in force: 6 April 2009: see SI 2009/642, r 1.

[CHAPTER 32

INTERIM DEBT RELIEF RESTRICTIONS ORDER]

NOTES

Amendment

Inserted by SI 2009/642, rr 4, 47.
Date in force: 6 April 2009: see SI 2009/642, r 1.

[6.257 Application for interim debt relief restrictions order]

[(1) Where the Secretary of State applies for an interim debt relief restrictions order under paragraph 5 of Schedule 4ZB to the Act, the court shall fix a venue for the hearing.

(2) Notice of an application for an interim debt relief restrictions order shall be given to the debtor at least 2 business days before the date set for the hearing unless the court directs otherwise.

(3) . . .]

NOTES

Amendment

Inserted by SI 2009/642, rr 4, 47.
Date in force: 6 April 2009: see SI 2009/642, r 1.
Para (3): revoked by SI 2010/686, r 2, Sch 1, para 428.
Date in force: 6 April 2010: see SI 2010/686, r 1; for transitional provisions see r 6(1), Sch 4, paras 1, 2(1)(b) thereto.

[6.258 The case against the debtor]

[(1) The Secretary of State shall file a report in court as evidence in support of any application for an interim debt relief restrictions order.

(2) The report shall include evidence of the debtor's conduct which is alleged to constitute the grounds for the making of an interim debt relief restrictions order and evidence of matters which relate to the public interest in making the order.

(3) Any evidence by persons other than the Secretary of State in support of an application for an interim debt relief restrictions order shall be by way of [a witness statement].]

NOTES

Amendment

Inserted by SI 2009/642, rr 4, 47.
Date in force: 6 April 2009: see SI 2009/642, r 1.
Para (3): words "a witness statement" in square brackets substituted by SI 2010/686, r 2, Sch 1, para 429.
Date in force: 6 April 2010: see SI 2010/686, r 1; for transitional provisions see r 6(1), Sch 4, paras 1, 2(1)(b), (2)–(4) thereto.

[6.259 Making an interim debt relief restrictions order]

[(1) The debtor may file in court any evidence which he wishes the court to take into consideration and may appear at the hearing for an interim debt relief restrictions order.

(2) The court may make an interim debt relief restrictions order against the debtor, whether or not the latter appears, and whether or not he has filed evidence.

(3) Where the court makes an interim debt relief restrictions order, as soon as reasonably practicable, it shall send two sealed copies of the order to the Secretary of State.

(4) As soon as reasonably practicable after receipt of the sealed copies of the order, the Secretary of State shall send a copy of the order to the debtor.]

NOTES

Amendment

Inserted by SI 2009/642, rr 4, 47.

Date in force: 6 April 2009: see SI 2009/642, r 1.

[6.260 Application to set aside an interim debt relief restrictions order]

[(1) A person subject to an interim debt relief restrictions order may apply to the court to set the order aside.

(2) An application to set aside an interim debt relief restrictions order shall be supported by [a witness statement] stating the grounds on which the application is made.

(3) Where an application is made to set aside an interim debt relief restrictions order under paragraph (1), the person making the application shall send to the Secretary of State, not less than [5 business] days before the hearing—

(a)   notice of his application;
(b)   notice of the venue;
(c)   a copy of his application; and
(d)   a copy of the supporting [witness statement].

(4) The Secretary of State may attend the hearing and call the attention of the court to any matters which seem to him to be relevant, and may himself give evidence or call witnesses.

(5) Where the court sets aside an interim debt relief restrictions order two sealed copies of the order shall be sent, as soon as reasonably practicable, to the Secretary of State by the court.

(6) As soon as reasonably practicable after receipt of the sealed copies of the order, the Secretary of State shall send a sealed copy of the order to the applicant.]

NOTES

Amendment

Inserted by SI 2009/642, rr 4, 47.

Date in force: 6 April 2009: see SI 2009/642, r 1.

Para (2): words "a witness statement" in square brackets substituted by SI 2010/686, r 2, Sch 1, para 430(1), (2).

Date in force: 6 April 2010: see SI 2010/686, r 1; for transitional provisions see r 6(1), Sch 4, paras 1, 2(1)(b), (2)–(4) thereto.

Para (3): words "5 business" in square brackets substituted by SI 2010/686, r 2, Sch 1, para 430(1), (3)(a).

Date in force: 6 April 2010: see SI 2010/686, r 1; for transitional provisions see r 6(1), Sch 4, para 1 thereto.

Para (3): in sub-para (d) words "witness statement" in square brackets substituted by SI 2010/686, r 2, Sch 1, para 430(1), (3)(b).

Date in force: 6 April 2010: see SI 2010/686, r 1; for transitional provisions see r 6(1), Sch 4, paras 1, 2(1)(b), (2)–(4) thereto.

[CHAPTER 33
DEBT RELIEF RESTRICTIONS UNDERTAKING]

NOTES

Amendment

Inserted by SI 2009/642, rr 4, 47.
Date in force: 6 April 2009: see SI 2009/642, r 1.

[6.261 Acceptance of debt relief restrictions undertaking]
[A debt relief restrictions undertaking [authenticated] by a person in relation to whom a debt relief order has been made shall be deemed to have been accepted by the Secretary of State for the purposes of paragraph 9 of Schedule 4ZB to the Act when the undertaking is [authenticated] by the Secretary of State.]

NOTES

Amendment

Inserted by SI 2009/642, rr 4, 47.
Date in force: 6 April 2009: see SI 2009/642, r 1.
Word "authenticated" in square brackets in both places it occurs substituted by SI 2010/686, r 2, Sch 1, para 1.
Date in force: 6 April 2010: see SI 2010/686, r 1; for transitional provisions see r 6(1), Sch 4, paras 1, 2(1)(b) thereto.

[6.262 Notification]
[As soon as reasonably practicable after a debt relief restrictions undertaking has been accepted by the Secretary of State, a copy shall be sent to the person who offered the undertaking and to the official receiver.]

NOTES

Amendment

Inserted by SI 2009/642, rr 4, 47.
Date in force: 6 April 2009: see SI 2009/642, r 1.

[6.263 Application under paragraph 9(3) of Schedule 4ZB to the Act to annul a debt relief restrictions undertaking.]
[(1) An application under paragraph 9(3)(a) or (b) of Schedule 4ZB to the Act shall be supported by [a witness statement] stating the grounds on which it is made.

(2) The applicant shall give notice of the application and the venue, together with a copy of the [witness statement] supporting his application to the Secretary of State at least 28 days before the date fixed for the hearing.

(3) The Secretary of State may attend the hearing and call the attention of the court to any matters which seem to him to be relevant, and may himself give evidence or call witnesses.

(4) The court shall send a sealed copy of any order annulling or varying the debt relief restrictions undertaking to the Secretary of State and the applicant.]

NOTES

Amendment

Inserted by SI 2009/642, rr 4, 47.

Date in force: 6 April 2009: see SI 2009/642, r 1.
Para (1): words "a witness statement" in square brackets substituted by SI 2010/686, r 2, Sch 1, para 431(1), (2).
Date in force: 6 April 2010: see SI 2010/686, r 1; for transitional provisions see r 6(1), Sch 4, paras 1, 2(1)(b), (2)–(4) thereto.
Para (2): words "witness statement" in square brackets substituted by SI 2010/686, r 2, Sch 1, para 431(1), (3).
Date in force: 6 April 2010: see SI 2010/686, r 1; for transitional provisions see r 6(1), Sch 4, paras 1, 2(1)(b), (2)–(4) thereto.

[PART 6A]

NOTES

Amendment

Inserted by SI 2003/1730, r 10, Sch 1, Pt 7, para 53.
Date in force: 1 April 2004: see SI 2003/1730, r 1(3).

[CHAPTER 1

GENERAL]

NOTES

Amendment

Inserted by SI 2003/1730, r 10, Sch 1, Pt 7, para 53.
Date in force: 1 April 2004: see SI 2003/1730, r 1(3).

[6A.1 The individual insolvency register; the bankruptcy restrictions register]

[(1) The Secretary of State shall create and maintain a register of matters relating to bankruptcies[, debt relief orders] and individual voluntary arrangements in accordance with the provisions of this Part (referred to in this Part as "the individual insolvency register").

[(2) The register—
- (a) referred to in paragraph 12 of Schedule 4A to the Act (referred to in this Part as "the bankruptcy restrictions register"), and
- (b) of the matters specified in paragraphs (b) and (c) of section 251W (referred to in this Part as "the debt relief restrictions register"),

shall be maintained in accordance with the provisions of this Part.]

(3) In this Part the "registers" means the registers referred to in paragraphs (1) and (2).

(4) The registers shall be open to public inspection on any business day between the hours of 9.00 am and 5.00 pm.

(5) Where an obligation to enter information onto, or delete information from, the registers arises under this Part, that obligation shall be performed as soon as is reasonably practicable after it arises.]

NOTES

Amendment

Inserted by SI 2003/1730, r 10, Sch 1, Pt 7, para 53.
Date in force: 1 April 2004: see SI 2003/1730, r 1(3).
Para (1): words ", debt relief orders" in square brackets inserted by SI 2009/642, rr 4, 48(a).
Date in force: 6 April 2009: see SI 2009/642, r 1.

Para (2): substituted by SI 2009/642, rr 4, 48(b).
Date in force: 6 April 2009: see SI 2009/642, r 1.

[CHAPTER 2

INDIVIDUAL INSOLVENCY REGISTER]

NOTES

Amendment

Inserted by SI 2003/1730, r 10, Sch 1, Pt 7, para 53.
Date in force: 1 April 2004: see SI 2003/1730, r 1(3).

[6A.2A Entry of information onto the individual insolvency register—individual voluntary arrangements]

[(1) This Rule applies where—
- (a) a voluntary arrangement has been accepted by the debtor's creditors; and
- (b) the Secretary of State has received—
  - (i) information under Rule 5.29(1) sent pursuant to paragraph (3) of that Rule; and
  - (ii) notice under Rule 5.34, Rule 5.45 or Rule 5.50.

(2) Subject to paragraph (3), the Secretary of State must enter onto the individual insolvency register—
- (a) the name and address of the debtor;
- (b) the date on which the arrangement was approved by the creditors;
- (c) the debtor's gender;
- (d) the debtor's date of birth;
- (e) any name by which the debtor was or is known, not being the name in which the debtor has entered into the voluntary arrangement;
- (f) as regards an arrangement other than under section 263A, the name and address of the supervisor;
- (g) as regards an arrangement under section 263A—
  - (i) that the official receiver is the supervisor; and
  - (ii) the address of the official receiver; and
- (h) a statement whether the arrangement—
  - (i) was completed in accordance with its terms; or
  - (ii) failed.

(3) Paragraph (4) applies where there is entered on the register information in respect of a voluntary arrangement—
- (a) of which the Secretary of State had been notified prior to this Rule coming into force; and
- (b) which has not been completed or terminated when this Rule comes into force.

(4) The Secretary of State must maintain on the register the information that the Secretary of State was required to enter on to the individual insolvency register immediately prior to the coming into force of this Rule.

(5) Paragraphs (2) and (4) are subject to Rules 5.67, 6A.3 and 6A.8.]

NOTES

Amendment

Inserted by SI 2003/1730, r 10, Sch 1, Pt 7, para 53.

Date in force: 1 April 2004: see SI 2003/1730, r 1(3).
Substituted, for r 6A.2 as previously enacted, by SI 2010/686, r 2, Sch 1, para 432.
Date in force: 6 April 2010: see SI 2010/686, r 1; for transitional provisions see r 6(1), Sch 4, para 1 thereto.

[6A.3 Deletion of information from the individual insolvency register—individual voluntary arrangements]

[The Secretary of State shall delete from the individual insolvency register all information concerning an individual voluntary arrangement where—
- (a) he receives notice under Rule 5.30(5) or Rule 5.46(4) of the making of a revocation order in respect of the arrangement; or
- (b) he receives notice under Rule 5.34(3) or Rule 5.50(3) of the full implementation or termination of the arrangement,

[and in either case a period of 3 months has elapsed from the receipt of the notice].]

NOTES

Amendment

Inserted by SI 2003/1730, r 10, Sch 1, Pt 7, para 53.
Date in force: 1 April 2004: see SI 2003/1730, r 1(3).
Words "and in either case a period of 3 months has elapsed from the receipt of the notice" in square brackets inserted by SI 2010/686, r 2, Sch 1, para 433.
Date in force: 6 April 2010: see SI 2010/686, r 1; for transitional provisions see r 6(1), Sch 4, para 1 thereto.

[6A.4 Entry of information onto the individual insolvency register—bankruptcy orders]

[(1) The Secretary of State shall enter onto the individual insolvency register any information that was required to be held on the register of bankruptcy orders maintained by the Secretary of State immediately prior to the coming into force of this Rule and which relates to a bankrupt who—
- (a) has not received his discharge on or before the date that this Rule comes into force; or
- (b) was discharged in the period of 3 months immediately preceding the coming into force of this Rule.

(2) Where the official receiver receives pursuant to Rule 6.34 or Rule 6.46 a copy of a bankruptcy order from the court, he shall cause to be entered onto the individual insolvency register—
- (a) the matters listed in Rules 6.7 and 6.38 with respect to the debtor as they are stated in the bankruptcy petition;
- (b) the date of the making of the bankruptcy order;
- (c) the name of the court that made the order; and
- (d) the court reference number as stated on the order.

(3) The official receiver shall cause to be entered onto the individual insolvency register as soon as reasonably practicable after receipt by him, the following information—
- (a) the name, gender, occupation (if any) and date of birth of the bankrupt;
- (b) the bankrupt's last known address;
- [(c) where a bankruptcy order or debt relief order has been made in the period of six years immediately prior to the day of the latest bankruptcy order made against the bankrupt (excluding for these purposes any bankruptcy order that was annulled or any debt relief order that was revoked), the date of whichever is the latest of them;]
- (d) any name by which the bankrupt was known, not being the name in which he was adjudged bankrupt;

Insolvency Rules 1986, reg 6A.4

(e) the address of any business carried on by the bankrupt and the name in which that business was carried on if carried on in a name other than the name in which the bankrupt was adjudged bankrupt;
(f) the name and address of any insolvency practitioner appointed to act as trustee in bankruptcy;
(g) the address at which the official receiver may be contacted; . . .
(h) the automatic discharge date under section 279[; and
(i) where a bankruptcy order is rescinded by the court, the fact that such an order has been made, the date on which it is made and (if different) the date on which it has effect].

(4) Where pursuant to Rule 6.176(5) or Rule 6.215(8) the official receiver receives a copy of an order suspending the bankrupt's discharge he shall cause to be entered onto the individual insolvency register—
(a) the fact that such an order has been made; and
(b) the period for which the discharge has been suspended or that the relevant period has ceased to run until the fulfilment of conditions specified in the order.

(5) Where pursuant to Rule 6.216(7) a copy of a certificate certifying the discharge of an order under section 279(3) is received by the official receiver, he shall cause to be entered onto the individual insolvency register—
(a) that the court has discharged the order made under section 279(3); and
(b) the new date of discharge of the bankrupt,
but where the order discharging the order under section 279(3) is subsequently rescinded by the court, the official receiver shall cause the register to be amended accordingly.

(6) Where a bankrupt is discharged from bankruptcy under section 279(1) or section 279(2), the official receiver shall cause the fact and date of such discharge to be entered in the individual insolvency register.

(7) This Rule is subject to [Rules 6.235B, 6A.5 and 6A.8].]

NOTES

Amendment
Inserted by SI 2003/1730, r 10, Sch 1, Pt 7, para 53.
Date in force: 1 April 2004: see SI 2003/1730, r 1(3).
Para (3): sub-para (c) substituted by SI 2009/642, rr 4, 49.
Date in force: 6 April 2009: see SI 2009/642, r 1.
Para (3): in sub-para (g) word omitted revoked by SI 2010/686, r 2, Sch 1, para 434(1), (2)(a).
Date in force: 6 April 2010: see SI 2010/686, r 1; for transitional provisions see r 6(1), Sch 4, para 1 thereto.
Para (3): sub-para (i) and word "; and" immediately preceding it inserted by SI 2010/686, r 2, Sch 1, para 434(1), (2)(b).
Date in force: 6 April 2010: see SI 2010/686, r 1; for transitional provisions see r 6(1), Sch 4, para 1 thereto.
Para (7): words "Rules 6.235B, 6A.5 and 6A.8" in square brackets substituted by SI 2010/686, r 2, Sch 1, para 434(1), (3).
Date in force: 6 April 2010: see SI 2010/686, r 1; for transitional provisions see r 6(1), Sch 4, para 1 thereto.

[6A.5 Deletion of information from the individual insolvency register—bankruptcy orders]
[. . . The Secretary of State shall delete from the individual insolvency register all information concerning a bankruptcy where—

(a) the bankruptcy order has been annulled pursuant to section 261(2)(a), 261(2)(b), 263D(3) or section 282(1)(b) [and a period of 3 months has elapsed since notice of the annulment was given to the Secretary of State];
(b) the bankrupt has been discharged from the bankruptcy and a period of 3 months has elapsed from the date of discharge;
(c) the bankruptcy order is annulled pursuant to section 282(1)(a) and [28 days have elapsed since notice of the annulment was given to the Secretary of State] under Rule 6.213(2); or
(d) the bankruptcy order is rescinded by the court under section 375 . . . the Secretary of State has received a copy of the order made by the court [and 28 days have elapsed since receipt of the copy of the order].]

NOTES

Amendment

Inserted by SI 2003/1730, r 10, Sch 1, Pt 7, para 53.
    Date in force: 1 April 2004: see SI 2003/1730, r 1(3).
First words omitted revoked by SI 2004/584, r 44.
    Date in force: 1 April 2004: see SI 2004/584, r 1(2).
In para (a) words from "and a period" to "Secretary of State" in square brackets inserted by SI 2010/686, r 2, Sch 1, para 435(1), (2).
    Date in force: 6 April 2010: see SI 2010/686, r 1; for transitional provisions see r 6(1), Sch 4, para 1 thereto.
In para (c) words "28 days have elapsed since notice of the annulment was given to the Secretary of State" in square brackets substituted by SI 2010/686, r 2, Sch 1, para 435(1), (3).
    Date in force: 6 April 2010: see SI 2010/686, r 1; for transitional provisions see r 6(1), Sch 4, para 1 thereto.
In para (d) word omitted revoked by SI 2010/686, r 2, Sch 1, para 435(1), (4)(a).
    Date in force: 6 April 2010: see SI 2010/686, r 1; for transitional provisions see r 6(1), Sch 4, para 1 thereto.
In para (d) words "and 28 days have elapsed since receipt of the copy of the order" in square brackets inserted by SI 2010/686, r 2, Sch 1, para 435(1), (4)(b).
    Date in force: 6 April 2010: see SI 2010/686, r 1; for transitional provisions see r 6(1), Sch 4, para 1 thereto.

[6A.5A Entry of information onto the individual insolvency register—debt relief orders]

[(1) This Rule is subject to [Rules 5A.18, 6A.5B and 6A.8].

(2) The official receiver shall cause to be entered onto the individual insolvency register as soon as reasonably practicable after the making of a debt relief order the following information relating to the order or to the debtor in respect of whom it has been made—
(a) as they are stated in the debtor's application—
   (i) the name, gender, occupation (if any) and date of birth of the debtor;
   (ii) the debtor's last known address;
   (iii) the name or names in which he carries or has carried on business, if other than his true name; and
   (iv) the nature of his business and the address or addresses at which he carries or has carried it on and whether alone or with others;
(b) the date of the making of the debt relief order;
(c) the reference number of the order;
(d) the date of the end of the moratorium period; and
(e) where a bankruptcy order or a debt relief order has been made in the period of six years immediately prior to the date of the latest debt relief

order made against the debtor (excluding for these purposes any bankruptcy order that was annulled or any debt relief order that was revoked), the date of whichever is the latest of them.

(3) Provided that information concerning a debt relief order has not been validly deleted under Rule 6A.5B, the official receiver shall also cause to be entered on the register in relation to the order—

(a) where the moratorium period is terminated early, the fact that such has happened, the date of early termination and whether the early termination is on revocation of the debt relief order or by virtue of any other enactment;

(b) where the moratorium period is extended, the fact that such has happened, the date on which the extension was made, its duration and the date of the new anticipated end of the moratorium period; or

(c) where the debtor is discharged from all qualifying debts, the date of such discharge.]

NOTES

Amendment

Inserted by SI 2009/642, rr 4, 50.
Date in force: 6 April 2009: see SI 2009/642, r 1.
Para (1): words "Rules 5A.18, 6A.5B and 6A.8" in square brackets substituted by SI 2010/686, r 2, Sch 1, para 436.
Date in force: 6 April 2010: see SI 2010/686, r 1; for transitional provisions see r 6(1), Sch 4, para 1 thereto.

[6A.5B Deletion of information from the individual insolvency register—debt relief orders]

[The Secretary of State shall delete from the individual insolvency register all information concerning a debt relief order where—

(a) the debt relief order has been revoked, or

(b) the debtor has been discharged from his qualifying debts,

and a period of 3 months has elapsed from the date of revocation or discharge.]

NOTES

Amendment

Inserted by SI 2009/642, rr 4, 50.
Date in force: 6 April 2009: see SI 2009/642, r 1.

[CHAPTER 3

BANKRUPTCY RESTRICTIONS REGISTER]

NOTES

Amendment

Inserted by SI 2003/1730, r 10, Sch 1, Pt 7, para 53.
Date in force: 1 April 2004: see SI 2003/1730, r 1(3).

[6A.6 Bankruptcy restrictions orders and undertakings—entry of information onto the bankruptcy restrictions register]
[(1) Where an interim bankruptcy restrictions order or a bankruptcy restrictions order is made against a bankrupt, the Secretary of State shall enter onto the bankruptcy restrictions register—
- [(a) the name, gender, occupation (if any) and date of birth of the bankrupt;
- (aa) the bankrupt's last known address;]
- (b) a statement that an interim bankruptcy restrictions order or, as the case may be, a bankruptcy restrictions order has been made against him;
- (c) the date of the making of the order, the court and the court reference number; and
- (d) the duration of the order.

(2) Where a bankruptcy restrictions undertaking is given by a bankrupt, the Secretary of State shall enter onto the bankruptcy restrictions register—
- [(a) the name, gender, occupation (if any) and date of birth of the bankrupt;
- (aa) the bankrupt's last known address;]
- (b) a statement that a bankruptcy restrictions undertaking has been given;
- (c) the date of the acceptance of the bankruptcy restrictions undertaking by the Secretary of State; and
- (d) the duration of the bankruptcy restrictions undertaking.

(3) This Rule is subject to [Rules 6.235B, 6A.7 and 6A.8].]

NOTES

Amendment

Inserted by SI 2003/1730, r 10, Sch 1, Pt 7, para 53.
Date in force: 1 April 2004: see SI 2003/1730, r 1(3).
Para (1): sub-paras (a), (aa) substituted, for sub-para (a), by SI 2004/584, r 45(a).
Date in force: 1 April 2004: see SI 2004/584, r 1(2).
Para (2): sub-paras (a), (aa) substituted, for sub-para (a), by SI 2004/584, r 45(b).
Date in force: 1 April 2004: see SI 2004/584, r 1(2).
Para (3): words "Rules 6.235B, 6A.7 and 6A.8" in square brackets substituted by SI 2010/686, r 2, Sch 1, para 437.
Date in force: 6 April 2010: see SI 2010/686, r 1; for transitional provisions see r 6(1), Sch 4, para 1 thereto.

[6A.7 Deletion of information from the bankruptcy restrictions register—bankruptcy restrictions orders and undertakings]
[In any case where an interim bankruptcy restrictions order or a bankruptcy restrictions order is made or a bankruptcy restrictions undertaking has been accepted, the Secretary of State shall remove from the bankruptcy restrictions register all information regarding that order or, as the case may be, undertaking after—
- (a) receipt of notification that the order or, as the case may be, the undertaking has ceased to have effect; or
- (b) the expiry of the order or, as the case may be, undertaking.]

NOTES

Amendment

Inserted by SI 2003/1730, r 10, Sch 1, Pt 7, para 53.
Date in force: 1 April 2004: see SI 2003/1730, r 1(3).

[CHAPTER 3A
DEBT RELIEF RESTRICTIONS REGISTER]

NOTES

Amendment

Inserted by SI 2009/642, rr 4, 51.
Date in force: 6 April 2009: see SI 2009/642, r 1.

[6A.7A Debt relief restrictions orders and undertakings—entries of information onto the debt relief restrictions register]

[(1) This Rule is subject to [Rules 5A.18, 6A.7B and 6A.8].

(2) Where an interim debt relief restrictions order or a debt relief restrictions order is made against a debtor, the Secretary of State shall enter onto the debt relief restrictions register—

- (a) the name, gender, occupation (if any) and date of birth of the debtor;
- (b) the debtor's last known address;
- (c) a statement that an interim debt relief restrictions order or, as the case may be, a debt relief restrictions order has been made against him;
- (d) the date of the making of the order and the order reference number; and
- (e) the duration of the order.

(3) Where a debt relief restrictions undertaking is given by a debtor, the Secretary of State shall enter onto the debt relief restrictions register—

- (a) the name, gender, occupation (if any) and date of birth of the debtor;
- (b) the debtor's last known address;
- (c) a statement that a debt relief restrictions undertaking has been given;
- (d) the date of the acceptance of the debt relief restrictions undertaking by the Secretary of State and reference number of the undertaking; and
- (e) the duration of the debt relief restrictions undertaking.]

NOTES

Amendment

Inserted by SI 2009/642, rr 4, 51.
Date in force: 6 April 2009: see SI 2009/642, r 1.
Para (1): words "Rules 5A.18, 6A.7B and 6A.8" in square brackets substituted by SI 2010/686, r 2, Sch 1, para 438.
Date in force: 6 April 2010: see SI 2010/686, r 1; for transitional provisions see r 6(1), Sch 4, para 1 thereto.

[6A.7B Deletion of information from the debt relief restrictions register—debt relief restrictions order and undertakings]

[In any case where an interim debt relief restrictions order or a debt relief restrictions order is made or a debt relief restrictions undertaking has been accepted, the Secretary of State shall remove from the debt relief restrictions register all information regarding that order or, as the case may be, undertaking after—

- (a) receipt of notification that the order or, as the case may be, undertaking has ceased to have effect; or
- (b) the expiry of the order or, as the case may be, undertaking.]

NOTES

Amendment

Inserted by SI 2009/642, rr 4, 51.
Date in force: 6 April 2009: see SI 2009/642, r 1.

[CHAPTER 4

RECTIFICATION OF REGISTERS]

NOTES

Amendment

Inserted by SI 2003/1730, r 10, Sch 1, Pt 7, para 53.
Date in force: 1 April 2004: see SI 2003/1730, r 1(3).

[6A.8 Rectification of the registers]
[(1) Where the Secretary of State becomes aware that there is any inaccuracy in any information maintained on the registers he shall rectify the inaccuracy as soon as reasonably practicable.

[(2) Where the Secretary of State receives notice of the date of the death of a person in respect of whom information is held on any of the registers, he shall cause the fact and date of the person's death to be entered onto the individual insolvency register and, as the case may be, the bankruptcy restrictions register or the debt relief restrictions register.]]

NOTES

Amendment

Inserted by SI 2003/1730, r 10, Sch 1, Pt 7, para 53.
Date in force: 1 April 2004: see SI 2003/1730, r 1(3).
Para (2): substituted by SI 2009/642, rr 4, 52.
Date in force: 6 April 2009: see SI 2009/642, r 1.

THE THIRD GROUP OF PARTS

PART 7

COURT PROCEDURE AND PRACTICE

CHAPTER 1

APPLICATIONS

7.1 Preliminary
This Chapter applies to any application made to the court under the Act or Rules except . . .—

    (a)   [an application for] an administration order under Part II,
    (b)   [a petition for] a winding-up order under Part IV, or
    (c)   [a petition for] a bankruptcy order under Part IX
of the Act.

NOTES

Initial Commencement

Specified date

Specified date: 29 December 1986: see r 0.1.

Amendment

Words omitted revoked by SI 2003/1730, r 11, Sch 1, Pt 8, para 54.
Date in force: 15 September 2003: see SI 2003/1730, r 1(2).
In para (a) words "an application for" in square brackets inserted by SI 2003/1730, r 11, Sch 1, Pt 8, para 54.
Date in force: 15 September 2003: see SI 2003/1730, r 1(2).
In para (b) words "a petition for" in square brackets inserted by SI 2003/1730, r 11, Sch 1, Pt 8, para 54.
Date in force: 15 September 2003: see SI 2003/1730, r 1(2).
In para (c) words "a petition for" in square brackets inserted by SI 2003/1730, r 11, Sch 1, Pt 8, para 54.
Date in force: 15 September 2003: see SI 2003/1730, r 1(2).

See Further

See further, in relation to the application of this rule, with modifications, in respect of bank administration and applications for bank administration: the Bank Administration (England and Wales) Rules 2009, SI 2009/357, rr 58–61.

7.2 . . .

. . .

NOTES

Amendment

Revoked by SI 2010/686, r 5.
Date in force: 6 April 2010: see SI 2010/686, r 1; for transitional provisions see r 6(1), Sch 4, para 1 thereto.

7.3 Form and contents of application

(1) Each application shall be in writing and shall state—

[(a) that the application is made under the Act;
(aa) the names of the parties;
(ab) the name of the bankrupt, or the debtor who or company which is the subject of the insolvency proceedings to which the application relates;
(ac) the court (and where applicable, the division or district registry of that court) in which the application is made;
(ad) where the court has previously allocated a number to the insolvency proceedings within which the application is made, that number;]
(b) the nature of the [remedy] or order applied for or the directions sought from the court;
(c) the names and addresses of the persons (if any) on whom it is intended to serve the application or that no person is intended to be served;
(d) where the Act or Rules require that notice of the application is to be given to specified persons, the names and addresses of all those persons (so far as known to the applicant); and
(e) the applicant's address for service.

(2) . . .

(3) The application must be [authenticated] by the applicant if he is acting in person or, when he is not so acting, by or on behalf of his solicitor.

NOTES

Initial Commencement

Specified date

Specified date: 29 December 1986: see r 0.1.

Amendment

Para (1): sub-paras (a), (aa)–(ad) substituted, for sub-para (a) as originally enacted, by SI 2010/686, r 2, Sch 1, para 439(1), (2)(a).
Date in force: 6 April 2010: see SI 2010/686, r 1; for transitional provisions and further effect see rr 6(1), 7, Sch 4, para 1, Sch 5 thereto.
Para (1): in sub-para (b) word "remedy" in square brackets substituted by SI 2010/686, r 2, Sch 1, para 439(1), (2)(b).
Date in force: 6 April 2010: see SI 2010/686, r 1; for transitional provisions and further effect see rr 6(1), 7, Sch 4, para 1, Sch 5 thereto.
Para (2): revoked by SI 2010/686, r 2, Sch 1, para 439(1), (3).
Date in force: 6 April 2010: see SI 2010/686, r 1; for transitional provisions and further effect see rr 6(1), 7, Sch 4, para 1, Sch 5 thereto.
Para (3): word "authenticated" in square brackets substituted by SI 2010/686, r 2, Sch 1, para 1.
Date in force: 6 April 2010: see SI 2010/686, r 1; for transitional provisions and further effect see rr 6(1), 7, Sch 4, paras 1, 2(1)(b), Sch 5 thereto.

Modification

References to solicitors etc modified to include references to bodies recognised under the Administration of Justice Act 1985, s 9, by the Solicitors' Incorporated Practices Order 1991, SI 1991/2684, arts 4, 5, Sch 1.

See Further

See further, in relation the application of this rule, with modifications, in respect of the procedure for the appointment of a bank liquidator and the operation of bank insolvency under the Banking Act 2009, Pt 2: the Bank Insolvency (England and Wales) Rules 2009, SI 2009/356, rr 3(3)–(8), 190.
See further, in relation to the application of this rule, with modifications, in respect of bank administration and applications for bank administration: the Bank Administration (England and Wales) Rules 2009, SI 2009/357, rr 58–61.

[7.3A Application under section 176A(5) to disapply section 176A]

[(1) An application under section 176A(5) shall be accompanied by [a witness statement] by the liquidator, administrator or receiver.

(2) The [witness statement] shall state—

    (a)   the type of insolvency proceedings in which the application arises;

    (b)   a summary of the financial position of the company;

    (c)   the information substantiating the applicant's view that the cost of making a distribution to unsecured creditors would be disproportionate to the benefits; and

    (d)   whether any other [office-holder] is acting in relation to the company and if so his address.]

NOTES

Amendment

Inserted by SI 2003/1730, r 11, Sch 1, Pt 8, para 55.
Date in force: 15 September 2003: see SI 2003/1730, r 1(2).
Para (1): words "a witness statement" in square brackets substituted by SI 2010/686, r 2, Sch 1, para 440(1), (2).

Date in force: 6 April 2010: see SI 2010/686, r 1; for transitional provisions and further effect see rr 6(1), 7, Sch 4, paras 1, 2(1)(b), (2)–(4), Sch 5 thereto.
Para (2): words "witness statement" in square brackets substituted by SI 2010/686, r 2, Sch 1, para 440(1), (3)(a).
Date in force: 6 April 2010: see SI 2010/686, r 1; for transitional provisions and further effect see rr 6(1), 7, Sch 4, paras 1, 2(1)(b), (2)–(4), Sch 5 thereto.
Para (2): in sub-para (d) word "office-holder" in square brackets substituted by SI 2010/686, r 2, Sch 1, para 440(1), (3)(b).
Date in force: 6 April 2010: see SI 2010/686, r 1; for transitional provisions and further effect see rr 6(1), 7, Sch 4, para 1, Sch 5 thereto.

See Further

See further, in relation the application of this rule, with modifications, in respect of the procedure for the appointment of a bank liquidator and the operation of bank insolvency under the Banking Act 2009, Pt 2: the Bank Insolvency (England and Wales) Rules 2009, SI 2009/356, rr 3(3)–(8), 191.

See further, in relation to the application of this rule, with modifications, in respect of bank administration and applications for bank administration: the Bank Administration (England and Wales) Rules 2009, SI 2009/357, rr 58–61.

7.4 Filing and service of application

(1) [An application must be filed with the court], accompanied by one copy and a number of additional copies equal to the number of persons who are to be served with the application.

[(2) Where an application is filed with the court in accordance with paragraph (1), the court must fix a venue for the application to be heard unless—

(a) it considers it is not appropriate to do so;

(b) the Rule under which the application is brought provides otherwise; or

(c) the case is one to which Rule 7.5A applies.]

(3) Unless the court otherwise directs, the applicant shall serve a sealed copy of the application, endorsed with the venue for the hearing, on the respondent named in the application (or on each respondent if more than one).

(4) The court may give any of the following directions—

(a) that the application be served upon persons other than those specified by the relevant provision of the Act or Rules;

(b) that the giving of notice to any person may be dispensed with;

(c) that notice be given in some way other than that specified in paragraph (3).

[(5) An application must be served at least 14 days before the date fixed for its hearing unless—

(a) the provision of the Act or the Rules under which the application is made makes different provision; or

(b) the case is one of urgency, to which paragraph (6) applies.]

(6) Where the case is one of urgency, the court may (without prejudice to its general power to extend or abridge time limits)—

(a) hear the application immediately, either with or without notice to, or the attendance of, other parties, or

(b) authorise a shorter period of service than that provided for by paragraph (5);

and any such application may be heard on terms providing for the filing or service of documents, or the carrying out of other formalities, as the court thinks [just].

NOTES

Initial Commencement

Specified date

Specified date: 29 December 1986: see r 0.1.

Amendment

Para (1): words "An application must be filed with the court" in square brackets substituted by SI 2010/686, r 2, Sch 1, para 441(1), (2).
Date in force: 6 April 2010: see SI 2010/686, r 1; for transitional provisions and further effect see rr 6(1), 7, Sch 4, paras 1, 2(1)(b), Sch 5 thereto.
Para (2): substituted by SI 2010/686, r 2, Sch 1, para 441(1), (3).
Date in force: 6 April 2010: see SI 2010/686, r 1; for transitional provisions and further effect see rr 6(1), 7, Sch 4, paras 1, 2(1)(b), Sch 5 thereto.
Para (5): substituted by SI 2010/686, r 2, Sch 1, para 441(1), (4).
Date in force: 6 April 2010: see SI 2010/686, r 1; for transitional provisions and further effect see rr 6(1), 7, Sch 4, paras 1, 2(1)(b), Sch 5 thereto.
Para (6): word "just" in square brackets substituted by SI 2010/686, r 2, Sch 1, para 1.
Date in force: 6 April 2010: see SI 2010/686, r 1; for transitional provisions and further effect see rr 6(1), 7, Sch 4, paras 1, 2(1)(b), Sch 5 thereto.

See Further

See further, in relation the application of this rule, with modifications, in respect of the procedure for the appointment of a bank liquidator and the operation of bank insolvency under the Banking Act 2009, Pt 2: the Bank Insolvency (England and Wales) Rules 2009, SI 2009/356, rr 3(3)–(8), 192.
See further, in relation to the application of this rule, with modifications, in respect of bank administration and applications for bank administration: the Bank Administration (England and Wales) Rules 2009, SI 2009/357, rr 58–61.

[7.4A Notice of application under section 176A(5)]

[An application under section 176A(5) may be made without the application being served upon or notice being given to any other party, save that notice of the application shall be given to any other [office-holder who is acting] in relation to the company including any member State liquidator.]

NOTES

Amendment

Inserted by SI 2003/1730, r 11, Sch 1, Pt 8, para 56.
Date in force: 15 September 2003: see SI 2003/1730, r 1(2).
Words "office-holder who is acting" in square brackets substituted by SI 2010/686, r 2, Sch 1, para 442.
Date in force: 6 April 2010: see SI 2010/686, r 1; for transitional provisions and further effect see rr 6(1), 7, Sch 4, para 1, Sch 5 thereto.

See Further

See further, in relation the application of this rule, with modifications, in respect of the procedure for the appointment of a bank liquidator and the operation of bank insolvency under the Banking Act 2009, Pt 2: the Bank Insolvency (England and Wales) Rules 2009, SI 2009/356, rr 3(3)–(8), 193.
See further, in relation to the application of this rule, with modifications, in respect of bank administration and applications for bank administration: the Bank Administration (England and Wales) Rules 2009, SI 2009/357, rr 58–61.

[7.5A Hearings without notice]

[Where the relevant provisions of the Act or the Rules do not require service of the application on, or notice of it to be given to, any person—

(a) the court may hear the application as soon as reasonably practicable without fixing a venue as required by Rule 7.4(2); or
(b) it may fix a venue for the application to be heard in which case Rule 7.4 must apply to the extent that it is relevant;
but nothing in those provisions is to be taken as prohibiting the applicant from giving such notice if the applicant wishes to do so.]

NOTES

Amendment

Substituted, for r 7.5 as originally enacted, by SI 2010/686, r 2, Sch 1, para 443.
Date in force: 6 April 2010: see SI 2010/686, r 1; for transitional provisions and further effect see rr 6(1), 7, Sch 4, paras 1, 2(1)(b), (2)–(4), Sch 5 thereto.

[7.6A Hearing of application]

[(1) Unless the court otherwise directs, the hearing of an application must be in open court.

(2) In the county court, the jurisdiction of the court to hear and determine an application may be exercised by the district judge (to whom any application must be made in the first instance) unless—
(a) a direction to the contrary has been given, or
(b) it is not within the district judge's power to make the order required.

(3) In the High Court, the jurisdiction of the court to hear and determine an application may be exercised by the registrar (to whom the application must be made in the first instance) unless—
(a) a direction to the contrary has been given, or
(b) it is not within the registrar's power to make the order required.

(4) Where the application is made to the district judge in the county court or to the registrar in the High Court, the district judge or the registrar may refer to the judge any matter which the district judge or registrar thinks should properly be decided by the judge, and the judge may either dispose of the matter or refer it back to the district judge or the registrar with such directions as that judge thinks just.

(5) Nothing in this Rule precludes an application being made directly to the judge in a proper case.]

NOTES

Amendment

Substituted, for r 7.6 as originally enacted, by SI 2010/686, r 2, Sch 1, para 443.
Date in force: 6 April 2010: see SI 2010/686, r 1; for transitional provisions and further effect see rr 6(1), 7, Sch 4, paras 1, 2(1)(b), (2)–(4), Sch 5 thereto.

[7.7A Witness statements—general]

[(1) Subject to Rule 7.9, where evidence is required by the Act or the Rules as to any matter, such evidence may be provided in the form of a witness statement unless—
(a) in any specific case a Rule or the Act makes different provision; or
(b) the court otherwise directs.

(2) The court may, on the application of any party to the matter in question order the attendance for cross-examination of the person making the witness statement.

(3) Where, after such an order has been made, the person in question does not attend, that person's witness statement must not be used in evidence without the leave of the court.]

NOTES

Amendment

Substituted, for r 7.7 as originally enacted, by SI 2010/686, r 2, Sch 1, para 443.
Date in force: 6 April 2010: see SI 2010/686, r 1; for transitional provisions and further effect see rr 6(1), 7, Sch 4, paras 1, 2(1)(b), (2)–(4), Sch 5 thereto.

7.8 Filing and service of [witness statements]

(1) Unless the provision of the Act or Rules under which the application is made provides otherwise, or the court otherwise allows—
  (a) if the applicant intends to rely at the first hearing on [evidence in a witness statement], he shall file [the witness statement with the] court and serve a copy . . . on the respondent, not less than 14 days before the date fixed for the hearing, and
  (b) where a respondent to an application intends to oppose it and to rely for that purpose on [evidence in a witness statement], he shall file [the witness statement with the] court and serve a copy . . . on the applicant, not less than [5 business] days before the date fixed for the hearing.

(2) . . .

NOTES

Initial Commencement

Specified date

Specified date: 29 December 1986: see r 0.1.

Amendment

Provision heading: words "witness statements" in square brackets substituted by SI 2010/686, r 2, Sch 1, para 444(1), (2).
Date in force: 6 April 2010: see SI 2010/686, r 1; for transitional provisions see r 6(1), Sch 4, paras 1, 2(1)(b), (2)–(4) thereto.
Para (1): in paras (a), (b) words "evidence in a witness statement" in square brackets substituted by SI 2010/686, r 2, Sch 1, para 444(1), (3)(a)(i).
Date in force: 6 April 2010: see SI 2010/686, r 1; for transitional provisions and further effect see rr 6(1), 7, Sch 4, paras 1, 2(1)(b), (2)–(4), Sch 5 thereto.
Para (1): in sub-paras (a), (b) words "the witness statement with the" in square brackets substituted by SI 2010/686, r 2, Sch 1, para 444(1), (3)(a)(ii).
Date in force: 6 April 2010: see SI 2010/686, r 1; for transitional provisions and further effect see rr 6(1), 7, Sch 4, paras 1, 2(1)(b), (2)–(4), Sch 5 thereto.
Para (1): in sub-paras (a), (b) words omitted revoked by SI 2010/686, r 2, Sch 1, paras 444(1), (3)(a)(iii).
Date in force: 6 April 2010: see SI 2010/686, r 1; for transitional provisions and further effect see rr 6(1), 7, Sch 4, paras 1, 2(1)(b), (2)–(4), Sch 5 thereto.
Para (1): in sub-para (b) words "5 business" in square brackets substituted by SI 2010/686, r 2, Sch 1, paras 444(1), (3)(b).
Date in force: 6 April 2010: see SI 2010/686, r 1; for transitional provisions and further effect see rr 6(1), 7, Sch 4, paras 1, 2(1)(b), Sch 5 thereto.
Para (2): revoked by SI 2010/686, r 2, Sch 1, para 444(1), (4).
Date in force: 6 April 2010: see SI 2010/686, r 1; for transitional provisions and further effect see rr 6(1), 7, Sch 4, paras 1, 2(1)(b), (2)–(4), Sch 5 thereto.

See Further

See further, in relation the application of this rule, with modifications, in respect of the procedure for the appointment of a bank liquidator and the operation of bank insolvency under the Banking Act 2009, Pt 2: the Bank Insolvency (England and Wales) Rules 2009, SI 2009/356, rr 3(3)–(8), 197.

See further, in relation to the application of this rule, with modifications, in respect of bank administration and applications for bank administration: the Bank Administration (England and Wales) Rules 2009, SI 2009/357, rr 58–61.

7.9 Use of reports

(1) A report may be filed in court instead of [a witness statement]—
- (a) in any case, by the official receiver (whether or not he is acting in any capacity mentioned in sub-paragraph (b)), or a deputy official receiver, or
- (b) unless the application involves other parties or the court otherwise orders, by—
    - (i) an administrator, a liquidator or a trustee in bankruptcy,
    - (ii) a provisional liquidator or an interim receiver,
    - (iii) a special manager, or
    - (iv) an insolvency practitioner appointed under section 273(2).

(2) In any case where a report is filed instead of [a witness statement], the report shall be treated for the purposes of Rule 7.8(1) and any hearing before the court as if it were [a witness statement].

[(3A) Where in insolvency proceedings a witness statement is made by an office-holder, the witness statement must state—
- (a) the capacity in which that office-holder is acting, and
- (b) the address at which that office-holder works.]

NOTES

Initial Commencement

Specified date

Specified date: 29 December 1986: see r 0.1.

Amendment

Para (1): words "a witness statement" in square brackets substituted by SI 2010/686, r 2, Sch 1, para 445(1), (2).
Date in force: 6 April 2010: see SI 2010/686, r 1; for transitional provisions and further effect see rr 6(1), 7, Sch 4, paras 1, 2(1)(b), (2)–(4), Sch 5 thereto.
Para (2): words "a witness statement" in square brackets in both places they occur substituted by SI 2010/686, r 2, Sch 1, para 445(1), (2).
Date in force: 6 April 2010: see SI 2010/686, r 1; for transitional provisions and further effect see rr 6(1), 7, Sch 4, paras 1, 2(1)(b), (2)–(4), Sch 5 thereto.
Para (3A): substituted, for para (3) as originally enacted, by SI 2010/686, r 2, Sch 1, para 445(1), (3).
Date in force: 6 April 2010: see SI 2010/686, r 1; for transitional provisions and further effect see rr 6(1), 7, Sch 4, paras 1, 2(1)(b), (2)–(4), Sch 5 thereto.

See Further

See further, in relation to the application of this rule, with modifications, in respect of bank administration and applications for bank administration: the Bank Administration (England and Wales) Rules 2009, SI 2009/357, rr 58–61.

7.10 Adjournment of hearing; directions

(1) The court may adjourn the hearing of an application on such terms . . . as it thinks [just].

(2) The court may at any time give such directions as it thinks [just] as to—
- (a) service or notice of the application on or to any person. . .;
- (b) whether particulars of claim and defence are to be delivered and generally as to the procedure on the application [including whether a hearing is necessary];

(c) . . .

(d) the matters to be dealt with in evidence.

[(3) The court may give directions as to the manner in which any evidence is to be adduced at a resumed hearing and in particular as to—

(a) the taking of evidence wholly or partly by witness statement or orally;

(b) the cross-examination of the maker of a witness statement; or

(c) any report to be made by an office-holder.]

NOTES

Initial Commencement

Specified date

Specified date: 29 December 1986: see r 0.1.

Amendment

Para (1): words omitted revoked by SI 2010/686, r 2, Sch 1, para 446(1), (2).
    Date in force: 6 April 2010: see SI 2010/686, r 1; for transitional provisions and further effect see rr 6(1), 7, Sch 4, para 1, Sch 5 thereto.
Para (1): word "just" in square brackets substituted by SI 2010/686, r 2, Sch 1, para 1.
    Date in force: 6 April 2010: see SI 2010/686, r 1; for transitional provisions and further effect see rr 6(1), 7, Sch 4, paras 1, 2(1)(b), Sch 5 thereto.
Para (2): word "just" in square brackets substituted by SI 2010/686, r 2, Sch 1, para 1.
    Date in force: 6 April 2010: see SI 2010/686, r 1; for transitional provisions and further effect see rr 6(1), 7, Sch 4, paras 1, 2(1)(b), Sch 5 thereto.
Para (2): in sub-para (a) words omitted revoked by SI 2010/686, r 2, Sch 1, para 446(1), (3)(a).
    Date in force: 6 April 2010: see SI 2010/686, r 1; for transitional provisions and further effect see rr 6(1), 7, Sch 4, para 1, Sch 5 thereto.
Para (2): in sub-para (b) words "including whether a hearing is necessary" in square brackets inserted by SI 2010/686, r 2, Sch 1, para 446(1), (3)(b).
    Date in force: 6 April 2010: see SI 2010/686, r 1; for transitional provisions and further effect see rr 6(1), 7, Sch 4, para 1, Sch 5 thereto.
Para (2): sub-para (c) revoked by SI 2010/686, r 2, Sch 1, para 446(1), (3)(c).
    Date in force: 6 April 2010: see SI 2010/686, r 1; for transitional provisions and further effect see rr 6(1), 7, Sch 4, para 1, Sch 5 thereto.
Para (3): inserted by SI 2010/686, r 2, Sch 1, para 446(1), (4).
    Date in force: 6 April 2010: see SI 2010/686, r 1; for transitional provisions and further effect see rr 6(1), 7, Sch 4, para 1, Sch 5 thereto.

See Further

See further, in relation the application of this rule, with modifications, in respect of the procedure for the appointment of a bank liquidator and the operation of bank insolvency under the Banking Act 2009, Pt 2: the Bank Insolvency (England and Wales) Rules 2009, SI 2009/356, rr 3(3)–(8), 199.

See further, in relation to the application of this rule, with modifications, in respect of bank administration and applications for bank administration: the Bank Administration (England and Wales) Rules 2009, SI 2009/357, rr 58–61.

[CHAPTER 1A

BLOCK TRANSFER OF CASES WHERE INSOLVENCY PRACTITIONER HAS DIED ETC]

NOTES

Amendment

Inserted by SI 2010/686, r 2, Sch 1, para 447.

Date in force: 6 April 2010: see SI 2010/686, r 1; for transitional provisions see r 6(1), Sch 4, para 1 thereto.

[7.10A Preliminary and interpretation]
[(1) The Rules in this Chapter relate to applications for a block transfer order.
(2) In this Chapter—
"outgoing office-holder" has the meaning in Rule 7.10B(1),
"replacement office-holder" has the meaning in Rule 7.10B(1),
"block transfer order" has the meaning in Rule 7.10B(2),
"substantive application" is that part of the application in Rule 7.10C(1)(c) and (d).]

NOTES

Amendment

Inserted by SI 2010/686, r 2, Sch 1, para 447.
Date in force: 6 April 2010: see SI 2010/686, r 1; for transitional provisions and further effect see rr 6(1), 7, Sch 4, para 1, Sch 5 thereto.

[7.10B Power to make a block transfer order]
[(1) This Rule applies where an individual who is acting as an office-holder ('the outgoing office-holder')—
- (a) dies,
- (b) retires from practice, or
- (c) is otherwise unable or unwilling to continue in office,

and it is expedient to transfer some or all of the cases in which the outgoing office-holder holds office to one or more office-holders ('the replacement office-holder') in a single transaction.

(2) In a case to which this Rule applies the court has the power to make an order, ('a block transfer order'), appointing a replacement office-holder in the place of the outgoing office-holder to be—
- (a) liquidator in any winding up (including a case where the official receiver is the liquidator by virtue of section 136 of the Act),
- (b) administrator in any administration,
- (c) trustee in a bankruptcy (including a case where the official receiver is the trustee by virtue of section 300 of the Act), or
- (d) supervisor of a voluntary arrangement under Part 1 or 8 of the Act.

(3) The replacement office-holder must be—
- (a) qualified to act as an insolvency practitioner, or
- (b) where the replacement office-holder is to be appointed supervisor of a voluntary arrangement under Part 1 or 8 of the Act—
  - (i) qualified to act as an insolvency practitioner, or
  - (ii) a person authorised so to act.]

NOTES

Amendment

Inserted by SI 2010/686, r 2, Sch 1, para 447.
Date in force: 6 April 2010: see SI 2010/686, r 1; for transitional provisions and further effect see rr 6(1), 7, Sch 4, para 1, Sch 5 thereto.

[7.10C Application for a block transfer order]

[(1) An application for a block transfer order may be made to the registrar or district judge for—
- (a) the transfer to the High Court of the cases specified in the schedule under paragraph (8);
- (b) the transfer of the cases back to the court from which they were transferred when a replacement office-holder has been appointed;
- (c) the removal of the outgoing office-holder by the exercise of any of the powers in paragraph (2);
- (d) the appointment of a replacement office-holder by the exercise of any of the powers in paragraph (3);
- (e) such other order or direction as may be necessary or expedient in connection with any of the matters referred to above.

(2) The powers referred to in paragraph (1)(c) are—
- (a) section 172(2) and Rule 7.10B(2) (winding up by the court);
- (b) section 108 (voluntary liquidation);
- (c) section 19, paragraph 88 of Schedule B1 to the Act and Rule 7.10B(2) (administration);
- (d) section 298 and Rule 7.10B(2) (bankruptcy);
- (e) section 7(5) and paragraph 39(6) of Schedule A1 to the Act (voluntary arrangement under Part 1 of the Act); and
- (f) section 263(5) (voluntary arrangement under Part 8 of the Act).

(3) The powers referred to in paragraph (1)(d) are—
- (a) section 168(3) and (5) and Rule 7.10B(2) (winding up by the court);
- (b) section 108 (voluntary liquidation);
- (c) section 13, paragraphs 63, 91 and 95 of Schedule B1 to the Act and Rule 7.10B(2) (administration);
- (d) sections 298 and 303(2) and Rule 7.10B(2) (bankruptcy);
- (e) section 7(5) and paragraph 39(6) of Schedule A1 to the Act (voluntary arrangement under Part 1 of the Act); and
- (f) section 263(5) (voluntary arrangement under Part 8 of the Act).

(4) Subject to paragraph (5), the application may be made by any of the following—
- (a) the outgoing office-holder (if able and willing to do so);
- (b) any person who holds office jointly with the outgoing office-holder;
- (c) any person who is proposed to be appointed as the replacement office-holder;
- (d) any creditor in a case subject to the application;
- (e) the recognised professional body or recognised body by which the outgoing office-holder is or was authorised; or
- (f) the Secretary of State.

(5) Where one or more outgoing office-holder in the schedule under paragraph (8) is an administrator, an application may not be made unless a person permitted to apply to replace that office-holder under section 13 or paragraph 63, 91 or 95 of Schedule B1 to the Act is the applicant or is joined as applicant in respect of the replacement of that office-holder.

(6) An applicant (other than the Secretary of State) must give notice of the application to the Secretary of State at least 5 business days before the hearing of the application.

(7) The following must be made a respondent to the application and served with it—
- (a) the outgoing office-holder (if not the applicant or deceased);
- (b) every person who holds office jointly with the outgoing office-holder; and

(c) such person as the registrar or district judge directs.
(8) The application must contain a schedule setting out—
  (a) the name of each case,
  (b) the identity of the court having jurisdiction when the application is made,
  (c) the case number (if any), and
  (d) the capacity in which the outgoing office-holder was appointed.
(9) The application must be supported by evidence—
  (a) setting out the circumstances which gave rise to it being expedient to appoint a replacement office-holder; and
  (b) exhibiting the written consent to act of each person who is proposed to be appointed as replacement office-holder.
(10) Where all the cases in the schedule under paragraph (8) are in a county court or more than one county court—
  (a) the application may be made to a district judge of a convenient county court having insolvency jurisdiction; and
  (b) this Rule applies with appropriate modifications.]

NOTES

Amendment

Inserted by SI 2010/686, r 2, Sch 1, para 447.
Date in force: 6 April 2010: see SI 2010/686, r 1; for transitional provisions and further effect see rr 6(1), 7, Sch 4, para 1, Sch 5 thereto.

[7.10D Action following application for a block transfer order]

[(1) The registrar or district judge may in the first instance consider the application without a hearing and make such order as the registrar or district judge thinks just.
(2) In the first instance, the registrar or district judge may do any of the following—
  (a) make an order directing the transfer to the High Court of those cases not already within its jurisdiction for the purpose only of the substantive application;
  (b) if the documents are considered to be in order and that the matter is straightforward, make an order on the substantive application;
  (c) give any directions which are considered to be necessary including (if appropriate) directions for the joinder of any additional respondents or requiring the service of the application on any person or requiring additional evidence to be provided; or
  (d) if an order is not made on the substantive application, give directions for the further consideration of the substantive application by the registrar or district judge or a judge of the Chancery Division.
(3) The applicant must ensure that a sealed copy of every order transferring any case to the High Court and of every order which is made on a substantive application is lodged with the court having jurisdiction over each case affected by such order for filing on the court file relating to that case.
(4) In any case other than an application relating to the appointment of an administrator, in deciding to what extent (if any) the costs of making an application under this Rule should be paid as an expense of the insolvency proceedings to which the application relates, the factors to which the court must have regard include—
  (a) the reasons for the making of the application;
  (b) the number of cases to which the application relates;
  (c) the value of assets comprised in those cases; and
  (d) the nature and extent of the costs involved.

(5) Where an application relates to the appointment of an administrator and is made by a person under section 13 or paragraph 63, 91 or 95 of Schedule B1 to the Act, the costs of making that application are to be paid as an expense of the administration to which the application relates unless the court directs otherwise.

(6) Any appointment made under this Rule must be notified—
- (a) to the Secretary of State as soon as reasonably practicable; and
- (b) to—
  - (i) the creditors, and
  - (ii) such other persons as the court may direct,

in such manner as the court may direct.

(7) Where the application was made to the district judge under Rule 7.10C(10) this Rule applies with appropriate modifications.]

NOTES

Amendment

Inserted by SI 2010/686, r 2, Sch 1, para 447.
Date in force: 6 April 2010: see SI 2010/686, r 1; for transitional provisions and further effect see rr 6(1), 7, Sch 4, para 1, Sch 5 thereto.

CHAPTER 2

TRANSFER OF PROCEEDINGS BETWEEN COURTS

7.11 General power of transfer

(1) Where winding-up or bankruptcy proceedings [or proceedings relating to a debt relief order] are pending in the High Court, the court may order them to be transferred to a specified county court.

(2) Where winding-up or bankruptcy proceedings [or proceedings relating to a debt relief order] are pending in a county court, the court may order them to be transferred either to the High Court or to another county court.

(3) In any case where [winding-up] proceedings are transferred to a county court, the transfer must be to a court which has jurisdiction to wind up companies . . ..

[(3A) In any case where bankruptcy proceedings or proceedings relating to a debt relief order are transferred to a county court, the transfer must be to a court which has jurisdiction in bankruptcy.]

(4) Where winding-up or bankruptcy proceedings [or proceedings relating to a debt relief order] are pending in a county court, a judge of the High Court may order them to be transferred to that Court.

[(4A) Solely for the purposes of Rule 7.10D (action following application for a block transfer order)—
- (a) the registrar may transfer to or from the High Court; and
- (b) the district judge of the county court to which the application is made may transfer to or from that county court,

any case in the schedule under Rule 7.10C(8).]

(5) A transfer of proceedings under this Rule may be ordered—
- (a) by the court of its own motion, or
- (b) on the application of the official receiver, or
- (c) on the application of a person appearing to the court to have an interest in the proceedings.

(6) A transfer of proceedings under this Rule may be ordered notwithstanding that the proceedings commenced before the coming into force of the Rules.

NOTES

Initial Commencement

Specified date

Specified date: 29 December 1986: see r 0.1.

Amendment

Para (1): words "or proceedings relating to a debt relief order" in square brackets inserted by SI 2009/642, rr 4, 54(a).
Date in force: 6 April 2009: see SI 2009/642, r 1.
Para (2): words "or proceedings relating to a debt relief order" in square brackets inserted by SI 2009/642, rr 4, 54(a).
Date in force: 6 April 2009: see SI 2009/642, r 1.
Para (3): words "winding-up" in square brackets inserted by SI 2009/642, rr 4, 54(b)(i).
Date in force: 6 April 2009: see SI 2009/642, r 1.
Para (3): words omitted revoked by SI 2009/642, rr 4, 54(b)(ii).
Date in force: 6 April 2009: see SI 2009/642, r 1.
Para (3A): inserted by SI 2009/642, rr 4, 54(c).
Date in force: 6 April 2009: see SI 2009/642, r 1.
Para (4): words "or proceedings relating to a debt relief order" in square brackets inserted by SI 2009/642, rr 4, 54(a).
Date in force: 6 April 2009: see SI 2009/642, r 1.
Para (4A): inserted by SI 2010/686, r 2, Sch 1, para 448.
Date in force: 6 April 2010: see SI 2010/686, r 1; for transitional provisions and further effect see rr 6(1), 7, Sch 4, para 1, Sch 5 thereto.

7.12 Proceedings commenced in wrong court

Where winding-up or bankruptcy proceedings [or proceedings relating to a debt relief order] are commenced in a court which is, in relation to those proceedings, the wrong court, that court may—

(a) order the transfer of the proceedings to the court in which they ought to have been commenced;

(b) order that the proceedings be continued in the court in which they have been commenced; or

(c) order the proceedings to be struck out.

NOTES

Initial Commencement

Specified date

Specified date: 29 December 1986: see r 0.1.

Amendment

Words "or proceedings relating to a debt relief order" in square brackets inserted by SI 2009/642, rr 4, 55.
Date in force: 6 April 2009: see SI 2009/642, r 1.

7.13 Applications for transfer

(1) An application by the official receiver for proceedings to be transferred shall be made with a report by him—

(a) setting out the reasons for the transfer, and

[(b) including a statement either that—

(i) the petitioner, or

(ii) the debtor in proceedings relating to a debt relief order, consents to the transfer, or that he has been given at least 14 days' notice of the official receiver's application].

(2) If the court is satisfied from the official receiver's report that the proceedings can be conducted more conveniently in another court, the proceedings shall be transferred to that court.

(3) Where an application for the transfer of proceedings is made otherwise than by the official receiver, at least 14 days' notice of the application shall be given by the applicant—

(a) to the official receiver attached to the court in which the proceedings are pending, and

(b) to the official receiver attached to the court to which it is proposed that they should be transferred.

NOTES

Initial Commencement

Specified date

Specified date: 29 December 1986: see r 0.1.

Amendment

Para (1): sub-para (b) substituted by SI 2009/642, rr 4, 56.
Date in force: 6 April 2009: see SI 2009/642, r 1.

7.14 Procedure following order for transfer

(1) Subject as follows, the court making an order under Rule 7.11 shall [as soon as reasonably practicable] send to the transferee court a sealed copy of the order, and the file of the proceedings.

(2) On receipt of these, the transferee court shall [as soon as reasonably practicable] send notice of the transfer to the official receivers attached to that court and the transferor court respectively.

(3) Paragraph (1) does not apply where the order is made by the High Court under Rule 7.11(4). In that case—

(a) the High Court shall send sealed copies of the order to the county court from which the proceedings are to be transferred, and to the official receivers attached to that court and the High Court respectively, and

(b) that county court shall send the file of the proceedings to the High Court.

(4) ...

NOTES

Initial Commencement

Specified date

Specified date: 29 December 1986: see r 0.1.

Amendment

Para (1): words "as soon as reasonably practicable" in square brackets substituted by SI 2009/642, rr 4, 5.
Date in force: 6 April 2009: see SI 2009/642, r 1; for transitional provisions see r 3 thereof.

Para (2): words "as soon as reasonably practicable" in square brackets substituted by SI 2009/642, rr 4, 5.
Date in force: 6 April 2009: see SI 2009/642, r 1; for transitional provisions see r 3 thereof.

Para (4): revoked by SI 2010/686, r 2, Sch 1, para 449.

Date in force: 6 April 2010: see SI 2010/686, r 1; for transitional provisions and further effect see rr 6(1), 7, Sch 4, para 1, Sch 5 thereto.

7.15 Consequential transfer of other proceedings

(1) This Rule applies where—
- [(a) the High Court has—
  - (i) made a bankruptcy order;
  - (ii) made a winding-up order;
  - (iii) appointed a provisional liquidator; or
  - (iv) appointed an interim receiver; or]
- (b) . . .
- (c) winding-up or bankruptcy proceedings have been transferred to that Court from a county court.

(2) A judge of any Division of the High Court may, of his own motion, order the transfer to that Division of any such proceedings as are mentioned below and are pending against the company or individual concerned ("the insolvent") either in another Division of the High Court or in a court in England and Wales other than the High Court.

(3) Proceedings which may be so transferred are those brought by or against the insolvent for the purpose of enforcing a claim against the insolvent estate, or brought by a person other than the insolvent for the purpose of enforcing any such claim (including in either case proceedings of any description by a debenture-holder or mortgagee).

(4) Where proceedings are transferred under this Rule, the registrar may (subject to [the] directions of the judge) dispose of any matter arising in the proceedings which would, but for the transfer, have been disposed of in chambers or, in the case of proceedings transferred from a county court, by the [district judge].

NOTES

Initial Commencement

Specified date

Specified date: 29 December 1986: see r 0.1.

Amendment

Para (1): sub-para (a) substituted by SI 2010/686, r 2, Sch 1, para 450(1), (2)(a).
Date in force: 6 April 2010: see SI 2010/686, r 1; for transitional provisions and further effect see rr 6(1), 7, Sch 4, para 1, Sch 5 thereto.

Para (1): sub-para (b) revoked by SI 2010/686, r 2, Sch 1, para 450(1), (2)(b).
Date in force: 6 April 2010: see SI 2010/686, r 1; for transitional provisions and further effect see rr 6(1), 7, Sch 4, para 1, Sch 5 thereto.

Para (4): word "the" in square brackets substituted by SI 2010/686, r 2, Sch 1, para 450(1), (3)(a).
Date in force: 6 April 2010: see SI 2010/686, r 1; for transitional provisions and further effect see rr 6(1), 7, Sch 4, para 1, Sch 5 thereto.

Para (4): words "district judge" in square brackets substituted by SI 2010/686, r 2, Sch 1, para 450(1), (3)(b).
Date in force: 6 April 2010: see SI 2010/686, r 1; for transitional provisions and further effect see rr 6(1), 7, Sch 4, para 1, Sch 5 thereto.

CHAPTER 3

SHORTHAND WRITERS

7.16 Nomination and appointment of shorthand writers

(1) In the High Court the judge [or registrar] and, in a county court, [a district judge] may in writing nominate one or more persons to be official shorthand writers to the court.

(2) The court may, at any time in the course of insolvency proceedings, appoint a shorthand writer to take down the evidence of a person examined under section 133, 236, [251N,] 290 or 366.

(3) Where the official receiver applies to the court for an order appointing a shorthand writer, he shall name the person he proposes for appointment. . ..

NOTES

Initial Commencement

Specified date

Specified date: 29 December 1986: see r 0.1.

Amendment

Para (1): words "or registrar" in square brackets inserted by SI 2010/686, r 2, Sch 1, para 451(1), (2)(a).
  Date in force: 6 April 2010: see SI 2010/686, r 1; for transitional provisions and further effect see rr 6(1), 7, Sch 4, paras 1, 2(1)(b), Sch 5 thereto.
Para (1): words "a district judge" in square brackets substituted by SI 2010/686, r 2, Sch 1, para 451(1), (2)(b).
  Date in force: 6 April 2010: see SI 2010/686, r 1; for transitional provisions and further effect see rr 6(1), 7, Sch 4, paras 1, 2(1)(b), Sch 5 thereto.
Para (2): reference to "251N," inserted by SI 2009/642, rr 4, 57.
  Date in force: 6 April 2009: see SI 2009/642, r 1.
Para (3): words omitted revoked by SI 2010/686, r 2, Sch 1, para 451(1), (3).
  Date in force: 6 April 2010: see SI 2010/686, r 1; for transitional provisions and further effect see rr 6(1), 7, Sch 4, paras 1, 2(1)(b), Sch 5 thereto.

See Further

See further, in relation the application of this rule, with modifications, in respect of the procedure for the appointment of a bank liquidator and the operation of bank insolvency under the Banking Act 2009, Pt 2: the Bank Insolvency (England and Wales) Rules 2009, SI 2009/356, rr 3(3)–(8), 200.
See further, in relation to the application of this rule, with modifications, in respect of bank administration and applications for bank administration: the Bank Administration (England and Wales) Rules 2009, SI 2009/357, rr 58–61.

7.17 Remuneration

(1) The remuneration of a shorthand writer appointed in insolvency proceedings shall be paid by the party at whose instance the appointment was made, or out of the insolvent estate, or otherwise, as the court may direct.

[(2) Any question arising as to the rates of remuneration payable under this Rule shall be determined by the court in its discretion.]

NOTES

Initial Commencement

Specified date

Specified date: 29 December 1986: see r 0.1.

Amendment

Para (2): substituted by SI 1993/602, r 3, Schedule, para 1.

See Further

See further, in relation the application of this rule, with modifications, in respect of the procedure for the appointment of a bank liquidator and the operation of bank insolvency under the Banking Act 2009, Pt 2: the Bank Insolvency (England and Wales) Rules 2009, SI 2009/356, rr 3(3)–(8), 201.

See further, in relation to the application of this rule, with modifications, in respect of bank administration and applications for bank administration: the Bank Administration (England and Wales) Rules 2009, SI 2009/357, rr 58–61.

7.18 . . .

. . .

NOTES

Amendment

Revoked by SI 2010/686, r 5.

Date in force: 6 April 2010: see SI 2010/686, r 1; for transitional provisions and further effect see rr 6(1), 7, Sch 4, para 1, Sch 5 thereto.

CHAPTER 4

ENFORCEMENT PROCEDURES

7.19 Enforcement of court orders

(1) In any insolvency proceedings, orders of the court may be enforced in the same manner as a judgment to the same effect.

(2) Where an order in insolvency proceedings is made, or any process is issued, by a county court ("the primary court"), the order or process may be enforced, executed and dealt with by any other county court ("the secondary court"), as if it had been made or issued for the enforcement of a judgment or order to the same effect made by the secondary court.

This applies whether or not the secondary court has jurisdiction to take insolvency proceedings.

[(3) Where a warrant for the arrest of a person is issued by the High Court, the warrant may be discharged by the county court where the person who is the subject of the warrant—

(a) has been brought before a county court exercising insolvency jurisdiction; and

(b) has given to the county court an undertaking which is satisfactory to the county court to comply with the obligations that apply to that person under the Act or the Rules.]

NOTES

Initial Commencement

Specified date

Specified date: 29 December 1986: see r 0.1.

Amendment

Para (3): inserted by SI 2010/686, r 2, Sch 1, para 452.

Date in force: 6 April 2010: see SI 2010/686, r 1; for transitional provisions and further effect see rr 6(1), 7, Sch 4, para 1, Sch 5 thereto.

See Further

See further, in relation the application of this rule, with modifications, in respect of the procedure for the appointment of a bank liquidator and the operation of bank insolvency under the Banking Act 2009, Pt 2: the Bank Insolvency (England and Wales) Rules 2009, SI 2009/356, rr 3(3)–(8), 202.
See further, in relation to the application of this rule, with modifications, in respect of bank administration and applications for bank administration: the Bank Administration (England and Wales) Rules 2009, SI 2009/357, rr 58–61.

7.20 Orders enforcing compliance with the Rules

(1) The court may, on application by the competent person, make such orders as it thinks necessary for the enforcement of obligations falling on any person in accordance with—

(a) [paragraph 47 of Schedule B1 to the Act or section] 47 or 131 (duty to submit statement of affairs in administration, administrative receivership or winding up),

(b) section 143(2) (liquidator to furnish information, books, papers, etc), or

(c) section 235 (duty of various persons to co-operate with office-holder).

(2) The competent person for this purpose is—

(a) under [paragraph 47 of Schedule B1 to the Act], the administrator,

(b) under section 47, the administrative receiver,

(c) under section 131 or 143(2), the official receiver, and

(d) under section 235, the official receiver, the administrator, the administrative receiver, the liquidator or the provisional liquidator, as the case may be.

(3) An order of the court under this Rule may provide that all costs of and incidental to the application for it shall be borne by the person against whom the order is made.

NOTES

Initial Commencement

Specified date

Specified date: 29 December 1986: see r 0.1.

Amendment

Para (1): in sub-para (a) words "paragraph 47 of Schedule B1 to the Act or section" in square brackets substituted by SI 2003/1730, r 11, Sch 1, Pt 8, para 57(a).
Date in force: 15 September 2003: see SI 2003/1730, r 1(2).
Para (2): in sub-para (a) words "paragraph 47 of Schedule B1 to the Act" in square brackets substituted by SI 2003/1730, r 11, Sch 1, Pt 8, para 57(b).
Date in force: 15 September 2003: see SI 2003/1730, r 1(2).

See Further

See further, in relation to the application of this rule, with modifications, in respect of bank administration and applications for bank administration: the Bank Administration (England and Wales) Rules 2009, SI 2009/357, rr 58–61.

7.21 Warrants (general provisions)

(1) A warrant issued by the court under any provision of the Act shall be addressed to such officer of the High Court or of a county court (whether or not having jurisdiction in insolvency proceedings) as the warrant specifies, or to any constable.

(2) The persons referred to in sections 134(2), 236(5), [251N(5),] 364(1), 365(3) and 366(3) (court's powers of enforcement) as the prescribed officer of the court are—

(a) in the case of the High Court, the tipstaff and his assistants of the court, and
(b) in the case of a county court, the [district judge] and the bailiffs.
(3) In this Chapter references to property include books, papers and records.

NOTES

Initial Commencement

Specified date

Specified date: 29 December 1986: see r 0.1.

Amendment

Para (2): reference to "251N(5)," inserted by SI 2009/642, rr 4, 58.
Date in force: 6 April 2009: see SI 2009/642, r 1.
Para (2): in sub-para (b) words "district judge" in square brackets substituted by SI 2010/686, r 2, Sch 1, para 453.
Date in force: 6 April 2010: see SI 2010/686, r 1; for transitional provisions and further effect see rr 6(1), 7, Sch 4, paras 1, 2(1)(b), Sch 5 thereto.

See Further

See further, in relation to the application of this rule, with modifications, in respect of bank administration and applications for bank administration: the Bank Administration (England and Wales) Rules 2009, SI 2009/357, rr 58–61.

7.22 Warrants under ss 134, 364

When a person [("the arrested person")] is arrested under a warrant issued by the court under section 134 (officer of company failing to attend for public examination), or section 364 (arrest of debtor or bankrupt)—

[(a) the officer apprehending the arrested person must give that person into the custody of—
 (i) the court in a case where the court is ready and able to deal with the arrested person, or
 (ii) where the court is not ready and able, the governor of the prison named in the warrant (or where that prison is not able to accommodate the arrested person, the governor of such other prison with appropriate facilities which is able to accommodate the arrested person), who must keep the arrested person in custody until such time as the court otherwise orders and must produce that person before the court at its next sitting; and]
(b) any property in the arrested person's possession which may be seized shall be—
 (i) lodged with, or otherwise dealt with as instructed by, whoever is specified in the warrant as authorised to receive it, or
 (ii) kept by the officer seizing it pending the receipt of written orders from the court as to its disposal,

as may be directed by the court in the warrant.

NOTES

Initial Commencement

Specified date

Specified date: 29 December 1986: see r 0.1.

Amendment

Words "("the arrested person")" in square brackets inserted by SI 2010/686, r 2, Sch 1, para 454(1), (2).
> Date in force: 6 April 2010: see SI 2010/686, r 1; for transitional provisions and further effect see rr 6(1), 7, Sch 4, para 1, Sch 5 thereto.

Para (a) substituted by SI 2010/686, r 2, Sch 1, para 454(1), (3).
> Date in force: 6 April 2010: see SI 2010/686, r 1; for transitional provisions and further effect see rr 6(1), 7, Sch 4, para 1, Sch 5 thereto.

7.23 Warrants under ss 236, [251N and] 366

(1) When a person is arrested under a warrant issued under section 236 (inquiry into insolvent company's dealings)[, 251N (the equivalent in relation to debt relief orders)] or 366 (the equivalent in bankruptcy) [("the arrested person")], the officer arresting him shall [as soon as reasonably practicable] bring him before the court issuing the warrant in order that he may be examined.

(2) If he cannot immediately be brought up for examination, the officer shall deliver him into the custody of the governor of the prison named in the warrant [(or where that prison is not able to accommodate the arrested person, the governor of such other prison with appropriate facilities which is able to accommodate the arrested person)], who shall keep him in custody and produce him before the court as it may from time to time direct.

(3) After arresting the person named in the warrant, the officer shall [as soon as reasonably practicable] report to the court the arrest or delivery into custody (as the case may be) and apply to the court to fix a venue for the person's examination.

(4) The court shall appoint the earliest practicable time for the examination, and shall—

(a) direct the governor of the prison to produce the person for examination at the time and place appointed, and

(b) [as soon as reasonably practicable] give notice of the venue to the person who applied for the warrant.

(5) Any property in the arrested person's possession which may be seized shall be—

(a) lodged with, or otherwise dealt with as instructed by, whoever is specified in the warrant as authorised to receive it, or

(b) kept by the officer seizing it pending the receipt of written orders from the court as to its disposal,

as may be directed by the court.

NOTES

Initial Commencement

Specified date

Specified date: 29 December 1986: see r 0.1.

Amendment

Provision heading: words "251N and" in square brackets inserted by SI 2009/642, rr 4, 59(a).
> Date in force: 6 April 2009: see SI 2009/642, r 1.

Para (1): words ", 251N (the equivalent in relation to debt relief orders)" in square brackets inserted by SI 2009/642, rr 4, 59(b).
> Date in force: 6 April 2009: see SI 2009/642, r 1.

Para (1): words "("the arrested person")" in square brackets inserted by SI 2010/686, r 2, Sch 1, para 455(1), (2).
> Date in force: 6 April 2010: see SI 2010/686, r 1; for transitional provisions and further effect see rr 6(1), 7, Sch 4, para 1, Sch 5 thereto.

Para (1): words "as soon as reasonably practicable" in square brackets substituted by SI 2009/642, rr 4, 5.

Date in force: 6 April 2009: see SI 2009/642, r 1; for transitional provisions see r 3 thereto.
Para (2): words from "(or where that" to "the arrested person)" in square brackets inserted by SI 2010/686, r 2, Sch 1, para 455(1), (3).
Date in force: 6 April 2010: see SI 2010/686, r 1; for transitional provisions and further effect see rr 6(1), 7, Sch 4, para 1, Sch 5 thereto.
Para (3): words "as soon as reasonably practicable" in square brackets substituted by SI 2009/642, rr 4, 5.
Date in force: 6 April 2009: see SI 2009/642, r 1; for transitional provisions see r 3 thereto.
Para (4): in sub-para (b) words "as soon as reasonably practicable" in square brackets substituted by SI 2009/642, rr 4, 5.
Date in force: 6 April 2009: see SI 2009/642, r 1; for transitional provisions see r 3 thereto.

See Further

See further, in relation the application of this rule, with modifications, in respect of the procedure for the appointment of a bank liquidator and the operation of bank insolvency under the Banking Act 2009, Pt 2: the Bank Insolvency (England and Wales) Rules 2009, SI 2009/356, rr 3(3)–(8), 205.
See further, in relation to the application of this rule, with modifications, in respect of bank administration and applications for bank administration: the Bank Administration (England and Wales) Rules 2009, SI 2009/357, rr 58–61.

7.24 Execution of warrants outside court's district

(1) This Rule applies where a warrant for a person's arrest has been issued in insolvency proceedings by a county court ("the primary court") and is addressed to another county court ("the secondary court") for execution in its district.

(2) The secondary court may send the warrant to the [district judge of another] county court (whether or not having jurisdiction to take insolvency proceedings) in whose district the person to be arrested is or is believed to be, with a notice to the effect that the warrant is transmitted to that court under this Rule for execution in its district at the request of the primary court.

(3) The court receiving a warrant transmitted by the secondary court under this Rule shall apply its seal to the warrant, and secure that all such steps are taken for its execution as would be appropriate in the case of a warrant issued by itself.

NOTES

Initial Commencement

Specified date

Specified date: 29 December 1986: see r 0.1.

Amendment

Para (2): words "district judge of another" in square brackets substituted by SI 2010/686, r 2, Sch 1, para 456.
Date in force: 6 April 2010: see SI 2010/686, r 1; for transitional provisions and further effect see rr 6(1), 7, Sch 4, paras 1, 2(1)(b), Sch 5 thereto.

7.25 Warrants under s 365

(1) A warrant issued under section 365(3) (search of premises not belonging to the bankrupt) shall authorise any person executing it to seize any property of the bankrupt found as a result of the execution of the warrant.

(2) Any property seized under a warrant issued under section 365(2) or (3) shall be—

    (a)   lodged with, or otherwise dealt with as instructed by, whoever is specified in the warrant as authorised to receive it, or

(b) kept by the officer seizing it pending the receipt of written orders from the court as to its disposal,

as may be directed by the warrant.

NOTES

Initial Commencement

Specified date
Specified date: 29 December 1986: see r 0.1.

CHAPTER 5
COURT RECORDS AND RETURNS

7.26 ...

...

NOTES

Amendment

Substituted, together with rr 7.27–7.31, by subsequent r 7.31A, by SI 2010/686, r 2, Sch 1, para 457.
    Date in force: 6 April 2010: see SI 2010/686, r 1; for transitional provisions and further effect see rr 6(1), 7, Sch 4, para 1, Sch 5 thereto.

7.27 ...

...

NOTES

Amendment

Substituted, together with rr 7.26, 7.28–7.31, by subsequent r 7.31A, by SI 2010/686, r 2, Sch 1, para 457.
    Date in force: 6 April 2010: see SI 2010/686, r 1; for transitional provisions and further effect see rr 6(1), 7, Sch 4, para 1, Sch 5 thereto.

7.28 ...

...

NOTES

Amendment

Substituted, together with rr 7.26, 7.27, 7.29–7.31, by subsequent r 7.31A, by SI 2010/686, r 2, Sch 1, para 457.
    Date in force: 6 April 2010: see SI 2010/686, r 1; for transitional provisions and further effect see rr 6(1), 7, Sch 4, para 1, Sch 5 thereto.

7.29 ...

...

NOTES

Amendment

Substituted, together with rr 7.26–7.28, 7.30, 7.31, by subsequent r 7.31A, by SI 2010/686, r 2, Sch 1, para 457.
   Date in force: 6 April 2010: see SI 2010/686, r 1; for transitional provisions and further effect see rr 6(1), 7, Sch 4, para 1, Sch 5 thereto.

7.30 . . .
. . .

NOTES

Amendment

Substituted, together with rr 7.26–7.29, 7.31, by subsequent r 7.31A, by SI 2010/686, r 2, Sch 1, para 457.
   Date in force: 6 April 2010: see SI 2010/686, r 1; for transitional provisions and further effect see rr 6(1), 7, Sch 4, para 1, Sch 5 thereto.

7.31 . . .
. . .

NOTES

Amendment

Substituted, together with rr 7.26–7.30, by subsequent r 7.31A, by SI 2010/686, r 2, Sch 1, para 457.
   Date in force: 6 April 2010: see SI 2010/686, r 1; for transitional provisions and further effect see rr 6(1), 7, Sch 4, para 1, Sch 5 thereto.

[7.31A Court file]

[(1) The court must open and maintain a file in any case where documents are filed with it under the Act or the Rules.

(2) Any documents which are filed with the court under the Act or the Rules must be placed on the file opened in accordance with paragraph (1).

(3) The following persons may inspect or obtain from the court a copy of, or a copy of any document or documents contained in, the file opened in accordance with paragraph (1)—

- (a) the office-holder in the proceedings;
- (b) the Secretary of State; and
- (c) any person who is a creditor of the company to which, or the individual to whom, the proceedings relate if that person provides the court with a statement in writing by confirming that that person is a creditor.

(4) The same right to inspect or obtain a copy of, or a copy of any document or documents contained in, the file opened in accordance with paragraph (1) is exercisable—

- (a) in proceedings under Parts 1 to 7 of the Act, by—
  - (i) an officer or former officer of the company to which the proceedings relate; or
  - (ii) a member of the company or a contributory in its winding up;
- (b) in proceedings with respect to a voluntary arrangement under Part 8 of the Act, by the debtor;
- (c) in bankruptcy proceedings, by—

(i) the bankrupt;
(ii) any person against whom a bankruptcy petition has been presented;
(iii) any person who has, in accordance with Chapter 1 of Part 6, been served with a statutory demand;
(d) in proceedings relating to a debt relief order, by the debtor.

(5) The right to inspect or obtain a copy of, or a copy of any document or documents contained in, the file opened in accordance with paragraph (1) may be exercised on that person's behalf by a person authorised to do so by that person.

(6) Any person who is not otherwise entitled to inspect or obtain a copy of, or a copy of any document or documents contained in, the file opened in accordance with paragraph (1) may do so if that person has the permission of the court.

(7) The court may direct that the file, a document (or part of it) or a copy of a document (or part of it) must not be made available under paragraph (3), (4) or (5) without the permission of the court.

(8) An application for a direction under paragraph (7) may be made by—
(a) the official receiver;
(b) the officer-holder in the proceedings; or
(c) any person appearing to the court to have an interest.

(9) Where any person wishes to exercise the right to inspect the file under paragraph (3), (4), (5) or (6), that person—
(a) if the permission of the court is required, must file with the court an application notice in accordance with these Rules; or
(b) if the permission of the court is not required, may inspect the file at any reasonable time.

(10) Where any person wishes to exercise the right to obtain a copy of a document under paragraph (3), (4), (5) or (6), that person must pay any prescribed fee and—
(a) if the permission of the court is required, file with the court an application notice in accordance with these Rules; or
(b) if the permission of the court is not required, file with the court a written request for the document.

(11) An application for—
(a) permission to inspect the file or obtain a copy of a document under paragraph (6); or
(b) a direction under paragraph (7),
may be made without notice to any other party, but the court may direct that notice must be given to any person who would be affected by its decision.

(12) If for the purposes of powers conferred by the Act or the Rules, the Secretary of State or the official receiver requests the transmission of the file of any insolvency proceedings, the court must comply with the request (unless the file is for the time being in use for the court's own purposes).]

NOTES

Amendment

Substituted, for rr 7.26–7.31 as originally enacted, by SI 2010/686, r 2, Sch 1, para 457. Date in force: 6 April 2010: see SI 2010/686, r 1; for transitional provisions and further effect see rr 6(1), 7, Sch 4, para 1, Sch 5 thereto.

7.32 . . .

. . .

NOTES

Amendment
Revoked by SI 2009/642, rr 4, 62.
Date in force: 6 April 2009: see SI 2009/642, r 1; for transitional provisions see r 3 thereof (as amended by SI 2010/686, r 8).

[CHAPTER 6
COSTS AND DETAILED ASSESSMENT]

NOTES

Amendment
Substituted by SI 1999/1022, r 3, Schedule, para 3.
Date in force: 26 April 1999: see SI 1999/1022, r 1.

[7.33A Application of Chapter 6]
[(1) This chapter applies in relation to costs in connection with insolvency proceedings.
(2) In this chapter a reference to costs includes charges and expenses.]

NOTES

Amendment
Substituted, for r 7.33 as previously enacted, by SI 2010/686, r 2, Sch 1, para 458.
Date in force: 6 April 2010: see SI 2010/686, r 1; for transitional provisions and further effect see rr 6(1), 7, Sch 4, para 1, Sch 5 thereto.

[7.34A Requirement to assess costs by the detailed procedure]
[(1) Where the costs of any person are payable as an expense out of the insolvent estate, the amount payable must be decided by detailed assessment unless agreed between the office-holder and the person entitled to payment.
(2) In the absence of such agreement as is mentioned in paragraph (1), the office-holder—
- (a) may serve notice requiring that person to commence detailed assessment proceedings in accordance with CPR Part 47; and
- (b) must serve such notice (except in an administrative receivership) where a liquidation or creditors' committee formed in relation to the insolvency proceedings resolves that the amount of the costs must be decided by detailed assessment.

(3) Detailed assessment proceedings must be commenced in the court to which the insolvency proceedings are allocated or, where in relation to a company there is no such court, any court having jurisdiction to wind up the company.
(4) Where the costs of any person employed by an office-holder in insolvency proceedings are required to be decided by detailed assessment or fixed by order of the court, the office-holder may make payments on account to such person in respect of those costs provided that person undertakes in writing—
- (a) to repay as soon as reasonably practicable any money which may, when detailed assessment is made, prove to have been overpaid; and
- (b) to pay interest on any such sum as is mentioned in sub-paragraph (a) at the rate specified in section 17 of the Judgments Act 1838 on the date

payment was made and for the period beginning with the date of payment and ending with the date of repayment.

(5) In any proceedings before the court (including proceedings on a petition), the court may order costs to be decided by detailed assessment.

(6) Unless otherwise directed or authorised, the costs of a trustee in bankruptcy or a liquidator are to be allowed on the standard basis for which provision is made in—
   (a)   CPR rule 44.4 (basis of assessment); and
   (b)   CPR rule 44.5 (factors to be taken into account when deciding the amount of costs).]

NOTES

Amendment

Substituted, for r 7.34 as previously enacted, by SI 2010/686, r 2, Sch 1, para 458.
Date in force: 6 April 2010: see SI 2010/686, r 1; for transitional provisions and further effect see rr 6(1), 7, Sch 4, para 1, Sch 5 thereto.

[7.35 Procedure where detailed assessment required]

[(1) Before making a detailed assessment of the costs of any person employed in insolvency proceedings by [the office-holder], the costs officer shall require a certificate of employment, which shall be endorsed on the bill and [authenticated] by [the office-holder].

(2) The certificate shall include—
   (a)   the name and address of the person employed,
   (b)   details of the functions to be carried out under the employment, and
   (c)   a note of any special terms of remuneration which have been agreed.

(3) Every person whose costs in insolvency proceedings are required to be decided by detailed assessment shall, on being required in writing to do so by the [office-holder], commence detailed assessment proceedings in accordance with CPR Part 47 (procedure for detailed assessment of costs and default provisions).

(4) If that person does not commence detailed assessment proceedings within 3 months of the requirement under paragraph (3), or within such further time as the court, on application, may permit, the [office-holder] may deal with the insolvent estate without regard to any claim by that person, whose claim is forfeited by such failure to commence proceedings.

(5) Where in any such case such a claim lies additionally against an [office-holder] in his personal capacity, that claim is also forfeited by such failure to commence proceedings.

(6) Where costs have been incurred in insolvency proceedings in the High Court and those proceedings are subsequently transferred to a county court, all costs of those proceedings directed by the court or otherwise required to be assessed may nevertheless, on the application of the person who incurred the costs, be ordered to be decided by detailed assessment in the High Court.]

NOTES

Initial Commencement

Specified date

Specified date: 29 December 1986: see r 0.1.

Amendment

Substituted by SI 1999/1022, r 3, Schedule, para 3.
Date in force: 26 April 1999: see SI 1999/1022, r 1.
Para (1): words "the office-holder" in square brackets in the first place they occur substituted by SI 2010/686, r 2, Sch 1, para 459(1), (2)(a).

Date in force: 6 April 2010: see SI 2010/686, r 1; for transitional provisions and further effect see rr 6(1), 7, Sch 4, para 1, Sch 5 thereto.
Para (1): word "authenticated" in square brackets substituted by SI 2010/686, r 2, Sch 1, para 1.
Date in force: 6 April 2010: see SI 2010/686, r 1; for transitional provisions and further effect see rr 6(1), 7, Sch 4, paras 1, 2(1)(b), Sch 5 thereto.
Para (1): words "the office-holder" in square brackets in the second place they occur substituted by SI 2010/686, r 2, Sch 1, para 459(1), (2)(b).
Date in force: 6 April 2010: see SI 2010/686, r 1; for transitional provisions and further effect see rr 6(1), 7, Sch 4, para 1, Sch 5 thereto.
Para (3): word "office-holder" in square brackets substituted by SI 2010/686, r 2, Sch 1, para 459(1), (3).
Date in force: 6 April 2010: see SI 2010/686, r 1; for transitional provisions and further effect see rr 6(1), 7, Sch 4, para 1, Sch 5 thereto.
Para (4): word "office-holder" in square brackets substituted by SI 2010/686, r 2, Sch 1, para 459(1), (3).
Date in force: 6 April 2010: see SI 2010/686, r 1; for transitional provisions and further effect see rr 6(1), 7, Sch 4, para 1, Sch 5 thereto.
Para (5): word "office-holder" in square brackets substituted by SI 2010/686, r 2, Sch 1, para 459(1), (3).
Date in force: 6 April 2010: see SI 2010/686, r 1; for transitional provisions and further effect see rr 6(1), 7, Sch 4, para 1, Sch 5 thereto.

See Further

See further, in relation the application of this rule, with modifications, in respect of the procedure for the appointment of a bank liquidator and the operation of bank insolvency under the Banking Act 2009, Pt 2: the Bank Insolvency (England and Wales) Rules 2009, SI 2009/356, rr 3(3)–(8), 213.

See further, in relation to the application of this rule, with modifications, in respect of bank administration and applications for bank administration: the Bank Administration (England and Wales) Rules 2009, SI 2009/357, rr 58–61.

[7.36 Costs of [officers charged with execution of writs or other process]]

[(1) Where [an enforcement officer, or other officer, charged with execution of the writ or other process;]—

(a) is required under section 184(2) or 346(2) to deliver up goods or money, or

(b) has under section 184(3) or 346(3) deducted costs from the proceeds of an execution or money paid to him,

the [office-holder] may require in writing that the amount of [the enforcement officer's or other officer's] bill of costs be decided by detailed assessment.'

(2) Where such a requirement is made, Rule 7.35(4) applies.

(3) Where, in the case of a deduction under paragraph (1)(b), any amount deducted is disallowed at the conclusion of the detailed assessment proceedings, the [enforcement officer] shall [as soon as reasonably practicable] pay a sum equal to that disallowed to the [office-holder] for the benefit of the insolvent estate.]

NOTES

Amendment

Substituted by SI 1999/1022, r 3, Schedule, para 3.
Date in force: 26 April 1999: see SI 1999/1022, r 1.
Provision heading: words "officers charged with execution of writs or other process" in square brackets substituted by SI 2005/527, r 42(a).
Date in force: 1 April 2005: see SI 2005/527, r 1(2).
Para (1): words "an enforcement officer, or other officer, charged with execution of the writ or other process;" and "the enforcement officer's or other officer's" in square brackets substituted by SI 2005/527, r 42(b).
Date in force: 1 April 2005: see SI 2005/527, r 1(2).

Para (1): word "office-holder" in square brackets substituted by SI 2010/686, r 2, Sch 1, para 460(1), (2).
    Date in force: 6 April 2010: see SI 2010/686, r 1; for transitional provisions and further effect see rr 6(1), 7, Sch 4, para 1, Sch 5 thereto.
Para (3): words "enforcement officer" in square brackets substituted by SI 2005/527, r 42(c).
    Date in force: 1 April 2005: see SI 2005/527, r 1(2).
Para (3): words "as soon as reasonably practicable" in square brackets substituted by SI 2009/642, rr 4, 5.
    Date in force: 6 April 2009: see SI 2009/642, r 1; for transitional provisions see r 3 thereof.
Para (3): word "office-holder" in square brackets substituted by SI 2010/686, r 2, Sch 1, para 460(1), (3).
    Date in force: 6 April 2010: see SI 2010/686, r 1; for transitional provisions and further effect see rr 6(1), 7, Sch 4, para 1, Sch 5 thereto.

See Further
See further, in relation the application of this rule, with modifications, in respect of the procedure for the appointment of a bank liquidator and the operation of bank insolvency under the Banking Act 2009, Pt 2: the Bank Insolvency (England and Wales) Rules 2009, SI 2009/356, rr 3(3)–(8), 214.
See further, in relation to the application of this rule, with modifications, in respect of bank administration and applications for bank administration: the Bank Administration (England and Wales) Rules 2009, SI 2009/357, rr 58–61.

[7.37A Petitions presented by insolvents]

[(1) This Rule applies where—
   (a)   a winding-up petition is presented by a company against itself;
   (b)   a bankruptcy petition is presented by a debtor against that debtor,
and references in this Rule to "the insolvent" are to be read as a reference to the company or the debtor.

(2) A solicitor acting in either of the cases mentioned in paragraph (1) must in the solicitor's bill of costs give credit for any sum or security received by the solicitor as a deposit from the insolvent on account of the costs and expenses to be incurred in respect of the filing and prosecution of the petition and the deposit must be noted by the costs officer on the final costs certificate.

(3) Where an order is made on a petition of a kind mentioned in paragraph (1) and prior to the presentation of that petition a petition had been presented by a creditor, no costs are allowed to the insolvent or that insolvent's solicitor out of that insolvent's estate unless the court considers that—
   (a)   the insolvent estate has benefited by the insolvent's conduct; or
   (b)   there are otherwise special circumstances justifying the allowance of costs.]

NOTES

Amendment
Substituted, for r 7.37 as previously enacted, by SI 2010/686, r 2, Sch 1, para 461.
    Date in force: 6 April 2010: see SI 2010/686, r 1; for transitional provisions and further effect see rr 6(1), 7, Sch 4, para 1, Sch 5 thereto.

[7.38 Costs paid otherwise than out of the insolvent estate]

[Where the amount of costs is decided by detailed assessment under an order of the court directing that those costs are to be paid otherwise than out of the insolvent estate, the costs officer shall note on the final costs certificate by whom, or the manner in which, the costs are to be paid.]

NOTES

Amendment

Substituted by SI 1999/1022, r 3, Schedule, para 3.
Date in force: 26 April 1999: see SI 1999/1022, r 1.

See Further

See further, in relation the application of this rule, with modifications, in respect of the procedure for the appointment of a bank liquidator and the operation of bank insolvency under the Banking Act 2009, Pt 2: the Bank Insolvency (England and Wales) Rules 2009, SI 2009/356, rr 3(3)–(8), 215.
See further, in relation to the application of this rule, with modifications, in respect of bank administration and applications for bank administration: the Bank Administration (England and Wales) Rules 2009, SI 2009/357, rr 58–61.

[7.39 Award of costs against official receiver or responsible insolvency practitioner]
[Without prejudice to any provision of the Act or Rules by virtue of which the official receiver is not in any event to be liable for costs and expenses, where [an office-holder or the official receiver where that official receiver is not acting as an office-holder] is made a party to any proceedings on the application of another party to the proceedings, he shall not be personally liable for costs unless the court otherwise directs.]

NOTES

Amendment

Substituted by SI 1999/1022, r 3, Schedule, para 3.
Date in force: 26 April 1999: see SI 1999/1022, r 1.
Words "an office-holder or the official receiver where that official receiver is not acting as an office-holder" in square brackets substituted by SI 2010/686, r 2, Sch 1, para 462.
Date in force: 6 April 2010: see SI 2010/686, r 1; for transitional provisions and further effect see rr 6(1), 7, Sch 4, para 1, Sch 5 thereto.

See Further

See further, in relation the application of this rule, with modifications, in respect of the procedure for the appointment of a bank liquidator and the operation of bank insolvency under the Banking Act 2009, Pt 2: the Bank Insolvency (England and Wales) Rules 2009, SI 2009/356, rr 3(3)–(8), 216.
See further, in relation to the application of this rule, with modifications, in respect of bank administration and applications for bank administration: the Bank Administration (England and Wales) Rules 2009, SI 2009/357, rr 58–61.

[7.40 Applications for costs]
[[(1) This Rule applies where a party to, or person affected by, any proceedings in an insolvency—
    (a) applies to the court for an order allowing his costs, or part of them, incidental to the proceedings; and
    (b) that application is not made at the time of the proceedings.
(2) The person concerned shall serve a sealed copy of his or her application—
    (a) in proceedings other than proceedings relating to a debt relief order—
        (i) on the [office-holder], and,
        (ii) in a winding up by the court or a bankruptcy, on the official receiver;
    (b) in proceedings relating to a debt relief order, on the official receiver.
(3) The [office-holder] and, where appropriate, the official receiver may appear on an application to which paragraph (2)(a) applies.

(3A) The official receiver may appear on an application to which paragraph (2)(b) applies.]

(4) No costs of or incidental to the application shall be allowed to the applicant unless the court is satisfied that the application could not have been made at the time of the proceedings.]

NOTES

Amendment

Substituted by SI 1999/1022, r 3, Schedule, para 3.
Date in force: 26 April 1999: see SI 1999/1022, r 1.
Paras (1)–(3), (3A): substituted, for paras (1)–(3) as previously enacted, by SI 2009/642, rr 4, 63.
Date in force: 6 April 2009: see SI 2009/642, r 1.
Para (2): in sub-para (a)(i) word "office-holder" in square brackets substituted by SI 2010/686, r 2, Sch 1, para 463(1), (2).
Date in force: 6 April 2010: see SI 2010/686, r 1; for transitional provisions and further effect see rr 6(1), 7, Sch 4, para 1, Sch 5 thereto.
Para (3): word "office-holder" in square brackets substituted by SI 2010/686, r 2, Sch 1, para 463(1), (3).
Date in force: 6 April 2010: see SI 2010/686, r 1; for transitional provisions and further effect see rr 6(1), 7, Sch 4, para 1, Sch 5 thereto.

See Further

See further, in relation the application of this rule, with modifications, in respect of the procedure for the appointment of a bank liquidator and the operation of bank insolvency under the Banking Act 2009, Pt 2: the Bank Insolvency (England and Wales) Rules 2009, SI 2009/356, rr 3(3)–(8), 217.
See further, in relation to the application of this rule, with modifications, in respect of bank administration and applications for bank administration: the Bank Administration (England and Wales) Rules 2009, SI 2009/357, rr 58–61.

[7.41 Costs and expenses of witnesses]

[(1) Except as directed by the court, no allowance as a witness in any examination or other proceedings before the court shall be made to the bankrupt [or the debtor] or an officer of the insolvent company to which the proceedings relate.

(2) A person presenting any petition in [a company insolvency or bankruptcy proceedings] shall not be regarded as a witness on the hearing of the petition, but the costs officer may allow his expenses of travelling and subsistence.]

NOTES

Amendment

Substituted by SI 1999/1022, r 3, Schedule, para 3.
Date in force: 26 April 1999: see SI 1999/1022, r 1.
Para (1): words "or the debtor" in square brackets inserted by SI 2009/642, rr 4, 64(a).
Date in force: 6 April 2009: see SI 2009/642, r 1.
Para (2): words "a company insolvency or bankruptcy proceedings" in square brackets substituted by SI 2009/642, rr 4, 64(b).
Date in force: 6 April 2009: see SI 2009/642, r 1.

See Further

See further, in relation the application of this rule, with modifications, in respect of the procedure for the appointment of a bank liquidator and the operation of bank insolvency under the Banking Act 2009, Pt 2: the Bank Insolvency (England and Wales) Rules 2009, SI 2009/356, rr 3(3)–(8), 218.

See further, in relation to the application of this rule, with modifications, in respect of bank administration and applications for bank administration: the Bank Administration (England and Wales) Rules 2009, SI 2009/357, rr 58–61.

[7.42 Final costs certificate]

[(1) A final costs certificate of the costs officer is final and conclusive as to all matters which have not been objected to in the manner provided for under the rules of the court.

(2) Where it is proved to the satisfaction of a costs officer that a final costs certificate has been lost or destroyed, he may issue a duplicate.]

NOTES

Amendment

Substituted by SI 1999/1022, r 3, Schedule, para 3.
Date in force: 26 April 1999: see SI 1999/1022, r 1.

See Further

See further, in relation the application of this rule, with modifications, in respect of the procedure for the appointment of a bank liquidator and the operation of bank insolvency under the Banking Act 2009, Pt 2: the Bank Insolvency (England and Wales) Rules 2009, SI 2009/356, rr 3(3)–(8), 219.

See further, in relation to the application of this rule, with modifications, in respect of bank administration and applications for bank administration: the Bank Administration (England and Wales) Rules 2009, SI 2009/357, rr 58–61.

CHAPTER 7

[PERSONS WHO LACK CAPACITY TO MANAGE THEIR AFFAIRS]

NOTES

Amendment

Chapter heading: substituted by SI 2007/1898, art 6, Sch 1, para 12(1), (4).
Date in force: 1 October 2007: see SI 2007/1898, art 1.

7.43 Introductory

(1) The Rules in this Chapter apply where in insolvency proceedings it appears to the court that a person affected by the proceedings is one who [lacks capacity within the meaning of the Mental Capacity Act 2005 to manage and administer his property and affairs] either—

(a) by reason of [lacking capacity within the meaning of the Mental Capacity Act 2005], or

(b) due to physical affliction or disability.

(2) The person concerned is referred to as "the incapacitated person".

NOTES

Initial Commencement

Specified date

Specified date: 29 December 1986: see r 0.1.

Amendment

Para (1): words from "lacks capacity" to "property and affairs" in square brackets substituted by SI 2007/1898, art 6, Sch 1, para 12(1), (5)(a).

Date in force: 1 October 2007: see SI 2007/1898, art 1.
Para (1): in sub-para (a) words "lacking capacity within the meaning of the Mental Capacity Act 2005" in square brackets substituted by SI 2007/1898, art 6, Sch 1, para 12(1), (5)(b).
Date in force: 1 October 2007: see SI 2007/1898, art 1.

See Further

See further, in relation the application of this rule, with modifications, in respect of the procedure for the appointment of a bank liquidator and the operation of bank insolvency under the Banking Act 2009, Pt 2: the Bank Insolvency (England and Wales) Rules 2009, SI 2009/356, rr 3(3)–(8), 220.
See further, in relation to the application of this rule, with modifications, in respect of bank administration and applications for bank administration: the Bank Administration (England and Wales) Rules 2009, SI 2009/357, rr 58–61.

7.44 Appointment of another person to act

(1) The court may appoint such person as it thinks [just] to appear for, represent or act for the incapacitated person.

(2) The appointment may be made either generally or for the purpose of any particular application or proceeding, or for the exercise of particular rights or powers which the incapacitated person might have exercised but for his incapacity.

(3) The court may make the appointment either of its own motion or on application by—

(a) a person who has been appointed by a court in the United Kingdom or elsewhere to manage the affairs of, or to represent, the incapacitated person, or

(b) any relative or friend of the incapacitated person who appears to the court to be a proper person to make the application, or

(c) the official receiver, or

(d) the person who, in relation to the proceedings, is the [office-holder].

(4) Application under paragraph (3) may be made [without notice to any other party]; but the court may require such notice of the application as it thinks necessary to be given to the person alleged to be incapacitated, or any other person, and may adjourn the hearing of the application to enable the notice to be given.

NOTES

Initial Commencement

Specified date

Specified date: 29 December 1986: see r 0.1.

Amendment

Para (1): word "just" in square brackets substituted by SI 2010/686, r 2, Sch 1, para 1.
Date in force: 6 April 2010: see SI 2010/686, r 1; for transitional provisions and further effect see rr 6(1), 7, Sch 4, paras 1, 2(1)(b), Sch 5 thereto.
Para (3): in sub-para (d) word "office-holder" in square brackets substituted by SI 2010/686, r 2, Sch 1, para 464(1), (2).
Date in force: 6 April 2010: see SI 2010/686, r 1; for transitional provisions and further effect see rr 6(1), 7, Sch 4, para 1, Sch 5 thereto.
Para (4): words "without notice to any other party" in square brackets substituted by SI 2010/686, r 2, Sch 1, para 464(1), (3).
Date in force: 6 April 2010: see SI 2010/686, r 1; for transitional provisions and further effect see rr 6(1), 7, Sch 4, paras 1, 2(1)(b) Sch 5 thereto.

See Further

See further, in relation the application of this rule, with modifications, in respect of the procedure for the appointment of a bank liquidator and the operation of bank insolvency under the Banking Act 2009, Pt 2: the Bank Insolvency (England and Wales) Rules 2009, SI 2009/356, rr 3(3)–(8), 221.

See further, in relation to the application of this rule, with modifications, in respect of bank administration and applications for bank administration: the Bank Administration (England and Wales) Rules 2009, SI 2009/357, rr 58–61.

[7.45A Witness statement in support of application]

[An application under Rule 7.44(3) must be supported by a witness statement made by a registered medical practitioner as to the mental or physical condition of the incapacitated person.]

NOTES

Amendment

Substituted, for r 7.45 as originally enacted, by SI 2010/686, r 2, Sch 1, para 465.
Date in force: 6 April 2010: see SI 2010/686, r 1; for transitional provisions and further effect see rr 6(1), 7, Sch 4, paras 1, 2(1)(b), (2)–(4), Sch 5 thereto.

7.46 Service of notices following appointment

Any notice served on, or sent to, a person appointed under Rule 7.44 has the same effect as if it had been served on, or given to, the incapacitated person.

NOTES

Initial Commencement

Specified date

Specified date: 29 December 1986: see r 0.1.

See Further

See further, in relation the application of this rule, with modifications, in respect of the procedure for the appointment of a bank liquidator and the operation of bank insolvency under the Banking Act 2009, Pt 2: the Bank Insolvency (England and Wales) Rules 2009, SI 2009/356, rr 3(3)–(8), 223.
See further, in relation to the application of this rule, with modifications, in respect of bank administration and applications for bank administration: the Bank Administration (England and Wales) Rules 2009, SI 2009/357, rr 58–61.

CHAPTER 8

APPEALS IN INSOLVENCY PROCEEDINGS

7.47 Appeals and reviews of court orders [in corporate insolvency]

(1) Every court having jurisdiction [for the purposes of Parts 1 to 4 of the Act and Parts 1 to 4 of the Rules,] may review, rescind or vary any order made by it in the exercise of that jurisdiction.

[(2) Appeals in civil matters in proceedings under Parts 1 to 4 of the Act and Parts 1 to 4 of the Rules lie as follows—

(a) to a single judge of the High Court where the decision appealed against is made by the county court or the registrar;

(b) to the Civil Division of the Court of Appeal from a decision of a single judge of the High Court.]

(3) A county court is not, in the exercise of its jurisdiction [for the purposes of Parts 1 to 4 of the Act and Parts 1 to 4 of the Rules], subject to be restrained by the order of any other court, and no appeal lies from its decision in the exercise of that jurisdiction except as provided by this Rule.

(4) Any application for the rescission of a winding-up order shall be made within [5 business] days after the date on which the order was made.

NOTES

Initial Commencement

Specified date
Specified date: 29 December 1986: see r 0.1.

Amendment
Provision heading: words "in corporate insolvency" in square brackets substituted by SI 2010/686, r 2, Sch 1, para 466(1), (2).
　　Date in force: 6 April 2010: see SI 2010/686, r 1; for transitional provisions and further effect see rr 6(1), 7, Sch 4, para 1, Sch 5 thereto.
Para (1): words "for the purposes of Parts 1 to 4 of the Act and Parts 1 to 4 of the Rules," in square brackets substituted by SI 2010/686, r 2, Sch 1, para 466(1), (3).
　　Date in force: 6 April 2010: see SI 2010/686, r 1; for transitional provisions and further effect see rr 6(1), 7, Sch 4, para 1, Sch 5 thereto.
Para (2): substituted by SI 2010/686, r 2, Sch 1, para 466(1), (4).
　　Date in force: 6 April 2010: see SI 2010/686, r 1; for transitional provisions and further effect see rr 6(1), 7, Sch 4, para 1, Sch 5 thereto.
Para (3): words "for the purposes of Parts 1 to 4 of the Act and Parts 1 to 4 of the Rules" in square brackets substituted by SI 2010/686, r 2, Sch 1, para 466(1), (5).
　　Date in force: 6 April 2010: see SI 2010/686, r 1; for transitional provisions and further effect see rr 6(1), 7, Sch 4, para 1, Sch 5 thereto.
Para (4): words "5 business" in square brackets substituted by SI 2010/686, r 2, Sch 1, para 466(1), (6).
　　Date in force: 6 April 2010: see SI 2010/686, r 1; for transitional provisions and further effect see rr 6(1), 7, Sch 4, para 1, Sch 5 thereto.

See Further
See further, in relation to the application of this rule, with modifications, in respect of bank administration and applications for bank administration: the Bank Administration (England and Wales) Rules 2009, SI 2009/357, rr 58–61.

7.48 Appeals in bankruptcy [by the Secretary of State]

(1) In bankruptcy proceedings, an appeal lies at the instance of the Secretary of State from any order of the court made on an application for the rescission or annulment of a bankruptcy order, or for a bankrupt's discharge.

(2) . . .

NOTES

Initial Commencement

Specified date
Specified date: 29 December 1986: see r 0.1.

Amendment
Provision heading: words "by the Secretary of State" in square brackets inserted by SI 2010/686, r 2, Sch 1, para 467(1), (2).
　　Date in force: 6 April 2010: see SI 2010/686, r 1; for transitional provisions and further effect see rr 6(1), 7, Sch 4, para 1, Sch 5 thereto.
Para (2): revoked by SI 2010/686, r 2, Sch 1, para 467(1), (3).
　　Date in force: 6 April 2010: see SI 2010/686, r 1; for transitional provisions and further effect see rr 6(1), 7, Sch 4, para 1, Sch 5 thereto.

[7.49A Procedure on appeal]

[(1) An appeal against a decision at first instance may only be brought with either the permission of the court which made the decision or the permission of the court which has jurisdiction to hear the appeal.

(2) An appellant must file an appellant's notice (within the meaning of CPR Part 52) within 21 days after the date of the decision of the court that the appellant wishes to appeal.

(3) The procedure set out in CPR Part 52 applies to any appeal to which this Chapter applies.]

NOTES

Amendment

Substituted, for r 7.49 as previously enacted, by SI 2010/686, r 2, Sch 1, para 468.
Date in force: 6 April 2010: see SI 2010/686, r 1; for transitional provisions and further effect see rr 6(1), 7, Sch 4, para 1, Sch 5 thereto.

7.50 Appeal against decision of Secretary of State or official receiver

[(1)] An appeal under the Act or the Rules against a decision of the Secretary of State or the official receiver shall be brought within 28 days of the notification of the decision.

[(2) In respect of a decision under Rule 6.214A(5)(b), an appeal shall be brought within 14 days of the notification of the decision.]

NOTES

Initial Commencement

Specified date

Specified date: 29 December 1986: see r 0.1.

Amendment

Para (1): numbered as such by SI 2003/1730, r 11, Sch 1, Pt 8, para 58.
Date in force: 1 April 2004: see SI 2003/1730, r 1(3).
Para (2): inserted by SI 2003/1730, r 11, Sch 1, Pt 8, para 58.
Date in force: 1 April 2004: see SI 2003/1730, r 1(3).

See Further

See further, in relation the application of this rule, with modifications, in respect of the procedure for the appointment of a bank liquidator and the operation of bank insolvency under the Banking Act 2009, Pt 2: the Bank Insolvency (England and Wales) Rules 2009, SI 2009/356, rr 3(3)–(8), 226.

CHAPTER 9

GENERAL

[7.51A Principal court rules and practice to apply]

[(1) The provisions of the CPR in the first column of the table in this Rule (including any related practice direction) apply to insolvency proceedings by virtue of the provisions of these Rules set out in the second column with any necessary modifications, except so far as inconsistent with these Rules.

Provisions of CPR	*Provisions of these Rules*
CPR Part 6 (except 6.30 to 6.51) (service of documents)	Chapter 3 of Part 12A
CPR Part 18 (further information)	Rules 7.60 and 9.2(3)(b)
CPR Part 31 (disclosure and inspection of documents)	Rules 7.60 and 9.2

CPR Part 37 (miscellaneous provisions about payments into court)	Rule 7.59
CPR Parts 44 and 47 (costs)	Chapter 6 of Part 7
CPR Part 52 (appeals)	Rule 7.49

(2) Subject to paragraph (3), the provisions of the CPR (including any related practice direction) not referred to in the table apply to proceedings under the Act and Rules with any necessary modifications, except so far as inconsistent with these Rules.

(3) All insolvency proceedings must be allocated to the multi-track for which CPR Part 29 makes provision, and accordingly those provisions of the CPR which provide for allocation questionnaires and track allocation do not apply.

(4) CPR Part 32 applies to a false statement in a document verified by a statement of truth made under these Rules as it applies to a false statement in a document verified by a statement of truth made under CPR Part 22.]

NOTES

Amendment

Substituted, for r 7.51 as previously enacted, by SI 2010/686, r 2, Sch 1, para 469.
Date in force: 6 April 2010: see SI 2010/686, r 1; for transitional provisions and further effect see rr 6(1), 7, Sch 4, para 1, Sch 5 thereto.

7.52 Right of audience

(1) Official receivers and deputy official receivers have right of audience in insolvency proceedings, whether in the High Court or a county court.

(2) . . .

NOTES

Initial Commencement

Specified date

Specified date: 29 December 1986: see r 0.1.

Amendment

Para (2): revoked by SI 2010/686, r 2, Sch 1, para 470.
Date in force: 6 April 2010: see SI 2010/686, r 1; for transitional provisions and further effect see rr 6(1), 7, Sch 4, para 1, Sch 5 thereto.

7.53 . . .

. . .

NOTES

Amendment

Revoked by SI 2010/686, r 5.
Date in force: 6 April 2010: see SI 2010/686, r 1; for transitional provisions and further effect see rr 6(1), 7, Sch 4, para 1, Sch 5 thereto.

7.54 . . .

. . .

Insolvency Rules 1986, reg 7.54

NOTES

Amendment

Revoked by SI 2010/686, r 5.
Date in force: 6 April 2010: see SI 2010/686, r 1; for transitional provisions and further effect see rr 6(1), 7, Sch 4, para 1, Sch 5 thereto.

7.55 Formal defects

No insolvency proceedings shall be invalidated by any formal defect or by any irregularity, unless the court before which objection is made considers that substantial injustice has been caused by the defect or irregularity, and that the injustice cannot be remedied by any order of the court.

NOTES

Initial Commencement

Specified date

Specified date: 29 December 1986: see r 0.1.

See Further

See further, in relation to the application of this rule, with modifications, in respect of bank administration and applications for bank administration: the Bank Administration (England and Wales) Rules 2009, SI 2009/357, rr 58–61.

7.56 [Service of orders staying proceedings]

Where in insolvency proceedings the court makes an order staying any action, execution or other legal process against the property of a company, or against the property or person of an individual debtor or bankrupt, service of the order may be effected by sending a sealed copy of the order to whatever is the address for service of the [claimant] or other party having the carriage of the proceedings to be stayed.

NOTES

Initial Commencement

Specified date

Specified date: 29 December 1986: see r 0.1.

Amendment

Provision heading: substituted by SI 2010/686, r 2, Sch 1, para 471(1), (2).
Date in force: 6 April 2010: see SI 2010/686, r 1; for transitional provisions and further effect see rr 6(1), 7, Sch 4, para 1, Sch 5 thereto.
Word "claimant" in square brackets substituted by SI 2010/686, r 2, Sch 1, para 471(1), (3).
Date in force: 6 April 2010: see SI 2010/686, r 1; for transitional provisions and further effect see rr 6(1), 7, Sch 4, para 1, Sch 5 thereto.

See Further

See further, in relation to the application of this rule, with modifications, in respect of bank administration and applications for bank administration: the Bank Administration (England and Wales) Rules 2009, SI 2009/357, rr 58–61.

7.57 . . .
. . .

NOTES

Amendment

Revoked by SI 2010/686, r 5.
Date in force: 6 April 2010: see SI 2010/686, r 1; for transitional provisions see r 6(1), Sch 4, para 1 thereto.

7.58 . . .

. . .

NOTES

Amendment

Revoked by SI 2010/686, r 5.
Date in force: 6 April 2010: see SI 2010/686, r 1; for transitional provisions see r 6(1), Sch 4, para 1 thereto.

[7.59 Payment into court]

[[CPR Part 37 (miscellaneous provisions about payments into court)] apply to money lodged in court under the Rules.]

NOTES

Amendment

Substituted by SI 1999/1022, r 3, Schedule, para 7.
Date in force: 26 April 1999: see SI 1999/1022, r 1.
Words "CPR Part 37 (miscellaneous provisions about payments into court)" in square brackets substituted by SI 2010/686, r 2, Sch 1, para 472.
Date in force: 6 April 2010: see SI 2010/686, r 1; for transitional provisions and further effect see rr 6(1), 7, Sch 4, para 1, Sch 5 thereto.

See Further

See further, in relation the application of this rule, with modifications, in respect of the procedure for the appointment of a bank liquidator and the operation of bank insolvency under the Banking Act 2009, Pt 2: the Bank Insolvency (England and Wales) Rules 2009, SI 2009/356, rr 3(3)–(8), 231.
See further, in relation to the application of this rule, with modifications, in respect of bank administration and applications for bank administration: the Bank Administration (England and Wales) Rules 2009, SI 2009/357, rr 58–61.

[7.60 Further Information and Disclosure]

[(1) Any party to insolvency proceedings may apply to the court for an order—
    (a)   that any other party
        (i)   clarify any matter which is in dispute in the proceedings, or
        (ii)   give additional information in relation to any such matter;

    in accordance with CPR Part 18 (further information); or
    (b)   to obtain disclosure from any other party in accordance with CPR Part 31 (disclosure and inspection of documents).

(2) An application under this Rule may be made without notice being served on any other party.]

NOTES

Amendment

Substituted by SI 1999/1022, r 3, Schedule, para 8.
Date in force: 26 April 1999: see SI 1999/1022, r 1.

See Further

See further, in relation the application of this rule, with modifications, in respect of the procedure for the appointment of a bank liquidator and the operation of bank insolvency under the Banking Act 2009, Pt 2: the Bank Insolvency (England and Wales) Rules 2009, SI 2009/356, rr 3(3)–(8), 232.

See further, in relation to the application of this rule, with modifications, in respect of bank administration and applications for bank administration: the Bank Administration (England and Wales) Rules 2009, SI 2009/357, rr 58–61.

7.61 Office copies of documents

(1) Any person who has under the Rules the right to inspect the court file of insolvency proceedings may require the court to provide him with an office copy of any document from the file.

(2) A person's rights under this Rule may be exercised on his behalf by his solicitor.

(3) An office copy provided by the court under this Rule shall be in such form as the registrar thinks appropriate, and shall bear the court's seal.

NOTES

Initial Commencement

Specified date

Specified date: 29 December 1986: see r 0.1.

Modification

References to solicitors etc modified to include references to bodies recognised under the Administration of Justice Act 1985, s 9, by the Solicitors' Incorporated Practices Order 1991, SI 1991/2684, arts 4, 5, Sch 1.

See Further

See further, in relation the application of this rule, with modifications, in respect of the procedure for the appointment of a bank liquidator and the operation of bank insolvency under the Banking Act 2009, Pt 2: the Bank Insolvency (England and Wales) Rules 2009, SI 2009/356, rr 3(3)–(8), 233.

See further, in relation to the application of this rule, with modifications, in respect of bank administration and applications for bank administration: the Bank Administration (England and Wales) Rules 2009, SI 2009/357, rr 58–61.

[CHAPTER 10

EC REGULATION—CREDITORS' VOLUNTARY WINDING UP—CONFIRMATION BY THE COURT]

NOTES

Amendment

Inserted by SI 2002/1307, rr 3(1), 9(1).
Date in force: 31 May 2002: see SI 2002/1307, r 1.

[7.62 Application for confirmation]
[(1) Where a company has passed a resolution for voluntary winding up, and no declaration under section 89 has been made [(or is deemed not to have been made in accordance with section 96)], the liquidator may apply to court for an order confirming the creditors' voluntary winding up for the purposes of the EC Regulation.

(2) The application shall be in writing [supported by a witness statement] by the liquidator (using [FORM 7.20] the same form) and shall state—
- (a) the name of the applicant,
- (b) the name of the company and its registered number,
- (c) the date on which the resolution for voluntary winding up was passed,
- (d) that the application is accompanied by all of the documents required under paragraph (3) which are true copies of the documents required, and
- (e) that the EC Regulation will apply to the company and whether the proceedings will be main proceedings, territorial proceedings or secondary proceedings.

(3) The liquidator shall file in court two copies of the application, together with one copy of the following—
- (a) a copy of the resolution for voluntary winding up referred to by section 84(3),
- (b) evidence of his appointment as liquidator of the company, and
- (c) a copy of the statement of affairs required under section 99.

(4) It shall not be necessary to serve the application on, or give notice of it to, any person.

(5) On an application under this Rule the court may confirm the creditors' voluntary winding up.

(6) If the court confirms the creditor's voluntary winding up—
- (a) it may do so without a hearing,
- (b) it shall affix its seal to the application.

(7) A member of the court staff may deal with an application under this Rule.

[(8) This Rule shall also apply where a company has moved to a voluntary liquidation in accordance with paragraph 83 of Schedule B1 to the Act [except that the material to be filed with the court under paragraph (3) must be a copy of the notice of moving from administration to creditors' voluntary liquidation sent by the administrator for the purposes of paragraph 83(3) that has been registered by the registrar of companies, together with the statement of affairs required under paragraph 47 of Schedule B1 to the Act].]]

NOTES

Amendment

Inserted by SI 2002/1307, rr 3(1), 9(1).
Date in force: 31 May 2002: see SI 2002/1307, r 1.
Para (1): words "(or is deemed not to have been made in accordance with section 96)" in square brackets inserted by SI 2010/686, r 2, Sch 1, para 473(1), (2).
Date in force: 6 April 2010: see SI 2010/686, r 1; for transitional provisions and further effect see rr 6(1), 7, Sch 4, para 1, Sch 5 thereto.
Para (2): words "supported by a witness statement" in square brackets substituted by SI 2010/686, r 2, Sch 1, para 473(1), (3).
Date in force: 6 April 2010: see SI 2010/686, r 1; for transitional provisions and further effect see rr 6(1), 7, Sch 4, paras 1, 2(1)(b), (2)–(4), Sch 5 thereto.
Para (8): inserted by SI 2003/1730, r 11, Sch 1, Pt 8, para 60.
Date in force: 15 September 2003: see SI 2003/1730, r 1(2).
Para (8): words from "except that the material" to "to the Act" in square brackets inserted by SI 2010/686, r 2, Sch 1, para 473(1), (4).

Date in force: 6 April 2010: see SI 2010/686, r 1; for transitional provisions and further effect see rr 6(1), 7, Sch 4, para 1, Sch 5 thereto.

Modification
Modified, in relation to a UK insurer, by the Insurers (Reorganisation and Winding Up) Regulations 2003, SI 2003/1102, reg 7(1), (2) and the Insurers (Reorganisation and Winding Up) Regulations 2004, SI 2004/353, reg 7.
Modified, in relation to a UK credit institution, by the Credit Institutions (Reorganisation and Winding up) Regulations 2004, SI 2004/1045, reg 6.

[7.63 Notice to member State liquidator and creditors in member States]
[Where the court has confirmed the creditors' voluntary winding up, the liquidator shall [as soon as reasonably practicable] give notice—
(a) if there is a member State liquidator in relation to the company, to the member State liquidator;
(b) in accordance with Article 40 of the EC Regulation (duty to inform creditors).]

NOTES

Amendment
Inserted by SI 2002/1307, rr 3(1), 9(1).
Date in force: 31 May 2002: see SI 2002/1307, r 1.
Words "as soon as reasonably practicable" in square brackets substituted by SI 2009/642, rr 4, 5.
Date in force: 6 April 2009: see SI 2009/642, r 1; for transitional provisions see r 3 thereof.

[CHAPTER 11

EC REGULATION—MEMBER STATE LIQUIDATOR]

NOTES

Amendment
Inserted by SI 2002/1307, rr 3(1), 9(1).
Date in force: 31 May 2002: see SI 2002/1307, r 1.

[7.64 Interpretation of creditor]
[(1) This Rule applies where a member State liquidator has been appointed in relation to a person subject to insolvency proceedings [other than proceedings relating to a debt relief order].

[(2) The member State liquidator has the same right to inspect or obtain from the court a copy of, or a copy of any document or documents contained in, the court file relating to the insolvency proceedings that is opened and maintained by the court under Rule 7.31A(1) as a creditor has under Rule 7.31A(3) and may appear at any hearing relating to those proceedings.]
(3) . . .
(4) [Paragraph (2) is] without prejudice to the generality of the right to participate referred to in paragraph 3 of Article 32 of the EC Regulation (exercise of creditor's rights).]

NOTES

Amendment

Inserted by SI 2002/1307, rr 3(1), 9(1).
Date in force: 31 May 2002: see SI 2002/1307, r 1.
Para (1): words "other than proceedings relating to a debt relief order" in square brackets inserted by SI 2009/642, rr 4, 65.
Date in force: 6 April 2009: see SI 2009/642, r 1.
Para (2): substituted by SI 2010/686, r 2, Sch 1, para 474(1), (2).
Date in force: 6 April 2010: see SI 2010/686, r 1; for transitional provisions and further effect see rr 6(1), 7, Sch 4, para 1, Sch 5 thereto.
Para (3): revoked by SI 2010/686, r 2, Sch 1, para 474(1), (3).
Date in force: 6 April 2010: see SI 2010/686, r 1; for transitional provisions and further effect see rr 6(1), 7, Sch 4, para 1, Sch 5 thereto.
Para (4): words "Paragraph (2) is" in square brackets substituted by SI 2010/686, r 2, Sch 1, para 474(1), (4).
Date in force: 6 April 2010: see SI 2010/686, r 1; for transitional provisions and further effect see rr 6(1), 7, Sch 4, para 1, Sch 5 thereto.

PART 8

PROXIES AND COMPANY REPRESENTATION

8.1 Definition of "proxy"

(1) For the purposes of the Rules, a proxy is an authority given by a person ("the principal") to another person ("the proxy-holder") to attend a meeting and speak and vote as his representative.

(2) Proxies are for use at creditors', company or contributories' meetings [summoned or called] under the Act or the Rules.

(3) Only one proxy may be given by a person for any one meeting at which he desires to be represented; and it may only be given to one person, being an individual aged 18 or over. But the principal may specify one or more other such individuals to be proxy-holder in the alternative, in the order in which they are named in the proxy.

(4) Without prejudice to the generality of paragraph (3), a proxy for a particular meeting may be given to whoever is to be the chairman of the meeting; and for a meeting held as part of the proceedings in a winding up by the court, or in a bankruptcy, it may be given to the official receiver.

[(5) A person given a proxy under paragraph (4) cannot decline to be the proxy-holder in relation to that proxy.

(6) A proxy requires the holder to give the principal's vote on matters arising for determination at the meeting, or to abstain, or to propose, in the principal's name, a resolution to be voted on by the meeting, either as directed or in accordance with the holder's own discretion.]

NOTES

Initial Commencement

Specified date

Specified date: 29 December 1986: see r 0.1.

Amendment

Para (2): words in square brackets inserted by SI 1987/1919, r 3(1), Schedule, Part 1, para 134(1).
Paras (5), (6): substituted for para (5) as originally enacted, by SI 1987/1919, r 3(1), Schedule, Part 1, para 134(2).

Insolvency Rules 1986, reg 8.1

See Further

See further, in relation the application of this rule, with modifications, in respect of the procedure for the appointment of a bank liquidator and the operation of bank insolvency under the Banking Act 2009, Pt 2: the Bank Insolvency (England and Wales) Rules 2009, SI 2009/356, rr 3(3)–(8), 234.

See further, in relation to the application of this rule, with modifications, in respect of bank administration and applications for bank administration: the Bank Administration (England and Wales) Rules 2009, SI 2009/357, rr 58–61.

8.2 Issue and use of forms

(1) When notice is given of a meeting to be held in insolvency proceedings, and forms of proxy are sent out with the notice, no form so sent out shall have inserted in it the name or description of any person.

(2) No form of proxy shall be used at any meeting except that which is sent out with the notice summoning the meeting, or a substantially similar form.

(3) A form of proxy shall be [authenticated] by the principal, or by some person authorised by him (either generally or with reference to a particular meeting). If the form is [authenticated] by a person other than the principal, the nature of the person's authority shall be stated.

NOTES

Initial Commencement

Specified date

Specified date: 29 December 1986: see r 0.1.

Amendment

Para (3): word "authenticated" in square brackets in both places it occurs substituted by SI 2010/686, r 2, Sch 1, para 1.

Date in force: 6 April 2010: see SI 2010/686, r 1; for transitional provisions and further effect see rr 6(1), 7, Sch 4, paras 1, 2(1)(b), Sch 5 thereto.

See Further

See further, in relation the application of this rule, with modifications, in respect of the procedure for the appointment of a bank liquidator and the operation of bank insolvency under the Banking Act 2009, Pt 2: the Bank Insolvency (England and Wales) Rules 2009, SI 2009/356, rr 3(3)–(8), 235.

See further, in relation to the application of this rule, with modifications, in respect of bank administration and applications for bank administration: the Bank Administration (England and Wales) Rules 2009, SI 2009/357, rr 58–61.

8.3 Use of proxies at meetings

(1) A proxy given for a particular meeting may be used at any adjournment of that meeting.

(2) Where the official receiver holds proxies for use at any meeting, his deputy, or any other official receiver, may act as proxy-holder in his place.

Alternatively, the official receiver may in writing authorise another officer of the Department to act for him at the meeting and use the proxies as if that other officer were himself proxy-holder.

(3) Where the responsible insolvency practitioner holds proxies to be used by him as chairman of a meeting, and some other person acts as chairman, the other person may use the insolvency practitioner's proxies as if he were himself proxy-holder.

[(4) Where a proxy directs a proxy-holder to vote for or against a resolution for the nomination or appointment of a person as the responsible insolvency practitioner, the proxy-holder may, unless the proxy states otherwise, vote for or against (as he thinks fit) any resolution for the nomination or appointment of that person jointly with another or others.

(5) A proxy-holder may propose any resolution which, if proposed by another, would be a resolution in favour of which by virtue of the proxy he would be entitled to vote.

(6) Where a proxy gives specific directions as to voting, this does not, unless the proxy states otherwise, preclude the proxy-holder from voting at his discretion on resolutions put to the meeting which are not dealt with in the proxy.]

NOTES

Initial Commencement

Specified date

Specified date: 29 December 1986: see r 0.1.

Amendment

Paras (4), (5), (6): inserted by SI 1987/1919, r 3(1), Schedule, Part 1, para 135.

See Further

See further, in relation the application of this rule, with modifications, in respect of the procedure for the appointment of a bank liquidator and the operation of bank insolvency under the Banking Act 2009, Pt 2: the Bank Insolvency (England and Wales) Rules 2009, SI 2009/356, rr 3(3)–(8), 236.

See further, in relation to the application of this rule, with modifications, in respect of bank administration and applications for bank administration: the Bank Administration (England and Wales) Rules 2009, SI 2009/357, rr 58–61.

8.4 Retention of proxies

(1) Subject as follows, proxies used for voting at any meeting shall be retained by the chairman of the meeting.

(2) The chairman shall deliver the proxies, [as soon as reasonably practicable] after the meeting, to the responsible insolvency practitioner (where that is someone other than himself).

NOTES

Initial Commencement

Specified date

Specified date: 29 December 1986: see r 0.1.

Amendment

Para (2): words "as soon as reasonably practicable" in square brackets substituted by SI 2009/642, rr 4, 5.

Date in force: 6 April 2009: see SI 2009/642, r 1; for transitional provisions see r 3 thereof.

See Further

See further, in relation the application of this rule, with modifications, in respect of the procedure for the appointment of a bank liquidator and the operation of bank insolvency under the Banking Act 2009, Pt 2: the Bank Insolvency (England and Wales) Rules 2009, SI 2009/356, rr 3(3)–(8), 237.

See further, in relation to the application of this rule, with modifications, in respect of bank administration and applications for bank administration: the Bank Administration (England and Wales) Rules 2009, SI 2009/357, rr 58–61.

8.5 Right of inspection

(1) The [office-holder] shall, so long as proxies lodged with him are in his hands, allow them to be inspected, at all reasonable times on any business day, by—
- (a) the creditors, in the case of proxies used at a meeting of creditors, and
- (b) a company's members or contributories, in the case of proxies used at a meeting of the company or of its contributories.

(2) The reference in paragraph (1) to creditors is—
- (a) in the case of a company in liquidation or of an individual's bankruptcy, those creditors who have proved their debts, and
- (b) in any other case, persons who have submitted in writing a claim to be creditors of the company or individual concerned;

but in neither case does it include a person whose proof or claim has been wholly rejected for purposes of voting, dividend or otherwise.

(3) The right of inspection given by this Rule is also exercisable—
- (a) in the case of an insolvent company, by its directors, and
- (b) in the case of an insolvent individual, by him.

(4) Any person attending a meeting in insolvency proceedings is entitled, immediately before or in the course of the meeting, to inspect proxies and associated documents [(including proofs) sent or given, in accordance with directions contained in any notice convening the meeting, to the chairman of that meeting or to any other person by a creditor, member or contributory for the purpose of that meeting.]

[(5) This Rule is subject to Rule 12A.51 (confidentiality of documents—grounds for refusing inspection).]

NOTES

Initial Commencement

Specified date

Specified date: 29 December 1986: see r 0.1.

Amendment

Para (1): words "office-holder" in square brackets substituted by SI 2010/686, r 2, Sch 1, para 475(1), (2).
Date in force: 6 April 2010: see SI 2010/686, r 1; for transitional provisions and further effect see rr 6(1), 7, Sch 4, para 1, Sch 5 thereto.

Para (4): words in square brackets substituted by SI 1987/1919, r 3(1), Schedule, Part 1, para 136.

Para (5): inserted by SI 2010/686, r 2, Sch 1, para 475(1), (3).
Date in force: 6 April 2010: see SI 2010/686, r 1; for transitional provisions and further effect see rr 6(1), 7, Sch 4, para 1, Sch 5 thereto.

See Further

See further, in relation the application of this rule, with modifications, in respect of the procedure for the appointment of a bank liquidator and the operation of bank insolvency under the Banking Act 2009, Pt 2: the Bank Insolvency (England and Wales) Rules 2009, SI 2009/356, rr 3(3)–(8), 238.
See further, in relation to the application of this rule, with modifications, in respect of bank administration and applications for bank administration: the Bank Administration (England and Wales) Rules 2009, SI 2009/357, rr 58–61.

8.6 Proxy-holder with financial interest

(1) A proxy-holder shall not vote in favour of any resolution which would directly or indirectly place him, or any associate of his, in a position to receive any remuneration out of the insolvent estate, unless the proxy specifically directs him to vote in that way.

[(1A) Where a proxy-holder has [authenticated] the proxy as being authorised to do so by his principal and the proxy specifically directs him to vote in the way mentioned in paragraph (1), he shall nevertheless not vote in that way unless he produces to the chairman of the meeting written authorisation from his principal sufficient to show that the proxy-holder was entitled so to [authenticate] the proxy.]

(2) This Rule applies also to any person acting as chairman of a meeting and using proxies in that capacity [under Rule 8.3]; and in its application to him, the proxy-holder is deemed an associate of his.

NOTES

Initial Commencement

Specified date

Specified date: 29 December 1986: see r 0.1.

Amendment

Para (1A): inserted by SI 1987/1919, r 3(1), Schedule, Part 1, para 137(1).

Para (1A): word "authenticated" in square brackets substituted by SI 2010/686, r 2, Sch 1, para 1.
Date in force: 6 April 2010: see SI 2010/686, r 1; for transitional provisions and further effect see rr 6(1), 7, Sch 4, paras 1, 2(1)(b), Sch 5 thereto.

Para (1A): word "authenticate" in square brackets substituted by SI 2010/686, r 2, Sch 1, para 1.
Date in force: 6 April 2010: see SI 2010/686, r 1; for transitional provisions and further effect see rr 6(1), 7, Sch 4, paras 1, 2(1)(b), Sch 5 thereto.

Para (2): words in square brackets inserted by SI 1987/1919, r 3(1), Schedule, Part 1, para 137(2).

See Further

See further, in relation the application of this rule, with modifications, in respect of the procedure for the appointment of a bank liquidator and the operation of bank insolvency under the Banking Act 2009, Pt 2: the Bank Insolvency (England and Wales) Rules 2009, SI 2009/356, rr 3(3)–(8), 239.
See further, in relation to the application of this rule, with modifications, in respect of bank administration and applications for bank administration: the Bank Administration (England and Wales) Rules 2009, SI 2009/357, rr 58–61.

8.7 Company representation

(1) Where a person is authorised . . . to represent a corporation at a meeting of creditors or of the company or its contributories, he shall produce to the chairman of the meeting a copy of the resolution from which he derives his authority.

(2) The copy resolution must be under the seal of the corporation, or certified by the secretary or a director of the corporation to be a true copy.

[(3) Nothing in this Rule requires the authority of a person to [authenticate] a proxy on behalf of a principal which is a corporation to be in the form of a resolution of that corporation.]

NOTES

Initial Commencement

Specified date

Specified date: 29 December 1986: see r 0.1.

Amendment

Para (1): words omitted revoked by SI 2010/686, r 2, Sch 1, para 476.
Date in force: 6 April 2010: see SI 2010/686, r 1; for transitional provisions and further effect see rr 6(1), 7, Sch 4, para 1, Sch 5 thereto.

Para (3): inserted by SI 1987/1919, r 3(1), Schedule, Part 1, para 138.

Para (3): word "authenticate" in square brackets substituted by SI 2010/686, r 2, Sch 1, para 1.
>Date in force: 6 April 2010: see SI 2010/686, r 1; for transitional provisions and further effect see rr 6(1), 7, Sch 4, paras 1, 2(1)(b), Sch 5 thereto.

See Further
>See further, in relation the application of this rule, with modifications, in respect of the procedure for the appointment of a bank liquidator and the operation of bank insolvency under the Banking Act 2009, Pt 2: the Bank Insolvency (England and Wales) Rules 2009, SI 2009/356, rr 3(3)–(8), 240.
>See further, in relation to the application of this rule, with modifications, in respect of bank administration and applications for bank administration: the Bank Administration (England and Wales) Rules 2009, SI 2009/357, rr 58–61.

[8.8 Interpretation of creditor]

[(1) This Rule applies where a member State liquidator has been appointed in relation to a person subject to insolvency proceedings.

(2) For the purposes of rule 8.5(1) (right of inspection of proxies) a member State liquidator appointed in main proceedings is deemed to be a creditor.

(3) Paragraph (2) is without prejudice to the generality of the right to participate referred to in paragraph 3 of Article 32 of the EC Regulation (exercise of creditor's rights).]

NOTES

Amendment
>Inserted by SI 2002/1307, rr 3(1), 9(2).
>Date in force: 31 May 2002: see SI 2002/1307, r 1.

PART 9

EXAMINATION OF PERSONS CONCERNED IN COMPANY AND INDIVIDUAL INSOLVENCY

9.1 Preliminary

[(1) The Rules in this Part apply to applications to the court for an order under—
- (a) section 236 (inquiry into company's dealings),
- (b) section 251N (debt relief orders—inquiry into dealings and property of debtor), or
- (c) section 366 (inquiry into bankruptcy, with respect to the bankrupt's dealings—including section 366 as it applies by virtue of section 368).]

(2) The following definitions apply—
- (a) the person in respect of whom an order is applied for is "the respondent";
- [(b) "the applicable section" is section 236, 251N or 366, according to whether the affairs of a company or those of a debtor in relation to a debt relief order or an application for a debt relief order or a bankrupt or (where the application under section 366 is made by virtue of section 368) a debtor in bankruptcy proceedings are in question;
- (c) the company or, as the case may be, the debtor in relation to a debt relief order or an application for a debt relief order, the bankrupt or debtor in bankruptcy proceedings concerned is "the insolvent";
- (d) "the applicant", in any application made under section 251N, means the official receiver].

NOTES

Initial Commencement

Specified date

Specified date: 29 December 1986: see r 0.1.

Amendment

Para (1): substituted by SI 2010/686, r 2, Sch 1, para 477.
Date in force: 6 April 2010: see SI 2010/686, r 1; for transitional provisions and further effect see rr 6(1), 7, Sch 4, para 1, Sch 5 thereto.
Para (2): sub-paras (b)–(d) substituted, for sub-paras (b), (c) as originally enacted, by SI 2009/642, rr 4, 66(b).
Date in force: 6 April 2009: see SI 2009/642, r 1.

See Further

See further, in relation to the application of this rule, with modifications, in respect of bank administration and applications for bank administration: the Bank Administration (England and Wales) Rules 2009, SI 2009/357, rr 58–61.

9.2 Form and contents of application

(1) The application shall be in writing [and specify] the grounds on which it is made.

[(2) The application must specify the name of the respondent.]

(3) It shall be stated whether the application is for the respondent—
   (a)   to be ordered to appear before the court, or
   [(b)   to be ordered to clarify any matter which is in dispute in the proceedings or to give additional information in relation to any such matter and if so CPR Part 18 (further information) shall apply to any such order, or]
   (c)   to submit [witness statements] (if so, particulars to be given of the matters to [be included]), or
   (d)   to produce books, papers or other records (if so, the items in question to be specified),
or for any two or more of those purposes.

(4) The application may be made [without notice to any other party].

NOTES

Initial Commencement

Specified date

Specified date: 29 December 1986: see r 0.1.

Amendment

Para (1): words "and specify" in square brackets substituted by SI 2010/686, r 2, Sch 1, para 478(1), (2).
Date in force: 6 April 2010: see SI 2010/686, r 1; for transitional provisions and further effect see rr 6(1), 7, Sch 4, paras 1, 2(1)(b), Sch 5 thereto.
Para (2): substituted by SI 2010/686, r 2, Sch 1, para 478(1), (3).
Date in force: 6 April 2010: see SI 2010/686, r 1; for transitional provisions and further effect see rr 6(1), 7, Sch 4, paras 1, 2(1)(b), Sch 5 thereto.
Para (3): sub-para (b) substituted by SI 1999/1022, r 3, Schedule, para 9.
Date in force: 26 April 1999: see SI 1999/1022, r 1.
Para (3): in sub-para (c) words "witness statements" in square brackets substituted by SI 2010/686, r 2, Sch 1, para 478(1), (4)(a).
Date in force: 6 April 2010: see SI 2010/686, r 1; for transitional provisions and further effect see rr 6(1), 7, Sch 4, paras 1, 2(1)(b), (2)–(4), Sch 5 thereto.

Para (3): in sub-para (c) words "be included" in square brackets substituted by SI 2010/686, r 2, Sch 1, para 478(1), (4)(b).
 Date in force: 6 April 2010: see SI 2010/686, r 1; for transitional provisions and further effect see rr 6(1), 7, Sch 4, paras 1, 2(1)(b), (2)–(4), Sch 5 thereto.
Para (4): words "without notice to any other party" in square brackets substituted by SI 2010/686, r 2, Sch 1, para 478(1), (5).
 Date in force: 6 April 2010: see SI 2010/686, r 1; for transitional provisions and further effect see rr 6(1), 7, Sch 4, paras 1, 2(1)(b), Sch 5 thereto.

See Further

See further, in relation the application of this rule, with modifications, in respect of the procedure for the appointment of a bank liquidator and the operation of bank insolvency under the Banking Act 2009, Pt 2: the Bank Insolvency (England and Wales) Rules 2009, SI 2009/356, rr 3(3)–(8), 242.

See further, in relation to the application of this rule, with modifications, in respect of bank administration and applications for bank administration: the Bank Administration (England and Wales) Rules 2009, SI 2009/357, rr 58–61.

9.3 Order for examination, etc

(1) The court may, whatever the purpose of the application, make any order which it has power to make under the applicable section.

(2) The court, if it orders the respondent to appear before it, shall specify a venue for his appearance, which shall be not less than 14 days from the date of the order.

(3) If he is ordered to submit [witness statements], the order shall specify—

(a) the matters which are to be dealt with in his [witness statements], and

(b) the time within which they are to be submitted to the court.

(4) If the order is to produce books, papers or other records, the time and manner of compliance shall be specified.

(5) The order must be served [as soon as reasonably practicable] on the respondent; and it must be served personally, unless the court otherwise orders.

NOTES

Initial Commencement

Specified date

 Specified date: 29 December 1986: see r 0.1.

Amendment

Para (3): words "witness statements" in square brackets in both places they occur substituted by SI 2010/686, r 2, Sch 1, para 479.
 Date in force: 6 April 2010: see SI 2010/686, r 1; for transitional provisions and further effect see rr 6(1), 7, Sch 4, paras 1, 2(1)(b), (2)–(4), Sch 5 thereto.
Para (5): words "as soon as reasonably practicable" in square brackets substituted by SI 2009/642, rr 4, 5.
 Date in force: 6 April 2009: see SI 2009/642, r 1; for transitional provisions see r 3 thereof.

See Further

See further, in relation the application of this rule, with modifications, in respect of the procedure for the appointment of a bank liquidator and the operation of bank insolvency under the Banking Act 2009, Pt 2: the Bank Insolvency (England and Wales) Rules 2009, SI 2009/356, rr 3(3)–(8), 243.

See further, in relation to the application of this rule, with modifications, in respect of bank administration and applications for bank administration: the Bank Administration (England and Wales) Rules 2009, SI 2009/357, rr 58–61.

9.4 Procedure for examination

(1) At any examination of the respondent, the applicant may attend in person, or be represented by a solicitor with or without counsel, and may put such questions to the respondent as the court may allow.

[(2) Unless the applicant objects, the following persons may attend the examination with the permission of the court and may put questions to the respondent (but only through the applicant)—

    (a)   any person who could have applied for an order under the applicable section; and

    (b)   any creditor who has provided information on which the application was made under section 236 or 366.]

[(3) If the respondent is ordered to clarify any matter or to give additional information, the court shall direct him as to the questions which he is required to answer, and as to whether his answers (if any) are to be made [in a witness statement].]

(4) . . .

(5) The respondent may at his own expense employ a solicitor with or without counsel, who may put to him such questions as the court may allow for the purpose of enabling him to explain or qualify any answers given by him, and may make representations on his behalf.

(6) There shall be made in writing such record of the examination as the court thinks proper. The record shall be read over either to or by the respondent and [authenticated] by him at a venue fixed by the court.

(7) The written record may, in any proceedings (whether under the Act or otherwise) be used as evidence against the respondent of any statement made by him in the course of his examination.

NOTES

Initial Commencement

Specified date

    Specified date: 29 December 1986: see r 0.1.

Amendment

    Para (2): substituted by SI 2010/686, r 2, Sch 1, para 480(1), (2).
        Date in force: 6 April 2010: see SI 2010/686, r 1; for transitional provisions and further effect see rr 6(1), 7, Sch 4, para 1, Sch 5 thereto.
    Para (3): substituted by SI 1999/1022, r 3, Schedule, para 10.
        Date in force: 26 April 1999: see SI 1999/1022, r 1.
    Para (3): words "in a witness statement" in square brackets substituted by SI 2010/686, r 2, Sch 1, para 480(1), (3).
        Date in force: 6 April 2010: see SI 2010/686, r 1; for transitional provisions and further effect see rr 6(1), 7, Sch 4, paras 1, 2(1)(b), (2)–(4), Sch 5 thereto.
    Para (4): revoked by SI 2010/686, r 2, Sch 1, para 480(1), (4).
        Date in force: 6 April 2010: see SI 2010/686, r 1; for transitional provisions and further effect see rr 6(1), 7, Sch 4, para 1, Sch 5 thereto.
    Para (6): word "authenticated" in square brackets substituted by SI 2010/686, r 2, Sch 1, para 1.
        Date in force: 6 April 2010: see SI 2010/686, r 1; for transitional provisions and further effect see rr 6(1), 7, Sch 4, paras 1, 2(1)(b), Sch 5 thereto.

See Further

    See further, in relation the application of this rule, with modifications, in respect of the procedure for the appointment of a bank liquidator and the operation of bank insolvency under the Banking Act 2009, Pt 2: the Bank Insolvency (England and Wales) Rules 2009, SI 2009/356, rr 3(3)–(8), 244.
    See further, in relation to the application of this rule, with modifications, in respect of bank administration and applications for bank administration: the Bank Administration (England

and Wales) Rules 2009, SI 2009/357, rr 58–61.

9.5 Record of examination

[(1) Unless the court otherwise directs, the written record of questions put to the respondent and the respondent's answers, and any witness statements submitted by the respondent in compliance with an order of the court under the applicable section, are not to be filed with the court.

(2) The documents set out in paragraph (3) are not open to inspection without an order of the court, by any person other than—

- (a) the applicant for an order under the applicable section, or
- (b) any person who could have applied for such an order in respect of the affairs of the same insolvent.

(3) The documents to which paragraph (2) applies are—

- (a) the written record of the respondent's examination;
- (b) copies of questions put to the respondent or proposed to be put to the respondent and answers to questions given by the respondent;
- (c) any witness statement by the respondent; and
- (d) any document on the court file as shows the grounds for the application for an order.]

(4) The court may from time to time give directions as to the custody and inspection of any documents to which this Rule applies, and as to the furnishing of copies of, or extracts from, such documents.

NOTES

Initial Commencement

Specified date

Specified date: 29 December 1986: see r 0.1.

Amendment

Paras (1)–(3): substituted by SI 2010/686, r 2, Sch 1, para 481.
Date in force: 6 April 2010: see SI 2010/686, r 1; for transitional provisions and further effect see rr 6(1), 7, Sch 4, para 1, Sch 5 thereto.

See Further

See further, in relation the application of this rule, with modifications, in respect of the procedure for the appointment of a bank liquidator and the operation of bank insolvency under the Banking Act 2009, Pt 2: the Bank Insolvency (England and Wales) Rules 2009, SI 2009/356, rr 3(3)–(8), 245.
See further, in relation to the application of this rule, with modifications, in respect of bank administration and applications for bank administration: the Bank Administration (England and Wales) Rules 2009, SI 2009/357, rr 58–61.

9.6 Costs of proceedings under ss 236, [251N and] 366

(1) Where the court has ordered an examination of any person under the applicable section, and it appears to it that the examination was made necessary because information had been unjustifiably refused by the respondent, it may order that the costs of the examination be paid by him.

(2) Where the court makes an order against a person under—

- (a) section 237(1) or 367(1) (to deliver up property in his possession which belongs to the insolvent), or
- (b) section 237(2) or 367(2) (to pay any amount in discharge of a debt due to the insolvent),

the costs of the application for the order may be ordered by the court to be paid by the respondent.

(3) Subject to paragraphs (1) and (2) above, the applicant's costs shall, unless the court otherwise orders, [be paid—
  (a)   in relation to a company insolvency, as an expense of the liquidation,
  (b)   in relation to an individual insolvency[, but not in proceedings relating to debt relief orders or applications for debt relief orders], out of the bankrupt's estate or (as the case may be) the debtor's property].

(4) A person summoned to attend for examination under this Chapter shall be tendered a reasonable sum in respect of travelling expenses incurred in connection with his attendance. Other costs falling on him are at the court's discretion.

(5) Where the examination is on the application of the official receiver otherwise than in the capacity of liquidator or trustee, no order shall be made for the payment of costs by him.

NOTES

Initial Commencement

Specified date

Specified date: 29 December 1986: see r 0.1.

Amendment

Provision heading: words "251N and" in square brackets inserted by SI 2009/642, rr 4, 68(a).
    Date in force: 6 April 2009: see SI 2009/642, r 1..
Para (3): words from "be paid— (a)" to "the debtor's property" in square brackets substituted by SI 2008/737, rr 3, 7(13).
    Date in force: 6 April 2008: see SI 2008/737, r 1(1); for transitional provisions see r 2 thereof.
Para (3): in sub-para (b) words from ", but not in" to "debt relief orders" in square brackets inserted by SI 2009/642, rr 4, 68(b).
    Date in force: 6 April 2009: see SI 2009/642, r 1.

See Further

See further, in relation the application of this rule, with modifications, in respect of the procedure for the appointment of a bank liquidator and the operation of bank insolvency under the Banking Act 2009, Pt 2: the Bank Insolvency (England and Wales) Rules 2009, SI 2009/356, rr 3(3)–(8), 246.
See further, in relation to the application of this rule, with modifications, in respect of bank administration and applications for bank administration: the Bank Administration (England and Wales) Rules 2009, SI 2009/357, rr 58–61.

PART 10

OFFICIAL RECEIVERS

10.1 Appointment of official receivers

Judicial notice shall be taken of the appointment under sections 399 to 401 of official receivers and deputy official receivers.

NOTES

Initial Commencement

Specified date

Specified date: 29 December 1986: see r 0.1.

10.2 Persons entitled to act on official receiver's behalf

(1) In the absence of the official receiver authorised to act in a particular case, an officer authorised in writing for the purpose by the Secretary of State, or by the official receiver himself, may, with the [permission] of the court, act on the official receiver's behalf and in his place—

(a) in any examination under section 133, 236, [251N,] 290 or 366, and

(b) in respect of any application to the court.

(2) In case of emergency, where there is no official receiver capable of acting, anything to be done by, to or before the official receiver may be done by, to or before the registrar [or district judge].

NOTES

Initial Commencement

Specified date

Specified date: 29 December 1986: see r 0.1.

Amendment

Para (1): word "permission" in square brackets substituted by SI 2010/686, r 2, Sch 1, para 1.
Date in force: 6 April 2010: see SI 2010/686, r 1; for transitional provisions and further effect see rr 6(1), 7, Sch 4, paras 1, 2(1)(b), Sch 5 thereto.

Para (1): in sub-para (a) reference to "251N," in square brackets inserted by SI 2009/642, rr 4, 69.
Date in force: 6 April 2009: see SI 2009/642, r 1.

Para (2): words "or district judge" in square brackets substituted by SI 2010/686, r 2, Sch 1, para 482.
Date in force: 6 April 2010: see SI 2010/686, r 1; for transitional provisions and further effect see rr 6(1), 7, Sch 4, paras 1, 2(1)(b), Sch 5 thereto.

10.3 Application for directions

The official receiver may apply to the court for directions in relation to any matter arising in insolvency proceedings.

NOTES

Initial Commencement

Specified date

Specified date: 29 December 1986: see r 0.1.

10.4 Official receiver's expenses

(1) Any expenses incurred by the official receiver (in whatever capacity he may be acting) in connection with proceedings taken against him in insolvency proceedings are to be treated as expenses of the insolvency proceedings.

"Expenses" includes damages.

(2) In respect of any sums due to him under paragraph (1) [in connection with insolvency proceedings other than proceedings relating to debt relief orders or applications for debt relief orders], the official receiver has a charge on the insolvent estate.

NOTES

Initial Commencement

Specified date

Specified date: 29 December 1986: see r 0.1.

Amendment

Para (2): words from "in connection with" to "debt relief orders" in square brackets inserted by SI 2009/642, rr 4, 70.
Date in force: 6 April 2009: see SI 2009/642, r 1.

PART 11

DECLARATION AND PAYMENT OF DIVIDEND (WINDING UP AND BANKRUPTCY)

11.1 Preliminary

(1) The Rules in this Part relate to the declaration and payment of dividends in companies winding up and in bankruptcy.

(2) The following definitions apply—

(a) "the insolvent" means the company in liquidation or, as the case may be, the bankrupt; and

(b) "creditors" means those creditors of the insolvent of whom the [office-holder] is aware. . ...

[(3) For the purposes of this Part, a member State liquidator appointed in relation to an insolvent is deemed to be a creditor.]

NOTES

Initial Commencement

Specified date

Specified date: 29 December 1986: see r 0.1.

Amendment

Para (2): in sub-para (b) word "office-holder" in square brackets substituted by SI 2010/686, r 2, Sch 1, para 483.
Date in force: 6 April 2010: see SI 2010/686, r 1; for transitional provisions and further effect see rr 6(1), 7, Sch 4, para 1, Sch 5 thereto.
Para (2): in sub-para (b) words omitted revoked by SI 2010/686, r 2, Sch 1, para 484.
Date in force: 6 April 2010: see SI 2010/686, r 1; for transitional provisions and further effect see rr 6(1), 7, Sch 4, para 1, Sch 5 thereto.
Para (3): inserted by SI 2002/1307, rr 3(1), 10(1).
Date in force: 31 May 2002: see SI 2002/1307, r 1.

See Further

See further, in relation to the application of this rule, with modifications, in respect of bank administration and applications for bank administration: the Bank Administration (England and Wales) Rules 2009, SI 2009/357, rr 58–61.

11.2 Notice of intended dividend

(1) Before declaring a dividend, the [office-holder] shall give notice of his intention to do so

[(a) to all creditors whose addresses are known to him and who have not proved their debts, and

(b) where a member State liquidator has been appointed in relation to the insolvent, to that person].

[(1A) Before declaring a first dividend the [office-holder] shall give notice of the intended dividend. As soon as reasonably practicable such notice—
(a) shall be gazetted; and
(b) may be advertised in such other manner as the [office-holder] thinks fit.]
[(1B) Paragraph (1A) shall not apply where the [office-holder] has previously, by notice [which has been gazetted], invited creditors to prove their debts.]
[(1C) In addition to the standard contents, a notice under paragraph (1A) must—
(a) state that the office-holder intends to declare a first dividend; and
(b) specify the date by which and place at which proofs must be lodged.]
(2) [Any notice under paragraph (1) and any notice of a first dividend under paragraph (1A)] shall specify a date ("the last date for proving") up to which proofs may be lodged. The date shall be the same for all creditors, and not less than 21 days from that of the notice.
(3) The [office-holder] shall in the notice state his intention to declare a dividend (specified as interim or final, as the case may be) within the period of [2] months from the last date for proving.

NOTES

Initial Commencement

Specified date

Specified date: 29 December 1986: see r 0.1.

Amendment

Para (1): word "office-holder" in square brackets substituted by SI 2010/686, r 2, Sch 1, para 483.
    Date in force: 6 April 2010: see SI 2010/686, r 1; for transitional provisions and further effect see rr 6(1), 7, Sch 4, para 1, Sch 5 thereto.
Para (1): sub-paras (a), (b) substituted by SI 2002/1307, rr 3(1), 10(2).
    Date in force: 31 May 2002: see SI 2002/1307, r 1.
Para (1A) (as inserted by SI 1987/1919, r 3(1), Schedule, Pt 1, para 139(2)): substituted by SI 2009/642, rr 4, 71(a).
    Date in force: 6 April 2009: see SI 2009/642, r 1; for transitional provisions see r 3 thereof.
Para (1A): word "office-holder" in square brackets in both places it occurs substituted by SI 2010/686, r 2, Sch 1, para 483.
    Date in force: 6 April 2010: see SI 2010/686, r 1; for transitional provisions and further effect see rr 6(1), 7, Sch 4, para 1, Sch 5 thereto.
Para (1B): inserted by SI 2009/642, rr 4, 71(b).
    Date in force: 6 April 2009: see SI 2009/642, r 1; for transitional provisions see r 3 thereof.
Para (1B): word "office-holder" in square brackets substituted by SI 2010/686, r 2, Sch 1, para 483.
    Date in force: 6 April 2010: see SI 2010/686, r 1; for transitional provisions and further effect see rr 6(1), 7, Sch 4, para 1, Sch 5 thereto.
Para (1B): words "which has been gazetted" in square brackets inserted by SI 2010/686, r 2, Sch 1, para 485(1), (2).
    Date in force: 6 April 2010: see SI 2010/686, r 1; for transitional provisions and further effect see rr 6(1), 7, Sch 4, para 1, Sch 5 thereto.
Para (1C): inserted by SI 2010/686, r 2, Sch 1, para 485(1), (3).
    Date in force: 6 April 2010: see SI 2010/686, r 1; for transitional provisions and further effect see rr 6(1), 7, Sch 4, para 1, Sch 5 thereto.
Para (2): words in square brackets substituted by SI 1987/1919, r 3(1), Schedule, Part 1, para 139(3).
Para (3): word "office-holder" in square brackets substituted by SI 2010/686, r 2, Sch 1, para 483.
    Date in force: 6 April 2010: see SI 2010/686, r 1; for transitional provisions and further effect see rr 6(1), 7, Sch 4, para 1, Sch 5 thereto.

Para (3): reference to "2" in square brackets substituted by SI 2010/686, r 2, Sch 1, para 485(1), (4).
> Date in force: 6 April 2010: see SI 2010/686, r 1; for transitional provisions and further effect see rr 6(1), 7, Sch 4, para 1, Sch 5 thereto.

See Further
> See further, in relation the application of this rule, with modifications, in respect of the procedure for the appointment of a bank liquidator and the operation of bank insolvency under the Banking Act 2009, Pt 2: the Bank Insolvency (England and Wales) Rules 2009, SI 2009/356, rr 3(3)–(8), 248.
> See further, in relation to the application of this rule, with modifications, in respect of bank administration and applications for bank administration: the Bank Administration (England and Wales) Rules 2009, SI 2009/357, rr 58–61.

11.3 Final admission/rejection of proofs

(1) The [office-holder] shall, within [5 business] days from the last date for proving, deal with every creditor's proof (in so far as not already dealt with) by admitting or rejecting it in whole or in part, or by making such provision as he thinks fit in respect of it.

(2) The [office-holder] is not obliged to deal with proofs lodged after the last date for proving; but he may do so, if he thinks fit.

[(3) In the declaration of a dividend no payment shall be made more than once by virtue of the same debt.

(4) Subject to Rule 11.11, where—
    (a)   a creditor has proved, and
    (b)   a member State liquidator has proved in relation to the same debt,
payment shall only be made to the creditor.]

NOTES

Initial Commencement

Specified date
> Specified date: 29 December 1986: see r 0.1.

Amendment
> Para (1): word "office-holder" in square brackets substituted by SI 2010/686, r 2, Sch 1, para 483.
>> Date in force: 6 April 2010: see SI 2010/686, r 1; for transitional provisions and further effect see rr 6(1), 7, Sch 4, para 1, Sch 5 thereto.
>
> Para (1): words "5 business" in square brackets substituted by SI 2010/686, r 2, Sch 1, para 486.
>> Date in force: 6 April 2010: see SI 2010/686, r 1; for transitional provisions and further effect see rr 6(1), 7, Sch 4, para 1, Sch 5 thereto.
>
> Para (2): word "office-holder" in square brackets substituted by SI 2010/686, r 2, Sch 1, para 483.
>> Date in force: 6 April 2010: see SI 2010/686, r 1; for transitional provisions and further effect see rr 6(1), 7, Sch 4, para 1, Sch 5 thereto.
>
> Paras (3), (4): inserted by SI 2002/1307, rr 3(1), 10(3).
>> Date in force: 31 May 2002: see SI 2002/1307, r 1.

See Further
> See further, in relation the application of this rule, with modifications, in respect of the procedure for the appointment of a bank liquidator and the operation of bank insolvency under the Banking Act 2009, Pt 2: the Bank Insolvency (England and Wales) Rules 2009, SI 2009/356, rr 3(3)–(8), 249.
> See further, in relation to the application of this rule, with modifications, in respect of bank administration and applications for bank administration: the Bank Administration (England and Wales) Rules 2009, SI 2009/357, rr 58–61.

11.4 Postponement or cancellation of dividend

If in the period of [2] months referred to in Rule 11.2(3)—

(a) the [office-holder] has rejected a proof in whole or in part and application is made to the court for his decision to be reversed or varied, or

(b) application is made to the court for the [office-holder's] decision on a proof to be reversed or varied, or for a proof to be expunged, or for a reduction of the amount claimed,

the [office-holder] may postpone or cancel the dividend.

NOTES

Initial Commencement

Specified date

Specified date: 29 December 1986: see r 0.1.

Amendment

Reference to "2" in square brackets substituted by SI 2010/686, r 2, Sch 1, para 487.
Date in force: 6 April 2010: see SI 2010/686, r 1; for transitional provisions and further effect see rr 6(1), 7, Sch 4, para 1, Sch 5 thereto.

Word "office-holder" in square brackets in both places it occurs substituted by SI 2010/686, r 2, Sch 1, para 483.
Date in force: 6 April 2010: see SI 2010/686, r 1; for transitional provisions and further effect see rr 6(1), 7, Sch 4, para 1, Sch 5 thereto.

In para (b) word "office-holder's" in square brackets substituted by virtue of SI 2010/686, r 2, Sch 1, para 483.
Date in force: 6 April 2010: see SI 2010/686, r 1; for transitional provisions and further effect see rr 6(1), 7, Sch 4, para 1, Sch 5 thereto.

See Further

See further, in relation the application of this rule, with modifications, in respect of the procedure for the appointment of a bank liquidator and the operation of bank insolvency under the Banking Act 2009, Pt 2: the Bank Insolvency (England and Wales) Rules 2009, SI 2009/356, rr 3(3)–(8), 250.

See further, in relation to the application of this rule, with modifications, in respect of bank administration and applications for bank administration: the Bank Administration (England and Wales) Rules 2009, SI 2009/357, rr 58–61.

11.5 Decision to declare dividend

(1) If the [office-holder] has not, in the [2-month] period referred to in Rule 11.2(3), had cause to postpone or cancel the dividend, he shall within that period proceed to declare the dividend of which he gave notice under that Rule.

(2) Except with the [permission] of the court, the [office-holder] shall not declare the dividend so long as there is pending any application to the court to reverse or vary a decision of his on a proof, or to expunge a proof or to reduce the amount claimed.

If the court gives [permission] under this paragraph, the [office-holder] shall make such provision in respect of the proof in question as the court directs.

NOTES

Initial Commencement

Specified date

Specified date: 29 December 1986: see r 0.1.

Amendment

Para (1): word "office-holder" in square brackets substituted by SI 2010/686, r 2, Sch 1, para 483.

Date in force: 6 April 2010: see SI 2010/686, r 1; for transitional provisions and further effect see rr 6(1), 7, Sch 4, para 1, Sch 5 thereto.

Para (1): word "2-month" in square brackets substituted by SI 2010/686, r 2, Sch 1, para 488.

Date in force: 6 April 2010: see SI 2010/686, r 1; for transitional provisions and further effect see rr 6(1), 7, Sch 4, para 1, Sch 5 thereto.

Para (2): word "permission" in square brackets in both places it occurs substituted by SI 2010/686, r 2, Sch 1, para 1.

Date in force: 6 April 2010: see SI 2010/686, r 1; for transitional provisions and further effect see rr 6(1), 7, Sch 4, paras 1, 2(1)(b), Sch 5 thereto.

Para (2): word "office-holder" in square brackets in both places it occurs substituted by SI 2010/686, r 2, Sch 1, para 483.

Date in force: 6 April 2010: see SI 2010/686, r 1; for transitional provisions and further effect see rr 6(1), 7, Sch 4, para 1, Sch 5 thereto.

See Further

See further, in relation the application of this rule, with modifications, in respect of the procedure for the appointment of a bank liquidator and the operation of bank insolvency under the Banking Act 2009, Pt 2: the Bank Insolvency (England and Wales) Rules 2009, SI 2009/356, rr 3(3)–(8), 251.

See further, in relation to the application of this rule, with modifications, in respect of bank administration and applications for bank administration: the Bank Administration (England and Wales) Rules 2009, SI 2009/357, rr 58–61.

11.6 Notice of declaration

(1) The [office-holder] shall give notice of the dividend to
- [(a) all creditors who have proved their debts, and
- (b) where a member State liquidator has been appointed in relation to the insolvent, to that person].

(2) The notice shall include the following particulars relating to the insolvency and the administration of the insolvent estate-
- (a) amounts realised from the sale of assets, indicating (so far as practicable) amounts raised by the sale of particular assets;
- (b) payments made by the [office-holder] in the administration of the insolvent estate;
- (c) provision (if any) made for unsettled claims, and funds (if any) retained for particular purposes;
- (d) the total amount to be distributed, and the rate of dividend;
- (e) whether, and if so when, any further dividend is expected to be declared.

[(2A) Where, in a winding up other than a members' voluntary winding up, the liquidator proposes to declare a dividend to unsecured creditors, the notice must also state the value of the prescribed part, except where the court has made an order under section 176A(5).]

(3) The dividend may be distributed simultaneously with the notice declaring it.

(4) Payment of dividend may be made by post, or arrangements may be made with any creditor for it to be paid to him in another way, or held for his collection.

(5) Where a dividend is paid on a bill of exchange or other negotiable instrument, the amount of the dividend shall be endorsed on the instrument, or on a certified copy of it, if required to be produced by the holder for that purpose.

NOTES

Initial Commencement

Specified date

Specified date: 29 December 1986: see r 0.1.

Amendment
> Para (1): word "office-holder" in square brackets substituted by SI 2010/686, r 2, Sch 1, para 483.
>> Date in force: 6 April 2010: see SI 2010/686, r 1; for transitional provisions and further effect see rr 6(1), 7, Sch 4, para 1, Sch 5 thereto.
>
> Para (1): sub-paras (a), (b) substituted by SI 2002/1307, rr 3(1), 10(4).
>> Date in force: 31 May 2002: see SI 2002/1307, r 1.
>
> Para (2): in para (b) word "office-holder" in square brackets substituted by SI 2010/686, r 2, Sch 1, para 483.
>> Date in force: 6 April 2010: see SI 2010/686, r 1; for transitional provisions and further effect see rr 6(1), 7, Sch 4, para 1, Sch 5 thereto.
>
> Para (2A): inserted by SI 2010/686, r 2, Sch 1, para 489.
>> Date in force: 6 April 2010: see SI 2010/686, r 1; for transitional provisions and further effect see rr 6(1), 7, Sch 4, para 1, Sch 5 thereto.

See Further
> See further, in relation the application of this rule, with modifications, in respect of the procedure for the appointment of a bank liquidator and the operation of bank insolvency under the Banking Act 2009, Pt 2: the Bank Insolvency (England and Wales) Rules 2009, SI 2009/356, rr 3(3)–(8), 252.
>
> See further, in relation to the application of this rule, with modifications, in respect of bank administration and applications for bank administration: the Bank Administration (England and Wales) Rules 2009, SI 2009/357, rr 58–61.

11.7 Notice of no, or no further, dividend

If the [office-holder] gives notice to creditors that he is unable to declare any dividend or (as the case may be) any further dividend, the notice shall contain a statement to the effect either—

(a) that no funds have been realised, or

(b) that the funds realised have already been distributed or used or allocated for defraying the expenses of administration.

NOTES

Initial Commencement

Specified date
> Specified date: 29 December 1986: see r 0.1.

Amendment
> Word "office-holder" in square brackets substituted by SI 2010/686, r 2, Sch 1, para 483.
>> Date in force: 6 April 2010: see SI 2010/686, r 1; for transitional provisions and further effect see rr 6(1), 7, Sch 4, para 1, Sch 5 thereto.

See Further
> See further, in relation the application of this rule, with modifications, in respect of the procedure for the appointment of a bank liquidator and the operation of bank insolvency under the Banking Act 2009, Pt 2: the Bank Insolvency (England and Wales) Rules 2009, SI 2009/356, rr 3(3)–(8), 253.
>
> See further, in relation to the application of this rule, with modifications, in respect of bank administration and applications for bank administration: the Bank Administration (England and Wales) Rules 2009, SI 2009/357, rr 58–61.

11.8 Proof altered after payment of dividend

(1) If after payment of dividend the amount claimed by a creditor in his proof is increased, the creditor is not entitled to disturb the distribution of the dividend; but he is entitled to be paid, out of any money for the time being available for the payment of any further dividend, any dividend or dividends which he has failed to receive.

(2) Any dividend or dividends payable under paragraph (1) shall be paid before the money there referred to is applied to the payment of any such further dividend.

(3) If, after a creditor's proof has been admitted, the proof is withdrawn or expunged, or the amount of it is reduced, the creditor is liable to repay to the [office-holder], for the credit of the insolvent estate, any amount overpaid by way of dividend.

NOTES

Initial Commencement

Specified date

Specified date: 29 December 1986: see r 0.1.

Amendment

Para (3): word "office-holder" in square brackets substituted by SI 2010/686, r 2, Sch 1, para 483.

Date in force: 6 April 2010: see SI 2010/686, r 1; for transitional provisions and further effect see rr 6(1), 7, Sch 4, para 1, Sch 5 thereto.

See Further

See further, in relation the application of this rule, with modifications, in respect of the procedure for the appointment of a bank liquidator and the operation of bank insolvency under the Banking Act 2009, Pt 2: the Bank Insolvency (England and Wales) Rules 2009, SI 2009/356, rr 3(3)–(8), 254.

See further, in relation to the application of this rule, with modifications, in respect of bank administration and applications for bank administration: the Bank Administration (England and Wales) Rules 2009, SI 2009/357, rr 58–61.

11.9 Secured creditors

(1) The following applies where a creditor re-values his security at a time when a dividend has been declared.

(2) If the revaluation results in a reduction of his unsecured claim ranking for dividend, the creditor shall [as soon as reasonably practicable] repay to the [office-holder], for the credit of the insolvent estate, any amount received by him as dividend in excess of that to which he would be entitled having regard to the revaluation of the security.

(3) If the revaluation results in an increase of his unsecured claim, the creditor is entitled to receive from the [office-holder], out of any money for the time being available for the payment of a further dividend, before any such further dividend is paid, any dividend or dividends which he has failed to receive, having regard to the revaluation of the security.

However, the creditor is not entitled to disturb any dividend declared (whether or not distributed) before the date of the revaluation.

NOTES

Initial Commencement

Specified date

Specified date: 29 December 1986: see r 0.1.

Amendment

Para (2): words "as soon as reasonably practicable" in square brackets substituted by SI 2009/642, rr 4, 5.

Date in force: 6 April 2009: see SI 2009/642, r 1; for transitional provisions see r 3 thereof.

Para (2): word "office-holder" in square brackets substituted by SI 2010/686, r 2, Sch 1, para 483.

Date in force: 6 April 2010: see SI 2010/686, r 1; for transitional provisions and further effect see rr 6(1), 7, Sch 4, para 1, Sch 5 thereto.

Para (3): word "office-holder" in square brackets substituted by SI 2010/686, r 2, Sch 1, para 483.

Date in force: 6 April 2010: see SI 2010/686, r 1; for transitional provisions and further effect see rr 6(1), 7, Sch 4, para 1, Sch 5 thereto.

See Further

See further, in relation the application of this rule, with modifications, in respect of the procedure for the appointment of a bank liquidator and the operation of bank insolvency under the Banking Act 2009, Pt 2: the Bank Insolvency (England and Wales) Rules 2009, SI 2009/356, rr 3(3)–(8), 255.

See further, in relation to the application of this rule, with modifications, in respect of bank administration and applications for bank administration: the Bank Administration (England and Wales) Rules 2009, SI 2009/357, rr 58–61.

11.10 Disqualification from dividend

If a creditor contravenes any provision of the Act or the Rules relating to the valuation of securities, the court may, on the application of the [office-holder], order that the creditor be wholly or partly disqualified from participation in any dividend.

NOTES

Initial Commencement

Specified date

Specified date: 29 December 1986: see r 0.1.

Amendment

Word "office-holder" in square brackets substituted by SI 2010/686, r 2, Sch 1, para 483.

Date in force: 6 April 2010: see SI 2010/686, r 1; for transitional provisions and further effect see rr 6(1), 7, Sch 4, para 1, Sch 5 thereto.

See Further

See further, in relation the application of this rule, with modifications, in respect of the procedure for the appointment of a bank liquidator and the operation of bank insolvency under the Banking Act 2009, Pt 2: the Bank Insolvency (England and Wales) Rules 2009, SI 2009/356, rr 3(3)–(8), 256.

See further, in relation to the application of this rule, with modifications, in respect of bank administration and applications for bank administration: the Bank Administration (England and Wales) Rules 2009, SI 2009/357, rr 58–61.

11.11 Assignment of right to dividend

(1) If a person entitled to a dividend gives notice to the [office-holder] that he wishes the dividend to be paid to another person, or that he has assigned his entitlement to another person, the [office-holder] shall pay the dividend to that other accordingly.

(2) A notice given under this Rule must specify the name and address of the person to whom payment is to be made.

NOTES

Initial Commencement

Specified date

Specified date: 29 December 1986: see r 0.1.

Amendment

Para (1): word "office-holder" in square brackets in both places it occurs substituted by SI 2010/686, r 2, Sch 1, para 483.

Date in force: 6 April 2010: see SI 2010/686, r 1; for transitional provisions and further effect see rr 6(1), 7, Sch 4, para 1, Sch 5 thereto.

See Further

See further, in relation the application of this rule, with modifications, in respect of the procedure for the appointment of a bank liquidator and the operation of bank insolvency under the Banking Act 2009, Pt 2: the Bank Insolvency (England and Wales) Rules 2009, SI 2009/356, rr 3(3)–(8), 257.

See further, in relation to the application of this rule, with modifications, in respect of bank administration and applications for bank administration: the Bank Administration (England and Wales) Rules 2009, SI 2009/357, rr 58–61.

11.12 Preferential creditors

(1) Subject as follows, the Rules in this Part apply with respect to any distribution made in the insolvency to preferential creditors, with such adaptations as are appropriate considering that such creditors are of a limited class.

(2) The notice by the [office-holder] under Rule 11.2, where a dividend is to be declared for preferential creditors, need only be given to those creditors in whose case he has reason to believe that their debts are preferential [and [notice] of the intended dividend need only be [gazetted] if the [office-holder] thinks fit].

NOTES

Initial Commencement

Specified date

Specified date: 29 December 1986: see r 0.1.

Amendment

Para (2): word "office-holder" in square brackets in both places it occurs substituted by SI 2010/686, r 2, Sch 1, para 483.

Date in force: 6 April 2010: see SI 2010/686, r 1; for transitional provisions and further effect see rr 6(1), 7, Sch 4, para 1, Sch 5 thereto.

Para (2): words from "and" to "thinks fit" in square brackets inserted by SI 1987/1919, r 3(1), Schedule, Pt 1, para 140.

Para (2): word "notice" in square brackets substituted by SI 2010/686, r 2, Sch 1, para 490(1), (2)(a).

Date in force: 6 April 2010: see SI 2010/686, r 1; for transitional provisions and further effect see rr 6(1), 7, Sch 4, para 1, Sch 5 thereto.

Para (2): word "gazetted" in square brackets substituted by SI 2010/686, r 2, Sch 1, para 490(1), (2)(b).

Date in force: 6 April 2010: see SI 2010/686, r 1; for transitional provisions and further effect see rr 6(1), 7, Sch 4, para 1, Sch 5 thereto.

See Further

See further, in relation the application of this rule, with modifications, in respect of the procedure for the appointment of a bank liquidator and the operation of bank insolvency under the Banking Act 2009, Pt 2: the Bank Insolvency (England and Wales) Rules 2009, SI 2009/356, rr 3(3)–(8), 258.

See further, in relation to the application of this rule, with modifications, in respect of bank administration and applications for bank administration: the Bank Administration (England and Wales) Rules 2009, SI 2009/357, rr 58–61.

11.13 Debt payable at future time

(1) Where a creditor has proved for a debt of which payment is not due at the date of the declaration of dividend, he is entitled to dividend equally with other creditors, but subject as follows.

[(2) For the purpose of dividend (and no other purpose) the amount of the creditor's admitted proof (or, if a distribution has previously been made to him, the amount remaining outstanding in respect of his admitted proof) shall be reduced by applying the following formula—]

$X / 1.05n$

[where—
- (a) "X" is the value of the admitted proof; and
- (b) "n" is the period beginning with the relevant date and ending with the date on which the payment of the creditor's debt would otherwise be due expressed in years and months in a decimalised form.

(3) In paragraph (2) "relevant date" means—
- (a) in the case of a winding up which was not immediately preceded by an administration, the date that the company went into liquidation;
- (b) in the case of a winding up which was immediately preceded by an administration, the date that the company entered administration; and
- (c) in the case of a bankruptcy, the date of the bankruptcy order.]

(3) . . .

NOTES

Initial Commencement

Specified date

Specified date: 29 December 1986: see r 0.1.

Amendment

Para (2) and first para (3): substituted, for para (2) as originally enacted, by SI 2005/527, r 43(1).
Date in force: 1 April 2005: see SI 2005/527, r 1(2); for transitional provisions in relation to any case where a company has entered administration or gone into liquidation, or a bankruptcy order has been made before that date see r 3(1) thereof.
Second para (3): revoked by SI 2005/527, r 43(2).
Date in force: 1 April 2005: see SI 2005/527, r 1(2); for transitional provisions in relation to any case where a company has entered administration or gone into liquidation, or a bankruptcy order has been made before that date see r 3(1) thereof.

See Further

See further, in relation the application of this rule, with modifications, in respect of the procedure for the appointment of a bank liquidator and the operation of bank insolvency under the Banking Act 2009, Pt 2: the Bank Insolvency (England and Wales) Rules 2009, SI 2009/356, rr 3(3)–(8), 259.
See further, in relation to the application of this rule, with modifications, in respect of bank administration and applications for bank administration: the Bank Administration (England and Wales) Rules 2009, SI 2009/357, rr 58–61.

PART 12

MISCELLANEOUS AND GENERAL

12.1 Power of Secretary of State to regulate certain matters

(1) Pursuant to paragraph 27 of Schedule 8 to the Act, and paragraph 30 of Schedule 9 to the Act, the Secretary of State may [, subject to the Act and the Rules, make regulations with respect to any matter provided for in the Rules as relates to the carrying out of the functions of a liquidator, provisional liquidator, administrator or

administrative receiver of a company, an interim receiver appointed under section 286, of the official receiver while acting as receiver or manager under section 287 or of a trustee of a bankrupt's estate, including, without prejudice to the generality of the foregoing, provision] with respect to the following matters arising in companies winding up and individual bankruptcy—

(a) the preparation and keeping by liquidators, trustees, provisional liquidators, interim receivers and the official receiver, of books, accounts and other records, and their production to such persons as may be authorised or required to inspect them;

(b) the auditing of liquidators' and trustees' accounts;

(c) the manner in which liquidators and trustees are to act in relation to the insolvent company's or bankrupt's books, papers and other records, and the manner of their disposal by the responsible [office-holder] or others;

(d) the supply—
 (i) in company insolvency, by the liquidator to creditors and members of the company, contributories in its winding up and the liquidation committee, and
 (ii) in [bankruptcy], by the trustee to creditors and the creditors' committee,

of copies of documents relating to the insolvency and the affairs of the insolvent company or individual (on payment, in such cases as may be specified by the regulations, of the specified fee);

(e) the manner in which insolvent estates are to be distributed by liquidators and trustees, including provision with respect to unclaimed funds and dividends;

(f) the manner in which moneys coming into the hands of a liquidator or trustee in the course of his administration are to be handled and. . . invested, and the payment of interest on sums which, in pursuance of regulations made by virtue of this sub-paragraph, have been paid into the Insolvency Services Account;

(g) the amount (or the manner of determining the amount) to be paid to the official receiver by way of remuneration when acting as provisional liquidator, liquidator, interim receiver or trustee.

(2) Any reference in paragraph (1) to a trustee includes a reference to the official receiver when acting as receiver and manager under section 287.

(3) Regulations made pursuant to paragraph (1) may—

(a) confer a discretion on the court;
(b) make non-compliance with any of the regulations a criminal offence;
(c) make different provision for different cases, including different provision for different areas[; and
(d) contain such incidental, supplemental and transitional provisions as may appear to the Secretary of State necessary or expedient].

NOTES

Initial Commencement

Specified date

Specified date: 29 December 1986: see r 0.1.

Amendment

Para (1): words from ", subject to the Act" to "the foregoing, provision" in square brackets substituted by SI 1987/1919, r 3(1), Schedule, Part 1, para 142(1).

Para (1): in sub-para (c) word "office-holder" in square brackets substituted by SI 2010/686, r 2, Sch 1, para 491.

Insolvency Rules 1986, reg 12.1

Date in force: 6 April 2010: see SI 2010/686, r 1; for transitional provisions and further effect see rr 6(1), 7, Sch 4, para 1, Sch 5 thereto.
Para (1): in sub-para (d)(ii) word "bankruptcy" in square brackets substituted by SI 2009/642, rr 4, 72.
Date in force: 6 April 2009: see SI 2009/642, r 1.
Para (1): in sub-para (f) words omitted revoked by SI 2001/763, r 2.
Date in force: 2 April 2001: see SI 2001/763, r 1.
Para (3): sub-para (d) inserted by SI 1987/1919, r 3(1), Schedule, Part 1, para 142(2).

See Further

See further, in relation to the application of this rule, with modifications, in respect of bank administration and applications for bank administration: the Bank Administration (England and Wales) Rules 2009, SI 2009/357, rr 58–61.

Subordinate Legislation

Insolvency (Amendment) Regulations 2000, SI 2000/485.
Insolvency (Amendment) Regulations 2001, SI 2001/762.
Insolvency (Amendment) Regulations 2004, SI 2004/472.
Insolvency (Amendment) Regulations 2005, SI 2005/512.
Insolvency (Amendment) Regulations 2008, SI 2008/670.
Insolvency (Amendment) Regulations 2009, SI 2009/482 (made under para (1)(g)).

12.2 Costs, expenses, etc

[(1)] All fees, costs, charges and other expenses incurred in the course of winding up[, administration] or bankruptcy proceedings are to be regarded as expenses of the winding up [or the administration] or, as the case may be, of the bankruptcy.

[(2) The costs associated with the prescribed part shall be paid out of the prescribed part.]

NOTES

Initial Commencement

Specified date

Specified date: 29 December 1986: see r 0.1.

Amendment

Para (1): numbered as such by SI 2003/1730, r 12, Sch 1, Pt 9, para 61(b).
Date in force: 15 September 2003: see SI 2003/1730, r 1(2).
Para (1): words ", administration" and "or the administration" in square brackets inserted by SI 2003/1730, r 12, Sch 1, Pt 9, para 61(a).
Date in force: 15 September 2003: see SI 2003/1730, r 1(2).
Para (2): inserted by SI 2003/1730, r 12, Sch 1, Pt 9, para 61(b).
Date in force: 15 September 2003: see SI 2003/1730, r 1(2).

See Further

See further, in relation to the application of this rule, with modifications, in respect of bank administration and applications for bank administration: the Bank Administration (England and Wales) Rules 2009, SI 2009/357, rr 58–61.

12.3 Provable debts

(1) Subject as follows, [in administration, winding up and bankruptcy], all claims by creditors are provable as debts against the company or, as the case may be, the bankrupt, whether they are present or future, certain or contingent, ascertained or sounding only in damages.

(2) The following are not provable—
    (a)   in bankruptcy, any fine imposed for an offence, and any obligation [(other than an obligation to pay a lump sum or to pay costs)] arising

under an order made in family < . . . > proceedings [or [any obligation arising] under a maintenance assessment made under the Child Support Act 1991];

(b) in [administration,] winding up or bankruptcy, any obligation arising under a confiscation order made under section 1 of the Drug Trafficking Offences Act 1986 [or section 1 of the Criminal Justice (Scotland) Act 1987] [or section 71 of the Criminal Justice Act 1988] [or under Parts 2, 3 or 4 of the Proceeds of Crime Act 2002].

"Fine" < . . . > and "family proceedings" have the meanings given by section 281(8) of the Act (which applies the Magistrates' Courts Act 1980 and the Matrimonial and Family Proceedings Act 1984.)

[(2A) The following are not provable except at a time when all other claims of creditors in the insolvency proceedings (other than any of a kind mentioned in this paragraph) have been paid in full with interest under section 189(2)[, Rule 2.88] or, as the case may be, section 328(4)—

[(a) in [an administration,] a winding up or a bankruptcy, any claim arising by virtue of section 382(1)(a) of the Financial Services and Markets Act 2000, not being a claim also arising by virtue of section 382(1)(b) of that Act;]

(c) in [an administration or] a winding up, any claim which by virtue of the Act or any other enactment is a claim the payment of which in a bankruptcy[, an administration] or a winding up is to be postponed.]

(3) Nothing in this Rule prejudices any enactment or rule of law under which a particular kind of debt is not provable, whether on grounds of public policy or otherwise.

NOTES

Initial Commencement

Specified date

Specified date: 29 December 1986: see r 0.1.

Amendment

Para (1): words "in administration, winding up and bankruptcy" in square brackets substituted by SI 2003/1730, r 12, Sch 1, Pt 9, para 62(a).
Date in force: 15 September 2003: see SI 2003/1730, r 1(2).
Para (2): in sub-para (a) words "(other than an obligation to pay a lump sum or to pay costs)" in square brackets inserted by SI 2005/527, r 44.
Date in force: 1 April 2005: see SI 2005/527, r 1(2); for transitional provisions in relation to any case where a company has entered administration or gone into liquidation, or a bankruptcy order has been made before that date see r 3(1) thereof.
Para (2): in sub-para (a) words omitted revoked by SI 1993/602, r 3, Schedule, para 2.
Para (2): in sub-para (a) words in square brackets beginning with the word "or" substituted by SI 1993/602, r 3, Schedule, para 2.
Para (2): in sub-para (a) words "any obligation arising" in square brackets inserted by SI 2005/527, r 44.
Date in force: 1 April 2005: see SI 2005/527, r 1(2); for transitional provisions in relation to any case where a company has entered administration or gone into liquidation, or a bankruptcy order has been made before that date see r 3(1) thereof.
Para (2): in sub-para (b) words "administration," and "or under Parts 2, 3 or 4 of the Proceeds of Crime Act 2002" in square brackets inserted by SI 2003/1730, r 12, Sch 1, Pt 9, para 62(b).
Date in force: 15 September 2003: see SI 2003/1730, r 1(2).
Para (2): in sub-para (b) words "or section 1 of the Criminal Justice (Scotland) Act 1987" in square brackets inserted by SI 1987/1919, r 3(1), Schedule, Pt 1, para 143(1).
Para (2): in sub-para (b) words "or section 71 of the Criminal Justice Act 1988" in square brackets inserted by SI 1989/397, r 3(1), Schedule, para 2.

Para (2): words omitted revoked by SI 1993/602, r 3, Schedule, para 3.

Para (2A): inserted by SI 1987/1919, r 3(1), Schedule, Pt 1, para 143(2).

Para (2A): words ", Rule 2.88" in square brackets inserted by SI 2003/1730, r 12, Sch 1, Pt 9, para 62(c).
  Date in force: 15 September 2003: see SI 2003/1730, r 1(2).

Para (2A): sub-para (a) substituted, for sub-paras (a), (b) as originally enacted, by SI 2001/3649, art 380.
  Date in force: 1 December 2001: see SI 2001/3649, art 1.

Para (2A): in sub-para (a) words "an administration," in square brackets inserted by SI 2003/1730, r 12, Sch 1, Pt 9, para 62(d).
  Date in force: 15 September 2003: see SI 2003/1730, r 1(2).

Para (2A): in sub-para (c) words "an administration or" and ", an administration" in square brackets inserted by SI 2003/1730, r 12, Sch 1, Pt 9, para 62(e).
  Date in force: 15 September 2003: see SI 2003/1730, r 1(2).

See Further

See further, in relation to the application of this rule, with modifications, in respect of bank administration and applications for bank administration: the Bank Administration (England and Wales) Rules 2009, SI 2009/357, rr 58–61.

12.4 . . .

. . .

NOTES

Amendment

Revoked by SI 2010/686, r 5.
  Date in force: 6 April 2010: see SI 2010/686, r 1; for transitional provisions and further effect see rr 6(1), 7, Sch 4, para 1, Sch 5 thereto.

[12.4A . . .]

. . .

NOTES

Amendment

Revoked by SI 2010/686, r 5.
  Date in force: 6 April 2010: see SI 2010/686, r 1; for transitional provisions and further effect see rr 6(1), 7, Sch 4, para 1, Sch 5 thereto.

12.5 . . .

. . .

NOTES

Amendment

Revoked by SI 2010/686, r 5.
  Date in force: 6 April 2010: see SI 2010/686, r 1; for transitional provisions and further effect see rr 6(1), 7, Sch 4, para 1, Sch 5 thereto.

12.6 . . .

. . .

NOTES

Amendment

Revoked by SI 2010/686, r 5.
Date in force: 6 April 2010: see SI 2010/686, r 1; for transitional provisions and further effect see rr 6(1), 7, Sch 4, para 1, Sch 5 thereto.

12.7 ...

...

NOTES

Amendment

Revoked by SI 2010/686, r 5.
Date in force: 6 April 2010: see SI 2010/686, r 1; for transitional provisions and further effect see rr 6(1), 7, Sch 4, para 1, Sch 5 thereto.

12.8 ...

...

NOTES

Amendment

Revoked by SI 2010/686, r 5.
Date in force: 6 April 2010: see SI 2010/686, r 1; for transitional provisions and further effect see rr 6(1), 7, Sch 4, para 1, Sch 5 thereto.

12.9 ...

...

NOTES

Amendment

Revoked by SI 2010/686, r 5.
Date in force: 6 April 2010: see SI 2010/686, r 1; for transitional provisions and further effect see rr 6(1), 7, Sch 4, para 1, Sch 5 thereto.

12.10 ...

...

NOTES

Amendment

Revoked by SI 2010/686, r 5.
Date in force: 6 April 2010: see SI 2010/686, r 1; for transitional provisions and further effect see rr 6(1), 7, Sch 4, para 1, Sch 5 thereto.

12.11 ...

...

Insolvency Rules 1986, reg 12.11

NOTES

Amendment

Revoked by SI 2010/686, r 5.
Date in force: 6 April 2010: see SI 2010/686, r 1; for transitional provisions and further effect see rr 6(1), 7, Sch 4, para 1, Sch 5 thereto.

12.12 ...

...

NOTES

Amendment

Revoked by SI 2010/686, r 5.
Date in force: 6 April 2010: see SI 2010/686, r 1; for transitional provisions and further effect see rr 6(1), 7, Sch 4, para 1, Sch 5 thereto.

12.13 ...

...

NOTES

Amendment

Revoked by SI 2010/686, r 5.
Date in force: 6 April 2010: see SI 2010/686, r 1; for transitional provisions and further effect see rr 6(1), 7, Sch 4, para 1, Sch 5 thereto.

12.14 ...

...

NOTES

Amendment

Revoked by SI 2010/686, r 5.
Date in force: 6 April 2010: see SI 2010/686, r 1; for transitional provisions and further effect see rr 6(1), 7, Sch 4, para 1, Sch 5 thereto.

12.15 ...

...

NOTES

Amendment

Revoked by SI 2010/686, r 5.
Date in force: 6 April 2010: see SI 2010/686, r 1; for transitional provisions and further effect see rr 6(1), 7, Sch 4, para 1, Sch 5 thereto.

[12.15A ...]

...

NOTES

Amendment

Revoked by SI 2010/686, r 5.
Date in force: 6 April 2010: see SI 2010/686, r 1; for transitional provisions and further effect see rr 6(1), 7, Sch 4, para 1, Sch 5 thereto.

12.16 . . .

. . .

NOTES

Amendment

Revoked by SI 2010/686, r 5.
Date in force: 6 April 2010: see SI 2010/686, r 1; for transitional provisions and further effect see rr 6(1), 7, Sch 4, para 1, Sch 5 thereto.

12.17 . . .

. . .

NOTES

Amendment

Revoked by SI 2010/686, r 5.
Date in force: 6 April 2010: see SI 2010/686, r 1; for transitional provisions and further effect see rr 6(1), 7, Sch 4, para 1, Sch 5 thereto.

12.18 False claim of status as creditor, etc

(1) Where the Rules provide for creditors, members of a company or contributories in a company's winding up a right to inspect any documents, whether on the court's file or in the hands of [an office-holder] or other person, it is an offence for a person, with the intention of obtaining a sight of documents which he has not under the Rules any right to inspect, falsely to claim a status which would entitle him to inspect them.

(2) A person guilty of an offence under this Rule is liable to imprisonment or a fine, or both.

NOTES

Initial Commencement

Specified date

Specified date: 29 December 1986: see r 0.1.

Amendment

Para (1): words "an office-holder" in square brackets substituted by SI 2010/686, r 2, Sch 1, para 492.
Date in force: 6 April 2010: see SI 2010/686, r 1; for transitional provisions and further effect see rr 6(1), 7, Sch 4, para 1, Sch 5 thereto.

See Further

See further, in relation the application of this rule, with modifications, in respect of the procedure for the appointment of a bank liquidator and the operation of bank insolvency under the Banking Act 2009, Pt 2: the Bank Insolvency (England and Wales) Rules 2009, SI 2009/356, rr 3(3)–(8), 278.

See further, in relation to the application of this rule, with modifications, in respect of bank administration and applications for bank administration: the Bank Administration (England and Wales) Rules 2009, SI 2009/357, rr 58–61.

12.19 ...
...

NOTES

Amendment

Revoked by SI 2010/686, r 5.
Date in force: 6 April 2010: see SI 2010/686, r 1; for transitional provisions and further effect see rr 6(1), 7, Sch 4, para 1, Sch 5 thereto.

12.20 ...
...

NOTES

Amendment

Revoked by SI 2010/686, r 5.
Date in force: 6 April 2010: see SI 2010/686, r 1; for transitional provisions and further effect see rr 6(1), 7, Sch 4, para 1, Sch 5 thereto.

12.21 Punishment of offences

(1) Schedule 5 to the Rules has effect with respect to the way in which contraventions of the Rules are punishable on conviction.

(2) In relation to an offence under a provision of the Rules specified in the first column of the Schedule (the general nature of the offence being described in the second column), the third column shows whether the offence is punishable on conviction on indictment, or on summary conviction, or either in the one way or the other.

(3) The fourth column shows, in relation to an offence, the maximum punishment by way of fine or imprisonment which may be imposed on a person convicted of the offence in the way specified in relation to it in the third column (that is to say, on indictment or summarily), a reference to a period of years or months being to a term of imprisonment of that duration.

(4) The fifth column shows (in relation to an offence for which there is an entry in that column) that a person convicted of the offence after continued contravention is liable to a daily default fine; that is to say, he is liable on a second or subsequent conviction of the offence to the fine specified in that column for each day on which the contravention is continued (instead of the penalty specified for the offence in the fourth column of the Schedule).

(5) Section 431 (summary proceedings), as it applies to England and Wales, has effect in relation to offences under the Rules as to offences under the Act.

NOTES

Initial Commencement

Specified date

Specified date: 29 December 1986: see r 0.1.

See Further

See further, in relation the application of this rule, with modifications, in respect of the procedure for the appointment of a bank liquidator and the operation of bank insolvency under the Banking Act 2009, Pt 2: the Bank Insolvency (England and Wales) Rules 2009, SI 2009/356, rr 3(3)–(8), 281.

See further, in relation to the application of this rule, with modifications, in respect of bank administration and applications for bank administration: the Bank Administration (England and Wales) Rules 2009, SI 2009/357, rr 58–61.

[12.22 . . .]
[. . .]

NOTES

Amendment

Inserted by SI 2003/1730, r 12, Sch 1, Pt 9, para 63.
Date in force: 15 September 2003: see SI 2003/1730, r 1(2).
Revoked by SI 2010/686, r 5.
Date in force: 6 April 2010: see SI 2010/686, r 1; for transitional provisions and further effect see rr 6(1), 7, Sch 4, para 1, Sch 5 thereto.

[PART 12A

PROVISIONS OF GENERAL EFFECT]

NOTES

Amendment

Inserted by SI 2010/686, r 4, Sch 3.
Date in force: 6 April 2010: see SI 2010/686, r 1; for transitional provisions and further effect see rr 6(1), 7, Sch 4, paras 1, 2(1)(c), 5(1), (2), Sch 5 thereto.

[CHAPTER 1

THE GIVING OF NOTICE AND THE SUPPLY OF DOCUMENTS—GENERAL]

NOTES

Amendment

Inserted by SI 2010/686, r 4, Sch 3.
Date in force: 6 April 2010: see SI 2010/686, r 1; for transitional provisions and further effect see rr 6(1), 7, Sch 4, para 1, Sch 5 thereto.

[12A.1 Application]

[(1) Subject to paragraphs (2) and (3), this Chapter applies where a notice or other document is required to be given, delivered or sent under the Act or the Rules by any person, including an office-holder.

(2) This Chapter does not apply to the service of—
  (a) any petition or application to the court;
  (b) any evidence in support of that petition or application; or
  (c) any order of the court.

(3) This Chapter does not apply to the submission of documents to the registrar of companies.]

Insolvency Rules 1986, reg 12A.1

NOTES

Amendment

Inserted by SI 2010/686, r 4, Sch 3.
Date in force: 6 April 2010: see SI 2010/686, r 1; for transitional provisions and further effect see rr 6(1), 7, Sch 4, para 1, Sch 5 thereto.

[12A.2 Personal delivery of documents]

[Personal delivery of a notice or other document is permissible in any case.]

NOTES

Amendment

Inserted by SI 2010/686, r 4, Sch 3.
Date in force: 6 April 2010: see SI 2010/686, r 1; for transitional provisions and further effect see rr 6(1), 7, Sch 4, para 1, Sch 5 thereto.

[12A.3 Postal delivery of documents]

[Unless in any particular case some other form of delivery is required by the Act, the Rules or an order of the court, a notice or other document may be sent by post in accordance with the rules for postal service in CPR Part 6 and sending by such means has effect as specified in those rules.]

NOTES

Amendment

Inserted by SI 2010/686, r 4, Sch 3.
Date in force: 6 April 2010: see SI 2010/686, r 1; for transitional provisions and further effect see rr 6(1), 7, Sch 4, para 1, Sch 5 thereto.

[12A.4 Non-receipt of notice of meeting]

[Where in accordance with the Act or the Rules, a meeting of creditors or other persons is summoned by notice, the meeting is presumed to have been duly summoned and held, notwithstanding that not all those to whom the notice is to be given have received it.]

NOTES

Amendment

Inserted by SI 2010/686, r 4, Sch 3.
Date in force: 6 April 2010: see SI 2010/686, r 1; for transitional provisions and further effect see rr 6(1), 7, Sch 4, para 1, Sch 5 thereto.

[12A.5 Notice etc to solicitors]

[Where under the Act or the Rules a notice or other document is required or authorised to be given, delivered or sent to a person, it may be given, delivered or sent instead to a solicitor authorised to accept delivery on that person's behalf.]

NOTES

Amendment

Inserted by SI 2010/686, r 4, Sch 3.

Date in force: 6 April 2010: see SI 2010/686, r 1; for transitional provisions and further effect see rr 6(1), 7, Sch 4, para 1, Sch 5 thereto.

[CHAPTER 2

THE GIVING OF NOTICE AND THE SUPPLY OF DOCUMENTS BY OR TO OFFICE-HOLDERS ETC]

NOTES

Amendment

Inserted by SI 2010/686, r 4, Sch 3.
Date in force: 6 April 2010: see SI 2010/686, r 1; for transitional provisions and further effect see rr 6(1), 7, Sch 4, paras 1, 2(1)(c), Sch 5 thereto.

[12A.6 Application]
[(1) Subject to paragraphs (2) to (4), this Chapter applies where a notice or other document is required to be given, delivered or sent under the Act or the Rules.
(2) This Chapter does not apply to the submission of documents to the registrar of companies.
(3) Rules 12A.10 to 12A.13 do not apply to—
(a) the filing of any notice or other document with the court; or
(b) the service of a statutory demand.]

NOTES

Amendment

Inserted by SI 2010/686, r 4, Sch 3.
Date in force: 6 April 2010: see SI 2010/686, r 1; for transitional provisions and further effect see rr 6(1), 7, Sch 4, paras 1, 2(1)(c), Sch 5 thereto.

[12A.7 The form of notices and other documents]
[Subject to any order of the court, any notice or other document required to be given, delivered or sent must be in writing and where electronic delivery is permitted a notice or other document in electronic form is treated as being in writing if a copy of it is capable of being produced in a legible form.]

NOTES

Amendment

Inserted by SI 2010/686, r 4, Sch 3.
Date in force: 6 April 2010: see SI 2010/686, r 1; for transitional provisions and further effect see rr 6(1), 7, Sch 4, paras 1, 2(1)(c), Sch 5 thereto.

[12A.8 Proof of sending etc]
[(1) Where in any insolvency proceedings a notice or other document is required to be given, delivered or sent by the office-holder, the giving, delivering or sending of it may be proved by means of a certificate that the notice or other document was duly given, delivered or sent.
(2) In the case of the official receiver the certificate may be given by—
(a) the official receiver; or
(b) a member of the official receiver's staff.

(3) In the case of a responsible insolvency practitioner the certificate may be given by—
  (a) the practitioner;
  (b) the practitioner's solicitor;
  (c) a partner or an employee of either of them.
(4) In the case of a notice or other document to be given, delivered or sent by a person other than the official receiver or a responsible insolvency practitioner, the giving, delivering or sending of it may be proved by means of a certificate by that person—
  (a) that the notice or document was given, delivered or sent by that person, or
  (b) that another person (named in the certificate) was instructed to give, deliver or send it.
(5) A certificate under this Rule may be endorsed on a copy or specimen of the notice or document to which it relates.]

NOTES

Amendment
  Inserted by SI 2010/686, r 4, Sch 3.
    Date in force: 6 April 2010: see SI 2010/686, r 1; for transitional provisions and further effect see rr 6(1), 7, Sch 4, paras 1, 2(1)(c), Sch 5 thereto.

[12A.9 Authentication]
[(1) A document or information given, delivered or sent in hard copy form is sufficiently authenticated if it is signed by the person sending or supplying it.
(2) A document or information given, delivered or sent in electronic form is sufficiently authenticated—
  (a) if the identity of the sender is confirmed in a manner specified by the recipient, or
  (b) where no such manner has been specified by the recipient, if the communication contains or is accompanied by a statement of the identity of the sender and the recipient has no reason to doubt the truth of that statement.]

NOTES

Amendment
  Inserted by SI 2010/686, r 4, Sch 3.
    Date in force: 6 April 2010: see SI 2010/686, r 1; for transitional provisions and further effect see rr 6(1), 7, Sch 4, paras 1, 2(1)(c), Sch 5 thereto.

[12A.10 Electronic delivery in insolvency proceedings—general]
[(1) Unless in any particular case some other form of delivery is required by the Act or the Rules or an order of the court and subject to paragraph (3), a notice or other document may be given, delivered or sent by electronic means provided that the intended recipient of the notice or other document has—
  (a) consented (whether in the specific case or generally) to electronic delivery (and has not revoked that consent); and
  (b) provided an electronic address for delivery.
(2) In the absence of evidence to the contrary, a notice or other document is presumed to have been delivered where—
  (a) the sender can produce a copy of the electronic message which—

(i) contained the notice or other document, or to which the notice or other document was attached, and
(ii) shows the time and date the message was sent; and
(b) that electronic message contains the address supplied under paragraph (1)(b).

(3) A message sent electronically is deemed to have been delivered to the recipient no later than 9.00am on the next business day after it was sent.]

NOTES

Amendment

Inserted by SI 2010/686, r 4, Sch 3.
Date in force: 6 April 2010: see SI 2010/686, r 1; for transitional provisions and further effect see rr 6(1), 7, Sch 4, paras 1, 2(1)(c), Sch 5 thereto.

[12A.11 Electronic delivery by office-holders]

[(1) Where an office-holder gives, sends or delivers a notice or other document to any person by electronic means, the notice or document must contain or be accompanied by a statement that the recipient may request a hard copy of the notice or document and specifying a telephone number, e-mail address and postal address which may be used to request a hard copy.

(2) Where a hard copy of the notice or other document is requested, it must be sent within 5 business days of receipt of the request by the office-holder.

(3) An office-holder must not require a person making a request under paragraph (2) to pay a fee for the supply of the document.]

NOTES

Amendment

Inserted by SI 2010/686, r 4, Sch 3.
Date in force: 6 April 2010: see SI 2010/686, r 1; for transitional provisions and further effect see rr 6(1), 7, Sch 4, paras 1, 2(1)(c), Sch 5 thereto.

[12A.12 Use of websites by office-holder]

[(1) This Rule applies for the purposes of sections 246B and 379B.

(2) An office-holder required to give, deliver or send a document to any person may (other than in a case where personal service is required) satisfy that requirement by sending that person a notice—
(a) stating that the document is available for viewing and downloading on a website;
(b) specifying the address of that website together with any password necessary to view and download the document from that site; and
(c) containing a statement that the person to whom the notice is given, delivered or sent may request a hard copy of the document and specifying a telephone number, e-mail address and postal address which may be used to request a hard copy.

(3) Where a notice to which this Rule applies is sent, the document to which it relates must—
(a) be available on the website for a period of not less than 3 months after the date on which the notice is sent; and
(b) must be in such a format as to enable it to be downloaded from the website within a reasonable time of an electronic request being made for it to be downloaded.

(4) Where a hard copy of the document is requested it must be sent within 5 business days of the receipt of the request by the office-holder.

(5) An office-holder must not require a person making a request under paragraph (4) to pay a fee for the supply of the document.

(6) Where a document is given, delivered or sent to a person by means of a website in accordance with this Rule, it is deemed to have been delivered—
- (a) when the document was first made available on the website, or
- (b) if later, when the notice under paragraph (2) was delivered to that person.]

NOTES

Amendment

Inserted by SI 2010/686, r 4, Sch 3.
Date in force: 6 April 2010: see SI 2010/686, r 1; for transitional provisions and further effect see rr 6(1), 7, Sch 4, paras 1, 2(1)(c), Sch 5 thereto.

[12A.13 Special provision on account of expense as to website use]

[(1) Where the court is satisfied that the expense of sending notices in accordance with Rule 12A.12 would, on account of the number of persons entitled to receive them, be disproportionate to the benefit of sending notices in accordance with that Rule, it may order that the requirement to give, deliver or send a relevant document to any person may (other than in a case where personal service is required) be satisfied by the office-holder sending each of those persons a notice—
- (a) stating that all relevant documents will be made available for viewing and downloading on a website;
- (b) specifying the address of that website together with any password necessary to view and download a relevant document from that site; and
- (c) containing a statement that the person to whom the notice is given, delivered or sent may at any time request that hard copies of all, or specific, relevant documents are sent to that person, and specifying a telephone number, e-mail address and postal address which may be used to make that request.

(2) A document to which this Rule relates must—
- (a) be available on the website for a period of not less than 12 months from the date when it was first made available on the website or, if later, from the date upon which the notice was sent, and
- (b) must be in such a format as to enable it to be downloaded from the website within a reasonable time of an electronic request being made for it to be downloaded.

(3) Where hard copies of relevant documents have been requested, they must be sent by the office-holder—
- (a) within 5 business days of the receipt by the office-holder of the request to be sent hard copies, in the case of relevant documents first appearing on the website before the request was received, or
- (b) within 5 business days from the date a relevant document first appears on the website, in all other cases.

(4) An office-holder must not require a person making a request under paragraph (3) to pay a fee for the supply of the document.

(5) Where a relevant document is given, delivered or sent to a person by means of a website in accordance with this Rule, it is deemed to have been delivered—
- (a) when the relevant document was first made available on the website, or
- (b) if later, when the notice under paragraph (1) was delivered to that person.

(6) In this Rule a relevant document means any document which the office-holder is first required to give, deliver or send to any person after the court has made an order under paragraph (1).]

NOTES

Amendment

Inserted by SI 2010/686, r 4, Sch 3.
Date in force: 6 April 2010: see SI 2010/686, r 1; for transitional provisions and further effect see rr 6(1), 7, Sch 4, paras 1, 2(1)(c), Sch 5 thereto.

[12A.14 Electronic delivery of insolvency proceedings to courts]

[(1) Except where paragraph (2) applies or the requirements of paragraph (3) are met, no petition, application, notice or other document may be delivered or made to a court by electronic means.

(2) This paragraph applies where electronic delivery of documents to a court is permitted by another Rule.

(3) The requirements of this paragraph are—
   (a) the court provides an electronic working scheme for the proceedings to which the document relates; and
   (b) the electronic communication is—
      (i) delivered and authenticated in a form which complies with the requirements of the scheme;
      (ii) sent to the electronic address provided by the court for electronic delivery of those proceedings; and
      (iii) accompanied by any payment due to the court in respect of those proceedings made in a manner which complies with the requirements of the scheme.

(4) In this Rule "an electronic working scheme" means a scheme permitting insolvency proceedings to be delivered electronically to the court set out in a practice direction.

(5) Under paragraph (3) an electronic communication is to be treated as delivered to the court at the time it is recorded by the court as having been received.]

NOTES

Amendment

Inserted by SI 2010/686, r 4, Sch 3.
Date in force: 6 April 2010: see SI 2010/686, r 1; for transitional provisions and further effect see rr 6(1), 7, Sch 4, paras 1, 2(1)(c), Sch 5 thereto.

[12A.15 Notice etc to joint office-holders]

[Where there are joint office-holders in insolvency proceedings, delivery of a document to one of them is to be treated as delivery to all of them.]

NOTES

Amendment

Inserted by SI 2010/686, r 4, Sch 3.
Date in force: 6 April 2010: see SI 2010/686, r 1; for transitional provisions and further effect see rr 6(1), 7, Sch 4, para 1, Sch 5 thereto.

[CHAPTER 3
SERVICE OF COURT DOCUMENTS]

NOTES

Amendment

Inserted by SI 2010/686, r 4, Sch 3.
Date in force: 6 April 2010: see SI 2010/686, r 1; for transitional provisions and further effect see rr 6(1), 7, Sch 4, para 1, Sch 5 thereto.

[12A.16 Application]

[(1) Subject to paragraph (2), this Chapter applies in relation to the service of—
- (a) petitions,
- (b) applications,
- (c) documents relating to petitions or applications, and
- (d) court orders,

which are required to be served by any provision of the Act or the Rules ("court documents").

(2) Rules 12A.17 to 12A.19 do not apply to the service of—
- (a) a winding-up petition,
- (b) a bankruptcy petition,
- (c) any document relating to such a petition, or
- (d) an administration, winding-up or bankruptcy order.

(3) For the purpose of the application by this Chapter of CPR Part 6 to the service of documents in insolvency proceedings—
- (a) an application commencing insolvency proceedings (including a winding-up petition, a bankruptcy petition or an administration application), or
- (b) an application within insolvency proceedings against a respondent,

is to be treated as a claim form.]

NOTES

Amendment

Inserted by SI 2010/686, r 4, Sch 3.
Date in force: 6 April 2010: see SI 2010/686, r 1; for transitional provisions and further effect see rr 6(1), 7, Sch 4, para 1, Sch 5 thereto.

[12A.17 Application of CPR Part 6 to service of court documents within the jurisdiction]

[Except where different provision is made in these Rules, CPR Part 6 applies in relation to the service of court documents within the jurisdiction with such modifications as the court may direct.]

NOTES

Amendment

Inserted by SI 2010/686, r 4, Sch 3.
Date in force: 6 April 2010: see SI 2010/686, r 1; for transitional provisions and further effect see rr 6(1), 7, Sch 4, para 1, Sch 5 thereto.

[12A.18 Service of orders staying proceedings]
[(1) This Rule applies where the court makes an order staying any action, execution or other legal process against—
  (a) the property of a company; or
  (b) the property or person of an individual debtor or bankrupt.

(2) Service within the jurisdiction of such an order as is mentioned in paragraph (1) may be effected by sending a sealed copy of the order to the address for service of the claimant or other party having the carriage of the proceedings to be stayed.]

NOTES

Amendment

Inserted by SI 2010/686, r 4, Sch 3.
Date in force: 6 April 2010: see SI 2010/686, r 1; for transitional provisions and further effect see rr 6(1), 7, Sch 4, para 1, Sch 5 thereto.

[12A.19 Service on joint office-holders]
[Where there are joint office-holders in insolvency proceedings, service on one of them is to be treated as service on all of them.]

NOTES

Amendment

Inserted by SI 2010/686, r 4, Sch 3.
Date in force: 6 April 2010: see SI 2010/686, r 1; for transitional provisions and further effect see rr 6(1), 7, Sch 4, para 1, Sch 5 thereto.

[12A.20 Application of CPR Part 6 to service of court documents outside the jurisdiction]
[CPR Part 6 applies to the service of court documents outside the jurisdiction with such modifications as the court may direct.]

NOTES

Amendment

Inserted by SI 2010/686, r 4, Sch 3.
Date in force: 6 April 2010: see SI 2010/686, r 1; for transitional provisions and further effect see rr 6(1), 7, Sch 4, para 1, Sch 5 thereto.

[CHAPTER 4

MEETINGS]

NOTES

Amendment

Inserted by SI 2010/686, r 4, Sch 3.
Date in force: 6 April 2010: see SI 2010/686, r 1; for transitional provisions and further effect see rr 6(1), 7, Sch 4, paras 1, 5(1), (2), Sch 5 thereto.

[12A.21 Quorum at meeting of creditors or contributories]

[(1) Any meeting of creditors or contributories in insolvency proceedings is competent to act if a quorum is present.

(2) Subject to the next paragraph, a quorum is—
- (a) in the case of a creditors' meeting, at least one creditor entitled to vote;
- (b) in the case of a meeting of contributories, at least two contributories so entitled, or all the contributories, if their number does not exceed two.

(3) For the purposes of this Rule, the reference to the creditor or contributories necessary to constitute a quorum is to those persons present or represented by proxy by any person (including the chairman) and in the case of any proceedings under Parts 1 to 7 of the Act includes corporations duly represented.

(4) Where at any meeting of creditors or contributories—
- (a) the provisions of this Rule as to a quorum being present are satisfied by the attendance of—
  - (i) the chairman alone, or
  - (ii) one other person in addition to the chairman, and
- (b) the chairman is aware, by virtue of proofs and proxies received or otherwise, that one or more additional persons would, if attending, be entitled to vote,

the meeting must not commence until at least the expiry of 15 minutes after the time appointed for its commencement.]

NOTES

Amendment

Inserted by SI 2010/686, r 4, Sch 3.
Date in force: 6 April 2010: see SI 2010/686, r 1; for transitional provisions and further effect see rr 6(1), 7, Sch 4, para 1, Sch 5 thereto.

[12A.22 Remote attendance at meetings of creditors]

[(1) This Rule applies to a request to the convener of a meeting under section 246A(9) or 379A(8) to specify a place for the meeting.

(2) The request must be accompanied by—
- (a) in the case of a request by creditors, a list of the creditors making or concurring with the request and the amounts of their respective debts in the insolvency proceedings in question,
- (b) in the case of a request by contributories, a list of the contributories making or concurring with the request and their respective values (being the amounts for which they may vote at the meeting),
- (c) in the case of a request by members, a list of the members making or concurring with the request and their voting rights, and
- (d) from each person concurring, written confirmation of that person's concurrence.

(3) The request must be made within 7 business days of the date on which the convener sent the notice of the meeting in question.

(4) Where the convener considers that the request has been properly made in accordance with the Act and this Rule, the convener must—
- (a) give notice to all those previously given notice of the meeting—
  - (i) that it is to be held at a specified place, and
  - (ii) as to whether the date and time are to remain the same or not;
- (b) set a venue (including specification of a place) for the meeting, the date of which must be not later than 28 days after the original date for the meeting; and

(c) give at least 14 days' notice of that venue to all those previously given notice of the meeting;

and the notices required by sub-paragraphs (a) and (c) may be given at the same or different times.

(5) Where—
- (a) a request to which this Rule relates is made in respect of a final meeting under section 106, 146 or 331;
- (b) an application is made under Rule 4.131 or 6.142 in respect of remuneration or expenses reported in the draft report for that meeting; and
- (c) the meeting cannot be held until the application (including any appeal) has been disposed of and any order of the court complied with,

paragraph (4)(a) does not apply and the duty to set a venue (including specification of a place) for the meeting applies in relation to the meeting when it is finally held.

(6) Where the convener has specified a place for the meeting in response to a request to which this Rule applies, the chairman of the meeting must attend the meeting by being present in person at that place.

(7) Rules 2.37(3), (4), (5) and (6), 4.61 and 6.87 (expenses of summoning meetings) do not apply to the summoning and holding of a meeting at a place specified in accordance with section 246A(9) or 379A(8).]

NOTES

Amendment

Inserted by SI 2010/686, r 4, Sch 3.
Date in force: 6 April 2010: see SI 2010/686, r 1; for transitional provisions and further effect see rr 6(1), 7, Sch 4, paras 1, 5(1), (2), Sch 5 thereto.

[12A.23 Action where person excluded]

[(1) In this Rule and Rules 12A.24 and 12A.25 an "excluded person" means a person who—
- (a) has taken all steps necessary to attend a meeting under the arrangements put in place to do so by the convener of the meeting under section 246A(6) or 379A(5); and
- (b) those arrangements do not permit that person to attend the whole or part of that meeting.

(2) Where the chairman becomes aware during the course of the meeting that there is an excluded person, the chairman may—
- (a) continue the meeting;
- (b) declare the meeting void and convene the meeting again;
- (c) declare the meeting valid up to the point where the person was excluded and adjourn the meeting.

(3) Where the chairman continues the meeting, the meeting is valid unless—
- (a) the chairman decides in consequence of a complaint under Rule 12A.25 to declare the meeting void and hold the meeting again; or
- (b) the court directs otherwise.

(4) Without prejudice to paragraph (2), where the chairman becomes aware during the course of the meeting that there is an excluded person, the chairman may, in the chairman's discretion and without an adjournment, declare the meeting suspended for any period up to 1 hour.]

NOTES

Amendment
Inserted by SI 2010/686, r 4, Sch 3.
Date in force: 6 April 2010: see SI 2010/686, r 1; for transitional provisions and further effect see rr 6(1), 7, Sch 4, paras 1, 5(1), Sch 5 thereto.

[12A.24 Indication to excluded person]
[(1) A person who claims to be an excluded person may request an indication of what occurred during the period of that person's claimed exclusion (an "indication").
(2) A request under paragraph (1) must be made as soon as reasonably practicable and, in any event, no later than 4.00 pm on the business day following the day on which the exclusion is claimed to have occurred.
(3) A request under paragraph (1) must be made to—
(a) the chairman, where it is made during the course of the business of the meeting; or
(b) the office-holder where it is made after the conclusion of the business of the meeting.
(4) Where satisfied that the person making the request is an excluded person, the person to whom the request is made under paragraph (3) must give the indication as soon as reasonably practicable and, in any event, no later than 4.00 pm on the business day following the day on which the request was made under paragraph (1).
(5) In this Rule and Rule 12A.25, "office-holder" has the meaning in Rule 13.9A.]

NOTES

Amendment
Inserted by SI 2010/686, r 4, Sch 3.
Date in force: 6 April 2010: see SI 2010/686, r 1; for transitional provisions and further effect see rr 6(1), 7, Sch 4, paras 1, 5(1), Sch 5 thereto.

[12A.25 Complaint]
[(1) Any person who—
(a) is, or claims to be, an excluded person; or
(b) attends the meeting (in person or by proxy) and considers that they have been adversely affected by a person's actual, apparent or claimed exclusion,
("the complainant") may make a complaint.
(2) The person to whom the complaint must be made ("the relevant person") is—
(a) the chairman, where it is made during the course of the meeting; or
(b) the office-holder, where it is made after the meeting.
(3) The relevant person must—
(a) consider whether there is an excluded person; and
(b) where satisfied that there is an excluded person, consider the complaint; and
(c) where satisfied that there has been prejudice, take such action as the relevant person considers fit to remedy the prejudice.
(4) Paragraph (5) applies where—
(a) the relevant person is satisfied that the complainant is an excluded person;
(b) during the period of the person's exclusion—
(i) a resolution was put to the meeting; and

(ii) voted on; and
(c) the excluded person asserts how the excluded person intended to vote on the resolution.

(5) Subject to paragraph (6), where satisfied that the effect of the intended vote in paragraph (4), if cast, would have changed the result of the resolution, the relevant person must—
(a) count the intended vote as being cast in accordance with the complainant's stated intention;
(b) amend the record of the result of the resolution; and
(c) where those entitled to attend the meeting have been notified of the result of the resolution, notify them of the change.

(6) Where satisfied that more than one complainant in paragraph (4) is an excluded person, the relevant person must have regard to the combined effect of the intended votes.

(7) The relevant person must notify the complainant in writing of any decision.

(8) A complaint must be made as soon as reasonably practicable and, in any event, no later than 4 pm on the business day following—
(a) the day on which the person was, appeared or claimed to be excluded; or
(b) where an indication is sought under Rule 12A.24, the day on which the complainant received the indication.

(9) A complainant who is not satisfied by the action of the relevant person may apply to the court for directions and any application must be made no more than 2 business days from the date of receiving the decision of the relevant person.]

NOTES

Amendment

Inserted by SI 2010/686, r 4, Sch 3.
Date in force: 6 April 2010: see SI 2010/686, r 1; for transitional provisions and further effect see rr 6(1), 7, Sch 4, paras 1, 5(1), Sch 5 thereto.

[12A.26 Remote attendance at meetings of creditors' committees and liquidation committees]

[(1) This Rule applies to any meeting of a creditors' committee or a liquidation committee held under these Rules.

(2) Where the office-holder considers it appropriate, the meeting may be conducted and held in such a way that persons who are not present together at the same place may attend it.

(3) Where a meeting is conducted and held in the manner referred to in paragraph (2), a person attends the meeting if that person is able to exercise any rights which that person may have to speak and vote at the meeting.

(4) For the purposes of this Rule—
(a) a person is able to exercise the right to speak at a meeting when that person is in a position to communicate to all those attending the meeting, during the meeting, any information or opinions which that person has on the business of the meeting; and
(b) a person is able to exercise the right to vote at a meeting when—
(i) that person is able to vote, during the meeting, on resolutions or determinations put to the vote at the meeting, and
(ii) that person's vote can be taken into account in determining whether or not such resolutions or determinations are passed at the same time as the votes of all the other persons attending the meeting.

(5) Where a meeting is to be conducted and held in the manner referred to in paragraph (2), the office-holder must make whatever arrangements the office-holder considers appropriate to—
- (a) enable those attending the meeting to exercise their rights to speak or vote, and
- (b) ensure the identification of those attending the meeting and the security of any electronic means used to enable attendance.

(6) Where in the reasonable opinion of the office-holder—
- (a) a meeting will be attended by persons who will not be present together at the same place, and
- (b) it is unnecessary or inexpedient to specify a place for the meeting,

any requirement under these Rules to specify a place for the meeting may be satisfied by specifying the arrangements the office-holder proposes to enable persons to exercise their rights to speak or vote.

(7) In making the arrangements referred to in paragraph (5) and in forming the opinion referred to in paragraph (6)(b), the office-holder must have regard to the legitimate interests of the committee members or their representatives attending the meeting in the efficient despatch of the business of the meeting.

(8) If—
- (a) the notice of a meeting does not specify a place for the meeting,
- (b) the office-holder is requested in accordance with Rule 12A.27 to specify a place for the meeting, and
- (c) that request is made by at least one member of the committee,

the office-holder must specify a place for the meeting.

(9) In this Rule, "the committee" means the creditors' committee or the liquidation committee.]

NOTES

Amendment

Inserted by SI 2010/686, r 4, Sch 3.
Date in force: 6 April 2010: see SI 2010/686, r 1; for transitional provisions and further effect see rr 6(1), 7, Sch 4, paras 1, 5(1), Sch 5 thereto.

[12A.27 Procedure for requests that a place for a meeting should be specified under Rule 12A.26]

[(1) This Rule applies to a request to the office-holder of a meeting under Rule 12A.26 to specify a place for the meeting.

(2) The request must be made within 5 business days of the date on which the office-holder sent the notice of the meeting in question.

(3) Where the office-holder considers that the request has been properly made in accordance with this Rule, the office-holder must—
- (a) give notice to all those previously given notice of the meeting—
  - (i) that it is to be held at a specified place, and
  - (ii) as to whether the date and time are to remain the same or not;
- (b) set a venue (including specification of a place) for the meeting, the date of which must be not later than 7 business days after the original date for the meeting; and
- (c) give 5 business days' notice of the venue to all those previously given notice of the meeting;

and the notices required by sub-paragraphs (a) and (c) may be given at the same or different times.

(4) Where the office-holder has specified a place for the meeting in response to a request to which this Rule applies, the chairman of the meeting must attend the meeting by being present in person at that place.]

NOTES

Amendment

Inserted by SI 2010/686, r 4, Sch 3.
Date in force: 6 April 2010: see SI 2010/686, r 1; for transitional provisions and further effect see rr 6(1), 7, Sch 4, paras 1, 5(1), Sch 5 thereto.

[CHAPTER 5

EFFECT OF INSOLVENCY ON EXECUTION—SPECIFIC PROVISIONS FOR NOTICES TO ENFORCEMENT OFFICERS ETC]

NOTES

Amendment

Inserted by SI 2010/686, r 4, Sch 3.
Date in force: 6 April 2010: see SI 2010/686, r 1; for transitional provisions and further effect see rr 6(1), 7, Sch 4, para 1, Sch 5 thereto.

[12A.28 Execution overtaken by judgment debtor's insolvency]

[(1) This Rule applies where execution has been taken out against property of a judgment debtor, and notice is given to the enforcement officer or other officer charged with the execution—

(a) under section 184(1) (that a winding-up order has been made against the debtor, or that a provisional liquidator has been appointed, or that a resolution for voluntary winding up has been passed); or

(b) under section 184(4) (that a winding-up petition has been presented, or a winding-up order made, or that a meeting has been called at which there is to be proposed a resolution for voluntary winding up, or that such a resolution has been passed); or

(c) under section 346(2) (that a judgment debtor has been adjudged bankrupt); or

(d) under section 346(3)(b) (that a bankruptcy petition has been presented in respect of the debtor).

(2) Subject to paragraph (3) and Rule 12A.29, the notice must be delivered to the office of the enforcement officer or of the officer charged with the execution—

(a) by hand, or

(b) by any other means of delivery which enables proof of receipt of the document at the relevant address.

(3) Where the execution is in a county court and the officer in charge of it is a district judge in that court, then if—

(a) there is filed in that court in respect of the judgment debtor a winding-up or bankruptcy petition, or

(b) there is made by that court in respect of the judgment debtor a winding-up order or an order appointing a provisional liquidator, or a bankruptcy order or an order appointing an interim receiver,

section 184 or 346 is deemed satisfied as regards the requirement of a notice to be served on, or given to, the officer in charge of the execution.]

NOTES

Amendment
Inserted by SI 2010/686, r 4, Sch 3.
Date in force: 6 April 2010: see SI 2010/686, r 1; for transitional provisions and further effect see rr 6(1), 7, Sch 4, para 1, Sch 5 thereto.

[12A.29 Notice to enforcement officers]
[(1) This Rule applies in relation to any provision of the Act or the Rules which makes provision for the giving of notice to an enforcement officer.

(2) Any such notice as is mentioned in paragraph (1) may be given by electronic means to any person who has been authorised to receive such notice on behalf of a specified enforcement officer or on behalf of enforcement officers generally.]

NOTES

Amendment
Inserted by SI 2010/686, r 4, Sch 3.
Date in force: 6 April 2010: see SI 2010/686, r 1; for transitional provisions and further effect see rr 6(1), 7, Sch 4, para 1, Sch 5 thereto.

[CHAPTER 6

FORMS]

NOTES

Amendment
Inserted by SI 2010/686, r 4, Sch 3.
Date in force: 6 April 2010: see SI 2010/686, r 1; for transitional provisions and further effect see rr 6(1), 7, Sch 4, paras 1, 2(1)(c), Sch 5 thereto.

[12A.30 Forms for use in insolvency proceedings]
[(1) Subject to the next Rule, the forms contained in Schedule 4 to these Rules must continue to be used in insolvency proceedings as provided for in specific Rules.

(2) The forms must be used with such variations, if any, as the circumstances may require.

(3) The Secretary of State, the official receiver or an insolvency practitioner may incorporate a barcode or other reference or recognition mark into any form in Schedule 4 to these Rules a copy of which is received by any of them or is sent to any person by any of them.]

NOTES

Amendment
Inserted by SI 2010/686, r 4, Sch 3.
Date in force: 6 April 2010: see SI 2010/686, r 1; for transitional provisions and further effect see rr 6(1), 7, Sch 4, paras 1, 2(1)(c), Sch 5 thereto.

[12A.31 Electronic submission of information instead of submission of forms to the Secretary of State, the Chief Land Registrar, office-holders, and of copies to the registrar of companies]

[(1) This Rule applies in any case where information in a prescribed form is required by the Rules to be sent by any person to the Secretary of State, the Chief Land Registrar, or an office-holder, or a copy of a prescribed form is to be sent to the registrar of companies.

(2) A requirement of the kind mentioned in paragraph (1) is treated as having been satisfied where—

- (a) the information is submitted electronically with the agreement of the person to whom the information is sent;
- (b) the form in which the electronic submission is made satisfies the requirements of the person to whom the information is sent (which may include a requirement that the information supplied can be reproduced in the format of the prescribed form);
- (c) that all the information required to be given in the prescribed form is provided in the electronic submission; and
- (d) the person to whom the information is sent can provide in legible form the information so submitted.

(3) Where information in a prescribed form is permitted to be sent electronically under paragraph (2), any requirement in the prescribed form that the prescribed form be accompanied by a signature is taken to be satisfied—

- (a) if the identity of the person who is supplying the information in the prescribed form and whose signature is required is confirmed in a manner specified by the recipient, or
- (b) where no such manner has been specified by the recipient, if the communication contains or is accompanied by a statement of the identity of the person who is providing the information in the prescribed form, and the recipient has no reason to doubt the truth of that statement.

(4) Where information required in prescribed form has been supplied to a person, whether or not it has been supplied electronically in accordance with paragraph (2), and a copy of that information is required to be supplied to another person falling within paragraph (1), the requirements contained in paragraph (2) apply in respect of the supply of the copy to that other person, as they apply in respect of the original.]

NOTES

Amendment

Inserted by SI 2010/686, r 4, Sch 3.
Date in force: 6 April 2010: see SI 2010/686, r 1; for transitional provisions and further effect see rr 6(1), 7, Sch 4, paras 1, 2(1)(c), Sch 5 thereto.

[12A.32 Electronic submission of information instead of submission of forms in all other cases]

[(1) Subject to paragraph (5), this Rule applies in any case where Rule 12A.31 does not apply, where information in a prescribed form is required by the Rules to be sent by any person.

(2) A requirement of the kind mentioned in paragraph (1) is treated as having been satisfied where—

- (a) the person to whom the information is sent has agreed—
  - (i) to receiving the information electronically and to the form in which it is to be sent; and
  - (ii) to the specified manner in which paragraph (3) is to be satisfied.

(b) all the information required to be given in the prescribed form is provided in the electronic submission; and

(c) the person to whom the information is sent can provide in legible form the information so submitted.

(3) Any requirement in a prescribed form that it be accompanied by a signature is taken to be satisfied if the identity of the person who is supplying the information and whose signature is required, is confirmed in the specified manner.

(4) Where information required in prescribed form has been supplied to a person, whether or not it has been supplied electronically in accordance with paragraph (2), and a copy of that information is required to be supplied to another person falling within paragraph (1), the requirements contained in paragraph (2) apply in respect of the supply of the copy to that other person, as they apply in respect of the original.

(5) This Rule does not apply in respect of a statutory demand.]

NOTES

Amendment

Inserted by SI 2010/686, r 4, Sch 3.
Date in force: 6 April 2010: see SI 2010/686, r 1; for transitional provisions and further effect see rr 6(1), 7, Sch 4, paras 1, 2(1)(c), Sch 5 thereto.

[CHAPTER 7

GAZETTE NOTICES]

NOTES

Amendment

Inserted by SI 2010/686, r 4, Sch 3.
Date in force: 6 April 2010: see SI 2010/686, r 1; for transitional provisions and further effect see rr 6(1), 7, Sch 4, para 1, Sch 5 thereto.

[12A.33 Contents of notices to be gazetted under the Act or Rules]

[(1) Except when paragraph (3) applies, where under the Act or the Rules a notice is gazetted, in addition to any content specifically required by the Act or any other provision of the Rules, the content of such a notice must be as set out in this Chapter.

(2) All notices published must specify insofar as it is applicable in relation to the particular notice—

(a) the name and postal address of the office-holder acting in the proceedings;

(b) the capacity in which the office-holder is acting and the date of appointment;

(c) either an e-mail address, or a telephone number, through which the office-holder may be contacted;

(d) the name of any person other than the office-holder (if any) who may be contacted regarding the proceedings;

(e) the number assigned to the office-holder by the Secretary of State; and

(f) the court name and any number assigned to the proceedings by the court.

(3) This paragraph applies to notices under Rule 4.228(2) (first excepted case).]

NOTES

Amendment

Inserted by SI 2010/686, r 4, Sch 3.
 Date in force: 6 April 2010: see SI 2010/686, r 1; for transitional provisions and further effect see rr 6(1), 7, Sch 4, para 1, Sch 5 thereto.

[12A.34 Gazette notices relating to companies]
[In addition to the information required by Rule 12A.33 a notice relating to a company must specify—
- (a) the registered name of the company;
- (b) its registered number;
- (c) its registered office, or if an unregistered company, the postal address of its principal place of business;
- (d) any principal trading address if this is different from its registered office;
- (e) any name under which it was registered in the 12 months prior to the date of the commencement of the proceedings which are the subject of the Gazette notice; and
- (f) any name or style (other than its registered name) under which—
  - (i) the company carried on business; and
  - (ii) any debt owed to a creditor was incurred.]

NOTES

Amendment

Inserted by SI 2010/686, r 4, Sch 3.
 Date in force: 6 April 2010: see SI 2010/686, r 1; for transitional provisions and further effect see rr 6(1), 7, Sch 4, para 1, Sch 5 thereto.

[12A.35 Gazette notices relating to bankrupts]
[In addition to the information required by Rule 12A.33 a notice relating to a bankruptcy must state,—
- (a) the bankrupt's full name and residential address;
- (b) any other address at which the bankrupt has resided in the period of 12 months preceding the making of the bankruptcy order;
- (c) the bankrupt's date of birth;
- (d) the bankrupt's occupation;
- (e) any other name by which the bankrupt has been known;
- (f) any name or style (other than the bankrupt's own name) under which—
  - (i) the bankrupt carried on business; and
  - (ii) any debt owed to a creditor was incurred.]

NOTES

Amendment

Inserted by SI 2010/686, r 4, Sch 3.
 Date in force: 6 April 2010: see SI 2010/686, r 1; for transitional provisions and further effect see rr 6(1), 7, Sch 4, para 1, Sch 5 thereto.

[12A.36 Omission of unobtainable information]
[Information required under this Chapter to be included in a notice to be gazetted may be omitted if it is not reasonably practicable to obtain it.]

NOTES

Amendment

Inserted by SI 2010/686, r 4, Sch 3.
Date in force: 6 April 2010: see SI 2010/686, r 1; for transitional provisions and further effect see rr 6(1), 7, Sch 4, para 1, Sch 5 thereto.

[12A.37 The Gazette—general]

[(1) A copy of the Gazette containing any notice required by the Act or the Rules to be gazetted is evidence of any facts stated in the notice.

(2) In the case of an order of the court notice of which is required by the Act or the Rules to be gazetted, a copy of the Gazette containing the notice may in any proceedings be produced as conclusive evidence that the order was made on the date specified in the notice.

(3) Where an order of the court which is gazetted has been varied, and where any matter has been erroneously or inaccurately gazetted, the person whose responsibility it was to procure the requisite entry in the Gazette must as soon as is reasonably practicable cause the variation of the order to be gazetted or a further entry to be made in the Gazette for the purpose of correcting the error or inaccuracy.]

NOTES

Amendment

Inserted by SI 2010/686, r 4, Sch 3.
Date in force: 6 April 2010: see SI 2010/686, r 1; for transitional provisions and further effect see rr 6(1), 7, Sch 4, para 1, Sch 5 thereto.

[CHAPTER 8

NOTICES ADVERTISED OTHERWISE THAN IN THE GAZETTE]

NOTES

Amendment

Inserted by SI 2010/686, r 4, Sch 3.
Date in force: 6 April 2010: see SI 2010/686, r 1; for transitional provisions and further effect see rr 6(1), 7, Sch 4, para 1, Sch 5 thereto.

[12A.38 Notices otherwise advertised under the Act or Rules]

[(1) Where under the Act or the Rules a notice may be advertised otherwise than in the Gazette, in addition to any content specifically required by the Act or any other provision of the Rules, the content of such a notice must be as set out in this Chapter.

(2) All notices published must specify insofar as it is applicable in relation to the particular notice—

- (a) the name and postal address of the office-holder acting in the proceedings to which the notice relates;
- (b) the capacity in which the office-holder is acting; and
- (c) either an e-mail address, or a telephone number, through which the office-holder may be contacted.]

NOTES

Amendment

Inserted by SI 2010/686, r 4, Sch 3.
Date in force: 6 April 2010: see SI 2010/686, r 1; for transitional provisions and further effect see rr 6(1), 7, Sch 4, para 1, Sch 5 thereto.

[12A.39 Non-Gazette notices relating to companies]

[In addition to the information required by Rule 12A.38, a notice relating to a company must state—

(a)   the registered name of the company;
(b)   its registered number;
(c)   any name under which it was registered in the 12 months prior to the date of the commencement of the proceedings which are the subject of the notice; and
(d)   any name or style (other than its registered name) under which—
      (i)   the company carried on business; and
      (ii)   any debt owed to a creditor was incurred.]

NOTES

Amendment

Inserted by SI 2010/686, r 4, Sch 3.
Date in force: 6 April 2010: see SI 2010/686, r 1; for transitional provisions and further effect see rr 6(1), 7, Sch 4, para 1, Sch 5 thereto.

[12A.40 Non-Gazette notices relating to bankrupts]

[In addition to the information required by Rule 12A.38, a notice relating to bankruptcy must state—

(a)   the bankrupt's full name and address;
(b)   any other address at which the bankrupt has resided in the period of 12 months preceding the making of the bankruptcy order;
(c)   the bankrupt's date of birth;
(d)   the bankrupt's occupation;
(e)   any other name by which the bankrupt has been known;
(f)   any name or style (other than the bankrupt's own name) under which—
      (i)   the bankrupt carried on business; and
      (ii)   any debt owed to a creditor was incurred.]

NOTES

Amendment

Inserted by SI 2010/686, r 4, Sch 3.
Date in force: 6 April 2010: see SI 2010/686, r 1; for transitional provisions and further effect see rr 6(1), 7, Sch 4, para 1, Sch 5 thereto.

[12A.41 Non-Gazette notices—other provisions]

[(1) The information required to be contained in a notice to which this Chapter applies must be included in the advertisement of that notice in a manner that is reasonably likely to ensure, in relation to the form of the advertising used, that a person reading, hearing or seeing the advertisement, will be able to read, hear or see that information.

(2) Information required under this Chapter to be included in a notice may be omitted if it is not reasonably practicable to obtain it.]

NOTES

Amendment

Inserted by SI 2010/686, r 4, Sch 3.
Date in force: 6 April 2010: see SI 2010/686, r 1; for transitional provisions and further effect see rr 6(1), 7, Sch 4, para 1, Sch 5 thereto.

[CHAPTER 9
NOTIFICATIONS TO THE REGISTRAR OF COMPANIES]

NOTES

Amendment

Inserted by SI 2010/686, r 4, Sch 3.
Date in force: 6 April 2010: see SI 2010/686, r 1; for transitional provisions and further effect see rr 6(1), 7, Sch 4, para 1, Sch 5 thereto.

[12A.42 Application of this Chapter]
[This Chapter applies where under the Act or the Rules information is to be sent or delivered to the registrar of companies.]

NOTES

Amendment

Inserted by SI 2010/686, r 4, Sch 3.
Date in force: 6 April 2010: see SI 2010/686, r 1; for transitional provisions and further effect see rr 6(1), 7, Sch 4, para 1, Sch 5 thereto.

[12A.43 Information to be contained in all notifications to the registrar]
[Where under the Act or the Rules a return, notice, or any other document or information is to be sent to the registrar of companies, that notification must specify—
- (a) the registered name of the company;
- (b) its registered number;
- (c) the nature of the notification;
- (d) the section of the Act or the Rule under which the notification is made;
- (e) the date of the notification;
- (f) the name and postal address of person making the notification;
- (g) the capacity in which that person is acting in respect of the company; and

the notification must be authenticated by the person making the notification.]

NOTES

Amendment

Inserted by SI 2010/686, r 4, Sch 3.
Date in force: 6 April 2010: see SI 2010/686, r 1; for transitional provisions and further effect see rr 6(1), 7, Sch 4, para 1, Sch 5 thereto.

[**12A.44 Notifications relating to the office of office-holders**]
[In addition to the information required by Rule 12A.43, a notification relating to the office of the office-holder must also specify—
(a) the name of the office-holder;
(b) the nature of the appointment held by the office holder
(c) the date of the event notified;
(e) where the notification relates to an appointment, the person, body or court making the appointment;
(f) where the notification relates to the termination of an appointment, the reason for that termination (for example, resignation); and
(e) the postal address of office-holder.]

NOTES

Amendment

Inserted by SI 2010/686, r 4, Sch 3.
Date in force: 6 April 2010: see SI 2010/686, r 1; for transitional provisions and further effect see rr 6(1), 7, Sch 4, para 1, Sch 5 thereto.

[**12A.45 Notifications relating to documents**]
[In addition to the information required by Rule 12A.43, a notification relating to a document (for example, a statement of affairs) must also specify—
(a) the nature of the document; and
(b) the date of the document; or
(c) where the document relates to a period of time (for example a report) the period of time to which the document relates.]

NOTES

Amendment

Inserted by SI 2010/686, r 4, Sch 3.
Date in force: 6 April 2010: see SI 2010/686, r 1; for transitional provisions and further effect see rr 6(1), 7, Sch 4, para 1, Sch 5 thereto.

[**12A.46 Notifications relating to court orders**]
[In addition to the information required by Rule 12A.43, a notification relating to a court order must also specify—
(a) the nature of the court order; and
(b) the date of the order.]

NOTES

Amendment

Inserted by SI 2010/686, r 4, Sch 3.
Date in force: 6 April 2010: see SI 2010/686, r 1; for transitional provisions and further effect see rr 6(1), 7, Sch 4, para 1, Sch 5 thereto.

[**12A.47 Returns or reports of meetings**]
[(1) In addition to the information required by Rule 12A.43, the notification of a return or a report of a meeting must specify—
(a) the purpose of the meeting including the section of the Act or Rule under which it was convened;

(b) the venue fixed for the meeting;
(c) whether a required quorum was present for the meeting to take place; and
(d) if the meeting took place, the outcome of the meeting (including any resolutions passed at the meeting).

(2) Where the return relates to the meeting required by section 94 or 106 (final meetings prior to dissolution), it must also specify the dates of the opening and close of the winding up.]

NOTES

Amendment

Inserted by SI 2010/686, r 4, Sch 3.
Date in force: 6 April 2010: see SI 2010/686, r 1; for transitional provisions and further effect see rr 6(1), 7, Sch 4, para 1, Sch 5 thereto.

[12A.48 Notifications relating to other events]

[In addition to the information required by Rule 12A.43, a notification relating to any other event (for example the coming in to force of a moratorium) must specify—
(a) the nature of the event including the section of the Act or Rule under which it took place; and
(b) the date the event occurred.]

NOTES

Amendment

Inserted by SI 2010/686, r 4, Sch 3.
Date in force: 6 April 2010: see SI 2010/686, r 1; for transitional provisions and further effect see rr 6(1), 7, Sch 4, para 1, Sch 5 thereto.

[12A.49 Notifications of more than one nature]

[A notification which includes a notification of more than one nature must satisfy the requirements applying in respect of each of those notifications.]

NOTES

Amendment

Inserted by SI 2010/686, r 4, Sch 3.
Date in force: 6 April 2010: see SI 2010/686, r 1; for transitional provisions and further effect see rr 6(1), 7, Sch 4, para 1, Sch 5 thereto.

[12A.50 Notifications made to other persons at the same time]

[(1) Where under the Act or the Rules a notice or other document is to be sent to another person at the same time that it is to be sent to the registrar of companies, that requirement may be satisfied by sending to that other person a copy of the notification sent to the registrar.

(2) Paragraph (1) does not apply—
(a) where a Form is prescribed for the notification to the other person; or
(b) where the notification to the registrar of companies is incomplete.]

NOTES

Amendment

Inserted by SI 2010/686, r 4, Sch 3.
Date in force: 6 April 2010: see SI 2010/686, r 1; for transitional provisions and further effect see rr 6(1), 7, Sch 4, para 1, Sch 5 thereto.

[CHAPTER 10
INSPECTION OF DOCUMENTS AND THE PROVISION OF INFORMATION]

NOTES

Amendment

Inserted by SI 2010/686, r 4, Sch 3.
Date in force: 6 April 2010: see SI 2010/686, r 1; for transitional provisions and further effect see rr 6(1), 7, Sch 4, para 1, Sch 5 thereto.

[12A.51 Confidentiality of documents—grounds for refusing inspection]

[(1) Where in insolvency proceedings the office-holder considers that a document forming part of the records of those proceedings—
- (a) should be treated as confidential, or
- (b) is of such a nature that its disclosure would be prejudicial to the conduct of the proceedings or might reasonably be expected to lead to violence against any person,

the office-holder may decline to allow it to be inspected by a person who would otherwise be entitled to inspect it.

(2) The persons to whom the office-holder may under this Rule refuse inspection include members of a liquidation committee or a creditors' committee.

(3) Where under this rule the office-holder determines to refuse inspection of a document, the person wishing to inspect it may apply to the court for that determination to be overruled and the court may either overrule it altogether or sustain it subject to such conditions (if any) as it thinks just.]

NOTES

Amendment

Inserted by SI 2010/686, r 4, Sch 3.
Date in force: 6 April 2010: see SI 2010/686, r 1; for transitional provisions and further effect see rr 6(1), 7, Sch 4, para 1, Sch 5 thereto.

[12A.52 Right to copy documents]

[Where the Act or the Rules confer a right for any person to inspect documents, the right includes that of taking copies of those documents, on payment—
- (a) in the case of documents on the court's file of proceedings, of the fee chargeable under any order made under section 92 of the Courts Act 2003, and
- (b) in any other case, of the appropriate fee.]

NOTES

Amendment

Inserted by SI 2010/686, r 4, Sch 3.

Date in force: 6 April 2010: see SI 2010/686, r 1; for transitional provisions and further effect see rr 6(1), 7, Sch 4, para 1, Sch 5 thereto.

[12A.53 Charges for copy documents]
[Except where prohibited by the Rules, a responsible insolvency practitioner or the official receiver is entitled to require the payment of the appropriate fee for the supply of documents requested by a creditor, member, contributory or member of a liquidation or creditors' committee.]

NOTES

Amendment
> Inserted by SI 2010/686, r 4, Sch 3.
> Date in force: 6 April 2010: see SI 2010/686, r 1; for transitional provisions and further effect see rr 6(1), 7, Sch 4, para 1, Sch 5 thereto.

[12A.54 Right to have list of creditors]
[(1) This Rule applies in the following proceedings—
  (a) administration;
  (b) winding up (other than a members' voluntary winding up); and
  (c) bankruptcy.

(2) A creditor or a member State liquidator has the right to require an office-holder to provide a list of the creditors and the amounts of their respective debts unless paragraph (5) applies.

(3) The office-holder on being required to furnish the list under paragraph (2)—
  (a) as soon as reasonably practicable must send it to the person requiring the list to be furnished; and
  (b) may charge the appropriate fee for doing so.

(4) The name and address of any creditor may be omitted from the list furnished under paragraph (3) where the office-holder is of the view that its disclosure would be prejudicial to the conduct of the proceedings or might reasonably be expected to lead to violence against any person provided that—
  (a) the amount of the debt in question is shown in the list; and
  (b) a statement is included in the list that the name and address of the creditor has been omitted in respect of that debt.

(5) Paragraph (2) does not apply where a statement of affairs has been—
  (a) delivered to the registrar of companies, in a winding up or an administration; or
  (b) filed with the court, in bankruptcy proceedings.]

NOTES

Amendment
> Inserted by SI 2010/686, r 4, Sch 3.
> Date in force: 6 April 2010: see SI 2010/686, r 1; for transitional provisions and further effect see rr 6(1), 7, Sch 4, para 1, Sch 5 thereto.

[CHAPTER 11

COMPUTATION OF TIME AND TIME LIMITS]

NOTES

Amendment

Inserted by SI 2010/686, r 4, Sch 3.
Date in force: 6 April 2010: see SI 2010/686, r 1; for transitional provisions and further effect see rr 6(1), 7, Sch 4, paras 1, 2(1)(c), Sch 5 thereto.

[12A.55 Time limits]

[(1) The provisions of CPR rule 2.8 (time) apply, as regards computation of time, to anything required or authorised to be done by the Rules.

(2) The provisions of CPR rule 3.1(2)(a) (the court's general powers of management) apply so as to enable the court to extend or shorten the time for compliance with anything required or authorised to be done by the Rules.]

NOTES

Amendment

Inserted by SI 2010/686, r 4, Sch 3.
Date in force: 6 April 2010: see SI 2010/686, r 1; for transitional provisions and further effect see rr 6(1), 7, Sch 4, paras 1, 2(1)(c), Sch 5 thereto.

[CHAPTER 12

SECURITY]

NOTES

Amendment

Inserted by SI 2010/686, r 4, Sch 3.
Date in force: 6 April 2010: see SI 2010/686, r 1; for transitional provisions see r 6(1), Sch 4, para 1 thereto.

[12A.56 Insolvency practitioners' security]

[(1) Wherever under the Rules any person has to appoint, or certify the appointment of, an insolvency practitioner to any office that person must, before making or certifying the appointment, be satisfied that the person appointed or to be appointed has security for the proper performance of that office.

(2) It is the duty—
    (a)   of the creditors' committee in—
        (i)   an administration,
        (ii)   an administrative receivership,
        (iii)   a bankruptcy, and
    (b)   of the liquidation committee in a winding up,
to review from time to time the adequacy of the responsible insolvency practitioner's security.

(3) In any insolvency proceedings the cost of the responsible insolvency practitioner's security shall be defrayed as an expense of the proceedings.]

NOTES

Amendment

Inserted by SI 2010/686, r 4, Sch 3.
Date in force: 6 April 2010: see SI 2010/686, r 1; for transitional provisions see r 6(1), Sch 4, para 1 thereto.

[CHAPTER 13

NOTICE OF ORDER UNDER SECTION 176A(5)]

NOTES

Amendment

Inserted by SI 2010/686, r 4, Sch 3.
Date in force: 6 April 2010: see SI 2010/686, r 1; for transitional provisions see r 6(1), Sch 4, para 1 thereto.

[12A.57 Notice of order under section 176A(5)]

[(1) Where the court makes an order under section 176A(5), it must as soon as reasonably practicable send two sealed copies of the order to the applicant and a sealed copy to any other office-holder.

(2) Where the court has made an order under section 176A(5), the liquidator, administrator or receiver must as soon as reasonably practicable, give notice to each creditor of whose address and claim the office-holder in question is aware.

(3) Paragraph (2) does not apply where the court directs otherwise.

(4) The court may direct that the requirement in paragraph (2) is complied with if a notice has been published by the liquidator, administrator or receiver which, in addition to containing the standard contents, states that the court has made an order disapplying the requirement to set aside the prescribed part. As soon as reasonably practicable the notice—
  (a) must be gazetted; and
  (b) may be advertised in such other manner as the liquidator, administrator, or receiver thinks fit.

(5) The liquidator, administrator or receiver must send a copy of the order to the registrar of companies as soon as reasonably practicable after the making of the order.]

NOTES

Amendment

Inserted by SI 2010/686, r 4, Sch 3.
Date in force: 6 April 2010: see SI 2010/686, r 1; for transitional provisions see r 6(1), Sch 4, para 1 thereto.

PART 13

INTERPRETATION AND APPLICATION

13.1 Introductory

This Part of the Rules has effect for their interpretation and application; and any definition given in this Part applies except, and in so far as, the context otherwise requires.

NOTES

Initial Commencement

Specified date

Specified date: 29 December 1986: see r 0.1.

See Further

See further, in relation to the application of this rule, with modifications, in respect of bank administration and applications for bank administration: the Bank Administration (England and Wales) Rules 2009, SI 2009/357, rr 58–61.

13.2 "The court"; "the registrar"

(1) Anything to be done under or by virtue of the Act or the Rules by, to or before the court may be done by, to or before a judge[, district judge] or the registrar.

(2) The registrar [or district judge] may authorise any act of a formal or administrative character which is not by statute his responsibility to be carried out by the chief clerk or any other officer of the court acting on his behalf, in accordance with directions given by the Lord Chancellor.

[(3A) "The registrar" means—
  (a) a Registrar in Bankruptcy of the High Court, or
  (b) where the proceedings are in the District Registry of Birmingham, Bristol, Caernarfon, Cardiff, Leeds, Liverpool, Manchester, Mold, Newcastle-upon-Tyne or Preston, a district judge attached to the District Registry in question.]

NOTES

Initial Commencement

Specified date

Specified date: 29 December 1986: see r 0.1.

Amendment

Para (1): words ", district judge" in square brackets inserted by SI 2010/686, r 2, Sch 1, para 493(1), (2).
  Date in force: 6 April 2010: see SI 2010/686, r 1; for transitional provisions and further effect see rr 6(1), 7, Sch 4, paras 1, 2(1)(b), Sch 5 thereto.
Para (2): words "or district judge" in square brackets inserted by SI 2010/686, r 2, Sch 1, para 493(1), (3).
  Date in force: 6 April 2010: see SI 2010/686, r 1; for transitional provisions and further effect see rr 6(1), 7, Sch 4, paras 1, 2(1)(b), Sch 5 thereto.
Para (3A): substituted for paras (3)–(5) as originally enacted, by SI 2010/686, r 2, Sch 1, para 493(1), (4).
  Date in force: 6 April 2010: see SI 2010/686, r 1; for transitional provisions and further effect see rr 6(1), 7, Sch 4, paras 1, 2(1)(b), Sch 5 thereto.

See Further

See further, in relation the application of this rule, with modifications, in respect of the procedure for the appointment of a bank liquidator and the operation of bank insolvency under the Banking Act 2009, Pt 2: the Bank Insolvency (England and Wales) Rules 2009, SI 2009/356, rr 3(3)–(8), 284.

See further, in relation to the application of this rule, with modifications, in respect of bank administration and applications for bank administration: the Bank Administration (England and Wales) Rules 2009, SI 2009/357, rr 58–61.

Insolvency Rules 1986, reg 13.3

13.3 "Give notice", etc

(1) ...

(2) ...

(3) ...

(4) Notice of the venue fixed for an application [made to the court] may be given by service of the sealed copy of the application under Rule 7.4(3).

NOTES

Initial Commencement

Specified date

Specified date: 29 December 1986: see r 0.1.

Amendment

Paras (1)–(3): revoked by SI 2010/686, r 2, Sch 1, para 494.
Date in force: 6 April 2010: see SI 2010/686, r 1; for transitional provisions and further effect see rr 6(1), 7, Sch 4, para 1, Sch 5 thereto.

Para (4): words "made to the court" in square brackets inserted by SI 2009/642, rr 4, 74(c).
Date in force: 6 April 2009: see SI 2009/642, r 1.

See Further

See further, in relation the application of this rule, with modifications, in respect of the procedure for the appointment of a bank liquidator and the operation of bank insolvency under the Banking Act 2009, Pt 2: the Bank Insolvency (England and Wales) Rules 2009, SI 2009/356, rr 3(3)–(8), 285.

See further, in relation to the application of this rule, with modifications, in respect of bank administration and applications for bank administration: the Bank Administration (England and Wales) Rules 2009, SI 2009/357, rr 58–61.

13.4 Notice, etc to solicitors

Where under the Act or the Rules a notice or other document is required or authorised to be given to a person, it may, if he has indicated that his solicitor is authorised to accept service on his behalf, be given instead to the solicitor.

NOTES

Initial Commencement

Specified date

Specified date: 29 December 1986: see r 0.1.

Modification

References to solicitors etc modified to include references to bodies recognised under the Administration of Justice Act 1985, s 9, by the Solicitors' Incorporated Practices Order 1991, SI 1991/2684, arts 4, 5, Sch 1.

See Further

See further, in relation the application of this rule, with modifications, in respect of the procedure for the appointment of a bank liquidator and the operation of bank insolvency under the Banking Act 2009, Pt 2: the Bank Insolvency (England and Wales) Rules 2009, SI 2009/356, rr 3(3)–(8), 286.

See further, in relation to the application of this rule, with modifications, in respect of bank administration and applications for bank administration: the Bank Administration (England and Wales) Rules 2009, SI 2009/357, rr 58–61.

13.5 Notice to joint liquidators, joint trustees, etc

Where two or more persons are acting jointly as the responsible insolvency practitioner in any proceedings, delivery of a document to one of them is to be treated as delivery to them all.

NOTES

Initial Commencement

Specified date

Specified date: 29 December 1986: see r 0.1.

See Further

See further, in relation to the application of this rule, with modifications, in respect of bank administration and applications for bank administration: the Bank Administration (England and Wales) Rules 2009, SI 2009/357, rr 58–61.

13.6 "Venue"

References to the "venue" for any proceeding or attendance before the court, or for a meeting, are to the time, date and place for the proceeding, attendance or meeting [or to the time and date for a meeting which is held in accordance with section 246A or 379A without any place being specified for it].

NOTES

Initial Commencement

Specified date

Specified date: 29 December 1986: see r 0.1.

Amendment

Words from "or to the" to "specified for it" in square brackets inserted by SI 2010/686, r 2, Sch 1, para 495.
Date in force: 6 April 2010: see SI 2010/686, r 1; for transitional provisions and further effect see rr 6(1), 7, Sch 4, paras 1, 2(1)(b), Sch 5 thereto.

See Further

See further, in relation to the application of this rule, with modifications, in respect of bank administration and applications for bank administration: the Bank Administration (England and Wales) Rules 2009, SI 2009/357, rr 58–61.

13.7 "Insolvency proceedings"

"Insolvency proceedings" means any proceedings under the Act or the Rules.

NOTES

Initial Commencement

Specified date

Specified date: 29 December 1986: see r 0.1.

See Further

See further, in relation to the application of this rule, with modifications, in respect of bank administration and applications for bank administration: the Bank Administration (England and Wales) Rules 2009, SI 2009/357, rr 58–61.

13.8 "Insolvent estate"

References to "the insolvent estate" are—
- (a) in relation to a company insolvency, the company's assets, and
- (b) in relation to [a bankruptcy or a petition for bankruptcy], the bankrupt's estate or (as the case may be) the debtor's property.

NOTES

Initial Commencement

Specified date

Specified date: 29 December 1986: see r 0.1.

Amendment

In para (b) words "a bankruptcy or a petition for bankruptcy" in square brackets substituted by SI 2009/642, rr 4, 75.
Date in force: 6 April 2009: see SI 2009/642, r 1.

See Further

See further, in relation to the application of this rule, with modifications, in respect of bank administration and applications for bank administration: the Bank Administration (England and Wales) Rules 2009, SI 2009/357, rr 58–61.

13.9 "Responsible insolvency practitioner", etc

(1) In relation to any insolvency proceedings, "the responsible insolvency practitioner" means—
- (a) the person [(other than the official receiver)] acting in a company insolvency, as supervisor of a voluntary arrangement under Part I of the Act, or as administrator, administrative receiver, liquidator or provisional liquidator;
- (b) the person [(other than the official receiver)] acting in an individual insolvency, as the supervisor of a voluntary arrangement under Part VIII of the Act, or as trustee or interim receiver;
- (c) . . ..

(2) . . .

[(3) A reference to an "authorised person" is a reference to a person who is authorised pursuant to section 389A of the Act to act as nominee or supervisor of a voluntary arrangement proposed or approved under Part I or Part VIII of the Act.]

NOTES

Initial Commencement

Specified date

Specified date: 29 December 1986: see r 0.1.

Amendment

Para (1): in sub-paras (a), (b) words "(other than the official receiver)" in square brackets inserted by SI 2010/686, r 2, Sch 1, para 496(1), (2)(a).
Date in force: 6 April 2010: see SI 2010/686, r 1; for transitional provisions and further effect see rr 6(1), 7, Sch 4, para 1, Sch 5 thereto.
Para (1): sub-para (c) revoked by SI 2010/686, r 2, Sch 1, para 496(1), (2)(b).
Date in force: 6 April 2010: see SI 2010/686, r 1; for transitional provisions and further effect see rr 6(1), 7, Sch 4, para 1, Sch 5 thereto.
Para (2): revoked by SI 2010/686, r 2, Sch 1, para 496(1), (3).
Date in force: 6 April 2010: see SI 2010/686, r 1; for transitional provisions and further effect see rr 6(1), 7, Sch 4, para 1, Sch 5 thereto.
Para (3): inserted by SI 2002/2712, r 7.

Date in force: 1 January 2003: see SI 2002/2712, r 1(1).

See Further
See further, in relation to the application of this rule, with modifications, in respect of bank administration and applications for bank administration: the Bank Administration (England and Wales) Rules 2009, SI 2009/357, rr 58–61.

[13.9A Office-holder]
["Office-holder" means in relation to insolvency proceedings any person who by virtue of any provision of the Act or the Rules holds an office in relation to those proceedings.]

NOTES

Amendment
Inserted by SI 2010/686, r 2, Sch 1, para 497.
Date in force: 6 April 2010: see SI 2010/686, r 1; for transitional provisions and further effect see rr 6(1), 7, Sch 4, paras 1, 5(3), Sch 5 thereto.

13.10 "Petitioner"
In winding-up and bankruptcy, references to "the petitioner" or "the petitioning creditor" include any person who has been substituted as such, or been given carriage of the petition.

NOTES

Initial Commencement

Specified date
Specified date: 29 December 1986: see r 0.1.

See Further
See further, in relation to the application of this rule, with modifications, in respect of bank administration and applications for bank administration: the Bank Administration (England and Wales) Rules 2009, SI 2009/357, rr 58–61.

13.11 "The appropriate fee"
"The appropriate fee" means—
    (a)   in Rule 6.192(2) (payor under income payments order entitled to clerical etc costs) [or Rule 6.193C(4) (payor under income payments agreement entitled to clerical etc costs)], 50 pence; and
    (b)   in other cases, 15 pence per A4 or A5 page, and 30 pence per A3 page.

NOTES

Initial Commencement

Specified date
Specified date: 29 December 1986: see r 0.1.

Amendment
In para (a) words from "or Rule 6.193C(4)" to "clerical etc costs)" in square brackets inserted by SI 2003/1730, r 13, Sch 1, Pt 10, para 64.
Date in force: 1 April 2004: see SI 2003/1730, r 1(3).

Insolvency Rules 1986, reg 13.11

See Further

See further, in relation to the application of this rule, with modifications, in respect of bank administration and applications for bank administration: the Bank Administration (England and Wales) Rules 2009, SI 2009/357, rr 58–61.

[13.12 "Debt", "liability" (winding up)]

[(1) "Debt", in relation to the winding up of a company, means (subject to the next paragraph) any of the following—

[(a) any debt or liability to which the company is subject—
  (i) in the case of a winding up which was not immediately preceded by an administration, at the date on which the company went into liquidation;
  (ii) in the case of a winding up which was immediately preceded by an administration, at the date on which the company entered administration;]

(b) any debt or liability to which the company may become subject after that date by reason of any obligation incurred before that date; and

(c) any interest provable as mentioned in Rule 4.93(1).

(2) For the purposes of any provision of the Act or the Rules about winding up, any liability in tort is a debt provable in the winding up, if either—

[(a) the cause of action has accrued—
  (i) in the case of a winding up which was not immediately preceded by an administration, at the date on which the company went into liquidation;
  (ii) in the case of a winding up which was immediately preceded by an administration, at the date on which the company entered administration]; or

(b) all the elements necessary to establish the cause of action exist at that date except for actionable damage.

(3) For the purposes of references in any provision of the Act or the Rules about winding up to a debt or liability, it is immaterial whether the debt or liability is present or future, whether it is certain or contingent, or whether its amount is fixed or liquidated, or is capable of being ascertained by fixed rules or as a matter of opinion; and references in any such provision to owing a debt are to be read accordingly.

(4) In any provision of the Act or the Rules about winding up, except in so far as the context otherwise requires, "liability" means (subject to paragraph (3) above) a liability to pay money or money's worth, including any liability under an enactment, any liability for breach of trust, any liability in contract, tort or bailment, and any liability arising out of an obligation to make restitution.

(5) This Rule shall apply where a company is in administration and shall be read as if[—

(a) references to winding up were references to administration,
(b) references to administration were references to winding up,
(c) references to going into liquidation were references to entering administration, and
(d) references to entering administration were references to going into liquidation].]

NOTES

Amendment

Substituted by SI 2006/1272, r 4.
  Date in force: 1 June 2006: see SI 2006/1272, r 1(2); for transitional provisions and further effect see r 3 thereof.
Para (1): sub-para (a) substituted by SI 2010/686, r 2, Sch 1, para 498(1), (2).

Date in force: 6 April 2010: see SI 2010/686, r 1; for transitional provisions and further effect see rr 6(1), 7, Sch 4, para 1, Sch 5 thereto.
Para (2): sub-para (a) substituted by SI 2010/686, r 2, Sch 1, para 498(1), (3).
Date in force: 6 April 2010: see SI 2010/686, r 1; for transitional provisions and further effect see rr 6(1), 7, Sch 4, para 1, Sch 5 thereto.
Para (5): sub-paras (a)–(d) substituted, for words in para (5) as originally enacted, by SI 2010/686, r 2, Sch 1, para 498(1), (4).
Date in force: 6 April 2010: see SI 2010/686, r 1; for transitional provisions and further effect see rr 6(1), 7, Sch 4, para 1, Sch 5 thereto.

See Further

See further, in relation the application of this rule, with modifications, in respect of the procedure for the appointment of a bank liquidator and the operation of bank insolvency under the Banking Act 2009, Pt 2: the Bank Insolvency (England and Wales) Rules 2009, SI 2009/356, rr 3(3)–(8), 291.

See further, in relation to the application of this rule, with modifications, in respect of bank administration and applications for bank administration: the Bank Administration (England and Wales) Rules 2009, SI 2009/357, rr 58–61.

[13.12A "Authorised deposit-taker and former authorised deposit-taker"]

[(1) "Authorised deposit-taker" means a person with permission under Part 4 of the Financial Services and Markets Act 2000 to accept deposits.

(2) "Former authorised deposit-taker" means a person who—

(a) is not an authorised deposit-taker,

(b) was formerly an authorised institution under the Banking Act 1987, or a recognised bank or a licensed institution under the Banking Act 1979, and

(c) continues to have liability in respect of any deposit for which it had a liability at a time when it was an authorised institution, recognised bank or licensed institution.

(3) Paragraphs (1) and (2) must be read with—

(a) section 22 of the Financial Services and Markets Act 2000;

(b) any relevant order under that section; and

(c) Schedule 22 to that Act.]

NOTES

Amendment

Inserted by SI 2001/3649, art 381.
Date in force: 1 December 2001: see SI 2001/3649, art 1.

See Further

See further, in relation to the application of this rule, with modifications, in respect of bank administration and applications for bank administration: the Bank Administration (England and Wales) Rules 2009, SI 2009/357, rr 58–61.

13.13 Expressions used generally

[(1) "Business day" means any day other than a Saturday, a Sunday, Christmas Day, Good Friday or a day which is a bank holiday in any part of [England and Wales] under or by virtue of the Banking and Financial Dealings Act 1971 . . ..]

(2) "The Department" means [the Department for Business, Innovation and Skills].

[(2A) "Duly authorised representative" means, in relation to a corporation, a person who is authorised by or under the constitution of the corporation to act on behalf of the corporation; and like expressions are to be construed accordingly.]

(3) "File in court [and file with the court]" means deliver to the court for filing.

(4) "The Gazette" means the London Gazette.

[(4A) "gazetted" means [advertised] once in the Gazette.]
[(4B) "Standard contents" means—
- (a) in relation to a notice to be gazetted, the contents specified in Rules 12A.33 to 12A.35; and
- (b) in relation to a notice to be advertised in any other way, the contents specified in Rules 12A.38 to 12A.40.]

(5) "General regulations" means regulations made by the Secretary of State under Rule 12.1.

[(6) "Practice direction" means a direction as to the practice and procedure of any court within the scope of the CPR.

(7) "Prescribed order of priority" means the order of priority of payments laid down by Chapter 20 of Part 4 of the Rules, or Chapter 23 of Part 6.]

[(8) "Centre of main interests" has the same meaning as in the EC Regulation.

(9) "Establishment" has the meaning given by Article 2(h) of the EC Regulation.

(10) "Main proceedings" means proceedings opened in accordance with Article 3(1) of the EC Regulation and falling within the definition of insolvency proceedings in Article 2(a) of the EC Regulation and
- (a) in relation to England and Wales . . . set out in Annex A to the EC Regulation under the heading "United Kingdom", and
- (b) in relation to another member State, set out in Annex A to the EC Regulation under the heading relating to that member State.

(11) "Member State liquidator" means a person falling within the definition of liquidator in Article 2(b) of the EC Regulation appointed in proceedings to which it applies in a member State other than the United Kingdom.

(12) "Secondary proceedings" means proceedings opened in accordance with Articles 3(2) and 3(3) of the EC Regulation and falling within the definition of winding-up proceedings in Article 2(c) of the EC Regulation, and
- (a) in relation to England and Wales . . ., set out in Annex B to the EC Regulation under the heading "United Kingdom", and
- (b) in relation to another member State, set out in Annex B to the EC Regulation under the heading relating to that member State.

(13) "Temporary administrator" means a temporary administrator referred to by Article 38 of the EC Regulation.

(14) "Territorial proceedings" means proceedings opened in accordance with Articles 3(2) and 3(4) of the EC Regulation and falling within the definition of insolvency proceedings in Article 2(a) of the EC Regulation, and
- (a) in relation to England and Wales . . ., set out in Annex A to the EC Regulation under the heading "United Kingdom", and
- (b) in relation to another member State, set out in Annex A to the EC Regulation under the heading relating to that member State.]

[(14A) "Winding-up proceedings" means winding-up proceedings within the meaning of Article 2(c) of the EC Regulation as listed under the United Kingdom entry in Annex B of that Regulation, except for bankruptcy and sequestration proceedings.]

[(15) "Prescribed part" has the same meaning as it does in section 176A(2)(a) [and the Insolvency Act 1986 (Prescribed Part) Order 2003].]

[(16) A "certificate of service" means a certificate of service verified by a statement of truth.

(17) A "statement of truth" means a statement of truth in accordance with CPR Part 22.

(18) A "witness statement" means a witness statement verified by a statement of truth in accordance with CPR Part 22.

(19) A fee or remuneration is charged when the work to which it relates is done.]

NOTES

Initial Commencement

Specified date

Specified date: 29 December 1986: see r 0.1.

Amendment

Para (1): substituted by SI 1999/1022, r 3, Schedule, para 14(a).
    Date in force: 26 April 1999: see SI 1999/1022, r 1.
Para (1): words "England and Wales" in square brackets substituted by SI 2010/686, r 2, Sch 1, para 499(1), (2)(a).
    Date in force: 6 April 2010: see SI 2010/686, r 1; for transitional provisions and further effect see rr 6(1), 7, Sch 4, para 1, Sch 5 thereto.
Para (1): words omitted revoked by SI 2010/686, r 2, Sch 1, para 499(1), (2)(b).
    Date in force: 6 April 2010: see SI 2010/686, r 1; for transitional provisions and further effect see rr 6(1), 7, Sch 4, para 1, Sch 5 thereto.
Para (2): words "the Department for Business, Innovation and Skills" in square brackets substituted by SI 2009/2748, art 8, Schedule, Pt 2, para 12.
    Date in force: 13 November 2009: see SI 2009/2748, art 1(2).
Para (2A): inserted by SI 2010/686, r 2, Sch 1, para 499(1), (3).
    Date in force: 6 April 2010: see SI 2010/686, r 1; for transitional provisions and further effect see rr 6(1), 7, Sch 4, para 1, Sch 5 thereto.
Para (3): words "and file with the court" in square brackets inserted by SI 2003/1730, r 13, Sch 1, Pt 10, para 66(a).
    Date in force: 15 September 2003: see SI 2003/1730, r 1(2).
Para (4A): inserted by SI 2009/642, rr 4, 76.
    Date in force: 6 April 2009: see SI 2009/642, r 1; for transitional provisions see r 3 thereof.
Para (4A): word "advertised" in square brackets substituted by SI 2010/686, r 2, Sch 1, para 499(1), (4).
    Date in force: 6 April 2010: see SI 2010/686, r 1; for transitional provisions and further effect see rr 6(1), 7, Sch 4, para 1, Sch 5 thereto.
Para (4B): inserted by SI 2010/686, r 2, Sch 1, para 499(1), (5).
    Date in force: 6 April 2010: see SI 2010/686, r 1; for transitional provisions and further effect see rr 6(1), 7, Sch 4, para 1, Sch 5 thereto.
Paras (6), (7): substituted, for para (6) as originally enacted, by SI 1999/1022, r 3, Schedule, para 14(b).
    Date in force: 26 April 1999: see SI 1999/1022, r 1.
Paras (8)–(14): inserted by SI 2002/1307, rr 3(1), 10(7).
    Date in force: 31 May 2002: see SI 2002/1307, r 1.
Para (10): in sub-para (a) words omitted revoked by SI 2010/686, r 2, Sch 1, para 499(1), (6).
    Date in force: 6 April 2010: see SI 2010/686, r 1; for transitional provisions and further effect see rr 6(1), 7, Sch 4, para 1, Sch 5 thereto.
Para (12): in sub-para (a) words omitted revoked by SI 2010/686, r 2, Sch 1, para 499(1), (6).
    Date in force: 6 April 2010: see SI 2010/686, r 1; for transitional provisions and further effect see rr 6(1), 7, Sch 4, para 1, Sch 5 thereto.
Para (14): in sub-para (a) words omitted revoked by SI 2010/686, r 2, Sch 1, para 499(1), (6).
    Date in force: 6 April 2010: see SI 2010/686, r 1; for transitional provisions and further effect see rr 6(1), 7, Sch 4, para 1, Sch 5 thereto.
Para (14A): inserted by SI 2010/686, r 2, Sch 1, para 499(1), (7).
    Date in force: 6 April 2010: see SI 2010/686, r 1; for transitional provisions and further effect see rr 6(1), 7, Sch 4, para 1, Sch 5 thereto.
Para (15): inserted by SI 2003/1730, r 13, Sch 1, Pt 10, para 66(b).
    Date in force: 15 September 2003: see SI 2003/1730, r 1(2).
Para (15): words "and the Insolvency Act 1986 (Prescribed Part) Order 2003" in square brackets inserted by SI 2010/686, r 2, Sch 1, para 499(1), (8).
    Date in force: 6 April 2010: see SI 2010/686, r 1; for transitional provisions and further effect see rr 6(1), 7, Sch 4, para 1, Sch 5 thereto.
Paras (16)–(19): inserted by SI 2010/686, r 2, Sch 1, para 499(1), (9).
    Date in force: 6 April 2010: see SI 2010/686, r 1; for transitional provisions see rr 6(1), 7, Sch 4, paras 1, 2(1)(b), (2)–(4), Sch 5 thereto.

See Further

See further, in relation the application of this rule, with modifications, in respect of the procedure for the appointment of a bank liquidator and the operation of bank insolvency under the Banking Act 2009, Pt 2: the Bank Insolvency (England and Wales) Rules 2009, SI 2009/356, rr 3(3)–(8), 292.

See further, in relation to the application of this rule, with modifications, in respect of bank administration and applications for bank administration: the Bank Administration (England and Wales) Rules 2009, SI 2009/357, rr 58–61.

13.14 Application

(1) Subject to paragraph (2) of this Rule, and save where otherwise expressly provided, the Rules apply—

(a) to . . . receivers appointed on or after the day on which the Rules come into force,

(b) to bankruptcy proceedings where the bankruptcy petition is presented on or after the day on which the Rules come into force, and

(c) to all other insolvency proceedings commenced on or after that day.

(2) The Rules also apply to winding-up and bankruptcy proceedings commenced before that day to which provisions of the Act are applied by Schedule 11 to the Act, to the extent necessary to give effect to those provisions.

NOTES

Initial Commencement

Specified date

Specified date: 29 December 1986: see r 0.1.

Amendment

Para (1): word omitted revoked by SI 1987/1919, r 3(1), Schedule, Part 1, para 152.

[13.15 Application of Insolvency Act 1986 and Company Directors Disqualification Act 1986]

[For the purposes of these Rules, any reference in the Act or the Company Directors Disqualification Act 1986 to "leave" of the court is to be construed as meaning "permission" of the court.]

NOTES

Amendment

Inserted by SI 2010/686, r 2, Sch 1, para 500.
Date in force: 6 April 2010: see SI 2010/686, r 1; for transitional provisions and further effect see rr 6(1), 7, Sch 4, para 1, Sch 5 thereto.

SCHEDULE 1
[SCHEME MANAGER'S] VOTING RIGHTS

NOTES

Amendment

Schedule heading: words "Scheme Manager's" in square brackets substituted by virtue of SI 2001/3649, art 378(3).
Date in force: 1 December 2001: see SI 2001/3649, art 1.

Rule 4.72(7)

1

This Schedule applies as does Rule 4.72.

2

In relation to any meeting at which the [scheme manager] is under Rule 4.72 entitled to be represented, the [scheme manager] may submit in the liquidation, instead of a proof, a written statement of voting rights ("the statement").

3

The statement shall contain details of—

    (a)   the names of creditors of the company in respect of whom an obligation of the [scheme manager] has arisen or may reasonably be expected to arise as a result of the liquidation or proposed liquidation;

    (b)   the amount of the obligation so arising; and

    (c)   the total amount of all such obligations specified in the statement.

4

The [scheme manager's] statement shall, for the purpose of voting at a meeting (but for no other purpose), be treated in all respects as if it were a proof.

5

Any voting rights which a creditor might otherwise exercise at a meeting in respect of a claim against the company are reduced by a sum equal to the amount of that claim in relation to which the [scheme manager], by virtue of its having submitted a statement, is entitled to exercise voting rights at that meeting.

6

The [scheme manager] may from time to time submit a further statement, and, if it does so, that statement supersedes any statement previously submitted.

NOTES

Initial Commencement

Specified date

    Specified date: 29 December 1986: see r 0.1.

Amendment

    Paras 2–6: words "scheme manager" in square brackets in each place they occur substituted by SI 2001/3649, art 378(3).
        Date in force: 1 December 2001: see SI 2001/3649, art 1.

See Further

    See further, in relation the application of this Schedule, with modifications, in respect of the procedure for the appointment of a bank liquidator and the operation of bank insolvency under the Banking Act 2009, Pt 2: the Bank Insolvency (England and Wales) Rules 2009, SI 2009/356, rr 3(3)–(8), 293, Schedule, para 1(a).

[SCHEDULE 2
ALTERNATIVE COURTS]

NOTES

Amendment

    Substituted by SI 1987/1919, r 3(1), Schedule, Pt 2, para 153, Pt 3.
    Schedule heading: substituted by SI 2009/642, rr 4, 77.

Insolvency Rules 1986, Sch 2

Date in force: 6 April 2009: see SI 2009/642, r 1.

[Rules 5A.21(2) and 6.40(3)]

NOTES

Amendment

Words "Rules 5A.21(2) and 6.40(3)" in square brackets substituted by SI 2009/642, rr 4, 77.

Date in force: 6 April 2009: see SI 2009/642, r 1.

[Debtor's own county court	Nearest full-time court
ABERDARE	CARDIFF
ABERYSTWYTH	CARDIFF
AYLESBURY	LUTON
BANBURY	LUTON or GLOUCESTER or READING
...	...
BARNSLEY	SHEFFIELD
BARNSTAPLE	EXETER
BARROW IN FURNESS	BLACKPOOL or PRESTON
BATH	BRISTOL
BEDFORD	LUTON
BLACKBURN	PRESTON
BLACKWOOD	CARDIFF
BOSTON	NOTTINGHAM
BRIDGEND	CARDIFF
...	...
[BURY	BOLTON]
BURNLEY	BOLTON or PRESTON
BURTON ON TRENT	LEICESTER or DERBY or NOTTINGHAM
BURY ST EDMUNDS	CAMBRIDGE
CANTERBURY	CROYDON or THE HIGH COURT (LONDON)

CARLISLE	PRESTON or BLACKPOOL
CARMARTHEN	CARDIFF
CHELMSFORD	SOUTHEND or THE HIGH COURT (LONDON)
CHELTENHAM	GLOUCESTER
CHESTERFIELD	SHEFFIELD
COLCHESTER	SOUTHEND or THE HIGH COURT (LONDON)
COVENTRY	BIRMINGHAM
CREWE	STOKE or CHESTER
DARLINGTON	MIDDLESBOROUGH
DEWSBURY	LEEDS
DONCASTER	SHEFFIELD
DUDLEY	BIRMINGHAM
DURHAM	NEWCASTLE
EASTBOURNE	BRIGHTON
GREAT GRIMSBY	HULL
...	...
GUILDFORD	CROYDON
HALIFAX	LEEDS
HARROGATE	LEEDS
HASTINGS	BRIGHTON
HAVERFORDWEST	CARDIFF
HEREFORD	GLOUCESTER
HERTFORD	LUTON
HUDDERSFIELD	LEEDS
IPSWICH	NORWICH or SOUTHEND
KENDAL	BLACKPOOL or PRESTON
KIDDERMINSTER	BIRMINGHAM

KING'S LYNN	NORWICH or CAMBRIDGE
LANCASTER	BLACKPOOL or PRESTON
LINCOLN	NOTTINGHAM
MACCLESFIELD	STOKE or MANCHESTER
MAIDSTONE	CROYDON or THE HIGH COURT (LONDON)
MEDWAY	CROYDON or THE HIGH COURT (LONDON)
MERTHYR TYDFIL	CARDIFF
MILTON KEYNES	LUTON
[MOLD	WREXHAM]
NEATH	CARDIFF
NEWBURY	READING
NEWPORT (GWENT)	CARDIFF
NEWPORT (IOW)	SOUTHAMPTON or PORTSMOUTH
NORTHAMPTON	LUTON
OXFORD	READING
PETERBOROUGH	CAMBRIDGE
PONTYPRIDD	CARDIFF
...	...
RHYL	BIRKENHEAD or CHESTER
...	...
SALISBURY	BOURNEMOUTH or SOUTHAMPTON
SCARBOROUGH	YORK or HULL or MIDDLESBOROUGH
SCUNTHORPE	HULL or SHEFFIELD
SHREWSBURY	STOKE
ST. ALBANS	LUTON

STAFFORD	STOKE
STOCKTON ON TEES	MIDDLES-BOROUGH
STOCKPORT	MANCHESTER
STOURBRIDGE	BIRMINGHAM
SUNDERLAND	NEWCASTLE
SWANSEA	CARDIFF
SWINDON	GLOUCESTER or READING
TAMESIDE	MANCHESTER
TAUNTON	EXETER or BRISTOL
TORQUAY	EXETER
TRURO	PLYMOUTH
TUNBRIDGE WELLS	CROYDON
WAKEFIELD	LEEDS
WARRINGTON	CHESTER or LIVERPOOL or MANCHESTER
WARWICK	BIRMINGHAM
WELSHPOOL	STOKE or CHESTER
...	...
WEYMOUTH	BOURNEMOUTH
WIGAN	BOLTON or MANCHESTER or PRESTON
WINCHESTER	SOUTHAMPTON
WORCESTER	GLOUCESTER
...	...
WREXHAM	BIRKENHEAD or STOKE or CHESTER
YEOVIL	EXETER or BRISTOL]

NOTES

Amendment

Substituted by SI 1987/1919, r 3(1), Schedule, Part 2, para 153, Part 3.

Entry relating to "Bangor" (omitted) revoked by SI 2010/686, r 2, Sch 1, para 501(1), (2). Date in force: 6 April 2010: see SI 2010/686, r 1; for transitional provisions see r 6(1), Sch 4, para 1 thereto.

Entry relating to "Bridgwater" (omitted) revoked by SI 2010/686, r 2, Sch 1, para 501(1), (3).
    Date in force: 6 April 2010: see SI 2010/686, r 1; for transitional provisions see r 6(1), Sch 4, para 1 thereto.
Entry relating to "Bury" inserted by SI 2010/686, r 2, Sch 1, para 501(1), (4).
    Date in force: 6 April 2010: see SI 2010/686, r 1; for transitional provisions see r 6(1), Sch 4, para 1 thereto.
Entry relating to "Great Yarmouth" (omitted) revoked by SI 2010/686, r 2, Sch 1, para 501(1), (5).
    Date in force: 6 April 2010: see SI 2010/686, rule 1.
Entry relating to "Mold" inserted by SI 2010/686, r 2, Sch 1, para 501(1), (6).
    Date in force: 6 April 2010: see SI 2010/686, r 1; for transitional provisions see r 6(1), Sch 4, para 1 thereto.
Entry relating to "Portmadoc" (omitted) revoked by SI 2010/686, r 2, Sch 1, para 501(1), (7).
    Date in force: 6 April 2010: see SI 2010/686, r 1; for transitional provisions see r 6(1), Sch 4, para 1 thereto.
Entry relating to "Rochdale" (omitted) revoked by SI 2010/686, r 2, Sch 1, para 501(1), (8).
    Date in force: 6 April 2010: see SI 2010/686, r 1; for transitional provisions see r 6(1), Sch 4, para 1 thereto.
Entry relating to "West Bromwich" (omitted) revoked by SI 2010/686, r 2, Sch 1, para 501(1), (9).
    Date in force: 6 April 2010: see SI 2010/686, r 1; for transitional provisions see r 6(1), Sch 4, para 1 thereto.
Entry relating to "Workington" (omitted) revoked by SI 2010/686, r 2, Sch 1, para 501(1), (10).
    Date in force: 6 April 2010: see SI 2010/686, r 1; for transitional provisions see r 6(1), Sch 4, para 1 thereto.

SCHEDULE 4
FORMS

Please note that none of the forms in this Schedule have been reproduced in this Handbook. Please consult The Insolvency Service website at http://www.insolvency.gov.uk/ to access the forms prescribed.
Rule 12.7

FORMS INDEX

PART 1: COMPANY VOLUNTARY ARRANGEMENTS

FORM NO / TITLE

1.1 . . .
[1.2 . . .
1.3 . . .
1.4 . . .
1.5 Nominee's statement of opinion
1.6 Statement of affairs
1.7 Statement of eligibility for a moratorium
1.8 Statement of consent to act by nominee
1.9 Documents to be submitted to court to obtain moratorium
1.10 [Advertisement of coming into force or ending of moratorium (for Gazette and other advertising)]
1.11 . . .
1.12 . . .
1.13 Notice to court of extension or further extension of moratorium
1.14 . . .
1.15 Nominee's notice to court of end of moratorium
1.16 . . .

1.17 Notice to court by nominee of withdrawal of consent to act
1.18 . . .
1.19 Notice to court of appointment of replacement nominee]

PART 2: ADMINISTRATION PROCEDURE

[2.1B Administration application
2.2B Statement of proposed administrator
2.3B . . .
2.4B Administration order
2.5B Notice of intention to appoint an administrator by holder of qualifying floating charge
2.6B Notice of appointment of an administrator by holder of qualifying floating charge
2.7B Notice of appointment of an administrator by holder of qualifying floating charge (For use in pursuance of Rule 2.19 of the Insolvency Rules 1986)
2.8B Notice of intention to appoint an administrator by company or director(s)
2.9B Notice of appointment of an administrator by company or director(s) (where a notice of intention to appoint has been issued)
2.10B Notice of appointment of an administrator by company or director(s) (where a notice of intention to appoint has not been issued)
2.11B . . .
2.12B Notice of administrator's appointment
2.13B Notice requiring submission of a statement of affairs
2.14B Statement of affairs
2.15B Statement of concurrence
2.16B . . .
2.17B . . .
2.18B Notice of extension of time period
2.19B Notice to attend meeting of creditors
2.20B Notice of a meeting of creditors
2.21B Creditor's request for a meeting
2.22B Statement of administrator's revised proposals
2.23B Notice of result of meeting of creditors
2.24B Administrator's progress report
2.25B Notice of conduct of business by correspondence
2.26B [Amended] Certificate of constitution of creditors' committee
2.27B . . .
2.28B . . .
2.29B . . .
2.30B Notice of automatic end of administration
2.31B . . .
2.32B Notice of end of administration
2.33B . . .
2.34B . . .
2.35B . . .
2.36B . . .
2.37B Notice of intention to resign as administrator
2.38B Notice of resignation by administrator
2.39B . . .
2.40B . . .]

PART 3: ADMINISTRATIVE RECEIVERSHIP

[3.1 Written acceptance of appointment by receiver

Insolvency Rules 1986, Sch 4

[3.1A [Notice of appointment of administrative receiver (for Gazette and other advertising)]]
[3.1B Notice requiring preparation and submission of administrative receivership statement of affairs]
3.2 Statement of affairs
3.3 . . .
3.4 . . .
3.5 . . .
3.6 Receiver or manager or administrative receiver's abstract of receipts and payments
3.7 . . .
3.8 . . .
3.9 Notice of resignation of administrative receiver pursuant to section 45(1) of Insolvency Act 1986
3.10 . . .

PART 4: COMPANIES WINDING UP

[4.1 Statutory demand under section 123(1)(a) or 222(1)(a) of the Insolvency Act 1986]
[4.2 Winding-up petition]
4.3 . . .
4.4 . . .
4.5 . . .
[4.6 Advertisement of winding-up petition]
4.7 Certificate that relevant provisions of Rules have been complied with
4.8 Order for [permission] to withdraw winding-up petition
4.9 Notice of intention to appear on petition
4.10 List of persons intending to appear on the hearing of the petition
[4.11 Order for winding up by the court]
[4.12 Order for winding up by the court following upon the cessation of the appointment of an administrator]
[4.13 Notice to official receiver of winding-up order]
[4.14 Petition by contributory]
[4.14A Notice to official receiver of appointment of provisional liquidator]
[4.15 Order of appointment of provisional liquidator]
[4.15A . . .]
[4.16 Notice requiring preparation and submission of statement of company's affairs]
[4.17 Statement of affairs]
[4.18 Statement of affairs]
[4.19 Statement of affairs]
4.20 . . .
4.21 Request by creditors for a meeting of the company's creditors (and contributories)
4.22 Notice to creditors of meeting of creditors
4.23 Notice to contributories of meeting of contributories
4.24 Request by contributory/contributories for a meeting of the company's contributories
[4.25 Proof of debt—general form]
4.26 . . .
4.27 Certificate of appointment of liquidator by meeting
4.28 Certificate of appointment of two or more liquidators by meeting
4.29 Order of court appointing liquidator
4.30 Order of court appointing two or more liquidators
4.31 . . .

4.32 Notice to court of resignation of liquidator following meeting of creditors
4.33 . . .
4.34 Order of court giving liquidator [permission] to resign
4.35 . . .
4.36 Notice to court of resignation of liquidator following [permission] of the court
4.37 Certificate of removal of liquidator
4.38 . . .
4.39 Order of court removing liquidator or directing liquidator to summon a meeting of creditors for purpose of his removal
4.40 . . .
4.41 Liquidator's application to the Secretary of State for his release
4.42 Notice to court of final meeting of creditors
4.43 . . .
4.44 . . .
4.45 Notice to official receiver or Secretary of State by liquidator on loss of qualification as insolvency practitioner
4.46 . . .
4.47 Certificate of constitution (amended certificate) of liquidation committee
4.48 . . .
4.49 . . .
4.50 . . .
4.51 . . .
[4.52 Liquidator's certificate of continuance of liquidation committee]
[4.53A Notice of disclaimer under section 178 of the Insolvency Act 1986]
4.54 Notice to elect
4.55 Notice of intended disclaimer to interested party
4.56 [Witness statement] of liquidator in support of application for call
4.57 Order giving [permission] to make a call
4.58 Notice of call sanctioned by the court or the liquidation committee to be sent to contributory
4.59 Order for payment of call due from contributory
4.60 Order of appointment of special manager
[4.61 Order of public examination]
4.62 Notice to official receiver by creditor requesting him to make application for the holding of a public examination
4.63 Notice to official receiver by contributory requesting him to make application for the holding of a public examination
[4.64 Order as to examination of person who lacks capacity to manage and administer his property and affairs or is suffering from a physical affliction or disability]
4.65 [Statement of truth verifying] record of the public examination
[4.66 Order of adjournment of public examination]
[4.67 Order appointing time for proceeding with public examination adjourned generally]
4.68 . . .
4.69 . . .
[4.70 Members' voluntary winding up declaration of solvency embodying a statement of assets and liabilities]
4.71 . . .
4.72 . . .
[4.73 Notice to the creditors of an insolvent company of the re-use of a prohibited name]
[4.74 Property subject to floating charge: notice of request to specified creditor for approval or authorisation of litigation expenses]

Insolvency Rules 1986, Sch 4

PART 5: INDIVIDUAL VOLUNTARY ARRANGEMENTS
[5.1 Order for stay pending hearing of application for interim order]
[5.2 Interim order of court under section 252 of the Insolvency Act 1986]
[5.3 Order extending effect of interim order]
[5.4 Alternative orders to be made at hearing to consider chairman's report]
[5.5 . . .]
[5.6 Voting form in relation to a proposal for a voluntary arrangement under section 263A of the Insolvency Act 1986
[5.7 Order of annulment under section 261 of the Insolvency Act 1986]]
[5.8 Order of annulment under section 263D of the Insolvency Act 1986]

PART 6: BANKRUPTCY
[6.1 Statutory demand under section 268(1)(a) of the Insolvency Act 1986—debt for liquidated sum payable immediately]
[6.2 Statutory demand under section 268(1)(a) of the Insolvency Act 1986—debt for liquidated sum payable immediately following a judgment or order of the court]
[6.3 Statutory demand under section 268(2) of the Insolvency Act 1986—debt payable at future date]
6.4 Application to set aside statutory demand
6.5 [Witness statement] in support of application to set aside statutory demand
6.6 Order setting aside statutory demand
[6.7 Creditor's bankruptcy petition on failure to comply with a statutory demand for a liquidated sum payable immediately]
[6.8 Creditor's bankruptcy petition on failure to comply with a statutory demand for a liquidated sum payable at a future date]
[6.9 Creditor's bankruptcy petition where execution or other process on a judgment has been returned unsatisfied in whole or part]
[6.10 Bankruptcy petition for default in connection with voluntary arrangement]
[6.11 [Certificate] of personal service of statutory demand]
6.12 [Certificate] of substituted service of statutory demand
[6.13A Statement of truth of statements in bankruptcy petition]
[6.14 Application for registration of a petition in bankruptcy against an individual under Land Charges Act 1972]
[6.15A Order for substituted service of a bankruptcy petition]
6.16 Substituted service of bankruptcy petition—notice in Gazette
[6.17A Certificate of personal service of bankruptcy petition]
[6.18A Certificate of substituted service of bankruptcy petition]
6.19 Notice by debtor of intention to oppose bankruptcy petition
6.20 Notice of intention to appear on bankruptcy petition
6.21 List of creditors intending to appear on hearing of the bankruptcy petition
6.22 Dismissal of bankruptcy petition
6.23 Order of adjournment of bankruptcy petition
6.24 Notice to debtor and creditors of order of adjournment of bankruptcy petition
[6.24A Order for substitution of petitioner on creditor's petition]
[6.24B Change of carriage order]
[6.25 Bankruptcy order on creditor's petition]
[6.26 Application for registration of a bankruptcy order against an individual under Land Charges Act 1972]
[6.27 Debtor's bankruptcy petition]
[6.28 Statement of affairs—debtor's petition]
6.29 Order of appointment of insolvency practitioner to prepare a report under section 274(1) of the Insolvency Act 1986
[6.30 Bankruptcy order on debtor's petition]

6.31 . . .
[6.32 Order of appointment of interim receiver]
[6.33A Statement of affairs (creditor's petition)]
6.34 Request by creditor(s) for a meeting of the bankrupt's creditors
6.35 Notice to creditors of meeting of creditors
6.36 Notice to bankrupt of meeting of creditors
[6.37 Proof of debt—general form]
6.38 Proof by existing trustee as a claim in later bankruptcy
6.39 . . .
6.40 Certificate of appointment of trustee by creditors' meeting
6.41 Certificate of appointment of two or more trustees by creditors' meeting
6.42 Order of court appointing trustee
6.43 Order of court appointing two or more trustees
6.44 Notice to court of resignation of trustee following meeting of creditors
6.45 Order of court giving trustee [permission] to resign
6.46 Notice to court of resignation of trustee following [permission] of the court
6.47 Certificate of removal of trustee
6.48 Order of court removing trustee or directing trustee to summon a meeting of creditors for the purpose of his removal
6.49 Trustee's application to the Secretary of State for his release
6.50 Notice to court of final meeting of creditors
6.51 Notice to official receiver by trustee on loss of qualification as insolvency practitioner
6.52 Certificate of constitution (amended certificate) of creditors' committee
6.53 . . .
6.54 Order of appointment of special manager
[6.55 Order for public examination of bankrupt]
6.56 Request by creditor(s) for the holding of a public examination of the bankrupt
[6.57 Order as to examination of bankrupt who lacks capacity to manage and administer his property and affairs or is suffering from a physical affliction or disability]
6.58 [Statement of truth verifying] record of the public examination of the bankrupt
[6.59 Order of adjournment of public examination of bankrupt]
[6.60 Order appointing time for proceeding with public examination of bankrupt adjourned . . .]
[6.61A Notice of disclaimer under section 315 of the Insolvency Act 1986]
6.62 Notice to elect
6.63 Notice of intended disclaimer to interested party
6.64 Notice to bankrupt of an application under section 310 of the Insolvency Act 1986 for an income payments order
6.65 Order for income claimed under section 310(3)(a) of the Insolvency Act 1986
6.66 Order for income claimed under section 310(3)(b) of the Insolvency Act 1986
6.67 Order converting income payments order made under section 310(1)(a) to an order under section 310(3)(b) of the Insolvency Act 1986
6.68 Discharge or variation of order for income claimed under section 310 of the Insolvency Act 1986
6.69 Order under section 369(l) of the Insolvency Act 1986
6.70 Order under section 369(2) of the Insolvency Act 1986
[6.71 Order of annulment under section 282 of the Insolvency Act 1986]
[6.72 Order of suspension of discharge under section 279(3) of the Insolvency Act 1986]
[6.73 Order of court lifting suspension of discharge]
6.74 Certificate that order suspending discharge has been lifted

Insolvency Rules 1986, Sch 4

6.75 Notice to court by bankrupt that he intends to dispute statements made by official receiver in his report under section 289(2) of the Insolvency Act 1986
6.76 Order granting absolute/suspended discharge under section 280(2)(b) or (c) of the Insolvency Act 1986
6.77 Certificate of discharge
[6.78 Notice to existing trustee of the presentation of a petition for a later bankruptcy]
6.79 Criminal bankruptcy petition
[6.79A Charging order under section 313 of the Insolvency Act 1986]
[6.80 Order to postal operator under section 371 of the Insolvency Act 1986]
[6.81 Variation of income payments agreement under section 310A of the Insolvency Act 1986
[6.82 Notice under section 279(2) of the Insolvency Act 1986]
[6.83 Notice to interested parties of a dwelling-house falling within section 283A of the Insolvency Act 1986]]
[6.84 Certificate issued pursuant to Rule 6.237B(1) of the Insolvency Rules 1986]

PART 7: COURT PROCEDURE AND PRACTICE

[7.1A]
7.2 . . .
7.3 . . .
7.4 . . .
7.5 . . .
7.6 . . .
7.7 . . .
7.8 . . .
7.9 . . .
7.10 . . .
7. 11 . . .
7.12 . . .
7.13 . . .
7.14 . . .
7.15 . . .
7.16 . . .
7.17 . . .
7.18 . . .
7.19 . . .
[7.20A Confirmation by court of creditors' voluntary winding up application and order]

PART 8: PROXIES AND COMPANY REPRESENTATION

8.1 Proxy—company or individual voluntary arrangements
8.2 Proxy—administration
8.3 Proxy—administrative receivership
8.4 Proxy—winding up by the court or bankruptcy
8.5 Proxy—members' or creditors' voluntary winding up

PART 9: EXAMINATION OF PERSONS CONCERNED IN COMPANY AND INDIVIDUAL INSOLVENCY

9.1 Order under section 236 or 366 of the Insolvency Act 1986

[PART 12: . . .
12.1 . . .]

804

Insolvency Rules 1986, Sch 4

NOTES

Initial Commencement

SPECIFIED DATE

Specified date: 29 December 1986: see r 0.1.

Amendment

Forms 1.1–1.4: revoked by SI 2010/686, r 2, Sch 1, para 502(1), (2)(a), (b)(i).
    Date in force: 6 April 2010: see SI 2010/686, r 1; for transitional provisions see r 6(1), Sch 4, paras 1, 6 thereto.
Forms 1.2–1.19: substituted, for forms 1.2–1.4 as originally enacted, by SI 2002/2712, r 8(1)(a), Schedule, Pt 5.
    Date in force: 1 January 2003: see SI 2002/2712, r 1(1).
Form 1.10: title substituted by SI 2009/642, rr 4, 78, Sch 2, para 1(a).
    Date in force: 6 April 2009: see SI 2009/642, r 1; for transitional provisions see r 3 thereof.
Forms 1.11, 1.12: revoked by SI 2010/686, r 2, Sch 1, para 502(1), (2)(a), (b)(i).
    Date in force: 6 April 2010: see SI 2010/686, r 1; for transitional provisions see r 6(1), Sch 4, paras 1, 6 thereto.
Form 1.14: revoked by SI 2010/686, r 2, Sch 1, para 502(1), (2)(a), (b)(i).
    Date in force: 6 April 2010: see SI 2010/686, r 1; for transitional provisions see r 6(1), Sch 4, paras 1, 6 thereto.
Form 1.16: revoked by SI 2010/686, r 2, Sch 1, para 502(1), (2)(a), (b)(i).
    Date in force: 6 April 2010: see SI 2010/686, r 1; for transitional provisions see r 6(1), Sch 4, paras 1, 6 thereto.
Form 1.18: revoked by SI 2010/686, r 2, Sch 1, para 502(1), (2)(a), (b)(i).
    Date in force: 6 April 2010: see SI 2010/686, r 1; for transitional provisions see r 6(1), Sch 4, paras 1, 6 thereto.
Forms 2.1B–2.40B: substituted, for Forms 2.1–2.4, 2.4A (inserted by SI 1987/1919, r 3(1), Schedule), 2.5–2.23, by SI 2003/1730, r 14(1)(a); for effect and the continuing operation of Forms 2.1–2.4, 2.4A, 2.5–2.23 see r 14(2)(a), (3) thereof.
    Date in force: 15 September 2003: see SI 2003/1730, r 1(2).
Form 2.3B: revoked by SI 2010/686, r 2, Sch 1, para 502(1), (2)(a), (b)(i).
    Date in force: 6 April 2010: see SI 2010/686, r 1; for transitional provisions see r 6(1), Sch 4, paras 1, 6 thereto.
Form 2.11B: revoked by SI 2010/686, r 2, Sch 1, para 502(1), (2)(a), (b)(i).
    Date in force: 6 April 2010: see SI 2010/686, r 1; for transitional provisions see r 6(1), Sch 4, paras 1, 6 thereto.
Forms 2.16B, 2,17B: revoked by SI 2010/686, r 2, Sch 1, para 502(1), (2)(a), (b)(i).
    Date in force: 6 April 2010: see SI 2010/686, r 1; for transitional provisions see r 6(1), Sch 4, paras 1, 6 thereto.
Forms 2.27B–2.29B: revoked by SI 2010/686, r 2, Sch 1, para 502(1), (2)(a), (b)(i).
    Date in force: 6 April 2010: see SI 2010/686, r 1; for transitional provisions see r 6(1), Sch 4, paras 1, 6 thereto.
Form 2.31B: revoked by SI 2010/686, r 2, Sch 1, para 502(1), (2)(a), (b)(i).
    Date in force: 6 April 2010: see SI 2010/686, r 1; for transitional provisions see r 6(1), Sch 4, paras 1, 6 thereto.
Forms 2.33B–2.36B: revoked by SI 2010/686, r 2, Sch 1, para 502(1), (2)(a), (b)(i).
    Date in force: 6 April 2010: see SI 2010/686, r 1; for transitional provisions see r 6(1), Sch 4, paras 1, 6 thereto.
Forms 2.39B, 2.40B: revoked by SI 2010/686, r 2, Sch 1, para 502(1), (2)(a), (b)(i).
    Date in force: 6 April 2010: see SI 2010/686, r 1; for transitional provisions see r 6(1), Sch 4, paras 1, 6 thereto.
Form 3.1A: title substituted by SI 2009/642, rr 4, 78, Sch 2, para 1(c).
    Date in force: 6 April 2009: see SI 2009/642, r 1; for transitional provisions see r 3 thereof.
Forms 3.3–3.5: revoked by SI 2010/686, r 2, Sch 1, para 502(1), (2)(a), (b)(i).
    Date in force: 6 April 2010: see SI 2010/686, r 1; for transitional provisions see r 6(1), Sch 4, paras 1, 6 thereto.
Forms 3.7, 3.8: revoked by SI 2010/686, r 2, Sch 1, para 502(1), (2)(a), (b)(i).

Date in force: 6 April 2010: see SI 2010/686, r 1; for transitional provisions see r 6(1), Sch 4, paras 1, 6 thereto.
Form 3.10: revoked by SI 2010/686, r 2, Sch 1, para 502(1), (2)(a), (b)(i).
Date in force: 6 April 2010: see SI 2010/686, r 1; for transitional provisions see r 6(1), Sch 4, paras 1, 6 thereto.
Form 4.2: substituted by SI 2002/1307, rr 3(1), 13, Schedule, Pt 2.
Date in force: 31 May 2002: see SI 2002/1307, r 1.
Form 4.3: revoked by SI 2005/527, r 49(1)(a), (2)(a).
Date in force: 1 April 2005: see SI 2005/527, r 1(2).
Forms 4.4, 4.5: revoked by SI 2010/686, r 2, Sch 1, para 502(1), (2)(a), (b)(i).
Date in force: 6 April 2010: see SI 2010/686, r 1; for transitional provisions see r 6(1), Sch 4, paras 1, 6 thereto.
Form 4.6: substituted by SI 2005/527, r 49(2)(c), Schedule, Pt B.
Date in force: 1 April 2005: see SI 2005/527, r 1(2).
Form 4.8: word "permission" in square brackets substituted by SI 2010/686, r 2, Sch 1, para 502(1), (4).
Date in force: 6 April 2010: see SI 2010/686, r 1; for transitional provisions and further effect see rr 6(1), 7, Sch 4, paras 1, 2(1)(b), 6, Sch 5 thereto.
Forms 4.11–4.14: substituted by SI 2005/527, r 49(2)(c), Schedule, Pt B.
Date in force: 1 April 2005: see SI 2005/527, r 1(2).
Form 4.15: substituted by SI 2002/1307, rr 3(1), 13, Schedule, Pt 2.
Date in force: 31 May 2002: see SI 2002/1307, r 1.
Form 4.15A: inserted by SI 2005/527, r 49(1)(b), (2)(b), Schedule.
Date in force: 1 April 2005: see SI 2005/527, r 1(2).
Form 4.15A: revoked by SI 2010/686, r 2, Sch 1, para 502(1), (2)(a), (b)(i).
Date in force: 6 April 2010: see SI 2010/686, r 1; for transitional provisions see r 6(1), Sch 4, paras 1, 6 thereto.
Forms 4.17–4.19: substituted by SI 2005/527, r 49(2)(c), Schedule, Pt B.
Date in force: 1 April 2005: see SI 2005/527, r 1(2).
Form 4.20: revoked by SI 2010/686, r 2, Sch 1, para 502(1), (2)(a), (b)(i).
Date in force: 6 April 2010: see SI 2010/686, r 1; for transitional provisions see r 6(1), Sch 4, paras 1, 6 thereto.
Form 4.25: substituted by SI 2004/584, r 46, Schedule.
Date in force: 1 April 2004: see SI 2004/584, r 1(2).
Form 4.26: revoked by SI 2010/686, r 2, Sch 1, para 502(1), (2)(a), (b)(i).
Date in force: 6 April 2010: see SI 2010/686, r 1; for transitional provisions see r 6(1), Sch 4, paras 1, 6 thereto.
Form 4.31: revoked by SI 2010/686, r 2, Sch 1, para 502(1), (2)(a), (b)(i).
Date in force: 6 April 2010: see SI 2010/686, r 1; for transitional provisions see r 6(1), Sch 4, paras 1, 6 thereto.
Form 4.33: revoked by SI 2010/686, r 2, Sch 1, para 502(1), (2)(a), (b)(i).
Date in force: 6 April 2010: see SI 2010/686, r 1; for transitional provisions see r 6(1), Sch 4, paras 1, 6 thereto.
Form 4.34: word "permission" in square brackets substituted by SI 2010/686, r 2, Sch 1, para 502(1), (4).
Date in force: 6 April 2010: see SI 2010/686, r 1; for transitional provisions and further effect see rr 6(1), 7, Sch 4, paras 1, 2(1)(b), 6, Sch 5 thereto.
Form 4.35: revoked by SI 2010/686, r 2, Sch 1, para 502(1), (2)(a), (b)(i).
Date in force: 6 April 2010: see SI 2010/686, r 1; for transitional provisions see r 6(1), Sch 4, paras 1, 6 thereto.
Form 4.36: word "permission" in square brackets substituted by SI 2010/686, r 2, Sch 1, para 502(1), (4).
Date in force: 6 April 2010: see SI 2010/686, r 1; for transitional provisions and further effect see rr 6(1), 7, Sch 4, paras 1, 2(1)(b), 6, Sch 5 thereto.
Form 4.38: revoked by SI 2010/686, r 2, Sch 1, para 502(1), (2)(a), (b)(i).
Date in force: 6 April 2010: see SI 2010/686, r 1; for transitional provisions see r 6(1), Sch 4, paras 1, 6 thereto.
Form 4.40: revoked by SI 2010/686, r 2, Sch 1, para 502(1), (2)(a), (b)(i).
Date in force: 6 April 2010: see SI 2010/686, r 1; for transitional provisions see r 6(1), Sch 4, paras 1, 6 thereto.
Forms 4.43, 4.44: revoked by SI 2010/686, r 2, Sch 1, para 502(1), (2)(a), (b)(i).
Date in force: 6 April 2010: see SI 2010/686, r 1; for transitional provisions see r 6(1), Sch 4, paras 1, 6 thereto.

Insolvency Rules 1986, Sch 4

Form 4.46: revoked by SI 2010/686, r 2, Sch 1, para 502(1), (2)(a), (b)(i).
　　Date in force: 6 April 2010: see SI 2010/686, r 1; for transitional provisions see r 6(1), Sch 4, paras 1, 6 thereto.
Forms 4.48–4.51: revoked by SI 2010/686, r 2, Sch 1, para 502(1), (2)(a), (b)(i).
　　Date in force: 6 April 2010: see SI 2010/686, r 1; for transitional provisions see r 6(1), Sch 4, paras 1, 6 thereto.
Form 4.52: substituted by SI 2003/1730, r 14(2)(c)(i), Sch 2, Pt C.
　　Date in force: 15 September 2003: see SI 2003/1730, r 1(2).
Form 4.53A: substituted, for Form 4.53 as previously enacted, by SI 2010/686, rr 2, 3, Sch 1, para 559, Sch 2.
　　Date in force: 6 April 2010: see SI 2010/686, r 1; for transitional provisions see r 6(1), Sch 4, paras 1, 6 thereto.
Form 4.56: words "Witness statement" in square brackets substituted by virtue of SI 2010/686, r 2, Sch 1, para 525(1), (2).
　　Date in force: 6 April 2010: see SI 2010/686, r 1; for transitional provisions see r 6(1), Sch 4, paras 1, 2(1)(b), (2)–(4), 6 thereto.
Form 4.57: word "permission" in square brackets substituted by SI 2010/686, r 2, Sch 1, para 502(1), (4).
　　Date in force: 6 April 2010: see SI 2010/686, r 1; for transitional provisions and further effect see rr 6(1), 7, Sch 4, paras 1, 2(1)(b), 6, Sch 5 thereto.
Form 4.64: substituted by virtue of SI 2007/1898, art 6, Sch 1, para 12(1), (6), (8), Sch 2, Pt 1.
　　Date in force: 1 October 2007: see SI 2007/1898, art 1.
Form 4.65: words "Statement of truth verifying" in square brackets substituted by virtue of SI 2010/686, r 2, Sch 1, para 526(1), (2).
　　Date in force: 6 April 2010: see SI 2010/686, r 1; for transitional provisions see r 6(1), Sch 4, paras 1, 2(1)(b), 6 thereto.
Forms 4.68, 4.69: revoked by SI 2010/686, r 2, Sch 1, para 502(1), (2)(a), (b)(i).
　　Date in force: 6 April 2010: see SI 2010/686, r 1; for transitional provisions see r 6(1), Sch 4, paras 1, 6 thereto.
Forms 4.71, 4.72: revoked by SI 2010/686, r 2, Sch 1, para 502(1), (2)(a), (b)(i).
　　Date in force: 6 April 2010: see SI 2010/686, r 1; for transitional provisions see r 6(1), Sch 4, paras 1, 6 thereto.
Form 4.73: inserted by SI 2007/1974, r 3(1), (3).
　　Date in force: 6 August 2007: see SI 2007/1974, r 1.
Form 4.74: inserted by SI 2008/737, rr 3, 6(a).
　　Date in force: 6 April 2008: see SI 2008/737, r 1(1); for transitional provisions see r 2 thereof.
Form 5.2: substituted by SI 2003/1730, r 14(2)(c)(i), Sch 2, Pt C.
　　Date in force: 15 September 2003: see SI 2003/1730, r 1(2).
Form 5.3: substituted by SI 2002/2712, r 8(2)(b), Schedule, Pt 6.
　　Date in force: 1 January 2003: see SI 2002/2712, r 1(1).
Form 5.4: substituted by SI 2003/1730, r 14(2)(c)(ii), Sch 2, Pt C.
　　Date in force: 1 April 2004: see SI 2003/1730, r 1(3).
Form 5.5: inserted by SI 2002/2712, r 8(1)(b).
　　Date in force: 1 January 2003: see SI 2002/2712, r 1(1).
Form 5.5: revoked by SI 2010/686, r 2, Sch 1, para 502(1), (2)(a), (b)(i).
　　Date in force: 6 April 2010: see SI 2010/686, r 1; for transitional provisions see r 6(1), Sch 4, paras 1, 6 thereto.
Forms 5.6–5.8: inserted by SI 2003/1730, r 14(1)(c).
　　Date in force: 1 April 2004: see SI 2003/1730, r 1(3).
Form 5.7: substituted by SI 2004/584, r 46, Schedule.
　　Date in force: 1 April 2004: see SI 2004/584, r 1(2).
Form 5.8: substituted by SI 2004/584, r 46, Schedule.
　　Date in force: 1 April 2004: see SI 2004/584, r 1(2).
Forms 6.1–6.3: substituted by SI 2003/1730, r 14(2)(c)(i), Sch 2, Pt C.
　　Date in force: 15 September 2003: see SI 2003/1730, r 1(2).
Form 6.5: words "Witness statement" in square brackets substituted by virtue of SI 2010/686, r 2, Sch 1, para 537(1), (2).
　　Date in force: 6 April 2010: see SI 2010/686, r 1; for transitional provisions see r 6(1), Sch 4, paras 1, 2(1)(b), (2)–(4), 6 thereto.
Forms 6.7, 6.8: substituted by SI 2002/1307, rr 3(1), 13, Schedule, Pt 2.

Date in force: 31 May 2002: see SI 2002/1307, r 1.
Form 6.9: substituted by SI 2005/527, r 49(2)(c), Schedule, Pt B.
Date in force: 1 April 2005: see SI 2005/527, r 1(2).
Form 6.10: substituted by SI 2002/1307, rr 3(1), 13, Schedule, Pt 2.
Date in force: 31 May 2002: see SI 2002/1307, r 1.
Form 6.11: word "Certificate" in square brackets substituted by virtue of SI 2010/686, r 2, Sch 1, para 540(1), (2).
Date in force: 6 April 2010: see SI 2010/686, r 1; for transitional provisions see r 6(1), Sch 4, paras 1, 2(1)(b), 6 thereto.
Form 6.12: word "Certificate" in square brackets substituted by virtue of SI 2010/686, r 2, Sch 1, para 540(1), (2).
Date in force: 6 April 2010: see SI 2010/686, r 1; for transitional provisions see r 6(1), Sch 4, paras 1, 2(1)(b), 6 thereto.
Form 6.13A: substituted, for Form 6.13 as previously enacted, by SI 2010/686, rr 2, 3, Sch 1, para 559, Sch 2.
Date in force: 6 April 2010: see SI 2010/686, r 1; for transitional provisions see r 6(1), Sch 4, paras 1, 2(1)(b), 6 thereto.
Form 6.15A: substituted, for Form 6.15 as previously enacted, by SI 2010/686, rr 2, 3, Sch 1, para 559, Sch 2.
Date in force: 6 April 2010: see SI 2010/686, r 1; for transitional provisions see r 6(1), Sch 4, paras 1, 6 thereto.
Form 6.17A: substituted, for Form 6.17 as previously enacted, by SI 2010/686, rr 2, 3, Sch 1, para 559, Sch 2.
Date in force: 6 April 2010: see SI 2010/686, r 1; for transitional provisions see r 6(1), Sch 4, paras 1, 2(1)(b), 6 thereto.
Form 6.18A: substituted, for Form 6.18 as previously enacted, by SI 2010/686, rr 2, 3, Sch 1, para 559, Sch 2.
Date in force: 6 April 2010: see SI 2010/686, r 1; for transitional provisions see r 6(1), Sch 4, paras 1, 2(1)(b), 6 thereto.
Form 6.24A: substituted by SI 2005/527, r 49(2)(c), Schedule, Pt B.
Date in force: 1 April 2005: see SI 2005/527, r 1(2).
Form 6.25: substituted by SI 2003/1730, r 14(2)(c)(i), Sch 2, Pt C.
Date in force: 15 September 2003: see SI 2003/1730, r 1(2).
Form 6.27: substituted by SI 2002/1307, rr 3(1), 13, Schedule, Pt 2.
Date in force: 31 May 2002: see SI 2002/1307, r 1.
Form 6.28: substituted by SI 2005/2114, art 2(18), Sch 18, Pt 1, para 1(1), (6), Pt 2.
Date in force: 5 December 2005: see SI 2005/2114, art 1.
Form 6.30: substituted by SI 2003/1730, r 14(2)(c)(ii), Sch 2, Pt C.
Date in force: 1 April 2004: see SI 2003/1730, r 1(3).
Form 6.31: revoked, with savings, by virtue of SI 2003/1730, r 14(2)(d), (4).
Date in force: 1 April 2004: see SI 2003/1730, r 1(3).
Form 6.32: substituted by SI 2002/1307, rr 3(1), 13, Schedule, Pt 2.
Date in force: 31 May 2002: see SI 2002/1307, r 1.
Form 6.33A: substituted, for Form 6.33 as previously enacted, by SI 2010/686, rr 2, 3, Sch 1, para 559, Sch 2.
Date in force: 6 April 2010: see SI 2010/686, r 1; for transitional provisions see r 6(1), Sch 4, paras 1, 6 thereto.
Form 6.37: substituted by SI 2004/584, r 46, Schedule.
Date in force: 1 April 2004: see SI 2004/584, r 1(2).
Form 6.39: revoked by SI 2010/686, r 2, Sch 1, para 502(1), (2)(a), (b)(i).
Date in force: 6 April 2010: see SI 2010/686, r 1; for transitional provisions see r 6(1), Sch 4, paras 1, 6 thereto.
Form 6.45: word "permission" in square brackets substituted by SI 2010/686, r 2, Sch 1, para 502(1), (4).
Date in force: 6 April 2010: see SI 2010/686, r 1; for transitional provisions and further effect see rr 6(1), 7, Sch 4, paras 1, 2(1)(b), 6, Sch 5 thereto.
Form 6.46: word "permission" in square brackets substituted by SI 2010/686, r 2, Sch 1, para 502(1), (4).
Date in force: 6 April 2010: see SI 2010/686, r 1; for transitional provisions and further effect see rr 6(1), 7, Sch 4, paras 1, 2(1)(b), 6, Sch 5 thereto.
Form 6.53: revoked by SI 2010/686, r 2, Sch 1, para 502(1), (2)(a), (b)(i).

Date in force: 6 April 2010: see SI 2010/686, r 1; for transitional provisions see r 6(1), Sch 4, paras 1, 6 thereto.

Form 6.57: substituted by virtue of SI 2007/1898, art 6, Sch 1, para 12(1), (7), (9), Sch 2, Pt 2.

Date in force: 1 October 2007: see SI 2007/1898, art 1.

Form 6.58: words "Statement of truth verifying" in square brackets substituted by virtue of SI 2010/686, r 2, Sch 1, para 552(1), (2).

Date in force: 6 April 2010: see SI 2010/686, r 1; for transitional provisions see r 6(1), Sch 4, paras 1, 2(1)(b), 6 thereto.

Form 6.60: word omitted revoked by virtue of SI 2010/686, r 2, Sch 1, para 554.

Date in force: 6 April 2010: see SI 2010/686, r 1; for transitional provisions see r 6(1), Sch 4, paras 1, 6 thereto.

Form 6.61A: substituted, for Form 6.61 as previously enacted, by SI 2010/686, rr 2, 3, Sch 1, para 559, Sch 2.

Date in force: 6 April 2010: see SI 2010/686, r 1; for transitional provisions see r 6(1), Sch 4, paras 1, 6 thereto.

Form 6.71: substituted by SI 2004/584, r 46, Schedule.

Date in force: 1 April 2004: see SI 2004/584, r 1(2).

Forms 6.72, 6.73: substituted by SI 2003/1730, r 14(2)(c)(ii), Sch 2, Pt C.

Date in force: 1 April 2004: see SI 2003/1730, r 1(3).

Form 6.79A: inserted by SI 1987/1919, r 3(1), Schedule, Pts 2, 4; substituted by SI 2004/584, r 46, Schedule.

Date in force: 1 April 2004: see SI 2004/584, r 1(2).

Form 6.80: substituted by SI 2005/527, r 49(2)(c), Schedule, Pt B.

Date in force: 1 April 2005: see SI 2005/527, r 1(2).

Forms 6.81–6.84: inserted by SI 2003/1730, r 14(1)(d).

Date in force: 1 April 2004: see SI 2003/1730, r 1(3).

Form 6.82: substituted by SI 2004/584, r 46, Schedule.

Date in force: 1 April 2004: see SI 2004/584, r 1(2).

Form 6.83: substituted by SI 2005/2114, art 2(18), Sch 18, Pt 1, para 1(1), (6), Pt 2.

Date in force: 5 December 2005: see SI 2005/2114, art 1.

Form 6.84: substituted by SI 2005/527, r 49(2)(c), Schedule, Pt B.

Date in force: 1 April 2005: see SI 2005/527, rule 1(2).

Form 7.1A: substituted, for Forms 7.1, 7.2 as previously enacted, by SI 2010/686, rr 2, 3, Sch 1, para 559, Sch 2.

Date in force: 6 April 2010: see SI 2010/686, r 1; for transitional provisions and further effect see rr 6(1), 7, Sch 4, paras 1, 2(1)(b), 6, Sch 5 thereto.

Form 7.2: substituted, together with Form 7.1 as previously enacted, by new Form 7.1A, by SI 2010/686, rr 2, 3, Sch 1, para 559, Sch 2.

Date in force: 6 April 2010: see SI 2010/686, r 1; for transitional provisions and further effect see rr 6(1), 7, Sch 4, paras 1, 2(1)(b), 6, Sch 5 thereto.

Forms 7.3–7.15: revoked by SI 2010/686, r 2, Sch 1, para 502(1), (2)(a), (b)(i).

Date in force: 6 April 2010: see SI 2010/686, r 1; for transitional provisions see r 6(1), Sch 4, paras 1, 6 thereto.

Forms 7.17–7.19: revoked by SI 2010/686, r 2, Sch 1, para 502(1), (2)(a), (b)(i).

Date in force: 6 April 2010: see SI 2010/686, r 1; for transitional provisions see r 6(1), Sch 4, paras 1, 6 thereto.

Form 7.20A: substituted, for Form 7.20 as previously enacted, by SI 2010/686, rr 2, 3, Sch 1, para 559, Sch 2.

Date in force: 6 April 2010: see SI 2010/686, r 1; for transitional provisions see r 6(1), Sch 4, paras 1, 6 thereto.

Form 12.1: inserted, together with Part 12 heading, by SI 2003/1730, r 14(1)(e).

Date in force: 15 September 2003: see SI 2003/1730, r 1(2).

Form 12.1: revoked by SI 2010/686, r 2, Sch 1, para 502(1), (2)(a), (b)(i).

Date in force: 6 April 2010: see SI 2010/686, r 1; for transitional provisions see r 6(1), Sch 4, paras 1, 6 thereto.

SCHEDULE 5
PUNISHMENT OF OFFENCES UNDER THE RULES
Rule 12.21

Note: In the fourth and fifth columns of this Schedule, "the statutory maximum" means the prescribed sum under section 32 of the Magistrates' Courts Act 1980 (c 43).

Rule creating offence	General nature of offence	Mode of prosecution	Punishment	Daily default fine (where applicable)
. . .	. . .	. . .	. . .	
In Part 2, [Rule 2.47(6)]	Administrator failing to send [a progress report]	Summary	[Level 3 on the standard scale]	[One-tenth of level 3 on the standard scale]
[Rule 2.111(3)]	Administrator failing to file a notice of automatic end of administration [and progress report]	Summary	[Level 3 on the standard scale]	[One-tenth of level 3 on the standard scale]
Rule 2.129(2)	[Failure to comply with] administrator's duties on vacating office	Summary	[Level 3 on the standard scale]	[One-tenth of level 3 on the standard scale]]
In Part 3, Rule 3.32(5)	Administrative receiver failing to send [requisite accounts of receipts and payments as receiver]	Summary	[Level 3 on the standard scale]	[One-tenth of level 3 on the standard scale]
. . .	. . .	. . .	. . .	
In Part 12, Rule 12.18	False representation of status for purpose of inspecting documents	1 On indictment	2 years or a fine, or both	
		2 Summary	6 months or the statutory maximum, or both	

NOTES

Initial Commencement

SPECIFIED DATE

Specified date: 29 December 1986: see r 0.1.

Amendment

Entry relating to Rule 1.30 (omitted) revoked by SI 2002/2712, r 9.
Date in force: 1 January 2003: see SI 2002/2712, r 1(1).
In entry relating to Rule 2.47(6) in column 1 words "Rule 2.47(6)" in square brackets substituted by SI 2003/1730, r 15(1)(a).
Date in force: 15 September 2003: see SI 2003/1730, r 1(2); for effect see rr 5(2)–(4), 15(2) thereof.
In entry relating to Rule 2.47(6) in column 2 words "a progress report" in square brackets substituted by SI 2010/686, r 2, Sch 1, para 560(1).
Date in force: 6 April 2010: see SI 2010/686, r 1; for transitional provisions see r 6(1), Sch 4, para 1 thereto.
In entries relating to Rules 2.47(6), 2.111(3), 2.129(2), 3.32(5) in column 4 words "Level 3 on the standard scale" in square brackets substituted by SI 2010/686, r 2, Sch 1, para 560(5).
Date in force: 6 April 2010: see SI 2010/686, r 1; for transitional provisions and further effect see rr 6(1), 7, Sch 4, paras 1, 2(1)(b), Sch 5 thereto.
In entries relating to Rules 2.47(6), 2.111(3), 2.129(2), 3.32(5) in column 5 words "One-tenth of level 3 on the standard scale" in square brackets substituted by SI 2010/686, r 2, Sch 1, para 560(6).
Date in force: 6 April 2010: see SI 2010/686, r 1; for transitional provisions and further effect see rr 6(1), 7, Sch 4, paras 1, 2(1)(b), Sch 5 thereto.
Entries relating to Rules 2.111(3), 2.129(2) inserted by SI 2003/1730, r 15(1)(b).
Date in force: 15 September 2003: see SI 2003/1730, r 1(2); for effect see rr 5(2)–(4), 15(2) thereof.
In entry relating to Rule 2.111(3) in column 2 words "and progress report" in square brackets inserted by SI 2010/686, r 2, Sch 1, para 560(2).
Date in force: 6 April 2010: see SI 2010/686, r 1; for transitional provisions see r 6(1), Sch 4, para 1 thereto.
In entry relating to Rule 2.129(2) in column 2 words "Failure to comply with" in square brackets inserted by SI 2010/686, r 2, Sch 1, para 560(3).
Date in force: 6 April 2010: see SI 2010/686, r 1; for transitional provisions see r 6(1), Sch 4, para 1 thereto.
In entry relating to Rule 3.32(5) in column 2 words "requisite accounts of receipts and payments as receiver" in square brackets substituted by SI 2010/686, r 2, Sch 1, para 560(4).
Date in force: 6 April 2010: see SI 2010/686, r 1; for transitional provisions see r 6(1), Sch 4, para 1 thereto.
Entry relating to Rule 5.30 (omitted) revoked by SI 2002/2712, r 9.
Date in force: 1 January 2003: see SI 2002/2712, r 1(1).

See Further

See further, in relation the application of this Schedule, with modifications, in respect of the procedure for the appointment of a bank liquidator and the operation of bank insolvency under the Banking Act 2009, Pt 2: the Bank Insolvency (England and Wales) Rules 2009, SI 2009/356, rr 3(3)–(8), 293, Schedule, para 1(b).
See further, in relation to the application of this rule, with modifications, in respect of bank administration and applications for bank administration: the Bank Administration (England and Wales) Rules 2009, SI 2009/357, rr 58–61.

Insolvency Rules 1986, Sch 6

[SCHEDULE 6
DETERMINATION OF INSOLVENCY OFFICE HOLDER'S REMUNERATION]

NOTES

Amendment

Inserted by SI 2004/584, r 47.
Date in force: 1 April 2004: see SI 2004/584, r 1(2).

[Rules 4.127A, 4.127B, 4.148B and 6.138A]

NOTES

Amendment

Inserted by SI 2004/584, r 47.
Date in force: 1 April 2004: see SI 2004/584, r 1(2).

[As regards the determination of the remuneration of trustees and liquidators the realisation and distribution scales are as set out in the table below—

The realisation scale		
(i)	on the first £5000 or fraction thereof	20%
(ii)	on the next £5000 or fraction thereof	15%
(iii)	on the next £90000 or fraction thereof	10%
(iv)	on all further sums realised	5%
The distribution scale		
(i)	on the first £5000 or fraction thereof	10%
(ii)	on the next £5000 or fraction thereof	7.5%
(iii)	on the next £90000 or fraction thereof	5%
(iv)	on all further sums distributed	2.5%.]

NOTES

Amendment

Inserted by SI 2004/584, r 47.
Date in force: 1 April 2004: see SI 2004/584, r 1(2).

See Further

See further, in relation the application of this rule, with modifications, in respect of the procedure for the appointment of a bank liquidator and the operation of bank insolvency under the Banking Act 2009, Pt 2: the Bank Insolvency (England and Wales) Rules 2009, SI 2009/356, rr 3(3)–(8), 293, Schedule, para 1(c).
See further, in relation to the application of this rule, with modifications, in respect of bank administration and applications for bank administration: the Bank Administration (England

and Wales) Rules 2009, SI 2009/357, rr 58–61.

Appendix II

The Legislative Reform (Insolvency) (Miscellaneous Provisions) Order 2010

SI 2010/18

LEGISLATIVE REFORM (INSOLVENCY) (MISCELLANEOUS PROVISIONS) ORDER 2010

Made 6th January 2010

Coming into force 6th April 2010

The Secretary of State for Business, Innovation and Skills makes the following Order, in exercise of the powers conferred by section 1 of the Legislative and Regulatory Reform Act 2006.

For the purposes of section 3(1) of that Act, he considers that the conditions in section 3(2) are satisfied, where relevant.

He has consulted in accordance with section 13(1) and (2) of that Act.

He laid a draft Order and an explanatory document before Parliament in accordance with section 14(1) of that Act.

Pursuant to section 15 of that Act, the super-affirmative resolution procedure (within the meaning of Part 1 of that Act) applies in relation to the making of the Order.

The period of 60 days referred to in section 18(2) of that Act has expired.

In accordance with section 18(2) of that Act, he has had regard to any representations, resolution and recommendations made during that period and in particular to the ninth report of the Delegated Powers and Regulatory Reform Committee.

In accordance with section 18(7) of that Act, he has laid a revised draft Order before Parliament together with a statement.

In accordance with section 18(8) of that Act, the revised draft Order has been approved by resolution of each House of Parliament.

1 Citation, commencement and extent

(1) This Order may be cited as the Legislative Reform (Insolvency) (Miscellaneous Provisions) Order 2010 and comes into force on 6th April 2010.

(2) Subject to paragraph (3), this Order extends to England and Wales and to Scotland.

(3) Articles 3(2), 5(7), 7, 8, 9, 10(2) and 11 do not extend to Scotland.

NOTES

Initial Commencement

Specified date

Specified date: 6 April 2010: see para (1) above.

---

2 Amendments to the Insolvency Act 1986

The Insolvency Act 1986 is amended as specified in articles 3 to 11 of this Order.

NOTES

Initial Commencement

Specified date

Specified date: 6 April 2010: see art 1(1).

Provisions relating to communication

3 Attendance at meetings and use of websites
(1) After section 246 insert—

"*Remote attendance at meetings*

246A Remote attendance at meetings
(1) Subject to subsection (2), this section applies to—
   (a) any meeting of the creditors of a company summoned under this Act or the rules, or
   (b) any meeting of the members or contributories of a company summoned by the office-holder under this Act or the rules, other than a meeting of the members of a company in a members' voluntary winding up.
(2) This section does not apply where—
   (a) a company is being wound up in Scotland, or
   (b) a receiver is appointed under section 51 in Chapter 2 of Part 3.
(3) Where the person summoning a meeting ("the convener") considers it appropriate, the meeting may be conducted and held in such a way that persons who are not present together at the same place may attend it.
(4) Where a meeting is conducted and held in the manner referred to in subsection (3), a person attends the meeting if that person is able to exercise any rights which that person may have to speak and vote at the meeting.
(5) For the purposes of this section—
   (a) a person is able to exercise the right to speak at a meeting when that person is in a position to communicate to all those attending the meeting, during the meeting, any information or opinions which that person has on the business of the meeting; and
   (b) a person is able to exercise the right to vote at a meeting when—
      (i) that person is able to vote, during the meeting, on resolutions put to the vote at the meeting, and
      (ii) that person's vote can be taken into account in determining whether or not such resolutions are passed at the same time as the votes of all the other persons attending the meeting.
(6) The convener of a meeting which is to be conducted and held in the manner referred to in subsection (3) shall make whatever arrangements the convener considers appropriate to—
   (a) enable those attending the meeting to exercise their rights to speak or vote, and
   (b) ensure the identification of those attending the meeting and the security of any electronic means used to enable attendance.
(7) Where in the reasonable opinion of the convener—
   (a) a meeting will be attended by persons who will not be present together at the same place, and
   (b) it is unnecessary or inexpedient to specify a place for the meeting,

any requirement under this Act or the rules to specify a place for the meeting may be satisfied by specifying the arrangements the convener proposes to enable persons to exercise their rights to speak or vote.

(8) In making the arrangements referred to in subsection (6) and in forming the opinion referred to in subsection (7)(b), the convener must have regard to the legitimate interests of the creditors, members or contributories and others attending the meeting in the efficient despatch of the business of the meeting.

(9) If—
- (a) the notice of a meeting does not specify a place for the meeting,
- (b) the convener is requested in accordance with the rules to specify a place for the meeting, and
- (c) that request is made—
  - (i) in the case of a meeting of creditors or contributories, by not less than ten percent in value of the creditors or contributories, or
  - (ii) in the case of a meeting of members, by members representing not less than ten percent of the total voting rights of all the members having at the date of the request a right to vote at the meeting,

it shall be the duty of the convener to specify a place for the meeting.

(10) In this section, "the office-holder", in relation to a company, means—
- (a) its liquidator, provisional liquidator, administrator, or administrative receiver, or
- (b) where a voluntary arrangement in relation to the company is proposed or has taken effect under Part 1, the nominee or the supervisor of the voluntary arrangement.

Use of websites

246B Use of websites

(1) Subject to subsection (2), where any provision of this Act or the rules requires the office-holder to give, deliver, furnish or send a notice or other document or information to any person, that requirement is satisfied by making the notice, document or information available on a website—
- (a) in accordance with the rules, and
- (b) in such circumstances as may be prescribed.

(2) This section does not apply where—
- (a) a company is being wound up in Scotland, or
- (b) a receiver is appointed under section 51 in Chapter 2 of Part 3.

(3) In this section, "the office-holder" means—
- (a) the liquidator, provisional liquidator, administrator, or administrative receiver of a company, or
- (b) where a voluntary arrangement in relation to a company is proposed or has taken effect under Part 1, the nominee or the supervisor of the voluntary arrangement.".

(2) After section 379 insert—

"Remote attendance at meetings

379A Remote attendance at meetings

(1) Where—
- (a) a bankruptcy order is made against an individual or an interim receiver of an individual's property is appointed, or
- (b) a voluntary arrangement in relation to an individual is proposed or is approved under Part 8,

this section applies to any meeting of the individual's creditors summoned under this Act or the rules.

(2) Where the person summoning a meeting ("the convener") considers it appropriate, the meeting may be conducted and held in such a way that persons who are not present together at the same place may attend it.

(3) Where a meeting is conducted and held in the manner referred to in subsection (2), a person attends the meeting if that person is able to exercise any rights which that person may have to speak and vote at the meeting.

(4) For the purposes of this section—
- (a) a person exercises the right to speak at a meeting when that person is in a position to communicate to all those attending the meeting, during the meeting, any information or opinions which that person has on the business of the meeting; and
- (b) a person exercises the right to vote at a meeting when—
  - (i) that person is able to vote, during the meeting, on resolutions put to the vote at the meeting, and
  - (ii) that person's vote can be taken into account in determining whether or not such resolutions are passed at the same time as the votes of all the other persons attending the meeting.

(5) The convener of a meeting which is to be conducted and held in the manner referred to in subsection (2) may make whatever arrangements the convener considers appropriate to—
- (a) enable those attending the meeting to exercise their rights to speak or vote, and
- (b) ensure the identification of those attending the meeting and the security of any electronic means used to enable attendance.

(6) Where in the reasonable opinion of the convener—
- (a) a meeting will be attended by persons who will not be present together at the same place, and
- (b) it is unnecessary or inexpedient to specify a place for the meeting,

any requirement under this Act or the rules to specify a place for the meeting may be satisfied by specifying the arrangements the convener proposes to enable persons to exercise their rights to speak or vote.

(7) In making the arrangements referred to in subsection (5) and in forming the opinion referred to in subsection (6)(b), the convener must have regard to the legitimate interests of the creditors and others attending the meeting in the efficient despatch of the business of the meeting.

(8) If—
- (a) the notice of a meeting does not specify a place for the meeting,
- (b) the convener is requested in accordance with the rules to specify a place for the meeting, and
- (c) that request is made by not less than ten percent in value of the creditors,

it shall be the duty of the convener to specify a place for the meeting.

Use of websites

379B Use of websites

(1) This section applies where—
- (a) a bankruptcy order is made against an individual or an interim receiver of an individual's property is appointed, or
- (b) a voluntary arrangement in relation to an individual is proposed or is approved under Part 8,

and "the office-holder" means the official receiver, the trustee in bankruptcy, the interim receiver, the nominee or the supervisor of the voluntary arrangement, as the case may be.

(2) Where any provision of this Act or the rules requires the office-holder to give, deliver, furnish or send a notice or other document or information to any person, that requirement is satisfied by making the notice, document or information available on a website—
- (a) in accordance with the rules, and
- (b) in such circumstances as may be prescribed.".

NOTES

Initial Commencement

Specified date
Specified date: 6 April 2010: see art 1(1).

Extent
Para (2) does not extend to Scotland: see art 1(3).

4 References to things in writing

(1) After section 436A (proceedings under EC Regulation: modified definition of property) insert—

"**436B References to things in writing**

(1) A reference in this Act to a thing in writing includes that thing in electronic form.

(2) Subsection (1) does not apply to the following provisions—
- (a) section 53 (mode of appointment by holder of charge),
- (b) section 67(2) (report by receiver),
- (c) section 70(4) (reference to instrument creating a charge),
- (d) section 111(2) (dissent from arrangement under s 110),
- (e) in the case of a winding up of a company registered in Scotland, section 111(4),
- (f) section 123(1) (definition of inability to pay debts),
- (g) section 198(3) (duties of sheriff principal as regards examination),
- (h) section 222(1) (inability to pay debts: unpaid creditor for £750 or more), and
- (i) section 223 (inability to pay debts: debt remaining unsatisfied after action brought).".

(2) Paragraph 111(2) of Schedule B1 is repealed.

NOTES

Initial Commencement

Specified date
Specified date: 6 April 2010: see art 1(1).

Provision relating to verification of documents

5 Affidavits

(1) In section 47(2) (statement of affairs to be submitted) for "affidavit" substitute "a statement of truth".

(2) In section 95 (effect of company's insolvency)—

(a) in subsection (4) omit "shall be verified by affidavit by the liquidator and"; and
(b) after that subsection insert—

"(4A) The statement as to the affairs of the company shall be verified by the liquidator—
    (a) in the case of a winding up of a company registered in England and Wales, by a statement of truth; and
    (b) in the case of a winding up of a company registered in Scotland, by affidavit.".

(3) In section 99 (directors to lay statement of affairs before creditors)—
    (a) in subsection (2) omit "shall be verified by affidavit by some or all of the directors and";
    (b) after that subsection insert—

"(2A) The statement as to the affairs of the company shall be verified by some or all of the directors—
    (a) in the case of a winding up of a company registered in England and Wales, by a statement of truth; and
    (b) in the case of a winding up of a company registered in Scotland, by affidavit."; and
    (c) in subsection (3)(a) for "or (2)" substitute ", (2) or (2A)".

(4) In section 131 (company's statement of affairs)—
    (a) in subsection (2) omit "shall be verified by affidavit by the persons required to submit it and"; and
    (b) after that subsection, insert—

"(2A) The statement shall be verified by the persons required to submit it—
    (a) in the case of an appointment of a provisional liquidator or a winding up by the court in England and Wales, by a statement of truth; and
    (b) in the case of an appointment of a provisional liquidator or a winding up by the court in Scotland, by affidavit.".

(5) In section 166(5)(b) (application to court where default in complying with section 98 or 99) for "or (2)" substitute ", (2) or (2A)".

(6) In section 236 (inquiry into company's dealings, etc)—
    (a) in subsection (3), for "an affidavit to the court containing" substitute "to the court"; and
    (b) after that subsection insert—

"(3A) An account submitted to the court under subsection (3) must be contained in—
    (a) a witness statement verified by a statement of truth (in England and Wales), and
    (b) an affidavit (in Scotland).".

(7) In section 366(1) (inquiry into bankrupt's dealings and property) omit "an affidavit" and substitute "a witness statement verified by a statement of truth".

NOTES

Initial Commencement

Specified date
Specified date: 6 April 2010: see art 1(1).

Extent
Para (7) does not extend to Scotland: see art 1(3).

Requirements relating to meetings

6 Removal of requirement for annual meetings in a members' voluntary and a creditors' voluntary winding up in England and Wales

(1) After section 92 (power to fill vacancy in office of liquidator) add—

"**92A Progress report to company at year's end (England and Wales)**

(1) Subject to sections 96 and 102, in the event of the winding up of a company registered in England and Wales continuing for more than one year, the liquidator must—

- (a) for each prescribed period produce a progress report relating to the prescribed matters; and
- (b) within such period commencing with the end of the period referred to in paragraph (a) as may be prescribed send a copy of the progress report to—
  - (i) the members of the company; and
  - (ii) such other persons as may be prescribed.

(2) A liquidator who fails to comply with this section is liable to a fine.".

(2) In section 93 (general company meeting at each year's end)—
- (a) in the heading, at the end, insert "(Scotland)"; and
- (b) in subsection (1) after "winding up", where it first occurs, insert "of a company registered in Scotland".

(3) After section 104 (vacancy in office of liquidator) add—

"**104A Progress report to company and creditors at year's end (England and Wales)**

(1) If the winding up of a company registered in England and Wales continues for more than one year, the liquidator must—

- (a) for each prescribed period produce a progress report relating to the prescribed matters; and
- (b) within such period commencing with the end of the period referred to in paragraph (a) as may be prescribed send a copy of the progress report to—
  - (i) the members and creditors of the company; and
  - (ii) such other persons as may be prescribed.

(2) A liquidator who fails to comply with this section is liable to a fine.".

(4) In section 105 (meetings of company and creditors at each year's end)—
- (a) in the heading, at the end, insert "(Scotland)"; and
- (b) in subsection (1) after "winding up", where it first occurs, insert "of a company registered in Scotland".

(5) In Schedule 10—
- (a) after the entry relating to section 89(6) insert—

"92A(2)	Liquidator failing to send progress report to members at year's end	Summary	Level 3 on the standard scale"; and

- (b) after the entry relating to section 99(3) insert—

"104A(2)	Liquidator failing to send progress report to members and creditors at year's end	Summary	Level 3 on the standard scale".

NOTES

Initial Commencement

Specified date
Specified date: 6 April 2010: see art 1(1).

7 Requirements in relation to meetings under sections 95 and 98 of the 1986 Act
In section 95(2A)(b) (effect of company's insolvency) and in section 98(1A)(b) (meeting of creditors), omit "by post".

NOTES

Initial Commencement

Specified date
Specified date: 6 April 2010: see art 1(1).

Extent
This article does not extend to Scotland: see art 1(3).

Reports in individual voluntary arrangements

8 Individual voluntary arrangements—removal of requirement to report to court
(1) In section 256A (debtor's proposal and nominee's report)—
    (a)   in subsection (2), for "to the court" substitute "under subsection (3)";
    (b)   in subsection (3), for "report to the court" substitute "report to the debtor's creditors".

(2) In section 257 (summoning of creditors' meeting), for subsection (1) substitute—

"(1) Where it has been reported to the court under section 256 or to the debtor's creditors under section 256A that a meeting of debtor's creditors should be summoned, the nominee (or the nominee's replacement under section 256(3) or 256A(4)) shall summon that meeting for the time, date and place proposed in the nominee's report unless, in the case of a report to which section 256 applies, the court otherwise directs.".

(3) In section 259 (report of decisions to court)—
    (a)   for subsection (1) substitute—

"(1) After the conclusion in accordance with the rules of the meeting summoned under section 257, the chairman of the meeting shall—
    (a)   give notice of the result of the meeting to such persons as may be prescribed, and
    (b)   where the meeting was summoned under section 257 pursuant to a report to the court under section 256(1)(aa), report the result of it to the court.";
    (b)   in subsection (2), for "debtor's proposal" substitute "voluntary arrangement proposed under section 256".

NOTES

Initial Commencement

Specified date
Specified date: 6 April 2010: see art 1(1).

Extent
This article does not extend to Scotland: see art 1(3).

9 Fast-track voluntary arrangements—notification of the Secretary of State

(1) In section 263C (result) for "report to the court" substitute "notify the Secretary of State".

(2) In section 263D (approval of voluntary arrangement) in subsection (1) for "reports to the court" substitute "notifies the Secretary of State".

(3) In section 263F (revocation) in subsection (3) for "makes his report to the court" substitute "notifies the Secretary of State".

NOTES

Initial Commencement

Specified date
Specified date: 6 April 2010: see art 1(1).

Extent
This article does not extend to Scotland: see art 1(3).

Powers of liquidator and trustee

10 Powers of liquidator exercisable with or without sanction in a winding up

(1) In Part 1 of Schedule 4 (powers exercisable with sanction), in paragraph 3, at the beginning insert "In the case of a winding up in Scotland,".

(2) In Part 3 of that Schedule (powers exercisable without sanction in any winding up), after paragraph 6, insert—

"6A
In the case of a winding up in England and Wales, power to compromise, on such terms as may be agreed—
(a) all calls and liabilities to calls, all debts and liabilities capable of resulting in debts, and all claims (present or future, certain or contingent, ascertained or sounding only in damages) subsisting or supposed to subsist between the company and a contributory or alleged contributory or other debtor or person apprehending liability to the company, and
(b) subject to paragraph 2 in Part 1 of this Schedule, all questions in any way relating to or affecting the assets or the winding up of the company, and take any security for the discharge of any such call, debt, liability or claim and give a complete discharge in respect of it.".

NOTES

Initial Commencement

Specified date
Specified date: 6 April 2010: see art 1(1).

Extent
Para (2) does not extend to Scotland: see art 1(3).

11 Powers of trustee exercisable with or without sanction in a bankruptcy

(1) In Part 1 of Schedule 5 (powers exercisable with sanction)—

(a) omit paragraph 6; and
(b) in paragraph 8 omit "or by the trustee on any person".
(2) In Part 2 of that Schedule (general powers), after paragraph 9, insert—

"9A

Power to refer to arbitration, or compromise on such terms as may be agreed, any debts, claims or liabilities subsisting or supposed to subsist between the bankrupt and any person who may have incurred any liability to the bankrupt.

9B

Power to make such compromise or other arrangement as may be thought expedient with respect to any claim arising out of or incidental to the bankrupt's estate made or capable of being made by the trustee on any person.".

NOTES

Initial Commencement

Specified date
Specified date: 6 April 2010: see art 1(1).

Extent
This article does not extend to Scotland: see art 1(3).

Transitional provisions

12 Transitional provisions
(1) Sections 92A and 104A of the Insolvency Act 1986 ("the 1986 Act") inserted by article 6 do not apply in respect of a company in voluntary winding up where the resolution to wind up was passed before 6th April 2010.
(2) The amendments to sections 93 and 105 of the 1986 Act made by article 6 do not apply in respect of a company in voluntary winding up where the resolution to wind up was passed before 6th April 2010.
(3) The amendments to sections 95 and 98 of the 1986 Act made by article 7 do not apply in respect of a company in voluntary winding up where the resolution to wind up was passed before 6th April 2010.
(4) Where a person agrees before 6th April 2010 to act as nominee in respect of a proposal for a voluntary arrangement under Part 8 of the 1986 Act by a debtor for a composition in satisfaction of his debts or for a scheme of arrangement of his affairs to a nominee under section 256A or 263B of the 1986 Act, the provisions of the 1986 Act relevant to a proposal under those sections as they were prior to the amendments made by this Order shall continue to apply to it.
(5) The amendments made to Schedules 4 and 5 to the 1986 Act by articles 10 and 11 respectively do not apply in respect of any proceedings under the 1986 Act where—
(a) in the case of a company in voluntary winding up, the resolution to wind up was passed before 6th April 2010;
(b) in the case of a company in voluntary winding up pursuant to paragraph 83 of Schedule B1 to the 1986 Act, the preceding administration commenced before 6th April 2010;
(c) in the case of a company in winding up following an order for the conversion of administration or a voluntary arrangement into winding up by virtue of article 37 of Council Regulation (EC) No 1346/2000 on insolvency proceedings, the order for conversion was made before 6th April 2010;
(d) in the case of a company being wound up by the court, the winding-up order was made before 6th April 2010;

(e) in the case of a bankruptcy, the debtor was adjudged bankrupt before 6th April 2010; and

(f) in the case of a bankruptcy following an order for the conversion of a voluntary arrangement into a bankruptcy by virtue of article 37 of Council Regulation (EC) No 1346/2000, the order for conversion was made before 6th April 2010.

NOTES

Initial Commencement

Specified date
Specified date: 6 April 2010: see art 1(1).

Ian Lucas
Minister for Business and Regulatory Reform
Department for Business, Innovation & Skills
6th January 2010

EXPLANATORY NOTE

(This note is not part of the Order)

This Order is made under section 1 of the Legislative and Regulatory Reform Act 2006 (c 51) (the "2006 Act"). It amends the Insolvency Act 1986 (c 45) (the "1986 Act").

Articles 3 and 4 make amendments to the 1986 Act relating to communications and meetings in insolvency proceedings.

Article 3(1) inserts a new section 246A (remote attendance at meetings) into Part 6 of the 1986 Act (miscellaneous provisions applying to companies which are insolvent or in liquidation). The new section allows those attending meetings in corporate insolvency proceedings to do so other than by physical attendance or by proxy in that it allows a person to attend a meeting using any form of technology which permits them to be heard and to vote at the meeting. Article 3(1) also inserts a new section 246B (use of websites) into the 1986 Act which allows an office-holder to use a website as a means of sending documents and information to others in the course of insolvency proceedings. As a consequence of section 9 of the 2006 Act (which prevents an Order under that Act making provision in relation to matters within the competence of the Scottish Parliament), sections 246A and 246B will have only limited application in relation to corporate insolvency proceedings in Scotland.

Article 3(2) introduces the equivalent amendments for individual insolvency in England and Wales by inserting new sections 379A and 379B into Part 10 of the 1986 Act (individual insolvency: general provisions).

Article 4 inserts a new section 436B (references to things in writing) into the 1986 Act which clarifies that references in the 1986 Act to documents or information "in writing" include documents or information in electronic form. As a consequence, the equivalent provision in Schedule B1 to the 1986 Act, which relates solely to administration, is repealed.

Article 5 removes requirements (in six sections of the 1986 Act) for documents in insolvency proceedings in England and Wales to be sworn by affidavit and replaces them with a requirement for the relevant documents to be verified by a statement of truth.

Article 6 relates to members' voluntary liquidation and creditors' voluntary liquidation. It amends sections 93 (general company meeting at each year's end) and 105 (meetings of company and creditors at year's end) of the 1986 Act and inserts new sections 92A (progress report to company at year's end (England and Wales)) and 104A (progress report to company and creditors at year's end (England and Wales)). The effect is that the requirement imposed upon liquidators to summon annual meetings of members and creditors for the purpose of laying an account of the liquidator's acts and dealings and of the conduct of the winding up during the preceding year (sections 93 and 105 of the 1986 Act) applies only to Scotland. In England and Wales, the requirement to summon a meeting is removed and replaced with a requirement to provide a progress report relating to matters prescribed in the Insolvency Rules 1986 to the members and creditors of the company as the case may be (sections 92A and 104A of the 1986 Act).

Article 7 amends sections 95 (effect of company's insolvency) and 98 (meeting of creditors) of the 1986 Act as they apply to England and Wales by removing the requirement for notice of the meeting to be sent to creditors "by post".

Article 8(1) relates to individual voluntary arrangements. It amends section 256A (debtor's proposal and nominee's report), so as to remove the requirement to submit a report to the court in those cases in which no application has been made to the court for an interim order. Paragraph (2) makes amendments to section 257 (summoning of creditors' meeting) consequential upon the amendment made to section 256A and removes the reference to a report made to the court under section 256A, replacing it with a report to the debtor's creditors. Paragraph (3) amends section 259 (report of decisions to court) as a consequence of the change made to section 256A. The amendment removes the reference to a report being made to the court under section 256A.

Article 9 amends provisions in respect of fast-track voluntary arrangements. Paragraph (1) amends section 263C (result) by substituting for a requirement that the official receiver report to the court whether the voluntary arrangement has been approved or rejected, a requirement to merely notify the Secretary of State of the same. Paragraph (2) amends section 263F (revocation) consequential upon the amendment made to section 263C by substituting a reference to notification of the Secretary of State for the reference to the official receiver's report to the court.

Articles 10 and 11 respectively amend Schedules 4 and 5 to the 1986 Act. They remove the requirement on liquidators and trustees in bankruptcy in England and Wales to obtain the sanction of creditors, company members or the court, as the case may be, for certain actions they propose to take as part of their conduct of the insolvency.

Article 12 contains transitional provisions in relation to the introduction of certain of the amendments made by the Order.

A full Regulatory Impact Assessment of the effect that this instrument will have on the costs of business and the voluntary sector is available from the Insolvency Service website (www.insolvency.gov.uk) and is annexed to the Explanatory Document which is available alongside the instrument on the OPSI website.

Appendix III

Commentary for stakeholders on the draft Insolvency Modernisation Rules

COMMENTARY FOR STAKEHOLDERS ON THE DRAFT
INSOLVENCY MODERNISATION RULES

1 INTRODUCTION

1.1 The draft Insolvency Rules which accompany this commentary (together with the draft Legislative Reform (Insolvency)(Miscellaneous Provisions) Order 2009, presently before Parliament) complete the implementation of the Government's modernisation proposals for insolvency law which began with the advertising amendment changes which came into effect in April 2009. They do not include any Rule changes relating to the present consultation about enhancing company rescue.

1.2 The purpose behind publishing a draft of the proposed Rule amendments now is to assist the insolvency profession and other stakeholders in their preparations for the changes that are expected to come into force with effect from 6th April 2010. The Rules amendments have been prepared with the benefit of extensive stakeholder input and they are not issued now for further consultation, which would delay the delivery timetable. Instead, we are seeking comments concerning any errors or drafting difficulties that may be found within the draft Rules. Please note that the draft Rules being published here are currently under review with the Insolvency Rules Committee and therefore may be subject to some further revision. They are published as a guide and are still work in progress. We are also expecting to include provisions facilitating the proposed extension of the pilot for electronic communications in insolvency proceedings at the Royal Courts of Justice.

1.3 The commentary that follows below provides an overview of the policy changes contained in the draft amendment Rules, to highlight particular issues and to explain methodologies adopted where this may not be readily apparent.

1.4 The project for modernisation of the Insolvency Rules will provide estimated annual savings of £42 million in the cost of administering insolvencies, the first phase of which were delivered in April 2009. These savings are expected to be passed on to creditors in the form of improved returns and the new e-delivery provisions will also provide for a significant reduction in the insolvency carbon footprint. The amendment Rules, by their nature, amend the Insolvency Rules 1986. They do not therefore include the restructuring or re-ordering changes which are planned for a new set of Insolvency Rules proposed for April 2011.

1.5 The Rules amendments adopt the now standard gender neutral drafting style (except we have continued to use the word "chairman", because that word is also to be found in unamended Rules: its continued use will be reconsidered in drafting the new Rules proposed for 2011). Wherever sensible they also apply the Civil Procedure Rules ("CPR") and adopt CPR language.

1.6 We have taken the opportunity presented by the significant amendment of much of what is currently in Part 12 of the Rules to create a new Part 12A, which includes much new material and some of the old which ought logically to be associated with it. Some of the old Part 12 however remains. We hope the creation of the new Part 12A will be seen as "user friendly".

1.7 Finally the amending Rules, for the most part, do not show the Rules being amended in their amended form. To assist stakeholders further the Insolvency Service

Commentary on draft Insolvency Modernisation Rules

has also produced a working document version of the Insolvency Rules 1986 as if they had been amended by the proposed "modernisation" Rules. We hope that you will find this helpful.

2. THEMES

2.1 The commentary is organised on a thematic basis, rather than on a rule by rule basis. The "themes" reflect the overarching policy themes contained in the modernisation programme. Under each theme reference to particular Rules may be given as examples of the changes being made under that theme.

2.2 The themes are –

The revised draft Legislative Reform (Insolvency)(Miscellaneous Provisions) Order 2009 (paragraph 3)

- Advertising Rule changes (paragraph 4)
- Standard contents for "gazetting" (paragraph 5)
- Standard contents for advertising otherwise than in the Gazette (paragraph 6)
- Meetings (paragraph 7)
- Official receiver (paragraph 8)
- Creditors' and liquidation committees (paragraph 9)
- Disclaimer procedure (paragraph 10)
- Court procedure and practice (paragraph 11)
- Applications for private examination under sections 236, 251N and 366 (paragraph 12)
- Public examination under sections 133(1) and 290(1) (paragraph 13)
- Filing in court: rationalisation and removal of unnecessary filings (paragraph 14)
- Affidavits (paragraph 15)
- Ex parte (paragraph 16)
- Leave of the court (paragraph 17)
- Deponents (paragraph 18)
- Parts 1 and 5 (CVAs and IVAs): miscellaneous modernisation and harmonisation (paragraph 19)
- Draft Legislative Reform (Insolvency)(Miscellaneous Provisions) Order 2009 (paragraph 20)
- Remuneration, expenses and reporting (paragraph 21)
- Provision of "receipts and payments" account on resignation of office holder (paragraph 22)
- Creditor and debtor bankruptcy petitions (paragraph 23)
- Block transfer orders (paragraph 24)
- Verification of a statement of affairs (paragraph 25)
- Claims and distributions (paragraph 26)
- Limited disclosure (paragraph 27)
- Amendments to Part 4 Chapter 22 (leave to act as director etc. of company with prohibited name) (paragraph 28)
- Part 3 (Administrative Receivership): miscellaneous amendments (paragraph 29)
- Amendments relating to the EC Regulation on Insolvency Proceedings (paragraph 30)
- Electronic delivery (paragraph 31)
- Service of court documents (paragraph 32)
- Prescribed forms (paragraph 33)
- Authentication (paragraph 34)
- Annulment Changes (paragraph 35)
- Insolvency Registers (paragraph 36)
- Victims of Violence (paragraph 37)
- Inland Revenue (paragraph 38)
- Deceased office-holders (paragraph 39)

- Definitions (paragraph 40)
- Schedule 2 (paragraph 41)
- Schedule 5 (paragraph (42)

3. LEGISLATIVE REFORM (INSOLVENCY)(MISCELLANEOUS PROVISIONS) ORDER 2009

3.1 The revised draft Legislative Reform (Insolvency)(Miscellaneous Provisions) Order 2009 the LRO) has been laid before Parliament for the secondary scrutiny phase.

3.2 The LRO aims to amend the Insolvency Act 1986 so as to reduce administrative burdens and thereby permit financial savings to be passed on to creditors.

3.3 Specifically, it aims to (a) permit certain new procedures, (b) remove certain burdensome requirements and (c) remove inconsistencies between the Act and the Rules.

3.4 The new procedures under (a) are-

(i) permitting remote attendance at meetings;
(ii) permitting the use of websites to communicate information.

3.5 The burdensome requirements to be removed in (b) are-

(i) removal of the requirement to hold annual meetings in creditors' and members' voluntary winding up in England and Wales;
(ii) removal of the requirement to report to court in certain voluntary arrangements;
(iii) the removal of the requirement for sanction for certain acts by the liquidator or trustee in bankruptcy.

3.6 The inconsistencies to be removed in (c) are-

(i) permitting things required by the Act to be in writing to be in electronic form;
(ii) removing the requirement for certain documents in the Act to be sworn by affidavit.

3.7 The items in (a) and (b)(i) and (ii) require either new rules or amendments to existing rules. Item (b)(iii) has no effect on the Rules.

3.8 The items in (c) allow the Rules to make uniform provision in certain areas without the need to make separate provision for matters where requirements under the Act are different.

4 ADVERTISING RULE CHANGES

4.1 The amending Rules contain a small number of amendments to the new advertising regime introduced in April 2009. These are mainly minor or technical changes but they do include some new advertising requirements. An example of a technical amendment can be found in respect of provisional liquidators in the amendments to Rule 4.31 removing the requirement to give notice of removal from office when a winding up order is made. An example of a new requirement to advertise can be found in the amendments to Rule 4.106.

5 STANDARD CONTENTS FOR "GAZETTING"

5.1 The amending Rules introduce "standard contents" provisions. These requirements are intended to ensure that all gazetted notices include the necessary information that readers of the gazetted notice may need in respect of the insolvency concerned. They are introduced in response to stakeholder representation. They are not expected to give rise to any increase in the cost of gazetting.

5.2 The expression "standard contents" is to be defined in Rule 13.13 and the "standard contents" provision is contained in the new Rules12A.31 to 12A.33. It works by applying in all cases where notices are gazetted, but it does not displace additional requirements as to contents contained in the Insolvency Act 1986 or the Rules. In order to assist users of the Rules we have adopted a drafting style in the main body of the Rules that reminds the reader, where additional contents are to be included, that these are additional to the standard contents. Good examples of this can be found in the amendments to Rules 1.40, 1.42 and 3.9.

6 STANDARD CONTENTS FOR ADVERTISING OTHERWISE THAN IN THE GAZETTE

6.1 The amending Rules introduce a new requirement as to standard contents for notices advertised otherwise than in the Gazette. These notices are discretionary on the part of the insolvency office-holder. The provisions are contained in new Rules 12A.36 to 12A.39. These requirements are a "cut down" version of the required minimum "standard contents" for gazetted notices reflecting the required minimum for these adverts and increasing the discretion available to an insolvency office-holder as to contents. These requirements apply in same way as those for gazetted notices. The definition "standard contents" includes the standard contents for advertising otherwise than in the Gazette.

6.2. The new advertising provisions introduce the possibility that advertisements might be contained in media other than newspapers. It therefore becomes important to ensure that where information must be provided it must be provided in a way that is likely to lead a person needing to hear, see or read the information to be able to do so. For that reason Rule 12A.39 (1) is introduced.

7 MEETINGS AND RESOLUTIONS

7.1 Inconsistencies are eliminated between various provisions relating to meetings, in particular of creditors, in different types of insolvency procedure, particularly in respect of the lodging of proofs and proxies and the adjournment of meetings; and the minimum period of notice for meetings is reduced from 21 to 14 days (other than final meetings in a liquidation or bankruptcy, where the minimum notice will be 28 days).

7.2 Restrictions on when company meetings in voluntary arrangements must be held are removed.

7.3 Resolutions may be adopted by correspondence in winding up and bankruptcy as already in administration.

7.4 Provision is also made facilitating remote attendance at meetings (see new Rules 12A.20-12A.25).

7.5 The power of the court to order that notice of a meeting be given by advertisement only, already present in liquidation and bankruptcy, is being extended to administration.

8 OFFICIAL RECEIVER

8.1 It is expressly provided that the official receiver may not be appointed liquidator or trustee in bankruptcy by a meeting of creditors, contributories or company members.

9 CREDITORS' AND LIQUIDATION COMMITTEES

9.1 Paragraph 57 of Schedule B1 to the Act (administration) provides for the establishment of a creditors' committee by a meeting of creditors. In Chapter 7 of Part 2 (administration procedure – the creditors' committee) the following amendments have been made. Rule 2.50 provides that any creditor of the company is eligible to be a member of the creditors' committee so long as his claim has not been rejected for the purpose of his entitlement to vote. This Rule has been amended to include the following additional eligibility criteria: a person's claim must not have been wholly rejected for the purpose of distribution or dividend; and that claim must not be fully secured.

9.2 Rule 2.52 provides that after the calling of the first meeting of the committee, the administrator must call a meeting if requested by a member of the committee. This Rule has been amended to provide that such a meeting must be held within 21 days of the request being received by the administrator. The current position is that the meeting must be held within 14 days of the receipt of the request.

9.3 Also in Rule 2.52, a new paragraph (4) provides that, in a case where the administrator has determined that a meeting should be held and conducted by remote means under new Rule 12A.20, the notice period of the meeting which must be given by the administrator to committee members is extended from 7 days to 10 days.

9.4 In Rule 2.57, paragraph (1)(c) has been amended to the effect that a person's membership of the creditors' committee is automatically terminated if that person ceases to be a creditor provided that a period of 3 months has elapsed from the date that he ceased to be a creditor.

9.5 In Rule 2.59, new paragraph (4) provides that a meeting of creditors may agree a resolution to appoint a new creditor to fill a vacancy in the membership of the creditors' committee.

9.6 Rule 2.61 provides for the agreement of resolutions by the committee. Paragraph (3) provides committee members with a right to request the administrator to summon a meeting to consider the matters raised by the resolution. That paragraph has been amended to provide that the request must be made within 10 days from the date of the administrator sending out the resolution.

9.7 Rule 2.64 has been amended to specify the persons who may deal with the company provided that any transactions in the course of such dealings are in good faith and for value. Other minor amendments have been made which are largely consequential on other changes that have been made to the Rules.

9.8 Equivalent amendments have been made to those mentioned above in relation to Chapter 7 of Part 2 to: Chapter 4 of Part 3 (administrative receivership – the creditors' committee); Chapter 12 of Part 4 (companies winding up – the liquidation committee); Chapter 13 of Part 4 (companies winding up – the liquidation committee where winding up follows immediately on administration) and Chapter 11 of part 6 (bankruptcy – the creditors' committee).

9.9 In addition, Rule 4.174 has been substituted with new Rule 4.174A which sets out the circumstances in which a creditors' committee established for the purposes of an administration continues in being as a liquidation committee.

9.10 Finally, provisions have been inserted into new Part 12A to allow creditors' and liquidation committee meetings to be attended by remote means.

10. DISCLAIMER PROCEDURE

10.1 Section 178 (power to disclaim onerous property) allows the liquidator of a company to disclaim any onerous property by giving a prescribed notice. The disclaimer operates so as to determine, as from the date of the disclaimer, the rights, interests and liabilities of the company in or in respect of the property.

10.2 In Chapter 15 of Part 4 (companies winding up) the following amendments have been made. In relation to filing a notice of disclaimer, a copy of the notice is no longer filed with the court. Instead, Rule 4.187 has been amended to provide that a copy of the notice must be sent to the registrar of companies and, in any case where the disclaimer is of registered land, a copy must also be sent to the Chief Land Registrar. In Rule 4.187(4), for the purposes of section 178, the date of the prescribed notice has been changed to the date the notice is authenticated by the liquidator. This means that the liquidator no longer has to wait for the notice to be endorsed by the court. Rule 4.190 has been substituted by new Rule 4.190A which replaces the duty to keep the court informed with a new requirement for the liquidator to keep certain records. Other minor amendments have been made which are largely consequential on other changes that have been made to the Rules.

10.3 Section 315 (disclaimer (general power)) is in similar terms to section 178 and allows the trustee in bankruptcy to disclaim any onerous property by giving a prescribed notice. In Chapter 14 of Part 6 (bankruptcy – disclaimer) equivalent amendments have been made to those mentioned above in relation to Chapter 15 of Part 4. The only difference being that in Part 6 the notice of disclaimer will continue to be filed with the court because there is no alternative repository in bankruptcy cases.

11 COURT PROCEDURE AND PRACTICE

11.1 In Part 7 (court procedure and practice), the following amendments have been made. References to county court registrars have been revised to refer instead to district judges. In relation to applications to court, the distinction between an ordinary application and an originating application has been removed. However, the distinction between the two types of applications is being maintained for court administrative purposes in the new Application Notice (Form 7.1A). Rule 7.6 has been replaced by new Rule 7.6A which provides that most hearings should be in open court.

11.2 In relation to enforcement procedures, certain amendments have been made to deal with problems relating to the delivery of bankrupts etc. to prison and the discharge of warrants. In particular, Rule 7.19 now makes provision to allow county courts to discharge High Court warrants. Rule 7.22 now provides that in the case of arrests under section 134 (officer of company failing to attend for public examination) or section 364 (arrest of debtor or bankrupt) the arrested person can be delivered to the court or, where the court is not ready to deal with that person, to the prison named in the warrant (or another prison if that prison cannot take the arrested person). In the case of arrests under section 236 (inquiry into insolvent company's dealings) or section 366 (the equivalent in bankruptcy), Rule 7.23 now permits a prisoner to be delivered either to the prison named in the warrant or, where that prison cannot accommodate the arrested person, such other prison which has appropriate facilities.

11.3 In relation to court records and returns, Rules 7.26, 7.28, 7.30 and 7.31 have been replaced by new Rule 7.31A. In particular, the new Rule provides specified persons with a right to receive a copy of the complete court file or copies of any particular documents. This replaces Rule 7.31 which provided specified persons with a right to inspect documents in the court file. Rule 7.31 placed an administrative burden on the court and did not accord with CPR Part 5.

11.4 Rules 7.26, 7.29, 7.53, 7.54 and 7.61 have been omitted as they do not seem to serve any useful purpose. Rule 7.58 has been omitted as security in court is covered by the CPR.

12 APPLICATIONS FOR PRIVATE EXAMINATION UNDER SECTIONS 236, 251N AND 366

12.1 Section 236 (inquiry into company's dealings, etc,) provides the court with a power to conduct an inquiry into a company's dealings. In particular, the court has the power, on the application by an office-holder (e.g. liquidator or official receiver), to summon to appear before it (a) any officer of the company; (b) any person known or suspected to have in his possession any property of the company or supposed to be indebted to the company; or (c) any person whom the court thinks capable of giving information concerning the promotion, formation, business, dealings, affairs or property of the company. The court has similar powers to conduct private examinations of specified persons under Section 251N (debt relief orders – inquiry into dealings and property of debtor) and 366 (inquiry into bankrupt's dealings and property).

12.2 Part 9 (applications for private examination – sections 236, 251N and 366) has been amended as follows. In particular, Rule 9.5 has been amended to expressly provide that copies of any questions put to the respondent or proposed to be put to the respondent are not open to inspection without an order of the court by specified persons. Other minor amendments have been made which are largely consequential on other changes that have been made to the Rules.

13 PUBLIC EXAMINATION UNDER SECTIONS 133(1) AND 290(1)

13.1 Section 133(1) (public examination of officers) provides that where a company is being wound up by the court, the official receiver may apply to court for the public examination of any person who (a) is or has been an officer of the company; (b) has acted as liquidator or administrator of the company or as receiver of manager; or (c) not being or having been any such person, is or has been concerned or has taken part, in the promotion, formation or management of the company.

13.2 Chapter 19 of Part 4 (companies winding up – public examination of company officers and others) is amended as follows. Rule 4.211 has been amended to provide that effective service of an order for public examination made by the court will be to a known address in accordance with any means permitted by new Part 12A. Service is no longer restricted to postal service in all cases.

13.3 In Rule 4.212(2) the requirement for the official receiver to give notice of the hearing of a public examination to every creditor and contributory of the company who is identified in the company's statement of affairs has been removed because it is unnecessary. All such creditors and contributories will be known to the official receiver who must serve them with a notice of the hearing by virtue of that knowledge pursuant to Rule 4.212(2)(c).

13.4 Rule 4.212(3) provides that, unless the court otherwise directs, at least 7 days must have elapsed since the examinee was served with the order for a public examination before the official receiver may exercise his discretion under this Rule to advertise notice of the order. Paragraph (3) has been amended to limit the 7 day protection so that it applies only to orders which relate to persons falling within section 133(1)(c) (public examination of officers). Other minor amendments have been made which are largely consequential on other changes that have been made to the Rules.

13.5 Section 290(1) (public examination of bankrupt) provides that where a bankruptcy order has been made, the official receiver may at any time before the discharge of the bankrupt apply to the court for public examination of the bankrupt.

13.6 Chapter 13 of Part 6 (bankruptcy – public examination of bankrupt) has been amended as follows. In Rule 6.172(3) an equivalent amendment has been made to that mentioned above in relation to Rule 4.212(2). Other minor amendments have been made which are largely consequential on other changes that have been made to the Rules.

14. FILING IN COURT: RATIONALISATION AND REMOVAL OF UNNECESSARY FILINGS

14.1 The aim of this theme is to reduce the burdens on the courts and their users by reducing the number of occasions when documents are filed in court; reducing the number of documents so filed; and, in corporate insolvency, substituting filing with the registrar of companies for filing in court where appropriate.

14.2 Most of the amendments are in Parts 4 and 6. However, there are also amendments to Parts 1, 2 and 5.

14.3 Where a filing is considered to serve no valuable purpose and is not required by the primary legislation, the requirement to file has been removed (e.g. Rules 1.26, 2.29, 2.47, 4.33, 4.42, 5.31, 6.60 and 6.65).

14.4 Filings solely with the registrar of companies occur in cases where removal of the concomitant requirement to file in court has left the registrar of companies as the sole depository (e.g. Rule 4.45).

14.5 In Rules 4.109 (action following acceptance of liquidator's resignation) and 4.116 (procedure on removal of liquidator) there is a new requirement for the documents in question to be filed with the registrar of companies as well as with the court. This is on account of the importance of the documents.

14.6 Where a petition is to be verified or a certificate of service is to be filed in court, the document served is to be described in sufficient detail for the served document to be identified (e.g. Rules 4.7, 4.12, 6.12). The effect is to avoid attaching a copy of the document served, of which the court already has a copy.

14.7 Also included in this theme is amendment to Rule 4.7 so that where the administrator files a winding up petition, the petition is no longer to be treated as if it were a petition filed by a contributory. This removes the need for a directions hearing prior to the hearing of the petition.

15 AFFIDAVITS

15.1 Throughout the Rules, references to affidavits have been removed. They have been replaced with a requirement for a statement of truth. In some cases this statement will be incorporated into the document to be verified and in others the reference to an affidavit is replaced by a reference to a witness statement supported by a statement of truth. There is a new definition in Rule 13.13 (expressions used generally) explaining that "statement of truth" has the same meaning as in the CPR.

15.2 Consequential changes have been made to references to "swear", "sworn", "oath" and "exhibited". In Parts 2 (administration procedure) and 4 (companies winding up) the discretionary requirement that a claim of debt must be verified by affidavit has been removed. In Part 6, the provision requiring a petition in respect of a moneylending transaction to be supported by an affidavit has been removed.

16 EX PARTE

16.1 Throughout the Rules, references to ex parte have been removed. They have been replaced with the phrase "without notice to any other party".

17 LEAVE OF THE COURT

17.1 Throughout the Rules, references to obtaining "leave" of the court have been replaced with references to obtaining "permission" of the court.

18 DEPONENTS

18.1 Throughout the Rules, references to deponents have been removed. Except in Part 3 (administrative receivership), they have been replaced with the phrase "person making the statement". In Part 3, they have been replaced with the term "nominated person" which is defined in that Part.

19 PARTS 1 AND 5 (CVAS AND IVAS): MISCELLANEOUS MODERNISATION AND HARMONISATION

19.1 Parts 1 and 5 mirror each other to a large extent. Where a rule in one part has a corresponding rule in the other part which differs, they have been amended in order to effect harmony, so far as possible. Where corresponding rules have been amended, they have been amended so far as possible to achieve harmony.

19.2 Miscellaneous amendments to Parts 1 and 5 have been incorporated. Examples are set out below:

- In Part 1, the proposal is to include details of other useful information (Rule 1.3(2)(r)).
- In Part 5, the proposal is to include details of any proposals in the preceding 2 years and their results (Rule 5.3(2)(s)). It is not considered appropriate to make corresponding provision in Part 1.
- In both Parts the, the statement of affairs is to accompany the proposal (Rules 1.5 & 5.5).
- In Part 1, the "nominee" has been substituted for references to the "convener" or "convenor" of a meeting (e.g. Rules 1.13 and 1.14).
- Rules 1.55 and 5.66 are new. The new rules give effect to regulation 36A of the Insolvency Regulations 1994 (S.I. 1994/2507) as regards voluntary arrangements.
- Majorities for creditors' meetings have been amended "three quarters or more" (Rules 1.19, 5.23 and 5.43).
- The office holder is to notify creditors of whose claim and address the office-holder is aware rather than of whom he is otherwise aware. (e.g. Rules 1.9 and 5.17).
- Defective drafting has been remedied (Rules 5.47(2) and 5.50(1)).

20 REMOVAL OF THE REQUIREMENT TO REPORT TO COURT IN CERTAIN VOLUNTARY ARRANGEMENTS

20.1 Two of the provisions of the LRO, (b)(ii) above relate to voluntary arrangements: one provision substitutes a requirement for the nominee to report to the creditors for the requirement to report to the court in a non-interim order individual voluntary arrangement; the other substitutes a requirement to give notice to the Secretary of State of the result of the creditors' consideration of the debtor's proposal in a fast-track voluntary arrangement for reporting it to the court.

20.2 New Rules 5.14A, 5.14B and the omission of Rules 5.15 and 5.16 give effect to the first provision.

20.3 As a consequence of the first provision, there is a distinction between individual voluntary arrangements where there has been an interim-order where the nominee continues to report to the court and non-interim order individual voluntary arrangements where there is no report to the court. There are numerous amendments giving effect to this. The form of words used to describe a non-interim order individual voluntary arrangement mirrors that in the draft LRO (e.g. Rules 5.34 and 5.55).

20.4 There are a number of amendments to give effect to the second provision (e.g. Rules 5.39 and 5.42).

21 REMUNERATION, EXPENSES AND REPORTS

21.1 The remuneration of office-holders may be set as a fixed amount instead of, or in addition to, a percentage of the value of property dealt with or a time charge. Remuneration may consist of a combination of any two, or all three, of these bases.

21.2 Scrutiny of office-holders' remuneration and expenses is made easier by enabling creditors to obtain further information. Expenses may be challenged as excessive as well as remuneration. Remuneration already received and expenses already incurred may be challenged within eight weeks of the report recording them.

21.3 Office-holders may seek a review of their remuneration if there is a change of circumstances.

21.4 Provision is made for an administrator or other qualified insolvency practitioner to be able to recover remuneration charged and expenses incurred before the formal start of the administration, of particular importance in what have become known as "pre-pack administrations".

21.5 Progress reports, already used in administration, are introduced into winding up and bankruptcy (but annually, not every six months as in administration). The report to be laid before the final meeting of creditors is brought into line with progress reports: and a draft of the final report must be sent to creditors eight weeks beforehand.

22. PROVISION OF "RECEIPTS AND PAYMENTS" ACCOUNT ON RESIGNATION OF OFFICE HOLDER

22.1 This theme is associated with the remuneration theme and the meetings theme. It affects winding up and bankruptcy.

22.2 A report with receipts and payments is to be submitted to the creditors' meeting to receive the liquidator's or trustee's resignation (Rules 4.108 and 6.126). Provision is made for the procedure to be followed where there is an ongoing challenge to the outgoing office-holder's remuneration. The resignation will be effective from the acceptance of the resignation (Rules 4.108, 4.108A, 6.126 and 6.126A). However, release can only be considered and effected once any challenge to remuneration has been resolved (Rules 4.108A and 6.126A). There are consequential amendments to Rules 4.109, 121, 122, 6.127 and 135.

23 CREDITOR AND DEBTOR BANKRUPTCY PETITIONS

23.1 These Rules have been amended to permit a creditor to present a petition against a non-resident debtor in that debtor's former local county court in certain circumstances.

24 BLOCK TRANSFER ORDERS

24.1 A new Chapter 1A is inserted into Part 7 between Chapter 1 (applications) and Chapter 2 (transfer of proceedings between courts). It is so placed because a block transfer order is a special type of application. Rule 7.11 is amended consequentially.

24.2 The Chapter builds on the provisions in paragraph 1.6 of the Practice Direction: Insolvency Proceedings as reflected in the 2007 draft Consolidation Rules and the subsequent decision in *Donaldson -v- O'Sullivan* [2008] EWCA Civ 879. It varies from the Practice Direction in the following respects: it allows the application to be made to the registrar in the first instance; an application may be made to a county court with insolvency jurisdiction where all the cases subject of the application are in the county court; not all the outgoing office-holder's cases need be subject of the block transfer order; the outgoing office-holder's cases may be transferred to more than one replacement office-holder.

24.3 *Donaldson* settled the law concerning block transfers as it relates to bankruptcy and winding up by the court. The powers under which the registrar may make the order reflect the decision in *Donaldson*.

25 VERIFICATION OF A STATEMENT OF AFFAIRS

25.1 In Part 1 (company voluntary arrangements), the provisions dealing with the verification of a statement of affairs have been amended to require that such statements are verified by a statement of truth made by at least one director.

26 CLAIMS AND DISTRIBUTIONS

26.1 The changes relating to claims and distributions are miscellaneous, with no overarching principle. Some inconsistencies between administration, administrative receivership, winding up and bankruptcy are eliminated (but not the differences in respect of the form of proof of debt, where there remains no prescribed form in administration, receivership or voluntary liquidation). Distribution of assets in kind is made more transparent.

27 LIMITED DISCLOSURE

27.1 Discrepancies between the existing provisions on limiting the public disclosure of information about creditors are eliminated, and the same principles on limited disclosure are applied uniformly to all types of insolvency procedure. Essentially, the court may order that information about creditors in statements of affairs and proposals for voluntary arrangements and administration may be omitted from what is filed at Companies House, sent to creditors generally or otherwise given wide publicity or circulation; and the grounds for omission are prejudice to the insolvency proceedings or the interests of the creditors in question.

28 AMENDMENTS TO PART 4 CHAPTER 22 (LEAVE TO ACT AS DIRECTOR ETC. OF COMPANY WITH PROHIBITED NAME)

28.1 Rule 4.227 is amended to provide for the service of an application for leave to use a prohibited name to be served on the Secretary of State who may make representations at the hearing of the application either in person or in writing.

28.2 Rule 4.228 is amended to remedy defective drafting.

29 PART 3 (ADMINISTRATIVE RECEIVERSHIP): MISCELLANEOUS AMENDMENTS

29.1 Rule 3.31 has been amended to mirror Rule 2.66 in order to achieve consistency.

29.2 In Rule 3.33, paragraph (3) was omitted on the basis that the Rule relates to resignation as distinct from vacation. Since an administrative receiver "vacates" office upon the making of the administration order, the paragraph is of no effect. Rule 3.35 applies for vacation of office on completion of the administrative receivership. It therefore does not apply where the company subsequently goes into administration. Therefore there is no requirement for an administrative receiver to give notice where the company subsequently goes into administration. Therefore Rule 3.33(3) is otiose.

30 THE EC REGULATION

30.1. The amending Rules include two classes of amendment relating to the EC Regulation on Insolvency Proceedings 2000 ("the EC Regulation"). Those in the first class relate to an application under Article 37 of the EC Regulation to convert insolvency proceedings opened as "primary proceedings" into "secondary proceedings". The amendments deal specifically with the requirement for there to be a witness statement accompanying the application to the court which should include the maker's opinion as to which winding up procedure the proceedings should be converted. In the first instance (which can be found in the amendment to Rules 1.31 to 1.33) the proceedings into which primary proceedings can be converted are listed as administration proceedings "limited to winding up", creditors' voluntary winding up and winding up by the court. In a second set (to be found in the amendments to Rules 2.130 to 2.132) proceedings into which the administration may be converted are listed out as creditors' voluntary winding up and winding up by the court. Provision is also now made to deal with the circumstance where the order limits the purposes of an administration to a "winding up through the administration". This reflects the fact that the wide purposes of administration generally must be restricted before they can fall within the more limited definition of administration now found in Annex B of the EC Regulation.

30.2. The second class of amendments also relates to the inclusion of certain administration proceedings within the definition of "secondary proceedings" within the EC Regulation. An example of this can be found in the amendments to Rule 2.4 where "secondary proceedings" are inserted between "main proceedings" and "territorial proceedings".

31 ELECTRONIC DELIVERY

31.1. One of the key facets of the modernisation reforms is to facilitate the delivery of documents electronically. With this in mind the amending Rules make a number of provisions facilitating the sending of documents by electronic means. The general principle found in Rules 12A.7 and 12A.10 is that documents may be delivered by electronic means provided that the recipient has consented and provides an electronic address. The provisions do not apply to petitions or applications to court, evidence in support of such applications or petitions or orders of the court; nor do certain other provisions apply to the filing of notices or other documents with the court, the submission of documents to the registrar of companies or to the service of a statutory demand. Uniformity is facilitated by the provision of the LRO. (Subject to the RCJ Pilot referred to in paragraph 1.2).

31.2. A new provision for the use of websites by office-holders occasioned by the LRO is now found in Rule 12A.11. However, a new provision is made in 12A.12 which allows the court, where it is satisfied the expense of sending notices under 12A.11 in specified circumstances is too onerous, to dispense with the requirement for notices to be sent on each and every occasion and instead allow the requirements to be satisfied by the sending of one notice alone to cover all circumstances. The justification for this is to reduce costs where because of the number of persons entitled to receive a notice on each occasion, the cost is disproportionate to the benefit of sending the notices every time.

31.3. New Rule 12A.13 simply repeats the requirement presently contained in the Rules that a document served on a single joint office-holder is to be treated as served on them all.

31.4 We have adopted the use of "hard copy" rather than "paper copy" in the Rules generally when referring to "paper" documents.

32 SERVICE OF COURT DOCUMENTS

32.1. Except for the serving of a winding up petition, a bankruptcy petition and any document relating to such an application or petition or the serving of an administration, winding up, or bankruptcy order, CPR Part 6 is to apply. But the provisions of CPR Part 6 relating to service outside the jurisdiction apply in every case (including bankruptcy petitions etc) so no bespoke Rule is now proposed for the Insolvency Rules. These Rules are now contained in Chapter 3 of the new Part 12A. (Subject to the RCJ Pilot referred to in paragraph 1.2).

33 FORMS

33.1. The approach adopted in the modernisation Rules is to start the move away generally from the prescription of forms in the Insolvency Rules. Instead the drafting approach adopted is to specify what information must be sent to a particular person (an information requirement) rather than to provide a form in which it is to be sent. The reason for this is that with the advent of the electronic age the use of prescribed forms – a concept heavily based on paper delivery – can get in the way of electronic delivery. It is ultimately the intention (when we come to the 2011 Rules) to dispense with "prescribed forms" wherever we can. This will not mean that forms are not produced by the Insolvency Service for use in supplying relevant information – it will just mean that is not the only "form" in which the information can be supplied. This should facilitate the use of electronic communication, in particular in the light of the provisions we have made in respect of website delivery and delivery of other Insolvency documents. This means that in these amending Rules –

- no new forms have been prescribed (only replacements)
- certain forms have been revoked where they no longer serve a useful purpose.

33.2 Old forms have however been retained or will be amended.

33.3 In order for the electronic provisions to work properly, there still needs to be "a fix" to deal with the submission of information which would otherwise have been submitted on a hard copy prescribed form. Our solution to this is found in Rules 12A.29 and 12A.30, which in effect allows the information which must be contained in a prescribed form to be sent electronically provided that minimum requirements are met.

33.4 Since the advent of the Companies Act 2006 any prescription as to the form and manner of delivery of information to the registrar of companies now falls properly to the registrar.

33.5 It has been agreed with Companies House that from April 2010 the rules which will apply to form and delivery of information to the registrar will be governed by registrar's rules. Those rules will prescribe any necessary forms and set out all the rules relating to the manner of delivery for this information. The Insolvency Rules will still determine the information requirements themselves but prescribed forms relating to this information have been removed from the Insolvency Rules. Any substantive provision to supply information to the registrar contained in the required content of a prescribed form, but not fully reflected in the Insolvency Rule to which it relates, has been placed in generic information requirements set out in Rules 12A.40 to 12A.48.

34 AUTHENTICATION

34.1 The Rules generally now adopt the concept of "authentication of a document" rather than requiring a "signature", again in order to facilitate electronic delivery. This provision can be found in Rule 12A.9 (and equivalents in Rules 12A.29 and 12A.30 for forms). In effect the provision follows that provided for by the Companies Act 2006. For paper documents a signature is sufficient authentication. For non-paper documents a document is sufficiently authenticated if the identity of the sender is confirmed in a manner specified by the recipient or where there is no such manner specified, if a communication contains or is accompanied by a statement of identity of the sender and the recipient has no reason to doubt the truth of that statement.

35 ANNULMENT CHANGES

35.1 Rule 5.55 has been amended so as to render more transparent the duration of the prescribed period referred to in section 261(2) of the Insolvency Act 1986.

35.2 Section 261(2)(b) permits the official receiver to make an application for annulment of a bankruptcy order "where the bankrupt has not made an application within the prescribed period". "Prescribed" in the 1986 Act means prescribed by rules. Whilst Rule 5.55(2) currently prohibits the official receiver from making an application before the expiry of 14 days from the date that the time period in section 262(3) for application under section 262(1) has expired, it does not itself prescribe any period within which the bankrupt might make an application, nor does it prescribe any period beyond the expiry of which the official receiver may make an application.

35.3 The duration of the period referred to in the current paragraph (2) may be deduced from the provisions of the 1986 Act referred to as consisting of the 28 days during which the decision of a creditors' meeting may be challenged beginning with the day that the report of the creditors' meeting is made to the court under section 259. To this is to be added the 14 days from the date upon which that period expires.

35.4 This amounts in total to 42 days which is reflected in these modernisation amendments.

35.5 In addition, Rule 6.211 has been amended to allow annulment where debts are secured for, to the satisfaction of the court, and to allow the court to take into account whether amounts in respect of post-commencement interest on the bankruptcy debts have been paid, which is of particular relevance where the payment is made by a third party. This latter amendment reflects case law on the subject (see *Harper v Buchler* [2004] BPIR, *Harper v Buchler (No.2)* [2005] BPIR, *Wilcox v Duckworth* [2005] BPIR).

36 INSOLVENCY REGISTERS

36.1 Part 6A of the Rules has been amended to reflect desired policy on the operation and maintenance of the insolvency registers. Rule 6A.2A seeks to make uniform provision for information to be displayed in respect of voluntary arrangements of all types. Rule 6A.3 extends the period of time for which information added to the register pursuant to Rule 6A.2A must remain on the register, prior to deletion by the Secretary of State following receipt of notice of either the making of a revocation order, or full implementation or termination of the voluntary arrangement. Rule 6A.4 requires additional information to be placed on the individual insolvency register by the official receiver in circumstances where a bankruptcy order has been rescinded by the court. Under Rule 6A.5, information on annulled bankruptcies will remain on the individual insolvency register for a period of between 28 days and three months. The insolvency registers have also been made subject to the court's discretion that information should either not be entered onto the register or should be deleted where there is a risk of harm to the subject of the information (see Victims of Violence below).

37 VICTIMS OF VIOLENCE

37.1 New Rules 5.67 and 6.235B have been added to the Rules to provide for an appropriate procedure to permit the court, on the application of the debtor, the supervisor, the official receiver (whether acting as a supervisor or otherwise) or the Secretary of State, to order that the details in respect of a debtor to be entered onto the individual insolvency register under Rule 6A are not to include details of the debtor's current address. The court is also permitted to order that details of the debtor's current address be removed from any part of the court file of the proceedings relating to the debtor, which is open to inspection, and be kept on a separate file not open to inspection. The provisions are to apply in any case where disclosure to other persons (whether to the public generally or to specific persons) of the current address or whereabouts of a debtor might reasonably be expected to lead to violence against the debtor or against a person who normally resides with the debtor as a member of the debtor's family.

38 INLAND REVENUE

38.1 References in the Rules to "Inland Revenue" have been amended to reflect the replacement of the Inland Revenue by HM Revenue and Customs.

39 DECEASED OFFICE-HOLDERS

39.1 Rules 2.124, 4.132, 4.133, 4.145 and 6.143 have been amended to reflect the fact that persons other than partners may be appointed as office-holders.

40 DEFINITIONS

40.1 The interpretation provisions contained in Part 0 and Part 13 of the Rules have been updated. Additionally, where in the Rules references are made to periods of less than 7 days, or an equivalent, these have been amended to business days in order to afford the relevant party a more appropriate period of time.

41 SCHEDULE 2

41.1 Schedule 2 has been amended to take account of changes in the alternative courts that may be utilised.

42 SCHEDULE 5

42.1 Schedule 5 has been amended to reflect current terminology. For example, reference is now made to "level 5 on the standard scale" rather than "the statutory maximum". The column identifying the 'General nature of offence' has also been amended to clarify the offence.

43 CONCLUSION

43.1 It is hoped that stakeholders will find this commentary useful.

©Crown copyright. Reproduced with permission.

Index

Adjournment of meetings
  discretionary, 3.43
  introduction, 3.40
  mandatory, 3.42
  proofs and proxies, and, 3.45
  time limit, 3.44
Administration
  administrator's proposals
    notice of deemed approval, 10.2
  advertising
    in the Gazette, 1.7
    other than in the Gazette, 1.12
  claims and distributions
    admission of proofs, 10.11
    appeal against a decision on proof, 10.6–10.7
    cancellation of dividend, 10.12
    definition of 'debt', 10.4
    disclosure of s 110 arrangements, 10.14
    distributions to members in specie, 10.15
    drawing a dividend, 10.16–10.21
    interest, 10.8
    introduction, 10.3
    notice of declaration of dividend, 10.13
    notice of intended dividend, 10.10
    office holders' powers, 10.22–10.23
    postponement of dividend, 10.12
    proof of claims, 10.5
    redemption of security by office holder, 10.9, 10.24
    rejection of proofs, 10.11
    Scotland, 10.16
  creditors' committees
    See also **Creditors' committees**
    overview, 4.1
  meetings
    See also **Meetings**
    overview, 3.1
  remuneration and expenses
    apportionment of set fee remuneration, 9.29
    basis of remuneration, 9.25–9.28
    creditor's claim that excessive, 9.38–9.39
    creditor's entitlement to information, 9.36–9.37
    introduction, 9.24

Administration – *cont.*
  remuneration and expenses – *cont.*
    new administrators, 9.30
    pre-administration costs, 9.31–9.35
    rent, 9.40–9.48
  Scotland
    creditors' committees, 4.12
Advertising
  Gazette, in the
    all cases, in, 1.6
    bankrupts, for, 1.8
    companies, for, 1.7
    general provisions, 1.9
    generally, 1.5
    introduction, 1.4
  introduction, 1.1–1.3
  liquidator's appointment, of, 1.14
  other than in the Gazette
    all cases, 1.10–1.11
    bankrupts, for, 1.13
    companies, for, 1.12
    introduction, 1.4
  Scotland, in, 1.15
  standard contents
    adverts in the Gazette, for, 1.5–1.9
    adverts other than in the Gazette, for, 1.10–1.14
    general, 1.4
    Scotland, in, 1.15
  transitional provisions, 1.16
Annual meetings
  voluntary liquidations, in, 3.30
Annulment of bankruptcy
  post-commencement interest, 10.33
  trustee's remuneration, 10.30–10.32
Annulment of bankruptcy orders
  individual voluntary arrangements, 6.32–6.34
Appeals
  chairman's decision, against, 3.38
Applications
  court procedure and practice, 5.2
  disclaimers
    bankruptcy, 7.10–7.11
    liquidation, 7.6–7.7
  interested party, by
    bankruptcy, 7.10–7.11

Index

Applications – *cont.*
  interested party, by – *cont.*
    liquidation, 7.6–7.7
Attendance at court
  court procedure and practice, 5.7
Authentication
  electronic communications, 2.6
Bankruptcy
  advertising
    in the Gazette, 1.8
    other than in the Gazette, 1.13
  annulment
    post-commencement interest, 10.33
    trustee's remuneration, 10.30–10.32
  bankrupt carrying on a business, 10.29
  claims and distributions
    admission of proofs, 10.11
    appeal against a decision on proof, 10.6–10.7
    cancellation of dividend, 10.12
    definition of 'debt', 10.4
    disclosure of s 110 arrangements, 10.14
    distributions to members in specie, 10.15
    drawing a dividend, 10.16–10.21
    interest, 10.8
    introduction, 10.3
    notice of declaration of dividend, 10.13
    notice of intended dividend, 10.10
    office holders' powers, 10.22–10.23
    postponement of dividend, 10.12
    proof of claims, 10.5
    redemption of security by office holder, 10.9, 10.24
    rejection of proofs, 10.11
    Scotland, 10.16
  creditors' committees
    See also **Creditors' committees**
    overview, 4.1
  disclaimer
    application by interested party, 7.10–7.11
    notice of disclaimer, 7.8
    records, 7.9
    transitional provisions, 7.12
  Individual Insolvency Register
    generally, 10.35–10.36
    information not to be included where persons at risk of violence, 10.37–10.43
  meetings
    See also **Meetings**
    overview, 3.1
  office holders' remuneration and expenses
    annulment applications, and, 10.30–10.32

Bankruptcy – *cont.*
  office holders' remuneration and expenses – *cont.*
    apportionment of set fee remuneration, 9.55
    basis of remuneration, 9.50–9.54
    creditor's claim that excessive, 9.58–9.60
    creditor's entitlement to information, 9.57
    introduction, 9.49
    new trustee, 9.56
  petitions
    amendment, 10.26
    service, 10.25
    withdrawal, 10.27–10.28
  public examination, 8.9–8.10
Bankruptcy orders
  annulment, 6.32–6.34
Bankruptcy petitions
  amendment, 10.26
  service, 10.25
  withdrawal, 10.27–10.28
Block transfer orders
  generally, 10.44–10.45
Certificates of constitution
  creditors' and liquidation committees, 4.3
Chairman
  appeals against decisions, 3.38
  discretion to allow a vote, 3.37
Civil Procedure Rules
  application to insolvency proceedings, 5.7
Claims and distributions
  admission of proofs, 10.11
  appeal against a decision on proof, 10.6–10.7
  cancellation of dividend, 10.12
  definition of 'debt', 10.4
  disclosure of s 110 arrangements, 10.14
  dividends
    cancellation, 10.12
    notice of declaration, 10.13
    notice of intended, 10.10
    postponement, 10.12
  drawing a dividend, 10.16–10.21
  interest, 10.8
  introduction, 10.3
  members in specie, to, 10.15
  notice of declaration of dividend, 10.13
  notice of intended dividend, 10.10
  office holders' powers, 10.22–10.23
  postponement of dividend, 10.12
  proof of claims
    admission, 10.11
    appeal against a decision, 10.6–10.7
    generally, 10.5
    rejection, 10.11

Index

Claims and distributions – *cont.*
  redemption of security by office holder, 10.9, 10.24
  rejection of proofs, 10.11
  Scotland, 10.16
Company voluntary arrangements (CVAs)
  content of proposals
    directors, by, 6.9–6.11
    insolvency practitioners, by, 6.12
  generally, 6.2–6.8
  improving visibility for creditors
    content of proposal made by directors, 6.9–6.11
    content of proposal made by insolvency practitioner, 6.12
    notice of moratorium, 6.16
    statement of affairs, 6.13–6.15
    time recording information, 6.17
  Individual Insolvency Register
    generally, 10.35–10.36
    information not to be included where persons at risk of violence, 10.37–10.43
  'insolvency proceedings', as, 6.3
  introduction, 6.1
  meetings
    See also **Meetings**
    overview, 3.1
  notice of moratorium, 6.16
  providing alternative and flexible tools to insolvency procedures
    delimitation of powers between joint supervisors, 6.24
    requisite majorities at creditors' meetings, 6.19–6.22
    summoning of meetings, 6.18
    supervisor's accounts and reports, 6.25–6.30
    suspension of meetings by chairman, 6.23
  statement of affairs, 6.13–6.15
  time recording information, 6.17
  transitional provisions, 6.36
Consent
  electronic communications, 2.4
Content of proposals
  company voluntary arrangements
    directors, by, 6.9–6.11
    insolvency practitioners, by, 6.12
  individual voluntary arrangements, 6.31
Court file and records
  inspection, 5.6
Court procedure and practice
  application of Civil Procedure Rules to insolvency proceedings, 5.7
  applications, 5.2
  attendance at court, 5.7
  court file, 5.6

Court procedure and practice – *cont.*
  delivery of arrested persons to prison, 5.4–5.5
  discharge of arrest warrants, 5.3
  enforcement, 5.3–5.5
  introduction, 5.1
  security in court, 5.7
  transitional provisions, 5.8
Creditors' committees
  certificate of constitution, 4.3
  first meeting, 4.4
  introduction, 4.1
  liquidation following administration, in, 4.10–4.11
  meetings
    first meeting, 4.4
    held at request of committee member, at, 4.5–4.6
    resolutions, 4.7
    termination of membership of committee, and, 4.8
  membership
    certificate of constitution, 4.3
    eligibility, 4.2
    termination, 4.8
  resolutions, 4.7
  Scotland, 4.12
  transitional provisions, 4.13
Delivery of arrested persons to prison
  court procedure and practice, 5.4–5.5
Discharge of arrest warrants
  court procedure and practice, 5.3
Disclaimer
  bankruptcy
    application by interested party, 7.10–7.11
    notice of disclaimer, 7.8
    records, 7.9
  introduction, 7.1–7.3
  liquidation
    application by interested party, 7.6–7.7
    notice of disclaimer, 7.4
    records, 7.5
    transitional provisions, 7.12
Disclosure
  s 110 arrangements, of, 10.14
Distributions
  admission of proofs, 10.11
  appeal against a decision on proof, 10.6–10.7
  cancellation of dividend, 10.12
  definition of 'debt', 10.4
  disclosure of s 110 arrangements, 10.14
  dividends
    cancellation, 10.12
    notice of declaration, 10.13
    notice of intended, 10.10

843

Distributions – *cont.*
dividends – *cont.*
postponement, 10.12
drawing a dividend, 10.16–10.21
interest, 10.8
introduction, 10.3
members in specie, to, 10.15
notice of declaration of dividend, 10.13
notice of intended dividend, 10.10
office holders' powers, 10.22–10.23
postponement of dividend, 10.12
proof of claims
admission, 10.11
appeal against a decision, 10.6–10.7
generally, 10.5
rejection, 10.11
redemption of security by office holder, 10.9, 10.24
rejection of proofs, 10.11
Scotland, 10.16
Dividends
distributions
cancellation, 10.12
notice of declaration, 10.13
notice of intended, 10.10
postponement, 10.12
EC Regulation on Insolvency Proceedings
generally, 10.49–10.50
Scotland, 10.51
Electronic communications
advantages, 2.10
authentication, 2.6
consent, 2.4
courts, with, 2.8–2.9
delivery, 2.7
failure of delivery notices, 2.13
general, 2.3
introduction, 2.1
practical considerations, 2.10–2.14
recipient to give consent, 2.4
right to request hard copy, 2.5
scope of application of provisions, 2.2
Scotland, 2.26
transitional provisions, 2.28
Enforcement
delivery of arrested persons to prison, 5.4–5.5
discharge of arrest warrants, 5.3
Examination
introduction, 8.1–8.2
private examination, 8.11–8.15
public examination
bankruptcy, in, 8.9–8.10
generally, 8.3–8.4
winding up, in, 8.5–8.8
transitional provisions, 8.16

Expenses and remuneration of office holder
administration
apportionment of set fee remuneration, 9.29
basis of remuneration, 9.25–9.28
creditor's claim that excessive, 9.38–9.39
creditor's entitlement to information, 9.36–9.37
introduction, 9.24
new administrators, 9.30
pre-administration costs, 9.31–9.35
rent, 9.40–9.48
bankruptcy
apportionment of set fee remuneration, 9.55
basis of remuneration, 9.50–9.54
creditor's claim that excessive, 9.58–9.60
creditor's entitlement to information, 9.57
introduction, 9.49
new trustee, 9.56
concept and approach, 9.2–9.6
introduction, 9.1
liquidation
apportionment of set fee remuneration, 9.15
basis of remuneration, 9.9–9.14
creditor's claim that excessive, 9.20–9.23
creditor's entitlement to information, 9.17–9.19
introduction, 9.8
new liquidators, 9.16
pre-administration costs, 9.31–9.35
Re Lundy Granite, 9.7
transitional provisions, 9.61–9.62
Gazetting
See also **Advertising**
all cases, in, 1.6
bankrupts, for, 1.8
companies, for, 1.7
general provisions, 1.9
generally, 1.5
introduction, 1.4
Individual Insolvency Register
bankruptcy, 10.35–10.36
information not to be included where persons at risk of violence
generally, 10.37–10.41
Scotland, 10.42–10.43
voluntary arrangements, 10.34
Individual voluntary arrangements (IVAs)
See also **Voluntary arrangements**
annulment of bankruptcy orders, 6.32–6.34
content of proposals, 6.31

Index

Individual voluntary arrangements (IVAs) – *cont.*
Individual Insolvency Register
generally, 10.35–10.36
information not to be included where persons at risk of violence, 10.37–10.43
nominee's reports, 6.35
transitional provisions, 6.36
'Insolvency proceedings'
voluntary arrangements, 6.3
Interest
claims and distributions, and, 10.8
Language and terminology
changes to Insolvency Rules, 10.48
Liquidation
See also **Liquidation committees**
advertising
in the Gazette, 1.7
other than in the Gazette, 1.12
claims and distributions
admission of proofs, 10.11
appeal against a decision on proof, 10.6–10.7
cancellation of dividend, 10.12
definition of 'debt', 10.4
disclosure of s 110 arrangements, 10.14
distributions to members in specie, 10.15
drawing a dividend, 10.16–10.21
interest, 10.8
introduction, 10.3
notice of declaration of dividend, 10.13
notice of intended dividend, 10.10
office holders' powers, 10.22–10.23
postponement of dividend, 10.12
proof of claims, 10.5
redemption of security by office holder, 10.9, 10.24
rejection of proofs, 10.11
Scotland, 10.16
creditors' committees
See also **Creditors' committees**
overview, 4.1
disclaimer
application by interested party, 7.6–7.7
notice of disclaimer, 7.4
records, 7.5
transitional provisions, 7.12
liquidation committees
See also **Liquidation committees**
overview, 4.1
meetings
See also **Meetings**
overview, 3.1

Liquidation – *cont.*
office holders' remuneration and expenses
apportionment of set fee remuneration, 9.15
basis of remuneration, 9.9–9.14
creditor's claim that excessive, 9.20–9.23
creditor's entitlement to information, 9.17–9.19
introduction, 9.8
new liquidators, 9.16
public examination 8.5–8.8
Liquidation committees
certificate of constitution, 4.3
composition when creditors have been paid in full, 4.9
first meeting, 4.4
introduction, 4.1
meetings
first meeting, 4.4
held at request of committee member, at, 4.5–4.6
resolutions, 4.7
termination of membership of committee, and, 4.8
membership
certificate of constitution, 4.3
eligibility, 4.2
termination, 4.8
resolutions, 4.7
transitional provisions, 4.13
Liquidators
advertising appointment, 1.14
remuneration and expenses
apportionment of set fee remuneration, 9.15
basis of remuneration, 9.9–9.14
creditor's claim that excessive, 9.20–9.23
creditor's entitlement to information, 9.17–9.19
introduction, 9.8
new liquidators, 9.16
Majority approval
CVA proposals, of
generally, 3.46
minutes or records of proceedings, 3.47
Meetings
adjournment
discretionary, 3.43
introduction, 3.40
mandatory, 3.42
proofs and proxies, and, 3.45
time limit, 3.44
annual meetings
voluntary liquidations, in, 3.30
appeals against chairman's decision, 3.38

845

Index

Meetings – *cont.*
  creditors' and liquidation committees
    first meeting, 4.4
    held at request of committee member, at, 4.5–4.6
    resolutions, 4.7
    termination of membership of committee, and, 4.8
  discretion of chairman to allow vote, 3.37
  introduction, 3.1
  majority approval of CVA proposals
    generally, 3.46
    minutes or records of proceedings, 3.47
  notice by advertisement only, 3.33
  notice periods, 3.31
  proofs and proxies for use
    adjourned meetings, and, 3.45
    generally, 3.35—3.37
  quorum, 3.39
  remote attendance
    creditors' committees, and, 3.19–3.23
    excluded persons, 3.14–3.18
    generally, 3.2
    liquidation committees, and, 3.19–3.23
    notice of meeting held by such means, 3.6
    practical considerations, 3.24—3.29
    'remote means', 3.3
    request for place to be specified, 3.7–3.13
    responsibilities of person summoning, 3.4–3.5
    Scotland, 3.57
  requisition, by, 3.34
  resolutions by correspondence, 3.32
  Scotland (administration)
    adjournment, 3.56
    entitlement to vote, 3.54
    notice by advertisement only, 3.55
    suspension, 3.56
  Scotland (CVAs)
    chairman as proxy holder, 3.50
    entitlement to vote, 3.51–3.52
    introduction, 3.48
    requisite majorities, 3.53
    summoning to consider CVA proposal, 3.49
  suspension, 3.40–3.41
  transitional provisions, 3.58 –3.60
Members in specie
  claims and distributions, and, 10.15
Nominee's reports
  individual voluntary arrangements, 6.35
Notice of declaration of dividend
  claims and distributions, and, 10.13
Notice of disclaimer
  bankruptcy, 7.8

Notice of disclaimer – *cont.*
  liquidation, 7.4
Notice of intended dividend
  claims and distributions, and, 10.10
Notice of meetings
  advertisement only, by, 3.33
  remote attendance, by, 3.6
Notice of moratorium
  company voluntary arrangements, 6.16
Office holders' remuneration and expenses
  administration
    apportionment of set fee remuneration, 9.29
    basis of remuneration, 9.25–9.28
    creditor's claim that excessive, 9.38–9.39
    creditor's entitlement to information, 9.36–9.37
    introduction, 9.24
    new administrators, 9.30
    pre-administration costs, 9.31–9.35
    rent, 9.40–9.48
  bankruptcy
    apportionment of set fee remuneration, 9.55
    basis of remuneration, 9.50–9.54
    creditor's claim that excessive, 9.58–9.60
    creditor's entitlement to information, 9.57
    introduction, 9.49
    new trustee, 9.56
  concept and approach, 9.2–9.6
  introduction, 9.1
  liquidation
    apportionment of set fee remuneration, 9.15
    basis of remuneration, 9.9–9.14
    creditor's claim that excessive, 9.20–9.23
    creditor's entitlement to information, 9.17–9.19
    introduction, 9.8
    new liquidators, 9.16
    pre-administration costs, 9.31–9.35
    Re Lundy Granite, 9.7
    transitional provisions, 9.61–9.62
Ordinary applications
  court procedure and practice, 5.2
Originating applications
  court procedure and practice, 5.2
Pre-administration costs
  office holders' remuneration and expenses, 9.31–9.35
Prescribed forms
  generally, 10.46
  Scotland, 10.47

Index

Private examination
  generally, 8.11–8.15
  transitional provisions, 8.16
Proof of claims
  admission, 10.11
  appeal against a decision, 10.6–10.7
  generally, 10.5
  rejection, 10.11
Proofs and proxies
  adjourned meetings, and, 3.45
  generally, 3.35—3.37
Public examination
  bankruptcy, in, 8.9–8.10
  generally, 8.3–8.4
  transitional provisions, 8.16
  winding up, in, 8.5–8.8
Quorum
  meetings, 3.39
Records
  disclaimer
    bankruptcy, 7.9
    liquidation, 7.5
Redemption of security by office holder
  claims and distributions, and, 10.9, 10.24
Remote attendance
  creditors' committees, and, 3.19–3.23
  excluded persons, 3.14–3.18
  generally, 3.2
  liquidation committees, and, 3.19–3.23
  notice of meeting held by such means, 3.6
  practical considerations, 3.24—3.29
  'remote means', 3.3
  request for place to be specified, 3.7–3.13
  responsibilities of person summoning, 3.4–3.5
  Scotland, 3.57
Remuneration and expenses of office holders
  administration
    apportionment of set fee remuneration, 9.29
    basis of remuneration, 9.25–9.28
    creditor's claim that excessive, 9.38–9.39
    creditor's entitlement to information, 9.36–9.37
    introduction, 9.24
    new administrators, 9.30
    pre-administration costs, 9.31–9.35
    rent, 9.40–9.48
  bankruptcy
    apportionment of set fee remuneration, 9.55
    basis of remuneration, 9.50–9.54
    creditor's claim that excessive, 9.58–9.60
    creditor's entitlement to information, 9.57

Remuneration and expenses of office holders – cont.
  bankruptcy – cont.
    introduction, 9.49
    new trustee, 9.56
  concept and approach, 9.2–9.6
  introduction, 9.1
  liquidation
    apportionment of set fee remuneration, 9.15
    basis of remuneration, 9.9–9.14
    creditor's claim that excessive, 9.20–9.23
    creditor's entitlement to information, 9.17–9.19
    introduction, 9.8
    new liquidators, 9.16
    pre-administration costs, 9.31–9.35
    Re Lundy Granite, 9.7
  transitional provisions, 9.61–9.62
Requisition
  meetings, 3.34
Resolutions
  correspondence, by, 3.1
  creditors' and liquidation committees, 4.7
Right to request hard copies
  electronic communications, 2.5
  website communication, 2.17
Scotland
  advertising, 1.15
  claims and distributions
    drawing a dividend in administration, 10.16–10.21
  creditors' committees, 4.12
  EC Regulation on Insolvency Proceedings, 10.51
  electronic communications, 2.26
  Individual Insolvency Register
    information not to be included where persons at risk of violence, 10.42–10.43
  meetings (administration)
    adjournment, 3.56
    entitlement to vote, 3.54
    notice by advertisement only, 3.55
    suspension, 3.56
  meetings (CVAs)
    chairman as proxy holder, 3.50
    entitlement to vote, 3.51–3.52
    introduction, 3.48
    requisite majorities, 3.53
    summoning to consider CVA proposal, 3.49
  remote attendance, 3.57
  prescribed forms, 10.47
  website communication, 2.27

847

Index

Security in court
court procedure and practice, 5.7
Statement of affairs
company voluntary arrangements, 6.13–6.15
Suspension
meetings, 3.40–3.41
Terminology
changes to Insolvency Rules, 10.48
Time recording information
company voluntary arrangements, 6.17
Trustees in bankruptcy
remuneration and expenses
apportionment of set fee remuneration, 9.55
basis of remuneration, 9.50–9.54
creditor's claim that excessive, 9.58–9.60
creditor's entitlement to information, 9.57
introduction, 9.49
new trustee, 9.56
Voluntary arrangements
content of proposals
directors, by, 6.9–6.11
insolvency practitioners, by, 6.12
generally, 6.2–6.8
improving visibility for creditors
content of proposal made by directors, 6.9–6.11
content of proposal made by insolvency practitioner, 6.12
notice of moratorium, 6.16
statement of affairs, 6.13–6.15
time recording information, 6.17

Voluntary arrangements – *cont.*
Individual Insolvency Register
generally, 10.35–10.36
information not to be included where persons at risk of violence, 10.37–10.43
'insolvency proceedings', as, 6.3
introduction, 6.1
meetings
See also **Meetings**
overview, 3.1
notice of moratorium, 6.16
providing alternative and flexible tools to insolvency procedures
delimitation of powers between joint supervisors, 6.24
requisite majorities at creditors' meetings, 6.19–6.22
summoning of meetings, 6.18
supervisor's accounts and reports, 6.25–6.30
suspension of meetings by chairman, 6.23
statement of affairs, 6.13–6.15
time recording information, 6.17
transitional provisions, 6.36
Website communications
delivery, 2.21
duration of availability, 2.19
general, 2.15–2.21
introduction, 2.1
practical considerations, 2.22–2.25
right to request hard copy, 2.17
scope of application of provisions, 2.2
Scotland, 2.27
transitional provisions, 2.28